COMMERCIAL LAW

By

ROBERT L. JORDAN
Professor of Law
University of California, Los Angeles

and

WILLIAM D. WARREN
Professor of Law
University of California, Los Angeles

THIRD EDITION

Westbury, New York
THE FOUNDATION PRESS, INC.
1992

Library of Congress Cataloging-in-Publication Data

Jordan, Robert L., 1928–
    Commercial law / by Robert L. Jordan and William D. Warren. — 3rd
ed.
        p.   cm. — (University casebook series)
    Includes index.
    ISBN 0–88277–984–2
    1. Commercial law—United States—Cases. I. Warren, William D.,
1924–   . II. Title. III. Series.
KF888.J67 1992
346.73'07—dc20
[347.3067]   92–7836

J. & W. Comm. Law 3rd Ed. UCB
2nd Reprint—1995

PREFACE

Much has happened in commercial law since our second edition in 1987. Two articles have been added to the Uniform Commercial Code: Article 2A (leases) and Article 4A (funds transfers). Article 3 has been completely rewritten and Article 4 has been heavily amended. Passage of the Expedited Funds Availability Act in 1987 led to promulgation by the Federal Reserve Board of Regulation CC which has made major changes in bank collection law. In 1990, the Permanent Editorial Board published a series of Commentaries on interpretation of certain UCC provisions. Of course, important new decisions continue to come down on the UCC and bankruptcy.

In this edition we have completely reorganized the materials on negotiable instruments and check collection. We have thoroughly integrated into these materials the changes made by revised Articles 3 and 4 and by new Article 4A. Greater emphasis has been placed on payment systems, particularly wire transfers, and on the bank-customer relationship. In recognition of the growing importance of standby letters of credit, we have expanded our coverage of this area and have placed the chapter on letters of credit immediately after the secured transactions materials. We have lengthened our treatment of the impact of bankruptcy on secured transactions. The avalanche of important new bankruptcy opinions continues.

Our approach in this third edition remains the same as in the prior two. Our aim is to teach rigorous statutory analysis. We offer a set of materials that can be tailored to meet the needs of almost any curriculum and to suit any pedagogical style. It is no coincidence that many of the opinions in this book were written by judges who had been law teachers, Breyer, Easterbrook, Peters, Posner and others. We find that they continue teaching effectively in their opinions.

We are particularly indebted to James Rubinfier who prepared the manuscript for publication.

ROBERT L. JORDAN
WILLIAM D. WARREN

April 1992

*

iii

ACKNOWLEDGMENTS

We gratefully acknowledge the permission extended to reprint excerpts from the following works:

Alces & Lloyd, An Agenda for Reform of the Article 9 Filing System, 44 Oklahoma Law Review 99, 110 (1991). Reprinted with the permission of the authors and the Oklahoma Law Review.

Baird, Standby Letters of Credit in Bankruptcy, 49 University of Chicago Law Review 130, 133–135 (1982). Reprinted with the permission of the author and the University of Chicago Law Review.

Brown, The Law of Personal Property 49–53, 514–515 (1975). Reprinted with permission of the author and the publisher, Clark Boardman Callaghan, 155 Pfingsten Road, Deerfield, IL. 60015. Toll-free 1–800–323–1336.

Clark & Clark, Regulation CC, Funds Availability and Check Collection (1988). Reprinted with the permission of the authors and publisher from Regulation CC, Funds Availability and Check Collection, 1988. Warren, Gorham & Lamont, 210 South Street, Boston, MA 02111. All rights reserved.

Cooper, Identifying a Personal Property Lease under the UCC, 49 Ohio State Law Journal 195, 245–246 (1988). Reprinted with the permission of the author and the Ohio State Law Journal.

Dolan, Good Faith Purchase and Warehouse Receipts: Thoughts on the Interplay of Articles 2, 7, and 9 of the UCC, 30 Hastings Law Journal 1, 2–3 (1978). Reprinted with the permission of the author and the Hastings Law Journal.

Fortgang & King, The 1978 Bankruptcy Code: Some Wrong Policy Decisions, 56 New York University Law Review 1148, 1165–1166, 1169 (1981). Reprinted with the permission of the authors and New York University Law Review.

Gilmore, Formalism and the Law of Negotiable Instruments, 13 Creighton Law Review 441, 446–450 (1979). Reprinted from the Creighton Law Review by permission. Copyright © 1979 by Creighton University School of Law.

Gilmore, Secured Transactions in Personal Property 24, 440, 787, 1220, 1226–1227 (1965). Reprinted with the permission of Little, Brown & Co.

Givray, UCC Survey, Letters of Credit, 44 Business Lawyer 1567, 1589, 1621 (1989). Reprinted with the permission of the author.

Givray, UCC Survey, Letters of Credit, 45 Business Lawyer 2381, 2404 (1990). Reprinted with the permission of the author.

ACKNOWLEDGMENTS

Plumb, Federal Tax Liens 10–11 (1972). Copyright © 1972 by the American Law Institute. Reprinted with the permission of the American Law Institute—American Bar Association Committee on Continuing Professional Education.

Reitz, Consumer Product Warranties under Federal and State Laws 22–23, 100–101 (2d ed. 1987). Copyright © 1987 by the American Law Institute. Reprinted with the permission of the American Law Institute—American Bar Association Committee on Continuing Professional Education.

Restatement, Restitution 55, 59–60 (1937). Copyright © 1937 by The American Law Institute. Reprinted with the permission of the American Law Institute.

Rosenthal, Negotiability—Who Needs It?, 71 Columbia Law Review 375, 378–381, 382–385 (1971). Copyright © 1971 by the Directors of the Columbia Law Review Association, Inc. All Rights Reserved. This article originally appeared at 71 Columb.L.Rev. 375 (1971). Reprinted by permission.

5 Uniform Laws Annotated, Uniform Commercial Code Forms and Materials, Forms 9:3200, 9:3201, 9:3202 (1990 Supp.). Reprinted with permission from Uniform Laws Annotated, Copyright © 1990 by West Publishing Co.

Wessman, Purchase Money Inventory Financing: The Case for Limiting Cross-Collateralization, 51 Ohio State Law Journal 1283, 1309 (1990). Reprinted with the permission of the author and the Ohio State Law Journal.

White & Summers, Uniform Commercial Code 526–528 (3d ed. 1988). Reprinted with the permission of the authors and West Publishing Company. Copyright © 1988 by West Publishing Co.

SUMMARY OF CONTENTS

*

TABLE OF CONTENTS

TABLE OF CONTENTS

TABLE OF CONTENTS

TABLE OF CONTENTS

xiii

TABLE OF CONTENTS

TABLE OF CONTENTS

TABLE OF CASES

Principal cases are in italic type. Non-principal cases are in roman type. References are to pages.

*

COMMERCIAL
LAW

*

Part I

SECURED TRANSACTIONS IN PERSONAL PROPERTY

PREFATORY NOTE

Credit is the lifeblood of today's business world and the commercial lawyer must know how to deal with it. Manufacturers borrow to buy the materials needed for processing; wholesale and retail merchants need credit to allow them to acquire the inventory they sell; and end-use buyers often pay for the products they buy on installment credit. The remarkably broad distribution of goods and services in this country has been made possible largely through a plentiful supply of secured credit made available by financial institutions. When this supply of credit contracts, the impact on the economy is marked.

It is fair to conclude that if secured credit had not developed, mass distribution of goods and services might never have occurred. This is true because the position of the unsecured creditor is so weak. If the debtor fails to pay, the unsecured creditor's legal remedies are restricted to bringing a law suit against the debtor, obtaining a judgment, and collecting the judgment by seizing the debtor's property and having it sold—a tedious and expensive process. On the other hand, a secured creditor contracts for an interest in the debtor's property and can often realize on this collateral without the delay and expense of a law suit. Moreover, although bankruptcy may wipe out an unsecured debt entirely, a secured creditor gets the benefit of the collateral despite the bankruptcy.

In this Part we introduce you to secured credit transactions law through the study of Article 9, the most innovative part of the Uniform Commercial Code. This Article is best understood against a brief historical background. Professor Grant Gilmore observes: "Until early in the nineteenth century the only security devices which were known in our legal system were the mortgage of real property and the pledge of chattels. Security interests in personal property which remained in the borrower's possession during the loan period were unknown. A transfer of an interest in personal property without delivery of possession was looked on as being in essence a fraudulent conveyance, invalid against creditors and purchasers." [1]

1. Gilmore, Secured Transactions in Personal Property 24 (1965). This introductory statement is largely based on Gilmore's extensive treatment of the

Not until a way could be found to allow the debtor to retain the possession and enjoyment of personal property collateral while paying off the debt would secured financing in personal property become economically significant. Two nineteenth century developments, one statutory and the other common law, legitimized nonpossessory personal property financing. Statutes allowed the creation of a mortgage in chattels in the possession of the mortgagor which was valid against creditors and purchasers so long as the chattel mortgagee spread the mortgage document on the public records. Meanwhile the courts were using the complex law of conditions to hold that a seller could sell a chattel to a buyer on condition that the buyer pay the price, and retake the property on the buyer's default. In contrast to the statutory chattel mortgage, the common law conditional sale was valid against third parties even though no public filing occurred.

Though the advent of the chattel mortgage and the conditional sale removed the traditional requirement that possession was required for the validity of secured transactions involving personal property, both these security devices were effective only when the collateral was static and the transaction was terminal. Neither device was sufficient when the collateral, as in the case of inventory or accounts receivable, would in the ordinary course of business be converted into cash or other proceeds in the hands of the debtor. In these cases the creditor required a security device that would attach automatically to the proceeds resulting from the sale of inventory or the collection of accounts, or would attach to the inventory or accounts acquired by the debtor as replacements for the original collateral.

The first half of the twentieth century saw the invention of a series of security devices—trust receipts, factors' liens, and assignments of accounts receivable—that gave secured creditors more or less effective security interests in shifting stocks of collateral like inventory and accounts. By the time drafting began on Article 9 in the late 40s, the leading commercial states had separate and wholly disparate laws on chattel mortgages, conditional sales, trust receipts, factors' liens, and assignments of accounts receivable. The law of chattel security was as provincial and nonuniform then as the law of real estate mortgages is today. Gilmore describes this body of law as one of "extraordinary complexity." [2]

The primary drafters of Article 9, Professors Grant Gilmore and Allison Dunham, went into the project resolved to junk the historical and conceptual categories that had characterized chattel security law and to strive for a functional approach to the area. Accordingly, instead of drafting revised and updated chattel mortgage or conditional sales acts, they set out to do a series of

history of chattel security devices in   **2.** Id. at 288.
volume 1 of his treatise.

separate statutes on each major type of financing: business equipment, consumer goods, agricultural products, inventory and accounts, and intangibles. As their work went forward they found that there were more similarities than differences among the various kinds of financing transactions. Hence, they decided to draft a unified statute, covering all secured transactions in personal property, that contained within it different rules for what were functionally different transactions.[3]

Article 9 does not abolish the pre-Code security devices, but it renders the formal distinctions among them irrelevant. Section 9–102(2) specifically states that Article 9 applies to security interests created by any of the traditional security devices. Lawyers and judges can and do continue to talk about chattel mortgages and conditional sales, but the old categories have no meaning except as a shorthand way of describing familiar transactions. The overriding statement is found in § 9–102(1) "* * * This Article applies (a) to any transaction (regardless of its form) which is intended to create a security interest in personal property. * * *" Comment 1 to § 9–102 states "* * * the principal test whether a transaction comes under this Article is: is the transaction intended to have effect as security?" The old labels no longer matter.

The terminology is simple. The person granting the credit may become a "secured party" (§ 9–105(1)(m)) by contracting for a "security interest" (§ 1–201(37)) in property called "collateral" (§ 9–105(1)(c)), to secure the "debtor's" (§ 9–105(1)(d)) obligation. The contract is a "security agreement" (§ 9–105(1)(*l*)). In order to assure the validity of the security interest against third parties, the secured party must "perfect" (§ 9–303(1)) the interest pursuant to Part 3. In certain instances this may be done by the secured party's filing a "financing statement" (§ 9–402) or by taking possession of the collateral. Different rules for perfection, priorities, and default apply depending on the kinds of transactions, e.g., whether "purchase money" (§ 9–107) or not, and the kinds of collateral, e.g., whether consumer goods, equipment, farm products, inventory (all defined in § 9–109) or fixtures (§ 9–313), or accounts or general intangibles (§ 9–106), or chattel paper, documents, or instruments (all defined in § 9–105).

3. Id. at § 9.2.

Chapter 1

CREATION AND PERFECTION OF SECURITY INTERESTS

A. INTRODUCTION

In this chapter we discuss the method by which the parties to a secured transaction may create and perfect an Article 9 security interest. Section 1–201(37) defines security interest as "an interest in personal property * * * which secures payment or performance of an obligation * * *." This broad definition encompasses any lien in personal property however it arises. A lien may be obtained in a number of ways. It may arise against the will of the debtor by judicial action taken by the creditor; it may arise by operation of law because of the status of the particular creditor; or it may arise as the result of a voluntary grant by the debtor. Liens in these three categories are usually referred to respectively as judicial liens, statutory liens and consensual liens.

Judicial liens are created in the litigation process in which the creditor seeks a money judgment on the debt. They may arise either before or after judgment. After a money judgment has been given by the court the creditor is entitled to seizure of the debtor's property to pay the debt, subject to certain exemptions which allow the debtor to protect some property from the reach of creditors. Sometimes the seizure is a physical taking of the property. In other cases the seizure is symbolic and occurs by the public filing of a document. But seizure, whether physical or symbolic, results in a transfer from the debtor to the creditor of an interest in the seized property and that interest is called a judicial lien. Some creditors may be able to acquire a judicial lien at the inception of the judicial action if the applicable law provides for prejudgment seizure, which is usually referred to as prejudgment attachment. Prejudgment judicial liens are severely limited in most states and the grounds for obtaining them varies widely among the various jurisdictions. Judicial liens are referred to in § 9–301(1)(b) and (3).

Statutory liens are not consensual and do not depend upon judicial action by the creditor. Rather, they are status liens. They are referred to in § 9–310. Certain creditors, favored by the state, are given the rights of secured creditors even though they did not bargain for security. There are many examples of statutory liens. Among the most common are those that arise in favor of creditors who have performed some service or otherwise gave

4

value which resulted in improvement or other benefit to the property to which the lien applies. Illustrations are the mechanic's and materialman's real property lien in favor of unpaid suppliers of services and goods used to improve the property, and the warehouseman's lien which allows an unpaid storer of goods to retain possession of the goods until the storage charges are paid. A more modern statutory lien that has become pervasive is the tax lien which allows the state or federal government to obtain a lien in all of the property of the taxpayer to secure payment of assessed taxes.

Consensual liens usually arise at the inception of a credit transaction and they are the subject of Article 9. Section 9–102(2) states that "this article applies to security interests created by contract * * *." Thus, when we refer to an Article 9 security interest we mean a consensual security interest. The drafters of the UCC selected the term "attachment" to denote when an Article 9 security interest is created. Attachment of the security interest means that it may be asserted against the debtor. But "perfection" of the security interest normally is necessary to make the security interest effective against third parties. The debtor after granting a security interest to Secured Party #1 may sell the collateral to Buyer or may grant a security interest in the same collateral to Secured Party #2. In most cases Secured Party #1 can have priority over Buyer or Secured Party #2 only if the security interest of Secured Party #1 was perfected. By requiring perfection the law accommodates the interests of the secured party and creditors of the debtor or other third parties who deal with the collateral. Since these third parties may not know that the debtor's assets are burdened with a security interest, it may be unfair for the secured party to assert rights against them based on the security interest if they have not been given some public notice of the security interest. To protect the interests of these third parties the secured party is not allowed, in most cases, to assert the security interest against these third parties unless the security interest is perfected. Section 9–303, which defines perfection, states that "a security interest is perfected when it has attached and when all of the applicable steps required for perfection have been taken." The "applicable steps" refer to some action by the secured party which gives notice of the security interest. There are two principal methods of perfection provided for by Article 9. The first method is possession of the collateral by the secured party. The absence of possession by the debtor is notice that somebody else may have an interest in the property. The second method is the filing in a designated public office of a notice of the secured transaction.

The concept of perfection is particularly important if the debtor goes into bankruptcy. Section 9–301(1) provides that "an unperfected security interest is subordinate to the rights of

* * * a person who becomes a lien creditor before the security interest is perfected * * *." "Lien creditor" is defined in § 9–301(3) to mean a creditor who has acquired a judicial lien. Under Bankruptcy Code § 544(a) the trustee in bankruptcy is given the rights and powers of a hypothetical creditor who obtains a judicial lien at the date of bankruptcy, and the trustee may avoid any transfer of property of the debtor that is avoidable by such a judicial lien creditor. The effect of § 9–301 and Bankruptcy Code § 544(a) is to make any unperfected security interest unenforceable in bankruptcy. The bulk of litigation concerning UCC security interests takes place in the federal bankrupcty courts. The adversaries are the secured party claiming the right under the Bankruptcy Code to remove the collateral from the debtor's estate and the trustee in bankruptcy seeking to avoid the security interest and to relegate the secured party to the status of an unsecured creditor.

The trustee in bankruptcy represents the debtor's unsecured creditors and the issue of the validity in bankruptcy of the security interest may have great impact on how the bankrupt debtor's assets are distributed, for a valid security interest has absolute priority in bankruptcy. It is not uncommon for secured creditors to claim all the assets in the debtor's bankruptcy estate, leaving nothing for unsecured creditors who may have extended vitally needed credit to the debtor.

Bankruptcy law has as one of its goals the equitable distribution of the debtor's estate. The drafters of Article 9 had as one of their goals that it should be easy for the parties to create valid security interests in any of the debtor's personal property. In the following cases we see what happens when these goals collide.

B. THE SECURITY AGREEMENT

Section 9–203(1)(a) provides that a security interest cannot attach until either the "debtor has signed a security agreement which contains a description of the collateral" or the secured party has taken possession of the collateral as in a pledge. Section 9–105(1)(*l*) defines "security agreement" as "an agreement which creates or provides for a security interest." Since the debtor cannot sign an agreement unless it is in writing, § 9–203(1)(a) is described in Comment 5 as "in the nature of a Statute of Frauds." This Comment notes that "this Article reduces formal requisites to a minimum" and refers to the requirement of a signed writing as a "simple formality." Nevertheless, the written security agreement requirement has generated much litigation. *Bollinger,* below, discusses the various views taken by the courts on this issue.

IN RE BOLLINGER CORP.

United States Court of Appeals, Third Circuit, 1980.
614 F.2d 924.

ROSENN, CIRCUIT JUDGE. This appeal from a district court review of an order in bankruptcy presents a question that has troubled courts since the enactment of Article Nine of the Uniform Commercial Code (U.C.C.) governing secured transactions. Can a creditor assert a secured claim against the debtor when no formal security agreement was ever signed, but where various documents executed in connection with a loan evince an intent to create a security interest? The district court answered this question in the affirmative and permitted the creditor, Zimmerman & Jansen, to assert a secured claim against the debtor, bankrupt Bollinger Corporation in the amount of $150,000. We affirm.

I.

The facts of this case are not in dispute. Industrial Credit Company (ICC) made a loan to Bollinger Corporation (Bollinger) on January 13, 1972, in the amount of $150,000. As evidence of the loan, Bollinger executed a promissory note in the sum of $150,000 and signed a security agreement with ICC giving it a security interest in certain machinery and equipment. ICC in due course perfected its security interest in the collateral by filing a financing statement in accordance with Pennsylvania's enactment of Article Nine of the U.C.C.

Bollinger faithfully met its obligations under the note and by December 4, 1974, had repaid $85,000 of the loan leaving $65,000 in unpaid principal. Bollinger, however, required additional capital and on December 5, 1974, entered into a loan agreement with Zimmerman & Jansen, Inc. (Z & J), by which Z & J agreed to lend Bollinger $150,000. Z & J undertook as part of this transaction to pay off the $65,000 still owed to ICC in return for an assignment by ICC to Z & J of the original note and security agreement between Bollinger and ICC. Bollinger executed a promissory note to Z & J, evidencing the agreement containing the following provision:

> *Security.* This Promissory Note is secured by security interests in a certain Security Agreement between Bollinger and Industrial Credit Company * * * and in a Financing Statement filed by [ICC] * * *, and is further secured by security interests in a certain security agreement to be delivered by Bollinger to Z and J with this Promissory Note covering the identical machinery and equipment as identified in the ICC Agreement and with identical schedule attached in the principal amount of Eighty-Five Thousand Dollars. ($85,000).

No formal security agreement was ever executed between Bollinger and Z & J. Z & J did, however, in connection with the promissory note, record a new financing statement signed by Bollinger containing a detailed list of the machinery and equipment originally taken as collateral by ICC for its loan to Bollinger.

Bollinger filed a petition for an arrangement under Chapter XI of the Bankruptcy Act in March, 1975 and was adjudicated bankrupt one year later. In administrating the bankrupt's estate, the receiver sold some of Bollinger's equipment but agreed that Z & J would receive a $10,000 credit on its secured claim.

Z & J asserted a secured claim against the bankrupt in the amount of $150,000, arguing that although it never signed a security agreement with Bollinger, the parties had intended that a security interest in the sum of $150,000 be created to protect the loan. The trustee in bankruptcy conceded that the assignment to Z & J of ICC's original security agreement with Bollinger gave Z & J a secured claim in the amount of $65,000, the balance owed by Bollinger to ICC at the time of the assignment. The trustee, however, refused to recognize Z & J's asserted claim of an additional secured claim of $85,000 because of the absence of a security agreement between Bollinger and Z & J. The bankruptcy court agreed and entered judgment for Z & J in the amount of $55,000, representing a secured claim in the amount of $65,000 less $10,000 credit received by Z & J.

Z & J appealed to the United States District Court for the Western District of Pennsylvania, which reversed the bankruptcy court and entered judgment for Z & J in the full amount of the asserted $150,000 secured claim. The trustee in bankruptcy appeals.

II.

Under Article Nine of the U.C.C., two documents are generally required to create a perfected security interest in a debtor's collateral. First, there must be a "security agreement" giving the creditor an interest in the collateral. Section 9–203(1)(b) contains minimal requirements for the creation of a security agreement. In order to create a security agreement, there must be: (1) a writing (2) signed by the debtor (3) containing a description of the collateral or the types of collateral. Section 9–203, Comment 1. The requirements of section 9–203(1)(b) further two basic policies. First, an evidentiary function is served by requiring a signed security agreement and second, a written agreement also obviates any Statute of Frauds problems with the debtor-creditor relationship. Id. Comments 3, 5. The second document generally required is a "financing statement," which is a document signed by both parties and filed for public record. The financing statement

This is wrong

This is wrong, may be

There may not a security int

serves the purpose of giving public notice to other creditors that a security interest is claimed in the debtor's collateral.

Despite the minimal formal requirements set forth in section 9–203 for the creation of a security agreement, the commercial world has frequently neglected to comply with this simple Code provision. Soon after Article Nine's enactment, creditors who had failed to obtain formal security agreements, but who nevertheless had obtained and filed financing statements, sought to enforce secured claims. Under section 9–402, a security agreement may serve as a financing statement if it is signed by both parties. The question arises whether the converse is true: Can a signed financing statement operate as a security agreement? The earliest case to consider this question was American Card Co. v. H.M.H. Co., 97 R.I. 59, 196 A.2d 150, 152 (1963) which held that a financing statement could *not* operate as a security agreement because there was no language *granting* a security interest to a creditor. Although section 9–203(1)(b) makes no mention of such a grant language requirement, the court in *American Card* thought that implicit in the definition of "security agreement" under section 9–105(1)(h) was such a requirement; some grant language was necessary to "create or provide security." This view also was adopted by the Tenth Circuit in Shelton v. Erwin, 472 F.2d 1118, 1120 (10th Cir. 1973). Thus, under the holdings of these cases, the creditor's assertion of a secured claim must fall in the absence of language connoting a grant of a security interest.

The Ninth Circuit in In re Amex-Protein Development Corp., 504 F.2d 1056 (9th Cir. 1974), echoed criticism by commentators of the *American Card* rule. The court wrote: "There is no support in legislative history or grammatical logic for the substitution of the word 'grant' for the phrase 'creates or provides for'." Id. at 1059–60. It concluded that as long as the financing statement contains a description of the collateral signed by the debtor, the financing statement may serve as the security agreement and the formal requirements of section 9–203(1)(b) are met. The tack pursued by the Ninth Circuit is supported by legal commentary on the issue. See G. Gilmore, Security Interests in Personal Property, § 11.4 at 347–48 (1965).

Some courts have declined to follow the Ninth Circuit's liberal rule allowing the financing statement alone to stand as the security agreement, but have permitted the financing statement, when read in conjunction with other documents executed by the parties, to satisfy the requirements of section 9–203(1)(b). The court in In re Numeric Corp., 485 F.2d 1328 (1st Cir. 1973) held that a financing statement coupled with a board of directors' resolution revealing an intent to create a security interest were sufficient to act as a security agreement. The court concluded from its reading of the Code that there appears no need to insist upon a separate document entitled "security agreement" as a prerequisite for an otherwise valid security interest.

> A writing or writings, regardless of label, which adequately describes the collateral, carries the signature of the debtor, and establishes that in fact a security interest was agreed upon, would satisfy both the formal requirements of the statute and the policies behind it.

Id. at 1331. The court went on to hold that "although a standard form financing statement by itself cannot be considered a security agreement, an adequate agreement can be found when a financing statement is considered together with other documents." Id. at 1332. * * *

More recently, the Supreme Court of Maine in Casco Bank & Trust Co. v. Cloutier, 398 A.2d 1224, 1231–32 (Me.1979) considered the question of whether composite documents were sufficient to create a security interest within the terms of the Code. Writing for the court, Justice Wernick allowed a financing statement to be joined with a promissory note for purposes of determining whether the note contained an adequate description of the collateral to create a security agreement. The court indicated that the evidentiary and Statute of Frauds policies behind section 9–203(1)(b) were satisfied by reading the note and financing statement together as the security agreement.

In the case before us, the district court went a step further and held that the promissory note executed by Bollinger in favor of Z & J, standing alone, was sufficient to act as the security agreement between the parties. In so doing, the court implicitly rejected the *American Card* rule requiring grant language before a security agreement arises under section 9–203(1)(b). The parties have not referred to any Pennsylvania state cases on the question and our independent research has failed to uncover any. But although we agree that no formal grant of a security interest need exist before a security agreement arises, we do not think that the promissory note standing alone would be sufficient under Pennsylvania law to act as the security agreement. We believe, however, that the promissory note, read in conjunction with the financing statement duly filed and supported, as it is here, by correspondence during the course of the transaction between the parties, would be sufficient under Pennsylvania law to establish a valid security agreement.

III.

We think Pennsylvania courts would accept the logic behind the First and Ninth Circuit rule and reject the *American Card* rule imposing the requirement of a formal grant of a security interest before a security agreement may exist. When the parties have neglected to sign a separate security agreement, it would appear that the better and more practical view is to look at the transaction as a whole in order to determine if there is a writing, or writings, signed by the debtor describing the collateral which demonstrates an intent to create a security interest in the collateral.[4] In connection with Z & J's loan of $150,000 to Bollinger, the relevant writings to be considered are: (1) the promissory note; (2) the financing statement; (3) a group of letters constituting the course of dealing between the parties. The district court focused solely on the promissory note finding it sufficient to constitute the security agreement. Reference, however, to the language in the note reveals that the note standing alone cannot serve as the security agreement. The note recites that along with the assigned 1972 security agreement between Bollinger and ICC, the Z & J loan is "further secured by security interests in a certain Security Agreement *to be delivered* by Bollinger to Z & J with this Promissory Note, * * *. (Emphasis added.) The bankruptcy judge correctly reasoned that "[t]he intention to create a separate security agreement negates any inference that the debtor intended that the promissory note constitute the security agreement." At best, the note is some evidence that a security agreement was contemplated by the parties, but by its own terms, plainly indicates that it is not the security agreement.

Looking beyond the promissory note, Z & J did file a financing statement signed by Bollinger containing a detailed list of all the collateral intended to secure the $150,000 loan to Bollinger. The financing statement alone meets the basic section 9–203(1)(b) requirements of a writing, signed by the debtor, describing the collateral. However, the financing statement provides only an inferential basis for concluding that the parties intended a security agreement. There would be little reason to file such a detailed financing statement unless the parties intended to create a security interest.[5] The intention of the parties to create a security interest may be gleaned from the expression of future intent to create one in the promissory note and the intention of the parties as expressed in letters constituting their course of dealing.

The promissory note was executed by Bollinger in favor of Z & J in December 1974. Prior to the consummation of the loan, Z &

4. We do not intend in anyway to encourage the commercial community to dispense with signing security agreements as a normal part of establishing a secured transaction. Lawsuits over the existence of a security agreement may be avoided by executing a separate security agreement conforming to the minimal requirements of section 9–203(1)(b). Our decision today only predicts, after our examination of the relevant case law, that Pennsylvania courts would adopt a pragmatic view of the issue raised here and recognize the intention of the parties expressed in the composite documents and not exalt form over substance.

5. Z & J would not have had to file a financing statement for the $65,000 covered by the 1972 security agreement between ICC and Bollinger, inasmuch as the assignee of a security interest is protected by the assignor's filing. Section 9–302(2).

J sent a letter to Bollinger on May 30, 1974, indicating that the loan would be made "provided" Bollinger secured the loan by a mortgage on its machinery and equipment. Bollinger sent a letter to Z & J on September 19, 1974, indicating:

> With your [Z & J's] stated desire to obtain security for material and funds advanced, it would appear that the use of the note would answer both our problems. Since the draft forwarded to you offers full collateralization for the funds to be advanced under it and bears normal interest during its term, it should offer you maximum security.

Subsequent to the execution of the promissory note, Bollinger sent to Z & J a list of the equipment and machinery intended as collateral under the security agreement which was to be, but never was, delivered to Z & J. In November 1975, the parties exchanged letters clarifying whether Bollinger could substitute or replace equipment in the ordinary course of business without Z & J's consent. Such a clarification would not have been necessary had a security interest not been intended by the parties. Finally, a letter of November 18, 1975, from Bollinger to Z & J indicated that "any attempted impairment of the collateral would constitute an event of default."

From the course of dealing between Z & J and Bollinger, we conclude there is sufficient evidence that the parties intended a security agreement to be created separate from the assigned ICC agreement with Bollinger. All the evidence points towards the intended creation of such an agreement and since the financing statement contains a detailed list of the collateral, signed by Bollinger, we hold that a valid Article Nine security agreement existed under Pennsylvania law between the parties which secured Z & J in the full amount of the loan to Bollinger.

IV.

The minimal formal requirements of section 9–203(1)(b) were met by the financing statement and the promissory note, and the course of dealing between the parties indicated the intent to create a security interest. The judgment of the district court recognizing Z & J's secured claim in the amount of $150,000 will be affirmed.

NOTE

A gross characterization of the conflict in the decisions regarding the existence of a valid security agreement follows:

The pro-secured-creditor view: The requirement of a written security agreement is merely evidentiary. If the creditor advances money to a debtor and the debtor signs a promissory note and a financing statement describing the collateral, this is enough to show intent to create a security interest; no additional formal security agreement is needed. Why else would the parties have done this unless they were entering into a secured transaction? *American Card* and its ilk are throwbacks to rigid, formalistic pre-Code thinking. *Bollinger* recognizes the clear intent of the parties even though the creditor was a little careless.

The pro-trustee-in-bankruptcy view: The secured creditor has a very strong position against other creditors in bankruptcy. Recognition of the security interest may clean out the bankrupt's estate, leaving nothing for others. Article 9 has made the formal requirements for creating a security so simple that Comment 5 to § 9–203 tells us that creditors no longer need the assistance that courts traditionally gave under the doctrine of equitable mortgages by which they upheld the validity of security interests even though the parties had failed to meet some formal requirement to validity. Since the Article 9 requirements for creating an enforceable security agreement are so minimal and the benefits conferred by secured-creditor status are so conspicuous, we should demand the creditor who seeks these benefits to comply clearly with these requirements. *American Card* merely requires that the writing contain some words unequivocally granting a security interest to the creditor. *Bollinger* is wrong in protecting the negligent creditor by finding a security agreement when the promissory note stated that a security agreement would subsequently be delivered to the debtor and none was. This is latter-day equitable mortgage thinking.

Most courts have adopted the pro-secured-creditor view as indicated in the authorities cited in *Bollinger.* See White & Summers, Uniform Commercial Code § 22–3 (3d ed. 1988).

MATTER OF MARTIN GRINDING & MACHINE WORKS, INC.

United States Court of Appeals, Seventh Circuit, 1986.
793 F.2d 592.

ESCHBACH, SENIOR CIRCUIT JUDGE.

The primary issue presented by this appeal is whether, under the Illinois Uniform Commercial Code, loan documents can supplement a security agreement to create a security interest in property inadvertently omitted from the security agreement's enumeration of secured collateral. The bankruptcy court dismissed a secured party's claim of a security interest in property not described in the security agreement. The district court affirmed the dismissal. For the reasons stated below, we hold that the loan documents cannot expand the scope of the security agreement and will affirm the district court's judgment.

I

In 1977 Martin Grinding & Machine Works, Inc. ("debtor") received a Small Business Administration ("SBA") guaranteed loan in the amount of $350,000 from Forest Park National Bank ("Bank"). In return, the debtor executed a security agreement dated October 7, 1977, granting the Bank a security interest in the debtor's machinery, equipment, furniture, and fixtures. The security agreement, however, inadvertently omitted inventory and accounts receivable from its description of the secured collateral. In addition to the security agreement, the debtor executed other loan documents (collectively referred to as "loan documents"),[1] each of which included inventory and accounts receivable as secured property.

In 1981 the debtor obtained a second SBA guaranteed loan from the Bank. This loan, in the amount of $233,000, also was secured by the October 7, 1977, security agreement.

In 1983 the debtor petitioned for voluntary reorganization under Chapter 11 of the Bankruptcy Code. The debtor denied that the Bank held a security interest in its inventory and accounts receivable. The Bank filed a complaint in bankruptcy court to determine the extent of the security interest. The bankruptcy court granted the debtor's motion to dismiss the complaint for failure to state a claim upon which relief could be granted. * * * The district court affirmed in an unpublished opinion. The Bank now appeals.

* * * The parties agree that the debtor has signed a security agreement, that value has been given, and that the debtor has rights in its inventory and accounts receivable. Moreover, they agree that the loan documents provided for a security interest in the debtor's inventory and accounts receivable, and that the security agreement did not describe inventory and accounts receivable as secured collateral. They, however, differ as to whether the Bank's security interest extends to collateral beyond that described in the security agreement to include inventory and accounts receivable. The Bank argues that the loan documents must be considered in determining the scope of its security interest. We disagree.

Allis–Chalmers Corp. v. Staggs, 117 Ill.App.3d 428, 432, 453 N.E.2d 145, 148 (1983), holds "that a broader description of collateral in a financing statement is ineffective to extend a security

---

1. The additional loan documents that described the debtor's inventory and accounts receivable as secured collateral were: (1) a SBA Authorization and Loan Agreement, dated October 7, 1977; (2) the debtor's Corporate Resolution, dated October 7, 1977; (3) a Note in the Principal Sum of $350,000, dated October 7, 1977; (4) an Authorization and Loan Agreement, dated February 24, 1981; (5) the debtor's Corporate Resolution, dated March 10, 1981; and (6) a Note in the Principal Sum of $233,000, dated March 20, 1981.

interest beyond that stated in the security agreement." In reaching this result, the court relied upon § 9–201, which provides that a security agreement is effective according to *its* terms, and upon § 9–203(1)(a), which states that a security interest is not effective against the debtor or third parties unless the debtor has signed a security agreement that contains a description of the collateral. 117 Ill.App.3d at 432, 453 N.E.2d at 148. The court reasoned that "a security interest cannot exist in the absence of a security agreement * * *, and it follows that a security interest is limited to property described in the security agreement." It also relied upon the Illinois Code Comment to § 9–110, which states that "[t]he security agreement and the financing statement are double screens through which the secured party's rights to collateral are viewed, and his rights are measured by the narrower of the two." We, therefore, conclude that, under Illinois law, a security interest attaches only to property described in the security agreement. Because the October 7, 1977, security agreement did not include inventory and accounts receivable, the Bank does not hold a security interest in this property.

* * *

Bank argues that, although the plaintiff in *Allis–Chalmers* relied upon only the financing statement to expand the scope of the security interest, the Bank relies not only upon the financing statement, but also upon the other loan documents. Nevertheless, *Allis–Chalmers*'s holding that a financing statement cannot extend a security interest beyond that stated in the security agreement is only an application of the general rule that parol evidence [2] cannot enlarge an unambiguous security agreement.

* * *

The October 7, 1977, security agreement is unambiguous on its face: it grants the Bank "a security interest in all machinery, equipment, furniture and fixtures * * * now owned and hereafter acquired by Debtor for use in Debtor's business, including without limitation the items described on Schedule 'A' attached hereto, together with all replacements thereof and all attachments, accessories and equipment now or hereafter installed therein or attached thereto." That the security agreement omits any mention of inventory and accounts receivable as secured collateral is unfortunate for the Bank, but does not make the agreement ambiguous. Since the security agreement is unambiguous on its face, neither the financing statement, nor the other loan documents can expand the Bank's security interest beyond that stated in the security agreement.

* * *

Thus, Illinois law provides that a security interest attaches to, and is enforceable against the debtor or a third party with respect

---

2. We use parol evidence to mean extrinsic evidence, whether oral or written. See 9 J. Wigmore, Evidence § 2400(2) (Chadbourn rev. 1981).

to, only property identified by the security agreement as secured collateral. This rule, however, works a result that is contrary to the parties' intentions when the parties agree that certain property would secure a loan, but the creditor inadvertently omits the property from the security agreement's enumeration of secured collateral.[3] We, therefore, might inquire what is the rule's rationale.

One answer, which was adopted by *Allis–Chalmers,* 117 Ill. App.3d at 432, 453 N.E.2d at 843–44, and the district court, is based upon the statutory definition of and requirements for a security agreement. A security agreement is "an agreement which creates or provides for a security interest." § 9–105(1). The agreement must be reduced to writing and must describe the secured collateral. § 9–203(1)(a). Therefore, if the written security agreement does not provide for a security interest in inventory and accounts receivable, then a security interest in inventory and accounts receivable does not exist. Although dictated by the statutory language, this answer does not consider the rule's effect upon commercial transactions.

Another answer, which was given by the bankruptcy court, see *Martin Grinding & Machine Works, Inc.,* 42 B.R. at 891–92, is that the rule promotes economy and certainty in secured transactions. The aim of Article 9 is to enable "the immense variety of present-day secured financing transactions * * * [to] go forward with less cost and with greater certainty." § 9–101 Uniform Commercial Code Comment. Accordingly, a purpose of the requisites for a security interest stated in § 9–203 is "evidentiary." § 9–203 Uniform Commercial Code Comment 3. "The requirement of [a] written record minimizes the possibility of future dispute as to the terms of a security agreement and as to what property stands as collateral for the obligation secured." Id.

The Code contemplates that a subsequent creditor that is considering extending credit to a debtor will examine any financing statements filed under the debtor's name to determine whether the debtor's property might be subject to a prior security interest. * * * If a financing statement gives notice of a prior

---

3. Indeed, the effect of excluding property from the security agreement's description of secured collateral is harsher than that of omitting such property from the financing statement's description of secured collateral. If the description of collateral contained in the security agreement is *narrower* than that in the financing statement, a security interest does not attach to the omitted property. Thus, a security interest would not be enforceable against either the debtor or a third party. However, if the description of collateral contained in the security agreement is *broader* than that in the financing statement, then a security interest would seem to attach to the omitted property, but would be unperfected. See B. Clark, The Law of Secured Transactions Under the Uniform Commercial Code ¶ 2.2[3], at S2–15 (1985 cumulative supp. no. 2). In this event, a security interest in the omitted property would be enforceable against the debtor, but would be subordinate to a third party's subsequently perfected security interest.

security interest, then the subsequent creditor can examine the security agreement to determine what property secures the debtor's existing obligations. The description of the secured collateral contained in the security agreement might be narrower than that in the financing statement.[4] Since parol evidence cannot enlarge a security interest beyond that stated by an unambiguous security agreement, then the subsequent creditor can rely upon the face of the security agreement to determine what property is subject to a prior security agreement.

However, if parol evidence could enlarge an unambiguous security agreement, then a subsequent creditor could not rely upon the face of an unambiguous security agreement to determine whether the property described in the financing statement, but not the security agreement, is subject to a prior security interest. Instead, it would have to consult the underlying loan documents to attempt to ascertain the property in which the prior secured party had taken a security interest. The examination of additional documents, which the admission of parol evidence would require, would increase the cost of, and inject uncertainty as to the scope of prior security interests, into secured transactions. * * * Therefore, although the rule excluding parol evidence works results contrary to the parties' intentions in particular cases, it reduces the cost and uncertainty of secured transactions generally.

We, therefore, conclude that the Bank does not hold a security interest in the debtor's inventory and accounts receivable. The district court thus correctly affirmed the bankruptcy court's dismissal of the Bank's claim.

NOTE

How can *Martin Grinding* be reconciled with *Bollinger?* In In re Maddox, 92 B.R. 707 (Bkrtcy.Tex.1988), there was no document entitled "security agreement." The court upheld the security interest under the *Bollinger* "composite document rule" by relying on the promissory note, financing statement, loan agreement, and

---

4. The discrepancy between the financing statement's and security agreement's descriptions of secured collateral might be inadvertent. Either the financing statement might have inadvertently included property that the parties did not intend would serve as secured collateral, or, as happened here, the security agreement might have accidentally omitted property that the parties intended would secure the obligation. The difference might also be intentional. The prior secured party might have filed a broad financing statement before it and the debtor agreed what property would secure the obligation in order to protect the priority of its security interest. * * * The prior secured party and the debtor might then agree that the obligation would be secured by only some of the property described in the financing statement. Therefore, that the description of secured collateral contained in the security agreement is narrower than that in the financing statement does not necessarily mean that the security agreement inadvertently omitted property that the parties had agreed would secure an obligation.

corporate resolution to show evidence of an agreement. The court distinguished *Martin Grinding* as follows:

> The parol evidence rule applied in *Martin Grinding* does not allow oral evidence or prior written evidence to vary the terms of a written agreement which the court has determined the parties intended as the full and final expression of their agreement. In *Martin Grinding* there was a written security agreement granting a security interest in four broad categories (machinery, equipment, furniture, fixtures). The financing statement covered these categories *and* inventory and accounts receivable. Because of the parol evidence rule, the written financing statement could not be used to vary the terms of the written security agreement. Martin Grinding & Machine Works, 793 F.2d 592 (7th Cir.1986). In the case before the Court, there is no single written agreement which the parties intended as the full and final expression of their agreement. Thus *Martin Grinding* and the parol evidence rule are inapplicable.

92 B.R. at 711–712.

C. DESCRIPTION OF THE COLLATERAL

---

1. SECURITY AGREEMENT

Section 9–203(1)(a) provides that the security agreement must contain a "description of the collateral." The bias of the Code toward a liberal interpretation of descriptions of collateral is set out in § 9–110, stating that "any description of personal property or real estate is sufficient whether or not it is specific if it reasonably identifies what is described," and in the Comment to that section which rejects the view "that descriptions are insufficient unless they are of the most exact and detailed nature, the so-called 'serial number' test." By and large the courts have gone along with this bias toward upholding descriptions of collateral.

Generic descriptions. Article 9 classifies the kinds of personal property collateral in generic categories: § 9–105 ("chattel paper," "deposit account," "document," "goods," "instrument"); § 9–106 ("account," "general intangibles"); § 9–109 ("consumer goods," "equipment," "farm products," "inventory"); § 9–306 ("proceeds"); § 9–313 ("fixtures"). These generic terms are so fundamental to the operation of Article 9 that the neophyte drafter sometimes believes that no description of collateral is complete without categorizing the collateral by use of one of the generic terms. This is not true. Whether generic descriptions are appropriate depends on whether they identify the collateral intended to be covered by the security interest. If a dealer in business machines sells a machine to a buyer in an isolated transaction and takes a security interest in the machine sold, the requirements of § 9–203(1)(a) are met by a specific description of the machine: kind of machine, brand name, model number, and so forth. There is no need to add the generic term "equipment" to the description. If the machine sold is described in the security agreement solely by the term "equipment," it is usually not adequately identified; the buyer may have several other items of equipment. Generic descriptions in a security agreement are accurate identifiers if the debtor grants a security interest in all its property within the generic category, "all inventory," or all of a specified kind of property within that category, "all inventory consisting of General Electric manufactured appliances." A typical description would be "all equipment located at debtor's place of business, including but not limited to the following:"

After-acquired collateral. Under Article 9 a security interest may not only apply to the collateral the debtor owns at the time the security interest is granted but also to later acquired collateral. Under § 9–204 no new security agreement is necessary when the collateral is later acquired if the security agreement provides that it applies to after-acquired collateral. In transactions like inventory financing in which goods are sold and replaced, or accounts financing in which accounts are collected and replaced, it is important that the security agreement cover later acquired inventory or accounts, lest the collateral liquidate over time leaving the secured creditor with a claim only to proceeds. In the usual inventory or accounts financing transactions the description of the collateral will include a phrase like "now owned or hereafter acquired." When the parties have left out after-acquired property clauses in situations like inventory or accounts financing transactions in which it is likely that they intended to include them, the courts have sometimes been willing to imply them. In American Employers Insurance Co. v. American Security Bank, 747 F.2d 1493 (D.C.Cir.1984), the court said "It is reasonable to read a security agreement granting an interest in all inventory or receivables to include after-acquired inventory or receivables." 747 F.2d at 1501. On the other hand, in In re Middle Atlantic Stud Welding Co., 503 F.2d 1133 (3d Cir.1974), in which the security agreement and the financing statement both described the collateral as "all of the debtor's accounts receivable," the court held that the security agreement did not cover after-acquired accounts because it would have been so easy for the secured party to refer explicitly to after-acquired property that the court should require it to do so. There was a strong dissent. In a case involving livestock collateral, the words "any and all increases, additions, accessions, substitutions and proceeds" were held to include after-acquired property in In re Grey, 902 F.2d 1479 (10th Cir.1990). The court said: "The fact that this security agreement provided a security interest in property which by its very nature rotated constantly and accordingly required a monthly update of the inventory of hogs * * * establishes the parties' intent to include after-acquired property * * *." 902 F.2d at 1481. On the other hand, in Graphic Resources, Inc. v. Thiebauth, 233 Neb. 592, 447 N.W.2d 28 (1989), in which the collateral was described as "All of Debtor's equipment, including replacement parts, additions, repairs, and accessories incorporated therein or affixed thereto," the court declined to hold that after-acquired property was covered.

Proceeds. "Proceeds" is defined as including "whatever is received upon the sale, exchange, collection or other disposition of collateral or proceeds." § 9–306(1). An earlier version of § 9–203 could have been read as requiring that the security agreement refer to proceeds if the intent of the parties was to include proceeds in the property covered by the security interest. In the 1972 amendments this provision was deleted and § 9–203(3) was added on the assumption that the parties intend to cover proceeds unless otherwise agreed. Section 9–306(2) provides that a security interest in collateral automatically passes to the proceeds of the disposition of that collateral.

PROBLEMS

The following fact situations are based on two cases that were decided by the same court with opinions by the same judge. He upheld the validity of the collateral description in one case and rejected it in the other. In your view which is the more vulnerable description? Can you distinguish the cases?

1. The security agreement granted a security interest in certain specifically described items, including an International truck, and contained the following omnibus clause:

> In addition to all the above enumerated items, it is the intention that this mortgage shall cover all chattels, machinery, equipment, tables, chairs, work benches, factory chairs, stools, shelving, cabinets, power lines, switch boxes, control panels, machine parts, motors, pumps, electrical equipment, measuring and calibrating instruments, office supplies, sundries, office furniture, fixtures, and all other items of equipment and fixtures belonging to the mortgagor, whether herein enumerated or not, now at the plant of [Debtor] located at 115–02 15th Ave. College Point, New York, and all chattels, machinery, fixtures, or equipment that may hereafter be brought in or installed in said premises or any new premises of the mortgagor, to replace, substitute for, or in addition to the above mentioned chattels and equipment with the exception of stock in trade.

The issue was whether the omnibus clause covered two Oldsmobile automobiles used in Debtor's business. The clause covered "equipment," a term defined in § 9–109(2). The two automobiles clearly are within the UCC definition. See In re Laminated Veneers Co., Inc., 471 F.2d 1124 (2d Cir. 1973).

2. The security agreement described the collateral as the following:

Items	Location, etc.
Machinery, equipment and fixtures; Molds, tools, dies, component parts including specifically the:	To be located either at the Debtor's plant in North Bergen, New Jersey; and in the case of the molds also at the plants of contractors who may be using said molds in the manufacture of products for the Debtor
1 x 1 two cavity cassette cover and base mold 2 x 2 four cavity cassette cover and base mold One twenty-four cavity roller mold One sixteen cavity hub mold	

The issue was whether the security agreement covered only the specifically described molds or whether it also covered other machinery and tools of the Debtor. If it were held to apply to other machinery and tools, could one identify which articles of machinery and tools were covered? See In re Sarex Corp., 509 F.2d 689 (2d Cir. 1975).

2. FINANCING STATEMENT

In order to understand the function of the description of collateral in a financing statement one must grasp the concept of notice filing. The authoritative statement on the subject is found in Comment 2 to § 9–402:

> This section adopts the system of "notice filing" which proved successful under the Uniform Trust Receipts Act. What is required to be filed is not, as under chattel mortgage and conditional sales acts, the security agreement itself, but only a simple notice which may be filed before the security interest attaches or thereafter. The notice itself indicates merely that the secured party who has filed may have a security interest in the collateral described. Further inquiry from the parties concerned will be necessary to disclose the complete state of affairs. Section 9–208 provides a statutory procedure under which the secured party, at the debtor's request, may be required to make disclosure. Notice filing has proved to be of great use in financing transactions involving inventory, accounts and chattel paper, since it obviates the necessity of refiling on each of a series of transactions in a continuing arrangement where the collateral changes from

day to day. Where other types of collateral are involved, the alternative procedure of filing a signed copy of the security agreement may prove to be the simplest solution. Sometimes more than one copy of a financing statement or of a security agreement used as a financing statement is needed for filing. In such a case the section permits use of a carbon copy or photographic copy of the paper, including signatures.

However, even in the case of filings that do not necessarily involve a series of transactions the financing statement is effective to encompass transactions under a security agreement not in existence and not contemplated at the time the notice was filed, if the description of collateral in the financing statement is broad enough to encompass them. Similarly, the financing statement is valid to cover after-acquired property and future advances under security agreements whether or not mentioned in the financing statement.

Section 9–402(1) provides that the financing statement must contain "a statement indicating the types, or describing the items, of collateral." Section 9–402(8) states "A financing statement substantially complying with the requirements of this section is effective even though it contains minor errors which are not seriously misleading." Thorp Commercial Corp. v. Northgate Industries, Inc., 654 F.2d 1245, 1248–1249 (8th Cir.1981), addresses the differing functions of descriptions of collateral in security agreements and financing statements.

> The security agreement and financing statement have different functions under the UCC. The security agreement defines what the collateral is so that, if necessary, the creditor can identify and claim it, and the debtor or other interested parties can limit the creditor's right in the collateral given as security. The security agreement must therefore describe the collateral. § 9–203(1). The financing statement, on the other hand, serves the purpose of putting subsequent creditors on notice that the debtor's property is encumbered. The description of collateral in the financing statement does not function to identify the collateral and define property which the creditor may claim, but rather to warn other subsequent creditors of the prior interest. The financing statement, which limits the prior creditor's rights vis-a-vis subsequent creditors, must therefore contain a description only of the type of collateral. § 9–402(1).

Before the UCC the secured party filed the security contract itself, e.g., the chattel mortgage agreement, to perfect a security interest, just as we record the real estate mortgage document today. The normal UCC case is one in which there are two documents, the security agreement and the financing statement. But there may be only one document, for the secured party may choose to file the security agreement as the financing statement.

Section 9–402(1) provides that a copy of the security agreement is sufficient as a financing statement if it is signed by the debtor and contains the information a financing statement is required to contain.

What is remarkable about the Code's notice filing system is how little information a financing statement—the only public document—need impart to third parties. It need only state the "types" of property covered; it need not tell where the property is kept or the amount of the indebtedness; and it may cover after-acquired property and future advances even though the financing statement never mentions these terms (Comment 2 to § 9–402), and proceeds even though the financing statement is silent on this subject as well (§ 9–306(3)(a)).

The courts have usually tested the adequacy of financing statement descriptions of collateral in the light of the purpose of notice filing. Thus, generic descriptions—"inventory," "accounts receivable," and "equipment"—have been generally approved by the cases. Given the paucity of information discoverable from the financing statement about the relationship of debtors and secured parties with respect to the type of collateral involved, how does one who wants to deal with a debtor gain the information necessary to make an informed decision?

It is clear that a potential Subsequent Creditor must learn from Debtor and Secured Party themselves what collateral is covered by the security agreement and how much debt is owing. If Debtor is seeking a loan from Subsequent Creditor, Debtor must cooperate with Subsequent Creditor who should demand to see the security agreement and note. But desperate debtors may lie and Subsequent Creditor cannot be safe without checking this information with Secured Party. However, Secured Party may have no incentive beyond business comity to make any disclosure to Subsequent Creditor.

Section 9–208 is designed to induce Secured Party to give information about its credit transaction with Debtor. Debtor may request that Secured Party approve Debtor's statement about the amount of the indebtedness and the extent of the collateral. The section imposes sanctions on Secured Party if it ignores the request. Note that this provision gives Subsequent Creditor no direct right to compel Secured Party to provide information. Only Debtor can activate the § 9–208 mechanism. Thus § 9–208 is of no use to a judgment creditor of Debtor looking for assets to seize; Debtor normally would have no interest in giving such a creditor information about Debtor's financial condition, let alone in helping the creditor gain information from Secured Creditor. Later we shall point out how limited § 9–208 is in assisting Subsequent Creditor in making credit decisions.

Would it be an abuse of the filing system if a creditor used for all its secured transactions a financing statement describing the collateral as "all of the debtor's personal property now owned or hereafter acquired"? In re JCM Cooperative, Inc., 8 UCC Rep. 247 (Bkrtcy.Mich.1970), involved a security agreement granting "a security interest * * * in the following collateral including the proceeds and products thereof: all other equipment now owned or hereafter acquired by Debtor * * * including but not limited to * * * all tangible, personal property now owned by the Debtor * * * including * * * the assets described on Schedule A attached hereto * * *." Schedule A listed items of equipment only. The financing statement described the collateral as "all tangible, personal property" of the debtor and also covered proceeds of collateral. The court held that the secured party had a perfected security interest in accounts receivable which were proceeds resulting from the sale of inventory.

In re Fuqua, 461 F.2d 1186 (10th Cir.1972), on the other hand, concerned a security agreement covering "All livestock, feed, and machinery to include but not limited to the following: [a specific enumeration of certain livestock]." The financing statement said: "This financing statement covers the following types (or items) of property: All Personal Property." The court held that the financing statement was invalid, saying "the phrase 'all personal property' does not even approach a description of property by type or description."

Can you reconcile the cases on the basis of the differences in the security agreements?

D. THE FILING SYSTEM

Section 9–303(1) provides: "A security interest is perfected when it has attached and when all of the applicable steps required for perfection have been taken. Such steps are specified in Sections 9–302, 9–304, 9–305 and 9–306. If such steps are taken before the security interest attaches, it is perfected at the time when it attaches." With respect to transactions in which the debtor is to have possession of the collateral (nonpossessory security interests), the common method of perfection is by filing a financing statement. § 9–302 and § 9–304. For transactions in which the secured party is to keep possession of the collateral—the traditional pledge transaction—the creditor's possession is sufficient public notice to perfect the security interest. § 9–305.

The kind of collateral is another variable in determining the appropriate act of perfection. In most instances a security interest in investment securities and negotiable instruments can be perfected only by possession because of their negotiable nature. § 9–304(1). At the other extreme, intangibles like accounts and general intangibles (§ 9–106) can be perfected only by filing because there is no physical embodiment of the property that can be pledged. Security interests in goods (§ 9–105(1)(h)), chattel paper (§ 9–105(1)(b)), and documents of title such as warehouse receipts and bills of lading (§ 9–105(1)(f)) may be perfected either by filing or by pledge. § 9–302(1), § 9–304(1) and § 9–305.

Still another variable is the purpose of the secured transaction. A purchase money security interest in consumer goods (with some exceptions) is perfected at the moment it attaches with no further act of filing or possession required. § 9–302(1)(d). Other secured transactions are outside the Code filing system because either the state or federal government maintains a separate registry for the transactions in question—state motor vehicle registration acts and the federal aircraft registration law are examples. § 9–302(3).

1. NAME OF DEBTOR

PEARSON v. SALINA COFFEE HOUSE, INC.

United States Court of Appeals, Tenth Circuit, 1987.
831 F.2d 1531.

STEPHEN H. ANDERSON, CIRCUIT JUDGE.

This is an appeal from the district court's reversal of an order by the bankruptcy court. The sole issue is whether the UCC–1 financing statements, filed by the appellant, Salina Coffee House ("SCH"), which listed the debtor, Beacon Realty Investment Company of Salina, d/b/a Hilton Inn ("Beacon"), under its trade name rather than under its legal name, are effective to protect SCH's security interest against a challenge by the debtor's trustee in bankruptcy. The district court, reversing the bankruptcy court, held that SCH's security interest was unperfected. We affirm.

SCH sold furnishings and kitchen equipment on credit to the debtor, Beacon, on several different occasions. On each occasion, SCH filed a financing statement covering the furnishings and equipment as required under § 9–402, except that it filed only in the debtor's trade name "Hilton Inn" and not in the debtor's partnership name, Beacon Realty Investment Company of Salina.

The parties stipulated to the facts. Under these facts, there is no evidence that Beacon ever did business in the partnership name or any trade name other than Hilton Inn. SCH was unaware of the existence of the partnership and assumed that Hilton Inn was a legal entity. All of the sales contracts and loan documentation between SCH and Beacon listed the purchaser/debtor as "Hilton Inn" and were signed by the hotel manager.

From 1981 until 1983, Beacon made payments, as Hilton Inn, to SCH in accordance with the sales contract. On December 8,

1983, Beacon filed a Chapter 11 bankruptcy petition which was later voluntarily converted to a Chapter 7 proceeding. John Pearson, the appointed trustee, filed a complaint challenging the validity of SCH's lien covering the equipment and furnishings sold to the Hilton Inn. Pearson claimed that the security interest held by SCH was unperfected because the financing statements listed Beacon's trade name without including the partnership's legal name. Pearson argued that since SCH's interest was unperfected, his statutory rights as trustee were superior to SCH's.

SCH responded that even if a creditor must generally file in the debtor's legal name, § 9–402(8) permits "minor errors which are not seriously misleading." It argued that the Hilton Inn trade name filing was not "seriously misleading" because Beacon had consistently and exclusively held itself out to the public under that trade name.

The bankruptcy court ruled that, under the conditions of this case, it was sufficient to file only in the trade name since "in an equity sense it seems extremely harsh to penalize Salina Coffee for failing to file in the undisclosed and unknown name of the partnership." Pearson v. Salina Coffee House, Inc. (In re Beacon Realty Inv. Co.), 44 B.R. 875, 879 (Bankr.D.Kan.1984), rev'd, 61 B.R. 538 (D.Kan.1986). The district court reversed, holding that allowing a creditor to file only in a trade name would place an impermissible burden "upon potential creditors to ascertain and search any number of trade names that may be used by a single debtor." Pearson v. Salina Coffee House, Inc., 61 B.R. 538, 541 (D.Kan.1986). The district court further held that the fact that no creditors were actually misled was not determinative since the trustee in bankruptcy is treated as an ideal hypothetical lien claimant as of the date of the bankruptcy and has priority over any unperfected interest.

The Bankruptcy Code confers on a trustee in bankruptcy the same rights that an ideal hypothetical lien claimant without notice possesses as of the date the bankruptcy petition is filed. 11 U.S.C. § 544(a). Section 544(a) allows the trustee to avoid any unperfected liens on property belonging to the bankruptcy estate. Under this provision, SCH will be an unsecured creditor in the debtor's bankruptcy unless its security interest in the debtor's furnishings and equipment was properly perfected.

Although the rights of the trustee as a lien creditor are governed by federal law, our determination of whether SCH possesses a perfected security interest which has priority over the trustee as a lien creditor is controlled by Kansas state law. * * * Kansas has adopted the UCC which requires that SCH file a financing statement to perfect its security interest in the furniture and equipment it sold to Beacon. The formal requirements concerning the contents of a financing statement are set forth in § 9–402. Subsection (7) provides:

> A financing statement sufficiently shows the name of the debtor if it gives the individual, partnership or corporate name of the debtor, whether or not it adds other trade names or the names of partners.

SCH correctly argues that this provision does not expressly answer whether filing solely in the debtor's trade name may also be sufficient under some circumstances.[1] The Official UCC Comment suggests that a trade name is not sufficient:

> Subsection (7) undertakes to deal with some of the problems as to who is the debtor. In the case of individuals, it contemplates filing only in the individual name, not in a trade name. In the case of partnerships it contemplates filing in the partnership name, not in the names of any of the partners, and not in any other trade names. Trade names are deemed to be too uncertain and too likely not to be known to the secured party or person searching the record, to form the basis for a filing system.[2]

Section 9–402 Official Comment 7 (1983). SCH argues that the Official Comment sets forth the general rule to which there are exceptions. The 1983 Kansas Comment to subsection (7) does not specifically mention partnerships, but it expressly rejects the sole use of the trade names of individuals and corporations:

> Perhaps the most important rule found in this subsection [(7)] is that a financing statement must be indexed in the name of the individual, not the trade name, when a sole proprietorship is involved * * *. Adding a trade name is neither necessary nor sufficient for perfection. If a corporate debtor is involved, the financing statement should show the corporate name. For example, if the debtor is the Carruthers Catfish Division of Associated Industries, Inc., the name should be shown as "Associated Industries, Inc." with an indexing following that name. See Official Comment 7. On the other hand, if a division or trade name is quite similar to the corporate name, use of the trade name in the financing statement might not be "seriously misleading" under § 9–402(8) and thus might pass muster. So it was in Records &

---

1. Without taking a position on the issue, White & Summers agree that the subsection does not answer the question of whether a trade name filing might be sufficient under some circumstances. See J. White & R. Summers, Uniform Commercial Code § 23–16, at 959 (2d ed. 1980). Prior to the 1972 revision of Article 9, § 9–402 did not expressly require any more than the signature of the debtor. Nonetheless, even under that version of the Code, courts held that the legal name was necessary. * * *

2. The Official Comment similarly rejects filings made in the trade name of a sole proprietor or a corporation. See Official Comment 7.

Tapes, Inc. v. Argus, Inc., 8 K.A.2d 255 [655 P.2d 133] (1982)
* * *.

§ 9–402, Kansas Comment 7.   Although the Kansas Comment does not discuss partnerships specifically, there is no reason to believe that the rule would be different than that for sole proprietors and corporations.   In each case, the name of the individual(s) or entity legally responsible for the debt must be used in the financing statement.

SCH argues that filing in the trade name, even if technically improper, is acceptable in this case under the provisions of subsection 9–402(8):

> A financing statement substantially complying with the requirements of this section is effective even though it contains minor errors which are not seriously misleading.[4]

§ 9–402(8).   Since the debtor has never held itself out to the public in any other name than "Hilton Inn," SCH argues that it was not seriously misleading under subsection (8) to file the financing statement in the trade name.

There are no rulings by the Kansas Supreme Court on subsections (7) and (8).   The Kansas Court of Appeals has considered these sections under circumstances where the debtor's trade name, which was similar to its corporate name, was incorrectly listed on a financing statement.   See Records & Tapes, Inc. v. Argus, Inc., 8 Kan.App.2d 255, 655 P.2d 133 (1982).   In *Records & Tapes*, the debtor's corporate name was "Argus, Inc."   Two financing statements were filed and each was secured, at least in part, by the same inventory.   The first statement was filed under the debtor's trade name, "Argus Tapes and Records."   The second statement was filed two months later under the name of "Argus, Inc. d/b/a Argus Tapes and Records."   The court held that the first financing statement, filed in the trade name, was sufficient to perfect the creditor's interest.   The court based its decision on the "minor errors" exception of subsection (8):

> If plaintiff had searched the record, it could not reasonably have been misled, and plaintiff does not claim it searched the record and was misled.   The thrust of plaintiff's argument is

---

4.   Official Comment 9 states that "[s]ubsection (8) is in line with the policy of this Article to simplify formal requisites and filing requirements and is designed to discourage the fanatical and impossibly refined reading of such statutory requirements in which courts have occasionally indulged themselves." The Kansas Comment adds that subsection (8) "embodies the notion that *de minimus* errors in a financing statement should not be fatal.   It promotes simplification and reduction of formal requisites by making financing statements effective even though they contain minor errors which are not seriously misleading to a third party searching the files * * *.   An example of a *de minimus* error might be the name of the debtor designated as 'ABC Corp.' rather than 'ABC Co., Inc.'   On the other hand, mistakenly designating 'ABC Corp.' as 'BCA Corp.' would probably be a substantial error since the indexing would be totally thrown off."

that since [the creditor] did not precisely list the debtor's exact legal name, [the creditor] had not perfected its lien and therefore plaintiff has priority. This is an oversimplification of the UCC, and we cannot agree.

Id. at 134. See also § 9–402, Kansas Comment 9 (1983). In *Records and Tapes,* the court quoted from the Fifth Circuit's decision in Brushwood v. Citizens Bank (In re Glasco, Inc.), 642 F.2d 793 (5th Cir. Unit B 1981), to support its reliance on the "minor errors" exception of subsection (8). In *Glasco,* the court held that filing under the trade name "Elite Boats Division of Glasco, Inc." as opposed to the legal corporate name "Glasco, Inc." was not seriously misleading. In a split decision, the court acknowledged that the filing was not cross-indexed under Glasco, Inc., but emphasized that the debtor did business only in the trade name. The court concluded that the filing was not misleading because a reasonably prudent creditor would have searched under the trade name as well as the legal corporate name. Id. at 1325.

Two years after the *Glasco* decision, the Fifth Circuit in National Bank v. West Texas Wholesale Supply Co. (In re McBee), 714 F.2d 1316 (5th Cir.1983), held that a filing under the trade name of a sole proprietor was sufficient under the facts of the case to perfect the security interest. In *McBee,* National Bank made a loan secured by the inventory of the business and filed its financing statement solely under the trade name "Oak Hill Gun Shop." Subsequent to this loan, two other lenders made loans secured by inventory in which they each filed a financing statement which included the legal name of the sole proprietor. McBee, the owner of the gunshop, later filed for bankruptcy and the trustee argued that National Bank's security interest in inventory was unperfected. Relying heavily on *Glasco,* the court held that the filing was not seriously misleading and, therefore, that National Bank's interest was perfected. Id. at 1325. Since it was first to file, National was given priority over the trustee and the other two creditors with perfected security interests.

Without citing *Tapes & Records* or the Kansas Comment, SCH bases its argument that its interest is perfected almost exclusively upon *Glasco* and *McBee. Tapes and Records* quoted from *Glasco* to support its conclusion that the filing under Argus Tapes and Records was not seriously misleading pursuant to subsection (8). The facts of *Tapes & Records,* however, are considerably different from the facts of *Glasco.* Unlike *Glasco, Tapes & Records* involved a trade name and corporate name which both shared an identical, less common first name, making it possible to discover the trade-name filing when searching the index for the legal name. The Kansas Comment cites *Tapes and Records* approvingly for the proposition that when a trade name is similar to the corporate name it may not be seriously misleading.

However, the 1983 Kansas Comment implicitly rejects the holdings of both *Glasco* and *McBee*. *McBee* involved a filing under a sole proprietor's trade name which bore no resemblance to the owner's name. The Kansas Comment emphasizes that "perhaps the most important rule" in subsection (7) "is that a financing statement *must* be indexed in the name of the individual, not the trade name, when a sole proprietorship is involved." § 9–402, Kansas Comment 7 (emphasis added).

In *Glasco*, the creditor filed in a debtor corporation's trade name. The Kansas Comment states that "[i]f a corporate debtor is involved, the financing statement should show the corporate name." Id. The example the Comment uses looks very similar to the facts of *Glasco*, but the Comment states that the corporate name should be used under such circumstances. It then offers an example of an erroneous trade name filing which looks very much like the situation involved in *Glasco*. Id.

We agree with the district court that under Kansas law "[i]t can hardly be said to be a 'minor error' or not 'seriously misleading' when a potential creditor of Beacon Realty Investment Co. searches the index under that name and finds no notice of a security interest because that notice is filed under 'Hilton Inn.' " *Pearson,* 61 B.R. at 540–41. Subsection (7), not subsection (8), must provide the basis to support SCH's claim. If subsection (7) is interpreted as requiring use of the legal name then use of the trade name fails unless it is coincidentally similar to the legal name so as to be not "seriously misleading." If, on the other hand, subsection (7) is read as permitting use of the trade name alone under some circumstances, then it is unnecessary to invoke the saving provisions of subsection (8) since no "error" was in fact made.

The rigid requirement that a debtor's legal name be used on the financing statement furthers the objectives of the UCC filing system for secured transactions. The purpose behind the filing provisions is to provide notice to subsequent creditors in a manner which will give such creditors confidence that they are aware of any prior security interests in the collateral that may be superior to their own interest. Clarity and certainty in lien perfection requirements are lost if equitable exceptions are created which permit trade name filings to replace filings in the legal name when the "equities" so dictate. The UCC provides that filing in the debtor's legal name is sufficient notice, although a creditor may, at its option, also file in the trade name(s) of the debtor. If use of the legal name is necessary to perfect the interest, then a creditor can be confident that all security interests with priority over its own interest will be located under the same name.[9] If a

---

9. Minor errors under subsection (8) do not alter this rule since, to be a minor error, it is usually assumed that the security interest will be discovered in the course of searching under the debtor's legal name. See, e.g., In re

trade name is ever deemed to be sufficient in *any* case where it bears no similarity to the debtor's legal name, then future creditors must *always* search under any and all trade names before assuring themselves that they have discovered prior interests. This is so because they will not know at the time they file a financing statement whether the equities will be in their favor if their priority is later contested in court by a creditor who filed in a trade name prior to their filing.

This is true even in a case such as this, where the debtor ceases doing business without ever operating in a name other than its trade name. Perfection occurs at the time the financing statement is properly filed or when the debtor receives the collateral, whichever occurs last. Under the position that SCH urges us to adopt, perfection could not be determined until an after-the-fact judicial inquiry revealed that all creditors had filed in the same trade name and possibly that no other persons were aware of the legal name. This hindsight approach to perfection threatens the simplicity the system was designed to achieve.

The bankruptcy court based its opinion primarily on the equities of this case, stating that it would be "extremely harsh" and "onerous" to hold that SCH's interest is unsecured. While the fact that no other creditor was actually misled in this case makes the result seem harsh, we are equally mindful of the mischief that would be created by allowing the trade name filing to be sufficient for perfection. If a creditor sues a debtor to recover its collateral, it is expected to sue in the debtor's legal name. It is not a serious burden to require the creditor to ascertain the legal name of the debtor at the time it files a financing statement as well. If a creditor inquires of a debtor as to its legal name and is intentionally misled, a different result might be appropriate. That is not the case here. "The secured creditor, as maker of the perfecting documents, is charged with the responsibility for their compliance. Therefore, any deviation which causes these documents to be seriously misleading is the burden of the creditor to bear." In re Hinson & Hinson, Inc., 62 B.R. 964, 968 (Bankr.W.D.Penn.1986). Although the language of subsection (7) itself does not definitively answer the question before us, the Kansas Comment states strongly that use of the debtor's trade name is "neither necessary nor sufficient for perfection." We agree with that Comment.

CONCLUSION

We hold that, under Kansas law, SCH's interest is unperfected. The rights conferred by § 544 of the Bankruptcy Code

Excel Stores, Inc., 341 F.2d 961 (2d Cir. 1965) (filing in "Excel Dep't Stores" instead of "Excel Stores, Inc."); McMillin v. First Nat'l Bank & Trust Co. (In re Fowler), 407 F.Supp. 799, 803 (W.D. Okla.1975).

give the trustee the power to avoid unperfected security interests. SCH, therefore, is an unsecured creditor of the bankruptcy estate.

NOTES

1. Having the correct name of the debtor on the financing statement is crucial to the Code's notice filing system because financing statements are indexed under the debtor's name. In many cases the courts have upheld financing statements even though the secured party erred somewhat in giving the debtor's correct name. In re Excel Stores, Inc., referred to in the principal case, is prototypic. The court upheld a description of the debtor as "Excel Department Stores" instead of "Excel Stores, Inc." finding the mistake to be in the category of "minor errors which are not seriously misleading." § 9–402(8). These cases seem to carry out the intent of the drafters expressed in Comment 9 to § 9–402 to reject "the fanatical and impossibly refined reading" of statutes like that typified by the *Haley* case cited in the Comment. In *Haley* the court held defective a notice describing the debtor, "E. R. Millen Co., Inc.," as "E. R. Millen Company" and signed "E. R. Millen, Trustee." The test worked out is the sensible one of whether a reasonable search of the records for the debtor's name would have found the financing statement in question.

2. States are increasingly computerizing UCC filing records. How would the reasonable search test apply to this case? The debtor's name in the financing statement was "Tri–State Moulded Plastics, Inc." At the time of debtor's bankruptcy the correct name of the debtor was "Tri–State Molded Plastics, Inc." It is undisputed that a computer search using the correct name of the debtor ("Molded") would not, because of the way the filing officer's computer was programmed, turn up filings using the incorrect name, "Moulded." It is also clear that a reasonable manual search of the records, though not possible under state law, would turn up the financing statement in question. Under these facts, the court in In re Tyler, 23 B.R. 806 (Bkrtcy.Fla.1982), found the financing statement to be insufficient. It said:

> It is arguable that errors should be judged strictly against the secured party, exactly because so little *is* required of the creditor. Errors in the debtor's name bring in additional concerns, because the debtor's name is the basis for the indexing on which the entire noticing system relies. It would seem that the nature of the particular recordation system must be another consideration because it necessarily affects whether an error in a name is actually misleading. For example, an intelligent human looking at an alphabetical list might be expected to see similar names which are in alphabetical proximity to each other and might be expected to investigate further. But if the recording officer's records are retriev-

able only by computer matching it may be unfeasible to locate any records except those filed under the absolutely identical name under which the search is made. Where filing is required in more than one location (as with state and county offices) the systems may differ. Is a name misleading or not where it can be found in one recording office but not another?

23 B.R. at 809.

IN RE SCOTT

United States Bankruptcy Court, W.D.Arkansas, 1990.
113 B.R. 516.

JAMES G. MIXON, BANKRUPTCY JUDGE.

On November 10, 1987, The Bank of Yellville, Arkansas (Bank) filed a complaint for foreclosure * * * against Shannon D. Scott and his wife, Patricia R. Scott d/b/a K/C Audio/Video Center of Camden. On November 18, 1987, Borg–Warner Acceptance Corporation of Arkansas (Borg–Warner) intervened in the foreclosure action claiming a security interest in the same property which was subject to the foreclosure action. On November 25, 1987, Shannon and Patricia Scott filed a counterclaim against the Bank for damages allegedly resulting from the improper issuance of a prejudgment writ of attachment. On November 27, 1987, Shannon and Patricia Scott (debtors) filed a voluntary petition for relief under the provisions of chapter 7 of the United States Bankruptcy Code. On February 1, 1988, the Bank removed the state court action to the Bankruptcy Court.

* * *

The parties have presented two issues to be determined: whether Borg–Warner or the Bank has a first lien on $24,947.66 of inventory; and whether the Bank is liable for damages resulting from the issuance and execution of a wrongful attachment.

I

LIEN PRIORITIES

The debtors purchased an audio/video business located in Camden, Arkansas, in June 1985. The assets of the business, including inventory, were purchased by the debtors in their individual capacities. As part of the purchase, the debtors obtained the right to continue to use the trade name of "KC Audio Video Center of Camden." To finance the purchase of the business, the debtors borrowed the sum of $185,000.00 from the Bank and executed a note to the Bank dated June 13, 1985. The note identified "Shannon D. Scott" and "Patricia R. Scott" as the borrowers and was executed by them in their individual capacities. To secure repayment of the note, the debtors executed a security agreement and financing statement dated June 13, 1985, granting to the Bank a security interest in all inventory, accounts receivable, machinery, equipment, furniture, and fixtures "now owned or hereafter acquired for use in Debtor's business as now conducted or hereafter to be conducted." The financing statement identified the debtors as "Shannon D. Scott or Patricia R. Scott DBA K/C Audio/Video Center of Camden," and was signed by "Shannon D. Scott" and "Patricia R. Scott," individually. The financing statement was properly filed with the Secretary of State of Arkansas and the Ouachita County Circuit Clerk on June 20, 1985, and August 8, 1985, respectively. The debtors also executed an inventory security agreement which identified the borrowers as "Shannon D. Scott and Patricia R. Scott d/b/a K/C Audio/Video Center of Camden." The inventory security agreement was signed "Shannon D. Scott" and "Patricia R. Scott."

On July 12, 1985, on the advice of their accountant, the debtors formed a corporation in which to conduct their business. The corporation was named "KC of Camden, Inc." Shannon Scott testified that all of the debtors' assets used in the business were transferred to the corporation. All but one share of the stock in the new corporation was issued to Shannon and Patricia Scott.

On July 17, 1985, Shannon Scott, as president of "K.C. of Camden, Inc.," executed a security agreement in favor of Borg-Warner granting a security interest in all inventory "now or hereafter owned" by the corporation. A financing statement in the name of "K.C. of Camden, Inc." was executed by Shannon Scott and Patricia Scott, on behalf of K.C. of Camden, Inc., and was properly filed of record with the Secretary of State of Arkansas and the Ouachita County Circuit Clerk on August 26, 1985, and August 27, 1985, respectively. The transaction between KC of Camden, Inc., and Borg-Warner was characterized by the parties as a floor plan arrangement, and Borg-Warner loaned the money to purchase relatively expensive items of inventory, such as stereo equipment, which were capable of specific identification through individual serial numbers. According to Shannon Scott, all of the inventory in which Borg-Warner claims a security interest was purchased with the loan proceeds from Borg-Warner and not with the proceeds from the sale of any preincorporation inventory in which the Bank claims a security interest.

The Bank did not become aware of the existence of the corporation until sometime in 1986 when financial information was submitted which made reference to the corporation. Charles Campbell, who became employed at the Bank in February 1987, testified that he was not alarmed when he learned that the business was being conducted in a corporate form because he felt the creation of the corporation was merely a name change. The Bank took no steps to obtain a new security agreement from the corporation or file a new financing statement in the name of the corporation.[3]

The Bank argues that its security interest extends not only to the property transferred to the corporation by the Scotts, but also to the inventory later acquired by the corporation with the proceeds of the Borg–Warner loan. Borg–Warner claims a security interest only in the inventory acquired by the corporation after its incorporation. Borg–Warner argues that the Bank has no security interest in this inventory for two reasons: first, the corporation never granted a security interest to the Bank in any of its property; and, second, even if the Bank were deemed to possess a security interest in the inventory acquired by the corporation, the security interest would not be perfected because the name on the Bank's financing statement is seriously misleading and is not sufficient notice of a claim of a security interest in property owned by KC of Camden, Inc.

The 1962 version of the Uniform Commercial Code did not deal specifically with the viability of a financing statement in situations where the debtor, postfiling, changed its name or business structure or transferred collateral to another. A uniform amendment, prepared by the Article 9 Review Committee in 1972 and adopted in Arkansas in 1973, sought to address the problem. Section 9–402(7), as amended in 1973, provides as follows:

> A financing statement sufficiently shows the name of the debtor if it gives the individual, partnership, or corporate name of the debtor, whether or not it adds other trade names or names of partners. Where the debtor so changes his name or in the case of an organization, its name, identity, or corporate structure that a filed financing statement becomes seriously misleading, the filing is not effective to perfect a security interest in collateral acquired by the debtor more than four (4) months after the change, unless a new appropriate financing statement is filed before the expiration of that time. A filed financing statement remains effective with respect to collateral transferred by the debtor even though the secured party knows of or consents to the transfer.

The language of the amended section 9–402(7) has been criticized as being ambiguous. See Burke, The Duty to Refile Under Section 9–402(7) of the Revised Article 9, 35 Bus.Law. 1083 (1980). The official comments to section 9–402(7) state, in part, as follows:

> [T]he principle sought to be achieved by the subsection is that after a change which would be seriously misleading, the old financing statement is not effective as to new collateral acquired more than four months after the change, unless a new

---

3. See § 9–402(2)(d) which purports to permit a secured party to file an effective financing statement without the debtor's signature to cover collateral acquired after a change of name or corporate structure.

appropriate financing statement is filed before the expiration of the four months. The old financing statement, if legally still valid under the circumstances, would continue to protect collateral acquired before the change and, if still operative under the particular circumstances, would also protect collateral acquired within the four months. Obviously, the subsection does not undertake to state whether the old security agreement continues to operate between the secured party and the party surviving the corporate change of the debtor.

One commentator's analysis described the section as follows:

> These two [the second and third] sentences address different issues and state different rules. The [second] refers to name changes and, for business organizations, changes in name, identity and corporate structure. The [third] sentence applies to transfers of collateral * * *.
>
> The basic import of each sentence is clear. According to the [second] sentence, if a name change or change in identity renders the financing statement seriously misleading, the filed financing statement (under the debtor's old name and now misleading) continues to perfect the creditor's interest in all collateral the debtor has or acquires within four months after the change. It is not effective to perfect a security interest in collateral the debtor acquires more than four months after the change. To maintain perfection regarding collateral the debtor acquires more than four months after the name change, the secured party must file a new, appropriate financing statement to reflect the change.

1 U.C.C. Serv. (MB) § 6.10[4], at 6–208 to –209 (1989) (footnotes omitted).

Under the facts present here, the debtors were conducting a business in their individual capacities, then created a corporation and transferred all of their business assets to the new entity. The new entity subsequently acquired inventory in its own name with the proceeds of a new loan from Borg–Warner. The loan proceeds were given, not to the individuals, but to the corporation, which in turn granted Borg–Warner a security interest in the new inventory. Borg–Warner properly perfected its security interest. No evidence of fraud or bad faith by any party was alleged or shown by the evidence, and Borg–Warner had no knowledge of the existence of the Bank's prior claim of a security interest.

Application of section 9–402(7) to property acquired by the corporation under these facts is difficult because a security interest cannot be created under Article 9 unless the debtor has signed a security agreement in favor of the secured party, value has been given and the debtor has rights in the collateral. See § 9–203(1) (a)–(c) * * *. A security interest in inventory is perfected when a valid financing statement, signed by the debtor, is properly filed.

See §§ 9–302, 9–401, 9–402. In this case no security agreement was executed by the corporation in favor of the Bank and no value was extended by the Bank to the corporation. Although the last sentence of section 9–402(7) permits the continued perfection of a security interest in collateral which is transferred to a new entity, new property acquired by the transferee corporation is, by definition, not collateral transferred by the debtor. Whether or not a financing statement is misleading so as to render a filing ineffective would appear to be legally irrelevant if there is no underlying security interest to perfect.

The author of one article acknowledges that it is technically impossible for section 9–402(7) to be construed to extend the security interest of a creditor to a transferee corporation's new inventory because of the absence of a security agreement. Knippenberg, Debtor Name Changes and Collateral Transfers Under 9–402(7): Drafting from the Outside–In, 52 Mo.L.Rev. 57, 106 (1987). See also Burke, supra, at 1094. Courts, however, have construed section 9–402(7) to extend to after-acquired property of the newly formed corporation in situations similar, if not identical, to the facts in this case.

Some cases have focused on whether the new entity's name was seriously misleading, and others have focused on whether the new entity was owned and controlled by the same individuals operating the old entity.[4] Some cases have specifically held that the secured creditor remained perfected as to property acquired by the new entity, while others have failed to address the distinction between property transferred to the new entity upon the corporate structure change and property subsequently acquired by the new entity.

For example, in Towers v. B.J. Holmes Sales Co. (In re West Coast Food Sales, Inc.), 637 F.2d 707 (9th Cir.1981), the court held that a security agreement executed by a sole proprietorship continued to be effective as to accounts receivable generated after the business incorporated. After noting other cases upholding a security interest in after-acquired property of a transferee debtor, the court abruptly concluded that the security interest must be recognized or else "a debtor would be able to evade the obligations of a validly executed security agreement by the simple expedient of an alteration in its business structure." Id. at 709.

---

4. One commentator who is critical of this construction argues that the basis for such decisions is an alter ego theory:

Many of the ∗ ∗ ∗ transfers of collateral cases seem to proceed upon the unstated premise that when collateral is transferred to a corporation that continues to be owned and operated by the same persons who controlled the transferor, the corporate identity may be disregarded and the case may be treated as though no transfer had occurred and only a name change is involved.

Burke, supra, at 1092.

In Houchen v. First Nat'l Bank of Pana (In re Taylorville Eisner Agency, Inc.), 445 F.Supp. 665 (S.D.Ill.1977), the court held that a creditor with a security interest in after-acquired property of a sole proprietorship remained perfected as to collateral transferred to a corporation formed by the business's owners, as well as property acquired by the corporation following the change. The court held that the "collateral" transferred encompassed after-acquired property but did not address the separate identity of the new entity acquiring the property.

In Bank of the West v. Commercial Credit Financial Services, Inc., 852 F.2d 1162 (9th Cir.1988), a parent corporation transferred one of its businesses from one of its wholly owned subsidiaries to another. Two creditors claimed an interest in the accounts generated from the sale of the business's inventory after the transfer. The court held that the first secured creditor, which held a security interest in the transferor subsidiary's after-acquired accounts, remained perfected as to accounts actually transferred and as to accounts subsequently generated by the transferee subsidiary. The court equated the transfer to a change in corporate structure that was governed by the second sentence of section 9–402(7). The court chose not to read section 9–402(7) rigidly and stated that the last sentence only applied to "bona fide transfers of collateral to third parties unrelated to the transferor," unlike the fact situation at hand. Id. at 1169–70 n. 6.

In Crocker Nat'l Bank v. Clark Equip. Credit Corp., 724 F.2d 696 (8th Cir.1984), the court held that a creditor's security interest in after-acquired inventory remained perfected following the reorganization of a business into a new corporation and the transfer of its assets. The court stated that the new corporation had agreed that the old corporation's creditors would retain their priority in property transferred and that the transfer amounted to a name change that was not misleading.

In Lieberman Music Co. v. Hagen, 2 U.C.C.Rep.Serv.2d (Callaghan) 718, 394 N.W.2d 837 (Minn.Ct.App.1986), the court held that a change in an organization from a sole proprietorship to a corporation did not render a financing statement misleading.

At least one case has attempted to reconcile the various provisions of the Uniform Commercial Code. In Citizens Sav. Bank v. Sac City State Bank, 33 U.C.C.Rep.Serv. (Callaghan) 98, 315 N.W.2d 20 (Iowa 1982), two banks claimed priority in the distribution of the liquidated assets of an auto dealership which changed its structure from a sole proprietorship to a corporation. The court held that the bank which had received a security agreement covering after-acquired property from the sole proprietorship did not have a perfected security interest in property acquired by the corporation for three reasons. First, the court stated that the incorporation created a distinct and different entity and was more than a mere name change. Second, the court stated that, for section 9–402(7) to apply, the debtor acquiring new collateral must be the same debtor which underwent a change, which was not the case since the sole proprietorship underwent a change and the new corporation acquired the new property. Finally, the court stated that the corporation could not be bound because it never granted a security interest to the bank or signed a financing statement as required by the Uniform Commercial Code.

In In re Edwards Equip. Co., 46 B.R. 689 (Bankr.W.D.Okla. 1985), the court stated in dicta that, if an original financing statement was executed by the debtor as a sole proprietorship and was subsequently amended to reflect the debtor's change to a corporation, the court doubted that a continuation statement referring to the amendment would continue to perfect the creditor's security interest in collateral listed only on the original financing statement. In In re Meyer–Midway, Inc., 65 B.R. 437 (Bankr.N.D.Ill.1986), two businesses granted security interests to a bank in their accounts receivable, then merged to form a new corporation. The court held that the bank remained perfected as to accounts receivable existing at the time of the merger, but not as to accounts receivable generated more than four months after the merger. The court stated it could not "infect" with perfection the property later acquired by the successor entity. Id. at 444.

Most of the cases which validate the existing security interest in the after-acquired collateral of the transferee appear to disregard the fact that the transferee is a separate entity which has not granted a security interest to the transferor's creditor. The transferee is typically owned by the former debtors. One commentator argues that the security interest in the transferee's after-acquired property ought to be validated under this so-called alter ego theory because this interpretation of section 9–402(7) produces a better result even though it requires the law to indulge in a legal fiction.[5]

While no satisfactory resolution of this issue may exist, the language of section 9–402(7) cannot properly be construed to dispense with the specific requirements of section 9–203(1) because, as Burke points out, section 9–402(7) "assumes the existence of a security interest to perfect." Burke, supra, at 1094. Nor can the requirements of section 9–203(1) be met by employing a legal

---

5. The commentator stated:

[I]t would be more consistent with the Code's aim to give filers certainty. In addition, changes in business form seem more analogous to name changes. If a debtor changes his name, the creditor continues to deal with the same person. So too, if the debtor incorporates, although his legal form has changed, the ultimate players remain the same * * *. Although at law, each entity is an entity unto itself and recognized at law, we all know the law indulges in legal fictions. If the creditor is still talking to, working with and loaning money to the same people, isn't the change in business form like a change in name?

1 U.C.C.Serv. (MB) § 6.10[5], at 6–218.

fiction that the new corporation is not a separate entity. Under state law, a corporate entity may be disregarded in appropriate circumstances, but here no allegation was made that the corporate entity should be disregarded and no facts warranting such action were shown. To require a searcher to determine to what extent a debtor entity is owned or controlled by owners of the transferor debtor would render the filing system of Article 9 unreliable. The potential structural variations of the new debtor are infinite.[6]

The Bank's claim of a security interest in the corporation's new inventory is, therefore, not sustainable because K.C. of Camden, Inc., has not executed a security agreement in favor of the Bank. See Citizens Sav. Bank v. Sac. City State Bank, 33 U.C.C. Rep.Serv. (Callaghan) at 107, 315 N.W.2d at 27–28. It is unnecessary to consider the alternative issue argued by the parties of whether the Bank's financing statement was seriously misleading. Borg–Warner is determined to have a valid first lien in the proceeds from the sale of the inventory in question.[7]

*   *   *

NOTES

1. The court in *Scott* concedes that several cases have held that the second sentence of § 9–402(7) should apply to cases in which debtors incorporate. This is a plausible reading of that provision. In *Scott* a husband and wife operating a business would seem to come within the definition of "organization" in § 1–201(28). And, despite Comment 28 to § 1–201, it might also be plausibly argued that a business operated as a sole proprietorship falls within the words "any other commercial entity." Thus,

---

6. As Burke stated:

If transfers are disregarded because of the management or ownership similarities of the transferor and the transferee, it will never be possible to determine how much change in ownership, control or business activity will result in recognition of the separate legal status of the transferee for purposes of creating and perfecting a security interest in the assets of the transferee. It is apparent that alter ego as a refiling theory is incompatible with the purpose of the filing rules of article 9 since it will not produce uniform filing or search rules that can be safely relied upon in structuring secured transactions.

Burke, supra, at 1092.

7. The result reached here is consistent with Burke's view:

With respect to new property acquired by the transferee, the secured creditor must establish both the exis-tence of security interest in the property and perfection of the security interest. Assuming that the secured creditor can establish the existence of a security interest in the property acquired by the transferee, the last sentence of section 9–402(7) clearly does not operate to perfect the security interest. The new property acquired by the transferee is by definition not "collateral transferred by the debtor," within the meaning of the last sentence of section 9–402(7); and a financing statement filed in the name of the transferor can not perfect a security interest in property acquired by the transferee. *As to new property acquired by the transferee after the transfer, the secured creditor should obtain a new security agreement signed by the transferee and file a new financing statement signed by the transferee.*

Burke, supra, at 1100 (emphasis added) (footnotes omitted).

under § 9–402(7), a sole proprietorship could be an organization whose "name, identity or corporate structure" has been changed. With respect to collateral acquired by the debtor after four months, if the second sentence of § 9–402(7) controls, the issue to be resolved would be whether the filed financing statement had become "seriously misleading." But in both Citizens Savings Bank v. Sac City State Bank, cited in the opinion, and *Scott*, the court held that § 9–203 had the effect of making § 9–402(7) (second sentence) inapplicable to any property acquired by the new entity after the incorporation because § 9–402(7) assumes the existence of a security interest and, without a security agreement from the new corporation, there would be no security interest in any newly acquired property. Thus it was irrelevant whether the reorganization made the financing statement seriously misleading. On this point, both White & Summers, Uniform Commercial Code § 22–19 (1988), and Clark, The Law of Secured Transactions under the Uniform Commercial Code ¶ 2.11[1][b][iv] (1988), are critical of *Sac City*. Clark observes "The trouble with *Sac City* is the court's failure to treat the transaction as a name change or business restructuring under the second sentence." (p. 2–117). White & Summers believes it possible and Clark considers it probable that either by contract or under corporation law, the successor entity would be liable on the security agreement of the predecessor entity. White & Summers sees no policy reason to insist on a new filing if the old filing gives adequate notice, as it did in *Sac City*, and concludes that when § 9–402(7) refers to "the debtor" it should mean both the predecessor and the successor entities.

With respect to collateral transferred by a single-proprietorship debtor to a successor corporation, *Sac City* held that the third sentence of § 9–402(7) applied; therefore, with respect to the property transferred and its proceeds, the secured party had no need to file a new financing statement in the name of the successor corporation no matter how misleading the old financing statement had become. Some of the case law and, apparently, White & Summers and Clark take the position that the second sentence of § 9–402(7) controls in this case so long as the successor entity is in substance the same party as the predecessor debtor. This would leave the third sentence of § 9–402(7) to apply only to transfers to independent third parties. But whether the dispute is governed by the second sentence or the third sentence, the result is the same with respect to transferred property. The security interest in the transferred collateral remains perfected after the transfer. § 9–306(2) and (3). The dispute concerning the interpretation of the second sentence of § 9–402(7) has importance only with respect to property acquired by the successor entity. With respect to that property the issue is whether, under § 9–203, a security interest in that property has been created.

2. By the third sentence of § 9–402(7) a financing statement filed by a creditor is effective to maintain perfection of a security interest in collateral even though it has been transferred by the original debtor to another person. This means that the creditor need not police the debtor to make sure that the collateral has not been disposed of. What is the policy basis of this rule? But the creditor is protected even in cases in which it knows that the collateral has been disposed of. What is the policy basis of this rule? What inquiries should a prospective secured creditor make with respect to the expected collateral? Referring to the last sentence of § 9–402(7), Permanent Editorial Board Commentary No. 3 explains:

> This sentence, which was added in the 1972 Official Text, was intended to resolve an ambiguity in the 1962 Code as to whether a secured party is required to file an amended or new financing statement when the collateral is transferred. Substantial policy arguments can be made on both sides of this issue. Those favoring a refiling obligation when collateral is transferred argue that, absent refiling in the name of the transferee, secured creditors searching in the name of the transferee could be misled since they would not discover a financing statement filed in the name of the transferor. Allowing a filing against the transferor to be effective against creditors of the transferee would thus promote hidden liens in violation of the public notice purposes of Article 9. Those who argue against a refiling obligation as to collateral transferred by the debtor point to the enormous policing responsibility that a refiling duty would impose on secured creditors of the transferor, most of whom have no continuing contact with the transferor after the secured transaction other than to receive installment payments on the secured indebtedness. A refiling obligation linked to the secured creditor's "notice" or "knowledge" of the transfer would create difficult problems of proof and would foster litigation with all of its resultant costs and uncertainties. Secured creditors of the transferee can protect themselves against filings in the name of prior owners of the collateral by tracing ownership of the collateral and searching in the name of prior owners. This tracing obligation, it is argued, is not an unreasonable burden to place on creditors of the transferee since they would have this responsibility anyway in order to insure that their debtor (the transferee) has rights in the collateral sufficient to grant a security interest.

> Balancing these competing policy concerns, the National Conference of Commissioners on Uniform State Laws and the American Law Institute, in adopting § 9–402(7), opted in favor of the no refiling rule as to collateral transferred by the debtor.

3. Are § 9–306(2) and § 9–402(7) inconsistent? The last sentence of 9–402(7) applies to a case in which the secured party consents to a transfer, but doesn't a secured party lose its security interest under § 9–306(2) if it authorizes the disposition of the collateral? Permanent Editorial Board Commentary No. 3 concludes that the two provisions are not inconsistent. A secured party loses it security interest in collateral under § 9–306(2) only if it authorizes disposition of the collateral free and clear of the security interest. If it authorizes disposition of the collateral subject to its security interest, its security interest continues in the collateral under § 9–306(2) and remains perfected under the last sentence of § 9–402(7). Comment 3 to § 9–306 and Comment 8 to § 9–402 were supplemented to clarify this issue.

See p. 757 for PEB comments

2. PLACE AND MECHANICS OF FILING

Place of Filing

Before the Code chattel mortgages and conditional sales contracts were, like real estate mortgages, filed locally. Central filing on a state-wide basis was used only for trust receipts in those states having the Uniform Trust Receipts Act and for accounts receivable and factor's liens in some states. Article 9 was a major breakthrough in the movement toward state-wide central filing, but disagreement on how far to go with central filing produced three alternatives to § 9–401(1).

The first alternative requires central filing in all cases except transactions involving timber, minerals, and fixtures. Even security interests in crops are filed centrally.

The second alternative requires central filing in all cases except transactions involving timber, minerals, and fixtures (subsection (1)(b)) as well as consumer goods and agricultural collateral (crops, farm accounts, farm equipment, and farm products) (subsection (1)(a)).

The third alternative provides that for those transactions that would be filed centrally under the second alternative there must be an additional local filing in the county where the debtor has an office or, if the debtor has no office, where the debtor resides.

The Code's theory of place of filing is expounded in Comment 4 to § 9–401:

> It is thought that sound policy requires a state-wide filing system for all transactions except the essentially local ones covered in paragraph (1)(a) of the Second and Third Alternatives and land-related transactions covered in paragraph (1)(b) of the Second and Third Alternatives. Paragraph (1)(c) so provides in both alternatives, as does paragraph (1)(b) in the First Alternative. In a state which has adopted either the Second or Third Alternative, central filing would be required

when the collateral was goods except consumer goods, farm equipment or farm products (including crops), or was documents or chattel paper or was accounts or general intangibles, unless related to a farm. Note that the filing provisions of this Article do not apply to instruments (see Section 9–304).

Thus in those states adopting the second alternative, one inquiring about filings with respect to a business debtor looks to a central filing system while one inquiring about filings with respect to a consumer or a farmer looks to a local filing system. How does a secured creditor avoid difficulties in applying the Code's place of filing rules?

Mechanics of Filing

In order to perfect a security interest by filing, the secured party must send the requisite number of copies of the financing statement to the filing officer with the filing fee. Commonly either Form UCC–1 (central filing) or Form UCC–2 (local filing) is utilized. The filing officer must give each statement a file number, mark it with the date and hour of filing, and index the form in the name of the debtor. § 9–403(4). The filing officer then returns a copy of the financing statement to the secured party as an acknowledgement of receipt. If the secured party employs a nonuniform form, for example, filing the security agreement, the filing officer is authorized by § 9–403(5) to charge a higher fee.

The secured party may amend the financing statement pursuant to § 9–402(4) by use of Form UCC–3. Both the debtor and the secured party must sign the amending form "to preclude either from adversely affecting the interests of the other." Comment 4 to § 9–402. The secured party may also release all or part of the collateral covered by a filed financing statement under § 9–406 by use of Form UCC–3.

Section 9–302(2) provides: "If a secured party assigns a perfected security interest, no filing under this Article is required in order to continue the perfected status of the security interest against creditors of and transferees from the original debtor." Hence, the filing of a statement of assignment (Form UCC–3) is permissive in terms of continuing the perfected security interest of the assignee against claimants from the debtor but is required before the assignee can become the secured party of record and entitled to file continuation, termination, or release statements. Comment to § 9–405.

Section 9–403(2) provides that a filed financing statement is effective for five years. It lapses at the end of five years unless under § 9–403(3) a continuation statement (Form UCC–3) is filed by the secured party within six months prior to the expiration of the five-year period. The 1972 amendment to § 9–403(2) cleared up the effect of lapse on junior secured parties and lien creditors of the debtor who acquired their interests before the lapse. This subsection now provides: "If the security interest becomes unperfected upon lapse, it is deemed to have been unperfected as against a person who became a purchaser or lien creditor before lapse." Hence, the junior interests are given priority over the lapsed security interests.

Since the effectiveness of a financing statement ends automatically after five years unless a continuation statement is filed, § 9–404(1) provides that, except in the case of consumer goods, the secured party has no duty to send the debtor a termination statement (Form UCC–3) after the debt is paid unless the debtor demands one. The debtor may do so if there is no further outstanding debt and no commitment on the part of the secured party to make advances or incur obligations. The debtor bears the burden of filing the termination statement. However in cases concerning consumer goods the secured party must file a termination statement either within a month after the debt is paid or within ten days after a written demand by the debtor.

Critique of State Filing Systems

A good filing system should provide a reliable, cheap, and fast process that allows: (1) secured creditors to enter information required to perfect, amend, assign, continue, or terminate their security interests, and (2) searchers to learn of the potential existence of security interests affecting a debtor's property. An elementary model, given the present state of the art, might be a central electronic on-line data bank in each state with connecting terminals in local filing places throughout the state where input of information by secured parties and retrieval of information by searchers may be instantaneous. Such a system would combine the convenience of local access with the reliability of central filing and, in doing so, would render the distinctions made between local and central filing in § 9–402(1) irrelevant. Moreover, the state systems should be connected in a manner that would allow national searches to be made.

A survey of UCC filing systems in the various states shows that we are far from this model today. See Alces & Lloyd, An Agenda for Reform of the Article 9 Filing System, 44 Okla.L.Rev. 99 (1991) ʾhereafter "Survey"). The provisions of Article 9 on filing were drafted in contemplation of a paper-based, manual search system. The huge increase in filings resulting from the business expansion of the last few decades has greatly overburdened this outdated system of data storage and retrieval. Delays in receiving responses to creditors' search requests are common in many states. Although in most states the delay is only a few days, in some states it is several weeks. (Survey p. 106) Prudent creditors will not make an advance until they know the state of the filings; transactions usually cannot go ahead until the search information is obtained. In consequence creditors have, in effect, privatized UCC filings by employing private firms to handle filings and searches. The expense of these firms is a hidden cost of the inadequacies of the present state central filing systems which have been starved for resources owing to budgetary constraints.

Some progress has been made. The Survey states:

> More than half of the states have some form of automated search process in their central filing systems. In many states unofficial searches can be conducted via commercial on-line services. Texas has recently introduced an on-line system that accommodates a wide variety of search strategies. Perhaps the most advanced filing system now in operation is the personal property registry in the province of British Columbia. The British Columbia system allows secured parties to file financing statements electronically at remote terminals in their offices. The original document is maintained by the secured party, and the computer at the central registry generates an additional hard copy which is mailed to the secured party as verification that its financing statement is properly on file. The filing fee is deducted from a deposit made by the secured party as a condition of being authorized to file in this manner. The system has been in effect since October 1990 and is reported to be working smoothly except for some minor problems that are being resolved through software enhancements.

Survey, p. 110.

Obviously much remains to be done in modernizing UCC filing systems. Although some statutory changes can make filing systems more efficient, for instance, cutting down on local filing requirements, most of the improvements must come through improved technology. Survey, pp. 110–113. The choice is whether to continue to build technologically modern private filing systems to supplement or effectively supplant the archaic public systems or to make the necessary investment to bring the public filing systems up to an efficient level. The latter course of action would require states to (1) charge enough for filing services to support a modern system, and (2) devote the filing fees exclusively to the filing system rather than divert these funds to meet the insatiable demands of operating a state government. So far states have been better at taking the first step than they have at taking the second.

Financing Statement for Central Filing

STATE OF ILLINOIS ✳

UNIFORM COMMERCIAL CODE — FINANCING STATEMENT — FORM UCC-1

INSTRUCTIONS:

1. PLEASE TYPE this form. Fold only along perforation for mailing.
2. Remove Secured Party and Debtor copies and send other 3 copies with interleaved carbon paper to the filing officer. Enclose filing fee.
3. If the space provided for any item(s) on the form is inadequate the item(s) should be continued on additional sheets, preferably 5'' x 8'' or 8'' x 10''. Only one copy of such additional sheets need be presented to the filing officer with a set of three copies of the financing statement. Long schedules of collateral, indentures, etc., may be on any size paper that is convenient for the secured party.

This STATEMENT is presented to a filing officer for filing pursuant to the Uniform Commercial Code.

Debtor(s) (Last Name First) and address(es)	Secured Party(ies) and address(es)	For Filing Officer (Date, Time, Number, and Filing Office)

1. This financing statement covers the following types (or items) of property:

ASSIGNEE OF SECURED PARTY

2. ☐ Products of Collateral are also covered.

———— Additional sheets presented.
———— Filed with Office of Secretary of State of Illinois.
———— Debtor is a transmitting utility as defined in UCC §9-105.

By:_____
Signature of (Debtor)
(Secured Party)✳

✳Signature of Debtor Required in Most Cases.
Signature of Secured Party in Cases Covered By UCC §9-402 (2)

(1) Filing Officer Copy - Alphabetical   This form of financing statement is approved by the Secretary of State.

STANDARD FORM — UNIFORM COMMERCIAL CODE — FORM UCC-1 — REV. 2-74

[B1132]

✳ 5 Uniform Laws Annotated, Uniform Commercial Code Forms and Materials, Form 9:3200 (1990 Supp.).

Financing Statement for Local Filing

STATE OF ILLINOIS *

UNIFORM COMMERCIAL CODE — FINANCING STATEMENT — FORM UCC-2

INSTRUCTIONS:

1. PLEASE TYPE this form. Fold only along perforation for mailing.
2. Remove Secured Party and Debtor copies and send other 3 copies with interleaved carbon paper to the filing officer. Enclose filing fee.
3. If the space provided for any item(s) on the form is inadequate the item(s) should be continued on additional sheets, preferably 5" x 8" or 8" x 10". Only one copy of such additional sheets need be presented to the filing officer with a set of three copies of the financing statement. Long schedules of collateral, indentures, etc., may be on any size paper that is convenient for the secured party.

This STATEMENT is presented to a filing officer for filing pursuant to the Uniform Commercial Code.

Debtor(s) (Last Name First) and address(es)	Secured Party(ies) and address(es)	For Filing Officer (Date, Time, Number, and Filing Office)

1. This financing statement covers the following types (or items) of property:

ASSIGNEE OF SECURED PARTY

2. (If collateral is crops) The above described crops are growing or are to be grown on:
   (Describe Real Estate)

3. (If applicable) The above goods are to become fixtures on (The above timber is standing on ...) (The above minerals or the like (including oil and gas) or accounts will be financed at the wellhead or minehead of the well or mine located on ...) (Strike what is inapplicable) (Describe Real Estate)

and this financing statement is to be filed in the real estate records. (If the debtor does not have an interest of record) The name of a record owner is

4. ☐ Products of Collateral are also covered.

_____ Additional sheets presented.

_____ Filed with Recorder's Office of_____ County, Illinois.

By_____
    Signature of (Debtor)
                (Secured Party)*

*Signature of Debtor Required in Most Cases:
Signature of Secured Party in Cases Covered By UCC §9-402 (2)

(1) Filing Officer Copy - Alphabetical   This form of financing statement is approved by the Secretary of State.

STANDARD FORM — UNIFORM COMMERCIAL CODE — FORM UCC-2 — REV. 4-73

[B1137]

* 5 Uniform Laws Annotated, Uniform Commercial Code Forms and Materials, Form 9:3201 (1990 Supp.).

Statement of Continuation, Partial Release, Assignment, Termination or Amendment

STATE OF ILLINOIS *
UNIFORM COMMERCIAL CODE
STATEMENTS OF CONTINUATION, PARTIAL RELEASE, ASSIGNMENT, ETC. — FORM UCC-3

INSTRUCTIONS:
1. PLEASE TYPE this form. Fold only along perforation for mailing.
2. Remove Secured Party and Debtor copies and send other 3 copies with interleaved carbon paper to the filing officer.
3. Enclose filing fee.
4. If the space provided for any item(s) on the form is inadequate the item(s) should be continued on additional sheets, preferably 5'' x 8'' or 8'' x 10''. Only one copy of such additional sheets need be presented to the filing officer with a set of three copies of Form UCC-3. Long schedules of collateral, etc., may be on any size paper that is convenient for the secured party.
5. At the time of filing, filing officer will return third copy as an acknowledgement.

This STATEMENT is presented to THE FILING OFFICER for filing pursuant to the Uniform Commercial Code:

Debtor(s) (Last Name First) and address(es)	Secured Party(ies) and address(es)	For Filing Officer (Date, Time, Number, and Filing Office)

This Statement refers to original Financing Statement No. _____
Date filed: _____, 19_____ Filed with _____

A. ☐ **CONTINUATION**..... The original financing statement between the foregoing Debtor and Secured Party, bearing the file number shown above, is still effective.
B. ☐ **PARTIAL RELEASE**.. From the collateral described in the financing statement bearing the file number shown above, the Secured Party releases the property indicated below.
C. ☐ **ASSIGNMENT**.......... The Secured Party certifies that the Secured Party has assigned to the Assignee whose name and address is shown below, Secured Party's rights under the financing statement bearing the file number shown above in the property indicated below.
D. ☐ **TERMINATION**....... The Secured Party certifies that the Secured Party no longer claims a security interest under the financing statement bearing the file number shown above.
E. ☐ **AMENDMENT**.......... The financing statement bearing the above file number is amended.
　　　　　　　　　　　　☐ To show the Secured Party's new address as indicated below;
　　　　　　　　　　　　☐ To show the Debtor's new address as indicated below;
　　　　　　　　　　　　☐ As set forth below:

_____ (Debtor)   _____ (Secured Party)
　　(Signature of Debtor, if required)

Dated: _____, 19_____   By _____
　　　　　　　　　　　　　　　　　　　　　　　　　　　　　(Signature of Secured Party)

(1) Filing Officer Copy - Alphabetical   This form of Financing Statement is approved by the Secretary of State.
STANDARD FORM — UNIFORM COMMERCIAL CODE — FORM UCC-3 REV. 4-73   [B1142]

*5 Uniform Laws Annotated, Uniform Commercial Code Forms and Materials, Form 9:3202 (1990 Supp.).

E. FILING ERRORS

BORG WARNER ACCEPTANCE CORP. v. ITT DIVERSIFIED CREDIT CORP.

Supreme Court of Minnesota, 1984.
344 N.W.2d 841.

YETKA, JUSTICE.

This is an appeal by Borg Warner Acceptance Corporation, a creditor holding a perfected blanket security interest in a debtor's inventory. The district court of Meeker County declared Borg Warner's interest junior to ITT Diversified Credit Corporation's purchase money interest in seven Crestliner boats, which were part of the debtor's inventory. ITT perfected its purchase money interest after Borg Warner had perfected its blanket lien. ITT requested a UCC search of the debtor's creditors from the Secretary of State's office, but the search failed to list Borg Warner as a creditor. Because it did not know Borg Warner was a prior creditor, ITT did not notify Borg Warner of its purchase money interest. Such notice is required by UCC § 9–312(3)(b) to give a subsequent purchase money lender priority over a conflicting security interest in the same collateral. When the debtor's business failed, ITT took possession of the seven Crestliner boats. Despite ITT's failure to notify Borg Warner of its purchase money interest, the district court held that ITT's interest was superior. We reverse and hold that the Borg Warner interest must prevail.

The facts have been stipulated by the parties. For convenience, we will outline the important dates:

8–21–75 Borg Warner files financing statement covering debtor's inventory.

2–13–76 Borg Warner files second financing statement covering debtor's inventory.

2–8–78 ITT files financing statement perfecting purchase money security interest in Crestliner boats.

ITT requests UCC search from Secretary of State in order to notify prior lenders of its purchase money interest.

2–10–78 ITT receives UCC search. List of creditors does not include Borg Warner. ITT gives notice as required by UCC § 9–312(3)(b) to other creditors, but does not notify Borg Warner of its purchase money interest.

9–27–78 Borg Warner perfects third security interest in inventory.

9–29–78—10–30–79 Seven Crestliner boats delivered to debtor.

3–27–79, 9–7–79, and 9–27–79 Borg Warner files three more financing statements in inventory.

7/80 ITT recovers possession of Crestliner boats.

The issue on appeal is whether a prior perfected security interest in inventory retains priority over a conflicting and subsequently perfected purchase money interest when the purchase money lender fails to notify the prior secured party because of a mistake by the filing officer. We hold that the prior interest does retain its priority.

[Section 9–312(3) grants priority in the Crestliner boats to ITT only if ITT gives notice to Borg Warner that it intends to acquire a purchase money security interest in the boats. Eds.]

In this case, ITT, the purchase money lender, failed to give notice to Borg Warner, the prior secured party, because the Secretary of State's office omitted Borg Warner from the list of secured parties it provided to ITT. The court below held that, in this situation, the "equities" and the purpose of § 9–312 favored giving ITT priority over Borg Warner.

We believe the trial court's decision was based on erroneous reasoning. The court stated that the equities favoring ITT were the facts that it took all the steps necessary to comply with § 9–312(3) and that it did, in fact, notify those creditors whose names were disclosed on the UCC report. However, Borg Warner also took all the steps necessary to perfect its security interest. Thus, the equities here are evenly balanced and do not support a decision for ITT any more than for Borg Warner.

* * *

Apart from the errors in the trial court's reasoning, we believe that placing the risk of mistakes by the filing officer on the later party to file in this situation is in accordance with the purpose of the Article 9 filing system. Article 9 establishes a system of notice filing whereby a creditor who properly files a financing statement can rely upon his prior secured position. In Borg-Warner Acceptance Corporation v. First National Bank of Pipestone, 307 Minn. 20, 238 N.W.2d 612 (1976), we recognized the Article 9 objective of promoting ease and certainty in the filing process. In that case, we held that evidence of subsequent conduct may not be introduced to vary the terms of a security agreement. *Id.* at 24, 238 N.W.2d at 614.

Other authority interpreting the UCC supports placing the risk of mistakes by the filing officer on the later party to file. The statute itself provides that a security interest is perfected upon tender of the filing fee or acceptance of the statement by the filing officer. § 9–403(1). The official comment to § 9–407 specifically states that the secured party therefore does not bear the risk of clerical errors:

> [U]nder Section 9–403(1) the secured party does not bear the risk that the filing officer will not properly perform his duties: under that Section the secured party has complied with the filing requirements when he presents his financing statement for filing and the filing fee has been tendered or the statement accepted by the filing officer.

§ 9–407 comment 1 (1972). This comment indicates that the drafters of the code anticipated filing errors and decided that, between two innocent parties, the last to file should bear the risk of such mistakes.

The rule stated in the comment has been followed by other courts and is discussed with approval by UCC authorities. See, e.g., In re Royal Electrotype Corporation, 485 F.2d 394 (3rd Cir. 1973); In re May Lee Industries, Inc., 380 F.Supp. 1, 2–3 (S.D.N.Y. 1974); Matter of Fowler, 407 F.Supp. 799, 803–04 (Bkrtcy.W.D. Okla.1975); J. White & R. Summers, Handbook of the Law Under the Uniform Commercial Code, § 23–15, p. 951 (2d Ed.1980); R. Henson, Handbook on Secured Transactions Under the Uniform Commercial Code, § 4–5, p. 66 (2d Ed.1979); 4 R. Anderson,

Anderson on the Uniform Commercial Code, § 9–403:5 (2d Ed. 1971).

Even though the comment apparently refers to mistakes made upon the initial presentation of the financing statement and tender of the filing fee, it is equally appropriate where errors occur later—as in this case where a UCC search fails to reveal a prior creditor. Accord, First National Bank of Sullivan County v. Mann, 22 U.C.C.Rep.Serv. 254 (Bkrtcy.E.D.Tenn.1977). To hold otherwise would require perfected inventory financers to review UCC filings prior to each new extension of credit. Article 9 clearly places this burden on new creditors and allows those who first take the necessary steps for perfection to rest assured in the priority of their security interests.

For the above reasons, we hold that ITT's purchase money interest in the seven Crestliner boats does not have priority over Borg Warner's security interest in the debtor's inventory. Reversed and remanded with instructions to enter judgment in favor of Borg Warner in accordance with this opinion.

NOTE

In In re Royal Electrotype Corp., cited in the principal case, the filing officer erred by listing the secured party as the debtor and the debtor as the secured party. The court held that under § 9–403(1) the secured party who submits a correct financing statement does not bear the risk of the filing officer's error. The fact that the secured party was given a receipt at the time of filing showing the error did not change the court's view. In re Flagstaff Foodservice Corp., 16 B.R. 132 (Bkrtcy.N.Y.1981), involved the failure of the filing officer to file a financing statement. The fact that the secured party had not received a copy of a properly stamped financing statement nor its canceled check for the filing fee by the time of the debtor's bankruptcy three years later did not impose a duty of investigation on the secured party. A subsequent creditor who is injured by a filing officer's error may seek recourse against the state, see, e.g., Hudleasco, Inc. v. State, 90 Misc.2d 1057, 396 N.Y.S.2d 1002 (Ct.Cl.1977), or the filing officer, see, e.g., Mobile Enterprises, Inc. v. Conrad, 177 Ind.App. 475, 380 N.E.2d 100 (1978), depending on the laws of the relevant state. In Borg-Warner Acceptance Corp. v. Secretary of State for the State of Kansas, 240 Kan. 598, 731 P.2d 301 (1987), the filing officer was held liable for negligence in the amount of $70,622, the value of the collateral lost because of the filing error. The Kansas legislature then added § 9–407(3) providing immunity from liability except for willful misconduct. A number of other states have also enacted legislation giving immunity for filing errors, e.g., Iowa, Kentucky, Minnesota, Missouri, Nebraska, North Dakota, Oklahoma and Wisconsin. 5 UCC Rep.Serv.2d 1211 (Editors'

Note) (1988). In Borg-Warner Acceptance Corp. v. Department of State, 433 Mich. 16, 444 N.W.2d 786 (1989), the court rejected a creditor's suit for damages for a filing error; the suit was based on breach of contract and the court found no consideration to support a contract.

IN RE MISTURA, INC.

United States Court of Appeals, Ninth Circuit, 1983.
705 F.2d 1496.

KILKENNY, CIRCUIT JUDGE.

McKesson Drug Company (McKesson) appeals from a decision of the bankruptcy appellate panel, 22 B.R. 60, reversing the court's determination that McKesson's lien in the personal property of Mistura, Inc. was superior to the lien of Lee and Ann Marcus (Marcuses). The bankruptcy appellate panel remanded for a new trial. We affirm.

The Marcuses sold a drug store to Mistura, Inc. taking back a security interest in the fixtures and personal property for the unpaid balance of the purchase price. They filed a financing statement on June 15, 1977. However, only the lien on fixtures, not the lien on personal property, was perfected because the Marcuses filed the statement with the Maricopa County Recorder, rather than the Arizona Secretary of State as required by Arizona law.

Subsequently, Mistura sought additional financing and obtained a loan from McKesson secured by the same collateral. McKesson properly perfected its security interest by filing a financing statement with the Arizona Secretary of State on September 5, 1979. Upon learning of their improper filing, the Marcuses filed a financing statement with the Secretary on September 12, 1980.

Absent the effect of UCC § 9–401(2), it is conceded that McKesson would prevail since it perfected its security interest prior to the Marcuses. However, the Marcuses contend that their good faith filing with the Maricopa County Recorder was effective against McKesson because it had knowledge of the contents of the improperly filed financing statement.

* * *

The sole issue on appeal is whether the bankruptcy appellate panel properly refused to accord substantial deference to the bankruptcy court's interpretation of UCC § 9–401(2) in reversing its determination that McKesson's lien was superior to the Marcuses.

UCC § 9–401(2) provides a careless creditor with some protection when a filing is made in good faith in an improper place. It provides:

A filing which is made in good faith in an improper place or not in all of the places required by this section is nonetheless effective with regard to any collateral as to which the filing complied with the requirements of this article and is also effective with regard to collateral covered by the financing statement against any person who has *knowledge of the contents of such financing statement.* [Emphasis added].

No Arizona courts have interpreted the requisite knowledge requirement in the above statute. Therefore, the bankruptcy court was obligated to sit as a state court and "look for guidance from * * * courts in other jurisdictions which have recently considered the issue." Lewis v. Anderson, supra, 615 F.2d at 781. Other jurisdictions, however, are not in accord as to the meaning or application of the phrase "knowledge of the contents of such financing statement."

Several courts have held knowledge of a creditor's prior security interest to be "knowledge of the contents of such financing statement." * * * This line of cases assumes that knowledge of the security interest provides the subsequent creditor with knowledge of the contents of the financing statement. Other courts, however, have reached the opposite result. * * *

It is clear that the courts have almost universally required actual, rather than constructive, knowledge of the general contents of the financing statement. However, the nature of the actual knowledge required varies substantially across a broad spectrum. To complicate matters, "the Code provides no further guidance as to where on the spectrum from 'should have found out' to 'actually eyeing the maverick [financing statement]' the correct solution lies." White and Summers, Handbook of the Law Under the Uniform Commercial Code, p. 949 (2d ed. 1980).

In the instant case, the bankruptcy court properly placed the burden of proof on the Marcuses to prove that McKesson had actual knowledge of the contents of the financing statement. However, it failed to further elaborate on the nature of the actual knowledge that was required to satisfy the provisions of UCC § 9–401(2). We find that without this determination, and in light of the divergence of views on the requisite nature of actual knowledge required, the statute was not properly construed.

Accordingly, we hold that the bankruptcy appellate panel did not err in refusing to give the bankruptcy court's interpretation the usual deference. * * * In addition, we hold that given an opportunity the Arizona Supreme Court would follow the line of cases holding that knowledge of the facts contained in a financing statement, even though learned in ignorance of the improperly filed financing statement, satisfies the requisite knowledge requirement of the statute. The statute by its terms requires "knowledge of the contents of such financing statement," but does not require an examination of the financing statement itself.

On remand, the Marcuses must prove that McKesson had actual knowledge of the contents of the financing statement, which generally includes the names of the debtors and creditors and an adequate description of the collateral. Any evidence, whether direct or circumstantial, "having any tendency to make the existence of" McKesson's knowledge of the Marcuses security interest and its contents "more probable * * * than it would be without the evidence" will not be excluded on the basis of relevance. FRE 401. This includes financial statements and other documents that McKesson would have examined prior to making the loan to Mistura.

NOTES

1. Suppose that instead of filing in the wrong place, the Marcuses had not filed at all. When McKesson perfected its security interest it knew of the Marcuses' security interest. Later the Marcuses filed in the proper place. Who has priority under § 9–312(5)? Change these facts so that McKesson is a judicial lien creditor. Who has priority under § 9–301(1)(b)? Why does the UCC make knowledge determinative under § 9–401(2) but irrelevant under § 9–301(1)(b) and § 9–312(5)?

2. Debtor granted a security interest in business equipment to First Bank which neglected to file a financing statement. Debtor then granted a security interest in the same collateral to Second Bank which erroneously filed a financing statement locally. The filing should have been made centrally. Then First Bank and Second Bank each found out about the transaction of the other and the filing by Second Bank. First Bank then filed centrally before Second Bank filed centrally. Who has priority? See § 9–401(2). According to First National Bank and Trust v. First National Bank, 582 F.2d 524, 526–527 (10th Cir.1978), First Bank should have priority.

F. RIGHTS IN COLLATERAL

In providing that a security interest does not attach unless the debtor has "rights in the collateral," § 9–203(1)(c) may be stating only the obvious. The phrase is not defined, and it is doubtful if any precise definition is possible. An owner of goods can create a security interest in the goods; a thief in possession cannot. It is clear that a debtor that has less than ownership of the collateral can create a security interest in the collateral, but it is not at all clear what relationship toward the collateral between the extremes of legal ownership and naked possession is sufficient. The rights-in-collateral rubric of § 9–203(1)(c) tells us nothing about the quantum of that relationship. We must look elsewhere for an answer.

Maxims like "no one can give what he has not" or "a creditor takes no greater rights than his debtor has" have been with us for a long time, and yet the books are full of cases in which transferors are found to have the power to pass on greater rights to their transferees than they had. Courts may find this power in the law of agency, fraud, estoppel, and other traditional bodies of law that § 1–103 explicitly, if somewhat gratuitously, states shall be used to supplement the UCC. They may also find that the transferor is given this power by specific Code provisions, e.g., § 2–403. One bit of guidance we find in the Code is that under § 1–201(32) and (33) a secured party enjoys the status of a "purchaser"; hence, provisions like § 2–403 that grant purchasers greater rights than their transferors apply to benefit secured parties.

The rights-in-collateral issue is significantly involved in the priority matters treated in the next chapter, and we will have more to say about it in that context. For now we briefly introduce you to the subject through the following two cases. As you read these cases and the cases in point in the next chapter, ask yourself whether the courts would have reached any different results had Article 9 said nothing at all about rights in collateral.

SWETS MOTOR SALES, INC. v. PRUISNER

Supreme Court of Iowa, 1975.
236 N.W.2d 299.

REES, JUSTICE. Plaintiff Swets Motor Sales, Inc., appeals from an order of trial court sustaining motion for summary judgment of defendant Chrysler Credit Corporation and therein adjudicating the latter's interest in certain automobiles to be superior to the interest of plaintiff. We affirm in part, reverse in part, and remand for appropriate proceedings in conformity with this opinion.

Plaintiff Swets Motor Sales, Inc., (hereinafter Swets), an Illinois automobile "wholesaler," sold used cars and trucks to defendant Pruisner, a retail automobile dealer at Waverly. Pursuant to an oral arrangement, plaintiff delivered vehicles to defendant Pruisner with unencumbered certificates of title and was paid by Pruisner at the time of delivery of the cars. Chrysler Credit Corporation, joined as a defendant in this action, financed defendant Pruisner's inventory under a floor planning arrangement which the parties have stipulated was a valid security agreement with filed financing statements covering new and used vehicles in Pruisner's possession.

From July 1973 until the end of September of the same year, Swets sold to Pruisner approximately 60 vehicles which were resold by Pruisner under the foregoing arrangement. In September 1973 four of Pruisner's checks written to plaintiff Swets, totalling approximately $31,000, were dishonored. Swets filed his petition at law and obtained a writ of attachment for the seizure of the vehicles then in Pruisner's possession, then amended his petition to an action sounding in equity, seeking a declaration that his interest in the automobiles was superior to that of Chrysler Credit Corporation. Chrysler Credit answered and counter-claimed against Swets, asserting therein that its interest in the vehicles was superior to that of plaintiff. It was stipulated that at the time of the issuance of the writ of attachment Chrysler Credit had in its possession the unencumbered titles to the vehicles in question.

Trial of the action commenced January 18, 1974, and on January 21, apparently after a substantial portion of the evidence had been presented, defendant Chrysler Credit moved for a summary judgment on the issue of priority of its security interest. Swets thereafter filed a resistance to such motion, alleging the existence of genuine issues of material fact regarding the possibility that, through fraud or mutual mistake, Swets' contract with Pruisner might be determined to be void. Swets also alleged the existence of genuine issues of material fact with respect to the proper valuation of the vehicles in question and Chrysler Credit's failure to minimize or mitigate damages.

On January 24 trial court sustained Chrysler Credit's motion for summary judgment and made various findings of fact and reached conclusions of law. In its findings of fact pertinent to this appeal was the trial court's determination the value of the attached vehicles was $9,300 at the date of the attachment and $5,100 on the date of the hearing. Trial court concluded as a matter of law that defendant Chrysler Credit Corporation had a right to assume defendant Pruisner's ownership of the vehicles in question from the latter's possession of unencumbered certificates of title. Trial court also concluded UCC § 2–403 precluded Swets from prevailing.

Accordingly, trial court decreed Chrysler Credit was entitled to possession of the vehicles under attachment and held valid title to them [with the exception of a certain Ford Torino automobile with which we are not concerned]. Trial court further found and adjudged the difference between the sum of $9,300 [which the court had determined to be the value of the vehicles at the time of attachment] and the subsequent sales price of the vehicles should be assessed against plaintiff Swets and paid out of its attachment bond.

* * *

It was stipulated by the parties to this action that defendant Chrysler Credit Corporation had a valid outstanding security agreement with defendant Pruisner covering new and used vehicles in the latter's possession at all times pertinent to the action. The Uniform Commercial Code provides the resolution of the priority problem in this case. Section 2–403 provides in pertinent part:

> "1. A purchaser of goods acquires all title which his transferor had or had power to transfer except that a purchaser of a limited interest acquires rights only to the extent of the interest purchased. A person with voidable title has power to transfer a good title to a good faith purchaser for value. When goods have been delivered under a transaction of purchase the purchaser has such power even though
>
> " * * *
>
> "b. the delivery was in exchange for a check which is later dishonored, * * *."

The above section of the Uniform Commercial Code indicates that despite the fact Pruisner tendered, for the purchase of the vehicles, a check which was subsequently dishonored, he could, nonetheless, transfer good title to a "good faith purchaser for value."

"Good faith" is defined in the Uniform Commercial Code as "honesty in fact in the conduct or transaction concerned." Section 1–201(19). Plaintiff did not, and does not now, present any factual question as to the good faith of defendant Chrysler Credit, whose security interest under the floor planning scheme predated the execution and delivery to plaintiff of the dishonored checks.

A purchaser is defined by section 1–201(33) as "a person who takes by purchase." Section 1–201(32) defines "purchase" as including "taking by sale, discount, negotiation, mortgage, pledge, lien, issue or reissue, gift or any other voluntary transaction creating an interest in property."

Section 1–201(44)(b) provides that a person gives "value" for rights if he acquires them "as security for or in total or partial satisfaction of a pre-existing claim." From the above definitions it is abidingly clear that we must conclude defendant Chrysler Credit acted in good faith and "gave value." It is equally clear that a secured party under Article 9 of the Uniform Commercial Code (§ 9–105(1)(i)) is a "purchaser" within the meaning of § 1–201(33) above. The central contention of Swets, however, is that if his contract with Pruisner were affected by fraud or mutual mistake, defendant Chrysler Credit would not be a secured party with respect to the vehicles in question in this case.

In support of this contention Swets directs our attention to § 9–204(1) which provides that a security interest cannot attach until there is agreement that it attach and value is given and the debtor has rights in the collateral. Swets argues that if the purchase by Pruisner was accomplished as a result of fraud or mutual mistake, Pruisner would have no "rights" in the collateral and, consequently, defendant Chrysler Corporation would be neither a secured party nor a purchaser. We find this contention to be without merit.

Particularly pertinent to our conclusion in this regard is our decision in Herington Livestock Auction Company v. Verschoor, 179 N.W.2d 491 (Iowa 1970). In *Herington* plaintiff had sold 84 head of cattle to a speculator, using an invoice which provided on its face: "The purchaser agrees that title of stock listed above shall be retained by us until check or draft in payment of same is paid." The speculator, in turn, delivered the cattle to defendant who, acting on the speculator's directions, sold them and tendered a check to the latter. Subsequently plaintiff was not paid for the cattle by the speculator, and brought an action against defendant for conversion. After a motion for judgment notwithstanding verdict had been resolved adversely to plaintiff, he appealed, claiming title to the cattle had not passed to the speculator, due to the reservation in the invoice.

We affirmed in *Herington*, holding that plaintiff seller could at most have reserved only a security interest in the cattle. Pertinent to our disposition of the appeal was Code section 2–401(2) which provides in material part:

> "Unless otherwise explicitly agreed title passes to the buyer at the time and place at which the seller completes his performance with reference to the physical delivery of the goods, despite any reservation of a security interest * * *."

In the matter before us here plaintiff did not even reserve a security interest in the vehicles in question. At the time of the delivery of the vehicles, Pruisner acquired sufficient rights in the same to permit Chrysler Credit Corporation's security interest to attach.

An almost identical analysis was employed by the Supreme Court of Nebraska under identical Uniform Commercial Code provisions in Jordan v. Butler, 182 Neb. 626, 156 N.W.2d 778, a case involving the respective rights of a defrauded initial seller and a subsequent good faith purchaser for value.

We also note that when goods have been delivered under a transaction of purchase the purchaser has power to transfer good title to a subsequent good faith purchaser for value even though the original delivery was procured through fraud punishable as larcenous under the criminal law. Section 2–403(1)(d).

We further observe § 2–702(2) provides that on a credit sale to an insolvent buyer, the seller has ten days to make reclamation, unless the buyer has misrepresented in writing his solvency within in three months prior, in which case the time limit does not apply. That section further provides: "Except as provided in this subsection the seller may not base a right to reclaim goods on the buyer's fraudulent or innocent misrepresentation of solvency or of intent to pay." There is no indication by plaintiff here that he pursued this remedy against Pruisner. For the implication drawn by the Tenth Circuit Court of Appeals from a plaintiff's failure to comply with an identical statute in a case quite similar to the one at bar, see United States v. Wyoming National Bank of Casper, 505 F.2d 1064 (10 Cir. 1974).

In summary, we conclude and hold:

(1) Trial court was correct in sustaining motion for summary judgment of defendant Chrysler Credit Corporation insofar as it sought an adjudication that its interest in the automobiles in question was senior and superior to plaintiff's claim of ownership thereto.

(2) Trial court erred in failing to find there was a genuine issue of material fact regarding the value of the automobiles at time of attachment of same, and accordingly erred in fixing the value of the cars at $9,300.

We therefore affirm trial court in its findings, conclusions and decree adjudicating the rights of plaintiff Swets in the automobiles in question to be junior and inferior to the claim of ownership of defendant Chrysler Credit Corporation. We reverse the judgment of trial court relative to the value of the vehicles and remand for further hearing and determination of the value of the same.

* * *

Affirmed in part, reversed in part and remanded for further proceedings.

KINETICS TECHNOLOGY INTERNATIONAL CORP. v. FOURTH NATIONAL BANK

United States Court of Appeals, Tenth Circuit, 1983.
705 F.2d 396.

SEYMOUR, CIRCUIT JUDGE.

Kinetics Technology International Corporation (KTI) brought this diversity action seeking damages for an alleged conversion of goods by Fourth National Bank of Tulsa (the Bank). The Bank admits taking possession of the goods from the custody of a third party, Oklahoma Heat Transfer Corporation (OHT), but claims a right to the goods arising under the Oklahoma version of the Uniform Commercial Code (hereinafter UCC or Code). For the reasons set out below, we affirm in part and reverse in part.

OHT, now defunct, was a manufacturer specializing in constructing heat exchangers to specifications supplied by its customers. On May 25, 1977, the Bank issued OHT a line of credit for $600,000, taking a security interest in OHT's inventory. On June

1, the Bank filed a financing statement covering, inter alia, "[a]ll inventory now or hereafter owned by the Debtor."

KTI is a company that designs and supplies process furnaces for the refinery and petrochemical industry. On August 18, 1977, it entered into a contract with OHT under which OHT was to build eight furnace economizers to KTI's specifications, in part from materials supplied by KTI, and in part from materials supplied by OHT. KTI was to ship to OHT certain specially designed and manufactured goods consisting of finned tubes, castings, fittings, and anchors (hereinafter referred to as the KTI Goods). OHT was to build eight box units (hereinafter referred to as the Box Units) from materials out of OHT's inventory, and then install the KTI Goods into the Box Units, resulting in eight completed furnace economizers. KTI agreed to make progress payments to OHT at various stages in the process. The purchase order form, supplied by KTI, provided that title to goods delivered to OHT by KTI would remain in KTI. Title to goods acquired by OHT from other sources for use in the KTI contract would pass to KTI upon the first progress (or other) payment made by KTI to OHT. KTI did not file under the UCC.

KTI procured the goods specified in the contract (the KTI Goods), and had them delivered to OHT. Delivery was complete by January 25, 1978. OHT began work on the contract. During this time, OHT's financial situation deteriorated, and it became necessary to seek additional financing from the Bank. The Bank agreed to make additional loans (separate from the line of credit), secured in part by specified accounts receivable of OHT. A loan was made to OHT on January 10, 1978, secured by the progress payments specified in the KTI–OHT contract. The Bank instructed KTI to make the first two progress payments directly to the Bank.

OHT's work on the contract reached the point at which OHT was entitled to the first two progress payments, a total of $42,600. Both payments, which KTI made on January 10 and January 19, 1978, were received by the Bank. OHT began work on the Box Units, but prior to their completion OHT management determined that the business' financial state could not support continued operation. On January 27, OHT shut down, and on January 30, OHT's management delivered the plant keys to the Bank. At that time, the Bank took possession and control of the plant where OHT's inventory, the Box Units, and the KTI Goods were located.

KTI demanded the surrender of the Box Units and the KTI Goods, but the Bank refused on the strength of its security interest in OHT's inventory, offering instead to sell the Box Units and the KTI Goods to KTI. Consequently, KTI filed this suit for conversion. A prolonged series of negotiations culminated in KTI's purchase of the Box Units and the KTI Goods on March 20, 1978.

KTI reserved the right to litigate all issues. After a trial to the bench, the court found that KTI was entitled both to the KTI Goods and to the Box Units, and awarded damages in the amount of $156,272.30 plus interest. Although we reach a similar result, we do so by a different route.

The Bank's argument for reversal is based on its status as a holder of a perfected security interest in OHT's inventory. The Bank asserts that both the KTI Goods and the Box Units were inventory collateral in OHT's hands, to which the Bank was entitled when OHT defaulted on the line of credit. The Bank contends that KTI's interest in the Box Units and in the KTI Goods amounted only to an unperfected security interest over which the Bank's perfected security interest had priority. KTI argues that the Bank's security interest was ineffective as to the goods at issue because, under the contract, KTI retained title and ownership rights in the KTI Goods and acquired title and ownership rights in the Box Units when it made the progress payments. The Bank asserts alternatively that even if the trial court was correct on the issue of liability, it erroneously computed the amount of damages.

I. Bank Security Interest in the KTI Goods

The Bank's claim to the KTI Goods is based on its perfected security interest in OHT's inventory. The Bank argues that when KTI had the KTI Goods delivered to OHT and OHT began work on the contract, the goods became inventory for the purposes of the Bank's security interest. The Bank insists that KTI's rights in the KTI Goods at most amounted to a retained, unperfected security interest. KTI bases its claim on its ownership of the goods as evidenced by the title retention clause in the contract, arguing that OHT was in the position of a bailee. Thus, KTI asserts, the goods were never part of OHT's inventory,[2] and therefore never became subject to the Bank's security interest.

The trial court examined the transaction between KTI and OHT to determine whether a "sale" by KTI to OHT had occurred when the KTI Goods were delivered to OHT. Finding none, it concluded that " 'Article Two has no application, and § 2–401(1) cannot operate to convert KTI's retention of title into a security interest under Article Nine.' " The court held additionally that, as a matter of law, " 'OHT has never had any interest in KTI's Goods other than that of a bailee.' " The court concluded that

2. The record shows that OHT believed these goods belonged to KTI and were not part of OHT's inventory. OHT had in fact reported to the Bank that there were goods in its plant that belonged to KTI. Additionally, no loans on the line of credit were made by the Bank after OHT received the KTI Goods. There is thus no question of a loan having been made in reliance on the KTI Goods as collateral.

KTI was entitled to possession of the KTI Goods notwithstanding the Bank's security interest.

In order for the Bank's security interest to include the KTI Goods and be enforceable, it must have attached to the goods. UCC § 9–203(1). A security interest attaches to collateral when (1) the debtor (here OHT) has signed a security agreement describing the collateral, (2) value has been given, and (3) the debtor has "rights in the collateral." Id. The first two requirements are met in this case. The issue here is whether OHT had sufficient rights in the collateral to meet the third requirement. The parties' disagreement is centered on whether OHT was a mere bailee of the KTI Goods, or instead had a greater property interest in them.

The phrase "rights in the collateral" is not defined in the UCC. The Code clearly does not require that a debtor have full ownership rights. See, e.g., tit. 12A, § 9–112. The Seventh Circuit has said that the requirement of "rights in the collateral" illustrates the general principal that " 'one cannot encumber another man's property in the absence of consent, estoppel, or some other special rule.' " In re Pubs, Inc., 618 F.2d 432, 436 (7th Cir.1980) (quoting First National Bank & Trust Co. v. McElmurray, 120 Ga.App. 134, 138, 169 S.E.2d 720, 724 (1969)).

In Amfac Mortgage Corp. v. Arizona Mall, 127 Ariz. 70, 618 P.2d 240 (Ct.App.1980), the debtor Mall had contracted with a third party for the construction of a shopping mall. The contract specified that the contractor would obtain the needed materials, and that title to the materials would pass to the Mall upon satisfaction of various conditions, including payment. Amfac loaned money to the Mall, taking a security interest in all materials to be incorporated in the Mall. The contractor acquired the materials and had them delivered, but prior to their incorporation and before any payments were made by the Mall to the contractor, the enterprise folded. Amfac brought an action to recover the unincorporated steel. The court, in deciding whether the Mall had had sufficient rights in the steel for Amfac's security interest to attach, stated that a debtor acquires sufficient rights when the debtor obtains possession of collateral pursuant to an agreement with the seller or manufacturer. Possession with contingent rights of ownership was held to be sufficient with or without payment on the contract. * * *

In Manger v. Davis, 619 P.2d 687 (Utah 1980), a consignment case, the Utah Supreme Court found that a debtor's "rights" in collateral must be in the nature of authority to subject the property to a security interest, and looked to the law of agency to resolve the issue. Id. at 690. In Connecticut Bank & Trust Co. v. Schindelman (In re Bosson), 432 F.Supp. 1013 (D.Conn.1977), the court found that under prevailing case law a debtor had sufficient rights when the debtor acquired possession of collateral pursuant

to a sales contract or like agreement. The court looked to principles of law external to the Code to find if such "rights" existed.
Id. at 1018.

Thus, it is clear that for a security interest to attach, a debtor
must have some degree of control or authority over collateral
placed in the debtor's possession. The Oklahoma Supreme Court,
in a case factually similar to the case before us, has said that the
requisite authority exists "where a debtor gains possession of
collateral pursuant to an agreement endowing him with any
interest other than naked possession." Morton Booth Co. v. Tiara
Furniture, Inc., 564 P.2d 210, 214 (Okl.1977). But see Chrysler
Corp. v. Adamatic, Inc., 59 Wis.2d 219, 208 N.W.2d 97, 104 (1973)
(bailee's possessory interest for limited purpose of repair not
sufficient "rights in the collateral"). The *Morton Booth* definition
strongly supports the Article Nine purpose of promoting certainty
in commercial loan transactions. *See* UCC, § 9–101, Official Comment. Otherwise, if a debtor received collateral from a third
party under an agreement giving the debtor authority to exercise
any outward indicia or manifestations of ownership or control, a
would-be creditor could easily be misled into making a loan under
an ineffective security agreement. For example, in *Morton Booth,*
the debtor, Tiara, contracted to build gun cabinets from materials
supplied primarily by Morton Booth, and then sell the completed
products to Morton Booth. Tiara, a furniture manufacturer, subsequently sought and received financing from the Small Business
Association, giving the participating banks a security interest in
Tiara's present and after-acquired inventory, which apparently
consisted of the same types of materials that were supplied it by
Morton Booth. *See* 564 P.2d at 211. Had the court found that
Tiara lacked sufficient "rights" in the Morton Booth-supplied
collateral for the banks' security interest to attach, the banks'
claim to the goods upon Tiara's default would have been defeated
by the sort of hidden-title subterfuge the Code was intended to
prevent.

This reason for the *Morton Booth* result is supported by
another feature of Article Nine. In this context, buyers such as
Morton Booth and KTI finance a debtor's operation by supplying
materials rather than money with which to buy materials. Such a
buyer-lender could easily protect itself from after-acquired property creditors of its contractor by filing an Article Nine purchase
money security interest in the goods supplied by it to the contractor, as well as those purchased or otherwise identified in the
contract by the contractor. See §§ 9–107, –312(3).[3] Requiring

3. * * * The general rule is that
priority between conflicting security interests in collateral is determined by
priority in time of filing or perfection,
or for unperfected interests, by time of
attachment, *id.* § 9–312(5). However,

§ 9–312(3) established an exception to
this general rule of first in time. Under § 9–312(3), the holder of a perfected
purchase money security interest in inventory enjoys priority over conflicting
security interests in the same inventory

buyers such as KTI to take this additional step—done easily and at minimal cost—thoroughly advances the Code policy of providing notice and certainty to inventory lenders.

In accordance with *Morton Booth Co.,* we conclude contrary to the district court that the Bank's perfected security interest in OHT's collateral attached to the KTI Goods.

*   *   *

NOTE

Litwiller Machine & Manufacturing, Inc. v. NBD Alpena Bank, 184 Mich.App. 369, 457 N.W.2d 163 (1990), follows *Kinetics*. In *Kinetics* KTI asserted that OHT was in possession of its goods as a bailee. For a somewhat comparable case in which a concurring opinion found the existence of a bailment, see In re Bristol Industries Corp., 690 F.2d 26, 30 (2d Cir.1982). A person in the position of KTI is sometimes referred to as a "financing buyer." See Jackson & Kronman, A Plea for the Financing Buyer, 85 Yale L.J. 1 (1975).

G.   PERFECTION BY POSSESSION

IN RE ROLAIN
United States Court of Appeals, Eighth Circuit, 1987.
823 F.2d 198.

EUGENE A. WRIGHT, CIRCUIT JUDGE.

We are asked to apply Minnesota law in this appeal arising from bankruptcy proceedings. The trustee in bankruptcy contends that the creditor bank has no perfected security interest in a negotiable instrument entrusted by the bank to an attorney agent. We find that there was a perfected security interest and affirm the judgment of the district court.

Norwest Bank loaned $163,000 to Rolain and a corporation of which he was president, United Wisconsin Properties. United Wisconsin executed a promissory note that was later partially guaranteed by United Corporations of Minnesota (UCM), its parent company. UCM's guarantee was secured by a note of one of its debtors, Owen. The Owen note was the collateral pledged by UCM to Norwest to secure the loan.

Norwest wished to perfect its security interest in the Owen note, which would require the bank or its agent to hold the

if the holder complies with certain procedures involving the giving of notice to competing secured parties. Id. See Comment, "Bailment for Processing": Article Nine Security Interest or Title Retention Contract? 61 Or.L.Rev. 441, 452–54 (1982) (arguing that such transactions are in effect buyer-financing devices intended to secure performance of contract and should be treated as Article Nine secured transactions).

document. Rolain was reluctant to let Norwest hold the note, however, because its terms were subject to a confidentiality agreement between himself and Owen. The parties agreed that the note would be held by Rolain's attorney, Mannikko, under a written agency agreement.

In November 1981, in consideration for Norwest extending the note's due date, UCM increased its guarantee of the note between Norwest and United Wisconsin. The agency agreement was amended accordingly. Rolain later filed for bankruptcy under Chapter VII and that proceeding was consolidated with those of the corporations owned by Rolain, including UCM and United Wisconsin.

Norwest moved in the bankruptcy court for a partial summary judgment that it had perfected its security interest in the Owen note. Bergquist, the trustee in bankruptcy, filed a cross-motion for summary judgment. The bankruptcy court granted the bank's motion and denied Bergquist's, and the district court affirmed.

* * *

A trustee may avoid transfers or encumbrances on property of the bankrupt estate. 11 U.S.C. § 544(a) (1982). The [Bankruptcy] Code vests him with the rights of a bona fide purchaser of real property from the debtor or a creditor having a judicial lien or an unsatisfied execution. Id. The trustee's rights under section 544 are derivative. They are those of a creditor under state law.
* * *

> Here, the applicable law is UCC § 9–305:
>
> *When Possession By Secured Party Perfects Security Interest Without Filing.*
>
> A security interest in letters of credit and advice of credit * * * goods, instruments (other than certificated securities), money, negotiable documents, or chattel paper may be perfected by the secured party's taking possession of the collateral. If such collateral other than goods covered by a negotiable document is held by a bailee, the secured party is deemed to have possession from the time the bailee receives notification of the secured party's interest.
>
> *   *   *   *   *   *   *   *   *

Comment 2 to this provision states:

> [p]ossession may be by the secured party himself or by an agent on his behalf: it is of course clear, however, that the debtor or a person controlled by him cannot qualify as such an agent for the secured party * * *.

The issue is whether Mannikko was under such control by Rolain that he could not serve as a bailee/agent under § 9–305.

The leading case on the issue of bailee/agent possession is In re Copeland, 531 F.2d 1195 (3d Cir.1976). The court held that an escrow agent, acting for the benefit of both parties, was a "bailee with notice" within the meaning of § 9–305 and that his possession perfected the creditor's security interest.   Id. at 1203–04. *Copeland* and subsequent cases explained that the purpose of the perfection requirement is to give notice to all current and potential creditors that the property was being used as collateral and could not be repledged.   * * *

Copeland noted that if the debtor or "an individual closely associated" with him holds the collateral, this would not sufficiently alert prospective creditors that the debtor's property is encumbered.   *Copeland,* 531 F.2d at 1204.   However, the holder of the document need not be under the sole control of the creditor. "[P]ossession by a third party bailee, who is not controlled by the debtor, which adequately informs potential lenders of the possible existence of a perfected security interest" satisfies the notice requirements of § 9–305.   Id.

Once the parties have designated an agent with no interest in the collateral, * * * and the collateral is delivered to him, the debtor no longer has unfettered use of the collateral and the notice function of section 9–305 is served by the agent's possession. * * *

Mannikko is a third party who asserts no interest in the collateral.   Because the Owen note was delivered to him under a written agency agreement, Rolain would not have unfettered use of it and could not repledge it.   If he did so, his lack of possession would notify the third party creditor that the note was encumbered.

Bergquist argues that a debtor's attorney may never be a suitable bailee because the attorney-client relationship necessarily means that the attorney is under the control of the client.   However, courts have held explicitly that attorneys may act as valid § 9–305 agents.   In *O.P.M. Leasing,* the debtor deposited money with its firm of lawyers to be held in escrow as security for performance under a lease contract.   46 B.R. at 664.   The court found that the law firm was a valid bailee.   Id. at 670; see also Barney v. Rigby Loan & Investment Co., 344 F.Supp. 694, 697 (D.Idaho 1972) (citing Henry v. Hutchins, 146 Minn. 381, 178 N.W. 807, 809 (Minn.1920) for proposition that debtor's attorney may serve as bailee or pledge holder).

The lawyers' possession of the security served " 'to provide notice to prospective third party creditors that the debtor no longer has unfettered use of [his] collateral.' "   *O.P.M. Leasing,* 46 B.R. at 670 (quoting *Ingersoll–Rand,* 671 F.2d at 844–45).   Because the debtor's attorneys had their client's consent and were acting as a fiduciary to the secured creditor, they were bound by the terms of the escrow agreement.   41 Bus.Law. at 1478.   Possession of the negotiable documents served notice to third parties that the documents were encumbered.   Id.

The same may be said here.   With Rolain's consent, Mannikko signed an agency agreement, promising to act as Norwest's agent in holding the note and perfecting Norwest's security interests.   He acted as a fiduciary to Norwest, was bound to respect the agency, and did so.

Bergquist argues that, even if a debtor's attorney may serve as a creditor's § 9–305 agent, the personal relationship between Rolain and Mannikko was so close that there was debtor control of the agent.   He says that the two engaged in business ventures, vacationed together, and confided in each other about personal matters.   Therefore, says Bergquist, Rolain controlled Mannikko and that Norwest and others were aware of that control.   The argument concludes that Mannikko's possession of the note did not put others on notice of the note's encumbrance.

This is unpersuasive.   Except for Rolain's claims, the record indicates nothing unusual about selecting Mannikko as Norwest's agent.   All parties agreed to the arrangement.   Indeed, it was desirable because Mannikko was one of the few persons whom both parties could trust to hold the note without disclosing its confidential terms.   There is no remaining question of material fact.

Norwest's security interest in the Owen note was perfected.

AFFIRMED.

NOTE: 1977 AMENDMENTS TO ARTICLE 8

The 1977 Amendments to Article 8 were the result of the breakdown in securities trading occasioned by the "paperwork crunch" of the late 1960s.   The unprecedented volume of shares sold overwhelmed the securities markets because each trade involved physical transfer of a share certificate.   A solution to this problem was to amend state business corporations codes to permit the issuance of stock in uncertificated form and to amend the UCC to deal with the issuance and transfer of uncertificated stock.   The latter was accomplished by the 1977 Amendments now enacted in almost all of the states.

With respect to secured transactions, the major change was the incorporation into Article 8 of provisions regarding the creation, perfection, and termination of security interests in all securities (defined in § 8–102(1)), both certificated and uncertificated. § 8–321 and § 8–313.   The definition of "instrument" in § 9–105 was amended to include a certificated, but not an uncertificated, security.   Section 9–203 (attachment) was amended to exclude security interests in securities.   Section 9–304 and § 9–305 as they applied to instruments were amended to exclude certificated securities. The effect is to make Article 8 control with respect to creation, perfection and termination of security interests in securities. Article 9 still governs other aspects of security interests in securities, e.g., choice of law (see § 9–103(6)), priorities, and default. § 8–321(3).

With respect to certificated shares, a security interest is both created and perfected when the debtor who has rights in collateral transfers the stock to a creditor who gives value. § 8–321(1) and (2). As Comment 2 to § 8–321 points out "an appropriate transfer will result not only in an enforceable security interest but also in one that is perfected. Under this section, an unperfected security interest in a security cannot be created." The debtor may make the requisite transfer under § 8–313(1) by giving possession of the certificate either to the creditor or its "financial intermediary," that is, a broker, bank, or other entity which maintains security accounts for its customers. In the case of stock in the possession of a bailee, § 8–313(1)(h) provides that the requisite transfer takes place when the debtor gives the bailee written notification signed by the debtor. The secured creditor may have the certificated security registered in its name if the debtor indorses the certificate for transfer. § 8–401. The secured creditor may then vote the shares and receive cash and stock distributions as the registered owner.

With respect to uncertificated shares, there can be no transfer by the traditional method of delivery of possession of the certificate because there is no certificate. Hence, under § 8–313(1)(b) transfer takes place when the security is registered to the secured party or its designee. Registration is accomplished by having the debtor who is the registered owner of the uncertificated security issue an "instruction" to the issuer. § 8–308(4). The secured party may be listed as the registered owner, thus gaining the right to vote the shares and receive dividends, or may elect to become a registered pledgee under § 8–108. In the case of a registered pledge, the registered owner continues to have all the rights of an owner except for the power to order a transfer. § 8–207(3). There can be no more than one registered pledgee at any time. § 8–108.

In many instances the pledgee of a certificated security will not become the registered owner because the agreement of the parties is that the debtor will continue to vote the shares and receive cash dividends. The concept of the registered pledge was introduced to allow the secured party of uncertificated stock to have the same rights as it would have as the pledgee of certificated stock that is not registered in its name. Comment to § 8–108. There is one difference in the rights of a pledgee of a certificated security and the registered pledgee of an uncertificated security. The former would not receive stock dividends or other distributions because the issuer does not know of, and need not consider, the rights of a nonregistered pledgee. Under § 8–207(6), the registered pledgee of an uncertificated security would receive securities issued in exchange for or distributed with respect to the uncertificated security as well as any money paid in exchange for or in redemption of that security. See the last paragraph of Comment 1 to § 8–207.

F.D.I.C. v. W. HUGH MEYER & ASSOCIATES, INC.

United States Court of Appeals, Fifth Circuit, 1989.
864 F.2d 371.

PATRICK E. HIGGINBOTHAM, CIRCUIT JUDGE:

In 1982, Hugh Meyer signed an agreement pledging some stock to the First National Bank of Midland. The pledge agreement entitled the bank to a security interest in the dividends upon the stock, but neither the bank nor the FDIC, the bank's successor in interest, registered the pledged shares in the bank's name. As a result, dividends from the pledged stock were delivered to Meyer. Among these dividends was a stock dividend worth about $500,000. Meyer eventually pledged these dividend shares to his law firm, Grambling & Mounce, to secure payment of a $125,000 retainer. Meyer then went bankrupt. His total indebtedness to the bank is in the neighborhood of $3 million. First Midland became insolvent and went into receivership. The FDIC sued Meyer and Grambling & Mounce to get the dividend shares. The district court held that the law firm had a perfected security interest in the shares up to the amount of its retainer, and that the FDIC was an unsecured creditor of the Meyer estate. The FDIC appeals. Because we find that possession is essential under Texas law to obtain a secured interest in securities, and because the bank never obtained possession of the contested securities, we affirm.

* * *

The bank, and later the FDIC, could have stopped Meyer from receiving dividends on the pledged stock by registering its holding of the pledged stock, or by putting a stop transfer order on the stock. The bank and the FDIC had on file forms, signed by Meyer, that would have permitted them to take these actions. The FDIC finally put a stop transfer order on the stock in June of 1985. But by that time, the horse was out of the barn.

The "horse," for purposes of this suit, is a 19,580 share stock dividend issued by Power Test in April 1985, and received by Meyer. Meyer claims, and the district court found, that he pledged and delivered this dividend stock to Grambling & Mounce in May 1985 as security for his promise to pay the firm's retainer.

* * *

The outcome of this case turns upon interpretation of Article 8 of the Uniform Commercial Code, as amended in 1977 and enacted into Texas law in 1983. * * * That article governs security interests in securities. The key question is whether the Code recognizes a security interest in stock shares—more precisely, in the language of the code, "certificated securities"—if the holder of the putative security interest has never possessed the shares. If not, then the FDIC is an unsecured creditor with respect to the dividend shares, and Grambling & Mounce is apparently the only secured creditor. Resolving this question of UCC law requires this court to write upon a rather clean slate.

There is a preliminary dispute between the parties as to the proper order of the issues. The FDIC asks the Court to consider first whether Grambling & Mounce took the stock as a bona fide purchaser, and then, if the Court finds that Grambling & Mounce did not, whether the FDIC had a perfected security interest in the stock. Meyer and the law firm contend that if the District Court was correct in its finding that the FDIC had no security interest in the stock and that Grambling & Mounce did have a perfected security interest, it is irrelevant whether or not Grambling & Mounce took without notice of any claims that the FDIC was trying to make.

We agree that we should first determine which, if any, parties developed security interests in the stock, and that we may thereby avoid the bona fides purchaser issue. Mere knowledge of a possible but as yet uncreated security interest does not suffice to defeat the perfected security interest of a later creditor. A contrary rule would undermine the "race of diligence among creditors" contemplated by the U.C.C. * * *

The FDIC suggested, at oral argument and without elaboration, that if the FDIC never developed a security interest in the contested shares, the bona fides issue was nonetheless relevant because "there was a conversion" of the shares. This argument begs the question. There can have been a conversion of an FDIC property interest only if the FDIC had such an interest. A mere unexercised contractual right to create a property interest is not itself a property interest. The question of whether the FDIC ever developed a security interest in the shares is thus necessarily antecedent to the question of whether a conversion occurred. Again, a contrary rule would undermine the incentives carefully established by the UCC's distinctions among secured interests, perfected secured interests, and other interests. If the FDIC never developed a security interest in the shares, and the law firm did develop a perfected security interest, it is plain that the district court's judgment is correct.

Article 8 of the Uniform Commercial Code, as amended in 1977 and enacted into Texas law in 1983, governs the creation and perfection of security interests in investment securities. The meaning of Article 8 is a question of law, and consequently we subject the district court's conclusions to *de novo* review. Under § 8–321(1), "A security interest in a security is enforceable and can attach only if it is transferred to the secured party or a person designated by him pursuant to a provision of § 8–313(1)." As applied to this case, the provision just quoted means that the FDIC, and similarly Grambling & Mounce, can claim a security interest in the contested stock only if it took that interest pursuant to a valid "transfer" as defined elsewhere in the Code.

The shares of Power Test dividend stock are certificated securities: that is, they are investment securities represented by physical certificates. Section 8–313(1)(a) specifies how one may effect a valid transfer of a security interest in such shares of stock. There must be a physical transfer of the shares from the pledgor to the pledgee: "Transfer of a security or a limited interest (including a security interest) therein to a purchaser occurs only at the time he or a person designated by him acquires possession of a certificated security."

* * *

Our analysis of this case thus depends upon the interaction between § 8–313(1)(a) and § 8–321. The implication of these two sections is that no party in this case can have acquired a security interest in shares of (certificated) stock without having taken actual possession of the stock certificates. The district court reached the same conclusion. Although there is little case law on this point, the relevant decisions do seem to assume that physical delivery is necessary to create a secured interest in certificated securities under the relevant provisions of Article 8. See, e.g., United States v. Doyle, 486 F.Supp. 1214, 1220 (D.Minn.1980) (applying amended version of UCC as enacted into Minnesota law; the case involves a "financial intermediary"). Every security interest transferred for value pursuant to § 8–313(1)(a), and thus any security interest created in this case, is a perfected security interest. § 8–321(2).

The FDIC proposes two ways to defeat this argument. First, the FDIC argues that an interaction between Article 8 and Article 9 gives it a perfected security interest in the dividend stock. Section 8–321(3)(b) provides, "A security interest in a security is subject to the provisions of Chapter 9, but no written security agreement signed by the debtor is necessary to make the security interest enforceable * * *. The secured party has the rights and duties provided under Section 9–207, to the extent they are applicable, whether or not the security is certificated, and, if certificated, *whether or not it is in his possession.*" The FDIC draws attention to the concluding phrase. Section 9–207 provides in part that "unless otherwise agreed, when collateral is in the secured party's possession the secured party may hold as additional security any increase or profits (except money) received from the collateral * * *." § 9–207(2)(c).

This argument appears question-begging. Section 9–207(2)(c) may mean only that *if* the pledgee receives increase or profit upon pledged collateral, the pledgee may rightfully keep the increase or profit. There is no dispute here that the FDIC could appropriately have retained the stock dividend as additional security had the FDIC ever received it. Rather, the issue is whether, given that Meyer received the stock dividend while the FDIC had a contractual claim upon it, the FDIC developed a security interest in the stock dividend. Section 9–207 does not appear to speak to that issue, and the FDIC does not cite any cases suggesting that the Section does so. Moreover, the FDIC's emphasis upon the concluding phrase in Section 8–321(3)(b) ("whether or not it is in his possession") is misplaced. On the FDIC's argument, the collateral referred to by that phrase is the base stock, and that stock was certainly in the FDIC's possession. The phrase is not a suggestion that a security interest in certificated securities can be obtained through means other than those specified in § 8–313. Rather, the phrase takes into account the possibility that a secured creditor might temporarily relinquish possession of the certificates after getting ahold of them.

Second, the FDIC asks the court to hold that its possession of the base stock impressed an "equitable lien" upon the dividend stock in favor of the FDIC. The FDIC bases this argument upon Powell v. Maryland Trust Co., 125 F.2d 260 (4th Cir.) cert. den. 316 U.S. 671, 62 S.Ct. 1046, 86 L.Ed. 1746 (1942) (interpreting Maryland law), and upon a line of cases interpreting *Powell*: Mathews v. Starr, 475 F.Supp. 37 (E.D.Va.1979) (following *Powell*) rev'd sub nom. In re Mathews, 626 F.2d 862 [Table], 29 U.C.C.Rept.Serv. 684 (4th Cir.1980) (ignoring *Powell*); In re Whitaker, 18 B.R. 314 (Bank.D.Kan.1982). The underlying ratio of *Powell* was that the stock dividend shares "were merely a part of the thing already pledged. They were not merely something which the Seaboard had agreed to pledge when they came into existence, but an essential part of what it had already pledged and which were subject, for that reason, to the pledge already created." 125 F.2d at 271. All parties to this suit apparently believe that the district court in the *Mathews* litigation accepted the equitable lien theory, and that the Fourth Circuit, in its unpublished opinion, rejected the theory and reversed *Powell sub silentio.*

In our view, the *Mathews* litigation does not necessarily overrule *Powell,* because *Mathews* involves Virginia law and *Powell* applies Maryland law. However, *Mathews* involved a stock split, not a stock dividend. 475 F.Supp. at 38. Whitaker likewise dealt with a stock split. 18 B.R. at 315. *Powell* also may have dealt with a stock split. Id.; see discussion of the character of the "stock dividend" in *Powell* as a mere record-keeping device which does not transfer profits to shareholders, 125 F.2d at 267; see also 18 B.R. at 317. Moreover, neither the *Mathews* cases nor *Powell* expressly considered the distinction between a contractual right to a stock dividend and a property (security) interest in the dividend. Finally, none of the cases was decided under the amended version of Article 8 of the U.C.C.

For these reasons, the cases cited by the FDIC do not justify application of the equitable lien theory in this case. Moreover, the Fourth Circuit's *Mathews* opinion, applying the unamended version of the U.C.C., rejected the equitable lien theory, even in the context of a stock split, precisely because possession is an absolute prerequisite to the creation of a security interest in stock shares. 626 F.2d 862, 29 U.C.C.Rept.Serv. at 686.

In summary, neither the language of the Texas code provisions nor any case law would favor reversing the district court's decision. The district court's ruling is consistent with the spirit of the U.C.C., which contemplates a "race of diligence among creditors." *Matter of E.A. Fretz Co., Inc.,* 565 F.2d at 371. This suit is the product of the FDIC's laxity. A diligent creditor would register its holdings, thereby guaranteeing its security and obviating the need for legal inquiry into the existence of an interest, or into the bona fides of a later claimant. Application of the general equitable theory proposed by the FDIC would be particularly inappropriate given the existence of a statutory scheme encouraging diligence, and given that the FDIC does not seek equity with "clean hands."

III

The district court concluded from the evidence that Grambling & Mounce possessed the shares and developed a perfected security interest in them. First Midland never possessed the shares. In light of the analysis developed above, the district court's determination that Grambling & Mounce has a perfected security interest in the shares while First Midland is an unsecured creditor is both consistent with the law and supported by the evidence. The decision of the district court is therefore

AFFIRMED.

NOTE

Hugh Meyer is discussed in Schroeder & Carlson, Security Interests Under Article 8 of the Uniform Commercial Code, 12 Cardozo L.Rev. 557, 620–625 (1990). Although the court believes that the FDIC is lax in not registering the shares so as to require that any stock dividend would be sent to it, Schroeder & Carlson point out that typically a pledgee does not register the shares in its name. The pledge agreement will provide that the debtor is entitled to the cash dividends until default, but the debtor will give the pledgee a stock power executed in blank which will allow the pledgee to transfer record ownership if it forecloses. Hence, until the stock power is exercised by the pledgee, both stock and cash dividends go to the debtor.

PROBLEMS

1. Debtor borrowed $10,000 from Bank and pledged a promissory note for $100,000 to secure the debt. Later Lender agreed to lend Debtor an additional $15,000. Debtor executed a security agreement granting Lender a security interest in the note in the possession of Bank. How can Lender perfect its security interest in the note? Is Bank a bailee under the second sentence of § 9–305? If so from whom should the notice come, Debtor or Lender? Must Bank agree to serve as a bailee? Note, Notice Problems in the Double–Pledge Situation: Can a Junior Pledgee Give Notice of a Security Interest to a Pledgee–Bailee under Section 9–305 of the Uniform Commercial Code?, 55 Fordham L.Rev. 809 (1987).

[handwritten margin note: – Take pcsscssion]

2. Change the collateral in Problem 1 to shares of stock represented by a certificate pledged to Bank. How may Lender perfect its security interest under Article 8?   § 8–313(h)(ii).

H. PERFECTION OF SECURITY INTERESTS IN CONSUMER GOODS

Article 9 was drafted at the dawn of the movement for reform of consumer credit law. By the end of the 40s a few states had retail installment sales acts and most had personal loan laws. Professor Gilmore recalls that at an early drafting stage it was contemplated that a number of the provisions found in retail installment sales acts would be incorporated into Article 9. Disclosure requirements and abolition of holding in due course with respect to consumer paper were examples of these provisions. It soon became apparent that no agreement could be reached on the desirability of these consumer protection provisions, and the final draft contained only a few remnants of the original grand scheme to protect the consumer debtor. The story is told in Gilmore, Security Interests in Personal Property § 9.2 (1965). The fall-back position taken was to provide in § 9–203(4) that Article 9 should be subordinate to those consumer protection laws passed in states that enacted the Code. This handed back to state legislatures the bone of contention concerning consumer credit protection on which they were to gnaw for the next 30 years. Section 9–206 also relinquished to the enacting states the determination of the validity of waiver of defenses clauses in consumer credit transactions.

Special protection for defaulting consumer debtors is found in § 9–505(1) and § 9–507(1). The most interesting vestige of the consumer protection phase of Article 9 is § 9–204(2) which greatly limits the effect of an after-acquired property clause in secured transactions involving consumer goods. The purpose of this section was to prevent a seller from adding on new sales to the balances of old ones merely by use of an after-acquired property clause in the original security agreement. But all a seller had to do to avoid this provision was to require the buyer to sign new security agreements at the time of subsequent sales. Nothing in Article 9 then prevented the seller from consolidating the sales and subjecting all the goods sold to the buyer to a security interest securing the combined balances of all the sales. This left the unfortunate buyer in the position described in Williams v. Walker-Thomas Furniture Co., 350 F.2d 445 (D.C.Cir. 1965), of being subjected to a lien on all property purchased until the last dollar of the consolidated balance was paid off. The solution to this abuse is found in Uniform Consumer Credit Code § 3.303 (1974) and other state statutes which allocate the debtor's payments entirely to discharging the debts first incurred, thus releasing from the seller's security interest each item sold as soon as the debtor's payments equal the debt arising from that sale. In short, there is no evidence that § 9–204(2) has been of any significance in protecting consumers. A business debtor is able to obtain loan credit by giving a floating lien on the debtor's assets. Why is this denied to an affluent consumer?

The major difference in the Code's treatment of consumer goods is that a purchase money security interest in consumer goods is automatically perfected at the time of attachment with no requirement of filing. § 9–302(1)(d). The reasons for this exception are: (1) consumer transactions are frequently small so the expense of filing can significantly add to the price that the consumer will have to pay; (2) consumer transactions are very numerous and they would unduly burden the filing system; (3) the pre-Code rule in most states did not require filing in conditional sale transactions; and (4) parties to consumer transactions are less likely to search the records. See Gilmore, Security Interests in Personal Property § 19.4 (1965).

However, the most important kind of consumer goods, motor vehicles, are specially treated. If the state does not have a certificate of title law perfection requires the filing of a financing statement. In states which have a certificate of title law perfection is accomplished by listing the security interest on the certificate of title. § 9–302(1)(d) and (3)(b). See White & Summers, Uniform Commercial Code § 24–17 (3d ed. 1988). Some states have similar requirements for boats. Security interests in airplanes must be recorded in the federal registry. See Sigman, The Wild Blue Yonder: Interests in Aircraft Under Our Federal System, 46 So.Cal.L.Rev. 316 (1973). A few states have set dollar limits above which filing is required for consumer goods.

PROBLEMS

1. Your client, Music Center, sells musical instruments of all kinds: strings (electric guitars are its best seller), pianos, brasses, and woodwinds. Music Center reserves a security interest in goods sold on credit. Some items run in excess of $1,000 in price, but most sales are between $50 and $200. Among its customers are amateur musicians: high school band and orchestra members and adults who play instruments for their own pleasure. Perhaps a fourth of Music Center's credit sales are made to professional musicians: members of professional performing groups and teachers who use their instruments in giving lessons. Advise your client how to set up workable operating procedures which will protect its security interest in goods sold. § 9–109(1) and (2), § 9–302(1)(d), and § 9–307(2). See also Strevell-Paterson Finance Co. v. May, 77 N.M. 331, 422 P.2d 366 (1967).

2. Manufacturer sold furniture to Retailer on credit, reserving a security interest in the furniture and its proceeds after it had been sold. Retailer sold furniture to numerous consumers, reserving a security interest in the furniture. Neither Manufacturer nor Retailer filed financing statements covering the furniture they sold. Does Manufacturer have a perfected security interest in the furniture that it sold to Retailer which is still in Retailer's possession? Does Retailer have a perfected security interest in furniture sold to consumers? See § 9–109(1) and (4).

I. MULTIPLE STATE TRANSACTIONS

We have examined the procedures for perfection of a security interest. This examination assumed that the transaction was governed by the law of a single jurisdiction. It is sometimes the case, however, that the law of more than one jurisdiction will apply to a secured transaction. There are two principal groups of cases. In one group the collateral subject to the security agreement may be located in more than one jurisdiction or it may have no fixed location, or the collateral may be an intangible and the debtor may operate in more than one jurisdiction. The problem is to determine in what jurisdiction a financing statement must be filed in order to perfect the security interest. A second group deals with the effect of the unauthorized removal by the debtor of collateral from the jurisdiction in which perfection of the security interest was made to another jurisdiction. The problem is to determine to what extent the perfected security interest will continue to be recognized as such after removal of the collateral to the second jurisdiction. Because the most common cases in the second group involve automobiles the problem is complicated by the fact of differences in the automobile registration laws of the various states. Section 9–103 deals with these matters. For an analysis of this section see Kripke, The "Last Event" Test for Perfection of Security Interests under Article 9 of the Uniform Commercial Code, 50 N.Y.U.L.Rev. 47 (1975).

1. ORDINARY GOODS

PROBLEM 1

In State A, Bank and Retailer executed a loan and security agreement under which Bank agreed to lend money to Retailer and Retailer agreed to give to Bank a security interest in all existing and after-acquired inventory of Retailer. In State A, Bank filed a financing statement covering inventory. Retailer's principal executive office is in State A but it has retail stores in State A and State B. After filing, Bank loaned money to Retailer under the agreement. At that time Retailer had inventory on hand in all of its stores. Is the security interest in Retailer's inventory perfected? Perfection is defined in § 9–303.

This case is governed by § 9–103(1)(b). In this case what is the "last event" referred to in that provision? Is the last event the same in the case of existing inventory and after-acquired inventory?

PROBLEM 2

Retailer in Problem 1 bought, for cash, goods for its inventory from Seller located in State C. The contract of sale provided for rail shipment of the goods F.O.B. Seller's plant in State C. The goods were shipped pursuant to the contract from Seller's plant in State C to one of Retailer's stores in State A. Must Bank make any further filing of a financing statement to perfect its security interest in this inventory?

Under § 2–401(2)(a) title to the goods passed from Seller to Retailer when the goods were delivered by Seller to the rail carrier in State C. What is the last event referred to in § 9–103(1) (b)?

Suppose in this case a creditor of Retailer acquired a judicial lien in the goods while they were still in State C in the possession of the rail carrier. Would the security interest of Bank in the goods prevail over the judicial lien of the creditor in State C? In this case what is the last event referred to in § 9–103(1)(b)?

PROBLEM 3

Seller sold industrial machinery to Buyer and delivery was made to Buyer at Seller's plant in State A. Buyer granted a security interest in the machinery to Seller as security for the price. Buyer had plants in State B and State C. The purchase agreement provided that the machinery was to be kept in Buyer's plant in State B until the price was fully paid. When Buyer took delivery of the machinery it immediately transported it to its plant in State C in violation of the agreement. The following day Seller filed in State B a financing statement covering the machinery. No financing statement was filed in either State A or State C. Later Buyer filed a petition in bankruptcy.

Read § 9–103(1)(c). Assume the machinery was never present in State B. Was the security interest of Seller perfected at the time of bankruptcy if bankruptcy occurred within 30 days of the time Debtor took delivery? Was it perfected if bankruptcy occurred 60 days after delivery? How does § 9–103(1)(b) bear on this question?

PROBLEM 4

Assume the same facts as Problem 3 except that the machinery was taken from State A to Buyer's plant in State B. Sometime later Buyer moved the machinery to Buyer's plant in State C. Seller filed its financing statement in State B before the machinery was moved from State B to State C. Buyer went into bankruptcy two months after the machinery entered State C. Was Seller's security interest perfected at the time of bankruptcy? § 9–103(1)(c) and § 9–103(1)(d)(i). If bankruptcy occurred six months after the machinery entered State C was the security interest perfected at the time of bankruptcy? Would your conclusions be different if the machinery had not been used by Buyer in State B but had simply been stored there for a few days prior to removal to State C?

The present § 9–103 resulted from the 1972 amendments to the Code. The case that follows, John Deere Co. v. Sanders, which was decided under the pre-1972 version of § 9–103, deals with the problem with which § 9–103(1)(d)(i) is concerned. In considering how Problem 4 and *John Deere* would be decided under § 9–103(1)(d)(i) note that that section gives a rule for deciding the question of when a perfected security interest becomes unperfected and a rule for deciding the rights of a third party who was a "purchaser" before the security interest became unperfected.

JOHN DEERE CO. v. SANDERS
Missouri Court of Appeals, Southern District, Division Three, 1981.
617 S.W.2d 606.

PER CURIAM. On September 18, 1979, plaintiff, John Deere Company, filed a petition in the Circuit Court of Pemiscot County, Missouri, for replevin of a John Deere combine. Defendant filed a motion to dismiss the petition on the grounds that it did not state facts to show plaintiff was entitled to relief. The trial court, on

February 11, 1980, entered an order sustaining the motion, and dismissed plaintiff's petition with prejudice. This appeal followed.

The basic factual allegations of the petition are as follows. On August 28, 1976, Danny Joe Grissom and Joe Grissom, who were residents of the state of Mississippi, purchased a John Deere combine from Rice's Equipment Company (Rice). The transaction occurred in Starkville, Oktibbeha County, Mississippi. The Grissoms executed a purchase money retail installment contract and security agreement for the balance of the purchase price, which amount, including finance charges, was $26,049.24. Rice, on the same day, for value received, assigned the contract and security agreement to plaintiff. On September 3, 1976, the security interest of plaintiff was perfected in Mississippi, by the filing of a financing statement in proper form, with the Clerk of the Chancery Court of Oktibbeha County, Mississippi.

The contract and security agreement, a copy of which was attached to the petition, provided that the Grissoms agreed to keep the combine in Oktibbeha County, Mississippi; would be in default if the Grissoms attempted to sell the combine; and, that in the event of default, the holder of the contract and agreement was authorized to take possession of the combine, and exercise other remedies provided by law. The Grissoms, in violation of the contract and security agreement and without the knowledge or consent of plaintiff, removed the combine from Oktibbeha County, Mississippi to the state of Missouri, where, on January 13, 1977, it was sold to Don Medlin in Pemiscot County, and was resold by Medlin to defendant J.W. Sanders on March 7, 1977. The petition does not state on what date the combine was removed from the state of Mississippi, but does state that the sales to Medlin and to Sanders both occurred within four months of the time that the combine was removed from the state of Mississippi.

The petition alleged that the sale of the combine from Medlin to defendant, within four months after the combine had been removed to Missouri, was subject to the security interest plaintiff had perfected in Mississippi; that defendant was in possession of the combine and refused to surrender possession of it to plaintiff; that plaintiff was legally entitled to immediate possession of the combine; that the combine had not been seized under any legal process; and, that plaintiff was in danger of losing its security interest unless it was given immediate possession of the combine or the property was otherwise secured. The petition also alleged that the present value of the combine was $24,000. The alleged facts in the petition were verified by plaintiff's affidavit.

The petition's prayer requested a prejudgment seizure of the combine, a judgment for its possession, and, in the event possession could not be obtained, that plaintiff be awarded a judgment of $24,000 against defendant.

* * *

The problem is whether the petition meets the requirement of Rule 99.03(b) by stating facts showing that the plaintiff is entitled to possession of the combine. The petition pleads that plaintiff has a properly perfected security interest in the state of Mississippi, that the Grissoms defaulted on their contract and removed the combine to Missouri, without the knowledge or consent of plaintiff, and that the combine was sold to Medlin and resold to defendant within four months after its removal from Mississippi to Missouri. Plaintiff's position is that the perfecting of its security interest in the state of Mississippi constituted constructive notice to Medlin and defendant in Missouri, and that defendant purchased the combine subject to the security interest of plaintiff. Defendant contends that plaintiff, by failing to reperfect its security interest by filing in Missouri, lost its preferential status, making its claim to the combine subordinate to that of defendant, who was an innocent purchaser. This is the issue on which battle was joined in the trial court, and is the only issue here.

There is no question that plaintiff's view was correct before Missouri adopted the Uniform Commercial Code. See Memphis Bank & Trust Co. v. West, 260 S.W.2d 866, 875 (Mo.App.1953); Finance Service Corporation v. Kelly, 235 S.W. 146, 147–148 (Mo. App.1921); and National Bank of Commerce v. Morris, 114 Mo. 255, 21 S.W. 511, 513 (1893). In these cases, the appellate court held, that based on the principles of comity, a chattel mortgage properly filed in the originating state gave constructive notice to innocent purchasers in Missouri, where the article was removed to Missouri without the knowledge or consent of the mortgagee, and where the mortgage had not been filed in Missouri prior to the time of its sale.

The only question remaining is whether Missouri's adoption of the Uniform Commercial Code (UCC) changed this rule of law. This question is one of first impression in Missouri. The pertinent portion of * * * § 9–103(3) * * * reads as follows:

> "If the security interest was already perfected under the law of the jurisdiction where the property was when the security interest attached and before being brought into this state, the security interest continues perfected in this state for four months and also thereafter if within the four-month period it is perfected in this state. The security interest may also be perfected in this state after the expiration of the four-month period; in such case perfection dates from the time of perfection in this state. If the security interest was not perfected under the law of the jurisdiction where the property was when the security interest attached and before being brought

into this state, it may be perfected in this state; in such case perfection dates from the time of perfection in this state."

This section was adopted by the Missouri Legislature in 1963, and has not been amended since.

The four-month protection period proviso set out in the statute has been interpreted two different ways. The first view gives the secured party four months of absolute protection in the removal state, and the second gives him four months of conditional protection, the condition being refiling in the removal state within that four-month period. The absolute protection version is favored by the overwhelming weight of authority in both cases and commentary. The absolute protection version is compatible with substantive law in Missouri that predated the enactment of § 9–103(3). The statute merely modified Missouri substantive law by limiting the period during which an out-of-state lienholder would have absolute priority over a Missouri purchaser to a period of four months, without reperfecting the security interest by filing in Missouri. * * *

On appeal, defendant agrees that the absolute protection rule is the majority view, but argues that Missouri should apply the minority view, i.e., the conditional protection approach, for the reason that the Uniform Commercial Code has been amended to make the conditional protection view the prevailing one. In 1972, the following code revision was made in Uniform Commercial Code Section 9–103(1)(d)(i):

> "(d) When collateral is brought into and kept in this state while subject to a security interest perfected under the law of the jurisdiction from which the collateral was removed, the security interest remains perfected, but if action is required by Part 3 of this Article to perfect the security interest,
>
> (i) if the action is not taken before the expiration of the period of perfection in the other jurisdiction or the end of four months after the collateral is brought into this state, whichever period first expires, the security interest becomes unperfected at the end of that period and is thereafter deemed to have been unperfected as against a person who became a purchaser after removal; * * *."

Defendant urges that to insure uniformity under the code we should adopt this interpretation as the correct one. The argument is ingenuous but not persuasive. What we are dealing with here is the interpretation of a state statute, which is § 9–103(3). We believe that a fair reading of this section mandates absolute protection of plaintiff's security interest that it had perfected in Mississippi for a period of four months from the time of the removal of the combine to Missouri, regardless of whether plaintiff had reperfected such interest by filing in Missouri. Defendant is asking us to judicially amend the statute to conform with the intent and meaning of the 1972 Uniform Commercial Code Revision. We decline to do so. The business of legislating should be left to the General Assembly. They have had eight years to adopt the proposed statutory revision, but have chosen not to do so. This being so, we do not believe that we should read into our present statute something that is not there.

* * *

The judgment of the trial court is reversed, and the cause is remanded to the trial court with directions to set aside its order of February 11, 1980, which order dismissed plaintiff's petition with prejudice, and to grant defendant sufficient time to file responsive pleadings to plaintiff's petition.

NOTE

Suppose during the four-month period after the collateral was removed to Missouri, John Deere Co. had made a written demand on the Grissoms to return the combine. There was no response, and John Deere Co. neither seized the combine nor filed in Missouri under § 9–402(2)(a). Has John Deere Co. taken the "action" called for in § 9–103(1)(d)(i)? The court in First National Bank v. John Deere Co., 409 N.W.2d 664 (S.D.1987), holds that an assertion of rights can constitute the requisite "action." The court in United States v. Handy & Harman, 750 F.2d 777 (9th Cir. 1984), strongly disagrees. What if John Deere Co. had filed suit for possession in Missouri during the four-month period but judicial officials had not yet seized the property within that period?

2. GOODS COVERED BY CERTIFICATES OF TITLE

Many states have certificate of title statutes covering automobiles, trailers, mobile homes, boats, tractors and the like, under which security interests in the goods are indicated on the certificate of title. In these states a security interest in the goods is perfected by complying with the certificate of title statute rather than by filing a financing statement under the UCC. § 9–302(3) (b). Collateral of this kind is covered by § 9–103(2).

Automobiles are registered in all states. In some states registration is accompanied by a certificate of title on which any security interest in the automobile is indicated. In others the registration of the automobile does not indicate property interests in the automobile. Cases under § 9–103(2) may arise when an automobile registered and subject to a perfected security interest in one state is taken to a second state where a new registration is obtained. The cases fall into three categories: 1. those in which the first state does not have a certificate of title statute but the second state does; 2. those in which the first state is a certificate of title state and the second is not; and 3. those in which both states have certificate of title statutes. Read Comment 4(a) and (b) to § 9–103.

The following case arose under the pre-1972 version of § 9–103. It discusses that statute as well as the changes made in the 1972 version. Consider how the case would have been decided under the 1972 Code. § 9–103(2)(c) and § 9–103(1)(d). The latter section refers to "action * * * required by Part 3 of this Article to perfect the security interest" that must be taken by the secured party prior to the expiration of the four months period. In the case of an automobile registered under a certificate of title statute, what is that action? Comment 4(d) and (e) to § 9–103.

IAC, LTD. v. PRINCETON PORSCHE–AUDI

Supreme Court of New Jersey, 1978.
75 N.J. 379, 382 A.2d 1125.

PASHMAN, J. The only question before the Court is whether the interest of a holder of a valid foreign lien remains superior to that of an innocent purchaser of the encumbered goods where the buyer is a dealer with respect to the goods and the purchase takes place within four months of the transfer of the property to New Jersey. Simply put, the issue is one of straightforward statutory construction involving [1962 UCC] § 9–103(3) and (4).

On August 2, 1976 Charles Ryan applied to IAC, Ltd., a Canadian corporation, to finance his purchase of a new Porsche automobile from Auto Hamer, Inc., a registered Porsche dealer located in Quebec, Canada. Ryan made a down payment of $5,700 and received financing for the purchase from IAC in the amount of $10,000. Later that day Auto Hamer was tendered the full purchase price and Ryan received his car.

Ryan had executed a conditional sales agreement with Auto Hamer in which title of the vehicle remained in the vendor until payment of the $10,000 loan principal and a $2,470.26 finance charge. The agreement further provided for an immediate assignment of the contract, title and all rights of the vendor to IAC. This contract fully complied with the applicable requirements of the Canadian Consumer Protection Act. According to the Appellate Division, "it is not disputed that * * * the security interest of plaintiff was perfected in Canada and that plaintiff thereby obtained a valid lien on the automobile under the law of Canada." 147 N.J.Super. 212, 215, 371 A.2d 84, 85 (App.Div.1977).

At some point between August 2 and August 6, 1976, Ryan acquired a certificate of registration in Quebec. This document did not require disclosure of the IAC security interest and no notation of the existence of the lien appeared on its face. Ryan then drove the vehicle to Trenton, New Jersey, where he changed the Canadian registration to one in New Jersey and acquired a certificate of title from the Division of Motor Vehicles. The New

Jersey certificate of title requires disclosure of any encumbrances on the vehicle. Nevertheless, as a result of Ryan's false representation that there were no such liens, he was issued a "clean" certificate of title.

On August 6, 1976 Ryan sold the car to defendant Princeton Porsche-Audi, a good faith purchaser without knowledge of the security interest, for $9,000. The vehicle had some 610 total miles on its odometer. Princeton Porsche-Audi would normally have paid $10,500 for a comparable vehicle in the wholesale market.

It is undisputed that at some point thereafter Princeton Porsche-Audi became aware of the lien. The exact time is contested, as is an alleged promise by defendant not to resell the auto. However, these factual disputes and the good faith of Princeton Porsche-Audi were disposed of by stipulation of the parties in order to permit summary disposition of the case. At any rate, an attempted sale to a Pennsylvania dealer fell through when the buyer received notice of the lien. Defendant then sold the automobile to a customer of its own.

Plaintiff abandoned any effort to regain possession of the automobile through replevin, and sought damages for conversion. IAC's motion for summary judgment on the issue of defendant's liability was granted. The Appellate Division reversed the grant of summary judgment. 147 N.J.Super. 212, 371 A.2d 84. We granted certification to consider this troublesome issue under the Uniform Commercial Code (U.C.C.) which had spawned inconsistent results across the country. 74 N.J. 277, 377 A.2d 681 (1977).

Resolution of this dispute turns on our interpretation of the applicable conflict of laws rule of the U.C.C., § 9–103(3), and the scope of the section which serves as an exception to that rule, § 9–103(4). These statutes provide, in pertinent part, as follows:

(3) If personal property * * * is already subject to a security interest when it is brought into this state, the validity of the security interest in this state is to be determined by the law (including the conflict of laws rules) of the jurisdiction where the property was when the security interest attached. * * * If the security interest was already perfected under the law of the jurisdiction where the property was when the security interest attached and before being brought into this state, the security interest continues perfected in this state for four months and also thereafter if within the four month period it is perfected in this state.

* * *

(4) * * * [I]f personal property is covered by a certificate of title issued under a statute of this state or any other jurisdiction which requires indication on a certificate of title of any security interest in the property as a condition of perfection,

then the perfection is governed by the law of the jurisdiction which issued the certificate.

The first section represents a compromise between the harsh common law rule under which a good faith purchaser would always lose against the claim of the secured party, and the equally undesirable rule which would permit such a purchaser to always prevail, with the consequent encouragement of fraud and theft. The four month period was deemed to be a reasonable time in which a vigilant creditor could locate the vehicle and register his lien in the new jurisdiction. The real issue is the meaning of the second section, 9–103(4), and the type of situation in which it applies. A commentator has noted the difficulties in interpreting this statutory provision.

> Subsection (4) suffers from an inherent ambiguity in that it is textually susceptible to two interpretations as to what point in time the property must be 'covered by a certificate of title' for the subsection to apply. Although not articulated in the decision, *Stamper* construes the statute to mean that subsection (4) applies only if the property is covered by a certificate of title (indicating the existence of a security interest) at the time it is brought into the enacting state (New Jersey). However, another possible interpretation is that subsection (4) applies if the property is covered by a certificate of title (indicating the existence of a security interest) at the time of the transaction under scrutiny * * * even though this may be subsequent to entry. [Comment, 47 Boston Univ.L.Rev. 430, 433 (1966)]

The case referred to in the note, The First Nat'l Bank of Bay Shore v. Stamper, 93 N.J.Super. 150, 225 A.2d 162 (Law.Div.1966), is still considered to be the leading case on the issue at bar. In *Stamper*, the court held that the conditional seller's assignee could recover from the defendant who had bought a used automobile from the conditional buyer. The conditional seller's security interest had been validly perfected in New York, and the conditional buyer had sold the car within four months of moving to New Jersey, under a "clean" certificate of ownership issued by the Division of Motor Vehicles. The conditional seller did not file his security interest within four months of the transfer of the vehicle to New Jersey. Nevertheless, the court found 9–103(3) applicable and the innocent purchaser from the conditional buyer was held liable.

Stamper relied heavily on Casterline v. General Motors Acceptance Corp., 195 Pa.Super. 344, 171 A.2d 813 (Super.Ct.1961); Churchill Motors, Inc. v. A. C. Lohman, Inc., 16 A.D.2d 560, 229 N.Y.S.2d 570 (App.Div.1962), and Al Maroone Ford Inc. v. Manheim Auto Assoc., Inc., 205 Pa.Super. 154, 208 A.2d 290 (Super.Ct. 1965). *Stamper* was in turn relied on by the trial court in the instant case. The Appellate Division herein questioned the validity of this authority. It noted that *Casterline* was concerned with transactions which took place before the enactment of U.C.C. 9–103(4) in Pennsylvania and had not even discussed the effect of that subsection. As recognized by the Appellate Division, *Churchill Motors* and *Al Maroone*, supra, erroneously relied on *Casterline*. The Appellate Division also rejected the comment of the Editorial Board of the Uniform Commercial Code with respect to subsection (4).

> Subsection 4 is new to avoid the possible necessity of duplicating perfection in the case of a vehicle subject to a certificate of title law requiring compliance therewith to perfect security interest. The certificate of title law requirements are adopted as the test for perfection.

This comment was also relied on by the *Stamper* court, but the Appellate Division refused to consider it because our legislature did not include it in the Code comments which follow § 9–103.

To compound our difficulties, the explanatory comment 7 to § 9–103 is not free of ambiguity.

> (7) Collateral other than accounts, contract rights, general intangibles and mobile equipment may be brought into this State subject to a security interest which has attached and may have been perfected under the laws of another jurisdiction. If the property is covered by a certificate of title, subsection (4) applies. In other cases, under subsection (3) this Article applies from the time the collateral comes into this state, except that (1) validity of the security interest is determined by the law of the jurisdiction where it attached (unless pursuant to an understanding of the parties the collateral is brought here within 30 days thereafter) and (2) if the security interest was perfected in the jurisdiction where the collateral was kept before being brought here, it continues perfected in this state for four months after the collateral is brought in, although the filing requirements of this Article have not been complied with here. After the four month period the secured party must comply with the perfection requirements of this Article (i.e., must file if filing is required).

The comment does not address the significance of the timing of the procurement of the certificate of title. Thus, neither the statute nor the commentary thereto clearly indicates whether § 9–103(3) or (4) applies under the facts at bar.

Insofar as the case law is concerned, the majority view is that if a security interest is perfected under the law of the jurisdiction in which it attaches, its priority cannot be defeated by the unauthorized securing of a "clean" certificate of title in another jurisdiction. * * * The Supreme Court of Texas held to the contrary in Phil Phillips Ford, Inc. v. St. Paul Fire & Mar. Ins. Co., 465

S.W.2d 933 (Tex.1971), ruling that once a Texas certificate of title issued, the applicable law was that of Texas and under its statutes only a lien actually noted on the certificate could be asserted against an innocent purchaser. As with the New Jersey statutes, the Texas statutory codification of the U.C.C. had omitted the comment to subsection (4) relied on in *Stamper*.

The 1972 amendments to Article 9 of the U.C.C. changed section 9–103. Some of the revisions were substantive, but the major purpose of the new section was one of clarification.

OFFICIAL REASONS FOR 1972 CHANGE

The section has been completely rewritten to clarify the relationship of its several provisions to each other and to other sections defining the applicable law. [Uniform Commercial Code (U.L.A.) § 9–103. (1977 pamphlet)]

Although our legislature has not yet enacted the 1972 amendments to Article 9, we believe it is appropriate to accord some deference to the views of the Code drafters where they might shed light on the instant problem. Under the reversed section 9–103, a professional buyer in the business of selling goods of the particular type involved, such as Princeton Porsche-Audi, would be defeated by the claim of the secured party, but a non-professional (consumer) buyer in such a position would prevail.

U.C.C. 9–103(2)(d), the amended code section provides:

If goods are brought into this state while a security interest therein is perfected in any manner under the law of the jurisdiction from which the goods are removed and a certificate of title is issued by this state and the certificate does not show that the goods are subject to the security interest or that they may be subject to security interests not shown on the certificate, the security interest is subordinate to the rights of a buyer of the goods who is not in the business of selling goods of that kind to the extent that he gives value and receives delivery of the goods after issuance of the certificate and without knowledge of the security interest.

The commentary to revised section 9–103, applicable to 9–103(2)(d), states:

(d) If a vehicle not described in the preceding paragraph (i.e., not covered by a certificate of title) is removed to a certificate state and a certificate is issued therefor, the holder of a security interest has the same 4-month protection, subject to the provision discussed in the next paragraph of Comment. (e) Where 'this state' issues a certificate of title on collateral that has come from another state subject to a security interest perfected in any manner, problems will arise if this state, from whatever cause, fails to show on its certificate the security interest perfected in the other jurisdiction. This state will have every reason, nevertheless, to make its certificate of title reliable to the type of person who most needs to rely on it. Paragraph (2)(d) of the section therefore provides that the security interest perfected in the other jurisdiction is subordinate to the rights of a limited class of persons buying the goods while there is a clean certificate of title issued by this state, without knowledge of the security interest perfected in the other jurisdiction. The limited class are buyers who are non-professionals, i.e., not dealers and not secured parties, because these are ordinarily professionals.

Turning to our statute in its present form, we feel constrained to differ with the Appellate Division's conclusion that under § 9–103(4) a professional buyer who purchases a vehicle with a clean certificate of title must prevail over the holder of a valid, but undisclosed, foreign lien. While we recognize that there is authority for this view, Phil Phillips Ford, Inc., supra, nevertheless we favor an interpretation of § 9–103(3) and (4) which protects the interest of the foreign lienholder. This position not only promotes interests of comity but also discourages the fraudulent conduct indirectly sanctioned by the Appellate Division's construction.

We agree with the observation of the Supreme Court of Washington with respect to the narrow scope of subsection (4).

> Does the subsection apply to all security interests, or only to those which attach after the certificate is issued? If it was meant to apply to all such interests, there is no way in which a person in the appellant's [a foreign lienholder from a non-title jurisdiction] position can protect himself. It would seem that if the draftsmen and the legislature had intended such a harsh result, the intent would have been more clearly expressed. [Associates Realty Credit Ltd. v. Brune, supra, 568 P.2d at 790]

Also pertinent is the succinct observation about subsection (4) in Judge Wright's special concurrence in General Motors Acceptance Corp. v. Long–Lewis Hardware Co., supra, 306 So.2d at 281, that "[i]t certainly was not intended to provide a loophole through which swindlers could pass and defeat a security interest legally perfected where it attached." Thus, we hold that § 9–103(4) should only be applied to goods which at the time of entry into this state are covered by a certificate of title. Section 9–103(3) should apply to all goods which are moved into New Jersey from non-certificate of title jurisdictions. If a certificate of title is subsequently acquired, § 9–103(3) remains applicable according to its terms.

With respect to professional buyers such as Princeton Porsche-Audi the four month grace period is absolute, and bona-fide status is no protection. Such buyers need look no further than the upper right hand corner of a Certificate of Ownership issued by New Jersey to know that a vehicle was once registered in another jurisdiction. Where such is the case, the alphabetic notation "Z" is prominently printed. Such a notation should put the buyer on notice that some investigation may be in order. To be completely safe without the necessity of further inquiries, the buyer should purchase such a vehicle only after four months have elapsed since the New Jersey registration date.

Since this case involves a professional buyer, it is not necessary for us to consider whether the same result would occur if an innocent consumer had purchased the automobile directly from Ryan. The 1972 amendments were primarily concerned with clarification of the meaning of 9–103, which was inartfully drafted in the 1962 version, and our holding is supportive of the purposes sought to be served by those amendments and in no sense constitutes a usurpation of the legislative function. However, since resolution of the issue is unnecessary to our disposition of this case, we reserve consideration thereof for an appropriate future case. Thus, our holding is limited to professional buyers in the application of the statute.

The judgment of the Appellate Division is reversed and the judgment of the trial court is reinstated.

PROBLEMS

1. Secured Party had a perfected security interest in Debtor's personal automobile under a certificate of title of State A. Secured Party retained possession of the certificate. Debtor took the automobile to State B and immediately registered it there. State B does not have a certificate of title statute. Assume that two months later Debtor a. sold the automobile to a car dealer; or b. sold the automobile to a non-dealer; or c. granted a security interest in the automobile. What are the rights of Secured Party? § 9–103(2)(b) and Comment 4(c) to § 9–103. How would your answer change if the rights of the third parties arose six months after the automobile entered State B?

2. Assume the same facts as in Problem 1 except that State B has a certificate of title statute and that Debtor obtained in that state a clean certificate of title. What are the rights of Secured Party? § 9–103(2)(b) and (d).

3. ACCOUNTS, GENERAL INTANGIBLES, AND MOBILE GOODS

In *Golf Course Builders*, the case that follows, the debtor granted a security interest in inventory classified in Article 9 as "mobile goods" (goods of a type which are normally used in more than one jurisdiction). The debtor had places of business in more than one state. The issue was to determine the state in which a financing statement had to be filed in order to perfect the security interest. The case was decided under the 1962 Official Text of Article 9 and § 9–103(2) was the governing provision. Under that provision filing had to be made in the state in which the debtor's "chief place of business" was located. Under the current Official Text of Article 9, filing would have to be made in the state in which the debtor "is located." § 9–103(3)(b). Under § 9–103(3)(d), a debtor with places of business in more than one state is located in the state in which the "chief executive office" of the debtor is located. The meaning of the quoted words is discussed in Comment 5(c) to § 9–103. The discussion by the court in *Golf Course Builders* is also relevant in determining the meaning of those words.

IN RE GOLF COURSE BUILDERS LEASING, INC.

United States Court of Appeals, Tenth Circuit, 1985.
768 F.2d 1167.

KERR, DISTRICT JUDGE.

* * *

The appellant, John B. Jarboe, Trustee for the bankrupt, Golf Course Builders Leasing, Inc., appeals from the decision of the district court reversing the ruling of the United States Bankruptcy Court for the Northern District of Oklahoma.

The facts of the case are not in dispute and many facts were stipulated in the bankruptcy pretrial order. Golf Course Builders Leasing, Inc. (GCB) was incorporated in Colorado in 1975 and later became domesticated to do business in Oklahoma on May 6, 1977 in connection with the filing of an unrelated lawsuit there. GCB was established by its sole shareholder, Lew Hammer, for the purpose of leasing heavy equipment to another corporation owned mainly by Hammer, Lew Hammer, Inc. (LHI). LHI was engaged in the business of general contracting and landscaping of golf courses.

The golf course landscaping business soon became unprofitable, but the heavy equipment which GCB leased was adaptable to mining operations. GCB began using the equipment for coal mining in Oklahoma in September of 1976. At that time, the equipment was moved to Oklahoma on the mineral lease sites, with the exception of two pieces of equipment still located on a previous job site in Idaho. This equipment, too, was later moved to Oklahoma for use in the coal mining operations.

In October of 1976, after mining operations had commenced, Lew Hammer and GCB obtained a loan from the United Bank of Denver (bank) in the amount of $50,000, providing to the bank as security an interest in GCB's accounts receivable. In January of

1977, Hammer, on behalf of GCB, obtained further financing from the bank, executing a $750,000 promissory note. In March 1977, another promissory note was executed to the bank for $50,000. The notes were secured by accounts receivable and inventory belonging to GCB. This inventory consisted mainly of "mobile goods" and "mobile equipment," as characterized by the Uniform Commercial Code. The funds were intended to be used in purchasing additional equipment for the mining operations and financing statements were timely filed by the bank in Colorado. On September 13, 1977 the bank filed additional financing statements in Oklahoma; however, on September 19, 1977 an involuntary bankruptcy petition was filed by GCB creditors seeking that GCB be declared bankrupt.

Pursuant to an agreement entered into in August of 1977 between GCB and Petroleum Reserve Corporation, GCB sold its equipment in October of 1977, with proceeds totaling $710,070.50. These proceeds were placed with the bank in accordance with a court approved stipulation. The proceeds from GCB's receivables amounted to $77,900, which the trustee held after collection. The trustee filed a complaint in bankruptcy court alleging that the bank was not entitled to the proceeds from the sale of the mobile equipment because it had not perfected its security interest in Oklahoma until after it had become aware of GCB's insolvent status.

With regard to the perfection of a security interest under the Uniform Commercial Code of both Colorado and Oklahoma, the provision concerning the conflict of laws on "mobile goods" is identical for each state. That language provides:

> (2) If the *chief place of business* of a debtor is in this state, this Article governs the validity and perfection of a security interest and the possibility and effect of proper filing with regard to general intangibles or with regard to goods of a type which are normally used in more than one jurisdiction (such as automotive equipment, rolling stock, airplanes, road building equipment, commercial harvesting equipment, construction machinery and the like) if such goods are classified as equipment or classified as inventory by reason of their being leased by the debtor to others. Otherwise, *the law* (including the conflict of laws rules) *of the jurisdiction where such chief place of business is located shall govern.* If the chief place of business is located in a jurisdiction which does not provide for perfection of the security interest by filing or recording in that jurisdiction, then the security interest may be perfected by filing in this state.

Okla.Stat. tit. 12A, § 9–103(2) (1972); Colo.Rev.Stat. § 4–9–103(2) (1973) (emphasis added).

The bankruptcy court in construing § 9–103(2), held that the "chief place of business" of GCB was Oklahoma, and that, therefore, Oklahoma was the proper place for filing financing statements and perfecting the bank's security interests in the mobile goods. Thus, the Colorado filings by the bank were ineffective. Further, the bankruptcy court held that the filings made by the bank in Oklahoma only a few days before bankruptcy proceedings were instituted constituted a voidable preference since the bank had reasonable cause to believe GCB was insolvent at the time.

Other portions of the bankruptcy court's holding concerning other security interests are not before this court on appeal.

The district court in reversing the decision of the bankruptcy court, found that the determination of "chief place of business" under § 9–103(2) was a question of law and that the bankruptcy court had erred in finding GCB's "chief place of business" to be Oklahoma. The district court held that as Colorado was GCB's "chief place of business," the bank had properly perfected its security interests in Colorado and should, therefore, have been adjudged a secured creditor. The district court never reached the voidable preference issue.

*   *   *

We agree with the district court that here the determination of GCB's "chief place of business" is a question of law, there being no dispute as to the facts. Furthermore, we conclude that the bankruptcy court erred in its legal conclusion that Oklahoma was the "chief place of business" because it misconstrued § 9–103(2), thus failing to apply the correct legal standard.

The bankruptcy court relied heavily and almost solely on the "volume of business" test set forth in Tatelbaum v. Commerce Investment Co., 257 Md. 194, 262 A.2d 494 (1970), 7 U.C.C. 406 (1970), in concluding that Oklahoma was GCB's "chief place of business." In *Tatelbaum,* the court determined that "chief place of business" under Maryland's § 9–401 relating to the recordation place of financing statement was analagous to that under § 9–103 and that it meant the place where the corporate debtor conducted the greatest volume of business activity. *Tatelbaum,* 262 A.2d at 498. The bankruptcy judge, after reviewing the facts, concluded that GCB conducted its greatest volume of business in Oklahoma and that Oklahoma was, therefore, the "chief place of business."

In the present case, it is undisputed that GCB's volume of business was greatest in Oklahoma. However, we agree with the district court's reliance on the Ninth Circuit case of In re J.A. Thompson & Son, Inc. v. Shepherd Machinery Co., 665 F.2d 941, 949–950 (9th Cir.1982), that volume of business may be a factor but it cannot be the only factor in determining "chief place of business."

The official comments to code section 9–103 are important in
providing guidance as to what the drafters of the code intended as
the "chief place of business" for multi-state operators. The official
comment by the drafters of the Uniform Commercial Code § 9–
103, comment 3 provides in part:

> 'Chief place of business' does not mean the place of incorpora-
> tion: it *means the place from which in fact the debtor manages
> the main part of his business operations.* This is the *place
> where persons dealing with the debtor would normally look for
> credit information, and is the appropriate place for filing.*
> The term 'chief place of business' is not defined in this Section
> or elsewhere in this Act. Doubt may arise as to which is the
> 'chief place of business' of a multi-state enterprise with decen-
> tralized, autonomous regional offices. A secured party in
> such a case may easily protect himself at no great additional
> burden by filing in each of several places. Although under
> this formula, as under the accounts receivable rule stated in
> subsection (1), there will be doubtful situations, the subsection
> states a rule which will be simple to apply in most cases,
> which will make it possible to dispense with much burden-
> some and useless filing, and which will operate to preserve a
> security interest in the case of non-scheduled operations.

(emphasis added).

The court in *Thompson,* relying on this official comment,
concluded that the drafters of the code "contemplated a two-fold
inquiry focusing first on the 'place from which * * * the debtor
manages the main part of his business operations,' and second, on
the reasonable expectations of creditors." *Thompson,* 665 F.2d at
949. Recognizing that confusion could emanate from use of the
concept "debtor's place of management," the *Thompson* court
examined the later revision of § 9–103 which utilizes the phrase
"chief executive office." Oklahoma, too, has adopted this newer
version of the code which states that "(d) a debtor shall be deemed
located at his place of business if he has one; at his *chief executive
office if he has more than one place of business;* otherwise at his
residence * * *." (emphasis added). This subsequent amendment and its legislative history, while not controlling, should be
given some weight in the construction of the earlier statute.
Glidden Co. v. Zdanok, 370 U.S. 530, 541, 82 S.Ct. 1459, 1468, 8
L.Ed.2d 671 (1962).

As the *Thompson* court noted, the focus is then placed on "the
location which serves as executive headquarters for the debtor's
multi-state operation, and not on the location which generates the
largest business volume." *Thompson,* 665 F.2d at 950. The court
suggested this creates stability in debtor-creditor relations because
a chief executive office is much less likely to change location than

changes which could result in the various volumes of business activity at different locations.

With regard to the second step of the inquiry concerning the reasonable expectations of the creditors, the Oklahoma comment provides that the purpose behind the rule "is that the state of the debtor's chief place of business is the place an interested party is likely to go for information." Okla.Stat. tit. 12A, § 9–103 comment subsec. 2. This is similar to the official comment which speaks in terms of where an interested party "would normally look for credit information."

Thus, we are persuaded that the analysis used by the *Thompson* court is a sound approach to determining "chief place of business" under § 9–103 and that the courts of Oklahoma, if faced with the issue of construing the phrase, would, like the district court, adopt the two-fold test of *Thompson*.

The undisputed facts of this case demonstrate that during the period of GCB's operations, Lew Hammer maintained the office for LHI at 2385 South Lipan Street, Denver, Colorado. From this office Hammer largely conducted the business of GCB. Hammer conducted much of the negotiations and business transactions for GCB from this Denver office, spending only an average of two days per week in Oklahoma supervising the mining operations there. There was no permanent office in Oklahoma for GCB. Rather, temporary office locations existed at each mine site; these temporary office locations in turn moved with the mining operations. All officers and directors of GCB were located in Colorado, and on the Oklahoma domestication certificate, Lew Hammer was named as the registered agent, listing his home address in Colorado.

All the financial records of GCB were maintained at the Denver office, including accounts receivable and invoices. Invoices were paid by the Denver office, even though at times they may have first been sent to a mine site office for approval by the mining supervisor. The payroll of GCB was prepared in the Denver office and forwarded to the mine site offices in Oklahoma. All monthly, quarterly, and annual reports were prepared at GCB's office in Denver and all of GCB's accountants were located in Colorado. GCB acquired all of its liability and worker's compensation insurance through the Denver office and much of the equipment owned by GCB was purchased or leased by Hammer through the Denver office.

Applying this two-fold inquiry, we agree with the district court that the conclusion to be drawn from these facts is that GCB's place of management and executive office was in Colorado. Furthermore, creditors seeking information would have likely looked to Lew Hammer, the president and key manager of GCB, who mainly worked and lived in Colorado and had access to GCB's financial records in Colorado.

We hold that Colorado was GCB's "chief place of business" and that the district court was correct in so concluding. Thus, the bank properly perfected its security interests in the "mobile goods" or equipment in Colorado. It is, therefore, unnecessary to reach the voidable preference issue concerning the filings made in Oklahoma.

The decision of the district court is, therefore,

AFFIRMED.

PROBLEMS

1. Retailer offers charge accounts to its customers under a credit agreement providing that a customer making purchases may either pay in full within 25 days after billing, without incurring a finance charge, or pay in monthly installments subject to a finance charge. At the time the purchase is made the customer signs the sales slip which contains an imprint of the buyer's name and account number and, immediately above the buyer's signature, the following statement: "I promise to pay the amount shown as the total subject to and in accordance with Retailer's credit agreement." Retailer normally retains these sales slips for at least a year. Retailer wishes to use its charge-account balances as collateral for a loan from Bank. Retailer's chief executive office is in State A, but all its retail outlets are in State B. How should Bank perfect a security interest in this collateral? In which state? § 9–105(1)(i) ("instrument"); § 9–106 ("accounts").

2. Debtor is in the business of collecting, storing, and selling credit information from public records. Its tradename is "Credit Eye". Debtor is fully computerized. Its credit information database and customer lists are stored on discs and tapes. Debtor wishes to use as collateral for a loan from Bank its tradename, database, and customer lists. Debtor's chief executive office is in State A but its field operations are all carried out in State B where the data is stored. How and where does Bank perfect a security interest in these items of collateral? § 9–106 ("general intangibles"); § 9–109(2) ("equipment"). Matter of Information Exchange, Inc., 98 B.R. 603 (Bkrtcy.Ga.1989); In re Emergency Beacon Corp., 23 U.C.C.Rep. 766 (S.D.N.Y.1977). For a discussion of the breadth of the term "general intangibles," see Clark, The Law of Secured Transactions Under the Uniform Commercial Code, ¶ 1.03[2] (2d ed. 1988).

3. Debtor, whose chief executive office is in State A, owns a hotel ("Hotel") in State B. Debtor wishes to borrow money from Bank and to grant a security interest in the collateral described in the cases set out below to secure the loan. Are these transactions governed by Article 9? § 9–104(j); § 9–106 ("accounts"). If so,

how and where would Bank perfect a security interest in this collateral?

    a. Debtor chose not to operate Hotel and leased it to Lessee for ten years for an agreed monthly rental. Debtor wishes to use its rights to the rental payments under the lease as collateral for the loan. In re Bristol Associates, Inc., 505 F.2d 1056 (3d Cir. 1974).

    b. Debtor operated Hotel and rented rooms to transient guests who stayed for visits averaging two to three nights. Debtor wishes to use its rights to the guest room receipts as collateral for the loan. In re Oceanview/Virginia Beach Real Estate Associates, 116 B.R. 57 (Bkrtcy.Va.1990).

Chapter 2

PRIORITIES

One of the most ambitious reforms accomplished by Article 9 was the creation of a comprehensive structure for determining priorities as between UCC secured parties and such competing claimants as other secured parties, buyers, judicial lien creditors (including trustees in bankruptcy), real property mortgagees, statutory lien creditors, and others. Although the priority rules had to be revised somewhat in the 1972 amendments, they have yielded a degree of predictability never before experienced in the chattel security area. However, some problems remain and doubtless others will emerge in time.

Article 9 works, but whether its priority rules operate fairly raises policy questions that will be addressed throughout this chapter. In greatly strengthening the position of the first party to file, has the Code been overly protective of banks and other institutional creditors at the expense of other meritorious claimants, or has the Code in fact succeeded in constructing an economically efficient system of priority allocation? The classic tension between efficiency and fairness is evident in this area.

A. THE FIRST–TO–FILE RULE

ALLIS–CHALMERS CREDIT CORP. v. CHENEY INVESTMENT, INC.
Supreme Court of Kansas, 1980.
227 Kan. 4, 605 P.2d 525.

PRAGER, JUSTICE. This is a dispute between two secured creditors over the priority of their security interests in an Allis-Chalmers combine. The facts in the case are undisputed and are covered generally by a stipulation of facts filed by the parties in district court. The factual circumstances giving rise to the controversy are set out in chronological order as follows: On November 16, 1970, Lloyd Catlin executed a retail installment contract to Ochs, Inc., a dealer for Allis-Chalmers Corporation, to cover the purchase price of an Allis-Chalmers combine identified as G–7754. This contract was in a total amount of $10,149.44 including the financing charge. There was no provision in the contract for future advances. In the course of the opinion, this will be referred to as contract # 1. This contract was assigned to plaintiff-appellant, Allis-Chalmers Credit Corporation, who financed the transaction. On November 27, 1970, a financing statement covering combine G–7754 was filed by Allis-Chalmers with the register of deeds of Barber County, Kansas.

On December 19, 1970, Cheney Investment Company, Inc., the defendant-appellee, made a cash advance to Lloyd Catlin, taking a security interest (chattel mortgage) in combine G–7754. On December 24, 1970, Cheney Investment filed a financing statement covering combine G–7754 with the Barber County register of deeds. In the course of the opinion, we will refer to the security interest of Cheney Investment as the chattel mortgage. On September 17, 1971, Catlin purchased a new Allis-Chalmers combine G–17992 from Highway Garage and Implement Company, another dealer of Allis-Chalmers. The retail installment contract which created the security interest included both the new combine, G–17992, and the used combine, G–7754. This contract will be referred to in the opinion as contract # 2. Contract # 2 provided that contract # 1 was cancelled and the notation "Payoff ACCC-Wichita $4,542.00" was written on its first page. The balance owing under contract # 1 was included in the purchase price stated in contract # 2. There was no other reference to the prior security agreement or financing statement. On September 29, 1971, Allis-Chalmers Credit Corporation, as assignee of contract # 2 from Highway Garage and Implement Company, filed a financing statement covering both the new combine G–17992 and the used combine G–7754. On February 16, 1972, Allis-Chalmers notified Cheney Investment of its claim to a senior security interest on combine G–7754, as Cheney had taken possession of that combine when Catlin defaulted on his loan payments to Cheney Investment.

On May 30, 1972, Allis-Chalmers and Cheney Investment executed a letter agreement to allow combine G–7754 to be returned to Catlin, the debtor, with each party to notify the other if Catlin defaulted on either financing agreement. On September 11, 1973, after several revisions and amendments to contract # 2, Catlin sold combine G–17992 and paid Allis-Chalmers $11,641.12, leaving an unpaid balance of $8,300. A new payment schedule was prepared for the balance owing plus a new finance charge. Thereafter, Catlin defaulted on his payments, both to Allis-Chalmers and to Cheney Investment. On March 1, 1974, Cheney Investment sold combine G–7754 at a chattel mortgage sale, having taken possession shortly after Catlin defaulted on the Allis-Chalmers obligation. Allis-Chalmers participated in the sale but was not the purchaser. The sale proceeds totaled $8,560. Subtracting the amount then owing to Cheney Investment and costs, there remained $2,111.80 to satisfy the security interest of Allis-Chalmers.

Following the above events, the plaintiff, Allis-Chalmers, brought this action against Cheney Investment for conversion of combine G–7754, claiming a senior and prior security interest. At that time, Catlin's indebtedness to Allis-Chalmers was in the amount of $8,650 plus interest. In its answer, Cheney Investment claimed a first and prior lien against the combine in the amount of $6,093.79 plus interest. All of the above facts were stipulated by the parties. In addition to the stipulation, the case was submitted on the deposition of Richard F. Ellis, vice-president of Allis-Chalmers. In his deposition, Ellis testified that contract # 1 between Ochs, Inc., and Lloyd Catlin was paid off and canceled at the time contract # 2 was executed and the balance owing on contract # 1 was carried forward and became a part of the consideration for contract # 2. He agreed that contract # 2 was a new and separate contract.

The district court held in favor of defendant Cheney Investment, reasoning that contract # 2 cancelled the prior contract # 1 and was thus an entirely new and separate agreement which created an entirely new and distinct security interest. In its memorandum decision, the trial court emphasized that contract # 1 was one involving only the sale of combine G–7754 and, since it contained no provision covering future advances or sales, it was a distinct and separate transaction from contract # 2. The trial court then concluded that the advances made under contract # 2, dated September 17, 1971, did not relate back and were not covered by the financing statement filed by Allis-Chalmers on November 27, 1970. Thus, it concluded that the intervening security interest of Cheney Investment, created by its chattel mortgage on December 19, 1970, and perfected by the filing of its financing statement on December 24, 1970, was a security interest, senior and prior to the security interest of Allis-Chalmers created by contract # 2 in September of 1971. The trial court entered judgment in favor of defendant Cheney Investment, and Allis-Chalmers has appealed to this court.

The question of priority presented in this case is one of first impression in this state under the Kansas Uniform Commercial Code. * * * The question of priorities between conflicting security interests is controlled by 9–312(5)(*a*). * * *

In this case, both of the parties have perfected their respective security interests. Simply stated, the issue to be determined is which of their security interests is entitled to priority over the other. Section 9–312(5)(*a*) governs the priority as between conflicting security interests. Prior to 1975, 9–312 provided in part as follows:

> "Priorities among conflicting security interests in the same collateral. (1) The rules of priority stated in the following sections shall govern where applicable:

* * *

"(5) In all cases not governed by other rules stated in this section * * * priority between conflicting security interests in the same collateral shall be determined as follows:

"(a) *In the order of filing if both are perfected by filing, regardless of which security interest attached first under section 9–204(1) and whether it attached before or after filing;"* (Emphasis supplied.)

* * *

The controversy arose in this case, as it has in other cases, because 9–312(5)(a), as originally adopted, did not have clear and specific language governing the right of a lender to include later advances made in subsequent transactions under the financing statement filed at the time of the original transaction. It should be noted that 9–204(5) provided that "[o]bligations covered by a security agreement may include future advances or other value whether or not the advances or value are given pursuant to commitment."

The issue as to the priority of the security interest of a lender, who made advances after the filing of the original financing statement, over the security interest of an intervening creditor came before a Rhode Island superior court in Coin-O-Matic Service Co. v. Rhode Island Hospital Trust Co., 3 U.C.C.Rptr.Serv. 1112 (R.I.Super.Ct.1966). The district court in the present case relied upon *Coin-O-Matic* in holding that the security interest of Cheney Investment was prior to the security interest of Allis-Chalmers. In *Coin-O-Matic*, the debtor gave a security interest in an automobile to the seller, who assigned the debt to Rhode Island Hospital Trust Company which filed a financing statement. One year later, the debtor gave Coin-O-Matic a security interest. It filed a financing statement. The following month, Rhode Island Hospital Trust Company loaned the debtor an additional sum of money, one-third of which was used to pay off the first note to Rhode Island Hospital Trust Company. The first note was cancelled, a new security agreement executed, and a new financing statement filed. When the debtor went into bankruptcy, both Coin-O-Matic Service Company and Rhode Island Hospital Trust Company claimed a prior security interest in the automobile. Rhode Island Hospital Trust Company argued that the first financing statement was sufficient to protect the second contract, as it effectively put the whole world on notice that the collateral was subject to present and future security interests in favor of the filing party. This argument was rejected by the Rhode Island superior court. The *Coin-O-Matic* court first recognized that giving the first-to-file priority in all subsequent transactions placed the lender in an unusually strong position. The court reasoned that, under such a holding, the debtor would be precluded from obtaining a second loan, even to pay off the first, because subsequent lenders would be reluctant to lend money based on the collateral already mort-

gaged, as their security interest would always be subject to preemption by a subsequent security agreement in favor of the first
creditor. The court stated that to construe the UCC to give the
first lender an interest in collateral for future advances, absent
future advance provisions in the security agreement, would render
information obtained under 9–204 irrelevant. The court noted
that the first creditor could easily protect future advances by
including a future advance provision as authorized by 9–204(5).

The ultimate conclusion in *Coin-O-Matic* was that a reasonable interpretation of 9–312(5)(*a*) should be that a "single financing
statement in connection with a security agreement, when no
provision is made for future advances, is not an umbrella for
future advances based upon new security agreements, notwithstanding the fact that involved is the same collateral." (3 U.C.C.
Rptr.Serv. at 1120.) This portion of the decision in *Coin-O-Matic*
caused controversy and widespread criticism of the rule announced therein.

The holding in *Coin-O-Matic*, requiring a future advance
clause in the original security instrument in order for future
advances to have 9–312 priority, has been rejected by the vast
majority of the jurisdictions in subsequent cases. In rejecting
Coin-O-Matic, those courts generally stress the "notice" or "red
flag" function of the code and hold that a financing statement on
file is notice to the entire world of present or *future* security
interests in the collateral. * * *

The rationale found in James Talcott, Inc. v. Franklin National Bank, 292 Minn. at 290–292, 194 N.W.2d at 784, well illustrates
the approach taken by those courts which have rejected the rule
adopted in *Coin-O-Matic*:

"Even where the parties originally contemplate a single debt,
secured by a single item of property or a single group of items,
the secured party and the debtor may enter into further
transactions whereby the debtor obtains additional credit and
the secured party is granted more security. The validity of
such arrangements as against creditors, trustees in bankruptcy, and other secured parties has been widely recognized by
many courts. * * *

"Using future-advance clauses and using after-acquired
property clauses in the original security agreement are not
the only means by which perfected security interests can be
obtained in subsequently contracted obligations or in goods
the debtor may later come to own. There is nothing exclusive
about § 9–204(3, 5). Parties may use future-advance and
after-acquired clauses, and they are a great convenience. But,
if they are not used, there is nothing in the code which
prevents the parties from accomplishing the same result by
entering into one or more additional security agreements.

"⁎ ⁎ ⁎ The better view holds that, where originally a security agreement is executed, an indebtedness created, and a financing statement describing the collateral filed, followed at a later date by another advance made pursuant to a subsequent security agreement covering the same collateral, the lender has a perfected security interest in the collateral not only for the original debt but also for the later advance."

Matter of Gruder, 89 Misc.2d at 481, 392 N.Y.S.2d at 206, reached the same result, quoting White & Summers, U.C.C. HB, § 25–4, at p. 908, as follows:

"We reject the *Coin-O-Matic* holding for three reasons. First, it provides little protection against overreaching, for a creditor can avoid the holding simply by including a future advance clause in his security agreement. Second, we suspect that the *Coin-O-Matic* court misunderstands commercial practice. We suspect that it is a rare banker who will lend against the same collateral which secures a prior loan; in our experience the commercial practice is for the second lender to pay off the first and so take a first priority as to all of the collateral. Finally, *Coin-O-Matic* conflicts with the most obvious and we think intended meaning of 9–312(5)(a); if the draftsmen had wished to qualify the rule as the *Coin-O-Matic* court did, they could have done so."

The only case supporting *Coin-O-Matic* called to our attention is Texas Kenworth v. First Nat. Bank of Bethany, 564 P.2d 222 (Okl. 1977). We have concluded that the district court in this case was not justified in relying upon the decision in *Coin-O-Matic*. The rule of *Coin-O-Matic* was immediately rejected by the UCC permanent editorial board. It conceded that under the 1962 code, as originally adopted, the position of an intervening creditor in reference to a subsequent advance by an earlier secured party was debatable. In order to clarify the matter, the editorial board suggested an amendment to 9–312 by the addition of a new subsection (7) which was subsequently adopted in various states. Subsection (7) was adopted by the Kansas legislature ⁎ ⁎ ⁎ effective January 1, 1976. The new subsection (7) is as follows:

"(7) If future advances are made while a security interest is perfected by filing or the taking of possession, the security interest has the same priority for the purposes of subsection (5) with respect to the future advances as it does with respect to the first advance. If a commitment is made before or while the security interest is so perfected, the security interest has the same priority with respect to advances made pursuant thereto. In other cases a perfected security interest has priority from the date the advance is made."

The issue has clearly been laid to rest in Kansas by the adoption of the new subsection (7) of 9–312 by the Kansas legislature in 1975. We note the official UCC comment to that section which states as follows:

> "7. The application of the priority rules to future advances is complicated. In general, since any secured party must operate in reference to the Code's system of notice, he takes subject to future advances under a priority security interest while it is perfected through filing or possession, whether the advances are committed or non-committed, and to any advances subsequently made 'pursuant to commitment' (Section 9–105) during that period."

Comment (7) is followed by example 5, which sets forth a hypothetical factual situation involving a question of priority which essentially presents the same issue to be decided in this case. It states:

> "Example 5. On February 1 A makes an advance against machinery in the debtor's possession and files his financing statement. On March 1 B makes an advance against the same machinery and files his financing statement. On April 1 A makes a further advance, under the original security agreement, against the same machinery (which is covered by the original financing statement and thus perfected when made). A has priority over B both as to the February 1 and as to the April 1 advance and it makes no difference whether or not A knows of B's intervening advance when he makes his second advance.

> "A wins, as to the April 1 advance, because he first filed even though B's interest attached, and indeed was perfected, before the April 1 advance. The same rule would apply if either A or B had perfected through possession. Section 9–204(3) and the Comment thereto should be consulted for the validation of future advances.

> "The same result would be reached even though A's April 1 advance was not under the original security agreement, but was under a new security agreement under A's same financing statement or during the continuation of A's possession."

Also note should be taken of the official UCC comment to 9–402, which states as follows:

> "However, even in the case of filings that do not necessarily involve a series of transactions the financing statement is effective to encompass transactions under a security agreement not in existence and not contemplated at the time the notice was filed, if the description of collateral in the financing statement is broad enough to encompass them. Similarly, the financing statement is valid to cover after-acquired property and future advances under security agreements whether or not mentioned in the financing statement."

It is clear that subsection (7) was adopted by the Kansas legislature to make it clear that 9–312(5)(a) should be applied to future advances made by the first creditor, whether such advances are "committed" or "noncommitted" thus making it immaterial whether or not there was a future advance provision in the original security agreement. We regard this amendment as a clarification of the original intent of the legislature when it adopted the Uniform Commercial Code in 1965.

On the basis of the reasoning set forth above, we hold that the security interest of Allis-Chalmers in combine G–7754 is prior and superior to the security interest of the defendant, Cheney Investment, Inc. Under the undisputed facts, the proceeds from the sale of the Allis-Chalmers combine G–7754 totaled $8,650. At the time the suit was filed, Catlin's indebtedness to Allis-Chalmers was in the total amount of $8,650 plus interest. Since the security interest of Allis-Chalmers equals or exceeds the amount of the net proceeds received from the sale of the combine, after expenses of sale, Allis-Chalmers is entitled to apply the net proceeds to its debt.

The judgment of the district court is reversed and the case is remanded to the district court with directions to enter judgment in favor of the plaintiff Allis-Chalmers, awarding it the net proceeds from the sale of combine G–7754, after deducting the expenses of sale, together with interest as allowed by law and for the costs of the action.

HOLMES, JUSTICE, dissenting.

I must respectfully dissent. In my opinion the trial court reached the right conclusion in this case and I would adopt the rule and reasoning set forth by the Rhode Island Superior Court in Coin-O-Matic Service Co. v. Rhode Island Hospital Trust Co., 3 U.C.C.Rptr.Serv. 1112 (R.I.Super.Ct.1966), cited and discussed in the majority opinion. The facts are adequately set forth by the majority and need not be repeated.

As noted by the majority, a basic theory behind the UCC is one of notice filing and that a notice when filed becomes a red flag to be heeded by all. However, the same applies to the filing made by defendant Cheney Investment, Inc. Their filing is also a red flag to all who might thereafter undertake dealings with the original debtor, Catlin. In the instant case it appears clear that the initial contract and obligation underlying the first filing by Allis-Chalmers was paid and satisfied at the time the second contract was entered into and a second financing statement filed. To say that, lacking a future advance clause as contemplated by the code, life could be breathed back into the first filing when the underlying obligation upon which it was based has been satisfied is difficult to accept.

The majority chooses to follow the majority rule that no future advance clause was necessary in the initial security instrument but concedes that the meaning of the statute (9–312[5]), upon which this conclusion rests, was debatable. The UCC permanent editorial board recognized the deficiency and recommended the addition of 9–312(7) to the code. Kansas adopted this new provision, to cover situations like the one before this court, in 1975. However, this case must be determined under the "debatable" meaning of the code prior to that amendment.

Plaintiff could have protected its future advances and its second contract by the notice filed under the first contract, if it had desired to do so, by complying with former 9–204(5) and including an after-acquired property and future advance clause in the original security agreement. The official UCC comment to 9–204(5) states in part:

> "8. Under subsection (5) collateral may secure future as well as present advances when the security agreement so provides. * * * In line with the policy of this Article toward after-acquired property interests this subsection validates the future advance interest, provided only that the obligation be covered by the security agreement."

* * *

In *Coin-O-Matic,* the court, after quoting section 9–312(5)(a), states at 1115–1120:

> "The defendant relies wholly upon what it considers the compelling literal meaning of the language of the section. That is to say, that having entered into a security transaction which covered the 1963 Chevrolet Greenbrier Station Wagon and having filed a financing statement it comes ahead of the plaintiff who had a security interest in the same collateral but whose filing of a financing statement was subsequent in time to the original filing and ahead of defendant's second filing. Obviously with respect to the original transaction there is no dispute that the prior filing of the financial statement would govern. But the defendant carries its argument a step further and contends that the original financing statement is an umbrella which gives the defendant a priority with respect to its second security transaction notwithstanding that the plaintiff's security interest was established in point of time prior to defendant's second security transaction.
>
> "The defendant contends that as long as there is a financing statement on file the whole world is given notice that the debtor is obligated; that there is a security interest in the particular collateral and that the debtor may at any time after the original transaction become further indebted and

enter into an additional security agreement with respect to the collateral. * * *

* * *

"It will be observed as already noted that the original conditional sales agreement * * * has no provision for future advances.

"Section 9–204, subsection (5) provides:

'Obligations covered by a security agreement may include future advances or other value whether or not the advances or value are given pursuant to commitment.'

Defendant contends that this provision merely permits a lender to include a provision for future advances in the original security agreement and that when this is so provided it obviates the necessity of executing subsequent security agreements with respect to the collateral in question but that it does not in any way affect the priority with respect to future advances as long as the financing statement covering the collateral in question is prior in time and additional security agreements are obtained with each new loan. * * * If this is so, it places a lender in an unusually strong position, vis-a-vis, the debtor and any subsequent lenders. In fact, it gives the lender a throttle hold on the debtor. For example, a debtor borrows $25,000.00 from a lender to be paid over a three-year period without any right of anticipation. The security is the equipment of the debtor. No provision is made for future advances. The financing statement is filed. The debtor reduces the obligation to $12,500.00 and now seeks to borrow an additional $5,000.00 The original lender is not interested in making a second loan. The debtor is in no position to pay off the loan without borrowing from another lender. The original lender does not desire to liquidate the obligation except in strict accordance with the agreement. Under the theory advanced by the defendant the original debtor cannot borrow from the second lender because no second lender can safely advance the money as long as there is a possibility that a future advance by the original lender would have priority in the collateral over the second lender. * * *

* * *

"Section 9–312(5) deals with priority between conflicting security interests in the same collateral and gives a priority in the order of the filing but that obviously does not relate to separate and distinct security transactions. Moreover, a careful examination of 9–312 and the other applicable provisions of the Code lead to the conclusion that the reasonable interpretation of 9–312 is that a security agreement which does not provide for future advances is a single transaction and in the case of subsequent security agreements there is required a new financing statement. That is to say, a single financing statement in connection with a security agreement when no provision is made for future advances is not an umbrella for future advances based upon new security agreements, notwithstanding the fact that involved is the same collateral."

In the instant case the parties appear to have considered the original transaction as a single transaction. No provision was made in the security agreement for future advances or after-acquired collateral. At the time of the second transaction a new combine was purchased, a new contract prepared, the old contract was paid off and cancelled. The case falls squarely within the rationale and holding of *Coin-O-Matic* and the opinion in that case is, in my opinion, a correct application of the UCC provisions as they existed prior to the 1975 amendment to the statute.

I would affirm the trial court with the proviso that any funds collected by Cheney Investments, Inc., in excess of the indebtedness due it together with appropriate costs, storage and other items properly included, be paid to plaintiff to apply on its claim against Catlin and the security.

SCHROEDER, C. J., and HERD, J., join the foregoing dissenting opinion.

PROBLEMS

1. On February 1 A advanced $30,000 on the security of D's equipment and filed an appropriate financing statement covering the equipment. When A refused to grant more credit, D induced B to advance $40,000 on the security of D's equipment. B filed an appropriate financing statement on June 15. Before making the loan to D, B had noted A's financing statement on the records and had requested that D submit to A under § 9–208 a statement requesting A's approval of the fact that only $30,000 had been loaned by A. A promptly approved the statement. B examined D's security agreement in favor of A and found that it did not contain a future advance clause. B assumed from the § 9–208 statement and the fact that neither A's financing statement nor security agreement mentioned future advances that A would not be loaning D more money on the security of D's equipment. But B was wrong, for in July A advanced another $60,000 to D pursuant to a new security agreement granting A a security interest in D's equipment. A did not file another financing statement. D's equipment is worth $100,000. What are the priorities between A and B? Would it matter if A had known about B's interest before making the second advance? Comment 7 to § 9–312. Does B have rights against A based on § 9–208(2)?

2. Debtor bought equipment with the proceeds of a loan from National Bank. To secure the loan Debtor granted a security

interest in the equipment to National Bank which filed an appropriate financing statement. Later, Debtor borrowed from Finance Co. and granted a security interest in the same equipment to Finance Co. which filed an appropriate financing statement. Debtor then defaulted on its debt to National Bank. To avoid repossession by National Bank Debtor borrowed money from State Bank. The loan to Debtor was made by State Bank's payment to National Bank of $10,000, the amount owed by Debtor to National Bank. Debtor granted a security interest in the same equipment to State Bank which filed an appropriate financing statement.

Debtor made some interest payments to State Bank on its loan debt and then defaulted. State Bank took possession of Debtor's equipment and sold it for $9,000. At the time of the sale Debtor owed State Bank $11,000, including unpaid interest, and owed Finance Co. $6,000. Finance Co. and State Bank both make claims to the $9,000 proceeds of the sale of equipment. Which has priority? In what way would your analysis of this problem differ if State Bank had taken an assignment of National Bank's security interest when it paid off the National Bank loan? § 9–302(2) and § 1–103. French Lumber Co., Inc. v. Commercial Realty & Finance Co., Inc., 346 Mass. 716, 195 N.E.2d 507 (1964).

3. Debtor granted Secured Party a security interest in certain equipment worth $100,000 to secure a loan of $30,000. The security agreement contained an after-acquired property clause and stated that the collateral would secure any future advances made but that Secured Party had no commitment to make future advances. Secured Party filed a financing statement on January 2. On July 1, Secured Party advanced an additional $40,000 to Debtor, pursuant to the original security agreement. What are the priorities of Secured Party with respect to the following persons?

a. Creditor of Debtor who obtained a judicial lien on the equipment on June 1. § 9–301(4).

b. Purchaser who bought the equipment from Debtor (who was not a dealer) on May 1. § 9–307(3).

4. "Advance" is not defined in the UCC, but the drafters of § 9–301(4) clearly intended the term to include a loan of money to the debtor. It is not clear, however, whether other kinds of value may be included in the term. Some debt owed to the secured party that arises after a third party acquires a judicial lien in the collateral may not result from a loan by the secured party to the debtor after the judicial lien arises. Examples are obligations to pay collection expenses and interest incurred or accrued after the judicial lien attaches. If those obligations arise under a commitment made by the debtor before the judicial lien attaches, does the language of § 9–301(4) limiting the priority of the secured creditor "only to the extent that it secures advances" mean that the

priority does not apply to the post-judicial lien collection expenses and interest? Comment 8 to § 9–301 and Permanent Editorial Board Commentary No. 2 address the issue. A discussion of the problem can also be found in Dick Warner Cargo Handling Corp. v. Aetna Business Credit, Inc., 746 F.2d 126 (2d Cir.1984).

B. THE PURCHASE MONEY PRIORITY

1. COLLATERAL OTHER THAN INVENTORY

IN RE PRIOR BROTHERS, INC.
Court of Appeals of Washington, 1981.
29 Wn.App. 905, 632 P.2d 522.

ROE, JUDGE. In 1974, Prior Brothers, Inc. (PBI) began financing its farming operations through the Bank of California, N. A. (Bank). The Bank's loans were secured by PBI's equipment and included any after-acquired property. On March 22, 1974, the Bank filed a financing statement perfecting its security interest. In April 1976, PBI needed a new tractor to use in its potato farming operation, as its tractor had broken down. A. Fred Prior, the president of PBI, contacted Jim Castle, a salesman at the International Harvester (IH) dealership in Sunnyside. On April 8, 1976, after considering various tractors, Prior signed a retail installment sales contract for a model 1066 IH tractor. In an affidavit Castle explained that Prior signed the contract "[i]n accordance with our customary practices," but that Prior took delivery of the tractor on approval and if PBI decided to purchase the tractor, it could do so by informing IH of its intention and sending a $6,000 down payment. Castle's recital of the arrangement is confirmed by Prior. The tractor was physically delivered to PBI sometime after April 8. On April 22, 1976, IH received a check for $6,000 from PBI. On April 27, 1976, IH filed a financing statement on the tractor.

Later, PBI went into voluntary receivership and its assets were ordered liquidated. On January 11, 1979, IH filed a complaint asking the court to declare its purchase money security interest [1] in the tractor had priority over the Bank's security interest. On December 13, 1979, IH moved for a summary judgment on its complaint. The trial court denied the motion and held the Bank's security interest had priority, as it was filed before IH's security interest,[2] and that IH had failed to perfect its security interest within the time period allowed by statute.[3]

---

1. UCC § 9–107.

2. UCC § 9–312(5).

3. UCC § 9–312(4).

IH appeals. It argues this was a sale on approval, UCC § 2–326(1)(a), PBI did not become a debtor [5] under the code until it had signaled its acceptance of the contract and made the down payment, and that it did not possess the tractor as a debtor until that time. Thus, it claims it had 10 days from April 22, 1976, the date it received PBI's down payment, to perfect its purchase money security interest. Since its financing statement was filed on April 27, 1976, 5 days after receipt of the down payment, it urges it did file within the 10 days allowed under section 9–312(4) and its security interest is thus prior to that of the Bank's.

Conversely, the Bank argues the sales contract signed by Prior on April 8, 1976, was the complete agreement between the parties and that the financing statement should have been filed within 10 days of April 8 in order to enjoy the protection of section 9–312(4).

This case was decided on a motion for summary judgment. Thus, our review is limited to deciding whether there are issues of material fact and whether judgment should have been entered as a matter of law. Because the contract includes an entire agreement clause, the Bank argues parol evidence was inadmissible to show the contract was one on approval. However, the trial court must hear all extrinsic evidence to determine whether the parties intended the agreement to be a final integration before it can apply the parol evidence rule. * * *

[The court's discussion of the parol evidence rule is omitted.]

Thus, we hold parol evidence is admissible to show a condition precedent to the contract between IH and PBI and remand for a determination whether the sale of the tractor was absolute or on approval. If the trial court finds the sale was absolute, i.e., took effect on April 8, 1976, it was correct in granting judgment to the Bank, as IH filed its security interest more than 10 days after PBI executed the contract. If, however, the trial court finds there was a sale on approval, with acceptance of the contract not occurring until April 22, 1976, it must then decide when PBI became a debtor in possession of collateral in order to determine when the 10-day grace period of section 9–312(4) had run. For the remainder of this opinion, we assume the sale between PBI and IH was a sale on approval accepted on April 22, 1976.

A purchase money security interest in collateral other than inventory has priority over other security interests in the same collateral if it is perfected within 10 days of when the "debtor receives possession of the collateral." UCC § 9–312(4). We do not believe PBI became a debtor in possession of the tractor collateral until it accepted the conditional contract of sale on April

---

5. UCC § 9–105(1)(d).

22, 1976.[9] Thus, IH's financing statement was timely filed on April 27, 1976.

* * * A sale on approval, which gives the purchaser the right to use and the option to purchase after a reasonable period of time, is a bailment. * * * In a bailment, title to the goods delivered remains in the bailor, while the bailee has possession only. * * *

Thus, a vendee on approval (such as PBI) owes an obligation to either buy the property subject to the sale or to reject it within a reasonable time. A sale on approval may appear to be a security interest under article 9. However, article 9 applies only to "any transaction * * * which is *intended* to create a security interest * * *" (Italics ours.) 9–102(1)(a). Attachment, which is evidenced by intent and which occurs (1) when the parties agree that it attaches, (2) when value is given, and (3) when the debtor has rights in the collateral, is necessary. 9–204(1) * * *. Here, PBI purported to grant IH a security interest in the tractor under the terms of the contract; thus, there was agreement subject to the condition precedent of approval. Value [12] was given by PBI when it sent IH the down payment of $6,000.

The third element necessary to show attachment is that the debtor have rights in the collateral. Collateral is "property subject to a security interest * * *" 9–105(1)(c). Here, until PBI accepted the contract by approving the sale, the tractor was not subject to a security interest and thus was not "collateral" until that time.

The final consideration in determining whether IH may rely on the priority of section 9–312(4) is when did PBI become a "debtor in possession" of the tractor. There are two lines of cases which consider this question in applying section 9–312(4). We believe that Brodie Hotel Supply, Inc. v. United States, 431 F.2d 1316 (9th Cir. 1970), and its progeny, which focus on the time the debtor/creditor relationship arose, is the better statement of the law.

In *Brodie,* Lyon took possession of restaurant equipment belonging to Brodie in June 1964, but did not execute a chattel mortgage to secure its unpaid purchase price until November 12, 1964. Brodie gave Lyon a bill of sale on that day but did not file a financing statement covering the equipment until November 23, 1964. Meanwhile, on November 2, 1964, Lyon borrowed money from the National Bank of Alaska, using the equipment as securi-

---

9. Because he may never approve the sale, a conservative and cautious prospective purchaser of goods taken on approval might not wish a financing statement filed upon delivery in which he is listed as a debtor and which could conceivably cover all after-acquired property. UCC § 9–404, which allows the debtor to demand a termination statement, is hardly an adequate answer.

12. UCC § 1–201(44).

ty for the loan. The bank filed a financing statement on November 4, 1964, and assigned its interest to the Small Business Administration (SBA). In a priority dispute between Brodie and the SBA, the question was when did Lyon become a debtor in possession of the equipment. The court held Lyon became a debtor on November 12, 1964 when he became obligated to pay the purchase price. "Until that obligation came into being, Lyon was not Brodie's debtor with power to mortgage the restaurant equipment as collateral for the unpaid purchase price." Brodie Hotel Supply, Inc. v. United States, supra at 1318. The court noted Lyon might have been liable for reasonable rental of the equipment or its return, but he did not owe performance of any obligation until November 12, the date on which he executed the chattel mortgage in Brodie's favor and Brodie gave him a bill of sale. Thus, Lyon was not a "person who owes payment or other performance of the obligation secured," 9–105(1)(d), until the sales transaction was completed.

The Ninth Circuit refined the *Brodie* holding in In re Ultra Precision Indus., Inc., 503 F.2d 414 (9th Cir. 1974). On March 3, 1967, Ultra executed a chattel mortgage on its after-acquired property in favor of National Acceptance Corporation. On April 30, June 30, and August 7, 1968, Ultra accepted delivery of three machines from Wolf Machinery Co. The agreement between Wolf and Ultra allowed Ultra to test the machines for a reasonable period. Ultra accepted two of the machines and executed a security agreement covering them on July 31, 1968; this security agreement was assigned and a financing statement filed on August 5, 1968. The third machine was accepted and a security agreement executed on October 23, 1968; the financing statement was filed on October 30, 1968. Ultra later declared bankruptcy. National asserted its priority in the three machines under the security agreements executed in 1967. Wolf argued it had perfected its purchase money security interests in the machines by filing within the 10 days allowed by section 9–312(4).

The issue again was when did Ultra become a debtor in possession of the collateral. National contended Ultra became a debtor when it received physical delivery of the machines. Wolf claimed Ultra was not a debtor until the terms of the proposed sale had been met and a security agreement executed and delivered. The court agreed with Wolf's position. Ultra did not become a debtor until it executed and delivered the security agreements, which occurred after it had tested the machines and accepted them. Before that time,

> Wolf held no definitive security interest in the machines which could be perfected by the filing of a Financing Statement, and * * * Ultra held no assignable legal interest in the machines which could fall into the grasp of National's after-acquired property security clause.

In re Ultra Precision Indus., Inc., supra at 417. In both *Brodie* and *Ultra,* the debtor had possession of the collateral before the sale of the goods was complete, i.e., before there was acceptance of the contract of sale. In both cases, the court looked to the time at which the relationship between the parties became that of debtor/ creditor to trigger the grace period of section 9–312(4). In the case at bench, the relationship between PBI and IH was in the first instance bailor/bailee; it did not become debtor/creditor until PBI accepted the tractor and tendered the down payment. Had PBI never approved the contract, it would never have become a debtor.

* * *

Some courts have held the critical inquiry under section 9– 312(4) is when the debtor received *possession* of the collateral. In James Talcott, Inc. v. Associates Capital Co., 491 F.2d 879 (6th Cir. 1974), Getz gave Talcott a security interest in after-acquired property which was filed on December 12, 1968. On February 17, 1969, Getz took delivery of a tractor from Highway Equipment Co. On February 25, 1969, Getz signed a lease agreement with an option to purchase on the tractor. A financing statement covering this tractor was filed on March 3, 1969. The lease/option agreement provided the lease dated back to the date of first possession. A second tractor was leased under similar terms; the lease was signed on April 22, 1969, and the financing statement filed on April 28, 1969. On October 27, 1969, Getz exercised the options and signed security agreements on both tractors. In a subsequent dispute between Talcott and Associates, the assignee of Highway, the court held Talcott's security interest had priority. Under the lease agreements, Getz owed an obligation to Highway on the date he received possession under the lease, not the date on which he signed the leases. In distinguishing *Brodie,* the *Talcott* court found this difference "critical."

In In re Automated Bookbinding Servs., Inc., 471 F.2d 546 (4th Cir. 1972), Automated had signed a chattel mortgage in favor of Finance Company of America (FCA), which included an after-acquired property clause, on November 20, 1968. FCA filed a financing statement on November 21, 1968. On January 30, 1970, Automated contracted to buy equipment from Hans Mueller Corp. (HMC), which retained a purchase money security interest in the equipment. The equipment was shipped in crates, which arrived at Automated between May 26 and June 2, 1970. Installation was completed sometime between June 13 and June 19; Automated acknowledged delivery and satisfaction on June 18, 1970. HMC filed a financing statement on June 15, 1970. In the dispute between HMC and FCA, the district court held HMC had timely perfected its interest, finding the critical time to be the time of the installation (June 13–19), rather than the time of delivery (June 2); Automated did not receive possession until the tender of delivery terms were completed. In re Automated Bookbinding

Servs., Inc., supra at 550. The Court of Appeals reversed, holding possession occurs when the debtor receives physical control of the collateral. In re Automated Bookbinding Servs., Inc., supra at 552. The court noted that tender of delivery under section 2–503 affects only the rights of the seller and buyer against each other.[13] Thus, "possession ＊ ＊ ＊ is not dependent upon completion of tender of delivery terms which affect only the buyer and seller of the goods." In re Automated Bookbinding Servs., Inc. supra at 553. To hold otherwise would allow sellers to postpone indefinitely the filing requirement by failing to comply with a tender of delivery term and still take advantage of the grace period of section 9–312(4).

Such a concern is not present when the triggering event is acceptance of a sale on approval. The buyer must give seasonable notice of acceptance. 2–327(1)(b); 1–204(3). He may not postpone acceptance indefinitely. The seller, extending the privilege, has no authority to rescind once he has granted it; he has no security interest to protect until there has been acceptance. The *Automated* court recognized that a situation in which the debtor receives possession before the goods are sold to him and the security agreement is entered into might produce a different result. See In re Automated Bookbinding Servs., Inc., supra at 553, n. 14 (distinguishing *Brodie*). We agree, as possession alone, without a concomitant obligation to perform, is not sufficient to call into play the provisions of article 9. Thus, it is when the purchaser of goods becomes a debtor, i.e., owes an obligation secured by the collateral, that the time period allowed under section 9–312(4) begins to run. When the sale is one on approval, that event takes place at the approval of the contract. For other transactions, different events will trigger the running of the 10-day period. See Rainier Nat'l Bank v. Inland Machinery Co., 29 Wash.App. 725, 739, 631 P.2d 389 (1981). (Execution of purchase agreement.)

Thus, if the trial court finds this was a sale on approval, until PBI approved purchase of the tractor, it was not a debtor under section 9–105(1)(d), nor was the tractor collateral under section 9–105(1)(c). Therefore, the 10-day period granted to purchase money secured creditors to file by section 9–312(4) did not commence to run until that time.

Judgment of the trial court is reversed and remanded for proceedings consistent with this opinion.

13. This is an added distinction between *Automated* and the case at bench. Although sales on approval are also covered by article 2, there is a specific provision in UCC § 2–326 which relates to the rights of the creditors of those who buy on approval.

Except as provided in subsection (3), goods held on approval are not subject to the claims of the buyer's creditors until acceptance; goods held on sale or return are subject to such claims while in the buyer's possession.

UCC § 2–326(2).

MUNSON, J., concurs.

MCINTURFF, CHIEF JUDGE (dissenting).

I respectfully dissent from the views expressed by the majority. Although there is no language in the contract to support Harvester's "on approval" argument, I will, for the sake of argument, assume that parol evidence plus the foregoing facts of this case describe a sale on approval. Thus, two questions are presented: (a) When did PBI become a "debtor", and (b) as a "debtor", when did PBI possess the "collateral"? The answer to these questions determines whether Harvester can take advantage of the PMSI priority outlined in 9–312(4).

In answer to the first question, the majority maintains PBI became a debtor only after making the first down payment. The parol evidence relative to a sale on approval does not purport to establish the date upon which PBI became obligated to perform under the written contract.[2] Rather, it merely establishes the condition which must be set aside before the written contract legally obligates PBI to perform. Harvester admits the conditions were satisfied and that the contract became legally binding. The determination of the date PBI became obligated to perform, once the contract became legally binding, should be made by reference to the written contract.

The April 8, 1976, contract provides in pertinent part:

7. UNPAID BALANCE (Amount Financed)
(Total of 5 and 6)   21,151.76

8. FINANCE CHARGE   5,708.68

ANNUAL PERCENTAGE RATE 12%

9. TOTAL OF PAYMENTS
(Total of 7 and 8)   26,860.44

10. DEFERRED PAYMENT PRICE
(Total of 3, 6 and 8)

DATE FINANCE CHARGE BEGINS TO ACCRUE
(If different than contract date)   /   /

2. The contract contained the following provisions:

"*Purchaser hereby purchases,* and seller hereby sells, subject to all terms, conditions and agreements contained herein, ⋆ ⋆ ⋆ the following described property, delivery, inspection and acceptance of which are hereby acknowledged by purchaser:

"⋆ ⋆ ⋆

"13. SECURITY INTEREST: In order to secure payment of the indebtedness contained herein, seller hereby retains, and purchaser hereby grants, a purchase money security interest under the Uniform Commercial Code in and to the above described property sold hereunder, ⋆ ⋆ ⋆

"14. ENTIRE AGREEMENT: Purchaser agrees that this contract ⋆ ⋆ ⋆ which he has read and to which he agrees, *contains the entire agreement* relating to the instalment sale of said property ⋆ ⋆ ⋆" (Italics mine.)

(Italics mine). From the foregoing, the date the finance charge began to accrue was the date of the contract, not acceptance. Hence, I would recognize PBI as the "debtor" within the purview of 9-105(1)(d), as of April 8, 1976, the date the contract was signed.

With regard to the second question, the majority maintains the tractor could not become "collateral" until PBI indicated its approval by making the down payment. I differ from this reasoning and conclude Harvester failed to come within the requirements of 9-312(4), by not filing within 10 days of the date PBI received possession.

When goods are sold "on approval", the seller retains title. 2-327(1)(a). The retention or reservation of title to goods by the seller, notwithstanding delivery of goods to the buyer, constitutes the reservation of the security interest. 1-201(37). From a commercial viewpoint, it seems clear that Harvester retained an interest in the tractor to secure PBI's performance of an obligation which existed legally on the date PBI took possession of the tractor. 1-201(37). When the parties agreed to a "sale on approval", PBI was then legally obligated to: (1) use the tractor only in a manner consistent with the utilization thereof; (2) approve or disapprove of the tractor within a reasonable period of time; and (3) either (a) approve the tractor and perform the terms of written contract, or (b) disapprove the tractor and return it to Harvester. 2-327(1)(a)–(c). Hence, Harvester's reservation of title was a device to secure PBI's obligation to return the tractor should the tractor not be approved. While it is true that 2-326(2) provides that goods held on approval are not subject to the claims of the buyer's creditors, this only assures the creditor if there is *no* sale, (which is not the case here) but has no applicability to extend the time period of 9-312(4). Thus, the tractor was "collateral" within the meaning of 9-105(1)(c) from the date of its delivery.

The majority relies upon Brodie Hotel Supply, Inc. v. United States, 431 F.2d 1316 (9th Cir. 1970), as favorable to its position. However, the Ninth Circuit held that *Brodie* had fulfilled the demands of the exception provided in section 9-312(4) because "Although Lyon might have been liable for the reasonable rental of the equipment ＊ ＊ ＊ he did not owe performance of an 'obligation secured' by the collateral in question until" the agreemeent had been executed. *Brodie,* supra at 1319. But *Brodie* is inapposite on the facts. Here, the executed agreement called for the obligation of interest on the contract to begin to accrue from the date of the contract. Thus, PBI is considered a debtor as of April 8, 1976.

In James Talcott, Inc. v. Associates Capital Co., 491 F.2d 879 (6th Cir. 1974), the court decided a similar issue. There, Getz, a heavy construction contractor, executed a promissory note to Talcott giving a security interest in all after-acquired property.

Subsequently, Getz negotiated with Highway Equipment Co. (Highway) for the sale of two Caterpillar tractors. One tractor was delivered to Getz on February 17, 1969; an agreement was signed on February 25, 1969, and Highway filed on March 3, 1969. Getz failed to make payments and a priority dispute arose. The court resolved the issue in favor of Talcott by stating:

> The only question that remains is when did Getz receive possession of the collateral as a "debtor" * * *
>
> The District Court answered this * * * by noting that "Getz's obligation was owed * * * on the date that he received possession * * * Perhaps the most telling exposure of the flaw in Highway's analysis was delivered by the District Court.
>
>> "*It would be a frustration of this purpose* [certainty in commercial transactions under the U.C.C.] *to hold that a purchase money secured party can deliver goods to his debtor, delay indefinitely before entering into a security agreement which binds the debtor retroactively as of the delivery date, and still obtain a perfected security interest by filing within ten days of the agreement.*"

(Italics mine.) *James Talcott, Inc.,* supra at 882–83. The court reasoned that regardless of when the agreement was entered into, Getz possessed the equipment as a debtor for more than 10 days prior to the filing of the statement. * * *

A similar result was reached in North Platte State Bank v. Production Credit Ass'n, 189 Neb. 44, 200 N.W.2d 1 (1972). There Gerald Tucker received an operating loan from Production Credit Association (PCA) and granted a security interest in all after-acquired livestock. He took delivery of some cattle from a third party with an agreement that payment and transfer of a bill of sale were to take place after the date of possession. He later borrowed funds from North Platte State Bank (to make payment). The bank took a security interest in the cattle. A priority dispute arose when Tucker defaulted on his payments to PCA. The Nebraska Supreme Court held that PCA had priority since the bank had failed to satisfy the requirements of section 9–312(4) by not filing within 10 days after Tucker took possession. *North Platte State Bank,* supra 200 N.W.2d at 6. The court noted: "[A]lthough [the bank] filed its statement within 10 days after it made its loan, the filing occurred almost 2 months after the cows had been delivered * * *" Id. Although the code does not define the term "possession" priority rules turn on the time of receipt of possession and not upon the time the debtor obtained rights in the collateral. See 2 P. Coogan, Secured Transactions Under the Uniform Commercial Code, § 19.02(3)(a) (1979). The rationale behind this approach was eloquently stated as follows:

We observe that the 10-day grace period in itself allows for a permissible flexibility in the practical aspects of consummating a purchase money transaction. By their nature grace periods must have a fixed time limit, or they become meaningless. We cannot extend judicially another grace period over the Code grace period. We cannot pile flexibility upon flexibility. The purchase money priority is an exception to the first to file rule, and it should be applied only in accordance with the limitations established by the Code. To interpret section 9–312(4), U.C.C., in the manner the Bank urges would not only be contrary to the plain meaning of the language used in the statute but would expose an original lender to such serious practical risks that the whole structure of the Code would be impaired or endangered, because the original lender could never feel sure that he could rely on his collateral in his future dealings with the debtor.

North Platte State Bank, supra 200 N.W.2d at 7. Moreover, the court in distinguishing *Brodie,* supra, stated:

The language and the reasoning of the *Brodie* case * * * have been seriously criticized. * * * see 27 The Business Lawyer, Kennedy, Secured Transactions, 755 at p. 768 (1972); and Comment, 49 N.C.L.Rev. 849 (1971).

Id.

The code's general purpose is to create a precise guide for commercial transactions under which businessmen can confidently predict the results of their dealings. Harvester merely had to file the agreement within 10 days of the tractor's delivery into possession of PBI for the protection of its interest pursuant to section 9–312(4). Its failure to take this simple, reasonable step should have resulted in the loss of its PMSI priority to the Bank of California.

For these reasons and for the rationale expressed in Rainier Nat'l Bank v. Inland Mach. Co., 29 Wash.App. 725, 631 P.2d 389 (filed June 30, 1981) (McInturff, C. J. dissenting) I would affirm the judgment of the superior court.

NOTES

1. More than half of the states have extended the ten-day period in § 9–312(4) to 20 days. Two have adopted a 15-day period and one a 21-day period. 3 Uniform Laws Annotated, 268–269 (Cum.Supp.1990). What is the policy basis for the purchase money exception of § 9–312(4) to the first-to-file rule of § 9–312(5)? Comment 3 to § 9–312.

2. Why does § 9–312(4) use the time at which the debtor "receives possession" to start the running of the 10-day grace period? Two other events could have been used: 1) the attach-

ment of the security interest, or 2) the debtor's acquiring rights in collateral. Professor Gilmore states: " 'Receives possession' is evidently meant to refer to the moment when the goods are physically delivered at the debtor's place of business—not to the possibility of the debtor's acquiring rights in the goods at an earlier point by identification or appropriation to the contract or by shipment under a term under which the debtor bears the risk." Gilmore, Security Interests in Personal Property 787 (1965).

Apparently, Gilmore believed that the possession test is better than a rights-in-collateral test because of the possibility that a debtor might acquire rights in collateral before taking possession of the collateral. In such a case it is easier to ascertain when possession is taken than it is to discover when rights in the collateral are acquired. What the commentators didn't discuss is the fact situation that has actually been happening, i.e., the debtor takes possession before acquiring rights in collateral. Does the possession test make sense in this kind of case? We have used *Prior Bros.* as the principal case not only because it poses a nice question but also because it sets out the other cases in point. The majority in *Prior* followed *Brodie* and *Ultra Precision* in giving priority to the purchase money interest. The dissenting opinion relied on *James Talcott, North Platte* and *Automated Bookbinding*. Can these two lines of authority be reconciled by a requirement that the financing statement be filed within 10 days after the time that the debtor acquired both possession and rights in the collateral?

3. A *seller* purchase money secured creditor (§ 9–107(a)) should be able to comply with the 10-day rule of § 9–312(4) because the seller controls when the debtor receives possession of the collateral sold. On the other hand, the possession test can cause operational difficulties for a *lender* purchase money secured creditor (§ 9–107(b)) because its loan officers may have no reliable way of determining when the debtor actually received possession short of communicating directly with the seller. What procedure would you advise loan officers to follow to be sure that the lender's purchase money priority is established?

PROBLEMS

1. On July 1 Seller sold goods to Debtor on unsecured credit. On July 7 Debtor borrowed $50,000 from Bank to pay Seller. Bank wrote the check to Seller and Debtor as joint payees and Debtor indorsed the check to Seller. Does Bank have a purchase money security interest when Debtor granted Bank a security interest in the goods to secure the debt? § 9–107(b).

2. Debtor borrowed $10,000 from Bank on July 1 for the purpose of buying a machine. Bank advanced the money by crediting Debtor's checking account. Bank filed a financing state-

ment on July 1. Debtor purchased the machine on July 3 and paid Seller by a check for $10,000 drawn on the checking account in Bank. Does Bank have a purchase money security interest in the machine? The balance in Debtor's account just before Bank credited the account was $15,000. When Debtor's check to Seller was paid the balance was $22,000. § 9–107(b).

3. At the beginning of the year Debtor granted Bank a security interest in all of Debtor's equipment then owned or after-acquired. Bank filed a financing statement covering equipment. In March Seller agreed to sell Debtor equipment for a price of $100,000, on terms calling for 20% down. Bank agreed to advance $20,000 to enable Debtor to buy the equipment. Bank wrote a check for $20,000 to Debtor and Seller as joint payees and Debtor indorsed it to Seller. Seller retained a security interest in the equipment which it perfected by filing upon delivery of the equipment to Debtor. What are the priorities as to the equipment between Bank and Seller and which UCC provision controls, § 9–312(4) or (5)? See Thet Mah & Associates, Inc. v. First Bank of North Dakota, 336 N.W.2d 134 (N.D.1983); Gilmore, Security Interests in Personal Property 784 (1965); Henson, Secured Transactions under the UCC 128 (1979).

4. Seller sold goods to Debtor who granted Seller a security interest in the goods sold to secure the unpaid portion of the price. Does Seller's security interest remain, in whole or in part, a purchase money security interest in the following cases?

a. Debtor found it difficult to make the required monthly payments. Seller accommodated Debtor's needs by reducing the amount of the monthly payments and extending the duration of the debt. The refinancing was done by cancelling the old security agreement and entering into a new security agreement embodying the new terms. In re Matthews, 724 F.2d 798 (9th Cir.1984), treated this transaction as a new loan, the proceeds of which were not used to acquire rights in the collateral; hence, the security interest was no longer purchase money. The court believed that this result was supported by the last sentence of Comment 2 to § 9–107. In re Billings, 838 F.2d 405 (10th Cir.1988), disagreed, holding that the refinancing did not extinguish the old obligation and create a new one.

b. Seller sold additional goods to Debtor. The parties entered into a new security agreement in which the old and new debts were consolidated and were secured by both the old and new collateral (cross-collateralization). In re Manuel, 507 F.2d 990 (5th Cir.1975), held that, as to the old collateral, Seller's security interest lost its purchase money character because, under § 9–107(a), the security interest in that property was not retained solely to secure "all or part of its price." The same principle would invalidate the purchase money nature of Seller's security interest in the new collateral as well. This view has come to be known as the "transformation" rule, in which a security interest in any item securing more than its own price is transformed into a nonpurchase money security interest. Pristas v. Landaus of Plymouth, Inc., 742 F.2d 797 (3d Cir.1984), rejected the transformation rule in favor of a "dual status" doctrine which holds that the presence of a nonpurchase money security interest does not destroy the purchase money aspect. A purchase money security interest can remain such "to the extent" (§ 9–107) that it secures the price of the goods even though it secures the price of other items as well.

For a thorough discussion of the meaning of purchase money under the UCC, see Wessman, Purchase Money Inventory Financing: The Case for Limited Cross–Collateralization, 51 Ohio St.L.J. 1283 (1990). The matter is further discussed in Note 2 on p. 128.

2. INVENTORY

Section 9–312(3) states requirements for establishing a purchase money priority in inventory quite different from those found in § 9–312(4) for other collateral. The first major difference is the notice requirement. A creditor who expects to acquire a purchase money security interest in a debtor's inventory must search the filing records and notify any prior holders of security interests in the debtor's inventory that it intends to do purchase money financing of inventory with the debtor. The notice requirement is explained in Comment 3 to § 9–312:

> The reason for the additional requirement of notification is that typically the arrangement between an inventory secured party and his debtor will require the secured party to make periodic advances against incoming inventory or periodic releases of old inventory as new inventory is received. A fraudulent debtor may apply to the secured party for advances even though he has already given a security interest in the inventory to another secured party. The notification requirement protects the inventory financer in such a situation: if he has received notification, he will presumably not make an advance; if he has not received notification (or if the other interest does not qualify as a purchase money interest), any advance he may make will have priority. Since an arrangement for periodic advances against incoming property is unusual outside the inventory field, no notification requirement is included in subsection (4).

The second difference is § 9–312(3)'s treatment of proceeds. Under § 9–312(4) the purchase money priority carries over to the proceeds of the original collateral, but under § 9–312(3) it is limited to cash proceeds received on or before delivery of the inventory to the buyer. This effectively deprives purchase money creditors of a priority in all of the usual proceeds from credit sales of inventory, e.g., accounts and chattel paper. The Reasons for 1972 Change, § 9–312, explains the drafters' decision:

> Perhaps the most debated subject under Article 9 has been the question whether between conflicting security interests a priority as to original collateral confers a priority as to proceeds. As indicated above, in the case of collateral other than inventory, e.g., equipment, it seems clear that the policy favoring the purchase money secured party in Section 9–312(4) should give him the first claim to the proceeds. This is so even though the security interests will have been perfected simultaneously when the proceeds arise and the debtor acquires rights therein.

> Proper policy is much less clear when the collateral involved is inventory and proceeds consisting of accounts. (Policy as to other types of receivables as proceeds is expressed in Sections 9–308 and 9–309). Accounts financing is more important in the economy than the financing of the kinds of inventory that produce accounts, and the desirable rule is one which makes accounts financing certain as to its legal position. Therefore, the rule proposed is that where a financing statement as to accounts is filed first (with or without related inventory financing), the security interest in accounts should not be defeated by any subsequent claim to accounts as proceeds of a security interest in inventory filed later. There is therefore no provision in Section 9–312(3) carrying forward to accounts any priority right in inventory, and proposed subsections (5) and (6) adhere firmly to the principle that a date of filing as to original collateral also defines the date of filing as to proceeds. Correspondingly, a financing statement as to inventory (carrying with it a claim to proceeds) which is filed first will under the same provisions have priority over a later-filed security interest in accounts.

SOUTHTRUST BANK v. BORG–WARNER ACCEPTANCE CORP.

United States Court of Appeals, Eleventh Circuit, 1985.
760 F.2d 1240.

TUTTLE, SENIOR CIRCUIT JUDGE:

Borg–Warner Acceptance Corporation ("BWAC") appeals from a decision of the district court denying its motion for summary judgment and granting summary judgment to Southtrust Bank ("the Bank") in a diversity suit. The Bank filed a declaratory judgment action to ascertain which of the parties has priority in the inventory of four debtors, Molay Brothers Supply Company, Inc., Gulf City Distributors, Inc., Standard Wholesale Supply Company and Crest Refrigeration, Inc. These debtors, which are no longer in existence, defaulted on obligations they owed to one or the other party.

Both the Bank and BWAC have perfected security interests in the inventory of the debtors. In each case, the Bank filed its financing statement first. BWAC contends that as a purchase money lender it falls within the purchase money security interest exception to the first to file rule and therefore is entitled to possession of the inventory. The Uniform Commercial Code (UCC) as adopted in both Alabama and Georgia, provides in pertinent part:

> A security interest is a "purchase money security interest" to the extent that it is:
>
> (a) Taken or retained by the seller of the collateral to secure all or part of its price; or
>
> (b) Taken by a person who by making advances or incurring an obligation gives value to enable the debtor to acquire rights in or the use of collateral if such value is in fact so used.

BWAC engages in purchase money financing. Here, BWAC purchased invoices from vendors who supplied inventory items to the debtors in question. The security agreements between BWAC and each of the debtors contained the following provision:

> In order to secure repayment to Secured Party of all such extensions of credit made by Secured Party in accordance with this Agreement, and to secure payment of all other debts or liabilities and performance of all obligations of Debtor to Secured Party, whether now existing or hereafter arising, Debtor agrees that Secured Party shall have and hereby grants to Secured Party a security interest in all Inventory of Debtor, whether now owned or hereafter acquired, and all Proceeds and products thereof.

The term "Inventory" was defined as "all inventory, of whatever kind or nature, wherever located, now owned or hereafter acquired * * * when such inventory has been financed by Borg–Warner Acceptance Corporation."

BWAC and the debtors employed a scheduled liquidation arrangement to reduce the debt owed BWAC. Under this arrangement a debtor was permitted to pay a percentage of the invoice each month, without regard to whether the item was actually sold. If an unpaid item was sold, then the remaining inventory served as collateral to secure the unpaid balance.

The key issue for decision by this Court is whether inclusion of an after-acquired property clause and a future advances clause in BWAC's security agreements converted its purchase money security interest (PMSI) into an ordinary security interest.

The district court held that inclusion of after-acquired property and future advances clauses ("the clauses") in the security agreement converted BWAC's PMSI into an ordinary security interest. The court relied on In re Manuel, 507 F.2d 990 (5th Cir. 1975) (holding, in a consumer bankruptcy context, that PMSI must be limited to the item purchased at time of the agreement and cannot exceed the price of that item); In re Norrell, 426 F.Supp. 435 (M.D.Ga.1977) (same); and In re Simpson, 4 U.C.C.Rep.Serv. 243 (W.D.Mich.1966) (inclusion of future advances clause in security agreement for farm equipment destroys PMSI).

BWAC argues that the cases relied on by the court are distinguishable. First, BWAC notes that almost all the cases following the "transformation" rule (i.e., inclusion of the clauses transforms a PMSI into an ordinary security interest) are consumer bankruptcy cases. It argues that the rationale of those cases, which is to protect the consumer, does not apply in commercial cases such as the case at bar. See In re Mid–Atlantic Flange, 26 U.C.C.Rep.Serv. 203, 208 (E.D.Pa.1979). BWAC argues that the policy considerations in a commercial setting, promoting commercial certainty and encouraging credit extension, do not support the application of the transformation rule. According to BWAC, applying the transformation rule to inventory financiers would require them to police inventory constantly and to see that inventory corresponds on an item-by-item basis with debt.

The Bank argues that the transformation rule is not a product of special bankruptcy considerations, and that if the drafters had intended to limit the rule to consumer transactions, they would have said so, as they did in other sections of the Code. The Bank contends that a holding that inclusion of the clauses destroys a PMSI would not have a serious negative effect on inventory financiers. It points out that such financiers could retain priority by obtaining a subordination agreement from the first-to-file creditor.

We see no reason to limit the holding of *In re Manuel* to consumer bankruptcy cases. In that case, the Fifth Circuit stated:

> A plain reading of the statutory requirements would indicate that they require the purchase money security interest to be in the item purchased, and that, as the judges below noted, the purchase money security interest cannot exceed the price of what is purchased in the transaction wherein the security interest is created * * *.

Id. at 993. Nothing in the language of U.C.C. § 9–312(3) or § 9–107 distinguishes between consumer and commercial transactions or between bankruptcy and nonbankruptcy contexts. We see no policy reasons for creating a distinction where the drafters have not done so.

Second, BWAC contends that the cases supporting the transformation rule involve situations in which the clauses were actually exercised, e.g., *Manuel* (agreement covered pre-existing debt);

Simpson (future advances actually made). BWAC argues that mere inclusion of the clauses does not void a PMSI. In re Griffin, 9 B.R. 880 (Bankr.N.D.Ga.1981) (when creditor is seller, mere existence of unexercised future advances clause does not destroy PMSI); *Mid Atlantic Flange* (same). We need not reach the issue of whether mere inclusion of unexercised future advances and after-acquired property clauses voids a PMSI because we find that BWAC exercised the clauses here. After entering the security agreements with the debtors, BWAC regularly purchased inventory for the debtors and now claims that the debtors' BWAC-financed inventory secures these purchases. This is an exercise of the future advances clause. Similarly, BWAC claims as collateral not only the inventory purchased at the time the security agreements were entered, but all BWAC-financed inventory. This is an exercise of the after-acquired property clause. We hold, therefore, that BWAC's exercise of the future advances and after-acquired property clauses in its security agreements with the debtors destroyed its PMSI.

We note, as did the district court, that BWAC retains a security interest in the goods. It merely loses its priority status as a purchase money secured lender. The concept of the floating lien under the U.C.C. remains intact. We hold, merely, that such a floating lien is inconsistent with a PMSI. A PMSI requires a one-to-one relationship between the debt and the collateral.

BWAC's final argument is that the court should adopt a "to the extent" rule, based on the literal language of UCC, § 9–107:

> A security interest is a "purchase money security interest" *to the extent* that it is * * * (b) Taken by a person who by making advances or incurring an obligation gives value to enable the debtor to acquire rights in or the use of collateral if such value is in fact so used. (emphasis added.)

Some courts have held that the clauses, even if exercised, do not invalidate a PMSI if there is some method for determining the extent of the PMSI. For example, in In re Staley, 426 F.Supp. 437 (M.D.Ga.1977), the court held that the PMSI was valid because the security agreement specified that payments be allocated first to items bought first. Thus, it was easy for the court to ascertain which items had been fully paid for and hence no longer served as collateral. Here, however, nothing in the contract or in state law allocates payments to particular items of inventory. BWAC, in fact, claims all BWAC-financed inventory as its collateral without regard to payments made by the debtors. We agree with the court in In re Coomer, 8 B.R. 351, 355 (Bankr.E.D.Tenn.1980), that

> Without some guidelines, legislative or contractual, the court should not be required to distill from a mass of transactions the extent to which a security interest is purchase money.

Unless a lender contractually provides some method for determining the extent to which each item of collateral secures its purchase money, it effectively gives up its purchase money status.

Because we hold that BWAC's exercise of the after-acquired property and future advances clauses in its security agreements voided its PMSI, we need not reach the other issues raised by the Bank. We also do not reach the issue raised by BWAC concerning the district court's reference to proceeds from sales of the inventory being held "in trust." Whether the proceeds are held "in trust" is relevant only to the issue of damages. The district court entered final judgment only on the claim for declaratory relief and referred the damage claim to a magistrate. Because no final judgment has been entered as to damages, that issue is not properly before this Court.

AFFIRMED.

NOTES

1. Before *Southtrust* we had thought that the incentive offered purchase money financers of inventory by § 9–312(3) was rather meager. On the debtor's default, a secured party who had filed a financing statement with respect to the debtor's inventory before the purchase money financer filed would take precedence in the proceeds of the inventory supplied by the purchase money financer, leaving the purchase money financer with only the unsold inventory remaining at the time of the debtor's default. But *Southtrust* casts doubt on whether the purchase money financer will even have priority with respect to the unsold inventory. *Southtrust* is very controversial. Wessman, Purchase Money Inventory Financing: The Case for Limited Cross–Collateralization, 51 Ohio.St.L.J. 1283 (1990) (hereafter "Wessman"), describes the reaction of commentators:

> Compare B. Clark, [The Law of Secured Transactions Under the Uniform Commercial Code] ¶ 3.09[3][a] at 3–99 [2d ed. 1988] (*Southtrust* "seems correct"); Hansford, The Purchase Money Security Interest in Inventory Versus the After–Acquired Property Interest—A "No Win" Situation, 20 U.Rich.L.Rev. 235, 262 (1986) (*Southtrust* reached proper result, even though basis for it is flawed); with Beard, The Purchase Money Security Interest in Inventory: If it Does Not Float, it Must Be Dead, 57 Tenn.L.Rev. 437, 444 (1990) (*Southtrust* is wholly inconsistent with the purpose, policy, and history of the Code); Marshall, Commercial Law (Annual Survey of Georgia Law), 37 Mercer L.Rev. 139, 155 (1985) (*Southtrust* decision "burdens inventory financing while furthering no apparent policy goals"); Aronov, supra note 114 at 45 (cases like *Southtrust* "are totally unjustified"); Smith, Secured Transactions, 41 Bus.Law. 1463, 1484–86 (criticizing

Southtrust on a number of grounds). See also, Lloyd, [Refinancing Purchase Money Security Interests, 53 Tenn.L.Rev. 1, 91 (1985)] (suggesting *Southtrust* is a trap for the unwary). 51 Ohio St.L.J. at 1309, note 203. Wessman is also critical of the case.

2. Whether a security interest is purchase money under § 9–107 is relevant in two other cases in addition to situations arising under § 9–312(3) and (4). Under § 9–302(1)(d) a purchase money security interest in consumer goods is perfected without possession or filing, and § 522(f)(2) of the Bankruptcy Code allows a trustee in bankruptcy to avoid a nonpossessory, nonpurchase money security interest in certain consumer goods. The great bulk of litigation on the meaning of § 9–107 has occurred in bankruptcy courts under § 522(f)(2). The distinction drawn in § 522(f)(2) between purchase money credit (e.g., a vendor retains a security interest in household goods sold to the debtor) and nonpurchase money credit (e.g., a personal loan company takes a security interest in household goods the debtor had already purchased to secure a loan made to the debtor) is based on Congressional hostility toward the personal finance business, thought to be creditors of last resort, whose security interests were considered in terrorem collection devices used to coerce necessitous debtors into paying the loan company in preference to other creditors or reaffirming debts discharged in bankruptcy.

Although the consumer context of both § 522(f)(2) and § 9–302(1)(d) is wholly foreign to the issue raised by § 9–312(3) of determining priorities between two sophisticated commercial financers, the court in *Southtrust* relies on these consumer cases for guidance and, of the conflicting lines of authorities discussed in Problem 4 on page 121, adopts the rigid rule that cross-collateralization destroys the purchase money nature of a transaction. As the court says, "A PMSI requires a one-to-one relationship between the debt and the collateral." Thus *Southtrust* reduces § 9–312(3) to awarding a reliable purchase money priority only if each sale is treated as a separate transaction. This, of course, is totally infeasible in any but big-ticket items like motor vehicles, and, even in these cases, *Southtrust* seems to require compliance with the paper-shuffling pre-Code regime that § 9–205 attempted to end.

3. In *Southtrust* the court suggests that a purchase money financer should protect its priority by an intercreditor subordination agreement with the first-to-file creditor. This is good advice; if *Southtrust* is good law, no purchase money financer is safe without such an agreement. Wessman, however, believes that there is usually little incentive on the part of the first-to-file creditor to subordinate its interest. 51 Ohio St.L.J. at 1338–1339. There is still another barrier to recognition of an effective purchase money priority in inventory under § 9–312(3). The follow-

ing is a covenant of the debtor taken from a standard loan and security agreement used in inventory financing by a leading financial institution:

> The Borrower is, and as to inventory to be acquired after the date hereof, shall be, the owner of all inventory and shall neither create nor suffer to exist any lien or encumbrance thereon or security interest therein * * * in favor of any person other than the Lender.

Assume that breach of this covenant constitutes an event of default which results in the debt secured by the inventory becoming immediately due and payable. In the light of this covenant, the first-to-file creditor may call its loan if the debtor even attempts to enter into purchase money financing with another creditor. Query: does § 9–312(3) have any commercial significance today?

C. CONSIGNMENT AND SALE OR RETURN

The classic sale "on consignment" refers to a transaction in the following form: The owner of goods—the consignor—gives possession of the goods to the consignee who acts as the consignor's agent in selling the goods. Sometimes the consignee is authorized to sell the goods and in other cases the consignee is authorized only to solicit offers to buy the goods and to convey the offer to the consignor who can accept or reject. In either case title to the goods remains with the consignor until the sale is made, and at that time title passes from the consignor directly to the purchaser. The consignee, who acts solely as an agent, may or may not be a dealer in goods like those consigned. Sometimes retention of title in what in form is a consignment sale is in fact a security interest. In that case the transaction is treated under Article 9 in the same way as other security-interest transactions. If the retention of title is not a security interest the agency relationship and the title of the consignor are recognized as such, subject to any rights that third parties dealing with the goods might have as a result of the giving up of possession to the consignee. These rights are found in Article 2.

Section 1–201(37) defines "security interest" as "an interest in personal property * * * which secures payment or performance of an obligation. * * * Unless a consignment is intended as security, reservation of title thereunder is not a 'security interest' * * *" This definition is meant to distinguish between "true consignments" and security interests that are consignments only in form. The key to the distinction can be found in the first part of the definition. A security interest can exist only if there is some obligation to be secured. If the consignee is obliged to purchase the goods from the consignor or to sell the goods and pay the price to the consignor, the transaction is treated as a credit sale of the goods by the consignor to the consignee and the retention of title is simply a security interest. Article 9 applies to the transaction as in other cases of purchase money security interests.

On the other hand, if the consignee is not liable for the price there can be no security interest because there is no obligation to secure. In this case the transaction is governed by Article 2 but by different terminology. The consignment sale transaction is treated as a "sale or return" the incidents of which are spelled out in § 2–326 and § 2–327. The first of these provisions states the conditions under which creditors of the consignee may treat the consigned goods as the property of the consignee. If the consignee is a merchant § 2–403(2) and (3) also apply. Section 9–114, which was added to the Code in 1972, applies only to true consignments and deals with conflicting claims to the goods between the consignor and a creditor of the consignee who has a security interest in inventory of the consignee.

Some transactions that are also covered by § 2–326 as sales or return do not take the agency or consignment form. For example, a manufacturer of a new product may have difficulty in finding dealers who will buy the product for their inventory because they don't know whether it will be readily salable. The manufacturer offers to supply the dealer with a quantity of the product which the dealer can sell for the dealer's account. The dealer can return any unsold products at any time and pays only for products not returned. The transaction can take two forms. Under the first alternative the transaction is set up as a present credit sale to the dealer who is given an option to sell back the goods to the manufacturer. In that case the goods become the property of the dealer and remain the dealer's property until they are returned pursuant to the resale option which requires repurchase by the manufacturer. As a second alternative, the transaction can be set up as a delivery of goods to the dealer without a present sale. In that case the goods remain the property of the manufacturer and the dealer simply holds the goods as bailee with the right to buy at any time. No sale by the manufacturer to the dealer occurs until the dealer resells to a customer. The dealer does not act as agent for the manufacturer in the sale to the customer. Rather, the dealer buys from the manufacturer and immediately resells to the customer as part of one transaction. But with respect to rights of creditors of the dealer, § 2–326(3) treats the second alternative like the first alternative. The transaction is deemed to be a "sale or return."

In the case of a true consignment or other sale or return that falls within subsection (3) of § 2–326, if the consignor or seller does not comply with paragraph (a), (b) or (c) the consequence under subsection (2) is that the goods in the possession of the dealer are "subject" to the claims of the dealer's creditors. This produces three results: 1. Creditors of the dealer can levy on the goods held by the dealer as though they were the property of the dealer; 2. If the dealer goes into bankruptcy the goods become part of the estate in bankruptcy by virtue of Bankruptcy Code § 544(a) which gives to the trustee in bankruptcy the rights of a creditor of the dealer who acquired a judicial lien in the goods at the time of bankruptcy. See, e.g., In re KLP, Inc., 7 B.R. 256 (Bkrtcy.Ga.1980); 3. The dealer, at the time possession of the goods is acquired, has sufficient "rights" in the goods to allow a security interest in the consignee's inventory to attach under § 9–203(1)(c). See In re Bildisco which follows. The consignor or seller normally gets protection from the claims of creditors of the dealer by filing a financing statement pursuant to § 9–408.

There are a few cases that have attempted to restrict "sale or return" transactions under § 2–326 to consignments by commercial sellers. An example is Founders Investment Corp. v. Fegett, 23 U.C.C.Rep. 903 (Ky.App.1978). In that case a non-commercial owner of a mobile home delivered it to a dealer for the purpose of having the dealer secure offers for its purchase and to submit them to the owner for approval. The dealer was to get a commission in the event of a sale. A creditor of the dealer levied on the mobile home and sold it. The court held that the owner simply made a bailment to the dealer not a sale or return under § 2–326. The court stated "We believe it would be an unjust and unwise policy to impose upon an *individual* owner, as distinguished from a *commercial* one, the deemed sale or return provision of § 2–326(3) unless the underlying facts indicate that a sale or return was intended or did, in fact, occur. Our decision does no disservice to the utilization of the Uniform Commercial Code between commercial dealers. It does reserve protection to the private individual owner vis-a-vis the commercial financier when such owner merely attempts, as in this case, to utilize the marketing or sales services of a commercial dealer with no intention of transferring any ownership interest to such dealer. Because transactions of the type in question are relatively few we do not think that commercial dealers or financiers will suffer unduly, but we do believe that the individual owner, to whom the loss in a given situation would be relatively more severe, will be afforded fair and reasonable protection." The court in Bischoff v. Thomasson, 400 So.2d 359 (Ala.1981), refused to follow *Founders* and referred to it and another case reaching a similar result as "maverick cases." Is the statement by the court in *Founders* persuasive as a statement of good public policy? Is there any basis for it in § 2–326?

IN RE BILDISCO
United States District Court, D.New Jersey, 1981.
11 B.R. 1019.

DEBEVOISE, DISTRICT JUDGE.   Gerber Industries, Inc. [Gerber]
appeals from an order of the Bankruptcy Court for the District of
New Jersey holding that goods consigned by Gerber to the debtor
Bildisco, a general partnership in the State of New Jersey [Bildis-
co], were subject to the claims of Bildisco's creditors.   Matter of
Bildisco, 7 B.R. 225 (U.S.Bkrtcy.Ct.N.J.1980).   For the reasons that
follow, the Bankruptcy Court's order is affirmed.

I.

In October, 1979, Bildisco and Gerber entered into a written
"Consignment Sale Agreement" which covered: "Consignment
inventories of goods manufactured and shipped by Gerber Industries Secured Party to Bildisco * * *".   On December 31, 1979,
Gerber filed a financing statement giving notice of that agreement; however, Gerber gave no actual notice of the consignment
agreement to Bildisco's secured creditors, nor did Gerber post a
sign at Bildisco's place of business declaring its ownership of the
goods.   Moreover, Bildisco was not generally known to its creditors to be a seller of goods on consignment.

Less than four months later, on April 14, 1980, Bildisco filed a
Voluntary Petition for Reorganization under Chapter 11 of the
Bankruptcy Code * * *.   On April 17, 1980, the Bankruptcy
Court entered a judgment establishing that by virtue of two
financing statements filed by appellee Congress Financial Corporation [Congress] with the Secretary of State on December 14, 1976
and on December 10, 1979, Congress held a valid and duly perfected security interest in various assets of the debtor.   Included in
these assets were the consigned Gerber products.   Gerber, however, was not a party to that proceeding.

On April 28, 1980, Gerber instituted an adversary proceeding
in the Bankruptcy Court against Bildisco and Congress, seeking
possession of the goods delivered to Bildisco pursuant to the
"Consignment Sale Agreement" and a determination that its
interest in the goods was paramount to that of Congress.

After a trial, the Bankruptcy Court, in a written opinion,
concluded that Gerber's failure to give written notice to Congress
of its intention to deliver goods on consignment to Bildisco rendered the goods subject to the rights of Bildisco's creditors.

* * *

III.

As its second ground for reversal, Gerber submits that the Bankruptcy Court erred when it treated the consignment as a security interest and applied the provisions of UCC § 9–312 which require that written notice be given by the holders of a purchase money security interest to parties claiming under an after-acquired property clause. Gerber argues that the consignment between itself and Bildisco was a "true" consignment and that, as such, the proper procedure under New Jersey's Uniform Commercial Code was to comply with § 2–326 and require a consignor to follow the "filing" provisions of Article 9 and not any other action for perfection. Since Gerber filed a financing statement on December 31, 1979 for its consignment inventory, Gerber concludes that its interests in the consigned goods are superior to that of Congress.

In its decision, the Bankruptcy Court, with little discussion, found the Gerber-Bildisco consignment agreement, like all consignments, to give a "kind of security interest" in the consignor. Matter of Bildisco, supra, at 227. Assuming the validity of that determination, section 9–312 of the Code would be applicable for it expressly assigns priorities among conflicting security claimants to the same collateral.

* * *

By virtue of Section 9–107, a security interest in the consigned goods would be a purchase money security interest since the rights in consigned goods are reserved "to secure all or part of its price". The consigned goods are "inventory" as defined by Section 9–109(4), which includes goods held "for sale or lease". Congress has a conflicting security interest in those goods. Thus, if Gerber's consignment to Bildisco creates a security interest, under Section 9–312(3) Gerber would be required, in addition to perfecting its security interest before the collateral reached the hands of the consignee, to notify Congress, as a known secured party, of its consignment. * * *

Gerber challenges the Bankruptcy Court's characterization of the consignment agreement as a security interest on the basis that the terms of the agreement, as well as the parties' conduct with respect to the agreement, evidence no intent to create security interests in the consigned goods. Gerber views the consignment as a "true consignment" by stressing that the agreement provides:

    for title to remain in Gerber;

    for the inventory to be clearly marked as Gerber's;

    for the inventory to be segregated from all other goods of the debtor;

    for periodic inspections of the inventory to be made by Gerber;

for monthly reports to be made by Bildisco;

for concurrent payments to be made by Bildisco to Gerber "for the merchandise sold from each such inventory sixty (60) days from the invoice date";

for the balance of inventory to be made by exchanging merchandise with inventory already delivered.

Characterization of the Gerber-Bildisco consignment, however, does not require resolution as it is not determinative of the outcome of this appeal. Even if the consignment at issue was intended to create a true consignment without any security interest in the consignor, the same policy considerations which require that a holder of a purchase money security interest give the secured creditors written notice of that interest are applicable to a true consignment and suggest that the same procedures be followed in order to prevent the consignee's creditors from establishing greater rights in the consigned goods.

Article 2 governs the relative rights of the parties in a true consignment situation. The relevant section [is] 2–326.

* * *

That section recognizes the ability of consignments to hide the consignor's interests to the detriment of creditors—even where the transaction is not intended to create a security interest—and thus requires the consignor to take one of three steps to perfect his rights. Failure to perform one of these steps makes the consignor's interest inferior to the claims of the consignee's creditors, while perfecting the interests renders the section inapplicable. This negative statement does not clarify the relationship between the prior-in-time secured creditor and the consignor. It may mean that perfection immunizes the consigned goods from all attacks made by creditors (including those prior in time) or only from those attacks by creditors whose claims were made after perfection (thus recognizing the basic law that prior in time is prior in right). It may also mean that an exception is recognized by giving the consignor, like the purchase money security interest holder, priority over an earlier created and perfected interest in after-acquired property, provided that actual notice of the consignment is given to prior in time secured parties. Thus, there was a gap in Section 2–326 at the time pertinent to this case.

Section 2–326 does not suggest how this matter of priority is to be handled, and no cases dealing directly with this point have been found. To fill the gap we should look to an analogous situation in the Code and the policy considerations underlying it— purchase money security interests and Section 9–312.

In considering the relationship of a secured party vis-a-vis a holder of a purchase money security interest, the drafters of the Code recognized that purchase money security interests may put secured parties with an after-acquired property clause in inventory to a serious disadvantage. These secured parties are quite susceptible to the loss of their collateral through the replacement of inventory on a purchase money security basis and, unless notified of this change, may be lulled into a false sense of security. If notified, however, the secured parties can protect their rights by acting quickly to correct or salvage the situation. To protect against an unfair dissipation of a creditor's collateral in inventory, the Code requires that actual notification be given. These considerations are equally applicable to all kinds of consignments.

Consignors, like holders of a purchase money security interest, enable a consignee secretly to replace inventory with goods on consignment and thereby undermine the secured party's position of priority in the inventory. Requiring that consignors, in addition to filing, check for and notify secured parties with conflicting interests of the consignment is a reasonable and workable answer for the problem at hand. Moreover, this resolution permits all consignments—those creating security interests and those which do not—to be treated in the same manner. See, Hawkland, Uniform Commercial "Code" Methodology, Univ. of Ill.Law Forum, vol. 1962, pp. 314–320 (1962).

Further support for the conclusion that the gap which existed in Section 2–326 should be filled by analogizing the situation to that covered in Section 9–312(3) is found in UCC 9–114, which was adopted by the New Jersey Legislature after the events in the instant case took place. * * * That section of the Code treats goods on consignment like purchase money security interests and requires both filing and actual notice to the prior in time secured party. While this legislation does not directly control the requirements for perfection applicable in the present case, it may be considered in seeking to determine how the New Jersey courts would have construed Section 2–326 * * *.

As the Bankruptcy Court pointed out, the authors of the amendment recognized that uncertainty existed under the Code as originally drafted whether the filing rule in Section 2–326(3) applicable to true consignments required only filing under Part 4 of Article 9 or also required notice to prior inventory secured parties of the debtor under Section 9–312(3). It could be argued, as Gerber does, that the amendment requiring notice demonstrates that prior to the amendment no notice was required. I think the better view is that prior to the amendment there was a gap in the law, and the manner in which that gap should be filled is suggested not only by the policy considerations referred to above but also by the statutory amendment which ultimately clarified the statute.

For these reasons, whether the consignment agreement between Bildisco and Gerber is viewed as a purchase money security interest or a true consignment, notice was required to give Gerber priority over Congress.

The order of the Bankruptcy Court will be affirmed.

NOTE

Suppose the consignor in *Bildisco* proved that the consignee was "generally known by his creditors to be substantially engaged in selling the goods of others." § 2–326(3)(b). Would that have changed the result? Does § 9–114 apply? In re State Street Auto Sales, Inc., 81 B.R. 215 (Bkrtcy.Mass.1988).

If § 9–114 applies to a consignment transaction, does it make any difference whether the transaction is treated as a true consignment or a credit sale secured by a security interest? Consider the following facts taken from GBS Meat Industry Pty. Limited v. Kress-Dobkin Co., Inc., 474 F.Supp. 1357 (W.D.Pa.1979). Finance Co. had a security interest in "all existing and hereafter acquired inventory and all proceeds of * * * the foregoing" of the debtor, Kress-Dobkin. Finance Co. perfected the security interest by filing a financing statement. Later Kress-Dobkin agreed to act as consignee of meat owned by GBS and to sell it in accordance with instructions by GBS. GBS agreed to pay Kress-Dobkin a commission on the sales. After receipt of the consigned meat Kress-Dobkin sold it pursuant to instructions of GBS but did not remit the proceeds. Instead, Kress-Dobkin paid the proceeds to Finance Co. GBS brought an action against Finance Co. for conversion of the proceeds of the sale of the consigned meat. GBS had not complied with any of the conditions set forth in § 2–326(3)(a), (b) and (c). Finance Co. conceded that the sale by GBS was a true consignment and that § 2–326 applied. The jury found that Finance Co. had actual knowledge that the meat was received by Kress-Dobkin on consignment. Finance Co. argued that since GBS had not complied with § 2–326(3)(a), (b) or (c), its security interest defeated the title of GBS and it was entitled to the proceeds of sale because its knowledge of the consignment was immaterial under § 2–326. The court, relying on Comment 2 to § 2–326, held in favor of GBS. The court stated " * * * where a secured creditor knows that the proceeds rightfully belong to a consignor, the consignor must have priority. Any other construction of § 2–326 would contravene the intent of that section and would sanction intentional conversion of goods or proceeds." Suppose the court had found that the transaction was not a true consignment, i.e., that the reservation of title by GBS had been a security interest. Since GBS did not file a financing statement its security interest would have been unperfected. Would knowledge by Finance Co. of the unperfected security interest of GBS have affected the right of Finance Co. to the meat? § 9–301(1)(a) and § 9–312(3) and (5).

Does the quoted language of the court apply to this situation as well?

D. BUYERS AND LESSEES

---

1. INVENTORY

A creditor with a perfected security interest in goods has priority over a buyer who buys the goods from the debtor (§ 9–301(1)(c)) unless either the secured party authorized the debtor to sell (§ 9–306(2)) or the buyer is a "buyer in ordinary course of business." § 9–307(1). Under § 1–201(9) a buyer in ordinary course of business means "a person who in good faith and without knowledge that the sale to him is in violation of the ownership rights or security interest of a third party in the goods buys in ordinary course from a person in the business of selling goods of that kind ∗ ∗ ∗." Section 9–307(1), which provides that a buyer in ordinary course of business takes free of a perfected security interest created by the seller even though the buyer knows of its existence, continues the rule that has traditionally protected the inventory buyer from one who has a security interest in the inventory. See generally Skilton, Buyer in the Ordinary Course of Business Under Article 9 of the Uniform Commercial Code (and Related Matters), 1974 Wis.L.Rev. 1.

Although courts often rely on § 9–307(1) in cases in which a buyer of inventory is awarded priority over the inventory financer, in fact, most inventory cases can be decided under § 9–306(2). Inventories are meant to be sold and normally the secured party has explicitly or implicitly authorized sale by the debtor. Thus, under § 9–306(2), the secured party has relinquished its security interest in the goods sold. Section 9–307(1) is usually important only in those cases in which authorization to sell is subject to certain conditions that were not met in the particular case. In those cases in which § 9–307(1) is relevant, if the buyer knows of the security interest does the buyer act in good faith as required by § 1–201(9)? This question is addressed in Comment 2 to § 9–307.

With respect to priority conflicts between secured parties and lessees, § 2A–307 sets out rules roughly parallel to the rules provided by Article 9 to govern priority between secured parties and buyers. A detailed critique of Article 2A's treatment of priority issues is found in Harris, The Rights of Creditors Under Article 2A, 39 Ala.L.Rev. 803 (1988). A creditor with a perfected security interest in goods of a debtor has priority over a lessee who subsequently leases the goods from the debtor unless the lessee is a "lessee in the ordinary course of business." § 2A–307(2)(c) and (3). This term is defined in § 2A–103(1)(*o*) as one who leases in ordinary course from a person in the business of selling or leasing goods of that kind. A lessee in ordinary course of business may take priority over a perfected security interest even though the security interest is perfected and the lessee knows of its existence. § 2A–307(3). The comparable provisions with respect to buyers are § 9–307(1) and § 1–201(9) ("buyer in ordinary course of business"). If the creditor has an unperfected security interest in goods subsequently leased, a lessee who gives value and takes delivery of the goods without knowledge of the unperfected security interest takes priority over that interest. § 2A–307(2)(b). Here the analogue is § 9–301(1)(c). But Comment 5 to § 2A–307 indicates that there is no provision in Article 2A comparable to the "relation-back rule" of § 9–301(2) which applies to buyers.

NATIONAL SHAWMUT BANK OF BOSTON v. JONES
Supreme Court of New Hampshire, 1967.
108 N.H. 386, 236 A.2d 484.

Action of replevin to recover possession of a 1964 Dodge Dart "270" station wagon. Defendant's motion for custody under RSA 536:5 was granted upon his filing a bond in the amount of $2,000.00 to secure payment of any judgment which might be rendered against him. According to an agreed statement of facts, Robert D. Wever of Hampton, New Hampshire, purchased the Dart from Wentworth Motor Company Inc. of Exeter on February 15, 1965 under a conditional sale contract for personal, family or household purposes. He executed a "Retail Installment Contract" which was assigned by Wentworth to the plaintiff. This contract was filed with the Town Clerk of Hampton pursuant to UCC § 9–401 on February 24, 1965. Sometime thereafter, without the consent of the plaintiff, Wever traded or sold the Dart to Hanson-Rock Inc. of Hampton, an automobile dealer in the business of selling new and used cars to the public. UCC § 1–201(9). Defendant, a resident of Hampton, purchased the Dart from Hanson-Rock on April 8, 1966 for good and sufficient consideration in good faith and without any actual knowledge of any security interest of the plaintiff or anyone else. Neither the defendant nor the Hampton National Bank from which he borrowed the purchase price examined or searched for any filing in the office of the town clerk. (It was agreed at argument that unless a search was made under the name Wever, the Retail Installment Contract could have been found only by examining all such contracts for the serial number of the vehicle.) An unpaid balance of $1,490.17 is still due under the installment contract.

The following questions were transferred without ruling by Leahy, C. J.:

1. Whether the defendant is liable to the plaintiff in the amount of $1,490.17, the amount outstanding under the Retail

Installment Contract executed by Robert Wever in favor of Wentworth Motors, Inc., and subsequently assigned to the plaintiff.

    2. Whether under the provisions of the Uniform Commercial Code in New Hampshire a buyer in ordinary course of business takes free of a perfected security interest created by a person other than the seller from whom the buyer purchased the goods.

    GRIMES, JUSTICE. Since Wever purchased for personal, family or household purposes, the Dart is classified as consumer goods. § 9–109. The plaintiff's security interest was perfected by filing the financing statement with the Town Clerk of Hampton where Wever resided, (§ 9–401(1)(a)), and continues when the collateral is sold without its consent as was the case here unless Article 9 provides otherwise. § 9–306(2). In the case of buyers of goods, § 9–307(1) does provide otherwise in certain instances, as follows:

    "A buyer in ordinary course of business (subsection (9) of Section 1–201) other than a person buying farm products from a person engaged in farming operations takes free of a security interest created by his seller even though the security interest is perfected and even though the buyer knows of its existence."

    Since defendant purchased in good faith without knowledge that the sale to him was in violation of the security interest of another and bought in the ordinary course from a person in the business of selling automobiles, he was a "buyer in the ordinary course of business." § 1–201(9). However, § 9–307(1) permits him to take free only of "a security interest created by his seller." The security interest of the plaintiff was not created by Hanson-Rock, Inc., the defendant's seller, but by Wentworth Motor Co., Inc. Defendant, therefore, does not take free of the plaintiff's security interest under this section. Neither does he take free of the security interest by reason of the provisions of § 9–307(2) relating to consumer goods even if he purchased for his own personal, family or household purposes (a fact not agreed upon) because "prior to the purchase, the secured party ＊ ＊ ＊ filed a financing statement ＊ ＊ ＊." These are the only two provisions of Article 9 under which a buyer of goods can claim to take free of a security interest where a sale, exchange or other disposition of the collateral was without the consent of the secured party. The defendant does not benefit from either one. Section 9–306(2) gives the court no leeway to create any other exceptions to its dictates and no custom, usage or agreement has been brought to our attention which would permit us to do so. § 1–102(2). ＊ ＊ ＊

    Defendant contends that § 2–403(1) provides an escape from plaintiff's security interest when it provides "＊ ＊ ＊ a person with a voidable title has power to transfer a good title to a good faith purchaser for value. ＊ ＊ ＊"

The contention has two answers. § 9–306(2) provides for the continuance of the security interest "except when this Article provides otherwise," thereby limiting any exceptions to those contained in Article 9; and § 2–403 itself provides that the rights of "lien creditors are governed by the Articles on Secured Transactions (Article 9) * * *." See also, § 2–402 which provides "(3) Nothing in this article shall be deemed to impair the rights of creditors of the seller (a) under the provisions of the Article on Secured Transactions (Article 9) * * *." It is clear, therefore, that a security interest in the case of a sale without consent was to be impaired only as provided in Article 9 and is unaffected by Article 2.

Our answer to question 1 is in the affirmative and to question 2 is in the negative.

Remanded.

NOTES

1. In Exchange Bank of Osceola v. Jarrett, 180 Mont. 33, 588 P.2d 1006 (1979), the Court upheld the view of the principal case but said: "This Court recognizes that this is a harsh result, since the purchaser * * * had no means to learn * * * that the property he purchased was subject to a security interest. It may be that legislative action is necessary to prevent such results in the future." 588 P.2d at 1009. Do you agree?

2. Assume the goods in the principal case had been a refrigerator and assume further that Wentworth had perfected a security interest without filing a financing statement pursuant to § 9–302(1)(d). Could Jones now prevail as against Wentworth's assignee under § 9–307(2)? New England Merchants National Bank of Boston v. Auto Owners Finance Co., 355 Mass. 487, 245 N.E.2d 437 (1969), answers in the negative. The court said:

> The crucial point is whether under § 9–307(2) the seller as well as the buyer must be a consumer. This subsection, as far as material, reads: "In the case of consumer goods * * * a buyer takes free of a security interest even though perfected if he buys without knowledge of the security interest, for value and for his own personal, family or household purposes * * * unless prior to the purchase the secured party has filed a financing statement covering such goods." Careful reading of the entire subsection leads to the conclusion that the opening phrase, "In the case of consumer goods," must require that the seller as well as the buyer be a consumer. If the buyer alone has to be a consumer, the opening phrase would be surplusage because of the subsequent provision that the buyer purchase "for his own personal, family or household purposes," which is nothing more than a repetition of the definition of consumer goods in § 9–109(1).

We hold that under § 9–307(2) both the buyer and seller must be consumers. The view has unanimous support in the authorities so far as they have come to our attention. In Everett Nat. Bank v. DeSchuiteneer, 109 N.H. 112, 244 A.2d 196 (1968), the same conclusion was squarely reached.

* * *

3. Although a seller need not file to perfect a security interest in consumer goods under § 9–302(1)(d), the security interest is cut off when the buyer sells the goods to another consumer buyer unless the seller had filed a financing statement. § 9–307(2). Thus filing as to consumer goods is irrelevant as to the rights of relatively sophisticated parties like creditors who normally use the filing system but is determinative as to the rights of a buyer of a used refrigerator at a garage sale who would never dream of examining the records. How can this be? When California adopted the UCC it omitted entirely § 9–307(2). Under the California Code a purchase money security interest in consumer goods is perfected for all purposes without filing.

PROBLEM

In State A, pursuant to an installment sale contract, Seller sold a piano to Buyer for personal use. Buyer granted Seller a security interest in the piano to secure payment of the price. Shortly thereafter Buyer moved to State B with the piano. Two months after moving to State B Buyer sold the piano to T, who had no knowledge that it was subject to a security interest. Buyer then defaulted on the installment sale contract with Seller.

(a) What are the rights of Seller and T to the piano if (1) T is a dealer in musical instruments who bought the piano as a trade-in, and (2) Seller never filed a financing statement in either State A or State B?

(b) What are the rights of Seller and T to the piano if (1) T is an individual who bought it for personal use and (2) Seller filed a financing statement in State A prior to the time the piano was removed from that state but did not file a financing statement within four months of the time that the piano entered State B? § 9–103(1)(d)(i) and (iii).

FARMERS & MERCHANTS BANK & TRUST v. KSENYCH

Supreme Court of South Dakota, 1977.
252 N.W.2d 220.

MORGAN, JUSTICE (on reassignment). Plaintiff-appellant, Farmers and Merchants Bank and Trust of Watertown, South Dakota (Bank), filed an action on October 24, 1974 against defendant-respondent, Nick Ksenych (Ksenych), seeking to recover a new 1974 Dodge pickup or its value. Ksenych counterclaimed for title to the vehicle. The case was submitted to the court on a Stipulation of Fact, the court's memorandum decision was delivered on June 19, 1975, and judgment entered July 11, 1975, finding against the Bank and declaring that title to the Dodge pickup belonged to Ksenych. The Bank appeals from the judgment. We affirm as to the result.

According to the stipulation of facts which has the status of special findings for the purpose of review, Williamson Dodge, a dealer in Dodge vehicles, entered into a "floor-plan" arrangement with the Bank. Under this arrangement Chrysler Motors Corporation would mail a draft drawn on the Bank covering Williamson Dodge's cost of a specific vehicle and would also mail the manufacturer's statement of origin for that vehicle to the Bank. Once the draft was drawn on the Bank, Williamson Dodge would then execute a note with the Bank. After Williamson Dodge sold the vehicle and deposited the proceeds of the sale with the Bank, the Bank would give Williamson Dodge the manufacturer's statement of origin for the vehicle. Through this arrangement Chrysler Motors agreed to transport a 1974 Dodge pickup to Williamson Dodge November 12, 1973. The manufacturer's statement of origin to the vehicle was retained by the Bank, and the vehicle was placed on Williamson Dodge's lot. On December 26, 1973 the Bank filed a financing statement with the Secretary of State, State of South Dakota, showing the debtor as Williamson Dodge and T. V. Williamson, Watertown, South Dakota and covering all "1974 Dodge vehicles."

On December 28, 1973 Williamson Dodge sold a new 1974 Dodge pickup to Ksenych for $5,000 cash, plus a trade-in. Williamson Dodge was to make an application for a certificate of title in Ksenych's name * * *. However, the certificate of title was never given to Ksenych since Williamson Dodge did not gain possession of the manufacturer's statement of origin when it failed to remit the proceeds of the Ksenych sale to the Bank. On January 5, 1974 Williamson Dodge closed its business with its remaining assets taken over by Williamson Dodge's secured creditors.

On October 24, 1974 the Bank, while asserting their superior interest in the collateral upon Williamson Dodge's default, filed this action to recover the 1974 Dodge pickup from Ksenych. Ksenych counterclaimed for clear title to the vehicle and responded by alleging that the purchase out of Williamson Dodge's inventory conveyed clear title to him according to the provisions of the Uniform Commercial Code.

The court ruled by its memo decision of June 19, 1975 that the Certificate of Title Act * * * controlled the outcome, not the Uniform Commercial Code, and that the Bank legally held title to the vehicle under [that Act]. He further held however that the Bank, by its conduct in clothing Williamson Dodge with the apparent authority to sell the vehicle, was estopped from asserting such title.

The first question on appeal as stated by the appellant is "Do the general provisions of the Uniform Commercial Code which protects buyers of encumbered consumer goods revoke [provisions of the Certificate of Title Act] which protect the lien of the holder of a security interest in a motor vehicle when the title documents are in his possession?" Respondent paraphrases this question to be whether or not the plaintiff's claim to the vehicle under [provisions of the Certificate of Title Act] is paramount and superior to the claim of defendant in said vehicle under the Uniform Commercial Code.

In certain particulars including those which relate to this action, [Article 9] relating to secured transactions under the Uniform Commercial Code and [provisions of the Certificate of Title Act] relating to registrations, liens and transfers under the motor vehicle code deal with the same subject matter and when statutes are in pari materia they should be considered concurrently whenever possible. If they can be made to stand together, effect should be given to both as far as possible.

In reviewing the legislative history of the statutes in question, we find no conflict that cannot be resolved while giving full force and effect to each. The sections in question which are part of [the Certificate of Title Act] titled "Registration, liens and transfers" will be referred to collectively as the Title Statutes. These statutes appear to have their inception in Chapter 229 of the Session Laws of 1951. Section 2 of that enactment at (4) provides that "no person, *except as provided in this chapter* (emphasis added) obtaining or getting possession of a motor vehicle shall acquire any right, title, claim, or interest in or to such motor vehicle, until he shall have had issued to him a certificate of title to such motor vehicle, or delivered to him a manufacturer's or importer's certificate for the same;" and goes on to provide "nor shall any waiver or estoppel operate in favor of such person against a person having possession of such certificate of title * * * for a valuable consideration." * * *

* * * reviewing the history of the enactments, it is not difficult to give reasonable interpretation to all of the provisions in accordance with the rule of pari materia, the object of which is to carry into effect the intention of the legislature and which proceeds upon the supposition that several statutes were governed by one spirit and policy and were intended to be consistent and harmonious in their several parts and provisions.

First of all, the provisions of [the Certificate of Title Act], including the reference to "waiver or estoppel", are subject to any

exceptions provided elsewhere in the chapter. We then find that
the provisions regarding the secured transactions were amended
in 1965 to except "trust receipt transactions." The trust receipt
was the principal device used in "floor-planning" arrangements.
The Trust Receipts Act was repealed by enactment of * * * the
Uniform Commercial Code effective July 1, 1967. The 1967 Legislature * * * amended the financing portion of the Title statutes
to substitute financing statement, the appropriate Uniform Commercial Code document, for trust receipt and substitute the provisions of the Uniform Commercial Code for the then repealed Trust
Receipts Act. The intent of the legislature to except floor-planning arrangements from the provisions of the Title statutes in
question is thus clearly documented.

The floor-planning arrangement between the Bank and Williamson as described in the stipulation of facts is clearly under the
provisions of the Uniform Commercial Code, and the defendant
who, the stipulation further discloses was a buyer in the ordinary
course of business, is entitled to the protection afforded by the
Uniform Commercial Code.

* * *

The respondent * * * contends that he is entitled to the
benefit of § 9–307(1), sale of goods in ordinary course of business,
which provides that a buyer in the ordinary course of business
other than a person buying farm products or a person engaged in
farming operations takes free of a security interest created by his
seller even though the security interest is perfected and even
though the buyer knows of its existence. The section which the
bank contends for is, as far as pertinent to this transaction,
confined to consumer goods which are defined as "used or bought
for use primarily for personal, family or household purposes."
The section the defendant relies on is restricted to "buyers in the
ordinary course of business" which under the provisions of § 1–
201(9) restricts the application to buyers (except pawnbrokers)
"from a person in the business of selling goods of that kind", thus,
in the terminology of the article is primarily restricted to inventory. It is obvious to us that the motor vehicle purchased constituted inventory as opposed to consumer goods and thus the provisions
of § 9–307(1) are applicable. It would seem that the bank was
originally of a similar view inasmuch as under the provisions of
§ 9–401 the proper place to file a financing statement to perfect a
security interest in consumer goods is in the office of the register
of deeds in the county of the debtor's residence and the proper
place to file in order to perfect a security interest in inventory is
in the office of the secretary of state, which as previously noted is
where the bank did indeed file its financing statement.

Having considered all of the applicable statutes together, we
are of the opinion that upon the sale of a new automobile from

inventory by a dealer in the ordinary course of business, the buyer takes free of any security interest under a floor-planning arrangement, even though perfected, and even though the buyer knows of the terms of the security agreement.

We therefore hold that the defendant was entitled to a judgment in his favor and against the bank under the provisions of the applicable Motor Vehicle Title Statutes and the Uniform Commercial Code. Having thus decided, we have no need to consider the second question presented in the appeal as to whether or not the plaintiff is estopped from asserting a superior claim upon which basis the trial court did enter judgment.

The trial court having reached the right result, regardless of the reasoning or theories on which it is predicated, its judgment will be affirmed.

NOTES

1. What result in the principal case if Dealer had been a used-car dealer? When a car was traded in owner would sign the transfer form on the back of the certificate of title with the name of the transferee left blank. When the vehicle was resold the dealer would fill in the name of the new buyer and send the old certificate of title to the state department of motor vehicles with an application signed by the new owner for issuance of a new certificate of title in the buyer's name. Suppose Bank had a blanket security agreement with Dealer covering used cars as well as new cars and a financing statement on file with the same description of collateral. However, before Bank would loan money on Dealer's used-car inventory it required Dealer to turn over possession of the certificate of title to it containing the indorsement of the previous owner. Dealer sold and delivered to Buyer a used car for $5,000 in cash, had Buyer sign an application for a new title, and promised Buyer that the new certificate of title would be mailed within three weeks. Actually Bank held the old certificate of title pursuant to a loan it had made to Dealer. When Dealer failed, Bank claimed the car in Buyer's possession. Compare Stroman v. Orlando Bank & Trust Co., 239 So.2d 621 (Fla.App.1970), and Correria v. Orlando Bank & Trust Co., 235 So. 2d 20 (Fla.App.1970), holding in favor of the buyer, with Sterling Acceptance Co. v. Grimes, 194 Pa.Super. 503, 168 A.2d 600 (1961) ("The purchaser of a used automobile knows that a certificate of title has been issued for the automobile and expects to have it produced at the time of sale, but the purchaser of a new vehicle expects no such certificate to exist.") and United Carolina Bank v. Sistrunk, 158 Ga.App. 107, 279 S.E.2d 272 (1981), holding against the buyer.

2. In Philko Aviation, Inc. v. Shacket, 462 U.S. 406, 103 S.Ct. 2476, 76 L.Ed.2d 678 (1983), Seller sold an airplane to First Buyer

who took possession of the airplane but did not receive the title documents or record his interest with the FAA. Later Seller sold to Second Buyer who received the title documents but not the airplane and recorded with the FAA. The lower court granted First Buyer a summary judgment on the ground that if an unrecorded transfer of an aircraft is valid under state law, it is valid against innocent third parties. The Court reversed on the basis of § 503(c) of the Federal Aviation Act, 49 U.S.C. § 1403(c):

> No conveyance or instrument the recording of which is provided for by [§ 503(a)(1)] shall be valid in respect of such aircraft * * * against any person other than the person by whom the conveyance or other instrument is made or given, his heir or devisee, or any person having actual notice thereof, until such conveyance or other instrument is filed for recordation in the office of the Secretary of Transportation.

The Court held that under this statute a failure to record invalidated the conveyance to First Buyer as against Second Buyer unless the latter had actual notice of the transfer. However, as between competing claimants both of whom had recorded with the FAA, the Court stated that state law may determine priority. "Although state law determines priorities, all interests must be federally recorded before they can obtain whatever priority to which they are entitled under state law." 462 U.S. at 413, 103 S.Ct. at 2480. For further developments in this case, see Shacket v. Philko Aviation, Inc., 841 F.2d 166 (7th Cir. 1988). In Matter of Gary Aircraft Corp., 681 F.2d 365 (5th Cir. 1982), the competing claimants were a secured creditor and a buyer in the ordinary course of business, both of whom had recorded with the FAA. The Court held for the buyer on the basis of state law. The Supreme Court denied certiorari. 462 U.S. 1131, 103 S.Ct. 3110, 77 L.Ed.2d 1366 (1983). Sigman, The Wild Blue Yonder: Interests in Aircraft under Our Federal System, 46 So.Cal.L.Rev. 316 (1973).

BANK OF THE WEST v. COMMERCIAL CREDIT FINANCIAL SERVICES, INC.

United States Court of Appeals, Ninth Circuit, 1988.
852 F.2d 1162.

THOMPSON, CIRCUIT JUDGE.

* * *

[In 1982, Bank of the West made a loan to Allied and was granted a security interest in all of Allied's existing and after-acquired inventory and accounts as well as proceeds of that collateral. The bank promptly filed a financing statement that perfected that security interest. In 1984 CCFS entered into a factoring agreement with BCI, which owned a beverage business. Under the agreement CCFS made loans to BCI. To secure the loans, BCI granted to CCFS a security interest in all of its existing and after-acquired inventory and accounts as well as proceeds of that collateral. CCFS promptly filed a financing statement that perfected that security interest. Later in 1984, BCI sold its beverage business to Allied. As part of the sale, BCI transferred assets to Allied. Among the assets were inventory and accounts in which CCFS had a perfected security interest. Both Bank of the West and CCFS claim priority with respect to the inventory and accounts transferred by BCI to Allied and to proceeds of that collateral, including accounts that arose as the result of sales of inventory by Allied after its purchase of the beverage business from BCI.]

* * *

B. *The Post–Transfer Security Interests*

1. *The Bank's Security Interest*

Bank of the West's security agreement with Allied granted the Bank a security interest in Allied's future-acquired inventory, accounts, and proceeds. * * * Bank of the West's security interest became perfected at the moment of attachment as a result of the Bank's financing statement naming Allied as its debtor, which was filed with the California Secretary of State on April 7, 1982. * * * In addition to its perfected security interest in assets actually transferred from BCI to Allied, because of the after-acquired property clause in its security agreement, Bank of the West had a perfected security interest in all inventory, accounts, and proceeds thereafter acquired by Allied.

2. *CCFS's Security Interest*

In its opinion, the district court concluded that it was unnecessary for it to determine whether CCFS's security interest remained perfected after the transfer. *Bank of the West,* 655 F.Supp. at 814. In light of our resolution of the priority dispute, we must address this question.

Two provisions of the commercial code are relevant to deciding whether CCFS's security interest continued after the transfer of the beverage business to Allied. We begin with section 9–306(2), which provides in pertinent part:

> Except where this division * * * otherwise provides, a security interest continues in collateral notwithstanding sale, exchange or other disposition thereof unless the disposition was authorized by the secured party in the security agreement or otherwise, and also continues in any identifiable proceeds including collections received by the debtor.

* * * Neither the factoring agreement nor the related security agreement expressly authorized BCI to transfer its assets to another corporation. There is no evidence to show that CCFS otherwise authorized this disposition of its collateral. California courts have made clear that implied authorizations of sales of the debtor's

collateral will not be found absent clear evidence based on the prior conduct of the parties. * * * Because there is no evidence that CCFS authorized BCI's disposition of the collateral, CCFS's security interest in the collateral actually transferred (inventory and accounts) and its proceeds continued after the transfer.

* * *

C. Resolving the Priority Dispute

Having concluded that both Bank of the West and CCFS had perfected security interests in the inventory and accounts actually transferred from BCI to Allied, as well as the inventory and accounts acquired by Allied after the July 1, 1984 transfer, we must decide which of these security interests is entitled to priority. The district court resolved this question by looking to section 9–312(5) * * *.

By applying section 9–312(5)(a) according to its literal language, the district court concluded that Bank of the West's security interest prevailed over that of CCFS. When BCI transferred the beverage business to Allied, Bank of the West's security interest attached under the after-acquired property clause in its security agreement. See § 9–203(1) and § 9–204(1). When Bank of the West's security interest attached, it automatically became perfected pursuant to the earlier filed financing statement naming Allied as its debtor. See § 9–303(1). Bank of the West's financing statement was filed on April 7, 1982. CCFS's financing statement was filed January 5, 1984, and its security interest became perfected on January 10, 1984 when BCI executed the factoring and related security agreements. Section 9–312(5) sets forth a "first to file or first to perfect" rule of priority. Because Bank of the West's financing statement was filed first, the district court concluded that the Bank's security interest prevailed over that of CCFS. Bank of the West, 655 F.Supp. at 817.

The situation we have described above has until this case been regarded by the commentators as only a hypothetical scenario. It is a scenario offered by the commentators, however, to illustrate a failure of the commercial code to resolve a priority dispute properly. See, e.g., B. Clark, The Law of Secured Transactions Under the Uniform Commercial Code ¶ 3.8[4] (1980); Harris, The Interaction of Articles 6 and 9 of the Uniform Commercial Code: A Study in Conveyancing, Priorities, and Code Interpretation, 39 Vand.L. Rev. 179, 222–25, 225 n. 182 (1986); Oldfather, Floor Plan Financing Under Article 9 of the Uniform Commercial Code, 14 U.Kan.L. Rev. 571, 582–84 (1966); Skilton, Security Interests in After– Acquired Property Under the Uniform Commercial Code, 1974 Wis.L.Rev. 925, 948. The difficulty noted by these commentators is this: Before the transfer from BCI to Allied, CCFS (the transferor's creditor) had a perfected security interest in the collateral. After the transfer, CCFS's perfected security interest suddenly is subordinated to the perfected security interest of Bank of the West (the transferee's creditor). CCFS, which had taken all steps required of it by the commercial code to announce its interest in the collateral *to potential creditors of the transferor* (BCI), now finds its security interest subordinated to that of the *transferee's* (Allied's) *creditor,* (Bank of the West), whose security interest came into play only because BCI made an unauthorized disposition of the collateral to which the Bank's security interest attached solely by operation of an after-acquired collateral clause. * * *

We agree with the commentators that applying section 9–312(5) to resolve this priority dispute produces an unsatisfactory result. The principal reason that section 9–312(5) fails to produce a proper result is that it does not appear the drafters contemplated what Professor Clark calls the "dual debtor dilemma." See B. Clark, supra, ¶ 3.8[4]. Certainly the official comments to the Uniform Commercial Code, which offer several illustrations of the operation of section 9–312(5), do not address the situation in which the competing security interests are between creditors of *different* debtors. See § 9–312(5) Uniform Commercial Code Comments 4– 8. In Mr. Coogan's seminal article, *The New UCC Article 9,* 86 Harv.L.Rev. 477 (1973), no mention of the dual debtor scenario is made in the thoughtful portion of the article addressing the drafters' reasons for adopting section 9–312(5). See id. at 507–11. Because section 9–312(5) does not contemplate the dual debtor scenario, we must resolve this priority dispute by returning to first principles.

As a general rule of construction, the commercial code "shall be liberally construed and applied to promote its underlying purposes and policies." § 1–102(1). The commercial code is intended to be flexible. "It is intended to make it possible for the law embodied in this Act to be developed by the courts in the light of unforeseen and new circumstances and practices. However, the proper construction of the Act requires that its interpretation and application be limited to its reason." Id. Uniform Commercial Code Comment 1. There are two reasons behind the rule of section 9–312(5)(a). First, the "first to file or first to perfect" rule serves to modify the common law notion of "first in time, first in right." Harris, supra, 39 Vand.L.Rev. at 222. Section 9–312(5) places a premium on prompt filing of financing statements as a means of protecting *future* creditors of the debtor. The financing statement alerts potential creditors that collateral against which they are contemplating making a loan already is encumbered. Thus, section 9–312(5)(a) penalizes a creditor who has a security interest but who does not promptly file a financing statement by awarding priority to a later creditor who acquires a security interest in the same collateral and who more promptly files a financing statement. The "first to file or first to perfect" rule of § 9–312(5)(a) thus addresses the problem of secret security interests that so concerned pre-Code courts. See id. But in the present case, the notice giving function of § 9–312(5)(a) does not apply. Bank of the West is a creditor of another debtor entity, and the Bank's interest in the collateral arises solely out of an after-acquired property clause. Bank of the West cannot claim that it has relied to its detriment on the absence of a filed financing statement by CCFS.

A second purpose behind section 9–312(5)(a) is an implied commitment to a secured creditor who has filed a financing statement that, absent special considerations such as a purchase money security interest, * * * no subsequent creditor will be able to defeat the complying creditor's security interest. This notion finds support in comment 5 to section 9–402(7), which reads in pertinent part: "The justification for this rule lies in the necessity of protecting the filing system—that is, of allowing the secured party who has first filed to make subsequent advances without each time having, as a precondition of protection, to check for filings later than his." * * * This has been described as the "claim staking" function of the financing statement. See Knippenberg, supra, 52 Mo.L.Rev. at 61 & n. 22. What this means is that by filing a proper financing statement in the proper place, a secured creditor has staked a claim to its collateral and knows that, absent special considerations, its claim will prevail against *subsequently arising* interests in the same property. By complying with the Code, the creditor is relieved of much of the responsibility of monitoring its debtor's collateral—the Code has allocated the burden of discovering prior filed financing statements to later lenders. Cf. § 9–402 Uniform Commercial Code Comment 8 ("[A]ny person searching the condition of ownership of a debtor must make inquiry as to the debtor's source of title, and must search in the name of a former owner if the circumstances seem to require it.").

Applying section 9–312(5)(a) to the present case serves neither of the rationales behind the "first to file or first to perfect" rule. The notice giving function is irrelevant because the creditor of a different debtor whose sole interest in disputed collateral arises from an after-acquired property clause has no incentive to check for financing statements against the property of another debtor. Certainly the burden is on a transferee's creditor to search the title to property, but this duty arises only when the transferee's creditor first appears on the scene after the transfer. Likewise, it makes no sense to use section 9–312(5)(a) to defeat CCFS's perfected security interest when CCFS has taken all steps required of it by the Code to proclaim its interest in the collateral. CCFS is entitled to rely on the Code's promise that a creditor who fully complies usually may expect its security interest to be given priority in a dispute with another secured creditor. To apply section 9–312(5)(a) to this case would produce an undesirable result that does not follow from the principles that the section is meant to promote.[8]

We think the correct result is reached in this case by applying the common sense notion that a creditor cannot convey to another more than it owns. Put another way, the transferee, Allied, cannot acquire any greater rights in the beverage business's assets than its transferor, BCI, had in them. Cf. § 2–403(1) ("A purchaser of goods acquires all title which his transferor had or had power to transfer except that a purchaser of a limited interest acquires rights only to the extent of the interest purchased."); see also B. Clark, supra, ¶ 3.8[4] (suggesting principles of section 2–403(1) apply to this situation); Harris, supra, 39 Vand.L.Rev. at 223, 225 n. 182 (same). Our analysis also finds direct support in the California Commercial Code. Section 9–312(1) provides, "The rules of priority stated in other sections of this chapter ＊ ＊ ＊ shall govern where applicable." And section 9–306(2) provides that a security interest follows collateral into the hands of a transferee when there is an unauthorized disposition by the transferor. ＊ ＊ ＊ The drafters tell us that "[i]n most cases when a debtor makes an unauthorized disposition of the collateral, the security interest, under ＊ ＊ ＊ this Article, continues in the original collateral in the hands of the purchaser or other transferee. That is to say, ＊ ＊ ＊ the transferee *takes subject to the security interest* ＊ ＊ ＊. Subsection 9–306(2) codifies this rule." § 9–306 Uniform Commercial Code Comment 3. If the transferee (Allied) takes the transferred collateral subject to the transferor's creditor's (CCFS's) security interest, certainly the transferee's creditor (Bank of the West) can have no greater rights in the

---

8. It is possible to argue, of course, that our analysis does violence to the interest of the transferee's creditor, whose security interest has been perfected by filing just the same as the transferor's creditor. But it is important to remember that the situation we consider is one in which the transferee's creditor's security interest attaches to the transferred collateral solely by operation of an after-acquired property clause. Although the Uniform Commercial Code expressly validates after-acquired property clauses, § 9–204(1), these "floating liens" still have not been whole-heartedly accepted by the drafters.

Subsection 1 makes clear that a security interest arising by virtue of an after-acquired property clause has equal status with a security interest in collateral in which the debtor has rights at the time value is given under the security agreement. That is to say: security interest in after-ac-

quired property is not merely an "equitable" interest; no further action by the secured party ＊ ＊ ＊ is required. This does *not* mean however *that the interest is proof against subordination or defeat* ＊ ＊ ＊.

§ 9–204 Uniform Commercial Code Comment 1 (emphasis added). To the extent our opinion results in holders of after-acquired property clauses not being able to prevail against the perfected security interest of a transferor's secured creditor, this is consistent with the drafters intention in validating after-acquired property clauses but not granting them an assurance of absolute priority in all cases.

For an excellent analysis of the monitoring burdens placed on creditors as they relate to the second sentence of section 9–402(7) and after-acquired property clauses, see Knippenberg, supra, 52 Mo.L.Rev. at 92–97.

collateral than does its debtor (Allied). Because section 9–402(7) preserves CCFS's perfected security interest in the collateral actually transferred as well as in the property acquired in the four months after the transfer, CCFS's security interest continues to be superior to Bank of the West's interest during this period, even though Bank of the West's interest also is perfected. This result is consistent with the principles of the filing system that we have previously discussed. If the notice giving function does not apply because Bank of the West has no reason to check for filings against BCI, the claim-staking function that protects CCFS should be enforced. CCFS has done all that the Code asks of it to protect its interest. Absent some countervailing consideration, CCFS should be entitled to rely on its perfected security interest.

* * *

PROBLEM

Debtor borrowed from Finance Co. and, to secure the debt, granted to Finance Co. a security interest in business equipment owned by Debtor. Finance Co. filed a financing statement covering business equipment. The security agreement prohibited Debtor from selling any collateral without permission of Finance Co. Debtor, without the consent or knowledge of Finance Co., made a cash sale of part of the business equipment to Equipment Dealer, a retailer of new and used business equipment. When Finance Co. learned of the sale it demanded that Equipment Dealer return the equipment. Is Finance Co. entitled to return of the equipment? Suppose that when Finance Co. made its demand Equipment Dealer had already sold the equipment to Buyer, who bought in the ordinary course of business. Is Finance Co. entitled to return of the equipment from Buyer?

Suppose Equipment Dealer had previously granted to Bank a security interest in all of Equipment Dealer's inventory whether then in existence or acquired thereafter. When Finance Co. demanded return of the equipment from Equipment Dealer, Bank made a claim to the equipment on the basis of its security interest in Equipment Dealer's inventory. As between Bank and Finance Co., who has priority? Does it matter whether Bank had filed before Finance Co.?

2. FARM PRODUCTS

Although farm products are frequently held by farmers as inventory, the inventory of a farmer is treated specially under the Code. Under § 9–109 "inventory" and "farm products" are mutually exclusive terms; if goods are held for sale by a farmer and the goods fall within the definition of farm products in § 9–109(3), they are excluded from the definition of inventory stated in § 9–109(4). The rights of persons who buy farm products from the farmer are also different under the UCC. Buyers of farm products are expressly excluded from the protection against perfected security interests which § 9–307(1) gives to buyers of inventory in ordinary course. The result under the UCC is that perfected security interests in farm products have priority over the rights of buyers unless the secured party has authorized sale under § 9–306(2). Since a perfected security interest in farm products is not cut off under § 9–307(1) even when sold to a buyer in ordinary course of business, subsequent buyers also take subject to the security interest. Agricultural products such as grain and cotton are "farm products" only if they are in the possession of a person engaged in farming operations. § 9–109(3). If a farmer sells bales of cotton to a cotton dealer, the cotton, in the hands of the dealer, becomes inventory. But a buyer of the cotton from the dealer gets no benefit from § 9–307(1). Under that section a buyer in ordinary course takes free of a perfected security interest only if the security interest was created by the dealer. Thus, innocent remote buyers could find themselves liable to the secured party in conversion after having already paid for the goods.

Why are buyers in ordinary course of farm products not given the same protection as buyers in ordinary course of inventory? Pre–Code law usually protected the chattel mortgagee of crops or livestock against the grain merchant or meatpacker who purchased from the mortgagor. Professor Gilmore states that the exclusion from § 9–307(1) of "a person buying farm products from a person engaged in farming operations" was the result of "bowing before the weight of case law authority." Gilmore, Security Interests in Personal Property 714 (1965). Professor Henson reports that in the process of drafting the 1972 amendments, the farm products exception was at one stage dropped from § 9–307(1) only to be restored by the Permanent Editorial Board. He notes that the federal government supported the farm products exception in its role as a major agricultural financer. Henson, Secured Transactions 144–145 (2d ed. 1979).

A large and confusing body of case law grew up around the interpretation of when a secured party has authorized sale under § 9–306(2) in farm products cases. One line of authority led by Clovis Nat. Bank v. Thomas, 77 N.M. 554, 425 P.2d 726 (1967), protected buyers even though the secured party had expressly prohibited sale without its written permission on the ground that the secured party had waived its rights by allowing previous sales without its written consent. Perhaps a majority of cases followed Garden City Production Credit Ass'n v. Lannan, 186 Neb. 668, 186 N.W.2d 99 (1971), and enforced clauses prohibiting sale without the consent of the secured party. In these cases policy arguments were heated; dissents were frequent. Volatility in the field is shown by the fact that in 1987 the Supreme Court of Nebraska overruled its own leading case, *Garden City,* in Farmers State Bank v. Farmland Foods, Inc., 255 Neb. 1, 402 N.W.2d 277 (1987).

Having failed to convince the Permanent Editorial Board of the need for change in the 1972 amendments, food processors and other agricultural buyer interests were more successful in the legislative forum. In the 1970s and 80s a substantial number of states enacted statutes affording buyers of farm products increased protection against secured creditors. California and Minnesota deleted from § 9–307(1) "other than a person buying farm products from a person engaged in farming operations," thus treating a security interest in farm products as an ordinary inventory lien subject to being cut off by a sale to a buyer in ordinary course. Other states allowed buyers of farm products to take free of security interests unless the secured party had notified the buyer of its security interest, relying on information obtained from the debtor or through a central registration of buyers. A number of states have established statewide central filing systems for financing statements covering farm products. For a compilation of these statutes see 3 Uniform Laws Annotated, Uniform Commercial Code § 9–307 (Cum.Supp.1990). The state legislation is discussed in Meyer, The 9–307(1) Farm Products Puzzle: Its Parts and Its Future, 60 N.D.L.Rev. 401 (1984).

By the mid–1980s state law on priorities in farm products collateral was hopelessly nonuniform. Although the federal agencies lending to farmers had opposed change in the farm products exception to § 9–307(1) in the 1972 amendments, Congress intervened on the part of buyers of agricultural products in the Food Security Act, 7 U.S.C. § 1631, which became effective in 1986, and preempted the UCC and other state statutes on security interests in farm products. Section 1631(d) states "Except as provided in subsection (e) * * * a buyer who in the ordinary course of business buys a farm product from a seller engaged in farming operations shall take free of a security interest created by the seller, even though the security interest is perfected; and the buyer knows of the existence of such interest." A similar provision in favor of commission merchants or selling agents is found in subsection (g). A person may protect its security interest in farm products against buyers, commission merchants or selling agents either by giving them notice, based on information obtained from debtors, or by filing notice with a central notice system established by the state in compliance with federal requirements. Section 1631(e) and (g)(2). Fry, Buying Farm Products: The 1985 Farm Bill Changes the Rules of the Game, 91 Com'l L.J. 433 (1986).

E. PROCEEDS

---

1. ACCOUNTS

PROBLEM

Debtor, a wholesaler of widgets, sells on open account to retailers. Bank made a loan to Debtor who executed a security agreement granting Bank a security interest in "all inventory of widgets now owned or hereafter acquired." Bank filed a financing statement with the same description of the collateral.

1. Debtor's inventory of widgets is located in a warehouse in State A, but its chief executive office is in State B. Bank filed its financing statement in State A. Does Bank have a perfected security interest in Debtor's inventory? Does Bank have a security interest in the accounts (§ 9–106) arising from the sale of Debtor's inventory? § 9–203(3) and § 9–306(2). Is it perfected? § 9–306(3), § 9–302, and § 9–103(3).

2. Change the facts by assuming that both Debtor's warehouse and chief executive office are in State A, and Bank filed its financing statement there. After Bank filed, Debtor obtained a loan from Financer pursuant to a security agreement which assigned to Financer "all accounts now owned or hereafter acquired." Financer filed a financing statement in State A describing the collateral in the same manner. Does Financer have priority over Bank with respect to Debtor's accounts? § 9–102(1) (b), § 9–312(5) and § 9–312(6). See Example 7 of Comment 8, to § 9–312.

3. Both Debtor's warehouse and chief executive office are in State A, and Bank filed its financing statement there. Before Bank filed, Debtor obtained a loan from Financer. Debtor executed a security agreement assigning all its accounts, then owned or thereafter acquired, to Financer who filed a financing statement in State A describing the collateral in the same manner. Financer filed before Bank. Does Financer have priority over Bank with respect to the accounts? See Example 8 of Comment 8 to § 9–312.

2. CHATTEL PAPER

REX FINANCIAL CORP. v. GREAT WESTERN BANK & TRUST

Court of Appeals of Arizona, Division 1, Department A, 1975.
23 Ariz.App. 286, 532 P.2d 558.

DONOFRIO, JUDGE.   This is an appeal from a judgment in favor of the appellee, Great Western Bank & Trust, on a motion to dismiss which was treated by the trial court as a motion for summary judgment under Rule 56 of the Arizona Rules of Civil Procedure, 16 A.R.S.   The trial court considered all of the pleadings, affidavits, other matters of record, and the oral arguments of counsel and determined that there was no genuine issue of material fact, in reaching its judgment.   For the reasons given below we affirm the judgment of the trial court.

The relevant facts are undisputed.   In December of 1971 appellant entered into an agreement with Liberty Mobile Home Centers, Inc., a dealer in mobile homes, under which appellant agreed to finance this dealer's inventory of mobile homes.   The dealer delivered to appellant certain manufacturer's certificates of origin on mobile homes to secure repayment of the loans, and gave appellant a security interest in the vehicles by way of a security agreement between the parties.   This appeal concerns four of those mobile homes.   The four mobile homes were sold by the dealer in the regular course of his business to certain individuals on security agreement contracts.   These four security agreement contracts were then sold and assigned to the appellee, Great Western, in the ordinary course of its business for a certain sum which was paid to the dealer.   Unfortunately, the dealer did not use these funds to pay off its outstanding loans owed to the appellant.

The basis for attacking a Rule 56 summary judgment ruling is that there were material factual issues disputed by the parties.   All facts considered by the trial court appear in the pleadings, affidavits, depositions, and of course, oral arguments of the parties.   On reviewing the record we are compelled to agree with the trial court that there were no material issues of fact, and that this was a question of law concerning the construction and application of U.C.C. § 9–308 concerning the priority between certain secured creditors and purchasers of chattel paper.

§ 9–308 states:

"A purchaser of chattel paper or a nonnegotiable instrument who gives new value and takes possession of it in the ordinary course of his business and without knowledge that the specific paper or instrument is subject to a security interest has priority over a security interest which is perfected under § 9–304 (permissive filing and temporary perfection). *A purchaser of chattel paper who gives new value and takes possession of it in the ordinary course of his business has priority over a security interest in chattel paper which is claimed merely as proceeds of inventory subject to a security interest (§ 9–306), even though he knows that the specific paper is subject to the security interest.* Added Laws 1967, Ch. 3, § 5." (Emphasis added.)

Since it was established that Great Western Bank had knowledge of the security interest claimed by Rex Financial Corporation in the four mobile homes, the second sentence of the foregoing section is the critical one for our purposes.

Appellant's first argument concerns the definition of "chattel paper" used in the above-mentioned sentence of § 9–308. Appellant argues that the manufacturer's certificates of origin, which remained in its possession, were a part of the chattel paper and were necessary ingredients along with the security agreements purchased by Great Western to make up the "chattel paper" which must be possessed by the purchaser. We do not agree. § 9–105(1)(b) defines "chattel paper" as:

> " 'Chattel paper' means a writing or writings which evidence both a monetary obligation and a security interest in or a lease of specific goods. When a transaction is evidenced both by such a security agreement or a lease and by an instrument or a series of instruments, the group of writings taken together constitutes chattel paper."

Appellant asserts that * * * the Motor Vehicle Code contemplate that a manufacturer's certificate of origin is a part of the "transaction" where chattel paper is purchased as in § 9–105(1)(b) above. We do not think that such comparison is relevant here. "Chattel paper" clearly must evidence "both a monetary obligation and a security interest in or a lease of specific goods." The manufacturer's certificates of origin do not meet this definition, and the trial court's construction of § 9–105(1)(b) was correct in the application to this factual situation. It was undisputed that Great Western gave "new value" for the four security agreements it purchased from the dealer, all in accordance with § 9–308.

The next requirement of § 9–308 which is attacked by appellant is the requirement that the purchase of the chattel paper be "in the ordinary course of *his business*." (emphasis added) Appellant maintains that this refers to a practice which "should have been followed" and not to the practice of this particular purchaser of chattel paper. Again we do not agree. The plain language of the statute refers to *"his business"* (meaning the purchaser of the chattel paper). It is undisputed that this purchase was the normal means used at Great Western to obtain this type of chattel paper. As was stated in the deposition of Mr. McFadden, a representative of Great Western, he expected the *dealer* to disburse funds to appellant to pay off the loans for the "floor plan" financing that the dealer had obtained from appellant. The term "buyer in the ordinary course of business" with its requirements of good faith, as used elsewhere in the Uniform Commercial Code, is to be distinguished from the use here of "[buyer] in the ordinary course of *his* business." In fact, § 9–308 (second sentence) allows the purchaser of the chattel paper to have priority even if he has knowledge of a prior security interest in the collateral. As noted by White and Summers in their Treatise on the Uniform Commercial Code, " * * * the later party is favored on the assumption that chattel paper is his main course but merely the frosting on the cake for the mere proceeds claimant." White and Summers, Uniform Commercial Code, Sec. 25–17, p. 951 (1972 Edition).

This brings us to the final issue raised by appellant: the fourth requirement of the second sentence of § 9–308, that the security interest claimed by appellant is claimed "merely as proceeds of inventory subject to a security interest." We find Comment 2 to this section of the U.C.C. (as found in the Final Report of the Permanent Editorial Board for the Uniform Commercial Code, Review Committee for Article 9, April 25, 1971) instructive on this issue. There it is stated:

> "Clause (b) of the section deals with the case where the security interest in the chattel paper is claimed merely as proceeds—i.e., on behalf of an inventory financer who has not by some new transaction with the debtor acquired a specific interest in the chattel paper. In that case a purchaser, even though he knows of the inventory financer's proceeds interest, takes priority provided he gives new value and takes possession of the paper in the ordinary course of his business."

We take this language to mean that the drafters of the Code contemplated a situation such as the instant one where the inventory financer, Rex Financial Corp., had a security interest in the collateral (mobile homes) and the proceeds upon sale. The record before us does *not* indicate that Rex entered into any new transaction with the debtor/dealer. The trial court had before it the security agreement between Rex and the dealer as well as the affidavit of Rex's president, and found that Rex's claim was merely to the proceeds of the inventory when sold. We do not find error in this construction and application of the term "mere proceeds of inventory" by the trial court. We think it is a reasonable interpretation of the record that the appellant, Rex, did *not* place a substantial reliance on the chattel paper in making the loan, but rather relied on the collateral (mobile homes) and the proceeds when the collateral was sold. The proceeds of the sale of these four mobile homes included the chattel paper sold by the dealer to Great Western. Rex could have protected itself by requiring all security agreements executed on sale of the mobile homes to be turned over immediately to Rex, or if sold, that all payments for the security agreements (chattel paper) be made to itself.

A case that aptly illustrates the operation of U.C.C. § 9–308 is Associates Discount Corporation v. Old Freeport Bank, 421 Pa. 609, 220 A.2d 621 (1966). In that case a finance company which purchased chattel paper from an auto dealer (in a factual situation somewhat similar to ours) prevailed over a bank which had "floor planned" the inventory of the dealer. The court found that the bank's claim was a mere proceeds claim to the chattel paper and that U.C.C. § 9–308 (second sentence) would operate to give priority to the purchaser of the chattel paper. The inventory financer's interest in the "proceeds" of the sale of the inventory had been shifted to the money paid by the purchaser of the chattel paper to the dealer. Another case in which the same result was obtained was Chrysler Credit Corporation v. Sharp, 56 Misc.2d 261, 288 N.Y.S.2d 525 (1968), a New York case, which again applied U.C.C. § 9–308 and held that the purchaser of an installment contract from an automobile dealer would prevail over a secured inventory financer.

The case of Price v. Universal C.I.T. Credit Corporation, 102 Ariz. 227, 427 P.2d 919 (1967), although decided before our state's adoption of the Uniform Commercial Code, is still instructive in the instant case. The court there held that an inventory financer who brought an action against, among others, the purchase money lender on the sale of an automobile should not have priority over the purchase money lender. The inventory financer sought to recover money loaned to the dealer on a "flooring loan" when the automobiles were sold out of trust. We realize that the Price case did not involve application of U.C.C. § 9–308, but it is indicative of the general feelings of our courts in the area of priorities between secured creditors and purchasers of chattel paper as proceeds of the sale of inventory collateral.

In any case, the construction and application of U.C.C. § 9–308 to undisputed facts is a question of law for the trial court which was reasonably determined in the instant case.

Affirmed.

PROBLEMS

1. Bank was granted a security interest in all inventory and chattel paper (whether then owned or after-acquired) of Debtor, a dealer in appliances. Bank filed a financing statement covering inventory and chattel paper. Debtor sold a refrigerator to a buyer

in ordinary course under an installment sale contract under which
Debtor was granted a security interest in the refrigerator. Debtor
assigned the installment sale contract to Bank which paid Debtor
new value. Bank did not take possession of the installment
contract. It left it with Debtor with instructions to collect the
installments and to remit to Bank. Debtor then assigned the
installment contract to Finance Co. which paid new value and
took possession of the paper. Finance Co. had actual knowledge of
Bank's financing statement. It did not know, however, that Debt-
or had assigned the installment contract to Bank. What are the
priorities of Bank and Finance Co. to the installment contract?

2. Debtor is an appliance dealer. Bank advanced $100,000
operating capital to Debtor and took a security interest, perfected
by filing, in all Debtor's inventory then owned or thereafter
acquired including all proceeds from the disposition of that collateral. Debtor sold a refrigerator to A for $1,000 and reserved a
security interest in the refrigerator for the unpaid price plus the
finance charge pursuant to an installment sale contract. Debtor
sold a washing machine and dryer unit to B for $1,000 and
accepted B's unsecured negotiable promissory note for the balance
of the price. Debtor leased a large screen television set to C for
one year at $100 per month rental. Debtor assigned and delivered
the installment contract, the promissory note, and the lease to
Finance Co. which paid cash to the Debtor less a 10% discount.
Finance Co. knew Bank was financing Debtor's inventory.

a. What are the priorities between Bank and Finance Co.
with respect to the contract, note, and lease? See § 9–308 and
§ 9–309. Would your answer change if Bank's security agreement
and financing statement specifically mentioned chattel paper and
instruments as primary collateral? What does "merely as proceeds" mean in § 9–308(b)?

b. What are the priorities between Bank and Finance Co.
with respect to Debtor's residual right to the television set? See
In re Leasing Consultants, Inc., 486 F.2d 367 (2d Cir. 1973); In re
Watertown Tractor & Equipment Co., Inc., 94 Wis.2d 622, 289
N.W.2d 288 (1980).

3. CASH PROCEEDS

HARLEY–DAVIDSON MOTOR CO. v. BANK OF NEW ENGLAND–OLD COLONY

United States Court of Appeals, First Circuit, 1990.
897 F.2d 611.

BREYER, CIRCUIT JUDGE.

A motorcycle manufacturer ("Harley") and a finance company ("ITT") loaned money to a motorcycle dealer ("Clemence") to help finance the dealer's *new* motorcycle inventory. To guarantee repayment they took and perfected a secured interest in the dealer's *entire*—new and used cycle—inventory and in all his motorcycle sale proceeds. Subsequently, a bank ("Old Colony") provided the dealer with a line of credit, primarily to help him buy *used* motorcycles. To guarantee repayment, the bank took and perfected a (junior) secured interest in the dealer's inventory. More importantly, the bank insisted that the dealer leave with it title documentation (which we shall refer to as "certificates") for particular used, and a few new, motorcycles. The bank released these certificates only as the dealer sold the individual cycles and repaid the bank's advances. The dealer went bankrupt.

The motorcycle manufacturer and the finance company brought this diversity action against the bank. They claim that the bank, by holding (as security for its advances) the title certificates of several new motorcycles, intentionally interfered with their senior "security agreement" contracts. They say the bank's practice caused the bankruptcy of the dealer, thereby preventing them from collecting all the money the dealer owed them and causing them to lose profits while they searched for a replacement dealer. They also claim that the bank's practice of holding the title certificates amounted to conversion, either (1) of the certificates themselves or (2) of motorcycle sale proceeds that the dealer consequently paid to the bank rather than to them.

The district court entered judgment for the bank on both sets of claims. The court, without hearing evidence, granted summary judgment for the bank on the conversion claim. 85 B.R. 1. After hearing evidence on the "contract interference" claim, it held for the bank on the ground that the plaintiffs failed to prove that the bank's practices caused the dealer's bankruptcy. The manufacturer and the finance company (Harley and ITT) now appeal. We conclude that the law entitles them to proceed to trial on one aspect of their "conversion" claims, but in all other respects we affirm the district court.

Background

To understand the basis for our conclusions, the reader must keep the following factual background in mind:

1.   The dealer, Richard J. Clemence, established his Harley–Davidson motorcycle dealership in 1982. The manufacturer, Harley, and the finance company, ITT, financed his acquisition of *new* motorcycles.

2.   Clemence signed written security agreements with both Harley and ITT. The agreements each contain four terms of particular importance here:

   a.   Each grants the secured party a secured interest in collateral that includes *all* Clemence's inventory, both new and used cycles, and the proceeds of their sale.

   b.   Each forbids Clemence (without the secured party's consent) to create another security interest in the collateral.

   c.   Each requires Clemence to pay back to the secured party the loan on any financed motorcycle immediately (e.g., within 24 hours) after Clemence sells the motorcycle.

   d.   Each defines "default" broadly to include Clemence's breaking of his promise not to encumber the collateral; and each permits the secured party to repossess the collateral upon default.

Harley and ITT each perfected its secured interest by filing financing statements with the Rhode Island Secretary of State in March 1982.

3.   Subsequently, Old Colony provided Clemence with a line of credit designed to help him buy used motorcycles—old motorcycles that customers would trade in when they bought new ones. As we have said, Old Colony secured repayment in two ways. First, it obtained a secured interest in Clemence's entire inventory of new and used cycles, an interest which it perfected by filing financing statements in September 1983 and December 1984. Old Colony's secured interest was junior to the previously perfected secured interests of Harley and ITT. Second, before making a particular advance (under its line of credit), Old Colony required Clemence to sign a document called "Trust Receipt and Promissory Note," which identified a specific motorcycle, the value of which equalled or exceeded the amount of the advance; and it required Clemence to deposit with it the title certificate for each such identified motorcycle. It returned the title certificate to Clemence only when he repaid the advance. Since Clemence could not sell a motorcycle without delivering the title certificate to the buyer, this practice assured Old Colony that Clemence would likely use any money from the sale of a motorcycle immediately to repay the advance.

4. As a practical matter, Old Colony's "certificate holding" practice did not conflict with Harley's and ITT's collection efforts so long as Old Colony held only *used* motorcycle certificates. Suppose, for example, that Clemence bought a new motorcycle from Harley for which it owed Harley (or ITT) $7,000. Suppose he sold the cycle for $5,000 cash plus a used (trade-in) cycle worth $6,000. He could pay Harley back the $7000 almost immediately by giving Harley the $5,000 cash he received from the buyer, plus, say, $2,000 that he borrowed from Old Colony on the strength of the used cycle. When Clemence later sold the used cycle, he would simultaneously repay Old Colony.

Suppose, however, that Old Colony loaned money against (and held the certificate for) a *new* motorcycle that Harley (or ITT) had financed. This could create a financially awkward situation. Suppose, as above, that Clemence bought a new cycle from Harley, for which he owed Harley $7,000. Assume he then borrowed, say, $4500 from Old Colony, using the same *new* cycle as collateral. And assume, as before, that Clemence sold the new cycle for $5,000 cash plus a used (trade-in) cycle worth $6,000. He would now immediately have to repay Old Colony $4500 to get back the new cycle's title certificate, and he would then have only $500 in cash left to repay Harley its $7000 loan. Even if Clemence could sell the used cycle immediately, or use the cycle to secure a further $6000 advance from Old Colony, he would still end up with $500 less than he needs to repay Harley: the "double financing" of the new cycle has created a financial problem. Harley and ITT say that such financial problems caused Clemence's bankruptcy.

5. From September 1983, when Old Colony provided Clemence with a $50,000 revolving line of credit, through October 1984, when Old Colony increased the line of credit to $75,000, until June 10, 1985, when Clemence filed for bankruptcy, Old Colony issued "trust receipts", and held title certificates, for 53 motorcycles. It returned 41 certificates to Clemence as he repaid the relevant advances. It turned over the remaining 12 certificates to Harley soon after Clemence filed for bankruptcy. Until January 1985 (with one irrelevant exception) it held only *used* cycle title certificates. Between January and June 1985, however, it took *eight certificates for new, Harley- or ITT-financed motorcycles*. At any one time it held a maximum of *four* such certificates, securing an advance to Clemence of $18,666.

* * *

The Proceeds

Harley and ITT make a second conversion claim. They point out that Clemence sold the 41 (mostly used, but a few new) motorcycles that he had pledged to Old Colony, simultaneously repaying Old Colony its advances and redeeming the motorcycle title certificates. Old Colony knew, however, that Harley and ITT had a perfected security interest in the "*proceeds*" arising from the sale of *all* Clemence's inventory. In taking and keeping the "proceeds" from these 41 sales, Old Colony (say Harley and ITT) was "converting" money that belonged to Harley and ITT.

In our view, this claim should have survived Old Colony's motion for summary judgment. The Uniform Commercial Code makes clear that a secured party may obtain a secured interest in "proceeds." See § 9–306. The Code defines "proceeds" as "whatever is received upon the sale, exchange, collection or other disposition of collateral or proceeds." § 9–306(1). It adds that a "security interest continues * * * in any identifiable proceeds * * *." § 9–306(2). The law also indicates that a secured party may bring an action for conversion to recover collateral that has found its way into the hands of a third party whose interest is inferior. See, e.g., § 9–306, comment 3 * * *.

The arguments that Old Colony makes to the contrary do not demonstrate a right to *summary* judgment on the claim. First, Old Colony argues that Harley and ITT have no legal right to recover *any* sale "proceeds" because (as Harley and ITT concede) prior to payment, Clemence *commingled* the sale money with other money that he kept in a single Old Colony bank account. They point to one knowledgeable commentator, writing when the Code was new, who suggests that, once a seller commingles "proceeds" with other money, the proceeds are no longer "identifiable," and therefore no longer count as "identifiable proceeds" that the Code permits a secured party to recover. See 1 G. Gilmore, Security Interests in Personal Property § 27.4, at 736 (1965).

The problem with this argument, however, is that the courts have subsequently, with virtual unanimity, rejected Professor Gilmore's early view. They have held that, in certain special circumstances, a secured party may trace "identifiable proceeds" through a commingled bank account and into the hands of a recipient who lacks the right to keep them. * * * For example, when a debtor, aware that his bank account balance would prove inadequate to pay both a secured creditor (a finance company) and another debt he owed (to the bank), told the bank to set off quickly the money the debtor owed it, and when the bank (knowing all) did so after regular banking hours, the court held that the finance company could use common law tracing rules to trace "proceeds" (in which it held a secured interest) through the debtor's bank account and into the hands of the bank. See *Universal C.I.T. Credit Corp.*, 358 F.Supp. at 323–24.

Courts, in justifying the use of tracing, have pointed out that the Code itself says that they are to supplement its provisions with general "principles of law and equity." § 1–103. * * * In deciding *when* to trace proceeds, they have distinguished between persons who take funds from a commingled account "in the ordinary course" of a debtor's business (where tracing and recovery are not appropriate), and recipients who have engaged in "fraudulent" or "collusive" or otherwise unfair behavior (where tracing and recovery are appropriate)—a distinction the courts base upon an official U.C.C. Comment to § 9–306, Comment 2(c), which reads as follows:

> Where cash proceeds are covered into the debtor's checking account and paid out in the operation of the debtor's business, recipients of the funds of course take free of any claim which the secured party may have in them as proceeds. What has been said relates to payments and transfers in ordinary course. The law of fraudulent conveyances would no doubt in appropriate cases support recovery of proceeds by a secured party from a transferee out of ordinary course or otherwise in collusion with the debtor to defraud the secured party.

In deciding *how* to trace "identifiable proceeds" through a commingled bank account, courts have used common law tracing rules. * * *

In sum, even though the courts have thus imposed rather strict limits as to *when* and *how* they will trace proceeds, the fact of commingling itself does not *automatically* bar recovery.

Second, Old Colony also argues here, as it argued in the district court, that a different subsection of U.C.C. § 9–306 limits Harley's and ITT's right to recover commingled proceeds in such a way as to preclude recovery in this case. That other subsection, § 9–306(4), says:

> In the event of insolvency proceedings instituted by or against a debtor, a secured party with a perfected security interest in proceeds has a perfected security interest only in the following proceeds:
>
> * * *
>
> (d) In all cash and deposit accounts of the debtor, in which proceeds have been commingled with other funds, but the perfected security interest under this subdivision (d) is
>
> * * *
>
> (ii) Limited to an amount not greater than the amount of any cash proceeds received by the debtor within (10) days before the institution of the insolvency proceedings [less certain sums already received] * * *.

* * * The district court, noting that Clemence had gone through "insolvency proceedings," agreed with Old Colony that this provision applied and that it limited Harley's and ITT's rights to recover "proceeds" to the proceeds that Clemence had received in the 10–day period prior to June 10, 1985, when he declared bankruptcy (which amount, the court thought, in respect to the 41

motorcycles, was zero). We do not accept this argument, however, because we believe that this provision does not apply to Harley's and ITT's "proceeds" claim.

The provision, on its face, speaks of circumstances in which a debtor is undergoing "insolvency proceedings," in which event it limits a "secured party with a perfected interest in proceeds" to an "interest only in the *following* proceeds." § 9–306(4). Given the initial "insolvency proceeding" limitation, the provision, as most naturally read, would seem to apply only to assets in the hands of the debtor at the time of the insolvency (or later), or conceivably to assets that a trustee might bring back into the hands of the debtor (a matter we need not decide). The provision's objective is to provide rules for dividing the funds in a debtor's commingled bank account that are more definite, more readily usable, than the common law tracing rules that, say, a bankruptcy court might otherwise try to apply. See, e.g., 2 J. White & R. Summers, supra, p. 16, § 25–10, at 463 ("In theory the secured creditor gives up the common law rights such as 'the lowest intermediate balance rule' in return for the claim he receives under [U.C.C. § 9–306(4)] subsection (d)."). What purpose would be served in applying the limitations of this provision to, say, briefly commingled "proceeds" that a third party knowingly (and outside the ordinary course of business) obtained from the debtor at a secured party's expense, many months *before* insolvency? The likely claimants are only the secured party and the third party (particularly where a bankruptcy trustee does not seek to bring the funds back into the estate). Why should the debtor's insolvency in such circumstances give the third party a better right to the money than it otherwise would have?

The district court feared that to hold that this "insolvency" provision applied only to commingled accounts in the debtor's possession (conceivably as augmented by a trustee's recovery actions) at the time of insolvency could produce different results depending upon whether a party brought his action in an "insolvency proceeding" or simply filed a common law tort action, say, in a state court. But that is not so. Irrespective of the *form* of a party's action, the court could find the party's right limited, or not limited, depending upon whether the party seeks recovery of money that remained in a commingled account when insolvency proceedings began, or that passed through a commingled account before insolvency.

For these reasons, we are not surprised to find that virtually all the courts that have considered the matter have concluded that the "insolvency" provision does not apply to a dispute between a secured party and a third party over money that was withdrawn from a commingled account *prior* to the institution of an insolvency proceeding. * * * see also B. Clark, The Law of Secured

Transactions under the Uniform Commercial Code § 10.03, at 10–35 n. 129 (2d ed. 1988). We believe Rhode Island would follow this authority.

Although we reject Old Colony's claims that the law prevents Harley and ITT from trying to prove its conversion of *any* proceeds, we note the existence of other legal principles that severely limit the kinds of factual showing that might warrant recovery, and which will severely limit Harley's and ITT's ability to recover here. First, the courts, using comment 2(c) to U.C.C. § 9–306 to determine *when* they should trace proceeds through a commingled account, have limited recovery to circumstances where the behavior of the third party, if not fraudulent, has at least seemed highly unfair or improper. Comment 2(c) explicitly excludes any judicial efforts to trace (as "identifiable" secured "proceeds") money "paid out [of a commingled account] in the [*ordinary course* of] operation of the debtor's business." § 9–306, comment 2(c) (emphasis added). That comment goes on explicitly to include transfers that are "fraudulent," or "otherwise in collusion with the debtor to defraud the secured party," *id.;* and, courts have recognized instances falling *between* these two sets of circumstances where tracing is appropriate, see, e.g., *Linn Cooperative Oil Co.,* 444 N.W.2d at 499; *Farmers and Merchants National Bank,* 766 P.2d at 330. If, however, courts too readily impose liability upon those who receive funds from the debtor's ordinary bank account—if, for example, they define "ordinary course" of business too narrowly—then ordinary suppliers, sellers of gas, electricity, tables, chairs, etc., might find themselves called upon to return ordinary payments (from a commingled account) to a debtor's secured creditor, say a financer of inventory. Indeed, we can imagine good commercial reasons for *not* imposing, even upon sophisticated suppliers or secondary lenders, who are aware that inventory financers often take senior secured interests in "all inventory plus proceeds," the complicated burden of contacting these financers to secure permission to take payment from a dealer's ordinary commingled bank account. See, e.g., Skilton, The Secured Party's Rights in a Debtor's Bank Account Under Article 9 of the Uniform Commercial Code, 1977 S.Ill.U.L.J. 120, 156–57 (cautioning against overenthusiastic application of restitution principles to ordinary secured transactions cases). These considerations indicate that "ordinary course" has a fairly broad meaning; and that a court should restrict the use of tracing rules to conduct that, in the commercial context, is rather clearly improper.

The record before us would not permit a finding that Old Colony acted unreasonably or improperly in simply lending Clemence money to finance his purchase of used motorcycles or asking Clemence to repay that money to Old Colony as he subsequently sold the old cycles. Consequently, the district court should not try to trace, through Clemence's commingled account, money that (1) arose from Clemence's sale of used motorcycles, (2) was repaid to redeem title certificates belonging to used motorcycles, and (3) represents repayment of advances that Clemence used to buy used motorcycles.

Second, courts, in deciding *how* to trace proceeds through commingled accounts, have used common law tracing rules. Those rules, at a minimum, prevent Harley and ITT from tracing into Old Colony's hands any "proceeds" that passed through Clemence's account at a time when, after withdrawal of funds to pay Old Colony, the account still contained enough money to pay any then current debt to Harley or ITT. The "lowest intermediate balance" rule, for example, would assume that any funds remaining in the account *after* an Old Colony payment withdrawal are the "proceeds" earmarked for Clemence's debts to Harley or ITT. Moreover, a later restoration of an account deficiency may stop a court from considering as "identifiable proceeds" money that was previously paid to Old Colony. (For explanation and application of these tracing rules, see, e.g., *Universal C.I.T. Credit Corp.*, 358 F.Supp. at 325–27; B. Clark, supra p. 29, ¶ 10.03, at 10–32 to 10–35; R. Hillman, J. McDonnell & S. Nickles, supra p. 26, ¶ 22.05[2], at 22–57 to 22–62.)

Despite these limiting legal principles, however, we cannot now say that Harley and ITT are entitled to *nothing*. The record does not foreclose the possibility that some of the "proceeds" arose from the sale of new (presumably "double financed") motorcycles, that Clemence paid this money into his commingled account, and that he subsequently transferred money to Old Colony from the account leaving the account insufficient to pay debts he then owed to Harley or ITT. We are not prepared to say now, without greater knowledge of the details surrounding such transfers, whether they did, or did not, amount to a transfer of "identifiable proceeds," out of the "ordinary course" of business, reflecting improper Old Colony behavior. We do believe that Harley and ITT have a right to prove the factual circumstances surrounding such transfers at trial.

For these reasons the judgment of the district court is

Affirmed in part; vacated and remanded in part.

NOTES

1. In 1990 Comment 9 was added to § 9–312. The Permanent Editorial Board Commentary No. 7 referred to in this comment states, in part:

ISSUE

Secured party A and secured party B each has a perfected security interest in the same account, chattel paper, or general intangible, with A having priority over B. If the account debtor makes payment to secured party B, directly or through the debtor, may A recover the payment from B?

* * *

B. Payment in Cash

The Code does not specifically address the right of B to retain a cash payment from the account debtor. Accordingly, resort must be had to the principles of law and equity. See § 1–103. Under those principles, when a person assigns the same claim to two persons and the assignee without priority (B) receives payment from the obligor, the assignee receiving payment owes a duty of restitution to the assignee having priority (A). But if B gave value for the assignment (as B must have, see § 9–203(1)(b)) and obtained the payment in good faith and without knowledge or reason to know of the prior assignment, then B may retain the payment. See Restatement, Second, Contracts § 342(b), Comment *e* & Illustration 3; see also Restatement of Restitution § 126, Comment *f* & Illustration 8. Cf. § 9–306 comment 2(c) (recipients of cash proceeds paid from the debtor's checking account in the operation of the debtor's business take free of a security interest in the proceeds). In determining whether B had reason to know of A's security interest, courts should apply § 9–309 by analogy. Otherwise, cash would be rendered less negotiable than a check.

Under § 9–309, invoked by analogy in the Commentary, the fact that A files before B becomes a holder of an instrument does not give B notice of A's security interest. What is the effect of Comment 9 to § 9–312 on Comment 2(c) of § 9–306? Is the decision in *Harley–Davidson* consistent with PEB Commentary No. 7?

2. In *Harley–Davidson*, Clemence deposited payments from buyers of motorcycles in a commingled deposit account and paid Old Colony from that account. These payments are "cash proceeds" under § 9–306(1) and are covered by the safe harbor provision of Comment 2(c) to § 9–306. How would the analysis change if Clemence had received checks in payment for the motorcycles and had indorsed the checks to Old Colony or had notified the buyers to send their checks directly to Old Colony? The checks are cash proceeds within § 9–306(1) but they are also instruments within § 9–308 and § 9–309. In 1990, Comment 3 was added to § 9–309 to address this issue. In Bank of the West v. Commercial Credit Financial Services, Inc., 655 F.Supp. 807 (N.D.Cal.1987), rev'd on other grounds, 852 F.2d 1162 (9th Cir.1988) (appearing on p. 146 of this casebook), Debtor granted a security interest in its accounts to Bank. Subsequently Debtor assigned its accounts to Factor. Debtor notified its account debtors to send their checks directly to Factor; most did, but a few sent their checks to Debtor

who indorsed them to Factor. The court held that Bank had
priority to the proceeds represented by the check payments and
rejected Factor's claim to priority based on its status as a holder in
due course of the checks. In Clark, U.C.C. Survey: Secured
Transactions, 43 Bus.Law 1425, 1464 (1988), the author approves
Bank of the West: "Although section 9–309 allows holders in due
course to take free from the claims of prior secured creditors, the
factor has no interest in the checks except as proceeds of the
accounts. On all points the case seems correct." Comment 3 to
§ 9–309 disapproves the result of *Bank of the West.* Which side
has the better policy argument? See the discussion in PEB
Commentary No. 7 supporting Comment 3.

3. In C.O. Funk & Sons, Inc. v. Sullivan Equipment, Inc., 89
Ill.2d 27, 59 Ill.Dec. 85, 431 N.E.2d 370 (1982), the Supreme Court
of Illinois made the following statement:

> Although the Code provides no guidance as to how pro-
> ceeds might be identified, § 1–103 directs that the Code be
> supplemented by "principles of law and equity," and this
> provision has been construed to permit application of a trac-
> ing theory known in the law of trusts as the "lowest interme-
> diate balance" rule. * * * see generally Skilton, The Se-
> cured Party's Rights In A Debtor's Bank Account Under
> Article 9 of the Uniform Commercial Code, 1977 So.Ill.U.L.J.
> 120, 140–43, 152–57). * * * As Professor Skilton notes
> (1977 So.Ill.U.L.J. 120, 133 n. 21), the argument that a pro-
> ceeds security interest terminates when those proceeds are
> deposited in a bank account since they can no longer be
> identified has found little favor with the courts.

> The rule, which operates on a common-sense view that
> dollars are fungible and cannot practically be earmarked in
> an account, provides a presumption that proceeds remain in
> the account as long as the account balance is equal to or
> greater than the amount of the proceeds deposited. The
> proceeds are "identified" by presuming that they remain in
> the account even if other funds are paid out of the account. If
> [the debtor] is likened to the trustee of a constructive trust
> imposed because he commingled funds, then the lowest-inter-
> mediate-balance rule directs that [the secured party's] pro-
> ceeds in [the debtor's] account are preserved to the greatest
> extent possible as the account is depleted. * * * Under the
> rule, however, if the balance of the account dips below the
> amount of deposited proceeds, [the secured party's] security
> interest in the identifiable proceeds abates accordingly. This
> lower balance is not increased if, later, other funds of the
> debtor are deposited in the account, i.e., the added amounts
> are not subject to an equitable lien, unless the latter deposits
> are made in restitution. (Restatement of Restitution sec. 212

(1937).) Thus the claimant has no priority over other creditors to any amount in excess of the lowest intermediate balance. (See Skilton, The Secured Party's Rights In A Debtor's Bank Account Under Article 9 of the Uniform Commercial Code, 1977 So.Ill.U.L.J. 120, 140.) In this case, [the secured party] cannot assert a security interest in proceeds superior to that asserted by the bank unless [the secured party] can show that those proceeds were preserved in [the debtor's] commingled account or that other inventory was purchased with those proceeds at a time, and to the extent, that those proceeds were identified in the account. The identification of the funds, as stated, is subject to the lowest intermediate balance of the account.

F. ASSERTION OF DEFENSES OF ACCOUNT DEBTOR AGAINST ASSIGNEE OF THE ACCOUNT

BANK OF WAUNAKEE v. ROCHESTER CHEESE SALES, INC.

United States Court of Appeals, Seventh Circuit, 1990.
906 F.2d 1185.

HARLINGTON WOOD, JR., CIRCUIT JUDGE.

Plaintiff-appellant Bank of Waunakee ("the Bank") appeals the district court's order granting defendant-appellee Rochester Cheese Sales, Inc.'s motion for summary judgment on the Bank's claim for collection of an account receivable. The Bank also appeals the district court's Order denying the Bank's Motion for Reconsideration, in which the Bank asserted that the court should vacate its earlier order and allow the Bank to pursue a conversion claim despite its failure to plead a conversion claim in its complaint.

I. FACTUAL BACKGROUND

Defendant-appellee Rochester Cheese Sales, Inc. ("RCS") is a Minnesota corporation that buys and resells cheese. Waunakee Kase Haus, Inc. ("Kase Haus") was in the business of purchasing and reprocessing various types of cheeses under its own label. As part of their business, RCS and Kase Haus each purchased cheese from particular sources and sold different types of cheese to these same sources. RCS and Kase Haus shared such a business relationship in 1987.

Kase Haus bought $46,970.47 worth of cheese from RCS on March 22, 1988; $50,094.59 worth of cheese on April 1, 1988; and $22,417.42 worth of cheese on May 24, 1988. Kase Haus wired $22,000.00 to RCS in May 1988 as partial payment. RCS purchased $41,863.55 worth of cheese from Kase Haus on May 6, 1988, and $80,326.20 worth of cheese on May 11, 1988. Larry Oliver, Kase Haus's manager, had the authority to make the sales to and purchases from RCS.

On June 10, 1988, Don Roberts, acting on behalf of RCS, initiated a telephone conference with Larry Oliver of Kase Haus to review the various outstanding invoices between RCS and Kase Haus. Roberts and Oliver determined that, taking into account all outstanding invoices, credits, shipping charge adjustments, weight adjustments, and payments received, RCS owed Kase Haus the total net sum of $22,643.69. On the same day, RCS issued and mailed a check to Kase Haus for the sum of $22,643.69 with the notation on the check register delivered with the check that the check "PAID IN FULL" the amount RCS owed Kase Haus. Kase Haus negotiated the RCS check without objection.

Several months before the transactions between Kase Haus and RCS, Kase Haus borrowed money from the Bank under several loan agreements. Kase Haus subsequently defaulted on its obligation under its loan agreements with the Bank. At the time the Bank filed its complaint, Kase Haus owed the Bank a sum in excess of $1,434,585.30. The Bank had a perfected security interest in Kase Haus's inventory and accounts receivable that provided in part:

VERIFICATION AND NOTIFICATION.

> Bank may verify Collateral in any manner, and Debtor shall assist Bank in so doing. *Upon default Bank may at any time and Debtor shall, upon request of Bank, notify the account debtors to make payment directly to Bank and Bank may enforce collection of, settle, compromise, extend or renew the indebtedness of such account debtors. Until account debtors are so notified, Debtor, as agent for Bank shall make collections on the Collateral ＊ ＊ ＊.*

(emphasis added). Prior to the transactions between RCS and Kase Haus, the Bank assigned its interest in Kase Haus's accounts receivable to another lender, CFC Capital Corporation ("CFC"). Kase Haus reported to CFC on the status of its accounts receivable on a weekly basis. CFC would then wire funds to Kase Haus through the Bank. CFC continued to advance money to Kase Haus throughout June 1988. When the Bank declared Kase Haus in default, it immediately notified CFC. The Bank purchased CFC's rights to Kase Haus's accounts receivable during August 1988.

On July 21, 1988, the Bank notified RCS that it expected RCS to make payments to the Bank for the amount it allegedly owed Kase Haus. RCS received a letter dated July 18, 1988, from the Bank's attorney that stated in part:

This brings us to the account of Rochester Cheese Sales as it is reflected on the records of Waunakee Kase Haus, Inc. and to the point of this correspondence. Account records reflect that on and between May 6, 1988 and May 11, 1988, Rochester Cheese Sales acquired cheese from the inventory of Waunakee Kase Haus, Inc. having a total value of $120,126.17. At this time, Waunakee Kase Haus, Inc. was indebted to Rochester Cheese Sales for purchases on account totalling $75,065.00. On June 9, 1988, this indebtedness increased to $97,482.48 reflecting a purchase made by Waunakee Kase Haus, Inc. on that date. It appears that on or after June 9, 1988, Rochester Cheese Sales tendered a check to Waunakee Kase Haus, Inc. for $22,643.69 and set off its accounts payable to Waunakee Kase Haus, Inc. with its account receivable from Waunakee Kase Haus, Inc. In so doing, it converted the collateral of the Bank of Waunakee to the extent of the amount of the set off; [*sic*] $97,482.48.

We are provided with no information that Rochester Cheese Sales at any time owned a security interest in the inventory of accounts of Waunakee Kase Haus, Inc. to secure payment of the account of Waunakee Kase Haus, Inc. Therefore, clearly, Rochester Cheese Sales was no more than a general, unsecured creditor of Waunakee Kase Haus, Inc. at the time of the set-off. Since the right of set-off in a creditor who does not have a security interest does not abrogate the security interest of a secured creditor, the offset taken by Rochester Cheese Sales was, in fact, a conversion. As such, Rochester Cheese Sales remains indebted to the Bank of Waunakee for the sum of $97,482.48.

On November 10, 1988, the Bank filed a complaint against RCS that contained a solitary claim for the collection of accounts receivable. * * * On March 15, 1989, RCS moved for summary judgment on the Bank's claim for the collection of accounts receivable. * * *

The district court granted RCS's summary judgment motion * * *. The district court found that there were no material facts in dispute and that RCS as an account debtor was entitled to set off amounts Kase Haus owed it against the amount it owed Kase Haus pursuant to section 9–318(1)(b) of the Wisconsin Uniform Commercial Code. * * *

The Bank alleges that the trial court erred in entering summary judgment on RCS's behalf on the grounds that (1) the documents it executed with Kase Haus did not constitute an assignment; (2) even if the Bank became a "de facto assignee" upon Kase Haus's default, section 9–318(1)(b) would not apply because the Bank did not acquire all right, title, and interest in Kase Haus's accounts receivable * * *.

A. *RCS's Right to Set Off*

Section 9–318(1) of the Wisconsin Uniform Commercial Code provides:

> (1) Unless an account debtor has made an enforceable agreement not to assert defenses or claims arising out of a sale as provided in § 9–206 the rights of an assignee are subject to:

> (a) All the terms of the contract between the account debtor and assignor and any defense or claim arising therefrom; and

> (b) Any other defense or claim of the account debtor against the assignor which accrues before the account debtor receives notification of the assignment.

* * * The Bank asserts that section 9–318 is inapplicable because the Bank's security interest in Kase Haus's accounts receivable was not an assignment of those accounts as collateral. Settled case law, however, contradicts both the Bank's allegation that section 9–318(1) does not apply and its post-summary judgment characterization of itself as anything less than an assignee of Kase Haus's accounts receivable. * * *

For purposes of section 9–318 and the equivalent statute in other states, the courts and the UCC have made no distinction between a party with a security interest in a debtor's accounts receivable and a party who is an assignee of a debtor's accounts receivable. Section 9–502 of the Wisconsin Uniform Commercial Code, which specifies the collection rights of a party with a security interest in collateral consisting of an account, chattel paper, contract right, general intangible, or instrument, states in part:

> When so agreed and in any event on default the secured party is entitled to notify an account debtor or the obligor on an instrument to make payment to him whether or not *the assignor* was theretofore making collections on the collateral, and also to take control of any proceeds to which he is entitled under § 9–306.

§ 9–502(1) (emphasis added). The UCC, which "is not a comprehensive codification of commercial law," 1 J. White & R. Summers, Uniform Commercial Code § 2, at 6 (3d ed. 1988), does not define "assignment." Nonetheless, treatment under section 9–318 of one with a security interest in an account receivable as an "assignee" of the account receivable is consistent with section 9–502's implicit description of a secured party who exercises his rights to collect on an "assignor's" accounts receivable as an assignee. The benefits that a secured creditor enjoys from the summary default remedy contained in section 9–502 are counterbalanced by the account debtor's right under section 9–318, to confront the secured creditor/assignee with any defenses or claims it had against the assignor. If we accepted the Bank's strict rules of construction for interpreting section 9–318, we also would have to find that the summary remedy in section 9–502 for one with a security interest in an account receivable is only available when the debtor is an "assignor" as strictly defined by the Bank.

The Bank's argument that it has priority to Kase Haus's assets because it perfected its security interest by prompt filing is inapposite. While a secured party who properly and promptly files thereby protects its security interest to the maximum possible extent, such protection is not absolute. For example, a perfected security interest is subordinate to the interest of a buyer in the ordinary course of business, even when the buyer is aware of the security interest. See § 9–307. Furthermore, a holder in due course of a negotiable instrument, a holder to whom a negotiable document of title has been duly negotiated, and a bona fide purchaser of a security take priority over an earlier security interest even though perfected. See § 9–309. As the New York Court of Appeals noted in In re Matter of Chase Manhattan Bank, 40 N.Y.2d at 593, 357 N.E.2d at 369, 388 N.Y.S.2d at 898, "the 'first to file' rule, designed to resolve situations where secured parties are competing in asserting superior rights, should not be controlling when the dispute is between a secured party and an account debtor." See also Central State Bank v. State, 73 Misc.2d 128, 129–30, 341 N.Y.S.2d 322 (N.Y.Ct.Cl.1973) (situation where account debtor sought set-off against secured creditor's claim to debtor/assignor's accounts receivable is "not a situation where two creditors with perfected interests are competing to subordinate the other's right to attach proceeds belonging to and held by the debtor"; account debtor may assert right to set off under UCC § 9–318).

The UCC counsels against hypertechnical rules of construction that undermine the UCC's underlying purposes and policies. Section 1–102 states that "Chapters 401 to 409 shall be liberally construed and applied to promote its underlying purposes and policies," which include efforts to "simplify, clarify and modernize the law governing commercial transactions." * * * Commentators have noted that a further purpose of the UCC is "simply that the law of commercial transactions be, so far as reasonable, liberal and nontechnical." 1 J. White & R. Summers, supra, at 14. We believe that our interpretation of section 9–318 approximates these objectives and sensibly reconciles the benefits to secured creditors/assignees found in section 9–502 with the safeguards available to account debtors under section 9–318. Under the Bank's proposed rendering of section 9–318, an account-debtor restaurant with a right to set off against the accounts receivable of a restaurant supplier would face the prospect of paying twice for its supplies in the event that the supplier defaults on a loan secured by a bank's security interest in the supplier's accounts receivable. A more sensible result would ensue from our reading of sections 9–308 and 9–502: the restaurant's claim against the assignor/supplier is set off against the bank's summary demand for payment on the assigned account. We therefore reject the Bank's claim that RCS may not rightfully raise the defense of set-off under section 9–318.

Subsection (1) of section 9–318 of the Wisconsin Uniform Commercial Code provides that an assignee's rights are subject to any defenses or claims of the account debtor arising out of the contract between the account debtor and the assignor, and "any other defense or claim of the account debtor against the assignor *which accrues before the account debtor receives notification of the assignment.*" (emphasis added). Subsection (26) of section 1–201 provides in part that "[a] person 'receives' a notice or notification when (a) it comes to his attention; or (b) it is duly delivered at the place held out by him as the place for receipt of such communications." Thus, in order to preclude RCS's right to set off under section 9–318, the Bank would have been obliged to notify RCS that it was the assignee of Kase Haus's accounts receivable. See 9 W. Hawkland, Uniform Commercial Code Series § 9–318:03, at 304–05 (1986). RCS first received notification from the Bank that it was the assignee of Kase Haus's accounts receivable and that RCS therefore was obliged to pay the Bank for any indebtedness arising from its transactions with Kase Haus on July 18, 1988. RCS's claim against Kase Haus arose and was settled well before RCS received the Bank's July 18, 1988, collection letter. The district court therefore did not err when it found that the protections of § 9–318 were available to RCS.

* * *

NOTES

1. In Michelin Tires (Canada), Ltd. v. First National Bank of Boston, 666 F.2d 673 (1st Cir.1981), Michelin agreed to make progress payments to a contractor, JCC, for construction of facilities relating to a tire plant. JCC assigned its rights under the contract to FNB, a bank. FNB requested that Michelin make payments directly to it. The mechanics of payment were that Michelin agreed to make payments when JCC submitted invoices for work completed. When invoices were submitted, JCC was required to certify that the work was done and that the subcontractors had been paid. JCC submitted invoices to Michelin accompanied by a fraudulent certification by JCC that it had paid its subcontractors. Relying on JCC's fraudulent representations that its subcontractors had been paid, Michelin paid FNB which then advanced a percentage to JCC. Later, JCC went into bankruptcy and Michelin sued FNB to recover the amounts paid FNB because

of JCC's fraudulent misrepresentations. The majority opinion denied Michelin recovery.

Under § 9–318(1) the assignee (FNB) stands in the shoes of the obligee (JCC) with respect to defenses or setoffs of the obligor (Michelin) against the obligee. Hence, if the facts had been that Michelin had not paid FNB and FNB had brought suit against Michelin for payment, Michelin clearly could have defended by raising the defense that JCC had defrauded it. The question in this case is whether the obligor (Michelin) could assert the fraud of the obligee (JCC) as the basis of an action against the assignee (FNB) to recover money that it had already paid to FNB. This issue is one of great importance to banks and other commercial lenders. It is one thing to allow obligors to defend against banks' suits by raising defenses they had against their obligees. Banks encounter debts they can't collect every day. But it is quite another thing to allow defrauded obligors to make banks disgorge money they have already collected in good faith. The prevailing view under pre-Code law was that obligors were not entitled to recover from assignees amounts already paid. Pre–Code law is important in interpreting § 9–318(1)(a) because Comment 1 says "Subsection (1) makes no substantial change in prior law." Despite this assurance in the Comment, the dissenting judge in *Michelin* believed that the use of the word "claim" in § 9–318(1)(a) connotes affirmative rights against the assignee and, therefore, that the Code intended to change the law in this area.

2. The court in *Michelin* supported its holding in favor of FNB by relying on § 14(2) of the Restatement of Restitution (1937):

> (2) An assignee of a non-negotiable chose in action who, having paid value therefor, has received payment from the obligor is under no duty to make restitution although the obligor had a defense thereto, if the transferee made no misrepresentation and did not have notice of the defense.

The Reporter's comment to Restatement § 14(2) is directly relevant to a case such as *Michelin* and to § 9–318(1). The comment is in part as follows:

> The rule stated in this Subsection presupposes that, had there been no payment, the assignee would have no rights against the payor. * * * The rule is based upon the principle that in determining whether or not one gives value it is immaterial whether he pays value at the time he acquires the title or has paid value at some prior time in order that he might acquire the title * * *. It is consistent with the rule that one who pays value for a transfer of property to be made in the future is a purchaser for value thereof if the property is subsequently transferred to him and that he is a bona fide

purchaser if, when he receives title, he has no notice of adverse interests.

The rule stated in this Subsection applies, and applies only, to those cases where there was a transaction between the payor and the assignor or some prior assignor from which a cause of action would have arisen but for failure of consideration, fraud, mistake, duress, the failure of a condition, or a similar defense. Thus the rule applies where a promise has been obtained by fraud or without consideration, or where the promise was conditional and the condition has not been performed. It also applies where there was a mistake common to both of the original parties to the transaction, a mistake for which there might have been rescission or reformation.

* * *

The rationale for the rule of Restatement § 14(2) would seem to be that if the account debtor and the assignee are both innocent parties and if there has been no unjust enrichment the court will leave the loss where it falls. If the assignor is insolvent and the account debtor has not yet paid, the loss falls on the assignee; if the account debtor has already paid the loss falls on the account debtor.

For a thorough discussion of Restatement § 14 see Palmer, The Law of Restitution, Vol. III 480–510 (1978).

G. ACCESSIONS

1. PRE–CODE LAW

The rights of a secured party can be affected by the law of accession, a venerable but imprecise doctrine of the law of property. The following is taken from Brown, The Law of Personal Property 49–53 (3d ed. W. Raushenbush 1975)

An accession is literally something added. In law the addition of new value to a chattel may raise some interesting and difficult questions, whether the addition of value is by labor or the addition of new materials or both combined. In general it may be postulated that the accession follows the title of the principal thing to which it is annexed. To put it another way, an owner of a chattel has title to lesser things united to that chattel either artificially or naturally. For example, in the case of domestic animals it is well settled that in the absence of an express or implied agreement to the contrary the owner of the mother acquires the ownership of the offspring.

The difficulty arises, however, when an accession is made by one person to the property of another. * * *

When the goods of two different owners are incorporated together, the title to the resulting product goes to the owner of the principal goods. Thus, if the owner of materials employs a mechanic or other artisan to make for him a garment, a wagon, or a boat, fabricating into the product the materials of both the employer and the employee, the title thereto before the final sale belongs to the owner of the principal goods. Such a result seems to accord both with reason and the intent of the parties. But even if a wrongdoer takes another's goods and attaches them to his principal materials he acquires title to the accession, and the mala fides of the converter seems immaterial. Thus, it may be supposed that if A steals B's paint, and with it paints A's automobile, both the automobile and the paint will belong to A.   *   *   *

It has been stated by the courts that the principle of accession does not apply when the attached articles can be separated and removed from the principal thing without damage to the latter. This principle is, however, frequently ignored, and the decisions of individual cases are found to turn on the presumed intention of the annexor and the equities of the particular situation.   *   *   *

Most of the more recent pre-Code cases regarding accessions to personal property involved automobiles. In the typical case the automobile was sold under a conditional sale to a buyer who after the sale added or replaced a part of the car. When the buyer subsequently defaulted on the conditional sale contract and the conditional vendor repossessed, the question presented was the right of the conditional vendor to the new part. Sometimes the conditional sale contract specifically provided that the vendor retained title to, or the benefit of, all repairs to the car, replacements of parts and accessions to the car. In other cases the contract was silent concerning accessions. The cases were usually determined by deciding whether the property involved was or was not an accession. An affirmative answer meant victory for the conditional vendor of the car and a negative answer meant defeat. But the courts did not use any consistent definition of "accession" in deciding the cases. Two situations can be contrasted:

Group #1. The conditional vendee of the car replaced the original tires or the original motor in the car with a new replacement which the vendee owned outright. When the conditional vendor repossessed the car the usual result was that with respect to the vendee the vendor was entitled to the new replacement parts whether or not there was a clause in the conditional sale contract specifically giving the vendor a right to accessions. The theory apparently was that replacement parts were similar to repairs in that they maintained the value of the car. Each benefits both the vendor and the vendee because the resulting enhancement of value of the car will tend to increase the proceeds when the car is resold after repossession. Thus more of the vendee's debt is paid and there is less liability for a deficiency judgment. See, e.g., Blackwood Tire & Vulcanizing Co. v. Auto Storage Co., 133 Tenn. 515, 182 S.W. 576 (1916); Purnell v. Fooks, 32 Del. 336, 122 A. 901 (1923).

Group #2. The conditional vendee replaced the original tires or motor with a new replacement purchased from a third party who sold the replacement part on conditional sale. In these cases the courts distinguished between parts that were readily detachable and those that were so incorporated into the car that they could not readily be detached without injury to the car. Tires and motors that were held to be accessions in Group #1 were almost always held not to be accessions in Group #2. See, e.g., Mossler Acceptance Co. v. Norton Tire Co., 70 So.2d 360 (Fla.1954); Sasia & Wallace, Inc. v. Scarborough Implement Co., 154 Cal.App.2d 308, 316 P.2d 39 (1957); Passieu v. B.F. Goodrich Co., 58 Ga.App. 691, 199 S.E. 775 (1938). Thus, the question of what constituted an accession was determined not so much by the nature of the property involved or its removability, but by the equities in the conflicting claims. The pre-Code cases are thoroughly discussed in Nickles, Accessions and Accessories under Pre-Code Law and UCC Article 9, 35 Ark.L.Rev. 111 (1981).

2. ACCESSIONS UNDER THE UCC

Rights concerning accessions are set forth in § 9–314. That section relates only to the rights of a person having a security interest in the accession vis-a-vis other persons having claims to the host goods to which the accession is made. Thus, cases falling in Group #1 in the preceding note are not affected by § 9–314. The term "accession" is neutral; it does not have the meaning that it was given in the pre-Code cases. It refers to "goods installed in or affixed to other goods." § 9–314(1). It applies equally to goods that are readily removable without damage to the host goods and to goods that cannot be removed without causing such damage. Whether or not the accession can be removed without damage to the host goods is still relevant (§ 9–314(4)) but this factor plays a significantly different role than it did in the pre-Code cases.

PROBLEMS

1. Dealer sold to Debtor on credit a tractor equipped with gasoline carburetion equipment and received a perfected security interest in the tractor at the time of sale. Later Seller sold to Debtor on credit butane carburetion equipment which was installed in the tractor as a substitute for the gasoline carburetion equipment, which was removed. Under the contract of sale Seller

received a security interest in the butane equipment to secure payment of the purchase price. Promptly after the equipment was installed Seller perfected the security interest by filing. Debtor defaulted on the contract with Dealer and Dealer repossessed the tractor. Under § 9–314 who had priority to the butane equipment when Dealer repossessed? Would it make any difference if Debtor had granted the security interest in the butane equipment after it was installed in the tractor? Would Seller's rights be any different if its security interest had not been perfected? Would the rights of Dealer be any different if its security interest in the tractor had not been perfected at the time the butane equipment was installed? Is knowledge or lack of knowledge by Seller of Dealer's security interest relevant? If Seller has a right under § 9–314 to remove the butane equipment, does it have to reimburse Dealer in any way?

2. A state statute provides as follows: "Every person who makes, alters or repairs any article of personal property at the request of the owner or legal possessor of the property has a possessory lien on the same for reasonable charges for work done and materials furnished, and may retain possession of the same until the charges are paid." Owner owns an automobile on which there is a perfected security interest in favor of Finance Co. Owner is having difficulty meeting the installment payments to Finance Co. Owner took the car to Mechanic and requested replacement of the engine. Mechanic told Owner that the job would cost $1,200, but nothing was said about the terms of payment. Mechanic replaced the engine and presented Owner with a bill for $900 for the new engine and $300 for labor. Owner is unable to pay all of the bill, but has offered to pay $300 down and $900 within 60 days if Mechanic releases the car. Owner is willing to sign a security agreement giving Mechanic a security interest in the engine. What should Mechanic do to protect against the possibility of nonpayment by Owner or repossession of the car by Finance Co.? § 9–310.

H. COMMINGLED AND PROCESSED GOODS

The doctrine of accession is also applicable to cases in which goods in which one person has a property interest are transformed by a second person into different goods. For example, suppose that A owns grapes which B, either innocently or knowingly, converts by taking them without A's consent. B then makes wine from the grapes. A, of course, has a cause of action to recover the value of the converted grapes. But, under the doctrine of accession, A probably has a valid claim to the wine as well, although the result is not certain. If B acted innocently and if B's labor accounted for a very large part of the value of the wine A's claim might be defeated to avoid an unconscionable windfall. See

Brown, The Law of Personal Property 51 (3d ed. W. Raushenbush 1975).

This doctrine can also be applied to secured transactions. Suppose A sells grapes to B and retains a purchase money security interest in the grapes. B then makes wine from the grapes. UCC § 9–315(1) applies to this case and it states the conditions under which A's security interest in the grapes is transformed into a security interest in the wine. Compare how the Code deals with this case and how it deals with an analogous case: the shifting of a security interest from the collateral disposed of by the debtor to the proceeds of the disposition. § 9–306(2).

Very few judicial decisions have dealt with the issue of the relative rights of a creditor having a security interest in raw materials and a creditor having a security interest in the product into which the raw materials were processed. One pre-Code case was Bancroft Steel Co., Inc. v. Kuniholm Manufacturing Co., 301 Mass. 91, 16 N.E.2d 78 (1938).

Bancroft was a supplier of steel to Industrial Hardware, which manufactured a product called a baby walker whose main component was steel. The steel was sold on a conditional sale contract which provided that Bancroft retained title to the steel "whether in the original, manufactured or completed state" until the steel was paid for. In UCC terminology Bancroft had a purchase money security interest in the steel that it supplied and a security interest in Industrial Hardware's inventory of partially completed and completed baby walkers made from steel not paid for.

Prior to making the conditional sale contract with Bancroft, Industrial Hardware had given to Kuniholm a chattel mortgage in all of Industrial Hardware's inventory of steel and partially completed and completed baby walkers.

Industrial Hardware defaulted on its debt to Kuniholm and had not paid for the steel purchased from Bancroft. Kuniholm took possession under the mortgage of all of Industrial Hardware's inventory of raw steel and finished and unfinished baby walkers. Bancroft claimed all the raw steel and finished and unfinished baby walkers.

The court held for Bancroft. With respect to the raw steel, Bancroft won because its reservation of title prevented Kuniholm's mortgage from attaching. If Industrial Hardware had no title in the steel it could not give to a mortgagee any interest in the steel superior to Bancroft's title. With respect to the finished and unfinished baby walkers the court noted that Bancroft's steel had been transformed in the manufacturing process and that paint and other material and component parts had been added to the steel. The issue was whether this transformation destroyed Bancroft's title to the steel. The court turned to the law of accession and noted that "by far the greater part of such finished product consisted of steel sold by [Bancroft] under the conditional sale contract." It then concluded that Bancroft did not lose title to its steel. Rather, "it acquired title to the lesser materials added."

How would *Bancroft* be decided under the UCC? Assume that the security interests of both Bancroft and Kuniholm had been perfected at the time Bancroft delivered the steel to Industrial Hardware, that the financing statements of each covered inventory, and that Kuniholm had filed its financing statement first. When Kuniholm repossessed the collateral after default it found unfabricated steel as well as partially completed and finished baby walkers. Consider the priorities of the parties to each class of inventory.

With respect to the unfabricated steel § 9–315 would not apply because the unfinished steel had not yet "become part of a product." Thus, the case would be decided under § 9–312(3) since each party had a security interest in inventory. If Bancroft had complied with the requirements of § 9–312(3) its purchase money security interest would prevail. Otherwise the security interest of Kuniholm would have priority under § 9–312(5) because it filed first.

Does the same rule of priority apply with respect to the partially completed and completed baby walkers? If the steel supplied by Bancroft had become part of the product—the baby walkers—and its identity had become lost, § 9–315 applies. If § 9–315 applies § 9–312 does not apply. § 9–312(1). At least with respect to finished baby walkers it would seem that the conditions of § 9–315(1)(a) have been met. But even if it can be argued that the steel maintained its identity in the partially completed and completed baby walkers, § 9–315(1)(b) should apply. Bancroft had a perfected security interest in the baby walkers. The security agreement granted to Bancroft a security interest in the steel "whether in the original, manufactured or completed state" and Bancroft's financing statement covering inventory covered both the unfinished steel and the resulting product. If § 9–315 applies the security interests of Bancroft and Kuniholm "rank equally according to the ratio of the cost of the goods to which each interest originally attached bears to the cost of the total product * * *" § 9–315(2). There are two difficulties in applying § 9–315. If the policy underlying § 9–312(3) is sound with respect to unfinished steel why should its priority rule be changed once the steel entered the manufacturing process? Even if the policy conflict between § 9–312(3) and § 9–315 can be resolved, is it possible to apply § 9–315(2)? That subsection contemplates a case in which a product is made up of several ingredients or components and in which security interests had attached to each of the ingredients or components prior to the time that they were welded into the product or mass. Comment 3 to § 9–315. An examination of the reported cases discloses no case of that kind arising under the UCC. But in the case at hand both Bancroft and Kuniholm had security interests in the same ingredient—the steel—and their security interests attached in perfected form at the same instant. How then can § 9–315(2) be applied? There is no hint of an answer in the Official Comments. Professor Gilmore, one of the principal drafters of Article 9, acknowledges the difficulty in applying that section to a case such as *Bancroft*, and he makes a valiant effort to make it make sense, largely by ignoring its language. Gilmore, Security Interests in Personal Property 851–856 (1965).

**NOTE: RELATIONSHIP BETWEEN
§ 9–314 AND § 9–315**

Suppose X, a manufacturer of bicycles, purchases components from various suppliers: seats from A, pedals from B and handlebars from C. Suppose X has outstanding loans from Bank secured by a perfected security interest in X's inventory of bicycles. Under § 9–314, if A, B and C sell components to X on credit they can obtain prior security interests in the components that they sell to X. If their security interests attach prior to the time that the components are affixed to the bicycles they will have priority over Bank. If their security interests are perfected they will also have priority over the subsequent parties listed in § 9–314(3). In the event of default the remedy of each is repossession of the collateral. Any components affixed to bicycles can be removed and returned to the original suppliers. § 9–314(4). Thus, there is no difficulty in resolving any conflicts between A, B or C and Bank and there are no conflicts among A, B and C. But because § 9–314 is subject to § 9–315(1), these results might be modified in some cases.

In cases in which § 9–315(1)(a) applies the remedy provided by § 9–314(4) is not feasible. If D supplies paint to X and the paint is applied to the bicycles D must as a practical matter lose any security interest that it may have had in the paint. The paint has effectively lost its identity as paint and has become an integral part of the bicycle. Removal of the paint obviously will produce no economic benefit. D's remedy must be found in a security interest in the bicycles under § 9–315(1)(a). Under that provision if D had a perfected security interest in the paint when it was applied to the bicycles D's interest continues in the bicycles, and although § 9–315 is not specific on the point, it would seem that the security interest should continue in perfected form. D in effect is given a modified right of accession even though its goods are not dominant. D's resulting security interest is then subject to the Delphian formula of § 9–315(2). D's problem is like that of the supplier of steel in *Bancroft*.

But can A, B and C also fall into the morass of § 9–315? If A filed a financing statement covering "bicycle seats," neither subsections (a) nor (b) of § 9–315(1) applies so A is left to its satisfactory remedy under § 9–314. But suppose A's financing statement covered "inventory," a term that covers both the bicycle seats and the bicycles. Does subsection (b) now apply? Comment 3 to § 9–315 states that A "is put to an election at the time of filing, by the last sentence of subsection (1), whether to claim under this section or to claim a security interest in one component under Section 9–314." But the comment does not say how the election is made. To talk of an election by A in this case is somewhat misleading. A cannot get a security interest in the bicycles unless X has agreed to grant it. A and X might have agreed in the security agreement that A's security interest applied both to the bicycle seats and the bicycles. In that event, if the financing statement covered inventory A would have a perfected security interest in the bicycles, and under the last sentence of § 9–315(1), it would have lost its security interest in the bicycle seats. But if the security agreement covered only the bicycle seats, the fact that the financing statement covered inventory should not result in A's getting a security interest in the bicycles. Thus, § 9–314 and not § 9–315 should apply.

Financing statements usually are made on Form UCC–1 which follows the information set forth in § 9–402(3). This form allows the person making the statement to indicate that "Products of Collateral Are Also Covered" by checking a box printed on the form. Comment 3 to § 9–315 apparently is referring to covering products in this manner when it refers to making an election at the time of filing. The financing statement is a document signed by the debtor, and by the checking of the products box the intent of the debtor to give a security interest in the bicycle is manifested. Thus, even if the security agreement relates only to bicycle seats, the financing statement might provide the basis for giving A a security interest in the bicycles. A, by filing the financing statement, is bound by the election. In the case of easily removable components it would seem a rare case in which it would be to the interest of the secured party to elect § 9–315 rather than § 9–314.

There are no reported cases that shed much light on the proper interpretation of § 9–315.

How does the analysis made in this Note change if we assume that Bank's security interest applied not only to X's inventory of bicycles, but also to its inventory of component parts?

I. FIXTURES

The following is taken from Brown, The Law of Personal
Property 514–515 (3d ed. W. Raushenbush 1975):

>   A fixture can best be defined as a thing which, although
> originally a movable chattel, is by reason of its annexation to,
> or association in use with land, regarded as a part of the land.
> The law of fixtures concerns those situations where the chat-
> tel annexed still retains a separate identity in spite of annexa-
> tion, for example a furnace or a light fixture. Where the
> chattel annexed loses such identity, as in the case of nails,
> boards, etc., the problem becomes one of accession, * * *.
> The question whether a particular article, formerly a chattel,
> has become part of the realty may arise in several different
> ways. (I) The owner of land and building may buy and install
> therein a new improvement—a furnace, a water heater, a gas
> range. He later sells or mortgages the real estate. Does the
> purchaser of the land, in absence of specific exclusions, obtain
> the above articles or any of them, or do they remain the
> personal property of the grantor? A similar problem arises
> when the landowner dies. Do the above articles pass to his
> heirs as part of the real estate, or are they personal property
> passing to the administrator? A related question is whether
> the article is subject to levy of execution or attachment, or to
> replevin, as personalty, or has become part of the real estate.
> Also, can the unpaid vendor of an article annexed to the
> realty claim a statutory mechanic's or construction lien for an
> improvement to the realty? (II) The owner of a chattel may
> annex it to the land of another, or to land in which another
> has an interest. The most common example of this is where a
> tenant for years attaches to the land of his landlord articles
> necessary or convenient for the tenant's trade or his domestic
> enjoyment. In this situation the question arises whether the
> tenant on the termination of his lease can remove from the
> premises those articles which he has attached, or whether
> they remain the property of the landlord. (III) Lastly the
> annexor of the chattel may not own the same, or his owner-
> ship may be encumbered by the security interest of another.
> When such a chattel is placed on the annexor's land or on
> land in which others have an interest, question inevitably
> arises as to the respective rights of the chattel owner and the
> landowner. * * * Much of the confusion in the law of
> fixtures is due, it is believed, to the attempt to consider
> together as analogous these three different fact situations,
> when in fact they are quite dissimilar. To attempt to discover
> an all-inclusive definition for a "fixture" or to posit tests for
> fixtures in all circumstances is not a profitable undertaking.
> The important quest is the determination of the rights of the

parties in the different type situations above outlined. Whether the particular article involved be denominated a fixture or not is of little importance.

Article 9 of the UCC is concerned with the conflict between holders of security interests in the chattel that becomes the fixture and a person with a property interest in the land. The 1962 Official Text of the UCC dealt with this problem in § 9–313 which we reproduce below.

Section 9–313. Priority of Security Interests in Fixtures.

(1) The rules of this section do not apply to goods incorporated into a structure in the manner of lumber, bricks, tile, cement, glass, metal work and the like and no security interest in them exists under this Article unless the structure remains personal property under applicable law. The law of this state other than this Act determines whether and when other goods become fixtures. This Act does not prevent creation of an encumbrance upon fixtures or real estate pursuant to the law applicable to real estate.

(2) A security interest which attaches to goods before they become fixtures takes priority as to the goods over the claims of all persons who have an interest in the real estate except as stated in subsection (4).

(3) A security interest which attaches to goods after they become fixtures is valid against all persons subsequently acquiring interests in the real estate except as stated in subsection (4) but is invalid against any person with an interest in the real estate at the time the security interest attaches to the goods who has not in writing consented to the security interest or disclaimed an interest in the goods as fixtures.

(4) The security interests described in subsections (2) and (3) do not take priority over

(a) a subsequent purchaser for value of any interest in the real estate; or

(b) a creditor with a lien on the real estate subsequently obtained by judicial proceedings; or

(c) a creditor with a prior encumbrance of record on the real estate to the extent that he makes subsequent advances

if the subsequent purchase is made, the lien by judicial proceedings is obtained, or the subsequent advance under the prior encumbrance is made or contracted for without knowledge of the security interest and before it is perfected. A purchaser of the real estate at a foreclosure sale other than an encumbrancer purchasing at his own foreclosure sale is a subsequent purchaser within this section.

(5) When under subsections (2) or (3) and (4) a secured party has priority over the claims of all persons who have interests in the real estate, he may, on default, subject to the provisions of Part 5, remove his collateral from the real estate but he must reimburse any encumbrancer or owner of the real estate who is not the debtor and who has not otherwise agreed for the cost of repair of any physical injury, but not for any diminution in value of the real estate caused by the absence of the goods removed or by any necessity for replacing them. A person entitled to reimbursement may refuse permission to remove until the secured party gives adequate security for the performance of this obligation.

You can see that subsections (2) through (5) of that section are almost identical to § 9–314, relating to accessions, which we have just examined. The belief of the drafters of Article 9 that the problem of resolving conflicts with respect to security interests in tires, batteries and other accessories in automobiles (§ 9–314) could be equated successfully to the problem of resolving conflicts regarding fixtures (§ 9–313) proved erroneous. In 1972, § 9–313 was drastically revised to its present form. The reasons for the changes are set forth by the Reporters for the 1972 Official Text as follows:

As the Code came to be widely enacted, the real estate bar came to realize the impact of the fixture provisions on real estate financing and real estate titles. They apparently had not fully appreciated the impact of these provisions of Article 9 on real estate matters during the enactment of the Code, because of the commonly-held assumption that Article 9 was concerned only with chattel security matters.

The treatment of fixtures in pre-Code law had varied widely from state to state. The treatment in Article 9 was based generally on prior treatment in the Uniform Conditional Sales Act, which, however, had been enacted in only a dozen states. In other states the word "fixture" had come to mean that a former chattel had become real estate for all purposes and that any chattel rights therein were lost. For lawyers trained in such states the Code provisions seemed to be extreme. Some sections of the real estate bar began attempting with some success to have Section 9–313 amended to bring it closer to the pre-Code law in their states. In some states, such as California and Iowa, Section 9–313 simply was not enacted.

Even supporters of Article 9 and of its fixture provisions came to recognize that there were some ambiguities in Section 9–313, particularly in its application to construction mortgages, and also in its failure to make it clear that filing of fixture security interests was to be in real estate records where they could be found by a standard real estate search.

Section 9–313 and related provisions of Part 4 have been redrafted to meet the legitimate criticisms and to make a substantial shift in the law in favor of construction mortgages. The specific changes are described in the 1972 Comments to Section 9–313, and the Comments to the several sections of Part 4.

The 1962 version did not define "fixture" a term which has never had a commonly-accepted definition and a term which, within a single jurisdiction, is often variously interpreted depending upon the nature of the dispute before the court. The application of the 1962 provision was thus uncertain because in different states it might or might not apply depending upon the local definition of fixture. The present version maintains this difficulty in that the "definition" of the term in subsection (1)(a) also depends on how the local real estate law treats the particular property involved. But most of the problems under the 1962 provision related to readily-removable factory and office machines and household appliances, and the 1972 provision deals specifically with these goods in subsection (4)(c).

IN RE PARK CORRUGATED BOX CORP.

United States District Court, D. New Jersey, 1966.
249 F.Supp. 56.

AUGELLI, DISTRICT JUDGE. This matter is before the Court on petition of Manufacturers Leasing Corporation (Manufacturers) for review of an order of the Referee in Bankruptcy (Referee), made on March 25, 1965, which denied Manufacturers' petition for reclamation of a certain machine from the Bankrupt herein, Park Corrugated Box Corp. (Park).

On February 8, 1965 Park filed a petition for an arrangement under Chapter XI of the Bankruptcy Act. Manufacturers was listed in Park's schedules as a security-holding creditor in the amount of $34,952.60. On March 8, Manufacturers filed its petition to reclaim from Park the machine above mentioned, which was used in the manufacture of corrugated boxes, and known as a "Hooper Combined Printer Slotter, Model WSG2P–200–E, size 50 × 103½ inches". On that date the Referee signed an order directed to James J. Murner, Jr., Receiver for Park, to show cause why that relief should not be granted.

On March 18, the Referee held a hearing on said order to show cause, and denied the petition for reclamation on the ground that the security agreement covering the machine was not properly filed with the Secretary of State, and that therefore Manufacturers was not a secured creditor entitled to reclamation. An order to this effect was entered on March 25, 1965. In the meantime, also on March 18, Park was adjudicated a bankrupt, and the Receiver, Murner, was thereafter appointed Trustee.

The Referee filed his opinion in this matter on June 14, 1965, and Manufacturers' petition for review was filed on June 28. The following are the facts disclosed by the record in this case.

On September 4, 1963, Manufacturers and Park entered into a "Conditional Sale and Security Agreement", whereby Park purchased the subject machine from Manufacturers for the sum of $47,405.00. The agreement stated that Manufacturers was to have a purchase money security interest in the collateral to secure the balance due, that Manufacturers was to have all the rights of a secured party under applicable state law, and that Manufacturers was to retain title to the collateral until the balance was paid in full.

The agreement between Manufacturers and Park was filed twice with the Register of Deeds of Passaic County, on September 10, 1963 and again on October 10, 1963. It had not been filed with the Secretary of State in Trenton, New Jersey.

Under the Uniform Commercial Code as adopted in New Jersey, § 9–401(1) provides that:

"The proper place to file in order to perfect a security interest is as follows:

(a) * * * (not applicable);

(b) when the collateral is goods which at the time the security interest attaches are or are to become fixtures, then in the office where a mortgage on the real estate concerned would be filed or recorded;

(c) in all other cases, in the office of the Secretary of State."

Manufacturers contends that the machine was a fixture, that under § 9–401(1)(b), the agreement was properly filed in the County Register's Office, and that therefore Manufacturers has a perfected security interest in the machine prior to the rights of the Trustee. The Trustee argues, as the Referee has found, that the machine was not a fixture, that under § 9–401(1)(c), the agreement should have been filed in the office of the Secretary of State, and that therefore Manufacturers' security interest was not perfected. The issue in this case is thus simply whether the machine in question is or is not a fixture within the meaning of § 9–401(1)(b).

§ 9–313(1) provides that the law of New Jersey determines whether and when goods become fixtures. The law in New Jersey concerning fixtures has most recently been reviewed in the case of Fahmie v. Nyman, 70 N.J.Super. 313, 175 A.2d 438 (App.Div.1961). In that case, the court discussed the two tests used in New Jersey to determine whether and when a chattel becomes a fixture. They are known as the "traditional test" and the "institutional doctrine."

Under the "traditional test", intention is the dominant factor. A chattel becomes a fixture when the party making the annexation intends a permanent accession to the freehold. This intention may be "inferred from the nature of the article affixed, the relation and situation of the party making the annexation, the structure and mode of annexation, and the purpose or use for which the annexation was made." 70 N.J.Super. at 317, 175 A.2d at 441.

The testimony before the Referee at the reclamation proceeding shows that there was no intention to annex the machine permanently to the freehold. A witness for Manufacturers testified that although the machine was annexed to the building, it could easily be removed in one hour without material physical damage to the building. He described the machine as being about 125 inches wide by 8 feet long, weighing 45,000 pounds, anchored by two or three leg screws on each side and connected to a 220 volt electric line. This same witness testified that a rigger could remove the machine quite easily by merely unbolting the screws, disconnecting the 220 volt line, jacking it up, putting it on rollers and taking it out. Park's president testified that the machine had been moved two or three times to other sections of the plant by employees of Park during the time it was located in the plant.

Under the "institutional doctrine", the test is whether the chattel is permanently essential to the completeness of the structure or its use. A chattel is a fixture if its severance from the structure would cause material damage to the structure or "prevent the structure from being used for the purposes for which it was erected or for which it has been adapted." Smyth Sales Corp. v. Norfolk B. & L. Ass'n, 116 N.J.L. 293, 298, 184 A. 204, 206, 111 A.L.R. 357 (E. & A. 1935). Thus, in Temple Co. v. Penn Mutual Life Ins. Co., 69 N.J.L. 36, 38, 54 A. 295 (Sup.Ct.1903), the Court stated, in holding lighting equipment and seats to be fixtures under the "institutional doctrine", that "[t]he building was erected and used as a theatre, and whatever was incorporated with the building to fit it for use as a theatre became part of the realty."

Again, the testimony before the Referee shows that the machine in question was not essential to the structure or its use, and that the severance of the machine would not prevent the structure from being used for the purposes for which it was erected or could be adapted. There was testimony that after the machine was removed from the building, the structure could be used for industrial uses generally; also testimony that different prior uses had been made of the structure. Thus, both before the machine was installed and after it was removed, the structure was and could be used for any number of different purposes. Cf. Fahmie v. Nyman, supra. Finally, there was attached to the agreement between the parties a statement by Manufacturers that the machine is "to be affixed to real property * * * by removable screw joints or otherwise, so as to be severable from the realty without material injury to the freehold."

While the machine in question does not appear to be a fixture under either the "traditional test" or the "institutional doctrine", Manufacturers makes the further contention that the machine is a "trade fixture" under New Jersey law, and therefore a "fixture" pursuant to § 9–401(1)(b). However, the term "trade fixture" is generally applied only in landlord and tenant cases to describe a chattel which the tenant has installed on the landlord's premises for trade purposes and which the tenant is allowed to remove if it can be severed without material injury to the freehold. Otherwise, the chattel would be a fixture and belong to the landlord. Crane v. Brigham, 11 N.J.Eq. 29 (Ch.1855); Handler v. Horns, 2 N.J. 18, 65 A.2d 523 (1949). Thus, a "fixture" is just the opposite of a "trade fixture" under landlord and tenant law; the latter can be removed by the tenant without material injury to the freehold. A "trade fixture" is not a fixture within the meaning of § 9–401(1) (b).

Since the machine here involved was not a fixture under § 9–401(1)(b), and the agreement between Manufacturers and Park was not filed in the office of the Secretary of State pursuant to § 9–401(1)(c), Manufacturers' security interest was not perfected prior to the filing of the Chapter XI petition. Therefore the Trustee's rights to the machine take priority over the rights of Manufacturers.

Under the circumstances, and for the reasons so well stated in the Referee's opinion, the order denying reclamation in this case will be affirmed. Counsel for the Trustee, on notice to counsel for Manufacturers, will please submit an appropriate order.

NOTES

1. Under the 1972 Code would the machine involved in *Park* fall within the definition of fixture in § 9–313(1)(a)? The court indicated that the machine was a "trade fixture" and used that term as an opposite of fixture; the first term referring to removable property and the second referring to nonremovable property. 1972 § 9–313(4)(c) covers readily removable factory machines like the machine in *Park*. Does this indicate an intention to treat such machines as fixtures for filing purposes? If a machine like that in *Park* is held not to be a fixture, a filing in the land records will not perfect the seller's security interest. § 9–401.

2. 1972 § 9–313 can be compared to § 9–312. Section 9–313(4)(b) states a residual first-to-file rule based on filings in the land records. Compare § 9–312(5). Section 9–313(4)(a) is an exception to the residual rule in favor of purchase money security interests in property that feed existing interests. Compare § 9–

312(4). Section 9–313(6) states a special rule for conflicts between financers under construction mortgages who provide the funds for the construction of a building (a purchase-money type interest) and purchase money security interests in property which become fixtures of the building. Compare § 9–312(3).

PROBLEMS

Answer the following problems on the basis of 1972 § 9–313.

1. Debtor, who owned a house that was unencumbered, replaced the furnace with a new one purchased from Vendor. The purchase was made by an installment-sale contract in which Vendor was granted a security interest in the furnace. Vendor filed a financing statement covering the furnace with the Secretary of State. Thereafter Debtor sold the house to Owner. Shortly after the sale Debtor left the jurisdiction and defaulted on the contract with Vendor. Vendor seeks to remove the furnace. Owner opposes removal. How is the conflict decided? § 9–313(4)(b) and § 9–313(7).

2. Suppose in Problem 1 that Debtor had purchased a kitchen range from Vendor instead of a furnace and that Vendor had made no filing of any kind. How would the conflict between Vendor and Owner be decided? § 9–313(4)(c).

3. Debtor owned and lived in a house on which there is a recorded mortgage in favor of Bank. Debtor bought a furnace from Vendor by an installment-sale contract in which Vendor was granted a security interest in the furnace. Five days after installing the furnace in the house Vendor made a fixture filing covering the furnace. Debtor then defaulted on the contract with Vendor. Vendor seeks to remove the furnace. Bank opposes removal. How is the conflict decided? § 9–313(4)(a) and § 9–313(8).

4. Lessee rented a house from Owner. When the central hot water heater irreparably broke down and Owner refused to replace it, Lessee bought a new one from Vendor and immediately installed it in the house. The purchase was made by an installment-sale contract in which Vendor was granted a security interest in the heater. Vendor initially made no filing with respect to the heater but a month after the sale, on the advice of counsel, Vendor made a fixture filing. Two months later Owner borrowed money from Bank and as security for the loan gave to Bank a mortgage on the house which was promptly recorded. Shortly thereafter Lessee defaulted on the contract with Vendor. Owner is also in default on the loan from Bank. Vendor seeks to remove the heater and Bank opposes removal. Assume that the heater can be removed without physical damage to the house by disconnecting it from the hot-water-pipe system that leads to hot-water outlets throughout the house. How is the conflict resolved apply-

ing § 9–313(4)(a) and (b) and § 9–313(7)?   Comment 4(b) to § 9–313.

5.   Consider how the conflict in Problem 4 is resolved if § 9–313(5) is applied and the following statute, which codifies common law rights, is in effect.

> "A tenant may remove from the demised premises, any time during the continuance of his term, anything affixed thereto for purposes of trade, manufacture, ornament, or domestic use, if the removal can be effected without injury to the premises, unless the thing has, by the manner in which it is affixed, become an integral part of the premises."   Calif.Civ. Code § 1019.

HOUSE v. LONG
Supreme Court of Arkansas, 1968.
244 Ark. 718, 426 S.W.2d 814.

W.B. PUTMAN, SPECIAL JUSTICE.

* * *

The defendant Long, a builder, had arranged for financing with Modern American Mortgage Company for approximately forty residences to be constructed primarily in Beverly Hills Addition to the City of Little Rock, Arkansas.   On each lot purchased by Long, purchase-money mortgages were given in amounts varying from $2,750.00 to $3,200.00, and in addition, separate construction money mortgages in the amount of $10,000.00 were given on each lot.   Both the purchase and construction money mortgages and the notes which they secured were subsequently assigned in trust to the appellant, A.F. House.   Construction was not begun until these mortgages were placed of record.

* * *

Cross-appellant, Arkansas Louisiana Gas Company, had entered into a separate contract with Long to sell a heating and air-conditioning unit, a cooling tower, a kitchen range and oven and to install the duct work in each house.   A blanket security agreement was executed on November 30, 1964, but was never recorded.   Security agreements on individual lots were also executed as the goods were delivered, but these also were not recorded.   It was not until December 27, 1965, approximately two months after construction had ceased and Long's insolvency was generally known, that additional security agreements were executed and recorded.

* * *

Arkansas Louisiana Gas Company has filed a cross-appeal asserting that the chancellor did not accord it the priority to which it is entitled.   We believe this point is well taken.   The trial court held that UCC § 9–312, dealing with priorities among conflicting security interests in the same collateral, was determinative of the rights of Arkansas Louisiana Gas Company. It was, however, stipulated that the kitchen range and oven were fixtures, and the chancellor held that the heating-air-conditioning units and cooling towers became fixtures when installed. We are of the opinion that under these circumstances, the applicable statute is UCC § 9–313 which is the provision of the Uniform Commercial Code designed to establish priority of security interests in fixtures. The appropriate provisions of that statute are as follows:

"(2) A security interest which attaches to goods before they become fixtures takes priority as to the goods over the claims of all persons who have an interest in the real estate except as stated in subsection (4).

"(4) The security interests described in subsections (2) and (3) do not take priority over

"(c) a creditor with a prior encumbrance of record on the real estate to the extent that he made subsequent advances if * * * the subsequent advance under the prior encumbrance is made or contracted for without knowledge of the security interest and before it is perfected."

Under this statute if Arkansas Louisiana's security interest in the goods, although not yet perfected, *attached* to the goods before they became fixtures, it would take priority, as to the goods only, over the prior recorded mortgages to the extent that advances were made under these mortgages before the goods were affixed to the realty.

UCC § 9–204(1) provides that a security interest attaches when there is an agreement that it attach and value is given and the debtor has rights in the collateral. The chancellor found that as between Arkansas Louisiana and Long, the security interest attached before the goods became fixtures.

All of the purchase money had been advanced before the goods became fixtures, and it is apparent from the record that some construction funds were advanced before and some were advanced afterward. In order to establish the extent to which Arkansas Louisiana is entitled to priority as to its goods which became fixtures, it will be necessary to determine in each case how much money had been advanced under the construction money mortgages before the goods became fixtures and how much was advanced thereafter.

* * *

It is argued that this permits a "secret lien" and results in inequities to the other lien holders. The answer to this is that there is no inequity in prohibiting a secured creditor from looking to security other than that upon which he relied when he decided to advance the money. Arkansas Louisiana's priority of security interests affects only the goods which became fixtures and not the remaining realty and improvements. UCC § 9–313(5) provides for the removal of the fixtures from the real estate in circumstances of this kind upon the posting of adequate security for the payment of damages resulting from the removal.

Appellant House argues, however, first: That Arkansas Louisiana's security interest attached at the time of the execution of the blanket security agreement on November 30, 1964, and that all the mortgage funds were advanced after that date; and, second: That this issue was raised by Arkansas Louisiana for the first time on appeal. We consider both of these arguments to be without merit. A security interest cannot attach under UCC § 9–204(1) until value is given and the debtor has rights in the collateral, and, in any event, it is important only to determine whether the security interest attached *before* the goods became fixtures. The significant time in determining the extent of priority is the time the goods were affixed to the real property, for it is only after this has been done that a prior mortgagee may be induced to make further advancements by seeing the fixtures in place.

* * *

This case must be reversed and remanded for determination of the amounts advanced under each construction money mortgage prior to and after the goods were affixed to the realty in question * * * and for establishment of priorities of liens on the fixtures and on the remaining real property in accordance with this opinion.

NOTES

1. How would House v. Long be decided under 1972 § 9–313? What would be the result if the Gas Company had made a fixture filing before the fixtures were installed? § 9–313(4)(a) and § 9–313(6).

2. Under § 1–201(37) an agreement that purports to be a lease may be a "true lease" or it may create a security interest. If the agreement creates a security interest, the transaction is governed exclusively by Article 9. See the next section for a detailed treatment of this issue. If the agreement is a true lease, Article 2A governs the transaction. One of the major policy decisions made in drafting Article 2A was that lessors should not have to file to perfect their interests. The one exception to this rule relates to leases of fixtures under § 2A–309. Section 2A–309(4)(a) and (b), in giving priority to a lessor making a fixture filing, is the analogue of § 9–313(4)(a) and (b). Under § 2A–309(7) if a fixture filing is not made, the interest of the lessor is subject to priority rules under the real estate law of the jurisdiction, which may give priority to a subsequent real estate claimant who had no knowledge or notice of the lessor's interest. But § 2A–309(5), in a few

specified situations, protects the interest of the lessor even if no fixture filing was made.

J. LEASES

Under pre-Code law the lease was sometimes used as a device for avoiding statutory filing requirements or default provisions applicable to conditional sales or chattel mortgages. It was used in transactions with respect to both consumer goods and industrial or business equipment. Any secured installment credit sale can be recast into the form of a lease. The buyer is given possession of the goods as lessee. The payments over the term of the lease which the lessee is required to pay are about equal to the installment purchase price of the goods. At the end of the term the lessee who has made all the rental payments is either entitled to keep the goods or may be given an option to purchase them at a price which is either nominal or far below the value of the goods. In the event of default the lessor, as owner of the goods, can simply reclaim them from the lessee. If the transaction is recognized as a lease the lessor not only avoids statutory filing and default requirements applicable to secured credit sales, but is protected against any sale of the goods by the lessee, any levy on the goods by creditors of the lessee, and the bankruptcy of the lessee.

In cases involving leases that were economically indistinguishable from a conditional sale the courts routinely treated them as conditional sales. Section 1 of the Uniform Conditional Sales Act treated as a conditional sale any lease or bailment under which "the bailee or lessee contracts to pay as compensation a sum substantially equivalent to the value of the goods, and by which it is agreed that the bailee or lessee is bound to become, or has the option of becoming the owner of such goods upon full compliance with the terms of the contract."

Sometimes transactions were cast in lease terms in order to avoid other statutory restraints applicable to sales, most notably usury or sales-finance statutes that put a limit on the amount of finance charges that could be imposed on the buyer. Today, the equipment-lease transaction is most likely to be designed to obtain a tax advantage which would not be available if the transaction were cast as a sale. In such cases the lessor of the goods might well comply with Article 9 requirements regarding filing or default while asserting that the transaction is nevertheless a lease for tax purposes. § 9–408.

"Lease" is defined in § 2A–103(j) as excluding a transaction creating a security interest. As we have seen, if an agreement in the form of a lease creates a security interest, Article 9 applies to all aspects of the agreement, including perfection, priority and default. If the agreement is a lease within § 2A–103(j), Article 2A applies to all aspects of the agreement. The issue of when a lease creates a security interest under former § 1–201(37) became one of the most litigated questions under the UCC. At the time Article 2A was drafted, § 1–201(37) was substantially amended to clarify the matter. The amendment is discussed in detail in Cooper, Identifying a Personal Property Lease under the UCC, 49 Ohio St. L.J. 195 (1988); Huddleson, Old Wine in New Bottles Under Article 2A—Leases, 39 Ala.L.Rev. 615 (1988). The efficacy of the sale/lease distinction is debated in Ayer, On the Vacuity of the Sale/Lease Distinction, 68 Iowa L.Rev. 667 (1983); Ayer, Further Thoughts on Lease and Sale, 1983 Ariz.St.L.J. 341; Mooney, The Mystery and Myth of "Ostensible Ownership" and Article 9 Filing: A Critique of Proposals to Extend Filing Requirements to Leases, 39 Ala.L.Rev. 683 (1988).

1. LEASE WITH OPTION TO PURCHASE OR RENEW

MATTER OF MARHOEFER PACKING CO.
United States Court of Appeals, Seventh Circuit, 1982.
674 F.2d 1139.

PELL, CIRCUIT JUDGE.

This appeal involves a dispute between the trustee of the bankrupt Marhoefer Packing Company, Inc., ("Marhoefer") and Robert Reiser & Company, Inc., ("Reiser") over certain equipment held by Marhoefer at the time of bankruptcy. The issue presented is whether the written agreement between Marhoefer and Reiser covering the equipment is a true lease under which Reiser is entitled to reclaim its property from the bankrupt estate, or whether it is actually a lease intended as security in which case Reiser's failure to file a financing statement to perfect its interest renders it subordinate to the trustee.

I

In December of 1976, Marhoefer Packing Co., Inc., of Muncie, Indiana, entered into negotiations with Reiser, a Massachusetts based corporation engaged in the business of selling and leasing food processing equipment, for the acquisition of one or possibly two Vemag Model 3007–1 Continuous Sausage Stuffers. Reiser informed Marhoefer that the units could be acquired by outright purchase, conditional sale contract or lease. Marhoefer ultimately acquired two sausage stuffers from Reiser. It purchased one under a conditional sale contract. Pursuant to the contract, Reiser retained a security interest in the machine, which it subsequently perfected by filing a financing statement with the Indiana Secretary of State. Title to that stuffer is not here in dispute. The other stuffer was delivered to Marhoefer under a written "Lease Agreement."

The Lease Agreement provided for monthly payments of $665.00 over a term of 48 months. The last nine months payments, totaling $5,985.00, were payable upon execution of the lease. If at the end of the lease term the machine was to be returned, it was to be shipped prepaid to Boston or similar destination "in the same condition as when received, reasonable wear and tear resulting from proper use alone excepted, and fully crated." The remaining terms and conditions of the agreement were as follows:

1. Any State or local taxes and/or excises are for the account of the Buyer.

2. The equipment shall at all times be located at

    Marhoefer Packing Co., Inc.
    1500 North Elm & 13th Street
    Muncie, Indiana

    and shall not be removed from said location without the written consent of Robert Reiser & Co. The equipment can only be used in conjunction with the manufacture of meat or similar products unless written consent is given by Robert Reiser & Co.

3. The equipment will carry a ninety-day guarantee for workmanship and materials and shall be maintained and operated safely and carefully in conformity with the instructions issued by our operators and the maintenance manual. Service and repairs of the equipment after the ninety-day period will be subject to a reasonable and fair charge.

4. If, after due warning, our maintenance instructions should be violated repeatedly, Robert Reiser & Co. will have the right to cancel the lease contract on seven days notice and remove the said equipment. In that case, lease fees would be refunded pro rata.

5. It is mutually agreed that in case of lessee, Marhoefer Packing Co., Inc., violating any of the above conditions, or shall default in the payment of any lease charge hereunder, or shall become bankrupt, make or execute any assignment or become party to any instrument or proceedings for the benefit of its creditors, Robert Reiser & Co. shall have the right at any time without trespass, to enter upon the premises and remove the aforesaid equipment, and if removed, lessee agrees to pay Robert Reiser & Co. the total lease fees, including all installments due or to become due for the full unexpired term of this lease agreement and including the cost for removal of the

equipment and counsel fees incurred in collecting sums
due hereunder.

6. It is agreed that the equipment shall remain personal
property of Robert Reiser & Co. and retain its character
as such no matter in what manner affixed or attached to
the premises.

In a letter accompanying the lease, Reiser added two option
provisions to the agreement. The first provided that at the end of
the four-year term, Marhoefer could purchase the stuffer for
$9,968.00. In the alternative, it could elect to renew the lease for
an additional four years at an annual rate of $2,990.00, payable in
advance. At the conclusion of the second four-year term, Marhoefer would be allowed to purchase the stuffer for one dollar.

Marhoefer never exercised either option. Approximately one
year after the Vemag stuffer was delivered to its plant, it ceased
all payments under the lease and shortly thereafter filed a voluntary petition in bankruptcy. On July 12, 1978, the trustee of the
bankrupt corporation applied to the bankruptcy court for leave to
sell the stuffer free and clear of all liens on the ground that the
"Lease Agreement" was in fact a lease intended as security within
the meaning of the Uniform Commercial Code ("Code") and that
Reiser's failure to perfect its interest as required by Article 9 of
the Code rendered it subordinate to that of the trustee. Reiser
responded with an answer and counterclaim in which it alleged
that the agreement was in fact a true lease, Marhoefer was in
default under the lease, and its equipment should therefore be
returned.

Following a trial on this issue, the bankruptcy court concluded that the agreement between Marhoefer and Reiser was in fact a
true lease and ordered the trustee to return the Vemag stuffer to
Reiser. The trustee appealed to the district court, which reversed
on the ground that the bankruptcy court had erred as a matter of
law in finding the agreement to be a true lease. We now reverse
the judgment of the district court.

II

The dispute in this case centers on section 1–201(37) of the
Uniform Commercial Code * * *. In applying this section, the
bankruptcy court concluded that "the presence of the option to
renew the lease for an additional four years and to acquire the
Vemag Stuffer at the conclusion of the second four-year term by
the payment of One Dollar ($1.00) did not, in and of itself, make
the lease one intended for security."

The district court disagreed. It held that the presence of an
option to purchase the stuffer for one dollar gave rise to a
conclusive presumption under clause (b) of section 1–201(37) that
the lease was intended as security. Although it acknowledged

that the option to purchase the stuffer for only one dollar would not have come into play unless Marhoefer chose to renew the lease for an additional four-year term, the district court concluded that this fact did not require a different result. "It would be anomalous," said the court, "to rule that the lease was a genuine lease for four years after its creation but was one intended for security eight years after its creation."

Reiser, relying on Peter F. Coogan's detailed analysis of section 1–201(37), Coogan, Hogan & Vagts, Secured Transactions Under the Uniform Commercial Code, ch. 4A, (1981) (hereinafter "Secured Transactions Under U.C.C."), argues that the district court erred in construing clause (b) of that section as creating a conclusive presumption that a lease is intended as security where the lease contains an option for the lessee to become the owner of the leased property for no additional consideration or for only nominal consideration. It contends that by interpreting clause (b) in this way, the district court totally ignored the first part of that sentence which states that "[w]hether a lease is intended as security is to be determined by the facts of each case." Reiser claims that because the totality of facts surrounding the transaction indicate that the lease was not intended as security, notwithstanding the presence of the option to purchase the stuffer for one dollar, the district court erred in reversing the bankruptcy court's determination.

We agree that the district court erred in concluding that because the Lease Agreement contained an option for Marhoefer to purchase the Vemag stuffer at the end of a second four-year term, it was conclusively presumed to be a lease intended as security. However, in our view, the district court's error lies not in its reading of clause (b) of section 1–201(37) as giving rise to such a presumption, but rather in its conclusion that clause (b) applies under the facts of this case.

The primary issue to be decided in determining whether a lease is "intended as security" is whether it is in effect a conditional sale in which the "lessor" retains an interest in the "leased" goods as security for the purchase price. 1C Secured Transactions Under U.C.C. § 29A.05[1][C], p. 2939. By defining the term "security interest" to include a lease intended as security, the drafters of the Code intended such disguised security interests to be governed by the same rules that apply to other security interests. See U.C.C., Art. 9. In this respect, section 1–201(37) represents the drafter's refusal to recognize form over substance.

Clearly, where a lease is structured so that the lessee is contractually bound to pay rent over a set period of time at the conclusion of which he automatically or for only nominal consideration becomes the owner of the leased goods, the transaction is in substance a conditional sale and should be treated as such. It is to this type of lease that clause (b) properly applies. Here, however, Marhoefer was under no contractual obligation to pay rent until such time as the option to purchase the Vemag stuffer for one dollar was to arise. In fact, in order to acquire that option, Marhoefer would have had to exercise its earlier option to renew the lease for a second four-year term and pay Reiser an additional $11,960 in "rent." In effect, Marhoefer was given a right to terminate the agreement after the first four years and cease making payments without that option ever becoming operative.

Despite this fact, the district court concluded as a matter of law that the lease was intended as security. It held that, under clause (b) of section 1–201(37), a lease containing an option for the lessee to purchase the leased goods for nominal consideration is conclusively presumed to be one intended as security. This presumption applies, the court concluded, regardless of any other options the lease may contain.

We think the district court's reading of clause (b) is in error. In our view, the conclusive presumption provided under clause (b) applies only where the option to purchase for nominal consideration necessarily arises upon compliance with the lease. See 1C Secured Transactions Under U.C.C. § 29.05[2][b] pp. 2947–49. It does not apply where the lessee has the right to terminate the lease before that option arises with no further obligation to continue paying rent. * * * For where the lessee has the right to terminate the transaction, it is not a conditional sale.

Moreover, to hold that a lease containing such an option is intended as security, even though the lessee has no contractual obligation to pay the full amount contemplated by the agreement, would lead to clearly erroneous results under other provisions of the Code. Under section 9–506 of the Code, for example, a debtor in default on his obligation to a secured party has a right to redeem the collateral by tendering full payment of that obligation. The same right is also enjoyed by a lessee under a lease intended as security. A lessee who defaults on a lease intended as security is entitled to purchase the leased goods by paying the full amount of his obligation under the lease. But if the lessee has the right to terminate the lease at any time during the lease term, his obligation under the lease may be only a small part of the total purchase price of the goods leased. To afford the lessee a right of redemption under such circumstances would clearly be wrong. There is no evidence that the drafters of the Code intended such a result.

We therefore hold that while section 1–201(37)(b) does provide a conclusive test of when a lease is intended as security, that test does not apply in every case in which the disputed lease contains an option to purchase for nominal or no consideration. An option of this type makes a lease one intended as security only when it necessarily arises upon compliance with the terms of the lease.

Applying section 1–201(37), so construed, to the facts of this case, it is clear that the district court erred in concluding that the possibility of Marhoefer's purchasing the stuffer for one dollar at the conclusion of a second four-year term was determinative. Because Marhoefer could have fully complied with the lease without that option ever arising, the district court was mistaken in thinking that the existence of that option alone made the lease a conditional sale. Certainly, if Marhoefer had elected to renew the lease for another term, in which case the nominal purchase option would necessarily have arisen, then the clause (b) test would apply.[6] But that is not the case we are faced with here. Marhoefer was not required to make any payments beyond the first four years. The fact that, at the conclusion of that term, it could have elected to renew the lease and obtain an option to purchase the stuffer for one dollar at the end of the second term does not transform the original transaction into a conditional sale.

This fact does not end our inquiry under clause (b), however, for the trustee also argues that, even if the district court erred in considering the one dollar purchase option as determinative, the lease should nevertheless be considered a conditional sale because the initial option price of $9,968 is also nominal when all of the operative facts are properly considered. We agree that if the clause (b) test is to apply at all in this case, this is the option that must be considered. For this is the option that was to arise automatically upon Marhoefer's compliance with the lease. We do not agree, however, that under the circumstances presented here the $9,968 option price can properly be considered nominal.

It is true that an option price may be more than a few dollars and still be considered nominal within the meaning of section 1–201(37). Because clause (b) speaks of nominal "consideration" and not a nominal "sum" or "amount," it has been held to apply not only where the option price is very small in absolute terms, but also where the price is insubstantial in relation to the fair market value of the leased goods at the time the option arises.[7]   *   *   *

Here, however, the evidence revealed that the initial option price of $9,968 was not nominal even under this standard. George Vetie, Reiser's treasurer and the person chiefly responsible for the

---

6. Reiser concedes that had Marhoefer elected to renew the lease after the first term, the transaction would have been transformed into a sale. George Vetie, Reiser's treasurer, testified that the renewal option was actually intended as a financing mechanism to allow Marhoefer to purchase the stuffer at the end of the lease if it desired to do so but was either unable or unwilling to pay the initial purchase price of $9,968.

7. The trustee argues that the determination of whether the option price is nominal is to be made by comparing it to the fair market value of the equipment at the time the parties enter into the lease, instead of the date the option arises. Although some courts have applied such a test, In re Wheatland Electric Products Co., 237 F.Supp. 820 (W.D. Pa.1964); In re Oak Mfg., Inc., 6 U.C.C. Rep. 1273 (Bankr.S.D.N.Y.1969), the better approach is to compare the option price with the fair market value of the goods at the time the option was to be exercised.

terms of the lease, testified at trial that the purchase price for the Vemag stuffer at the time the parties entered into the transaction was $33,225. He testified that the initial option price of $9,968 was arrived at by taking thirty percent of the purchase price, which was what he felt a four-year-old Vemag stuffer would be worth based on Reiser's past experience.

The trustee, relying on the testimony of its expert appraiser, argues that in fact the stuffer would have been worth between eighteen and twenty thousand dollars at the end of the first four-year term. Because the initial option price is substantially less than this amount, he claims that it is nominal within the meaning of clause (b) and the lease is therefore one intended as security.

Even assuming this appraisal to be accurate, an issue on which the bankruptcy court made no finding, we would not find the initial option price of $9,968 so small by comparison that the clause (b) presumption would apply. While it is difficult to state any bright line percentage test for determining when an option price could properly be considered nominal as compared to the fair market value of the leased goods, an option price of almost ten thousand dollars, which amounts to fifty percent of the fair market value, is not nominal by any standard.

Furthermore, in determining whether an option price is nominal, the proper figure to compare it with is not the actual fair market value of the leased goods at the time the option arises, but their fair market value at that time as anticipated by the parties when the lease is signed. 1C Secured Transactions Under U.C.C. § 29A.05[2][b], p. 2953. Here, for example, Vetie testified that his estimate of the fair market value of a four-year-old Vemag stuffer was based on records from a period of time in which the economy was relatively stable. Since that time, a high rate of inflation has caused the machines to lose their value more slowly. As a result, the actual fair market value of a machine may turn out to be significantly more than the parties anticipated it would be several years earlier. When this occurs, the lessee's option to purchase the leased goods may be much more favorable than either party intended, but it does not change the true character of the transaction.

We conclude, therefore, that neither option to purchase contained in the lease between Marhoefer and Reiser gives rise to a conclusive presumption under section 1–201(37)(b) that the lease is one intended as security. This being so, we now turn to the other facts surrounding the transaction.

III

Although section 1–201(37) states that "[w]hether a lease is intended as security is to be determined by the facts of each case," it is completely silent as to what facts, other than the option to purchase, are to be considered in making that determination. Facts that the courts have found relevant include the total amount of rent the lessee is required to pay under the lease, * * *; whether the lessee acquires any equity in the leased property, * * *; the useful life of the leased goods, * * *; the nature of the lessor's business, * * *; and the payment of taxes, insurance and other charges normally imposed on ownership * * *. Consideration of the facts of this case in light of these factors leads us to conclude that the lease in question was not intended as security.

First, Marhoefer was under no obligation to pay the full purchase price for the stuffer. Over the first four-year term, its payments under the lease were to have amounted to $31,920. Although this amount may not be substantially less than the original purchase price of $33,225 in absolute terms, it becomes so when one factors in the interest rate over four years that would have been charged had Marhoefer elected to purchase the machine under a conditional sale contract.[8] The fact that the total amount of rent Marhoefer was to pay under the lease was substantially less than that amount shows that a sale was not intended. 1 Secured Transactions Under U.C.C. § 4A.01.

It is also significant that the useful life of the Vemag stuffer exceeded the term of the lease. An essential characteristic of a true lease is that there be something of value to return to the lessor after the term. 1C Secured Transactions Under U.C.C. § 29A.05[2][c], p. 2959. Where the term of the lease is substantially equal to the life of the leased property such that there will be nothing of value to return at the end of the lease, the transaction is in essence a sale. In re Lakeshore Transit–Kenosha, Inc., supra. Here, the evidence revealed that the useful life of a Vemag stuffer was eight to ten years.

Finally, the bankruptcy court specifically found that "there was no express or implied provision in the lease agreement dated February 28, 1977, which gave Marhoefer any equity interest in the leased Vemag stuffer." This fact clearly reveals the agreement between Marhoefer and Reiser to be a true lease. See Hawkland, The Impact of the Uniform Commercial Code on Equipment Leasing, 1972 Ill.L.Forum 446, 453 ("The difference between a true lease and a security transaction lies in whether the lessee acquires an equity of ownership through his rent payments."). Had Marhoefer remained solvent and elected not to exercise its option to renew its lease with Reiser, it would have received

8. The bankruptcy court found that Reiser was originally willing to sell Marhoefer the stuffer under a conditional sale contract the terms of which would have been $7,225 down and monthly installments of $1,224 over a twenty-four month period. The total payments under such an agreement would have amounted to $36,601, substantially more than the amount Marhoefer was required to pay over four years under the lease.

nothing for its previous lease payments. And in order to exercise that option, Marhoefer would have had to pay what Reiser anticipated would then be the machine's fair market value. An option of this kind is not the mark of a lease intended as security. See In re Alpha Creamery Company, 4 U.C.C.Rep. 794, 798 (Bankr.W.D. Mich.1967).

Although Marhoefer was required to pay state and local taxes and the cost of repairs, this fact does not require a contrary result. Costs such as taxes, insurance and repairs are necessarily borne by one party or the other. They reflect less the true character of the transaction than the strength of the parties' respective bargaining positions. * * *

IV

We conclude from the foregoing that the district court erred in its application of section 1–201(37) of the Uniform Commercial Code to the facts of this case. Neither the option to purchase the Vemag stuffer for one dollar at the conclusion of a second four-year term, nor the initial option to purchase it for $9,968 after the first four years, gives rise to a conclusive presumption under clause (b) of section 1–201(37) that the lease is intended as security. From all of the facts surrounding the transaction, we conclude that the agreement between Marhoefer and Reiser is a true lease. The judgment of the district court is therefore reversed.

NOTES

1. Both the former version of § 1–201(37) discussed in *Marhoefer* and the revised version, § 1–201(37) (first (d)), provide that a "lease" is actually a sale with a security interest in the goods sold if the lessee has an option to become the owner of the goods by paying nominal consideration. The "lessor" has reserved no residual interest in the goods. Case law extended this principle to cases, like those cited in *Marhoefer,* in which the option price is so insubstantial in relation to the fair market value of the goods that the lessee would have "no sensible alternative" to the exercise of the option. Peco, Inc. v. Hartbauer Tool & Die Co., 262 Or. 573, 500 P.2d 708 (1972). Suppose Dealer leased a piano to Lessee on a month-to-month basis for a rental of $25 per month with an option to purchase at any time for $1,500 with the right to apply all rentals paid against the $1,500 purchase option amount. If Lessee continues the lease for five years, total rental payments made by Lessee equals the $1,500 purchase amount. The useful life of a piano is indefinite and is normally far more than five years. Thus, at some point before the expiration of the five-year period Lessee could purchase the piano for an amount far less than the value of the piano at that time. At that point Lessee would have no sensible alternative to exercising the purchase option. Several

cases held that such a lease creates a security interest. In re J.A. Thompson & Son, Inc., 665 F.2d 941 (9th Cir.1982); Stanley v. Fabricators, Inc., 459 P.2d 467 (Alaska 1969); United Rental Equipment Co. v. Potts & Callahan Contracting Co., 231 Md. 552, 191 A.2d 570 (1963). In his article, Leases of Equipment and Some Other Unconventional Security Devices: An Analysis of UCC Section 1–201(3) and Article 9, 5 Duke L.J. 909 (1973), Peter Coogan argues that a lease should not be held to create a security interest if the lessee has the right to terminate before an amount equivalent to the purchase price is paid. Crumley v. Berry, 298 Ark. 112, 766 S.W.2d 7 (1989) (week-to-week lease of kitchen appliances), follows Coogan's view and holds a transaction like the piano lease above to be a true lease. What view does § 1–201(37) take on this issue?

2. How would revised § 1–201(37) deal with facts like those in *Marhoefer* if the $9,968 option price, viewed at the inception of the transaction, was below the predictable fair market value of the goods at the end of the first four-year term of the lease? Is the old no-sensible-alternative test still relevant? Comment 37 to § 1–201 (10th paragraph) states: "A fixed price purchase option in a lease does not of itself create a security interest. This is particularly true if the fixed price is equal to or greater than the reasonably predictable fair market value of the goods at the time the option is to be performed. A security interest is created only if the option price is nominal * * *. There is a set of purchase options whose fixed price is less than fair market value but greater than nominal that must be determined on the facts of each case to ascertain whether the transaction in which the option is included creates a lease or a security interest." Professor Cooper, in Identifying a Personal Property Lease under the UCC, 49 Ohio St.L.J. 195 (1988), criticizes this Comment:

> The second unresolved issue is the absence of any guidance in the Proposed Amendment describing when the amount of an option to buy or renew is nominal. An option payment that is less than the anticipated fair market value is not necessarily nominal under the Proposed Amendment. The troubling language in the Official Comment, which notes that there is a category of options whose price is less than fair market value but greater than nominal, pinpoints this problem, but offers little guidance. The comment merely provides that these must be determined "on the facts of each case." Given what the courts have done when left with this slim guidance under the current version of Section 1–201(37), this gap in the definition of nominal value could create the same problems which the Proposed Amendment is intended to resolve.

> Remember that nominal value is only relevant when there is an option to purchase the goods, or to renew the lease

to the end of economic life. In other words, we need a definition of nominal that will address a transfer of all remaining residual value, and recognize that transfer of this value for sufficient payment does not make the initial transaction a disguised security interest. For example, it would be preferable to provide that an option payment less than the anticipated fair market rent or value is nominal when it would not induce a reasonable lessor to transfer the residual outside of the context of the lease agreement. If no reasonable lessor would transfer the entire residual in exchange for the option payment, absent a prior lease relationship between the lessor and lessee, then the option payment is not compensating the lessor for the value of the residual, but is completing payment, and the transaction is a security interest, and was from the inception. This test, or any similar test which gives the courts guidance as to the operation of the section, is better than the "other facts" guidance offered by the Official Comment.

49 Ohio St.L.J. 245–246.

Huddleson, Old Wine in New Bottles: UCC Article 2A—Leases, 39 Ala.L.Rev. 615, 628–631 (1988), describes the efforts of the drafters to agree on some percentage formula to define what is nominal consideration, e.g., no greater than 10% of the original value of the goods or less than 75% of the reasonably predictable fair market value of the goods at the time the option was to be exercised. Eventually efforts to arrive at a percentage formula were abandoned.

3. The court in *Marhoefer* in part III of the opinion cites facts that courts have relied on to find whether a lease creates a security interest. Facts tending to show a security interest include whether the lessee is obliged to pay taxes, insurance and other charges showing ownership. Compare § 1–201(37) (second (b)).

2. LEASE WITHOUT OPTION TO PURCHASE OR RENEW

IN RE ASPEN IMPRESSIONS, INC.
United States Bankruptcy Court, E.D.Pa., 1989.
94 B.R. 861.

BRUCE I. FOX, BANKRUPTCY JUDGE:

I have before me a motion by Provident Savings Bank for determination of priority among encumbrance holders, for relief from the automatic stay in the chapter 11 case, and to compel payment of an administrative claim. The motion is challenged by

Bucks County Bank and Trust, a secured creditor. In dispute are the proceeds of a sale of equipment from the debtor's estate, which proceeds are currently being held in escrow pending resolution of this dispute. Provident's argument presents alternate theories in support of its motion: first, that the subject document entitled "Equipment Lease" is a true lease, as opposed to a security agreement for sale[3], second, should I find that the document represents a security agreement, the movant instead argues that it holds a purchase money security interest, which was duly perfected in a way to give it priority over Bucks County Bank.

I.

At the hearing the debtor's president, John M. Sisk, testified that Aspen Impressions attempted to purchase a particular printing press from its manufacturer, Didde Graphics, in November, 1985. After various negotiations, Didde Graphics declined to sell its press to Aspen Impressions, Inc. (the debtor probably not having sufficient cash and requesting a financing arrangement from the seller, to which Didde did not agree). A description of the press sought to be purchased and its price is found in the document "Machine Order & Contract," dated November 15, 1985, which was signed by a Didde salesman and John Sisk, for Aspen, and which was offered into evidence.

Mr. Sisk further testified that, upon the failure of his negotiations with Didde Graphics, he entered into an agreement with an entity known as High Tech Funding, Inc. (Ex. P–3), which agreement is denominated a "lease." This document identifies Aspen Impressions, Inc. as the lessee of one printing press, serial number 410–0012, the supplier being Didde Graphics. The lease was signed by the lessor, High Tech, and by Sisk for the debtor; it is dated April 15, 1986. The "Equipment Lease Schedule" states that the duration of the lease is 84 months, the monthly rent payment being $8,355.00 (with two monthly payments due in advance). Thus, $701,820.00 would have been paid by the end of this seven year payment schedule.

Exhibit P–4, an "Invoice revised (3–19–86)" by Didde Graphics, evinces a sale to High Tech Funding of a printing press, serial number 410–0012. This invoice calls for shipment to Aspen on March 17, 1986. The unit price of the press is listed as $409,600.00. Advance payments of $40,112.50 had been received by Didde; the payment terms for the balance are undisclosed by the invoice.

On the same day that High Tech signed its lease agreement with the debtor it assigned that lease to Provident; testimony

3. The parties agree that if it is a true lease, the movant would be entitled to the proceeds.

showed that Provident "bought the lease [from High Tech] and gave them money for it." [N.T. at 14, 17].

Thereafter, on April 23, 1986, Bucks County Bank made loans and advances and extensions of credit to the debtor. To secure these obligations the debtor granted Bucks County Bank a security interest in, among other things, the debtor's existing and future equipment and machinery. (Ex. B–4.) Bucks County Bank filed a UCC–1 financing statement on May 2, 1986 with the Secretary of the Commonwealth of Pennsylvania perfecting this security interest; another UCC–1 statement concerning this security interest was filed on May 5, 1986 with the Prothonotary of Montgomery County, Pa. (Exs. B–3 and B–5.) Provident, as assignee of High Tech, filed a financing statement covering the subject printing press against the debtor with the Commonwealth on April 25, 1986, (Ex. P–2); it also filed, on May 5, 1986, a statement concerning this property with the Prothonotary of Montgomery County, Pa.

The debtor filed its petition in bankruptcy under chapter 11 on April 4, 1988. The subject press was sold at auction for, approximately, $180,000.00. Bucks County Bank is currently holding these funds in escrow, pending resolution of the instant controversy.

II.

The initial question posed is whether the "lease" agreement between High Tech and the debtor, which was subsequently (if not simultaneously) assigned by High Tech to Provident, is a true lease or a lease intended as security for the conditional sale of the equipment. A brief review of the distinction between leases and conditional sales contracts is thus in order.

Generally, true leases cover the temporary lease of property for a price, and require the leased item's return to the lessor. Leases intended as security, however, are conditional sales of equipment with a reservation of title to provide security. "In a conditional sales agreement, the lessee-purchaser generally assumes the risks and obligations associated with the benefits of ownership; 'rental' payments compensate the lessor-seller for the capital outlay plus interest and usually a profit by the end of the lease's term." In re Loop Hospital Partnership, 35 B.R. 929, 931 (Bankr.N.D.Ill.1983). If it is determined that the instant agreement is a true lease, then Provident retains a reversionary ownership interest in the press and is entitled to the proceeds of the sale of that equipment.

In determining whether the lease agreement is "intended as security," reliance is to be placed, according to Section 1–201(37) of the Uniform Commercial Code, upon "the facts of each case."

This section ✳ ✳ ✳ helps identify when such a security interest exists. Specifically, the statute provides:

> Whether a lease is intended as security is to be determined by the facts of each case; however:
>
> (1) the inclusion of an option to purchase does not of itself make the lease one intended for security; and
>
> (2) an agreement that upon compliance with the terms of the lease the lessee shall become or has the option to become the owner of the property for no additional consideration or for a nominal consideration does make the lease one intended for security.

This section indicates that while an express option to buy does not automatically create a security interest, a lease with an option to purchase for nominal or no additional consideration creates one as a matter of law.

✳ ✳ ✳

The agreement currently under review, however, contains no option to purchase; indeed, the document expressly denies the lessee the option to buy the equipment. *See* Ex. P–3, paragraph **XXX** ("lessee shall have no option to purchase or otherwise acquire title or ownership of any of the equipment and shall have only the right to use the same under and subject to the terms and provisions of the lease"). Thus, the agreement does not conform to either statutory subdivision cited above, and its character must be determined by examining the "facts of [this] case." § 1–201(37).

III.

It is generally agreed that, just as the inclusion of a purchase option in a lease does not, of itself, imply a secured installment sale, the exclusion of one does not automatically imply a true lease. ✳ ✳ ✳ Thus, even though nothing in the agreement may permit purchase at nominal consideration, a security interest nonetheless may be found. ✳ ✳ ✳ As the UCC does not create an absolute standard by which to categorize a "no-option" instrument, some courts have earmarked persuasive facts as indicative of the parties' intentions, and hence revealing the true character of the instrument. I am persuaded that the better analysis distinguishes true leases from security interests by examining whether there is a realistic residual value in the leased property upon the conclusion of the contract.

Above I noted that the mere existence of a purchase option is not dispositive of this question. The price at which a purchase option may be exercised is subject to judicial scrutiny, as this sum must be of "nominal" consideration. Where the option price is nominal or substantially less than the fair market value of the equipment at the end of the contract's term, the option effectively acts as consideration for the passing of title from the lessor-seller to the lessee-purchaser; such a lease is a conditional sales agreement. * * * White & Summers, Handbook & the Law Under the Uniform Commercial Code, 881 (2d ed. 1980) ("White and Summers") ("if the option price amounts to 25% (or more) of the total list price, then it would appear that the lessee has been paying true rent rather than 'building up an equity,' and it would not follow that the only sensible course for him would be to exercise his option."). The more nominal the purchase option (relative to the fair market value at the time of exercise) or the more favorable the exercise terms, the more likely is the conclusion that the lease was really one intended to accomplish the transfer of a title interest.

* * *

The rationale underlying such a conclusion is that a significant enough option advantage to the benefit of the lessee almost insures a purchase election decision. * * * Courts and commentators have characterized this as the "economic realities test," which provides that if at the end of the lease term the only sensible course economically for the lessee would be for him or her to exercise the option, the transaction is really a secured installment sale. * * * The question at bottom becomes whether the lessor has, in effect, at the end of the instrument's term, surrendered any claim to the residual value of the leased goods.

* * *

This rationale also underlies agreements containing no option to purchase, which might simply reflect an intent for title to pass with no additional consideration because the property is expected to have no market value at the expiration of the lease term. * * * The salient factor, then, is the relationship of the amount paid towards the equipment over the life of the agreement to the property's fair market value at the end of the lease.

The agreement in dispute here calls upon the debtor/lessee to make 84 monthly payments of $8,355.00 to the lessor; thus $701,820.00 will have been paid at the end of the seven year term. The 1986 invoice of sale of this equipment to the lessor shows a sale price of $409,600.00.[8] Thus, at first blush it appears, as Bucks County Bank argues, that Provident in effect lent $410,000.00 to the debtor for the purchase of this equipment, the sum to be repaid in 84 installments at roughly a 17% rate of return.

However, the issue of whether there exists residual ownership in the lessor must be addressed with an understanding of the equipment's fair market value at the end of the lease term. Id. The above argument presupposes that the useful life of the press is

8. As noted above, the press itself was sold as part of this bankruptcy in 1988 for, approximately, $180,000.00. No valuation testimony was offered.

seven years; that is, that the fair market value of the press at the end of the lease term approaches zero. ＊ ＊ ＊

In this case, as it is the objector who desires to have the purported lease declared a security agreement, the burden of persuasion rests upon Bucks County Bank. Here, having heard no evidence as to the anticipated fair market value of the press at the conclusion of the lease term, I have no basis upon which to conclude that no residual value would exist in the property upon the conclusion of the contract. In re Loop Hospital Partnership, 35 B.R. at 936 ("The Court cannot imply an option [where none exists] because the debtor has not established that its rental payments were intended to compensate the creditor for the equipment's fair market value in 1986, when the agreement would expire."). See also In re Pacific Express, Inc., 780 F.2d at 1485 (where "lease" included no purchase option, "lessee" paid sums equivalent to original value plus interest, and evidence showed that the equipment would be rendered obsolescent by the end of the lease period, the transaction is that of an installment sale).[9] Cf. *Matter of Fashion Optical, Ltd.,* 653 F.2d at 1390 (where instrument gave option to purchase at end of five years' term, option price fixed in terms of fair market value at end of term, but no evidence presented from which to infer such value, there was no way for court to tell whether the consideration requirement of section 1–201(37) has been contravened).

My reliance upon the significance of residual value is supported by the American Law Institute's recent approval of an addition to the UCC, "Article 2A–Leases." This article provides, *inter alia,* standardized provisions for drawing distinctions between true leases and those intended as secured transactions or sales. This in part is accomplished by an amendment to current UCC Section 1–201(37) "in order to re-assert the significance of residual value as the touchstone of the common law definition of a true lease." *Naples,* at 349 (criticizing courts' reliance on other factors). Specifically, Section 1–201(37) as amended would read as follows:

＊ ＊ ＊

I am cognizant of the fact that, as noted above, courts have earmarked a number of other factors which will indicate the

---

9. The sole fact that the debtor was paying, in effect, 17 per cent interest on a purchase price does not, of itself, establish the existence of an agreement intended for security. No evidence was offered as to the lessor's cost of funds; moreover, at the time of contracting the debtor was in some economic straits, and was not in a strong bargaining position. Thus, the 17 per cent interest payments arguably may have been intended to compensate the lessor for taking the risk of the transaction. Compare Leasing Service Corp. v. American Nat'l Bank & Trust Co., 19 U.C.C.Rep. Serv. at 259–260, (court held that where no evidence of anticipated useful life of the equipment was presented and the contract contained no option to purchase, but where total rental payments exceeded the initial cost of the equipment by 37 per cent, no residual proprietary rights remained with the "lessor").

existence of a security interest in the disguise of a lease. These factors include whether the lessee is required to insure the items on behalf of the lessor for a value equal to the total rental payments; if risk of loss or damage is on the lessee; if lessee is to pay for taxes, repairs, damage and maintenance; whether there exist default provisions governing acceleration and resale; and whether the goods are fixtures impractical to remove. ＊ ＊ ＊ This list is not exhaustive; and not one factor alone conclusively creates a security agreement in the absence of an option. Instead, these decisions weigh these various factors and decide, looking at the totality of the objective facts, what the intent of the parties was. I find, however, that these factors are, at best, inconclusive of the issue as they can all legitimately appear in true leases. ＊ ＊ ＊ I agree that the "better indicator of intended ownership is the parties' anticipation of the fair market value at the end of the agreement." In re Loop Hospital Partnership, 35 B.R. at 936.

Finally, then, as no evidence of the anticipated fair market value of the equipment at the end of the lease term was presented, I cannot conclude that the agreement is anything other than what it purports to be, a true lease of personal property.

＊　＊　＊

NOTES

1. The court in *Aspen* states the issue to be whether the lessor has retained residual value in the leased property. Thus if the term of the lease is as long as or longer than the economic life of the goods, the lease creates a security interest; the lessor has retained no residual value. § 1–201(37) (first a). Why is it not equally true that there is a security interest if the lessee is obligated to pay the full cash price of the property ($409,600) plus a 17% finance charge as in this case? § 1–201(37) (second a). Would any rational lessee be willing to pay the full value of the goods in rentals if the lease is not for the economic life of the goods? Comment 37 to § 1–201 states: "Subparagraph (a) has no statutory derivation; it states that a full payout lease does not *per se* create a security interest."

2. The transaction in *Aspen* is an example of the popular equipment lease transaction. In a recent year over $310 billion in equipment lease receivables were estimated to be outstanding. Naples, A Review and Analysis of the New Article 2A Leases Amendment to the UCC and Its Impact on Secured Creditors, Equipment and Finance Lessors, 93 Com'l L.J. 342, 343 note 2 (1988). The lease in *Aspen* would be classified as a "finance lease" under § 2A–103(1)(g). See Comment (g) to § 2A–103 for a description of the attributes and consequences of a finance lease.

3. OPEN–END LEASE

IN RE TULSA PORT WAREHOUSE CO.

United States Court of Appeals, Tenth Circuit, 1982.
690 F.2d 809.

SEYMOUR, CIRCUIT JUDGE.

We are once again called upon to consider a question proven to be a prime source of litigation in the field of commercial law: when is a purported lease in fact a security agreement subject to the requirements of Article 9 of the Uniform Commercial Code (UCC)?

In this case, Tulsa Port Warehouse Company (bankrupt or lessee) entered into four automobile "Non-Maintenance Lease Agreements" with defendant Chuck Naiman Buick Company (lessor), which were subsequently assigned to defendant General Motors Acceptance Corporation (GMAC). Following the bankruptcy of the lessee, the trustee in bankruptcy and GMAC engaged in the classic battle to determine the priority of their interests in the vehicles. It is undisputed that GMAC did not comply with the requirements of Article 9 relating to the perfection of a security interest. If the leases are in fact security agreements, GMAC's interest in the automobiles is subordinate to that of the trustee under * * * § 9–301(1)(b), (3). The bankruptcy court resolved the issue in favor of the trustee, and the district court affirmed that decision.

Under the open-end leases [1] at issue, which are identical in all pertinent respects, the bankrupt leased the automobiles for commercial or business use for either a twenty-four or thirty-six month period. The monthly charge was determined as follows: first, the agreed depreciated value of the vehicle at the end of the lease term was deducted from the original value; second, to this remainder, designated "total amount of fixed monthly rentals for the lease term to be credited against original value," was added the item "total amount of fixed monthly rentals *not* to be credited against original value." The lease agreements did not further identify this latter amount or indicate how it was calculated.[2]

1. The lessor uses closed-end and open-end leases. Under the closed-end leases, the lessee returns the vehicle to the lessor at the end of the lease term and the obligations of both come to an end. Under the open-end lease, however, the relationship between the lessor and lessee does not end. Rather, it involves the sale of the vehicle and an adjustment between the lessor and lessee based on the sales price, as more fully described hereinafter.

2. The bankruptcy court held that this item "euphemistically describes ordinary interest without disclosure as to its rate." The district court also found the amount to constitute interest.

Finally, the sum of these two items was divided by the number of months in the lease term to produce the amount due monthly.[3]

The open-end leases contain no option to purchase. Each lease includes termination and default provisions under which the lessee is obligated at termination to return the vehicle to the lessor. At that time, the lessor is required to dispose of the vehicle at wholesale in a commercially reasonable manner. If the amount realized at this sale exceeds the agreed depreciated value, the lessee receives the surplus. If the sale amount is less than the agreed depreciated value, the lessee is liable to the lessor for the deficit.

In Oklahoma, "[w]hether a lease is intended as security is to be determined by the facts of each case." UCC § 1–201(37). This court has recently set out the analytical framework for determining whether an agreement is a true lease or a secured transaction. Steele v. Gebetsberger *(In re Fashion Optical, Ltd.)*, 653 F.2d 1385, 1388–89 (10th Cir.1981). We pointed out that when a lease does not contain a purchase option, the lease "will still be deemed one intended as security if the facts otherwise expose economic realities tending to confirm that a secured transfer of ownership is afoot." Id. at 1389.

In considering the persistent lease versus secured transfer question, the courts have identified a number of significant factors tending to suggest that a sale has occurred: (1) whether the lease creates an equity in the lessee * * *; (2) whether the lessee is obligated to provide comprehensive insurance in favor of the lessor * * *; (3) whether the lessee pays sales tax * * *; (4) whether the lessee pays all taxes, maintenance, and repairs * * *; and (5) whether the lessee holds the lessor harmless * * *.

With respect to the creation of an equity interest in the lessee in this case, the bankruptcy court and the district judge approved the discussion in Bill Swad Leasing Co. v. Stikes *(In re Tillery)*, 571 F.2d 1361 (5th Cir.1978). In *Tillery*, the court considered an open-end lease agreement substantially similar to the ones before us and concluded that "[t]he termination formula recognizes the equity of the 'Lessee,' in the vehicle because he is required to bear

---

3. For example, under one of the 36 month leases for a Buick Regal, the monthly rental was computed as follows:

1.	Original value of vehicle	$7,798.00
2.	Agreed depreciated value at end of lease term	3,450.00
3.	Total amount of fixed monthly rentals for the full base term to be credited against original value	4,348.00
4.	Total amount of fixed monthly rentals *not* to be credited against original value	1,730.96
5.	Fixed monthly rental charges	6,078.96
6.	Sales or use tax	243.00
7.	Total monthly rental charge	$6,321.96
8.	Monthly rental payments	$ 175.61

the loss or receive the gain from its wholesale disposition." Id. at 1365. Although defendants argue vigorously on appeal that *Tillery* was wrongly decided, we agree with its analysis on this issue.

Moreover, many of the other factors tending to indicate that a lease is in reality a secured transaction are present in this case. The lessee is required to obtain comprehensive insurance in favor of the lessor; pay sales tax and all other licenses, registration, and title fees; pay for all maintenance and repairs; and indemnify the lessor against all loss. As a practical matter, the lessee holds all the incidents of ownership except bare legal title.

Defendants conceded at oral argument that there is no economic difference to the lessor between the lease arrangement here and a secured transfer of property. Under the lease, the lessor is assured of receiving the entire original value of the vehicle plus an amount that realistically must be viewed as interest. The fact that a portion of the original value may be paid by a third party wholesale purchaser after termination of the lease is of no economic significance to the lessor, particularly when the surplus or deficit from this sale is borne by the lessee. We agree with the trial judge's conclusion that "[t]he practical effect of this arrangement is the same as if lessee purchased the car, then sold it two or three years later and used the proceeds to pay off the note."

In sum, we conclude that the agreements were transfers of property subject to a security interest. One purpose of Article 9 of the UCC is to provide notice of such prior interests to third parties dealing with personal property. To promote that end, buyer and seller should be prevented "from masquerading their secured installment sale as a 'lease,' thereby placing it beyond the reach of UCC provisions governing secured transactions." *Fashion Optical,* 653 F.2d at 1388.

Judgment affirmed.

NOTES

1. Apparently some motor vehicle lessors wanted § 1–201(37) to provide that open-end leases are true leases, but the drafters decided not to include special provisions on open-end leases. Huddleson, Old Wine in New Bottles: UCC Article 2A—Leases, 39 Ala. L.Rev. 615, 638–641 (1988). How would *Tulsa Port Warehouse* be decided under revised § 1–201(37)?

2. Each year new cases appear on the issue whether a lease creates a security interest. Has the UCC taken the correct approach in making filing depend on the sometimes difficult issue of when a lease creates a security interest under § 1–201(37)? With respect to consignments we have found that the Code requires filing in most cases to protect the consignor's interest against the consignee's creditors even though no security interest is created.

§ 2–326(3)(c). Filing is also required in sales of accounts and chattel paper. § 9–102(1)(b). Should the same approach be taken in the leasing area with filing required for all leases of personal property in which the term of the lease exceeds a certain period of time? See the Uniform Consumer Credit Code definition of "consumer lease" as a "lease of goods * * * which is for a term exceeding four months." UCCC § 1.301(14) (1974). The issue was extensively debated in the course of drafting Article 2A and the decision was made not to require filing for true leases. See Mooney, The Mystery and Myth of "Ostensible Ownership" and Article 9 Filing: A Critique of Proposals to Extend Filing Requirements to Leases, 39 Ala.L.Rev. 683 (1988).

K. REAL PROPERTY INTERESTS

ARMY NATIONAL BANK v. EQUITY DEVELOPERS, INC.

Supreme Court of Kansas, 1989.
245 Kan. 3, 774 P.2d 919.

SIX, JUSTICE:

This case presents a first impression issue involving a mortgagee's transfer and assignment of notes and mortgages as security for its own borrowing. We are requested to establish the appropriate controlling law to be applied in the determination of the relative priorities of competing interests. The issue is centered within the relationship of Article 9 of the Uniform Commercial Code, Kansas real estate recording statutes, the perfection of an Article 9 UCC instrument secured by real estate, and priority to foreclose a real estate mortgage. The parties involved are commercially sophisticated entities.

The defendants, Equibank Corporation (Equibank) and Federal Deposit Insurance Corporation (FDIC), appeal from the trial court's judgment holding that Army National Bank (Army) and its assignee, Maryville Bancshares, Inc., had a superior interest in the proceeds of the foreclosure of mortgages on the "Greenbrook project" in Wichita, Kansas. Army's and Maryville Bancshares' interest arose out of Army's participation in loans made by Equibank to the developers of Greenbrook and a subsequent subordination agreement between Army and Equibank. The FDIC was substituted as the real party in interest in place of the Bank of Kansas City (BOKC) by order of the district court. BOKC was a credit lender of Equibank. Equibank assigned and gave possession of nine promissory notes by Equity Developers Inc., (EDI) the developers of Greenbrook, secured by mortgages on the subject property, to BOKC.

The questions to be considered in this appeal are: * * * (2) Did BOKC have a prior, perfected security interest in the EDI notes and mortgages, giving it priority in the proceeds of the mortgages? (3) Does the Uniform Commercial Code apply to security interests taken in promissory notes, which are in turn secured by real estate mortgages? * * *

We vacate the judgment of the trial court and remand for further proceedings.

* * *

Equibank Corporation is a company that exists to provide loan participations for nonaffiliated banks (banks that are not affiliated with Equibank, with each other, or with a large holding company). On August 31, 1983, Equibank entered into a participation agreement with Army National Bank. According to Joseph Archias, President of Equibank, the participation agreement established the participation relationship between Equibank and the participating bank; however, it was not necessary for a particular project or loan to be specified at the time of agreement.

On May 15, 1984, EDI, which was developing an area in Wichita called "Greenbrook," executed and delivered to Equibank nine construction notes in the aggregate amount of $1,943,000. According to Archias, neither Army nor Equibank had heard of EDI in August of 1983. The notes were secured by mortgages on the Greenbrook property. The mortgages were recorded by Equibank with the Sedgwick County Register of Deeds on June 15, 1984. On June 7, 1984, Equibank had executed a note in favor of Traders Bank of Kansas City (predecessor in interest to BOKC) in the amount of $800,000. The note listed the nine EDI notes as security for the note and "all other indebtedness owing to the bank," but no security agreement or assignment was made at that time. Equibank, previously, had executed a note to BOKC for $200,000.

On June 27, 1984, Equibank and Army executed a "certificate of participation" in which Army participated in the loan to EDI in the amount of $1,000,000. According to Archias, at the time the initial participation by Army matured on November 1, 1984, Army had advanced $943,000 pursuant to the certificate of participation. Army agreed to continue, but indicated that it was not interested in increasing its participation beyond $1,000,000. Archias testified that, at the November 1 meeting, he told the representatives of Army that Equibank would obtain additional funds to finish the Greenbrook project through Equibank's line of credit at BOKC. According to Steve Hamilton, who was vice president and senior loan officer of Army at the time of the November 1 meeting (and is now president and chief executive officer of Army), there was "nothing that was said that gave any rise to a secured interest by the Bank of Kansas City."

On November 16, 1984, Equibank pledged, endorsed, and delivered the nine EDI notes and executed assignments of the nine EDI mortgages to BOKC. These assignments were not recorded with the register of deeds until February 12, 1986. Under the terms of the participation agreement between Army and Equibank, instruments executed by the borrower with respect to the loan were to be deposited with an independent custodian. Equibank never deposited the EDI notes with the custodian. The record does not indicate that Army ever inquired if Equibank had done so. Army did not request to see the notes.

EDI experienced financial difficulties. During the spring of 1985, Army and Equibank negotiated to work out the problems. On May 20, 1985, Army and Equibank entered into an agreement in which Army agreed to advance additional money to complete the Greenbrook project. Equibank agreed to subordinate its interest in the EDI notes and mortgages to the interest of Army. In addition, the title to the Greenbrook property was conveyed to Greenbrook Development Corporation, an affiliate of Equibank.

On July 22, 1985, Equibank executed another certificate of participation on behalf of Army in the amount of $417,686 in a loan made to Greenbrook Development Corporation. In addition, Joseph Archias personally guaranteed the debt. Greenbrook Development executed a promissory note and mortgage to Equibank in the amount of $735,000 in September 1985.

Greenbrook Development Corporation subsequently abandoned the project. In November of 1985, an action was brought against EDI for the enforcement of a mechanic's lien on the Greenbrook project. In addition to EDI, Greenbrook Development, Equibank, Army, and a number of other lien holders were named as defendants.

Army subsequently filed an action to foreclose the real estate mortgages on the Greenbrook property and to determine the various interests of the parties. Army's standing to foreclose is not at issue in this litigation. Army's action named all the parties in the mechanic's lien suit and BOKC. The two cases were consolidated. The many claims arising out of various mechanic's liens on the property were disposed of or settled prior to trial. The case proceeded to trial on the issue of the priorities of Army and BOKC.

* * *

2. *Security Interests in Promissory Notes Secured by Real Estate Mortgages—Application of the Uniform Commercial Code*

* * *

Equibank argues that BOKC had a prior perfected security interest under Article 9 of the Uniform Commercial Code and, consequently, an interest in the nine notes and mortgages superior to that of Army. We agree.

* * *

Pursuant to § 9–304(1), a security interest in instruments may only be perfected by possession of the instrument. There is no dispute that BOKC took possession of the EDI notes. BOKC also satisfied the attachment and enforcement requirements of § 9–203 in that BOKC took possession of the notes and mortgages and extended credit to Equibank. Equibank, as sole payee named on the notes and mortgages, had rights in the collateral.

We next consider the key question in this appeal: Is the priority to foreclose a mortgage securing a note, which has been transferred and delivered with its mortgage assigned by a mortgagee as security for its own borrowing, controlled by the Uniform Commercial Code or by state real estate law?

Although Article 9 applies to BOKC's security interest in the EDI notes, its effect on the EDI mortgages requires further analysis. * * *

§ 9–104 states, in part:

"This article does not apply * * *

(j) except to the extent that provision is made for fixtures in section 9–313, to the creation or transfer of an interest in or lien on real estate, including a lease or rents thereunder."

In contrast, § 9–102(3) states:

"The application of this article to a security interest in a secured obligation is not affected by the fact that the obligation is itself secured by a transaction or interest to which this article does not apply."

According to Professors White and Summers, the issue of perfection of security interests in instruments secured by real estate mortgages has created conflict in the case law; however, a consensus is now emerging. 2 White and Summers Uniform Commercial Code 270 (3d ed. 1988).

White and Summers endorse the analysis made in In re Kennedy Mortgage Co., 17 B.R. 957 (Bankr.D.N.J.1982). In *Kennedy,* an involuntary bankruptcy action was brought against Kennedy Mortgage Company (Kennedy). Kennedy was engaged in the business of obtaining funds for mortgage applicants and processing mortgage applications. Kennedy established a line of credit with the First National Bank of Boston (First) similar to the arrangement between Equibank and BOKC. As collateral, Kennedy delivered five promissory notes secured by mortgages and executed assignments of the mortgages to First. The mortgages were properly recorded in accordance with state law, but the assignments to First were not recorded. Several of Kennedy's other creditors disputed First's claim that it had a perfected security interest in the notes and mortgages. The bankruptcy court held "that it is not necessary under the Uniform Commercial Code or the Bankruptcy Code or State Statutes for an assignee of a mortgage to record the assignment of the mortgage in order to have a secured status." 17 B.R. at 962.

The court gave several rationales for its decision. First, the recording statutes are designed to protect the mortgagee as against other creditors of the mortgagor, not to protect one creditor of the mortgagee as against another creditor of the mortgagee. The recording statutes are also designed to establish the rights of individuals affected by the chain of title on the real estate. The court also cited the impact that requiring recording of assignments of mortgages would have on the mortgage financing industry. It said that the sources of funds that mortgage brokers now have would be disrupted and the availability of funds would be reduced. Finally the court said: "Without the manifestation of the debt, usually evidenced by a note or bond, the mortgage instrument itself is subject to attack. The lien of a mortgage is regarded as no greater than the actual debt secured." 17 B.R. at 965.

The *Kennedy* case was analyzed with approval in Krasnowiecki, Miller & Ziff, The Kennedy Mortgage Co. Bankruptcy Case: New Light Shed on the Position of Mortgage Warehousing Banks, 56 Am.Bankr.L.J. 325, 338 (1982):

> "Persons seeking to acquire rights *in the mortgage* must know that they will have no right to enforce the mortgage unless they have a right to enforce the underlying obligation. The law is very clear on this point. People who deal in mortgages are not ordinary consumers. Surely it is not too much to expect them to inquire where the note is. Furthermore, quite apart from the mortgage law which says that the mortgage cannot be enforced except for the obligation, there can be no doubt that the UCC covers security interests in mortgage notes and that possession of the note is sufficient to perfect an interest in it. This fact must be widely known in the trade. Therefore, anyone who gives value for or asserts a claim against a mortgage should inquire where the note is. Indeed, the courts have uniformly held that possession of the note puts everyone who deals with a record mortgagee on notice of the outstanding claim."

The recording acts were not intended to apply as to entities who deal in the mortgage paper itself, but to protect the mortgagor and those dealing with the underlying land. 56 Am.Bankr. L.J. at 346. We agree.

White and Summers adopt Krasnowiecki's view that the parties to these transactions live in two separate worlds, that of the mortgagee and that of the mortgagor. 2 White and Summers, Uniform Commercial Code 271 (3d ed. 1988).

For a listing of cases consistent with *Kennedy Mortgage* in recognizing that the lender perfects a security interest when the lender takes possession of the note, see 2 White and Summers, Uniform Commercial Code 272 n. 18 (3d ed. 1988).

The Official Comment 4 to § 9–102 states:

"An illustration of subsection (3) is as follows:

The owner of Blackacre borrows $10,000 from his neighbor, and secures his note by a mortgage on Blackacre. This Article is not applicable to the creation of the real estate mortgage. Nor is it applicable to a sale of the note by the mortgagee, even though the mortgage continues to secure the note. However, when the mortgagee pledges the note to secure his own obligation to X, this Article applies to the security interest in an instrument even though the instrument is secured by a real estate mortgage. This Article leaves to other law the question of the effect on rights under the mortgage of delivery or non-delivery of the mortgage or of recording or nonrecording of an assignment of the mortgagee's interest."

Prior to 1962, this comment was worded somewhat differently. It originally suggested that both the note and the mortgage were covered under Article 9. The language referring to the mortgage was deleted and the sentence about leaving to other law the effects on rights under the mortgage was added. Clark, The Law of Secured Transactions Under the Uniform Commercial Code ¶ 1.08[10][a], p. 1–112 n. 372. Kansas has adopted these amendments.

* * *

Professor Clark has addressed the issue of the application of Article 9 to security interests in notes secured by real estate:

"The notes may be of little value as personal obligations of the homeowners; their real worth comes from the mortgages that secure them. Therefore, in addition to taking possession of the notes, Bank must make sure that the mortgage documents are properly recorded under state real estate law. Perfecting as to the notes may not perfect as to the underlying real estate, which is excluded from the ambit of Article 9. Conversely, the fact that the real estate recording is not covered by Article 9 does not alter the fact that Article 9 applies to the note itself, so that possession is critical." Clark, The Law of Secured Transactions Under the Uniform Commercial Code ¶ 7.04 at pp. 7–9 to 7–10.

Our view is that the mortgage follows the note. A perfected claim to the note is equally perfected as to the mortgage. This view is supported by Professors Nelson and Whitman in their text. See Nelson and Whitman, Real Estate Finance Law 370 (2d ed. 1985).

The parties cite In re Maryville Sav. & Loan Corp., 743 F.2d 413 (6th Cir.1984), aff'd on reh. 760 F.2d 119 (6th Cir.1985). In *Maryville,* a bank made a loan to Maryville for which Maryville assigned promissory notes and deeds of trust to the bank as collateral. The bank did not take possession of the notes, but it did record the assignment with the register of deeds in the county in which the real estate was located. The bank argued that it had a perfected security interest because it had duly recorded the assignment as required by real property law. The trustee in bankruptcy argued that the bank's failure to take possession of the notes rendered the interest unperfected pursuant to Article 9 of the UCC. The bankruptcy court found for the trustee, but was reversed by the district court. 743 F.2d at 415.

The Sixth Circuit Court of Appeals first noted that both the bankruptcy court and the district court assumed that the UCC applied either to the entirety of the transaction or that it did not apply at all. 743 F.2d at 415. The court said that Comment 4 to § 9–102 of the UCC indicates that the security interest in the promissory note should be analyzed separately from the interest created in the deed of trust. "[W]e conclude that article nine applies to the plaintiff's security interest but only in the promissory notes themselves. Since plaintiff did not take possession of the notes, plaintiff's security interest in the notes was not perfected." 743 F.2d at 416–17.

The court concluded that the bank's interest in the deeds of trust was perfected. The original opinion did not explain the effect of this holding. 743 F.2d at 417. The parties moved for clarification as to the proper handling of the funds paid to the trustee on the promissory notes at issue. 760 F.2d at 120.

White and Summers are critical of the *Maryville* decision. They argue that splitting the perfection of the note and the mortgage would have the effect of requiring the mortgagor to pay twice in order to get free and clear title to his property because one creditor will have claim to the note and the other will have a mortgage that will not be discharged by payment to the note holder.

> "Every conceivable proposition, good or bad, has a champion in the cases. In our view, *Kennedy Mortgage* is the correct analysis. One in possession of the note should be regarded as having a perfected security interest in that note, with the mortgage to follow it. Absent possession of the note, the trustee prevails. Such an outcome facilitates lending and, at least with respect to sophisticated persons, protects subsequent parties who will necessarily ask to see the negotiable instrument." 2 White and Summers, Uniform Commercial Code 273–74 (3d ed. 1988).

We reason that a mortgage cannot exist separately from the note it secures. A mortgage without a note is worthless. In our view, the problem with splitting the perfection of the note and the mortgage is that Article 9 would be applicable to the security interest in the note and real property law would be applicable to the security interest in the mortgage. We can foresee that in priority contests one party would have a perfected interest in the note and another party would have a perfected interest in the mortgage. The result could be a situation where the creditor of the assigning mortgagee is left with either a note absent its security or a mortgage which may be worthless.

The parties also cite two related cases, Matter of Staff Mortg. & Inv. Corp., 550 F.2d 1228 (9th Cir.1977), and In re Staff Mortg. & Inv. Corp., 625 F.2d 281 (9th Cir.1980). Both cases arose out of the bankruptcy of Staff, which was in the business of buying and selling promissory notes secured by trust deeds. In each of the cases, Staff had borrowed money from the plaintiffs and the loans were secured by pledges of promissory notes secured by trust deeds. In both cases the assignments were recorded in the appropriate county, but Staff retained possession of the documents. The Ninth Circuit Court of Appeals held that, although the recording may have served as notice to interested parties who checked the county records, it was not sufficient to perfect a security interest in the instruments pursuant to the Uniform Commercial Code. 550 F.2d at 1230. "Perfection of a security interest in an instrument can only occur with the actual possession of the instrument by the secured party or by an agent or bailee on his behalf." 625 F.2d at 283.

We reason that the mortgagee's creditor would be perfected by possession as to other creditors of the mortgagee, but would be required to record its interest in order to be perfected as to creditors of the mortgagor. This approach is in accordance with the purposes of the recording acts: to protect the interests of the mortgagor. The creditors of the mortgagee should inquire as to the whereabouts of the underlying promissory note.

We read § 9–104(j) in connection with the plain meaning of § 9–102(3) and hold that Article 9 of the UCC governs the collateral assignment of the real property interests, the mortgages, securing the nine notes as well as governing the collateral assignment of the notes. See Landmark Land Co., Inc. v. Sprague, 529 F.Supp. 971, 977 (S.D.N.Y.1981); In re Atlantic Mortg. Corp., 69 B.R. 321 (Bankr.E.D.Mich.1987).

*   *   *

3. *Army National's Interest in the EDI Notes and Mortgages*

*   *   *

The trial court found that Army had no notice of the assignment of the mortgages to BOKC. There was substantial competent evidence to support the trial court's finding. In our view, however, the fact of Army's lack of notice of the mortgages' assignment to BOKC does not affect BOKC's priority.

Army appears to have been careless in its dealings with Equibank. In May 1985, Army knew that there were problems with the Greenbrook project but it agreed to advance more money to Equibank and to the project without either inquiring as to the whereabouts of the EDI notes or requesting Equibank to deposit them with an independent custodian as set out in the participation agreement.

The testimony indicated that Archias, the president of Equibank, assured the Army representatives that BOKC did not have a claim on the project. Apparently, Army trusted Archias. We note that apparently BOKC also trusted Archias. BOKC finally recorded the Equibank assignments February 12, 1986, after the recording of the Army–Equibank subordination agreement (May 31, 1985) and the Greenbrook Development Corporation–Equibank mortgage (February 7, 1986).

* * *

We do not agree that Army's rights in the EDI notes and mortgages arose on June 15, 1984, the date the mortgages were recorded. As of June 15, 1984, all that existed between Army and Equibank was the participation agreement, which did not contemplate any specific loan. It merely set out the conditions by which Army might participate in a loan in the future. It was not until June 27, 1984, when the first participation certificate was executed, that Army advanced any money to purchase a participation in the EDI loan.

Army argues that it was a bona fide purchaser for value by virtue of its purchase of the participation certificate on June 27, 1984. It contends that, because of this status, it took free of any unperfected security interest that BOKC might have had at the time. Army, however, neither took possession of the collateral, recorded its interest, nor required Equibank to deposit the collateral with an independent custodian as contemplated by the agreement. The participation agreement states that Army is purchasing an undivided fractional interest in the *loan,* not in the notes and mortgages. Army does not advance a persuasive legal argument as to why it should be given bona fide purchaser status.

As between BOKC's security interest in the notes and mortgages and Army's interest by virtue of its participation in the loans to EDI, BOKC has priority.

* * *

NOTE

Assume that Army had merely lent money to Equibank and, as security, had taken assignments of the notes and mortgages. It recorded the assignments in the appropriate real estate records before BOKC either: (1) took possession of the notes, or (2) recorded the assignments. In either case would Army have priority over BOKC as to the notes and mortgages? Section 3–302 states "Public filing or recording of a document does not of itself constitute notice of a defense, claim in recoupment, or claim to the instrument."

L. CONFLICTING INTERESTS NOT GOVERNED BY ARTICLE NINE

1. SUBROGATION

CANTER v. SCHLAGER

Supreme Judicial Court of Massachusetts, 1971.
358 Mass. 789, 267 N.E.2d 492.

BRAUCHER, JUSTICE. This is an action of contract brought by the trustee in bankruptcy of Zef Parabicoli & Sons, Inc. (the contractor) against S. Lawrence Schlager, Judith R. Schlager, Alba A. Jameson and Arlene T. Vecchi (the owners) for money owed under a written construction contract. In May, 1963, the contractor agreed with the owners to build a post office on their property in Wellesley for a price later amended to $109,000. By the amendment the work was to be substantially completed by July 1, 1964, and time was to be of the essence. In accordance with the contract, the contractor provided performance and payment bonds, and in its application for the bonds assigned to the surety, Maryland Casualty Company, all payments due or to become due under the contract. No financing statement with respect to the assignment was filed under the Uniform Commercial Code. The surety appears to be the real defendant in this action, under an agreement to indemnify the owners.

Work began in January, 1964, and by June 26, 1964, the owners had paid the contractor $66,650. On June 26, 1964, an involuntary petition in bankruptcy was filed against the contractor, but by order of the referee in bankruptcy the contractor continued to operate under the supervision of a receiver. On August 1, 1964, the Post Office Department accepted the building and began to pay rent under a lease from the owners. On October 27, 1964, the contractor was adjudicated a bankrupt and the plaintiff, who had been the receiver, was appointed trustee.

The owners refused to pay a requisition in the amount of $27,990 submitted by the contractor on July 1, 1964, for work completed up to that date. On July 21, there was a conference of representatives of the Post Office Department, the surety, the contractor, its receiver and the owners; the attorney for the surety, at the request of the owners and with the approval of the contractor, agreed that the surety would assume responsibility for completion. Late in September, the contractor submitted a final requisition in the amount of $42,850, which the owners refused to pay. In October, 1964, the surety paid more than $60,000 to subcontractors who had furnished labor and materials for the building. On August 30, 1965, the owners paid the balance of the contract price, less more than $5,000 in disputed "back charges," to the surety in the net amount of $36,630.11. The owners now contend that payment to the surety discharged any obligation to the plaintiff.

The judge, sitting without a jury, held that the surety's claim to the contract balance was not subject to the Uniform Commercial Code and found for the owners. We agree.

1. If the surety were claiming the balance due under the contract by virtue of the assignment to it in the contractor's bond application, it would be fairly arguable that it was claiming a "security interest" in a "contract right." UCC §§ 1–201(37), 9–102, 9–106. If there were such a security interest, it would be subordinate to the rights of a person who became a lien creditor without knowledge of the security interest and before it was perfected, and a trustee in bankruptcy would ordinarily have the rights of such a lien creditor. UCC §§ 9–301(1)(b), 9–301(3). Bankruptcy Act, § 70, sub. c., 11 U.S.C.A. § 110(c) (1964). To perfect a security interest, a financing statement must be filed unless the case is within one of several exceptions. UCC § 9–302(1). We do not pass on the question whether the assignment to the surety in this case was excepted as "a transfer of a contract right to an assignee who is also to do the performance under the contract," UCC § 9–104(f), or "an assignment of accounts or contract rights which does not alone or in conjunction with other assignments to the same assignee transfer a significant part of the outstanding accounts or contract rights of the assignor * * *." UCC § 9–302(1)(e). See Gilmore, Security Interests in Personal Property, §§ 10.5, 19.6.

2. The surety makes an alternative claim, not resting on the assignment to it by the contractor, that it is subrogated to the rights of the contractor to the contract balance, to the rights of the owners, and to the rights of the subcontractors it paid. Such claims are not superseded by the Uniform Commercial Code. Section 1–103 of the Code provides in part, "Unless displaced by the particular provisions of this chapter, the principles of law and equity * * * shall supplement its provisions." "No provision of the Code purports to affect the fundamental equitable doctrine of subrogation." French Lumber Co. Inc. v. Commercial Realty &

Finance Co. Inc., 346 Mass. 716, 719, 195 N.E.2d 507, 510. "Of basic importance is the general rule of Section 9–102(2) that Article 9 'applies to security interests *created by contract.*' (Emphasis supplied.) Rights of subrogation, although growing out of a contractual setting and ofttimes articulated by the contract, do not depend for their existence on a grant in the contract, but are created by law to avoid injustice. Therefore, subrogation rights are not 'security interests' within the meaning of Article 9." Jacobs v. Northeastern Corp., 416 Pa. 417, 429, 206 A.2d 49, 55.

Our conclusion that filing under the Code is unnecessary to preserve the priority of a surety's right of subrogation over the rights of a construction contractor's trustee in bankruptcy is reinforced by decisions of other courts. * * * The Uniform Commercial Code is to be "liberally construed and applied to promote its underlying purposes and policies," which include a purpose and policy "to make uniform the law among the various jurisdictions." § 1–102.

3. The plaintiff here argues that we should "establish a degree of certainty (indeed, even a degree of sanity) to the determination of priorities among claimants to construction contract proceeds" by enunciating "an absolute requirement that sureties engaged in bonding construction projects perfect security interests in their assignment by filing." See Notes, 4 B.C.Ind. & Commercial L.Rev. 748, 755; 65 Col.L.Rev. 927, 933. We find that the draftsmen and sponsors of the Uniform Commercial Code did not overlook the problems of construction contract sureties. The 1952 Official Draft included § 9–312(7), subordinating the surety's interest to a later interest taken by a party who gave new value to enable the debtor to perform his obligation; that provision was deleted in 1953, with an explanation by the editorial board that representatives of the surety companies had complained that it changed settled law and that the problem should be left to agreements for subordination.[27] See National Shawmut Bank v. New

---

27. "The Surety Companies' representatives convincingly took the position that subsection (7) as it stands is a complete reversal of the case law not only of the Supreme Court of the United States but also of the highest courts of most of the states. * * *

"The typical case involved is a case in which a surety company, as a prerequisite to the execution of a performance bond, requires a contractor to make an assignment of all moneys coming to the contractor from the owner. Later, the contractor goes to a bank and obtains a loan presumably or actually for the purpose of enabling him to perform his contract.

"Under the cited case law, the surety's rights come first as to the funds owing by the owner unless the surety has subordinated its right to the bank. Subsection (7) of the Code as written would reverse the situation and give the bank priority in all cases.

"Under existing case law, both the contractor and the bank are in a position to bargain with the surety which may or may not be willing to subordinate its claim. Under subsection (7), as written in the Code the surety company would have nothing to bargain about." Recommendations of the Editorial Board for Changes in the Text and Comments of the Uniform Commercial Code, Official Draft, Text and Com-

Amsterdam Cas. Co. Inc., 411 F.2d 843, 846, c. 4 (1st Cir.). The 1952 proposal did not include a requirement of filing to perfect rights of subrogation, and we do not believe we should insert a requirement omitted by legislative draftsmen who considered the problem. It is possible for parties dealing with a construction contractor to be ignorant of the existence of a surety bond. * * * But it could well be a rational legislative judgment that the practice of furnishing performance and payment bonds in connection with construction contracts is so common and so well known that a requirement of public filing is unnecessary. * * *

4. The plaintiff argues that, even if "the anachronistic doctrine of equitable subrogation still has vitality," the surety has only the rights of those to whose rights it would be subrogated, and that they had none. Under Pearlman v. Reliance Ins. Co., 371 U.S. 132, 141, 83 S.Ct. 232, 9 L.Ed.2d 190, and similar cases, the surety may stand in the shoes of either (1) the contractor whose obligations are discharged, (2) the owners to whom it was bound, or (3) the subcontractors whom it paid. So far as the trustee in bankruptcy asserts the rights of the contractor, any one of these three bases of subrogation should be sufficient. Regardless of whether the contractor was aggrieved by the delay in payment of his requisition of $27,990 submitted July 1, 1964, or his final requisition of $42,850 submitted late in September, 1964, he could not avoid the surety's right to reimbursement for more than $60,000 paid by the surety to discharge his obligations in October, 1964. Nor could he avoid recoupment by the owners for amounts properly paid by them to the subcontractors. See American Bridge Co. of N. Y. v. Boston, 202 Mass. 374, 377, 88 N.E. 1089; Berkal v. M. De Matteo Constr. Co., 327 Mass. 329, 334, 98 N.E.2d 617. A different case might be presented if it were found that the owners or the surety, to induce the contractor to continue, promised after trouble arose to make payments regardless of offsets. * * * There is no such showing here.

* * *

The plaintiff is not helped by Bankruptcy Act § 70, sub. c, 11 U.S.C.A. § 110(c) (1964), giving him the rights of a judgment creditor of the bankrupt with a lien by legal proceedings. Such rights date from June 26, 1964, when the petition in bankruptcy was filed; the surety's right dates back to the date of its bond. * * * Hence the right of subrogation prevails over the rights of a lien creditor such as the trustee in bankruptcy. * * *

5. The plaintiff complains that the surety improperly yielded to the owners' claims of more than $5,000 of "back charges." The

ments Edition, pp. 24–25, April 30, 1953. See Uniform Commercial Code § 9–312(7), Official Draft, Text and Comments Edition, 1952; Cramer, Uniform Commercial Code: Surety v. Lend-er, 3 Forum 295, 300–302. In Gilmore, Security Interests in Personal Property § 36.7, it is erroneously stated that the offending provision "disappeared, without official explanation."

surety paid more than $60,000 of debts owed by the contractor, and was reimbursed $36,630.11. In these circumstances, if $5,000 more was owed, it should have been paid to the surety rather than to the plaintiff.

There was no error.

Exceptions overruled.

NOTE

Transamerica Insurance Co. v. Barnett Bank, 540 So.2d 113 (Fla.1989), marshals the authorities on subrogation and agrees with the analysis of Justice Braucher in *Canter*.

2. SUBORDINATION

It is not uncommon for an institutional debtor, usually a corporation, to have classes of unsecured debt. For example, an unsecured creditor may have agreed that its debt shall be subordinated to the debt of another unsecured creditor. The purpose of the subordination agreement is usually to allow the debtor to obtain credit which might otherwise not be available. The effect of subordination is to transfer to the favored creditor the amount that would otherwise have gone to the subordinated creditor in any insolvency distribution. Subordination agreements are enforceable in bankruptcy. Bankruptcy Code § 510(a). To the extent that the favored creditor enjoys a priority with respect to the assets of the debtor it can be argued that the creditor has an interest in personal property of the debtor which secures payment of the obligation, and thus has a security interest as defined by § 1–201(37). But this "security interest" is different from conventional security interests in that it does not affect any creditor except those who have subordinated their claims. Thus, it would serve little purpose to make enforceability of subordination agreements depend upon perfection under Article 9. Because the status of subordination agreements under Article 9 was not clear, the UCC was amended in 1966 to add § 1–209 as an optional provision to make it clear that subordination agreements do not come within § 1–201(37). The comment to § 1–209 discusses the problem in detail. See also § 9–316.

3. SETOFF

NATIONAL ACCEPTANCE CO. OF AMERICA v. VIRGINIA CAPITAL BANK

United States District Court, E.D.Virginia, 1980.
498 F.Supp. 1078.

CLARKE, DISTRICT JUDGE. This diversity action was brought pursuant to 28 U.S.C. § 1332 by two creditors of Concrete Structures, Inc., a Virginia corporation recently the subject of bankruptcy proceedings under Chapter XI of the Bankruptcy Act. Claiming a prior, perfected security interest in certain funds deposited in several deposit accounts maintained by Concrete Structures in the Virginia Capital Bank, the plaintiffs allege that the Bank unlawfully appropriated these funds to set-off certain debts owed to the Bank by Structures. Evidence was submitted by the parties in support of their various positions at a hearing held before this Court on June 19, 1980, and the matter is ripe for a determination on the merits. The following opinion represents the Court's findings of fact and conclusions of law under Fed.R. Civ.P. 52(a).

Although certain facts relating to this controversy were recited by the Court in a previous Order denying the Bank's motion for summary judgment, 491 F.Supp. 1269 (1980), a more complete picture of the circumstances surrounding this case can now be drawn. Concrete Structures, Inc. was at all relevant times engaged in the business of manufacturing and distributing concrete blocks and prestressed concrete building materials. Beginning in 1964, National Acceptance Company of America (NAC), a Delaware corporation, lent Structures various amounts of money pursuant to certain loan and security agreements and other financing documents. A significant portion of these loans were made as part of an accounts receivable financing arrangement whereby NAC agreed to lend Structures a certain percentage of the face amount of Structures' accounts receivable. NAC reserved the right reasonably to reject unsound accounts which might be tendered by Structures for financing, and took a security interest in the financed accounts and in other collateral. For its part, Structures was obligated to submit all payments received from customers in payment of any account financed under this arrangement directly to NAC.

During the period January 1, 1978, to June 30, 1978, NAC continued to lend money pursuant to these financing arrangements. These transactions were governed by a Loan and Security Agreement dated January 5, 1973; an Extension Agreement dated October 1, 1976, which extended payments on certain outstanding loans; an Accounts Rider dated November 18, 1977; and an Inventory Rider dated November 18, 1977. Under the Loan and Security Agreement, Structures granted NAC a security interest in the following collateral to secure loans made under these agreements:

(a) existing and future accounts, chattel paper, contract rights and instruments (sometimes hereinafter individually and collectively referred to as "Accounts"), whether Accounts are acceptable or unacceptable to Lender and whether Accounts are scheduled to Lender on Schedules of Accounts or not, and all goods whose sale, lease or other disposition by Borrower has given rise to any Accounts and which goods have been returned to or repossessed or stopped in transit by Borrower;

(b) presently owned and hereafter acquired inventory ("Inventory");

(c) presently owned and hereafter acquired general intangibles, goods (other than Inventory), equipment, vehicles and fixtures, together with all accessions, parts and appurtenances thereto appertaining or attached or kept or used or intended for use in connection therewith and all substitutions, renewals, improvements and replacements of and additions thereto (sometimes hereinafter individually and collectively referred to as "Equipment") and all Equipment described in Equipment Rider attached hereto;

(d) presently owned and hereafter acquired Inventory evidenced by warehouse receipts (whether negotiable or nonnegotiable) now or at any time or times hereafter issued by any bailee in Lender's name or negotiated to Lender evidencing such bailee's possession of any Inventory now or at any time or times hereafter deposited with such bailee;

and all proceeds and products of and accessions to all of the foregoing described properties and interests in properties.

* * *

It is agreed that this security interest was duly perfected and remained so throughout all relevant times. As of June 1978, when Structures instituted bankruptcy proceedings, Structures was indebted to NAC in an amount exceeding the funds in dispute in this action, under the various financing arrangements governed by the Loan and Security Agreement and related documents.

At the time it instituted bankruptcy proceedings, Structures also was indebted to the other plaintiff in this action, Mitsubishi International Corporation. For some period prior to April 1976, Mitsubishi had been selling steel products to Concrete Structures on open account. Concrete Structures fell behind in its payments on this account and in April 1976, it issued a note promising to pay Mitsubishi the sum of $210,415.20 by July 23, 1976, according to a schedule of payments established in the note. However, Concrete Structures soon failed to meet this schedule of payments and on June 1, 1976, Concrete Structures and Mitsubishi entered into a security agreement to secure "payment and performance of all liabilities and obligations of [Concrete Structures] to [Mitsubishi] of any kind and description, direct or indirect, absolute or contingent, due or to become due, now existing or hereafter arising and howsoever evidenced or acquired and whether joint, several or joint and several. * * *" Under this security agreement, which was duly perfected by the recording of a financing statement, Mitsubishi acquired a security interest in:

> (a) Debtor's inventory including all goods and merchandise, raw materials, goods in process, finished goods, goods in transit now owned or hereafter acquired and the proceeds thereof.

> (b) Debtor's accounts receivable and notes receivable and contract rights including all sais [sic] accounts [sic] receivable and notes receivable and contract rights outstanding as of this date and all future accounts receivable and notes receivable, and contract rights and proceeds thereof.[1]

As of June 30, 1978, Structures remained indebted to Mitsubishi in the amount of $278,298.65, exclusive of interest.

In December 1977, Concrete Structures opened several deposit accounts with Virginia Capital Bank, including accounts 010–716–6 and 010–722–0, the two accounts at issue in this litigation. Thereafter, on March 21, 1978, the Bank loaned Concrete Structures $40,249.92, payable in installments over a two-year period. The Bank took as security nineteen vehicles listed in an accompanying security agreement. On April 4, 1978, the Bank made a demand loan of $12,000 to Concrete Structures. This loan was unsecured. A third loan, in the amount of $50,000, was made by the Bank on or about April 27, 1978,[2] to refinance an outstanding loan previously made to Concrete Erectors, Inc., a subsidiary of Structures. The Bank concedes that, although this April 27 loan ostensibly was secured by an interest in the accounts receivable of Concrete Erectors, this security interest was never perfected.

Almost immediately Structures encountered difficulty in meeting its obligations to the Bank under the terms of these loans. Beginning on June 1, 1978, Structures' impending insolvency

---

1. In a later subordination agreement between Mitsubishi and the other plaintiff, National Acceptance Company of America (NAC), Mitsubishi's security interest in inventory and in accounts and contract rights, both present and future, arising from the sale of concrete blocks manufactured by Concrete Structures was subordinated to NAC's security interest. This subordination agreement was entered into in October 1977 and was perfected on December 8, 1977.

2. While the plaintiffs urge that this loan was made not to Concrete Structures, but to a sister corporation, Concrete Erectors, we need not decide this question in light of our holding which is dispositive of the issues presented even if it is assumed that this loan was attributable to Concrete Structures.

became apparent, and without notice to or the authorization of the plaintiffs, the Bank made the following debits to Structures' deposit accounts to satisfy that company's remaining indebtedness under the loans:

Account No. 010–716–6

6/1/78	$10,000.00	
6/5/78	5,000.00	
6/6/78	5,000.00	
6/7/78	22,829.94	
6/16/78	6,151.67	
6/19/78	5,505.53	
	$54,487.14	$54,487.14

Account No. 010–722–0

6/12/78	$ 6,000.00	
6/19/78	18,840.62	
	$24,840.62	$24,840.62
Total		$79,327.76

There is no dispute that the entire balance of these accounts at the time of these set-offs was attributable to funds derived from cash sales of inventory, collections of accounts receivable, or funds wired by NAC to Structures pursuant to their loan agreements.

Actuated in part by this drain of its operating funds, Structures filed a petition for an arrangement under Chapter XI of the Bankruptcy Act on or about June 29, 1978. The Bank received notice of these proceedings and was listed as a general creditor of Structures. In connection with these bankruptcy proceedings, the plaintiffs entered into an Inter-Creditor Agreement, approved by the Bankruptcy Court, in which the plaintiffs agreed upon a plan for sharing any proceeds of certain of Structures' pre-bankruptcy accounts which might be collected in this litigation.

On July 19, 1979, NAC brought the present action, contending that the funds in the accounts set-off by the Bank represented identifiable proceeds of collateral secured by its loan and security agreement with Structures, that its security interest expressly extended to these proceeds and was superior to any interest of the Bank, and that it was entitled to these funds by reason of Structures' default on its obligations to NAC evidenced by its petition in bankruptcy. Mitsubishi later intervened also alleging that it had a prior security interest in the proceeds deposited in the accounts set-off by the Bank, and that it was entitled to these funds by reason of Structures' default. The Complaints demanded return of the sums and that judgment be entered against the Bank for the amount of the funds appropriated from these accounts by the

Bank, plus interest from the dates of the set-offs. The Complaints also seek punitive damages and an award of attorney's fees.

The first point we must consider is whether the plaintiffs had a security interest in the funds set-off by the Bank. There is not much question that the funds in the accounts did not fall within the first generation of collateral listed in the various security agreements. Therefore, these funds could be covered by these agreements only if found to be proceeds of the enumerated collateral. "Proceeds," as defined by section 9–306(1) of the Uniform Commercial Code includes "whatever is received upon the sale, exchange, collection or other disposition of collateral or proceeds." This definition is to be given a flexible and broad content.

[The court found the funds to be identifiable proceeds.]

We come now to the key issue in this action: whether the Bank's right of set-off was subordinate to the plaintiffs' security interest in the proceeds deposited in Structures' deposit accounts. In this diversity action, the answer to this issue is, of course, governed by the law of Virginia. Virginia law long ago recognized the common-law right of a bank, as a debtor of its depositors, to set-off a matured debt owed to the bank by a depositor against funds on deposit. * * * Although often referred to as a "banker's lien," this right of set-off is not properly a lien upon a depositor's account. Rather, it is "a mere right of the bank to retain in its own possession property the title of which (absolute or special) is, or, in the case of negotiable paper, purports to be, in one against whom the bank has some demand until that demand is satisfied." Nolting v. National Bank of Va., 99 Va. 54, 60–61, 37 S.E. 804, 806 (1901), quoting, 1 Morse, Banks, § 323. This right, however, is not absolute. Virginia adheres to the majority rule that if the bank can be charged with knowledge of the interest of a third party in a deposit account, or notice of facts sufficient to put it on inquiry that such an interest exists, it may not apply the account to satisfy a debt owed by the depositor. * * * If called upon to evaluate this case under the common-law doctrine of set-off in Virginia, therefore we would be put to the task of determining whether the Bank had either actual knowledge of the plaintiffs' interests in Structures' deposit accounts, or notice of facts sufficient to put the Bank to a further inquiry as to the existence of such interests.

It is not clear, however, whether this common-law approach to the present priority issue has been altered by Virginia's adoption of Article 9 of the Uniform Commercial Code, which establishes a comprehensive scheme of rules governimg secured transactions and the relative dignity of conflicting interests in collateral. Section 9-104(i) of the Code states:

This title does not apply * * * to any right of set-off.
* * *

Two views of this language have been espoused. Several jurisdictions have held that this exclusion was intended to indicate only that a right of set-off arises under state law as a result of the parties' status, without regard to compliance with the Code, and not that an otherwise extant right of set-off is exempt from Article 9's rules concerning priority of interests in collateral. * * * These courts find support for this conclusion in the remarks of a principal reporter of Article 9, Professor G. Gilmore, who has stated the following view of this exclusion:

> This exclusion is an apt example of the absurdities which result when draftsmen attempt to appease critics by putting into a statute something that is not in any sense wicked but is hopelessly irrelevant. Of course a right of set-off is not a security interest and has never been confused with one: the statute might as appropriately exclude fan dancing. A bank's right of set-off against a depositor's account is often loosely referred to as a "banker's lien," but the "lien" usage has never led anyone to think that the bank held a security interest in the bank account. Banking groups were, however, concerned lest someone, someday, might think that a bank's right of set-off, because it was called a lien, was a security interest. Hence the exclusion, which does no harm except to the dignity and self-respect of the draftsmen.

This position could also be supported by reference to section 9–306(4) of the Code which provides in pertinent part:

> (4) In the event of insolvency proceedings instituted by or against a debtor, a secured party with a perfected security interest in proceeds has a perfected security interest only in the following proceeds:
>
> * * *
>
> (d) in all cash and deposit accounts of the debtor, in which proceeds have been commingled with other funds, but the perfected security interest under this paragraph (d) is
>
> (i) subject to any right of setoff * * *.

Arguably, this provision would be unnecessary if the relative priority of any right of set-off was unaffected by Article 9 because all perfected security interests, and not merely those recognized under section 9–306(4)(d), would be equally "subject to any right of setoff." [5]

---

5. Section 9–306(4)(d)(i) does not create a right of set-off. Rather, it continues any right of set-off which might otherwise exist under prior state law. * * * This section, however, is not applicable in this case. That exception applies only "in the event of insolvency proceedings." The present proceedings, while occasioned by Structures' insolvency, are not insolvency proceedings, defined at section 1–201(22) of the Code, as "any assignment for the benefit of creditors or other proceedings intended to liquidate or rehabilitate the estate of the person involved." * * *

Further support could be found in another exclusion under section 9–104(h) which provides:

> This title does not apply * * * to a right represented by a judgment (other than a judgment taken on a right to payment which was collateral. * * *

The priority of a judgment lien creditor's interest in secured property clearly is governed by the various priority rules of Article 9, notwithstanding this exclusion. See, e.g., U.C.C. § 9–301(1)(b) (stating that an unperfected security interest is subordinate to the rights of a lien creditor without knowledge of the security interest and before it is perfected).

Other jurisdictions and commentators have disagreed with this interpretation of section 9–104(i), declaring instead that this provision renders inapplicable not only those portions of Article 9 governing the creation of security interests, but also the various priority provisions of that Article. * * *

Other indications as to the scope of the exclusion of rights of setoff, may be gleaned from several sources in the commentary accompanying Article 9. The first such indication is found in the Official Comment to section 9–101, the first sentence of which states:

> This Article sets out a comprehensive scheme for the regulation of *security interests* in personal property and fixtures.

As noted above, a bank's right of set-off is not a "security interest" within the meaning of Article 9, leaving one to speculate that interests in property other than security interests are beyond the scope of all portions of Article 9. See also U.C.C. § 1–201(37) (defining "security interest" as "an interest in personal property or fixtures which secures payment or performance of an obligation"). That this distinction between security interests and the interest such as that represented by rights of set-off underlies the exclusion of set-off rights from Article 9 under section 9–104(i) is confirmed by paragraph 8 of the Official Comment to section 9–104, which states:

> The remaining exclusions go to other types of claims which do not customarily serve as commercial collateral: judgments under paragraph (h), *set-offs under paragraph (i)* and tort claims under paragraph (k).

No Virginia case has been uncovered aligning that jurisdiction with either of these two schools of thought concerning the scope of section 9–104(i). Nor is any decisive interpretive guidance provided by the Virginia Comments to that provision or other portions of Article 9. It is fortunate, therefore, that this Federal Court is not called upon to resolve this ambiguity of state law in this action, for the result we would reach under either interpretation is the same: The set-off accomplished by the Bank was improper and constituted a conversion of the property of at least one of the plaintiffs, NAC. We need not go further and decide whether it also constituted a conversion of property in which Mitsubishi had a superior interest. The security interest of each of the plaintiffs in the deposit accounts exceeded the amount set-off by the Bank. In view of their October 1978, Inter-Creditor Agreement as to the distribution of certain proceeds collected by NAC in this action, and the subordination agreement previously entered into by the plaintiffs, it is sufficient to determine that NAC's interest prevails, leaving it to the plaintiffs to distribute the proceeds in accordance with their agreement.

As stated previously, NAC possessed a perfected security interest in all of the funds set-off by the Bank, while the Bank's position was that of an unsecured general creditor. If we were to follow the lead of those jurisdictions which have narrowly construed section 9–104(i) of the Code, our decision in this case would be governed by the cornerstone principle underlying the Code's complex priority scheme, stated in section 9–201:

> Except as otherwise provided by this act a security agreement is effective according to its terms between the parties, against purchasers of the collateral and against creditors.

This section states the fundamental rule that "the secured creditor, even an unperfected secured creditor, has greater rights in his collateral than any other creditor unless Article Nine provides otherwise." White & Summers, Handbook of the Law Under the Uniform Commercial Code 901 (1972). There being nothing in Article 9 providing otherwise, the Bank's unsecured interest would be subordinate to the secured interest of NAC.   *   *   *

Alternatively, were we to conclude that section 9–104(i) precludes application of any portion of Article 9 to this controversy, we are persuaded that the Bank was sufficiently aware of NAC's interest in the deposit accounts to prohibit it from appropriating the funds from those accounts to satisfy its own claims.

At the time the deposit accounts were opened at the Bank, principals of Structures disclosed to the Bank's President, Harry Grymes, that various amounts of money would be wired into these accounts by NAC, pursuant to an accounts receivable financing arrangement. At least some aspects of this financing arrangement were conveyed to Mr. Grymes at a later meeting between he, Jack Lacy, Chief Administrative Officer of Structures, and Hyman Kanes, a former executive officer of NAC. While NAC's security interests may not have been specifically mentioned at these meetings, Mr. Grymes clearly was acquainted with the relations between NAC and Structures and the source of at least some of the funds deposited in the accounts, wired by NAC. Mr. Grymes conceded that he knew of these arrangements in his testimony.

The Bank's Cashier, Richard Wyatt, who worked closely with Mr. Grymes on the Structures' accounts and loans, testified that he knew in the early part of 1978, prior to the dates of the set-offs, that funds were being wired to Structures' accounts, and that there was a strong likelihood that these funds arose from an accounts receivable financing arrangement. Mr. Wyatt explained that he understood the mechanics of accounts receivable financing, and that he suspected that there were security agreements supporting the financing arrangement between Structures and NAC.

Notwithstanding this knowledge, Bank officials made the various loans later satisfied by set-offs without any effort to search the appropriate records to determine whether any security agreements or financing statements had been filed covering Structures' assets by NAC or any other entity. Such a search would have uncovered the interests held by both plaintiffs. Nor did it take the logical step of inquiring of Structures' officers whether any such security agreement existed and whether any interest in funds in the accounts had been conveyed to Structures' other creditors. The Bank failed even to ascertain whether its own purported security interests taken to secure payment of these loans had been properly perfected.

In short, the Bank chose to ignore evidence which would have led a reasonable man to conclude that the funds deposited in the deposit accounts were encumbered by the liens of third parties, or at least to inquire whether such interests existed. This knowledge or notice was sufficient to preclude any right of set-off it might otherwise have had and rendered its actions unlawful under Virginia commonlaw. See Peoples Nat. Bank v. Coleman, supra; Federal Reserve Bank v. State & City Bank, supra.

For these reasons, we conclude that the Bank converted property belonging to NAC when it set-off $79,327.76 from Structures' deposit accounts numbered 010–716–6 and 010–722–0 in June 1978, and that these funds must be returned to NAC. For the reasons stated previously, we need not decide whether the Bank had knowledge or notice of Mitsubishi's interest in these accounts.

* * *

NOTE

The principal case was affirmed in part and reversed in part and remanded in 673 F.2d 1314 (4th Cir. 1981), an unpublished opinion. A portion of the opinion appears in 32 UCC Rep.Serv. 987. The opinion does not discuss the setoff issue. The Court of Appeals decided that certain of the funds in the bank account that the District Court had treated as proceeds were not proceeds.

M. FEDERAL TAX LIENS

PLUMB, FEDERAL TAX LIENS
Pp. 10–11 (3d ed. 1972)

Circumstances Under Which, and Time When, a Lien Comes into Being

Taxpayer's possible ignorance of lien's existence.—It is quite possible that a financially troubled taxpayer, who has deferred payment of an assessed tax, will not know whether or when a tax lien has been imposed upon all of his property. This is because, initially, the general tax lien is usually of the *secret* variety. It arises automatically on the occurrence of certain events and without notification to the taxpayer. Eventually, in one of the Government's written demands for payment, the delinquent taxpayer will be informed of the Government's power to file notice of a lien. But before that, the secret lien has become firmly entrenched and no mention is made of this by the Government. Even if the latter does later file notice of this lien in an appropriate office, a copy of that notice will not usually be forwarded to the taxpayer, though it is quite possible that a collection officer will call it to his attention in the course of subsequent negotiations for payment.

Formalities which "trigger" a lien: In general.—The fact that the Government may or may not file a *notice* of its lien in appropriate public records has nothing whatever to do with the validity of the lien against the taxpayer himself. With a so-called secret lien, the Government's rights against the taxpayer's property will be preserved against all but subsequent purchasers, mechanic's lienors, judgment lien creditors, and holders of security interests. (Int.Rev.Code of 1954, § 6323 [26 U.S.C.A.] ed.)

As against the taxpayer and creditors who fail to measure up to the standards just described, it is only essential to the creation of a valid lien that the taxpayer "neglects or refuses to pay * * * after demand." (Int.Rev.Code of 1954, § 6321 [26 U.S.C.A.] ed.) If these two requirements were met, the lien—arising because of the neglect or refusal to pay after demand—relates back to the earlier assessment date. The assessment itself was the only essential formal prerequisite to an otherwise valid demand.

In the following problem and case we examine the conflict between federal tax liens and Article 9 security interests. The subject is governed by the Federal Tax Lien Act.

PROBLEM

On October 1 Debtor and Bank entered into a security agreement in which Debtor granted to Bank a security interest in all its inventory, accounts, and equipment, then owned or thereafter acquired, and all proceeds thereof. The agreement contained an optional future advances clause. Bank filed a proper financing statement on October 1 and advanced $10,000 at that time. The Government filed a notice of tax lien on November 1; Bank had no actual knowledge of the tax lien at any time relevant to this problem. On November 10 and December 27, Debtor assigned newly acquired accounts to Bank, and on each occasion Bank advanced $10,000. Debtor's inventory continued to turn over after November 1 at the normal rate and its value was about the same throughout the period relevant to this problem. Debtor acquired new equipment on November 10 and December 27. What are the priorities as between the Government and Bank with respect to Debtor's inventory, accounts, and equipment? Int.Rev.Code § 6323(c) and (d). On the priority as between optional future advances and judgment liens, see § 9–301(4). How would your answer to the priorities problem differ if Bank had failed to file a financing statement? See Int.Rev.Code § 6323(h)(1) for the definition of "security interest." Consider the following case.

TEXAS OIL & GAS CORP. v. UNITED STATES
United States Court of Appeals, Fifth Circuit, 1972.
466 F.2d 1040.

GOLDBERG, CIRCUIT JUDGE.

We enter with some trepidation the tortured meanderings of federal tax lien law, intersected now by the somewhat smoother byway of the Uniform Commercial Code. Standing at this vantage-point in the instant case, we must decide the disposition of a fund of the taxpayer-debtor's accounts receivable that is claimed both by the Government under its tax lien authority and by the lender under the aegis of the Uniform Commercial Code. Amendments to the tax lien statutes in 1966 give us some shelter in our decision; under this lien-to we conclude that the tax lien must take priority over the claim of the private lien holder, and we affirm the judgment of the lower court, D.C., 340 F.Supp. 409.

The real parties in interest in this appeal are the Pecos Bank and the Internal Revenue Service. The nominal appellant Texas Oil & Gas Corporation, is merely the stakeholder in an interpleader action to determine the allocation of competing claims against $14,690.10, which Texas Oil & Gas admittedly owes for services rendered by the taxpayer, Hilton R. Blackmon, d/b/a Blackie's Oil & Gas Field Services. Internal Revenue's claim to the fund is based upon federal tax liens duly filed against the taxpayer in Pecos County, Texas, on February 27, 1970, for almost $55,000 in unpaid withholding and FICA taxes assessed in 1969. See 26 U.S. C.A. §§ 6321, 6323(f).

Pecos Bank claims an interest in the fund by virtue of a security agreement between the bank and taxpayer-debtor executed on March 25, 1967, and duly filed and perfected on March 29, 1967. * * * Pursuant to that security agreement the bank agreed to advance money at various times to the taxpayer-debtor in exchange for a security interest in taxpayer-debtor's accounts receivable.[1] As is frequently the case in so-called "open" agreements, the amount of money to be loaned and the times at which the money was to be advanced were not specified in the contract. See 26 U.S.C.A. § 6323(c)(4), relating to obligatory disbursement agreements. Under the contract the lender's eventual acquisition of the accounts receivable were uncertain, contingent upon the performance of services by the taxpayer-debtor. The bank's security interest, however, attached automatically to any new accounts receivable without additional filing or perfection required by the bank. UCC § 9–204. Taxpayer agreed to factor his accounts receivable with the bank as soon as the accounts receivable arose in consideration for the loans. The bank continued to make loans and to factor taxpayer's accounts receivable under the agreement until October 15, 1970. Taxpayer-debtor completed his services to the plaintiff, Texas Oil & Gas, during the months of September, October, and November of 1970, apparently pursuant to a contract entered into in September.

During December of 1969 and January of 1970, the Government assessed federal withholding and FICA liabilities against Blackie's for the preceding tax year, 1969. A tax lien notice was duly filed on February 27, 1970, and the United States attempted to enforce part of its lien by serving notice of levy on Texas Oil & Gas. The bank first became aware of the tax lien on October 22, 1970, and shortly thereafter served notice on Texas Oil & Gas that it too claimed Blackie's accounts receivable. This interpleader action by Texas Oil & Gas followed. F.R.Civ.Proc. 22.

Tax liens have had a mixed history in the law. See generally Coogan, "The Effect of the Federal Tax Lien Act of 1966 Upon Security Interests Created Under the Uniform Commercial Code," 81 Harv.L.Rev. 1369 (1968); United States v. Vermont, 2 Cir.1963,

---

1. The agreement between taxpayer-debtor and the bank provides for a continuing security interest in "[a]ll accounts, contract rights, chattel paper, instruments, general intangibles and rights to payment of every kind now or at any time hereafter arising out of the business of the debtor; all interest of the debtor in any goods, the sale or lease of which shall have given or shall give rise to any of the foregoing."

317 F.2d 246 (Friendly, J.), aff'd, 1964, 377 U.S. 351, 84 S.Ct. 1267, 12 L.Ed.2d 370. For the past two decades, however, the federal tax lien has held the upper hand in its battles with competing private liens. The genesis of that advantage, as it applies to the instant case, appears to be United States v. Security Trust & Savings Bank, 1950, 340 U.S. 47, 71 S.Ct. 111, 95 L.Ed. 53. Prior to Security Trust, the courts had carved out a doctrine concerning the priority granted to a federal tax lien in competition with a private lien in situations in which the taxpayer-debtor was insolvent. 31 U.S.C.A. § 191.[2] Under the tax lien law as it developed for insolvent taxpayer-debtors, a private lien competing with a federal tax lien had to be "choate" and perfected. See Spokane County v. United States, 1929, 279 U.S. 80, 49 S.Ct. 321, 73 L.Ed. 621; see generally Kennedy, "The Relative Priority of the Federal Government: The Pernicious Career of the Inchoate and General Lien," 63 Yale L.J. 905 (1954); Kennedy, "From Spokane to Vermont: The Campaign of the Federal Government Against the Inchoate Lien," 50 Iowa L.Rev. 724 (1965). Choateness, a concept entirely court-made, see Plumb, "Federal Liens and Priorities-Agenda for the Next Decade," 77 Yale L.J. 228, 230 (1967), requires that the private lien holder establish the identity of the lienor, the property subject to the lien, and the fixed amount of the lien. See, e.g., United States v. New Britain, 1953, 347 U.S. 81, 74 S.Ct. 367, 98 L.Ed. 520; United States v. Pioneer American Insurance Co., 1963, 374 U.S. 84, 83 S.Ct. 1651, 10 L.Ed.2d 770. The choateness requirement has generally been harsh in insolvency situations. See, e.g., United States v. Gilbert Associates, Inc., 1953, 345 U.S. 361, 73 S.Ct. 701, 97 L.Ed. 1071, where the Supreme Court indicated that only possession or reduction to judgment would allow a private lien to prevail over a competing federal tax lien. But United States v. Security Trust, supra, marked the first time in which the Supreme Court applied the choateness doctrine to a competing lien situation in which the debtor was not insolvent. And in United States v. R.F. Ball Construction Co., 1958, 355 U.S. 587, 78 S.Ct. 442, 2 L.Ed.2d 510, the Supreme Court applied its choateness doctrine to a situation in which the private lien, an assignment of sums due for performance of a subcontract which was competing with a federal tax lien, had been created entirely by contract between private parties. See especially United States v. R.F. Ball, supra (Whittaker, J., dissenting), and United States v. Pioneer American Insurance Co., 1963, 374 U.S. 84, 83 S.Ct. 1651, 10 L.Ed.2d 770, for an explanation of the rather abbreviated opinion of the majority in United States v. R.F. Ball, supra.[3] Prior to Ball the choateness doctrine had been applied

2. This statute is generally known as R.S. 3466 even though it is part of the Code.

3. "The Court has never held that mortgagees [under section 6323(a)] face a less demanding test of perfection than other interests when competing with a federal lien. Indeed United States v. R.F. Ball Constr. Co. . . . stands for just the contrary." United States v.

only to statutory liens or to liens created by attachment or garnishment. At the same time that the Supreme Court was extending the perimeters of the types of private liens that were subject to the choateness doctrine, it also gave some indication that the doctrine would not operate as severely when applied to the private liens newly-added to the choateness test as it had when applied to federal priority under the insolvency statute. See United States v. New Britain, supra; Coogan, 81 Harv.L.Rev. at 1378–1379. Even for that proposition, however, there is some conflicting authority from the Supreme Court. In United States v. White Bear Brewing Co., 1956, 350 U.S. 1010, 76 S.Ct. 646, 100 L.Ed. 871, a majority of the Supreme Court reversed a lower court conclusion that a federal tax lien did not have priority over a statutory mechanics' lien " * * * even though the mechanics' lien was specific, prior in time, perfected in the sense that everything possible under state law had been done to make it choate, and was being enforced before the federal tax lien arose." United States v. White Bear Brewing, 350 U.S. at 1010, 76 S.Ct. at 646, 100 L.Ed. at 871 (Douglas, J., dissenting). Two later opinions appear to reaffirm the intimation in United States v. R.F. Ball, supra, that the choateness tests were not so severe for liens arising under section 6321 as they were for liens arising under R.S. 3466. See Crest Finance Co. v. United States, 1961, 368 U.S. 347, 82 S.Ct. 384, 7 L.Ed.2d 342, and United States v. Vermont, 1964, 377 U.S. 351, 84 S.Ct. 1267, 12 L.Ed.2d 370.

Against this historical background Congress in 1966 amended the tax lien provisions of section 6323 in a number of ways. The amendments are:

> " * * * in part an attempt to conform the lien provisions of the internal revenue laws to the concepts developed in this Uniform Commercial Code. It represents an effort to adjust the provisions in the internal revenue laws relating to the collection of taxes of delinquent persons to the more recent developments in commercial practice (permitted and protected under State law) and to deal with a multitude of technical problems which have arisen over the past 50 years."

S.Rep. No. 1708, 89th Cong., 2d Sess. (1966); see also H.R.Rep. No. 1884, 89th Cong., 2d Sess., U.S.Code Cong. & Admin.News, p. 3722 (1966). We must construe but a small part of these amendments for purposes of this appeal, primarily the amendments to section 6323(c).[5]

Pioneer American Insurance Co., 374 U.S. at 89, 83 S.Ct. at 1656, 10 L.Ed.2d at 775.

5. "(c) *Protection for certain commercial transactions financing agreements, etc.—*

(1) *In general.*—To the extent provided in this subsection, even though notice of a lien imposed by section 6321 has been filed, such lien shall not be valid with respect to a security interest which came into existence after tax lien filing but which—

The parties have submitted their own theories of this case, and we find ourselves in the not too unusual position of rejecting large parts of both theories. It is the Government's general position, as we understand it, that the usual tests of choateness in non-insolvency situations would operate to give priority to the tax lien. The bank attempts to turn elements of the choateness doctrine back on the Government. It argues that taxpayer-debtor's accounts receivable became subject to the liens of the bank and of the Government at the same time. In effect, the bank concedes that it does not come within the protective perimeters of section 6323(c), but it contends that it should divide the accounts receivable with the Government upon a mathematical formula consonant with its own theory of simultaneous attachment.

The tax lien statute itself narrows the issue in this appeal considerably. Section 6323(c), truncated somewhat, provides that a section 6321 lien " * * * shall not be valid with respect to a security interest which came into existence after tax lien filing but which * * * is in qualified property covered by the terms of a written agreement entered into before tax lien filing and constituting * * * a commercial transactions financing agreement * * * and * * * is protected under local law against a judg-

(A) is in qualified property covered by the terms of a written agreement entered into before tax lien filing and constituting—

   (i) a commercial transactions financing agreement,

   (ii) a real property construction or improvement financing agreement, or

   (iii) an obligatory disbursement agreement, and

(B) is protected under local law against a judgment lien arising, as of the time of tax lien filing, out of an unsecured obligation.

(2) *Commercial transactions financing agreement.*—For purposes of this subsection—

(A) *Definition.*—The term 'commercial transactions financing agreement' means an agreement (entered into by a person in the course of his trade or business)—

   (i) to make loans to the taxpayer to be secured by commercial financing security acquired by the taxpayer in the ordinary course of his trade or business, or

   (ii) to purchase commercial financing security (other than inventory) acquired by the taxpayer in the ordinary course of his trade or business; but such an agreement shall be treated as coming within the term only to the extent that such loan or purchase is made before the 46th day after the date of tax lien filing or (if earlier) before the lender or purchaser had actual notice or knowledge of such tax lien filing.

(B) *Limitation on qualified property.*—The term 'qualified property', when used with respect to a commercial transactions financing agreement, includes only commercial financing security acquired by the taxpayer before the 46th day after the date of tax lien filing.

(C) *Commercial financing security defined.*—The term 'commercial financing security' means (i) paper of a kind ordinarily arising in commercial transactions, (ii) accounts receivable, (iii) mortgage on real property, and (iv) inventory.

(D) *Purchaser treated as acquiring security interest.*—A person who satisfies subparagraph (A) by reason of clause (ii) thereof shall be treated as having acquired a security interest in commercial financing security.

    * * * ''

26 U.S.C.A. § 6323(c).

ment lien arising, as of the time of tax lien filing, out of an unsecured obligation." "Security interest" is defined generally for section 6323 by section 6323(h)(1):

> *"Definitions.*—For purposes of this section and section 6324—

> (1) Security interest.—The term 'security interest' means any interest in property acquired by contract for the purpose of securing payment or performance of an obligation or indemnifying against loss or liability. A security interest exists at any time (A) if, at such time, the property is in existence and the interest has become protected under local law against a subsequent judgment lien arising out of an unsecured obligation, and (B) to the extent that, at such time, the holder has parted with money or money's worth."

However, section 6323(c)(1) appears to have qualified that general definition. Unlike the "security interest" contemplated by section 6323(h)(1)(A), a section 6323(c) interest need not always be "in existence" at the standard point-in-time reference to "existence" of section 6323(h)(1)(A), for section 6323(c) by its terms contemplates certain limited types of property acquired after the point-in-time reference, which is "as of the time of tax lien filing" for purposes of section 6323(c)(1)(B). A security interest cannot be "perfected" until it "attaches," UCC § 9–303, and the interest cannot attach prior to the time that the "debtor has rights in the collateral," UCC § 9–204(1). By definition, the debtor in section 6323(c) situations often does not attain "rights in the collateral" until after the tax lien filing, and it is to that problem that section 6323(c) directs its attention. See Young, "Priority of the Federal Tax Lien," 34 U.Chi.L.Rev. 723 (1967); Coogan, 81 Harv.L.Rev. at 1397, 1404–1405; but cf. United States v. Strollo, 67–1 U.S.Tax. Cas. 83,162 (Fla.Dist.Ct.App.1966), where it appears that a security interest in the after-acquired property in question (contract rights) did not attach immediately under the existing (pre-Uniform Commercial Code) Florida law. In addition, to qualify as a "security interest" under section 6323(h)(1)(A) and section 6323(c)(1)(B), the security interest must be "protected under local law against a subsequent judgment lien arising out of an unsecured obligation." The phrase "protected against a judgment lien" is not a term of art easily adaptable to the sometimes equally unartful language of the Uniform Commercial Code. See Hearings before the House Ways and Means Comm. on H.R. 11256 and H.R. 11290, 89th Cong., 2d Sess. (1966), for a suggested alternative to the present "judgment lien" test; cf. Mellinkoff, "The Language of the Uniform Commercial Code," 77 Yale L.J. 185 (1967). In the context of section 6323(c), however, "protected against a judgment lien" does not raise the problems that might occur in other sections of the tax lien amendments. See, e.g., 26 U.S.C.A. § 6323(d); Coogan, 81 Harv.L.Rev. 1369, supra; Plumb, 77 Yale L.J. 228, supra. A security interest in after-acquired accounts receivable "is perfected when it has attached," UCC § 9–303, and the interest attaches automatically if the lender has taken "all of the applicable steps required for perfection" under UCC § 9–302 to § 9–306. At the same time, a perfected security interest "is protected by local law" against a person who does not become "a lien creditor * * * before it [the security interest] is perfected," UCC § 9–301(1)(b).[6] Because a judgment creditor, like a secured creditor, cannot attach his lien to the debtor's after-acquired accounts receivable until the accounts receivable come into existence regardless of whether he has taken all the necessary actions for perfection under state law, the judgment lien could not possibly become perfected *before* the security holder's interest becomes perfected. At the most, the judgment lien could become perfected at the same time that the security interest becomes perfected, but that circumstance does not alter the security holder's priority under the Uniform Commercial Code.[7]

The agreement in question in the instant case was also a "commercial transactions financing agreement" contemplated by section 6323(c)(2)(A)(i) of the 1966 amendments:

> "[A]n agreement (entered into by a person in the course of his trade or business)—

> (i) to make loans to taxpayer to be secured by commercial financing security acquired by the taxpayer in the ordinary course of his trade or business * * *"

However, the protection given to a private lien in competition with a Government tax lien for after-acquired property secured pursuant to a non-obligatory disbursement agreement is a limited protection. Congress was understandably unwilling, as a general proposition, to allow a taxpayer-debtor to lock in his property for an indefinite period of time pursuant to a security agreement for advances that he could draw upon a will. Section 6323(c), as amended, represents the limited exceptions to that general proposition in the context of the courts' choateness doctrines:

---

6. A so-called judgment lien is not a term specifically contemplated by the Uniform Commercial Code, see UCC § 9–104(h). But the judgment lien, as a standard against which a security interest competing with a federal tax lien is measured by section 6323, is properly analogous to a "lien creditor" if the judgment holder has actually acquired a lien under applicable state law:

"A 'lien creditor' means a creditor who has acquired a lien on the property involved by attachment, levy or the like. * * *"

UCC § 9–301(3).

7. Under Texas law it is possible that a judgment lien could attach automatically upon entry of judgment to property existing prior to the date of judgment on which a writ of attachment had been levied. See Tex.Stat. Ann. Art. 300; Midway National Bank of Grand Prairie v. West Texas Wholesale Co., 447 S.W.2d 709 (Tex.Civ.App. 1969). The writ of attachment, however, cannot be levied upon after-acquired property. See Tex.Stat.Ann. Art. 288; Smith & Co. v. Whitfield, 67 Tex. 124, 2 S.W. 822 (1887); Shaw v. Frank, 334 S.W.2d 476 (Tex.Civ.App.1959). See also Miss.Code Ann. § 1555.

"[S]uch an agreement shall be treated as coming within the term [commercial transactions financing agreement] only to the extent that such loan or purchase is made before the 46th day after the date of the tax lien filing or (if earlier) before the lender or purchaser had actual notice or knowledge of such tax lien filing."

26 U.S.C.A. § 6323(c)(2); see section 6323(c)(4) with regard to funds advanced and property secured pursuant to obligatory disbursement agreements. Based on the above language alone, there is a position intermediate between that argued by the bank and that advanced by the Government, namely, that the bank would maintain a priority over the Government tax lien for property acquired after the filing of the tax lien but acquired pursuant to loans actually advanced prior to or within 45 days after the filing of the tax lien. For funds advanced after the 45 day period, the Government would take priority. Such a reading of section 6323(c)(4) would allow a commercial lender to claim only collateral for which it actually disbursed funds within the 45 day time period after the filing of the tax lien, thus preventing a security agreement on after-acquired property that might allow the commercial lender to take an infinite security interest in after-acquired property by contracting for a large paper loan and for protracted actual advancing of the loan funds. The history of the statute however, will not support that reading.

It appears clear that Congress contemplated not only that the funds must actually be advanced prior to or within 45 days of the filing of the tax lien, but also that the secured property must be "acquired" within that period:

"The term 'qualified property', when used with respect to a commercial transactions financing agreement, includes only commercial financing security *acquired* by the taxpayer before the 46th day after the date of tax lien filing."

26 U.S.C.A. § 6323(c)(2)(B) [emphasis added]. The Senate Finance Committee in reporting the 1966 amendments concluded that " * * * protection is afforded only where the loan or purchase is made not later than 45 days after the tax lien filing * * * and only where the * * * accounts receivable * * * are *acquired* before the 45 days have elapsed." S.Rep. No. 1708, supra, U.S. Code Cong. & Admin.News, p. 3729 (1966) [emphasis added]. Although it is not clear from the record whether the bank in the instant case had actually advanced funds to the taxpayer-debtor within the 45 day "grace" period, it is undisputed that none of the accounts receivable came into existence prior to April 13, 1970, 45 days after the filing of the tax lien.

Arguably, the bank could claim that its security interest was "acquired" when the loan agreement was reached. See 2 G. Gilmore, Security Interests in Personal Property § 45.5 (1965). In order to maintain that argument, however, the lender would have to contend that at the time of the tax lien filing "the debtor [had] rights in the collateral" in the present, even though the security itself might exist only in the future. UCC § 9–204(1). This problem, of course, ultimately relates to the choateness doctrine as it applies to the instant case.

The Supreme Court has maintained the integrity of the choateness doctrine, such as it is, throughout a number of amendments to the tax lien statutes:

> "The predecessor to § 6323 was first enacted by Congress in 1912 in order to protect mortgagees, purchasers and judgment creditors against a secret lien for assessed taxes and to postpone the effectiveness of the tax lien as against these interests until the tax lien was filed. H.R.Rep. No. 1018, 62nd Cong., 2d Sess. [An amendment prompted, it appears, by the Supreme Court's decision in United States v. Snyder, 1892, 149 U.S. 210, 13 S.Ct. 846, 37 L.Ed. 705]. The section dealt with the federal lien only and it did not purport to affect the time at which local liens were deemed to arise or to become choate or to subordinate the tax lien to tentative, conditional or imperfect state liens. Rather, we believe Congress intended that if out of the whole spectrum of state-created liens, certain liens are to enjoy the preferred status granted by § 6323, they should at least have attained the degree of perfection required of other liens *and be choate for the purpose of the federal rule.*"

United States v. Pioneer American Insurance Co., 1963, 374 U.S. 84, 89, 83 S.Ct. 1651, 1655, 10 L.Ed.2d 770, 775 [emphasis added]. It is settled law that the " * * * effect of a [state-created] lien in relation to a provision of federal law for the collection of debts owing the United States is always a federal question," whether or not the state law would classify the private lien as specific and perfected. United States v. Security Trust, 340 U.S. 47 at 49, 71 S.Ct. 111 at 113, 95 L.Ed. 53 at 56.

> "Otherwise a State could affect the standing of federal liens, contrary to the established doctrine, simply by causing an inchoate lien to attach at some arbitrary time even before the amount of the tax, assessment, etc., is determined."

United States v. New Britain, 347 U.S. 81 at 86, 74 S.Ct. 367 at 371, 98 L.Ed. 520 at 526. See also United States v. Acri, 1954, 348 U.S. 211, 75 S.Ct. 239, 99 L.Ed. 264; United States v. Waddill, Holland & Flinn, 1945, 323 U.S. 353, 65 S.Ct. 304, 89 L.Ed. 294. Thus, although a state's conclusion that a particular lien is specific and perfected " * * * is entitled to weight, it is subject to reexamination by this [federal] Court." United States v. Security Trust, 340 U.S. at 49–50, 71 S.Ct. at 113, 95 L.Ed. at 56. However, if state law itself would determine that a particular lien was not "acquired" or choate, in the federal sense of the terms, that determination would be "practically conclusive." Illinois ex rel. Gordon v. Campbell, 1946, 329 U.S. 362, 371, 67 S.Ct. 340, 345, 91 L.Ed. 348, 355. The Texas version of the Uniform Commercial Code provides that " * * * the debtor has no rights * * * in an account until it comes into existence." Tex.Bus. & Comm.Code Ann. § 9.204(b)(4). The Uniform Commercial Code uses only the word "account," which is defined as " * * * any right to payment for goods sold or leased or for services rendered which is not evidenced by an instrument or chattel paper." UCC § 9–106. Although "account" may be somewhat narrower than "account receivable," See Coogan, 81 Harv.L.Rev. at 1407, the difference between the two commercial terms is not substantive for purposes of the instant case. See also UCC § 9–103, comment 2, which appears to interchange the terms "account" and "account receivable" as their transactional genesis is contemplated by the section. Both terms contemplate " * * * rights * * * for services rendered * * *" by the debtor that create a debt owing to the debtor by another party. See UCC § 9–106, comment; Chester v. Jones, 386 S.W.2d 544 (Tex.Civ.App.1965); Mellinkoff, 77 Yale L.J. at 198–199. Thus, it is unlikely under Texas law that the money owed to taxpayer-debtor by Texas Oil & Gas could be considered "acquired" accounts or accounts receivable at the time of the filing of the tax lien or 45 days later on April 13, 1970, for prior to that date taxpayer-debtor had neither entered into a contract with Texas Oil & Gas nor rendered services. Even if the payment owing to taxpayer-debtor from Texas Oil & Gas could be considered "acquired" accounts receivable under Texas law by April 13, 1970, it also appears that state law would conclude that the bank's security interest could not finally attach until the accounts receivable came into existence, that is, until the services were rendered and the debt became owing. In addition, the performance by the taxpayer-debtor that underlies the accounts receivable in issue could not be considered a "contract right" at the time the tax lien was filed, for there was no contract between taxpayer-debtor and Texas Oil & Gas in existence at that time. See UCC § 9–106, § 9–204(1); see also, Plumb, 77 Yale L.J. at 666; Young, "Priority of the Federal Tax Lien", U.Chi.L.Rev. 723, 743–748 (1967).

The most substantial present interest that the bank could claim in the accounts receivable at the time of the tax lien filing or within 45 days thereafter was that of a "general intangible." See UCC § 9–106. But the legislative history of the 1966 amendments to the tax lien statutes expressly excludes "general intangibles" from classification as "qualified property" of commercial financing security. H.R.Rep. No. 1884, 89th Cong., 2d Sess. 42 (1966); 26 U.S.C.A. § 6323(c)(2)(B).

Thus it appears that even state law would not render the bank's security interest in taxpayer-debtor's accounts receivable sufficient to pass muster under the federal standards of choateness. The accounts receivable were simply not "acquired" at the required point in time, in this case within 45 days of the filing of the tax lien. This is not to imply in any way that the bank's security interest in the accounts receivable was not sufficiently perfected under state law. As we have pointed out earlier, it appears clear that no other action was required to maintain the bank's security interest in the future accounts receivable of tax-payer-debtor, UCC § 9–204(1), save that the accounts had to come into existence.

Regardless of state law, it appears even clearer that federal law would not consider the bank's interest sufficiently choate to defeat the federal tax lien. In two cases that followed United States v. Security Trust, supra, the Supreme Court indicated a continued unwillingness to protect a private lien holder for nonobligatory agreements entered into prior to the filing of a tax lien but becoming fixed after the filing. United States v. Pioneer American Insurance Co., 1963, 374 U.S. 84, 83 S.Ct. 1651, 10 L.Ed. 2d 770; United States v. Equitable Life Assurance Society, 1966, 384 U.S. 323, 86 S.Ct. 1561, 16 L.Ed.2d 593. Both cases involved the priority to be attached to attorneys' fees that accrued pursuant to mortgages that were admittedly superior to the federal tax lien. In *Pioneer American,* state law provided that the attorneys' fees became enforceable as an indemnity contract immediately upon default of the mortgage, and the default and the suit to foreclose the mortgage both occurred prior to the filing of the tax lien. Nevertheless, the Supreme Court held that the attorneys' lien was inchoate because it had not been reduced to a fixed amount at the time the tax lien was filed (pre-1966 amendments). In *Equitable Life* the attorneys' fees awarded pursuant to a foreclosure of the superior private mortgage, were based under state law upon a fixed percentage of the mortgage, which was a known sum. The Supreme Court nonetheless concluded that Equitable's lien was inchoate, reasoning that there was no presently existing lien for attorneys' fees when the tax lien was filed because the mortgage had not been in default at the filing date. In both *Equitable Life* and *Pioneer American* the fact that the final transaction on which the private lien was allegedly based was not yet in existence at the time of the tax lien filing played an important role in the Court's reasoning. In the instant case, it is true that the bank had done all it could do under the Uniform Commercial Code to secure its interest in taxpayer-debtor's accounts receivable. However, that conclusion simply does not answer the case law as it has developed in the area of tax liens. However "complete" a lender's perfection may be under state recording laws and however "specific" state law might deem that interest to be, it is federal law that determines the extent to which that state determination will protect a private lien from a federal tax lien. It appears clear from the case law that an account receivable not yet "acquired" at the time of the filing of a tax lien because the final transaction creating the account receivable was not yet in existence cannot be considered choate, save for those accounts receivable now protected by section 6323(c). The Senate Finance Committee, speaking generally of the 1966 amendments, concluded that:

> " *   *   * [i]n the case of commercial transactions financing, the protection generally is afforded even though the property underlying the lien is not yet in existence or is turned over within a short time (45 days) after the tax lien filing as long as the loan *   *   * is made within this time."

S.Rep. No. 1708. Thus, it appears that Congress separated the transactions of lending and "acquiring" the secured collateral, requiring that both transactions be completed within 45 days of the filing of a tax lien. Since the accounts receivable were not "acquired" for purposes of the federal tax lien statutes until the work was performed for Texas Oil & Gas, the bank in the instant case simply does not come within the judicial or statutory protection afforded to private lien holders in competition with federal tax liens.

* * *

Of course we realize that this disposition does not afford the protection that commercial lenders who deal with after-acquired property might prefer. As the law appears to stand, the commercial lender must check the applicable records every 45 days or else seriously jeopardize his security under the varying degrees of rigor promulgated by the choateness doctrine. Even that 45 day grace period is probably of minimal efficacy. Commercial lenders might often be lulled into a false sense of security with debtors who are doing badly, for it might appear to the lender that such a debtor is unlikely to have any income to tax. Yet it is precisely in these circumstances that back taxes are likely to accrue. In addition, the lender would most likely not have the entire 45 day period in which to act unless he were lucky enough to discover the tax lien filing almost immediately after it was filed. Finally, there is often not a great deal that the lender can do to protect his advances even after he discovers the tax lien in time. Of course, he has little control over the actual receipt of after-acquired property by the taxpayer-debtor, which is usually subject to contracts and contingencies entirely within the authority of the taxpayer-debtor and various third-parties. The lender can attempt to substitute other existing collateral for his interest in after-acquired property if the taxpayer-debtor has any substitutable assets and if there is sufficient time. Of course, however difficult the present amendments to the tax lien statutes might be to commercial lenders, the amendments offer greater protection to certain categories of lien holders and liens than were afforded by prior doctrines. But the whole genesis and historicity of section 6323(c) appears to have been to give only a slight handicap (45 days) to a private lien holder. The bank here did not establish its case under the choateness doctrine or under these statutory amendments, and the judgment of the district court awarding the accounts receivable fund to the Government by virtue of its tax lien is affirmed.

Affirmed.

ON PETITION FOR REHEARING AND PETITION FOR REHEARING EN BANC

PER CURIAM. The Petition for Rehearing is denied and no member of this panel nor Judge in regular active service on the Court having requested that the Court be polled on rehearing en banc, (Rule 35 Federal Rules of Appellate Procedure; Local Fifth Circuit Rule 12) the Petition for Rehearing En Banc is denied.

NOTES

1. To what extent has the choateness doctrine been limited by the tax lien statute? What would the result have been in *Texas Oil & Gas* if Taxpayer had entered into the contract to perform the services within the 45–day period but had not performed the services until after that period had ended? The security agreement described contract rights as well as accounts. Under § 9–106, as it was when this case was decided, "contract right" was defined to mean "any right to payment under a contract not yet earned by performance." The 1972 revision of § 9–106 deleted the term "contract right" and redefined "account" to include rights to payment whether or not earned by performance. The legislative history indicates that contract rights are included in the phrase "paper of a kind ordinarily arising in commercial transactions" in the definition of "commercial financing security" (IRC § 6323(c)(2)(C)). H.R.Rep. No. 1884, 89th Cong. 2d Sess. 42 (1966). If the contract had been entered into during the 45–day period, Taxpayer arguably has acquired the requisite "commercial financing security."

In Pine Builders, Inc. v. United States, 413 F.Supp. 77 (E.D. Va.1976), Taxpayer granted Creditor a security interest in the present and future contract rights and accounts arising out of a contract Taxpayer entered into in 1974 to install carpets for Account Debtor in a large number of apartments. Creditor filed its financing statement in July of 1974. In February of 1975 the IRS filed the first of a series of tax lien notices. Some of the carpeting was not completed until after the tax lien notice had been filed. Both Creditor and IRS claimed funds that Account Debtor owed Taxpayer, apparently, in part for services Taxpayer had performed after the IRS had filed. The court indicated that Creditor would prevail over IRS for the funds on the ground that the contract entered into in 1974 was property in existence at the time IRS filed within § 6323(h)(1) even though the contract was performed after filing by Taxpayer's installation of the carpets. The court relied on Creedon, Assignments for Security and Federal Tax Liens, 37 Fordham L.Rev. 535 (1969), contending that contract rights, even though unperformed, qualify for the priority of § 6323(c).

Had the contract in *Texas Oil & Gas* been made during the 45–day period and performed later, Judge Goldberg apparently would not have awarded priority to Bank because the security interest would not have been choate until the performance was completed and the money was owed to Taxpayer. In *Pine Builder* the court disposed of this view in a footnote: "The Court acknowledges the argument presented in the briefs relative to federal lien priority 'choateness'. However, we have serious doubts about its applicability under FTLA Code § 6323, which we find to be controlling in this case." 413 F.Supp. at 80, fn. 1.

2. In insolvency cases the federal priority for tax claims is established by R.S. § 3466 (31 U.S.C. § 3713). There is no legislatively established federal priority in noninsolvency cases, and the courts have purported to determine priorities of federal tax claims on the basis of "first in time, first in right." United States v. New Britain, 347 U.S. 81, 74 S.Ct. 367, 98 L.Ed. 520 (1954). Actually, as pointed out in *Texas Oil & Gas,* the Supreme Court in a line of cases commencing in 1950 has substantially subverted the first-in-time doctrine by embracing the concept that a prior lien must be subordinated to a subsequent federal tax lien if it was "inchoate." The Court applied the inchoate test to attachment liens in United States v. Security Trust & Sav. Bank, 340 U.S. 47, 49, 71 S.Ct. 111, 112, 95 L.Ed. 53 (1950); to local tax liens in United States v. New Britain, supra; to mechanic's liens in United States v. Colotta, 350 U.S. 808, 76 S.Ct. 82, 100 L.Ed. 725 (1955); to landlord's liens in United States v. Scovil, 348 U.S. 218, 75 S.Ct. 244, 99 L.Ed. 271 (1955); and to contractual liens in United States v. R.F. Ball Const. Co., 355 U.S. 587, 78 S.Ct. 442, 2 L.Ed.2d 510 (1958), and in United States v. Pioneer American Ins. Co., 374 U.S. 84, 83 S.Ct. 1651, 10 L.Ed.2d 770 (1963).

3. Among the loudest protests against the Supreme Court's doctrine of inchoate liens were those from mechanic's lienors. In a series of cases commencing in the 1950s, the Court held federal tax liens prior to mechanic's liens not only when the federal lien had arisen after the work of improvement had begun or after notice of the mechanic's lien had been filed, but even after suit had been brought to foreclose the mechanic's lien. United States v. Hulley, 358 U.S. 66, 79 S.Ct. 117, 3 L.Ed.2d 106 (1958); United States v. Vorreiter, 355 U.S. 15, 78 S.Ct. 19, 2 L.Ed.2d 23 (1957); United States v. White Bear Brewing Co., 350 U.S. 1010, 76 S.Ct. 646, 100 L.Ed. 871 (1956); United States v. Colotta, 350 U.S. 808,

76 S.Ct. 82, 100 L.Ed. 725 (1955). How has the statute dealt with this problem? See Int.Rev.Code § 6323(a) and (h)(2).

4. In United States v. Pioneer American Ins. Co., 374 U.S. 84, 83 S.Ct. 1651, 10 L.Ed.2d 770 (1963), a mortgage note assumed by the taxpayers in 1958 obligated them to pay reasonable attorney's fees in the event of default and the placing of the note in the hands of an attorney for collection. In October, 1960, taxpayers defaulted and in March, 1961, the mortgagee sued to foreclose the mortgage and sought in addition to the principal and interest a reasonable attorney's fee. The United States filed notice of tax liens in November, 1960, and January, 1961. In November, 1961, the decree of foreclosure was entered which fixed the amount of the attorney's fee at $1,250; the mortgage holder was given priority over the federal tax lien for principal, interest, and the attorney's fee. The Supreme Court held that the federal tax lien was prior to the mortgagee's attorney's fee because the mortgagee's claim to the fee was inchoate until the amount was fixed by the court in November, 1961. See also United States v. Equitable Life Assurance Society, 384 U.S. 323, 86 S.Ct. 1561, 16 L.Ed.2d 593 (1966). What result under the 1966 statute? See Int.Rev.Code § 6323(e).

PROBLEM

Debtor manufactures truck trailers. Bank loaned money to Debtor and took a duly perfected security interest in "all items of personal property, wherever situated, including but not limited to: cars, trucks, inventory, accounts receivable, equipment used in connection with manufacturing, tools, finished products, work in process, now owned or purchased as a replacement, or purchased as new equipment in the future." Later the IRS filed a tax lien against Debtor in the appropriate place. On the 45th day after the filing of the tax lien Debtor had in its possession some finished and some unfinished truck trailers. After this date Debtor sold some of the finished trailers and took in exchange trade-ins and cash which it segregated in a deposit account. It expended labor and added parts after the 45th day to complete the unfinished trailers. The parts added were acquired by Debtor after the 45th day. What are the priorities of the Bank and the IRS in (1) the deposit account holding proceeds, (2) the trailers traded-in, and (3) the trailers finished after the 45–day period? See Donald v. Madison Industries, Inc., 483 F.2d 837 (10th Cir.1973)?

N. PRIORITIES AND EQUITIES

We believe the Article 9 priority rules have been extremely successful. They have on a nationwide basis afforded a level of predictability never before attained in secured transactions. But they are a rather spare, minimal set of principles, refreshingly different from the Internal Revenue Code approach utilized in some statutes in which numbing detail is used to provide for all foreseeable contingencies. Article 9 priority rules are efficient but some courts have found them unfair and have invoked § 1–103 which invites courts to supplement the UCC by reference to "principles of law and equity" and § 1–203 which imposes the obligation of good faith. Whether courts are going too far in their quest for fairness at the cost of certainty is an issue that will be debated forever. See 2 White & Summers, Uniform Commercial Code § 25–20 (3d ed., Practitioner's Edition, 1988), entitled "Weird Cases: The Creeping Infestation of Article 9 Priority Rules by 'Principles of Law and Equity'." A brief discussion of some recent cases follows.

In Grossmann v. Saunders, 237 Va. 113, 376 S.E.2d 66 (1989), the court reaffirmed that knowledge by a second secured party of a prior unperfected security interest is not a relevant consideration in establishing priorities under § 9–312(5), but said: "Although lack of notice is not a prerequisite to the operation of [§ 9–312(5)], [§ 1–203] provides that '[e]very contract or duty within this act imposes an obligation of good faith in its performance or enforcement.' Accordingly, allegations and proof of a 'leading on, bad faith or inequitable conduct' on the part of a secured party may affect the priorities, established under [§ 9–312(5)] by estopping the assertion of a priority." 376 S.E.2d at 72. The court sent the case back to the trial court for an evidentiary hearing on whether the second secured party acted in good faith. Since the only evidence of bad faith the court mentions is knowledge of the prior security interest, the opinion raises the question whether the second secured party's knowledge of the prior unperfected security interest shows bad faith.

In Northern Production Credit Association v. Ed Duggan, Inc., 821 P.2d 788 (Colo.1991), PCA held a perfected security interest in the assets of a livestock feeder. A supplier sold feed corn to the feeder on unsecured credit with the knowledge and consent of PCA, and was owed $101,000 when the feeder failed. The supplier sued PCA on the theory of unjust enrichment. PCA contended that recovery on unjust enrichment was inconsistent with the carefully crafted priority system of Article 9. The court recognized the principle that if a secured creditor is benefitted by an extension of unsecured credit to the debtor and the secured creditor initiated or encouraged the extension, the secured creditor may be liable to the unsecured creditor on the theory of unjust enrichment. A contrary view is taken by Peerless Packing Co. v. Malone & Hyde, Inc., 180 W.Va. 267, 376 S.E.2d 161 (1988).

A number of cases have applied equitable estoppel to defeat perfected security interests. See, *e.g.,* Citizens State Bank v. Peoples Bank, 475 N.E.2d 324 (Ind.App.1985). But in Daniel v.

Stevens, 183 W.Va. 95, 394 S.E.2d 79 (1990), the court refused to apply the doctrine in a case in which an employee of a secured creditor falsely represented to the buyer of the collateral that the security interest had been released, noting that the buyer should have examined the record rather than relying on oral representations about the record. The court stated strong reservations about the wisdom of upsetting the UCC priority rules by use of equitable estoppel. In re Howard's Appliance Corp., 874 F.2d 88 (2d Cir. 1989), must represent the high-water mark of equitable tampering with UCC priorities rules. Secured Party perfected a security interest in Debtor's collateral by filing in New York where the collateral was then located. Without notifying Secured Party, Debtor began to store new collateral in New Jersey. Although Secured Party's traffic department knew of the New Jersey location because it shipped goods there, its credit department was never notified and Secured Party did not file in New Jersey. When Debtor filed in bankruptcy, Debtor claimed that Secured Party lost its priority in the New Jersey collateral. This seems an easy case under § 9–103(1); Secured Party loses unless it perfects in New Jersey. But in an astonishing opinion, the Second Circuit held for Secured Party by imposing a constructive trust on the New Jersey collateral for the benefit of Secured Party on the ground that Debtor had deliberately misled Secured Party about the location of the collateral; had Secured Party been notified it would have filed in New Jersey and prevailed. By storing collateral in New Jersey, Debtor had deprived Secured Party of its interest in the collateral; the constructive trust restores that interest to Secured Party. If this opinion is taken seriously, it significantly undermines § 9–103(1) and offers a boon to desperate litigators in attacking UCC priority rules.

Chapter 3

DEFAULT

A. MEANING OF DEFAULT

A secured creditor can proceed against the collateral only when the "debtor is in default under a security agreement." § 9–501(1). Article 9 does not define default, leading Professor Gilmore to observe that default is, within reason, "whatever the security agreement says it is." 2 Gilmore, Security Interests in Personal Property 1193 (1965). The great variety of commercial and consumer transactions falling within Article 9's broad scope yields almost infinite variations in the kinds of events that the security agreement may define as defaults.

In all instances agreements make failure to make required payments a default. Other commonly-found events of default are the death, dissolution, insolvency or bankruptcy of the debtor, and the debtor's breach or failure to perform any of the agreements, covenants, representations, or warranties contained in the agreement. If the collateral is tangible personal property the debtor will typically agree to insure the collateral, keep it in good condition, not remove or transfer the collateral, and not permit loss, theft, damage, or destruction, or levy, seizure, or attachment of the collateral. If the collateral is accounts, the debtor may agree that it owns all accounts free and clear of any claims of others, that the account debtor has accepted delivery of the goods giving rise to the account, and that all accounts are binding obligations of the account debtor. In commercial lending transactions events of default may include the debtor's failure to maintain net worth or working capital ratios or any other material adverse change in the debtor's financial position. If the creditor is concerned that its enumeration of specific events of default is not adequate to protect against unforeseen occurrences that might impair the debtor's prospect of payment, it may contract for the right to declare a default whenever it deems itself insecure. See § 1–208.

In failing to define default, Article 9 leaves for resolution by contract law the crucial issue of when a creditor can proceed against the collateral. In commercial transactions, seizure of the collateral may effectively close the debtor's business. In consumer cases, repossession of the debtor's automobile, furniture, or appliances may alter drastically the debtor's standard of living. In most instances economic considerations restrain creditors from proceeding against collateral as other than a last resort, utilized only after all other collection efforts by way of workout arrangements have failed. Creditors understandably prefer payment from debtors, even though delayed, to the expense of foreclosing on collateral.

In leaving the definition of default to the agreement of the parties, Article 9 assumed that debtors and creditors could look after their own interests. However the consumer movement of the 1960s and 1970s rejected this assumption in consumer transactions on the ground that there was a disparity in bargaining position between creditors and consumer debtors. For example, § 5.109 of the Uniform Consumer Credit Code (1974) defines default as follows:

> An agreement of the parties to a consumer credit transaction with respect to default on the part of the consumer is enforceable only to the extent that:

> (1) the consumer fails to make a payment as required by agreement; or

> (2) the prospect of payment, performance, or realization of collateral is significantly impaired; the burden of establishing the prospect of significant impairment is on the creditor.

B.   ACCELERATION

1.   FUNCTION OF ACCELERATION

Since a security interest secures the performance of an obligation, usually to pay money, the extent to which the secured party can resort to the collateral upon default depends on the amount of the obligation. If the debt is payable in installments the agreement between the creditor and the debtor commonly provides that upon default by the debtor the creditor may accelerate the due date of the debt not yet payable, so that the entire debt becomes immediately payable. Thus, default in one installment payment could lead to acceleration of the entire unpaid debt. But if the debtor is in default on one or more installments and the agreement does not provide for acceleration the secured party may sell or otherwise realize on the collateral under § 9–504(1) only to the extent of the amount of the unpaid installments. General Electric Credit Corp. v. Bankers Commercial Corp., 244 Ark. 984, 429 S.W.2d 60 (1968). Moreover, in such a case the debtor may redeem under § 9–506 by paying only the amount of the overdue installments plus other amounts required by the statute. If the default is other than a failure to make a payment, there may be no amount then due, absent an acceleration clause. Hence, failure to include an acceleration clause may be very costly to a secured creditor. If in such a case the collateral is repossessed and sold before all installments are due, the proceeds of sale can be applied to satisfy only the amount of the installments then due, and the surplus must be returned to the debtor. § 9–504(1) and (2). Although the secured creditor would retain a security interest in the money returned to the debtor as proceeds of the disposition of the collateral (§ 9–306(2)), the practical difficulty of tracing cash proceeds renders the creditor effectively unsecured after foreclosure. The equally unappealing alternative is for the creditor to wait until all payments are due before repossessing.

2. INSECURITY CLAUSES

The most commonly litigated issue regarding acceleration in secured transactions involves insecurity clauses. If a creditor is given the right by agreement to accelerate "at will" or "when it deems itself insecure," § 1–208 provides that the creditor may "do so only if he in good faith believes that the prospect of payment or promise is impaired." The burden of establishing the creditor's lack of good faith is imposed by § 1–208 on the debtor. Section 1–201(19) defines "good faith" in subjective terms as "honesty in fact in the conduct or transaction concerned." The Comment to § 1–208 indicates that the thrust of that section is to bar a creditor from acting whimsically or capriciously in accelerating a debtor's loan. Given the potentially disastrous consequences to the business debtor of having the debt accelerated and the collateral seized, the need for barring arbitrary action on the part of the creditor in making the crucial acceleration decision is great.

However, § 1–208, read literally, is a weak instrument for achieving the intended goal. The aggrieved debtor, whose loan has been called, whose property has been taken, and whose business has been ruined, is given the unenviable task under § 1–208 of bringing a lawsuit and proving that the creditor did not honestly believe that it was insecure. Under this interpretation, § 1–208 does not wash. Whim and caprice are antonyms not for honesty but for rationality. If debtors are to be protected against arbitrary acceleration by creditors, an objective standard of good faith seems preferable. The majority opinion in Universal C.I.T. Credit Corp. v. Shepler, 164 Ind.App. 516, 329 N.E.2d 620 (1975), concluded: "If the good faith provision of [§ 1–208] in conjunction with the good faith definition of [§ 1–201(19)] is to have any real effect, the subjective test will have to be modified." 329 N.E.2d at 623.

The mischief may be laid at the door of § 1–201(19) which attempts to impose a subjective good faith test on a business world that has come increasingly to be held to higher standards by judges and juries. A number of courts have declined to read § 1–201(19) and § 1–208 as they are written and have injected some degree of objectivity into the meaning of good faith. An example is Yankton Production Credit Association v. Larsen, 219 Neb. 610, 365 N.W.2d 430 (1985). Professor Gilmore encouraged this view: "The creditor has the right to accelerate if, under all the circumstances, a reasonable man, motivated by good faith, would have done so." 2 Gilmore, Security Interests in Personal Property 1197 (1965). Other cases read § 1–208 as it is written and purport to accept the subjective interpretation of good faith. An example is Farmers Cooperative Elevator, Inc. v. State Bank, 236 N.W.2d 674 (Iowa 1975).

Reading the decisions taking both views, one is struck with the difficulty of saying with any certainty whether the results in any of these cases would have changed whether a subjective or objective definition of good faith were employed. *Farmers Cooperative* is a leading case for the subjective standard of good faith. In that case the bank decided to accelerate the debtor's secured loan on the basis of an insecurity clause and to set off against the debtor's deposit account. The court strongly rejected the debtor's contention that the bank should be held to a standard of reasonableness. But, in showing that the bank had acted honestly, the court listed enough factors to lead one to believe that the bank had acted quite reasonably as well.

The commercial law establishment that shaped the UCC in the late 40s probably intended in drafting § 1–201(19) and § 1–208 that creditors acting under insecurity clauses should be granted much leeway so long as they acted honestly. See Braucher, The Legislative History of the Uniform Commercial Code, 58 Colum.L. Rev. 798, 812–813 (1958). Several decades later ideas about creditor responsibility to deal fairly with debtors have changed. Ironically, one of the chief instruments that the courts have seized upon to impose higher standards of conduct on creditors is the implied covenant of good faith imposed on all UCC transactions by § 1–203. It is highly unlikely that these courts, in their zeal to force creditors to treat debtors fairly will look kindly upon a bank, for example, that draws the mantle of § 1–201(19) about itself and answers that although it may have acted unreasonably in terminating the debtor's business, it did so honestly.

3. GOOD FAITH AND FAIR DEALING

Acceleration can spell disaster for a debtor. Upon acceleration an unsecured creditor can proceed to judgment and levy on the debtor's assets; a secured creditor can immediately repossess. This usually closes the debtor's business and often brings on bankruptcy. If default is what the security agreement says it is, and if, as is commonly the case, the creditor writes the security agreement, what safeguard does a debtor have against improper acceleration by a creditor? In the following case and notes we briefly discuss some of the legal doctrines utilized by debtors in acceleration and related cases. These doctrines have different substantive content but they are often, for the sake of convenience, lumped together as the creditor's duty of good faith and fair dealing. In the following case the debtor looks to § 1–208 for protection.

GREENBERG v. SERVICE BUSINESS FORMS INDUSTRIES, INC.

United States Court of Appeals, Tenth Circuit, 1989.
882 F.2d 1538.

Before LOGAN, BRORBY, and EBEL, CIRCUIT JUDGES.

PER CURIAM.

Service Business Forms Industries, Inc. (Service Business) and Service Computer Forms Industries, Inc. (Service Computer), defendants, appeal the district court's order granting plaintiffs partial summary judgment on their claim for recovery of an accelerated debt allegedly due under Service Business' promissory note. The district court determined that there were no material issues of fact as to Service Business' default under the terms of the promissory note and that plaintiffs properly exercised their right to accelerate the unpaid principal balance and accrued interest. On appeal, defendants contend there are genuine issues of fact regarding each of its defenses.

Plaintiffs are co-trustees of the Mal Greenberg Testamentary Trust (the Trust). On October 29, 1982, plaintiffs entered into a stock redemption agreement with Service Computer, a Nevada corporation presently owned and operated by Carolyn and Laurance Wolfberg. The Wolfbergs are the sister and brother-in-law of Robert Greenberg (Greenberg), a plaintiff and a trustee of the Trust. Under the stock redemption agreement, the Trust transferred all the shares it owned in Service Computer back to the company in exchange for $102,000. Of this amount, $2,000 was to be paid at closing and $100,000 was to be paid pursuant to the promissory note at issue here.

Pursuant to the stock redemption agreement, Service Business, an affiliate of Service Computer which is also operated by the Wolfbergs, executed a $100,000 promissory note on October 29, 1982, the closing date of the stock redemption agreement. The note provided for annual payments to be calculated on a twenty-year amortization schedule with full payment to be made on the tenth anniversary of the note's execution. The note further stated that the Trust had the option to accelerate the debt and demand full payment if Service Business defaulted on any of its obligations under the note. The note did not specify a specific due date for the annual payments. In addition to this written agreement, Service Business alleged that Greenberg promised to execute a disclaimer of any interest he had as a beneficiary under the Trust. Greenberg denied that he ever made such an agreement.

By April, 1986, Service Business had made only one payment on the note, in the amount of $5,000. As a result of further negotiation between the parties, Greenberg executed a written disclaimer in favor of Service Computer under which Greenberg disclaimed any interest he might have through inheritance in the family jewelry. The disclaimer was conditioned on Service Business' payment of all past due amounts owing under the promissory note and upon its "timely payment" of all future installments. The disclaimer also failed to designate a specific date for the future annual payments. Thereafter, Service Business paid $43,231.86 on June 26, 1986, which included partial payment of the 1986 installment. On November 6, 1986, not having received the payment from Service Business which they considered due on October 29, 1986, plaintiffs sent Service Business a notice of their intention to accelerate payment of the note. On November 14, 1986, and again on October 29, 1987, Service Business tendered payment of the installment amount owing, calculated as of the anniversary date of the note. On both occasions, plaintiffs refused to accept the payments.

Plaintiffs brought this action to recover the accelerated amount of the principal and accrued interest under the note. In its answer, defendants raised several defenses, including waiver, estoppel, and lack of default under the terms of the note. Defendants also filed a counterclaim, alleging failure of consideration by virtue of Greenberg's refusal to execute a disclaimer of any interest in the Trust funds. Plaintiffs moved for summary judgment and, after a hearing, the district court granted partial summary judgment in their favor. The court found that the terms of the contract clearly designated the payments to be due on October 29th of each year, by virtue of the date of the note's execution and the fact that annual payments were calculated on the basis of a twenty-year amortization. The court further held that there were no material issues of fact as to waiver, estoppel, or default and found that Business Service had defaulted on its payment obligations, that the Trust had the right to accelerate the balance owing upon default, and that the Trust properly exercised its right to accelerate. The court ruled, however, that there were material issues of fact regarding the issue of whether Service Business received full consideration for the stock redemption agreement with the Trust because Greenberg allegedly failed to issue a disclaimer of any interest as beneficiary under the Trust. This last issue was presented to the jury, which returned a verdict in favor of Greenberg and the Trust.

On appeal, Service Business contends that there are several genuine issues of fact which precluded the granting of partial summary judgment. First, Service Business contends that it did not default on its obligations under the note because the document did not specify a date on which payment was due, and argues under Oklahoma law that payment was thereby due within a reasonable time. We disagree. Oklahoma statute dictates that contracts are to be interpreted according to the intent of the parties at the time the instrument was executed. * * * Intent must be determined by construing the contract as a whole, and the court must construe the contract so as to give effect to each provision. * * * The language of the note setting the date of final payment as October 29, 1992, and the method for calculating the amount of annual payments clearly indicate that the parties intended that payments were to have been made on the anniversary date of the note.

Second, Service Business asserts that plaintiffs did not accelerate the note in good faith. Service Business claims the duty of good faith arises both under the Uniform Commercial Code (UCC) § 1–208 and under the common law doctrine of good faith in the performance of a contract. Section 1–208 provides:

> A term providing that one party * * * may accelerate payment or performance or require collateral or additional collateral "at will" or "when he deems himself insecure" or in words of similar import shall be const ᵈd to mean that he shall have power to do so only if he in good faith believes that the prospect of payment or performance is impaired. The burden of establishing lack of good faith is on the party against whom the power has been exercised.

* * * In finding that plaintiffs properly exercised their power of acceleration, the district court implicitly found that the good faith requirement set forth in § 1–208 does not apply to notes that permit acceleration at the option of the holder upon default by the debtor. We agree.

The only Oklahoma case we have located which addresses the question of whether the good faith requirement under the UCC applies to acceleration on default clauses is Knittel v. Security State Bank, Mooreland, Okla., 593 P.2d 92 (Okla.1979). The case did not directly address the issue; however, it upheld a challenged jury instruction which stated that the good faith requirement under § 1–208 did not apply to an acceleration on default clause. Id. at 97. Because a court must determine whether a challenged jury instruction properly states the applicable law, * * * it logically follows that *Knittel* supports the position that the UCC good faith requirement does not apply to acceleration on default clauses.

Several states have similarly held that the UCC good faith requirement is not applicable when the acceleration clause is based on an event in the debtor's complete control. * * * But see Brown v. AVEMCO Inv. Corp., 603 F.2d 1367, 1375–80 (9th Cir. 1979) (comparing the applicability of UCC § 1–208 on "default" acceleration clauses as opposed to "insecurity" acceleration clauses under Texas law). Because of the ruling in *Knittel* and the general consensus in other jurisdictions, we conclude that Oklahoma would not apply the good faith requirement in § 1–208 to the acceleration on default clause at issue in this case.

Service Business also claims that plaintiffs failed to perform their contract in good faith under common law equitable principles. Service Business relies on Brown v. AVEMCO Inv. Corp., in which the Ninth Circuit applied the common law doctrine of good faith to a due-on-lease clause contained in a security agreement executed in conjunction with a promissory note.[2] 603 F.2d at 1375–79. In reversing a jury verdict in favor of the creditor, the court noted that, under Texas law, acceleration clauses are designed to protect a creditor from conduct or events that jeopardize or impair the creditor's security. Id. at 1376. The court held that the jury should have been instructed on the issue of the creditor's good faith in exercising the due-on-lease clause when evidence existed that it inequitably desired to take advantage of a technical default, not because it in good faith feared its security was impaired. Id. at 1379. This decision was based on Texas case law which clearly mandated that equitable considerations should be applied when a creditor exercises an optional right to accelerate for the sole purpose of receiving the entire payment rather than for the purpose of protecting its debt. Id. We must determine whether Oklahoma would likewise impose an equitable duty on a creditor to not use the power of acceleration when its security is not impaired.

The Oklahoma Supreme Court has ruled on two occasions that an acceleration clause contained in a mortgage will not be enforced where the conduct of the mortgagee has been unconscionable or inequitable. Continental Fed. Sav. & Loan Ass'n v. Fetter, 564 P.2d 1013, 1019 (Okla.1977); Murphy v. Fox, 278 P.2d 820, 826 (Okla.1955). In *Continental,* the court denied a bank's request to accelerate and foreclose on a mortgage based on a due-on-transfer clause when the bank refused to consent to a transfer solely because the mortgagor would not pay a substantial transfer fee. The transfer fee was an additional condition unilaterally imposed

---

2. Under the security agreement, the creditor, AVEMCO, had the option to accelerate the entire debt if the debtor leased the property, an airplane, without its written consent. In 1973, the debtor leased the airplane to a third party and also executed an option to purchase. The debtor sent notice of the agreement to AVEMCO. Two years later, the lessee exercised its option to purchase and tendered full payment of the remainder owing under the promissory note. AVEMCO, after two years of inaction, refused the tendered payment and instead exercised its option to accelerate under the due-on-lease clause but also demanded an additional sum for the cost of insurance premiums. After the debtor refused to pay the additional amount, AVEMCO repossessed the airplane and sold it for a higher profit. 603 F.2d at 1369.

by the bank and was not contained in the original mortgage agreement. The court held the bank's conduct in demanding additional payment was unconscionable and denied its requested relief. 564 P.2d at 1019.

In *Murphy*, the court refused to permit a mortgagee to accelerate the maturity of a promissory note because the court found that the mortgagee had attempted to hinder timely payment by the mortgagor and had encouraged its default. 278 P.2d at 824. The court determined that this conduct was motivated solely by the mortgagee's desire to accelerate the maturity of the entire debt and held that the technical default of tendering late payment of taxes was insufficient to justify acceleration when the mortgagee had acted unconscionably. Id. at 826.

According to our reading of these cases, whether the Oklahoma court permits acceleration depends on the conduct of the mortgagee and whether he has dealt fairly with the debtor or has acted oppressively or unconscionably. This view is consistent with that of several other jurisdictions. See Phipps v. First Fed. Sav. & Loan Ass'n, 438 N.W.2d 814, 819 (S.D.1989) (an acceleration clause will be enforced absent fraud, bad faith, or other conduct on part of the mortgagee which would make it unconscionable to enforce the clause); Key Int'l Mfg., Inc. v. Stillman, 103 A.D.2d 475, 480 N.Y.S.2d 528, 530 (1984) (absent some element of fraud, exploitative overreaching or unconscionable conduct by the creditor, the court should enforce an acceleration clause), aff'd as modified, 66 N.Y.2d 924, 498 N.Y.S.2d 795, 489 N.E.2d 764 (1985); Bowen v. Danna, 637 S.W.2d at 564 (a court in equity can relieve a debtor from the hardship of acceleration based on accident, mistake, fraud, or inequitable conduct of the creditor); First Fed. Sav. & Loan Ass'n v. Ram, 135 Ariz. 178, 659 P.2d 1323, 1325 (Ct.App. 1982) (same); Ciavarelli v. Zimmerman, 122 Ariz. 143, 593 P.2d 697, 698–99 (Ct.App.1979) (same).

Nothing in the record warrants an application of these equitable principles in the instant case. Plaintiffs did not exercise their option to accelerate after a considerable delay. See, e.g., *Brown*, 603 F.2d at 1379; Caspert v. Anderson Apartments, Inc., 196 Misc. 555, 94 N.Y.S.2d 521, 526 (Sup.Ct.1949). Nor did the default concern a technical, secondary obligation such as payment of taxes.[3] Rather, the default violated the essence of the written agreement, timely payment of principal and interest.[4] Finally, no

3. In *Murphy*, the court discussed several cases from other jurisdictions which considered a technical default to be a failure to comply with a secondary obligation such as payment of taxes or assessments as opposed to a default on payment of principal or interest. See 278 P.2d at 825. Generally, these cases consider a default in payment of a principal or interest payment to be a substantial breach rather than a technical default. See e.g., Graf v. Hope Bldg. Corp., 254 N.Y. 1, 171 N.E. 884, 885–86 (1930).

4. The court in Continental Federal Savings & Loan Association v. Fetter stated:

evidence was presented that Greenberg attempted to hinder or otherwise cause the default so as to make his conduct unconscionable. Defendants had complete control over the event which triggered plaintiffs' right to accelerate. The mere fact that the plaintiffs' interest might not have been in jeopardy, without some misconduct on the part of the plaintiffs, does not warrant a refusal to enforce an acceleration clause which was a bargained-for element of the contract between the parties. Under the circumstances of this case, we conclude that there are no material issues of fact under the applicable Oklahoma law regarding the enforceability of the acceleration clause and the issue of good faith.

Service Business also asserts that plaintiffs waived their right to accelerate through their prior acceptance of late payments. Ordinarily, prior acceptance of late payments only waives the right to accelerate as to those past installments. McGowan v. Pasol, 605 S.W.2d 728, 732 (Tex.Civ.App.1980). When a creditor establishes a prior course of dealing in accepting late payments, the creditor is estopped from declaring total debt due on future defaults. Id. Estoppel does not apply, however, when the obligor gives the debtor notice that the terms of the agreement will be enforced in the future. Id.; Dunn v. General Equities of Iowa, Ltd., 319 N.W.2d 515, 517 (Iowa 1982); see also Sternberg v. Mason, 339 So.2d 373, 376 (La.Ct.App.1976) (waiver rule has no application where obligee made frequent demands for punctual payment or accepted tardy payment as a result of unwilling or forced indulgence). Because Service Business or its officers received adequate notice by virtue of the disclaimer executed in April, 1986, that the trustees demanded all future payments to be made timely, no material issue of fact exists on the issue of waiver.

* * *

The judgment of the United States District Court for the Western District of Oklahoma is AFFIRMED.

NOTES

1. Section 1–208 relates to clauses allowing a creditor to accelerate "at will" or "when he deems himself insecure." Under such clauses, the creditor can accelerate even if there is no default

[A]cceleration clauses are bargained-for elements of mortgages and notes to protect the mortgagee from risks connected with transfer of the mortgaged property. The underlying rationale for an acceleration clause is to insure that a responsible party is in possession, to protect the mortgagee from unanticipated risks, and to afford the lender the right to be assured of the safety of his security. However, an action to accelerate and foreclose a mortgage is an equitable proceeding, and the equitable powers of the court will not be invoked to impose an extreme penalty on a mortgagor with no showing that he *has violated the substance of the agreement.*

564 P.2d at 1017–18 (footnote omitted) (emphasis added).

by the debtor. To protect the debtor, § 1–208 prohibits acceleration unless the creditor has a good faith belief that the prospect of
payment had been impaired. Brown v. Avemco Investment Corp.,
discussed in *Greenberg,* applied the § 1–208 prohibition to a case in
which the acceleration was based on a default by the debtor. In
Brown the debtor breached a clause prohibiting lease of the
collateral without the secured party's consent. This was clearly a
default under the contract, but the court held the secured party's
acceleration and repossession to be wrongful because there was no
basis for a belief on the part of the secured party that its prospect
of payment was impaired. *Brown* seems wrong and *Greenberg*
seems right on the reach of § 1–208, but debtors have found other
sources of law to safeguard them from what they conceive to be
improper acts of acceleration and repossession by creditors. Section 1–203 imposes an obligation of good faith in the performance
or enforcement of every contract within the UCC. Moreover,
Restatement of Contracts (Second) § 205 provides that every contract imposes upon each party a duty of good faith and fair dealing
in its performance and enforcement.

2. In a number of cases decided in the 1980s debtors were
awarded damages from the creditor for economic harm for action
apparently permitted by the contract between the parties, but
which was deemed to be arbitrary and unfair to the debtor and
thus in violation of § 1–203.

In Alaska Statebank v. Fairco, 674 P.2d 288 (Alaska 1983), a
toy store was in default on its debt to a bank. After negotiations
were entered into for a workout, the bank without notice seized its
collateral, the inventory of the store, and refused to honor the
debtor's checks. The debtor was allowed to reopen its business
only by agreeing to terms it had previously rejected. Alleging
that the bank had breached its duty of good faith under § 1–203 in
closing the store in order to coerce the debtor into putting up
additional security, the debtor sued for wrongful repossession and
dishonor of checks. Although the debtor was clearly in default
when the bank acted, the trial court, sitting without a jury, held
for the debtor on the ground that the existence of negotiations
between the parties modified the written agreement so as to
require the bank to give notice to the debtor before closing its
business and dishonoring its checks. Punitive damages were
awarded. The Supreme Court of Alaska affirmed.

Just as a creditor can close a debtor's business by calling a
loan and seizing collateral, it can have the same effect by refusing
to make a further advance of credit. In K.M.C. Co., Inc. v. Irving
Trust Company, 757 F.2d 752 (6th Cir.1985), the issue was whether
a major bank had violated its § 1–203 covenant of good faith in
refusing to make an advance to a wholesale grocer wholly dependent upon the bank's financing when the advance was within the

debtor's agreed loan limit, was fully secured, and was vital to the debtor's survival. The jury found the bank liable for breach of contract and gave $7,500,000 in damages. The Sixth Circuit affirmed, holding that the obligation of good faith compelled the bank, if it wished to curtail its financing with the debtor, to make the requested advance and give the debtor a period of time to seek alternative financing unless there were "valid business reasons" precluding the bank from doing so. The bank's loan officer's subjective belief that there were valid reasons for not making the advance was not enough. "[T]here must be at least *some* objective basis upon which a reasonable loan officer in the exercise of his discretion would have acted in that manner." (Emphasis in original.) 757 F.2d at 761.

A more limited view of the role of good faith in lender liability cases is presented in Kham & Nate's Shoes No. 2, Inc. v. First Bank, 908 F.2d 1351 (7th Cir.1990). Bank gave Debtor a $300,000 line of credit reserving the right to cancel at its discretion. After Bank had advanced $75,000 it refused to advance more funds and Debtor failed. The lower court held Bank's refusal was inequitable conduct and justified equitable subordination of its claim in bankruptcy. In reversing the lower court, Judge Easterbrook, speaking for the court, said:

> Firms that have negotiated contracts are entitled to enforce them to the letter, even to the great discomfort of their trading partners, without being mulcted for lack of "good faith". Although courts often refer to the obligation of good faith that exists in every contractual relation, e.g., UCC § 1–203; Jordan v. Duff & Phelps, Inc., 815 F.2d 429, 438 (7th Cir. 1987), this is not an invitation to the court to decide whether one party ought to have exercised privileges expressly reserved in the document. "Good faith" is a compact reference to an implied undertaking not to take opportunistic advantage in a way that could not have been contemplated at the time of drafting, and which therefore was not resolved explicitly by the parties. When the contract is silent, principles of good faith—such as the UCC's standard of honesty in fact, UCC § 1–201(19), and the reasonable expectations of the trade, UCC § 2–103(b) (a principle applicable, however, *only* to "merchants", which Bank is not)—fill the gap. They do not block use of terms that actually appear in the contract.

> We do not doubt the force of the proverb that the letter killeth, while the spirit giveth life. Literal implementation of unadorned language may destroy the essence of the venture. Few people pass out of childhood without learning fables about genies, whose wickedly literal interpretation of their "masters" wishes always leads to calamity. Yet knowledge that literal enforcement means some mismatch between the

parties' expectation and the outcome does not imply a general duty of "kindness" in performance, or of judicial oversight into whether a party had "good cause" to act as it did. Parties to a contract are not each others' fiduciaries; they are not bound to treat customers with the same consideration reserved for their families. Any attempt to add an overlay of "just cause"—as the bankruptcy judge effectively did—to the exercise of contractual privileges would reduce commercial certainty and breed costly litigation. The UCC's requirement of "honesty in fact" stops well short of the requirements the bankruptcy judge thought incident to contractual performance. "[I]n commercial transactions it does not in the end promote justice to seek strained interpretations in aid of those who do not protect themselves." James Baird Co. v. Gimbel Bros., Inc., 64 F.2d 344, 346 (2d Cir.1933) (L. Hand, J.).

908 F.2d at 1357.

3. Does the obligation of good faith limit a creditor's right to call a loan if the note is "payable on demand?" Section 1–208 should not apply. The Comment to that section states: "Obviously this section has no application to demand instruments or obligations whose very nature permits call at any time with or without reason." In Centerre Bank v. Distributors, Inc., 705 S.W.2d 42 (Mo.App.1985), the court rejected the debtor's contention that § 1–203 limited the creditor's discretion in calling the note:

> The imposition of a good faith defense to the call for payment of a demand note transcends the performance or enforcement of a contract and in fact adds a term to the agreement which the parties had not included. The additional term would be that the note is not payable at any time demand is made but only payable when demand is made if such demand is made in good faith. The parties by the demand note did not agree that payment would be made only when demand was made in good faith but agreed that payment would be made whenever demand was made. Thus § 1–203 has no application because it does not relate to the performance or enforcement of any right under the demand note but in fact would add an additional term which the parties did not agree to. This court is not willing to rewrite the agreement which Distributors made that the demand note which it executed could be called for payment at any time by adding a provision that payment could only be demanded in good faith.

705 S.W.2d at 48. In Reid v. Key Bank of Southern Maine, Inc., 821 F.2d 9 (1st Cir.1987), the court, faced with what appeared to be an unambiguous demand clause, invoked the good faith doctrine to limit the creditor's discretion in calling the loan because other

terms of the contract indicated that the parties did not intend a true demand note.

4. The most significant element in the lender liability cases of the 1980s was the success of debtors in imposing punitive damages on lenders. The barrier was that ordinarily punitive damages are not appropriate in breach of contract cases. Nonetheless a number of cases found sufficient tortious conduct on the part of lenders to justify punitive damages. Other cases found punitive damages inappropriate.

C. REPOSSESSION

PENNEY v. FIRST NATIONAL BANK OF BOSTON
Supreme Judicial Court of Massachusetts, 1982.
385 Mass. 715, 433 N.E.2d 901.

O'CONNOR, JUSTICE. Frederick Penney, a commercial fisherman who borrowed money from the defendant bank, appeals from a summary judgment for the bank on his complaint and from an award of attorney's fees in favor of the bank on its counterclaim. We affirm.

On March 28, 1975, Penney borrowed $32,802.39 from the bank, and executed a promissory note and a security agreement involving a lobster boat. The back of the note provided that upon default all obligations would become immediately due and payable without notice or demand and the holder would then have the rights and remedies of a secured party under the Uniform Commercial Code of Massachusetts (UCC).

The security agreement provided as follows: "Borrower may have possession and use of the Collateral until default. Upon the happening of any of the following events or conditions, namely: (a) default in the payment or performance of any of the obligations * * * contained or referred to herein or in any note evidencing any of the obligations * * *, thereupon, and as long as such default continues Bank may declare all of the Obligations to be immediately due and payable, and Bank shall then have * * * in addition to all other rights and remedies, the rights and remedies of a secured party under the Uniform Commercial Code of Massachusetts, including without limitation thereto the right to take immediate possession of the Collateral * * *. Bank will give Borrower at least five days' prior written notice of the time and place of any public sale of the Collateral or of the time after which any private sale thereof is to be made." Penney's obligation was guaranteed by William Regan, who agreed to pay in the event Penney defaulted.

On March 4, 1976, Penney executed another note, payable to the bank on demand, in the amount of $4,244.40. This note also expressly gave the bank the rights and remedies of a secured party under the UCC.

Penney defaulted on both notes. On July 29, October 11, November 4, and December 30, 1977, the bank wrote to Penney demanding full payment of all sums due. Penney made some further payments after each letter except the last, but he remained in default on both notes throughout that period. The bank brought an action on Regan's guaranty and on August 25, 1977, attached Regan's real estate in the amount of $18,500. The bank never exercised its remedies against Regan. The bank seized the lobster boat without prior notice on January 19, 1978, at which time Penney's total indebtedness to the bank was approximately $19,000. The bank notified Penney five days later of the repossession, of its intention to sell the boat, and of his right to redeem. Penney did not exercise his right to redeem, and the boat was sold at public auction for $13,500. Penney asserts by affidavit that as a result of the repossession he lost $34,000 worth of fishing equipment which was at sea.

Penney commenced this action to recover for the losses he alleges resulted from a wrongful seizure and sale of the boat. He claims that the seizure and sale violated G.L. c. 93A, § 2, and his due process rights secured by the Fourteenth Amendment to the Constitution of the United States. The bank answered and counterclaimed for the balance due on the two notes together with interest, costs and attorney's fees. The bank's motion for summary judgment on the counterclaim was allowed by agreement, subject to later assessment of interest, costs, and attorney's fees, on the condition that no execution would issue until Penney's action was decided. The bank then moved for summary judgment on Penney's action and the motion was allowed, based on pleadings, affidavits, a deposition, admissions, and answers to interrogatories. Thereafter, interest, costs, and attorney's fees were assessed in connection with the counterclaim. Penney appeals from the summary judgment on his complaint and from the assessment of attorney's fees on the counterclaim. Penney claims that the award of attorney's fees in connection with the bank's defense against his complaint was erroneous.

1. *Constitutionality of § 9–503.* We interpret the security agreement as neither adding to nor detracting from the bank's right to repossess without notice under UCC § 9–503. Penney attacks that section as violating the due process guarantees of the Fourteenth Amendment. Section 9–503 provides in pertinent part that "[u]nless otherwise agreed a secured party has on default the right to take possession of the collateral. In taking possession a secured party may proceed without judicial process if this can be

done without breach of the peace or may proceed by action." The Fourteenth Amendment by its terms applies only to the States. In order for the Fourteenth Amendment to be invoked against a private actor, the government must not only act but must be "significantly involved" in the actor's underlying conduct. Moose Lodge No. 107 v. Irvis, 407 U.S. 163, 173, 92 S.Ct. 1965, 1971, 32 L.Ed.2d 627 (1972), quoting from Reitman v. Mulkey, 387 U.S. 369, 380, 87 S.Ct. 1627, 1633, 18 L.Ed.2d 830 (1967). Penney argues that the Legislature's enactment of § 9–503 was sufficient State action to render unconstitutional a private party's self-help repossession in reliance thereon.

Neither this court nor the United States Supreme Court has reached this precise question. The constitutionality of UCC § 9–503 has been considered in many other jurisdictions, however, and has been almost uniformly held to involve no State action. * * *

Flagg Bros. v. Brooks, 436 U.S. 149, 98 S.Ct. 1729, 56 L.Ed.2d 185 (1978), is persuasive authority for the proposition that there is no State action in mere legislative authorization of creditors' self-help remedies that do not involve the participation of any governmental employees. In *Flagg Bros.*, the Court rejected a due process attack on a warehouseman's sale, pursuant to UCC § 7–210, of another's goods to satisfy overdue storage charges because the sale involved no State action. Section 9–503, like § 7–210, authorizes but does not compel private action and does not delegate a function traditionally reserved to the State. *Id.* at 161–162, 164–166, 98 S.Ct. at 1736, 1737–1738. * * *

We hold that self-help repossession by a private party pursuant to § 9–503, does not involve State action and does not violate the Fourteenth Amendment. Our holding is consonant with our decision in Debral Realty, Inc. v. DiChiara, 383 Mass. 359, Mass. Adv.Sh. (1981) 1140, 420 N.E.2d 343, where we held that the lis pendens procedure under G.L. c. 184, § 15, does not violate due process.

2. *Consumer Protection Act violations.* Penney contends that summary judgment was improper even if § 9–503 is constitutional. He argues that the bank's repossession without prior notice in the circumstances presented here constituted an "unfair or deceptive" act entitling him to damages under G.L. c. 93A, §§ 2 & 11. * * *

Penney asserts that there are four facts, each of which is either established or subject to substantial dispute, that show a violation of c. 93A when taken together. These are (1) that the bank repossessed without notice (2) when it had previously attached real property with a value in excess of the attachment under the guaranty (3) leaving a balance owed of $600 over the attachment amount (4) when it knew or should have known Penney had equipment at sea that he would be unable to retrieve.

* * *

Regulation XV of the regulations promulgated by the Attorney General pursuant to c. 93A, provides in pertinent part that an act or practice is a violation of c. 93A, § 2, if it is oppressive or otherwise unconscionable in any respect. * * * We therefore consider whether the bank's repossession without notice was in any way unconscionable or oppressive.

In Zapatha v. Dairy Mart, Inc., 381 Mass. 284, 408 N.E.2d 1370, we considered the meaning of "unconscionable" in UCC § 2–302, which authorizes a court to refuse to enforce any clause of a contract that the court finds "to have been unconscionable at the time it was made." Penney argues that under Regulation XV the security agreement was unconscionable at the time it was made and that its enforcement by repossession without notice was also unconscionable. Our consideration in *Zapatha* of unconscionability with respect to contract terms, within the meaning of UCC § 2–302, is helpful not only to our determination whether the provisions in the notes and security agreement here were unconscionable but also to our determination whether the repossession was unconscionable within the meaning of Regulation XV. In *Zapatha*, we said, "Because there is no clear, all-purpose definition of 'unconscionable,' nor could there be, unconscionability must be determined on a case by case basis (see Commonwealth v. Gustafsson, 370 Mass. 181, 187 [346 N.E.2d 706] [1976]), giving particular attention to whether, at the time of the execution of the agreement, the contract provision could result in unfair surprise and was oppressive to the allegedly disadvantaged party." *Zapatha*, supra 381 Mass. at 292–293, 408 N.E.2d 1370. "The fact that particular conduct is permitted by statute or by common law principles should be considered, but it is not conclusive on the question of unfairness," Schubach v. Household Fin. Corp., 375 Mass. 133, 137, 376 N.E.2d 140 (1978), nor is it conclusive as to fairness that conduct is expressly permitted by a contract between the parties, Fortune v. National Cash Register Co., 373 Mass. 96, 104–105, 364 N.E.2d 1251 (1977).

UCC § 9–503, permits self-help repossession independent of similar contractual permission. Accordingly, neither the act of repossession nor a contract permitting it is per se unconscionable. Furthermore, the security agreement specifically provides that Penney "may have possession and use of the Collateral *until default*" and that upon default the bank shall have "the rights and remedies of a secured party under the Uniform Commercial Code of Massachusetts, *including without limitation thereto the right to take immediate possession of the Collateral*" (emphasis added). Regardless of whether Penney was familiar with the provisions of § 9–503, he was fairly put on notice of the bank's unconditional right to take immediate possession upon default. In addition, the contract provision for notice before sale, together with the lack of provision for notice before repossession, fairly implied that notice was not a prerequisite to repossession. There was no potential for unfair surprise in the note and security agreement provisions allowing immediate repossession upon default. If Penney was surprised by the repossession, he was not surprised unfairly.

There was no oppression in including in the notes and security agreement a provision confirming the remedies available under § 9–503. We view the question of oppression as directed to the substantive fairness to the parties of permitting the repossession provisions as written. See *Zapatha*, supra 381 Mass. at 295, 408 N.E.2d 1370. The right of repossession without notice was reasonably related to the bank's need for assurance that the collateral would be available to it in the event of default. The risk to the bank of having a right of repossession only after notice to Penney was not disproportionate to Penney's risk of loss upon repossession without notice. In light of the bank's commercial needs, it was not unfair to impose upon Penney the practical requirement that after default he limit the amount of his equipment at sea or that he make arrangements for retrieving it other than by means of the collateral.

Penney argues that it was unfair for the bank to repossess the boat when it knew or should have known that Penney might have fishing equipment at sea worth thousands of dollars, and when it had an attachment in the amount of $18,500 on land with an equity of $35,000 owned by Regan, the guarantor. What we have said in the preceding paragraph disposes of the contention that it was unfair to repossess without notice, apart from the attachment, and we know of no authority or sound reason for requiring that a creditor exhaust his rights against a guarantor before proceeding against the debtor's property. We hold that the facts established here require that neither the contractual provisions permitting self-help repossession, nor the implementation thereof, are "oppressive or otherwise unconscionable" within the meaning of the Attorney General's Regulation XV. The bank's motion for summary judgment on Penney's complaint was properly allowed.

3. *Attorney's fees.* Penney challenges the award of any attorney's fees incurred by the bank to defend the wrongful repossession and c. 93A claims * * *.

Each note provided that Penney would pay all costs of collection and attorney's fees paid or incurred by the bank in enforcing the note on default. The order of the judge allowing the bank's motion for summary judgment on its counterclaim with the assent of both parties provided that no execution was to issue until resolution of Penney's claims or further order of the court. Defense of Penney's claims was therefore essential to collection on the notes, and the attorney's fees incurred for that defense were incurred by the bank in enforcing the notes. In addition, those fees were required to withstand attack upon the repossession and sale of the boat, which were an integral part of the collection process. They were expenses of the collection process and so were within the fee provisions of the notes.

Judgments affirmed.

NOTES

1. The right of self-help repossession, set out in § 9–503, is the creditor's most cherished weapon. It is cheap, fast, and effective. On the other hand, in allowing creditors to act extra-judicially, this remedy is particularly offensive to debtor groups which claim that it is subject to abuse. The revolution in creditors' remedies law occasioned by Sniadach v. Family Finance Corp., 395 U.S. 337, 89 S.Ct. 1820, 23 L.Ed.2d 349 (1969), threatened the legality of self-help repossession. Both creditor and debtor groups threw maximum resources into a series of test cases that raged across the country throughout the 70s. But, as *Penney* indicates, the creditors won all of the battles and the great debtor-creditor issue of the decade never reached the United States Supreme Court. See Burke & Reber, State Action, Congressional Power and Creditors' Rights: An Essay on the Fourteenth Amendment, 47 So.Cal.L.Rev. 1 (1973); McCall, The Past as Prologue: History of the Right to Repossess, 47 So.Cal.L.Rev. 58 (1973).

2. The secured party has the rights and remedies provided for in Part 5 of Article 9 even though the security agreement is silent on the subject. § 9–501(1). Hence, it is possible that the secured party has the right of self-help repossession without knowledge of that fact by the debtor. But other law may apply. For example, Maryland has enacted a statute making self-help repossession a crime unless the security agreement specifically authorizes the remedy. Maryland Code, Art. 27, § 343. See Opinion of the Attorney General of Maryland, 32 U.C.C.Rep. 359 (1980).

3. There are two questions in repossession cases: (1) Was the creditor entitled to repossession? (2) Has the debt been accelerated? The first depends on whether there has been a default, for a creditor may repossess under § 9–503 only if the debtor is in default. The second usually depends on whether there is an acceleration clause and whether it has been triggered. Acceleration determines the amount of the debt that is due at the time of repossession. That amount determines how much the debtor must pay to redeem (§ 9–506) and the amount the creditor receives from the proceeds of the sale (§ 9–504(1)).

Was the Creditor Entitled to Repossession? In *Penney* the bank seized the lobster boat without prior notice. The debtor asserted that, in consequence, he lost $34,000 of fishing equipment that was left out at sea. If there has been a default, Article 9 imposes no duty on the creditor to give notice of intention to repossess. In the usual case, as in *Penney,* the existence of a default is clear because the debtor is behind in payments on the debt. However, in some cases the existence of default may depend on notice to the debtor. In Mechanics National Bank v. Killeen, 377 Mass. 100, 384 N.E.2d 1231 (1979), the debt, secured by shares of stock, was evidenced by a note that provided that the debtor's obligation "shall, at the option of Bank, become immediately due and payable upon * * * Bank deeming itself insecure." The court held that the bank had no right to sell the collateral until it had notified the debtor that it had accelerated the debt and had given the debtor a reasonable opportunity to satisfy the accelerated obligation. Until that was done there was no default. Accord: Manufacturers Hanover Leasing Corp. v. Ace Drilling Co., 726 F.Supp. 966 (S.D.N.Y.1989).

Has the Debt Been Accelerated? This should depend on the wording of the acceleration clause. In Fulton National Bank v. Horn, 239 Ga. 648, 238 S.E.2d 358 (1977), the security agreement said: "In the event of a default, any of the Liabilities [any indebtedness owed the bank, whether due or to become due] may, at the option of the Bank and without demand or notice of any kind, be declared, by Bank, and thereupon immediately shall become due and payable and Bank may [repossess] * * *." The court said:

> Where the parties agree that in the event of default the creditor "may declare" acceleration, the exercise of the option to declare acceleration must be communicated to the debtor or manifested by some affirmative act sufficient to constitute notice to the debtor of acceleration * * * but where the parties agree that in the event of default the creditor "may declare" acceleration "without notice" to the debtor * * * notice of declaration of acceleration need not be communicated to the debtor.

238 S.E.2d at 360.

Even if the security agreement does not allow the creditor to accelerate without giving notice to the debtor, the creditor can nevertheless repossess without notice so long as there has been an event of default such as a missed payment. After repossession the creditor can notify the debtor of its decision to accelerate, the accelerated amount owing, and its intentions about disposition of the collateral.

4. In *Penney* if the bank had known that its failure to give the debtor notice of repossession would result in the loss to the

debtor of $34,000 of fishing equipment, would the good faith requirement of § 1–203 have imposed a duty of notice on the bank? Should § 1–203 require that notice of repossession be given in any case in which there is no danger of the debtor's removing, concealing, or dissipating the collateral?

5. Some consumer protection statutes prevent the creditor from accelerating or repossessing until the debtor is notified of the right to cure a default within a stated number of days. See, e.g., Uniform Consumer Credit Code § 5.110 and § 5.111 (1974); Wis. Stat.Ann. § 425.104 and § 425.105 (1988).

PROBLEM

Cobb bought a truck from Mack for $28,886, of which $23,886 was to be paid pursuant to an installment contract calling for 48 monthly payments of $497.63 each. The installment contract provided that time was of the essence and that if Cobb failed to pay any installment when due the full balance would become due thereby giving Mack the right to repossess without notice or demand. It also stated "Any waiver of any breach or default shall not constitute a waiver of any other subsequent breach or default." Cobb's payment record was irregular almost from the start. For two years he was always at least two payments in default and there were times when he made no payments for three or more months. When Cobb was particularly delinquent Mack would send him form letters, couched in the stilted language of the bill collector, that if he didn't get current Mack would "terminate his financial agreement" or "pursue a course of action outlined in your contract." Mack never mentioned the crude word "repossession" and consistently accepted Cobb's late payments, assessing late charges respecting these payments. With Cobb still two payments behind and only $2,000 remaining unpaid, Mack had had enough and repossessed the truck. Cobb sued for conversion because Mack had failed to notify him that strict compliance would be required in the future after late payments had been accepted. Mack defended on the basis of the nonwaiver provisions of the contract. What result? See Cobb v. Midwest Recovery Bureau Co., 295 N.W.2d 232 (Minn.1980), and Nevada National Bank v. Huff, 94 Nev. 506, 582 P.2d 364 (1978).

WILLIAMS v. FORD MOTOR CREDIT CO.

United States Court of Appeals, Eighth Circuit, 1982.
674 F.2d 717.

BENSON, CHIEF JUDGE.

In this diversity action brought by Cathy A. Williams to recover damages for conversion arising out of an alleged wrongful repossession of an automobile, Williams appeals from a judgment notwithstanding the verdict entered on motion of defendant Ford

Motor Credit Company (FMCC). In the same case, FMCC appeals a directed verdict in favor of third party defendant S & S Recovery, Inc. (S & S) on FMCC's third party claim for indemnification. We affirm the judgment n.o.v. FMCC's appeal is thereby rendered moot.

In July, 1975, David Williams, husband of plaintiff Cathy Williams, purchased a Ford Mustang from an Oklahoma Ford dealer. Although David Williams executed the sales contract, security agreement, and loan papers, title to the car was in the name of both David and Cathy Williams. The car was financed through the Ford dealer, who in turn assigned the paper to FMCC. Cathy and David Williams were divorced in 1977. The divorce court granted Cathy title to the automobile and required David to continue to make payments to FMCC for eighteen months. David defaulted on the payments and signed a voluntary repossession authorization for FMCC. Cathy Williams was informed of the delinquency and responded that she was trying to get her former husband David to make the payments. There is no evidence of any agreement between her and FMCC. Pursuant to an agreement with FMCC, S & S was directed to repossess the automobile.

On December 1, 1977, at approximately 4:30 a.m., Cathy Williams was awakened by a noise outside her house trailer in Van Buren, Arkansas.[2] She saw that a wrecker truck with two men in it had hooked up to the Ford Mustang and started to tow it away. She went outside and hollered at them. The truck stopped. She then told them that the car was hers and asked them what they were doing. One of the men, later identified as Don Sappington, president of S & S Recovery, Inc., informed her that he was repossessing the vehicle on behalf of FMCC. Williams explained that she had been attempting to bring the past due payments up to date and informed Sappington that the car contained personal items which did not even belong to her. Sappington got out of the truck, retrieved the items from the car, and handed them to her. Without further complaint from Williams, Sappington returned to the truck and drove off, car in tow. At trial, Williams testified that Sappington was polite throughout their encounter and did not make any threats toward her or do anything which caused her to fear any physical harm. The automobile had been parked in an unenclosed driveway which plaintiff shared with a neighbor. The neighbor was awakened by the wrecker backing into the driveway, but did not come out. After the wrecker drove off, Williams returned to her house trailer and called the police, reporting her car as stolen. Later, Williams commenced this action.

2. Cathy Williams testified that the noise sounded like there was a car stuck in her yard.

The case was tried to a jury which awarded her $5,000.00 in damages. FMCC moved for judgment notwithstanding the verdict, but the district court, on Williams' motion, ordered a nonsuit without prejudice to refile in state court. On FMCC's appeal, this court reversed and remanded with directions to the district court to rule on the motion for judgment notwithstanding the verdict. The district court entered judgment notwithstanding the verdict for FMCC, and this appeal followed.

§ 9–503 provides in pertinent part:

> Unless otherwise agreed, a secured party has on default the right to take possession of the collateral. In taking possession, a secured party may proceed without judicial process if this can be done without breach of the peace. * * *[4]

In Ford Motor Credit Co. v. Herring, 27 U.C.C.Rep. 1448, 267 Ark. 201, 589 S.W.2d 584, 586 (1979), which involved an alleged conversion arising out of a repossession, the Supreme Court of Arkansas cited § 9–503 and referred to its previous holdings as follows:

> In pre-code cases, we have sustained a finding of conversion only where force, or threats of force, or risk of invoking violence, accompanied the repossession. * * *

The thrust of Williams' argument on appeal is that the repossession was accomplished by the risk of invoking violence. The district judge who presided at the trial commented on her theory in his memorandum opinion:

> Mrs. Williams herself admitted that the men who repossessed her automobile were very polite and complied with her requests. The evidence does not reveal that they performed any act which was oppressive, threatening or tended to cause physical violence. Unlike the situation presented in Manhattan Credit Co. v. Brewer, supra, it was not shown that Mrs. Williams would have been forced to resort to physical violence to stop the men from leaving with her automobile.

In the pre-Code case Manhattan Credit Co. v. Brewer, 232 Ark. 976, 341 S.W.2d 765 (1961), the court held that a breach of peace occurred when the debtor and her husband confronted the creditor's agent during the act of repossession and clearly objected to the repossession, 341 S.W.2d at 767–68. In *Manhattan,* the court examined holdings of earlier cases in which repossessions were deemed to have been accomplished without any breach of the peace, id. In particular, the Supreme Court of Arkansas discussed

---

4. It is generally considered that the objectives of this section are (1) to benefit creditors in permitting them to realize collateral without having to resort to judicial process; (2) to benefit debtors in general by making credit available at lower costs * * *; and (3) to support a public policy discouraging extrajudicial acts by citizens when those acts are fraught with the likelihood of resulting violence * * *.

the case of Rutledge v. Universal C.I.T. Credit Corp., 218 Ark. 510, 237 S.W.2d 469 (1951). In *Rutledge,* the court found no breach of the peace when the repossessor acquired keys to the automobile, confronted the debtor and his wife, informed them he was going to take the car, and immediately proceeded to do so. As the *Rutledge* court explained and the *Manhattan* court reiterated, a breach of the peace did not occur when the "Appellant [debtor-possessor] did not give his permission but he did not object." *Manhattan,* supra, 341 S.W.2d at 767–68; *Rutledge,* supra, 237 S.W.2d at 470.

We have read the transcript of the trial. There is no material dispute in the evidence, and the district court has correctly summarized it. Cathy Williams did not raise an objection to the taking, and the repossession was accomplished without any incident which might tend to provoke violence. * * *

Appellees deserve something less than commendation for the taking during the night time sleeping hours, but it is clear that viewing the facts in the light most favorable to Williams, the taking was a legal repossession under the laws of the State of Arkansas. The evidence does not support the verdict of the jury. FMCC is entitled to judgment notwithstanding the verdict.

The judgment notwithstanding the verdict is affirmed.

HEANEY, CIRCUIT JUDGE, dissenting.

The only issue is whether the repossession of appellant's automobile constituted a breach of the peace by creating a "risk of invoking violence." See Ford Motor Credit Co. v. Herring, 267 Ark. 201, 589 S.W.2d 584, 586 (1979). The trial jury found that it did and awarded $5,000 for conversion. Because that determination was in my view a reasonable one, I dissent from the Court's decision to overturn it.

Cathy Williams was a single parent living with her two small children in a trailer home in Van Buren, Arkansas. On December 1, 1977, at approximately 4:30 a.m., she was awakened by noises in her driveway. She went into the night to investigate and discovered a wrecker and its crew in the process of towing away her car. According to the trial court, "she ran outside to stop them * * * but she made no *strenuous* protests to their actions." (Emphasis added.) In fact, the wrecker crew stepped between her and the car when she sought to retrieve personal items from inside it, although the men retrieved some of the items for her. The commotion created by the incident awakened neighbors in the vicinity.

Facing the wrecker crew in the dead of night, Cathy Williams did everything she could to stop them, short of introducing physical force to meet the presence of the crew. The confrontation did not result in violence only because Ms. Williams did not take such steps and was otherwise powerless to stop the crew.

The controlling law is the UCC, which authorizes self-help repossession only when such is done "without breach of the peace * * *." § 9–503. The majority recognizes that one important policy consideration underlying this restriction is to discourage "extrajudicial acts by citizens when those acts are fraught with the likelihood of resulting violence." Supra, at 719. Despite this, the majority holds that no reasonable jury could find that the confrontation in Cathy Williams' driveway at 4:30 a.m. created a risk of violence. I cannot agree. At a minimum, the largely undisputed facts created a jury question. The jury found a breach of the peace and this Court has no sound, much less compelling, reason to overturn that determination.

Indeed, I would think that sound application of the self-help limitation might require a directed verdict in favor of Ms. Williams, but certainly not against her. If a "night raid" is conducted without detection and confrontation, then, of course, there could be no breach of the peace. But where the invasion is detected and a confrontation ensues, the repossessor should be under a duty to retreat and turn to judicial process. The alternative which the majority embraces is to allow a repossessor to proceed following confrontation unless and until violence results in fact. Such a rule invites tragic consequences which the law should seek to prevent, not to encourage. I would reverse the trial court and reinstate the jury's verdict.

NOTES

1. What would the court have Cathy Williams do to show her lack of consent?

2. In Thompson v. Ford Motor Company, quoted in the principal case, the automobile sought by the seller was found in a repair garage. The garageman refused to allow the seller to take the vehicle unless he had obtained the debtor's consent. The seller lied in telling the garageman that he had the debtor's consent. The court said "Merely to connive to repossess does not make [the seller] liable * * * *" On similar facts the same result was reached in K.B. Oil Co. v. Ford Motor Credit Co., Inc., 811 F.2d 310 (6th Cir. 1987). In Reno v. General Motors Acceptance Corp., 378 So.2d 1103 (Ala.1979), the finance company repossessed an automobile from the parking lot of a grocery supermarket where the debtor worked by use of a duplicate key obtained from the dealer who had sold the installment contract to the finance company. The court held that there was no breach of the peace because possession was obtained without fraud, artifice, stealth, or trickery. The same court found a breach of the peace when the "repo man" induced the debtor to drive his car to the dealer's office to discuss whether his payments were in arrears.

While the debtor was inside discussing the account, his car was removed. Ford Motor Credit Co. v. Byrd, 351 So.2d 557 (Ala.1977).

3. If the collateral is in an enclosed area the creditor must either obtain the consent of the debtor to take the property or must resort to judicial process. Replevin statutes allow levying officers to use force to enter and seize the collateral. The following provisions are found in the California Code of Civil Procedure § 514.010:

> (c) If the specified property or any part of it is in a private place, the levying officer shall at the time he demands possession of the property announce his identity, purpose, and authority. If the property is not voluntarily delivered, the levying officer may cause any building or enclosure where the property may be located to be broken open in such a manner as he reasonably believes will cause the least damage and may call upon the power of the county to aid and protect him, but, if he reasonably believes that entry and seizure of the property will involve a substantial risk of death or serious bodily harm to any person, he shall refrain from seizing the property and shall promptly make a return to the court from which the writ issued setting forth the reasons for his belief that the risk exists. In such case, the court shall make such orders as may be appropriate.

> (d) Nothing in this section authorizes the levying officer to enter or search any private place not specified in the writ of possession or other order of the court.

PROBLEM

Seller sold Buyer a tractor and Buyer fell in default. When Seller demanded payment, Buyer was unable to pay and said that he would not give up possession of the tractor unless Seller established his right to repossess by judicial proceedings. He said that "someone would get hurt" if an attempt was made to repossess without "proper papers." Seller filed suit in Washington but was unable to locate the tractor. Later he located the tractor in Oregon and contacted the local sheriff, requesting him to accompany him in retaking the tractor. Proceeding to the site of the tractor was a convoy made up of Seller's car, his mechanic in a pickup, a lo-boy truck to transport the tractor, and the sheriff's official car. The sheriff was in uniform, wearing his badge and sidearms. The sheriff, who had seen the contract, informed Buyer that Seller had the right to repossess and said, "We come to pick up the tractor." Buyer asked whether the sheriff had the proper papers to take the tractor and the sheriff replied, "No." Buyer protested the repossession but offered no physical resistance because, as he later testified, he didn't think he could disregard the order of a sheriff. Seller testified that he had the sheriff present

to prevent anticipated violence. Is Seller liable in conversion?
See Stone Machinery Co. v. Kessler, 1 Wn.App. 750, 463 P.2d 651
(1970).

D. DISPOSAL OF COLLATERAL

---

1. RESALE OF COLLATERAL

The law has long struggled with the problem of how to strike
a fair balance between the interest of the foreclosing creditor in
being able to realize on collateral quickly and cheaply and the
rights of the defaulting debtor in having a fair disposition of the
property. The traditional view was to require a public sale to the
highest cash bidder after public notice of the sale. As in the
foreclosure of real estate mortgages, if the creditor complied with
all of the procedural requirements, the sale was a valid termination of all the debtor's rights in the collateral even though the
price obtained for the property might be only a fraction of what
the debtor thought the property was worth. The Uniform Conditional Sales Act was an example of the assimilation of the procedures for disposition on default of personal property to the rigid
procedures long used in the foreclosure of real property mortgages.

The drafters of the Code wanted something better than the
"sale on the courthouse steps" held before a listless audience of
courthouse loiterers or, still worse, before a conniving group of
professional public sale bidders colluding to keep the bids down.
In Part 5 of Article 9, they strove to loosen up the disposition
process and make it more businesslike to get a better return.
They encouraged the creditor to resell in private sales at market
prices. But as a balance to this freedom of action the creditor was
held to a post-audit standard of "commercial reasonableness" in
all aspects of the realization process with strict accountability for
failure to meet this flexible standard.

a. DEBTOR'S RIGHT TO NOTICE AND
COMMERCIALLY REASONABLE RESALE

MATTER OF EXCELLO PRESS, INC.
United States Court of Appeals, Seventh Circuit, 1989.
890 F.2d 896.

EASTERBROOK, CIRCUIT JUDGE.

* * *

I

Excello Press was a commercial printer in Elk Grove, Illinois; now it is a bankrupt. It filed under Chapter 11 in October 1985.

* * *

In late 1980 Metlife Capital Credit Corp. sold Excello two web presses (web presses print on continuous rolls of paper), an M110 and an M1000, for a little more than $3 million to be paid over ten years. Metlife retained a security interest. By the time of the bankruptcy Excello still owed Metlife about $2.7 million. Metlife attempted to collect from Excello under Article Nine of the Uniform Commercial Code, which governs a debtor's default under a security agreement. See U.C.C. § 9–501(1). The parties agree that New York's interpretation of the UCC governs, as the contract provides.

To liquidate its collateral, Metlife required a modification of the automatic stay imposed by § 362(a) of the Bankruptcy Code. On April 4, 1986, the bankruptcy court entered an agreed order, which permitted Metlife to sell the two presses. Metlife promised to remove them from Excello's plant by April 30. The agreement also capped Metlife's deficiency claim at $900,000 should the presses fetch less than the $2.7 million debt—as they did. Metlife sold each press privately for $550,000, the M1000 on April 23 and the M110 in June. This left Excello's debt at more than $1.6 million, U.C.C. § 9–504(2), and Metlife filed the maximum claim of $900,000, to which Excello and its unsecured creditors' committee objected. The bankruptcy court held a hearing in November to resolve the dispute.

Over three days of testimony, Metlife argued that it had sold the presses in a commercially reasonable fashion, had received the fair market value, and was entitled to its deficiency judgment. Four witnesses testified that Metlife began to look for buyers in December 1985. Harris, the manufacturer, was enlisted to help in the marketing effort. More than 30 of the 150 largest printers were solicited, as were 13 other prospects and nine brokers in 15 states. Metlife introduced an appraisal dated March 1985, filed as part of the bankruptcy petition, estimating that the two presses together were worth $1.2 million. Excello owned one each of the same models clear of liens; it valued these at $1.55 million, the difference likely reflecting that each of Excello's presses could print five colors. (Metlife's could print only four.) Excello sold these presses at a public auction and received a total of $950,000. The difference might have tracked a change in the market, but the only testimony on the state of the market for presses of this kind was excluded as hearsay. Finally, Metlife observed that the cap on its deficiency judgment gave it every incentive to maximize the return on the presses. Its deficiency judgment was going to be

$900,000 unless it managed to get more than $1.8 million for the two presses, which was unlikely. So every extra cent received on the sale would go straight to its treasury, while the estate would pay out less than 100 cents on the dollar for any judgment, already limited by the cap, it obtained. (Metlife's $900,000 claim is worth only about $200,000.)

At the close of Metlife's case, Judge James granted judgment in Excello's favor. * * * Excello argued that Metlife had not proved that it had given notice and conducted a commercially reasonable sale as required by the UCC. Metlife had mailed a written notice on April 23, the day before the first sale was finalized, simply stating that it was selling the presses, without indicating when. Relying on Executive Financial Services, Inc. v. Garrison, 722 F.2d 417 (8th Cir.1983) (Missouri law), Judge James predicted that New York would establish that only written notice would satisfy the command that "reasonable notification of the time after which any private sale or other intended disposition is to be made shall be sent by the secured party to the debtor". U.C.C. § 9–504(3). The April 23 notice was not "reasonable notification", he found. When notice is not given, New York law creates a presumption that the collateral's fair market value at the time of the sale is equal to the amount of the debt. Judge James concluded that Metlife had not overcome this presumption. He would not consider the price Metlife had received at its sale because he rejected Metlife's employees' testimony about the sale as coming from biased parties. The other evidence was not enough to convince him that the presses were worth less than $2.7 million (the amount of the debt): the appraisal was almost two years old, the testimony about the market from Metlife employees was inadmissible hearsay, the prices paid at the auction of the Excello presses were "immaterial". What was missing? "[T]estimony of persons familiar with the business to apprise the Court of what is a fair market price of available goods—or available market for these goods".

Judge James reiterated these determinations when he denied Metlife's motion for reconsideration, and added a new ground for disregarding the price obtained from the sale: because Metlife hadn't given notice, it could not use the price achieved at the sale as evidence of market value. On this view, whether the sale had been conducted in a commercially reasonable fashion is irrelevant. 83 B.R. 539, 543 (Bankr.N.D.Ill.1988).

The district court affirmed. 90 B.R. 335 (N.D.Ill.1988). The judge found it unnecessary to determine whether New York would require written notice, because Metlife had not shown that it gave adequate oral notice. Agreeing that New York would require Metlife to rebut a presumption that the presses had a market value of $2.7 million, he deferred to the bankruptcy court's determination that the presumption had not been overcome and did not decide whether New York would prohibit recovery in the absence of notice. He relied on Colorado Leasing Corp. v. Borquez, 738 P.2d 377, 380 (Colo.App.1986) (interpreting Colorado law), for the proposition that prices from sales that violate any provision of § 9–504(3) are not evidence of fair market value.

* * *

Metlife contends that written notice is not a precondition to a deficiency judgment and that the district court erred when it found that no oral notice had been given. Even if the notice was inadequate, Metlife continues, the bankruptcy judge erred in finding that the fair market value of the presses had not been established. Excello replies that factual findings should not be disturbed unless clearly erroneous * * * which it submits they are not.

II

The outcome turns on U.C.C. § 9–504(3), which sets out a secured party's obligations in disposing of collateral:

> Disposition of the collateral may be by public or private proceedings * * * [E]very aspect of the disposition including the method, manner, time, place and terms must be commercially reasonable. Unless collateral is perishable or threatens to decline speedily in value or is of a type customarily sold on a recognized market * * * reasonable notification of the time after which any private sale or other intended disposition is to be made shall be sent by the secured party to the debtor if he has not signed after default a statement renouncing or modifying his right to notification of the sale.

The UCC doesn't define either "commercially reasonable" or "reasonable notification"; it also does not explain how these obligations relate to an action for deficiency. In order to sort this dispute out, we must look at how this subsection fits into the rest of Article Nine.

A

Both of the courts below started by asking whether Metlife had given "reasonable notification", assuming the answer would affect recovery of the deficiency. The significance of notice is not so obvious, however. The Code and its official comments are silent about the effect of noncompliance with § 9–504(3) on a deficiency action; the drafters of Article Nine did not consider the question. Grant Gilmore, 2 Security Interests in Personal Property § 44.9.4 at 1264 (1965). The only provision speaking to the debtor's entitlements is § 9–507(1): "If the disposition has occurred the debtor * * * has a right to recover from the secured party any loss caused by a failure to comply with the provisions of this Part." Perhaps this remedy for non-compliance is exclusive—if the secured party has not fulfilled its obligations, the debtor can counter-claim for or obtain a set-off of any damages suffered in consequence of a commercially unreasonable sale or inadequate notice. Some courts have construed Article Nine this way.

* * *

This approach is a logical outgrowth of the common law's allocation of responsibilities. An action for deficiency is one form of action for payment of a debt: the sale of the collateral is partial satisfaction. In the traditional debt action, the plaintiff need only establish that a debt is owed and its amount. Payment is an affirmative defense. A debtor's challenge to the disposition of collateral is a complaint that the payment, in the form of the repossessed collateral, is worth more than the credit given by the lender: there is no question that the debtor owes the lender, only how much of the debt has been repaid.

Attractive as this might be, it is a minority position among the states, and New York has evinced little interest in it. New York courts, in line with the majority of the other states' courts, say that compliance with § 9–504(3) is part of the creditor's proof in a deficiency action. And even though there is nothing in the Code about who shall have the burden of persuasion with respect to compliance, these courts are nearly unanimous in assuming without discussion that it belongs to the secured party. * * * Pursuing the analogy to the debt action, this is akin to placing on the creditor the burden of proving non-payment.

If secured parties are not likely to maximize the price obtained for repossessed collateral then it might be sound to place on them the burdens of production and persuasion, supplying an incentive to do so. A belief that secured parties consistently do not maximize has been deployed in support of a conclusion that all deficiency judgments should be barred. Philip Shuchman, Profit on Default: An Archival Study of Automobile Repossession and Resale, 22 Stan.L.Rev. 20 (1969) (study of 89 car repossessions in Connecticut). But why shouldn't they maximize? Even if the secured party could be assured of a judgment for the full deficiency, why would it forgo a dollar today for the chance to enforce a deficiency judgment tomorrow? The UCC provides that the proceeds from the sale of the collateral are applied first to the expenses incurred in its disposition; the remainder goes to satisfy the debt. U.C.C. § 9–504(1)(a). So even if the return after expenses is small, the secured party will expend every cost-justified effort because it prefers money now to judgment later. See Alan Schwartz, The Enforceability of Security Interests in Consumer Goods, 26 J.L. & Econ. 117, 126–27 (1983) (demonstrating that rational creditors will maximize sale prices of repossessed collateral). Add the uncertainty of recovery in litigation and this preference for cash grows stronger. That the debtor has defaulted is an indication that it is unlikely to be good for all of any judgment the creditor is able to get. See White & Summers, 2 Uniform Commercial Code § 27–14 at 612. This case illustrates the point. Every dollar extra that Metlife got for the presses went straight into its pockets. Even if its possible judgment had not been capped at $900,000—$700,000 less than it was owed after selling the presses—it still would not have recovered more than 22¢ on the dollar. What reason could Metlife have had to do anything but maximize the resale price? True, it would have had little incentive to maximize any surplus (which must be paid to the debtor under § 9–502(2)), but all agree that the majority of cases, like this one, involve creditors who are under-secured.

One treatise argues that secured parties should bear the burden because they are in control of the procedures called into question. White & Summers, 2 Uniform Commercial Code § 27–16 at 617–18. This, however, is at best a reason to impose on them the burden of production, not the burden of persuasion. At least one court has adopted this approach. Karlstad State Bank v. Fritsche, 374 N.W.2d 177 (Minn.App.1985). Another justification for laying the burden on the creditor might be that the creditor as plaintiff must prove every element of its case, including compliance with § 9–504(3). But this begs the question: *why* is compliance with § 9–504(3) an "element" of the claim? One only need think about the situation where the lender is over-secured and the debtor is owed the surplus to see the problem. If enough money is realized from the sale of the collateral to cover the debt, the debtor may have to sue the lender under § 9–507(1) if it thought the surplus was not as great as it could have been. Many courts say that the debtor, as plaintiff, must prove that the creditor has not complied with § 9–504(3). * * * Yet there is no reason to make the burden of persuasion turn on the amount realized at the sale or the sequence of pleadings.

Despite our doubt that the courts of New York have fully considered the subject, we have no doubt about how New York's courts would approach the question if this case were pending there. Although no New York court has given reasons, and although the cases seem to reflect assumptions about a subject that has not been argued by the parties, a pervasive assumption is good evidence about how the courts will decide. New York regularly, albeit without explanation, lays the burden on the secured creditor. What happens when this burden is not met, however, is less clear.

B

Excello argues that Metlife did not comply with the notice requirement of § 9–504(3) because written notice is required and

Metlife didn't give it. The UCC does not provide any definition of "reasonable notification", and, as with most of the issues raised in this appeal, the Court of Appeals of New York has not addressed the subject. Metlife points to several trial court decisions applying New York law holding that oral notification achieving actual notice is sufficient under § 9–504(3). * * * The bankruptcy judge disregarded these cases and agreed with Excello, relying on a case from the Eighth Circuit construing Missouri law. The Eighth Circuit focused on the phrase "shall be sent":

> It is difficult to believe that, in choosing this language, the draftsmen contemplated oral notice as being sufficient. * * * Section 9–504 requires that the secured party "send" notice and 1–201(38) tells us that ' "Send" in connection with any writing or notice means to deposit in the mail or deliver for transmission by any other usual means of communication with postage provided for and properly addressed * * *.' It is most difficult to fit an oral message into the quoted language. Rather the subsection seems to contemplate mail or telegraphic notice.

Executive Financial Services, Inc. v. Garrison, 722 F.2d 417, 418–19 (8th Cir.1983), quoting from White & Summers, Uniform Commercial Code § 26–10 at 1112 (2d ed. 1980). Yet the UCC also provides that a person has "notice" of a fact "when (a) he has actual knowledge of it; or (b) he has received a notice or notification of it; or (c) from all the facts and circumstances known to him at the time in question he has reason to know that it exists." U.C.C. § 1–201(25). The very next section of Article Nine implies that the drafters did not use "send" to imply "written". U.C.C. § 9–505(2) ("[w]ritten notice * * * shall be sent * * *"). See MBank Dallas, N.A. v. Sunbelt Manufacturing, Inc., 710 S.W.2d 633 (Tex.App.1986) (§ 9–504(3) therefore allows oral notice). "Send" can mean "give", which may be done orally. There is little reason to rely on the definition of "send" over that of "notice" in order to impose the additional requirement of a writing. The purposes of the notice requirement are to allow the debtor to ensure that the sale is commercially reasonable, find another buyer, or redeem the debt. * * * If the debtor knew enough to monitor the sale, that is sufficient. Did Excello receive notice in time to come up with another buyer or to request information on Metlife's plans so as to challenge them? If so, then Metlife fulfilled its obligation to provide "reasonable notification".

Unfortunately, this question remains unanswered. The district court's determination that Excello did not have actual notice flowed not from the facts but from its assumption that New York would follow Spillers v. First National Bank, 81 Ill.App.3d 199, 36 Ill.Dec. 477, 480, 400 N.E.2d 1057, 1060 (4th Dist.1980) ("It therefore became the duty of [the secured party] to notify petitioner of all and every proposed private sale, or sales. Simply being aware of an impending sale is insufficient.") (citation omitted). *Spillers* read the phrase "any private sale" in "reasonable notification of the time after which any private sale or other intended disposition is to be made" to mean "all and every proposed private sale". Ibid. But this ignores the "after which" language. Notice of a private sale need only let the debtor know how much time he has before the collateral will be sold, not to whom or even if a definite buyer is lined up. To be reasonable, notice must assure that the debtor has sufficient time to take appropriate action to protect its interests. Fitzpatrick v. Bank of New York, 124 Misc.2d 732, 480 N.Y.S.2d 157, 159 (2d Dept.1983); U.C.C. § 9–504(3) Official Comment 5. Notice provides time for the debtor to protect itself: to bid on the collateral, to find other buyers, to get involved in the process of selling it. There is nothing in § 9–504(3) which requires the creditor to tell the debtor anything more than the "time after which" the disposition will occur, so any notice after the first one indicating "the time after which" would be redundant. "Reasonable notification" does not relieve the debtor of all responsibility to act to defend its self-interest; the secured party need not put forth a steady stream of notices, while the debtor sits back and does nothing. Similarly, Excello's contention that they had to be notified of the time and place of the sale is silly. Knowing time and place is helpful for a public sale where monitoring the actual bidding and presentation of the collateral is feasible—indeed it is required by § 9–504(3). When a sale is private, by contrast, the debtor needs to know how much time it has to scare up buyers, which is why the statute requires the creditor to tell the debtor the "time after which" the sale may occur, and why only one notice is required.

Metlife believes that its notice of April 23 was "reasonable notification" of the sale of the second press, which did not occur until June. But the notice baldly stated that the presses were going to be sold, without giving a "time after which" the sale was to occur. So Excello did not know how long it had to procure buyers, at least from the written notice. Metlife also urges us to rule that it gave "reasonable notification" because Excello had actual notice. By February 28, Excello knew that Metlife intended to sell the presses through a private sale rather than Excello's public auction. Excello helped Metlife identify potential buyers, and on several occasions assisted Metlife in demonstrating the presses to interested prospects, both proving, according to Metlife, that Excello had plenty of time to act. Since removing the presses from the debtor's plant was a very expensive proposition and likely to decrease the presses' value, Excello must have known that Metlife had a strong incentive to close a sale before April 30. All of this, Metlife argues, is enough to find that Excello had actual notice. That's a strong logical case, but whether a party actually knows something is a question of fact. And Excello has not had an opportunity to put in any evidence. Since this case must be remanded in light of the standards set out in Part II(C), we leave this question to be considered in the first instance by the bankruptcy court.

C

Excello presses on us an argument that the bankruptcy court rejected and the district court did not reach: that New York would bar a deficiency judgment if notice were inadequate. Several states have taken this position * * *. We agree with the bankruptcy court, however, that New York would apply what has been termed the middle-of-the-road position (between barring a deficiency and leaving the debtor only a counterclaim under § 9–507(1)):

> [D]espite failure of the secured party to give notice of sale of the security to the debtor as provided by the statute, and even despite the creditor's failure to conduct the sale in a commercially reasonable manner, the creditor may still recover a deficiency judgment * * * except that in such cases the secured creditor must prove the amount of his deficiency and that the fair value of the security was less than the amount of the debt. This is sometimes expressed by stating that in such cases there is a presumption that the security was equal to the debt and that the secured party has the burden of proof to overcome such presumption.

Security Trust Co. v. Thomas, 59 A.D.2d 242, 399 N.Y.S.2d 511, 513 (4th Dept.1977) * * * New York's highest court has not spoken on this issue. While one can never be sure of predictions of state law, we do not believe that New York would abandon the other Departments' more recent decisions and return to a rule that makes it even harder to recover deficiencies. Other states have not been stampeding toward an absolute bar; the states seem to be about evenly divided. Although the absolute bar rule has the virtue of predictability, it produces a penalty out of line with the gravity of the omission; moreover, to the extent notice includes oral notice and actual knowledge, the absolute bar rule does not deliver on its promise of easy administration. We therefore conclude that the most recent appellate cases in New York are the best evidence of what New York's highest court would do.

Yet given that the secured party bears the burden of proving compliance with § 9–504(3), does this "rebuttable presumption" change anything? Not unless one takes the extra step, as bankruptcy and district courts did, of refusing to consider the price obtained after a sale without notice. This was, we believe, a step unauthorized by state law, for there is a substantial difference between discounting the weight of evidence and refusing to consider evidence. There may be good reason to discount the evidentiary value of the price, and to require other evidence of the fair market value, when the sale was not commercially reasonable: the price from a commercially unreasonable sale doesn't reveal much about the collateral's market value. And there may be good reason for believing that the failure to give notice decreases the likelihood that the sale was commercially reasonable, because lack of notice may remove from the process the party (the debtor) with the best ability to find buyers (and a good incentive to do so).

Even after discount, though, the sale conveys information. If despite the lack of notice the sale was commercially reasonable, the price is more than merely informative. The product of a commercially reasonable sale *is* the fair market value. If the secured party can prove that the sale was commercially reasonable, it has proved the market value of the collateral. The bankruptcy court misunderstood the relation between the reasonableness of the sale and the market price when it said that the price from a sale without notice could be ignored, so that "Metlife's argument that its disposition of the presses was commercially reasonable becomes moot." 83 B.R. at 543. The price obtained in a commercially reasonable sale is not *evidence* of the market value, which can be discounted or thrown out. It *is* the market value. Whether the sale was commercially reasonable thus is the central inquiry. See Bankers Trust Co. v. J.V. Dowler & Co., 47 N.Y.2d 128, 417 N.Y.S.2d 47, 50–51, 390 N.E.2d 766, 769 (1979) ("the touchstone of its obligations as a secured party was to dispose of the collateral in a 'commercially reasonable' manner"). The third-party evidence (such as an appraiser's estimate), which the bankruptcy judge thought essential to establish the market value and which the district court called superior "direct evidence", 90 B.R. at 339, is at best second-best. What someone pays in a commercially reasonable sale is the market price; an appraisal (that is, what an expert thinks someone would pay in a commercially reasonable sale) is useful only when the price of such a sale cannot be got at directly. If a creditor is able to meet the burden of proving that the sale was commercially reasonable, it has "rebutted the presumption", notice or not.

Lack of notice may make a difference, but only because it is suggestive on the question whether the sale was conducted in a commercially reasonable fashion. The UCC gives it no talismanic significance and allows the omission of notice when other devices protect the debtor. See § 9–504(3), excusing notice when the sale takes place on a "recognized market" or notice is too expensive. In the end, the "principal limitation on the secured party's right to dispose of the collateral is the requirement that he proceed in good faith (Section 1–203) and in a commercially reasonable manner." U.C.C. § 9–507 Official Comment 1. Whether a sale was commercially unreasonable is, like other questions about "reasonableness", a fact-intensive inquiry; no magic set of procedures will immunize a sale from scrutiny. * * * Failure to give notice is evidence of commercially unreasonable behavior. It might indicate that the secured creditor was trying to avoid the debtor's monitoring and call for closer scrutiny; yet the omission might have been innocent, a result of a speedy sale needed to maximize the return, or irrelevant (if the debtor had knowledge anyway). The choice of public versus private sale also depends on the circumstances. Judge James seemed to think that a public auction (such as that conducted by Excello) is always commercially reasonable, so that Metlife could be censured for proceeding otherwise. The right inquiry is whether a particular method of sale was the commercially reasonable way to proceed under *these* circumstances with *this* equipment. * * * And a party's good faith may be taken into account in evaluating whether the sale was on the up-and-up. * * *

Some courts have talked about the possibility of a separate "proceeds test" to hold that the shortfall of the proceeds (compared with the debt) makes a sale commercially unreasonable without regard to the creditor's efforts to obtain a price as high as possible. * * * A low price may signal the need for close scrutiny. A large deficiency might indicate the search for buyers had been inadequate; or it might simply reflect a greatly depreciated piece of collateral. Sumner v. Extebank, 88 A.D.2d 887, 452 N.Y.S.2d 873, 875 (1st Dept.1982) ("The low price paid and the lack of bidders were not the result of a commercially unreasonable sale, but were rather indicative of the lack of demand for a disabled vessel.") * * * So the "proceeds test" is simply another part of looking at the circumstances of the sale. Once the sale is shown to have been commercially reasonable, though, the size of the deficiency is irrelevant. U.C.C. § 9–507(2) ("The fact that a better price could have been obtained by a sale at a different time or in a different method from that selected by the secured party is not of itself sufficient to establish that the sale was not made in a commercially reasonable manner.") * * *

In the end, the court must decide what a reasonable business would have done to maximize the return on the collateral. It must consult "[c]ustoms and usages that actually govern the members of a business calling day-in and day-out [that] not only provide a creditor with standards that are well recognized, but tend to reflect a practical wisdom born of accumulated experience." *Bankers Trust Co.*, 417 N.Y.S.2d at 51, 390 N.E.2d at 769. That inquiry, abjured in the first instance by the bankruptcy court, must be the center of attention on remand.

D

In addition to deciding that commercial reasonableness is irrelevant, Judge James also looked at Metlife's evidence and suggested that it is insufficient. It is unclear to us that the judge gave this independent weight, but to the extent the judge meant this to be a finding of fact, we hold it clearly erroneous. Judge James said that the sale was commercially unreasonable because Metlife had not presented the testimony of disinterested third parties on the question of valuation; he disregarded the testimony of two Metlife employees who described what Metlife had done to procure the best possible price. There is no general rule in deficiency actions, or any others, that interested parties cannot provide competent testimony. A judge may not say: "In my court, the testimony of the parties counts for naught." Triers of fact must evaluate the testimony with greater specificity; some interested witnesses will be credible and others not so, and the court must try to determine which is which rather than reject everything out of hand.

The bankruptcy judge paid scant attention to aspects of this record that seem to us important to any evaluation of the commercial reasonableness of a sale, such as Metlife's exhaustive search for buyers and the need to move the presses by the end of April. The bankruptcy judge rejected Excello's own 1985 appraisal of these two presses at $1.2 million as too old, an unsupported decision: there is no evidence that the market had changed since the time it was made, and presses one year older are worth less unless the market rose in the interim (which no evidence supports). Although Judge James said that the price Excello received for its five-color presses is immaterial, 83 B.R. at 543, he gave no reasons and it is hard to see what they might be. Other things equal, five-color presses are worth more than four-color presses; no evidence suggests that the five-color presses were in worse shape. Excello had placed a greater value on its presses than on Metlife's in its bankruptcy schedules. The bankruptcy judge did not discuss why Excello's presses might have fetched less at what he presumed was a commercially reasonable auction than Metlife obtained from its private sale. Metlife knew in advance that its recovery was capped, which gave it every reason to conduct a commercially reasonable sale. Judge James did not mention this. There was also no explanation how Metlife could have been expected to receive $700,000 more than it did for the presses; all it had to do was show that the market value was less than $1.8 million to be entitled to a $900,000 deficiency judgment, and there is no evidence that the presses were worth anything near that.

III

To summarize, the main question in a deficiency action is the commercial reasonableness of the disposition of the collateral, with the secured party bearing the burden of persuasion. Oral notification producing actual knowledge is "notice". If the debtor did not receive notice, the court may use the omission (along with other factors) to inform its assessment of commercial reasonableness. Only if the secured party cannot establish the commercial reasonableness of its sale need it try to prove market value using secondary evidence, such as appraisals and sales of similar equipment. Because the bankruptcy and district judges cut short these inquiries, the judgment is reversed, and the case is remanded to the bankruptcy court for proceedings consistent with this opinion.

RIPPLE, CIRCUIT JUDGE, dissenting.

[Opinion omitted]

NOTES

1. **The Remedy.** Although, as the court states, the "rebuttable presumption" rule may be the majority rule, there is a large number of states subscribing to the "absolute bar" rule under which a creditor loses any right to a deficiency judgment if it fails to comply with the notice requirement. An Arkansas case, Norton v. National Bank of Commerce, 240 Ark. 143, 398 S.W.2d 538 (1966), had been considered a leading case for the rebuttable presumption rule, but Arkansas has now adopted the absolute bar rule, First State Bank v. Hallett, 291 Ark. 37, 722 S.W.2d 555 (1987). On the other hand, California, whose courts have been among the staunchest adherents of the absolute bar theory, has amended § 9–502 and § 9–504 to reject the absolute bar rule in commercial cases in which the required notice has been given but the disposition has not been conducted in a commercially reasonable manner. The amendments, enacted in 1990, are subject to a five-year "sunset" provision; unless the legislature acts to extend the duration of the amendments, they expire after 1995.

2. **Public or Private Sale.** The court makes the point that secured creditors have strong incentive to get the highest price obtainable at a private sale disposition. Does a secured creditor have the same incentive at a public sale? Under § 9–504(3) a secured creditor may buy at its own public sale but may not buy at its private sale unless "the collateral is of a type customarily sold in a recognized market or is of a type which is the subject of widely distributed standard price quotations." Comment 1 to § 9–504 says, "Although public sale is recognized, it is hoped that private sale will be encouraged where, as is frequently the case, private sale through commercial channels will result in higher realization on collateral for the benefit of all parties." Actually,

in allowing the secured party to buy at a public sale § 9–504(3) encourages creditors to opt for public sales. If there are no higher bids the secured creditor may acquire the property at a public sale without laying out any cash at all merely by bidding the amount of the debt. Then the creditor may dispose of the property in any manner.

The notice requirement of § 9–504(3) varies depending upon whether the sale is public or private. If the sale is public the notice must give the time and place of the sale; if private, the notice need only state the time after which the private sale is to be held.

Article 9 offers only the barest hint about what is meant by a public or private sale. Comment 1 to § 9–504 refers to § 2–706, and Comment 4 to that section says, "By 'public' sale is meant a sale by auction. A 'private' sale may be effected by solicitation and negotiation conducted either directly or through a broker." Should a public sale be interpreted to include a regularly scheduled dealer's auction even though the general public is not admitted? John Deery Motors, Inc. v. Steinbronn, 383 N.W.2d 553 (Iowa 1986), answered in the negative: "Because the concepts of 'public' sale and 'private' sale are presented without explicit legislative definition, we look to the dictionary for their meaning. A public sale is one that is 'accessible to or shared by all members of the community.' Webster's Third New International Dictionary 1836 (1976). The ordinary meaning of the word 'private,' on the other hand, is something 'intended for or restricted to the use of a particular person or group or class,' the converse of something 'freely available to the public.' Id. at 1804. The automobile auction in the present case was restricted to automobile dealers. Sale at that auction was not public in character." 383 N.W.2d at 555.

If Article 9 allows, in fact encourages, the creditor to opt for a public sale aren't we back where we started before the Code: a funereal auction on the courthouse steps with the only people present being the local public-sale vultures and the secured creditor prepared to bid the amount of the debt? Not if the court takes to heart the admonition of § 9–504(3) that "every aspect of the disposition including the method, manner, time, place and terms must be commercially reasonable." In Farmers Bank v. Hubbard, 247 Ga. 431, 276 S.E.2d 622 (1981), the creditor sold a tractor and trailer at public sale after advertisement and notice. The creditor sued for a deficiency judgment. The court said, "In passing, however, we note that it was not shown that selling a tractor-trailer on the courthouse steps was commercially reasonable, where there was no evidence that tractor-trailers are customarily sold on the courthouse steps where the sale occurred. We note further that there was no evidence as to what a dealer in used tractor-trailers would have paid for the tractor-trailer or what an auctioneer would have been able to sell it for. That is to say, courthouse sales may not be commercially reasonable as to all types of collateral, especially where there are better recognized means of marketing the particular collateral involved." 276 S.E.2d at 627. See also In re Frazier, 93 B.R. 366 (Bkrtcy.Tenn. 1988) (public sale inappropriate for sale of Lear Jet).

3. **Written or Oral Notice.** As the court notes in *Excello Press*, the cases are in conflict on whether § 9–504(3) requires written notice. It states "[R]easonable notification of the time and place of any public sale or reasonable notification of the time after which any private sale or other intended disposition is to be made shall be *sent* by the secured party to the debtor;" (Emphasis added.) See Executive Financial Services, Inc. v. Garrison, 722 F.2d 417 (8th Cir. 1983) (written notice required); Hall v. Owen County State Bank, 175 Ind.App. 150, 370 N.E.2d 918 (1977) (oral notice allowed); McKee v. Mississippi Bank & Trust Co., 366 So.2d 234 (Miss. 1979) (written notice required); DeLay First National Bank & Trust Co. v. Jacobson Appliance Co., 196 Neb. 398, 243 N.W.2d 745 (1976) (written notice required); Crest Investment Trust, Inc. v. Alatzas, 264 Md. 571, 287 A.2d 261 (1972) (oral notice allowed).

4. **Commercially Reasonable Test.** Article 9 is generally very favorable to secured creditors but, in applying the "commercially reasonable" test of § 9–504(3), some courts have imposed standards of conduct on secured creditors that would have been unthinkable under pre-Code procedure-oriented foreclosure laws. An example is Liberty National Bank & Trust v. Acme Tool Division of the Rucker Co., 540 F.2d 1375 (10th Cir. 1976), referred to in the principal case. The court described Liberty Bank's actions in selling an oil rig as follows:

> It had no previous experience in selling an oil rig and so the officers inquired or investigated as to the usual manner of such sales. Liberty was told that the ordinary method for selling a drilling rig was to employ an auctioneer to move the rig to a convenient location to clean and paint it and then notify interested persons and, in addition, advertise the sale in trade journals and newspapers. The bank followed none of these suggestions. Indeed, it sold the rig without any professional help. Notices were sent to 16 creditors, including Taurus, and to some 19 other companies. Mrs. Bailey did not receive notice except information furnished by her son-in-law. The rig was neither cleaned, painted nor dismantled. Liberty did not move it to a convenient site, but sold it at the place where it had been near Perryton, Texas. The sale was conducted by an attorney for Liberty who had never conducted an auction of an oil rig or oil field equipment and who lacked

experience in the oil business. The attorney was assisted by a
Liberty Bank officer who knew something about oil production, but was not acquainted with the drilling of wells. Some
40 or 50 people appeared for the sale, but few made bids. In
fact, after the price reached $37,000, there were only two
bidders. The final sale price, $42,000, was sufficient to pay off
the Taurus note and pay the expenses of the sale, but left
little for the other creditors. The rig had been appraised at
$60,000 to $80,000.

The successful bidder was Raymond Hefner of Bonray Oil
Company and Miller & Miller Auctioneers. In June 1972,
Miller & Miller sold the equipment for $77,705.50.

540 F.2d at 1377–78.

In deciding that the sale was not conducted in a commercially
reasonable manner (it was held in a snowstorm in Perryton,
Texas), the court quoted the District Court's finding of fact:

> The proper way to sell the rig and related equipment
> would have been to contract with a professional auctioneer, or
> to follow the same steps and procedures a professional auc-
> tioneer follows in disposing of equipment of this type which is
> to clean and paint the equipment, prepare a brochure and
> mail it to the proper people; advertise in trade journals,
> regional newspapers and the Wall Street Journal; move the
> equipment to a convenient location, and offer the equipment
> on a piece by piece basis as well as in one lot. The Court finds
> that the rig and related equipment were not sold by Liberty
> Bank in the usual manner in a recognized market, nor in
> conformity with reasonable commercial practices among oil
> field equipment dealers.

540 F.2d at 1378.

Section 9–504(1) allows a creditor to dispose of collateral "in
its then condition *or* following any commercially reasonable preparation." (Emphasis added.) Doesn't this language give the creditor an option whether to repair and refurbish or to sell the
collateral in its present state? Is this option taken away from the
creditor in some situations by the dictate of § 9–504(3) that every
aspect of the disposition must be commercially reasonable? A
leading credit lawyer, speaking of cases like *Liberty*, says, "Clearly
the most significant development under part 5 of Article 9 has
been the trend evidenced by a series of decisions to impose upon
secured creditors a duty to make reasonable efforts to refurbish or
repair repossessed collateral before sale." Burke, Uniform Commercial Code Annual Survey—Secured Transactions, 32 Bus.Law.
1133, 1161 (1977).

When California was considering adoption of the Code in the
early 60s, creditors were wary of the uncertainties inherent in the

commercial reasonableness standard. Hence they persuaded the legislature to add to § 9–504(3) requirements that notice be given at least five days before sale and that the notice be published in a "newspaper of general circulation." If a creditor complies with the statutory notice requirements is the sale immune from attack on the ground of lack of commercial reasonableness with respect to notice? In American Business Credit Corp. v. Kirby, 122 Cal.App.3d 217, 175 Cal.Rptr. 720 (1981), the court held that the creditor had not conducted a commercially reasonable resale when notice of sale was published in the Los Angeles Daily Journal. Although that newspaper met the statutory requirement in California's version of § 9–504(3) of "a newspaper of general circulation," still the creditor should have provided the court with proof that "it had exposed the potential sale to at least a substantial number of potential buyers." The creditor did not show that people who read the Daily Journal were potential buyers of the equipment being sold. Thus, in California if a judgment creditor has property of the judgment debtor sold by the sheriff, publication in the Daily Journal would meet the statutory requirement that notice be published in a "newspaper of general circulation," Cal. Civ. Code § 701.540(f), and the sale could not be overturned on the notice issue. But if a secured party gives notice in the same manner when selling collateral under § 9–504(3), the sale may be attacked as not meeting the commercially reasonable standard.

PROBLEMS

1. Debtor is a retail automobile dealer and Secured Party finances Debtor's inventory. The following clause appears in the security agreement: "Debtor further agrees that if Secured Party shall solicit bids from three or more other dealers in the type of property repossessed by Secured Party hereunder, any sale by Secured Party of such property to the bidder submitting the highest cash bid therefor shall be deemed to be a commercially reasonable means of disposing of the same." Debtor contends the clause is an invalid attempt at a pre-default waiver barred by § 9–501(3) and § 9–504(3). Secured Party asserts that it is a valid exercise of § 9–501(3) ("but the parties may by agreement determine the standards by which the fulfillment of these rights and duties is to be measured if such standards are not manifestly unreasonable"). Who is right? See Ford Motor Credit Co. v. Solway, 825 F.2d 1213 (7th Cir.1987).

2. On August 1, Debtor purchased a used car from Dealer for $1,595 plus finance charges, payable under an installment sale contract under which Dealer was granted a security interest in the car. The car immediately developed mechanical problems and Debtor had to return the car several times for repairs. On August 25, after paying only one partial installment Debtor refused to

make additional payments and surrendered the car to Dealer. After making a demand for payment which was ignored Dealer sent written notice to Debtor that after October 15 the car would be sold at private sale. The car was purchased by Dealer at a private sale to itself on October 16. The sale took place by means of an interoffice exchange of papers by which Debtor was credited with $900, the proceeds of the sale. Debtor was also credited with the amount of the down payment and first installment payment totalling $95. Dealer then brought an action against Debtor for a deficiency judgment of $600 ($1,595 – $995).

Dealer testified that the $900 value was based on the wholesale value for used cars of the same model, year etc. stated in the then current market reporter or "blue book" used by used car dealers in the area. Dealer resold the car to a retail customer for $1,495 a few weeks after Debtor surrendered the car.

How much is Dealer entitled to recover from Debtor? Would your answer differ if Dealer had sold the car surrendered by Debtor to another used car dealer for $900 and used that sale as the basis for its deficiency judgment claim? See Vic Hansen & Sons, Inc. v. Crowley, 57 Wis.2d 106, 203 N.W.2d 728 (1973).

NOTE: RESALE AT WHOLESALE OR RETAIL?

In In re Ford Motor Co., 27 UCC Rep. 1118 (1979), the Federal Trade Commission examined the practice of an automobile dealer with respect to repossessed automobiles of crediting the debtor with the wholesale value of the automobile and then reselling the car at retail. This practice was that normally followed in the used car business. It held that the debtor's right to any surplus realized by the secured party on resale of collateral under § 9–504(2) must be measured by the retail resale price obtained by the dealer reduced only by the direct expenses incurred in the repossession and resale, with no allowance for overhead or lost profit. Failure of the auto dealer to calculate surpluses on that basis was held to be an unfair trade practice under Section 5 of the Federal Trade Commission Act. The decision was reversed on the basis that the Commission should have proceeded by rule making rather than adjudication. Ford Motor Co. v. Federal Trade Commission, 673 F.2d 1008 (9th Cir. 1981). See Professor Kripke's critique of the FTC position in 32 UCC Rep. 4 (1982).

With reference to whether a creditor may sell at wholesale or retail Judge Posner stated in Contrail Leasing Partners, Ltd. v. Consolidated Airways, Inc., 742 F.2d 1095 (7th Cir.1984):

> Official Comment 2 to UCC § 9–507 states that the secured creditor is not required to resell the collateral at retail rather than wholesale. Although it is true that Indiana has not enacted the official comments, as some states have, see, e.g., Piper Acceptance Corp. v. Yarbrough, 702 F.2d 733, 735

(8th Cir.1983) (Arkansas), no negative inference can be drawn; and even without the comment, it is pretty clear that section 9–507 does not require sale in a retail market. It provides that if the creditor "sells the collateral in the usual manner *in any recognized market therefor* * * * he has sold in a commercially reasonable manner." § 9–507(2), Ind.Code § 26–1–9–507(2) (emphasis added). Wholesale markets are recognized markets for most goods, including aircraft, as we know from the *Piper* case; and an ironclad rule against selling collateral at wholesale rather than retail would make no sense. Although retail prices tend to be higher than wholesale prices, this is because it costs more to sell at retail. Not only can there be, therefore, no presumption that the net gains to the seller are different at the two levels, but economic theory implies that returns at the two levels will tend toward equality, since until they are equalized dealers will have incentives to enter at the level where the higher returns are being earned and by entering will bid those returns down.

742 F.2d at 1101.

b. GUARANTORS

A great deal of litigation has been occasioned by the uncertain status of guarantors with respect to § 9–504. Insiders of corporate debtors frequently sign guaranties of the corporation's debts. If guarantors are "debtors" within the meaning of § 9–105(d) they enjoy the protections of § 9–504(3) with respect to a right to reasonable notification and a commercially reasonable disposition of the collateral. But § 9–105(d), drafted at a time when guaranty agreements were as common as they are today, does not mention guarantors, and the Comment to § 9–105(d) is silent on this subject as well. Moreover, guaranty agreements typically contain extensive waivers of any rights on the part of the guarantor to compel the creditor to proceed first against the principal debtor or its collateral before proceeding against the guarantor. Sometimes guaranty agreements include a specific waiver of any right to receive reasonable notification of a sale of the collateral or to question the manner in which the sale is carried out. Apart from Article 9, courts have usually enforced waivers by a guarantor considered to be knowledgeable about business matters if the waiver was knowingly made. With respect to notice and the right to have a commercially reasonable sale, does § 9–501(3) change this traditional rule, even though nothing is said either in the text of the provision or in the Comment about guarantors? The following case discusses these issues.

MAY v. WOMAN'S BANK

Supreme Court of Colorado, 1991.
807 P.2d 1145.

JUSTICE KIRSHBAUM delivered the Opinion of the Court.

*   *   *

I

In 1983 and 1984, May was the president and principal shareholder of the LaBoca chain of retail clothing stores. During that period of time LaBoca entered into a series of financial transactions with the Bank. In connection with those transactions, the Bank obtained a security interest in LaBoca's inventory, accounts receivable, furniture, fixtures and equipment. In addition, May executed a continuing guaranty in which she personally "guarantee[d] absolutely and unconditionally" the payment of all debts of LaBoca to the Bank. May also executed two promissory notes and deeds of trust in favor of the Bank against properties she owned. In October 1984, all of LaBoca's debts to the Bank were consolidated into a single promissory note secured by LaBoca's assets, the guaranty and the two deeds of trust on May's properties.

In June of 1985, LaBoca filed a petition for reorganization under Chapter 11 of the United States Bankruptcy Code. The Bank obtained permission from the bankruptcy court to replevy and liquidate LaBoca's assets. After disposing of those assets, the Bank commenced foreclosure actions under the May deeds of trust to recover a claimed deficiency. May then instituted this action, alleging that the Bank's negligence in failing to conduct the sale of LaBoca's assets in a commercially reasonable manner, as required by section 9–504(3) of the [Uniform Commercial Code (the "Code")] was the cause of any deficiency owed to the Bank.

The Bank filed a motion for summary judgment, asserting that uncontroverted facts established that by executing the continuing guaranty May had waived any right she might have had to rely upon the Code's provisions concerning the disposition of collateral. The trial court granted the Bank's motion, and the Court of Appeals affirmed the trial court's judgment.

II

May contends that the Code prohibits a guarantor from waiving the right to insist upon disposition of collateral in a commercially reasonable manner. The Bank asserts that the Code's provision prohibiting a debtor from waiving such right is not applicable to a guarantor of a secured transaction. We agree with May.

A

Section 9–504(3) of the Code provides specific protections to debtors with respect to the disposition of property pledged to secure a debt * * *. This section requires a secured party to provide a debtor with reasonable notice of any disposition of collateral after default unless the debtor, after such default, specifically, knowingly and in writing releases the creditor from such obligation. * * * The section also expressly requires a creditor to dispose of collateral in a commercially reasonable manner.

The creation of these obligations of creditors affords debtors with corresponding rights. The Code contains the following pertinent provisions with respect to a debtor's right to require that collateral be disposed of in a commercially reasonable manner:

> To the extent that they give rights to the debtor and impose duties on the secured party, the rules stated in the subsections referred to below may not be waived or varied except as provided with respect to compulsory disposition of collateral (subsection (3) of section 9–504 and section 9–505) * * * but the parties may by agreement determine the standards by which the fulfillment of these rights and duties is to be measured if such standards are not manifestly unreasonable:

> * * *

> (b) Subsection (3) of section 9–504 and subsection (1) of section 9–505 which deal with disposition of collateral * * *.

§ 9–501(3) * * * These provisions prohibit a debtor from releasing a secured party from the obligation to dispose of collateral in a commercially reasonable manner. * * * While the Code authorizes waiver of the right to receive reasonable notice of the disposition of collateral after default, it prohibits waiver of the right to demand a commercially reasonable disposition of the collateral.

This distinction emphasizes the significance of the requirement in section 9–504(3) that collateral be disposed of in a commercially reasonable manner. To assure confidence in the integrity and fairness of such transactions, debtors, creditors and third party purchasers must all be able to assume that the collateral will not be disposed of in an unreasonable manner. A contrary rule would encourage inequitable, collusive and fraudulent manipulations of sales of collateral by creditors, third parties and debtors.

The obligations and rights established by the above-quoted provisions of the Code further several additional public policy goals. Requiring a creditor to give a debtor reasonable notice of any disposition of collateral permits the debtor to pursue alternative means to ensure satisfaction of the debt, promotes economic efficiency, and tends to reduce the potential deficiency for which the debtor might be liable.   *   *   *

B

The Bank does not challenge the foregoing legal principles. The Bank contends, however, that as a guarantor rather than a debtor, May is not prohibited from waiving her right to require disposition of the collateral in a commercially reasonable manner. We do not agree with this argument.

The term "debtor" is defined by the Code as follows:

> "Debtor" means the person who owes payment or other performance of the obligation secured, whether or not he owns or has rights in the collateral, and includes the seller of accounts or chattel paper. Where the debtor and the owner of the collateral are not the same person, the term "debtor" means the owner of the collateral in any provision of the article dealing with the collateral, the obligor in any provision dealing with the obligation, and may include both where the context so requires *   *   *.

§ 9–105(1)(d) *   *   * In First National Bank v. Cillessen, 622 P.2d 598 (Colo.App.1980), the Court of Appeals considered the question of whether a co-maker of a corporate note should be deemed a debtor for purposes of section 9–504(3)'s requirement of notice after default. Relying in part on the broad definition of the term "debtor" contained in section 9–105(1)(d) of the Code, the court answered that question in the affirmative. The court noted that all persons who might ultimately be determined liable for any deficiency in a loan transaction have equally strong interests in minimizing the extent of their potential liabilities. *Cillessen* at 600–01.

Questions of whether a guarantor should be deemed a debtor for purposes of state commercial code provisions requiring notice and commercially reasonable disposition of collateral and whether such a guarantor is prohibited from waiving the rights to require reasonable notice after default and commercially reasonable disposition of collateral have been addressed by many courts. Almost all of those courts have answered such questions affirmatively.

*   *   *

The majority rule recognizes that the interests of guarantors and debtors in matters affecting the disposition of collateral are substantially similar. In addition, the rule encourages guarantors to participate in commercial transactions, thus facilitating the creation of flexible loan arrangements. These are important policies the Code was designed to accomplish.

It is also noteworthy that a guarantor who pays a creditor obtains a right of subrogation of all rights the creditor has against the debtor, including the creditor's right to dispose of collateral. * * * Several courts have indicated that non-waivable defenses established by commercial codes are available to a debtor in a reimbursement action instituted by a guarantor who has paid or been adjudicated liable for a deficiency. * * * A rule requiring a guarantor who has paid a deficiency to dispose of collateral in a commercially reasonable manner, but denying that same guarantor the irrevocable right to insist that the creditor adhere to the same standard, would encourage creditors to dispose of collateral in commercially unreasonable ways and avoid any sanctions for such conduct by seeking recovery for the deficiency solely from the guarantor.

In the present case, May contends that the Bank's sale of LaBoca's assets was conducted in a commercially unreasonable manner. Her claim alleges a breach of the Bank's duty of care. As provided by section 1–102(3), "the obligations of good faith, diligence, reasonableness, and care prescribed by this title may not be disclaimed by agreement * * *." Id. A waiver of the requirement of a commercially reasonable sale would be tantamount to a waiver of the obligations of good faith, reasonableness and care—a disclaimer that is prohibited by sections 1–102(3) and 9– 504(3). * * *

Based on the language and structure of the Code, the policy objectives it seeks to achieve and the reasoning underlying those decisions illustrative of the majority rule, we conclude that a guarantor is entitled to the rights established by sections 9–501(3) and 9–504(3) of the Code, including the non-waivable right to require a creditor to dispose of collateral in a commercially reasonable manner. As one noted commentator has observed, "[a]ny other rule would encourage creditor misbehavior in the holding of a foreclosure sale, since the creditor would be safe in the knowledge that the guarantor would pick up the tab for any deficiency." B. Clark, The Law of Secured Transactions Under the Uniform Commercial Code § 4.03(3)(b) at 4–43 (2d ed. 1988).

C

Emphasizing the fact that the guaranty executed by May authorizes the Bank to seek satisfaction of LaBoca's debts from May prior to any disposition of the collateral, the Bank argues that the document must be construed to relieve it of any obligation to dispose of the collateral in a commercially reasonable manner. The Bank finds support for this argument in First Commercial Corp. v. Geter, 37 Colo.App. 391, 547 P.2d 1291 (1976), wherein a panel of our Court of Appeals concluded that because an absolute guaranty may be immediately enforced without first seeking satisfaction of the debt from the principal obligor or from disposition of any collateral, the defense of commercially unreasonable disposition of collateral is not available to a guarantor defending a suit by a creditor seeking recovery of a deficiency remaining on the debt.

We have concluded that a guarantor is to be deemed a debtor for purposes of the protections afforded by section 9–504(3) of the Code. In addition, in Cooper Investments v. Conger, 775 P.2d 76 (Colo.App.1989), another panel of the Court of Appeals, relying on First National Bank v. Cillessen, 622 P.2d 598 (Colo.App.1980), concluded that section 9–501(3) of the Code prohibits a guarantor from waiving the commercial reasonableness requirement of section 9–504(3) of the Code. *Conger* at 80. The reasoning and results of *Conger* and *Cillessen* are consistent with our decision today. To the extent *Geter* expresses a contrary view, we disapprove of that decision.

D

In view of our conclusion that May was prohibited by the Code from waiving her right to require commercially reasonable disposition of the collateral, we need not address the Bank's argument that by executing the guaranty May waived any right she might have had to require disposition of the property in a commercially reasonable manner. May has asserted that the deficiency claimed by the Bank exceeds any amount she might actually owe because the Bank disposed of the collateral in a commercially unreasonable manner. It is undisputed that the amount of May's liability is based primarily, if not completely, upon the amount the Bank received from the sale of the collateral. The language, structure and underlying policies of the Code would be substantially undermined if May were prohibited from challenging the claimed deficiency on the ground that the sale of the collateral was not conducted in a commercially reasonable manner. We conclude that May is entitled to rely upon that right as a defense to the Bank's action, and that section 9–501(3) of the Code prohibits any waiver of that right. The trial court and the Court of Appeals erred in adopting a contrary view.

III

For the above-stated reasons, the decision of the Court of Appeals is reversed and the case is remanded to that court with instructions to vacate the judgment of the trial court and remand the case to the trial court for further proceedings.

NOTE

In Chrysler Credit Corp. v. Curley, 753 F.Supp. 611 (E.D.Va. 1990), guarantors waived the usual suretyship defenses and any right to receive notice of the disposition of the collateral as well as any right to object to the commercial reasonableness of the disposition of the collateral. In the face of Virginia authority holding that a guarantor is a debtor under § 9–504(3) and is entitled to the protections of that section, the court held that § 9–501(3) does not prohibit guarantors from waiving their rights to these protections. The court believed that the traditional view favoring enforceability of waivers against guarantors should not be displaced in the absence of explicit statutory direction and it found no such direction because § 9–501(3) failed to mention guarantors. The court cited other cases that drew a distinction between a guarantor's status as a debtor under § 9–504(3) and under § 9–501(3).

2. RETENTION OF COLLATERAL IN SATISFACTION OF DEBT

LAMP FAIR, INC. v. PEREZ–ORTIZ

United States Court of Appeals, First Circuit, 1989.
888 F.2d 173.

BREYER, CIRCUIT JUDGE.

* * *

I.

Relevant Background Facts

* * *

a. On July 1, 1985, Pedro Perez Ortiz and Lamp Fair, Inc., made a contract. Perez Ortiz bought Lamp Fair's lighting fixture store located in Orange, Connecticut. Perez Ortiz promised to pay $327,000; in return he received furniture, fixtures, equipment, inventory, goodwill, and covenants not to compete.

b. Perez Ortiz paid Lamp Fair $50,000 at the time of the sale. He signed notes promising to pay the remaining $277,000 over time. He and Lamp Fair also signed a Security Agreement, intended to make certain that Perez Ortiz would pay this money. The Security Agreement gave Lamp Fair a secured interest in the store as collateral for the notes.

c. After a few months had passed, Perez Ortiz decided he could not, or would not, pay the additional money he owed under the contract and notes. On December 26, 1985, he returned the store—inventory, fixtures, and all—to Lamp Fair.

d. Lamp Fair immediately began to operate the store. In January 1986 Lamp Fair sent Perez Ortiz a bill for $131,000, which, it said, represented the difference between a) the money Perez Ortiz still owed under the contract and notes,

and b) the value of the store and inventory, which he had
returned.

   e. Perez Ortiz refused to pay the $131,000. Lamp Fair then
brought this suit.

After a trial before a magistrate, the district court entered a
judgment in Lamp Fair's favor and against Perez Ortiz for
$65,000. Both sides now appeal.

II.

The Law

    Perez Ortiz argued at trial that his return of the store in
December, and Lamp Fair's acceptance of the store, amounted to a
rescission of the July contract. That is to say, it amounted to an
agreement between the parties that Lamp Fair would accept the
store back and, in return, would forgive Perez Ortiz's still outstanding debt. The magistrate found, however, that there was no
such rescission or new agreement. He found that Lamp Fair,
while accepting the store, did not promise to forgive any still
outstanding debt. The magistrate's conclusion on this issue was
not "clearly erroneous," and we accept it as lawful.

    If there was no rescission of the contract, however, the origi-
nal contract, notes and, in particular, the Security Agreement
govern the legal relation between the parties. The Security
Agreement set out what would happen if Perez Ortiz defaulted on
his obligation to pay the remainder of the purchase price (as he
did). It provided that Lamp Fair could require Perez Ortiz to
assemble the collateral, and that Lamp Fair could then take
possession of it (i.e., the store), which is just what happened. The
Agreement also provided that Lamp Fair would have "all the
remedies of a Secured Party under the Uniform Commercial Code
of Connecticut." In light of this last statement in the Agreement
the magistrate should have looked to the Uniform Commercial
Code (as adopted by Connecticut) to determine whether or not
Lamp Fair was entitled to more than it had already received—the
$50,000 down payment, the monthly payments through December,
and the returned store. The magistrate failed to do this. We
have examined Connecticut law ourselves, however, and we conclude that Lamp Fair cannot recover a deficiency.

A.

    Article 9 of the Uniform Commercial Code sets forth the
remedies available to a secured party. It gives a secured party,
such as Lamp Fair, three basic options after default. See 2 J.
White and R. Summers, Uniform Commercial Code 570. (3d ed.
1988). Each of these options, while permitting the creditor under
some circumstances to obtain the collateral, contains safeguards to

assure the debtor that the secured party will not take unfair advantage of the situation and that the value of the collateral will be fairly ascertained.

1. *Judgment.* The secured party may simply sue on the note itself; that is to say, he "may reduce his claim to judgment * * * by any available judicial procedure." U.C.C. § 9–501(1). At a judicial sale of the debtor's property (which would not be governed by the Code), the secured party may buy the collateral himself, and he can look to the debtor's other property to satisfy any remaining debt. U.C.C. § 9–501(5), § 9–501 comment 6. A secured party choosing this option may take possession of the collateral prior to obtaining judgment, but only to preserve it as security for the debt. Kimura v. Wauford, 104 N.M. 3, 715 P.2d 451, 453 (1986). He does not own the collateral; he may use it only "for the purpose of preserving the collateral or its value" for future disposition. U.C.C. § 9–207(4); Wade v. Sport Concession Enterprises, Inc., 138 Ga.App. 17, 225 S.E.2d 488, 489 (1976). It would be "unfair to the debtor to allow a creditor to take possession at all, if the creditor never intended to dispose of the security." *Kimura,* 715 P.2d at 454.

Lamp Fair cannot look to this "judgment option" to support its claim to a "deficiency judgment," because Lamp Fair did not choose this option. The record makes clear that Lamp Fair has not sought a judicial sale of the store, nor did Lamp Fair take possession of the store simply for the purpose of preserving it or its value for future disposition. Rather, Lamp Fair intended to keep the store for its own use, and to obtain a deficiency judgment as well.

2. *Retention.* The secured party's second option after default is to "retain the collateral in satisfaction of the obligation." U.C.C. § 9–505(2). The Code makes clear, however, that retention of the collateral normally *completely satisfies* the debt; the secured party *must abandon* any claim for deficiency (unless the debtor signs a written statement permitting such a claim, which Perez Ortiz did not do). U.C.C. § 9–505, comment 1 * * *. The Code also states that the secured party must give notice of its intention to retain the collateral in satisfaction of the obligation, so that the debtor may object to retention and demand that the collateral be sold. Lamp Fair did not give this notice; it did not consciously choose this option.

3. *Disposition.* Section 9–504 sets forth the secured creditor's remaining option. It says that he "may sell, lease or otherwise dispose of any or all of the collateral * * * by public or private proceedings." After doing so, he must "account to the debtor for any surplus," and "the debtor is liable for any deficiency." Every aspect of the disposition must be "commercially reasonable." In addition, the secured creditor must give the debtor

notice of when the sale or other disposition will take place. The secured creditor can buy the collateral himself at any "public sale," but he cannot buy it at a "private sale" unless the collateral is "of a type customarily sold in a recognized market or * * * the subject of widely distributed standard price quotations." U.C.C. § 9–504(1)–(3). These rules in part seek to protect the debtor, for they help prevent the creditor from acquiring the collateral himself at less than its true value or unfairly understating its value to obtain a greater-than-warranted deficiency judgment. * * *

B.

Given these provisions of Connecticut law, Lamp Fair, in our view, cannot both retain the collateral and also obtain a deficiency judgment. We can reach this conclusion through either of two alternative lines of reasoning.

First, the majority of courts that have dealt with this issue would simply hold that Lamp Fair's conduct in retaining and operating the store on a permanent basis brings the transaction within the scope of the § 9–505(2) "retention option," irrespective of whether or not Lamp Fair consciously chose to invoke this option. See, e.g., Shultz v. Delaware Trust Co., 360 A.2d 576, 578 (Del.Super.1976) (retention of collateral for five years may be found to be in satisfaction of obligation despite secured party's protestations to the contrary); Millican v. Turner, 503 So.2d 289, 291 (Miss.1987) (adopting "majority position" that creditor who retains collateral for unreasonably long period is deemed to have retained in satisfaction); Swanson v. May, 40 Wash.App. 148, 697 P.2d 1013, 1015–16 (1985) (same); Schmode's, Inc. v. Wilkinson, 219 Neb. 209, 361 N.W.2d 557, 559 (1985) (secured party who used collateral for nearly three years elected to retain in satisfaction); Haufler v. Ardinger, 28 U.C.C.Rep.Serv. 893, 896–97 (Mass.App. 1979) (use of collateral for 38 months is election to retain barring deficiency); In re Boyd, 73 B.R. 122, 124–25 (Bankr.N.D.Tex.1987) (use of collateral for three months deemed retention in satisfaction). See also 2 J. White and R. Summers, Uniform Commercial Code 588. These courts reason that the Code intends "to put the creditor to an election to either sell the repossessed collateral pursuant to Section 9.504 or to retain the collateral in complete satisfaction of the debt pursuant to Section 9.505." Tanenbaum v. Economics Laboratory, Inc., 628 S.W.2d at 771–72 (creditor who retained and then scrapped collateral deemed to have retained in satisfaction of debt). The secured creditor cannot both avoid a more "objective," market-based, valuation of the collateral and also obtain an additional "deficiency judgment" remedy (unless the debtor expressly consents).

We note, however, that a minority of courts, including the Second Circuit in a rather different context, have written that § 9–505(2) does not apply when the secured creditor, wishing it not to apply, does not fulfill its procedural prerequisites (i.e., does not give notice). See Warnaco, Inc. v. Farkas, 872 F.2d 539, 544–45 (2d Cir.1989) (Winter, J.) (predicting Connecticut would not follow cases applying § 9–505(2) where creditor did not give written notice of intent to retain collateral in satisfaction of debt); S.M. Flickinger Co. v. 18 Genesee Corp., 71 A.D.2d 382, 423 N.Y.S.2d 73, 76 (1979); In re Nardone, 70 B.R. 1010, 1016–17 (Bankr.D.Mass. 1987). In effect, these courts have refused to "force" § 9–505(2) upon an unwilling secured creditor. Since Lamp Fair wishes to obtain a deficiency judgment, it is such an "unwilling creditor."

Our second, alternative, line of reasoning would accept this minority view; it would start from *Warnaco's* premise that § 9–505(2)'s "retention option" does not apply because an unwilling Lamp Fair did not give the required notice. Following this line of reasoning, we should note that the transaction must fall within the scope of the remaining "disposition option." This option, under § 9–504, does permit a creditor to obtain a deficiency judgment. But, regardless, Lamp Fair failed to satisfy § 9–504's preconditions for obtaining such a judgment because Lamp Fair did not "sell, lease or otherwise dispose" of the store. Lamp Fair did not hold a "public sale," at which it could have bid for the collateral. Nor could it have purchased the collateral itself by means of "private sale," for the store is not of the "type customarily sold in a recognized market or * * * the subject of widely distributed standard price quotations." And, whatever the meaning of the words "otherwise dispose of," they do not include permanent retention of the collateral for the secured party's own use. Appeal of Copeland, 531 F.2d 1195, 1207 (3d Cir.1976). Cf. National Equipment Rental, Ltd. v. Priority Electronics Corp., 435 F.Supp. 236, 240 (E.D.N.Y.1977) (repossession and conversion to own use by plaintiff's agent not "disposition" under § 9–504, so § 9–505 applies); Black's Law Dictionary 423 (5th ed. 1979) (defining "disposition" as "transferring to the care or possession of another * * * parting with, alienation of, or giving up property"). (Consider, as well, the contrasting use of "disposition" in section 9–504 and "retention" in section 9–505. *Copeland*, 531 F.2d at 1207.)

We concede that this last point (that § 9–504 does not foresee a creditor's *both* retaining the collateral (without public or private sale) *and* obtaining a deficiency judgment) is not absolutely clear in the Code. Conceivably, one could argue the contrary by pointing out that the Code elsewhere gives a remedy to a debtor when a secured creditor holds his collateral and will not dispose of it. (To be specific, § 9–507(1) says:

If it is established that the secured party is not proceeding in accordance with the provisions of this Part disposition may be ordered or restrained on appropriate terms and conditions.)

One might reason that where the creditor keeps the collateral and where the debtor does not use § 9–507(1) to force its disposition, the creditor then may proceed under § 9–504 to collect a deficiency judgment. (In any such proceeding the creditor might have to overcome a special "rebuttable presumption" that the collateral was worth at least as much as the debt. Savings Bank of New Britain v. Booze, 34 Conn.Supp. 632, 382 A.2d 226, 228–29 (1977) (creating "presumption" as a penalty for creditor's failure to fulfill § 9–504's notice requirements); Connecticut Bank and Trust Company, N.A. v. Incendy, 207 Conn. 15, 540 A.2d 32, 38 (1988) (adopting *Booze*).) This retention-plus-deficiency-judgment-plus-presumption theory does not strike us as a very plausible analysis of § 9–504, however. And, we have found only one court that has taken this last-mentioned course, allowing a deficiency judgment (while imposing a "rebuttable presumption") where the creditor simply retained the collateral. S.M. Flickinger Co. v. 18 Genesee Corp., 71 A.D.2d 382, 423 N.Y.S.2d 73, 76 (1979) (court divided 3–2). Every other case we have found has denied the creditor the deficiency judgment. See, e.g., H.V. Funding, Inc. v. Ernest Varkas & Sons, Inc., 140 Misc.2d 587, 531 N.Y.S.2d 484, 486 (1988) (agreeing with *Flickinger* dissenters and denying deficiency). The Third Circuit, for example, has said that to permit a deficiency judgment "would contravene the Code's mandate that an effective election to retain the collateral results in a complete discharge of the underlying obligation," *Appeal of Copeland,* 531 F.2d at 1207, a mandate that permits the creditor to obtain a deficiency judgment only with the "collateral valuation" safeguards that a "commercially reasonable" sale under § 9–504 or a judicial sale make possible.

We need not decide which alternative line of reasoning Connecticut would follow, whether Connecticut would hold 1) that § 9–505(2) governs, or 2) that the transaction falls within the scope of, but fails to meet the necessary prerequisites of, § 9–504. Either way the law denies Lamp Fair its deficiency judgment. We can predict with reasonable assurance, Meredith v. Winter Haven, 320 U.S. 228, 236–38, 64 S.Ct. 7, 11–13, 88 L.Ed. 9 (1943), that Connecticut would follow one or the other of these paths to this result. Therefore the judgment of the district court must be

Reversed.

NOTES

1. In Reeves v. Foutz & Tanner, Inc., 94 N.M. 760, 617 P.2d 149 (1980), two uneducated Navajos with limited ability to understand English pawned jewelry with a lender as security for a

thirty-day loan. The jewelry was worth much more than the amount borrowed. The debtors defaulted and the lender sent each of them a notice of intent to retain the collateral. Neither debtor objected and the lender sold the jewelry in the regular course of its business for more than the amount of the debt. The debtors contended that the lender could not sell the collateral without complying with § 9–504 and returning the surplus to the debtors. The court held that § 9–505(2) cannot be employed by a secured party that intends to resell the collateral. Thus, in the court's view, § 9–505(2) can be used only by a secured party who intends to retain the collateral for its own use. Is this a reasonable interpretation of the intent of § 9–505(2)? It is possible that a secured party might want to retain collateral seized from the debtor for the secured party's own use. *Lamp Fair* is such a case, but cases of that kind are not at all typical. Normally, the secured party is a financial institution that loaned money or a merchant that sold the collateral to the debtor. Retention for use with respect to such secured parties is not a commercial reality. Professor Gilmore explained the rationale of § 9–505(2) as follows: "The best and simplest way of liquidating any secured transaction, default having occurred, is for the secured party to keep the collateral as his own free of the debtor's equity, waiving any claim to a deficiency judgment. This avoids the tricky and difficult problem of arriving at a fair valuation of the collateral as well as the expense and delay involved in sale or other methods of foreclosure, judicial or nonjudicial. The land mortgagee's right to a decree of strict foreclosure and the common law conditional seller's right to forfeit the buyer's equity on retaking of the goods (which automatically barred the seller's claim for the unpaid balance of the price) were both illustrations of this approach." Gilmore, Security Interests in Personal Property 1220 (1965). The problem in *Reeves* was that the § 9–505(2) remedy was not used by the secured party as a convenient way of squaring accounts with the debtors but rather as a way of gaining an unconscionable windfall. Since the trial court found that the secured party acted in bad faith in disposing of the collateral, what remedy is appropriate? § 1–203.

2. Professor Gilmore's prescience is shown by his comment on § 9–505(2). "Now what is to happen when a secured party makes a proposal to retain, say, a million dollars' worth of collateral in satisfaction of a hundred-thousand-dollar debt—or a thousand dollars' worth of collateral in satisfaction of a hundred-dollar debt—and, through oversight in the million-dollar case or ignorance in the thousand-dollar case, no one who is qualified to object does so within the statutory time limits? The courts will do what they always have done and always will do. If fraud is alleged by someone who has standing to complain of it, the allegation will be inquired into. If the fraud is proved, the offending transaction

will be set aside and the court will devise an appropriate remedy."
Gilmore, Security Interests in Personal Property 1226–27 (1965).

3. RIGHTS OF JUNIOR LIENORS

LOUIS ZAHN DRUG CO. v. BANK OF OAK BROOK TERRACE

Appellate Court of Illinois, 1981.
95 Ill.App.3d 435, 50 Ill.Dec. 959, 420 N.E.2d 276.

NASH, JUSTICE. In this appeal we consider whether plaintiff, a junior secured creditor, has stated a cause of action pursuant to sections 9–504(1)(c) or section 9–507(1) of the Uniform Commercial Code against defendant, a senior secured creditor, and others, to recover damages for the alleged improper disposition of the collateral which secured their respective loans to the debtor. ✶ ✶ ✶ Defendants' motion to dismiss ✶ ✶ ✶ the complaint was granted by the trial court and plaintiff appeals.

✶ ✶ ✶ plaintiff alleged that prior to June 6, 1977, defendant Bank of Oak Brook Terrace (Bank) loaned $25,000 to George Meringolo and GJM Enterprises, Inc. (debtor). According to a financing statement filed on June 6, 1977, the loan was secured by a security interest in "inventory, fixtures, equipment now owned or hereafter acquired [by the debtor]." On December 20, 1977, plaintiff loaned $82,282.82 to the debtor and, according to a financing statement filed on January 9, 1978, plaintiff was given a security interest in

> "All fixtures, furnishings, fittings, utensils, tools and equipment signs, prescription records and files, stock in trade, inventory, pharmaceuticals, drugs, sundry products, lease hold improvements, accounts receivable, proceeds, franchises, contract rights, good will, assignment of store lease, including, but not limited to, all other goods, wares, merchandise, furniture, fixtures, equipment, appliances, prescriptions and miscellaneous items, now existing or hereafter acquired by debtor ✶ ✶ ✶."

The debtor subsequently defaulted on the obligations to both plaintiff and defendant.

After the debtor defaulted, plaintiff attempted to find purchasers for the business and defendants, Harold Shapiro and Donald Warsaw (Buyers), expressed an interest in purchasing it for $70,000. Plaintiff alleged that prior to October 20, 1978, it entered "into negotiations with the defendant [Bank], with an intent to obtain a settlement of the first lien position of the defendant [Bank] ✶ ✶ ✶ by way of verbal and written communications with said Bank ✶ ✶ ✶ ." At about the same time, plaintiff began negotiations with defendant American National Bank & Trust Co., as Trustee (Trustee) which held legal title to the debtor's premises, and its rental agent, defendant Triangle Management Co., in order to assure that the Buyers would be able to obtain a lease of the premises. James Guido was alleged to be the beneficial owner of the premises and also a major shareholder and chairman of the board of the defendant Bank. Plaintiff alleged it also received another offer to purchase the business for $100,000 and then invited the buyers to reconsider their previous bid. When plaintiff did not hear from them, it resumed its attempts to consummate a sale of the business to the high bidder.

Plaintiff alleges that on October 30, 1978, the bank had, without notice to plaintiff, obtained a renunciation of rights in the collateral from the debtor and sold the entire inventory assets, fixtures and equipment of the debtor's business for $70,000 to others. The complaint asserts that the sale was commercially unreasonable "in that, among other things, a higher price could have been obtained" and that the Bank, the Buyers, and Triangle Management Co. "did enter into a conspiracy" to defraud plaintiff. Plaintiff further alleged that the bank had failed to exercise good faith in its dealings with plaintiff concerning the sale, in failing to give notice of it, and in failing to disclose the relationship between the Bank, the beneficiaries of the trust under which title to the premises was held, and Triangle Management Co. Plaintiff also alleged that although the Bank had received payment in full for its loan, it had refused to account for the balance of the funds received or to pay over any excess amount to the plaintiff. Plaintiff prayed that the sale be held commercially unreasonable and that damages be awarded pursuant to UCC § 9–507(1).

* * *

Section 9–504(1) of the Uniform Commercial Code describes a secured party's right to dispose of collateral after default and provides that the proceeds of the disposition shall be applied first (a) to the expenses incurred, then (b) to satisfaction of the principal indebtedness secured, and then (c) to

> "the satisfaction of indebtedness secured by any subordinate security interest in the collateral if written notification of demand therefor is received before distribution of the proceeds is completed. * * *"

With certain exceptions not pertinent here

> "* * * notification shall be sent to any other secured party from whom the secured party [who is making the disposition] has received (before sending his notification to the debtor or before the debtor's renunciation of his rights) written notice of a claim of an interest in the collateral. * * *" (UCC § 9–504(3).)

Section 9–504(3) further provides that the "[s]ale or other disposition may be as a unit or in parcels and at any time and place and on any terms but every aspect of the disposition including the method, manner, time, place, and terms must be commercially reasonable." The Code also provides a remedy if a secured party fails to proceed in accordance with its provisions in the disposition of collateral:

> "If it is established that the secured party is not proceeding in accordance with the provisions of this Part disposition may be ordered or restrained on appropriate terms and conditions. If the disposition has occurred the debtor or *any person* entitled to notification or *whose security interest has been made known to the secured party prior to the disposition* has a right to recover from the secured party any loss caused by a failure to comply with the provisions of this Part. * * *"
> (UCC § 9–507(1).) (Emphasis supplied.)

Thus, in seeking to impose liability upon a secured party under the remedies provided by section 9–507, plaintiff must allege facts showing it is "a person entitled to notification" or that its security interest was "made known" to defendant prior to disposition of the collateral.

The essential question presented by defendant's motion to dismiss the complaint in the trial court and by the arguments of the parties on appeal is whether plaintiff, as a secondary secured party, must allege it gave notice *in writing* to defendant in order to proceed under section 9–507, or whether allegations that plaintiff's security interest was otherwise "made known" to defendant before disposition are sufficient. Plaintiff relies upon the allegations in the complaint that plaintiff and defendant bank had negotiated in an attempt to settle the bank's first lien against the collateral and did so by both written and verbal communications. It contends that by these means plaintiff's security interest was made known to defendant prior to sale of the collateral giving plaintiff standing to now assert the sale was commercially unreasonable and to seek damages pursuant to section 9–507. Defendant contends, however, that a secondary secured party such as plaintiff may not complain about any aspect of the sale of the collateral unless it has given written notice of its claim or interest before sale and plaintiff's complaint failed to allege it did so.

Prior to the 1972 amendments of Article 9 of the Uniform Commercial Code, a secured party wishing to dispose of collateral was under a duty to give notice to any person who had a security interest in the collateral who had filed a financing statement with the Secretary of State. He was also required to give notice to any other person known to him to have a security interest in the collateral. Under the 1972 amendments the notice requirements were eased to the extent that a selling secured party need not notify other secured parties of a proposed disposition of collateral unless such parties had first given him written notice of a claim of interest in the collateral. It necessarily follows that a subordinate secured party who has failed to give the requisite written notice of his claim cannot be heard to complain if he is not notified in advance of the disposition of the collateral and may not seek satisfaction of his indebtedness from the proceeds of the disposition pursuant to section 9–504(1)(c). * * *

It does not necessarily follow, however, that the failure of a subordinate secured party to give written notice of a claim of interest in the collateral forecloses him from contesting the commercial reasonableness of the sale and seeking damages if proven. While the amendments to section 9–504(3) eased the notice requirements of the selling secured party, the provisions of section 9–507(1) giving a secured party whose security interest has been "made known" to the selling secured party an action for damages was not affected by the amendments. We note that the commentators to section 9–507 have reasoned that its language "whose security interest has been made known" to the other secured party may be read to mean "made known in writing", but that is not what it says. Had the legislature intended that an action for damages was to be limited to subordinate secured parties whose interest had been made known to the selling secured party "in writing", as it did so limit their rights under section 9–504(1)(c), it could easily have done so. The legislature clearly chose, however, to retain the existing remedy in favor of other secured parties whose interest was made known to the selling party prior to disposition of the collateral. Those subordinate secured parties who have given written notice of their claim against the collateral are entitled to receive notice of its proposed disposition and also to satisfaction of their claim from any surplus in the proceeds. The remedy sought by plaintiff arises after disposition and is granted to the debtor, any person entitled to notification (being those who have given written notice of their claim), or [any person] whose security interest has been made known to the selling party. If, as urged by defendant, the remedy extends only to those secured parties in the third category who have given notice in writing it would be redundant as such parties are already included within the second category.

One of the purposes of the Code requirement that a sale of collateral be conducted in a commercially reasonable manner is to protect the interests of other secured parties. The selling party is not required to search out and give notice of an intended disposition to all other secured parties, but as to those from whom it has received written notice of their claim of an interest in the collateral prior to the time distribution of the proceeds has been completed, the holder of the subordinate security interest would be entitled to seek satisfaction of its indebtedness from any surplus remaining of the proceeds of sale after payment of expenses and the primary indebtedness.

In the event the subordinate secured party has not given the notice required by section 9–504(3) then he would not be entitled to receive the notice provided by that section from the principal secured party. As we have noted, however, the subordinate secured party is not without remedy as section 9–507(1) provides that any person whose security interest has been made known to the secured party prior to disposition of the collateral may recover for losses caused by a failure to comply with the Act.

Under somewhat analogous circumstances, this court in Blackhawk Production Credit Association v. Meridian Implement Co. (1980), 82 Ill.App.3d 93, 37 Ill.Dec. 387, 402 N.E.2d 277, considered the rights of a secured party holding a subordinate security interest where the party with the superior security interest retained the collateral in full satisfaction of the debtor's obligation to it. Under section 9–505(2) if a secured party retains the collateral in satisfaction of its obligation, it is required to send notice to any other secured party from whom it has received written notice of a claim of an interest in the collateral and if another secured party objects in writing within 21 days thereafter, the collateral must be disposed of under section 9–504. In *Blackhawk* we held that a secured party was not authorized by section 9–505 to retain collateral in satisfaction of unsecured as well as secured debts and, therefore, the failure of the holder of a subordinate security interest to serve written notice on the senior secured party prior to the repossession of the collateral did not preclude his recovery since his security interest was *made known* to the senior secured party before the subsequent sale of the collateral. The wrongful disposition of the collateral in that case which gave rise to a claim under section 9–507(1) was the sale of the collateral after the primary secured party had received notification of the interest of the junior secured party.

Similarly, it has been said that mere knowledge by the selling secured party of the interest of another secured party in the collateral is sufficient to subject him to liability under section 9–507(1), if he fails to dispose of the collateral in a commercially reasonable manner. See Liberty National Bank & Trust Co. of Oklahoma City v. Acme Tool Division of the Rucker Co. (10th Cir. 1976), 540 F.2d 1375, 1382.

We conclude that a subordinate secured party's security interest in the collateral need not be made known in writing to the selling secured party in order to challenge a disposition under section 9–507 on the grounds it was commercially unreasonable where the interest was otherwise made known to the secured party prior to disposition.

While plaintiff does not and need not allege that its security interest was made known to the Bank in writing in order to maintain an action under section 9–507, its complaint must set forth facts which if proven show that the selling secured party had been informed of plaintiff's interest prior to the disposition of the collateral. It may not be inferred from plaintiff's allegation that it negotiated with the Bank seeking to settle the Bank's first lien that the Bank became aware of plaintiff's junior secured status. A complaint will not withstand a motion to dismiss under section 45 of the Civil Practice Act unless it at least minimally allege facts setting forth the essential elements of a cause of action ＊ ＊ ＊.

The trial court dismissed the complaint finding it lacked necessary allegations that plaintiff had given written notice to the Bank of its claim of an interest in the collateral. As we have determined written notice is not required to preserve a remedy pursuant to section 9–507(1), the court erred in dismissing [the complaint] on that ground. ＊ ＊ ＊ A complaint should not be dismissed unless it clearly appears that no set of facts can be proved which will justify a recovery ＊ ＊ ＊ and plaintiff may wish to amend its complaint in an effort to supply the deficiencies we have discussed.

For these reasons the judgment of the trial court will be reversed and the cause remanded for further proceedings in accordance with the views expressed herein.

NOTES

1. What is the loss that must be shown in order for a junior secured party to recover damages under § 9–507(1)? In McGowen v. Nebraska State Bank, 229 Neb. 471, 427 N.W.2d 772 (1988), the senior secured party failed to notify the junior secured party of the sale of the collateral. The junior contended that it was damaged by the lack of notice because it was deprived of the profit that could have been realized by buying the collateral at the senior's sale and subsequently selling it at a higher price. The court decided in favor of the senior:

> We hold that the "loss" envisioned by § 9–507(1), as to junior lienholders, refers to the loss of any surplus proceeds due to an improper disposition of the collateral. Surplus proceeds in this case means the difference between the fair market value of the collateral, if sold at a proper sale, and the amount required to satisfy the senior lien. Thus, a junior lienholder can only be said to suffer a loss due to lack of notice if a commercially reasonable sale would have produced an amount in excess of the senior lien.

427 N.W.2d at 775. River Valley State Bank v. Peterson, 154 Wis. 2d 442, 453 N.W.2d 193 (App.1990), is in accord. See Nickles, Rights and Remedies Between U.C.C. Article 9 Secured Parties

With Conflicting Security Interests in Goods, 68 Iowa L.Rev. 217 (1983).

2. The court in *Louis Zahn* discussed Blackhawk Production Credit Ass'n v. Meridian Implement Co. The facts were as follows: Seller sold Debtor a tractor and obtained a purchase money security interest for the balance of the price. Later Debtor granted Lender a security interest in the same tractor. Although Lender knew of Seller's senior interest, it did not send Seller written notice of its claim of an interest in the collateral. In July 1976 Seller repossessed the tractor and entered into an agreement with Debtor to retain the tractor in full satisfaction of both the remaining secured debt and an additional unsecured debt owed by Debtor to Seller. The two debts amounted to a total of over $20,000. Seller knew nothing of Lender's interest until the spring of 1977 when Lender demanded that Seller either sell the tractor pursuant to § 9–504 or pay over to Lender the difference between the value of the tractor and the unpaid balance secured by Lender's senior security interest. Seller refused Lender's demand and sold the tractor in ordinary course of its business. Lender sued Seller under § 9–507(1).

In allowing Lender to recover more than $11,000 from Seller the court stated that Seller could retain possession under § 9–505(2) only in satisfaction of the secured debt. Any value of the tractor in excess of the secured debt had to be used to pay off Lender's security interest and not to satisfy Debtor's unsecured debt to Seller. The court acknowledged that Lender could have avoided the problem by promptly notifying Seller of its claim to the collateral. It held that the word "disposition" in the second sentence of § 9–507(1)—" * * * any person entitled to notification or whose security interest has been made known to the secured party prior to the disposition has a right to recover from the secured party * * *"—refers to the eventual sale of the collateral by the secured party and not the act of strict foreclosure pursuant to § 9–505(2). Do you agree with that interpretation? If that interpretation is correct what would Seller have had to do to protect itself against possible claims of unknown secured parties?

3. The rights of junior secured parties in personal property do not receive the degree of protection under Article 9 that like interests in real property receive. Perhaps this reflects the fact that junior security interests are not as important in personal property financing as in real property financing. Under Article 9, the junior secured party is entitled to receive notification of disposition of the collateral by the senior secured party (§ 9–504(3)) and to share in the proceeds of disposition (§ 9–504(1)(c)) only if the senior secured party received prior written notice of the junior security interest. The junior secured party may recover damages from the senior secured party for wrongful disposition of

the collateral (§ 9–507(1)) only if the senior secured party received prior written notice or had knowledge of the junior security interest.

A holder of a judicial lien enjoys none of these rights. Section 9–504(1)(c) applies only to holders of junior security interests. Although the definition of security interest in § 1–201(37) is broad enough to include nonconsensual liens, the holder of a judicial lien is not the holder of a security interest as the term is used in § 9–504(1)(c). That section would appear to be restricted to Article 9 security interests which must be created by contract. § 9–102(2). Judicial lienholders are treated separately under Article 9 as "lien creditors." § 9–301(3). Section 9–311 recognizes that a judicial lien creditor may reach the debtor's interest in collateral and § 9–301(1)(b) subordinates a judicial lien creditor's interest to a prior perfected security interest. Any further rights of the judicial lien creditor in the collateral as against those of the secured party are left to other state law. See Justice, Secured Parties and Judgment Creditors—The Courts and Section 9–311 of the Uniform Commercial Code, 30 Bus. Law. 433 (1975). For example, under California Code of Civil Procedure § 720.210 through § 720.290 a secured party whose security interest has priority over the judicial lien can require that the levying officer release the property to the secured party unless the judicial lien creditor pays the claim of the secured party or posts a bond in lieu of payment. If the secured party gets possession of the collateral, it can be disposed of pursuant to § 9–504 or § 9–505 without accounting to the holder of the judicial lien.

4. ACCOUNTS RECEIVABLE AND CHATTEL PAPER

MAJOR'S FURNITURE MART, INC. v. CASTLE CREDIT CORP.

United States Court of Appeals, Third Circuit, 1979.
602 F.2d 538.

GARTH, CIRCUIT JUDGE: This appeal requires us to answer the question: "When is a sale—not a sale, but rather a secured loan?" The district court held that despite the form of their Agreement, which purported to be, and hence was characterized as, a sale of accounts receivable, the parties' transactions did not constitute sales. Major's Furniture Mart, Inc. v. Castle Credit Corp., 449 F.Supp. 538 (E.D.Pa.1978). No facts are in dispute, and the issue presented on this appeal is purely a legal issue involving the interpretation of relevant sections of the Uniform Commercial Code and their proper application to the undisputed facts presented here.

The district court granted plaintiff Major's motion for summary judgment. Castle Credit Corporation appeals from that order. We affirm.

Major's is engaged in the retail sale of furniture. Castle is in the business of financing furniture dealers such as Major's. Count I of Major's amended complaint alleged that Major's and Castle had entered into an Agreement dated June 18, 1973 for the financing of Major's accounts receivable; that a large number of transactions pursuant to the Agreement took place between June 1973 and May 1975; that in March and October 1975 Castle declared Major's in default under the Agreement; and that from and after June 1973 Castle was in possession of monies which constituted a surplus over the accounts receivable transferred under the Agreement. Among other relief sought, Major's asked for an accounting of the surplus and all sums received by Castle since June 1, 1976 which had been collected from the Major's accounts receivable transferred under the Agreement.

The provisions of the June 18, 1973 Agreement which are relevant to our discussion provide: that Major's shall from time to time "sell" accounts receivable to Castle, and that all accounts so "sold" shall be with full recourse against Major's. Major's was required to warrant that each account receivable was based upon a written order or contract fully performed by Major's.[3] Castle in its sole discretion could refuse to "purchase" any account. The amount paid by Castle to Major's on any particular account was the unpaid face amount of the account exclusive of interest [4] less a fifteen percent "discount"[5] and less another ten percent of the unpaid face amount as a reserve against bad debts.[6]

3. The parties do not dispute that their rights are governed by the law of Pennsylvania. The Pennsylvania Uniform Commercial Code, and in particular § 9–105, classifies the accounts receivable which are the subject of the agreement as "chattel paper."

4. According to Major's brief, the "face amount" of its customers' installment payment agreements included (1) the retail cost of the furniture purchased (amount financed), (2) the total amount of interest payable by the customer over the life of the customer's installment payment agreement, and (3) insurance charges.

5. The 15% "discount" was subsequently increased unilaterally by Castle to 18% and thereafter was adjusted monthly to reflect changes in the prime rate (Appellee's Supplemental Appendix 3b–4b).

6. It becomes apparent from a review of the record that the amount which Castle actually paid to Major's on each account transferred was the unpaid face amount exclusive of interest and exclusive of insurance premiums less 28% (18% "discount" and 10% reserve).

In its brief on appeal, Castle sets out the following summary of the transactions that took place over the relevant period. It appears that the face amount of the accounts which were "sold" by Major's to Castle was $439,832.08, to which finance charges totalling $116,350.46 and insurance charges totalling $42,304.03 were added, bringing the total amount "purchased" by Castle to $598,486.57. For these "purchases" Castle paid Major's $316,107. Exclusive of any surplus as determined by the district court Castle has retained $528,176.13 which it has received as a result of customer collections and repurchases by Major's. Collection costs were found by the district court to be $1,627.81.

Under the Agreement the reserve was to be held by Castle without interest and was to indemnify Castle against a customer's failure to pay the full amount of the account (which included interest and insurance premiums), as well as any other charges or losses sustained by Castle for any reason.

In addition, Major's was required to "repurchase" any account "sold" to Castle which was in default for more than 60 days. In such case Major's was obligated to pay to Castle

> an amount equal to the balance due by the customer on said Account plus any other expenses incurred by CASTLE as a result of such default or breach of warranty, less a rebate of interest on the account under the "Rule of the 78's."
> * * * [7]

Thus essentially, Major's was obligated to repurchase a defaulted account not for the discounted amount paid to it by Castle, but for a "repurchase" price based on the balance due by the customer, plus any costs incurred by Castle upon default.

As an example, applying the Agreement to a typical case, Major's in its brief on appeal summarized an account transaction of one of its customers (William Jones) as follows:

> A customer Jones of Major's (later designated Account No. 15,915) purchased furniture from Major's worth $1700.00 (or more). He executed an installment payment agreement with Major's in the total face amount of $2549.88, including interest and insurance costs. * * * Using this piece of chattel paper, * * * Major's engaged in a financing transaction with Castle under the Agreement. * * * Major's delivered the Jones' chattel paper with a $2549.88 face amount of Castle together with an assignment of rights. Shortly thereafter, Castle delivered to Major's cash in the amount of $1224.00. The difference between this cash amount and the full face of the chattel paper in the amount of $2549.88, consisted of the following costs and deductions by Castle:
>
> 1. $180.00 discount credited to a "reserve" account of Major's.
>
> 2. $300.06 "discount" (actually a prepaid interest charge).
>
> 3. $30.85 for life insurance premium.

---

7. The Rule of 78 is "the predominant method used to determine refunds of unearned finance charges upon prepayment of consumer debts." Hunt, James H., "The Rule of 78: Hidden Penalty for Prepayment in Consumer Credit Transactions," 55 B.U.L.Rev. 331, 332 (1975). That article points out that the Rule of 78 allocates a disproportionately large portion of finance charges to the early months of a credit transaction which produces a hidden penalty for prepayment, although the extent of the penalty diminishes as the term of the debt nears expiration.

Apparently a rebate of insurance premiums was provided as well as a rebate of interest.

4. $77.77 for accident and health insurance premium.

5. $152.99 for property insurance premium.

6. $588.27 interest charged to Jones on the $1700 face of the note.

Thus, as to the Jones' account, Castle received and proceeded to collect a piece of chattel paper with a collectible face value of $2549.88.   Major's received $1224.00 in cash.

As we understand the Agreement, if Jones in the above example defaulted without having made any payments on account, the very least Major's would have been obliged to pay on repurchase would be $1,700 even though Major's had received only $1,224 in cash on transfer of the account and had been credited with a reserve of $180.   The repurchase price was either charged fully to reserve or, as provided in the Agreement, 50% to reserve and 50% by cash payment from Major's.   In the event of bankruptcy, default under the agreement or discontinuation of business, Major's was required to repurchase all outstanding accounts immediately.   *   *   *

Under the Agreement, over 600 accounts were transferred to Castle by Major's of which 73 became delinquent and subject to repurchase by Major's.   On March 21, 1975, Castle notified Major's that Major's was in default in failing to repurchase delinquent accounts.   Apparently to remedy the default, Major's deposited an additional $10,000 into the reserve.   After June 30, 1975, Major's discontinued transferring accounts to Castle.   On October 7, 1975 Castle again declared Major's in default (App. 53).

Major's' action against Castle alleged that the transaction by which Major's transferred its accounts to Castle constituted a financing of accounts receivable and that Castle had collected a surplus of monies to which Major's was entitled.   We are thus faced with the question which we posed at the outset of this opinion: did the June 18, 1973 Agreement create a *secured interest* in the accounts, or did the transaction constitute a *true sale* of the accounts?   The district court, contrary to Castle's contention, refused to construe the Agreement as one giving rise to the sales of accounts receivable.   Rather, it interpreted the Agreement as creating a security interest in the accounts which accordingly was subject to all the provisions of Article 9 of the U.C.C.   It thereupon entered its order of June 13, 1977 granting Major's' motion for summary judgment and denying Castle's motion for summary judgment.   This order was ultimately incorporated into the court's final judgment entered May 5, 1978 which specified the amount of surplus owed by Castle to Major's.   It was from this final judgment that Castle appealed.

Castle on appeal argues (1) that the express language of the Agreement indicates that it was an agreement for the sale of accounts and (2) that the parties' course of performance and course of dealing compel an interpretation of the Agreement as one for the sale of accounts. Castle also asserts that the district court erred in "reforming" the Agreement and in concluding that the transaction was a loan. In substance these contentions do no more than reflect Castle's overall position that the Agreement was for an absolute sale of accounts.

Our analysis starts with Article 9 of the Uniform Commercial Code which encompasses both *sales* of accounts and *secured interests* in accounts. Thus, the Pennsylvania counterpart of the Code "applies * * * (a) to any transaction (regardless of its form) which is intended to create a security interest in * * * accounts * * *; and also (b) to any sale of accounts * * *" § 9–102. The official comments to that section make it evident that Article 9 is to govern *all* transactions in accounts. Comment 2 indicates that, because "[c]ommercial financing on the basis of accounts * * * is often so conducted that the distinction between a security transfer and a sale is blurred," that "sales" as well as transactions "intended to create a security interest" are subject to the provisions of Article 9. Moreover, a "security interest" is defined under the Act as "any interest of a buyer of accounts." § 1–201(37). Thus even an outright buyer of accounts, such as Castle claims to be, by definition has a "security interest" in the accounts which it purchases.

Article 9 of the Pennsylvania Code is subdivided into five parts. Our examination of Parts 1–4, §§ 9–101 to 9–410, reveals no distinction drawn between a sale and a security interest which is relevant to the issue on this appeal. However, the distinction between an outright sale and a transaction intended to create a security interest becomes highly significant with respect to certain provisions found in Part 5 of Article 9. That part pertains to default under a "security agreement." § 9–501, et seq.

The default section relevant here, which distinguishes between the consequences that follow on default when the transaction *secures an indebtedness* rather than a *sale,* provides:

> A secured party who by agreement is entitled to charge back uncollected collateral or otherwise to full and limited recourse against the debtor and who undertakes to collect from the account debtors or obligors must proceed in a commercially reasonable manner and may deduct his reasonable expenses of realization from the collections. *If the security agreement secures an indebtedness, the secured party must account to the debtor for any surplus,* and unless otherwise agreed, the debtor is liable for any deficiency. But, *if the underlying transaction was a sale of accounts,* contract rights, or chattel paper, *the debtor is entitled to any surplus* or is

liable for any deficiency *only if the security agreement so provides.*

§ 9–502(2) (emphasis added).

Thus, if the accounts were transferred to Castle *to secure Major's' indebtedness,* Castle was obligated to account for and pay over the surplus proceeds to Major's under § 9–502(2), as a debtor's (Major's') right to surplus in such a case cannot be waived even by an express agreement. § 9–501(3)(a). On the other hand, if a *sale of accounts* had been effected, then Castle was entitled to all proceeds received from all accounts because the June 18, 1973 Agreement does not provide otherwise.

However, while the Code instructs us as to the consequences that ensue as a result of the determination of "secured indebtedness" as contrasted with "sale," the Code does not provide assistance in distinguishing between the character of such transactions. This determination, as to whether a particular assignment constitutes a sale or a transfer for security, is left to the courts for decision. § 9–502, Comment 4. It is to that task that we now turn.

* * *

The comments to § 9–502(2) (and in particular Comment 4) make clear to us that the presence of recourse in a sale agreement without more will not automatically convert a sale into a security interest. Hence, one of Major's arguments which is predicated on such a *per se* principle attracts us no more than it attracted the district court. The Code comments however are consistent with and reflect the views expressed by courts and commentators that "[t]he determination of whether a particular assignment constitutes a [true] sale or a transfer for security is left to the courts." § 9–502, Comment 4. The question for the court then is whether the *nature* of the recourse, and the true nature of the transaction, are such that the legal rights and economic consequences of the agreement bear a greater similarity to a financing transaction or to a sale.

[The court's discussion of other cases is omitted.]

Hence, it appears that in each of the cases cited, despite the express language of the agreements, the respective courts examined the parties' practices, objectives, business activities and relationships and determined whether the transaction was a sale or a secured loan only after analysis of the evidence as to the true nature of the transaction. We noted earlier that here the parties, satisfied that there was nothing other than the Agreement and documents bearing on their relationship (Part III, supra), submitted to the court's determination on an agreed record. The district court thereupon reviewed the Agreement and the documents as they reflected the conduct of the parties to determine whether

Castle treated the transactions as sales or transfers of a security interest. In referring to the extremely relevant factor of "recourse"[12] and to the risks allocated, the district court found:

> In the instant case the allocation of risks heavily favors Major's claim to be considered as an assignor with an interest in the collectibility of its accounts. It appears that Castle required Major's to retain all conceivable risks of uncollectibility of these accounts. It required warranties that retail account debtors—e.g., Major's customers—meet the criteria set forth by Castle, that Major's perform the credit check to verify that these criteria were satisfied, and that Major's warrant that the accounts were fully enforceable legally and were "fully and timely collectible." It also imposed an obligation to indemnify Castle out of a reserve account for losses resulting from a customer's failure to pay, or for any breach of warranty, and an obligation to repurchase any account after the customer was in default for more than 60 days. Castle only assumed the risk that the assignor itself would be unable to fulfill its obligations. Guaranties of quality alone, or even guarantees of collectibility alone, might be consistent with a true sale, but Castle attempted to shift all risks to Major's, and incur none of the risks or obligations of ownership. It strains credulity to believe that this is the type of situation, referred to in Comment 4, in which "there may be a true sale of accounts * * * although recourse exists." When we turn to the conduct of the parties to seek support for this contention, we find instead that Castle, in fact, treated these transactions as a transfer of a security interest.

449 F.Supp. at 543.

Moreover, in looking ot the conduct of the parties, the district court found one of the more significant documents to be an August 31, 1973 letter written by Irving Canter, President of Castle Credit, to Major's. As the district court characterized it, and as we agree:

> This letter, in effect, announces the imposition of a floating interest rate on loans under a line of credit of $80,000 per

---

12. Gilmore, in commenting on the Code's decision to leave the distinction between a security transfer and a sale to the courts, would place almost controlling significance on the one factor of recourse. He states:

If there is no right of charge-back or recourse with respect to uncollectible accounts and no right to claim for a deficiency, then the transaction should be held to be a sale, entirely outside the scope of Part 5. If there is a right to charge back uncollectible accounts (a right, as § 9–502 puts it, of "full or limited recourse") or a right to claim a deficiency, then the transaction should be held to be for security and thus subject to Part 5 as well as the other Parts of the Article.

II Gilmore, Security Interests in Personal Property, § 44.4 at 1230.

Here, of course, the Agreement provided Castle with full recourse against Major's.

month, based upon the fluctuating prime interest rate. The key portion of the letter states:

> Accordingly, your volume for the month of September cannot exceed $80,000. Any business above that amount will have to be paid for in October. I think you'll agree that your quota is quite liberal. The surcharge for the month of September will be 3% of the principal amount financed which is based upon a $9\frac{1}{2}\%$ prime rate. On October 1, and for each month thereafter, the surcharge will be adjusted, based upon the prime rate in effect at that time as it relates to a $6\frac{1}{2}\%$ base rate. * * *

This unilateral change in the terms of the Agreement makes it obvious that Castle treated the transaction as a line of credit to Major's—i.e., a loan situation. Were this a true sale, as Castle now argues, it would not have been able to impose these new conditions by fiat. Such changes in a sales contract would have modified the price term of the agreement, which could only be done by a writing signed by all the parties.

449 F.Supp. at 543.

It is apparent to us that on this record none of the risks present in a true sale is present here. Nor has the custom of the parties or their relationship, as found by the district court, given rise to more than a debtor/creditor relationship in which Major's' debt was secured by a transfer of Major's' customer accounts to Castle, thereby bringing the transaction within the ambit of § 9–502. To the extent that the district court determined that a surplus existed, Castle was obligated to account to Major's for that surplus and Major's' right to the surplus could not be waived, § 9–502(2). Accordingly, we hold that on this record the district court did not err in determining that the true nature of the transaction between Major's and Castle was a secured loan, not a sale.

* * *

The judgment of the district court will be affirmed.

NOTES

1. The only transaction covered by Article 9 which is not a true secured transaction is the sale of accounts and chattel paper. § 1–201(37) and § 9–102(1)(b). The fact that it is difficult to distinguish between an outright sale and a security transfer of accounts or chattel paper is one of the reasons the Code covers such sales. Comment 2 to § 9–102. Another reason is that in some states some form of public notice was probably needed to protect the buyer of accounts or chattel paper against creditors of the seller and other buyers or transferees of the account or chattel paper, and Article 9's provisions on perfection and priority per-

form that function admirably. Gilmore, Security Interests in Personal Property § 8.7 (1965).

2. Comment 1 to § 9–502 explains the advantage the accounts creditor has over the creditor whose collateral is tangible property in realizing on the collateral. We have seen the difficulties encountered in realizing on tangible personal property. The selling creditor must be concerned about refurbishing or repairing the property, selling it in the proper market, and getting a decent price even though the liquidation value of used goods may seem disproportionately low compared to their original cost. In short, the selling creditor must make sure that goods were disposed of in a manner that a reviewing court years later will deign to call commercially reasonable. Contrast the position of the accounts or chattel paper creditor. If the financing arrangement calls for account debtors to pay the accounts creditor directly, the creditor continues to collect after the default of the debtor-assignor. If the financing arrangement calls for account debtors to pay the debtor-assignor, § 9–502 (and invariably the security agreement) allows the creditor-assignee to notify the account debtors to make their payments directly to the creditor-assignee in the future. Under § 9–318(3) the account debtors must comply. If the accounts are good, the creditor-assignee collects one hundred cents on the dollar and does so virtually without additional expense. If the accounts or chattel paper creditor does not choose to collect them, the creditor may dispose of the collateral by sale under § 9–504.

If the assignment of accounts or chattel paper is a secured transaction, the collecting creditor-assignee must protect the debtor's interest in the collateral. The creditor-assignee must act in a commercially reasonable manner and cannot simply settle with account debtors for just enough to pay off the secured debt. But if an outright sale of accounts or chattel paper has taken place and the assignor is neither liable for a deficiency nor entitled to a surplus, Part 5 of Article 9 has no application. Since the accounts or chattel paper are the property of the assignee and the debtor has no interest in them, the assignee can deal with the accounts or chattel paper in any way desired. Gilmore, Security Interests in Personal Property § 44.4 (1965).

Chapter 4

SECURITY INTERESTS IN BANKRUPTCY

A. OVERVIEW OF BANKRUPTCY

---

1. INTRODUCTION

As stated in the preceding chapters, Article 9, though a state statute, is frequently a key element of federal bankruptcy cases. No lawyer can competently advise on the planning of secured transactions or on the enforcement of security interests arising from these transactions without a detailed understanding of the Bankruptcy Code's impact on Article 9 security interests. Our coverage of this broad subject is roughly divided into two parts. First, we very briefly discuss the way Article 9 security interests are treated by the Bankruptcy Code. Here we offer an overview of bankruptcy law, note the effect of the automatic stay, and discuss the status of secured claims under Chapter 7 and Chapter 11 of the Bankruptcy Code. Second, and in more detail, we deal with the effect of the debtor's filing in bankruptcy on the validity of Article 9 security interests. Here we discuss the "strong arm" clause, fraudulent transfers, preferences and equitable subordination.

Bankruptcy law is federal law. The applicable statute is the Bankruptcy Reform Act of 1978 which went into effect in 1979 replacing the Bankruptcy Act of 1898. We will refer to the 1978 Act as the Bankruptcy Code. Amendments to the Bankruptcy Code occur frequently. The Bankruptcy Code is supplemented by the Bankruptcy Rules which govern procedures in the United States Bankruptcy Courts.

Although bankruptcy is federal law the rights in bankruptcy of debtors and creditors are governed in large part by rights under applicable state law. Liens, which are created by state law, are of paramount importance in bankruptcy. The creditor whose debt is secured by a lien in the debtor's property has absolute priority with respect to that property over other creditors who have no liens, or whose liens are of lower priority. Usually bankrupts are insolvent, i.e., the value of their assets is less than their debts, and, particularly in the case of business debtors, the debtor's property is normally encumbered. The result in many of these cases is that the bulk of the bankrupt's assets is applied to the payment of secured debts. Much of bankruptcy law is concerned

332

with striking an equitable balance between the rights of secured and unsecured creditors to the debtor's assets. Toward this end bankruptcy law allows some liens which are valid outside bankruptcy to be invalidated in the bankruptcy proceedings, thus demoting the lienholder from the status of secured creditor to that of unsecured creditor. Sometimes the bankruptcy law recognizes the validity of a lien but the rights of the lienholder are restricted in some fashion in order to enhance the rights of unsecured creditors.

Under the early law bankruptcy was exclusively a creditor's remedy, and in modern times bankruptcy is still an important, though little used, creditor's remedy. Some creditors who would receive little or nothing in payment of their claims outside bankruptcy may be able to obtain substantial payment if the debtor is in bankruptcy. Creditors can, under some circumstances, force a debtor into bankruptcy by filing a petition in involuntary bankruptcy against a debtor. The most common ground for obtaining involuntary bankruptcy is that "the debtor is generally not paying such debtor's debts as such debts become due * * *." § 303(h) (1). Involuntary bankruptcy, however, is relatively uncommon. Bankruptcy today is most important as a debtor's remedy. The overwhelming majority of bankruptcies occur by voluntary act of debtors who are seeking relief from the demands of their creditors.

Outside of bankruptcy there is often little relief for a debtor who is unable to pay creditors. Creditors with security interests may be threatening to sell collateral. Other creditors may have obtained, or are threatening to obtain, judicial liens in the debtor's property. Although state law may allow the debtor to protect exempt property from execution or attachment, that law may not apply to some property that the debtor vitally needs. Most debtors that are not natural persons cannot protect any property from creditors. For debtors beset by creditors bankruptcy can provide instant and dramatic relief. The paragraphs that follow provide a brief description of the principal characteristics of voluntary bankruptcy proceedings.

The United States is divided into 91 judicial districts. Each of these districts comprises either a state or a part of a state, the District of Columbia, or Puerto Rico. In each district there is a United States Bankruptcy Court with one or more bankruptcy judges. There are also United States Trustees, each of whom is assigned to one or more of the judicial districts. The function of the United States Trustee, who is a salaried employee appointed by the Attorney General, is to supervise the administration of bankruptcy cases. The duties of a United States Trustee are stated in 28 U.S.C. § 586.

2. TYPES OF BANKRUPTCY

The debtor can choose two types of bankruptcy. The first, and most simple type, is a bankruptcy liquidation under Chapter 7 of the Bankruptcy Code. In a liquidation bankruptcy all of the property of the debtor owned at the date of bankruptcy becomes part of the bankruptcy estate. § 541. A debtor who is an individual is entitled to exempt certain property from the bankruptcy estate. The exempt property is released to the debtor. The property that may be exempted is in most cases determined by the law of the state of the debtor's domicile and consists of property that is exempt from judicial liens in that state. In some cases the debtor has the option of electing to exempt property listed in § 522(d). The trustee in bankruptcy must also dispose of property in which a lienholder or other person such as a co-owner has a property interest. In some cases that property is released by the trustee. In other cases the property is sold by the trustee and the property interest of the lienholder or other person is satisfied from the proeeds of sale. Any remaining property of the estate is sold by the trustee and the proceeds are applied to payment of claims of the debtor's creditors and the expenses of the bankruptcy proceedings. A debtor who is an individual normally will be discharged of personal liability on all or most prebankruptcy debts. The ability of an individual to obtain a discharge of prebankruptcy debts is one of the most important characteristics of modern bankruptcy law. The overextended debtor can get a "fresh start" by having personal liability on prebankruptcy debts wiped out while being allowed to retain all exempt property. Debtors other than individuals—corporations and partnerships— do not need this fresh start. An insolvent organization can simply be dissolved and liquidated by distributing all its assets to creditors. Thus, in Chapter 7, only an individual can be discharged. § 727(a)(1).

In the second type of bankruptcy the assets of the debtor need not be liquidated. This type of bankruptcy is usually referred to as reorganization or rehabilitation bankruptcy and is governed by Chapter 11, Chapter 12, or Chapter 13 of the Bankruptcy Code. Chapter 13 can be used only by a debtor who is "an individual with regular income that owes, on the date of the filing of the petition, noncontingent, liquidated, unsecured debts of less than $100,000 and noncontingent, liquidated, secured debts of less than $350,000 * * *." § 109(e). The great advantage of Chapter 13 is that the debtor can get the benefits of discharge without losing nonexempt property. The debtor is required to formulate a plan under which the debtor proposes to pay, in whole or in part, some or all prebankruptcy debts over a period of time which is usually three years. Creditors are paid in accordance with the plan normally from postbankruptcy earnings although the plan could provide for a liquidation of some assets. The plan need not be approved by creditors. If the plan is confirmed by the bankruptcy court creditors are bound by its terms. § 1327(a). But a plan cannot be confirmed over the objection of a creditor unless certain requirements are met. With respect to a secured claim the plan must provide either for surrender of the collateral to the secured creditor or, if no surrender is made, for retention of the lien by the creditor and deferred payments of no less than the amount of the secured claim plus interest to compensate for the delay in payment. § 1325(a)(5). With respect to an unsecured claim the plan must provide for payments of not less than the amount that would have been paid on the claim if the bankruptcy had been in Chapter 7 plus interest to compensate for the delay in payment. § 1325(a)(4). In addition, if the plan does not propose payment in full of unsecured claims the plan must provide for the payment of all of the debtor's "disposable income" for three years. § 1325(b)(1). Disposable income means total income received by the debtor less the amount necessary for the maintenance or support of the debtor and the debtor's dependents. § 1325(b)(2). When all payments are completed the debtor is entitled to a discharge of those debts (with some exceptions) that are provided for in the plan. § 1328(a). Under some circumstances the debtor can obtain a discharge even if payments under the plan have not been completed if the failure to complete the plan is not the fault of the debtor. § 1328(b).

Chapter 11 can be used by both individuals and organizations, whether or not the debtor is engaged in business, but it is designed primarily for business organizations. It resembles Chapter 13 in that the debtor is normally allowed to retain its assets and to continue operation of its business. The debtor proposes a plan of reorganization under which creditors will be paid, usually over a period of time, from assets of the estate or postconfirmation earnings of the debtor. Unlike Chapter 13, confirmation of a plan in Chapter 11 is usually made after it has been accepted by the various classes of creditors and stockholder interests of the debtor. Acceptance by a class is accomplished by a vote of members of the class in specified majorities. Under some circumstances a plan can be confirmed even though not all classes accept the plan. Upon confirmation of the plan the debtor, whether an individual or an organization, is normally given a discharge of all preconfirmation debts. In return, creditors and stockholder interests have rights that are given to them by the plan. There are various provisions in Chapter 11 designed to protect the interests of creditors and stockholder interests who did not accept the plan.

Chapter 12 was added to the Bankruptcy Code in 1986 to provide for the rehabilitation of "family farmers" defined in § 101. Chapter 12 is similar to Chapter 13, but it incorporates some elements of Chapter 11. It is specifically designed to make it easier for family farmers who are threatened with loss of their farms to restructure their debts in bankruptcy while continuing to operate their farms.

3. PETITION IN BANKRUPTCY AND THE AUTOMATIC STAY

Voluntary bankruptcy, or a "voluntary case" as it is called in the Bankruptcy Code, is commenced by the debtor's filing in the Bankruptcy Court of a petition in bankruptcy. § 301. In addition to the petition the debtor must file various statements and schedules of information including a statement of assets and liabilities with descriptions of each and a list of creditors identified by name and address.

The filing of the petition in bankruptcy operates as an automatic stay against a variety of acts taken against the debtor or with respect to property of the bankruptcy estate. § 362(a). Among the most important acts which are stayed are the following: the commencement or continuation of judicial proceedings against the debtor to recover a prebankruptcy claim; the enforcement of any prebankruptcy judgment against the debtor or against property of the estate; any act to obtain possession of property of the estate or property held by the estate; and any act to create, perfect or enforce any lien against property of the estate. The stay even applies to informal acts to collect a prebankruptcy debt such as dunning letters, telephone calls and the like. There are some exceptions to the very broad scope of the stay, but the stay effectively insulates the debtor from any kind of action to collect prebankruptcy debts. Under § 362(d), a creditor can get relief from the stay in some cases, but the effect of the stay is to require all collection action to be made through or with the consent of the bankruptcy court. The importance of the automatic stay cannot be overemphasized. Frequently the primary purpose of the filing of a bankruptcy petition is to obtain the benefit of the stay.

4. TRUSTEE IN BANKRUPTCY

In a Chapter 7 bankruptcy the bankruptcy estate is administered by a trustee in bankruptcy who can be either an individual or a corporation. § 321. The duties of the trustee are listed in § 704. The principal duty of the trustee is to collect the property of the estate, to reduce it to money by selling it, and to apply the proceeds to payment of expenses of the bankruptcy and claims of creditors. The collecting of the property of the estate sometimes requires the trustee to recover property of the debtor that was transferred before bankruptcy in transactions that are avoidable in bankruptcy because in violation of some bankruptcy policy. These "avoiding powers" of the trustee are one of the most important aspects of bankruptcy. In asserting these powers the trustee acts primarily for the benefit of unsecured creditors. The trustee also has wide powers of investigation of the financial affairs of the debtor and may oppose discharge of the debtor if the circumstances warrant. The trustee may also examine the validity of claims of creditors and may oppose improper claims. The trustee, who must be a disinterested person, is a fiduciary although the Bankruptcy Code does not specify the nature of the fiduciary relationship. The trustee's duties, particularly those of collecting, holding and disposing of property of the estate, are exercised on behalf of creditors generally, but often the trustee must oppose some creditors to benefit others. Basically the job of the trustee is to maximize the assets available for payment to general unsecured creditors.

Promptly after a Chapter 7 case is commenced an interim trustee in bankruptcy is appointed by the United States Trustee. In each district there is a panel of persons qualified to serve as trustees. The interim trustee is appointed from this panel. § 701.

There is a trustee in bankruptcy in a case under Chapter 12 or Chapter 13 but the trustee's duties are somewhat different. The only property of the bankruptcy estate that normally comes into the hands of the trustee is the earnings of the debtor that are the source of the payments under the plan. The primary duty of the trustee is to disburse to creditors payments due under the plan. The trustee is either appointed by the bankruptcy court to serve in the particular case or is a "standing trustee" appointed by the court to act generally in Chapter 12 or Chapter 13 cases filed in the district. Normally there is no trustee in bankruptcy in a Chapter 11 case. Rather, the debtor continues in possession of its property as a "debtor in possession" that exercises the powers of a trustee in bankruptcy. § 1107(a) and § 1108. A trustee in bankruptcy is appointed in a Chapter 11 case only in unusual cases such as those involving fraud or gross mismanagement by the debtor. § 1104(a).

5. CLAIMS IN BANKRUPTCY

In Chapter 7, after the trustee in bankruptcy has collected the bankruptcy estate and has sold it, the proceeds are applied to the payment of bankruptcy expenses and the claims of creditors. A claim is the basis for a distribution from the bankruptcy estate. A "proof of claim," which is a written statement setting forth a creditor's claim, is normally filed by the creditor. § 501 and Bankruptcy Rule 3001. Creditor is defined by § 101 to mean an entity (also defined in § 101) holding a claim that arose before the filing of the petition in a voluntary case. Thus, rights against the debtor that arise after bankruptcy are not treated as claims in bankruptcy. There are a few exceptions to this statement.

A claim can be paid only if it is "allowed." Allowance of a claim means simply that it has been recognized by the court as valid in the amount claimed. If there is a dispute concerning a claim the court must determine whether the claim should be allowed. Section 502 contains detailed provisions governing allowance and disallowance. Any claim can be dealt with in bankruptcy except to the extent that a claim is specifically excepted. The exceptions are stated in § 502(b), (d), and (e).

Claims are classified as either secured or unsecured. Suppose the debtor owes Bank $20,000 and the debt is secured by a security interest in collateral of the debtor on which there are no other liens. The collateral, because it was owned by the debtor, is part of the bankruptcy estate. § 541(a)(1). If Bank's security interest is valid in bankruptcy Bank has a secured claim to the extent that its debt is covered by value of the collateral. To the extent that its debt is not covered by value of the collateral, Bank has an unsecured claim. § 506(a). For example, if the collateral has a value of $30,000 Bank is oversecured and it has a secured claim of $20,000; if the collateral has a value of $15,000 Bank is undersecured and it has a secured claim of $15,000 and an unsecured claim of $5,000. The value of the collateral is determined by the bankruptcy court.

6. DISTRIBUTION OF ASSETS TO UNSECURED CREDITORS

In Chapter 7, after the trustee has disposed of property of the estate in satisfaction of secured claims the remaining property will be distributed pursuant to § 726 which states an order of priority among the various claimants. First, distribution is made in payment of expenses and claims that have priority under § 507. First priority is for administrative expenses described in § 503. After administrative expenses have been paid priority claims of creditors are paid. These claims are ranked in seven additional priority categories by § 507. The most important are certain claims of employees of the debtor which have a third and fourth priority and certain claims for taxes which have a seventh priority. After all priority claims have been paid in their order of priority, distribution is made pursuant to § 726 to the remaining creditors. With some exceptions these claims are paid on a pro rata basis to the extent of the property available.

Priorities also apply to cases under Chapters 11, 12 and 13. Under Chapters 12 and 13 the plan must provide for payment in full of all priority claims, but deferred payment can be made, with interest, over the period of the plan. A Chapter 11 plan must provide for payment in full of all priority claims. Administrative expenses and second priority claims must be paid in cash on the effective date of the plan. Others can be paid, with interest, over the period of the plan.

7. DISCHARGE

In Chapter 7, a debtor who is an individual will normally receive a discharge from prebankruptcy debts. § 727(b). For individuals the primary purpose of filing a petition in Chapter 7 bankruptcy is to obtain this discharge. In some cases, however, the debtor is not entitled to a discharge. The various grounds for denying a discharge to a debtor in Chapter 7 are set forth in § 727(a). A debtor is not entitled to a discharge if the debtor has received a discharge under Chapter 7 in a case commenced within six years of the time the current case was commenced. The other grounds stated for denying discharge refer to misconduct by the debtor. This reflects the fact that bankruptcy is an equitable proceeding and that a debtor guilty of certain inequitable conduct should not enjoy the benefit of a discharge. Even in cases in which the debtor is entitled to discharge, not all debts are dischargeable. Discharge is a benefit to the debtor and a concomitant loss to the creditor. The theory of bankruptcy is that a qualified debtor is entitled to the "fresh start" that discharge provides, but in some cases the creditor may have equities which are greater than those of the debtor. In those cases the law provides that the debt of that creditor is not discharged. In effect that creditor can participate in the distribution of the debtor's property, but to the extent that the creditor's debt has not been satisfied the creditor will have a claim against the debtor that survives bankruptcy. Debts that are excepted from a Chapter 7 discharge are described in § 523(a).

Chapter 11, 12 and 13 have their own discharge provisions. Corporations and partnerships can be discharged in Chapter 11 and Chapter 12. Section 727(a) applies only to Chapter 7 discharges. Section 523 has only limited effect in Chapters 11 and 13. It applies only to individuals in Chapter 11 and only some of the § 523 exceptions apply to a Chapter 13 discharge if the debtor completes payments under the plan.

B. SECURED CLAIMS IN BANKRUPTCY

---

1. NATURE OF SECURED CLAIM AND SURVIVAL OF LIEN

The act of commencing a bankruptcy case by the filing of a petition in bankruptcy creates the bankruptcy estate. Section 541, which defines the estate, applies both to Chapter 7 liquidations and to reorganizations and rehabilitations under Chapters 11, 12 and 13. Section 541(a)(1), which is the basic provision, states that the estate includes "all legal or equitable interests of the debtor in property as of the commencement of the case." Under § 541(a)(7) the estate also includes "any interest in property that the estate acquires after the commencement of the case." The latter provision is particularly important in Chapter 11 cases in which the estate is a business that will continue to be operated after bankruptcy.

In Chapter 7 cases involving a debtor who is a natural person, an important corollary to § 541(a)(1) is that as a general rule property which is obtained by the debtor after bankruptcy is commenced is not property of the estate and thus is not available for the enforced payment of prebankruptcy claims. Defining property of the estate is also important because that property falls under the jurisdiction of the bankruptcy court and the automatic stay of § 362 prevents third parties from taking any action to recover property of the estate without resorting to the bankruptcy court.

In Chapter 7 an unsecured claim is a right to receive a share of the bankruptcy estate to the extent that the estate has not been exhausted by superior competing claims. A secured claim is very different. It is a claim to specific property, the creditor's collateral, rather than a claim to share in the distribution of the bankruptcy estate. If the secured claim exhausts the economic value of the collateral, the holder of the secured claim is entitled to the collateral itself. The holder of the secured claim can assert this right to the collateral by requesting the bankruptcy court for relief from the automatic stay. § 362(d). Relief from the stay means that the holder of the secured claim may resort to nonbankruptcy remedies to obtain possession of the collateral such as UCC § 9–503. In this case it is not necessary for the holder of the secured claim to file a proof of claim under § 501. In many cases the holder of the secured claim may be able to obtain the collateral without resort to § 362(d). The property right of the claimant may be recognized in other ways. In a Chapter 7 case if there is no economic value in property of the estate above the value of liens, the trustee in bankruptcy will normally abandon the property either to the debtor or to the holder of the secured claim. § 554. No formal proof of claim is required. The property interest of the holder of a secured claim is also recognized in § 725 which states that " * * * before final distribution of property of the estate under section 726 * * * the trustee * * * shall dispose of any property in which an entity other than the estate has an interest, such as a lien * * *."

In Chapter 7, if the amount of the secured claim is less than the value of the collateral, the holder of the claim is not entitled to the collateral itself. Rather, the trustee in bankruptcy may sell the property free of the lien (§ 363(b) and (f)(3)) but the property interest of the holder of the secured claim is recognized by § 363(e) which requires adequate protection of the secured claim. In practice, this means that the holder of the secured claim is paid the value of the claim from the proceeds of the sale.

If property of the estate that is subject to a lien is released to the debtor or to the lienholder and the debtor is given a discharge under § 727(b), the effect is to discharge the debtor from liability on the debt which is secured by the lien. How does this affect the rights of the lienholder? The theory of discharge has always been that it affects only the personal liability of the debtor. It does not affect the debt itself which remains unpaid. If third parties are liable on the debt they remain liable. For example, a surety or other guarantor is liable even through the principal debtor is released as a result of the discharge. This is specifically recognized in § 524(e). Nor is an insurance carrier's liability affected by the discharge of the insured. Similarly, if the debt is secured by property of a third party that property can be reached to the full extent of the security agreement. The same rule applies if the discharged debt was secured by a lien in the debtor's property. The debt and the lien continue to exist after bankruptcy even though the debtor may have been discharged from personal liability to pay the debt and even though the creditor did not file a proof of claim in bankruptcy. This principle was recognized in Long v. Bullard, 117 U.S. 617, 6 S.Ct. 917, 29 L.Ed. 1004 (1886), a case antedating the Bankruptcy Act of 1898. In that case, Long received a discharge in bankruptcy and retained as exempt property a homestead that was subject to a mortgage in favor of Bullard. Bullard did not file proof of the mortgage debt in the bankruptcy. After bankruptcy, Bullard brought a foreclosure action. Long defended on the ground that the discharge prevented foreclosure under the mortgage. This defense was rejected in the state court which stated that "there could be no personal recovery against [Long] upon the note, but that the property could be subjected to the payment of the amount due, as the discharge of Long in bankruptcy did not release the lien of the mortgage." The court entered a decree for sale of the property. The Supreme Court of the United States affirmed the decree. Chief Justice Waite stated:

> * * * the discharge releases the bankrupt only from debts which were or might have been proved, and * * * debts secured by mortgage or pledge can only be proved for the balance remaining due after deducting the value of the security, unless all claim upon the security is released. Here the creditor neither proved his debt in bankruptcy nor released his lien. Consequently his security was preserved notwithstanding the bankruptcy of his debtor. * * * The dispute in the court below was as to the existence of the lien

at the time of the commencement of the proceedings in bankruptcy. That depended entirely on the state laws, as to which the judgment of the state court is final and not subject to review here. * * *

117 U.S. at 620–621.

Section 506(d), which was amended in the 1984 Amendments, was meant to preserve the rule of Long v. Bullard. The House Report on the Bankruptcy Reform Act of 1978 states with respect to the original version of § 506(d): "Subsection (d) permits liens to pass through the bankruptcy case unaffected. However, if a party in interest requests the court to determine and allow or disallow the claim secured by the lien under section 502 and the claim is not allowed, then the lien is void to the extent that the claim is not allowed." 1978 U.S.Code Cong. & Admin.News 6313. Section 506(d) in both its original and amended form is phrased negatively. It states when a lien is void. Only by negative inference does it indicate that a lien not void under § 506(d) will survive bankruptcy. It assumes that the rule of Long v. Bullard preserves a lien if the lien is not void under § 506(d) and is not avoided by some other provision of the Code.

Section 506(d) may be illustrated by the hypothetical cases that follow. Debtor granted Creditor a security interest in goods of Debtor to secure a debt. At the time of Debtor's Chapter 7 bankruptcy the amount of the debt was $8,000 and the goods had a value of only $5,000. The trustee in bankruptcy abandoned any claim to the property and Creditor did not file a proof of claim. Debtor obtained a discharge of the $8,000 debt owed to Creditor. If the security interest was not otherwise avoided in bankruptcy, the security interest is enforceable after bankruptcy unless § 506(d) makes it void because no other provision of the Bankruptcy Code avoids it. If Creditor had filed a proof of secured claim in bankruptcy the claim would have been allowed in the amount of $5,000 because that was the value of the property. § 506(a). Creditor could also have filed proof of an unsecured claim for $3,000. Each claim would have been allowed because we are assuming that the $8,000 was a valid debt and that the value of the property was $5,000. Under § 506(d) Creditor's security interest secured a claim of Creditor, but it did not secure "an allowed secured claim" because under § 502 a claim cannot be allowed unless proof of the claim is filed. Thus, the first clause of § 506(d), if literally read, would make Creditor's security interest void if the unless clause does not apply. But in this case the unless clause would save Creditor's security interest. Creditor's claim was not an allowed secured claim only because Creditor did not file a proof of claim. § 506(d)(2).

In some cases, however, § 506(d), if literally read, would either nullify or reduce the amount of liens that are valid under state law and otherwise indefeasible in bankruptcy. Section 506(a) states that a creditor with a claim secured by a lien on property has a secured claim "to the extent of the value of such creditor's interest in the estate's interest in such property." It is important to understand that having a claim secured by a lien and having a secured claim are different concepts. It is possible for a creditor to have a valid lien in property of the estate without having a secured claim. In order for a lien to give rise to a secured claim the lien must have present monetary value. For example, suppose Creditor A and Creditor B each have claims of $10,000 against Debtor, and each is secured by a perfected security interest in the same collateral owned by Debtor. If the collateral is worth no more than $10,000 and the security interest of Creditor B is subordinate to the security interest of Creditor A, the security interest of Creditor B has no present monetary value and Creditor B does not have a secured claim even though the subordinated lien is valid under nonbankruptcy law. Literally read, § 506(d) applies in this case. Because Creditor B's lien secures a claim that is not an allowed secured claim the lien is avoided by the bankruptcy under the first clause of § 506(d). Under this reading of § 502(d), the lien is not saved by the unless clause because this case is not covered by either § 506(d)(1) or (2). Creditor B has only an unsecured claim for $10,000 and has no rights with respect to the debt against either Debtor or the property after Debtor is discharged.

Another example of the effect of a literal reading of § 506(d) follows: Debtor, an individual, bought a house for $100,000 which was financed by a first mortgage of $80,000 to a lender. Debtor spent $30,000 in remodeling the house, all of which was financed by a second mortgage on the house to another lender. As the result of the closing of a factory that was the principal employer in the town in which Debtor lived, real property values dropped precipitously. When Debtor filed in Chapter 7 the house was worth no more than $75,000 and the unpaid amount of the first mortgage debt was $78,000. The house will be abandoned to Debtor by the trustee in bankruptcy whether or not it is exempt property, because Debtor's ownership interest in the house has no present value. Personal liability on the first mortgage debt can be discharged in bankruptcy, but the mortgage will survive bankruptcy. If the house is sold in a foreclosure sale for its maximum value of $75,000 or less, all of the proceeds of sale go to the first mortgagee. But Debtor may not want to lose the house. If Debtor is able to continue making the monthly payments on the first mortgage, § 506(d), if literally read, would allow Debtor to save the house. In a case like this it is likely that the first mortgagee will agree not to foreclose if Debtor agrees to waive discharge of the mortgage debt by "reaffirming" it under § 524(c). Thus, Debtor could keep the house as long as the monthly payments are

made. But for Debtor to obtain the full benefit of this agreement
with the first mortgagee it is necessary that the second mortgage
be avoided in bankruptcy. A reduction in the first mortgage debt
by payments after bankruptcy or an increase in value of the house
in the event that economic conditions in the town substantially
improve could give to Debtor a substantial equity in the house. If
the second mortgage is not avoided, any increase in value of the
house above the amount of the first mortgage will be captured by
the second mortgagee. Literally read, § 506(d) nullifies that mortgage because the second mortgage had no present value at the
time of the bankruptcy and is not a lien that secures a secured
claim. If at the time of bankruptcy the house had a resale value
of § 90,000, there was value in the collateral above the claim of
the first mortgage ($78,000), and the second mortgagee would have
a secured claim of $12,000. Because § 506(d) starts with the
words "To the extent that," a lien could be partially avoided or
pared down under § 506(d), and the remainder of the second
mortgagee's lien could be avoided.

A literal reading of § 506(d) and the foregoing description of
the effect of § 506(d) was supported by most of the courts to which
the issue was presented, including Gaglia v. First Federal Savings
& Loan Ass'n, 889 F.2d 1304 (3d Cir.1989). The 10th Circuit, in In
re Dewsnup, 908 F.2d 588 (10th Cir.1990), declined to follow
Gaglia which it acknowledged as representing the majority view.
In the Tenth Circuit case, the Chapter 7 debtors owed a debt of
$120,000 secured by a lien under a deed of trust on two parcels of
farm land owned by the debtors and having a value of $39,000.
The trustee in bankruptcy abandoned the land to the debtor under
§ 554(a) because it had no value to the estate. The debtors sought
to use § 506(d) to nullify the lien to the extent it exceeded the
value of the property and to then redeem the land by paying the
lienor $39,000, the amount of the lienor's secured claim. In
refusing to grant the relief sought by the debtors, the court read
the phrase "in which the estate has an interest" appearing in the
first sentence of § 506(a) to mean that § 506(d) was not meant to
apply to property which had ceased to be property of the estate
when it was abandoned by the trustee in bankruptcy. Under that
reading, § 506(d) could be used to avoid liens only with respect to
property administered by the estate. The court concluded that
§ 506(d) "was intended to facilitate valuation and disposition of
property in the reorganization chapters of the Code."

Because of the conflict between the views expressed by the
Third Circuit in Gaglia and the Tenth Circuit in Dewsnup, the
Supreme Court of the United States granted certiorari in Dewsnup. In Dewsnup v. Timm, ___ U.S. ___, 112 S.Ct. 773, ___ L.Ed.
2d ___ (1992), by a 6–2 vote it affirmed the result reached by the
Tenth Circuit but it used a different rationale. In an astonishing
opinion by Justice Blackmun which provoked a fulminating dis-

sent by Justice Scalia, the Court, despite the apparent clarity of the language of § 506(d), found that it does not mean what it apparently says. The Court noted that under Long v. Bullard a lien passed through bankruptcy unaffected and expressed reluctance to interpret the Bankruptcy Code as changing this venerable rule unless its language was unambiguous. The Court pointed out that the legislative history spoke of a purpose to preserve the rule of Long v. Bullard and referred only to avoidance of liens when the claim secured by the lien is not allowed. But the Court did not explain how the language of § 506(d) was ambiguous. The Court held that "§ 506(d) does not allow petitioner to 'strip down' respondents' lien, because respondents' claim is secured by a lien and has been fully allowed pursuant to § 502." Under the Court's reading, a lien is voided under § 506(d) only if the claim that the lien secures is not an allowed claim. To arrive at this result, the Court simply expunges the word "secured" in the introductory clause of § 506(d) and holds that the term "allowed secured claim" in § 506(d) means something different from what it does in § 506(a). The Court stated: "Were we writing on a clean slate, we might be inclined to agree with [the debtor] that the words 'allowed secured claim' must take the same meaning in § 506(d) as in § 506(a). But, given the ambiguity in the text, we are not convinced that Congress intended to depart from the pre-Code rule that liens pass through bankruptcy unaffected." The Court went on to state that it expresses "no opinion as to whether the words 'allowed secured claim' have different meaning in other provisions of the Bankruptcy Code."

How will the Supreme Court decision in *Dewsnup* affect the hypothetical cases discussed above?

2. PREBANKRUPTCY LIENS ON PROPERTY ACQUIRED AFTER BANKRUPTCY

Section 9–204(1) allows a security agreement to provide for a security interest in property to be acquired by the debtor in the future. If a debtor has signed a security agreement before bankruptcy providing for a security interest in after-acquired property, what is the effect of the security agreement on property acquired after bankruptcy? Bankruptcy Code § 552(a), which applies only to consensual liens, states that "property acquired by the estate or by the debtor after the commencement of the case is not subject to any lien resulting from any security agreement entered into by the debtor before the commencement of the case" unless, under § 552(b) the property is "proceeds, product, offspring, rents, or profits" of property acquired before bankruptcy. This provision is particularly important in Chapter 11 reorganizations of corporations in which the debtor in possession continues to operate a business after bankruptcy. In Chapter 11, property described in

§ 552(a) is property of the estate under § 541(a)(7); property described in § 552(b) is also property of the estate. § 541(a)(6). If an individual files in Chapter 7, property acquired by the debtor after bankruptcy is property of the debtor and the effect of § 552(a) is to free this property from the prebankruptcy security agreement.

IN RE BUMPER SALES, INC.
United States Court of Appeals, Fourth Circuit, 1990.
907 F.2d 1430.

CHAPMAN, CIRCUIT JUDGE:

This appeal stems from the district court's affirmance of the bankruptcy court's order granting to the appellee/cross-appellant Marepcon Financial Corporation (Marepcon), t/a Norshipco Financial Corporation (Norshipco), a post-petition security interest in the inventory, receivables and other assets of debtor Bumper Sales, Inc. (Bumper Sales), to the detriment of appellant/cross-appellee Unsecured Creditors' Committee (the Committee). We affirm.

In order to expand its inventory of car and truck bumpers, Bumper Sales borrowed from Marepcon, a small asset-based lender whose trade name is Norshipco, about $510,000 in the form of two promissory notes, one for $110,000 dated December 8, 1987, and another for $400,000 dated March 9, 1988. In return, Bumper Sales agreed to give Marepcon a security interest in "all of ＊ ＊ ＊ [Bumper Sales'] inventory, accounts receivable, contract rights, furniture, fixtures and equipment, general intangibles, now owned or hereafter-acquired and the proceeds from said collateral," as stipulated by the parties.

＊　＊　＊

When Bumper Sales filed for Chapter 11 bankruptcy on July 22, 1988, the principal remaining due to Marepcon was $499,964.88. At that time, the value of Bumper Sales' inventory, which consisted solely of finished bumpers, was $769,000. Bumper Sales continued to operate the business as debtor-in-possession. ＊ ＊ ＊ The parties stipulated that, during the post-petition period, Bumper Sales did not borrow any outside funds or incur any outside debt; that Bumper Sales used *only* Marepcon's cash collateral—the cash proceeds of inventory secured under Marepcon's security interest—to finance new inventory; and that Bumper Sales would not have been able to reorganize without the use of the cash collateral.

On March 31, 1989, Marepcon filed a Motion to Condition Use, Sale or Lease of Collateral and Proceeds, declaring a claim of $500,000 against Bumper Sales and asserting a security interest in

Bumper Sales' inventory, accounts receivable, general intangibles, furniture, fixtures, equipment, and proceeds. The motion sought adequate protection for this security interest. The Committee filed an objection to the motion * * * contending that any post-petition lien had been lost by Marepcon's failure to condition use of the collateral. The bankruptcy court held that Marepcon had a valid and properly perfected security interest in Bumper Sales' pre-petition inventory and receivables, among other assets, and their proceeds, and that this security interest continued post-petition to the extent of Marepcon's unpaid claim. As a result, the court granted Marepcon a lien on Bumper Sales' pre- and post-petition collateral. The U.S. District Court for the Eastern District of Virginia affirmed the bankruptcy court, and the Committee appeals.

* * *

We now address the crux of the Committee's appeal: whether Marepcon has a security interest in Bumper Sales' post-petition assets. This issue is partly answered easily, because the Committee does not contest that Marepcon holds a security interest in the pre-petition collateral (i.e., that held as of the bankruptcy filing on July 22, 1988) remaining in Bumper Sales' hands at the time of Marepcon's motion for adequate protection on March 31, 1989. It was stipulated that the total amount of inventory at the time of the filing was $769,000. Mr. Waters, the former Executive Vice President of Marepcon, testified that the total cost of goods sold, and hence total amount of inventory released, during this period was at most $464,000 and at least $168,000, making the inventory remaining at the time of the motion between $305,000 ($769,000–$464,000) and $601,000 ($769,000–168,000). Adding the undisputed value of pre-petition equipment of $74,000 and pre-petition receivables of $11,215.57, Marepcon's security interest extends to at least $390,215.57 ($305,000 + $74,000 + $11,215.57) of Bumper Sales' post-petition assets. Given that Marepcon's total claim against Bumper Sales amounts to $486,957.69, the remainder of this opinion is devoted to the issue whether the $96,742.12 balance is secured.

The Committee maintains that Marepcon's security interest does not cover Bumper Sales' post-petition inventory and accounts, because Section 552(a) of the Bankruptcy Code invalidates the operation of after-acquired clauses in bankruptcy. Section 552(a) states as follows:

> Except as provided in subsection (b) of this section, property acquired by the estate or by the debtor after the commencement of the case is not subject to any lien resulting from any security agreement entered into by the debtor before the commencement of the case.

11 U.S.C. § 552(a) (1988). This subsection was "designed to facilitate the debtor's 'fresh start' by allowing the debtor to acquire
postpetition assets free of prepetition liabilities" and thereby offer
"postpetition accounts receivable and inventory as collateral" to
new creditors. In re Photo Promotion Associates, Inc., 53 B.R.
759, 763 (Bankr.S.D.N.Y.1985).

In response, Marepcon asserts that Section 552(b), which
carves out an exception to Section 552(a), applies:

> (b) Except as provided in section[ ] 363 * * * of this title, if
> the debtor and an entity entered into a security agreement
> before the commencement of the case and if the security
> interest created by such security agreement extends to proper-
> ty of the debtor acquired before the commencement of the
> case and to proceeds * * * of such property, then such
> security interest extends to such proceeds * * * acquired by
> the estate after the commencement of the case to the extent
> provided by such security agreement and by applicable
> nonbankruptcy law, except to any extent that the court, after
> notice and a hearing and based on the equities of the case,
> orders otherwise.

11 U.S.C. § 552(b) (1988). Marepcon correctly explains that, according to Section 552, "[p]roceeds coverage, but not after-acquired
property clauses, are valid under title 11." In re Gross–Feibel Co.,
Inc., 21 B.R. 648, 649 (Bankr.S.D.Ohio 1982) (quoting 124 Cong.
Rec. H11, 097–98 (Sept. 28, 1978) (remarks of Rep. Edwards);
S17,414 (Oct. 6, 1978) (remarks of Sen. DeConcini)). Marepcon
contends that its security interest extends to Bumper Sales' post-
petition inventory and accounts because they are proceeds of
Bumper Sales' pre-petition inventory and accounts, pointing out
that Bumper Sales' post-petition inventory was financed solely by
the proceeds of its pre-petition inventory and accounts.[8]

The issue before us, then, is whether Bumper Sales' post-
petition inventory and accounts are after-acquired property or
proceeds. In order to determine the applicability of the exception
in Section 552(b), we must undertake a four-part inquiry. First, is
there a pre-petition security agreement that by its terms extends
to Bumper Sales' pre-petition inventory, accounts and proceeds?
Second, did Bumper Sales receive the proceeds of the pre-petition
inventory and accounts after the filing of the petition? Third, is
Bumper Sales' post-petition inventory second generation proceeds
of pre-petition inventory and accounts, and are Bumper Sales'
post-petition accounts proceeds of post-petition inventory?
Fourth, did Marepcon's consent to Bumper Sales' use of the

---

8. While the Committee challenges
Marepcon's security interest in post-petition accounts arising from post-petition inventory, the Committee concedes
that Marepcon has a security interest.

proceeds of pre-petition inventory and accounts to purchase post-petition inventory destroy Marepcon's security interest?

Under the first inquiry, it is clear that Marepcon has a security interest that was created before Bumper Sales filed its petition for bankruptcy and that covers inventory, accounts and proceeds. Under the second inquiry, the parties do not deny that Bumper Sales received the proceeds of pre-petition inventory after the filing of the petition. Thus, the basic factual prerequisites of Section 552(b) are met.

Under the third inquiry, we encounter difficulties in construing the Bankruptcy Code, because Section 552(b) fails to establish the parameters of "proceeds." Two interpretations are possible. One infers from the absence of a Code definition and from Section 552(b)'s language limiting any security interest "to the extent provided by * * * applicable nonbankruptcy law" that Congress intended to defer to state law, i.e., to the UCC. See 4 Collier on Bankruptcy ¶ 552.02 at 552–11 (15th Ed.1989). The other interpretation relies primarily on the legislative history stating that "[t]he term 'proceeds' is not limited to the technical definition of that term in the UCC, but covers any property into which property subject to the security interest is converted." H.R.Rep. No. 95–595, 95th Cong., 1st Sess. 377 (1977), U.S.Code Cong. & Admin. News 1978, pp. 5787, 6333. This view encourages a broader coverage of proceeds than in the UCC. See, e.g., 2 Norton Bankr. L. and Prac. § 38.03 at 38–2 (1981) (proceeds includes "property into which the prepetition property is converted, property derived from the prepetition property, and income from the prepetition property that is acquired by the estate after the commencement of the case."). However, we believe that Section 552(b)'s express reference to "nonbankruptcy law" should take priority over a vague and isolated piece of legislative history. We also note that the judicial creation of a definition for "proceeds," broader post-petition than pre-petition, would produce arbitrary and potentially inequitable results. As a result, we hold that the UCC's definition and treatment of proceeds applies to Section 552 of the Bankruptcy Code. This is consistent with the unstated rule of the many courts that have looked to the UCC in applying Section 552 of the Code. * * *

Turning to the UCC, we start with Section 9–306(2), which states that a security interest in collateral continues in any proceeds of such collateral: "Except where this title otherwise provides, a security interest * * * continues in any identifiable proceeds including collections received by the debtor." * * * Section 9–306(1) explains what is included: " 'Proceeds' includes whatever is received upon the sale, exchange, collection or other disposition of collateral or proceeds * * *. Money, checks, deposit accounts, and the like are 'cash proceeds.' " * * * Thus, the funds received by Bumper Sales from the sale of its inventory and collection of accounts are cash proceeds, and Marepcon's security interest in Bumper Sales' pre-petition inventory and accounts continues in the cash proceeds, so long as they are identifiable. But there is no doubt that the cash proceeds are identifiable, because the parties have stipulated that Bumper Sales used only these cash proceeds to finance its operations during bankruptcy. Since only these proceeds were used, they are conclusively identifiable.

* * *

Under Section 9–306(3)(b), a security interest in proceeds remains perfected * * * if "a filed financing statement covers the original collateral and the proceeds are identifiable cash proceeds." In this case, we have already shown that Marepcon has a security interest in the pre-petition inventory and accounts and that the cash proceeds of such inventory and accounts are identifiable. As a result, Marepcon has a security interest in the cash proceeds. However, Bumper Sales subsequently used the cash proceeds to finance new inventory, which was both after-acquired property and proceeds. This presents an apparent conflict between Section 552(a), which cuts off after-acquired property clauses, and Section 552(b), which continues security interests in proceeds. Professor Clark describes this collision and offers a solution:

> What happens when the proceeds or final products are sold by the estate and the cash is used to manufacture new inventory, particularly in a rehabilitation proceeding? A literal reading of § 552 would suggest that the general rule applies and the floating lien is cut off. In other words, a bright line is drawn between first-generation proceeds and after-acquired property. Such a result, however, could completely deprive the secured party of his pre-petition perfected security interest. Therefore, the term "proceeds" should be read broadly—as in U.C.C. § 9–306—to include after-acquired property, at least where inventory and accounts are concerned and there is no improvement in position. This is nothing more than a post-petition substitution of collateral.

Clark, The Law of Secured Transactions under the Uniform Commercial Code, ¶ 6.6[3] at 6–47 (1980).

We agree that Section 552(b) covers second generation proceeds, even if they are in the form of inventory, because such proceeds are clearly contemplated by the UCC. Section 9–306(1) states that proceeds includes the proceeds of proceeds: " 'Proceeds' includes whatever is received upon the sale, exchange, collection or other disposition of collateral *or proceeds.*" * * * As a result, "after-acquired property will frequently qualify as second-generation proceeds, as when a dealer sells an appliance and reinvests the cash proceeds in new inventory." Clark, The Law of Secured Transactions under the Uniform Commercial Code, ¶ 10.1[2] at 10–4 (1980). The fact that Section 552(a) denies the validity of after-acquired property clauses in bankruptcy does not affect this reasoning. Accordingly, the courts have held that, when a secured party has a pre-petition security interest in a crop in Year 1, its security interest extends to the post-petition proceeds of that crop as well as to the post-petition crop in Year 2 and its proceeds if the Year 2 crop is financed with the proceeds of the Year 1 crop. In re Heims, 65 B.R. 112 (Bankr.N.D.Iowa 1986); In re Hugo, 58 B.R. 903 (Bankr.E.D.Mich.1986). See also J. Catton Farms v. First Nat'l Bank of Chicago, 779 F.2d 1242, 1247 (7th Cir.1985). The only requirement is that the second generation proceeds be traceable to the original collateral, which, as discussed above, the parties have stipulated is true in this case. Therefore, we hold that Marepcon has a properly perfected security interest in Bumper Sales' post-petition inventory as well as in any post-petition accounts and cash generated therefrom.[12]

Under the fourth inquiry, the Committee argues that Marepcon's consent to Bumper Sales' use of the proceeds to purchase inventory destroyed Marepcon's security interest in the proceeds. In particular, the Committee claims that Marepcon's consent precludes its right to trace proceeds under Section 9–306(2) of the UCC. In effect, the Committee argues that Marepcon's failure to condition its consent on the grant of a post-petition lien on Bumper Sales' inventory under Section 363 precludes its security interest in the post-petition inventory and the proceeds thereof. We disagree.

* * *

The Committee's argument under Section 363 is premised on the fact that Section 552(b) is expressly subject to the provisions of Section 363 of the Code. This section deals in part with the use of cash collateral, which includes the proceeds of property subject to a pre-petition security interest; under this definition, the cash proceeds of Bumper Sales' pre-petition inventory and accounts secured by Marepcon are cash collateral. In particular, the Committee claims that Marepcon consented to the use of its cash collateral pursuant to section 363(c)(2), which states that a debtor may not use cash collateral without the secured party's consent. The Committee insists that Marepcon's failure to seek a court order conditioning the use of cash collateral under Section 363(e) is fatal to its claim.

12. Our holding is further supported by the fact that Marepcon's security interest in post-petition inventory does not prejudice the Committee in any way, again because the post-petition inventory was produced entirely with the proceeds of Marepcon's pre-petition collateral, not with any of the debtor's unencumbered assets to which the Committee, as unsecured creditors, might have had a claim in bankruptcy.

However, we see nothing in Section 363 that alters the rule established under Section 9–306 of the UCC by requiring a secured party to obtain a court order to preserve rights in the proceeds of cash collateral. Indeed, Section 363 deals with the antecedent issue whether the debtor may even use the cash collateral in the first place, an important determination because the use of cash collateral "may involve a complete consumption of the [secured party's] collateral." 3 Collier Bankruptcy Practice Guide, ¶ 41.04 at 41–13 (1990). However, Section 363 does not concern the issue whether the debtor's use affects the secured party's interest in the proceeds of the cash collateral. The latter issue depends on the application of Section 9–306. As a result, Marepcon's consent to Bumper Sales' use of the cash collateral under Section 363(c)(2) does not affect Marepcon's security interest in the proceeds of the cash collateral. Of course, Marepcon could have prevented the litigation of this issue by seeking a court order under Section 363(e), but Marepcon did not lose its security interest by failing to do so.

V

For the above reasons, the holding of the district court is Affirmed.

C. AUTOMATIC STAY AND ADEQUATE PROTECTION

----

1. INTRODUCTION

When a debtor goes into bankruptcy the automatic stay has a major impact on the rights of an Article 9 secured party. Section 362(a)(4) and (5) stay any act of a prepetition secured creditor to enforce its security interest in property of the estate or of the debtor. Accordingly a creditor having an Article 9 security interest is barred by the stay from availing itself of its rights under § 9–503 to repossess by either self-help or judicial process. If the creditor is a pledgee or has retaken possession of the collateral before the debtor's petition, it may not realize on the collateral by either a nonjudicial or judicial sale after the petition. If sale of the collateral had already been completed before the petition, the debtor would have no right under the UCC to redeem, and the stay is inapplicable because the property sold is no longer either property of the estate or of the debtor. This would also be true if, before the debtor's petition, the debtor had already relinquished all rights in the collateral under § 9–505(2).

Since the automatic stay abruptly halts any effort by a secured creditor to realize on its collateral, perhaps the most litigated issue under the Bankruptcy Code has been the rights of secured creditors to have the stay modified or lifted under § 362(d) so that they can assert their rights under state law to realize on collateral. We have seen that in Chapter 7, with respect to an undersecured creditor, either the trustee should abandon the property under § 554 or the court should grant the creditor's motion to lift the stay under § 362(d). The debtor has no equity in the property and the trustee has nothing to gain for the estate in selling the property. When the stay is lifted or the property is abandoned the secured party may take possession of the collateral and sell it as if the bankruptcy had not occurred. But if the creditor is oversecured, the stay should not be lifted and the trustee should sell, pay the creditor the amount of its secured claim, and distribute the surplus to the unsecured creditors.

2. CHAPTER 11

Balancing the secured party's rights against those of the reorganizing debtor under Chapter 11 has been very difficult. The automatic stay is effective from the date of the petition in bankruptcy until the plan of reorganization is confirmed and the debtor is discharged. § 362(c). Since this interim period between petition and confirmation is always at least several months and, in complex cases, may be several years, determining the rights of the debtor in possession and the secured party to the collateral during this period is of cardinal importance to each side. The debtor in possession cannot reorganize its business unless it can continue to operate the business. In order to do so it usually must use the very assets that are subject to the secured party's security interest, and § 363(c) allows the debtor in possession to use this property. Thus acts of secured parties to realize on their collateral must be stayed for some period of time after the debtor files its petition. The question of how long the stay may be continued is answered by § 362(d) which states the grounds that a secured party can use to have the stay lifted. In a Chapter 11 case it is not enough for the secured party to show that the security interest exhausts the full value of the collateral. Even if the debtor had no equity in the property the creditor is not entitled to relief under § 362(d)(2) if the collateral is necessary to an effective reorganization. If the debtor in possession can show that the collateral is needed in the reorganization, the stay must be lifted under (d)(1) if the secured party is not given adequate protection of its security interest in the collateral. Moreover, the debtor may use the collateral under § 363(c) only so long as the secured party is adequately protected. § 363(e). Under § 362(g) the debtor bears the burden of proof on all issues under § 362(d) except that of the existence of the debtor's equity in the property.

In most cases the debtor can make a convincing case that the collateral is needed in the reorganization, leaving as the crucial issue under both § 362(d)(1) and § 363(e) whether the secured party's interest in the collateral is adequately protected. Adequate protection is not defined in the Bankruptcy Code but § 361 states three ways in which adequate protection can be provided. In a case in which the collateral will depreciate because of use during the interim period, the debtor may be able to adequately protect the interest of an undersecured creditor by making periodic payments under § 361(1) to cover the value of the depreciation. Or, if the debtor owns other unencumbered property, the secured party may be protected from loss caused by depreciation by being given an additional or replacement lien on the debtor's other property under § 361(2).

Suppose the collateral is not depreciating and no decrease in value can be proved to have resulted from the stay. This is often the case if the collateral is real property. Can the debtor in possession retain the collateral for the entire period between petition and confirmation without compensating an undersecured creditor for losses resulting from the delay, caused by the bankruptcy, of the creditor's realization on the collateral? This issue split the circuits and was not resolved until the decision by the Supreme Court in United Savings Association of Texas v. Timbers of Inwood Forest Associates, Ltd., 484 U.S. 365, 108 S.Ct. 626, 98 L.Ed.2d 740 (1988).

The House Report stated with respect to the meaning of adequate protection: "Secured creditors should not be deprived of the benefit of their bargain." 1978 U.S.Code Cong. & Ad.News at 6295. The secured creditor's bargain is that upon default by the debtor the creditor may take possession of the collateral, sell it, and reinvest the proceeds. In *Timbers* the secured party contended that it was entitled to its "opportunity costs," that is, the interest return it would have received from the reinvested proceeds. On some points the law is clear. A secured creditor is entitled to postfiling interest on the amount of the obligation to the extent the value of the collateral covers the interest claim. § 506(b). Unsecured creditors receive no postfiling interest on their claims. § 502(b). If an undersecured creditor is denied immediate payment of the secured claim because of bankruptcy, should the resulting interest loss be treated like the postfiling interest loss of an unsecured creditor, or is a secured creditor entitled to special compensation because the creditor's collateral is being used by the debtor in possession for the benefit of the estate? Does the "indubitable equivalent" language of § 361(3) require that the secured party be compensated for its lost opportunity costs resulting from the stay as well as for any loss in the value of the collateral?

The stakes were high. Debtors saw imposition of the duty to compensate undersecured creditors for what was, in effect, a market interest rate on the value of the collateral as a killing burden to be borne by cash-strapped debtors attempting to reorganize. Creditors saw loss of opportunity costs as a deprivation of a vital economic benefit for which they had bargained. They predicted that failure to compensate for lost opportunity costs would reward debtors for even more stalling in getting plans of reorganization confirmed. The Supreme Court rejected the arguments of the creditors, concluding that if Congress had intended to give undersecured creditors interest on the value of their collateral it would have said so in § 506(b). But in favoring debtors on the opportunity costs issue, the Court gave creditors some help on the delay problem:

> Section 362(d)(2) also belies petitioner's contention that undersecured creditors will face inordinate and extortionate delay if they are denied compensation for interest lost during the stay as part of "adequate protection" under § 362(d)(1). Once the movant under § 362(d)(2) establishes that he is an undersecured creditor, it is the burden of the debtor to establish that the collateral at issue is "necessary to an effective reorganization." See § 362(g). What this requires is not merely a showing that if there is conceivably to be an effective reorganization, this property will be needed for it; but that the property is essential for an effective reorganization *that is in prospect.* This means, as many lower courts, including the en banc court in this case, have properly said, that there must be a "reasonable possibility of a successful reorganization within a reasonable time." * * * The cases are numerous in which § 362(d)(2) relief has been provided within less than a year from the filing of the bankruptcy petition. And while the bankruptcy courts demand less detailed showings during the four months in which the debtor is given the exclusive right to put together a plan, see 11 U.S.C. § 1121(b), (c)(2), even within that period lack of any realistic prospect of effective reorganization will require § 362(d)(2) relief.

108 S.Ct. at 632–633. (Italics in original.)

D. SECURED CLAIMS UNDER CHAPTER 11 PLAN

A case under Chapter 7 ends with the secured party either being paid the amount of its secured claim after a trustee's sale of the collateral or, if the collateral is abandoned or the stay is lifted, having the right to sell the collateral under state law. In either case the secured party has the right to make a credit bid for the amount of its debt (that is, offset the amount of the debt against the purchase price of the collateral) and buy the collateral at the foreclosure sale. § 363(k). A case under Chapter 11 ends with

confirmation by the court of a plan of reorganization, usually one
proposed by the debtor. Typically, the plan will provide for
retention by the debtor of collateral needed by the reorganized
enterprise and for payment, in full or in part, of secured and
unsecured claims under the terms of the plan, often over a period
of years.

A Chapter 11 plan can be confirmed by a court only if (1) all
classes of impaired claims vote to accept the plan (§ 1129(a)), or (2)
the plan complies with the requirements of § 1129(b), in which
case the court must confirm the plan even though one or more
classes of impaired claims have not accepted the plan. The latter
case is popularly referred to as "cramdown." The great majority
of cases in which Chapter 11 plans are confirmed are those under
§ 1129(a) in which all classes of impaired claims have accepted the
plan. This acceptance by creditors is often obtained only after
prolonged bargaining. Secured parties have a strong position
from which to bargain. Since each secured creditor is usually the
only member of its class, it can bar confirmation of the entire plan
until either the debtor pays the amount of its secured claim or any
lesser amount that the secured party is willing to accept. If the
secured party does not accept the plan, cramdown can occur under
§ 1129(b)(2)(A) only if the secured party receives the economic
value of its secured claim under the terms of the plan.

E. THE STRONG ARM CLAUSE

There are a number of provisions in the Bankruptcy Code
pursuant to which some security interests and other liens can be
nullified by the trustee or the debtor. Among these avoiding
powers one of the most important is § 544(a), which is commonly
referred to as the strong arm clause. The power of the trustee
under § 544(a) is based on the power, under nonbankruptcy law, of
a hypothetical creditor or purchaser to avoid the transfer. The
avoiding power under § 544(a) is directed at secret liens and other
secret transfers. Subparagraph (1) of § 544(a) is the provision
that applies to Article 9 security interests.

The primary effect of § 544(a) is to invalidate in bankruptcy
unperfected Article 9 security interests and unrecorded mortgages
on real property. Under § 9–301(1)(b) an unperfected security
interest, although enforceable against the debtor under § 9–203, is
subordinated to the rights of a person who acquires a judicial lien
in the collateral. Under § 544(a)(1) the trustee in bankruptcy is
given, when bankruptcy commences, the rights of a hypothetical
creditor who obtained a judicial lien at that time on all property of
the debtor. That section states that the trustee may avoid any
transfer that is "voidable" by the hypothetical judicial lien creditor. Although § 9–301(1)(b) speaks in terms of "subordination" of
the unperfected security interest rather than avoidance of the

security interest, it is clear that the effect of § 544(a)(1) is to invalidate the security interest if it was unperfected at the time of bankruptcy. Section 546(b) and § 362(b)(3) allow perfection after bankruptcy to defeat the rights of the trustee under § 544(a) in cases in which the applicable nonbankruptcy law gives retroactive effect to the perfection. An example is § 9–301(2). If a purchase money security interest is perfected by filing within ten days of the debtor's taking of possession of the collateral the security interest is good in bankruptcy even if the debtor goes into bankruptcy before the filing is made.

F. FRAUDULENT TRANSFERS

1. HISTORICAL ORIGINS

One of the earliest statements of fraudulent conveyance law is contained in a famous decision of the Star Chamber, Twyne's Case, 3 Coke 80b, 70 Eng.Rep. 809 (1601), which was decided under the Statute of 13 Elizabeth c. 5 (1570), "an act against fraudulent deeds, alienations, &c." Pierce owed 400 pounds to Twyne and 200 pounds to C. C brought an action against Pierce on the debt. While the case was pending Pierce made a general conveyance of all his goods, worth 300 pounds, to Twyne in satisfaction of the debt owed to him. The conveyance was made in secret and Pierce retained possession of the goods, which included sheep. Notwithstanding the conveyance, Pierce sold some of the goods "and he shore the sheep, and marked them with his own mark." When C got judgment against Pierce he tried to levy on the goods of Pierce. Twyne resisted the levy claiming the goods as his own. The court held that the conveyance to Twyne was fraudulent. The case is famous for its listing of the "six badges of fraud" which the court described as follows: 1. The conveyance "had the signs and marks of fraud" because it was "general, without exception of his apparel, or any thing of necessity;" 2. Pierce "continued in possession and used them as his own; and by reason thereof he traded and trafficked with others, and defrauded and deceived them;" 3. The conveyance was made in secret and therefore was suspicious; 4. The conveyance was made while C's action against Pierce was pending; 5. There "was a trust between the parties, for [Pierce] possessed all, and used them as his proper goods and fraud is always apparelled and clad with a trust, and a trust is the cover of fraud;" and 6. The deed of conveyance recited that it "was made honestly, truly and bona fide" and unusual clauses always induce suspicion.

In Twyne's Case the court held that it was not a sufficient defense that the conveyance was for good consideration because it was not bona fide. The court emphasized that the conveyance was

accompanied by a trust by which it apparently meant that Pierce
retained possession and the benefit of the goods. What could
Twyne have done to assure the validity of the conveyance? The
court gave the following advice:

> " * * * and therefore, reader, when any gift shall be to
> you in satisfaction of a debt, by one who is indebted to others
> also; 1st, Let it be made in a public manner, and before the
> neighbours, and not in private, for secrecy is a mark of fraud.
> 2nd, Let the goods and chattels be appraised by good people to
> the very value, and take a gift in particular in satisfaction of
> your debt. 3rd, Immediately after the gift, take the posses-
> sion of them; for continuance of the possession in the donor, is
> a sign of trust. And know, reader, that the said words of the
> proviso, on a good consideration, and *bona fide*, do not extend
> to every gift made *bona fide*; and therefore there are two
> manners of gifts on a good consideration, *scil.* consideration of
> nature or blood, and a valuable consideration. As to the first,
> in the case before put; if he who is indebted to five several
> persons, to each party in twenty pounds, in consideration of
> natural affection, gives all his goods to his son, or cousin, in
> that case, forasmuch as others should lose their debts, &c.
> which are things of value, the intent of the Act was, that the
> consideration in such case should be valuable; for equity
> requires, that such gift, which defeats others, should be made
> on as high and good consideration as the things which are
> thereby defeated are; and it is to be presumed, that the
> father, if he had not been indebted to others, would not have
> dispossessed himself of all his goods, and subjected himself to
> his cradle; and therefore it shall be intended, that it was
> made to defeat his creditors; and if consideration of nature or
> blood should be a good consideration within this proviso, the
> statute would serve for little or nothing, and no creditor would
> be sure of his debt."

Many of the principles of Twyne's Case survive in modern
law. It is common for state law to provide that creditors of a
seller in possession of goods may treat as fraudulent a sale of the
goods if not accompanied by a change of possession. See, e.g.,
West's Ann.California Civil Code § 3440 and § 2–402(2). Section
9–301(1)(b) is based on a similar principle. A security interest
cloaked in secrecy will not prevail over the rights of creditors of
the debtor levying on the collateral. The secured party is required to perfect the security interest by giving creditors some
observable indication that it has been granted either by filing a
financing statement or taking possession of the collateral. The
most important state law regarding fraudulent conveyances had
been the Uniform Fraudulent Conveyance Act ("UFCA"). The
UFCA was promulgated by the National Conference of Commissioners on Uniform State Laws in 1918 and was adopted in 25

jurisdictions. In 1938 the substance of the UFCA was also made a part of the Bankruptcy Act in a new § 67d. In 1979 the National Conference appointed a committee to revise the UFCA to take into account changes made in the Bankruptcy Code and to harmonize the UFCA with other laws such as the Model Business Corporation Act and the UCC which contained provisions that conflicted with, or affected, provisions of the UFCA. As a result the National Conference in 1984 approved a Uniform Fraudulent Transfer Act ("UFTA") to replace the UFCA. At the time this is written the UFTA has been adopted in 24 states and ten states still have the UFCA.

It is important to understand that, in spite of their names, the UFCA and UFTA invalidate some conveyances that are not fraudulent if that word is used in its ordinary sense to denote activity that is dishonest or deceitful. You should also note that these statutes may invalidate obligations of the debtor as well as conveyances or transfers of property.

2. RELATIONSHIP OF STATE FRAUDULENT TRANSFER LAW AND BANKRUPTCY

What is the effect of state fraudulent transfer law in bankruptcy? Assume that the UFTA is in effect in the state in which all transactions by a bankrupt debtor occurred. Before bankruptcy the debtor made a transfer of property that was fraudulent within the meaning of the UFTA. Under § 7 of that Act creditors of the debtor may have the transfer set aside. But once the debtor has filed in bankruptcy the right of creditors to set aside a fraudulent conveyance is lost. If the fraudulent conveyance is not avoided in bankruptcy there will be a net loss to the bankruptcy estate because the property conveyed could have been used to pay the creditors having the right to set aside the conveyance. To avoid this loss § 544(b) gives to the trustee in bankruptcy the right to avoid any transfer that could be avoided outside of bankruptcy by any creditor with an unsecured claim in the bankruptcy.

The action of the trustee in avoiding the transfer is not simply for the benefit of the creditor whose right is the basis of the trustee's action. Rather, it is for the benefit of the estate. § 550(a) and § 541(a)(3). The latter point is very significant and has been part of bankruptcy law since the celebrated case, Moore v. Bay, 284 U.S. 4, 52 S.Ct. 3, 76 L.Ed. 133 (1931). That case involved the validity of a chattel mortgage that had not been promptly recorded. Under the appliable state law some unsecured creditors of the mortgagor had priority over the mortgagee's claim because of the late recording and because advance public notice of the mortgage had not been given as required by law. Some of these creditors had claims in bankruptcy. Other unsecured creditors with claims in the bankruptcy did not, under the state law, have priority over the mortgagee. The Supreme Court held that the chattel mortgage was void in bankruptcy. By this decision all creditors, whether or not they had rights under the state law, got the benefit of the avoidance. The principle of Moore v. Bay was first codified by the enactment of § 70e of the Bankruptcy Act, and subsequently by the enactment of § 544(b) and § 550(a) of the Bankruptcy Code.

The principle of Moore v. Bay can have dramatic effects. Assume the debtor made a transfer of property worth $1,000,000 and that under the state law one creditor, with a claim of $100, can avoid the transfer because some duty to that creditor had not been performed. Assume no other creditor has the right under the state law to attack the transfer, that under the state law the creditor with the $100 claim is entitled to have that claim paid from the property transferred, and that the transfer is otherwise valid. The effect in bankruptcy, if the $100 claim still exists, is that the entire $1,000,000 transfer is voidable by the trustee under § 544(b).

The UFCA or the UFTA is in effect in two-thirds of the states and the other states have judicial or other statutory law defining fraudulent conveyances. To the extent that law allows a creditor to avoid a transfer, the trustee in bankruptcy may proceed under § 544(b).

Section 548 is substantially similar to the UFTA. The trustee in bankruptcy has the choice of attacking a fraudulent transfer either under § 548 or under the state fraudulent transfer law by using § 544(b). In most cases in which the state law is the UFTA it does not make any difference which route is taken, but there are some cases in which the trustee's rights will differ under the two bodies of law. One limitation of § 548 is that the transfer must have occurred within one year before bankruptcy. If the trustee is relying on the rights of a creditor under the state law the transfer can be avoided so long as the right of the creditor is not barred by the state statute of limitations, which under UFTA § 9 may be as long as four years.

3. TRANSFERS FOR LESS THAN REASONABLY EQUIVALENT VALUE

PROBLEM

Debtor was an officer of Bank who embezzled large amounts of money from Bank over a period of years. The embezzled money was used to pay Debtor's gambling debts. Debtor's aged mother is entirely dependent upon Debtor for her support. When it became apparent to Debtor that his criminal activities would soon be discovered, Debtor's house and investment securities were transferred to Debtor's mother so that she would have a place to live and a source of income. None of the transferred property was purchased with embezzled money. After the transfer Debtor had insufficient assets to pay the debt of Bank. Debtor's mother had no knowledge of Debtor's debt to Bank or of the purpose of the transfer. What are the rights of Bank against Debtor's mother under § 548?

MATTER OF BUNDLES

United States Court of Appeals, Seventh Circuit, 1988.
856 F.2d 815.

RIPPLE, CIRCUIT JUDGE.

In this appeal, we must decide whether a debtor in bankruptcy may set aside under section 548(a)(2) of the Bankruptcy Code (the Code), the sale of his personal residence upon foreclosure of the mortgage. The bankruptcy court and the district court held that he could not. We reverse and remand for further proceedings.

I

Background

A. *Statutory Background*

Section 548 of the Code provides in pertinent part:

§ 548. Fraudulent transfers and obligations

(a) The trustee may avoid any transfer of an interest of the debtor in property, or any obligation incurred by the debtor, that was made or incurred on or within one year before the date of the filing of the petition, if the debtor voluntarily or involuntary—

*   *   *

(2)(A) received less than a reasonably equivalent value in exchange for such transfer or obligation; and

(B)(i) was insolvent on the date that such transfer was made or such obligation was incurred, or became insolvent as a result of such transfer or obligation;

*   *   *

This provision sets forth four elements that must be established before a debtor may set aside a transfer of property. These are: (1) the debtor had an interest in the property transferred; (2) the debtor was insolvent at the time of the transfer or became insolvent as a result of the transfer; (3) the transfer occurred within one year of the filing of the bankruptcy petition; and (4) the transfer was for less than a "reasonably equivalent value." The parties agree that the debtor has established each of these elements except the last. Therefore, the only issue before us is whether the debtor received less than a reasonably equivalent value for the property in question.

B. *Facts*

The facts are stipulated. The debtor-appellant Donald Eugene Bundles has maintained a residence in Indianapolis, Indiana since 1964. Sometime in 1984 and 1985, due to various financial and health problems, Mr. Bundles was unable to meet his mortgage payments. On March 4, 1985, the mortgagee, Indiana National Bank (INB), commenced an action in state court seeking foreclosure of Mr. Bundles' residence. On July 10, 1985, the state court entered a default judgment against Mr. Bundles in the amount of $4,696.46. In addition, an IRS tax lien against the real estate was reduced to a personal judgment against Mr. Bundles in the amount of $2,666. A sheriff's sale of Mr. Bundles' residence was scheduled and held on September 11, 1985, after proper notice and in compliance with Indiana foreclosure law. As of this date, Mr. Bundles was insolvent. The property was purchased at the sale by William J. Baker for $5,066.80. The value of the property at this time was $15,500.[3] On September 12, 1985, Sheriff James L. Wells of Marion County executed a deed to Mr. Baker conveying Mr. Bundles' residence to him. The deed to the property was recorded on September 24, 1985.

On September 25, 1985, after the foreclosure and sale of his residence, Mr. Bundles filed a voluntary petition under Chapter 13 of the Code. Thereafter, on November 14, 1985, he filed a complaint in the bankruptcy court to set aside the foreclosure sale as a fraudulent conveyance. The complaint named as defendants Mr. Baker, the purchaser of his home; INB, the foreclosing mortgagee; and James C. Wells in his official capacity as the Sheriff of Marion County, Indiana.

*   *   *

II

Discussion

We must interpret the phrase "reasonably equivalent value" as applied to a foreclosure sale. Our task is complicated by the fact that reasonably equivalent value is not defined in section 548 or in any other provision of the Code. The courts addressing this issue have expressed a variety of viewpoints. Nevertheless, two basic lines of authority, each espousing a different interpretation of reasonably equivalent value as that term is used in section

---

3. The parties' stipulation of facts provides that the property was worth $15,500 on November 14, 1985, the date that Mr. Bundles filed his complaint to set aside the conveyance in the bankruptcy court. * * * At oral argument, the appellant indicated that this figure was arrived at after each party had his own appraisal done and a single figure was agreed upon.

548(a)(2)(A), have developed. We begin by reviewing the cases on either side of this difference of opinion among the courts.

A.

The two seminal cases in this area are Durrett v. Washington National Insurance Co., 621 F.2d 201 (5th Cir.1980), and Lawyers Title Insurance Co. v. Madrid (In re Madrid), 21 B.R. 424 (Bankr. 9th Cir.1982), aff'd on other grounds, 725 F.2d 1197 (9th Cir.), cert. denied, 469 U.S. 833, 105 S.Ct. 125, 83 L.Ed.2d 66 (1984). Their precise holdings have ultimately come to be less important than the analytical approach that each has fostered in subsequent cases. Courts have interpreted *Durrett* as standing for the position that reasonably equivalent value in the foreclosure context should be determined as a set percentage of the fair market value of the property, with 70 percent being the appropriate benchmark. Similarly, courts have interpreted *Madrid* as representing the position that the sale price obtained at a regularly conducted, noncollusive foreclosure sale should be presumed conclusively to be the reasonably equivalent value for purposes of section 548(a)(2) (A). Bankruptcy courts have followed both approaches. * * * The bankruptcy court and the district court in this case both followed *Madrid*. Because of the influential impact of *Durrett* and *Madrid* on subsequent judicial interpretation of section 548(a)(2) (A), a more thorough discussion of these two cases is in order.

Durrett was decided under section 67(d) of the former Bankruptcy Act, 11 U.S.C. § 107(d), which employed the term "fair consideration" rather than "reasonably equivalent value." In reversing the trial court's determination that a sale price of 57.7 percent of the fair market value of the property on the date of the foreclosure sale was a fair equivalent, the Fifth Circuit stated that it had been unable to locate a decision of any court that approved a transfer for less than 70 percent of the market value of the property. *Durrett*, 621 F.2d at 203. The court's reference to 70 percent has led other courts and commentators to read that opinion as establishing a fixed percentage mark—the so-called "*Durrett* 70 percent rule." However, the Fifth Circuit's actual approach in *Durrett* is one of simply analyzing the question of reasonably equivalent value in terms of whether the foreclosure sale price is some acceptable percentage of the fair market value of the property.

Durrett is certainly not without its critics. In *Madrid*, a bankruptcy panel of the Ninth Circuit was the first court to reject *Durrett's* percentage rule and to articulate a different standard. The *Madrid* court noted that the only case cited by the Fifth Circuit in support of its holding involved a voluntary transfer of real property by the debtor corporation to the mother of the principal stockholder of the debtor corporation. 21 B.R. at 426 (the case was Schafer v. Hammond, 456 F.2d 15 (10th Cir.1972)). The *Madrid* court opined that, "[h]owever valid it may be to hold that less than 70 percent of fair market value is not a fair equivalent for a private transfer to an insider, application of that standard to regularly conducted public sales is questionable." Id. Its own research, the court observed, did not reveal any cases, other than the Fifth Circuit's decisions in *Durrett* and Abramson v. Lakewood Bank & Trust Co., 647 F.2d 547 (5th Cir.1981) (per curiam), cert. denied, 454 U.S. 1164, 102 S.Ct. 1038, 71 L.Ed.2d 320 (1982), where a nonjudicial foreclosure sale was set aside on fraudulent conveyance grounds. Furthermore, the *Madrid* court was concerned that the *Durrett* approach would alter radically state foreclosure law under which the mere inadequacy of price is usually insufficient to upset a foreclosure sale. Id. at 427. Consequently, the court reasoned that "[t]he law of foreclosure should be harmonized with the law of fraudulent conveyances." Id.

Based on the above analysis, the *Madrid* court held that "the consideration received at a non-collusive and regularly conducted foreclosure sale" should be presumed to be the reasonable equivalent value for purposes of section 548. Id. Applying this holding to the facts before it, the *Madrid* court upheld a foreclosure sale where the debtor received a price between 64 and 67 percent of the market value of the property at the time of the sale. The bankruptcy panel's opinion in *Madrid* was affirmed by the Ninth Circuit on different grounds. 725 F.2d 1197 (9th Cir.1984). Nevertheless, its reasoning has been followed, as we have noted already, by several bankruptcy courts, and recently was adopted in dictum by the Sixth Circuit in In the Matter of Winshall Settlor's Trust, 758 F.2d 1136, 1139 (6th Cir.1985) ("the better view is that reasonable equivalence for the purposes of a foreclosure sale under § 548(a)(2)(A) should be consonant with the state law of fraudulent conveyances").

B.

We begin our analysis, as did the bankruptcy court and the district court, with the language of the statute. Section 548(a)(2) (A) provides that a transfer of the debtor's property may be set aside if it is transferred for less than a reasonably equivalent value. It makes no distinction between sales that do and sales that do not comply with state law. If we take the statute at its face value, we must conclude that its unambiguous language requires the reviewing court to make an independent assessment of whether reasonable equivalence was given.

Our analysis of the statutory language is not altered by the legislative history of the BAFJA. This legislative history, consisting of an exchange between two Senators recorded after the BAFJA was passed, indicates only that the amendments were not intended to resolve the so-called "*Durrett* issue." [8] Furthermore, one of the proposed amendments to the BAFJA dealt specifically with the *Durrett–Madrid* debate and adopted the *Madrid* irrebuttable presumption rule. This amendment, however, was not included in the bill that ultimately became law.* Accordingly, we believe that the most reasonable interpretation of the legislative history is that Congress did not legislate an irrebuttable presumption in the case of mortgage foreclosure sales.

* * *

We realize that much of the debate over this issue has centered on policy considerations that favor one result over the other.[12] However, " 'the meaning of a statute must, in the first

---

8. The legislative history, cited to us by the parties and relied on by the bankruptcy court, is as follows:

Mr. DeCONCINI. Apparently there may have been some misunderstanding regarding the effect of certain technical amendments made by the recently enacted bankruptcy legislation * * * which amended the definition of transfer * * * to add the phrase "and foreclosure of the debtor's equity of redemption," * * * [and amended] section 548(a) * * * to add the phrase "voluntarily or involuntary." A question has arisen whether these amendments somehow support the position taken * * * in *Durrett* * * *. My understanding is that these provisions were not intended to have any effect one way or the other on the so called Durrett issue. Is my understanding correct?

Mr. DOLE. The Senator's understanding is indeed correct. * * * In deference to Senator METZENBAUM's position, Senator THURMOND agreed to delete from his amendment all provisions dealing with the Durrett issue * * *. Consequently, no provision of the bankruptcy bill passed by this body was intended to intimate any view one way or the other regarding the correctness of the position taken * * * in the Durrett case, or regarding the correctness of the position taken by * * * Madrid, * * * which reached a contrary result.

* * * [T]he amendment should not be construed to in any way codify Durrett or throw a cloud over noncollusive foreclosure sales.

* * * Finally, neither of the [amendments] purport to deal with the question of whether a noncollu-

sive, regularly conducted foreclosure sale should be deemed to be for a reasonably equivalent value.

Mr. DeCONCINI. Then I am correct in concluding that parties in bankruptcy proceedings who seek avoidance of prepetition foreclosure sales would find no support for their arguments in these amendments?

Mr. DOLE. The Senator's conclusion is correct.

130 Cong.Rec.S. 13771–S.13772 (No. 131, Pt. II, Oct. 5, 1984).

* [Eds. The failed amendment granted an irrebuttable presumption of reasonably equivalent value to any mortgagee or third-party purchaser who purchases mortgaged property at a regularly conducted non-collusive foreclosure sale for a price equal to the full amount of the mortgage debt.]

12. The central policy concern expressed in the opinions is that permitting avoidance of foreclosure sales under § 548(a)(2) would have a negative effect on the foreclosure market. This concern was best voiced by Judge Clark in his dissenting opinion in *Abramson*, 647 F.2d 547. Judge Clark believed that the *Durrett* rule would "cast a cloud upon mortgages and trust deeds" and that this cloud would "naturally inhibit a purchaser other than the mortgagee from buying at foreclosure" thereby tending to "depress further the prices of foreclosure sales and thus increase the potential size of the deficiency in each foreclosure." Id. at 550 (Clark, J., dissenting). But see Schuckman, Data on the Durrett Controversy, 9 Cardozo L.Rev. 605 (1987) (arguing that there is no empirical evidence that the effect of the *Durrett* rule on the foreclosure market has been to reduce participation in foreclosure sales, in-

instance, be sought in the language in which the act is framed, and if that is plain, and if the law is within the constitutional authority of the law-making body which passed it, the sole function of the courts is to enforce it according to its terms.' " Central Trust Co. v. Official Creditors' Comm. of Geiger Enters., 454 U.S. 354, 359–60, 102 S.Ct. 695, 698, 70 L.Ed.2d 542 (1982) (per curiam) (quoting Caminetti v. United States, 242 U.S. 470, 485, 37 S.Ct. 192, 194, 61 L.Ed. 442 (1917)). It is beyond our scope of review to consider the policy implications of permitting the debtor to set aside the foreclosure of his home. Any change deemed desirable on policy grounds should be addressed to Congress rather than to this court. Our duty is simply to interpret the language of the statute. * * *

Implying an irrebuttable presumption would be inconsistent with that language. Such a reading, in effect, creates an exception to the trustee's avoiding powers under section 548(a)(2)(A)—an exception not otherwise found in the statute—for property sold at a foreclosure sale. See In re Madrid, 21 B.R. at 428 (Volinn, J., dissenting) ("By concluding that a regularly conducted sale in the absence of collusion satisfies the 'reasonably equivalent value' test, the majority has excised vital language from § 548 in order to create an exception to the statute where a forced sale of the debtor's property is involved."); Richardson v. Gillman (In re Richardson), 23 B.R. 434, 446 (Bankr.D.Utah 1982) ("fixing an irrebuttable presumption of reasonable equivalence for non-collusive, regularly conducted public sales proscribes the factual inquiry into 'reasonable equivalence' which Section 548(a)(2) was designed to facilitate"). Moreover, an irrebuttable presumption has the effect of reading good faith into section 548(a)(2)(A); as long as the sale is conducted in good faith and in accordance with state law, the sale price is conclusively presumed to be a reasonably equivalent value. This result is inconsistent with section 548(a)(2)'s purpose of permitting the trustee to avoid transfers as constructively fraudulent, irrespective of the parties' actual intent. * * * Finally, an irrebuttable presumption renders section 548(a)(2) merely duplicative of other Code provisions, such as section 548(a)(1) (permitting avoidance for actual intent to defraud) and section 544(b) (permitting avoidance where state law would allow it) * * * We therefore conclude that section 548(a) (2)(A) establishes a federal basis—independent of state law—for setting aside a foreclosure sale.

C.

Having determined that there is a federal statutory basis for avoiding a foreclosure sale under section 548(a), we are confronted

crease mortgage interest rates or reduce the amount of individual mortgage
loans). * * *

with the problem of defining that federal standard. As Justice Brandeis once observed, "[v]alue is a word of many meanings." Missouri ex rel. Southwestern Bell Tel. Co. v. Public Serv. Comm'n, 262 U.S. 276, 310, 43 S.Ct. 544, 554, 67 L.Ed. 981 (1923) (Brandeis, J., concurring). A good example of this observation is in the Code where value is defined differently throughout. For instance, section 522(a)(2) refers to "fair market value as of the date of the filing of the petition," and section 506(a) refers to value "determined in light of the purpose of the valuation and of the proposed disposition or use of such property." The definition of value found in section 548 is not very useful for our purposes. It defines value as "property, or satisfaction or securing of a present or antecedent debt of the debtor, but does not include an unperformed promise to furnish support to the debtor or to a relative of the debtor * * *." If anything is clear from the various uses of the word "value" in the Code, it is that Congress did not mean fair market value when it used the term reasonably equivalent value. On the other hand, Congress' conscious use of a federal standard suggests that it did not believe that the expedient of relying entirely on state foreclosure law would protect adequately federal interests. "State law's sanction of exchanges in foreclosures which are not reasonably equivalent gives effect to state contract and foreclosure policy but may overlook the interests of other creditors of the debtor." In re Richardson, 23 B.R. at 447.

In our view, in defining reasonably equivalent value, the court should neither grant a conclusive presumption in favor of a purchaser at a regularly conducted, non-collusive foreclosure sale, nor limit its inquiry to a simple comparison of the sale price to the fair market value. Reasonable equivalence should depend on all the facts of each case. This middle ground has been adopted by several of the bankruptcy courts. * * *

The implementation of this approach requires case-by-case adjudication. In determining whether property was sold for reasonably equivalent value, the bankruptcy court must, of course, be mindful constantly of the purpose of section 548's avoiding powers—to preserve the assets of the estate. * * * This consideration requires that, in determining reasonably equivalent value, the court must focus on what the debtor received in return for what he surrendered.

* * * Consequently, it is appropriate to consider, as a starting point, the fair market value. However, the fact that the sale was the result of a foreclosure rather than an arm's length transaction between a willing buyer and a willing seller is also of considerable importance. Therefore, the bankruptcy court must focus ultimately on the fair market value as affected by the fact of foreclosure. As a practical matter, the foreclosure sale price is the only means of measuring the effect of foreclosure on the value of

the property. Indeed, in usual circumstances, it would be appropriate to permit a *rebuttable* presumption that the price obtained at the foreclosure sale represents reasonably equivalent value. However, the bankruptcy court also must examine the foreclosure transaction in its totality to determine whether the procedures employed were calculated not only to secure for the mortgagee the value of its interest but also to return to the debtor-mortgagor his equity in the property. The bankruptcy court therefore must consider such factors as whether there was a fair appraisal of the property, whether the property was advertised widely, and whether competitive bidding was encouraged.

The inquiry outlined in the foregoing paragraph is necessarily a fact-specific one; it will require the bankruptcy court to draw upon its expertise in evaluating the economic forces at play in a specific case. Once that determination is made, we must accord it great deference. On the other hand, we shall expect the bankruptcy court, while recognizing that it alone has the responsibility to determine whether the transaction meets the federal standard of reasonably equivalent value, to accord respect to the state foreclosure sale proceedings. While the sale price determined in the foreclosure proceeding cannot be considered conclusive with respect to the issue of federal law before the bankruptcy court, it is an important element in the analysis of that question.

Conclusion

We hold that the sale price at a regularly conducted, noncollusive foreclosure sale cannot automatically be deemed to provide a reasonably equivalent value within the meaning of section 548(a) (2)(A). We therefore reverse the judgment of the district court and remand to the bankruptcy court for further proceedings not inconsistent with this opinion.

NOTES

1. In inviting the bankruptcy court to examine whether there was a fair appraisal, whether the property was advertised widely, and whether competitive bidding was authorized, is the court employing a commercially reasonable resale test similar to that in § 9–504(3) in determining reasonably equivalent value in a foreclosure case? Among the cases that have explicitly adopted the commercially reasonable test is In re Lindsay, 98 B.R. 983 (Bktcy.Cal.1989). It relies on *Bundles*.

2. An approach similar to that taken by the lower courts in *Bundles* is reflected in § 3(b) of the Uniform Fraudulent Transfer Act. The UFTA adopts the terminology of § 548(a)(2)(A) in using the term "reasonably equivalent value" instead of the term "fair consideration" used in the UFCA and the Bankruptcy Act. Under UFTA § 3(b) "a person gives a reasonably equivalent value if the

person acquires an interest of the debtor in an asset pursuant to a regularly conducted, noncollusive foreclosure, exercise of a power of sale, or other procedure for the acquisition or disposition of the interest of the debtor upon default under a mortgage, deed of trust, or other security agreement or contract." The official comment to that section states that it was meant to reject the fair value rule of *Durrett* and to adopt the view of the intermediate appellate court in *Madrid*.

It is interesting to speculate about what would happen in a Chapter 7 case if under the facts of *Bundles* the trustee in bankruptcy sold the property in liquidation of the estate. Isn't the trustee likely to sell the property in a sale that resembles a public foreclosure sale? If the trustee sells at a public auction is it likely that the property will be sold for a price that exceeds that obtained in a typical foreclosure sale?

PROBLEMS

Section 548(a)(2) states a traditional rule. An insolvent debtor cannot be allowed to prejudice its creditors by transferring its property or incurring obligations within a year of bankruptcy unless it receives reasonably equivalent value. As the court states in *Bundles* "the bankruptcy court must, of course, be mindful constantly of the purpose of section 548's avoiding powers—to preserve the assets of the estate." 856 F.2d at 824. We sketch out in abbreviated form two elementary examples of modern applications of the rule.

1. Owner agreed to sell Buyer all the stock of Corporation on credit if Buyer could provide adequate collateral. Buyer offered Owner a security interest in the stock of Corporation, but Owner demanded a security interest in Corporation's assets. Buyer complied, but within a year after the security interest was given Corporation's business operations failed and Corporation filed in bankruptcy under Chapter 7. The trustee in bankruptcy sought to avoid Owner's security interest in Corporation's assets under § 548(a)(2). Assume that the trustee could prove that the reason Corporation failed was the existence of Owner's security interest on all its assets which precluded Corporation from obtaining the credit from financial sources that it needed to survive. Should the trustee prevail? Why would Owner prefer a security interest in Corporation's assets rather than its stock? What if Owner had demanded cash, Buyer had borrowed the money from Bank, and Corporation had given Bank a security interest in all of its assets to secure the loan. Could the trustee invalidate the Bank's security interest if it could prove that Bank knew what Buyer intended to do with the money? The problems raised by these facts have been considered by a number of cases in recent years.

Perhaps the best known is United States v. Tabor Court Realty Corp., 803 F.2d 1288 (3d Cir.1986).

2. Parent Corporation is a holding company, and its only assets are the stock of its various subsidiaries which are operating companies with tangible assets. Parent Corporation sought a loan from Bank and offered as collateral a security interest in all its assets. Bank demanded that Subsidiary Corporation, one of Parent's wholly owned subsidiaries, guarantee Parent's obligation. Subsidiary complied, but its business failed and it filed a petition in bankruptcy under Chapter 7 within a year after the guaranty was given. Counting the guaranty as a liability equal to the amount of the loan to Parent, Subsidiary became insolvent when it gave the guaranty. Can the trustee in bankruptcy avoid the guaranty under § 548? Leading cases on the issue of "up-stream" guaranties (subsidiary guarantees obligation of parent) or "cross-stream" guaranties (one subsidiary of parent guarantees obligation of another subsidiary) are Rubin v. Manufacturers Hanover Trust Co., 661 F.2d 979 (2d Cir.1981) and Matter of Xonics Photochemical, Inc., 841 F.2d 198 (7th Cir.1988).

G. PREFERENCES

---

1. CONCEPT OF A PREFERENCE

An insolvent debtor who is unable to pay all unsecured creditors in full may prefer one of the creditors by transferring property to the creditor to pay or secure the debt owed. The debtor might make payment of the debt in cash or in kind or may grant a security interest in the debtor's property to secure the previously existing debt. Sometimes the transfer is involuntary. This might occur if the creditor acquires a judicial lien in the debtor's property under a writ of execution or pursuant to a statute allowing prejudgment attachment. For the most part the obtaining of an advantage by one creditor over another in this manner is valid under nonbankruptcy law. Under the common law a transfer by an insolvent debtor in payment of a debt was not a fraudulent conveyance even if the effect or the purpose of the transfer was to make it more difficult for other creditors to obtain payment of their debts. The rule is stated in Shelley v. Boothe, 73 Mo. 74 (1880), as follows: "A debtor may give a preference to a particular creditor or set of creditors by a direct payment or assignment, if he does so in payment of his or their just demands, and not as a mere screen to secure the property to himself. The pendency of another creditor's suit is immaterial, and the transaction is valid though done to defeat that creditor's claim." Thus, a preferential payment of a bona fide debt does not violate UFTA § 4(a)(1) (actual fraud). Nor can it violate UFTA § 4(a)(2) (without reasonably equivalent value) because satisfaction of an antecedent debt is "value." UFTA § 3(a).

State debt collection law is characterized by a race of diligence among creditors. The first to obtain a transfer of title of the debtor's property or a lien in the debtor's property is paid in full to the extent of the property interest received by the creditor. But the rule in bankruptcy is different.

In a bankruptcy liquidation secured claims are paid first. Then unsecured claims are paid according to a system of priorities stated in § 507. With some exceptions stated in § 726 unsecured claims without priority are paid pro rata. Once bankruptcy has occurred this scheme of distribution cannot be altered by actions of the debtor or the debtor's creditors. The debtor's property becomes property of the estate under the control of the bankruptcy court and creditors are prohibited from taking any action under nonbankruptcy law to obtain payment of their claims. § 362. But the distribution contemplated by the Bankruptcy Code can be frustrated by transactions occurring before bankruptcy. For example, an unsecured creditor who would receive ten cents on the dollar in the impending bankruptcy of the debtor might try to avert that result by obtaining a judicial lien in the debtor's property before the debtor can file the petition in bankruptcy. Or, the debtor might voluntarily favor an unsecured creditor by paying the debt in some measure greater than ten cents on the dollar or by granting to the creditor a security interest in the debtor's property.

Section 547 is designed to undo certain prebankruptcy transactions the effect of which is to frustrate the distribution scheme set forth in the Bankruptcy Code. It allows the trustee in bankruptcy to avoid certain transfers of the debtor's property. These transfers are known as voidable preferences. The five elements of a voidable preference are set forth in subsection (b) of § 547. Subsection (c) of § 547 applies to certain transfers which are within the definition of voidable preferences under subsection (b), but which are insulated from attack by the trustee because they are not deemed to violate the policy which § 547 is designed to carry out. Section 547(b)(3) requires that the debtor be insolvent at the time of the transfer. Section 547(f) creates a presumption that the debtor was insolvent during the 90 days immediately preceding the date of filing of the petition in bankruptcy. This means that the party against whom the presumption is made— normally the recipient of the preference—must come forward with some evidence to rebut the presumption. Since the burden of proving all elements of a preference rests with the party seeking avoidance—normally the trustee in bankruptcy—if the presumption is rebutted the trustee must prove insolvency by a preponderance of the evidence. With respect to § 547(c) the burden of proof is on the recipient of the preference who is seeking the exception from § 547(b) that that subsection provides. § 547(g).

If the trustee in bankruptcy avoids a preferential transfer under § 547(b) the result is that the property transferred by the debtor to the creditor can be recovered for the benefit of the estate. § 550(a). If the preference occurred when the debtor paid a debt in cash the trustee is entitled to recover an equivalent amount which then becomes part of the bankruptcy estate. § 541(a)(3). Suppose the preference occurred when the creditor obtained a lien in the debtor's property to secure the debt either by voluntary act of the debtor or against the will of the debtor as in the case of a judicial lien. Assume that the property to which the lien applies is property of the bankruptcy estate. In that case avoidance of the preference usually means that the creditor's lien is nullified. The effect of nullification is to increase the value of property of the estate in the amount of the value of the nullified lien.

Sometimes simple nullification of a lien will not benefit the estate. Suppose property of the estate worth $10,000 is burdened by two liens, valid outside of bankruptcy, in favor of Creditor A and Creditor B, each of whom is owed $10,000. Assume that under the nonbankruptcy law the lien of Creditor A has priority over the lien of Creditor B, but that the lien of Creditor A is avoidable under § 547(b) while the lien of Creditor B is indefeasible in bankruptcy. If the lien of Creditor A is nullified the effect is to benefit Creditor B. The junior lien of Creditor B had no value before nullification while it has a value of $10,000 after nullification. But we have seen that the purpose of allowing the trustee to recover preferential transfers is to benefit the estate, i.e., to increase the value of the estate for the benefit of creditors generally. If the effect of avoidance of a lien is to simply shift the benefit of the preference from one creditor to another creditor this bankruptcy purpose is frustrated. To prevent this result § 551 provides that the "transfer avoided * * * is preserved for the benefit of the estate." The transfer avoided is the lien obtained by Creditor A. Thus, the lien is automatically preserved but the benefit of the lien is shifted from Creditor A to the bankruptcy estate. The effect is to maintain Creditor B in a junior lien status thereby increasing the value of the estate by $10,000.

PROBLEMS

1. On May 1 Smith was indebted to Jones on an overdue unsecured loan made the previous year. On that date Smith paid Jones cash equal to the amount due on the loan. At the time of payment Smith had other debts which were not being paid and which exceeded Smith's assets. On July 15 Smith filed a petition in bankruptcy under Chapter 7. Answer the following questions

on the basis of § 547(b) without considering whether any exception under § 547(c) applies.

(a) Is the trustee in bankruptcy entitled to recover from Jones the amount received from Smith? § 547(b) and § 550(a). Does it matter whether or not Jones knew of Smith's financial condition at the time payment was received? Who has the burden of proving that Smith was insolvent? § 101 ("insolvent") and § 547(f)?

(b) Would your answers to (a) be different if Smith had filed in bankruptcy on August 15? § 101 ("insider" and "relative").

(c) Suppose that on May 1 Smith had not paid the loan and that Jones on that date had obtained a prejudgment attachment lien on business property of Smith with a value exceeding the amount due on the loan. When the petition in bankruptcy was filed on July 15 Smith's assets included the property on which Jones had an attachment lien. What are the rights of the trustee in bankruptcy? § 547(b) and § 101 ("transfer").

2.   Bank made a one-year loan of $10,000 to Debtor on September 1, 1990 and to secure the loan Debtor granted Bank a security interest in equipment owned by Debtor. Bank promptly perfected by filing a financing statement. On November 1, 1991 Debtor paid Bank $10,000 plus interest in discharge of the debt. Debtor filed a petition in bankruptcy on December 1, 1991. Debtor was insolvent on November 1, 1991 and at all times thereafter. Was the payment to Bank on November 1, 1991 a transfer on account of an antecedent debt? § 547(b)(2). Can the transfer be avoided by the trustee in bankruptcy under § 547(b)? What is the effect of § 547(b)(5)? Assume that the value of the equipment was greater than the payment made to Bank and that there were no other security interests or liens in the equipment superior to the security interest of Bank. Would the outcome of the case be different if Bank had been undersecured at the time it received payment from Debtor?

NOTE: THE PREFERENCE PERIOD

Under § 547(b)(4) a transfer cannot be a voidable preference unless it occurs within what we can call the "preference period." The preference period can be one of two lengths depending upon the identity of the recipient of the transfer. If the transferee is an insider, defined in § 101, the preference period is one year before the date of the filing of the petition in bankruptcy. If the transferee is not an insider the preference period is 90 days before the filing of the petition. Section 547(b) was amended in 1984, but § 547(b)(4)(A) was not changed. That provision has always allowed any transfer to be avoided if it occurred during the 90-day period before bankruptcy and if the requirements of subparagraphs (1), (2), (3) and (5) were met. Section 547(b)(4)(B) applies to transfers occurring between 90 days and one year before bankruptcy. Before the 1984 amendment, a transfer that occurred during the § 547(b)(4)(B) period could be avoided only if two additional requirements were met. The transferee had to be an insider and the transferee must have had "reasonable cause to believe the debtor was insolvent at the time of such transfer." We will discuss the reasonable cause to believe requirement later in this chapter. In the 1984 amendment the reasonable cause to believe requirement was dropped from § 547(b)(4)(B). The net result is that the same standards for avoidance now apply to both insiders and other transferees. The only difference is that the preference period for insiders is longer. A transfer to an insider can be avoided if it occurred within one year before bankruptcy and if the requirements of § 547(b)(1), (2), (3) and (5) are met.

2. INSIDER PREFERENCES UNDER STATE LAW AND THE BANKRUPTCY CODE

Previously we noted the common law rule that a preferential transfer by an insolvent debtor in payment of a debt is not fraudulent. Thus, a debtor who cannot pay all creditors may discriminate in favor of some to the detriment of others. Although the debtor may not dissipate assets by gratuitous transfers there is no duty to treat creditors equally. In a few states the common law rule has been changed by statute.

Preferences by an insolvent corporation present an independent issue. If the preference is made to a creditor who is not an officer, director or affiliate of the corporation the normal common law rule applies. See, e.g., Amussen v. Quaker City Corp., 18 Del. Ch. 28, 156 A. 180 (1931). There are a few cases to the contrary. But if the preference is made to a director or comparable insider of the corporation the general rule is that the preference can be recovered for the benefit of the creditors of the corporation. See, e.g., Pennsylvania Co. v. South Broad St. Theatre Co., 20 Del.Ch. 220, 174 A. 112 (1934). The reason for the rule was stated by the court in the latter case as follows: "The principle upon which the rule rests that forbids a director-creditor to enjoy a preference over others in the circumstance of the company's insolvency, is variously stated. By most of the authorities it is posited on the so-called 'trust fund theory' by which capital assets are said to constitute a trust fund for creditors. By others it is said to be based on the inequity of allowing a director to take advantage of the superior means of information which he enjoys over other creditors, conjoined as it is with a power or influence which enables the possessor to reap a personal advantage over others whose claims are equally meritorious."

The rule against insider preferences by an insolvent corporation has been extended by some courts to cover a preference made to a creditor whose debt was guaranteed by an insider. In Davis v. Woolf, 147 F.2d 629 (4th Cir.1945), the corporation was obligated to construct a building. Its obligation was guaranteed by a completion bond on which Woolf was liable. The corporation got into financial difficulty which prevented completion of the building. In order to facilitate completion of the building by the corporation and thus relieve himself of his obligation on the completion bond, Woolf loaned $18,000 to the corporation, and as security he was given a mortgage on the corporation's property which fully secured the debt. The building was completed and the corporation eventually went into bankruptcy. The trustee in bankruptcy attempted to avoid the mortgage under § 70e of the Bankruptcy Act, which was the predecessor to Bankruptcy Code § 544(b) and was similar in effect to that provision. The trustee argued that because the mortgage was an illegal preference under state law, it could under that law have been avoided by creditors who had claims in bankruptcy. Under § 70e the trustee succeeded to the rights of those creditors. The court stated that when a surety advances an insolvent principal debtor funds to satisfy the guaranteed debt and the principal debtor transfers property to the surety to indemnify or reimburse the surety, a preference to the surety is made. The effect of the transaction is the same as though the principal debtor had paid the guaranteed debt with its funds in order to relieve the surety of its obligation. In both cases the surety has suffered no loss and the insolvent principal debtor has lost property equal to the obligation satisfied. The court stated that the trustee's action under § 70e was meritorious if he could prove that Woolf was a director of the corporation at the time the mortgage was granted and that the corporation was then insolvent.

The Uniform Fraudulent Transfer Act, in § 5(b), adopts the common law rule applicable to insolvent corporations, but expands it so that it is a general rule applicable to preferences paid by any debtor to an insider, a term defined in UFTA § 1(7) to "include" the persons stated. The definition is based on § 101 ("insider") although there are minor differences between the two sections. The official comment to UFTA § 1(7) makes clear that that section, like § 101 ("insider"), is not meant to be limited to the persons stated. A court would be free to find that other persons are insiders if they "have the kind of close relationship intended to be covered by the term 'insider.'" UFTA § 5(b) does not have any effect on preferences to insiders during the year before bankruptcy because they are already voidable under § 547(b). However, it allows the trustee to attack, under § 544(b), insider preferences made before the start of the one-year period. Avoidability under UFTA § 5(b) depends upon the insider's having had "reasonable cause to believe that the debtor was insolvent," a requirement that no longer exists under § 547(b).

Suppose an insolvent corporation at the behest of X, a director of the corporation, pays a debt owing to Y which had been guaranteed by X. Against whom can the payment be recovered? In Arnold v. Knapp, 75 W.Va. 804, 84 S.E. 895 (1915), the court treated the payment as an unlawful preference to X, the director, on the theory that the payment was made for X's benefit. Could the payment also be recovered from Y? Several cases like Arnold v. Knapp have arisen under the Bankruptcy Code. One of those cases follows. It was not decided, however, on principles of corporation law or fraudulent transfer law. Rather, it involved § 547(b)(4)(B).

LEVIT v. INGERSOLL RAND FINANCIAL CORP.

United States Court of Appeals, Seventh Circuit, 1989.
874 F.2d 1186.

EASTERBROOK, CIRCUIT JUDGE.

We must decide a question no other appellate court has addressed: whether payments to creditors who dealt at arms' length with a debtor are subject to the year-long preference-recovery period that [Bankruptcy Code] § 547(b)(4)(B) provides for "inside" creditors, when the payments are "for the benefit of" insiders, § 547(b)(1). The bankruptcy court in this case answered "no", 58 B.R. 478 (Bankr.N.D.Ill.1986), and the district court "yes", 86 B.R. 545 (N.D.Ill.1988). * * *

I

In 1980 V.N. Deprizio Construction Co. was awarded contracts to do $13.4 million of work on the extension of Chicago's subway system to O'Hare Airport. By 1982 the company was in financial trouble. Because Mayor Byrne wanted the line open before the primary election for that office in February 1983, the City made the firm extraordinary loans of $2.5 million; the firm in turn donated $3,000 to the Mayor's campaign fund. Neither outlay achieved its purpose. The line wasn't finished on time, and Byrne lost. These and other dealings by Richard N. Deprizio, the firm's president, including suspicions of affiliation with organized crime, led the United States Attorney to open an investigation. In April 1983 Deprizio Co. filed a petition under the Bankruptcy Code of 1978. Other firms finished the subway, which opened in 1984.

As the investigation continued and Deprizio's indictment was imminent, word circulated that he might "sing". So in January 1986 Deprizio was lured to a vacant parking lot, where an assassin's gun and the obligations of a lifetime were discharged together. Corporations are not so easily liquidated.

Deprizio Co. had borrowed money from many sources other than the City of Chicago, including Ingersoll Rand Financial Corp., CIT Group/Equipment Financing, Inc., and Melrose Park Bank & Trust. Richard Deprizio co-signed the note to the Bank. Richard and his brothers, Robert and Edward, all insiders of the firm, also guaranteed its debts to other lenders. ("Insider", a term to which we return, includes officers of the debtor and the officers' relatives.) As the district court observed "the record is devoid of detail" concerning these guarantees. Details are potentially important, because CIT maintains on appeal that no insider guaranteed any of the firm's debts to it. The Trustee does not contest this but maintains that inside creditors received a benefit from payments to CIT because insiders had guaranteed debt secured by collateral in which CIT held the senior interest.

* * *

Payments out of the ordinary course in the 90 days before filing a bankruptcy petition may be recovered for the estate under §§ 547 and 550. Creditors then receive shares determined by statutory priorities and contractual entitlements rather than by their ability to sneak in under the wire. Payments to or for the benefit of an insider during a full year, not just 90 days, may be recovered by virtue of § 547(b)(4)(B). The Trustee filed adversary proceedings against the lenders * * *—none of them insiders— seeking to recover payments made more than 90 days but within the year before the filing. The Trustee reasoned that the payments made to these outside creditors were "for the benefit" of inside co-signers and guarantors, because every dollar paid to the outside creditor reduced the insider's exposure by the same amount.

Without deciding whether any of the payments was preferential within the meaning of § 547 or worked to the benefit of any insider, the bankruptcy judge denied the Trustee's request. Judge Eisen concluded that any transfer to an outside creditor for the benefit of an insider should be treated as two transfers: one being the money, and the other the benefit. A transfer may be recovered under § 550(a) only to the extent it is avoidable under § 547. The monetary transfer to the outsider is not avoidable, Judge Eisen concluded, when made more than 90 days before the filing. Thus it may not be recovered from the outsider, even though the benefit to the insider may be recovered from the insider.

On an interlocutory appeal to the district court, Judge Plunkett reversed. He concluded that payment is only one transfer, although a transfer may create benefits for many persons. If the insider receives a benefit, then the transfer is avoidable under § 547(b)(4)(B) if made within a year of the bankruptcy and does not qualify for the exclusions in § 547(c). * * * Section 550(a), as Judge Plunkett read it, allows the Trustee to recover the transfer from either the recipient or the indirect beneficiary, at the Trustee's option. The district court remanded the case so that the bankruptcy court could determine whether the payments identified by the Trustee occurred, whether an insider received a benefit from any particular payment, and whether any of them was protected by § 547(c). Judge Plunkett certified the question under 28 U.S.C. § 1292(b), and we granted leave to appeal.

II

Many bankruptcy and district judges have addressed the question we confront,[2] as have commentators.[3] A majority of judges have concluded that insiders' guarantees do not expose outside lenders to an extended preference-recovery period, frequently because they believe that recovery would be inequitable when ordinarily outside creditors need restore only preferences received within the 90 days before bankruptcy. The commentators are evenly divided.

A

Six sections of the Bankruptcy Code supply the texts. * * *

Section 547(b) uses three terms of art: "creditor", "insider", and "transfer", and the definition of "creditor" brings in a fourth: "claim". Section 101 defines each. * * * Finally there is § 550, which specifies who is liable for a transfer avoided under § 547. * * * The Trustee's argument for extended recovery

---

2. Five cases answer "yes": the district court's decision here plus In re Robinson Bros. Drilling, Inc., 97 B.R. 77 (W.D.Okla.1988), appeal pending, No. 88–8089 (10th Cir.); In re Coastal Petroleum Corp., 91 B.R. 35 (Bankr.N.D.Ohio 1988); In re W.E. Tucker Oil, Inc., 42 B.R. 897 (Bankr.W.D.Ark.1984); In re Big Three Transportation, Inc., 41 B.R. 16 (Bankr.W.D.Ark.1983). These cases answer "no" on the ground that extended preference recovery would be inequitable: In re T.B. Westex Foods, Inc., 96 B.R. 77 (Bankr.W.D.Tex.1989) (alternative holding); In re Midwestern Companies Inc., 96 B.R. 224 (Bankr.W.D.Mo. 1988); In re C–L Cartage Co., 70 B.R. 928 (Bankr.E.D.Tenn.1987); In re Aerco Metals, Inc., 60 B.R. 77 (Bankr.N.D.Tex. 1985); In re R.A. Beck Builder, Inc., 34 B.R. 888 (Bankr.W.D.Pa.1983); In re Duccilli Formal Wear, Inc., 8 Bankr.Ct. Dec. (CRR) 1180 (Bankr.S.D.Ohio 1982); In re Cove Patio Corp., 19 B.R. 843 (Bankr.S.D.Fla.1982); In re Church Buildings & Interiors, Inc., 14 B.R. 128 (Bankr.W.D.Okla.1981). Two answer "no" on the ground that insider and outsider receive different "transfers", only one of which may be recovered:

the bankruptcy judge's opinion in our case and In re Mercon Industries, Inc., 37 B.R. 549 (Bankr.E.D.Pa.1984). (Midwestern adopts this view as an alternative holding.)

3. Compare Lawrence P. King, 4 Collier on Bankruptcy ¶ 550.02 at 550–8 (15th ed. 1987), and Vern Countryman, The Trustee's Recovery in Preference Actions, 3 Bankruptcy Developments J. 449, 464 (1986), both saying "no" on grounds of equity, with Isaac Nutovic, The Bankruptcy Preference Laws: Interpreting Code Sections 547(c)(2), 550(a)(1), and 546(a)(1), 41 Bus.Law. 175, 186–99 (1985), and Thomas E. Pitts, Jr., Insider Guaranties and the Law of Preferences, 55 Am.Bankr.L.J. 343 (1981), both answering "yes". See also Phillip I. Blumberg, The Law of Corporate Groups: Bankruptcy Law § 9.03 (1985 & Supp.1988), contending that the answer should depend on whether the insider is solvent. A student note suggests still another approach. Note, The Interplay Between Sections 547(b) and 550(a)(1) of the Bankruptcy Code, 89 Colum.L.Rev. 530 (1989).

from outside creditors flows directly from these interlocked provisions.

Suppose Firm borrows money from Lender, with payment guaranteed by Firm's officer (Guarantor). Section 101(30)(B)(ii) renders Guarantor an "insider". Guarantor is not Firm's creditor in the colloquial sense, but under § 101(9) of the Code any person with a "claim" against Firm is a "creditor", and anyone with a contingent right to payment holds a "claim" under § 101(4)(A). A guarantor has a contingent right to payment from the debtor: if Lender collects from Guarantor, Guarantor succeeds to Lender's entitlements and can collect from Firm. So Guarantor is a "creditor" in Firm's bankruptcy. A payment ("transfer") by Firm to Lender is "for the benefit of" Guarantor under § 547(b)(1) because every reduction in the debt to Lender reduces Guarantor's exposure. Because the payment to Lender assists Guarantor, it is avoidable under § 547(b)(4)(B) unless one of the exemptions in § 547(c) applies. Once the transfer is avoided under § 547, the Trustee turns to § 550 for authority to recover. "Section 547(b)(4) distinguishes according to [whether Guarantor is an "insider"], but § 550 does not. It says that if a transfer is recoverable by the trustee, it may be recovered from *either* the 'initial transferee' (Lender) or the 'entity for whose benefit such transfer was made' (Guarantor)." Bonded Financial Services, Inc. v. European American Bank, 838 F.2d 890, 894 (7th Cir.1988) (emphasis in original). So Lender may have to repay transfers received during the year before filing, even though Lender is not an insider.

Judge Plunkett accepted this chain of reasoning. The creditors seek to break it at three links. First, they observe that § 550(a) allows the trustee to recover only "to the extent that a transfer is avoided under" § 547. Viewing each payment as two "transfers"—one to Lender, another to Guarantor—they insist that the only transfer avoidable under § 547 is the one to Guarantor. Second, several of the lenders say that the insiders are not "creditors" for particular debts. Third, CIT submits that payment of a non-guaranteed loan backed by a senior security interest does not produce a "benefit" for an inside guarantor of a junior secured creditor. The district court did not consider this third argument, and we do not pursue it (although we discuss it briefly at the close of this opinion); it should be resolved in the first instance by the bankruptcy court.

* * *

III

Now for the principal question: whether the Trustee may recover from an outside creditor under § 550(a)(1) a transfer more than 90 days before the filing that is avoided under § 547(b) because of a benefit for an inside creditor. The textual argument, which we have already given, is simple. Section 547(b) defines which transfers are "avoidable". No one doubts that a transfer to Lender produces a "benefit" for Guarantor. After § 547 defines which transfers may be avoided, § 550(a) identifies who is responsible for payment: "the initial transferee of such transfer *or* the entity for whose benefit such transfer was made" (emphasis added). This gives the trustee the option to collect from Lender, Guarantor, or both, subject only to the proviso in § 550(c) that there can be but one satisfaction.

More than language lies behind this approach. The trustee's power to avoid preferences (the "avoiding power") is essential to make the bankruptcy case a *collective* proceeding for the determination and payment of debts. Any individual creditor has a strong incentive to make off with the assets of a troubled firm, saving itself at potential damage to the value of the enterprise. Many a firm is worth more together than in pieces, and a spate of asset-grabbing by creditors could dissipate whatever firm-specific value the assets have. Like fishers in a common pool, creditors logically disregard the fact that their self-protection may diminish aggregate value—for if Creditor A does not lay claim to the assets, Creditor B will, and A will suffer for inaction. All creditors gain from a rule of law that induces each to hold back. The trustee's avoiding powers serve this end in two ways: first, they eliminate the benefit of attaching assets out of the ordinary course in the last 90 days before the filing, so that the rush to dismember a firm is not profitable from a creditor's perspective; second, the avoiding powers assure each creditor that if it refrains from acting, the pickings of anyone less civil will be fetched back into the pool. See Thomas H. Jackson, Avoiding Powers in Bankruptcy, 36 Stan. L.Rev. 725, 727–31, 756–68 (1984).

How long should this preference-recovery period be? If one outside creditor knows that the firm is in trouble, others will too. Each major lender monitors both the firm and fellow lenders. If it perceives that some other lender is being paid preferentially, a major lender can propel Firm into bankruptcy. Reasonably alert lenders can act with sufficient dispatch to ensure that the perceived preference is recoverable even when the preference period is short. Section 547(b) makes 90 days the rule, time enough (Congress concluded) for careful creditors to protect themselves (and when one does, small unsecured trade creditors get the benefits too).

Insiders pose special problems. Insiders will be the first to recognize that the firm is in a downward spiral. If insiders and outsiders had the same preference-recovery period, insiders who lent money to the firm could use their knowledge to advantage by paying their own loans preferentially, then putting off filing the petition in bankruptcy until the preference period had passed.

Outside creditors, aware of this risk, would monitor more closely, or grab assets themselves (fearing that the reciprocity that is important to the pooling scheme has been destroyed), or precipitate bankruptcy at the smallest sign of trouble, hoping to "catch" inside preferences before it is too late. All of these devices could be costly. An alternative device is to make the preference-recovery period for insiders longer than that for outsiders. With a long period for insiders, even the prescient managers who first see the end coming are unlikely to be able to prefer themselves in distribution.

Loans from insiders to their firms are not the only, or even the most important, concern of outside creditors. Insiders frequently guarantee other loans. If the firm folds while these loans are outstanding, the insiders are personally liable. So insiders bent on serving their own interests (few managers hold outside lenders' interests of equal weight with their own!) could do so by inducing the firm to pay the guaranteed loans preferentially. If the preference-recovery period for such payments were identical to the one for outside debts, this would be an attractive device for insiders. While concealing the firm's true financial state, they would pay off (at least pay down) the debts they had guaranteed, while neglecting others. To the extent they could use private information to do this more than 90 days ahead of the filing in bankruptcy, they would make out like bandits. The guaranteed loans would be extinguished, and with them the guarantees. True, it is logically possible to recover from the insider the value of the released guarantee, even if the trustee could not reach the proceeds in the hands of the outside lender. But it is hard to determine the value of a released guarantee, and anyway insiders might think that they would be more successful resisting the claims of the trustee than the hounds of the outside creditors. So an extended recovery period for payments to outside creditors that benefit insiders could contribute to the ability of the bankruptcy process to deter last-minute grabs of assets. The outsiders who must kick into the pool when the trustee uses the avoiding powers retain their contractual entitlements; all the trustee's recovery does is ensure that those entitlements (as modified by any statutory priorities)—rather than the efforts of insiders to protect their own interests, or the cleverness of outsiders in beating the 90–day deadline—determine the ultimate distribution of the debtor's net assets.

A

The bankruptcy court bridled at the extended preference period for outside creditors. Treating each payment as two transfers, one to Lender and the other to Guarantor, Judge Eisen concluded that § 550(a) limits the trustee to recovery from Guarantor. Section 550(a) allows recovery only "to the extent that a transfer is avoided" under § 547, and the two-transfer approach implies that the transfer to Lender has not been "avoided" at all. Judge Plunkett disagreed with this approach; so do we.

The two-transfer approach equates "transfer" with "benefit received". Both Lender and Guarantor gain from payment, and each receives a "transfer" to the extent of the gain. The Code, however, equates "transfer" with payments made. Section 101 * * * says that a transfer is a disposition of property. Sections 547 and 550 both speak of a transfer being avoided; avoidability is an attribute of the transfer rather than of the creditor. While the lenders want to define transfer from the recipients' perspectives, the Code consistently defines it from the debtor's. A single payment therefore is one "transfer", no matter how many persons gain thereby.

Section 550(a) allows recovery "to the extent that a transfer is avoided" not because a single payment may be many "transfers" but because on occasion less than all of a given transfer is "avoided". Section 547(b)(5) provides that a transfer is avoidable only to the extent it gives the creditor more than it would have received in a liquidation under Chapter 7. Several portions of § 547(c) also contemplate avoiding part of a transfer. Section 547(c)(1), for example, excludes from recovery the portion of a transfer supported by contemporaneous new value. So if Lender receives an asset worth $100 and infuses $80 of new capital, only $20 of the transfer is avoidable. The "to the extent that a transfer is avoided" language in § 550(a) ensures that the trustee recovers only the $20 and not the $100 in such a case.[7]

There is no greater support for the two-transfer approach in the legislative history than in the text and structure of the Code. The features of the Code important to us were substantially revised by the Conference Committee, which did not issue a report. Managers of the legislation read into the Congressional Record identical statements explaining the Conference Committee's work, but these statements do not address the subject at hand.

The parties agree that there is no helpful legislative history. They draw different inferences from this, however. The creditors say that we must infer that Congress meant to preserve the practice, under the Bankruptcy Act of 1898, of recovering payments only from those to whom the transfer represented a preference, see Dean v. Davis, 242 U.S. 438, 443, 37 S.Ct. 130, 131, 61 L.Ed. 419 (1917) (dictum), on the theory that if Congress made a change as momentous as this, surely someone would have said so. Frequently the pre–1978 practice will be informative. * * * Yet "[i]t is not the law that a statute can have no effects which are not

---

7. The legislative history supports this understanding. See, e.g., H.R.Rep. No. 95–595, 95th Cong., 1st Sess. 375–76 (1977); S.Rep. No. 95–989, 95th Cong., 2d Sess. 90 (1978), U.S.Code Cong. & Admin.News 1978, pp. 5787, 5876, 5963, 6331, 6332.

explicitly mentioned in its legislative history". Pittston Coal Group v. Sebben, 488 U.S. 105, 109 S.Ct. 414, 420–21, 102 L.Ed.2d 408 (1988). * * * When Congress makes wholesale changes in the text and structure of the law, it is fatuous to pretend that a silent legislative history means that existing practices should continue unchanged. The 1978 Code separates the identification of avoidable transfers (§ 547) from the identification of those who must pay (§ 550), a structural change with no antecedents in the 1898 Act.[8] It also creates for the first time the principle that transfers may be recoverable from either transferee or beneficiary—something introduced to § 550(a)(1) in the Conference Committee, too late for comment in the usual committee reports.[9] Changes of this character show that the pre–1978 practice is not a useful guide to interpreting the relation between §§ 547 and 550. * * *

Applying the longer preference-recovery period to outside creditors would not put the Code in conflict with fundamental policies reflected in both state and federal law * * *. An extended recovery period is consistent with the structure of the Code and does not subvert any of its functions. A longer period when insiders reap benefits by preferring one outside creditor over another facilitates the operation of bankruptcy as a collective process and ensures that each creditor will receive payment according to the Code's priorities and non-bankruptcy entitlements. Silence in the legislative history therefore does not require or authorize a court to depart from the text and structure of the Code. * * *

B

The creditors do not argue that even if the Code extends the preference period, the extension should not be enforced because "inequitable". Perhaps our rebuff to "equity" arguments in other

---

8. This separation was well thought out and discussed at length in the legislative history, although without discussing all of its consequences. See the references in note 7 above.

9. And obviously too late for comment in the Report of the Commission on the Bankruptcy Laws of the United States, H.R.Doc. No. 137, 93d Cong., 1st Sess. (1973). This Report has influenced the interpretation of the many features of the 1978 Code it proposed and discussed in detail. As the creditors observe, the Report does not mention the possibility that outside lenders could be subject to an extended preference-recovery period on account of insiders' guarantees. The Report discussed (and discarded) a proposal to make transfers avoidable on account of benefits to insiders, reasoning that this was implicit under current law. Report pt. II at 170; See National Bank of Newport v. National Herkimer County Bank, 225 U.S. 178, 184, 32 S.Ct. 633, 635, 56 L.Ed. 1042 (1912). The creditors ask us to infer that the "benefit" language in the Code did not change the law. But it is not the "benefit" language of § 547(b)(1), the possibility discussed by the *Report*, that makes the change; it is the novel text of § 550(a)(1), allowing recovery from either transferee or beneficiary, that underlies the Trustee's claim. Because that change did not happen until five years after the *Report*, its silence on the subject is not informative.

bankruptcy cases is responsible. See Bonded Financial, 838 F.2d at 894–95, and, e.g., In re Iowa R.R., 840 F.2d 535, 536 (7th Cir. 1988); In re Chicago, Milwaukee, St. Paul & Pacific R.R., 791 F.2d 524, 528 (7th Cir.1986); Boston & Maine Corp. v. Chicago Pacific Corp., 785 F.2d 562, 566 (7th Cir.1986). See also, e.g., Norwest Bank Worthington v. Ahlers, 485 U.S. 197, 108 S.Ct. 963, 968–69, 99 L.Ed.2d 169 (1988) ("whatever equitable powers remain in the bankruptcy courts must and can only be exercised within the confines of the Bankruptcy Code"); Official Committee v. Mabey, 832 F.2d 299, 301–02 (4th Cir.1987); Guerin v. Weil, Gotshal & Manges, 205 F.2d 302, 304 (2d Cir.1953) (A. Hand, J.). "There is a basic difference between filling a gap left by Congress' silence and rewriting rules that Congress has affirmatively and specifically enacted." Mobil Oil Corp. v. Higginbotham, 436 U.S. 618, 625, 98 S.Ct. 2010, 2015, 56 L.Ed.2d 581 (1978). Bankruptcy laws are not special cases, as *Ahlers* demonstrates.[10]   *   *   *

Nonetheless, "equity" arguments have captivated a majority of the bankruptcy judges and several of the commentators who have spoken on this subject (see notes 2 and 3 above). So it is worth pointing out that even if equity arguments were admissible, they would not help the creditors' cause. Rules of law affecting parties to voluntary arrangements do not operate "inequitably" in the business world—at least not once the rule is understood. Prices adjust. If the extended preference period facilitates the operation of bankruptcy as a collective debt-adjustment process, then credit will become available on slightly better terms. If a longer period has the opposite effect, creditors will charge slightly higher rates of interest and monitor debtors more closely. In either case creditors will receive the competitive rate of return in financial markets—the same risk-adjusted rate they would have received with a 90–day preference-recovery period. A rule may injure debtors and creditors by foreclosing efficient business arrangements and increasing the rate of interest low-risk borrowers must pay, see In re Thompson, 867 F.2d 416, 419 (7th Cir.1989); In re Patterson, 825 F.2d 1140, 1142 (7th Cir.1987); In re Erickson, 815 F.2d 1090, 1094 (7th Cir.1987), but inefficiency is not inequity. At all events, in what sense is it "inequitable" to recapture payments to creditors that may have been favored only because payment reduced insiders' exposure (recall that the insiders select which debts to pay first), then distribute these monies according to statutory priorities and contractual entitlements? In what sense is it "inequitable" to require the outside lenders to pursue the inside guarantors for any shortfall, when they bargained for exactly that recourse? See also 86 B.R. at 552–53.

10. Whatever force the assertion in Bank of Marin v. England, 385 U.S. 99, 103, 87 S.Ct. 274, 277, 17 L.Ed.2d 197 (1966), that "equitable principles govern the exercise of bankruptcy jurisdiction" may have had under the 1898 Act, this approach has no place under the Code to the extent the statute addresses the question.

Our creditors press a cousin to "equity" arguments: "policy" arguments. According to the creditors, an extended preference period will force lenders to precipitate bankruptcy filings at the slightest sign of trouble in order to prevent erosion of their positions. The lenders paint a bleak picture of firms driven under when the problems could have been worked out—if only the lenders knew that they would keep what they receive in the "workout". Workouts often involve guarantees, and if these mean longer preference periods, then workouts may become less common (and formal bankruptcy more common). It is not clear to us that bankruptcy proceedings are more costly than workouts. See Olympia Equipment Leasing Co. v. Western Union Telegraph Co., 786 F.2d 794, 802–03 (7th Cir.1986) (concurring opinion). It's not as though the filing of a bankruptcy petition closes the firm and heaves its workers into the streets. A firm with positive cash flows will continue operating in bankruptcy; the court simply sorts out the financial claims to the enterprise. Creditors are free to compromise their claims inside of bankruptcy, just as they are outside it.[11] So the fear of bankruptcy replacing some workouts does not lead us to shy away from an ordinary reading of the statute.

For what it may be worth, we doubt that an extended preference-recovery period will cause a stampede from workouts to bankruptcies. Unless there is a "preference", there is nothing for the trustee to avoid. Most of the tales of woe presented by the creditors do not involve preferences in light of § 547(b)(5), which says that a transfer is a preference only to the extent the creditor got more than it would have received in a liquidation, and § 547(c), which specifies situations that do not create avoidable preferences.

* * *

Consider some of the transactions the lenders use to illustrate what they view as pernicious consequences of an extended preference-recovery period:

- A fully-secured creditor with an insider's guarantee to boot is paid off nine months before bankruptcy and releases its security interest. The debtor uses the property as security for a new loan. The trustee recovers the payment as a preference, and the creditor has been stripped of its security. The trustee confronts two obstacles in such a case. First, if the creditor was fully secured, then payment does not produce a benefit for the

---

11. To a substantial extent a corporate bankruptcy is nothing but an orderly forum for private adjustments. Often these adjustments could be made at least cost if the firm were sold intact and the proceeds divided according to contractual and statutory entitlements, see Douglas G. Baird, The Uneasy Case for Corporate Reorganization, 15 J. Legal Studies 127 (1986), but even when the court rather than an auction market resolves questions of valuation, it is serving a function equally important in a private workout.

inside guarantor, whose exposure was zero. The preference-recovery period therefore would be only 90 days.
Second, under § 547(b)(5) a transfer is avoidable only to
the extent the creditor received more than it would have
in a Chapter 7 liquidation. A fully-secured creditor will
be paid in full under Chapter 7, so there is no avoidable
preference in this case with or without a guarantee by an
insider. If, on the other hand, the security covered only
90% of the debt, then only the remaining 10% of the
payment is avoidable as a preference.

- A creditor financing the debtor's inventory and receivables makes many loans and receives many payments
during the year before the filing. The trustee seeks to
recover all of these. Under § 547(c)(5), however, the
trustee must show that the lender improved its position
relative to other creditors during the preference period.
See In re Ebbler Furniture & Appliances, Inc., 804 F.2d 87
(7th Cir.1986). Ordinary financing arrangements do not
produce such an effect.

- A creditor makes an unsecured loan guaranteed by an
insider and requires monthly payments over a number of
years. The trustee seeks to recover all of the payments
during the year before the filing. To the extent the
debtor paid on time, the creditor is protected by the
current version of § 547(c)(2), the "ordinary course" rule.
(The state of things for payments before the amendment
is less clear, as we have mentioned.)

- Lender # 1 extends credit and takes security. It is so
over-secured that Lender # 2 is willing to make a second
loan and take a junior security interest. This second loan
(but not the first) is backed up by an insider's guarantee.
Every payment to Lender # 1 increases the amount of
security available for Lender # 2, which produces a benefit to Guarantor by reducing his exposure. Cf. In re
Prescott, 805 F.2d 719, 731 (7th Cir.1986). The trustee
seeks to recover all payments to Lender # 1 during the
year before the filing, even though Lender # 1 did not
negotiate for an insider's guarantee. This appears to be
the Trustee's position vis-à-vis CIT. If the payments had
been made after the 1984 amendments, then § 547(c)(2)
would prevent recovery. Even under the pre–1984 law
that applies to this case, we have substantial doubt that
the payments to Lender # 1 are avoidable transfers. By
assumption Lender # 1 is over-secured, so its position has
not been improved relative to a Chapter 7 liquidation,
§ 547(b)(5). The benefit in such a case is negligible at
best, so the case for recapture is weak. *Bonded Finan-*

cial, 838 F.2d at 895. Because neither the bankruptcy court nor the district court considered this question in detail, we do not resolve it, but the Trustee has an uphill battle.

In light of these exclusions, there is no reason to use ambulatory arguments of "equity" or "policy" to defeat the Trustee's claims in this case. Congress has considered and addressed specifically the situations that most concern lenders. If these exclusions and exemptions are not "enough", creditors should complain to Congress.

* * *

NOTE

Since the decision in *Levit,* some lenders have followed a practice of requiring the guarantor, at the time of entering into the guaranty, to waive all rights of reimbursement, indemnification, and subrogation against the debtor. Does that practice avoid the result in *Levit?* Could the trustee in bankruptcy prevail by bringing an action against the lender under § 548 or § 544(b) based on state law regarding transfers for the benefit of an insider of an insolvent corporation? If a waiver of rights against the debtor were made, would the insider guarantor have more or less incentive to pressure the debtor to pay the guaranteed claim before other claims? See Katzen, *Deprizio* and Bankruptcy Code Section 550: Extended Preference Exposure Via Insider Guarantees and Other Perils of Initial Transferee Liability, 45 Bus.Law. 511, 529 (1990).

PROBLEM

Bank has a perfected security interest in all the business equipment of D Corporation to secure a $200,000 loan. D needed additional operating capital but Bank declined to make further advances. Innis, a director of D, came to its aid with a $100,000 loan secured by a perfected security interest in all of D's business equipment. D was late in paying Bank and Bank began to press D to pay off its loan. On January 2, D paid Bank in full. Bank returned D's note and gave D a termination statement signed by Bank which D filed immediately in the UCC filing records. § 9–404(1). On July 1, D filed a petition in bankruptcy. D was insolvent on January 2 and at all times thereafter. On January 2 and at all times thereafter D's business equipment was worth $200,000. May the trustee in bankruptcy recover $100,000 from Bank as a voidable preference?

3. CONTEMPORANEOUS EXCHANGES

Section 547(b)(2) states as one element of a voidable preference that the transfer be "for or on account of an antecedent debt." Thus, if an insolvent buyer buys goods and pays for them at the time of sale by transferring money or other property to the seller, there is no preference because the buyer's obligation to pay for the goods and the transfer of the buyer's property to satisfy the obligation arise contemporaneously. But suppose there is a short delay between the time the obligation is incurred and the transfer of property in payment of the obligation. Does the short delay make the debt antecedent? The issue was considered by the Supreme Court in the case of Dean v. Davis, 242 U.S. 438, 37 S.Ct. 130, 61 L.Ed. 419 (1917). On September 3 the debtor obtained a loan from Dean on the debtor's promise to secure the loan by a mortgage on all of his property. The proceeds of the loan were used by the debtor to pay a debt owed to a bank. The mortgage was executed on September 10 and recorded the next day. Within a few days a petition for involuntary bankruptcy was filed against the debtor. The trustee in bankruptcy brought an action to set aside the mortgage. Both the district court and the court of appeals held that the mortgage was voidable as a fraudulent conveyance. The court of appeals also held that the mortgage could be avoided as a preference under Section 60b of the Bankruptcy Act. The Supreme Court, in reversing the court of appeals on the latter point stated: "The mortgage was not voidable as a preference under § 60b. Preference implies paying or securing a pre-existing debt of the person preferred. The mortgage was given to secure Dean for a substantially contemporaneous advance. The bank, not Dean, was preferred. The use of Dean's money to accomplish this purpose could not convert the transaction into a preferring of Dean, although he knew of the debtor's insolvency." Section 547(c)(1) codifies this holding of the Supreme Court. If the parties intend a contemporaneous exchange of a loan for a mortgage and the transfer of the debtor's property represented by the mortgage is delayed only a short time the exchange is substantially contemporaneous and the mortgage cannot be avoided. Does this analysis apply to the problems that follow?

PROBLEMS

1. On April 1, Debtor, while in New York, called Bank which is located in Los Angeles and requested an immediate emergency loan. On that day Bank wired $10,000 to Debtor on the understanding that Debtor, upon returning to Los Angeles, would sign a security agreement granting Bank a security interest in collateral owned by Debtor and located in Los Angeles. On April 4, Debtor returned to Los Angeles and immediately signed a security agree-

ment granting a security interest in the collateral to Bank. The same day Bank filed a financing statement covering the collateral. On June 20, Debtor filed a petition in bankruptcy. If Debtor was insolvent on April 1 and at all times thereafter, can Bank's security interest be avoided as a preference? § 547(b) and § 547(c) (1).

2. Bank made an unsecured demand loan to Debtor on the morning of April 1. Bank believed that Debtor was financially sound. Later that day Bank received a credit report indicating that Debtor was in financial difficulty and might be insolvent. Bank immediately talked to Debtor who acknowledged the truth of the credit report. When Bank demanded immediate repayment of the loan, Debtor offered instead to secure the loan by a mortgage on real property worth more than the amount of the loan. Bank agreed and the mortgage was executed on the evening of April 1 and recorded the next day. If Debtor was insolvent on April 1 and filed a petition in bankruptcy on June 1 can the mortgage be avoided as a preference? § 547(b) and § 547(c)(1).

3. On April 1, Bank loaned $10,000 to Debtor by crediting that amount to Debtor's checking account. The loan agreement signed on that day provided that the $10,000 would be used to buy described equipment in which Debtor granted a security interest to Bank. Bank filed a financing statement covering equipment of Debtor on April 1. On April 7, Debtor bought the equipment described in the loan agreement. On June 20, Debtor filed a petition in bankruptcy. Under § 547(e)(2) and (3) when did a transfer of property of the Debtor occur? If Debtor was insolvent on April 1 and at all times thereafter can Bank's security interest be avoided under § 547(b)? Is avoidance prevented under § 547(c) (1)? Is avoidance prevented under § 547(c)(3)? Would your answers be different if Debtor had acquired the equipment on April 30?

4. ORDINARY COURSE PAYMENTS

Preference law reflects the oft stated, though inconsistently followed, policy in favor of equal treatment of creditors. Justification for taking away from the preferred creditor an advantage that was lawfully obtained under nonbankruptcy law was often expressed in terms of unfair conduct by the debtor and the preferred creditor. We can find this notion as far back as the 16th century Case of Bankrupts, 2 Coke 25a, 76 Eng.Rep. 331 (1584), in which the court stated " * * * there ought to be an equal distribution * * * but if, after the debtor becomes a bankrupt, he may prefer one * * * and defeat and defraud many other poor men of their true debts it would be unequal and unconscionable, and a great defect in the law * * *." The court was referring to the conduct of the debtor in that case, but in many cases the preferred creditor will be a person who because of a special relationship to the debtor, is able to obtain an advantage not obtainable by others.

The characterization of preference in terms of unconscionability or fraud has had an important influence on the development of preference law. The classic preference situation is that of a privileged creditor—perhaps an insider—with knowledge of and influence over the affairs of the debtor who, seeing that the debtor is sinking in insolvency, gets payment before the debacle becomes manifest. But the typical preference situation today more often than not does not fit this classic pattern. A debtor in trouble usually will try to hide insolvency and often succeeds for an extended period of time. The debtor pays bills as long as possible hoping that somehow the crisis will pass. Many, if not most, creditors who are paid shortly before bankruptcy are not taking advantage of any special status that they have and indeed may not be aware that the debtor is in any financial difficulty. Is there any basis for treating differently the creditor who takes payment of a debt knowing that other creditors will go unpaid and the creditor who receives a windfall without knowledge that it is a windfall?

This distinction was made in the Bankruptcy Act. Under Bankruptcy Act § 60b a preferential transfer could be avoided by the trustee only if the creditor had at the time when the transfer was made "reasonable cause to believe that the debtor [was] insolvent." Under this standard the preferred creditor could lose the preference only if the creditor was on notice of the fact that receipt of property of the debtor would prejudice the rights of other creditors. Under the Bankruptcy Act preferential transfers resulting from judicial liens obtained against insolvent debtors within the four-month period before filing of the petition were separately treated by § 67a and were nullified. Although it was not necessary to prove that the creditor had reasonable cause to believe that the debtor was insolvent at the time the lien was obtained, any creditor who obtains a judicial lien is not an innocent recipient of payment of a debt. Debtors who allow their property to be subjected to judicial liens are frequently in financial difficulty, and judicial seizure of a debtor's property is often followed by bankruptcy. Thus, under the Bankruptcy Act a creditor whose preference was avoided usually had had notice that some advantage over other creditors was being obtained.

The Commission on the Bankruptcy Laws of the United States recommended to Congress that proof of "reasonable cause to believe" be eliminated as a requirement for the avoidance of a preference. The recommendation was adopted in § 547(b). The reasons for this change have been described as follows:

The Commission on the Bankruptcy Laws of the United States, in its report submitted to Congress, was first to recommend the elimination of this requirement. During the congressional hearings that were held both on the bill prepared by the Commission and a companion bill, there was testimony critical of the former requirement. The criticism was twofold. First, it was said that reasonable cause to believe was an unnecessary burden to impose upon the trustee in bankruptcy. Invariably, the transferee alleged that he did not know or have reason to know that the debtor was insolvent, thus creating a litigable issue in every case, with the burden of proof resting on the trustee in bankruptcy. As a result, many preferential transfers were not avoided, thereby undermining a basic tenet of the bankruptcy law—equitable distribution of a debtor's assets among its unsecured creditors. Second, it was said that the requirement had no logical basis in the law of voidable preferences. The main elements of a preference were set forth in section 60a: (1) a transfer of the debtor's property, (2) made within four months before bankruptcy, (3) for an antecedent debt, (4) at a time when the debtor was insolvent, and (5) the effect of which was to permit the transferee to receive a greater portion of its debt than other creditors in the same class would receive. When one reviewed these elements, an intention on the part of the debtor, or intention or knowledge on the part of the creditor, seemed to be irrelevant factors.

Fortgang & King, The 1978 Bankruptcy Code: Some Wrong Policy Decisions, 56 N.Y.U.L.Rev. 1148, 1165–1166 (1981).

In spite of the difficulties that the reasonable cause to believe requirement may have caused, it also performed a useful function. It is normally the case that in the 90-day period before bankruptcy the debtor has paid many unsecured debts of a recurring nature as they become due. An individual debtor, for example, pays utility bills and credit card purchases, and may be paying for previously rendered personal services such as those of doctors and dentists. A business debtor normally purchases inventory and supplies, as well as services of employees and other suppliers, on short term unsecured credit which may call for payment for various periods of time ranging from 10 or 20 days to as long as six months. The debtor may pay these obligations in ordinary course as they become due, but if the debtor was insolvent when payment was made all payments become preferences if the debtor goes into bankruptcy within 90 days. Under the Bankruptcy Act preferential payments of this kind were not voidable because the creditor normally would not have any cause to believe that the debtor was insolvent. Was that a desirable result?

One vital goal of any commercial law regime is certainty and finality of transactions. If large numbers of ordinary commercial transactions are subject to being upset by later legal proceedings, all transactions of that type become more expensive. Creditors must charge for the increased risk and expense incident to those transactions. There is general consensus in favor of avoiding preferences made in out-of-the-ordinary transactions in which a creditor seeks, and is given, favored treatment by a debtor in obvious financial difficulty. It is not so clear that transactions by an insolvent debtor in paying debts as they mature should be avoided solely because an incidental result is that the creditors have been preferred over others who did not have the good fortune of being paid before bankruptcy. If a doctrine designed to obtain equality for all creditors interferes with normal commercial practices and significantly adds to the cost of ordinary commercial transactions, the cost of the equality may be too high. Fortgang and King give a dramatic example:

> Another problem which surfaced shortly after promulgation of the Bankruptcy Code involves the issuance of commercial paper that is backed by a bank-issued letter of credit. Traditionally, the benefits to the issuer of using commercial paper backed by a bank letter of credit were lower interest costs and a better market for the notes. The latter advantage derived from the fact that the agencies that rate commercial paper based their rating on the creditworthiness of the bank issuing the letter of credit, not on the creditworthiness of the issuer of the commercial paper. Because banks generally are entitled to a higher rating than the issuers of the commercial paper, this financing technique was a very useful one. Little difficulty ensued if the issuer of commercial paper began a bankruptcy proceeding under the former Bankruptcy Act. Usually, any payments that had been made on the commercial paper within four months prior to that proceeding could not be upset as preferential because the holders of the commercial paper did not have reasonable cause to believe that the issuer was insolvent at the time the payments were made.

> Under the Bankruptcy Code, the situation has been dramatically changed; the benefits of this very useful conventional financing arrangement have been destroyed. Essentially, the elimination of the "reasonable cause to believe" requirement has caused rating agencies to base their ratings on the creditworthiness of the issuer as well as on the creditworthiness of the bank issuing the letter of credit backing the commercial paper. Without that requirement, payments by the issuer to a holder of commercial paper may be deemed voidable preferences, a determination that will inevitably come after the expiration of the letter of credit (which usually is tied to the date of payment of the commercial paper). Thus, the issuer of the letter of credit will have no liability to

the holder, and the holder will be left without recourse to the backing bank.

56 N.Y.U.L.Rev. at p. 1169.

In the Bankruptcy Code Congress attempted to alleviate the effects of dropping the reasonable cause to believe requirement by adopting § 547(c)(2). The purpose of that section was to insulate from avoidance preferential transfers resulting from certain ordinary course transactions of the type outlined above. As originally adopted § 547(c)(2) read as follows:

> (c) The trustee may not avoid under this section a transfer—

>> (2) to the extent that such transfer was—

>>> (A) in payment of a debt incurred in the ordinary course of business or financial affairs of the debtor and the transferee;

>>> (B) made not later than 45 days after such debt was incurred;

>>> (C) made in the ordinary course of business or financial affairs of the debtor and the transferee; and

>>> (D) made according to ordinary business terms;

In 1984, § 547(c)(2) was amended to take its present form, which is virtually identical to the original provision except for the dropping of subparagraph (B) which required that payment be no more than 45 days after the debt was incurred. The 1984 amendment also added § 547(c)(7).

The former § 547(c)(2) was effective in excluding from avoidance many ordinary course payments, but the 45 day provision in subparagraph (B) caused difficulty. First, it failed to take into account the very high proportion of short term financing that calls for payment beyond 45 days. Second, the courts had great difficulty in dealing with the requirement that the 45 day period start with the time that the "debt was incurred." Two examples illustrate the problem. 1. The debtor receives an invoice that covers a series of purchases of goods or services, as in the case of a telephone bill covering a series of long distance calls or a bill covering a series of credit card transactions made over the preceding month. The debtor pays the bill within 30 days of its receipt. Some of the transactions covered by the bill occurred more than 45 days before the creditor received payment from the debtor. Was the debt incurred at the time the debtor was billed or at the time the individual transactions occurred? 2. The debtor owed debt payable in equal monthly installments. Each installment was divided between a payment for interest on the outstanding debt for the previous month and a payment to reduce the principal. If the debtor paid an installment within 30 days of the time the installment was due, was the payment covered by former

§ 547(c)(2)? Is the analysis different depending upon whether the payment is on account of accrued interest or on account of principal? As a result of the 1984 amendment these difficult issues are no longer relevant.

PROBLEM

About five years ago Debtor Corporation borrowed from Bank $400,000 to be used for working capital. The loan was secured by a security interest in equipment of Debtor which was perfected by Bank. At the time the resale value of the equipment was somewhat more than $400,000, but since that time there has been a substantial decline in the value of the collateral because of obsolescence. The loan bore interest payable monthly and had a maturity of 90 days. It was the understanding of the parties that the loan would be renewed at maturity from time to time for additional 90-day periods if the financial situation of Debtor was satisfactory to Bank. The loan was regularly renewed over the years and was increased from time to time as the business of Debtor expanded. At the most recent maturity date the outstanding principal balance was $950,000. Shortly before the maturity date Bank examined the financial affairs of Debtor and discovered that Debtor had suffered very grave financial reversals during the previous 90 days. In fact, Bank determined that Debtor was not paying some of its creditors and was probably insolvent at that time. Bank requested that the loan be repaid at the due date, but Debtor was unable to pay. Bank and Debtor then made the following transaction on the due date of the loan. Debtor paid the monthly interest of about $11,500 and paid $450,000 of the principal. Bank renewed the loan for its unpaid principal amount of $500,000 for an additional 90-day period, but the interest rate was increased substantially. The affairs of Debtor continued to decline. Debtor failed to make any further interest payments to Bank. Two months after the renewal Debtor filed a petition in bankruptcy under Chapter 7. The trustee in bankruptcy brought an action against Bank to recover the $450,000 and $11,500 payments which Debtor had made to Bank when the loan was renewed. Is the trustee entitled to recover under the present version of § 547?

UNION BANK v. WOLAS

Supreme Court of the United States, 1991.
__ U.S. __, 112 S.Ct. 527, 116 L.Ed.2d 514.

JUSTICE STEVENS delivered the opinion of the Court.

Section 547(b) of the Bankruptcy Code authorizes a trustee to avoid certain property transfers made by a debtor within 90 days before bankruptcy. The Code makes an exception, however, for transfers made in the ordinary course of business, § 547(c)(2). The question presented is whether payments on long-term debt may qualify for that exception.

On December 17, 1986, ZZZZ Best Co., Inc. (Debtor) borrowed seven million dollars from petitioner, Union Bank (Bank).[1] On July 8, 1987, the Debtor filed a voluntary petition under Chapter 7 of the Bankruptcy Code. During the preceding 90–day period, the Debtor had made two interest payments totalling approximately $100,000 and had paid a loan commitment fee of about $2,500 to the Bank. After his appointment as trustee of the Debtor's estate, respondent filed a complaint against the Bank to recover those payments pursuant to § 547(b).

The Bankruptcy Court found that the loans had been made "in the ordinary course of business or financial affairs" of both the Debtor and the Bank, and that both interest payments as well as the payment of the loan commitment fee had been made according to ordinary business terms and in the ordinary course of business. As a matter of law, the Bankruptcy Court concluded that the payments satisfied the requirements of § 547(c)(2) and therefore were not avoidable by the trustee. The District Court affirmed the Bankruptcy Court's summary judgment in favor of the Bank.

Shortly thereafter, in another case, the Court of Appeals held that the ordinary course of business exception to avoidance of preferential transfers was not available to long-term creditors. In re CHG International, Inc., 897 F.2d 1479 (CA9 1990). In reaching that conclusion, the Court of Appeals relied primarily on the policies underlying the voidable preference provisions and the state of the law prior to the enactment of the 1978 Bankruptcy Code and its amendment in 1984. Thus, the Ninth Circuit concluded, its holding in CHG International, Inc. dictated a reversal in this case. 921 F.2d 968, 969 (1990).[5] The importance of the question of law decided by the Ninth Circuit, coupled with the fact that the Sixth Circuit had interpreted § 547(c)(2) in a contrary manner, In re Finn, 909 F.2d 903 (1990), persuaded us to grant the Bank's petition for certiorari. * * *

---

1. The Bankruptcy Court found that the Bank and Debtor executed a revolving credit agreement on December 16, 1986, in which the Bank agreed to lend the Debtor $7 million in accordance with the terms of a promissory note to be executed and delivered by the Debtor. * * * On December 17, 1986, the Debtor executed and delivered to the Bank a promissory note in the principal sum of $7 million. The promissory note provided that interest would be payable on a monthly basis and would accrue on the principal balance at a rate of .65% per annum in excess of the Bank's reference rate.

5. In so holding, the Ninth Circuit rejected the Bank's argument that the revolving line of credit in this case was not "long-term" because it was for less than one year. 921 F.2d 968, 969 (1990). Because we hold that the ordinary course of business exception applies to payments on long-term as well as short-term debt, we need not decide whether the revolving line of credit was a "long-term" debt.

I

We shall discuss the history and policy of § 547 after examining its text. In subsection (b), Congress broadly authorized bankruptcy trustees to "avoid any transfer of an interest of the debtor in property" if five conditions are satisfied and unless one of seven exceptions defined in subsection (c) is applicable. In brief, the five characteristics of a voidable preference are that it (1) benefit a creditor; (2) be on account of antecedent debt; (3) be made while the debtor was insolvent; (4) be within 90 days before bankruptcy; and (5) enable the creditor to receive a larger share of the estate than if the transfer had not been made. Section 547 also provides that the debtor is presumed to have been insolvent during the 90–day period preceding bankruptcy. § 547(f). In this case, it is undisputed that all five of the foregoing conditions were satisfied and that the interest and loan commitment fee payments were voidable preferences unless excepted by subsection (c)(2).

The most significant feature of subsection (c)(2) that is relevant to this case is the absence of any language distinguishing between long-term debt and short-term debt.   *   *   *

Instead of focusing on the term of the debt for which the transfer was made, subsection (c)(2) focuses on whether the debt was incurred, and payment made, in the "ordinary course of business or financial affairs" of the debtor and transferee. Thus, the text provides no support for respondent's contention that § 547(c)(2)'s coverage is limited to short-term debt, such as commercial paper or trade debt. Given the clarity of the statutory text, respondent's burden of persuading us that Congress intended to create or to preserve a special rule for long-term debt is exceptionally heavy. United States v. Ron Pair Enterprises, Inc., 489 U.S. 235, 241–242 (1989). As did the Ninth Circuit, respondent relies on the history and the policies underlying the preference provision.

II

The relevant history of § 547 contains two chapters, one of which clearly supports, and the second of which is not inconsistent with, the Bank's literal reading of the statute. Section 547 was enacted in 1978 when Congress overhauled the Nation's bankruptcy laws. The section was amended in 1984. For purposes of the question presented in this case, the original version of § 547 differed in one significant respect from the current version: it contained a provision that the ordinary course of business exception did not apply unless the payment was made within 45 days of the date the debt was incurred. That provision presumably excluded most payments on long-term debt from the exception. In

1984 Congress repealed the 45–day limitation but did not substitute a comparable limitation. * * *

Respondent contends that this amendment was intended to satisfy complaints by issuers of commercial paper [10] and by trade creditors [11] that regularly extended credit for periods of more than 45 days. Furthermore, respondent continues, there is no evidence in the legislative history that Congress intended to make the ordinary course of business exception available to conventional long-term lenders. Therefore, respondent argues, we should follow the analysis of the Ninth Circuit and read § 547(c)(2) as protecting only short-term debt payments. Cf. In re CHG International, 897 F.2d, at 1484.

We need not dispute the accuracy of respondent's description of the legislative history of the 1984 amendment in order to reject his conclusion. For even if Congress adopted the 1984 amendment to redress particular problems of specific short-term creditors, it remains true that Congress redressed those problems by entirely deleting the time limitation in § 547(c)(2). The fact that Congress may not have foreseen all of the consequences of a statutory enactment is not a sufficient reason for refusing to give effect to its plain meaning. Toibb v. Radloff, 501 U.S. ___, 111 S.Ct. 2197, 115 L.Ed.2d 145 (1991).

Respondent also relies on the history of voidable preferences prior to the enactment of the 1978 Bankruptcy Code. The text of the preference provision in the earlier Bankruptcy Act did not specifically include an exception for payments made in the ordinary course of business. The courts had, however, developed what is sometimes described as the "current expense" rule to cover situations in which a debtor's payments on the eve of bankruptcy did not diminish the net estate because tangible assets were obtained in exchange for the payment. See Marshall v. Florida National Bank of Jacksonville, 112 F.2d 380, 382 (CA5 1940); 3 Collier On Bankruptcy ¶ 60.23, p. 873 (14th ed. 1977). Without such an exception, trade creditors and other suppliers of necessary goods and services might have been reluctant to extend even short-term credit and might have required advance payment instead, thus making it difficult for many companies in temporary distress to have remained in business. Respondent argues that Congress

---

10. Because payments to a commercial paper purchaser within 90 days prior to bankruptcy may be preferential transfers under § 547(b), a purchaser could be assured that the payment would not be avoided under the prior version of § 547(c)(2) only if the commercial paper had a maturity of 45 days or less. Commercial issuers thus complained that the 45–day limitation lowered demand for commercial paper with a maturity in excess of 45 days. * * *

11. Trade creditors stated that normal payment periods in many industries exceeded 45 days and complained that the arbitrary 45–day limitation in § 547(c)(2) deprived these trade creditors of the protection of the ordinary course of business exception to the trustee's power to avoid preferential transfers. * * *

enacted § 547(c)(2) in 1978 to codify that exception, and therefore the Court should construe § 547(c)(2) as limited to the confines of the current expense rule.

This argument is not compelling for several reasons. First, it is by no means clear that § 547(c)(2) should be construed as the statutory analogue of the judicially crafted current expense rule because there are other exceptions in § 547(c) that explicitly cover contemporaneous exchanges for new value.[13] Those provisions occupy some (if not all) of the territory previously covered by the current expense rule. Nor has respondent directed our attention to any extrinsic evidence suggesting that Congress intended to codify the current expense rule in § 547(c)(2).

The current expense rule developed when the statutory preference provision was significantly narrower than it is today. To establish a preference under the Bankruptcy Act, the trustee had to prove that the challenged payment was made at a time when the creditor had "reasonable cause to believe that the debtor [was] insolvent." 11 U.S.C. § 96(b) (1976 ed.). When Congress rewrote the preference provision in the 1978 Bankruptcy Code, it substantially enlarged the trustee's power to avoid preferential transfers by eliminating the reasonable cause to believe requirement for transfers made within 90 days of bankruptcy and creating a presumption of insolvency during that period. * * * At the same time, Congress created a new exception for transfers made in the ordinary course of business, § 547(c)(2). This exception was intended to "leave undisturbed normal financial relations, because it does not detract from the general policy of the preference section to discourage unusual action by either the debtor or his creditors during the debtor's slide into bankruptcy." H.R.Rep. No. 95–595, at 373.

In light of these substantial changes in the preference provision, there is no reason to assume that the justification for narrowly confining the "current expense" exception to trade creditors before 1978 should apply to the ordinary course of business exception under the 1978 Code. Instead, the fact that Congress carefully reexamined and entirely rewrote the preference provision in 1978 supports the conclusion that the text of § 547(c)(2) as enacted reflects the deliberate choice of Congress.[15]

---

13. Thus, for example, § 547(c)(1) exempts a transfer to the extent that it was a "contemporaneous exchange for new value given to the debtor," and § 547(c)(4) exempts a transfer to a creditor "to the extent that, after such transfer, such creditor gave new value to or for the benefit of the debtor * * *."

15. Indeed, the House Committee Report concludes its discussion of the trustee's avoidance powers with the ob-

servation that the language in the preference section of the earlier Bankruptcy Act was "hopelessly complex" and had been "subject to varying interpretations. The bill undoes the numerous amendments that have been heaped on section 60 during the past 40 years, and proposes a unified and coherent section to deal with the problems created by prebankruptcy preferential transfers." H.R.Rep. No. 95–595, p. 179 (1977). Respondent's assumption that § 547(c)(2)

III

The Bank and the trustee agree that § 547 is intended to serve two basic policies that are fairly described in the House Committee Report. The Committee explained:

"A preference is a transfer that enables a creditor to receive payment of a greater percentage of his claim against the debtor than he would have received if the transfer had not been made and he had participated in the distribution of the assets of the bankrupt estate. The purpose of the preference section is two-fold. First, by permitting the trustee to avoid prebankruptcy transfers that occur within a short period before bankruptcy, creditors are discouraged from racing to the courthouse to dismember the debtor during his slide into bankruptcy. The protection thus afforded the debtor often enables him to work his way out of a difficult financial situation through cooperation with all of his creditors. Second, and more important, the preference provisions facilitate the prime bankruptcy policy of equality of distribution among creditors of the debtor. Any creditor that received a greater payment than others of his class is required to disgorge so that all may share equally. The operation of the preference section to deter 'the race of diligence' of creditors to dismember the debtor before bankruptcy furthers the second goal of the preference section—that of equality of distribution." Id., at 177–178.

As this comment demonstrates, the two policies are not entirely independent. On the one hand, any exception for a payment on account of an antecedent debt tends to favor the payee over other creditors and therefore may conflict with the policy of equal treatment. On the other hand, the ordinary course of business exception may benefit all creditors by deterring the "race to the courthouse" and enabling the struggling debtor to continue operating its business.

Respondent places primary emphasis, as did the Court of Appeals, on the interest in equal distribution. See In re CHG International, 897 F.2d, at 1483–1485. When a debtor is insolvent, a transfer to one creditor necessarily impairs the claims of the debtor's other unsecured and undersecured creditors. By authorizing the avoidance of such preferential transfers, § 547(b) empowers the trustee to restore equal status to all creditors. Respondent thus contends that the ordinary course of business exception should be limited to short-term debt so the trustee may order that preferential long-term debt payments be returned to the estate to be distributed among all of the creditors.

was intended to preserve pre-existing law is at war with this legislative history.

But the statutory text—which makes no distinction between short-term debt and long-term debt—precludes an analysis that divorces the policy of favoring equal distribution from the policy of discouraging creditors from racing to the courthouse to dismember the debtor. Long-term creditors, as well as trade creditors, may seek a head start in that race. Thus, even if we accept the Court of Appeals' conclusion that the availability of the ordinary business exception to long-term creditors does not directly further the policy of equal treatment, we must recognize that it does further the policy of deterring the race to the courthouse and, as the House Report recognized, may indirectly further the goal of equal distribution as well. Whether Congress has wisely balanced the sometimes conflicting policies underlying § 547 is not a question that we are authorized to decide.

IV

In sum, we hold that payments on long-term debt, as well as payments on short-term debt, may qualify for the ordinary course of business exception to the trustee's power to avoid preferential transfers. We express no opinion, however, on the question whether the Bankruptcy Court correctly concluded that the Debtor's payments of interest and the loan commitment fee qualify for the ordinary course of business exception, § 547(c)(2). In particular, we do not decide whether the loan involved in this case was incurred in the ordinary course of the Debtor's business and of the Bank's business, whether the payments were made in the ordinary course of business, or whether the payments were made according to ordinary business terms. These questions remain open for the Court of Appeals on remand.

The judgment of the Court of Appeals is reversed and the case is remanded for further proceedings consistent with this opinion.

It is so ordered.

JUSTICE SCALIA, concurring.

I join the opinion of the Court, including Parts II and III, which respond persuasively to legislative-history and policy arguments made by respondent. It is regrettable that we have a legal culture in which such arguments have to be addressed (and are indeed credited by a Court of Appeals), with respect to a statute utterly devoid of language that could remotely be thought to distinguish between long-term and short-term debt. Since there was here no contention of a "scrivener's error" producing an absurd result, the plain text of the statute should have made this litigation unnecessary and unmaintainable.

5. SECURITY INTERESTS IN INVENTORY AND ACCOUNTS

---

a. UNDER THE BANKRUPTCY ACT

Bankruptcy Act § 60a(2) provided: " *   *   * a transfer of property other than real property shall be deemed to have been made or suffered at the time when it became so far perfected that no subsequent lien upon such property obtainable by legal or equitable proceedings on a simple contract could become superior to the rights of the transferee."

In adopting a perfection test for when a transfer was made for preference purposes § 60a(2) seemed to threaten the validity in bankruptcy of security interests in inventory and accounts receivable. Suppose Debtor, an appliance retailer, signed a security agreement on February 1 granting a security interest to Bank to secure a loan made at the same time. The collateral was all of Debtor's inventory then owned or thereafter acquired. Bank immediately filed a financing statement covering inventory. Under the UCC the security interest attached, with respect to any item of inventory, when all of the following conditions were met: (1) Debtor signed the security agreement; (2) Bank gave value to Debtor; and (3) Debtor had rights in the item of inventory. § 9–203. The first two conditions were satisfied on February 1 when the loan was made and the agreement signed. The third condition was satisfied at various times. With respect to inventory owned on February 1 it was satisfied on that date. With respect to after-acquired inventory it was satisfied when the inventory was acquired. Section 9–303 states that a security interest is perfected when it has attached and when all of the applicable steps required for perfection have been taken. The step normally taken to perfect a security interest in inventory is the filing of a financing statement. Thus, under the UCC whenever Debtor acquired an item of inventory after February 1 a security interest in that item attached and when it attached it was perfected. Filing of the financing statement occurred on February 1 but perfection with respect to the inventory covered by the financing statement could not occur until the inventory was acquired. Suppose in our example that Debtor's inventory completely turned over every 60 days and that Debtor filed in bankruptcy on December 1. If that is so all inventory on hand at the date of bankruptcy was not on hand at the beginning of the preference period. Assume that Bank did not make any loans to Debtor after February 1 and that the original loan was unpaid at the date of bankruptcy. Under the UCC the security interest of Bank in inventory at the date of bankruptcy attached and was perfected during the preference period and it secured a debt that arose on February 1. Under Bankruptcy Act § 60a(2) the apparent result was that the transfer of Debtor's property represented by the security interest was made when the security interest attached and was perfected during the preference period. Thus, if Debtor was insolvent at the time of the transfer and Bank had reason to know of the insolvency the security interest was a voidable preference under § 60b.

There were various arguments that could be made to avert the result just stated. One argument was based on § 9–108 which applied to a case such as our hypothetical and which stated that the security interest in after-acquired inventory "shall be deemed to be taken for new value and not as security for an antecedent debt." Few bankruptcy lawyers thought that this section had any validity because it was rather obviously an attempt by the state law to define "antecedent debt" in the Bankruptcy Act, a matter of federal not state law. Other arguments, that had a better chance of success, were based on the "entity theory" and "substitution theory" of inventory and accounts receivable collateral. They are discussed in Grain Merchants of Indiana, Inc. v. Union Bank & Savings Co., 408 F.2d 209 (7th Cir.1969). The court in that case surprised and confounded almost all of the bankruptcy bar by its unorthodox reading of § 60a(2). That reading differed very much with the analysis just made.

Grain Merchants involved accounts receivable rather than inventory but the analysis made above also applies to accounts. On September 17, 1965 Debtor signed a security agreement giving Bank a security interest in its present and future accounts. Bank promptly filed a financing statement. Bank made periodic advances to Debtor. The last was made on September 20, 1966. Debtor filed a petition in bankruptcy on October 27, 1966. The trustee in bankruptcy argued that any security interest in accounts that came into existence after September 20 was a transfer on account of an antecedent debt and voidable under § 60b because the transfer occurred when Debtor acquired rights in the new accounts. At that point the after-acquired property clause automatically granted a security interest in these accounts to Bank which did not give new value in exchange.

The court held that no preference occurred because the transfer took place at the time Bank filed its financing statement in September 1965. But how could accounts that did not arise until 1966 be transferred in 1965? The court said "This is, [the interpretation of § 60a(2)] in the first instance, a question of priorities between creditors rather than a question of complete perfection in the abstract." 408 F.2d at 212. Hence, the issue is not when Bank's security interest in an after-acquired account becomes perfected under Article 9 but when it becomes "so far perfected" that no subsequent lien could have priority over it. The issue is priority not perfection. Nobody can obtain a lien in an account until the account comes into existence and under the UCC as soon as any account in *Grain Merchants* came into existence it was instantly burdened with the perfected security interest of Bank. Under § 9–301(1)(b) a judicial lien in an account can have priority over a security interest in that account only if the security interest is unperfected at the time the judicial lien attaches. Thus, in *Grain Merchants* no judicial lien could ever have priority over Bank's security interest in an after-acquired account because the security interest was born perfected. From this the court concluded that the "transfer" occurred at the time Bank filed its financing statement. Since filing occurred before the beginning of the preference period no avoidable preference was involved.

In DuBay v. Williams, 417 F.2d 1277 (9th Cir.1969), on facts similar to those of *Grain Merchants,* the court followed the *Grain Merchants* theory. Judge Hufstedler stated: " 'Transfer' for the purpose of section 60a(2) is thus equated with the act by which priority over later creditors is achieved and not with the event which attaches the security interest to a specific account." 417 F.2d at 1287.

The court in *Grain Merchants* bolstered its view with two additional theories. The first is a metaphorical confection known as the entity or Mississippi River theory. Under this theory the collateral is considered to be an entity apart from the individual accounts or items of inventory that it comprises. It is like a river that is recognized as continually existing even though the water of which it is made is constantly changing. Old accounts are paid and disappear, new accounts are acquired, but old man entity just keeps rollin' along. Since the entity was in existence before the beginning of the preference period, no preferential transfer took place.

The court's entity theory makes more sense as an application of its second alternative theory, the substitution theory. Under this theory we look at the effect of the transfer in depleting the estate of the debtor available for other creditors. A typical preference case is one in which a debtor who owes a creditor $10,000 takes that amount from a bank account that was available to all creditors and pays it to the preferred creditor. Since that creditor is preferred the amount of the debtor's property available to other creditors is depleted. On the other hand, if the creditor has a perfected security interest in the debtor's $10,000 machine to secure a $7,500 debt and, during the preference period, debtor sells the old machine and replaces it with another machine of the same value in which creditor acquires a security interest, the estate of the debtor has not been depleted. There was a transfer to the secured creditor when the security interest in the new machine was granted but the transfer was a contemporaneous exchange with the secured creditor because the creditor gave new value when it released its indefeasible security interest in the old machine. As the court says concerning the facts in *Grain Merchants:* "Since the relative positions of the Bank and the debtor were unaltered by the exchanges, the debtor's other creditors cannot be considered harmed by the transactions with the Bank." 408 F.2d at 217.

Because of the enactment of the Bankruptcy Code the limits of *Grain Merchants* and *DuBay* were never fully tested. Suppose Bank loaned Debtor $100,000 and was granted a security interest in all of Debtor's business equipment then owned or after-acquired. Bank immediately filed a financing statement covering equipment. Six months later a fire destroyed all of Debtor's equipment. The loss was not insured. Debtor then bought new equipment to replace the old. Two months later Debtor filed in bankruptcy. Under the UCC, Bank obtained a perfected security interest in the new equipment at the instant that Debtor acquired it. Thus no judicial lien could be superior to Bank's security interest. Would the *Grain Merchants* court have held that under the Bankruptcy Act there was no preference because Bank filed its financing statement before the start of the preference period? The substitution theory and the entity theory would not apply in this case. Did the *Grain Merchants* court intend that the substitution theory and the entity theory should be a limitation on its reading of § 60a(2)? *DuBay* said nothing about the substitution and entity theories. Judge Hufstedler based the result solely on a reading of § 60(a)(2). Under that reading no preference to Bank would result in the equipment case. However, it must be conceded that neither *DuBay* nor *Grain Merchants* concerned cases in which the secured creditor's interest increased during the preference period. Perhaps those courts would have found ways to deal with the equipment hypothetical case had those facts been before them.

Thwarted by the courts, the bankruptcy bar took their case to Congress. In speaking of § 547(e)(3), the House and Senate Reports say: "This provision, more than any other in the section, overrules *DuBay* and *Grain Merchants.* * * * " House Report, pp. 374–75 (1977); Senate Report, p. 89 (1978). But § 547(c)(5) has the effect of insulating security interests on after-acquired inventory and accounts from attack as voidable preferences so long as the creditor's position is not improved during the 90–day period. We suspect that in time courts would have refined the doctrine of *DuBay* and *Grain Merchants* to approximate the result of § 547(c) (5) which in effect adopts the substitution theory described in *Grain Merchants.*

b. UNDER BANKRUPTCY CODE § 547(c)(5)

The legislative history of the Bankruptcy Code is not very helpful in determining the precise meaning of § 547(c)(5). The House and Senate Reports explaining this provision state the following:

> Paragraph (5) codifies the improvement in position test, and thereby overrules such cases as * * * Grain Merchants of Indiana, Inc. v. Union Bank and Savings Co. * * * A creditor with a security interest in a floating mass, such as inventory or accounts receivable, is subject to preference attack to the extent he improves his position during the 90–day period before bankruptcy. The test is a two-point test, and requires determination of the secured creditor's position 90 days before the petition and on the date of the petition. If new value was first given after 90 days before the case, the date on which it was first given substitutes for the 90–day point.

1978 U.S.Code Cong. & Admin.News 5874.

Accounts receivable and inventory normally turn over within a short period of time. It is likely that at the date of bankruptcy some receivables or inventory on hand were acquired by the debtor within the 90–day period. Since a security interest in this new collateral was, by virtue of § 547(e)(3), a transfer to the secured party when it was acquired by the debtor there might have been a voidable preference under § 547(b) if the debtor was insolvent at the time. Section 547(c)(5) is a limited exemption from this rule. A typical case to which § 547(c)(5) applies is as follows: Secured Party is secured by all accounts receivable of Debtor; at the beginning of the 90–day period the debt was $100,000 and at the date of bankruptcy the debt was $90,000; at the beginning of the 90–day period there were $60,000 in receivables; during the 90–day period Debtor increased its receivables so that on the date of bankruptcy they amounted to $70,000. To the extent of $50,000 Secured Party has a valid secured claim and to the extent of $20,000 Secured Party's security interest is disallowed because preferential. The test is stated in terms of the amount of the reduction of the amount by which the debt exceeded the value of the security interest from the beginning of the 90–day period to the date of bankruptcy. At the beginning of the period the deficiency was $40,000 ($100,000 debt minus $60,000 collateral) and at bankruptcy the deficiency was reduced to $20,000 ($90,000 debt minus $70,000 collateral). Secured Party has a valid security interest except to the extent of the $20,000 by which the deficiency was reduced.

Section 547(c)(5) is a variation of the substitution theory of *Grain Merchants*. It says in effect that it is not important whether the items making up the mass of inventory or accounts receivable at bankruptcy were or were not identical to the items making up the mass at the beginning of the 90–day period so long as the volume has not changed. Within that limitation any new item that came into existence within the 90–day period is treated as a substitute for an item that was disposed of by the debtor during the same period. This provision seems workable when applied to accounts receivable but it causes difficulty when applied to inventory. To calculate the reduction of the deficiency (or in other words improvement of position) it is necessary to value the security interest which in turn requires a valuation of the collateral. Since accounts are simply claims against third parties they are normally valued at face value, i.e., the amount owed by the account debtors, reduced by some amount that reflects the fact that some accounts will turn out to be uncollectible or will entail collection costs. A financer that lends money on the basis of accounts as collateral normally would assume that accounts will be liquidated by collection rather than sale to a third party. The most obvious definition of "value" in § 547(c)(5) as applied to accounts would seem to be either face value or face value less a discount for estimated uncollectibility or costs of collection. Professor Neil B. Cohen in his article, Value Judgments: Accounts Receivable Financing and Voidable Preferences Under the New Bankruptcy Code, 66 Minn.L.Rev. 639, 664 (1982), suggests a number of other possible definitions of value and states that the appropriate comparison under § 547(c)(5) should be between "the proceeds of the receivables actually liquidated after bankruptcy and the amount which would have been obtained if the receivables serving as collateral ninety days earlier had been liquidated in the same manner. In other words, if the receivables at bankruptcy were liquidated by collection, the comparison should be with the amounts actually collected from receivables serving as collateral ninety days before bankruptcy. If the receivables were liquidated by sale, the comparison should be with the amount which would have been received had the receivables serving as collateral ninety days before bankruptcy been sold."

The valuation problem in § 547(c)(5) regarding inventory is more complex. If the unit value of inventory is constant and the number of units of inventory on hand at the date of bankruptcy is greater than the number of units on hand at the beginning of the preference period, § 547(c)(5) can be properly applied to make voidable as a preference the improvement in position represented by the increased number of units. But in some cases the value of a secured party's collateral may increase during the preference period without the increase being preferential. To take a case not covered by § 547(c)(5) suppose Secured Party has an indefeasible security interest in a piece of equipment. With Secured Party's consent the equipment is sold during the 90–day period. Secured

Party gets a perfected security interest in the identifiable cash proceeds. § 9–306(2) and (3). Because of § 547(e)(3) the attachment of the security interest to the cash is considered to be a transfer to Secured Party when Debtor received the cash. But a security interest that passes from the original collateral to the cash proceeds is not preferential because the case can be analyzed simply as a contemporaneous exchange in which the proceeds are substituted for the original collateral. Whether or not the original collateral appreciated in value from the time of the original secured transaction would be immaterial. That increase was not the result of any transfer from the debtor. Under the UCC security interests attach to property of the debtor not to the value represented by the property. It seems quite clear that if a secured party has a security interest in a unit of oil which doubles in value because of a change in world oil prices the secured party is entitled to the benefit of the increase in value. The security interest is in the unit of oil not in its value. As is the case generally with owners of property interests, the secured party takes the risk, and gets the benefit, of any change in value of the interest owned. Section 547(c)(5) does not seem to be directed at this kind of problem. Rather it seems more likely that the case of an increase in the number of units of inventory may have been in mind when it was written. If § 547(c)(5) is read to be applicable to any improvement of position regardless of whether it results from a transfer from the debtor, it has been argued that there is no voidable preference because of the phrase "to the prejudice of the creditors holding unsecured claims." The theory is that the increase in value was not given to the secured party by the use of assets otherwise available to unsecured creditors. Unsecured creditors never had any claim to the asset that increased in value so the increase in value doesn't hurt them. Collier on Bankruptcy ¶ 547.13 (15th ed. 1987).

But there is a limitation to the conclusions just expressed. Sometimes an increase in value of inventory is the result of an investment in labor or materials. The best example is a security interest in inventory consisting of unfinished goods. As those goods are transformed into finished goods by new value contributed by the debtor § 547(c)(5) may properly be read to mean that the secured party is the recipient of preferential transfers from the debtor to the extent of the new value. Collier on Bankruptcy ¶ 547.13 (15th ed. 1987).

The case that follows considers the question of how the inventory of a retailer should be valued for the purposes of Section 547(c)(5).

IN RE EBBLER FURNITURE & APPLIANCES, INC.

United States Court of Appeals, Seventh Circuit, 1986.
804 F.2d 87.

FLAUM, CIRCUIT JUDGE.

This suit involves an issue of first impression in this circuit. We are asked to define the word "value" as used in § 547(c)(5). We affirm the bankruptcy court and district court in their use of "cost" as the proper measurement in this case. However, we remand this case for further proceedings to determine the precise amount of the preference payment that the defendant received.

I.

The present action is by the trustee in bankruptcy under §§ 547(b) and (c)(5) (1986), to recover preference payments received by the defendant. Ebbler Furniture and Appliance, Inc. ("Ebbler"), filed a voluntary petition for relief pursuant to the Chapter 7 liquidation provisions of the Bankruptcy Code.

The appellant, Alton Bank & Trust Co. ("the Bank"), was the inventory financier for Ebbler. * * *

II.

A.

When a court reviews a bankruptcy court decision on appeal the court must adopt the bankruptcy court's findings of fact unless clearly erroneous. In re Kimzey, 761 F.2d 421, 423 (7th Cir.1985); In re Evanston Motor Company, Inc., 735 F.2d 1029, 1031 (7th Cir. 1984). The clearly erroneous rule does not apply to review of the bankruptcy court's conclusions of law. In re Kimzey, 761 F.2d 421, 423 (7th Cir.1985).

This case involves a mixed question of fact and law. The definition of value in § 547(c)(5) is a legal question, which depends on factual determinations made by the bankruptcy court. The factual determinations are subject to the clearly erroneous standard; but the manner in which these factual conclusions implicate the legal definition of value is subject to a *de novo* review. We note, however, that by deferring to these initial factual determinations, subject to review by the district courts, we are not abdicating our role as the reviewer of the definition of value adopted by the lower courts.

B.

The issue presented is the interpretation of "value" as used in § 547(c)(5) of the Bankruptcy Code. Section 547(c)(5) applies to situations where a secured creditor does not have sufficient collateral to cover his outstanding debt. Subparagraph five (5) codifies the "improvement in position test" and overrules an earlier line of cases such as Grain Merchants of Indiana, Inc. v. Union Bank & Savings Co., 408 F.2d 209 (7th Cir.), cert. denied, 396 U.S. 827, 90 S.Ct. 75, 24 L.Ed.2d 78 (1969). Section 547(c)(5) prevents a secured creditor from improving its position at the expense of an unsecured creditor during the 90 days prior to filing the bankruptcy petition. See generally 4A Collier on Bankruptcy ¶ 547.41, p. 547–133 (15th ed.).

The first step in applying section 547(c)(5) is to determine the amount of the loan outstanding 90 days prior to filing and the "value" of the collateral on that day. The difference between these figures is then computed. Next, the same determinations are made as of the date of filing the petition. A comparison is made, and, if there is a reduction during the 90 day period of the amount by which the initially existing debt exceeded the security, then a preference for section 547(c)(5) purposes exists. See generally 4A Collier on Bankruptcy ¶ 547.41. The effect of section 547(c)(5) is to make the security interest voidable to the extent of the preference. Id. at p. 547–134. Of course, if the creditor is fully secured 90 days before the filing of the petition, then that creditor will never be subject to a preference attack. Id.; see also Matter of Missionary Baptist Foundation, 796 F.2d 752, 760 n. 11 (5th Cir.1986).

C.

The language of section 547(c)(5), the "value of all security interest for such debt," was purposely left without a precise definition. See generally H.R. No. 595, S.Rep. No. 989, 95th Cong., 2d Sess., reprinted in 1978 U.S.Code Cong. & Ad.News, 5787, 6176; N. Cohen, "Value" Judgments: Account Receivable Financing and Voidable Preferences Under the New Bankruptcy Code, 66 Minn. L.Rev. 639, 653 (1982) (hereinafter "Cohen"); In re Beattie, 31 B.R. 703, 714 (W.D.N.C.1983). Furthermore, it has been persuasively argued that the other Bankruptcy Code sections' definitions of "value" would not be useful for section 547(c)(5) purposes. Cohen, supra, at 651–654. Thus, the only legislative guidance is "that we are to determine value on case-by-case basis, taking into account the facts of each case and the competing interests in the case." Matter of Lackow Bros., Inc., 752 F.2d 1529, 1532 (11th Cir.1985)

* * *

The method used to value the collateral is crucial in determining whether or not the bank received a preference. The Bank urges that we adopt an "ongoing concern" [2] value standard, which,

---

2. The authors of Collier on Bankruptcy suggest that in a liquidation case under chapter 7, "it would seem that liquidation value should be used, al-though other standards of value may be appropriate under certain circumstances. In a case under chapter 9, 11, or 13, it would seem that a going con-

in this case, would be cost plus a 60% mark-up. The Bank relies on *Lackow Bros.,* supra, as authority for the use of this definition of value. We find *Lackow Bros.* readily distinguishable. There, the only evidence of value before the court was ongoing concern value. As the Eleventh Circuit stated: "The only evidence in the record of value for the ninetieth day prior to the filing of the bankruptcy is the ongoing concern value; therefore, this is the *only* standard of valuation that can be applied to determine if Creditor's position improved * * *." *Lackow Bros.* at 1532.

Another view as to how value should be defined is proposed by Professor Cohen. He proposes an after-the-fact determination of value. In his article discussing accounts receivable, Cohen argues that the courts should look at the actual manner in which the collateral was liquidated, i.e. cost or ongoing concern. Whatever method is used to dispose of the collateral, Cohen argues, should be used to value the collateral 90 days before the filing of the bankruptcy petition. *Cohen,* supra, at 664. At least one circuit has found Cohen's reasoning useful, though not necessarily adopting it as a rigid rule. Matter of Missionary Baptist Foundation, 796 F.2d 752, 761–62 (5th Cir.1986).

In *Missionary Baptist Foundation,* supra, the appellate court remanded to the district court for factual determinations as to whether or not the bank improved its position during the preference period. Id. at 761. The court noted, however, that merely remanding for factual findings may not be sufficient in light of the ambiguous meaning of "value" in section 547(c)(5). Id. at 761–62. The Fifth Circuit quoted with approval Cohen's admonition of an individualized approach in defining value and his hindsight solution of the problem. We follow the Fifth Circuit's lead and hold that under section 547(c)(5) value should be defined on a case by case basis, with the factual determinations of the bankruptcy court controlling.

D.

In the present case we affirm the bankruptcy court's use of cost as the method for valuing the collateral for section 547(c)(5) purposes. * * *

EASTERBROOK, CIRCUIT JUDGE, concurring.

This case involves the meaning of "value" under § 547(c)(5). I join the court's opinion, which concludes that the statute does not require bankruptcy judges to use one universal definition. The

cern value should be used although liquidation value may be appropriate in certain cases." 4A Collier on Bankruptcy ¶ 547.41, at 547–135; *Lackow Bros.,* 752 F.2d at 1532. We deem it inappropriate to bind this circuit to these distinctions at the present time. We note, however, that the Eleventh Circuit has cited this distinction, although commenting that it "is not set in cement." Id. We believe that the definition of "value" should be individualized and variable enough so as to be tailored to each situation.

history of condemnation litigation shows that a single definition of "value" is not within judicial grasp. Still, we need not leave bankruptcy judges and litigants adrift. Security interests must be appraised with some frequency in bankruptcy litigation. The greater the uncertainty in the legal rule, the harder it is to settle pending cases. "Anything goes" is not a durable rule. The parties cannot know their entitlements until bankruptcy, district, and appellate courts have spoken. One important function of appellate courts is to provide additional clarity, when that is reasonably possible. It is possible here. The bankruptcy judge did better than to avoid an abuse of discretion. He decided the case correctly.

"Value" is defined for a purpose, which sets limits on the admissible standards of appraisal even though it does not govern all cases. Section 547(c)(5) requires the court to find whether the secured creditor improved its position at the expense of other investors during the 90 days before the filing of the petition in bankruptcy. This calls for two appraisals, one on the day of filing and one 90 days earlier, using the same method each time, to see whether there was an improvement in position. The only standard that might plausibly be used in this case is wholesale cost of goods, because that is the only standard that could have been applied on both dates.

Wholesale cost is also the appropriate standard as a rule because wholesale and retail goods are different things. A furniture store, a supermarket, or the manufacturer of a product (the three situations are identical) uses raw materials purchased at wholesale to produce a new item. In the retailing business the difference between the wholesale price and the retail price is the "value added" of the business. It is the amount contributed by storing, inspecting, displaying, hawking, collecting for, delivering, and handling warranty claims on the goods. This difference covers the employees' wages, rent and utilities of the premises, interest on the cost of goods, bad debts, repairs, the value of entrepreneurial talent, and so on. The increment of price is attributable to this investment of time and other resources. The Bank does not have a security interest in these labors. It has an interest only in its merchandise and cash on hand.* The value of its interest depends on what the Bank could do, outside of bankruptcy, to realize on its security. See Thomas H. Jackson, Avoiding Powers in Bankruptcy, 36 Stan.L.Rev. 725, 756–77 (1984). What it could do is seize and sell the inventory. It would get at most the wholesale price—maybe less because the Bank would sell

* The Bank's interest in the proceeds of sales is not the same as an interest in the whole retail price for unsold inventory. An ongoing financing arrangement provides for operating expenses, too, to come out of proceeds. The security interest on any given day covers only identified proceeds, an asset that is identifiable and significantly smaller than the wholesale or retail value of the entire inventory.

the goods "as is" and would not offer the wholesaler's usual services to its customer. The Bank does not operate its own furniture store, and if it did it would still incur all the costs of retailing the goods, costs that would have to be subtracted from the retail price to determine the "value" of the inventory on the day the Bank seized it. Cf. Contrail Leasing Partners, Ltd. v. Consolidated Airways, Inc., 742 F.2d 1095, 1101 (7th Cir.1984); Uniform Commercial Code § 9–504(1)(a).

To give the Bank more than the wholesale value is to induce a spate of asset-grabbing among creditors, which could make all worse off. If the Bank gets the whole increment of value (from wholesale to retail) during the last 90 days, other creditors may respond by watching the debtor closely and propelling it into bankruptcy when it has a lower inventory (and therefore less "markup" for the Bank to seize). The premature filing may reduce the value of the enterprise. There are other defensive measures available to creditors. The principal function of § 547(c)(5) is to reduce the need of unsecured creditors to protect themselves against the last-minute moves of secured creditors. It would serve this function less well if goods subject to a security interest were appraised at their retail price.

Too, the Bank's security interest does not reach the "going concern" value of the debtor; it had security in the *goods,* not in the *firm.* To value the inventory in a way that reflects "going concern" value is to give the Bank something for which it did not contract. At all events, this wrinkle does not make a difference. If Ebbler had been sold as a going venture 90 days before the filing of the bankruptcy petition, the buyer of the business would have paid only wholesale price for Ebbler's inventory. If Ebbler had been at the peak of health, the buyer would have paid no more for inventory. A buyer would not have paid retail, because it would have had to invest the additional time and money necessary to obtain the retail price. So whether Ebbler is valued as a defunct business or as a going business sold to a hypothetical buyer on the critical date, wholesale is the right valuation, because it reflects the price that a willing buyer would pay after arms'-length negotiation. (The "going concern" value of Ebbler is reflected in its name, reputation, customer list, staff, and so on—things in which the Bank did not have a security interest.)

To put this differently, a willing buyer of a flourishing retail or manufacturing business will not pay more than the wholesale price for inventory of goods or parts on hand, because this buyer could purchase the same items on the market from the original sellers. Why pay Ebbler $500 for a sofa when you can get the same item for $200 from its manufacturer? Nothing would depend on whether Ebbler planned to stay in business. The court therefore properly does not allow the outcome of this case to turn on the fact that Ebbler chose a Chapter 7 liquidation rather than a Chapter 11 reorganization. Chapter titles are of little use in valuing assets under § 547(c)(5). A "liquidation" may be a sale of the business en bloc as an ongoing concern, and a "reorganization" may be a transition from one line of business to another.

The difference between the wholesale and retail prices of the inventory is the compensation that the other factors of production—the employees, landlords, utilities, etc.—obtain for their services. To appraise Ebbler's inventory at "retail" is to award to the Bank the entire value of the work done during the last 90 days by these other creditors of Ebbler. It is to allow the Bank to improve its position at their expense. Because a valuation at "retail" would produce exactly the consequence that § 547(c)(5) is designed to avert, the bankruptcy court wisely chose to appraise the goods at wholesale. The court leaves to another day the question whether retail price is ever an appropriate measure of value under § 547(c)(5). The observation that the bankruptcy court has leeway, however, does not imply that the court's discretion should be exercised without reference to the function of § 547(c)(5) and the limits of the security interest.

6. SECURITY INTERESTS IN CASH PROCEEDS

Under § 9–306(2) if collateral is disposed of, the secured party is given a security interest in identifiable proceeds resulting from the disposition. If the proceeds are "cash proceeds," defined in § 9–306(1) as "money, checks, deposit accounts and the like," the security interest is continuously perfected. § 9–306(3)(b). Although the Code does not state how the key word "identifiable" is to be defined, some cases do not cause difficulty. If an undeposited check was given by a buyer in payment for a purchase of collateral the check is identifiable as cash proceeds. Similarly, with respect to currency or deposit accounts (§ 9–105(1)(e)) there is no problem of identification if there is no commingling of proceeds and nonproceeds. The meaning of "identifiable" in the case of commingling, however, is not clearly indicated by § 9–306. The courts, however, have allowed secured parties to identify cash proceeds in a commingled account by tracing rules in effect in the jurisdiction. § 1–103. See *Harley–Davidson*, p. 161 and Note 3 on p. 170.

The problem of interpretation of "identifiable" in § 9–306(2) is complicated by the fact that § 9–306(4) contains a detailed statement of the secured party's rights to proceeds, and particularly rights in commingled deposit accounts, in the event debtor is in an insolvency proceeding, which in most cases means bankruptcy. Since the question of rights to cash proceeds will usually arise in bankruptcy, subsection (4) is of paramount importance. The two cases that follow interpret this provision. Both cases were decided under the Bankruptcy Act and *Gibson Products* assumes that the applicable preference rule regarding floating liens is that stated in *Grain Merchants,* discussed on pp. 402–404.

MATTER OF GIBSON PRODUCTS OF ARIZONA

United States Court of Appeals, Ninth Circuit, 1976.
543 F.2d 652.

HUFSTEDLER, CIRCUIT JUDGE. On this appeal we must referee a collision between the "proceeds" provision of the Uniform Commercial Code (U.C.C. § 9–306(4)) [1] and the bankruptcy trustee's power to avoid preferences under Section 60 of the Bankruptcy Act. The provisions collide under circumstances that place the creditor, asserting a perfected security interest in the debtor's bank account, in the dimmest equitable light: If the creditor prevails, it receives $19,505.27 from the debtor's account on proof that the debtor, within ten days of the insolvency, deposited $10 in the account from the sale of a hair dryer in which the creditor had a perfected security interest. The district court affirmed the bankruptcy judge's order awarding $19,505.27 to the secured creditor. We reverse because we conclude that the operation of U.C.C. Section 9–306(4)(d) created a voidable preference by the transfer to the creditor of a perfected security interest in the cash deposited in the debtor's account that exceeded the amount of the creditor's proceeds.

The creditor, Arizona Wholesale Supply Co. ("Wholesale") sold General Electric and Proctor-Silex appliances to the debtor, Gibson Products of Arizona ("Gibson"). Wholesale has a perfected security interest in the appliances. On January 13, 1972, Gibson initiated Chapter XI proceedings. During the ten-day period immediately preceding the institution of these proceedings, Gibson deposited $19,505.27 in its bank account. During the same period, Gibson deposited in the account $10 from the sale of a Proctor-Silex dryer.[3] At the time insolvency proceedings were instituted, Gibson was indebted to Wholesale in the amount of $28,800 for the appliances it had sold to Gibson and for which it has perfected security interests.

* * *

The proceeds section of the Code generally follows the pre-Code law that a security interest continues in any identifiable

1. * * * We also use the text of U.C.C. § 9–306 prior to the 1972 amendments because Arizona did not adopt the 1972 amendments until 1975, effective January 1, 1976, a date long after this litigation began. * * * The 1972 amendments, even if applicable, do not affect the issues in this case.

3. No other sales during the 10-day period were proved, regardless of the

disposition of the proceeds. Under these circumstances, some alternative interpretations of U.C.C. § 9–306(4)(d) were not advanced and are not before us. Wholesale tried, but failed to prove that the proceeds from the sale of some television sets were also deposited in the account during the ten-day period.

proceeds received by the debtor from the sale or other disposition of the collateral. The Code's new twist is extending the creditor's security interest to commingled funds without specifically tracing the creditor's proceeds into the fund, when the debtor has become insolvent. (U.C.C. § 9–306(4)(d).) No collision between the proceeds provision of the Code and the preference sections of the Bankruptcy Act occurs when the creditor's perfected security interest in his collateral is attached to the proceeds from the sale or other disposition of the collateral if (1) his interest was initially perfected in the collateral more than four months before bankruptcy, and (2) he can identify the proceeds to which his security interest has attached. Under these circumstances, the creditor has priority over later creditors when he first perfected his security interest, and his priority relates back to his initial perfection. (Cf. DuBay v. Williams (9th Cir. 1969) 417 F.2d 1277, 1286–87.) The problem arises in the U.C.C. Section 9–306(4)(d) situation because that subsection gives the secured creditor a perfected security interest in the entire amount deposited by the debtor within ten days before bankruptcy without limiting the interest to the amount that can be identified as the proceeds from the sale of the creditor's collateral. With respect to the funds that are not the creditor's proceeds, the creditor has no security interest except that conferred by U.C.C. Section 9–306(4)(d). His interest in these nonproceeds arises upon the occurrence of two events: (1) insolvency proceedings instituted by or against a debtor, and (2) commingling of some of the proceeds from his collateral with the debtor's cash on hand or with other deposits in this debtor's bank account. His security interest is limited to an "amount not greater than the amount of any cash proceeds received by the debtor within ten days before institution of the insolvency proceedings" and is subject to the additional set-offs in Section 9–306(4)(d).

The draftsmen's intent was not to deliver a security bonanza to any secured creditor. As Professor Gilmore observes: "It goes without saying that a provision of state law which purported to give a secured creditor greater rights in the event his debtor's estate was administered in bankruptcy than he would have apart from bankruptcy would be invalid. However, * * * § 9–306(4) does not in the least aim at such a result. Indeed, § 9–306(4) is the reverse of such a statute, since it sharply cuts back the secured party's rights when insolvency proceedings are initiated." (2 G. Gilmore, Security Interests in Personal Property 45.9, at 1337–38 (1965). The intent was to eliminate the expense and nuisance of tracing when funds are commingled and to limit the grasp of secured creditors to the amount received during the last ten days before insolvency proceedings, which, the draftsmen assumed, would usually be less than the same creditor could trace if he had a grip on the entire balance deposited over an unlimited time. (Id. at 1340.) On that assumption, awarding a perfected security interest to the secured creditor, good for a short time on the entire balance, gives the secured creditor no windfall to the detriment of general creditors. On our facts, the contrary is true.

When confronted with an analogous situation, the Seventh Circuit limited the secured creditor's interest to those proceeds in the bank account traceable to the sale of the creditor's collateral. The Seventh Circuit's theory was that the term "any cash proceeds" used in Section 9–306(4)(d) does not refer to all receipts from any source deposited in the bank account, but, instead, refers to "proceeds" as defined in Section 9–306(1), and thus the phrase means "cash proceeds from the sale of collateral in which the creditor had a security interest." (Fitzpatrick v. Philco Finance Corp. (7th Cir. 1974) 491 F.2d 1288, 1291–92.)

Although we reach a similar result, we reject the Seventh Circuit's reasoning because, in our view, that construction impermissibly bends the language and structure of Section 9–306. The general definition of "proceeds" in Section 9–306(1) cannot be transplanted into Section 9–306(4) shorn of its statutory freight. The statute divides "proceeds" into two categories, "identifiable" and "commingled," i.e., nonidentifiable proceeds, and alters the reach of a perfected security interest, depending upon whether the proceeds are identifiable or nonidentifiable. (Compare § 9–306(4) (a), (b), (c) with § 9–306(4)(d).) Section 9–306(4)(d) deals only with nonidentifiable cash proceeds. If the cash proceeds could be "identified," i.e., had not been commingled, the secured party would have a perfected security interest in the whole fund under Section 9–306(4)(b), just as he did in pre-Code days, without any of the limitations imposed by Section 9–306(4)(d). Under the Code scheme, the secured creditor also has a perfected security interest under subsection (d) when he cannot identify his proceeds in the commingled fund, as long as he can show that some of his proceeds were among those in the commingled fund. (See Section 9–306, Comment in U.C.C.Rep.Serv., Current Materials, 9306, at 60 (1968); Gilmore, supra, § 45.9, at 1336–37.)

We leave the language of Section 9–306(4) as it was drafted and apply Section 60 of the Bankruptcy Act to resolve the problem. As defined by Section 60a(1), a preference is "[1] a transfer * * * of the property of a debtor [2] to or for the benefit of a creditor [3] for or on account of an antecedent debt, [4] made or suffered by such debtor while insolvent and [5] within four months before the filing * * * [of bankruptcy], [6] the effect of which transfer will be to enable such creditor to obtain a greater percentage of his debt than some other creditor of the same class." Section 60a(2) of the Bankruptcy Act provides that "a transfer of property * * * shall be deemed to have been made or suffered at the time when it became so far perfected that no subsequent lien upon such property obtainable by legal or equitable proceedings on a simple contract could become superior to the rights of the transferee." As we held in DuBay v. Williams, supra, 417 F.2d at 1287:

> " 'Transfer' for the purpose of section 60a(2) is thus equated with the act by which priority over later creditors is achieved and not with the event which attaches the security interest to a specific account."

With respect to Wholesale's security interest in the proceeds from the sale of the collateral, no later creditor could obtain priority over Wholesale from the time its financing statement was filed and further perfected pursuant to Section 9–306(3), at least until Wholesale's proceeds were commingled with that of other secured creditors or with cash from other sources deposited in Gibson's bank account. Wholesale's security interest in those proceeds relates back to its initial financing statement. (Cf. Du-Bay v. Williams, supra, 417 F.2d at 1287–88.) However, Wholesale had no interest in cash other than its own proceeds, and hence no priority over later creditors in such cash, until (1) some part of Wholesale's proceeds were deposited with other cash in Gibson's bank account, (2) within ten days of Gibson's filing its Chapter XI petition. The effect of Section 9–306(4) is thus to transfer to Wholesale a security interest in the cash in Gibson's bank account which does not derive from the sale of its collateral. In this situation, the act that gives Wholesale priority and the events that attach the security interest to the question asset occur at the same time. The transfer cannot occur earlier than ten days before the institution of bankruptcy. The transfer of the excess, above the wholesaler's proceeds, is a preference unless we can say that the transfer was neither for nor on account of an antecedent debt. We cannot avoid the conclusion that the transfer was on account of an antecedent debt. Wholesale could not qualify for Section 9–306(4) treatment absent the antecedent debt; moreover, the transfer does not happen unless the debt owed exceeds the payments made to the creditor during the ten-day period before the bankruptcy petition has been filed.

The result is that Wholesale cannot successfully assert its claim under U.C.C. Section 9–306(4)(d) to thwart the trustee's power to set that interest aside as a preference. However, the conclusion does not necessarily also follow that the creditor loses his security interest both in the proceeds from the sale of his collateral and in the nonproceeds in the debtor's bank account. In his contest with the trustee, he only loses his claim to the amounts in excess of his proceeds because only that amount is a preference. His security interest in the whole account, subject to the limitations of U.C.C. Section 9–306(4), is valid except that the trustee can avoid it. To the extent that a creditor is able to identify his proceeds to trace their path into the commingled funds, he will be able to defeat *pro tanto* the trustee's assertion of a preference.

By this construction of Section 60 of the Bankruptcy Act and Section 9–306(4) of the U.C.C., we do violence neither to statute nor to substantial justice among the parties. The creditor's security interest in the whole account under Section 9–306(4) is *prima facie* valid, except as to the trustee, and, as to him, the creditor's security interest is presumptively preferential. The creditor can rebut the presumption by appropriately tracing his proceeds. We think that it is fair to place the burden on the creditor to identify his own proceeds and thus to defeat, in whole or in part, the trustee's claim of preference. The creditor is in a better position than the trustee to trace his proceeds; moreover, if the creditor wants to avoid both the limitations of U.C.C. Section 9–306(4)(d) and the burden of proof in a potential contest with the trustee, all he needs to do is to prevent commingling of his proceeds and thus to follow U.C.C. Section 9–306(4)(a)–(c).

Reversed and remanded for further proceedings consistent with the views herein expressed.

MATTER OF GUARANTEED MUFFLER SUPPLY CO.

United States Bankruptcy Court, N.D. Georgia, 1980.
5 B.R. 236.

A. D. KAHN, BANKRUPTCY JUDGE. Before the court is Plaintiff/ Trustee's motion for "judgment on the pleadings regarding the specific issue of law whether the application of UCC § 9–306(4)(d) (1962) shall be limited by National Bank of Georgia's having to trace the proceeds from the disposition of each piece of [property in which NBG holds a valid security interest]." The court will interpret the Trustee's motion to constitute a request for a ruling that would limit a secured party's proceeds claim under UCC § 9– 306(4)(d)[1] to those proceeds which are appropriately identified as having been collected upon disposition of property which is validly encumbered by the secured party's lien. For the reasons outlined below, the court is inclined to grant the Trustee's request.

1. As pointed out by previous order, the 1962 version of the U.C.C. governs the instant case. * * *

The applicable provision provides, in pertinent part, as follows:

(4) In the event of insolvency proceedings instituted by or against a debtor, a secured party with a perfected security interest in proceeds has a perfected security interest

* * *

(d) in all cash and bank accounts of the debtor, if other cash proceeds have been commingled or deposited in a bank account, but the perfected security interest under this paragraph (d) is

(i) subject to any right of set-off; and (ii) limited to an amount not greater than the amount of any cash proceeds received by the debtor within 10 days before the institution of the insolvency proceedings and commingled or deposited in a bank account prior to the insolvency proceedings less the amount of cash proceeds received by the debtor and paid over to the secured party during the 10-day period.

As explained more fully by court order entered November 27, 1979 (reported at 1 B.R. 324, 27 U.C.C.Rep. 1217), the relationship between the above-named parties was initiated in 1976 when Defendant National Bank of Georgia (NBG) took a security interest in all inventory and accounts owned by a predecessor partnership of the corporate Bankrupt. Some two years later, after the corporation was formed and the assets of the old partnership were transferred to the new entity, Defendant Hamilton took a security interest in all inventory and accounts of the newly formed corporation.

In March of 1979, the corporation filed a petition in bankruptcy, but the lien-holding Defendants and the Trustee could not resolve their conflicting claims to property of the estate. The Trustee, therefore, commenced the above-styled proceeding to resolve the conflict.

Although Defendant Hamilton's lien on property of the estate is subordinate to those claims which NBG validly asserts to the same property (see UCC § 9–312(5) and order entered February 6, 1980), the court made clear in its November 1979 order that NBG's lien on property of the estate is limited to the following: (1) partnership accounts and inventory which survived until the date of bankruptcy; (2) proceeds collected by the partnership upon sale of the accounts and inventory; and (3) proceeds collected by the now bankrupt corporation upon its sale of partnership property encumbered by NBG's lien. These limitations are imposed upon NBG's lien because NBG failed to obtain a security interest in property of the corporate entity and because no party has urged the court to pierce the corporate veil.

Of tremendous practical significance is the fact that NBG may assert a lien on property which is alleged to constitute proceeds only after it is shown that the property is indeed the fruit obtained upon disposition of NBG's collateral. This requirement is otherwise known as the requirement that proceeds be "identifiable." UCC § 9–306 (1962) * * *.

Since NBG's claim to property of the estate is largely rooted in U.C.C. article 9 proceeds theory, the court declared in its November order that the general U.C.C. restrictions placed upon proceeds rights should apply not only to NBG's claims to proceeds collected by the partnership, but also to NBG's claims to proceeds collected by the corporate Bankrupt, (otherwise known as the "transferee's proceeds"). One such restriction discussed in the order was the one found in U.C.C. § 9–306(4)(d) (1962) which "eliminates secured parties' rights in cash proceeds which are on hand as of the date of a bankruptcy unless a secured party can show that the cash was collected within ten days before bankruptcy or that the cash was not mingled with [non-proceeds] cash." In

Re Guaranteed Muffler Supply Co., Inc., 1 B.R. 324, 329, 27 U.C.C. Rep. 1217, 1224 (Bkrtcy.N.D.Ga.1979).

That characterization of the nature of U.C.C. § 9–306(4)(d) implicitly answers the question posed by the Trustee's motion. The court's view of § 9–306(4)(d) as a provision which RESTRICTS secured parties' claims to proceeds is an implicit rejection of any interpretation of § 9–306(4)(d) through which secured parties obtain greater lien rights than they would in the absence of § 9–306(4)(d).

Admittedly, at least one court has taken the position that U.C.C. § 9–306(4)(d) "gives the secured creditor a perfected security interest in the entire amount [of cash proceeds] deposited [or received] by the debtor within ten days before bankruptcy without limiting the interest to the amount that can be identified as the proceeds from the sale of the creditor's collateral." In Re Gibson Products of Arizona, 543 F.2d 652, 655 (9th Cir.), cert. denied 430 U.S. 946, 97 S.Ct. 1586, 51 L.Ed.2d 794 (1976). The *Gibson Products* court elaborated on its position by stating that "with respect to the funds that are not the creditor's proceeds, the creditor has no security interest except that conferred by UCC Section 9–306(4)(d)." Id. at 655.

It is this court's position that the *Gibson Products* view misinterprets the language and logic of the UCC proceeds section.[3] Although the *Gibson Products* court ultimately relied upon bankruptcy preference law to invalidate that portion of the secured party's claim to proceeds conferred solely by § 9–306(4)(d), this court is of the opinion that there is absolutely no conflict between § 9–306(4)(d) and the Bankruptcy Act.[4] Accord Fitzpatrick v. Philco Finance Corp., 491 F.2d 1288 (7th Cir. 1974). To create a false conflict in this circumstance is not only to raise complicated questions involving the meaning of a preferential "transfer," [5] but also to cause unnecessary argument about the extent to which portions of the UCC are to be invalidated as disguised state priorities or voidable statutory liens. See In Re Dexter Buick—GMG Truck Co., 2 B.R. 242 (Bkrtcy. D.R.I.1980).

The point of departure between the position taken by this court and the Ninth Circuit *Gibson Products* panel is rooted in conflicting views about the very nature of secured parties' rights

---

3. Leading commentators have referred to the *Gibson Products* view as "not defensible." J. White & R. Summers, Uniform Commercial Code 1016 (2d ed. 1980).

4. Although the instant case is governed by the old Bankruptcy Act, the proceeds analysis which appears herein is relevant in cases pending under the new Bankruptcy Code. See especially 11 U.S.C. § 552.

5. The existence of a "transfer" is a prerequisite to the finding of a voidable preference. See, e.g., First Nat'l Bank of Clinton v. Julian, 383 F.2d 329, 334 (8th Cir. 1967) (proceeds claims which arose within four months of bankruptcy held not to constitute a transfer, since the proceeds claims which arose during the four-month period were a mere surrogate for the original collateral, in which the secured party had lost its lien).

to proceeds. Such rights are obtained by authority of UCC § 9–306(2), which states that an article nine lien "continues in collateral notwithstanding [an unauthorized] sale, and also continues in any identifiable proceeds * * *." This important provision makes proceeds claims, by definition, depend upon a showing that the property claimed is identified as the fruit of a sale or other disposition of the original collateral. Thus, a right to proceeds of any kind, whether in bankruptcy or not, arises out of the language of § 9–306(2); the limitations upon "cash proceeds" listed in § 9–306(4)(d)(ii), therefore include, by definition, the identifiability limitations which apply to all claims made to all proceeds.[6] To require that proceeds claims be so limited is consistent with the fact that the exercise of lien rights is confined to specific property which the debtor has chosen to make available as a surrogate for his own performance.

Accordingly, the Trustee's motion is hereby GRANTED. No secured party in this proceeding may claim property of the estate on the basis of U.C.C. article nine proceeds theory unless the property is shown to have been collected upon the disposition of property in which the secured party held a valid lien.

NOTE

In Ford Motor Credit Co. v. Troy Bank & Trust Co., 76 B.R. 836 (M.D.Ala.1986), Bank had a perfected security interest in Dealer's inventory, except for new automobiles, and the proceeds from the sale of that inventory. Financer had a security interest in Dealer's new automobile inventory and the proceeds from the sale of that inventory. Dealer commingled the proceeds from the sale of both kinds of collateral in its bank account and filed in bankruptcy. Both secured parties claimed the proceeds in the account from the sale of their collateral. The court noted that § 9–306(4)(d) prescribes how a single creditor's interest is to be determined in a commingled account but is silent on how to treat multiple security interests. Since the security interests were in different collateral, the first-to-file rule of § 9–312(5) was inapplicable. The court stated:

> * * * the fairer and more logical reading of subsection (4)(d) is that competing creditors obtain their perfected interest at the same time under the subsection; the subsection's transformation of the nature of a secured creditor's perfected interests occurs when insolvency proceedings are initiated against the debtor, and this is simultaneous for all such creditors. It then follows that, there being a tie for all secured creditors under

6. As the Seventh Circuit has pointed out, state law which governs the creation of consensual liens on personalty "also limits the application [of such liens] to co-mingled proceeds in the event of insolvency * * *." Fitzpatrick v. Philco Finance Corp., 491 F.2d 1288, 1291 (7th Cir. 1974).

subsection (4)(d), the appropriate division of the bank account should be pro-rata. * * * first, each creditor is to determine how much it is entitled to as a secured creditor with a perfected interest according to the formula set forth in subsection (4)(d); second, the two creditors are then to prorate the * * * bank account between themselves accordingly * * *.

76 B.R. at 839.

PROBLEM

Secured Party has a perfected security interest in all of the inventory of Debtor. During the ten days preceding Debtor's filing of a petition in bankruptcy Debtor received $20,000 in proceeds of inventory all of which was deposited into Debtor's checking account. Assume that application of the lowest-intermediate-balance rule set forth in *Funk*, p. 170, will determine that at the beginning of the 10-day period the balance of $3,000 in Debtor's checking account was made up of $1,000 of proceeds deposited before the 10-day period and $2,000 of nonproceeds. During the 10-day period no payments were made by Debtor to Secured Party and Debtor made the following deposits to the account and payments to third parties from the account.

	Deposit Proceeds	Deposit Nonproceeds	Payment to Third Parties	Balance
Day 1				$ 3,000
3	$9,000			12,000
5	9,000			21,000
6			$20,000	1,000
7		$20,000		21,000
9	2,000			23,000

Secured Party and the trustee in bankruptcy both make claims to Debtor's checking account. How much goes to each by applying § 9–306(4)(d)? Assuming that Debtor was insolvent at all times during the 10-day period, is any amount to which Secured Party is entitled under § 9–306(4)(d) voidable as a preference? If a judgment creditor of Debtor had obtained a judicial lien on Debtor's checking account just prior to the filing of the petition in bankruptcy what would the priorities have been between the judgment creditor and Secured Party to the $23,000 balance? § 9–306(2). Is Secured Party's security interest in the deposit account subject to attack under Bankruptcy Code § 544(a)?

7. FALSE PREFERENCES: DELAYED PERFECTION OF SECURITY INTERESTS

We have already dealt with the problem of secured creditors who give credit to a debtor in what is a secured transaction but in which there is some delay between the time the credit is granted and the time that the security interest attaches to secure the credit. Since the attaching of the security interest is a transfer of property of the debtor on account of the antecedent debt arising from the credit, there is a prima facie voidable preference if the other elements of § 547(b) are present. If the delay is very short the security interest may, under some circumstances, be saved by § 547(c)(1). If the credit was for the purpose of enabling the debtor to acquire the collateral which secures the debt the security interest may be saved if there was compliance with § 547(c)(3). In all of these cases the problem arises because of a delay in the creation of the security interest.

A superficially similar but entirely distinct problem arises when the granting of the credit and the creation of the security interest are contemporaneous, but there is a delay between the creation, or attachment, of the security interest and the perfection of the security interest. There is no true preference in these cases because the transfer of the security interest to the creditor was not on account of an antecedent debt. The problem of delayed perfection is the evil of the secret lien. The classic case is that of a debtor in financial difficulty who wants to conceal from general creditors the true state of the debtor's financial condition. The debtor obtains an emergency loan from a creditor and grants to that creditor a mortgage on real property or a security interest in personal property to secure the loan. The property involved might well be most of the debtor's previously unencumbered assets. If public notice of the transaction were given by recording the mortgage or filing a financing statement with respect to the security interest, the result might be that other creditors would be deterred from giving to the debtor further unsecured credit because of the absence of unencumbered assets. To avoid this result the creditor might be induced not to record the mortgage or file the financing statement. Essentially the issue is fraud on creditors, not preference. Usually, an unrecorded mortgage of real property has priority over the claim of a creditor who subsequently levies on the property. The holder of an unperfected security interest in personal property takes a greater risk by not promptly perfecting because an unperfected Article 9 security interest does not have priority over a subsequent judicial lien. But in either case the creditor can protect the lien by promptly perfecting at the first sign that other creditors may either levy on assets of the debtor or file a petition for involuntary bankruptcy against the debtor. In the classic case, the creditor is an insider with access to information that provides some assurance that the creditor will have sufficient advance notice of facts that will allow the creditor to perfect in time.

It is understandable that there should be a policy against secret liens, and such a policy was expressed in the Bankruptcy

Act. However, the technique used in the Bankruptcy Act to address the evil was unusual. Instead of dealing with the problem directly as a case of fraud on creditors, Congress discouraged the secret lien by a provision in Bankruptcy Act § 60a, the preference section. Since 1950, Bankruptcy Act § 60a(2) provided as follows:

> (2) For the purposes of subdivisions (a) and (b) of this section, a transfer of property other than real property shall be deemed to have been made or suffered at the time when it became so far perfected that no subsequent lien upon such property obtainable by legal or equitable proceedings on a simple contract could become superior to the rights of the transferee. A transfer of real property shall be deemed to have been made or suffered when it became so far perfected that no subsequent bona fide purchase from the debtor could create rights in such property superior to the rights of the transferee. If any transfer of real property is not so perfected against a bona fide purchase, or if any transfer of other property is not so perfected against such liens by legal or equitable proceedings prior to the filing of a petition initiating a proceeding under this title, it shall be deemed to have been made immediately before the filing of the petition.

This 1950 provision was the culmination of a series of amendments to § 60, dating as far back as 1903, designed to deal with the problem of secret liens. The effect of § 60a(2) was to convert what was not in fact a preferential lien into a preferential lien by a conclusive presumption that the lien became effective at the time it was perfected rather than at the time it was actually created. Certain grace periods were allowed for the creditor to perfect. If the creditor didn't perfect within these periods the effect was that the lien was treated as having been given for an antecedent debt. This technique of turning secret liens into false preferences was carried over into the Bankruptcy Code. The relevant provision is § 547(e)(2). The meaning of § 547(e)(2) is clarified in § 547(e)(1) which defines the term "perfected" and in § 547(e)(3) which in effect defines the earliest time a transfer can occur.

Section 547(e)(2) was designed to eliminate the evils of the secret lien, and it is effective in that regard. Unfortunately, it also has had the effect of ensnaring many hapless secured creditors who, through no fault of their own, were unable to perfect within the strict ten-day time limit.

IN RE ARNETT

United States Court of Appeals, Sixth Circuit, 1984.
731 F.2d 358.

MILES, DISTRICT JUDGE.

This is an appeal in bankruptcy. Plaintiff, the trustee in bankruptcy, appeals the order of the district court, 17 B.R. 912, affirming the decision of the bankruptcy court declining to set aside as a preferential transfer the security interest held by defendant-appellee Security Mutual Finance Corporation ("Security Mutual") in property of the debtors in bankruptcy and co-defendants-appellees in this proceeding, Burton and Charlotte Arnett.

On December 10, 1980, the Arnetts obtained a consolidation loan from Security Mutual, granting to Security Mutual a lien on their 1978 Volkswagen, which was at that time subject to a prior perfected lien held by defendant-appellee American National Bank ("ANB"). The loan obtained from Security Mutual thus included an amount sufficient to pay off the prior security interest. On December 10 or 11, 1980, Security Mutual mailed a check for the outstanding balance of the lien to ANB, requesting ANB to release its lien and forward the certificate of title to the vehicle to Security Mutual. ANB deposited the check on December 19, 1980. Because of the delayed holiday mails and employee absences, however, ANB did not release its lien and forward the certificate of title until January 9, 1981. Upon receiving the release, Security Mutual applied to the State of Tennessee Department of Motor Vehicles to note its lien on the certificate, as required by T.C.A. 55–3–119. The lien was perfected on January 12, 1981, 33 days after the granting of the security interest to Security Mutual.

On February 25, 1981, the Arnetts filed a voluntary petition for relief under Chapter 7 of the Bankruptcy Code. The trustee filed suit to set aside Security Mutual's lien on the Volkswagen as a voidable preference under § 547(b). The parties agreed to allow the vehicle to be sold to the debtors for $3,601.47 pending the outcome of this proceeding.

The bankruptcy judge ruled that Security Mutual's perfection of its security interest was "substantially contemporaneous" with the loan transaction, notwithstanding the 33-day hiatus and thus, that the transaction fell within the exception to the trustee's avoidance powers found at § 547(c)(1). See, In re Arnett, 13 B.R. 267 (Bkrtcy.E.D.Tenn.1981). The trustee unsuccessfully appealed to the district court, which upheld the bankruptcy court's decision. This appeal followed.

The sole issue before this Court is whether a delay of 33 days in perfection of a security interest is a "substantially contemporaneous exchange" under § 547(c)(1), thus excepted from the trustee's avoidance powers. Although the lower courts have been wrestling with this problem for some time, the issue has not yet been addressed by any of the circuit courts of appeals.

*   *   *

Relying on §§ 547(c)(3) and 547(e)(2)(A) and (B), the trustee contends that the contemporaneous exchange exception is inapplicable beyond 10 days of creation of Security Mutual's security interest, and thus, that the lien may be avoided. Section 547(c)(3), the so-called "enabling loan" provision, excepts from the trustee's avoidance powers security interests in property acquired by the debtor which are perfected within 10 days of creation. Section 547(e)(2) establishes when the "transfer" of a security interest is deemed to occur:

> (2) For the purposes of this section, except as provided in paragraph (3) of this subsection, a transfer is made—

> > (A) at the time such transfer takes effect between the transferor and the transferee, if such transfer is perfected at, or within 10 days after, such time;

> > (B) at the time such transfer is perfected, if such transfer is perfected after such 10 days;

Not persuaded that the 10-day limit established by the above two sections was incorporated *sub silentio* into the contemporaneous exchange exception, both the bankruptcy judge and the district judge ruled that "contemporaneity" is a question of fact to be evaluated in light of the parties' intent, the reasons for delay, and the risks of fraud and misrepresentation. The construction given to section 547(c)(1) by the lower courts in this case requires examination of all circumstances surrounding the transaction giving rise to the transfer. Thus, where delayed perfection of a security interest may be satisfactorily explained, and in the absence of dilatoriness or negligence on the part of a transferee, the transfer may still be found "substantially contemporaneous" with the exchange of new value to the debtor, regardless of the lapse of time.

*   *   *

Two elements are crucial to the establishment of the contemporaneous exchange exception: 1. The parties must intend that the exchange be substantially contemporaneous; 2. the exchange must *in fact* be substantially contemporaneous. § 547(c)(1); Butz v. Pingel, 17 B.R. 236 (Bkrtcy.S.D.Ohio 1982). There is no dispute here that the parties intended a contemporaneous exchange when the loan was obtained through the granting of a security interest to Security Mutual. Further, the parties do not dispute that the "transfer" here pertinent occurred when Security Mutual perfected its security interest 33 days later. In any case, section 547(e)(2) resolves any doubt by providing that the "transfer" of a security interest not perfected until after 10 days is deemed to occur at the date of perfection. Moreover, under Tennessee law, Security Mutual's lien was invalid until recorded on a certificate of title. T.C.A. 55–3–114, 123, 125, 126. Thus, the key inquiry is whether the exchange was "in fact" substantially contemporaneous.

The issue has frequently arisen in the context of the relationship between section 547(c)(1) and (c)(3). As previously noted, section 547(c)(3) excepts from avoidance so-called "enabling loans", or "purchase money loans", and prescribes a 10-day limit for perfection of security interest taken in such transactions. Some purchase-money lenders, having failed to meet the prescribed 10-day deadline, have argued that perfection of the purchase-money security interest was nonetheless substantially contemporaneous with the giving of "new value" to the debtor. See, e.g. In re Davis, 22 B.R. 644 (Bkrtcy.M.D.Ga.1982); In re Enlow, 20 B.R. 480 (Bkrtcy.Ind.1982); In re Burnette, 14 B.R. 795 (Bkrtcy.E.D.Tenn. 1981); In re Christian, 8 B.R. 816 (Bkrtcy.M.D.Fla.1981); In re Merritt, 7 B.R. 876 (Bkrtcy.W.D.Mo.1980).

As *Davis* notes, one line of cases holds that section 547(c)(1) is merely cumulative with section 547(c)(3), so that a transfer which occurs more than 10 days after the cash advance, thus not qualifying under section 547(c)(3), may nonetheless be deemed substantially contemporaneous under section 547(c)(1). In re Burnette, supra; In re Hall, 14 B.R. 186 (Bkrtcy.S.D.Fla.1981). Judge Kelley, the presiding bankruptcy judge in both this case and in Burnette, has concluded that section 547(c)(3) is simply one type of contemporaneous exchange, and that section 547(c)(1), although not intended to reach the transfer of security interests, may be read broadly to cover such situations as the present. In re Burnette, supra, at 802–803. The practical effect of an expansive reading in the "enabling loan" context is to give creditors "two bites at the apple." In re Davis, supra at 647.

Most courts, however, have concluded that an expansive reading of section 547(c)(1) renders section 547(c)(3) redundant and superfluous in the enabling loan context, and thus, is an unwarranted and erroneous construction. In re Murray, 27 B.R. 445 (Bkrtcy.Tenn.1983); In re Davis, supra; In re Vance, 22 B.R. 26 (Bkrtcy.D.Idaho 1982); In re Enlow, supra; In re Merritt, supra. These courts have been persuaded that Congress intended section 547(c)(3) to be the exclusive provision applicable in the enabling loan context. "Expressio unius est exclusius alterius."

Although this case does not involve an "enabling loan", we are also persuaded that expansion of section 547(c)(1)'s reference to contemporaneity beyond 10 days in the context of transfers of security interests is erroneous. The particular problems posed by the delay between creation and perfection of security interests were well recognized by Congress. One of the principal purposes of the Bankruptcy Reform Act is to discourage the creation of "secret liens" by invalidating all transfers occurring within 90 days prior to the filing of the petitions. Thus, creditors are discouraged from waiting until the debtor's financial troubles become all-too-manifest before recording security interests. Section 547(e)(2)(A) and (B) reflect this concern by providing that a transfer of a security interest relates back to the date of the underlying transaction if perfection occurs no more than 10 days afterwards; if perfection occurs more than 10 days later, the transfer is deemed to occur at the date of perfection.

The lower courts' broad reading of section 547(c)(1) effectively negates section 547(e)(2). Assuming the interval between creation and perfection to straddle the 90-day cutoff, although a security interest is perfected more than 10 days after the underlying transaction, and is thus voidable as a preference, the transfer might still be preserved if it is found to be part of a "substantially contemporaneous" exchange. Such hopeless conflict cannot have been intended by Congress.

Further, the evidentiary problems inherent in an expansive reading of section 547(c)(1) embody a Pandora's box of evils, even if no risk of fraud or misrepresentation was present in this case.

> [S]uch a stance invites litigation over the question when in fact a transfer is "substantially contemporaneous". There are no objective standards for determining this fact and the courts are having great difficulty in determining the issue, creating much uncertainty in the law. In re Vance, supra at 28.

The lower courts noted that the facts of this case cry out for application of the contemporaneous exchange exception. However, the lower courts' conviction that delayed perfection of the security interest resulted from fortuitous circumstances entirely beyond Security Manual's control and unattributable to negligence is not entirely well-founded. Under Tennessee's expedited title procedure, T.C.A. 55–3–114, discharge of a lien may be noted upon the certificate of title within 72 hours from demand.* Thus,

---

* Several states have adopted expedited title procedures similar to Tennessee's. Florida also permits recordation of the lien on the certificate within 72 hours after demand. F.S.A. § 319.323. Colorado requires the authorized agent of the county to deliver within 48 hours the certificate of title upon which a lien has been noted to the state director of motor vehicles, C.R.S.A. 42–6–122, and Ohio requires the county clerk to notify the registrar of motor vehicles of the notation of lien on the same day as the certificate is presented for notation of the lien, R.C.O. 4505.01 et seq.

In a variation upon these truly expedited procedures, other states require lienholders whose liens have been discharged to execute a release of the lien within a certain period of time after demand, typically 10 to 30 days, and to then file the release with the pertinent authority. Generally, such states have adopted, or follow the pattern established by, the Uniform Motor Vehicle Certificate of Title and Anti-Theft Act.

* * *

In yet another variation a few states merely require the lienholder to "immediately" execute a release upon satisfaction of the lien. Pennsylvania, 75 Pa. C.S.A. § 1135; Maryland, Ann.Code 1957 Tr. § 13–2092. Iowa requires a release of a junior lien to be noted on the same day as the title is delivered to the county treasurer for such recorda-

Security Mutual is to some extent responsible for its own predicament. Although there can be no doubt that the parties' clear intent to effectuate a contemporaneous exchange was frustrated, the statute nonetheless requires that the exchange *in fact* be contemporaneous. Section 547(c)(1)(B). The lower courts' interpretation places too little emphasis on the necessity of temporal proximity between the loan and the transfer of the security interest.

> If the sole test is the intention of the parties as required in § 547(c)(1)(A), then it would be necessary for the Court to conduct extensive factual inquiries into situations which would lend themselves to collusion and the fabrication of evidence, and perhaps render the preference section inoperable against all but the most flagrant violations. The purpose of adding the requirement of § 547(c)(1)(B) is to avoid the inherent evidentiary difficulties of § 547(c)(1)(A) by requiring that the parties' conduct bears out their intentions. Butz v. Pingel, supra at 238–239.

In light of the explicit grace periods provided for perfection of security interests in sections 547(e)(2) and 547(c)(3), Congress has clearly struck the balance in favor of repose in this area of the law. Case-by-case development of the contemporaneous exchange exception would quickly result in uncertainty and protracted litigation, delaying, not expediting, the satisfaction of creditors' claims and the debtor's return to financial health. The policies of discouraging creditors "from racing to the Courthouse to dismember the debtor during his slide into bankruptcy" and facilitating equality of distribution would be severely eroded under the lower courts' construction of the statute. H.R.595.

In conclusion, we believe the District Court and the Bankruptcy Court erred in ruling that Security Mutual's perfection of its security interest 33 days after granting a loan to the Arnetts was part of a substantially contemporaneous exchange of new value. Section 547(e)(2)(B) explicitly provides that a security interest perfected more than 10 days after its creation does not relate back and is deemed to have occurred on the date of perfection. The applicability of section 547(c)(1) to delayed perfection of security interests is thus limited to 10 days. The transfer of Security Mutual's security interest is not excepted from the trustee's avoidance powers, and may be set aside as a voidable preference.

* * *

Reversed and remanded for further proceedings.

tion. I.C.A. § 321.50(3). The remaining states do not fit these general patterns of establishing time limits to insure prompt recordation or discharge of liens upon motor vehicle certificates of title.

WELLFORD, CIRCUIT JUDGE, dissenting:

I would affirm District Judge Frank Wilson and the Bankruptcy Judge in this case. I agree with them that the credit transaction involved comes within the meaning of a "contemporaneous exchange" under § 547(c)(1), and that Security Mutual Finance Corporation's perfecting of its lien and security interest, although delayed, was excepted from the preference provisions of § 547(b). Not only is it clear that the transaction in dispute was intended to be contemporaneous, but appellee Security Mutual acted diligently under the circumstances to protect its security position under the law.

Judge Wilson deemed it to be essentially, a question of fact as to whether a transaction extending beyond ten days is "substantially contemporaneous" under the law. The Bankruptcy Court decided the question in accordance with the clear intent of the parties. The result reached, in my view, was in accord with legislative purpose and with sound authority. * * *[1]

I conclude that § 547(c)(1) of the applicable Bankruptcy Act preserves the principles set out in Dean v. Davis, 242 U.S. 438, 37 S.Ct. 130, 61 L.Ed. 419 (1917), and National City Bank v. Hotchkiss, 231 U.S. 50, 34 S.Ct. 20, 58 L.Ed. 115 (1913). Whether a transaction is "substantially contemporaneous" contemplates factors other than a ten day limitation, it calls for consideration of the intention of the parties and other surrounding circumstances, including the equities of the particular case. I disagree with Judge Miles' conclusion that "Congress has clearly struck the balance in favor of repose in this area * * *." This area of the law is far from "clear," and the better authority, including the decision of Judge Wilson herein, indicates precisely to the contrary.

NOTES

1. There is a certain Alice-in-Wonderland flavor to *Arnett* and to the many other cases that have presented the same issue. The court assumed that the making of the loan and the creation of the security interest both occurred on December 10. Under this assumption the transaction was in fact a contemporaneous exchange. But the argument addressed was whether the actually contemporaneous exchange, which was made noncontemporaneous by § 547(e)(2), should nevertheless be considered contemporaneous under § 547(c)(1) because it was substantially contemporaneous! The result reached in *Arnett* was undoubtedly a correct reading of the statute, but one is left with some doubts whether that result can be supported as a policy matter. The inflexible ten-day rule of § 547(e)(2) may make some sense if perfection occurs by the act of

1. There was no "race to the courthouse" here to dismember the debtor.

the secured party in presenting to a filing officer a document that the secured party controls. This is the norm in cases of perfection by filing a financing statement under the UCC (§ 9–403(1)) or in cases of filing a real property mortgage for recording. Ten days for perfection would normally be adequate in those cases. But perfection of security interests in automobiles is not usually done by filing a financing statement. Most states have certificate of title laws. Under the Tennessee statute involved in *Arnett* perfection is effective from the time of receipt by the filing officer of the request by the secured party for the notation of lien on the certificate of title, Personal Loan & Finance Corp. of Memphis v. Guardian Discount Co., 206 Tenn. 221, 332 S.W.2d 504 (1960); however, in *Arnett* when the secured party made the loan the certificate of title was in the possession of a prior secured party. It was necessary first to pay off the prior secured creditor, to obtain release of the prior lien and to obtain the certificate of title before submitting the certificate to the filing officer with the request for notation of the lien. It may have been possible to accomplish all of this in ten days, but it certainly would have been difficult. In some states it may have been impossible without the close cooperation of the prior secured party. See the court's long footnote summarizing the various state laws. What public policy is served by requiring heroic efforts to meet the ten-day deadline? Certainly, the scenario in *Arnett* bears little resemblance to the secret lien evil that gave rise to the false preference doctrine which § 547(e)(2) carries forward.

2.   In re Busenlehner, 918 F.2d 928 (11th Cir.1990), involved a finance company that perfected a purchase money security interest in an automobile 13 days after the security interest attached and within 90 days of the debtor's bankruptcy. The trustee in bankruptcy contended that the security interest should be avoided as a preference because perfection occurred more than ten days after attachment. State law (Georgia) provided that a security interest in a motor vehicle is perfected as of the time of attachment if the act of perfection occurred within 20 days of attachment. The court sustained the security interest under § 547(c)(3). The court held that under § 547(e)(1)(B) no creditor could have acquired a judicial lien having priority over the security interest because, under state law, perfection within 20 days related back to the date of attachment. Thus under § 547(c)(3)(B) the security interest was perfected within the ten day period; in fact, it was, retroactively, perfected at the time of attachment.

In re Hamilton, 892 F.2d 1230 (5th Cir.1990), was decided under the Texas version of § 9–301(2) in which the 10–day rule of the Official Text was extended to 20 days. A secured party perfected a security interest in an automobile more than ten days but less than 20 days after attachment. Unlike Georgia law, the Texas law with respect to security interests in motor vehicles merely prescribes a method for perfection (issuance of a receipt preliminary to notation of a lien on a certificate of title) and does not include a priority rule giving retroactive effect to perfection. The court considered the effect of § 9–301(2) which provided for retroactive effect of perfection within a 20–day period after attachment. The court applied § 547(c)(3) because the security interest was purchase money and, almost without analysis, concluded that the ten-day rule of § 547(c)(3) was in conflict with the 20–day rule of § 9–301(2) and that the Bankruptcy Code provision must prevail over state law. The court implied that its position was supported by the fact that all the courts of appeal had agreed with *Arnett* in refusing to allow § 547(c)(1) to extend the ten-day rule of § 547(e) (2)(B).

In both *Busenlehner* and *Hamilton* the courts assumed that § 547(c)(3) (enabling loans) applied because the security interests were purchase money. But this provision was intended to address the delayed attachment problem in which the creditor advances value first and the debtor uses this money to acquire the collateral later, rather than the delayed perfection issue raised in these two cases. In both of these cases the giving of value and the grant of the security interest in existing collateral were contemporaneous and there was no delayed attachment issue. A delayed perfection problem was involved only because § 547(e)(2) dates a transfer at the time of perfection rather than the time of attachment and artificially turns a contemporaneous exchange into a transfer on account of an antecedent debt.

These two cases should be decided as delayed perfection cases in which the grant of a security interest may be deemed preferential if under § 547(e)(2) the transfer is not perfected at the time of attachment or within ten days of this time. *Busenlehner* invokes § 547(e)(1)(B) to conclude that the ten-day limit of § 547(e)(2) never comes into play because under the priority rule of Georgia (similar to that of § 9–301(2)) a secured party who perfects within 20 days is superior to intervening creditors; hence, the security interest was deemed perfected when it attached. This view that the existence of a preference depends on priority rules is the same rationale that prevailed in *Grain Merchants*, discussed on pp. 402–404, and allowed the court to achieve what it saw as the desirable result of saving floating liens in bankruptcy. Doubtless the court in *Busenlehner* saw its decision as also achieving a good result because the ten-day period of § 547(e)(2) is often too short a period in which to perfect security interests in states requiring notation of the lien on a certificate of title. But it seems quite unlikely that Congress intended § 547(e) to cede the issue of when a delayed perfection is a preference to state legislatures which could enact 90–day or even 180–day relation back provisions as well as those of 20–day in length.

H. EQUITABLE SUBORDINATION

1. INTRODUCTION

Bankruptcy courts are courts of equity and as such may "sift the circumstances surrounding any claim" in order to avoid unfairness in distributing the assets of the estate among claimants. Pepper v. Litton, 308 U.S. 295, 308 (1939). Thus, bankruptcy courts may depart from the basic rule of equality of distribution and subordinate some claims and interests to others in the exercise of their equitable powers.

The Bankruptcy Act made no specific reference to equitable subordination. Bankruptcy Code § 510(c) merely authorizes the court to subordinate claims and interests "under principles of equitable subordination." The great bulk of equitable subordination cases in bankruptcy have concerned the activities of fiduciaries or "insiders" (§ 101), usually the officers, directors, or controlling stockholders of corporations. Cases such as Pepper v. Litton allow subordination because of fraudulent conduct by stockholders. Other cases subordinate the claims of insiders against the debtor corporation because of undercapitalization and inequitable conduct.

Pepper v. Litton involved a claim of about $30,000 for accumulated salary, dating back at least five years, by Litton who was the sole or dominant stockholder of Dixie Splint Coal Company. The court held that the claim could be disallowed or subordinated in the bankruptcy of Dixie Splint because of fraudulent conduct by Litton. The salary claim was asserted for the first time after Pepper brought action against Dixie Splint for an accounting of royalties due to Pepper. While the Pepper action was pending Litton caused Dixie Splint to confess judgment on Litton's action. "Execution was issued on this judgment the same day but no return was made thereon, Litton waiting 'quietly until the outcome of the Pepper suit was definitely known.'" When Pepper obtained judgment Dixie Splint obtained suspension of execution by Pepper for 90 days to permit an appeal although no appeal was ever made. During the 90–day period Litton levied on his judgment. "Litton 'had no intention of trying to satisfy his confessed judgment' against his corporation 'unless and until it became necessary to do so'; he was using it 'only as a shield against the Pepper debt.' Thus, when execution and levy were made * * * no steps were taken for over two months towards a sale of the property on which levy had been made." When Pepper levied on her judgment Litton caused the sheriff "who seems to have been cooperating with Litton" to sell the property on which Litton had levied. Litton purchased the property at the execution sale for

$3,200. "The next step in the 'planned and fraudulent' scheme was the formation by Litton of 'another of his one-man corporations' * * * to which Litton transferred the property he had acquired at the execution sale at a valuation [fixed by the board of directors at over $20,000] to be paid for in stock of the new company." As the "third step in Litton's scheme" Dixie Splint filed in bankruptcy two days after Litton's execution sale. "This step, according to the findings below, was 'plainly for the sole purpose of avoiding payment of the Pepper debt.'" The court concluded:

> * * * Litton allowed his salary claims to lie dormant for years and sought to enforce them only when his debtor corporation was in financial difficulty. Then he used them so that the rights of another creditor were impaired. Litton as an insider utilized his strategic position for his own preferment to the damage of Pepper. Litton as the dominant influence over Dixie Splint Coal Company used his power not to deal fairly with the creditors of that company but to manipulate its affairs in such a manner that when one of its creditors came to collect her just debt the bulk of the assets had disappeared into another Litton company. Litton, though a fiduciary, was enabled by astute legal maneuvering to acquire most of the assets of the bankrupt not for cash or other consideration of value to creditors but for bookkeeping entries representing at best merely Litton's appraisal of the worth of Litton's services over the years.

2. DOMINANT CREDITORS

When a business debtor fails, its relationship with its dominant creditor, usually a bank, may come under scrutiny. The close relationship between debtor and bank may lead other creditors to attempt to hold the bank liable for the debts of the failed debtor as though they were joint venturers. If the debtor files in bankruptcy, the trustee in bankruptcy may attempt to subordinate the bank's claims to those of the other creditors on this same ground. The following quotation from In re Teltronics Services, Inc., 29 B.R. 139, 170–171 (Bkrtcy.N.Y.1983), raises some of the difficulties facing creditors who exert control over their debtors.

> The general rule that a creditor is not a fiduciary of his debtor is not without exception. In the rare circumstance where a creditor exercises such control over the decision-making processes of the debtor as amounts to a domination of its will, he may be held accountable for his actions under a fiduciary standard. See In re Prima Co., 98 F.2d 952, 965 (7th Cir.1938); * * *. Accordingly, several commentators have admonished creditors to avoid becoming overly involved in the debtor's management:

Where the creditor controls the corporate debtor by voting control of its stock, dominant influence in its management or ability otherwise to control its business affairs, the creditor may have a fiduciary duty to its corporate debtor.

* * *

* * * [W]henever a creditor interferes in the business affairs of a financially troubled corporate debtor, it risks the possibility that such interference may provide a basis for the equitable adjustment of its claims against the debtor, the imposition of statutory liability or the imposition of liabilities at common law.

Douglas–Hamilton, Creditor Liabilities Resulting from Improper Interference with the Management of a Financially Troubled Debtor, 31 Bus.Lawy. 343, 352, 365 (1975).

* * * [O]nce the creditor is not satisfied with simply insulating himself from the risk of loss of capital and interest, and instead insists upon affirmative participation in the entrepreneurial effort being financed * * * he has entered into a relationship whose expected extraordinary economic benefit justifies the requirement of special obligations.

* * *

With affirmative conduct thus has come voluntary assumption of duty, and the fact that the creditor's motives are not altruistic will strengthen arguments for the imposition of liability.

Bartlett & Lapatin, The Status of a Creditor as a Controlling Person, 28 Mercer L.Rev. 639, 655–57 (1977).

MATTER OF CLARK PIPE & SUPPLY CO.

United States Court of Appeals, Fifth Circuit, 1990.
893 F.2d 693.

E. GRADY JOLLY, CIRCUIT JUDGE:

Treating the suggestion for rehearing en banc filed in this case by Associates Commercial Corporation ("Associates"), as a petition for panel rehearing, we hereby grant the petition for rehearing. After re-examining the evidence in this case and the applicable law, we conclude that our prior opinion was in error. We therefore withdraw our prior opinion and substitute the following:

* * *

I

Clark Pipe and Supply Company, Inc., ("Clark") was in the business of buying and selling steel pipe used in the fabrication of offshore drilling platforms. In September 1980, Associates and Clark executed various agreements under which Associates would make revolving loans secured by an assignment of accounts receivable and an inventory mortgage. Under the agreements, Clark was required to deposit all collections from the accounts receivable in a bank account belonging to Associates. The amount that Associates would lend was determined by a formula, i.e., a certain percentage of the amount of eligible accounts receivable plus a certain percentage of the cost of inventory. The agreements provided that Associates could reduce the percentage advance rates at any time at its discretion.

When bad times hit the oil fields in late 1981, Clark's business slumped. In February 1982 Associates began reducing the percentage advance rates so that Clark would have just enough cash to pay its direct operating expenses. Clark used the advances to keep its doors open and to sell inventory, the proceeds of which were used to pay off the past advances from Associates. Associates did not expressly dictate to Clark which bills to pay. Neither did it direct Clark not to pay vendors or threaten Clark with a cutoff of advances if it did pay vendors. But Clark had no funds left over from the advances to pay vendors or other creditors whose services were not essential to keeping its doors open.

One of Clark's vendors, going unpaid, initiated foreclosure proceedings in February and seized the pipe it had sold Clark. Another attempted to do so in March. * * * When a third unpaid creditor initiated foreclosure proceedings in May, Clark sought protection from creditors by filing for reorganization under Chapter 11 of the Bankruptcy Code.

The case was converted to a Chapter 7 liquidation on August 31, 1982, and a trustee was appointed. In 1983, the trustee brought this adversary proceeding against Clark's lender, Associates. The trustee sought the recovery of alleged preferences and equitable subordination of Associates' claims. Following a one-day trial on August 28, 1986, the bankruptcy court entered judgment on April 10, 1987, and an amended judgment on June 9, 1987. The court required Associates to turn over $370,505 of payments found to be preferential and subordinated Associates' claims. The district court affirmed on May 24, 1988. 87 B.R. 21.

II

[The part of the opinion concerning the alleged preference is omitted.]

III

The second issue before us is whether the bankruptcy court was justified in equitably subordinating Associates' claims. This court has enunciated a three-pronged test to determine whether and to what extent a claim should be equitably subordinated: (1) the claimant must have engaged in some type of inequitable conduct, (2) the misconduct must have resulted in injury to the creditors of the bankrupt or conferred an unfair advantage on the claimant, and (3) equitable subordination of the claim must not be inconsistent with the provisions of the Bankruptcy Code. Missionary Baptist I, 712 F.2d at 212. Three general categories of conduct have been recognized as sufficient to satisfy the first prong of the three-part test: (1) fraud, illegality or breach of fiduciary duties; (2) undercapitalization; and (3) a claimant's use of the debtor as a mere instrumentality or alter ego. Id.

In essence, the bankruptcy court found that once Associates realized Clark's desperate financial condition, Associates asserted total control and used Clark as a mere instrumentality to liquidate Associates' unpaid loans. Moreover, it did so, the trustee argues, to the detriment of the rights of Clark's other creditors.

Associates contends that its control over Clark was far from total. Associates says that it did no more than determine the percentage of advances as expressly permitted in the loan agreement; it never made or dictated decisions as to which creditors were paid. Thus, argues Associates, it never had the "actual, participatory, total control of the debtor" required to make Clark its instrumentality under Krivo Industrial Supply Co. v. National Distillers & Chemical Corp., 483 F.2d 1098, 1105 (5th Cir.1973), modified factually, 490 F.2d 916 (5th Cir.1974) (elaborated in Valdes v. Leisure Resource Group, 810 F.2d 1345, 1354 (5th Cir. 1987)). If it did not use Clark as an instrumentality or engage in any other type of inequitable conduct under *Missionary Baptist I*, argues Associates, then it cannot be equitably subordinated.

A

We first consider whether Associates asserted such control over the activities of Clark that we should consider that it was using Clark as its mere instrumentality. In our prior opinion, we agreed with the district court and the bankruptcy court that, as a practical matter, Associates asserted total control over Clark's liquidation, and that it used its control in a manner detrimental to the unsecured creditors. Upon reconsideration, we have concluded that we cannot say that the sort of control Associates asserted over Clark's financial affairs rises to the level of unconscionable conduct necessary to justify the application of the doctrine of equitable subordination.[5] We have reached our revised conclusion primarily because we cannot escape the salient fact that, pursuant to its loan agreement with Clark, Associates had the right to

---

5. The question whether a creditor's conduct is so unconscionable as to require equitable subordination as a remedy is a conclusion of law, reviewable de novo. See, e.g. Wegner v. Grunewaldt, 821 F.2d 1317, 1322–23 (8th Cir.1987).

reduce funding, just as it did, as Clark's sales slowed. We now conclude that there is no evidence that Associates exceeded its authority under the loan agreement, or that Associates acted inequitably in exercising its rights under that agreement.

We think it is important to note at the outset that the loan and security agreements between Associates and Clark, which are at issue here, were executed in 1980, at the inception of their relationship. There is no evidence that Clark was insolvent at the time the agreements were entered into. Clark was represented by counsel during the negotiations, and there is no evidence that the loan documents were negotiated at anything other than arm's length or that they are atypical of loan documents used in similar asset-based financings.

The loan agreement between Associates and Clark established a line of credit varying from $2.2 million to approximately $2.7 million over the life of the loan. The amount that Associates would lend was determined by a formula: 85% of the amount of eligible accounts receivables plus 60% of the cost of inventory. Under the agreement, Clark was required to deposit all collections from the accounts receivable in a bank account belonging to Associates. Associates would, in turn, readvance the agreed-upon portion of those funds to Clark on a revolving basis. The agreement provided that Associates could reduce the percentage advance rates at any time in its discretion.

When Clark's business began to decline, along with that of the oil patch generally, Associates advised Clark that it would reduce the advance ratio for the inventory loan by 5% per month beginning in January 1982. After that time, the company stopped buying new inventory and, according to the Trustee's expert witness, Clark's monthly sales revenues amounted to less than one-fifth of the company's outstanding accounts payable. Clark prepared a budget at Associates' request that indicated the disbursements necessary to keep the company operating. The budget did not include payment to vendors for previously shipped goods. Associates' former loan officer, Fred Slice, testified as to what he had in mind:

> If he [the comptroller of Clark] had had the availability [of funds to pay a vendor or other trade creditor] that particular day, I would have said, "Are you sure you've got that much availability, Jim," because he shouldn't have that much. The way I had structured it, he wouldn't have any money to pay his suppliers.
>
> * * *
>
> But you know, the possibility that—this is all hypothetical. I had it structured so that there was no—there was barely enough money—there was enough money, if I did it right, enough money to keep the doors open. Clark could

continue to operate, sell the inventory, turn it into receivables, collect the cash, transfer that cash to me, and reduce my loans.

And, if he had ever had availability for other things, that meant I had done something wrong, and I would have been surprised. To ask me what I would have done is purely hypothetical[;] I don't think it would happen. I think it's so unrealistic, I don't know.

Despite Associates' motive, which was, according to Slice, "to get in the best position I can prior to the bankruptcy, i.e., I want to get the absolute amount of dollars as low as I can by hook or crook," the evidence shows that the amount of its advances continued to be based on the applicable funding formulas. Slice testified that the lender did not appreciably alter its original credit procedures when Clark fell into financial difficulty.

In our original opinion, we failed to focus sufficiently on the loan agreement, which gave Associates the right to conduct its affairs with Clark in the manner in which it did. In addition, we think that in our previous opinion we were overly influenced by the negative and inculpatory tone of Slice's testimony. Given the agreement he was working under, his testimony was hardly more than fanfaronading about the power that the agreement afforded him over the financial affairs of Clark. Although his talk was crass (e.g., "I want to get the absolute dollars as low as I can, by hook or crook"), our careful examination of the record does not reveal any conduct on his part that was inconsistent with the loan agreement, irrespective of what his personal motive may have been.

Through its loan agreement, every lender effectively exercises "control" over its borrower to some degree. A lender in Associates' position will usually possess "control" in the sense that it can foreclose or drastically reduce the debtor's financing. The purpose of equitable subordination is to distinguish between the unilateral remedies that a creditor may properly enforce pursuant to its agreements with the debtor and other inequitable conduct such as fraud, misrepresentation, or the exercise of such total control over the debtor as to have essentially replaced its decision-making capacity with that of the lender. The crucial distinction between what is inequitable and what a lender can reasonably and legitimately do to protect its interests is the distinction between the existence of "control" and the exercise of that "control" to direct the activities of the debtor. As the Supreme Court stated in Comstock v. Group of Institutional Investors, 335 U.S. 211, 229, 68 S.Ct. 1454, 1463, 92 L.Ed. 1911 (1948): "It is not mere existence of an opportunity to do wrong that brings the rule into play; it is the unconscionable use of the opportunity afforded by the domination to advantage itself at the injury of the subsidiary that deprives the wrongdoer of the fruits of his wrong."

In our prior opinion, we drew support from In re American Lumber Co., 5 B.R. 470 (D.Minn.1980), to reach our conclusion that Associates' claims should be equitably subordinated. Upon reconsideration, however, we find that the facts of that case are significantly more egregious than we have here. In that case, the court equitably subordinated the claims of a bank because the bank "controlled" the debtor through its right to a controlling interest in the debtor's stock. The bank forced the debtor to convey security interests in its remaining unencumbered assets to the bank after the borrower defaulted on an existing debt. Immediately thereafter, the bank foreclosed on the borrower's accounts receivable, terminated the borrower's employees, hired its own skeleton crew to conduct a liquidation, and selectively honored the debtor's payables to improve its own position. The bank began receiving and opening all incoming mail at the borrower's office, and it established a bank account into which all amounts received by the borrower were deposited and over which the bank had sole control. The bankruptcy court found that the bank exercised control over all aspects of the debtor's finances and operation including: payments of payables and wages, collection and use of accounts receivable and contract rights, purchase and use of supplies and materials, inventory sales, a lumber yard, the salaries of the principals, the employment of employees, and the receipt of payments for sales and accounts receivable.

Despite its decision to prohibit further advances to the debtor, its declaration that the debtor was in default of its loans, and its decisions to use all available funds of the company to offset the company's obligations to it, the bank in *American Lumber* made two specific representations to the American Lumbermen's Credit Association that the debtor was not in a bankruptcy situation and that current contracts would be fulfilled. Two days after this second reassurance, the bank gave notice of foreclosure of its security interests in the company's inventory and equipment. Approximately two weeks later the bank sold equipment and inventory of the debtor amounting to roughly $450,000, applying all of the proceeds to the debtor's indebtedness to the bank.

Associates exercised significantly less "control" over the activities of Clark than did the lender in *American Lumber*. Associates did not own any stock of Clark, much less a controlling block. Nor did Associates interfere with the operations of the borrower to an extent even roughly commensurate with the degree of interference exercised by the bank in *American Lumber*. Associates made no management decisions for Clark, such as deciding which creditors to prefer with the diminishing amount of funds available. At no time did Associates place any of its employees as either a director or officer of Clark. Associates never influenced the removal from office of any Clark personnel, nor did Associates ever request Clark to take any particular action at a shareholders meeting. Associates did not expressly dictate to Clark which bills to pay, nor did it direct Clark not to pay vendors or threaten a cutoff of advances if it did pay vendors. Clark handled its own daily operations. The same basic procedures with respect to the reporting of collateral, the calculation of availability of funds, and the procedures for the advancement of funds were followed throughout the relationship between Clark and Associates. Unlike the lender in *American Lumber,* Associates did not mislead creditors to continue supplying Clark. Cf. American Lumber, 5 B.R. at 474. Perhaps the most important fact that distinguishes this case from *American Lumber* is that Associates did not coerce Clark into executing the security agreements after Clark became insolvent. Instead, the loan and security agreements between Clark and Associates were entered into at arm's length prior to Clark's insolvency, and all of Associates' activities were conducted pursuant to those agreements.

Associates' control over Clark's finances, admittedly powerful and ultimately severe, was based solely on the exercise of powers found in the loan agreement. Associates' close watch over Clark's affairs does not, by itself, however, amount to such control as would justify equitable subordination. In re W.T. Grant, 699 F.2d 599, 610 (2d Cir.1983). "There is nothing inherently wrong with a creditor carefully monitoring his debtor's financial situation or with suggesting what course of action the debtor ought to follow." In re Teltronics Services, Inc., 29 B.R. 139, 172 (Bankr.E.D.N.Y. 1983) (citations omitted). Although the terms of the agreement did give Associates potent leverage over Clark, that agreement did not give Associates total control over Clark's activities. At all material times Clark had the power to act autonomously and, if it chose, to disregard the advice of Associates; for example, Clark was free to shut its doors at any time it chose to do so and to file for bankruptcy.

Finally, on reconsideration, we are persuaded that the rationale of In re W.T. Grant Co., 699 F.2d 599 (2d Cir.1983) should control the case before us. In that case, the Second Circuit recognized that

> a creditor is under no fiduciary obligation to its debtor or to other creditors of the debtor in the collection of its claim. [citations omitted] The permissible parameters of a creditor's efforts to seek collection from a debtor are generally those with respect to voidable preferences and fraudulent conveyances proscribed by the Bankruptcy Act; apart from these there is generally no objection to a creditor's using his bargaining position, including his ability to refuse to make fur-

ther loans needed by the debtor, to improve the status of his existing claims.

699 F.2d at 609–10. Associates was not a fiduciary of Clark, it did not exert improper control over Clark's financial affairs, and it did not act inequitably in exercising its rights under its loan agreement with Clark.

B

Finally, we should note that in our earlier opinion, we found that, in exercising such control over Clark, Associates engaged in other inequitable conduct that justified equitable subordination. Our re-examination of the record indicates, however, that there is not really any evidence that Associates engaged in such conduct. Our earlier opinion assumed that Associates knew that Clark was selling pipe to which the suppliers had a first lien, but the issue of whether the vendors had a first lien on the pipe was not decided by our court until a significantly later time. In addition, although the trustee made much of the point on appeal, after our re-study of the record, we conclude that it does not support the finding that Associates encouraged Clark to remove decals from pipe in its inventory.

We also note that the record is devoid of any evidence that Associates misled other Clark creditors to their detriment. See, e.g., Matter of CTS Truss, Inc., 868 F.2d 146, 149 (5th Cir.1989) (lender did not represent to third parties that additional financing was in place or that debtor was solvent, when the opposite was true).

When the foregoing factors are considered, there is no basis for finding inequitable conduct upon which equitable subordination can be based. We therefore conclude that the district court erred in affirming the bankruptcy court's decision to subordinate Associates' claims.

* * *

NOTES

1. The court in *Clark* adopts the test formulated in In re Mobile Steel Co., 563 F.2d 692 (5th Cir.1977), that states three threshold requirements for invoking equitable subordination: (1) the claimant must be engaged in inequitable conduct; (2) the misconduct must have injured other creditors or conferred an unfair advantage on the claimant; and (3) equitable subordination of the claim must not be inconsistent with the provisions of the bankruptcy laws. Since *Mobile Steel,* virtually all equitable subordination cases have repeated these standards as accepted doctrine. However, these criteria, though embraced by the courts as a guide through the uncertainties of equitable subordination, are so imprecise as to leave the field as unpredictable as before.

In recent years several opinions have extended the doctrine of equitable subordination in order to subordinate tax penalties even though the IRS was guilty of no inequitable conduct. In the Matter of Virtual Network Services Corporation, 902 F.2d 1246 (7th Cir.1990), is a leading case on the subject and marshals the authorities. The basis for subordinating a penalty claim is that it is unfair to punish other innocent creditors for the acts of the debtor. Section 726(a)(4) automatically subordinates noncompensatory penalties in Chapter 7 cases. The result of the *Virtual Network* extension of equitable subordination is to allow courts to subordinate penalty claims in Chapter 11 cases as well. But the principle stated in *Virtual Network* goes beyond merely subordinating penalties: "It is clear that in principle, equitable subordination no longer requires, in all circumstances, some inequitable conduct on the part of the creditor." 902 F.2d at 1250. A lawyer representing creditor interests was quoted as saying: "A recent and possibly disturbing trend is that some courts have suggested that you don't need inequitable conduct [to invoke equitable subordination]. It is a frightening thing for lenders because there's no real standard there. It's at the judge's discretion." Wall Street Journal, p. B4, col. 4, June 20, 1991.

2. In Kham & Nate's Shoes No. 2, Inc. v. First Bank of Whiting, 908 F.2d 1351 (7th Cir.1990), Bank opened a $300,000 line of credit for Debtor which permitted Bank to cancel at its discretion. After advancing $75,000, of which Debtor repaid $10,000, Bank refused to make further advances. The lower court equitably subordinated Bank's $65,000 claim on the ground that Bank's refusal to extend further credit was inequitable conduct. In overruling the lower court, Judge Easterbrook, speaking for the court, stated:

> "Inequitable conduct" in commercial life means breach *plus* some advantage-taking, such as the star who agrees to act in a motion picture and then, after $20 million has been spent, sulks in his dressing room until the contract has been renegotiated.
>
> *   *   *
>
> Bank did not break a promise at a time Debtor was especially vulnerable, then use the costs and delay of obtaining legal enforcement of the contract as levers to a better deal. Debtor and Bank signed a contract expressly allowing the Bank to cease making further advances. The $300,000 was the maximum loan, not a guarantee. The Bank exercised its contractual privilege after loaning Debtor $75,000; it made a clean break and did not demand improved terms. It had the right to do this for any reason satisfactory to itself.
>
> *   *   *
>
> Although Bank's decision left Debtor scratching for other sources of credit, Bank did not create Debtor's need for funds,

and it was not contractually obliged to satisfy its customer's desires. The Bank was entitled to advance its own interests, and it did not need to put the interests of Debtor and Debtor's other creditors first. To the extent K.M.C. Co., Inc. v. Irving Trust Co., 757 F.2d 752, 759–63 (6th Cir.1985), holds that a bank must loan more money or give more advance notice of termination than its contract requires, we respectfully disagree. First Bank of Whiting is not an eleemosynary institution. It need not throw good money after bad, even if other persons would catch the lucre.

* * *

Debtor stresses, and the bankruptcy judge found, that Bank would have been secure in making additional advances. Perhaps so, but the contract did not oblige Bank to make all advances for which it could be assured of payment. *Ex post* assessments of a lender's security are no basis on which to deny it the negotiated place in the queue. Risk must be assessed *ex ante* by lenders, rather than *ex post* by judges. If a loan seems secure at the time, lenders will put up the money; their own interests are served by making loans bound to be repaid. What is more, the bankruptcy judge's finding that Bank would have been secure in making additional advances is highly questionable. The judgment of the market vindicates Bank. If more credit would have enabled Debtor to flourish, then other lenders should have been willing to supply it. Yet no one else, not even the SBA, would advance additional money to Debtor.

908 F.2d at 1357–1358.

Chapter 5

LETTERS OF CREDIT

A. INTRODUCTION

A generation ago, letter of credit law was primarily a part of international transactions involving documentary sales of goods. Article 5 of the UCC was drafted in the context of that type of transaction. Today, letters of credit are used to provide what is functionally a bank guaranty of debt arising from a very wide variety of transactions. The term "standby letter of credit" is used to refer to this type of guaranty. No business lawyer can competently advise clients without a working knowledge of this rapidly growing body of letter of credit law.

The UCC Permanent Editorial Board has initiated a revision of Article 5 which was drafted in what now must be regarded as the stone age of letters of credit. A useful critique of current letter of credit law with recommendations for amendments to Article 5 is found in Task Force on the Study of U.C.C. Article 5, 45 Bus.Law. 1521–1646 (1990) (hereafter "Task Force Study"). General references are found in Dolan, Law of Letters of Credit (1984), and in Chapter 19 of White & Summers, Uniform Commercial Code (3d ed. 1988).

BAIRD, STANDBY LETTERS OF CREDIT IN BANKRUPTCY
49 U. of Chi.L.Rev. 130, 133–135 (1982).

I. THE LETTER-OF-CREDIT TRANSACTION

A. Background

As recently as twenty years ago, letters of credit were used principally in international sales. No seller willingly sends its goods across national borders unless it is confident it will be paid, because no seller welcomes the prospect of having its goods in the care of unknown parties in a foreign port, where finding a new buyer may be impossible and bringing a legal action extremely difficult. The letter of credit as we now know it arose in the middle of the nineteenth century in response to this problem.

Although letter-of-credit transactions vary, their basic structure can be stated briefly. In a typical letter-of-credit transaction, a seller specifies that payment be made with a letter of credit in its favor. The buyer (known as the "customer" in the letter-of-

445

credit transaction) contracts with the bank to issue the letter. The bank, knowing the creditworthiness of its customer, is willing to issue the letter for a small fee, typically some fraction of one per cent of the price of the goods. The bank sends the letter to the seller, promising to pay the full price of the goods when the seller presents it with a draft and the documents specified in the letter. These documents typically include a negotiable bill of lading.

This arrangement benefits all parties to the transaction. The seller can manufacture goods to the buyer's order, confident it will be paid regardless of what befalls the buyer, because it can rely on the bank's commitment. The buyer that secures the letter of credit is better off than if it had advanced cash to the seller, because it does not become liable for the price until a trustworthy party (the bank) has possession of a negotiable document of title. The bank, in turn, earns a fee for issuing the letter and exposes itself to only a small risk, because it can readily assess the creditworthiness of its customer and, as the holder of a negotiable bill of lading, it has a perfected security interest in the goods involved in the transaction.

The linchpin of the letter-of-credit transaction is the unique legal relationship between the bank and the beneficiary.[16] Unlike a guarantor, the bank is primarily liable whenever the beneficiary presents a draft and documents that conform to the letter. Unlike its counterpart in a third-party beneficiary contract, the bank may not invoke the defenses its customer might have on the underlying contract. Moreover, the status of a beneficiary of a letter of credit is radically different from that of a payee of a check, who has no right to compel payment from the drawee bank. In the letter-of-credit transaction, the beneficiary does have the right to compel payment, and once the letter of credit is issued, the customer is powerless to stop payment in the absence of fraud. This difference exists because a letter of credit, unlike a negotiable instrument such as a check, is a binding and irrevocable obligation of the bank itself, not of the customer who procured it. The legal relationship between bank and beneficiary is governed by special principles which, like the law merchant in an earlier era, are nearly uniform throughout the world.

16. In their discussion of the legal relationship created by the letter of credit, Professors White and Summers note that a letter of credit is not like other devices creating legal obligations, but rather that

a letter of credit is a letter of credit. As Bishop Butler once said, "Everything is what it is and not another thing." Thus, when a beneficiary sues an issuer for refusal to honor drafts drawn pursuant to a letter of credit, his theory is not that of breach of contract, nor does he sue "on a negotiable instrument." Rather, he sues "on a letter of credit."

J. White & R. Summers, supra note 15, § 18–2, at 715 (footnotes omitted).

B. The Standby Letter of Credit

The archetypal letter-of-credit transaction described above is the means by which the parties pay one another if the underlying transaction takes place as planned. Standby letters of credit, in contrast, are never drawn upon if the transaction runs smoothly. For example, a builder might require a developer to have a bank issue a letter of credit in its behalf to ensure payment if the developer defaults. Such a letter of credit might require that the bank honor the builder's draft when accompanied by an architect's certificate that the building was finished and a statement by the builder that it had not been paid. In this kind of transaction, the bank usually will issue the letter only if the developer gives it a security interest in some property to which the bank will have recourse if the letter is drawn upon. If all goes well, the builder never presents its draft because it has been paid on schedule by the developer. If the developer defaults, however, the builder is still assured payment under the letter of credit. The bank then must seek reimbursement from the developer or enforce its security interest.

The parties to this transaction might employ a standby letter of credit in a different way. The developer might want to ensure that any money it advances to the builder is used to build the building. The developer could require the builder to have its bank issue a letter of credit in the developer's favor. Such a letter might provide that the developer's draft, accompanied by its statement that the builder had defaulted on its obligations, would be honored by the bank. Unlike the negotiable document of title specified in the usual commercial letter-of-credit transaction, the documents in the standby letter-of-credit transaction have no intrinsic value. For this reason, the bank is likely to insist that the builder give it a security interest as a condition of the letter's issuance.

Standby letters of credit also are used in transactions involving sales of goods. A supplier of raw materials, for example, might prefer to have a letter of credit in its favor from the buyer's bank rather than a security interest in the goods. Alternatively, a buyer of manufactured goods might want to protect itself when it advances money to finance its seller's purchase of raw materials. Such a buyer risks more in the event of default than one who sells on credit, because the buyer cannot easily acquire a purchase money security interest in the raw materials its seller uses. As the beneficiary of a standby letter of credit issued by the seller's bank, however, the buyer obtains equivalent protection.

A business that wishes to raise money may issue commercial paper backed by a standby letter of credit. This type of transaction involves larger dollar amounts than other uses of letters of credit. The business's bank may be more willing to accept the risk of its customer's insolvency than will the buyers of commercial paper. The buyers, however may be willing to extend cash to the business if they can rely on the bank to ensure repayment. The letter of credit makes it easy for all of the parties to allocate among themselves the risk of the business's failure. The business acquires the cash it needs, the bank lends its credit to the business without having to supply cash, and the buyers of commercial paper enjoy a relatively safe investment. As in the other letter-of-credit transactions, all parties directly involved benefit.

B. SOURCES OF LETTER OF CREDIT LAW

The Uniform Customs and Practice for Documentary Credits (UCP) antedated Article 5 of the UCC. It is an international trade code drafted by the International Chamber of Commerce. The latest version is dated 1983. Article 1 of the UCP states expansively: "These articles apply to all documentary credits, including, to the extent to which they may be applicable, standby letters of credit, and are binding on all parties thereto unless otherwise expressly agreed." Since the ICC has no authority to make law binding on U.S. courts, the UCP, unless expressly incorporated into the letter of credit, functions only as trade usage. But if the UCP is incorporated into the letter of credit it becomes a part of the contract and is enforceable as such. The official text of Article 5 contains no reference to the UCP. Since several provisions of Article 5 conflict with the UCP, problems of primacy arise when the UCP has been incorporated into the letter of credit. However, this problem is lessened because Article 5 allows the parties to vary the terms of several of its provisions by agreement.

The balance between the UCP and Article 5, always an uncertain one, has been tilted strongly in favor of the UCP in the leading letter of credit state, New York. Banking interests in that state blocked passage of Article 5 until § 5–102(4) was added. It provides: "Unless otherwise agreed, this Article 5 does not apply to a letter of credit or a credit if by its terms or by agreement, course of dealing or usage of trade such letter of credit or credit is subject in whole or in part to the Uniform Customs and Practice for Commercial Documentary Credits fixed by the Thirteenth or by any subsequent Congress of the International Chamber of Commerce." Note that this amendment does not say that the UCP prevails over Article 5 in cases of conflict; it says that Article 5 has no application at all if the letter of credit incorporates the UCP. Since New York banks typically make the letters of credit they issue, both domestic and foreign, subject to the UCP, Article 5 has only marginal application in New York and a few other states that have followed its lead.

When Article 5 was drafted the archetypal letter of credit was the "commercial" letter of credit in which the credit was issued by a bank on which the seller could draw drafts for the price of goods upon presentment of a bill of lading. Not until many years after the drafting of Article 5 did the explosion of standby letters of credit occur. Among the questions being examined in the on-going revision of Article 5 is how appropriate the provisions of Article 5 are to govern standby letter of credit transactions. Certainly Article 5's present coverage is broad enough to encompass standby letters of credit. Section 5–102(1) and Comment 1 to that section make clear that Article 5 applies to any case in which a credit is payable upon presentment to the issuer by the beneficiary of a draft or other demand for payment in compliance with the conditions of the credit. Article 5 applies to a case in which a movie star presents a demand for payment accompanied by a statement that her work on a movie is completed as well as to the traditional documentary sale discussed in Chapter 14 in which the seller presents a bill of lading along with a draft. However, § 5–115 providing for damages for wrongful dishonor by an issuer speaks in terms of the traditional sale of goods transaction.

C. FORMAL REQUIREMENTS

TRANSPARENT PRODUCTS CORP. v. PAYSAVER CREDIT UNION

United States Court of Appeals, Seventh Circuit, 1988.
864 F.2d 60.

EASTERBROOK, CIRCUIT JUDGE.

Uncertain of the difference between a line of credit and a letter of credit, the president of Paysaver Credit Union signed this document on the Credit Union's letterhead:

Transparent Products Corporation

Bensenville, IL. 60101

RE: Thomas Wells

Gentlemen:

We hereby establish our letter of credit at the request of Thomas Wells of 1003 South 23rd Avenue, Maywood and of Titan Tool of 1315 South 3rd Avenue, Maywood up to the aggregate amount of fifty-thousand dollars ($50,000).

At the time Paysaver signed this document, Titan Tool owed Transparent some $33,000 on open account credit for plastics. Titan wanted to buy another $61,000 worth, but Transparent had balked unless Titan's creditworthiness could be assured. Wells, an employee of Titan who had a $50,000 certificate of deposit with Paysaver, procured this document. Transparent apparently deemed it insufficient assurance of payment and did not sell additional goods to Titan. Some 13 months later Titan, then a debtor in bankruptcy, still had not paid the original $33,000. Transparent demanded that Paysaver make good the debt. Transparent believes that the document guarantees Titan's general debts; Paysaver believes that the document is a mish-mash with no legal effect.

The district court concluded after a trial (at which the president of Paysaver allowed that he did not understand how letters of credit differed from lines of credit) that the document is a letter of credit. The court then held, in part on the basis of the intent underlying Paysaver's decision to send the document, that Transparent's delay in making a demand equitably estopped it from collecting. The injection of such considerations into the enforcement of letters of credit is unprecedented and would be most unfortunate. The district court did not find that Transparent deceived Paysaver or otherwise induced detrimental reliance on an unkept promise; it found only that Transparent tarried unduly. Letters of credit are designed to provide assurance of payment and could not serve that purpose if the beneficiary risked being denied payment for withholding a demand "for too long" while attempting to collect from the primary debtor. We need not consider, however, whether principles of estoppel are forever beyond the pale when dealing with letters of credit, for Paysaver defends its judgment on the ground that the document is not one.

Letters of credit facilitate commercial transactions by providing the assurance of a reliable party that a debt will be paid quickly and with no fuss. Letters often provide that the issuer will pay on presentation of shipping documents, relieving the seller of the risk of nonpayment (or delayed payment) while shifting to the buyer the risk that the goods will be defective and it will need to pursue the seller. Standby letters of credit do not contemplate immediate payment by the issuer but serve as assurance if the debtor does not pay. Guarantee letters of credit serve a role similar to more conventional guarantees of debt, but with the promise that the issuer will pay on demand rather than balk and precipitate litigation to determine whether the underlying debt was due (a common event when guarantees are issued by officers or shareholders of the debtor), and with the additional benefit of enabling banks to stand behind their customers' transactions when they are forbidden to issue straight guarantees. See generally Cassondra E. Joseph, Letters of Credit: The Developing Concepts and Financing Functions, 94 Banking L.J. 816 (1977). In any of these cases, the issuer specifies conditions under which payment will be made. The Uniform Commercial Code defines "credit" by reference to these conditions. The definition has two stages. Section 5–102 * * * establishes the scope of Article 5 (governing letters of credit), and § 5–103(1) defines "credit":

5–102.　Scope.　(1) This Article applies

(a) to a credit issued by a bank if the credit requires a documentary draft or a documentary demand for payment;　and

(b) to a credit issued by a person other than a bank if the credit requires that the draft or demand for payment be accompanied by a document of title;　and

(c) to a credit issued by a bank or other person if the credit is not within subparagraphs (a) or (b) but conspicuously states that it is a letter of credit or is conspicuously so entitled.

5–103.　Definitions.　(1) In this Article unless the context otherwise requires

(a) "Credit" or "letter of credit" means an engagement by a bank or other person made at the request of a customer and of a kind within the scope of this Article (Section 5–102) that the issuer will honor drafts or other demands for payment upon compliance with the conditions specified in the credit.　A credit may be either revocable or irrevocable.　The engagement may be either an agreement to honor or a statement that the bank or other person is authorized to honor.

Transparent relies on § 5–102(1)(c), observing that the document conspicuously calls itself a "letter of credit".　(A statement is "conspicuous" if it is "so written that a reasonable person against whom it is to operate ought to have noticed it."　UCC § 1–201(10). Paysaver, which wrote this short letter, had to notice its own words.)　But § 5–102(1)(c) applies only to "a credit", and under § 5–103(1)(a) a "credit" is an "engagement" to "honor drafts or other demands for payment upon compliance with the conditions" stated.　The document Paysaver signed does not engage to do anything, under any conditions.

Sections 5–102 and 5–103, taken together with §§ 5–104 and 5–105 (saying that there are no formal requirements), show that a letter of credit need not be supported by consideration or contain any magic words or expiration date.　They show with equal force that a letter of credit is an "engagement" to pay on the occurrence of specified events or the presentation of specified documents.　A document engaging to do nothing and mentioning no events is simply a stray piece of paper.　*　*　*

The title controls only when the document contains the terms appropriate to the substance of such an instrument.　The letter Paysaver signed is no different in principle from a pumpkin on which "$50,000" and "letter of credit" had been stencilled.　Just as calling a sports car a "principal residence" will not permit the owner to take the deduction for interest under the tax laws, so calling a pumpkin a "letter of credit" will not make it one. This harmonizes our views with Board of Inland Revenue v. Haddock, in which String, J., concluded that a cow bearing the words "To the London and Literary Bank, Ltd.: Pay to the Collector of Taxes, who is no gentleman, or Order, the sum of fifty-seven pounds (and may he rot!). £57/0/0", was a negotiable instrument.[2] The judge observed that the writing included all the terms necessary for negotiability, and that the cow could be endorsed over to any willing holder.

Insistence on having terms—a concrete "engagement"—is not mere pedantry. Letters of credit give assurance of payment; to promote the reliability of the device, courts do not look beneath the surface of the documents to discover side agreements, plumb the intent of the parties, and the like. Yet only such a detour could flesh out the document written by Paysaver. If this letter were viewed as an ordinary contract, it would be unenforceable on the ground that the undertaking is hopelessly indefinite. A document too vague to be enforced as a contract is an implausible candidate for an Article 5 letter of credit.

Consider what is missing. One item is the term most important to any letter of credit: specification of the circumstances requiring the issuer to pay. Transparent believes that the document commits Paysaver to make good Titan's existing debt. Yet letters of credit to guarantee payment of prior debts are rare. One could see the document alternatively as an undertaking to make good on any new transaction, such as the $61,000 sale under discussion. A letter with this meaning would not stand behind the $33,000 accrued debt. Only speculation or a detailed inquiry into oral negotiations—both anathema in letter of credit transactions—could supply the missing term. Contrast Bank of North Carolina, N.A. v. Rock Island Bank, 570 F.2d 202 (7th Cir.1978) (holding an undertaking to be a letter of credit because it contained detailed terms on which payment would occur).

Another missing or confusing item is the customer. The document is captioned "RE: Thomas Wells". Wells was an employee of Titan and not indebted to Transparent. Counsel for Transparent conceded at oral argument that it had no claim against Wells personally. Only the recitation that the document was issued "at the request of" Titan in addition to that of Wells offers support for application to Titan's transactions. If we must choose between reading the document as standing behind Wells or standing behind Titan, where the former is what the caption says and the latter is a felony (given limitations on credit unions' activities, 12 U.S.C. § 1757), the choice is simple. Transparent

2. This enlightening case does not appear in the official reports, perhaps because it is the invention of A.P. Herbert, Uncommon Law 201–06 (1935), but given what *does* appear in the official reports, Board of Inland Revenue v. Haddock has its attractions.

balked (as well it should) when asked whether a document saying something like "at the request of Exxon Corp., we undertake to assume the obligations of Titan Tool" would allow Transparent to invoke the letter of credit to collect a debt due from Exxon. Transparent suggested that we dip beneath the surface of *this* document to see that the negotiations leading to its issuance grew out of commercial dealings between Transparent and Titan, but we have explained already why courts do not consider parol evidence when evaluating letters of credit.

The document is silent or obscure on every significant question. Such writings do not promote certainty in commercial transactions. Why a credit union put the words "letter of credit" to a document is beyond us; perhaps the National Credit Union Administration ought to have a few words with the management at the Paysaver Credit Union. Whatever this document may be, it is not a "credit" under §§ 5–102 and 5–103 of the UCC.

AFFIRMED.

NOTES

1. The court finds the writing deficient as a credit under § 5–103(1)(a) because, among other things, it does not specify the circumstances requiring the issuer to pay. Typically letters of credit will state specific conditions on the issuer's undertaking to pay, like the presentment of a document of title for goods, a construction completion certificate, or a representation that the customer (the person who requests issuance of the letter of credit) is in default on its obligation to the beneficiary (the person in whose favor the credit is issued). These documents will usually be accompanied by a draft drawn by the beneficiary on the issuing bank payable "at sight" (that is on presentment) to the order of the beneficiary. A sight draft is merely a demand for payment that may be negotiable in form, thus conferring upon the beneficiary the power to transfer the draft to a third person who may take the rights of a holder in due course discussed in the next chapter. Would the writing be a credit within § 5–103(1)(a) if the only condition to payment stated was the beneficiary's act of drawing a draft on the issuer or otherwise making a demand for payment of the issuer?

2. Section 5–103(1)(a) says "A credit may be either revocable or irrevocable." Since a revocable letter of credit may be rendered worthless by the unilateral act of revocation on the part of the issuer, beneficiaries should take care to see that the term "irrevocable letter of credit" appears in the credit. But what is the consequence if the credit is silent on the issue? Comment 1 to § 5–103 waffles, and refers the issue to the courts for decision with only the vague standards of § 1–205 on course of dealing and usage of the trade as guidance. The courts, noting the illusory

aspects of a revocable letter of credit, have sensibly read in a presumption of irrevocability in cases covered by Article 5. See, e.g., Data General Corp., Inc. v. Citizens National Bank, 502 F.Supp. 776 (D.Conn.1980). On the other hand Article 7 of the UCP states that in the absence of an indication in the credit that it is irrevocable, the credit shall be deemed revocable. Thus if the credit incorporates the UCP and is silent on irrevocability, disaster may await the beneficiary, as Pete Beathard of the Chicago Winds of the World Football League found to his dismay in Beathard v. Chicago Football Club, Inc., 419 F.Supp. 1133 (N.D.Ill. 1976). But in Conoco, Inc. v. Norwest Bank Mason City, N.A., 767 F.2d 470 (8th Cir.1985), the court, noting that a revocable letter of credit would be "meaningless," managed to find irrevocability in a credit subject to the UCP on the basis of wording to the effect that the credit would remain in force for six months.

3. One of the problems that has arisen with respect to standby letters of credit is whether the use of a letter of credit as a general guaranty device conflicts with federal and state laws forbidding banks from guaranteeing the obligations of others. For example, in New Jersey Bank v. Palladino, 77 N.J. 33, 389 A.2d 454 (1978), Palladino sought a loan from New Jersey Bank which was willing to make the loan only if the borrower produced "some sort of collateral or support for the note." Palladino obtained a letter from First State Bank addressed to New Jersey Bank which stated that First State Bank would "assume the obligation" arising from a note signed by Palladino in the amount of $50,000, and that First State Bank would honor the commitment upon notice that the loan had not been paid. The New Jersey statute denied power to First State Bank to "guarantee the obligations of others" subject to an exception which allowed it "to issue letters of credit authorizing holders thereof to draw drafts upon it." The court noted that Article 5 of the UCC applies "to a credit issued by a bank if the credit requires a documentary draft or a documentary demand for payment." § 5–102(1)(a). "Documentary demand for payment" is defined as a demand "honor of which is conditioned upon the presentation of a document or documents" and "document" is defined as "any paper including * * * notice of default and the like." § 5–103(1)(b). The court held that the letter of First State Bank was a letter of credit within these definitions, stating that the notice of default was intended by the parties to be a written notice and therefore was a "document." The court noted that this "standby letter of credit" was "akin to a guaranty, for the bank's sole function is to act as surety for its customer's failure to pay," but it followed cases decided in other jurisdictions holding that standby letters of credit fall within the exception to the prohibition against banks acting as sureties. A dissenting opinion stated that the standby letter of credit was in substance identical to a guaranty and that to allow its use was to erode the

statutory policy against bank guaranties. It also stated: "The difference between conventional letters of credit and the standby variety in terms of bank solvency is clear. In the former, typically used to finance sales of goods, the issuing bank's obligation arises only on the delivery of shipping documents evidencing title to the goods. The bank is therefore secure. In the standby letter of credit situation, by the time the bank is called upon to meet the demand of the beneficiary there has typically been a default of the bank customer to the beneficiary and there is no practicable recourse by the bank because of the insolvency of the customer." Banking regulations limit the amount of obligations banks can incur in issuing standby letters of credit. White & Summers, Uniform Commercial Code § 19–3 (3d ed. 1988). For a discussion of standby letters of credit see Verkuil, Bank Solvency and Guaranty Letters of Credit, 25 Stan.L.Rev. 716 (1973).

D. ISSUER'S OBLIGATION TO PAY

1. THE STRICT COMPLIANCE RULE

AMERICAN COLEMAN CO. v. INTRAWEST BANK
United States Court of Appeals, Tenth Circuit, 1989.
887 F.2d 1382.

BARRETT, SENIOR CIRCUIT JUDGE.

* * *

In this diversity case, the American Coleman Company (American Coleman), plaintiff below, appeals from the district court's order granting summary judgment on behalf of the defendant below, Intrawest Bank of Southglenn, N.A., the predecessor to the United Bank of Southglenn, N.A. (Bank). The court dismissed, with prejudice, American Coleman's action for damages for an alleged wrongful dishonor of a request for payment pursuant to a letter of credit.

In 1984, American Coleman sold some real property located in Littleton, Colorado, to James E. Gammon (Gammon) and the South Santa Fe Partnership (the Partnership) and took a note secured by a first deed of trust on the property. The note and deed of trust were dated November 16, 1984, but not recorded until November 21, 1984. The terms of the repayment of the note required Gammon and the Partnership to post a letter of credit, of which American Coleman would be the beneficiary. The Bank, on behalf of its customer, Gammon and Associates, established a "Clean, Irrevocable Letter of Credit" in amount of $250,000 in favor of American Coleman. It was dated February 15, 1985, and was to expire on November 15, 1986. In consideration, the Bank received from Gammon a letter of credit fee and a second deed of trust on the Littleton property under a reimbursement contract whereby Gammon was to repay Bank for all payments made by Bank to American Coleman pursuant to the letter of credit. The letter of credit arrangement, once established, is often referred to as a statutory obligation on the part of the issuer (Bank) to honor drafts drawn by the beneficiary (American Coleman) that comply with the terms of the letter of credit. The transaction is separate and independent from the underlying business transaction between the beneficiary (American Coleman) and the Bank's customer (Gammon and Associates) which is contractual in nature. * * * A letter of credit is not an evidence of indebtedness; it is merely a promise by a bank to lend money under certain circumstances. * * *

The Bank was to make funds available to American Coleman pursuant to its sight drafts to be accompanied by the "[o]riginal Letter of Credit and your signed written statement that Jim Gammon and Associates is in default on the Note and Security Agreement dated November 21, 1984, between American Coleman and Jim Gammon and Associates." * * * The above reference to a note and security agreement dated November 21, 1984, was an error, inasmuch as no such documents ever existed. The record does not resolve the dispute relative to the party responsible for the error. However, on November 16, 1984, Gammon and Associates executed and delivered to American Coleman a note in the principal sum of $1,037,500 secured by a first deed of trust on the Littleton property sold which were recorded on November 21, 1984.

Thereafter, on December 31, 1985, and on May 16, 1986, American Coleman requested payments of $75,000, respectively, under the letter of credit. Both of these requests included the original letter of credit and the specific default language previously referred to, i.e., "Jim Gammon and Associates is in default on the Note and Security Agreement dated November 21, 1984, between American Coleman and Jim Gammon and Associates." Thus, a balance of $100,000 remained available to be drawn on under the letter of credit when on November 13, 1986, American Coleman tendered to Bank a sight draft in amount of $100,000 with the following statement appended thereto:

> [T]he American Coleman Company informs you that Jim Gammon and Associates is in default on the Note and Security Agreement dated November 21, 1984, and the Promissory Note dated November 16, 1984, between American Coleman and Jim Gammon and Associates.

Bank formally dishonored the draft on November 17, 1986, two days after the letter of credit expired because (1) the amount requested was in advance of any default, and (2) no default could occur until November 16, 1986. Bank did not give as a reason for dishonor the fact that the wording of American Coleman's request was not in strict compliance with the terms of the letter of credit.

In the district court, both parties moved for summary judgment, agreeing that there was no genuine dispute of material fact relative to Bank's liability for its dishonor of American Coleman's request of November 13, 1986, for the balance of funds under the letter of credit. Bank contended that the fact that the note was not then in default constituted a valid ground for dishonor and, further, that dishonor was proper because American Coleman's request was not in strict compliance with the terms of the letter of credit. American Coleman argued that Bank should be estopped from raising the defense of strict compliance because Bank had not asserted this defense at the time of dishonor. Further, should Bank not be estopped, American Coleman contended that its request for funds was in strict compliance with the terms of the letter of credit. In considering the cross-motions for summary judgment, the district court relied upon the pleadings, the briefs, affidavits and other documentation.

The district court found/concluded that Bank was not estopped from raising the defense of strict compliance and that American Coleman's request of November 13, 1986, was not in strict compliance with the terms of the letter of credit. The court did not reach the issue whether the original reason given by the Bank, i.e., that the note was not yet in default, was a valid ground for dishonor.

On appeal, American Coleman contends that the district court's decision was erroneous, contrary to law, and an abuse of discretion in the court's holdings that: (1) the note was not yet in default, (2) the demand was not in strict compliance, technically or literally, with the terms of the letter of credit, (3) the Bank was not estopped from raising lack of strict compliance as a reason for dishonor, and (4) the beneficiary (American Coleman) was not misled, and could not have cured the defect because Bank was allowed, pursuant to § 5–112(1)(a), to defer payment or dishonor for three banking days.

* * *

I.

American Coleman argues that the district court was clearly erroneous in finding/concluding that the Note of November 16, 1984, was not yet in default when the November 13, 1986, demand for payment was made by American Coleman upon Bank. The record shows, however, that the district court made no such finding.

It is true that after the draft of November 13, 1986, was submitted Bank did inform American Coleman that it would not fund the letter of credit because the Note was not in default and could not be in default until November 16, 1986. Because this was the only ground relied upon by Bank to dishonor the draft, American Coleman argued, unsuccessfully, that Bank should be estopped from raising the defense of strict compliance in the district court action because it failed to assert the issue of nonconformity at the time it dishonored the draft.

The district court plainly did not find/conclude that the Note of December 16, 1984, was in default. In the district court's Memorandum Opinion and Order of December 17, 1987, the court stated:

> Since I conclude that the bank is not estopped from raising the defense of strict compliance, and since I further find that American Coleman's request for funds was not in strict compliance with the terms and conditions of the letter of credit, I need not reach the issue of whether the original reason given by the bank (that the note was not yet in default) was a valid ground for dishonor.

II.

American Coleman contends that the district court erred in holding that the doctrine of strict compliance required American Coleman, as beneficiary of the letter of credit from Bank, as issuer, to literally and technically adhere to the requirements of the letter of credit. The district court found/concluded:

> In the present case, it is clear that American Coleman's request for payment presented November 13, 1986 was not in technical or literal compliance with the terms of the letter of credit. American Coleman's reference to two different notes could easily have caused the bank's documents examiner some confusion. Accordingly, because I conclude that the rule of strict compliance, as it is applied in Colorado, requires literal compliance with the terms and requirements set forth in the letter of credit, and there was no such literal compliance in this case * * *.

The district court recognized that many courts refuse to allow an issuing bank to dishonor a demand for payment when the nonconformity between the language contained in the draft or demand and the terms contained in the letter of credit is trivial or technical. The court observed that the Colorado Supreme Court has not as yet ruled on the distinction between traditional strict compliance versus substantial compliance, and particularly so where the deviation is "[a]s minor and technical as in this case." Even so, based upon Colorado National Bank v. Board of County Commissioners, 634 P.2d 32, 40 (Colo.1981) ("To maintain the commercial vitality of the letter of credit device, strict compliance with the terms of the letter of credit is required"); Guilford Pattern Works, Inc. v. United Bank of Boulder, 655 F.Supp. 378, 379–80 (D.Colo.1987) ("Colorado courts have held that in order to maintain the commercial validity of the vehicle of letters of credit, strict compliance with the terms and conditions is necessary."), and other cases and authorities, the district court reasoned that the Colorado Supreme Court "[w]ould shun the non-standard of substantial compliance and would require literal and technical adherence to the requirements of the letter of credit." We agree.

§ 5–114(1) provides:

> An issuer must honor a draft or demand for payment which complies with the terms of the relevant credit, regardless of whether the goods or documents conform to the underlying contract for sale or other contract between the customer and the beneficiary. The issuer is not excused from honor of such a draft or demand by reason of an additional general term that all documents must be satisfactory to the issuer, but an issuer may require that specified documents must be satisfactory to it.

In Raiffeisen–Zentralkasse Tirol v. First National Bank, 671 P.2d 1008 (Colo.App.1983), the court held that the obligation of the issuer of a letter of credit to honor the letter is wholly separate from the beneficiary's compliance with the terms of the underlying contract and is dependent solely on the terms and conditions contained in the letter of credit. This separation is supportive of the rule laid down in Colorado National Bank v. Board of County Commissioners, supra, that strict compliance with the terms of a letter of credit is required to maintain the commercial vitality of the letter of credit device. Failure on the part of Bank to oversee careful compliance with the terms of the letter of credit would have prohibited Bank from collecting the funds paid to the beneficiary (American Coleman) from its customer, the Partnership (Jim Gammon and Associates). * * * The duty of the issuing Bank is ministerial in nature, confined to checking the presented documents carefully against what the letter of credit requires. * * *

The district court found that the language in American Coleman's draft of November 13, 1986, referring to "[T]he Note and Security Agreement dated November 21, 1984, *and the Promissory Note dated November 16, 1984*, between American Coleman and Jim Gammon and Associates" was not in strict compliance because of the extra language that was included. We agree.

It has been observed that most courts apply the "strict compliance" standard which leaves "no room for documents which are almost the same or which will do just as well." A minority of the courts hold that a beneficiary's "reasonable" or "substantial" performance of the letter of credit's requirement will do. However, no matter how one reads the cases, strict compliance endures as the central test. White & Summers, Uniform Commercial Code, Third Edition (1988), Vol. 2, § 19–5, p. 31. The authors state that cases applying the "reasonable" or "substantial" compliance standard "[a]re so few and their notion so inherently fuzzy that they give little or no clue as to what might be 'reasonable' or 'substantial' compliance."

While it is apparent from the cases that minute discrepancies which could not possibly mislead a document examiner are usually disregarded, this does not constitute a retreat from the strict compliance standard applicable in this case inasmuch as the district court found that "[A]merican Coleman's reference to two different notes could easily have caused the bank's documents examiner some confusion." We agree.

We hold that the district court did not err in applying the strict compliance standard. We reject American Coleman's argument that reference in the November 13, 1986, draft to the second note was mere "surplusage." The apparent existence of two promissory notes supports the district court's finding that Bank could have been misled by American Coleman's November 13, 1986, draft. American Coleman's contention that Bank could not have been misled by the draft because Bank drafted the letter of credit is without support in this record. The deposition testimony of American Coleman representative Joseph E. McElroy demonstrates that American Coleman's attorney assisted in drafting the letter of credit. There is no other evidence in the record on appeal relative thereto.

III.

American Coleman contends that the district court was clearly erroneous in holding that Bank was not estopped from raising the defense of lack of strict compliance as a reason for its dishonor of the November 13, 1986, draft.

The district court recognized that in Colorado the general rule is that "[w]hen an issuer of a letter of credit formally places its refusal to pay upon specified grounds, it is held to have waived all other grounds," quoting from Colorado National Bank v. Board of County Commissioners, 634 P.2d 32, 41 (Colo.1981). However, the district court relied upon that same case for the proposition that the waiver-estoppel rule "[i]s limited to situations where the statements have misled the beneficiary who would have cured the defect but relied on the stated grounds to its injury."

The district court relied on Colorado National Bank v. Board of County Commissioners, supra, for its ruling that Bank was not estopped from raising a ground for dishonor in defense of suit brought by American Coleman even though it failed to state such ground at the time of dishonor.

In Colorado National Bank v. Board of County Commissioners, the letter of credit provided for a 15–day sight draft. However, the beneficiary submitted a demand draft on the day the letter of credit was to expire. Bank gave several reasons for dishonor, but did not rely upon the fact that the beneficiary had presented a demand draft in lieu of the required 15–day sight draft. Even so, the court held that the bank was not estopped from raising this ground in defense of the suit because the non-conforming demand draft was presented on the same day that the letter of credit expired. The court observed that under § 5–112(1)(a) a bank called upon to honor a draft or demand for payment under a letter of credit may defer payment or dishonor until the close of the third banking day following receipt of the documents. Thus, the court reasoned that the beneficiary could not have cured the defect since any subsequent presentment would have been untimely. Accordingly, the beneficiary could not have detrimentally relied on the bank's failure to state the discrepancy as a ground for dishonor.

We agree with the district court's conclusion that the facts of the instant case are quite similar to those in *Colorado National* and that American Coleman cannot be said to have detrimentally relied on Bank's failure to state the strict compliance discrepancy as one ground for dishonor, and that Bank is not estopped from raising the doctrine of strict compliance in its defense. November 13, 1986, was a Thursday. Three banking days thereafter would extend to November 18, 1986, just one day after Bank gave formal notice of dishonor. American Coleman could not have submitted another draft before the note expired. § 5–112(1) provides, in pertinent part:

> A bank to which a documentary draft or demand for payment is presented under a credit may without dishonor of the draft, demand or credit (a) defer honor until the close of the third banking day following receipt of the documents
> *　*　*.

American Coleman insists that the letter of credit in this case is clearly denominated a "clean" letter of credit as distinguished from a "documentary" letter of credit and that, accordingly, the three-banking-day rule does not apply. We agree that this statute applies only to a documentary draft or demand for payment. We disagree with American Coleman's contention that simply because the letter of credit here was denominated "Clean Irrevocable Letter of Credit", it was treated by the parties as such.

§ 5–103(1)(b) defines a "documentary draft" or a "documentary demand for payment" as one honor of which is conditioned upon the presentation of a document or documents. "Document" is defined therein as any paper, including invoice, certificate, notice of default, and the like. In the case at bar, American

Coleman was required under the terms of the letter of credit to present the original letter of credit (a document) and a notice of default (a document) with each draft. American Coleman's effort to restrict the definition of "documentary draft" to documents of title or shipping invoices must fail.

We AFFIRM.

NOTES

1. The plight of the issuing bank is described by Givray, Letters of Credit, 44 Bus.Law. 1567, 1589 (1989):

> Consider the letter of credit department in a large bank. When the presented documents arrive, they are routed to an examining clerk. He pulls the related letter of credit from the bank's files and lays it next to the presented documents. He compares these documents against the letter's requirements and decides whether compliance has occurred. This happens daily for many sets of documents. Some are presented against a commercial letter, others against a standby. Yet the routine stays the same. It must move along steadily.
>
> Each time, the examiner has only the letter's words and the face of the presented documents to go by. Much may be going on outside these papers. For example, a presented certificate may swear customer's default even though such default is being honestly disputed. Or a bill of lading may show goods loaded on a ship that later sank in a storm. Or perhaps some practice in customer's or beneficiary's industry shades the meaning of a presented document and none of the papers before the examiner explain such practice. The document examiner is ill-equipped to deal with outside events like these. He has no lawyer by his side. He will probably have little or no command of any industry practice not within banking spheres. Nor can he afford the expense, risk, and delay of any elaborate reasoning as he checks the presented papers against the letter's requirements. For the letter of credit to work quickly as a cheap and sure device, then, the examiner must disregard outside influences like these as he routinely asks, "From what appears on their face, do the presented documents meet all the letter's requirements?"

2. Article 5 takes no explicit position on the strict/substantial compliance dispute. Most decisions embrace the strict compliance rule, but this leaves open the question whether strict compliance requires literal adherence. The district court in *American Coleman* saw Colorado law as demanding "literal and technical adherence to the requirements of the letter of credit." The Task Force Study, 45 Bus.Law. 1527, 1609 (1990), proposes the following solution: "The strict compliance standard as practiced by banks should be utilized. Properly understood, strict compliance means

what a knowledgeable diligent document checker would have accepted as being in facial compliance with the terms of the credit." Under this test should the decision in *American Coleman* be different? The triggering event for the bank's obligation to pay was presentment to the bank of a sight draft accompanied by a written statement by the beneficiary that the "Note and Security Agreement dated November 21, 1984" was in default. Even though there was no such note, the beneficiary's statement contained the required representation, and the bank would surely have incurred no liability to its customers for wrongful payment if it had paid the draft. Perhaps because of its unease about representing that the customers were in default on a non-existent note, the beneficiary added the fatal words "and the Promissory Note dated November 16, 1984", which described the true note on which the customers were actually in default. Should a diligent and knowledgeable document checker have dishonored? In Beyene v. Irving Trust Co., 762 F.2d 4 (2d Cir.1985), the terms of the letter of credit called for presentment of a bill of lading on which the party to be notified was to be the buyer, *Sofran.* The name that actually appeared on the bill of lading was *Soran.* The court held that the misspelling was a material discrepancy that entitled the bank to dishonor the letter of credit.

3. Matter of Coral Petroleum, Inc., 878 F.2d 830 (5th Cir. 1989), presented the issue of whether impossibility excuses strict compliance with a letter of credit. Seller sold Buyer 31,000 barrels of West Texas Intermediate crude oil for $880,400 and required Buyer to obtain a standby letter of credit in a form acceptable to Seller for the price. Bank issued the letter of credit under Buyer's instructions that the credit would be payable upon receipt of certain documents including (1) a statement by Seller that West Texas Intermediate oil had been delivered to Buyer and (2) a copy of the shipper's transfer order showing transfer to Buyer of 31,000 barrels of "WTNM SO or SR." Buyer's instructions were mistaken. West Texas Intermediate crude is a sweet oil (meaning not containing certain undesirable elements found in sour oil), but WTNM SO or SR refers to sour oil. Thus, the letter of credit required two documents that were contradictory: a shipper's order showing transfer of sour oil to Buyer and a statement that sweet oil had been delivered to Buyer. After Buyer filed in bankruptcy under Chapter 11, Seller demanded payment under the letter of credit. Bank refused to pay because Seller's demand was accompanied by a shipper's order showing transfer of sweet oil to Buyer. Seller had inspected the letter of credit before accepting it and did not ask that the erroneous description be corrected. Seller argued that the terms of the credit were impossible to perform. Seller could not deliver sweet oil to Buyer and procure a shipper's transfer order showing that sour oil had been delivered. Seller also argued that the letter of credit was ambiguous and the

ambiguity should be construed against Bank. The court held that the letter of credit was not ambiguous. The fact that it was impossible for Seller to comply did not excuse compliance by Seller. Bank is not required to know the meaning of technical trade terms used in the letter of credit. Moreover, Seller was negligent in accepting a letter of credit with requirements that could not be met. In Givray, Letters of Credit, 45 Bus.Law. 2381, 2404 (1990), it is wryly suggested that issuers add a conspicuous legend stating "Please examine this letter of credit at once. If you feel unable to meet any of its requirements, either singly or together, please contact customer immediately to see if the letter of credit can be amended. Otherwise, you risk losing payment under this letter of credit for failure to comply strictly with its terms as written."

4. Was the strict compliance rule properly applied in the following cases?

Seller in accord with instructions from Buyer shipped goods to Columbus, Indiana. Payment was to be made under a letter of credit issued by Bank. The letter of credit mistakenly stated the place of delivery as Scottsdale, Arizona. Bank had issued the letter of credit without checking the financial status of Buyer. When Seller presented its demand for payment Bank refused on the ground that shipment was not made to the destination stated in the letter of credit. At that time Bank had reason to believe that Buyer would not be able to reimburse Bank for any payment made under the letter of credit. Both Buyer and Seller requested Bank to amend the letter of credit to reflect the correct destination point. Bank refused. The court stated: "In this action, [Seller] plainly relied upon the letter of credit issued by [Bank]. The point of delivery, [Seller] alleges, is of no concern to [Bank]. [Bank] did not have a security interest in the goods, and [Bank's] ability to collect from its customer will not be prejudiced by changing delivery from Arizona to Indiana. [Bank's] sole reason for refusal to amend the letter of credit was simply to rescue itself from its poor judgment when the letter was issued. On these facts, the conduct of [Bank] is inequitable." Nevertheless, the court found that Bank had no duty to amend the letter of credit and could refuse payment because the terms of the letter of credit had not been satisfied. AMF Head Sports Wear, Inc. v. Ray Scott's All–American Sports Club, 448 F.Supp. 222 (D.Ariz.1978).

In Board of Trade of San Francisco v. Swiss Credit Bank, 597 F.2d 146 (9th Cir.1979), a letter of credit called for presentment of various documents including a "full set clean on board bills of lading" which according to expert testimony referred to ocean shipment. An initial shipment was made by air and an air way bill (bill of lading) was presented in support of the draft which was paid. Two subsequent shipments were also made by air and air way bills were again presented in support of the draft. This time the issuing bank refused to pay stating that the letter of credit required ocean shipment. The court held that if the expert testimony was correct the letter of credit required ocean shipment and the issuing bank did not wrongfully dishonor the credit.

In United States Industries, Inc. v. Second New Haven Bank, 462 F.Supp. 662 (D.Conn.1978), the letter of credit required a certificate that the demand for payment represented money owing for goods duly shipped to Buyer for which payment was demanded and not received within seven days of shipment. Seller, on the morning of the last day of the term of the credit, presented a certificate that the demand for payment represented money owing for goods duly shipped to Buyer for which payment was not received within seven days of shipment. The certificate did not expressly state that payment had been demanded; however, invoices accompanying the certificate clearly showed that demand had been made. The court held that the documents presented complied with the credit because on their face they put Issuer "on notice that [Seller] had made the required demand for payment."

In First National Bank of Atlanta v. Wynne, 149 Ga.App. 811, 256 S.E.2d 383 (1979), the letter of credit required a draft marked "Drawn Under The First National Bank of Atlanta Credit No. S–3753." Beneficiary presented a draft without the quoted phrase but the letter transmitting the draft referred to Credit No. S–3753 and the original letter of credit No. S–3753 was enclosed. Issuer refused to pay. In holding in favor of Beneficiary the court stated: "Accordingly, we hold that if from all the documents presented to the issuer by the beneficiary there is substantial compliance *and* there is no possibility that the documents submitted could mislead the issuer to its detriment, there has been compliance with the letter of credit."

2. WAIVER AND ESTOPPEL

Under § 5–112(1) an issuer has until the close of the third banking day after receipt of the documents to pay. If the issuer fails to pay within this period it is liable for damages for dishonor (§ 5–115) if the beneficiary's tender of documents strictly complies with the terms of the letter of credit. However, the strict compliance rule has been ameliorated by case holdings that the issuer has either waived its right to assert the strict compliance rule or is estopped to do so. For waiver to apply it must be shown that the issuer was giving up a known right. The usual statement of estoppel is that it must be shown that the party asserting the estoppel lacked knowledge of the facts, was without means to discover them, relied on the actions of the party sought to be charged, and changed position in reliance thereon.

PROBLEMS

How would the *American Coleman* court have decided that case if the facts had been these:

Case #1. Beneficiary presented three drafts for payment to Issuer, two before Customer's bankruptcy and the third after its bankruptcy. Each time the draft was accompanied by the same nonconforming document referring to "the Promissory Note dated November 16, 1984." The first two times Issuer paid the draft without objection after receiving permission of Customer to pay despite the nonconformity. The third time Issuer dishonored the draft on the ground that the document did not comply with the terms of the letter of credit. Has Issuer wrongfully dishonored?

Case #2. The facts are the same as Case #1 except that when the documents were presented the first two times, Beneficiary asked Issuer whether the documents were in order. Issuer said "yes." Does this additional fact change the result in Case #1?

Case #3. Before expiration of the letter of credit, Beneficiary presented a draft to Issuer accompanied by the nonconforming statement referring to "the Promissory Note dated November 16, 1984." Shortly before the close of business on the third banking day Bank notified Beneficiary that it was dishonoring the draft because of noncompliance of the documents but Bank failed to explain why the documents did not comply. Beneficiary contended that Issuer had wrongfully dishonored because of its failure to point out a discrepancy that Beneficiary could easily have cured by presenting a document making no reference to the note of November 16, 1984. Has Issuer wrongfully dishonored?

Case #4. Before expiration of the letter of credit, Beneficiary presented a draft to Issuer accompanied by the nonconforming statement referring to the note dated November 16, 1984. On the day after presentment Issuer notified Beneficiary that it was dishonoring for two specified reasons neither of which involved the nonconforming reference to the note of November 16, 1984. When Beneficiary sued Issuer for wrongful dishonor, Issuer sought to rely on the nonconforming reference to the note of November 16, 1984 to excuse nonpayment. May it do so?

Case #5. Would the results change in any of these four cases if Issuer can show that Beneficiary knew it was submitting a nonconforming document?

NOTE

There are major differences between the UCC's approach in § 5–112, as construed by cases like *American Coleman,* and the UCP provisions summarized below by the Task Force Study, 45 Bus.Law. at 1600:

U.C.P. Article 16(c) provides:

The issuing bank shall have a reasonable time in which to examine the documents and to determine as above whether to take up or to refuse the documents.

U.C.P. Article 16(d) provides:

If the issuing bank decides to refuse the documents, it must give notice to that effect without delay by telecommunication or, if that is not possible, by other expeditious means, to the bank from which it received the documents (the remitting bank), or to the beneficiary, if it received the documents directly from him. Such notice must state the discrepancies in respect of which the issuing bank refuses the documents and must also state whether it is holding the documents at the disposal of, or is returning them to, the presenter (remitting bank or the beneficiary, as the case may be). The issuing bank shall then be entitled to claim from the remitting bank refund of any reimbursement which may have been made to that bank.

U.C.P. Article 16(e) provides:

If the issuing bank fails to act in accordance with the provisions of paragraphs (c) and (d) of this article and/or fails to hold the documents at the disposal of, or to return them to, the presenter, the issuing bank shall be precluded from claiming that the documents are not in accordance with the terms and conditions of the credit.

How would *American Coleman* and the Problems have been decided if these provisions of the U.C.P. had applied in those cases?

3. ISSUER'S RIGHT TO REIMBURSEMENT FROM CUSTOMER

If the issuer wrongfully dishonors a letter of credit, it is liable in damages to the beneficiary. § 5–115. But if it has paid a letter of credit that it should not have paid, it may jeopardize its right of reimbursement against its customer under § 5–114. Section 5–114(1) provides: "An issuer must honor a draft or demand for payment which complies with the terms of the relevant credit regardless of whether the goods or documents conform to the underlying contract for sale or other contract between the customer and the beneficiary." Unless the issuer's reimbursement agree-

ment with the customer specifies otherwise the issuer's statutory
right of reimbursement under § 5–114(3) arises only if it has "duly
honored a draft or demand for payment." Under § 5–114(2), the
issuer, acting in good faith, may pay a "draft or demand for
payment despite notification from the customer of fraud, forgery
or other defect not apparent on the face of the documents," and
Comment 3 to § 5–114 treats such a payment as included within
the meaning of "duly honored."

The credit risk that the issuer takes with respect to reimbursement may vary depending on whether the credit is the
traditional commercial letter of credit (payment against a bill of
lading) or a standby letter of credit. Commercial letters of credit
are meant to be paid in every case and, when the issuer has paid,
it receives possession of the bill of lading which the customer must
obtain in order to get the goods from the carrier. The issuer,
almost always a commercial bank in commercial letter of credit
cases, will usually not turn over the bill of lading to the customer
unless it can obtain reimbursement from the customer or it has
decided to grant credit to the customer. But standby letters are
meant to be paid only in the event of the customer's default on a
contract with the beneficiary. When the issuer pays it receives no
bill of lading or like document that the customer must have. If
the issuer pays a standby letter of credit, it has effectively made a
loan to the customer, and the reimbursement agreement will
resemble a loan agreement. In order to secure the customer's
reimbursement obligation, the issuer will typically take a security
interest in the customer's assets.

If the customer wants payment to be made in spite of a
nonconformity, normally the issuer will pay. The issuer is entitled to reimbursement because the customer has waived the nonconformity. On the other hand, the issuer may be reluctant to
pay if the customer does not want the letter of credit to be paid.
The issuer may not want to offend its customer. If an issuer pays
a letter of credit over a customer's objection, its right to reimbursement under § 5–114(3), in the absence of contrary agreement, depends on whether the issuer has "duly honored." What
"duly honored" means usually arises when the issuer has paid a
letter of credit in a case in which the tender of documents does not
meet the strict compliance test. Under § 5–109(2) an issuer owes
a customer the duty of examining the "documents with care so as
to ascertain that on their face they appear to comply with the
terms of the credit." Does observance by the courts of the strict
compliance rule in cases in which a beneficiary sues an issuer for
wrongful dishonor necessarily mean that the same test governs
when a customer sues an issuer for wrongful payment? In Bank
of Cochin Ltd. v. Manufacturers Hanover Trust Co., 612 F.Supp.
1533, 1538 (S.D.N.Y.1985), Judge Cannella spoke to this issue as
follows:

Courts and commentators have noted, however, that New York appears to maintain a bifurcated standard of compliance. * * * This approach calls for a strict compliance standard when the bank is sued by the beneficiary for wrongful dishonor but allows for a substantial compliance test when the bank is sued by the customer for wrongful honor. The stated rationale for the bifurcated standard is that it accords the bank flexibility in reacting to "a crossfire of pressures * * * especially in times of falling commodity prices," J. White & R. Summers, Handbook of the Law Under the Uniform Commercial Code, § 18–6, at 731–32 (quoting State of N.Y. Law Revision Comm'n, Study of Uniform Commercial Code: Article 5—Documentary Letters of Credit, at 66 (1955), reprinted in 3 State of N.Y. Law Revision Comm'n, Report of the Law Revision Comm'n for 1955, at 1634 ["N.Y.U.C.C. Study"], by limiting the liability burden on the bank, which might otherwise be caught between the "rock of a customer insisting on dishonor for highly technical reasons, and the hard place of a beneficiary threatening to sue for wrongful dishonor." B. Clark, The Law of Bank Deposits, Collection and Credit Cards, ¶ 8.5[4], at 8–48 (1981).

An example of the kind of case in which this bifurcated standard might apply is that in which the demand for payment was fraudulent and the supporting documents were forgeries. The issuer, however, was not aware that the documents were not genuine and was not negligent in accepting them as genuine. Risk of falsification of documents is placed on the customer by § 5–109(2). The customer, nevertheless, seeks to avoid reimbursement of the issuer on the basis of some nonconformity on the face of the documents. For example, in Bank of New York & Trust Co. v. Atterbury Brothers, 226 App.Div. 117, 234 N.Y.S. 442 (1st Dept. 1929), the issuer paid a draft on the basis of a forged bill of lading. The customer refused to reimburse the issuer on the ground that the letter of credit called for a draft by Arthur James Brown. The signature on the draft was "A. James Brown," but in fact that signature was by Arthur James Brown. The letter of credit also required documents covering "casein" while the documents presented covered "ground casein." Despite these discrepancies, which the court described as "trivial," the issuer was allowed reimbursement.

Prudent issuers will safeguard themselves against liability for wrongful payment by including exculpatory clauses in the reimbursement agreement designed to allow them to obtain reimbursement even though they pay a letter of credit in a case in which the documents do not strictly comply with the letter of credit. Some reimbursement agreements go so far as to provide that the issuer shall never be liable for the "form, sufficiency, accuracy, genuineness, falsification, legal effect, correctness or validity of any documents." White & Summers, Uniform Commercial Code § 19–8 (3d ed. 1988), questions whether this would not be limited by § 1–102(3) which invalidates the disclaimer of "the obligations of good faith, diligence, reasonableness and care prescribed by this Act."

4. DAMAGES FOR WRONGFUL DISHONOR

It is a basic principle of letter of credit law that the letter of credit contract between an issuer and a beneficiary is independent of the underlying contract between the beneficiary and the customer. Comment 1 to § 5–114. It might seem to follow that if the issuer wrongfully dishonors a letter of credit, the beneficiary should be able to recover the face amount of the credit from the issuer, often on summary judgment, leaving the customer to litigate with the beneficiary in a separate action over any amount the beneficiary has received in excess of its right of recovery on the underlying contract. But, at least in cases in which the beneficiary is a seller of goods, § 5–115 limits the beneficiary's recovery by requiring it to deduct from the face amount of the credit any amount realized by it upon disposition of the goods in the underlying sales transaction. In the case of an anticipatory repudiation the beneficiary selling goods has the same rights against the issuer that a seller has against a buyer under § 2–610. Hence, in these cases, § 5–115 requires reference to the underlying sales contract to prevent a beneficiary from receiving double recovery. It is clear that § 5–115 was drafted with the traditional commercial letter of credit transaction in mind, but it would also apply to require a reduction in recovery of the face amount of the credit in a case in which a standby letter of credit is involved if the beneficiary is the seller of goods. What is not clear is how § 5–115 applies to cases of standby letters of credit in which there is no underlying sale of goods.

PROBLEM

Customer planned to develop a recreational community. County approval of Customer's subdivision was conditional on Customer's agreement to provide a standby letter of credit to the County (Beneficiary) to ensure that Customer would complete roads and related improvements in accordance with subdivision design specifications. The required letter of credit was obtained from Issuer. Customer never commenced construction of the roads or other improvements and Issuer wrongfully dishonored the letter of credit. Beneficiary sued Issuer for the face amount of the letter of credit plus interest from the date of the demand for payment. Issuer defended on the ground that Beneficiary would receive a windfall since it had not expended or committed itself to expend any funds to complete the road improvements. What result? Colorado National Bank v. Board of County Commissioners, 634 P.2d 32 (Colo.1981). See Dolan, Law of Letters of Credit 9–13 (1984).

E. FRAUD IN THE TRANSACTION

INTRAWORLD INDUSTRIES, INC. v. GIRARD TRUST BANK

Supreme Court of Pennsylvania, 1975.
461 Pa. 343, 336 A.2d 316.

ROBERTS, JUSTICE.

This appeal requires us to review the trial court's denial of a preliminary injunction to restrain honor of a draft under an international letter of credit. A precise statement of the facts, which are complex, is necessary for a proper understanding.

On February 11, 1972, a lease was executed by Intraworld Industries, Inc., a corporation headquartered in Wilkes–Barre, Pennsylvania, and Paulette Cymbalista, a citizen of Switzerland and resident of Italy. Cymbalista agreed to lease to Intraworld the Hotel Carlton, a luxury hotel located in St. Moritz, Switzerland, for a term of 15 years at an annual rental of 800,000 Swiss francs, payable in semi-annual installments.[2] The lease provided that Intraworld was required to prepay the rent for the initial 18–month period. Intraworld was also obligated to procure, within the first 100 days of the term, a performance bond in the amount of $500,000 "to insure to lessor the payment of the rent."[3]

Intraworld entered into possession of the hotel on May 1, 1972. Shortly thereafter, Intraworld assigned its interest in the lease to its subsidiary, Vacanze In Paradiso Hotels, S.A., a Swiss corporation.[4]

At a later time, Intraworld and Cymbalista executed an addendum to the lease (to which the parties have referred by its German title "Nachtrag"). The Nachtrag cancelled Intraworld's obligation to procure a performance bond and substituted a duty to provide letters of credit issued by "the Girard Trust Company of Philadelphia" in order to guarantee rental payments one year in advance. Two letters of credit were specifically required, each in the amount of $100,000, maturing in November, 1973, and May,

---

2. The lease contained a formula for the adjustment of the annual rental with respect to changes in the value of the Swiss franc. At the time of the execution of the lease, the annual rental was approximately equivalent to $200,000.

3. The record does not establish whether Intraworld performed its obligation to procure a performance bond.

The lease also provided: "This agreement shall be governed by the Swiss law. The competent forum shall be in Saint Moritz Court."

4. For convenience we will refer to the lessee as Intraworld.

1974, to secure the rent due at those times. After each rental payment, Intraworld was to provide a new letter of credit "in order that the lessor remains secured one years [sic] rent in advance." The Nachtrag also provided:

"In the event the lessee should not fulfill its obligation to pay, so that the letter of credit must be used, * * * then the lessor can terminate the lease immediately without further notice. In this case, the lessor retains the rent paid or guaranteed for the following year as a stipulated penalty for non-performance of the contract from the lessee, in doing so the lessor retains the right to make a claim for additional damages not covered by the stipulated penalty."

On September 1, 1972, Intraworld and the Girard Trust Bank, Philadelphia, entered into an agreement to provide the letters of credit required by the Nachtrag. Girard agreed to

"issue a letter of credit * * * in the amount of $100,000 under which the Lessor may draw a sight draft on [Girard] for payment of the sum due under said lease (a) on November 10, 1973 and (b) May 10, 1974. Under the terms of such letter of credit, payments will be made if the Lessor presents a draft as provided in such letter of credit. Each such letter of credit will expire * * * on the twentieth day after the payment under said lease is due." [6]

In accordance with the agreement, Girard issued two irrevocable letters of credit on September 5, 1972. Each authorized Cymbalista to draw a draft on Girard in the amount of $100,000.00 if Intraworld failed to pay the rent when due.[7]

6. The agreement also provided: "This agreement shall be construed in accordance with the law of the State of Pennsylvania and the Acts of Congress of the United States affecting transactions under the provisions hereof."

7. "IRREVOCABLE LETTER OF CREDIT

NO. 35798

Date: September 5, 1972
"Amount: $100,000.00
"Beneficiary: Paulette Cymbalista
                c/o Carlton Hotel
                St. Moritz, Switzerland
"For account of: Intraworld Industries, Inc.
                116 South Main Street
                Wilkes Barre, PA 18701

"Madam:

"You are hereby authorized to draw on us at sight the sum of One Hundred Thousand and 00/100 Dollars United States Currency ($100,000.00) due on November 10, 1973 under a lease, a copy of which is attached to both Beneficiary's copy

and Bank's copy of this letter of credit as Exhibit 1, available by your draft for said amount, accompanied by:

"1. Simple receipt for amount drawn.

"2. A signed statement of the drawer of the draft to the effect that the drawer is the lessor under said lease and that the lessee thereunder has not paid the installment of rent due under said lease on November 10, 1973 within 10 days after said installment was due and payable.

"This credit expires on November 30, 1973.

"Drafts under this credit must contain the clause 'drawn under Credit No. 35798 of Girard Trust Bank, dated September 5, 1972.'

"Girard Trust Bank hereby agrees with the drawers, endorsers and bona fide owners of the bills drawn strictly in compliance with the terms of this

In the summer of 1973, the relationship between Cymbalista and Intraworld began to go awry. Norbert Cymbalista, Paulette's husband, visited the hotel in August and, after discussions with the manager, became very concerned over the hotel's financial condition. He discovered that there were unpaid bills in excess of $100,000, that all telephone and Telex communications had been cut off for nonpayment of bills, and that the filing of mechanics liens against the hotel was imminent. After a trans-Atlantic telephone call, the Cymbalistas travelled to the United States within several days of Norbert's discoveries to attempt to resolve the hotel's difficulties with Intraworld. However, as Norbert testified,

"I tried to reach [the president of Intraworld] innumerable times by telephone and each time his secretary answered that he would call me back and he never did. I stayed a whole month in the United States trying continually to reach him and it was never possible."

On August 20, 1973, apparently while the Cymbalistas were in the United States, their Swiss counsel sent a letter to Intraworld reciting the unpaid bills, erosion of the Carlton's reputation, and internal corporate difficulties (apparently of Intraworld's Swiss subsidiary). It concluded:

"Based upon [Swiss law] and in reference to the provisions of the Lease Contract, we herewith extend to you a final time limit up to September 15, 1973 in order to:

(a) to pay all due debts,

(b) to supply the necessary means to safeguard proper management of the business,

(c) to complete the Board of Directors according to the law.

Within this time limit you must prove to the Hotel Owners that the aforementioned measures have been effectuated. Should you [fail to?] comply with this demand within the time-limit, the Lease Contract will be regarded as void."

Intraworld's Swiss counsel replied to the August 20 letter (but this reply is not in the record). Finding this reply unsatisfactory, Cymbalista's Swiss counsel answered on September 18, 1973:

"As [Intraworld] did not comply with our demand within this time-limit, we regard the leasing contract as terminated effective from 15 September 1973 * * *. From now on, the proprietor will have direct and sole control over the hotel real estate respective to the hotel management."

credit that the same will be duly honored upon presentation.

"Except so far as otherwise express- ly stated, this credit is subject to the uniform customs and practices for documentary credits (1962 revision),

International Chamber of Commerce Brochure No. 222."

Credit No. 35799 was identical to 35798, except that it applied to the rent due on May 10, 1974, and expired on May 30, 1974.

Further correspondence was exchanged by Swiss counsel, including, apparently, a demand on November 3 for the rent due in November. On November 7, 1973, Intraworld's Swiss counsel wrote to Cymbalista's counsel:

"You state on behalf of the lessor that [Intraworld] has the obligation to pay * * * rent by November 1. My client [Intraworld], who is presently in close contact with their American Bank [Girard], however, have [sic] informed me that the payment of the rent can be made up to November 10 * * * My client informed me further that accordingly these payments shall be legally undertaken by the 'Girard Trust Bank' * * * [M]y client cannot agree with your position according to which the lease contract can be considered as terminated either because of [Swiss law] or because of the terms of the lease agreement * * *."

That letter was followed on November 9, 1973, by another from Intraworld's counsel to Cymbalista's counsel in which he stated:

"If the transfer of the rent from the United States should not be made in timely fashion, your client [Cymbalista] is at liberty to obtain payment by way of the guarantee contracts [i.e., letters of credit]. In any event, there exist the two guarantee contracts, valid until November 30, 1973 and May 30, 1974, respectively, in order to preserve the rights of your client."

The rent due on November 10, 1973, was not paid by Intraworld. Accordingly, on November 21, 1973, Cymbalista's American counsel presented to Girard a draft drawn on Girard for $100,000 under Credit No. 35798. The draft was accompanied, all parties agree, by documentation that conformed to the terms of the credit. In his letter to Girard, Cymbalista's counsel stated:

"Your attention is directed to correspondence dated November 7 and November 9, 1973, copies of which are attached, in which Swiss counsel representing the Lessee invites the Lessor to draw upon the Letters of Credit; our client, as Lessor, takes the position that the lease * * * has terminated for various reasons, including the failure timely to pay the amount due pursuant to the 'Nachtrag' * * *."

Girard informed Intraworld on November 21 that it intended to honor the draft. Intraworld immediately filed an action in equity in the Court of Common Pleas of Philadelphia seeking injunctive relief prohibiting Girard from honoring the draft. Cymbalista filed a petition to intervene, which was granted by the trial court.

The November action was terminated on December 6, 1973, by agreement of all parties. Pursuant to the agreement, Girard placed $100,000 in escrow with a Swiss bank, with entitlement to that fund to be determined by the courts of Switzerland.

The situation remained unchanged for about six months. The rent due on May 10, 1974, was not paid. On May 21, 1974, Cymbalista's American counsel presented to Girard a draft for $100,000 under Credit No. 35799, accompanied by conforming documentation. Girard immediately advised Intraworld that it intended to honor the draft.

On May 24, Intraworld filed this equity action in the Court of Common Pleas of Philadelphia. It sought preliminary and permanent injunctions restraining Girard from honoring Cymbalista's draft under the letter of credit. The court issued a preliminary restraining order and set a date for a hearing. Cymbalista again petitioned for leave to intervene, which the court granted on May 29.

After the filing of additional pleadings, including preliminary objections and an amended complaint, a hearing was held and testimony taken on May 30 and 31, 1974. On July 11, the trial court issued a memorandum and decree in which it denied a preliminary injunction. Intraworld has appealed to this Court. We affirm.

*   *   *

Girard's obligations to Cymbalista are "subject to" the Uniform Customs and Practice. However, the UCP "is by definition a recording of practice rather than a statement of legal rules," and therefore does not purport to offer rules which govern the issuance of an injunction against honor of a draft. Harfield, Practice Commentary, N.Y.U.C.C., § 5–114 (McKinney's Consol.Laws, c. 38, 1964).

All parties have briefed and argued the case on the assumption that the Pennsylvania Uniform Commercial Code controls, and with this assumption we agree.

The great utility of letters of credit flows from the independence of the issuer-bank's engagement from the underlying contract between beneficiary and customer. Long-standing case law has established that, unless otherwise agreed, the issuer deals only in documents. If the documents presented conform to the requirements of the credit, the issuer may and must honor demands for payment, regardless of whether the goods conform to the underlying contract between beneficiary and customer. Absent its agreement to the contrary, the issuer is, under the general rule, not required or even permitted to go behind the documents to determine if the beneficiary has performed in conformity with the underlying contract.

*   *   *

This principle of the issuer's right and obligation to honor upon presentation of conforming documents has been codified in § 5–114:

> "(1) An issuer must honor a draft or demand for payment which complies with the terms of the relevant credit regardless of whether the goods or documents conform to the underlying contract for sale or other contract between the customer and the beneficiary. * * *

> "(2) Unless otherwise agreed when documents appear on their face to comply with the terms of a credit but a required document * * * is forged or fraudulent or there is fraud in the transaction

> *   *   *   *   *   *   *   *   *

> "(b) in all other cases as against its customer, an issuer acting in good faith may honor the draft or demand for payment despite notification from the customer of fraud, forgery or other defect not apparent on the face of the documents but a court of appropriate jurisdiction may enjoin such honor."

Intraworld seeks to enjoin honor under § 5–114(2)(b) on the basis that there is "fraud * * * not apparent on the face of the documents." It points to what it believes are two respects in which Cymbalista's demand for payment and supporting documentation are false and fraudulent, although conceding that the documents on their face conform to the credit. First, it contends that Cymbalista's statement (as required by the credit) that "lessee * * * has not paid the installment of rent due under said lease on May 10, 1974," is false and fraudulent because, after Cymbalista purported to terminate the lease in September, 1973, Intraworld was not obligated to pay rent and because the statement failed to disclose the termination of the lease. Second, it argues that the demand is fraudulent because Cymbalista is not seeking rent at all (as, Intraworld contends, she represents in the documents) but rather the "stipulated penalty" pursuant to the Nachtrag.

In light of the basic rule of the independence of the issuer's engagement and the importance of this rule to the effectuation of the purposes of the letter of credit, we think that the circumstances which will justify an injunction against honor must be narrowly limited to situations of fraud in which the wrongdoing of the beneficiary has so vitiated the entire transaction that the legitimate purposes of the independence of the issuer's obligation would no longer be served. A court of equity has the limited duty of

> "guaranteeing that [the beneficiary] not be allowed to take unconscientious advantage of the situation and run off with

plaintiff's money on a *pro forma* declaration which has *absolutely no basis in fact.*"

Dynamics Corp. of America v. Citizens and Southern National Bank, 356 F.Supp. 991, 999 (N.D.Ga.1973) (emphasis supplied).

The leading case on the question of what conduct will justify an injunction against honor is Sztejn v. J. Henry Schroder Banking Corp., 177 Misc. 719, 31 N.Y.S.2d 631 (Sup.Ct.1941). In that case as here, the customer sought an injunction against the issuer of a letter of credit restraining honor of a draft drawn by the beneficiary. The customer had contracted to purchase a quantity of bristles from the beneficiary and arranged to have the issuer issue a letter of credit in favor of the beneficiary. The credit required that the draft be accompanied by an invoice and bill of lading.

The beneficiary placed fifty cases of merchandise on a steamship and obtained a bill of lading describing the material as bristles. The beneficiary then drew a draft and presented it, along with the required documents, through a collecting bank. The customer's complaint alleged that the material shipped was not bristles as described in the documents, but rather "cowhair, other worthless material and rubbish [shipped] with intent to simulate genuine merchandise and defraud the plaintiff * * *."

The collecting bank moved to dismiss the complaint for failure to state a cause of action. The court, assuming the pleaded facts to be true, denied the motion. The court recognized that the issuer's obligation was independent from the underlying contract between customer and beneficiary. That independence is predicated, however, on the genuineness of the documents. The court noted:

> "This is not a controversy between the buyer and seller concerning a mere breach of warranty regarding the quality of the merchandise; on the present motion, it must be assumed that the seller has intentionally failed to ship any goods ordered by the buyer."

177 Misc. at 721, 31 N.Y.S.2d at 634. When the beneficiary has intentionally shipped no goods at all, the court held, the documentation was not genuine and therefore the predicate of the independence of the issuer's engagement was removed.

We conclude that, if the documents presented by Cymbalista are genuine in the sense of having some basis in fact, an injunction must be refused. An injunction is proper only if Cymbalista, comparable to the beneficiary in *Sztejn*, has no bona fide claim to payment under the lease. Dynamics Corp. of America v. Citizens and Southern National Bank, 356 F.Supp. 991, 999 (N.D.Ga.1973). Of course, neither the trial court nor this Court may attempt to determine Cymbalista's actual entitlement to payment under the lease. Such is not the proper standard for the grant or denial of an injunction against honor. Moreover, questions of rights and obligations under the lease are required by the lease to be determined under Swiss law in the courts of Switzerland. See Dynamics Corp. of America v. Citizens and Southern National Bank, supra.

On this record, we are unable to conclude that Intraworld established that Cymbalista has no bona fide claim to payment or that the documents presented to Girard have absolutely no basis in fact. Intraworld's argument rests on the basic premise that the lease was terminated in September, 1973. From this premise Intraworld asserts the falsity of Cymbalista's representations that she is the lessor and that the rent was due and unpaid. However, Intraworld did not attempt to prove to the trial court that, under Swiss law, Cymbalista's attempted termination was effective. In fact, Intraworld's Swiss counsel informed Cymbalista's counsel on November 7, 1973, that Intraworld "cannot agree with your position according to which the lease contract can be considered as terminated * * *." Counsel added that Cymbalista was "at liberty to obtain payment by way of" the letters of credit. Thus, Intraworld failed to prove that, under Swiss law, Cymbalista had no bona fide claim to rent under the lease despite Intraworld's repudiation of termination.

Intraworld's argument that Cymbalista fraudulently concealed the purported termination from Girard is unpersuasive. When presenting the draft and documents to Girard in November, 1973, Cymbalista's American counsel candidly admitted that "our client, as Lessor, takes the position that the lease has terminated * * * for various reasons * * *." In addition, Girard was a party to the first equity action and its counsel joined the agreement which terminated that action. Cymbalista could reasonably have assumed in May, 1974, that Girard was fully aware of the positions of both Intraworld and Cymbalista.

Intraworld's further contention that Cymbalista's demand was fraudulent in that she was not seeking "rent" at all but the "stipulated penalty" pursuant to the Nachtrag is more substantial but, under scrutiny, also fails. It argues that payment under the credit was permitted only for "rent," and that Cymbalista (as she concedes) was in fact seeking the "stipulated penalty," which is not "rent." Intraworld concludes that Cymbalista was fraudulently attempting to draw under the credit for satisfaction of an obligation not secured by the credit. There are two flaws in this argument.

First, we are not persuaded that the credit was issued for payment of "rent," narrowly defined, only. The letter of credit (see note 7 supra) authorized Cymbalista to draw "the sum * * * due * * * under [the] lease," without specifying that the "sum due" contemplated was only "rent." The letter required that a draft must be accompanied by Cymbalista's statement that "the lessee * * * has not paid the installment of rent due under said lease." This is not equivalent to a limitation on availability of the credit only for nonpayment of rent; in fact, such nonpayment of rent is precisely the condition which triggers Cymbalista's entitlement to the "stipulated penalty." In short, Intraworld has failed to persuade us that the letter of credit was not available to Cymbalista for satisfaction of the "stipulated penalty."

Second and more important, the Nachtrag does not, in our view, create the sharp distinction between "rent" and "stipulated penalty" that Intraworld hypothesizes. It provides that "[i]n the event the lessee should not fulfill its obligation to pay, so that the letter of credit must be used," then the lessor was entitled to terminate the lease and "retain the *rent* paid or *guaranteed* [by the letters of credit] for the following year as a stipulated penalty for non-performance of the contract * * *." (Emphasis supplied.) Because Intraworld did fail to pay the rent due on November 10, 1973, and May 10, 1974, Cymbalista could reasonably and in good faith have concluded that she had the right to draw on the credit for the "rent * * * guaranteed for the following year."

Whether Intraworld was in fact obligated to pay the rent nonpayment of which triggered Cymbalista's right to retain the "rent guaranteed" by the credit or whether Cymbalista is not entitled to the "stipulated penalty" for some other reason are questions to be decided under Swiss law in the courts of Switzerland. We hold only that Intraworld failed to establish that Cymbalista lacked a bona fide claim to the "rent * * * guaranteed * * * as a stipulated penalty" or that her demand under the credit lacked some basis in fact. Therefore, her documented demand was not shown to be fraudulent because she was seeking satisfaction of the "stipulated penalty."

In summary, we are unable to conclude on this record that Intraworld succeeded in proving that Cymbalista had no bona fide claim for payment under the lease and that her documented demand had absolutely no basis in fact. Accordingly, it is clear that there is an apparently reasonable ground for refusing an injunction.

In addition, Intraworld alleged in its complaint and contends in this Court that Girard's decision to honor Cymbalista's draft was not formed in good faith. Intraworld asserts that Girard's bad faith constituted an additional ground justifying an injunction. It is clear that an issuer of a letter of credit must act in good faith, see §§ 5–114(2)(b), 5–109(1). However, we are not persuaded that issuer bad faith is a circumstance justifying an injunction against honor; in most if not all instances of issuer bad faith, it would seem that a customer would have an adequate remedy at law in a claim against the issuer or a defense against the issuer's claim for reimbursement. In any event, in this case Intraworld has failed to prove the existence of bad faith on the part of Girard. It has proved no more than that Girard failed to resolve the dispute over the rights and obligations of the parties to the lease in Intraworld's favor. This Girard was not obligated to do. Its obligations included a careful scrutiny of the documents, but once it determined that the documents conformed to the requirements of the credit, it bore no responsibility for the performance of the lease obligations or the genuineness of the documents. § 5–109(1) (a) & (2). It would, we think, place an issuer in an intolerable position if the law compelled it to serve at its peril as an arbitrator of contract disputes between customer and beneficiary.

* * *

NOTES

1. In order to enjoin payment of a letter of credit, a customer must meet the usual requirements for injunctive relief. "To get a temporary injunction, customer typically must show (i) irreparable harm, (ii) probability of success on the 'fraud' merits, (iii) a balance of hardships tipping decidedly in favor of the injunction's issuance, and (iv) no public interest disfavoring the injunction." Givray, Letters of Credit, 44 Bus.Law. 1567, 1621 (1989). If the beneficiary is solvent and subject to service of process, doesn't the customer usually have an adequate remedy at law by suing the beneficiary who has fraudulently obtained payment from the issuer for damages? See Dolan, Law of Letters of Credit ¶ 7.04[1] (1984).

2. Empowering customers to enjoin payment of letters of credit on the grounds that the documents were forged or fraudulent or that there was "fraud in the transaction" under § 5–114(2) is an important exception to the independence principle of § 5–114(1) that insulates the beneficiary's right to be paid on the letter of credit from its rights on the underlying contract. Is this exception justified in the light of the function of letters of credit? The beneficiary's bargain under a letter of credit is to be paid promptly upon presenting the issuer with proper documentation. In inducing the customer to provide a letter of credit, the beneficiary has achieved the great tactical advantage of making sure that in sales transactions it will be a paid seller and in loan transactions a paid lender. Letters of credit are used only by sophisticated parties, and the customer must realize that in furnishing a letter of credit it is undertaking the burden of initiating litigation against a paid beneficiary to recover any payment the beneficiary is not entitled to under the underlying contract. "Pay now, litigate later" is the axiom of letters of credit.

Section 5–114(2) frustrates the expectation of the beneficiary for prompt payment; it lessens the advantage that the beneficiary has achieved in inducing the customer to provide a letter of credit. In doing so has § 5–114(2) significantly undermined the usefulness of letters of credit? No one is troubled by limiting the beneficiary's right to prompt payment in cases in which it presents forged documents or delivers junk, as in the *Sztejn* case, a decision that led to the drafting of § 5–114(2). But "fraud in the transaction" can plausibly be interpreted to include not only the letter of credit transaction but also the underlying transaction. White & Summers, Uniform Commercial Code § 19–7 (3d ed. 1988). And it is a rare customer who, having been bested in a business deal and facing the uphill battle of suing to get its money back if the letter of credit is paid, cannot find some "fraud in the transaction."

The breadth of the undefined term "fraud in the transaction" has left to the courts the difficult task of determining when it would be appropriate to allow customers to enjoin payment to fraudulent beneficiaries and when it would be a subversion of the independence principle to grant such an injunction. Commentators believe that on the whole the courts have done a good job of line drawing in the fraud cases. *Intraworld* has become the leading case in its interpretation of the meaning of "fraud in the transaction." It's two oft-quoted tests severely narrow the ambit of § 5–114(2): (1) An injunction is proper only if the customer can prove that the beneficiary "has no bona fide claim to payment," or the documents presented "have absolutely no basis in fact"; and (2) "the circumstances which will justify an injunction against honor must be narrowly limited to situations of fraud in which the wrongdoing of the beneficiary has so vitiated the entire transaction that the legitimate purposes of the independence of the issuer's obligation would no longer be served."

How should the *Intraworld* tests be applied to the following Problem?

PROBLEM

A letter of credit issued by Bank provided for payment by Bank of invoices for goods purchased by Customer from Beneficiary upon presentment of the invoices and a certificate of Beneficiary that the invoices had not been paid. The letter of credit covered only goods shipped by Beneficiary before September 1. On October 9, Customer and Beneficiary met and agreed that all unpaid invoices dated before September 11 would be paid by Customer's wiring the payment to Beneficiary rather than by the Beneficiary's presenting the invoices to Bank. Six days after the meeting Customer wired enough money to Beneficiary to pay all pre-September 11 invoices. But Beneficiary, in apparent violation of the agreement, allocated the wire payment to invoices dated after September 11, and used the letter of credit to draw on Bank for several pre-September 11 invoices. In doing so Beneficiary

submitted its certificate that the invoices had not been paid.
When Customer learned of this, it urged Bank not to pay the
letter of credit, contending that Beneficiary was defrauding Bank
and Customer by drawing on invoices that it knew were already
paid.   Bank dishonored the letter of credit.   Beneficiary sued
Bank for wrongful dishonor and justified its conduct by stating its
understanding of the agreement with Customer to be that Beneficiary had to apply the wire payment to pre-September 11 invoices
only if Customer had sent the payment on October 10, and
Customer did not do so.   If you were Bank's counsel would you
have advised Bank to dishonor the letter of credit in this case?   If
Customer had applied to your court for an injunction against
payment of the letter of credit by Bank, would you have issued the
injunction?   The facts are based on Roman Ceramics Corp. v.
Peoples National Bank, 714 F.2d 1207 (3d Cir.1983).

F. LETTERS OF CREDIT IN BANKRUPTCY

If a standby letter of credit is to be useful as the functional
equivalent of a guaranty, it must pass muster in bankruptcy.   So
far it has.   The initial question is whether the automatic stay of
Bankruptcy Code § 362(a) restrains the beneficiary from drawing
on the issuer after the customer's bankruptcy.   If it does, the
utility of letters of credit is greatly impaired for the beneficiary
would be forced to go through the expensive and time-consuming
procedure to lift the stay under § 362(d).   The usual letter of
credit transaction involves three contracts: the letter of credit
between the issuer and the beneficiary;   the underlying contract
between the customer and the beneficiary;   and the reimbursement contract between the customer and the issuer.   There is no
question that the automatic stay precludes any action by the
beneficiary against the customer on the underlying contract as
well as any action by the issuer against the customer on the
reimbursement agreement.

That § 362(a) does not stay the beneficiary's draw against the
issuer was decided in In re Page, 18 B.R. 713 (D.D.C.1982), and has
been widely accepted.   In that case the customer granted security
interests in its assets to issuer to secure its obligation to reimburse
the issuer if the issuer had to pay the letter of credit.   The
bankruptcy court held that unless payment of the letter of credit
were enjoined, the issuer, after payment, would be able to realize
on its security interest in debtor's property, thereby reducing the
assets available to the other creditors.   The district court reversed
on the ground that before the customer had filed in bankruptcy
the issuer already had a perfected security interest in the customer's assets to secure its contingent claim for reimbursement.   In
its payment of the letter of credit, the issuer merely liquidated its
claim against the customer for reimbursement, and customer's

other creditors are no worse off because the property of the customer's bankruptcy estate has not been depleted. The letter of credit was not, of course, property of the customer's estate. The court demonstrated its respect for the importance of the independence principle of letters of credit law: "Moreover, enjoining the payment of the letter of credit, even temporarily, would frustrate the commercial purposes of letters of credit to the detriment of financial institutions as well as their customers. *   *   * If payment on a letter of credit could be routinely delayed by the filing of a Chapter 11 petition the intended substitution of a bank for its less credit-worthy customer would be defeated." 18 B.R. at 717.

The more difficult problems concerning letters of credit in bankruptcy have arisen in the area of voidable preferences law as illustrated in the following case.

MATTER OF COMPTON CORP.

United States Court of Appeals, Fifth Circuit, 1987.
831 F.2d 586.

JERRE S. WILLIAMS, CIRCUIT JUDGE:

This is a bankruptcy preference case in which a bankruptcy trustee seeks to recover a transfer made via a letter of credit for the benefit of one of the debtor's unsecured creditors on the eve of bankruptcy. The bankruptcy court and the district court found there to be no voidable preference. We reverse.

I. *Factual Background*

In March 1982, Blue Quail Energy, Inc., delivered a shipment of oil to debtor Compton Corporation. Payment of $585,443.85 for this shipment of oil was due on or about April 20, 1982. Compton failed to make timely payment. Compton induced Abilene National Bank (now MBank–Abilene) to issue an irrevocable standby letter of credit in Blue Quail's favor on May 6, 1982. Under the terms of the letter of credit, payment of up to $585,443.85 was due Blue Quail if Compton failed to pay Blue Quail this amount by June 22, 1982. Compton paid MBank $1,463.61 to issue the letter of credit. MBank also received a promissory note payable on demand for $585,443.85. MBank did not need a security agreement to cover the letter of credit transaction because a prior 1980 security agreement between the bank and Compton had a future advances provision. This 1980 security agreement had been perfected as to a variety of Compton's assets through the filing of several financing statements. The most recent financing statement had been filed a year before, May 7, 1981. The letter of credit on its face noted that it was for an antecedent debt due Blue Quail.

On May 7, 1982, the day after MBank issued the letter of credit in Blue Quail's favor, several of Compton's creditors filed an involuntary bankruptcy petition against Compton. On June 22, 1982, MBank paid Blue Quail $569,932.03 on the letter of credit after Compton failed to pay Blue Quail.

In the ensuing bankruptcy proceeding, MBank's aggregate secured claims against Compton, including the letter of credit payment to Blue Quail, were paid in full from the liquidation of Compton's assets which served as the bank's collateral. Walter Kellogg, bankruptcy trustee for Compton, did not contest the validity of MBank's secured claim against Compton's assets for the amount drawn under the letter of credit by Blue Quail. Instead, on June 14, 1983, trustee Kellogg filed a complaint in the bankruptcy court against Blue Quail asserting that Blue Quail had received a preferential transfer under § 547 through the letter of credit transaction. The trustee sought to recover $585,443.85 from Blue Quail pursuant to § 550.

Blue Quail answered and filed a third party complaint against MBank. On June 16, 1986, Blue Quail filed a motion for summary judgment asserting that the trustee could not recover any preference from Blue Quail because Blue Quail had been paid from MBank's funds under the letter of credit and therefore had not received any of Compton's property. On August 27, 1986, the bankruptcy court granted Blue Quail's motion, agreeing that the payment under the letter of credit did not constitute a transfer of debtor Compton's property but rather was a transfer of the bank's property. The bankruptcy court entered judgment on the motion on September 10, 1986. Trustee Kellogg appealed this decision to the district court. On December 11, 1986, the district court affirmed the bankruptcy court ruling, holding that the trustee did not establish two necessary elements of a voidable transfer under § 547. The district court agreed with Blue Quail and the bankruptcy court that the trustee could not establish that the funds transferred to Blue Quail were ever property of Compton. Furthermore, the district court held that the transfer of the increased security interest to MBank was a transfer of the debtor's property for the sole benefit of the bank and in no way benefitted Blue Quail. The district court therefore found no voidable preference as to Blue Quail. The trustee is appealing the decision to this Court.

II. *The Letter of Credit*

It is well established that a letter of credit and the proceeds therefrom are not property of the debtor's estate under § 541. * * * When the issuer honors a proper draft under a letter of credit, it does so from its own assets and not from the assets of its customer who caused the letter of credit to be issued. * * * As a result, a bankruptcy trustee is not entitled to enjoin a post petition payment of funds under a letter of credit from the issuer to the beneficiary, because such a payment is not a transfer of debtor's property (a threshold requirement under § 547(b)). A case apparently holding otherwise, In re Twist Cap, Inc., 1 B.R. 284 (Bankr.Fla.1979), has been roundly criticized and otherwise ignored by courts and commentators alike.

Recognizing these characteristics of a letter of credit in a bankruptcy case is necessary in order to maintain the independence principle, the cornerstone of letter of credit law. Under the independence principle, an issuer's obligation to the letter of credit's beneficiary is independent from any obligation between the beneficiary and the issuer's customer. All a beneficiary has to do to receive payment under a letter of credit is to show that it has performed all the duties required by the letter of credit. Any disputes between the beneficiary and the customer do not affect the issuer's obligation to the beneficiary to pay under the letter of credit.

Letters of credit are most commonly arranged by a party who benefits from the provision of goods or services. The party will request a bank to issue a letter of credit which names the provider of the goods or services as the beneficiary. Under a standby letter of credit, the bank becomes primarily liable to the beneficiary upon the default of the bank's customer to pay for the goods or services. The bank charges a fee to issue a letter of credit and to undertake this liability. The shifting of liability to the bank rather than to the services or goods provider is the main purpose of the letter of credit. After all, the bank is in a much better position to assess the risk of its customer's insolvency than is the the service or goods provider. It should be noted, however, that it is the risk of the debtor's insolvency and not the risk of a preference attack that a bank assumes under a letter of credit transaction. Overall, the independence principle is necessary to insure "the certainty of payments for services or goods rendered regardless of any intervening misfortune which may befall the other contracting party." In re North Shore, 30 B.R. at 378.

The trustee in this case accepts this analysis and does not ask us to upset it. The trustee is not attempting to set aside the post petition payments by MBank to Blue Quail under the letter of credit as a preference; nor does the trustee claim the letter of credit itself constitutes debtor's property. The trustee is instead challenging the earlier transfer in which Compton granted MBank an increased security interest in its assets to obtain the letter of credit for the benefit of Blue Quail. Collateral which has been pledged by a debtor as security for a letter of credit is property of the debtor's estate. In re W.L. Mead, 42 B.R. at 59. The trustee claims that the direct transfer to MBank of the increased security interest on May 6, 1982, also constituted an indirect transfer to Blue Quail which occurred one day prior to the filing of the involuntary bankruptcy petition and is voidable as a preference under § 547. This assertion of a preferential transfer is evaluated in Parts III and IV of this opinion.

It is important to note that the irrevocable standby letter of credit in the case at bar was not arranged in connection with Blue Quail's initial decision to sell oil to Compton on credit. Compton arranged for the letter of credit after Blue Quail had shipped the oil and after Compton had defaulted in payment. The letter of credit in this case did not serve its usual function of backing up a contemporaneous credit decision, but instead served as a back up payment guarantee on an extension of credit already in jeopardy. The letter of credit was issued to pay off an antecedent unsecured debt. This fact was clearly noted on the face of the letter of credit. Blue Quail, the beneficiary of the letter of credit, did not give new value for the issuance of the letter of credit by MBank on May 6, 1982, or for the resulting increased security interest held by MBank. MBank, however, did give new value for the increased security interest it obtained in Compton's collateral: the bank issued the letter of credit.

When a debtor pledges its assets to secure a letter of credit, a transfer of debtor's property has occurred under the provisions of § 547. By subjecting its assets to MBank's reimbursement claim in the event MBank had to pay on the letter of credit, Compton made a transfer of its property. The broad definition of "transfer" under § 101 is clearly designed to cover such a transfer. Overall, the letter of credit itself and the payments thereunder may not be property of debtor, but the collateral pledged as a security interest for the letter of credit is.

Furthermore, in a secured letter of credit transaction, the transfer of debtor's property takes place at the time the letter of credit is issued (when the security interest is granted) and received by the beneficiary, not at the time the issuer pays on the letter of credit. * * *

The transfer to MBank of the increased security interest was a direct transfer which occurred on May 6, 1982, when the bank issued the letter of credit. Under § 547(e)(2)(A), however, such a transfer is deemed to have taken place for purposes of § 547 at the time such transfer "takes effect" between the transferor and transferee if such transfer is perfected within 10 days. The phrase "takes effect" is undefined in the Bankruptcy Code, but under Uniform Commercial Code Article 9 law, a transfer of a security interest "takes effect" when the security interest attaches. Because of the future advances clause in MBank's 1980 security agreement with Compton, the attachment of the MBank's security interest relates back to May 9, 1980, the date the security agreement went into effect. The bottom line is that the direct transfer of the increased security interest to MBank is artificially deemed to have occurred at least by May 7, 1981, the date MBank filed its final financing statement, for purposes of a preference attack against the bank.[4] This date is well before the 90 day window of § 547(b)(4)(A). This would protect the bank from a preference attack by the trustee even if the bank had not given new value at the time it received the increased security interest.[*] MBank is therefore protected from a preference attack by the trustee for the increased security interest transfer under either of two theories: under § 547(c)(1) because it gave new value and under the operation of the relation back provision of § 547(e)(2)(A). The bank is also protected from any claims of reimbursement by Blue Quail because the bank received no voidable preference.

The relation back provision of § 547(e)(2)(A), however, applies only to the direct transfer of the increased security interest to MBank. The indirect transfer to Blue Quail that allegedly resulted from the direct transfer to MBank occurred on May 6, 1982, the date of issuance of the letter of credit. The relation back principle of § 547(e)(2)(A) does not apply to this indirect transfer to Blue Quail. Blue Quail was not a party to the security agreement between MBank and Compton. So it will not be able to utilize the relation back provision if it is deemed to have received an indirect transfer resulting from the direct transfer of the increased security interest to MBank. Blue Quail, therefore, cannot assert either of the two defenses to a preference attack which MBank can claim. Blue Quail did not give new value under § 547(c)(1), and it received a transfer within 90 days of the filing of Compton's bankruptcy petition.[5]

4. UCC § 9–312(7) specifies that for purposes of priority among competing secured parties, the security interest for a future advance has the same priority as the security interest for the first advance. Conflicting security interests rank according to priority in time of filing or perfection. UCC § 9–312(5).

[*] [Editors' Note: The "relation back" theory of the Court is not supported by the Bankruptcy Code. The Court is correct in stating that the phrase "at the time such transfer takes effect" in § 547(e)(2)(A) refers to the time the security interest "attaches" under the UCC. The time of attachment is governed by UCC § 9–203. In this case attachment occurred when three events occurred: (1) value was given by MBank; (2) the debtor had rights in the collateral; and (3) the debtor signed a security agreement providing for the security interest. The second and third events occurred before May 6, but MBank did not give value with respect to the transfer challenged by the trustee in bankruptcy until the letter of credit was issued on May 6. Thus, under § 547(e)(2)(A), the transfer could not

have occurred before May 6. Under UCC § 9–303, the security interest that attached on May 6 was perfected at the time it attached because the filing of a financing statement—the applicable step required for perfection—had already occurred before May 6. Because May 6 is the day of both attachment and perfection, the result under § 547(e)(2)(A) is that the transfer from the debtor to MBank occurred on May 6. It is irrelevant under § 547 that UCC § 9–312(5) and (7) date the priority of MBank with respect to the May 6 transaction from the time MBank filed its financing statement. § 547(e)(2)(A) refers to the time of attachment and perfection, not to the date of priority. There is no avoidable preference in this case, however. The Court correctly holds that the giving of value by MBank and the transfer by the debtor to MBank were a contemporaneous exchange under § 547(c)(1).]

5. Nor does Blue Quail have the protection of the § 547(c)(2) "ordinary course of business" preference exception. Getting a standby letter of credit issued to cover a debt several weeks

III. *Direct/Indirect Transfer Doctrine*

The federal courts have long recognized that "[t]o constitute a preference, it is not necessary that the transfer be made directly to the creditor." National Bank of Newport v. National Herkimer County Bank, 225 U.S. 178, 184 (1912). "If the bankrupt has made a transfer of his property, the *effect* of which is to enable one of his creditors to obtain a greater percentage of his debt than another creditor of the same class, circuity of arrangement will not avail to save it." Id. (Emphasis added). To combat such circuity, the courts have broken down certain transfers into two transfers, one direct and one indirect. The direct transfer to the third party may be valid and not subject to a preference attack. The indirect transfer, arising from the same action by the debtor, however, may constitute a voidable preference as to the creditor who indirectly benefitted from the direct transfer to the third party.

This is the situation presented in the case before us. The term "transfer" as used in the various bankruptcy statutes through the years has always been broad enough to cover such indirect transfers and to catch various circuitous arrangements. Katz v. First National Bank of Glen Head, 568 F.2d 964, 969 n. 4, (2nd Cir.), cert. denied, 434 U.S. 1069 (1978). The new Bankruptcy Code implicitly adopts this doctrine through its broad definition of "transfer." [6] Examining the case law that has developed since the *National Bank of Newport* case yields an understanding of what types of transfers the direct/indirect doctrine is meant to cover.

In Palmer v. Radio Corporation of America, 453 F.2d 1133 (5th Cir.1971), a third party purchased from the debtor a television station for $40,000 cash and the assumption of certain liabilities of the debtor, including unsecured claims by creditor RCA. This Court found the direct transfer from the debtor to the third party purchaser constituted an indirect preferential transfer to creditor RCA. We found that the assumption by the third party purchaser of the debt owed by the debtor to RCA and the subsequent payments made thereunder constituted a voidable transfer as to RCA. The court noted that such indirect transfers as this had long been held to constitute voidable preferences under bankruptcy laws. 453 F.2d at 1136.

* * *

In Virginia National Bank v. Woodson, 329 F.2d 836 (4th Cir. 1964), the debtor had several overdrawn accounts with his bank.

---

past due does not constitute ordinary course of business.

6. "Transfer" means every mode, direct or *indirect*, absolute or conditional, voluntary or involuntary, of disposing of or parting with property or with an interest in property, including retention of title as a security interest and foreclosure of the debtor's equity of redemption. § 101 (emphasis added). See also the Notes of the Committee on the Judiciary under 11 U.S.C. 101 ("The definition of transfer is as broad as possible.")

The debtor talked his sister into paying off $8,000 of the overdrafts in exchange for an $8,000 promissory note and an assignment of some collateral as security. The debtor's sister made the $8,000 payment directly to the bank. The $8,000 technically was never part of the debtor's estate. The court, however, held that the payment of the $8,000 by the sister to the bank was a preference as to the bank to the extent of the value of the collateral held by the sister. The court noted that the measure of the value of a voidable preference is diminution of the debtor's estate and not the value of the transfer to the creditor.

In the *Woodson* case the sister was secured only to the extent the pledged collateral had value; the remainder of her loan to her brother was unsecured. Swapping one unsecured creditor for another unsecured creditor does not create any kind of preference. The court held that a preference in such a transaction arises only when a secured creditor is swapped for an unsecured creditor. Only then is the pool of assets available for distribution to the general unsecured creditors depleted because the secured creditor has priority over the unsecured creditors. Furthermore, the court held that the bank and not the sister had received the voidable preference and had to pay back to the trustee an amount equal to the value of the collateral.

* * *

IV. *The Direct/Indirect Doctrine in the Context of a Letter of Credit Transaction*

The case at bar differs from the cases discussed in Part III supra only by the presence of the letter of credit as the mechanism for paying off the unsecured creditor. Blue Quail's attempt to otherwise distinguish the case from the direct/indirect transfer cases does not withstand scrutiny.

In the letter of credit cases discussed in Part II supra, the letters of credit were issued contemporaneously with the initial extension of credit by the beneficiaries of the letters. In those cases the letters of credit effectively served as security devices for the benefit of the creditor beneficiaries and took the place of formal security interests. The courts in those cases properly found there had been no voidable transfers, direct or indirect, in the letter of credit transactions involved. New value was given contemporaneously with the issuance of the letters of credit in the form of the extensions of credit by the beneficiaries of the letters. As a result, the § 547(c)(1) preference exception was applicable.

The case at bar differs from these other letter of credit cases by one very important fact: the letter of credit in this case was issued to secure an antecedent unsecured debt due the beneficiary of the letter of credit. The unsecured creditor beneficiary gave no new value upon the issuance of the letter of credit. When the issuer paid off the letter of credit and foreclosed on the collateral securing the letter of credit, a preferential transfer had occurred. An unsecured creditor was paid in full and a secured creditor was substituted in its place.

The district court upheld the bankruptcy court in maintaining the validity of the letter of credit issued to cover the antecedent debt. The district court held that MBank, the issuer of the letter of credit, could pay off the letter of credit and foreclose on the collateral securing it. We are in full agreement. But we also look to the impact of the transaction as it affects the situation of Blue Quail in the bankrupt estate. We hold that the bankruptcy trustee can recover from Blue Quail, the beneficiary of the letter of credit, because Blue Quail received an indirect preference. This result preserves the sanctity of letter of credit and carries out the purposes of the Bankruptcy Code by avoiding a preferential transfer. MBank, the issuer of the letter of credit, being just the intermediary through which the preferential transfer was accomplished, completely falls out of the picture and is not involved in this particular legal proceeding.

MBank did not receive any preferential transfer—it gave new value for the security interest. Furthermore, because the direct and indirect transfers are separate and independent, the trustee does not even need to challenge the direct transfer of the increased security interest to MBank, or seek any relief at all from MBank, in order to attack the indirect transfer and recover under § 550 from the indirect transferee Blue Quail.

We hold that a creditor cannot secure payment of an unsecured antecedent debt through a letter of credit transaction when it could not do so through any other type of transaction. The purpose of the letter of credit transaction in this case was to secure payment of an unsecured antecedent debt for the benefit of an unsecured creditor. This is the only proper way to look at such letters of credit in the bankruptcy context. The promised transfer of pledged collateral induced the bank to issue the letter of credit in favor of the creditor. The increased security interest held by the bank clearly benefitted the creditor because the bank would not have issued the letter of credit without this security. A secured creditor was substituted for an unsecured creditor to the detriment of the other unsecured creditors.

* * *

The precise holding in this case needs to be emphasized. We do not hold that payment under a letter of credit, or even a letter of credit itself, constitute preferential transfers under § 547(b) or property of a debtor under § 541. The holding of this case fully allows the letter of credit to function. We preserve its sanctity and the underlying independence doctrine. We do not, however, allow an unsecured creditor to avoid a preference attack by utilizing a letter of credit to secure payment of an antecedent debt. Otherwise the unsecured creditor would receive an indirect preferential transfer from the granting of the security for the letter of credit to the extent of the value of that security. Our holding does not affect the strength of or the proper use of letters of credit. When a letter of credit is issued contemporaneously with a new extension of credit, the creditor beneficiary will not be subject to a preferential attack under the direct/indirect doctrine elaborated in this case because the creditor will have given new value in exchange for the indirect benefit of the secured letter of credit. Only when a creditor receives a secured letter of credit to cover an unsecured antecedent debt will it be subject to a preferential attack under § 547(b).

* * *

PROBLEM

Customer and Beneficiary entered into a gasoline exchange agreement. Beneficiary agreed to transfer 200,000 barrels of gasoline to Customer in May, and Customer agreed to transfer the same quantity of gasoline to Beneficiary in June. Beneficiary requested that Customer supply it with a letter of credit securing Customer's obligation to transfer the gasoline to Beneficiary. The required letter was issued to Beneficiary by Bank which fully secured its right of reimbursement against Customer by taking a perfected security interest in Customer's assets. Beneficiary transferred the required amount of gasoline to Customer in May and Customer reciprocated in June. After Beneficiary received the last of the gasoline from Customer, it cancelled its letter of credit. When Beneficiary cancelled the letter of credit, Bank released its security interest in Customer's property. In July Customer filed a petition in bankruptcy. It is clear that Customer was insolvent at the time it transferred the gasoline to Beneficiary in June. The trustee in bankruptcy now sues to avoid Customer's transfers of gasoline to Beneficiary as voidable preferences under § 547(b). Beneficiary defends on the ground that Customer's creditors were not damaged by Customer's transfers to Beneficiary because these transfers did not reduce the assets of Customer's estate. What result? § 547(b)(5) and § 547(c)(1). The facts are based on Matter of Fuel Oil Supply & Terminaling, Inc., 837 F.2d 224 (5th Cir.1988). Is the result different if Bank had not taken a security interest in Customer's property to secure its right of reimbursement?

Part II

NEGOTIABLE INSTRUMENTS

———

Chapter 6

NEGOTIABILITY AND HOLDERS IN DUE COURSE

———

A. INTRODUCTION

The law of negotiable instruments is based in large part on common law doctrine developed primarily in the last half of the eighteenth century and the first half of the nineteenth century. This law was codified in Great Britain in 1882 in the Bills of Exchange Act and in 1896 in the United States in the Uniform Negotiable Instruments Law, usually referred to as the NIL. In 1952 the American Law Institute and the National Conference of Commissioners on Uniform State Laws promulgated the Uniform Commercial Code. Article 3 of the Code eventually displaced the NIL as the primary statute governing negotiable instruments. Article 4 of the Code complements Article 3 with respect to collection of negotiable instruments by banks and also governs the bank-customer relationship with respect to some matters relating to instruments. In 1990 a Revised Article 3 was promulgated to take the place of the original Article 3. At the same time conforming amendments to Articles 1 and 4 were promulgated. Revised Article 3 and the conforming amendments to Articles 1 and 4 have been enacted in a number of states and it is anticipated that Revised Article 3 will eventually displace the original Article 3. Revised Article 3 is not a radical departure from the earlier statute; the principal concepts of traditional negotiable instruments law have been preserved. But Revised Article 3 differs from the original Article 3 with respect to a number of important substantive areas. In addition, no attempt was made to preserve the language of the original Article 3. As a result, the drafting style reflected in Revised Article 3 is quite different from that of the previous statute.

Since almost all of the negotiable instruments cases reprinted in this book were decided under the original Article 3 or 4, we include the text of the particular section involved to the extent reference to the statutory language is necessary to understand the

492

point at issue. Revised Article 3 is accompanied by a "Table of Disposition of Sections in Former Article 3" which indicates the section of Revised Article 3 which governs the issue addressed by a section of the original Article 3. In reading cases reprinted in this book, this table should be consulted because the result reached in the case may be different if the same facts are governed by Revised Article 3. In the text of this book other than the reprinted cases, references to sections of Article 3 or 4 are to Revised Article 3 or 4 unless the contrary is stated.

B. CONCEPT OF NEGOTIABILITY

---

1. HISTORICAL ORIGIN

Professor Gilmore sketches the background of negotiable instruments law in the following quotation from his article "Formalism and the Law of Negotiable Instruments," 13 Creighton L.Rev. 441, 446–450 (1979)

> Our law of negotiable instruments dates from the late eighteenth century. * * * Lord Mansfield and his colleagues in the late eighteenth century were faced with radically new problems for which they devised radically new solutions.
>
> The radically new problems all stemmed from the industrial revolution and the vastly increased number of commercial transactions which it spawned. When goods were shipped, they had to be paid for. The idea that the payments could be made in metallic currency, chronically in short supply, was ludicrous. The primitive banking system could not cope with the situation: the bank check which—a hundred years later—became the universal payment device was unknown. In effect the merchants and the bankers invented their own paper currency. The form which they used was an old one: the so-called bill of exchange which was an order issued by one person (the drawer) to a second person (the drawee) directing the drawee to pay a specified sum of money at a specified time to a third person (the holder). Frequently these bills, drawn by sellers on buyers, represented the purchase price of goods sold. In a more sophisticated and somewhat later variant a mercantile banking house issued what came to be called a letter of credit to a customer. The letter authorized the customer to draw on the bankers for the purchase price of goods which he intended to buy: Through the first half of the nineteenth century Yankees trading out of Boston, armed with their letters of credit which were frequently issued by English houses, roamed the Far East assembling their precious and fabulously profitable cargoes of silks

and teas and spices, paying for them with drafts on London. For half a century these bills or drafts were an indispensable supplement to the official currencies and were indeed used as currency: the bills which showed up in litigation had, as the case reports tell us, passed from hand to hand in a long series of transactions. And a draft on a ranking London house was a much safer as well as a much more convenient thing to have than a bag-full of clipped Maria Theresa dollars. These bills moved in a world-wide market, typically ending up in the possession of people who knew nothing about the transaction which had given rise to the bill, had no way of finding out anything about the transaction and, in any case, had not the slightest interest in it.

Against that background, the courts, English and American, put together, in not much more than half a century, the law of negotiable instruments almost exactly as we know it today. Indeed anyone who has mastered the current American formulation of the subject in Article 3 of the Uniform Commercial Code will have a startling sense of *deja vu*—I suppose this is *deja vu* in reverse—if he then goes back to the mid-nineteenth century treatises: time seems to have been suspended, nothing has changed, the late twentieth century law of negotiable instruments is still a law for clipper ships and their exotic cargoes from the Indies. The *deja vu* is false, a sort of floating mirage—but I will return to that later.

In putting together their law of negotiable instruments, the courts assumed that the new mercantile currency was a good thing whose use should be encouraged. Two quite simple ideas became the foundation pieces for the whole structure. One was the good faith purchase idea. The stranger who purchased the bill in the market was entitled to do so without inquiry into the facts of the underlying transaction or of previous transfers of the bill and without being affected by them: if he bought the bill for value, in good faith and in the ordinary course of business, he held it free both of underlying contract defenses and of outstanding equities of ownership. The other idea which, the first time you run into it, sounds like nonsense—the legal mind at its worst—was even more basic to the structure and indeed was what gave the completed edifice its pure and almost unearthly beauty. That was the idea that the piece of paper on which the bill was written or printed should be treated as if it—the piece of paper—was itself the claim or debt which it evidenced. This idea came to be known as the doctrine of merger—the debt was merged in the instrument. At one stroke it drastically simplified the law of negotiable instruments, to the benefit of both purchasers and the people required to pay the instruments. Under merger theory the only way of transferring the debt represented by the bill was by physical delivery of the bill itself to the transferee. The courts also worked out an elaborate set of rules on when the transferor was required to endorse, as well as deliver, the bill and on what liabilities to subsequent parties he assumed by endorsing. When these formalities— delivery and endorsement—had been accomplished—but not until then—the transfer became a negotiation and the transferee a holder. Only the holder—the person physically in possession of the bill under a proper chain of endorsements— was entitled to demand payment of the bill from the party required to pay it; only payment to such a holder discharged the bill as well as the underlying obligation. Merger theory was also of immense importance from the point of view of the paying party: not only did he know whom he was supposed to pay—the holder—but, under another aspect of the theory, he was entitled to pay (and get his discharge) even if he knew, to state an extreme case, that the holder he paid had acquired the bill by fraud or trickery from a previous holder. Parties with claims adverse to the holder were required to fight their own battles; they could not involve the payor by serving notice on him not to pay.

2. MERGER DOCTRINE

---

a. NEGOTIATION AND TRANSFER

Under the merger doctrine described by Professor Gilmore the right to enforce or receive payment of an instrument is the exclusive right of the holder of the instrument. Although the notion that the right to enforce an instrument results from possession by a holder remains a central concept of Article 3, merger doctrine is attenuated in some cases. This is reflected in § 3–301 which defines "person entitled to enforce" to include some nonholders. The following cases illustrate § 3–301 and some basic concepts and terminology regarding negotiation and transfer of instruments.

Case # 1. John Doe signs a note and delivers it to Rachel Roe. The note reads as follows:

> I promise to pay $1,000 on April 1, 1993 to the bearer of this note.

The note is "issued" by Doe, the "maker," when it is delivered to Roe. § 3–105(a) and § 3–103(a)(5). The note is "payable to bearer." § 3–109(a). When Roe receives possession, she becomes the bearer of the note as well as its holder. § 1–201(5) and (20). Normally, Roe is also the owner of the note. But the right of Roe to receive or enforce payment is based on the fact that Roe is the holder of the note, not on Roe's ownership. § 3–301.

Suppose Roe loses the note and it is found by Peter Poe who takes possession of it. By obtaining possession Poe does not become the owner of the note, but Poe becomes the holder of the note and thereby obtains the right to enforce it. § 3–301. The transfer of possession which resulted in Poe's becoming a holder is described in § 3–201(a) as a negotiation of the note. Typically, negotiation is the result of a voluntary transfer of possession, but § 3–201(a) applies to any transfer of possession, voluntary or involuntary.

Case # 2. John Doe signs a note and delivers it to Rachel Roe. The note reads as follows:

I promise to pay $1,000 on April 1, 1991 to the order of Rachel Roe.

In this case the note is not payable to bearer. Rather, it is "payable to order" and therefore is "payable to an identified person." § 3–109(b). Upon delivery of the note to Roe, she becomes its holder because she has possession and she is the person identified in the note as its payee. § 1–201(20). In Case # 1 we saw that a finder or thief can obtain the right to enforce a note payable to bearer simply by obtaining possession of it. That rule does not apply if an instrument is payable to an identified person. Negotiation of such an instrument also requires transfer of possession, but an indorsement by the holder is necessary as well. § 3–201(b). Thus, the note payable to Roe cannot be negotiated, i.e. nobody else can become its holder, unless she indorses it.

Suppose Roe does not lose the note. Rather, she sells it to Peter Poe for cash and delivers the note to him. In this case no negotiation to Poe occurs unless Roe indorses the note. Indorsement is defined in § 3–204(a) and can be made for several purposes. The most important purpose is to negotiate the instrument. An indorsement is normally made on the reverse side of the instrument and can consist of a signature alone or a signature accompanied by other words. An indorsement by Roe consisting of her signature preceded by the words "Pay to Peter Poe" identifies a person to whom it makes the note payable and is called a "special indorsement." § 3–205(a). An indorsement by Roe consisting solely of her signature does not identify a person to whom is makes the note payable and is called a "blank indorsement." § 3–205(b). The effect of a blank indorsement is to make the note payable to bearer. § 3–205(b) and § 3–109(c). If either indorsement is made, Poe becomes the holder when he obtains possession of the note (§ 1–201(20)) and may enforce the note as holder. If Roe indorses in blank, Poe can negotiate the note to somebody else either by delivery alone or by delivery plus Poe's special indorsement. § 3–205(b) and § 3–109(c). If Roe indorses specially, Poe must indorse the note in order to negotiate it and may indorse either specially or in blank. § 3–205(a).

Although the right to enforce an instrument is normally obtained as a result of negotiation, the right to enforce an instrument can also be obtained in some transactions in which negotiation does not occur. Suppose Roe delivers the note to Poe without indorsing it. What rights does Poe obtain? Because Roe's purpose in delivering the note is to give Poe the right to enforce it, Roe has "transferred" the note to Poe. § 3–203(a). Transfer means that there has been a conveyance by the transferor to the transferee of the transferor's right to enforce the instrument. This transfer can occur only by "delivery," a voluntary transfer of possession (Section 1–201(14)), plus an intent by the transferor to give to the transferee the right to enforce. Since the note was not indorsed by Roe, Poe cannot enforce the note in his own right as holder and cannot negotiate the note to somebody else. But as a result of the transfer from Roe, Poe obtains Roe's right as holder to enforce the note. This result is commonly referred to as the "shelter doctrine." Armed with that right and possession of the note, Poe becomes a person entitled to enforce the note under clause (ii) of the first sentence of § 3–301. In addition Poe, as a buyer of the note for value, obtains a specifically enforceable right to have Roe indorse the note so that Poe can become its holder. § 3–203(c).

If, by transfer, Poe acquires Roe's right as holder to enforce the note, why is it important whether Poe, in enforcing the note, is asserting his own right as holder or a right to enforce derived from Roe's right as holder? Read Comments 2 through 4 to § 3–203 as well as § 3–308(b) and the first two paragraphs of Comment 2 to § 3–308.

b. ENFORCEMENT BY NONHOLDERS

If there is a holder of an instrument, only the holder is entitled to enforce the instrument. But sometimes there is no holder. We have just discussed one case of that kind arising under § 3–203(a). An instrument payable to an identified person is sold and delivered by the holder to the buyer, but the seller neglects to indorse. After the delivery to the buyer, neither the buyer nor the seller is the holder. In another category of cases, usually relating to unindorsed instruments payable to an identified person, the holder loses the instrument, the instrument is stolen from the holder, or the instrument is destroyed while in the possession of the holder. This category of cases is governed by § 3–309.

The two cases that follow consider the enforceability of instruments if the person seeking enforcement either is not in possession of the instrument or is in possession of an instrument payable to someone else. Consider these cases under § 3–301 and § 3–308.

INVESTMENT SERVICE CO. v. MARTIN BROTHERS CONTAINER & TIMBER PRODUCTS CORP.

Supreme Court of Oregon, 1970.
255 Or. 192, 465 P.2d 868.

DENECKE, JUSTICE.

* * *

On May 22 the defendant, Martin Bros., drew a check on its account in a Tennessee bank, payable to the order of Quinco, Inc. The next day Quinco deposited the check in its checking account in U.S. National Bank of Oregon (US). US sent the check through the Federal Reserve Bank system to the Tennessee drawee bank for collection. After deposit of the check and before its collection, US paid checks drawn by Quinco on its US checking account. Before presentment of the check to the Tennessee Bank, Martin Bros. ordered the Tennessee bank to stop payment of the check. The Tennessee bank did so and returned the check dishonored to US. US charged the amount of this check back against Quinco's account, which resulted in the account being overdrawn.

On June 8, in response to a request from Quinco, US sent the check to Quinco's attorney. The attorney requested the check so that he could commence an action for Quinco against the drawer, Martin Bros., on the check. There was no direct evidence of any agreement accompanying the delivery of the check to Quinco's attorney.

Quinco commmenced an action on June 15 for the entire face amount of the check, $2,937. The complaint alleged that Quinco "now holds said check." Sometime thereafter Quinco became bankrupt and a trustee was appointed. Quinco's lawsuit was dismissed for lack of prosecution about six months after the judgment in the present case.

Shortly after Quinco filed its lawsuit, it executed and delivered to US a document entitled "Assignment." This was done entirely on the initiative of Quinco's attorney.

On September 20 Investment Service Co. commenced this litigation as assignee of US's interest in the check. Since US's rights in the check are determinative here, we shall refer to US as plaintiff instead of Investment Service Co. Prior to the April trial of this litigation, US asked Quinco's attorney for the check. US received the check in March, and it was received in evidence in this litigation.

The principal issue in the case is whether the plaintiff bank can recover as a holder in an action on the check after it unconditionally returned physical possession of the check to the payee, with whom the check reposed at the time the bank commenced this action, and charged the check back to the payee's account.

When US initially received the check from Quinco, US became a "holder" of the check within the meaning of Oregon's Uniform Commercial Code (UCC) § 1–201(20). * * * US was in possession of the check and the check was properly indorsed. * * *

US initially proceeded upon the ground that it was a holder in due course and the defendant contested this status. On appeal, however, whether or not plaintiff is a holder in due course is immaterial because defendant challenges only US's status as a holder and does not assert any defense which would relieve it of an obligation to pay an ordinary holder.

If US had retained possession of the check from the time the check was returned dishonored, US would have been able to recover from the defendant drawer. The difficulty is created because US delivered the check to Quinco. The issue is whether US retained sufficient rights in the check to maintain this action.

Under §§ 51 and 191 of the Negotiable Instruments Law (NIL) the general law was that one could not maintain an action on a bill or note unless the plaintiff had possession of the bill or note.

* * *

"The owner of an instrument who is not in possession cannot sue thereon for he is not the holder under section 51 nor a transferee under section 49." Britton, Bills and Notes, 184 (2d ed. 1961).

Gilmore emphasizes the need for possession by the following illustration:

> " * * * Take first the case of a negotiable instrument: if A wishes to make a transfer of the instrument to B, the only effective method is a delivery of the instrument to B. So long as B holds the instrument in pledge (assuming the transfer to have been for security), no one can acquire superior rights to the instrument or against the obligor through anything A may do. If, however, A, retaining possession of the instrument, delivers to B a written declaration that he has transferred the instrument to B and holds it as B's property, B's possession of the written declaration may given him rights against A but will not protect him against subsequent good faith purchasers of the instrument from A or against A's creditors and will not even give him the right to collect the instrument from the obligor. * * *" 1 Gilmore, Security Interests in Personal Property, § 1.2, 11 (1965).

* * *

Lost instruments were treated under the NIL as an exception to the rule that possession is a prerequisite to recovery:

> " * * * While a person out of possession normally cannot sue on the instrument, an exception exists in favor of the

holder or owner who lost the instrument or from whom it was stolen. The holder of a lost instrument may sue thereon." Britton, supra, at 184.

* * *

The UCC is probably more exacting on the requirement of possession as a prerequisite than was the NIL. As stated, the NIL provides that to begin an action under usual circumstances one must be a holder and to be a holder one must be in possession. Although no exceptions to this principle were expressed in the NIL, the courts made exceptions such as in the case of a lost or pledged instrument. The UCC does contain an express exception to the requirement that one must have possession of an instrument to maintain an action thereon. That exception is UCC § 3–804, providing that an owner of a lost instrument can maintain an action upon the instrument if he can prove the instrument is lost. Under the usual rules of statutory construction the specification of one exception to the requirement of possession leads to a construction of the entire statute that no other exceptions to the requirement of possession are intended. This construction is fortified by the official comment to UCC § 3–804.

* * *

That part of the comment that is particularly significant is that the owner of a lost instrument is not a "holder" because he is not in possession. Also, if one is not in possession for some cause other than because the instrument is lost he cannot be a "holder." Except for UCC § 3–804, just referred to, and other provisions not here material, one cannot maintain an action upon the instrument if he is not a "holder." Thus possession of the instrument is a prerequisite to maintaining an action on it with the sole exception here material of UCC § 3–804. This exception is clearly of no avail to plaintiff.

Two reasons are the probable basis for the requirement of possession. The most important is the danger of exposing the drawer to double liability if the drawer is required to pay one who does not have physical possession of the note.

* * *

In the instance of an instrument claimed lost, the comment to UCC § 3–804, concerning lost instruments, states: "If the claimant testifies falsely, or if the instrument subsequently turns up in the hands of a holder in due course, the obligor may be subjected to double liability."

In the instant case payment by the defendant to US at the time US instituted this action could have resulted in double liability for Martin Bros. Payment to US would not have been a bar to Quinco's recovery on the check based upon Quinco's then existing rights as a holder. Since Quinco was the payee, it could, upon reacquisition of the check, strike all the endorsements. UCC § 3–208. In that event, US would no longer be a holder, not only because US no longer had possession, but also because the check was no longer endorsed to US. To be a holder, the instrument must be "issued or indorsed to him [the person claiming to be a holder] or to his order or to bearer or in blank." UCC § 1–201(20). Payment to US would not be payment to a holder * * * and, therefore, payment to US would not discharge the drawer.

*   *   *

In addition, one in the position of Quinco at the outset of this litigation could negotiate the note to a holder in due course. In that event, the holder in due course could have enforced the check against the drawer and the fact that the drawer had already paid US would not have prevented recovery by the holder in due course. *   *   *

The other reason for the requirement of possession as a prerequisite to recovery on a negotiable instrument is the necessity for simplicity and clarity in the law of commercial paper in order to facilitate commercial dealings. The basic principle of commercial dealings in negotiable instruments is that one who presents an instrument which on its front and back establishes the right of payment is entitled to be paid and one who cannot make such a showing is not entitled to be paid. Exceptions to this should be rare; the UCC expresses only one, UCC § 3–804, concerning lost instruments.

*   *   *

We hold that under the UCC, as well as the NIL, the plaintiff must prove the instrument is in its possession if it is not shown to be lost.

*   *   *

Lastly, US contends that at the time of the trial it was a holder having physical possession of the check and that the time of trial, rather than the time of the commencement of the action is the relevant time. US did have possession at the time of trial; however, we conclude that the relevant time was the commencement of the action.

Dolin v. Darnall, supra (115 N.J.L. 508, 181 A. 201, 102 A.L.R. 454), expressly held that possession of the negotiable instrument at the commencement of the action was essential and it was not sufficient that the plaintiff subsequently obtained possession by the time of trial. Johnson v. United Securities Corporation, 194 A.2d 132 (D.C.Mun.App.1963), followed Dolin v. Darnall, supra (115 N.J.L. 508, 181 A. 201):

> "Without proof that appellee was in possession of the note at the time it commenced the action, it could not maintain the action as a holder of the note. Regaining possession of the

note after commencing the action would not cure the defect. * * *." 194 A.2d at 133.

On the other hand, Professor Britton states: "It is probably sufficient if the plaintiff is the holder at the time of trial."

* * *

Our decisions are to the effect that a cause of action or suit must exist at the commencement of the litigation and litigation is premature if a necessary element of the cause of action does not occur until after the commencement of the action. We have not found an articulation of the reasons for such policy but presume that it is to discourage speculative litigation.

* * *

Affirmed.

O'CONNELL, JUSTICE (dissenting). The record shows that plaintiff introduced the check into evidence at the time of the trial. It is clear, then, that the bank was the holder of the check at that time. And I understand that the majority of the court would concede that the bank could have brought the action if the check had come into its possession prior to the commencement of the action. So the decision in this case is made to rest solely upon the extremely technical ground that the elements of a cause of action must exist at the commencement of the action and the defect is not cured by evidence at the trial which supplies the missing element in the cause of action.

Whatever may be said in defense of this rule, I do not think that it should be applied when it is asserted by the defendant for the first time on appeal. If defendant had set up this defense at the time of trial, plaintiff would simply have refiled his action and the cause of action would have then been good. As it is, plaintiff is denied relief on appeal on technical grounds which plaintiff can readily circumvent by filing a new action and, as I understand the majority opinion, plaintiff will be entitled to recover as a holder of the check.

PERRY, C.J., joints in this dissent.

SMATHERS v. SMATHERS

Court of Appeals of North Carolina, 1977.
34 N.C.App. 724, 239 S.E.2d 637.

In separate actions plaintiff seeks to recover on two promissory notes, each of which was signed by defendants and made payable to the order of John H. Smathers. Although the notes were not indorsed, plaintiff alleged she is presently the owner and holder of the notes by assignment. Defendants answered and admitted that they executed the notes to John H. Smathers, who was the father of the male defendant, but alleged that it was the understanding of the parties that defendants would not have to pay the notes and that they were only for record in the later settlement of the John H. Smathers Estate. Defendants also denied that plaintiff is the owner of the notes. The two actions were consolidated for trial and were tried by the court without a jury.

At trial, plaintiff introduced the notes in evidence and stipulated that they had never been indorsed by the payee. Plaintiff testified that the notes had been given to her husband by his father, John H. Smathers, the payee, and that they came to her as result of her husband's death three years ago. There was also evidence that John H. Smathers had died and that First Union National Bank was executor of his estate.

At conclusion of the evidence, the court entered judgment finding "as a matter of law that the plaintiff is the owner and holder of the two promissory notes being sued on and pursuant to UCC § 3–301 is entitled to enforce payment in her own name." From judgment for plaintiff for the amount of the notes plus interest, defendants appeal.

PARKER, JUDGE. UCC § 1–201(20) defines a "holder" as "a person who is in possession of a document of title or an instrument or an investment security drawn, issued or indorsed to him or to his order or to bearer or in blank." The notes upon which plaintiff sues were not drawn, issued or indorsed to her or to her order or to bearer or in blank. Therefore, plaintiff is not the holder of the notes * * * and the trial court erred in according her the rights of a holder under UCC § 3–301.

* * *

UCC § 3–201(1) provides in part that "[t]ransfer of an instrument vests in the transferee such rights as the transferor has therein * * *." However, subsection (3) of that section provides that until the instrument is indorsed "there is no presumption that the transferee is the owner." Referring to this clause of subsection (3), [the] Official Comment * * * to Section 3–201 of the U.C.C. states:

> The final clause of subsection (3), which is new, is intended to make it clear that the transferee without indorsement of an order instrument is not a holder and so is not aided by the presumption that he is entitled to recover on the instrument provided in Section 3–307(2). The terms of the obligation do not run to him, and he must account for his possession of the unindorsed paper by proving the transaction through which he acquired it.

In the present case, the plaintiff testified to some of the circumstances under which she obtained possession of the notes, but the trial court made no findings of fact with respect thereto. Indeed, the trial court, which heard this case without a jury, made no findings of fact whatsoever as it was required to do by G.S. 1A–1, Rule 52(a)(1). Instead, it based its judgment for the plaintiff entirely upon its finding "as a matter of law that the plaintiff is the owner and holder" of the notes. Since we have found that legal conclusion was in error, defendants are entitled to a new trial. Upon a new trial, plaintiff may be able to establish that she is the transferee of the notes and thus under UCC § 3–201(1) has such rights as her transferor had therein. This may include the right to maintain an action to enforce payment of the notes, subject, however, to any defenses which defendants could have asserted against her transferor.

New Trial.

c. DISCHARGE

A corollary to the merger doctrine that the right to enforce an instrument is the exclusive right of the holder was that the person obliged to pay the instrument discharges the obligation by paying the holder. Revised Article 3 reflects this corollary in a modified form in § 3–602(a). The obligor who pays the holder is assured that nobody else can obtain a right to enforce the instrument if the obligor obtains surrender of the instrument from the holder at the time of payment. § 3–501(a) and (b)(2). But there is also a corollary to the discharge rule: payment to a person who is not the holder might not result in discharge. This corollary is considered in *Lambert* which follows.

LAMBERT v. BARKER
Supreme Court of Virginia, 1986.
232 Va. 21, 348 S.E.2d 214.

COCHRAN, JUSTICE.

The central question in this appeal is whether payment by the obligors of a note to a party not in possession of the note discharged the obligation of the makers and precluded recovery on the note by the party in possession.

The facts surrounding the underlying transactions are substantially undisputed. In May 1978, William K. Barker and Barbara R. Barker acquired from Robert O. Davis, Jr., property located at 2610 Monument Avenue, Richmond. As part of the consideration for their purchase, the Barkers executed a note, secured by a second deed of trust on the property, in the principal amount of $20,300 payable to Davis, or order, in monthly installments.

In December 1978, the Barkers conveyed the property to S. David Beloff, who in turn conveyed it to Charles P. Harwood, Jr.,

and Ann G. Harwood in January 1979. The Harwoods, uniting in
the deed from Beloff, expressly agreed to pay the Barker note.
Pursuant to a loan agreement dated November 1, 1979, Davis
transferred this note, along with certain other notes, to Katherine
W. Lambert (who signed her name as Kathleen), Trustee for Cecil-
Waller & Sterling, Inc. (Lambert), to secure a loan from Cecil-
Waller & Sterling to Davis in the amount of $197,234.72. The
loan agreement between Davis and Lambert provided that the
monthly installments on the Barker note would continue to be
payable to Davis, while any prepayment was to be made to
Lambert.

In February 1980, the Harwoods conveyed the property to
Bryce A. Bugg and Nancy S. Bugg. At closing, Davis provided an
affidavit in which he falsely asserted that he was the noteholder
but that the Barker note was lost. The sum of $18,446.17 was
withheld from the sale proceeds and paid to Davis, purportedly in
satisfaction of the note.

In 1981, Lambert instituted this action against the Barkers
and the Harwoods to recover $18,497.94 on the note, together with
interest, costs, and attorney's fees. Alleging the note was in
default and this amount represented the unpaid balance, Lambert
claimed she was entitled to payment as the holder of the note.

The Barkers and Harwoods filed their separate grounds of
defense denying liability on the ground that the Harwoods' payment to Davis satisfied the note in full. They also filed third-
party motions for judgment against the attorney who represented
the Buggs in their purchase from the Harwoods and against his
law firm, alleging negligence and breach of fiduciary duty in
failing properly to discharge the obligation of the note by paying
the holder.

After a hearing at which Lambert tendered the note in her
possession indorsed by Davis, the trial court granted a motion for
summary judgment filed by the Barkers and the Harwoods and
dismissed a motion for summary judgment filed by Lambert. The
court ruled that UCC § 9–318(3) was controlling and required
Lambert to give notice to both the Barkers and the Harwoods of
the pledge of the note. Finding no such notice had been given, the
court ruled that Lambert could not "question" payments by the
Barkers or the Harwoods made directly to Davis. Accordingly,
the court dismissed both the principal action and the third-party
motions for judgment. Lambert appealed the court's dismissal of
her action against the Barkers.

[Omitted is the part of the opinion in which the Court held
that UCC § 9–318(3) was inapplicable.]

The Barkers contend, as they did below, that payment to
Davis discharged their liability as makers of the note. The right
of a party to payment, however, depends upon his status as a

holder. UCC § 3–301. A holder is one who is in possession of an instrument issued or indorsed to him or his order, to bearer, or in blank. UCC § 1–201(20) * * *. Payment or satisfaction discharges the liability of a party only if made to the holder of the instrument. * * * Because payment in satisfaction of the instrument must be made to a party in possession in order to discharge the payor's liability, no notice is required for the protection of the payor. Rather, the payor may protect himself by demanding production of the instrument and refusing payment to any party not in possession unless in an action on the obligation the owner proves his ownership.

Payment to an authorized agent of the holder will also satisfy the requirement of payment to the holder, resulting in discharge. UCC § 1–103 (agency principles supplement UCC provisions); Security Company v. Juliano, Inc., 203 Va. 827, 833, 127 S.E.2d 348, 352 (1962) * * *. But the burden of proving an agency relationship rests on the party claiming payment as a defense.

> One making payment to an agent has the burden of showing that the agent has either express or apparent authority to receive such payment upon behalf of his principal, and the evidence to that effect must be clear and convincing. If payment is made to a party who does not have in hand the obligation, the debtor takes the risk of such party having the authority to make collection.

Security Company, 203 Va. at 833, 127 S.E.2d at 352 * * *.

It is clear that Davis was not the holder of the Barker note at the time of payment, as the note was not in his possession. By delivering the note, indorsed in blank, to Lambert, Davis negotiated the instrument and made Lambert the holder. * * * Payment to Davis could therefore discharge the Barkers' liability only if Davis were the authorized agent of Lambert. Moreover, it was the Barkers' responsibility to raise and establish this affirmative defense. *Security Company,* 203 Va. at 833, 127 S.E.2d at 352. The Barkers, however, never asserted payment to Lambert; nor did they allege that payment to Davis constituted payment to Lambert under an actual or implied agency theory. Having failed properly to assert a defense of payment to Lambert, the noteholder, the Barkers were not entitled to summary judgment. To the contrary, Lambert was entitled to judgment against the Barkers upon their failure to raise a valid defense.

The Barkers contend that, even if Lambert were the holder of the note, she was not a holder in due course under UCC § 3–302 and therefore did not take the instrument free from defenses under UCC § 3–305. Because the Barkers failed properly to assert the defense of payment to Lambert, Lambert's status— whether as a holder in due course or not in due course—does not affect this result.

The amount payable on the note is not controverted. Accordingly, we will reverse the judgment of the trial court and enter final judgment in favor of Lambert.

3. GOOD FAITH PURCHASE: FREEDOM FROM CLAIMS AND DEFENSES

a. CLAIMS OF OWNERSHIP

The doctrine that a good faith purchaser for value takes an instrument free both of defenses arising from the transaction giving rise to the instrument and claims of ownership to the instrument can be traced to two seminal cases. The first, Miller v. Race, 1 Burr. 452, 97 Eng.Rep. 398 (K.B. 1758), presented the question of title to a stolen promissory note issued by the Bank of England for the payment of 21 pounds ten shillings to "William Finney or bearer, on demand." On December 11 Finney mailed the note to one Odenharty but that night the note was stolen from the mails by a robber. The next day, in the words of Lord Mansfield, "an inn-keeper took it, bona fide, in his business from a person who made an appearance of a gentleman. Here is no pretence or suspicion of collusion with the robber: for this matter was strictly inquired and examined into at the trial; and is so stated in the case 'that he took it for a full and valuable consideration, in the usual course of business.' Indeed if there had been any collusion, or any circumstances of unfair dealing; the case had been much otherwise. If it had been a note for 1000 [pounds] it might have been suspicious: but this was a small note for 21 [pounds] 10 [shillings] only: and money given in exchange for it." On December 13 Finney, having learned of the robbery, "applied to the Bank of England 'to stop the payment of this note:' which was ordered accordingly, upon Mr. Finney's entering into proper security 'to indemnify the bank.' " Plaintiff then delivered the note for payment to defendant, a clerk of the Bank of England. Defendant refused to pay or to redeliver the note to Plaintiff. In an action in trover judgment for the amount of the note was given to Plaintiff. Lord Mansfield in holding that Plaintiff, the good faith purchaser, had acquired good title to the note superior to that of Finney said "A banknote is constantly and universally, both at home and abroad, treated as money, as cash; and paid and received, as cash; and it is necessary, for the purposes of commerce, that their currency should be established and secured."

Notes of the kind involved in Miller v. Race were the ancestors of modern English currency and similar in form. A modern ten-pound note reads as follows "I promise to pay the bearer on demand the sum of ten pounds." The promise to pay is signed by the Chief Cashier of the Bank of England "For the Governor and

Company of the Bank of England." Commercial transactions would be seriously impeded if money, or its equivalent, could not be accepted without question as to whether the taker was acquiring good title to it. The rule of Miller v. Race might have been explained as being simply a recognition of this fact in the case of certain bank obligations which, de facto, were taken as the equivalent of money. But the rule was also applied to the obligations of individuals to which the rationale of "money equivalent" was less persuasive.

The second case, Peacock v. Rhodes, 2 Doug. 633, 99 Eng.Rep. 402 (K.B. 1781), involved a bill of exchange, payable on issue to "William Ingham, or order" and subsequently indorsed by Ingham in blank. Neither the drawer nor the drawee was a bank. The bill, indorsed in blank, was stolen and negotiated to plaintiff, a mercer who "received the bill from a man not known, who called himself William Brown, and, by that name, indorsed the bill to the plaintiff, of whom he bought cloth, and other articles in the way of the plaintiff's trade as a mercer, in his shop at Scarborough, and paid him that bill, the value whereof the plaintiff gave to the buyer in cloth and other articles, and cash, and small bills."

Lord Mansfield stated that the case was within the rule of Miller v. Race. "The holder of a bill of exchange, or promissory note, is not to be considered in the light of an assignee of the payee. An assignee must take the thing assigned, subject to all the equity to which the original party was subject. If this rule applied to bills and promissory notes, it would stop their currency. The law is settled, that a holder, coming fairly by a bill or note, has nothing to do with the transaction between the original parties; unless, perhaps, in the single case (which is a hard one, but has been determined) of a note won at play. I see no difference between a note indorsed blank, and one payable to bearer. They both go by delivery, and possession proves property in both cases. The question of mala fides was for the consideration of the jury. The circumstances, that the buyer and also the drawers were strangers to the plaintiff, and that he took the bill for goods on which he had a profit, were grounds of suspicion, very fit for their consideration. But they have considered them, and have found it was received in the course of trade, and, therefore, the case is clear, and within the principle of *   *   * Miller v. Race *   *   *."

Miller v. Race and Peacock v. Rhodes both involved good faith purchasers for value who took free of claims of ownership, but the words of Lord Mansfield in Peacock v. Rhodes—"the holder *   *   * has nothing to do with the transaction between the original parties"—applied as well to defenses that the drawer of the bill may have had against the original payee of the bill. Thus, the good faith purchaser took free of defenses as well.

The common law doctrine of these cases was codified in the NIL and in Article 3 with different terminology. The early cases spoke of a holder who was a good faith purchaser for value. In Article 3 this holder is referred to as a "holder in due course," a term defined in § 3–302(a). This definition is discussed in Comments 1 and 2 to § 3–302. The rule of Miller v. Race is restated in § 3–306. A person taking an instrument, other than a person with rights of a holder in due course, is subject to a "property or possessory right" in the instrument or its proceeds. Thus, if a check is stolen from the payee of the check or possession is obtained from the payee by fraud, the payee has a claim to the check or, if the check is paid, to the proceeds of the check. But that claim cannot be asserted against a person having rights of a holder in due course.

b. ORDINARY DEFENSES

The extent to which a holder takes free of defenses is governed by § 3–305(a) and (b). Subsection (a) states that the right to enforce an instrument is subject to defenses described in paragraphs (1) and (2) of that subsection and claims in recoupment described in paragraph (3). Subsection (b) of § 3–305 is a limitation on subsection (a). The right of a holder in due course to enforce an instrument is subject to the defenses stated in subsection (a)(1)—the so-called "real defenses"—but is not subject to the "ordinary" defenses stated in subsection (a)(2) or claims in recoupment described in subsection (a)(3).

Section § 3–305(a)(2) refers to defenses that are specifically stated in other sections of Article 3. Those defenses and the sections in which they are found are listed in the first paragraph of Comment 2 to § 3–305. Subsection (a)(2) also refers to the common law defenses applicable to simple contracts which are not enumerated. The principal common law defenses are fraud, misrepresentation, and mistake in the issuance of the instrument.

c. REAL DEFENSES

Section § 3–305(a)(1) lists the defenses that may be asserted against even a holder in due course. These defenses are discussed in Comment 1 to § 3–305. With the exception of the defense of discharge in an insolvency proceeding, all of the real defenses refer to an instrument that is made unenforceable in order to carry out some public policy of the state not related to the law of negotiable instruments, or to an instrument which does not represent a contract of the person who signed the instrument.

d. CLAIMS IN RECOUPMENT

Restatement (Second) of Contracts § 336(2) states: "The right of an assignee is subject to any defense or claim of the obligor which accrues before the obligor receives notification of the assignment, but not to defenses or claims which accrue thereafter * * *." Suppose A promises to pay $1,000 to B in return for a promise by B to deliver goods to A. B assigns to C the right of B to receive $1,000 from A. A receives no notification of the assignment. If A's promise to pay B was induced by B's fraud or if B failed to deliver the goods as promised, A has a defense to the obligation to pay B. The defense can be asserted against C, the assignee. Change the facts. Suppose there was no fraud by B and B tendered the goods to A, who accepted them. A has no defense to the obligation to pay for the goods. But suppose A has a claim against B to receive $600. If C demands payment of $1,000 from A, A can assert the $600 claim as a reduction of the amount owing to C from $1,000 to $400.

If A's promise to pay is a negotiable instrument and the instrument is negotiated to C, § 3–305 rather than the Restatement governs the rights of A and C. Subsection (a)(2) of § 3–305 applies to the defense of fraud or failure to deliver the goods. Subsection (a)(3) applies to A's $600 claim against B if A's claim arose from the transaction that gave rise to the instrument and is therefore a claim in recoupment. Furthermore, the rights of C depend upon whether C is a holder in due course. § 3–305(b). Claims in recoupment are discussed in Comment 3 to § 3–305.

PROBLEM

Merchant sold and delivered goods to Plumber who accepted them and, as payment of the price, delivered to Merchant a negotiable note of Plumber to pay $10,000 to the order of Merchant. The note was payable one year after the date it was issued. Merchant immediately negotiated the note to Finance Co. A month after the sale and delivery of the goods by Merchant, Plumber, at the request of Merchant, repaired and replaced water pipes and plumbing fixtures at Merchant's place of business. Plumber's bill for this work was $8,000. When Plumber's note became due Finance Co. demanded payment. Plumber refused to pay for the following reasons: (1) Merchant had not paid the $8,000 owed for the work performed by Plumber; (2) some of the goods sold by Merchant to Plumber were defective and, as a result of the defects, Plumber incurred losses of over $4,000. How much is Finance Co. entitled to recover from Plumber if Finance Co. is a holder in due course? How much is Finance Co. entitled to recover if Finance Co. is not a holder in due course?

C. FORMAL REQUISITES OF NEGOTIABLE INSTRUMENTS

Merger theory and the ability of a good faith purchaser for value to take free of claims and defenses with respect to the instrument were based on a separation of the right to payment represented by the instrument from the transaction giving rise to the instrument. But merger theory assumed that the terms of the instrument were not inconsistent with separation from the underlying transaction, and that the terms of the right to receive payment could be determined simply by examination of the instrument itself. Thus the consequences of negotiability were applied by the common-law courts only if the instrument met certain criteria that satisfied these assumptions. The definition of negotiable instrument is found in Revised Article 3 in § 3–104(a), and this definition differs only slightly from the requisites for negotiability stated in the NIL and the original Article 3.

The definition of negotiable instrument in § 3–104 defines the scope of Revised Article 3. § 3–102(a). The most important elements of that definition can be briefly described. Only an "order" or "promise" can qualify as a negotiable instrument. "Order" is defined in § 3–103(a)(6) as a written instruction to pay money signed by the person giving the instruction. "Promise" is defined in § 3–103(a)(9) as a written undertaking to pay money signed by the person undertaking to pay. Thus, a negotiable instrument is always a signed writing that promises or orders payment of money. Negotiable instruments fall into two categories: drafts and notes. An instrument is a draft if it is an order and is a note if it is a promise. § 3–104(e). Checks are the most common examples of drafts. § 3–104(f). Certificates of deposit are considered to be notes. § 3–104(j).

Because the rules applicable to negotiable instruments and the rules applicable to ordinary contracts can produce dramatically different results in some cases, it is imperative that both the person issuing a promise or order to pay money and the person to whom the promise or order is issued be able to know in advance whether Article 3 or ordinary contract law will apply. The various requirements of § 3–104(a) are designed to provide mechanical tests to allow that determination to be made. One particularly important requirement is that the order or promise be "payable to bearer or to order," a term explained in § 3–109. Thus, a technical and wholly formal distinction is made between a promise to pay "to John Doe" and a promise to pay "to the order of John Doe." The second promise may be a negotiable instrument if it otherwise qualifies under § 3–104. The first promise cannot be a negotiable instrument. Because of this distinction, the issuer of a promissory note payable to an identified person can easily avoid the consequences of negotiability by avoiding use of the words of negotiability: "to order" or "to bearer." Another device for avoiding the effects of Article 3 is provided by § 3–104(d). These devices for excluding an order or promise from Article 3 are discussed in Comments 2 and 3 to § 3–104.

Three of the requisites of a negotiable instrument relate to the certainty of the obligation to pay. First, the order or promise to pay must be "unconditional," a term explained in § 3–106. An examination of that provision discloses that some promises or orders that are in fact conditional are deemed to be unconditional while others that are in fact unconditional are deemed to be conditional for the purposes of § 3–104(a). The Comment to § 3–106 is a guide to the rather arbitrary distinctions and refinements of § 3–106. Second, the order or promise must be payable on demand or at a definite time, a requirement explained in § 3–108. Third, the order or promise must be to pay a "fixed amount of money, with or without interest or other charges described in the promise or order." The quoted language differs from § 3–104(1)(b) of the original Article 3 which used the phrase "sum certain in money." Taylor v. Roeder, which follows, discusses the problem of variable interest rates under the original Article 3. How is this issue resolved under Revised Article 3? § 3–112(b).

TAYLOR v. ROEDER
Supreme Court of Virginia, 1987.
234 Va. 99, 360 S.E.2d 191.

Russell, Justice.

The dispositive question in this case is whether a note providing for a variable rate of interest, not ascertainable from the face of the note, is a negotiable instrument. We conclude that it is not.

The facts are undisputed. VMC Mortgage Company (VMC) was a mortgage lender in Northern Virginia. In the conduct of its business, it borrowed funds from investors, pledging as security the notes secured by deeds of trust which it had obtained from its borrowers. Two of these transactions became the subject of this suit. Because they involve similar facts and the same question of law, they were consolidated for trial below and are consolidated in a single record here * * *.

In the first case, Olde Towne Investment Corporation of Virginia, Inc., on September 11, 1979, borrowed $18,000 from VMC, evidenced by a 60–day note secured by a deed of trust on land in Fairfax County. The note provided for interest at "[t]hree percent (3.00%) over Chase Manhattan Prime to be adjusted monthly." The note provided for renewal "at the same rate of interest at the option of the makers up to a maximum of six (6) months in sixty (60) day increments with the payment of an additional fee of [t]wo (2) points." The note was renewed and extended to November 11, 1980, by a written extension agreement signed by Olde Towne and by VMC.

In May 1981, Frederick R. Taylor, Jr., as trustee for himself and other parties, entered into a contract to buy from Olde Towne the land in Fairfax County securing the $18,000 loan. Taylor's title examination revealed the VMC deed of trust. He requested the payoff figures from VMC and forwarded to VMC the funds VMC said were due. He never received the cancelled Olde Towne note, and the deed of trust was not released.

In the second case, Richard L. Saslaw and others, on December 31, 1979, borrowed $22,450 from VMC evidenced by a 12–month note secured by deed of trust on Fairfax County land. This note also bore interest at "3% over Chase Manhattan prime adjusted monthly." Interest was to be "payable quarterly beginning April 1, 1980." In November 1980, Virender and Barbara Puri entered into a contract to purchase from Saslaw, et al., the land subject to the last-mentioned deed of trust. The Puris designated the same Frederick R. Taylor, Jr., as their settlement attorney. Taylor's title examination revealed VMC's deed of trust. Taylor again requested a payoff figure from VMC. At settlement, Saslaw objected to the figure, communicated with VMC and received VMC's agreement to an adjusted figure. Taylor paid the adjusted amount to VMC. Again, Taylor failed to receive the cancelled Saslaw note, and the Saslaw deed of trust was not released.

Cecil Pruitt, Jr., was a trustee of a tax-exempt employees' pension fund. He invested some of the pension fund's assets with VMC, receiving as collateral pledges of certain secured notes that VMC held. The Saslaw note was pledged and delivered to him on January 25, 1980; the Olde Towne note was pledged and delivered to him on September 12, 1980. No notice was given to the makers, or to Taylor, that the notes had been transferred, and all payments on both notes were made to and accepted by VMC.

VMC received and deposited in its account sufficient funds to pay both notes in full, but never informed Pruitt of the payments and made no request of him for return of the original notes. In February 1982, VMC defaulted on its obligation to Pruitt for which both notes had been pledged as collateral. In May 1982, VMC filed a bankruptcy petition in federal court.

Learning that the properties securing both notes had been sold, Pruitt demanded payment from the respective original makers as well as the new owners of the properties, contending that he was a holder in due course. The makers and new owners took the position that they had paid the notes in full. Pruitt caused William F. Roeder, Jr., to qualify as substituted trustee under both deeds of trust and directed him to foreclose them. Taylor and the Puris filed separate bills of complaint against Roeder, trustee, seeking to enjoin the foreclosure sales. The chancellor entered a temporary injunction to preserve the *status quo* and heard the consolidated cases *ore tenus*. By letter opinion incorporated into a final decree entered February 3, 1984, the chancellor found for the defendant and dissolved the injunctions. We granted the complainants an appeal. The parties have agreed on the record that foreclosure will be withheld while the case is pending in this Court.

Under the general law of contracts, if an obligor has received no notice that his debt has been assigned and is in fact unaware of the assignment, he may, with impunity, pay his original creditor and thus extinguish the obligation. His payment will be a complete defense against the claim of an assignee who failed to give him notice of the assignment. * * *

Under the law of negotiable instruments, continued in effect under the Uniform Commercial Code, the rule is different: the makers are bound by their contract to make payment to the *holder.* * * * Further, a holder in due course takes the instrument free from the maker's defense that he has made payment to the original payee, if he lacks notice of the payment and has not dealt with the maker. UCC § 3–305. Thus, the question whether the notes in this case were negotiable is crucial.

UCC § 3–104(1) provides, in pertinent part:

> Any writing to be a negotiable instrument within this title must

> * * *

> (b) contain an unconditional promise or order to pay a sum certain in money * * *.

The meaning of "sum certain" is clarified by UCC § 3–106:

> (1) The sum payable is a sum certain even though it is to be paid

> (a) with stated interest or by stated installments; or

> (b) with stated different rates of interest before and after default or a specified date; or

> (c) with a stated discount or addition if paid before or after the date fixed for payment; or

> (d) with exchange or less exchange, whether at a fixed rate or at the current rate; or

> (e) with costs of collection or an attorney's fee or both upon default.

> (2) Nothing in this section shall validate any term which is otherwise illegal.

Official Comment 1, which follows, states in part:

> It is sufficient [to establish negotiability] that at any time of payment the holder is able to determine the amount then

payable *from the instrument itself* with any necessary computation * * *. The computation must be one which can be
made *from the instrument itself without reference to any
outside source,* and this section does not make negotiable a
note payable with interest "at the current rate."

(Emphasis added.) UCC § 3–107 provides an explicit exception to
the "four corners" rule laid down above by providing for the
negotiability of instruments payable in foreign currency.

We conclude that the drafters of the Uniform Commercial
Code adopted criteria of negotiability intended to exclude an
instrument which requires reference to any source outside the
instrument itself in order to ascertain the amount due, subject
only to the exceptions specifically provided for by the U.C.C.
* * *

The appellee points to the Official Comment to UCC § 3–104.
Comment 1 states that by providing criteria for negotiability
"within this Article," * * * "leaves open the possibility that
some writings may be made negotiable by other statutes or by
judicial decision." The Comment continues: "The same is true as
to any new type of paper which commercial practice may develop
in the future." The appellee urges us to create, by judicial
decision, just such an exception in favor of variable-interest notes.

Appellants concede that variable-interest loans have become a
familiar device in the mortgage lending industry. Their popularity arose when lending institutions, committed to long-term loans
at fixed rates of interest to their borrowers, were in turn required
to borrow short-term funds at high rates during periods of rapid
inflation. Variable rates protected lenders when rates rose and
benefitted borrowers when rates declined. They suffer, however,
from the disadvantage that the amount required to satisfy the
debt cannot be ascertained without reference to an extrinsic
source—in this case the varying prime rate charged by the Chase
Manhattan Bank. Although that rate may readily be ascertained
from published sources, it cannot be found within the "four
corners" of the note.

Other courts confronted with similar questions have reached
differing results. See, e.g., A. Alport & Son, Inc. v. Hotel Evans,
Inc., 65 Misc.2d 374, 376–77, 317 N.Y.S.2d 937, 939–40 (1970) (note
bearing interest at "bank rates" not negotiable under U.C.C.);
Woodhouse, Drake and Carey, Ltd. v. Anderson, 61 Misc.2d 951,
307 N.Y.S.2d 113 (1970) (note providing for interest at "8½% or at
the maximum legal rate" was not usurious. Inferentially, the
note was negotiable.); Farmers Production Credit Ass'n v. Arena,
145 Vt. 20, 23, 481 A.2d 1064, 1065 (1984) (variable-interest note
not negotiable under U.C.C.).

The U.C.C. introduced a degree of clarity into the law of
commercial transactions which permits it to be applied by laymen

daily to countless transactions without resort to judicial interpretation. The relative predictability of results made possible by that clarity constitutes the overriding benefit arising from its adoption. In our view, that factor makes it imperative that when change is thought desirable, the change should be made by statutory amendment, not through litigation and judicial interpretation. Accordingly, we decline the appellee's invitation to create an exception, by judicial interpretation, in favor of instruments providing for a variable rate of interest not ascertainable from the instrument itself.

In an alternative argument, the appellee contends that even if the notes are not negotiable, they are nevertheless "symbolic instruments" which ought to be paid according to their express terms. Those terms include the maker's promises to pay "to VMC Mortgage Company *or order,*" and in the event of default, to make accelerated payment "at the option of the *holder.*" The emphasized language, appellee contends, makes clear that the makers undertook an obligation to pay any party who held the notes as a result of a transfer from VMC. Assuming the abstract correctness of that argument, it does not follow that the makers undertook the further obligation of making a monthly canvass of all inhabitants of the earth in order to ascertain who the holder might be. In the absence of notice to the makers that their debt had been assigned, they were entitled to the protection of the rule in *Evans v. Joyner* in making good-faith payment to the original payee of these non-negotiable notes.

Accordingly, we will reverse the decree and remand the cause to the trial court for entry of a permanent injunction against foreclosure.

COMPTON, JUSTICE, dissenting.

The majority views the Uniform Commercial Code as inflexible, requiring legislative action to adapt to changing commercial practices. This overlooks a basic purpose of the Code, flexibility and adaptability of construction to meet developing commercial usage.

According to § 1–102(1), the UCC "shall be liberally construed and applied to promote its underlying purposes and policies." One of such underlying purposes and policies is "to permit the continued expansion of commercial practices through custom, usage and agreement of the parties." § 1–102(2)(b). Comment 1 to this section sets out clearly the intention of the drafters:

> "This Act is drawn to provide flexibility so that, since it is intended to be a semi-permanent piece of legislation, it will provide its own machinery for expansion of commercial practices. *It is intended to make it possible for the law embodied in this Act to be developed by the courts in light of unforeseen and new circumstances and practices.* However, the proper

construction of the Act requires that its interpretation and application be limited to its reason." (Emphasis added).

The majority's rigid interpretation defeats the purpose of the Code. Nowhere in the UCC is "sum certain" defined. This absence must be interpreted in light of the expectation that commercial law continue to evolve. The § 3–106 exceptions could not have been intended as the exclusive list of "safe harbors," as the drafters anticipated "unforeseen" changes in commercial practices. Instead, those exceptions represented, at the time of drafting, recognized conditions of payment which did not impair negotiability in the judgment of businessmen. To limit exceptions to those existing at that time would frustrate the "continued expansion of commercial practices" by freezing the Code in time and requiring additional legislation whenever "unforeseen and new circumstances and practices" evolve, regardless of "custom, usage, and agreement of the parties."

> "The rule requiring certainty in commercial paper was a rule of commerce before it was a rule of law. It requires commercial, not mathematical, certainty. An uncertainty which does not impair the function of negotiable instruments in the judgment of business men ought not to be regarded by the courts * * *. The whole question is, do [the provisions] render the instruments so uncertain as to destroy their fitness to pass current in the business world?" *Cudahy Packing Co. v. State National Bank of St. Louis,* 134 F. 538, 542, 545 (8th Cir.1904).

Instruments providing that loan interest may be adjusted over the life of the loan routinely pass with increasing frequency in this state and many others as negotiable instruments. This Court should recognize this custom and usage, as the commercial market has, and hold these instruments to be negotiable.

The majority focuses on the requirement found in Comment 1 to § 3–106 that a negotiable instrument be self-contained, understood without reference to an outside source. Our cases have interpreted this to mean that reference to terms in another agreement which materially affect the instrument renders it non-negotiable. See, e.g., McLean Bank v. Nelson, Adm'r, 232 Va. 420, 350 S.E.2d 651 (1986) (where note was accepted "pursuant" to a separate agreement, reference considered surplusage and the note negotiable); Salomonsky v. Kelly, 232 Va. 261, 349 S.E.2d 358 (1986) (where principal sum payable "as set forth" in a separate agreement, all the essential terms did not appear on the face of the instrument and the note was nonnegotiable).

The commercial market requires a self-contained instrument for negotiability so that a stranger to the original transaction will be fully apprised of its terms and will not be disadvantaged by terms not ascertainable from the instrument itself. For example, interest payable at the "current rate" leaves a holder subject to claims that the current rate was established by one bank rather than another and would disadvantage a stranger to the original transaction.

The rate which is stated in the notes in this case, however, does not similarly disadvantage a stranger to the original agreement. Anyone coming into possession could immediately ascertain the terms of the notes; interest payable at three percent above the prime rate established by the Chase Manhattan Bank of New York City. This is a third-party objective standard which is recognized as such by the commercial market. The rate can be determined by a telephone call to the bank or from published lists obtained on request. * * *

Accordingly, I believe these notes are negotiable under the Code and I would affirm the decision below.

NOTES

1. In Miller & Harrell, The Law of Modern Payment Systems and Notes 37 (1985), the authors suggest that we scrap the traditional formal requirements of negotiability and adopt the following:

(1) Any writing to be a negotiable instrument within this article must

(a) be signed by the maker or drawer;

(b) be for the payment, or evidence a right to the payment, of money; and

(c) be of a type which in the ordinary course of business is transferred by delivery with any necessary endorsement or assignment.

This is similar to the definition of "instrument" in § 9–105(1)(i). Why does § 3–104 reject this functional test of negotiability in favor of the traditional, somewhat mechanical tests incorporated in § 3–104(a)? Comment 2 to § 3–104.

2. Under § 3–104(a)(1) a promissory note which says "I promise to pay Payee" is not a negotiable instrument, but a check which says "Pay to Payee" is a negotiable instrument under § 3–104(c). Why draw this distinction? The original Article 3 included § 3–805 which provided: "This Article applies to any instrument whose terms do not preclude transfer and which is otherwise negotiable within this Article but which is not payable to order or to bearer, except that there can be no holder in due course of such an instrument." Why was this provision dropped in Revised Article 3? What body of law governs promissory notes lacking words of negotiability? These issues are discussed in Comment 2 to § 3–104.

D. REQUIREMENTS FOR STATUS AS HOLDER IN DUE COURSE

---

1. GOOD FAITH AND NOTICE

To qualify as a holder in due course under § 3–302 a holder must, among other requirements, have taken the instrument in good faith and without notice of any defense against or claim to it on the part of any person. The meaning of good faith as applied to negotiable instruments has varied over the years. The law prior to the adoption of the NIL is traced by the Court in Howard National Bank v. Wilson, 96 Vt. 438, 120 A. 889 (1923):

> Prior to the Negotiable Instruments Act, two distinct lines of cases had developed in this country. The first had its origin in Gill v. Cubitt, 3 B. & C. 466, 10 E.C.L. 215, where the rule was distinctly laid down by the court of King's Bench that the purchaser of negotiable paper must exercise reasonable prudence and caution, and that, if the circumstances were such as ought to have excited the suspicion of a prudent and careful man, and he made no inquiry, he did not stand in the legal position of a bona fide holder. The rule was adopted by the courts of this country generally and seem to have become a fixed rule in the law of negotiable paper. Later in Goodman v. Harvey, 4 A. & E. 870, 31 E.C.L. 381, the English court abandoned its former position and adopted the rule that nothing short of actual bad faith or fraud in the purchaser would deprive him of the character of a bona fide purchaser and let in defenses existing between prior parties, that no circumstances of suspicion merely, or want of proper caution in the purchaser, would have this effect, and that even gross negligence would have no effect, except as evidence tending to establish bad faith or fraud. Some of the American courts adhered to the earlier rule, while others followed the change inaugurated in Goodman v. Harvey. The question was before this court in Roth v. Colvin, 32 Vt. 125, and, on full consideration of the question, a rule was adopted in harmony with that announced in Gill v. Cubitt, which has been adhered to in subsequent cases, including those cited above. Stated briefly, one line of cases including our own had adopted the test of the reasonably prudent man and the other that of actual good faith. It would seem that it was the intent of the Negotiable Instruments Act to harmonize this disagreement by adopting the latter test. That such is the view generally accepted by the courts appears from a recent review of the cases concerning what constitutes notice of defect. Brannan on Neg.Ins. Law, 187–201. To effectuate the general purpose of the act to

make uniform the Negotiable Instruments Law of those states which should enact it, we are constrained to hold (contrary to the rule adopted in our former decisions) that negligence on the part of the plaintiff, or suspicious circumstances sufficient to put a prudent man on inquiry, will not of themselves prevent a recovery, but are to be considered merely as evidence bearing on the question of bad faith. 96 Vt. at 452–453, 120 A. at 894.

Gill v. Cubitt, referred to in the above quotation and decided by the Court of King's Bench in 1824, is reminiscent of Miller v. Race. It involved a stolen bill of exchange purchased by plaintiff without any inquiry about the title of the transferor. The court decided that the circumstances under which the purchase was made should have caused plaintiff to be suspicious about the transferor. Because plaintiff did not make inquiries about the title of the transferor, he did not qualify as a bona fide purchaser and was subject to the defense of theft pleaded by defendants who were the acceptors of the bill. Thus, good faith and notice of the claim to the instrument were part of one package. The NIL and the UCC, however, both treat good faith and notice as two separate concepts, and this has caused some difficulties of analysis. The NIL required that a taker to be a holder in due course must take in "good faith" and without "notice of any infirmity or defect in the title of the person negotiating it." (Section 52.) Good faith was not defined but notice was defined in Section 56: "To constitute notice of an infirmity in the instrument or defect in the title of the person negotiating the same, the person to whom it is negotiated must have had actual knowledge of the infirmity or defect, or knowledge of such facts that his action in taking the instrument amounted to bad faith." Professor Britton agrees with the conclusion in *Howard National Bank,* that the effect of the NIL provisions, as interpreted by the courts, was to reject Gill v. Cubitt and to adopt a test of subjective good faith. Britton, Bills and Notes 246 (2d ed. 1961).

The UCC, during its development, at first departed from the NIL approach and then, in part, returned to it. Section 1–201(19), the general definition applicable to all articles of the UCC, defines "good faith" as "honesty in fact in the conduct or transaction concerned." This is a purely subjective standard. The 1952 draft of the UCC in § 2–103(1)(b) applicable to sale of goods transactions added an objective standard of conduct by merchants. It stated that " 'Good faith' in the case of a merchant includes observance of reasonable commercial standards." The 1952 draft also added an objective standard of conduct for purchasers of instruments. Section 3–302(1)(b) of that draft provided as follows: "in good faith including observance of the reasonable commercial standards of any business in which the holder may be engaged." The apparent purpose was to return to the rule of Gill v. Cubitt which required the exercise of reasonable prudence and caution in taking an instrument with respect to which there may be indications of a possible defense or claim. The comment to this section said: "The 'reasonable commercial standards' language added here and in comparable provisions elsewhere in the Act, e.g., Section 2–103, merely makes explicit what has long been implicit in case-law handling of the 'good faith' concept. A business man engaging in a commercial transaction is not entitled to claim the peculiar advantages which the law accords the good faith purchaser— called in this context holder in due course—on a bare showing of 'honesty in fact' when his actions fail to meet the generally accepted standards current in his business, trade or profession. The cases so hold; this section so declares the law."

But in the later versions of the UCC the objective standard of good faith in both Article 2 and Article 3 was changed. With respect to Article 2, in the 1962 Official Text, § 2–103(1)(b) was changed to read as follows: "Good faith" in the case of a merchant means honesty in fact and the observance of reasonable commercial standards of fair dealing in the trade." Although this definition is an objective standard of good faith it relates to fairness rather than prudence and caution which were the focus of the 1952 draft of § 2–103(1)(b). In the 1962 Official Text, § 3–302(1)(b) was amended to drop the words "including observance of the reasonable commercial standards of any business in which the holder may be engaged." The apparent purpose of this change in § 3–302(1)(b) was to return to the subjective standard of the NIL, the so-called "pure heart" doctrine. But this purpose was not achieved. The 1962 Official Text of § 3–302(1)(c) provided: "without notice * * * of any defense against or claim to [the instrument] on the part of any person." The NIL applied the good or bad faith standard to the concept of "notice." The purchaser had notice of a defense or claim to the instrument only if the purchaser had "knowledge of such facts that his action in taking the instrument amounted to bad faith." The UCC has always had an objective standard of notice. Section 1–201(25) states that a person has notice of a fact when "from all the facts and circumstances known to him at the time in question he has reason to know that it exists." Thus, through § 3–302(1)(c) and § 1–201(25) the result reached in Gill v. Cubitt, on the same facts can easily be reached under the 1962 Official Text of Article 3. Since 1962 until adoption of Revised Article 3 in 1990, no changes to the Official Text of Article 3 were made with respect to this issue. Most cases probably involve situations in which the facts relevant to the issue of good faith are the same facts giving rise to notice of a defense or claim. In those cases the issue of whether good faith is subjective or objective seems academic. See Littlefield, Good Faith Purchase of Commercial Paper: The Failure of the Subjective Test, 39 S.Cal. L.Rev. 48 (1966).

Revised Article 3 adopts a new definition of good faith in § 3–103(a)(4). This definition applies to both Article 3 and Article 4. It differs from the definition of good faith in § 1–201(19) by referring not only to honesty in fact but also to "observance of reasonable commercial standards of fair dealing." Although the quoted words may have importance with respect to other sections of Article 3 or Article 4 in which good faith is an issue, these words do not change the standard of the original Article 3 for determining holder-in-due-course status. Section 3–302(a)(2) continues the previous Article 3 requirement that the instrument be taken both in good faith and without notice of claims or defenses. Good faith does not relate to the issue of notice of claims and defenses. Since § 1–201(25), which defines notice, has not been amended, the result reached in Gill v. Cubitt would also be reached under Revised Article 3 on the same facts.

KAW VALLEY STATE BANK & TRUST CO. v. RIDDLE

Supreme Court of Kansas, 1976.
219 Kan. 550, 549 P.2d 927.

FROMME, JUSTICE. This action was brought by The Kaw Valley State Bank and Trust Company (hereinafter referred to as Kaw Valley) to recover judgment against John H. Riddle d/b/a Riddle Contracting Company (hereafter referred to as Riddle) on two notes and to determine the priority of conflicting security agreements. The two notes were covered by separate security agreements and were given to purchase construction equipment. The Planters State Bank and Trust Company (hereinafter referred to as Planters) held a note and security interest on the same and other construction equipment acquired by Riddle. Kaw Valley had acquired the two notes and the security agreements by assignment from Co-Mac, Inc. (hereinafter referred to as Co-Mac), a dealer, from whom Riddle purchased the construction equipment.

In a trial to the court Kaw Valley was found not to be a holder in due course of one of the notes. Its claim on said note, totaling $21,904.64, was successfully defended on the grounds of failure of consideration. It was stipulated at the trial that none of the construction equipment for which the note was given had ever been delivered by Co-Mac. Kaw Valley has appealed.

* * *

Prior to the transactions in question Riddle had purchased construction equipment and machinery from the dealer, Co-Mac. A number of these purchases had been on credit and discounted to Kaw Valley by Co-Mac. Including the Riddle transactions, Kaw Valley had purchased over 250 notes and security agreements from Co-Mac during the prior ten year period. All were guaranteed by Co-Mac and by its president personally.

In May, 1971, Riddle negotiated for the purchase of a model 6–c Caterpillar tractor, a dozer and a used 944 Caterpillar wheel tractor with a two yard bucket. Riddle was advised that this machinery could be delivered but it would first be necessary for Co-Mac to have a signed note and security agreement to complete the transaction. An installment note, security agreement and acceptance of delivery of the machinery was mailed to Riddle. These were signed and returned to Co-Mac. Ten days later, the machinery not having been delivered, Riddle called Co-Mac and inquired about purchasing a D–8 Caterpillar and a #80 Caterpillar scraper in place of the first machinery ordered. Co-Mac agreed to destroy the May 11, 1971 papers and sell this larger machinery to Riddle in place of that previously ordered.

The sale of this substitute machinery was completed and the machinery was delivered after the execution of an additional note and security agreement. However, the May 11, 1971 papers were not destroyed. The note had been discounted and assigned to Kaw Valley prior to the sale of the substitute machinery. Thereafter Co-Mac, who was in financial trouble, made regular payments on the first note to Kaw Valley. The note was thus kept current by Co-Mac and Riddle had no knowledge of the continued existence of that note. The 6–c Caterpillar tractor, dozer and the used 944 Caterpillar wheel tractor were never delivered to Riddle. Riddle received no consideration for the May 11, 1971 note and no lien attached under the security agreement because the machinery never came into possession of Riddle. (See UCC § 9–204.) The debtor never had rights in any of the collateral.

On February 24, 1972, representatives of Riddle, Co-Mac and Kaw Valley met for the purpose of consolidiating the indebtedness of Riddle on machinery notes held by Kaw Valley and guaranteed by Co-Mac. Riddle was behind in some of his payments and wanted to consolidate the notes and reduce his monthly payments to $4,500.00. Kaw Valley disclosed eight past due machinery notes, each representing separate purchase transactions by Riddle. Riddle objected to one of these notes dated July 16, 1971, because the machinery purchased under this particular transaction had been previously returned to Co-Mac.

It was agreed by Kaw Valley that Riddle did not owe for this machinery because of the previous settlement between Co-Mac and Riddle. Kaw Valley cancelled the $5,000.00 balance shown to be due from Riddle.

Thereupon a renewal note and security agreement for $44,557.70 dated February 24, 1972, was drawn consolidating and renewing the seven remaining notes. Riddle then asked Kaw Valley if this was all that it owed the bank and he was assured that it was. The renewal note was then executed by Riddle.

It was not until March 12, 1972, that Riddle was advised by Kaw Valley that it held the note and security agreement dated May 11, 1971, which Riddle believed had been destroyed by Co-Mac. This was within a week after a receiver had been appointed to take over Co-Mac's business affairs. Riddle explained the machinery had never been delivered and Co-Mac promised to destroy the papers. No demand for payment of the May 11, 1971 note was made on Riddle until this action was filed.

Prior to the time this action was filed, Riddle executed a note and granted a security agreement in all of its machinery and equipment to Planters. This included the machinery covered in the previous consolidation transaction of February 24, 1972, with Kaw Valley and Co-Mac.

Subsequently Kaw Valley obtained possession of the machinery covered by the February 24 transaction by court order. Thereupon by agreement in writing between Kaw Valley, Planters and Riddle an immediate sale of the collateral covered in the February 24 transaction was held. By the terms of this agreement the first $22,200.00 in proceeds was to be paid to Kaw Valley in full satisfaction of the note of February 24, 1972. The money received from the sale in excess of this amount was to be paid to the Merchants National Bank to hold as escrow agent, awaiting a determination of entitlement by the court.

At the time of the trial the $22,200.00 had been received by Kaw Valley and the balance of the proceeds of the agreed sale amounting to $25,371.15 was in the hands of the escrow agent.

In the court's memorandum of decision filed November 19, 1974, the court found:

> "That the proceeds remaining in plaintiff's possession from the agreed equipment sale are $25,371.15. The plaintiff claims $21,904.64 of same is due on the transaction of May 11, 1971. The parties agree that the excess of $3,466.51 should be paid to defendant Planters State Bank to apply on its August 28, 1972 claim;"

On December 20, 1974, the court entered the following pay-out order:

> "TO THE CLERK OF THE DISTRICT COURT:

> "Now on this 20th day of December 1974, you are ordered to pay to The Planters State Bank and Trust Company the sum of $3,466.51 now in your hands, having been paid by the Kaw Valley State Bank and Trust Company, pursuant to the Journal Entry of Judgment entered herein on November 19, 1974."

Although it does not appear who initiated the order, the $3,466.51 was paid to and accepted by Planters leaving the disputed proceeds of the sale ($21,904.64) in the hands of either the escrow agent or the court.

* * *

The primary point on appeal questions the holding of the trial court that Kaw Valley was not a holder in due course of the note and security agreement dated May 11, 1971.

UCC § 3–306 provides that unless a holder of an instrument is a holder in due course he takes the instrument subject to the defenses of want or failure of consideration, nonperformance of any condition precedent, nondelivery or delivery for a special purpose. It was undisputed in this case that Riddle received no consideration after executing the note. The machinery was never delivered and he was assured by Co-Mac that the papers would be destroyed. The parties so stipulated. If Kaw Valley was not a holder in due course the proven defense was a bar to recovery by Kaw Valley.

UCC § 3–302 states that a holder in due course is a holder who takes the instrument (1) for value, (2) in good faith and (3) without notice of any defense against it. It was not disputed and the court found that Kaw Valley took the note for value so the first requirement was satisfied. The other requirements were subject to dispute. The trial court concluded:

> "Kaw Valley State Bank and Trust Company is not a holder in due course of the note and security agreement, dated May 11, 1971 for the reason that it did not establish in all respects that it took said instruments in good faith and without notice of any defense against or claimed to it on the part of John H. Riddle, and Kaw Valley State Bank and Trust Company therefor took said instruments subject to the defense of failure of consideration. [Citations omitted.]"

So we are confronted with the question of what is required for a holder to take an instrument "in good faith" and "without notice of defense." We will consider the two parts of the question in the order mentioned.

"Good faith" is defined in UCC § 1–201(19) as "honesty in fact in the conduct or transaction concerned." The first draft of the Uniform Commercial Code (U.C.C.) as proposed required not only that the actions of a holder be honest in fact but in addition it required the actions to conform to *reasonable commercial standards*. This would have permitted the courts to inquire as to whether a particular commercial standard was in fact reasonable. (See Uniform Commercial Code, Proposed Final Draft [1950], § 1–201, 18, p. 30.) However, when the final draft was approved the test of reasonable commercial standards was excised thus indicating that a more rigid standard must be applied for determining "good faith." * * *

From the history of the Uniform Commercial Code it would appear that "good faith" requires no actual knowledge of or participation in any material infirmity in the original transaction.

The second part of our question concerns the requirement of the U.C.C. that a holder in due course take the instrument without notice of any defense to the instrument. UCC § 1–201(25) provides:

"A person has 'notice' of a fact when

"(a) he has actual knowledge of it; or

"(b) he has received a notice or notification of it; or

"(c) from all the facts and circumstances known to him at the time in question he has reason to know that it exists. A person 'known' or has 'knowledge' of a fact when he has actual knowledge of it. 'Discover' or 'learn' or a word or phrase of similar import refers to knowledge rather than to reason to know. The time and circumstances under which a notice or notification may cease to be effective are not determined by this act."

As is apparent from reading the above statute the standard enunciated is not limited to the rigid standard of actual knowledge of the defense. Reason to know appears to be premised on the use of reasonable commercial practices. * * * Since "good faith" and "no notice of defense" are both required of a holder to claim the status of a holder in due course it would appear that the two standards are not in conflict even though the standards of conduct may be different.

There is little or no evidence in the present case to indicate that Kaw Valley acted dishonestly or "not in good faith" when it purchased the note of May 11, 1971. However, as to "notice of defense" the court found from all the facts and circumstances known to Kaw Valley at the time in question it had reason to know a defense existed. The court found:

"During the period 1960 to May, 1971, plaintiff purchased from Co-Mac over 250 notes and secured transactions and held at any given time between $100,000.00 and $250,000.00 of such obligations. All of which were guaranteed by Co-Mac and personally guaranteed by D. J. Wickern, its president. Conant Wait personally handled most if not all of such transactions for plaintiff. Mr. Wait was aware that Co-Mac was making warranties and representation as to fitness to some purchasers of new and used equipment. Mr. Wait further knew that some transactions were in fact not as they would appear to be in that the money from Kaw Valley would be used by Co-Mac to buy the equipment that was the subject matter of the sale. Further, that delivery to the customer of said purchased equipment was sometimes delayed 60 to 90 days for repairing and/or overhauling of same. The plaintiff obviously on many transactions was relying on Co-Mac to insure payment of the obligations and contacted Co-Mac to collect delinquent payments. Some transactions involved delivery of coupon books to Co-Mac rather than the debtor so Co-Mac could bill service and parts charges along with the secured debt. Co-Mac collected payments directly from debtors in various transactions and paid plaintiff. Plaintiff did not concern itself with known irregularities in the transactions as it clearly was relying on Co-Mac;

"The coupon book on the May 11, 1971 transaction was not sent to defendant Riddle; no payments on same were made by defendant Riddle; the payments were made by Co-Mac until January 25, 1972; prior to early March, 1972, defendant Riddle did not know plaintiff had the May 11, 1971 secured transaction; knowledge of said transaction came to defendant Riddle on March 12, 1972 when Mr. Wait contacted defendant Riddle's manager; that Co-Mac had shortly before been placed in receivership; that no demand for any payment on said transaction was made by plaintiff to defendant Riddle until September 1972."

To further support its holding that Kaw Valley had reason to know that the defense existed the court found that when Kaw Valley, Co-Mac and Riddle met on February 24, 1972, to consolidate all of Riddle's past due notes Kaw Valley recognized Co-Mac's authority to act for it. Co-Mac had accepted return of the machinery on one of the eight transactions and Kaw Valley recognized its authority as their agent to do so and cancelled the $5,000.00 balance remaining due on the note held by the bank.

The cases dealing with the question of "reason to know a defense exists" seem to fall into four categories.

The first includes those cases where it is established the holder had information from the transferor or the obligor which disclosed the existence of a defense. In those cases it is clear if the holder takes an instrument having received prior or contemporaneous notice of a defense he is not a holder in due course. (Billingsley v. Mackay, 382 F.2d 290 [5th Cir. 1967].) Our present case does not fall in that category for there is no evidence that Co-Mac or Riddle informed Kaw Valley that the machinery had not been delivered when the note was negotiated.

The second group of cases are those in which the defense appears in an accompanying document delivered to the holder with the note. For example, when a security agreement is executed concurrently with a note evidencing an indebtedness incurred for machinery to be delivered in the future. In such case the instrument may under certain circumstances disclose a defense to the note, such as nondelivery of the machinery purchased. (See also Commerce Trust Company v. Denson, 437 S.W.2d 94 [Mo.App. 1968], and HIMC Investment Co. v. Siciliano, 103 N.J.Super. 27, 246 A.2d 502, for other examples.) Our present case does not fall in this category because Riddle had signed a written delivery acceptance which was handed to Kaw Valley along with the note and security agreement.

A third group of cases are those in which information appears in the written instrument indicating the existence of a defense, such as when the note on its face shows that the due date has passed or the note bears visible evidence of alteration and forgery or the note is clearly incomplete. (See E. F. Corporation v. Smith, 496 F.2d 826 [10th Cir. 1974]; Srochi v. Kamensky, 118 Ga.App. 182, 162 S.E.2d 889; and Winter & Hirsch, Inc. v. Passarelli, 122 Ill.App.2d 372, 259 N.E.2d 312.) In our present case the instrument assigned bore nothing unusual on its face and appeared complete and proper in all respects.

In the fourth category of cases it has been held that the holder of a negotiable instrument may be prevented from assuming holder in due course status because of knowledge of the business practices of his transferor or when he is so closely aligned with the transferor that transferor may be considered an agent of the holder and the transferee is charged with the actions and knowledge of the transferor.

Under our former negotiable instruments law containing provisions similar to the U.C.C. this court refused to accord holder in due course status to a machinery company receiving notes from one of its dealers because of its knowledge of the business practices of the dealer and the company's participation and alignment with the dealer who transferred the note. (International Harvester Co. v. Watkins, 127 Kan. 50, Sly. 3, 272 P. 139, 61 A.L.R. 687.)

In Unico v. Owen, 50 N.J. 101, 232 A.2d 405, the New Jersey court refused to accord holder in due course status to a financing partnership which was closely connected with the transferor and had been organized to finance the commercial paper obtained by the transferor and others. The financing partnership had a voice in setting the policies and standards to be followed by the transferor. Under such circumstances the court found that the holder must be considered a participant in the transaction and subject to defenses available against the payee-transferor. In United States Finance Company v. Jones, 285 Ala. 105, 229 So.2d 495, it was held that a finance company purchasing a note from a payee for fifty percent of its face value did not establish holder in due course status and must be held subject to defenses inherent in the original transaction. Other jurisdictions have followed the rationale of Unico. See American Plan Corp. v. Woods, 16 Ohio App.2d 1, 240 N.E.2d 886, where the holder supplied forms to the payee, established financing charges and investigated the credit of the maker of the note; Calvert Credit Corporation v. Williams, 244 A.2d 494 (D.C.App.1968), where the holder exerted total control over payee's financial affairs; and Jones v. Approved Bancredit Corp., 256 A.2d 739 (Del.1969), where ownership and management of the holder and payee were connected.

In the present case Kaw Valley had worked closely with Co-Mac in over 250 financing transactions over a period of ten years. It knew that some of these transactions were not for valuable consideration at the time the paper was delivered since the bank's money was to be used in purchasing the machinery or equipment represented in the instruments as already in possession of the maker of the note. Kaw Valley had been advised that delivery to Co-Mac's customers was sometimes delayed from 60 to 90 days. Kaw Valley continued to rely on Co-Mac to assure payment of the obligations and contacted it to collect delinquent payments. Some of these transactions, including the one in question, involved the use of coupon books to be used by the debtor in making payment on the notes. In the present case Kaw Valley did not notify Riddle that it was the holder of the note. It delivered Riddle's coupon book to Co-Mac as if it were the obligor or was authorized as its collection agent for this transaction.

Throughout the period from May 11, 1971, to February 25, 1972, Kaw Valley received and credited the monthly payments knowing that payments were being made by Co-Mac and not by Riddle. Then when Riddle's loans were consolidated, the May 11, 1971 transaction was not included by Kaw Valley, either by oversight or by intention, as an obligation of Riddle. Co-Mac occupied a close relationship with Kaw Valley and with its knowledge and consent acted as its agent in collecting payments on notes held by Kaw Valley. The working relationship existing between Kaw Valley and Co-Mac was further demonstrated on February 24, 1972, when the $5,000.00 balance due on one of Riddle's notes was cancelled when it was shown that the machinery for which the note was given had previously been returned to Co-Mac with the understanding that no further payments were due.

UCC § 3–307(3) provides:

> "After it is shown that a defense exists a person claiming the rights of a holder in due course has the burden of establishing that he or some person under whom he claims is in all respects a holder in due course."

In the present case the court found that the appellant, Kaw Valley, had not sustained its burden of proving that it was a holder in due course. Under the evidence in this case the holder failed to advise the maker of the note of its acquisition of the note and security agreement. It placed the payment coupon book in the hands of Co-Mac and received all monthly payments from them. A close working relationship existed between the two companies and Co-Mac was clothed with authority to collect and forward all payments due on the transaction. Agency and authority was further shown to exist by authorizing return of machinery to Co-Mac and terminating balances due on purchase money paper. We cannot say under the facts and circumstances known and participated in by Kaw Valley in this transaction it did not at the time in question have reason to know that the defense existed. This was a question of fact to be determined by the trier of fact which if supported by substantial competent evidence must stand.

* * *

The judgment is affirmed.

PROBLEMS

1. On October 16, 1969, $8,000,000 of United States Treasury Bills in bearer form were stolen from Morgan Bank. On October 28, 1969, when the theft was discovered, Morgan Bank sent a "notice of lost securities," describing the stolen bills by serial number, to bankers and brokers throughout the country. Third Bank, upon receiving the notice placed the notice in its lost securities file. On January 30, 1970 Third Bank made loans totalling $82,000 to Bialkin. As collateral for the loans it took two treasury bills each with a face amount of $50,000. The two bills were among those stolen from Morgan Bank and were listed in the notice of lost securities. The officer of Third Bank who approved the loan to Bialkin did not check the lost securities file of Third Bank. He testified that he was not aware of its existence. Third Bank later discovered that the treasury bills had been stolen and reported it to law enforcement authorities. Morgan Bank then sued to recover the bills.

Treasury bills come within the definition of "investment securities" that are governed by Article 8 of the UCC rather than Article 3. § 3–102(a). In this case Third Bank would defeat the claim of Morgan Bank if it qualified as a bona fide purchaser. The treasury bills in this case are now known as "certificated securities." § 8–102(1)(a). A bona fide purchaser of a certificated security, defined in § 8–302, is essentially the same as a holder in due course of a negotiable instrument. Did Third Bank have notice of the claim of Morgan Bank to the bills? § 1–201(25), (26), and (27). This problem is based on the facts, slightly modified, of Morgan Guaranty Trust Co. of New York v. Third National Bank of Hampden County, 529 F.2d 1141 (1st Cir. 1976).

2. In December 1957 Fazzari was induced by fraud to sign a promissory note for $400 payable to the order of Wade. After discovering the fraud, in January 1958, Fazzari notified all of the local banks of the fraud. He personally spoke to the cashier of Odessa Bank and advised him not to purchase the note because he

had been "tricked" by Wade. Three months later Odessa Bank, acting through its cashier, purchased the note. The cashier admitted that Fazzari had told him about the note in January but testified that at the time the note was purchased in April he had forgotten the incident. Did Odessa Bank take the note as a holder in due course? § 1–201(25) and the Comment to that provision. This problem is based on the facts of First National Bank of Odessa v. Fazzari, 10 N.Y.2d 394, 223 N.Y.S.2d 483, 179 N.E.2d 493 (1961).

2. OVERDUE OR IRREGULAR INSTRUMENTS

Section 3–302(a) incorporates two traditional rules: holder in due course status cannot be attained if the instrument is taken with notice that it is overdue or if the instrument is so irregular or incomplete as to call into question its authenticity. These doctrines are rooted in the law of good faith and may be viewed as special applications of the suspicious circumstances rule of Gill v. Cubitt. But for a long time they have enjoyed independent status, and NIL § 52 adopted them as separate requirements for holder in due course status in addition to the good faith requirement.

Under the common-law view, the fact that an instrument was overdue or irregular or incomplete was notice that something was wrong. But the fact that an instrument is overdue does not point to any particular defense or claim or, for that matter, to the existence of any defense or claim at all. Most notes are probably overdue because the makers can't pay them. Most checks that are still out more than 90 days (§ 3–304(a)(2)) have not been collected because the holder hasn't deposited them. In the range of possibilities raised in the mind of one purchasing an overdue instrument, it is doubtful that the likelihood of a defense rises very high or that the possibility of a claim of ownership by a prior party is considered at all. The fact that an instrument bears an obvious alteration does warn a taker of the possibility of a fraudulent alteration but not of defenses or claims wholly unrelated to the alteration.

Why shouldn't a purchaser who is willing to pay good money for an overdue or irregular or incomplete instrument be entitled to holder in due course status? Perhaps the question is better phrased in terms of why should such a holder be accorded that status. The answer to these questions may depend upon whether one looks upon holder in due course status to be the norm or whether it should be seen as something unusual to be given only when a clear commercial benefit is achieved. If negotiability is a doctrine to promote the free flow of instruments, what social or economic gain is achieved by encouraging the currency of stale, irregular or incomplete instruments?

PROBLEMS

1. S agreed to sell real property to B for $58,000, of which $6,500 was to be a down payment. When making the down payment, B insisted that S execute a promissory note to B's order for the amount of $6,500 as evidence of indebtedness for any sums B might be called upon to expend to pay off any claims or liens with respect to the property of which B was not aware. In time B expended $4,244 in paying these claims. The note, which was executed by S on March 25 and due 75 days after date, was indorsed without recourse to Plaintiff on September 1 for a total consideration of $3,067. S refused to pay the note and Plaintiff brought suit. How much is Plaintiff entitled to recover—$6,500, $4,244, or $3,067? § 3–203(b), § 3–302(a), § 3–117, and § 3–305(a). See also Brock v. Adams, 79 N.M. 17, 439 P.2d 234 (1968).

2. Payee sold a house to Maker and as partial payment of the price took a promissory note for $5,000 payable in monthly instalments over a five year period. When Payee's reserve army unit was called to active duty Payee asked Banker to collect the note during Payee's indefinite absence. Banker insisted that Payee indorse the note in blank and turn over possession of both the note and mortgage. Later Maker fell in default on the payments and Banker, who was also in financial difficulties, sold the note to Purchaser for value. Purchaser knew that four payments had not been made but had no knowledge of the circumstances under which Banker had taken the note. After Payee returned and learned of Banker's actions, Payee asserted a claim of ownership against Purchaser and sued to retake possession of the note. What result? Justice v. Stonecipher, 267 Ill. 448, 108 N.E. 722 (1915). § 3–304(b)(1) and § 3–306.

3. In payment of goods, Maker signed a negotiable note in the amount of $10,000 and mailed it to Payee. The note should have been payable in the amount of $20,000. Payee noticed the discrepancy and called Maker's attention to it. Maker told Payee to change the $10,000 to $20,000. Payee did so by erasing and typing over. The alteration was crudely done and very obvious. Payee then sold the note to Holder. Holder noticed the alteration but accepted Payee's truthful explanation of the circumstances under which it was made. When Holder demanded payment Maker refused, stating that Payee never delivered the goods for which the note was given. Is Holder subject to the defense of Maker? Suppose Holder, before completing the transaction, had called Maker and that Maker had verified that the $20,000 figure was correct. How does this affect your answer? § 3–302(a)(1) and § 3–305(a).

3. NEGOTIABILITY IN CONSUMER TRANSACTIONS

a. INTRODUCTION

Whether the doctrine of negotiability in all its vigor is necessary or desirable when applied to modern negotiable instruments—promissory notes and checks—has been challenged. See Gilmore, The Good Faith Purchase Idea and the Uniform Commercial Code: Confessions of a Repentant Draftsman, 15 Ga.L.Rev. 605 (1981). Consider the following observations of Professor Albert J. Rosenthal taken from his article, Negotiability—Who Needs It? 71 Colum.L.Rev. 375, 378–381 (1971):

> The negotiable promissory note of today is quite a different instrument, serving different purposes, and the consequences of its negotiability are quite different in impact. By far the most commonly employed variety of the species today is the note given by the installment purchaser of goods to reflect the unpaid portion of the purchase price. Typically, such a note is transferred just once, from the dealer to the lender (usually either a finance company or a bank), and thereafter remains in the possession of the latter or its lawyers until it is either paid off or offered in evidence in court. Its negotiable character is of no importance with respect to claims of ownership, as it is unlikely to be lost or stolen. Even if it is, the last indorsement will have been a special indorsement to the order of the lender; without the genuine further indorsement of the latter there can be no subsequent holder, much less a holder in due course.

> The only significant consequence of the negotiability of such a note is that it cuts off the defenses of the maker. If, for example, the purchaser gives the note in payment for a refrigerator, the finance company is entitled to full payment regardless of whether the refrigerator fails to work or whether its sale was accomplished through fraudulent misrepresentations or, indeed, whether it was ever delivered at all. And it may be small comfort to the buyer, forced to pay the finance company in full, to know that he has a cause of action against the seller, which may at best be collectible with difficulty and may in many cases be worthless because the seller is insolvent or has left town.

> A promissory note of this kind, and a consequence of negotiability that works in this fashion, are a far cry from the stolen Bank of England note, and the protection accorded its purchaser, in Miller v. Race. Whether the finance company should be allowed to prevail free of the maker's defenses raises questions that ought to be decided on their own merits,

and not merely through the absent-minded application of a doctrine created to meet an entirely different situation.

The social evils flowing from negotiability in this circumstance have become manifest, and there has been a clear trend in both the courts and the legislatures toward amelioration of its consequences. In particular, the unfairness to the poorest members of the community of the law governing consumer installment purchases has generated a reaction that is giving rise to a major alteration in it. This departure is being accomplished, not by modification of the provisions of Article 3 of the Code, but by legislative action forbidding the use of negotiable instruments in consumer installment transactions and by judicial attempts to stretch the facts to deny holder in due course status to finance companies. Since the installment buyer can be similarly harmed even without a negotiable instrument if there is a clause in his purchase contract waiving, as against an assignee of his obligation, any defenses on the contract that he may have, legislatures and courts have also been moving in the direction of declaring such clauses invalid.

It is not clear whether the apparent weakness in the opposition to these changes springs from a lack of genuine need on the part of sellers or lenders for continuation of the power to cut off buyers' defenses. While there has been ground to believe that where this protection is denied, credit nevertheless will remain available, a recent study suggests that this may not be so.

If an exception is carved out, should it be limited to consumer paper, or should it be applied to promissory notes across the board? Thus far, the demand for reform has been confined largely to the former. While there may be small commercial purchasers also in need of similar protection, and while there may be other situations in which unfair advantage seems to be taken of makers of promissory notes, there does not appear in such cases to be a resulting social problem of comparable dimension. On the other hand, we need to know more about the range of other uses to which promissory notes are put in today's economy, and about the circumstances in which the cutting off of claims and defenses in connection with such notes serves legitimate needs or works undue hardship.

* * *

b. THE JUDICIAL RESPONSE

UNICO v. OWEN

Supreme Court of New Jersey, 1967.
50 N.J. 101, 232 A.2d 405.

FRANCIS, J. The issue to be decided here is whether plaintiff Unico, a New Jersey partnership, is a holder in due course of defendant's note. If so, it is entitled to a judgment for the unpaid balance due thereon, for which this suit was brought. The District Court found plaintiff was not such a holder and that it was therefore subject to the defense interposed by defendant, maker of the note, of failure of consideration on the part of the payee, which endorsed it to plaintiff. Since it was undisputed that the payee failed to furnish the consideration for which the note was given, judgment was entered for defendant. The Appellate Division affirmed, and we granted plaintiff's petition for certification in order to consider the problem. 47 N.J. 241, 220 A.2d 114 (1966).

The facts are important. Defendant's wife, Jean Owen, answered an advertisement in a Newark, N.J. newspaper in which Universal Stereo Corporation of Hillside, N.J., offered for sale 140 albums of stereophonic records for $698. This amount could be financed and paid on an installment basis. In addition the buyer would receive "without separate charge" (as plaintiff puts it) a Motorola stereo record player. The plain implication was that on agreement to purchase 140 albums, the record player would be given free. A representative of Universal called at the Owens' home and discussed the matter with Mr. and Mrs. Owen. As a result, on November 6, 1962 they signed a "retail installment contract" for the purchase of 140 albums on the time payment plan proposed by Universal.

Under the printed form of contract Universal sold and Owen bought "subject to the terms and conditions stipulated in Exhibit 'A' hereto annexed and printed on the other side hereof and made part hereof, the following goods * * *: 12 stereo albums to be delivered at inception of program and every 6 months thereafter until completion of program," a "new Motorola consolo [sic]" and "140 stereo albums of choice * * *." The total cash price was listed as $698; a downpayment of $30 was noted; the balance of $668, plus an "official fee" of $1.40 and a time price differential of $150.32, left a time balance of $819.72 to be paid in installments. Owen agreed to pay this balance in 36 equal monthly installments of $22.77 each beginning on December 12, 1962, "at the office of Universal Stereo Corp., 8 Hollywood Avenue, Hillside, N.J., or any other address determined by assignee." The contract provided:

> "If the Buyer executed a promissory note of even date herewith in the amount of the time balance indicated, said note is

not in payment thereof, but is a negotiable instrument separate and apart from this contract even though at the time of
execution it may be temporarily attached hereto by perforation or otherwise."

It was part of Universal's practice to take notes for these
contracts, and obviously there was no doubt that it would be done
in the Owen case. Owen did sign a printed form of note which
was presented with the contract. The name of Universal Stereo
Corporation was printed thereon, and the note provided for the
monthly installment payments specified. On the reverse side was
an elaborate printed form of endorsement which began "Pay to
the order of Unico, 251 Broad St., Elizabeth, New Jersey, with full
recourse;" and which contained various waivers by the endorser,
and an authorization to the transferee to vary the terms of the
note in its discretion in dealing with the maker.

Exhibit "A", referred to as being on the reverse side of the
contract, is divided into three separate parts, the body of each part
being in very fine print. The *first* section sets out in 11 fine print
paragraphs the obligations of the buyer and rights of the seller.
Under paragraph 1 the seller retains title to the property until the
full time price is paid. Here it may be noted that Universal
recorded the contract in the Union County Register's Office a few
days after its execution. Paragraph 2 says that the term "Seller"
as used shall refer to the party signing the contract as seller "or *if
said party has assigned said contract, any holder of* said contract."
(Emphasis added). It is patent that Universal contemplated assigning the contract forthwith to Unico, and it was so assigned.
Of course, it was a bilateral executory contract, and since under
the language just quoted "assignee" and "seller" have the same
connotation, the reasonable and normal expectation by Owen
would be that performance of the delivery obligation was a condition precedent to his undertaking to make installment payments.
* * * Universal sought under paragraph 5 to deprive Owen of
his right to plead failure of consideration against its intended
assignee, Unico. The paragraph provides:

> "Buyer hereby acknowledges notice that the contract may be
> assigned and that assignees will rely upon the agreements
> contained in this paragraph, and agrees that the liability of
> the Buyer to any assignee shall be immediate and absolute
> and not affected by any default whatsoever of the Seller
> signing this contract; and in order to induce assignees to
> purchase this contract, the Buyer further agrees not to set up
> any claim against such Seller as a defense, counterclaim or
> offset to any action by any assignee for the unpaid balance of
> the purchase price or for possession of the property."

The validity and efficacy of this paragraph will be discussed
hereinafter. At this point it need only be said that the design of

Universal in adopting this form of contract and presenting it to buyers, not for bargaining purposes but for signature, was to get the most and give the least. Overall it includes a multitude of conditions, stipulations, reservations, exceptions and waivers skillfully devised to restrict the liability of the seller within the narrowest limits, and to leave no avenue of escape from liability on the part of the purchaser.

The *second* part of Exhibit "A" is entitled in large type, "Assignment and dealer's recommendation. This must be executed by the dealer." There follows an elaborate fine-print form of assignment of the contract and the rights thereunder to Unico, which name is part of the printed form. It is signed by Murray Feldman, President of Universal.

The *third* part of Exhibit "A" is entitled "Guaranty." It is a printed form signed by Murray Feldman, as President, and Rhea M. Feldman, as Secretary, of Universal, and also as individuals guaranteeing payment of the sums due under Owen's contract to Unico.

As Exhibit "A" appears in the appendix, the Owen note referred to above is not now attached to the contract. The record is not clear as to just how it was attached originally, i.e., by a perforated line or otherwise; indication from the agreement itself is that it was attached, and was removed after execution and after or upon endorsement to Unico. In any event it was presented to and executed by Owen with the contract, and in view of the result we have reached in the case, whether it was attached or simply presented to Owen for signature with the contract is of no particular consequence.

At this point the hyper-executory character of the performance agreed to by Universal in return for the installment payment stipulation by Owen must be noted. Owen's time balance of $819.72 was required to be paid by 36 monthly installments of $22.77 each. Universal's undertaking was to deliver 24 record albums a year until 140 albums had been delivered. Completion by the seller therefore would require $5\frac{1}{3}$ years. Thus, although Owen would have fully paid for 140 albums at the end of three years, Universal's delivery obligation did not have to be completed until $2\frac{1}{3}$ years thereafter. This means that 40% of the albums, although fully paid for, would still be in the hands of the seller. It means also that for $2\frac{1}{3}$ years Universal would have the use of 40% of Owen's money on which he had been charged the high time-price differential rate. In contrast, since Universal discounted the note immediately with Unico on the strength of Owen's credit and purchase contract, the transaction, so far as the seller is concerned, can fairly be considered as one for cash. In this posture, Universal had its sale price almost contemporaneously with Owen's execution of the contract, in return for an executory performance to extend over 5⅓ years. And Unico acquired Owen's note which, on its face and considered apart from the remainder of the transaction, appeared to be an unqualifiedly negotiable instrument. On the other hand, on the face of things, by virtue of the ostensibly negotiable note and the waiver or estoppel clause quoted above which was intended to bar any defense against an assignee for the seller's default, Owen had no recourse and no protection if Universal defaulted on its obligation and was financially worthless.

Owen's installment note to Universal for the time balance of $819.72 is dated November 6, 1962. Although the endorsement on the reverse side is not dated, Unico concedes the note was received on or about the day it was made. The underlying sale contract was assigned to Unico at the same time, and it is admitted that Owen was never notified of the assignment.

Owen received from Universal the stereo record player and the original 12 albums called for by the contract. Although he continued to pay the monthly installments on the note for the 12 succeeding months, he never received another album. During that period Mrs. Owen endeavored unsuccessfully to communicate with Universal, and finally ceased making payments when the albums were not delivered. Nothing further was heard about the matter until July 1964, when the attorney for Unico, who was also one of its partners, advised Mrs. Owen that Unico held the note and that payments should be made to it. She told him the payments would be resumed if the albums were delivered. No further deliveries were made because Universal had become insolvent. Up to this time Owen had paid the deposit of $30 and 12 installments of $22.77 each, for a total of $303.24. Unico brought this suit for the balance due on the note plus penalties and a 20% attorney's fee.

Owen defended on the ground that Unico was not a holder in due course of the note, that the payment of $303.24 adequately satisfied any obligation for Universal's partial performance, and that Universal's default and the consequent failure of consideration barred recovery by Unico. As we have said, the trial court found plaintiff was not a holder in due course of the note and that Universal's breach of the sales contract barred recovery.

I.

This brings us to the primary inquiry in the case. Is the plaintiff Unico a holder in due course of defendant's note?

The defendant's note was executed on November 6, 1962. The Uniform Commercial Code was adopted by the Legislature in 1961 (L.1961, c. 120), but it did not become operative until January 1, 1963. The note, therefore, is governed by the Uniform Negotiable Instruments Law. Section 52 thereof defined a holder in due course as one who (among other prerequisites) took the instrument "in good faith and for value." If plaintiff is not a holder in due course it is subject to the defense of failure of consideration on the part of Universal, both under the Negotiable Instruments Law, § 58, and the Uniform Commercial Code, § 3–306(c).

In the field of negotiable instruments, good faith is a broad concept. The basic philosophy of the holder in due course status is to encourage free negotiability of commercial paper by removing certain anxieties of one who takes the paper as an innocent purchaser knowing no reason why the paper is not as sound as its face would indicate. It would seem to follow, therefore, that the more the holder knows about the underlying transaction, and particularly the more he controls or participates or becomes involved in it, the less he fits the role of a good faith purchaser for value; the closer his relationship to the underlying agreement which is the source of the note, the less need there is for giving him the tension-free rights considered necessary in a fast-moving, credit-extending commercial world.

We are concerned here with a problem of consumer goods financing. Such goods are defined in the Uniform Commercial Code as those used or bought for use primarily for personal, family or household purposes. § 9–109(1). Although the Code as such is not applicable in this case, the definition is appropriate for our purposes. And it is fair to say also that in today's society, sale of such goods and arrangements for consumer credit financing of the sale are problems of increasing state and national concern. The consumer-credit market is essentially a process of exchange, the general nature of which is shaped by the objectives and relative bargaining power of each of the parties. In consumer goods transactions there is almost always a substantial differential in bargaining power between the seller and his financer, on the one side, and the householder on the other. That difference exists because generally there is a substantial inequality of economic resources between them, and of course, that balance in the great mass of cases favors the seller and gives him and his financer the power to shape the exchange to their advantage. Their greater economic resources permit them to obtain the advice of experts; moreover, they have more time to reflect about the specific terms of the exchange prior to the negotiations with the consumer; they know from experience how to strengthen their own position in consumer-credit arrangements; and the financer-creditor is better able to absorb the impact of a single imprudent or unfair exchange. See Curran, Legislative Controls as a Response to Consumer-Credit Problems, 8 B.C.Ind. and Com.L.Rev. 409, 435–437 (1967).

Mass marketing in consumer goods, as in many other commercial activities, has produced standardized financing contracts.

Henningsen v. Bloomfield Motors, Inc., 32 N.J. 358, 389, 161 A.2d 69, 75 A.L.R.2d 1 (1960). As a result there is no real arms-length bargaining between the creditor (seller-financer) and the consumer, beyond minimal negotiating about amount of credit, terms of installment payment and description of the goods to be purchased, all of which is accomplished by filling blanks left in the jungle of finely printed, creditor-oriented provisions. In the present case the purchase contract was a typical standardized finely printed form, focused practically in its entirety upon the interests of the seller and its intended assignee. Little remained to be done but to describe the stereo record player and to fix the price and terms of installment payment by filling in the blanks. Even as to the matter inserted in the blanks, it cannot be said that there was any real bargaining; the seller fixed the price of the albums, and, as we shall see, the plaintiff Unico as the financer for Universal established the maximum length of the installment payment period under its contract with Universal. The ordinary consumer goods purchaser more often than not does not read the fine print; if he did it is unlikely that he would understand the legal jargon, and the significance of the clauses is not explained to him. This is not to say that all such contracts of adhesion are unfair or constitute imposition. But many of them are, and the judicial branch of the government within its sphere of operation in construing and applying such contracts must be responsive to equitable considerations. As the late Mr. Justice Frankfurter said in United States v. Bethlehem Steel Corp., 315 U.S. 289, 326, 62 S.Ct. 581, 599, 86 L.Ed. 855, 876 (1942):

> "But is there any principle which is more familiar or more firmly embedded in the history of Anglo-American law than the basic doctrine that the courts will not permit themselves to be used as instruments of inequity and injustice? Does any principle in our law have more universal application than the doctrine that courts will not enforce transactions in which the relative positions of the parties are such that one has unconscionably taken advantage of the necessities of the other?"

And see, Henningsen v. Bloomfield Motors, 32 N.J. at 388, 390, 161 A.2d 69; 1 Corbin on Contracts, § 128 (1963). Just as the community has an interest in insuring (usually by means of the legislative process) that credit financing contracts facilitating sales of consumer goods conform to community-imposed standards of fairness and decency, so too the courts, in the absence of controlling legislation, in applying the adjudicatory process must endeavor, whenever reasonably possible, to impose those same standards on principles of equity and public policy. An initial step in that direction of unquestioned need, and fortunately of common judicial acceptance, is the view that consumer goods contracts and their concurrent financing arrangements should be construed most strictly against the seller who imposed the contract on the buyer, and against the finance company which participated in the transaction, directly or indirectly, or was aware of the nature of the seller's consumer goods sales and installment payment operation.

The courts have recognized that the basic problem in consumer goods sales and financing is that of balancing the interest of the commercial community in unrestricted negotiability of commercial paper against the interest of installment buyers of such goods in the preservation of their normal remedy of withholding payment when, as in this case, the seller fails to deliver as agreed, and thus the consideration for his obligation fails. Many courts have solved the problem by denying to the holder of the paper the status of holder in due course where the financer maintains a close relationship with the dealer whose paper he buys; where the financer is closely connected with the dealer's business operations or with the particular credit transaction; or where the financer furnishes the form of sale contract and note for use by the dealer, the buyer signs the contract and note concurrently, and the dealer endorses the note and assigns the contract immediately thereafter or within the period prescribed by the financer. * * * Other courts have said that when the financer supplies or prescribes or approves the form of sales contract, or conditional sale agreement, or chattel mortgage as well as the installment payment note (particularly if it has the financer's name printed on the face or in the endorsement), and all the documents are executed by the buyer at one time and the contract assigned and note endorsed to the financer and delivered to the financer together (whether or not attached or part of a single instrument), the holder takes subject to the rights and obligations of the seller. The transaction is looked upon as a species of tripartite proceeding, and the tenor of the cases is that the financer should not be permitted "to isolate itself behind the fictional fence" of the Negotiable Instruments Law, and thereby achieve an unfair advantage over the buyer * * *.

Before looking at the particular circumstances of the above cases, it seems advisable to examine into the relationship between Universal and the financer Unico.

Unico is a partnership formed expressly for the purpose of financing Universal Stereo Corporation, and Universal agreed to pay all costs up to a fixed amount in connection with Unico's formation. The elaborate contract between them, dated August 24, 1962, recited that Universal was engaged in the merchandising of records and stereophonic sets, and that it desired to borrow money from time to time from Unico, "secured by the assignment of accounts receivable, promissory notes, trade acceptances, conditional sales contracts, chattel mortgages, leases, installment contracts, or other forms of agreement evidencing liens." Subject to conditions set out in the agreement, Unico agreed to lend Universal up to 35% of the total amount of the balances of customers' contracts assigned to Unico subject to a limit of $50,000, in return for which Universal submitted to a substantial degree of control of its entire business operation by the lender. As collateral security for the loans, Universal agreed to negotiate "to the lender" all customers' notes listed in a monthly schedule of new sales contracts, and to assign all conditional sale contracts connected with the notes, as well as the right to any monies due from customers.

Specific credit qualifications for Universal's record album customers were imposed by Unico; requirements for the making of the notes and their endorsement were established, and the sale contracts had to be recorded in the county recording office. All such contracts were required to meet the standards of the agreement between lender and borrower, among them being that the customer's installment payment term would not exceed 36 months and "every term" of the Unico-Universal agreement was to "be deemed incorporated into all assignments" of record sales contracts delivered as security for the loans. It was further agreed that Unico should have all the rights of Universal under the contracts as if it were the seller, including the right to enforce them in its name, and Unico was given an irrevocable power to enforce such rights.

In the event of Universal's default on payment of its loans, Unico was authorized to deal directly with the record buyers with respect to payment of their notes and to settle with and discharge such customers. Unico was empowered to place its representatives on Universal's premises with full authority to take possession of the books and records; or otherwise, it could inspect the records at any time; and it was given a "special property interest" in such records. Financial statements were required to be submitted by Universal "at least semiannually"; and two partners of Unico were to be paid one-quarter of one per cent interest on the loans as a management service charge, in addition to the interest to be paid Unico. Significant also in connection with the right to oversee Universal's business is a warranty included in the contract. It warrants that Universal owns free and clear "all merchandise referred to and described in [the sales] contracts, * * * at the time of making the sale creating such contracts." Obviously this was not the fact, otherwise Universal would not have discontinued shipping records to its customers, such as Owen. If Universal did not have such a store of records, as warranted, Unico might well have had reason to suspect its borrower's financial stability.

This general outline of the Universal-Unico financing agreement serves as evidence that Unico not only had a thorough knowledge of the nature and method of operation of Universal's business, but also exercised extensive control over it. Moreover, obviously it had a large, if not decisive, hand in the fashioning and supplying of the form of contract and note used by Universal, and particularly in setting the terms of the record album sales agreement, which were designed to put the buyer-consumer in an unfair and burdensome legal strait jacket and to bar any escape no matter what the default of the seller, while permitting the note-holder, contract-assignee to force payment from him by enveloping itself in the formal status of holder in due course. To say the relationship between Unico and the business operations of Universal was close, and that Unico was involved therein, is to put it mildly. There is no case in New Jersey dealing with the contention that the holder of a consumer goods buyer's note in purchasing it did not meet the test of good faith negotiation because the connection between the seller and the financer was as intimate as in this case.   *   *   *

There is a conflict of authority in other jurisdictions (Annotation, 44 A.L.R.2d 8 (1955)), but we are impelled for reasons of equity and justice to join those courts which deny holder in due course status in consumer goods sales cases to those financers whose involvement with the seller's business is as close, and whose knowledge of the extrinsic factors—i.e., the terms of the underlying sale agreement—is as pervasive, as it is in the present case. Their reasoning is particularly persuasive in this case because of the unusual executory character of the seller's obligation to furnish the consideration for the buyer's undertaking.

In Commercial Credit Corp. v. Orange County Mach. Wks., 34 Cal.2d 776, 214 P.2d 819 (1950), Machine Works was in the market for a press. Ermac Company knew of one which could be purchased from General American Precooling Corporation for $5000, and offered to sell it to Machine Works for $5500. Commercial Credit was consulted by Ermac, and agreed to finance the transaction by taking an assignment of the contract of sale between Ermac and Machine Works. For a substantial period before this time, Ermac had obtained similar financing from Commercial Credit and had some blank forms supplied to it by the latter. By a contract written on one of these forms, which was entitled "Industrial Conditional Sales Contract," Ermac agreed to sell and Machine Works bound itself to purchase the press.

The terms of the contract were very much like those in the case now before us. The purchase price was to be paid in 12 equal monthly installments, "evidenced by my note of even date to your order." As to the note, the contract said:

> "Said note is a negotiable instrument, separate and apart from this contract, even though at the time of execution it may be temporarily attached hereto by perforation or otherwise."

544   NEGOTIABLE INSTRUMENTS   Pt. II

It provided also, as in our case:

> "This contract may be assigned and/or said note may be
> negotiated without notice to me and when assigned and/or
> negotiated shall be free from any defense, counterclaim or
> cross complaint by me."

The note originally was the latter part of the printed form of
contract, but could be detached from it at a dotted or perforated
line.

Machine Works made the required down payment to Ermac,
which in turn under its contract with Commercial assigned the
contract and endorsed the note to the latter. Commercial then
gave its check to Ermac for $4261. Ermac sent its check to
Precooling Corporation, which refused to deliver the press to
Machine Works when the check was dishonored. Commercial
sued Machine Works as a holder in due course of its note to
Ermac. Machine Works contended Commercial was not entitled
to the status of such a holder because the sales contract and
attached note should be construed as constituting a single document. Machine Works contended also that the finance company
was a party to the original transaction rather than a subsequent
purchaser, that it took subject to all equities and defenses existing
in its favor against Ermac, and that the claimed negotiability of
the note was destroyed when it and the conditional sales agreement were transferred together as one instrument.

The Supreme Court of California said the fact that the contract and note were physically attached at the time of transfer to
Commercial would not alone defeat negotiability. But the court
pointed out that Commercial advanced money to Ermac (with
which it had dealt previously and whose "credit had been checked
and financial integrity demonstrated"), with the understanding
that the agreement and note would be assigned and endorsed to it
immediately; and that "[i]n a very real sense, the finance company was a moving force in the transaction from its very inception,
and acted as a party to it." In deciding against Commercial, the
court said:

> "When a finance company actively participates in a transac-
> tion of this type from its inception, counseling and aiding the
> future vendor-payee, it cannot be regarded as a holder in due
> course of the note given in the transaction and the defense of
> failure of consideration may properly be maintained. Ma-
> chine Works never obtained the press for which it bargained
> and, as against Commercial, there is no more obligation upon
> it to pay the note than there is to pay the installments
> specified in the contract."

In the case before us Unico was brought into existence to
finance all Universal's sales contracts, and it was a major factor in
establishing the terms upon which the financing and installment

payment of the resulting notes and installment delivery of the record albums were to be engaged in. As in the case just cited, it too was "in a very real sense" a party not only to the Owen contract, but to all others similarly procured by Universal.

* * *

The *Martin* case, decided by the Supreme Court of Florida, is frequently cited by the courts of other states. Martin purchased a deep freezer and meat saw from an appliance dealer on an installment payment conditional sale agreement. He executed the agreement and a note (attached thereto by perforations) for payment of the balance due in monthly installments. On the following day the sale agreement and note were assigned and endorsed respectively to the plaintiff-finance company. The freezer turned out to be an outmoded model and otherwise totally unfit for Martin's purposes, and when neither the dealer nor the financer remedied the defects he declined to make further payments on the note.

The finance company prepared and furnished to the dealer the printed forms of conditional sale agreement and promissory note employed in the transaction. The forms designated the financer as the specific assignee of the contract and note; its office was designated as the place of payment of the note installments; it investigated and approved Martin's credit, agreed to purchase his contract and note, and by written assignment took the contract and note contemporaneously from the dealer.

In deciding that the finance company was not a holder in due course, the court declared it saw no reason why the concurrent execution of such a contract along with a promissory note, whether the note is a separate piece of paper or is attached to the contract by perforations, of itself should in any way affect "any of the characteristics of the note which give it commercial value." But, referring to the conflicting decisions in various states, it said that in situations such as the one before it, the better rule is that the note and the contract should be considered as one instrument. It approved the language of the Arkansas Supreme Court in Commercial Credit Co. v. Childs, supra, to the effect that the financer was so closely connected with the entire transaction that it could not be heard to say that it, in good faith, was an innocent purchaser for value; rather, to all intents and purposes it was a party to the agreement and instrument from the beginning.

The finance company in *Martin*, as in this case, contended that to deny it holder in due course status would seriously affect the mode of transacting business in Florida. In answer, the Court said:

> "It may be that our holding here will require some changes in business methods and will impose a greater burden on the finance companies. We think the buyer—Mr. & Mrs. General Public—should have some protection somewhere along the

line. We believe the finance company is better able to bear the risk of the dealer's insolvency than the buyer and in a far better position to protect his interests against unscrupulous and insolvent dealers." 63 So.2d at p. 653.

In our judgment the views expressed in the cited cases provide the sound solution for the problem under consideration. Under the facts of our case the relationship between Unico and Universal, and the nature of Unico's participation in Universal's contractual arrangements with its customers, if anything are closer and more active than in any of those cases, and in justice Unico should not be deemed a holder in due course of the Owen note. Adoption of such a rule is consistent in theory with the Court of Errors and Appeals' holding in General Contracts etc. Corp. v. Moon Carrier Corp., 129 N.J.L. 431, 435, 29 A.2d 843 (E. & A.1943), where it was said that where a note refers to or is accompanied by a collateral contemporaneous agreement, or the purchaser has actual knowledge of the collateral agreement, he takes subject to its contents and conditions. Moreover, although as we have already noted, the Uniform Commercial Code is not applicable because its effective date was subsequent to Owen's note, the principle we now espouse is consistent with § 3–119 thereof. That section provides that:

"As between the obligor and his immediate obligee or any transferee the terms of an instrument may be modified or affected by any other written agreement executed as a part of the same transaction, except that a holder in due course is not affected by any limitation of his rights arising out of the separate written agreement if he had no notice of the limitation when he took the instrument."

For purposes of consumer goods transactions, we hold that where the seller's performance is executory in character and when it appears from the totality of the arrangements between dealer and financer that the financer has had a substantial voice in setting standards for the underlying transaction, or has approved the standards established by the dealer, and has agreed to take all or a predetermined or substantial quantity of the negotiable paper which is backed by such standards, the financer should be considered a participant in the original transaction and therefore not entitled to holder in due course status. We reserve specifically the question whether, when the buyer's claim is breach of warranty as distinguished from failure of consideration, the seller's default as to the former may be raised as a defense against the financer. Cf. Eastern Acceptance Corp. v. Kavlick, 10 N.J.Super. 253, 77 A.2d 49 (App.Div.1950).

II.

Plaintiff argues that even if it cannot be considered a holder in due course of Owen's note, it is entitled to recover regardless of the failure of consideration on the part of Universal, because of the so-called waiver of defenses or estoppel clause contained in the sale contract. The clause says:

> "Buyer hereby acknowledges notice that this contract may be assigned and that assignees will rely upon the agreements contained in this paragraph, and agrees that the liability of the Buyer to any assignee shall be immediate and absolute and not affected by any default whatsoever of the Seller signing this contract; and in order to induce assignees to purchase this contract, the Buyer further agrees not to set up any claim against such Seller as a defense, counterclaim or offset to any action by any assignee for the unpaid balance of the purchase price or for possession of the property."

This provision is the fifth of 11 fine print paragraphs on the reverse side of the sale contract. The type is the same as in the other clauses; there is no emphasis put on it in the context, and there is no evidence that it was in any way brought to Owen's attention or its significance explained to him. But regardless, we consider that the clause is an unfair imposition on a consumer goods purchaser and is contrary to public policy.

The plain attempt and purpose of the waiver is to invest the sale agreement with the type of negotiability which under the Negotiable Instruments Law would have made the holder of a negotiable promissory note a holder in due course and entitled to recover regardless of the seller-payee's default.

In our judgment such a clause in consumer goods conditional sale contracts, chattel mortgages, and other instruments of like character is void as against public policy for three reasons: (1) it is opposed to the policy of the Negotiable Instruments Law which had established the controlling prerequisites for negotiability, and provided also that the rights of one not a holder in due course were subject to all legal defenses which the maker of the instrument had against the transferor. § 58; (2) it is opposed to the spirit of N.J.S. 2A:25–1, N.J.S.A., which provides that an obligor sued by an assignee "shall be allowed * * * all * * * defenses he had against the assignor or his representatives before notice of such assignment was given to him." (It is conceded here that plaintiff gave no notice of the assignment to defendant); and (3) the policy of our state is to protect conditional vendees against imposition by conditional vendors and installment sellers.

Section 9–206(1) of the Uniform Commercial Code (Secured Transactions) deals with this problem. It provides:

> "Subject to any statute or decision which establishes a different rule for buyers of *consumer goods,* an agreement by a buyer that he will not assert against an assignee any claim or defense which he may have against the seller is enforceable by an assignee who takes his assignment for value, in good

faith and without notice of a claim or defense, except as to defenses of a type which may be asserted against a holder in due course of a negotiable instrument under the Chapter on Commercial Paper (Chapter 3). A buyer who as part of one transaction signs both a negotiable instrument and a security agreement makes such an agreement." (Emphasis ours).

In this section of the Code, the Legislature recognized the possibility of need for special treatment of waiver clauses in consumer goods contracts. Such contracts, particularly those of the type involved in this case, are so fraught with opportunities for misuse that the purchasers must be protected against oppressive and unconscionable clauses. And section 9–206 in the area of consumer goods sales must as a matter of policy be deemed closely linked with section 2–302 which authorizes a court to refuse to enforce any clause in a contract of sale which it finds is unconscionable. We see in the enactment of these two sections of the Code an intention to leave in the hands of the courts the continued application of common law principles in deciding in consumer goods cases whether such waiver clauses as the one imposed on Owen in this case are so one-sided as to be contrary to public policy. Cf. Williams v. Walker-Thomas Furniture Co., 121 U.S. App.D.C. 315, 350 F.2d 445, 448–449 (1965). For reasons already expressed, we hold that they are so opposed to such policy as to require condemnation. As the New Jersey Study Comment to section 2–302 indicates, the practice of denying relief because of unconscionable circumstances has long been the rule in this state.

* * *

For the reasons stated, we hold the waiver clause unenforceable and invalid against Owen.

III.

We agree with the result reached in the tribunals below. Plaintiff offered no proof in the trial court to show that the value of the 12 albums Owen received before breach of the contract by Universal, together with that of the record player at the time of the breach (assuming its value was material in view of the seller's representation that there was to be no charge for it), was in excess of the $303.24 paid by Owen under the contract. Moreover, there has been no suggestion throughout this proceeding that plaintiff is entitled to a partial recovery on the note in its capacity as an assignee thereof. Accordingly, the judgment for the defendant is affirmed.

NOTE

Cases such as *Unico* are given effect under Revised Article 3. § 3–302(g) and Comment 7 to § 3–302.

c. THE LEGISLATIVE RESPONSE

Consumer Credit Sales

Consumer credit sales are regulated in most states by statute. Most states have taken the position that the holder in due course doctrine should be abrogated with respect to notes given by buyers to sellers of consumer goods or services. One approach taken is to prohibit the taking of a negotiable note from the buyer and to invalidate waiver of defenses clauses in the installment sale contract. The Uniform Consumer Credit Code, in effect in 11 jurisdictions, is an example of this kind of legislation. The 1974 Official Text provides as follows:

Section 3.307 [Certain Negotiable Instruments Prohibited]

With respect to a consumer credit sale or consumer lease, [except a sale or lease primarily for an agricultural purpose,] the creditor may not take a negotiable instrument other than a check dated not later than ten days after its issuance as evidence of the obligation of the consumer.

Section 3.404 [Assignee Subject to Claims and Defenses]

(1) With respect to a consumer credit sale or consumer lease [, except one primarily for an agricultural purpose], an assignee of the rights of the seller or lessor is subject to all claims and defenses of the consumer against the seller or lessor arising from the sale or lease of property or services, notwithstanding that the assignee is a holder in due course of a negotiable instrument issued in violation of the provisions prohibiting certain negotiable instruments (Section 3.307).

(2) A claim or defense of a consumer specified in subsection (1) may be asserted against the assignee under this section only if the consumer has made a good faith attempt to obtain satisfaction from the seller or lessor with respect to the claim or defense and then only to the extent of the amount owing to the assignee with respect to the sale or lease of the property or services as to which the claim or defense arose at the time the assignee has notice of the claim or defense. Notice of the claim or defense may be given before the attempt specified in this subsection. Oral notice is effective unless the assignee requests written confirmation when or promptly after oral notice is given and the consumer fails to give the assignee written confirmation within the period of time, not less than 14 days, stated to the consumer when written confirmation is requested.

* * *

(4) An agreement may not limit or waive the claims or defenses of a consumer under this section.

The Federal Trade Commission has promulgated rules (16 C.F.R. Part 433—Preservation of Consumers' Claims and Defenses) designed to prevent the use of the holder-in-due-course doctrine in sales of consumer goods or services. The rules also apply to leases of consumer goods. References to "seller" also include a lessor. Any "consumer credit contract," a term which includes a promissory note, arising out of such a sale or lease must contain a bold-faced legend stating in effect that any holder of the contract is subject to all claims and defenses that the debtor has against the seller of the goods or services. The effect of the legend is to cause any assignee of the note or sales contract to take subject to the buyer's claims and defenses against the seller. Failure by a seller to include the legend is an unfair or deceptive act or practice under Section 5 of the Federal Trade Commission Act. Under that Act, the seller is subject to a civil suit by the FTC in which the court may "grant such relief as the court finds necessary to redress injury to consumers * * * resulting from the rule violation * * *. Such relief may include, but shall not be limited to, rescission or reformation of contracts, the refund of money or return of property, the payment of damages, and public notification respecting the rule violation * * * except that nothing in this subsection is intended to authorize the imposition of any exemplary or punitive damages." 15 U.S.C. § 57b(a)(1) and (b). Under Revised Article 3, a promissory note bearing the FTC legend can be a negotiable instrument if it otherwise complies with § 3–104(a) but there cannot be a holder in due course of the note. § 3–106(d) and Comment 3 to § 3–106.

Purchase Money Loans

Under traditional law, a financer who loans money directly to a debtor for the purpose of buying goods or services is not subject to claims or defenses the buyer may have against the seller. However, the purchase money loan transaction bears a close functional resemblance to the assigned paper transaction discussed above. In both cases the seller desires to get cash as soon as possible; the buyer has no cash to pay; and the financer is willing to provide the money. In the purchase money loan, the financer makes a direct loan to the buyer; in the assigned paper case, the financer buys the buyer's credit contract from the seller. Customs differ among the states: in some, consumer goods financing is done by purchase money loans, but in most the assigned-paper transaction predominates.

If financers are subject to consumer defenses in assigned-paper transactions, incentive is present to convert to purchase money loans to free financers of consumer defenses. By the latter part of the 1960s consumer representatives began to advocate subjecting purchase money lenders to consumer claims and defenses in situations in which there was a sufficiently close relationship between the seller and the lender to warrant doing so. But how close must this relation be? The task of defining the requisite relationship has been difficult.

Under the FTC rule referred to above the seller is guilty of an unfair or deceptive act if it accepts the proceeds of a purchase money loan (§ 433.2(b)) unless the loan agreement between the debtor and the purchase money lender contains the requisite notice. If the loan agreement contains the notice, the lender thereby subjects itself to defenses arising out of the sale. Section 433.1(d) defines purchase money loan to include two cases: (1) the seller refers the buyers to the lender, or (2) the seller is affiliated with the lender by common control, contract or business arrangement (defined in Section 433.1(f) as "any understanding, procedure, course of dealing, or arrangement, formal or informal, between a creditor and a seller, in connection with the sale of goods or services to consumers or the financing thereof"). It is not at all clear what constitutes affiliation by business arrangement. In the very common case of the secured loan the loan is made for a particular purpose and the lender will be aware that a particular seller is involved in the transaction, but, without more, this should not mean that the lender's right to repayment is subject to any defenses that the borrower has against the seller. There is no problem in the case in which the seller steers the buyer to the lender or the case in which the lender will make loans only if the proceeds are used to purchase from the particular seller. Suppose the buyer of an automobile from a dealer shows that the lender has made numerous loans to borrowers who used the proceeds to purchase automobiles from the same dealer. Have the lender and the dealer become affiliated by an informal course of dealing? Must the seller in each case inquire about the buyer's source of funds to determine whether the required legend was required and was in fact made? 1 White & Summers, Uniform Commercial Code 724–727 (3d ed., Practitioner's Edition, 1988).

Compare the following provision of the Uniform Consumer Credit Code (1974 Official Text) dealing with the same problem.

Section 3.405 [Lender Subject to Claims and Defenses Arising from Sales and Leases]

(1) A lender, except the issuer of a lender credit card, who, with respect to a particular transaction, makes a consumer loan to enable a consumer to buy or lease from a particular seller or lessor property or services [, except primarily for an agricultural purpose,] is subject to all claims and defenses of the consumer against the seller or lessor arising from that sale or lease of the property or services if:

(a) the lender knows that the seller or lessor arranged for the extension of credit by the lender for a commission, brokerage, or referral fee;

(b) the lender is a person related to the seller or lessor, unless the relationship is remote or is not a factor in the transaction;

(c) the seller or lessor guarantees the loan or otherwise assumes the risk of loss by the lender upon the loan;

(d) the lender directly supplies the seller or lessor with the contract document used by the consumer to evidence the loan, and the seller or lessor has knowledge of the credit terms and participates in preparation of the document;

(e) the loan is conditioned upon the consumer's purchase or lease of the property or services from the particular seller or lessor, but the lender's payment of proceeds of the loan to the seller or lessor does not in itself establish that the loan was so conditioned; or

(f) the lender, before he makes the consumer loan, has knowledge or, from his course of dealing with the particular seller or lessor or his records, notice of substantial complaints by other buyers or lessees of the particular seller's or lessor's failure or refusal to perform his contracts with them and of the particular seller's or lessor's failure to remedy his defaults within a reasonable time after notice to him of the complaints.

* * *

4. TRANSACTIONS WITH FIDUCIARIES

Under § 3–306 a holder in due course of an instrument takes free of "a claim of a property or possessory right in the instrument or its proceeds." For example, a claim to the instrument or its proceeds may arise if a fiduciary, in breach of fiduciary duty, negotiates the instrument for value. The negotiation of the instrument may be the means used by the fiduciary to misappropriate funds of the person to whom the fiduciary duty is owed. The claim of that person falls within the language of § 3–306. Under § 3–302(a)(2), the person to whom the instrument is negotiated cannot be a holder in due course if the instrument was taken with notice of the claim. Section 3–307 governs cases of negotiation of instruments in breach of fiduciary duty. It states rules for determining when the person taking the instrument has notice of breach of fiduciary duty. It also states that notice of breach of fiduciary duty is notice of the claim of the person to whom the fiduciary duty was owed. Consider how the following case would have been decided if Revised Article 3 had been in effect when the transactions occurred.

SMITH v. OLYMPIC BANK

Supreme Court of Washington, 1985.
103 Wn.2d 418, 693 P.2d 92.

DORE, JUSTICE.

We hold that, where a bank allows a check that is made payable to a guardian to be deposited in a guardian's personal account instead of a guardianship account, the bank is not a holder in due course under the Uniform Commercial Code (UCC) because it has notice that the guardian is breaching his fiduciary duty.

Facts

Charles Alcombrack was appointed guardian for his son Chad Stephen Alcombrack who was then 7 years old and the beneficiary of his grandfather's life insurance policy. The insurance company issued a check for $30,588.39 made payable to "Charles Alcombrack, Guardian of the Estate of Chad Stephen Alcombrack a Minor". The attorney for the son's estate directed the father to take the check, along with the letters of guardianship issued to the father, to the bank and open up a guardianship savings and checking account. The father, however, did not follow the attorney's instructions. Instead, he took the check, without the letters of guardianship, to the bank and opened a personal checking and a personal savings account. The following was printed on the back of the check:

> By endorsement of this check the payee acknowledges receipt of the amount thereof in full settlement of all claims resulting from the death of Roy Alcombrack, certificate holder under Group Life Policy No. 9,745,632

/s/ Charles Alcombrack

Guardian of the Estate of Chad Stephen Alcombrack, a minor

Despite the above written notice that the check was payable to the father in his guardianship capacity, the bank allowed the father to place the entire amount in newly opened personal accounts. On the same day that the father opened his accounts, the attorney for the guardian called a trust officer from Olympic Bank and inquired as to the fees the bank charged for maintaining guardianship accounts. Responding to the attorney's questions, the trust officer wrote the attorney, specifically mentioning the "Estate of Chad Alcombrack".[1]

1. The following is the letter sent by the trust officer to the guardian's attorney:

"October 30, 1975

"Mr. Charles A. Schaaf, Attorney
Suite 707, Hoge Building
Seattle, Washington 98104

"Reference: Estate of Chad Alcombrack

"Dear Mr. Schaaf:

"This is a follow up to our telephone conversation of October 28, 1975. The information you requested on the performance of our common trust

The father, and later his new wife, used all but $320.60 of the trust money for their own personal benefit. Bank records disclosed how the estate money was withdrawn: five withdrawals were made to cash or into the father's checking account (total— approximately $16,000); one withdrawal paid off an unsecured personal loan made by the bank to the father (approximately $3,000); seven debits to the account were made by the bank exercising its right of offset to make payments on or pay off personal loans by the bank to the father (total—approximately $12,500).

After the depletion of the son's estate, J. David Smith was appointed successor guardian. He received a judgment against the father and instituted this suit against the bank. The trial court granted summary judgment in favor of the bank. The Court of Appeals reversed and remanded, holding that the trial court should determine the factual issue whether the bank was a holder in due course.

Argument

Olympic Bank claims that it is a holder in due course (HIDC) and, as such, is not subject to the claims of the petitioner. In order to qualify as a HIDC, the bank must meet five requirements. It must be (1) a holder (2) of a negotiable instrument, (3) that took the instrument for value (4) in good faith and (5) without notice that it was overdue, dishonored, or of any defense or claim to it on the part of any person. ∗ ∗ ∗ We need not decide whether the bank met the first four conditions as we hold that the bank took the check with notice of an adverse claim to the instrument and, therefore, is not a holder in due course. Consequently, the bank is liable to the petitioner.[4]

A purchaser has notice of an adverse claim when "he has knowledge that a fiduciary has negotiated the instrument in payment of or as security for his own debt or in any transaction for his own benefit or otherwise in breach of duty." UCC § 3-304(2). Thus, the issue raised by this case is whether the bank had knowledge that the guardian was breaching his fiduciary duty when it allowed him to deposit a check, made payable to him in his guardianship capacity, into his personal accounts. As to this

funds will be available in about four weeks. October 31st is the end of our fiscal year. If this is not too long for you to wait, please let me know and I will send you a copy of our annual report.

"Our fee for handling a Guardianship account is, eight tenths ($^8/_{10}$) of one percent (1%), minimum of $350.00 per year."

4. UCC § 3-306 sets forth the liabilities of one who accepts a check and who is not a holder in due course.

"Unless he has the rights of a holder in due course any person takes the instrument subject to

"(a) all valid claims to it on the part of any person; and

"(b) all defenses of any party which would be available in an action on a simple contract; ∗ ∗ ∗ "

issue, Von Gohren v. Pacific Nat'l Bank, 8 Wash.App. 245, 505
P.2d 467 (1973) is persuasive and controlling. In *Von Gohren,* it
was held that a bank had notice that an employee was breaching
her fiduciary duty when it allowed her to deposit third-party
checks payable to her employer in her personal account. The
bank was put on notice despite the fact that the employer had
authorized the employee to draw checks against his account and
also to endorse checks made payable to him and deposit such
checks into his account. The court held that notice need not
always consist of actual knowledge of a breach of a fiduciary duty,
but can be predicated upon reasonable commercial standards.
The court concluded by stating:

> It is our view that since defendant had notice of the claim
> by virtue of UCC § 3–304(2), and since it is undisputed that
> defendant did nothing to investigate Mrs. Martin's authority
> to negotiate checks payable to her employer, we must hold as
> a matter of law it did not act in accordance with reasonable
> commercial standards.

Von Gohren, at 255, 505 P.2d 467. The same conclusion is mandated in the present case.

Here, the bank knew it was dealing with guardianship funds.
The check was payable to the father as guardian and not to him
personally. The father endorsed it in his guardianship capacity.
The bank received a call from the guardian's attorney inquiring
about the fee the bank charged for guardianship accounts, and a
trust officer for the bank replied in a letter referring to the
"Estate of Chad Alcombrack".

Reasonable commercial practices dictate that when the bank
knew that the funds were deposited in a personal account instead
of a guardianship account, it also knew that the father was
breaching his fiduciary duty. The funds lost the protection they
would have received in a guardianship account when they were
placed in a personal account. If the funds had been placed in a
guardianship account, the bank would not have been allowed to
exercise its set-off rights which amounted to approximately
$12,500. * * * Nor would it have been permitted to accept a
check, drawn on the guardianship account, from the father in
satisfaction of the father's unsecured personal loan in the amount
of approximately $3,000. Nor could the father, or bank, have
authorized his new wife to write checks against the guardianship
account without court approval. * * * A fiduciary has a duty to
ensure that trust funds are protected. * * * Here, the father
breached his duty.

While this is the first time, under the Uniform Commercial
Code, that we have held a bank liable for allowing a guardian to
deposit trust funds in a personal account, we have held a bank
liable in a pre-Code case for allowing a trustee to breach his

fiduciary duty. * * * In addition, other jurisdictions have held banks liable under similar circumstances using the Code * * * and without using the Code * * *. The policy reasons for holding a bank liable are compelling—especially in the situation presented in this case. The ward has no control of his own estate. He must rely on his guardian and on the bank for the safekeeping of his money. In order to protect the ward, the guardian and bank must be held to a high standard of care. For the guardian, this means that he must deposit guardian funds in a guardianship account. For the bank, it means that when it receives a check made payable to an individual as a guardian, it must make sure that the check is placed in a guardianship account. This will not place an undue burden on either banks or guardians and will have the beneficial effect of protecting the ward.

* * *

NOTE

A view contrary to Smith v. Olympic Bank is expressed in Matter of Knox, 64 N.Y.2d 434, 488 N.Y.S.2d 146, 477 N.E.2d 448 (1985), a case also involving a father who was guardian of the property of a minor son. Robert, the son, was injured when he was four years old. An action brought on behalf of Robert for damages was settled and a check was issued to the father as guardian of the property of the son. The check was negotiated to a bank and $11,000 of the proceeds of the check was deposited in the personal account of the father in the bank. The amount deposited in the account was eventually spent in the purchase of a house for the family and for other family expenses. The family included three other children besides Robert and the parents. The family was impoverished and the father stated that the money was spent to "give Robert as well as the rest [of the family] the same kind of normal life that any family enjoys." Eventually an action was brought against the father by a guardian ad litem appointed for Robert to recover the funds that had been misappropriated by the father. The bank was joined in the action and the trial court entered judgment against both. The bank appealed and the Appellate Division reversed the judgment against the bank. In affirming the Appellate Division, the Court of Appeals, one judge dissenting, stated:

In Bradford Trust Co. v. Citibank, 60 N.Y.2d 868, 470 N.Y.S.2d 361, 458 N.E.2d 820, we held that "there is no requirement that a check payable to a fiduciary be deposited to a fiduciary account, and the fact that the instrument was not so deposited may not, without more, be relied upon as establishing a wrongful payment on the part of the depositary bank" * * *. Our decision was grounded upon the Uniform Commercial Code which provides that "[a]n instrument made payable to a named person with the addition of words describing him * * * as [a] fiduciary for a specified person or purpose is payable to the payee and may be negotiated, discharged or enforced by him" (Uniform Commercial Code § 3–117[b]), and that mere knowledge that the "person negotiating the instrument is or was a fiduciary" does not of itself give the purchaser of a negotiable instrument notice of any claims or defenses (Uniform Commercial Code § 3–304[4][e]). The conduct with which [the bank] is charged—having negotiated a check payable to [the father] in a fiduciary capacity without requiring deposit of the check in a fiduciary account—is thus permissible.

In general, a bank may assume that a person acting as a fiduciary will apply entrusted funds to the proper purposes and will adhere to the conditions of the appointment * * *. A bank is not in the normal course required to conduct an investigation to protect funds from possible misappropriation by a fiduciary, unless there are facts—not here present—indicating misappropriation * * *. In this event, a bank may be liable for participation in the diversion, either by itself acquiring a benefit, or by notice or knowledge that a diversion is intended or being executed * * *. No facts are before this court suggesting that [the bank] had notice that [the father] intended to, or did in fact, use the settlement proceeds for improper purposes. Consequently, [the bank] cannot be charged with the misappropriation.

PROBLEM

Little Corporation has about 100 stockholders and conducts its manufacturing operations in Centerville, a small city. Little has a checking account in Centerville Bank. The agreement between Little and the bank provides that the bank is authorized to honor checks drawn on the account if signed in the name of Little by either the President or Treasurer of Little. Doe, the President of Little, was involved in the following transactions:

Case # 1. Doe's personal credit card was used to pay for automobile rentals, restaurant meals, and hotel accommodations. All of the credit card charges were incurred for the personal benefit of Doe and were not related to any business purpose of Little. Doe wrote a check drawn on Little's checking account and sent it to the issuer of the credit card to pay the monthly bill that included the charges.

Case # 2. Doe bought a small but expensive rug from Merchant and paid for it by writing a check drawn on Little's checking account. The rug was delivered to Doe at the store.

Case # 3. Doe went to Clothier's store and bought several suits that were custom tailored to Doe's measurements. Doe paid by writing a check drawn on Little's checking account. Before accepting the check, Clothier asked Doe why a check of the corporation was being used to pay for the clothing. Doe answered, "The suits are a present from a grateful employer for five years of faithful service by yours truly."

Case # 4. Doe wrote a $1,000 check drawn on Little's account payable to Doe. Doe indorsed the check in blank and deposited it to Doe's account in Depositary Bank by delivering it to a teller who knew Doe personally and knew that Doe was President of Little.

In each of the foregoing cases, Doe committed a breach of fiduciary duty to Little in writing the check on Little's account. When Little discovered the defalcations it brought actions to recover the proceeds of the checks written by Doe and paid from Little's account. The actions were brought against the issuer of the credit card in Case # 1, against Merchant in Case # 2, against Clothier in Case # 3, and against Centerville Bank in Case # 4. State your opinion whether Little is entitled to recover in each case. § 3–306, § 3–307, § 1–201(25) and (27), and Comment 2 to § 3–307.

5. THE FEDERAL HOLDER IN DUE COURSE DOCTRINE

CAMPBELL LEASING, INC. v. FEDERAL DEPOSIT INSURANCE CORP.

United States Court of Appeals, Fifth Circuit, 1990.
901 F.2d 1244.

CLARK, CHIEF JUDGE:

I.

Appellants Campbell Leasing, Inc., Eagle Airlines, Inc., and George A. Day challenge the district court's entry of summary judgment on a promissory note in favor of the Federal Deposit Insurance Corporation (FDIC) and NCNB Texas National Bank (NCNB). We affirm in part, vacate in part, and remand for further proceedings.

II.

On February 16, 1984, Campbell Leasing, Inc. (Campbell Leasing) executed a promissory note in the amount of $136,804.24, plus interest, payable to RepublicBank Brownwood (RepublicBank). To secure payment of the note, Campbell Leasing granted RepublicBank a security interest in a 1979 Piper airplane. RepublicBank also obtained the personal guarantee of George A. Day (Day).

In May of 1986, Campbell Leasing defaulted on the note. RepublicBank accelerated the maturity of the note after Campbell Leasing failed to cure its default. On June 12, 1986, RepublicBank seized the airplane but did not gain possession of its maintenance records or flight logs. The seizure prompted appellants to file this lawsuit. RepublicBank counterclaimed for payment of the note, plus interest, costs, and attorneys' fees.

On July 29, 1988, the successor to RepublicBank, First RepublicBank Brownwood, N.A. (First RepublicBank), was declared insolvent and closed. The Comptroller of Currency appointed the FDIC as receiver. The FDIC entered into a purchase and assumption agreement with a federally established bridge bank, which purchased the promissory note, security agreement, and guarantee at issue in this case. The bridge bank became NCNB Texas National Bank.

In August of 1988, the FDIC and NCNB removed the case to federal court and filed a motion for summary judgment. The district court subsequently permitted the parties to amend their pleadings. In their amended complaint, the appellants asserted: (1) that prior to seizing the airplane RepublicBank had agreed to a novation wherein Tex–Star Airlines, Inc. (Tex–Star) executed a note to RepublicBank for the purchase of the plane, thereby relieving Campbell Leasing and Day of their obligations under the Campbell Leasing note; (2) that RepublicBank was guilty of trespass and conversion in connection with the seizure of the airplane; (3) that after seizing the plane, RepublicBank failed to deal with the appellants fairly and in good faith and tortiously interfered with their attempts to lease the plane to a third party; (4) that RepublicBank failed to maintain the plane and dispose of it in a commercially reasonable manner; (5) that RepublicBank had elected to retain the plane in satisfaction of Campbell Leasing's debt, and (6) that RepublicBank had caused Day to suffer mental and emotional distress.

The district court granted summary judgment for NCNB and the FDIC, concluding that all of the appellants' claims and affirmative defenses were barred by the federal common-law doctrine announced in D'Oench, Duhme & Co. v. Federal Deposit Insurance Corporation, 315 U.S. 447, 62 S.Ct. 676, 86 L.Ed. 956 (1942) and the holder in due course doctrine announced in Federal Deposit Insurance Corporation v. Wood, 758 F.2d 156 (6th Cir.), cert. denied, 474 U.S. 944, 106 S.Ct. 308, 88 L.Ed.2d 286 (1985). The court entered judgment against Campbell Leasing and Day jointly and severally for the amount due on the note, plus interest, and awarded the FDIC and NCNB costs and attorneys' fees. The court also foreclosed the lien on the plane and its attachments and directed the appellants to deliver the maintenance records and log books to the

FDIC and NCNB. Finally, the court ordered the airplane sold and the amount of the judgment reduced by the proceeds.

The appellants now challenge the district court's entry of summary judgment. At oral argument, the appellants waived all but the following contentions: (1) the *D'Oench, Duhme* doctrine is unconstitutional; (2) the federal holder in due course doctrine does not bar their claims against RepublicBank, and if it does bar those claims it is unconstitutional; and (3) the FDIC and NCNB have not acted in a commercially reasonable manner regarding the maintenance and sale of the airplane. We affirm in part, vacate in part, and remand.

III.

A.   *The* D'Oench, Duhme *Doctrine.*

The appellants concede that the *D'Oench, Duhme* doctrine bars their claim that the promissory note was extinguished in a transaction involving Tex–Star, because the transaction was not documented in RepublicBank's records. They argue instead that the *D'Oench, Duhme* doctrine violates their rights under the fifth amendment by depriving them of valuable property—their defense to liability on the note—without just compensation or due process of law. We disagree.

The *D'Oench, Duhme* doctrine is "a common law rule of estoppel precluding a borrower from asserting against the FDIC defenses based upon secret or unrecorded 'side agreements' that alter the terms of facially unqualified obligations." Bell & Murphy & Assoc. v. Interfirst Bank Gateway, N.A., 894 F.2d 750, 753 (5th Cir.1990). Even borrowers who are innocent of any intent to mislead banking authorities are covered by the doctrine if they lend themselves to an arrangement which is likely to do so. Id. at 753–54. The doctrine thus "favors the interests of depositors and creditors of a failed bank, who cannot protect themselves from secret agreements, over the interests of borrowers, who can." Id. at 754.

In this case, the appellants were in a position to protect themselves by ensuring that the alleged Tex–Star transaction was adequately documented in RepublicBank's records. They failed to do so. Because the absence of documentation was likely to mislead banking authorities as to the value of the Campbell Leasing note, the appellants are estopped from asserting against the FDIC and NCNB any claims relating to the Tex–Star transaction. Id.

The *D'Oench, Duhme* doctrine does not deprive the appellants of property without just compensation. The appellants have simply deprived themselves of certain defenses to liability by failing to protect themselves in the manner required by the *D'Oench, Duhme* doctrine. See United States v. Locke, 471 U.S. 84, 107–08,

105 S.Ct. 1785, 1799, 85 L.Ed.2d 64 (1985) (upholding a federal provision extinguishing mineral interests for failure to make a timely annual filing). The government has never been required "to compensate [property owners] for the consequences of [their] own neglect." Texaco, Inc. v. Short, 454 U.S. 516, 530, 102 S.Ct. 781, 792, 70 L.Ed.2d 738 (1982).

Nor have the appellants been denied due process. The *D'Oench, Duhme* doctrine is a federal common law rule of general applicability that was established long before the appellants' claims arose. Because the appellants had "a reasonable opportunity both to familiarize themselves with [its] general requirements and to comply with those requirements," due process has been satisfied. *Locke,* 471 U.S. at 108, 105 S.Ct. at 1799. We conclude that the *D'Oench, Duhme* doctrine does not violate the takings clause or the due process clause of the fifth amendment.

B. The Federal Holder In Due Course Doctrine.

The federal holder in due course doctrine bars the makers of promissory notes from asserting various "personal" defenses against the FDIC in connection with purchase and assumption transactions involving insolvent banks. *Wood,* 758 F.2d at 161; see also FSLIC v. Murray, 853 F.2d 1251, 1256 (5th Cir.1988). The protection extends to subsequent holders of the notes. See id.

This doctrine is grounded in the federal policy of "bringing to depositors sound, effective, and uninterrupted operation of the [nation's] banking system with resulting safety and liquidity of bank deposits." S.Rep. No. 1269, 81st Cong., 2d Sess., *reprinted in* 1950 U.S.CODE CONG. & ADMIN.NEWS 3765, 3765–66. The most effective way for the FDIC to implement this policy when a bank becomes insolvent is by arranging a purchase and assumption transaction rather than by liquidating the bank. *Wood,* 758 F.2d at 160–61; see also Murray, 853 F.2d at 1256–57. If the FDIC were required to determine the value of the bank's notes in light of all possible "personal" defenses, a purchase and assumption transaction could not take place in the timely fashion necessary to ensure "uninterrupted operation" of the bank and the "safety and liquidity of deposits." Thus, the FDIC as a matter of federal common law enjoys holder in due course status in order to effectively perform its congressionally mandated function.

In this case, the appellants assert various defenses and counterclaims to liability on the note. They contend that RepublicBank tortiously interfered with their efforts to lease the Piper airplane to a third party and delayed too long after the plane's seizure before attempting to sell it. They maintain that the note could have been completely discharged absent RepublicBank's wrongful actions. They also claim that RepublicBank elected to keep the airplane in full satisfaction of the note and caused Day to suffer mental and emotional distress. Because these are "personal" rather than "real" defenses to liability on the note, * * * the FDIC and NCNB as holders in due course acquired the note free of these claims. * * *

The appellants challenge this conclusion, contending that the federal holder in due course doctrine does not apply to this case because the FDIC was not acting in its corporate capacity. See *Wood,* 758 F.2d at 161. They also argue that the FDIC and NCNB do not qualify as holders in due course under Texas law because they acquired the note in a bulk transaction by legal process and had notice that the note was overdue. * * * We reject these contentions.

We find no logical reason to limit federal holder in due course protection to the FDIC in its corporate capacity, to the exclusion of its receivership function. In its corporate capacity, the FDIC is obligated to protect the depositors of a failed bank, while the FDIC as receiver must also protect the bank's creditors and shareholders. Gilman v. FDIC, 660 F.2d 688, 690 (6th Cir.1981); see generally 12 U.S.C. § 1821. In both cases, the holder in due course doctrine enables the FDIC to efficiently and effectively fulfill its role, thus minimizing the harm to depositors, creditors, and shareholders. See *Wood,* 758 F.2d at 160–61; *Murray,* 853 F.2d at 1256. For example, the doctrine prevents note makers from gaining absolute priority over a failed bank's assets, by asserting "personal" claims as defenses or setoff to their notes, to the detriment of the bank's other creditors and potentially its depositors. *Wood,* 758 F.2d at 160–61; see also *Murray,* 853 F.2d at 1256–57. We conclude that the FDIC enjoys holder in due course status as a matter of federal common law whether it is acting in its corporate or its receivership capacity. * * *

In addition, the FDIC and subsequent note holders enjoy holder in due course status whether or not they satisfy the technical requirements of state law. The court in *Wood* assumed that the FDIC did not qualify as a holder in due course under state law, yet it still held that the FDIC was entitled to the protections of a holder in due course as a matter of federal common law. See 758 F.2d at 158. We reached the same conclusion with respect to the FSLIC. *Murray,* 853 F.2d at 1256. This rule "promotes the necessary uniformity of law in this area while it counters individual state laws that would frustrate [basic FDIC objectives]." Id.

However, the district court erred in granting summary judgment against the appellants on all their claims. The appellants have a statutory right to continue their action against the FDIC as receiver for First RepublicBank on their claims of tortious interference with contract, breach of the Campbell Leasing security agreement, and intentional infliction of mental and emotional distress. 12 U.S.C. § 1821(d)(6)(A). While the holder in due course doctrine prevents the appellants from asserting these claims as a set-off to liability on the note, it does not prevent the appellants from trying these claims to the district court, liquidating the amount of damages, and subsequently receiving a pro-rata share of First RepublicBank's remaining assets along with the bank's other creditors. See id. § 1821(d)(11)(A)(ii). We therefore must vacate that part of the district court's judgment dismissing the appellants' breach of contract and tort claims and remand for additional proceedings.

In light of these statutory provisions, we reject the appellants' further contention that application of the holder in due course doctrine violates due process or amounts to an unconstitutional taking of property without just compensation.

> A negotiable instrument is subject to transfer at any time, and the maker must always be aware that the transferee may be a holder in due course. From the maker's view, there is no difference between his bank failing and the note going to the * * * FDIC, and his bank failing after selling the note to a holder in due course.

Wood, 758 F.2d at 161. The appellants have not been denied the opportunity to assert their claims because they may pursue them against the FDIC as receiver for First RepublicBank. The appellants have "therefore suffer[ed] no prejudice." *Murray,* 853 F.2d 1256–57.

* * *

6. VALUE

---

a. INTRODUCTION

If Thief steals a negotiable instrument from Owner and sells it to unsuspecting Holder it may make sense to give Holder rights in the instrument at the expense of Owner. One or the other must bear a loss. Although each is equally innocent the negotiability doctrine tips the scales in favor of Holder in order to carry out a policy objective of encouraging free commerce in instruments. But if Holder has paid nothing for the instrument, denial of the right to defeat Owner's title results in no loss to Holder except the loss of a windfall. Thus, if Thief makes a gift of the instrument to Holder it seems unfair to allow Holder to profit at the expense of Owner. Since it is not necessary to impose a loss on Owner in order to carry out the objective of encouraging free commerce in instruments, Holder loses. Section 3–302(a)(2)(i) provides that only a holder who takes the instrument for value can be a holder in due course. Taking for value is defined in § 3–303(a). Although the taking for value requirement can be explained in part by distinguishing between loss and windfall, this distinction is not always clearly apparent in the cases covered by § 3–303(a). The problems that follow illustrate the cases covered by that section. In each problem, and the cases that follow, you might ask yourself the question whether the holder-in-due-course doctrine is necessary in order to protect some interest of the holder or whether the doctrine simply confers on the holder a windfall. If there is a windfall, is the result justified by commercial necessity? You might also ask the question whether, if the doctrine did not exist, the taking of the instrument in the particular transaction would have been discouraged.

PROBLEMS

1. On April 1, Drawer wrote a check to the order of Payee and delivered it to Payee. Issue of the check was induced by fraudulent representations of Payee. Drawer discovered the fraud on April 2 and immediately ordered the drawee bank to stop payment of the check. § 4–403. On April 3, Payee negotiated the check to Seller in payment of the purchase price of goods to be delivered by Seller on April 10. On April 5, payment of the check was refused by the drawee bank and the dishonored check was returned to Seller. On April 6, Seller demanded payment of the check from Drawer. § 3–414(b). Drawer refused to pay on the ground that issuance of the check was obtained as the result of fraud by Payee. Is the defense of Drawer good against Seller? § 3–305(a)(2) and (b). Did Seller give consideration for the check? § 3–303(b). Did Seller give value for the check? § 3–303(a).

2. Change the facts in Problem 1 in one respect. Assume there was no contract of sale between Seller and Payee. Rather, Seller had sold and delivered goods to Third Party on February 1 and Third Party failed to pay for them. Payee negotiated the check to Seller on April 3 in payment of Third Party's obligation to pay for the goods. Did Seller give value for the check? § 3–303(a)(3).

b. RIGHTS OF DEPOSITARY BANK IN DEPOSITED CHECK

Checks are usually deposited by the payee in the payee's bank. That bank is referred to in § 4–105(2) as the "depositary bank." The payee's bank is also referred to as a "collecting bank" if the check is not drawn on the payee's bank. § 4–105(5). The depositary bank normally credits the account of the depositor in the amount of the check and forwards the check to the drawee for payment. The drawee is referred to in § 4–105(3) as the "payor bank." The depositary bank is considered to be acting as the agent of the depositor in obtaining payment of the deposited check. § 4–201. The credit to the depositor's account is normally provisional in nature. When the check is paid by the payor bank, this provisional credit becomes final, i.e., the credit represents a debt owed by the depositary bank to the depositor, § 4–215(d). If the check is not paid by the payor bank, the depositary bank has the right to "charge back," i.e., cancel the provisional credit. § 4–214(a).

Frequently, the depositary bank will also be a creditor of the depositor because of a past transaction such as a loan. If a debt owing by the depositor to the depositary bank is past due, the depositary bank may exercise a common-law right to set off against the debt any amounts which the bank owes the depositor. For example, if the depositor owes the depositary bank $1,000 on a past-due loan and there is an $800 final credit balance in the depositor's checking account, the depositary bank may simply wipe out the $800 balance by applying it to reduce the $1,000 loan balance.[1] In addition to this right of setoff a depositary bank has a closely-related common-law right known as a banker's lien.[2] For

1. The bank's right of setoff may be limited by statute. For example, Calif. Financial Code § 864 limits setoffs with respect to certain consumer-type installment debt owed to the bank.

2. Restatement, Security § 62 provides as follows: "General possessory liens exist in favor of * * * (c) a banker, as security for the general balance due him from a customer, upon commercial paper and other instruments which can be used as the basis of credit and which are deposited with him in the regular course of business." Some states have codified the common-law lien. For example, a California statute provides: "A banker, or a savings and loan association, has a general lien, dependent on possession, upon all property in his or her hands belonging to a customer, for the balance due to the banker or savings and loan association from the customer in the course of the business." Civil Code § 3054(a). The lien may be important to the bank in the event of the depositor's insolvency. In Goggin v. Bank of America, 183 F.2d 322 (9th Cir. 1950), the depositor owed the bank $600,000 on a loan. At the time of the depositor's bankruptcy the bank held commercial paper delivered by the depositor for collection and credit to its general deposit account. After bankruptcy and after written notice by the depositor attempting to terminate the authority of the bank to act as agent for collection, the bank collected the commercial paper. In an action by the receiver of the depositor's estate in bankruptcy to recover the proceeds for the estate, it was held (a) that the bank had a banker's lien on the commercial

paper at the date of bankruptcy, (b) that the authority of the bank to collect the paper was not affected by either bankruptcy or the attempt of the depositor to revoke the bank's authority, and (c) that the bank was entitled to apply the proceeds to reduction of the loan balance. This case was decided under the Bankruptcy Act. Under the present Bankruptcy Code the right of the bank to enforce its lien after bankruptcy would be affected by the automatic stay pursuant to Bankruptcy Code § 362(a)(7). If the bank had collected the paper before bankruptcy it would have had in bankruptcy a right of setoff with respect to the mutual debts existing at the time of bankruptcy. This right of setoff is subject to certain limitations. Bankruptcy Code § 553. In *Goggin* the setoff after bankruptcy was based on the bank's lien existing at the time of bankruptcy.

The banker's lien may also be the basis for cutting off claims of third parties to the paper deposited by the depositor. In *Wyman v. Colorado National Bank*, 5 Colo. 30 (1879), plaintiff drew a draft on a drawee in London payable to the order of First Bank with which plaintiff had an account. Plaintiff's intent was to have First Bank collect the draft and deposit the proceeds to plaintiff's account. First Bank indorsed the draft and sent it to Second Bank with orders to collect it. At that time First Bank was indebted to Second Bank on an overdraft. Second Bank sent the draft to London for collection. After the draft was paid but before Second Bank was paid the proceeds Second Bank was notified that the draft was

example, if the depositor owes the depositary bank $1,000 on a past-due loan and deposits a check to the depositor's account in the regular course of business, the depositary bank has a lien in the check as security for the $1,000 debt. Although the bank when it forwards the check to the payor bank for payment acts as agent for the depositor, it also has a property interest in the check represented by the lien. Thus, the depositary bank can collect the check and apply the proceeds to the debt owed by the depositor. Since the taking of an instrument for an antecedent debt is value, the depositary bank could attain the rights of a holder in due course. These two related but separate common-law rights—setoff and banker's lien—are preserved under § 1–103. Comment 1 to § 4–210. The two common-law rights are frequently confused. It is not uncommon for a court to refer to the banker's lien as a right of setoff or to refer to the right of setoff as a banker's lien. When a depositary bank is asserting a right in an uncollected check it is relying on a lien. A setoff can occur only if there are mutual debts. There can be no present right of setoff with respect to an uncollected check because until collected the check does not represent a debt of the depositary bank to the depositor.

Depositary banks may acquire rights as holders in due course under other provisions of the UCC. Suppose there is no debt owing by the depositor when the check is deposited. Whether the depositary bank has given value for the check is determined under § 4–211 which states that the bank has given value to the extent it has a security interest in the check. Section 4–210 states rules for determining when a security interest arises. This security interest is in addition to the bank's common-law banker's lien. Comment 1 to § 4–210. By virtue of § 4–210 the depositary bank has a security interest under subsection (a)(1) if the check is deposited and the resulting credit is withdrawn, under subsection (a)(2) if the check is deposited and the depositor is given the right to withdraw the credit, and under (a)(3) if the bank makes a loan or cash payment based on the check. In these cases the bank is

the property of plaintiff and that First Bank had failed. The court held that Second Bank got a lien on the draft immediately upon receipt of the draft and became a holder for value without notice of plaintiff's claim, thereby cutting off the claim. In effect Second Bank took the draft as security for the antecedent debt represented by the overdraft. Compare UCC § 3–303(a)(2) and (3). The issue in cases like *Wyman* is whether the deposited paper "belongs" to the customer making the deposit. For example, if Second Bank had been aware that First Bank was acting solely as collecting agent with respect to the draft the lien would not have attached. But in cases of undisclosed agency there is no notice of the claim of the owner of the item and the apparent ownership of the paper by the depositor has been recognized by some courts as sufficient to allow the lien to attach.

A rationale for the banker's lien is stated in Gibbons v. Hecox, 105 Mich. 509, 513, 63 N.W. 519, 520 (1895). "The reason for allowing the lien is that any credit which a bank gives by discounting notes or allowing an overdraft to be made is given on the faith that money or securities sufficient to pay the debt will come into the possession of the bank in the due course of future transactions."

treated as though it were a lender to the depositor taking as security a security interest in the check. In the case in which the depositor is not allowed to withdraw the funds, the bank does not have a security interest and is not a holder in due course. It has committed no funds and is fully protected by its ability to charge back the depositor's account in the event the check is not paid by the payor bank.

In most cases the depositor has an existing credit balance in the account when a deposit is made and there may be a series of deposits and withdrawals from the account. In those cases, whether credit for a particular check has been withdrawn cannot be determined except by applying some mechanical tracing rule. Such a rule is provided by the last sentence of § 4–210(b) which states that "credits first given are first withdrawn." This rule is usually referred to as the first-in-first-out or FIFO rule.

PROBLEM

The table shows debits and credits made to Depositor's checking account in Depositary Bank. Withdrawals were made by payment by Depositary Bank of checks drawn by Depositor on the account. Deposits were made either in cash or by third-party checks payable to Depositor as indicated.

Date		Debit	Credit	Balance
Nov. 1	Existing balance			4,000
Nov. 2	Deposit by check		5,000	9,000
Nov. 3	Withdrawal	4,000		5,000
Nov. 4	Deposit in cash		6,000	11,000
Nov. 5	Withdrawal	5,000		6,000
Nov. 6	Received notice of dis-honor of check deposit-ed on Nov. 2			
Nov. 7 (A.M.)	Withdrawal	3,000		3,000
Nov. 7 (P.M.)	Charge-back of Nov. 2 credit	5,000		(2,000)

The check deposited on November 2 was not paid by the payor bank because the drawer had stopped payment. § 4–403(a). Depositary Bank received notice of dishonor of the check on November 6. Depositor is insolvent. Depositary Bank brings an action against the drawer of the November 2 check to recover the amount of the check. § 3–414(b). The drawer defends by asserting that no consideration was given for the check. § 3–303(b). Assume that Depositary Bank is a holder in due course if it gave value for the check. Did Depositary Bank give value? § 4–210(a) (1) and (b). Is the result in this problem consistent with the case discussed in Comment 2 to § 3–303? That case is governed by § 3–303(1)(a), under which the unperformed promise of performance is not value. The rationale is that until performance is made the promisor will not suffer any out-of-pocket loss and dishonor of the check excuses performance by the promisor. In this problem, is holder-in-due-course status necessary to protect Depositary Bank against an out-of-pocket loss when Depositary Bank received notice of dishonor on November 6? § 4–214(a).

Section 4–210(a)(1) refers not only to cases in which a credit has been withdrawn, but also to cases in which the credit has been "applied." The latter term refers to cases in which the credit has been used by the bank to pay an obligation to itself or to make a payment to a third party. This provision is considered in the cases that follow. When these cases were decided, the current § 4–210(a)(1) and § 4–211 appeared in slightly different form as § 4–208(1)(a) and § 4–209 of the pre–1990 Article 4.

LAUREL BANK & TRUST CO. v. CITY NATIONAL BANK OF CONNECTICUT

Superior Court of Connecticut, Appellate Session, 1976.
33 Conn.Sup. 641, 365 A.2d 1222.

SPONZO, JUDGE. In this action the facts may be summarized as follows: The plaintiff and the defendant were at all times pertinent to this case commercial banks duly authorized to conduct business in this state and had checking account facilities available for their respective customers. On March 27, 1973, and for some time prior thereto, one A. S. Maisto maintained two checking accounts with the plaintiff. One account was No. O–41190–6 and was conducted under the name of "Tony's Sunoco," and the other account, No. O–41233–3, was maintained under the name of "B & D Automotive." On the same date A. S. Maisto had an account with the defendant at its office in the town of Cheshire.

Between the hours of 1 p. m. and 2 p. m. on March 27, 1973, Maisto purchased from the defendant an official check, or cashier's check, in the amount of $3446. That cashier's check was paid for with two checks plus cash. One of the checks was in the amount of $2585.50 and was drawn by Maisto on the account No. O–41190–6 that was maintained with the plaintiff. In order to draw an official check, the defendant's teller had to obtain the approval of an officer. As a result of that requirement, an officer of the defendant bank telephoned the plaintiff bank and was assured by an unknown person in the bookkeeping department that "Maisto's check for an amount over $2500 was good at this time." The defendant then issued its official check to Maisto.

On March 27, 1973, at about 4:15 p. m., that cashier's check together with other items, all of which totaled $9501, were deposited by Maisto with the plaintiff in account No. O–41233–3, which at the time of deposit was overdrawn to the extent of $21,079.43. That transaction was entered as a check deposit in the plaintiff's bookkeeping record for March 28, 1973, since all banking transactions occurring after 3 p. m. are recorded as received on the next day. The deposit of $9501 was provisionally credited by the plaintiff to the B & D Automotive account, No. O–41233–3, subject to later withdrawal or reversal of credit, and the overdrawn balance was reduced by that amount.

On March 28, 1973, the plaintiff returned the check in the amount of $2585.50 to the defendant because of insufficient funds. The plaintiff presented the official or cashier's check in the amount of $3446 to the defendant through normal bank collection procedures and the defendant dishonored the check in that it stopped payment thereon. The check was returned to the plaintiff unpaid, remains unpaid to date, and is the subject matter of this action. The signature of the drawer on the cashier's check has been admitted.

The trial court concluded that the plaintiff was a mere holder of the cashier's check because it did not establish that it took the check for value. It also concluded that the defendant established a defense of want of consideration because the $2585.50 check which was one of the items used to purchase the cashier's check was subsequently dishonored. Accordingly, the court rendered judgment for the plaintiff in the amount of $860.50, the difference between the $3446 cashier's check and the $2585.50 check. The plaintiff has appealed from that judgment.

* * *

Since the signature on the cashier's check has been admitted, the mere production of the instrument would entitle the plaintiff to recover, even if it were a mere holder, unless the defendant sustained its burden of establishing a want or failure of consideration. * * * Once a defendant meets his burden of proving that a defense exists, in order to prevail the person claiming the rights of a holder in due course has the burden of establishing that he, or the person under whom he claims, is in all respects a holder in due course. * * *

A cashier's check is a bill of exchange drawn by a bank as drawer upon itself as drawee and made to the order of a payee who, as in this case, may also be the purchaser of the check. * * * With respect to the issuing bank's ability to stop payment on a cashier's check, analogies to a customer's right to stop payment on an ordinary check are inapposite and confusing. * * * The proper approach is to view the issuing bank, acting in its dual role as drawer and drawee, as the equivalent of a maker of a negotiable promissory note payable on demand. * * *

It is clear that the defendant bank did establish the failure of consideration for issuance of the cashier's check, because the check drawn on the plaintiff which Maisto transferred in payment for the cashier's check was returned for insufficient funds. That defense of want of consideration would be effective against a party who was not a holder in due course. * * * If the plaintiff was a mere holder, the trial court was correct in concluding that the defendant had sustained its burden of proving that there was a partial want of a consideration to the extent of $2585.50 and in awarding a judgment in favor of the plaintiff in the amount of $860.50 after deducting the sum of $2585.50 from the cashier's check in the amount of $3446.

Since the plaintiff alleged in its reply that it was a holder in due course, it assumed the burden of establishing that it was in all respects a holder in due course. * * * To be a holder in due course, the plaintiff must have taken the cashier's check for value, in good faith, and without notice that it was overdue or dishonored or that there was any defense against it or claim to it on the part of any person. * * *

The plaintiff contends that the deposit of $9501 made on March 28, 1973, was a cash deposit. That contention has no merit because the unchallenged finding of the court is that it was a check deposit. The principal issue in this case is whether the provisional credit made by the plaintiff against the B & D Automotive account, which was overdrawn in the amount of $21,079.43, constituted value * * *. The credit entered was subject to a later withdrawal or reversal of the credit by the plaintiff. The trial court concluded that no value was given because the credit was not extended irrevocably. That conclusion was erroneous.

UCC § 3–303(b) provides that a holder takes for value "when he takes the instrument in payment of or as security for an antecedent claim against any person whether or not the claim is due * * *." UCC § 4–208(1)(a) elaborates on that concept and provides that "[a] bank has a security interest in an item and any accompanying documents or the proceeds of either * * * in case of an item deposited in an account to the extent to which credit given for the item has been withdrawn or applied * * *." UCC § 4–209 completes that thought, stating that "[f]or purposes of determining its status as a holder in due course, the bank has given value to the extent that it has a security interest in an item provided that the bank otherwise complies with the requirements of section 3–302 on what constitutes a holder in due course."

In order to comprehend how the plaintiff became a holder for value under the provisions of the statutes referred to, it is necessary to state the parameters of the security interest with relation to the value concept. It is clear that if a depositor's account is not overdrawn and he deposits a check which is credited to his account but not drawn on, then no value is given. * * * It is clear under UCC § 4–208(1)(a) that a bank has given value and is a holder in due course to the extent that a depositor actually draws against a check given for collection, even if the check is later dishonored. It is immaterial that the bank takes the check for collection only and can charge back against the depositor's account the amount of the uncollected item. * * *

The reason for that rule is to prevent the hindrance to commercial transactions which would result if depository banks refused to permit withdrawal prior to clearance of checks. By giving the bank a security interest in the amount credited prior to notice of a stop payment order or other notice of dishonor, UCC §§ 4–208 and 4–209 allow continuation of that common practice while protecting the bank as a holder in due course. * * *

While Maisto did not draw upon the deposit of $9501, the deposit was applied to his overdraft or antecedent debt on a provisional basis. Under the circumstances it appears that where the plaintiff applied the deposit, even provisionally, to Maisto's overdrawn account, it gave value and thus cut off the defense of want of consideration. In a leading case, Bath National Bank v. Sonnenstrahl, Inc., 249 N.Y. 391, 394, 164 N.E. 327, 328, it was stated: "Though title to a draft left by a depositor with the bank for collection does not pass absolutely to the bank where the full amount of the draft was credited to the depositor, 'for convenience and in anticipation of its payment,' and 'the bank could have cancelled the credit, as it clearly accepted no risk on the paper,' yet if the depositor 'had overdrawn, and this draft had been credited to cover the overdraft, or if the company had drawn against the draft, the bank could hold the paper until the account was squared.' It would then be a holder for value. St. Louis & San Francisco Ry. Co. v. Johnston, 133 U.S. 566, 10 S.Ct. 390, 33 L.Ed. 683."

[handwritten margin note: Application of proceeds results in giving value]

UCC § 4–201(1) provides, in part, that "[u]nless a contrary intent clearly appears and prior to the time that a settlement given by a collecting bank for an item is or becomes final as provided in subsection (3) of section 4–211 and sections 4–212 and 4–213 the bank is an agent or subagent of the owner of the item and any settlement given for the item is provisional. * * * [A]ny rights of the owner to proceeds of the item are subject to rights of a collecting bank such as those resulting from outstanding advances on the item and valid rights of setoff." That provision, which makes the bank an agent of its customer, is to be construed harmoniously with UCC § 4–208(1) which does not derogate from the banker's general common-law lien or right of setoff against indebtedness owing in deposit accounts.

In the present case, the plaintiff's action in provisionally crediting a $9501 deposit to the antecedent debt of the depositor was an exercise of its common-law right of setoff, UCC § 4–208(1) and also gave the plaintiff a security interest sufficient to constitute value. In Sandler v. United Industrial Bank, 23 A.D.2d 567, 256 N.Y.S.2d 442, a check was deposited in an account which was overdrawn and the bank credited the deposit in part to repay the overdrawn account and applied the balance to a new item presented for payment. The maker of the check died that evening and his bank returned his check unpaid. The court held that the collecting bank became a holder for value prior to the maker's death. See Bowling Green, Inc. N. H. v. State Street Bank & Trust Co. of Boston, 307 F.Supp. 648, 654–55 (D.Mass.).

To make a collecting bank a holder for value where it applies a deposit to an overdrawn account is a result consistent with logic and good banking practice. If an account is overdrawn, it is highly doubtful that a bank would pass over an opportunity to erase or reduce the overdraft. That opportunity arises when the customer makes a deposit. The bank credits or sets off the overdraft and waits for final settlement as a holder for value. If the check is dishonored, the bank may then reverse the provisional granting of credit to the overdraft and proceed not only against its customer but also against the drawee bank. If it can proceed against the drawee bank, the latter can then recover from its customer.

The trial court erred in concluding that the plaintiff was not a holder for value when it applied Maisto's deposit, which included the cashier's check in the amount of $3446, to an overdraft in his account, subject to reversal upon dishonor.

There is error, the judgment is set aside and the matter is remanded for a trial limited to the issue of whether the plaintiff took the cashier's check in good faith and without notice that it was overdue, dishonored or that there was any defect or defense.

NOTES

1. *Laurel Bank* represents an orthodox analysis of former § 4–208(1)(a) (now § 4–210(a)(1)). A contrary analysis of that provision was made by the New York Court of Appeals in Marine Midland Bank New York v. Graybar Electric Co., Inc., 41 N.Y.2d 703, 395 N.Y.S.2d 403, 363 N.E.2d 1139 (1977). Dynamics was indebted to the bank on a loan. A check of Graybar payable to Dynamics was deposited in Dynamics' account with the bank which forwarded it for collection. On the day of the deposit the credit given for the check was "set off" against Dynamics' loan debt to the bank. The check was not paid because Graybar had stopped payment. The bank then brought an action against Graybar as drawer of the check. Under the court's analysis of the case the bank's rights to recover the amount of the check depended upon whether it was a holder in due course and this in turn depended upon whether the bank took the check for value. The court analyzed this issue as follows:

> As to value, the bank contends that it took the July 25 check for value because under the Uniform Commercial Code

"A holder takes the instrument for value (a) to the extent that * * * he acquires a *security interest in or a lien on the instrument* * * * or (b) when he takes the instrument in *payment of or as security for an antecedent claim* against any person whether or not the claim is due" (Uniform Commercial Code, § 3–303; emphasis added). Further, the bank notes that the Uniform Commercial Code accords to it a "security interest" in a check "to the extent to which credit given for the item is withdrawn or *applied*" * * *. Thus, the bank's position is that, by its setoff, it took the check in payment of its antecedent loan, and also that by applying the credit for the check to the loan, the bank acquired a security interest therein. For these reasons, the bank argues that it has given value under the Uniform Commercial Code * * *.

Dynamics argues that a bank and its depositor must "bilaterally" agree, either expressly or impliedly, to the creation of a security interest in an item. Examples of an implied agreement are said to be participating in the withdrawal of funds, or applying the credit which the bank has given for the item prior to collection. Furthermore, Dynamics argues, the bank must give value unconditionally and irrevocably by actually extinguishing the depositor's debt upon receipt of the check, even though not yet collected. Dynamics is thus arguing that under the circumstances presented here the bank has not given value.

A bank, of course, gives value to the extent that a credit given for an item is withdrawn by the party whose account was credited * * *. Value is also given by a holder when it takes a check in payment of, or as security for, an antecedent debt * * *. Long before the enactment of the Uniform Commercial Code, however, the entry of a credit on a bank's books was held not to be parting with value under circumstances manifesting that the pre-existing debt or a part thereof was not, in fact, extinguished in consideration for the item for which the credit was given (see Sixth Nat. Bank of City of N. Y. v. Lorillard Brick Works Co., Sup., 18 N.Y.S. 861, affd., 136 N.Y.S. 667, 33 N.E. 335). The basis for that decision was that the bookkeeping entry of the credit was not a parting with value * * *.

These events present somewhat of a hybrid situation in that the bank first gave Dynamics a credit for the Graybar check and then applied this credit, by way of setoff, to Dynamics' indebtedness to it. A literal reading of the Uniform Commercial Code suggests that under § 4–208(1)(a) the net result of the credit followed by the setoff is that the bank had taken the check for value. The difficulty with this analysis is, however, that the credit given to Dynamics' account was provisional because the bank could and did reverse the credit after notice of the stop payment order, thereby reinstating that portion of the loan against which the credit was set off.

Considering first the credit given to Dynamics' account for the Graybar check, it is established that the giving of a provisional credit is not a parting with value under the Uniform Commercial Code. In discussing the notion that it is not necessary to give holder in due course status to one who has not actually paid value, the Official Commentary to the Uniform Commercial Code cites as an illustration "the bank credit not drawn upon, which can be and is revoked when a claim or defense appears" * * *.

* * *

Turning then to the argument that by applying the credit by way of setoff to Dynamics' indebtedness the bank gave value, the following is relevant. The clearest instance of giving value in this sort of case is where a bank actually extinguishes a debt by, for example, parting with a note in exchange for a check and then seeking to collect on the check * * *. With respect to UCC § 4–208(1)(a), however, one text has suggested that its purpose was to give "the bank protection in any case in which it is not clear that the bank purchased the item outright, but in which it is clear that the bank has done something, of advantage to the depositor, more than giving the depositor a mere credit on the bank's books" (Clarke, Bailey & Young, Bank Deposits and Collections [1963], p. 56). Here, the bank argues that by applying the credit to Dynamics' indebtedness it was giving value as contemplated under UCC § 4–208.

This argument should be rejected. To say that the bank was doing something of advantage to Dynamics by applying the credit to that depositor's indebtedness is to ignore what actually occurred. The bank was merely seeking to protect itself and not giving value, in any traditional sense, or under the Uniform Commercial Code. Since the credit given to the Dynamics account was not, as noted, available to Dynamics, there is no reason for allowing the bank to benefit from this credit, particularly since the bank reinstated that portion of the debt against which the credit was applied upon learning that payment was not to be forthcoming on the check. Under this analysis the bank is in no worse position than any other creditor, and the bank's unilateral agreement to take the credit for the indebtedness, conditioned on payment of the check for which the credit was given, is recognized for what it was—an attempt to recoup its losses.

This is not to diminish the bank's right of setoff of mutual debts in a bankruptcy situation * * *. Nor is this holding intended to suggest that the setoff was impermissible simply because the check was uncollected at the time of the setoff * * *. Rather, this determination is based on the conclusion that what the bank did was merely give a provisional credit for the Graybar check. That the bank unilaterally agreed to apply this provisional credit to Dynamics' indebtedness should not elevate the transaction to the level of those instances where value is considered to be given under the Uniform Commercial Code. Therefore, since the bank did not give value, it is not a holder in due course and cannot recover on the check.

The Court of Appeals suggests that an antecedent debt can constitute value only in cases in which the debt was "extinguished" in consideration of the instrument for which the credit was given. Taking a personal check for an underlying obligation does not normally "extinguish" the obligation. Under § 3–310(b) the underlying obligation is suspended until the check is presented; if the check is dishonored the obligation revives. It is a rare case indeed in which a personal check is accepted in absolute payment of an obligation. Thus, in the normal case, the check is taken as provisional payment. This is similar to the provisional credit given by the depositary bank for an uncollected check. In both cases the credit given for the check is reversed if the check is not paid. But, under § 3–310(b), the person taking the check may sue on it and there is no indication in the UCC that the fact that the debt was not extinguished affects the taking-for-value question. One of the arguments against recognizing an antecedent debt as value is that the creditor taking the instrument is often given a windfall. The creditor may not have made any detrimental reliance and if the instrument is not enforceable the creditor is in no worse position than before taking the instrument. This argument was rejected by the drafters of the NIL and the UCC. Before New York adopted the NIL, the common-law rule in that state did not recognize an antecedent debt as value for holder-in-due-course purposes. See Kelso & Co. v. Ellis, 224 N.Y. 528, 121 N.E. 364 (1918). *Marine Midland* appears to be a step backward in the direction of the old New York doctrine.

2. Earlier, when we were discussing the concept of negotiability, we quoted from Professor Rosenthal's article questioning the desirability of the doctrine of negotiability. Here we include another section of that article in which he considers the negotiability of checks. This is from Negotiability—Who Needs It? 71 Colum.L.Rev. 375, 382–385 (1971).

To begin with, negotiability normally plays almost no part with respect to checks. While some checks are cashed at a grocery store or across the counter at a bank, the overwhelming majority of checks are deposited by the payee for collection at his own bank, which, acting merely as the depositor's agent for that purpose, sends the check through banking channels to the drawee bank where it is presented for payment. If paid, the check is so marked and is ultimately returned to the drawer along with his monthly statement; if the check is dishonored, a slip setting forth the reason is attached to it and goes with it back through banking channels to the payee.

There is no holder in due course (except perhaps the payee himself) of such a check since, even though such other requirements as good faith and lack of notice may be met, the bank would not have given value for the check. Any dispute between drawer and payee will, therefore, simply be between themselves, with no one else in a position to assert special rights.

Let us now modify the case of a relatively poor buyer purchasing a refrigerator on installments, and substitute a middle-class consumer paying for it with his personal check. If the refrigerator fails to work properly, if its defect is immediately apparent, if the buyer's attempts to get redress from the seller prove unavailing, and if the buyer moves with sufficient alacrity, he can often stop payment on his check before it has cleared through his own bank. The buyer and seller will then be in a position themselves to resolve their dispute on the merits, with the buyer having the tactical advantage that the seller will have to bring suit in order to collect if the matter cannot be resolved without litigation.

Suppose, however, the bank in which the seller-payee deposits the check allows him to draw against it before it has been collected. This is not standard practice, but it does occur with some frequency. When the check is presented to the drawee bank for payment, it is dishonored because of the stop payment order. This time, however, the depositary bank is given the status of holder in due course "to the extent to which credit for the item has been withdrawn or applied," or "if it makes an advance on or against the item." To this extent, the drawer cannot assert against the bank the defense that the sale of the refrigerator was fraudulent. Although the stop payment order is effective, its utility to the drawer is defeated, since he is liable to the depositary bank.

* * *

If the depositary bank were to grant credit to the payee by allowing withdrawals before collection, and if it were to do this in reliance upon its knowledge of the *drawer's* financial standing or reputation, there might be good reason to protect the depositary bank in this fashion. Typically, however the depositary bank pays no attention to the identity of the drawer; in fact, it does not even know whether the drawer's signature is genuine. It will often allow or refuse to allow withdrawals against the check before collection solely on the basis of its relations with and knowledge of the creditworthiness of its own customer, the payee. If payment is stopped, and the depositary bank cannot recover its advances by charging the amount back against the payee's account, but is permitted to hold the drawer liable, the bank receives a windfall: in such cases, it picks up the liability of the drawer, which by hypothesis it had not counted upon when it made its decision to allow withdrawals before collection.

The fact that the depositary bank would not normally be relying upon the drawer's credit may be seen in the improbable combination of circumstances that have to coincide for the drawer's liability to matter. First, the bank's customer, the payee, must have allowed his account to drop to the point at which some of his withdrawals cannot be charged against other funds in the account but must be regarded as advances against the uncollected check. Second, the payee must be insolvent, or at least his assets must not be readily amenable to collection. Third, the drawer has to be solvent and available, and his signature genuine. Fourth, the check must be dishonored. Finally, for the doctrine to make any ultimate difference, the drawer must have a legitimate defense on the check that is good against the payee, but is not of a type that can be asserted against a holder in due course. Only if all of these elements coincide is the bank's position improved by virtue of its becoming a holder in due course. It must therefore be a rare case indeed in which the bank's decision to extend credit before the check is collected can be regarded as having been made in reliance upon its ability to cut off the defenses of the drawer. Neither banks specifically, nor commerce in general, seem to need the rule declaring the bank to be a holder in due course. Where the bank relies entirely on the identity and credit of the payee in allowing withdrawals, it should shock no one's conscience if the bank were limited to the payee as a source of reimbursement.

* * *

BOWLING GREEN, INC. v. STATE STREET BANK & TRUST CO.

United States Court of Appeals, First Circuit, 1970.
425 F.2d 81.

COFFIN, CIRCUIT JUDGE. On September 26, 1966, plaintiff Bowling Green, Inc., the operator of a bowling alley, negotiated a United States government check for $15,306 to Bowl-Mor, Inc., a manufacturer of bowling alley equipment. The check, which plaintiff had acquired through a Small Business Administration loan, represented the first installment on a conditional sales contract for the purchase of candlepin setting machines. On the following day, September 27, a representative of Bowl-Mor deposited the check in defendant State Street Bank and Trust Co. The Bank immediately credited $5,024.85 of the check against an overdraft in Bowl-Mor's account. Later that day, when the Bank learned that Bowl-Mor had filed a petition for reorganization under Chapter X of the Bankruptcy Act, it transferred $233.61 of Bowl-Mor's funds to another account and applied the remaining $10,047.54 against debts which Bowl-Mor owed the Bank. Shortly thereafter Bowl-Mor's petition for reorganization was dismissed and the firm was adjudicated a bankrupt. Plaintiff has never received the pin-setting machines for which it contracted. Its part payment remains in the hands of defendant Bank.

Plaintiff brought this diversity action to recover its payment from defendant Bank on the grounds that the Bank is constructive trustee of the funds deposited by Bowl-Mor. In the court below, plaintiff argued that Bowl-Mor knew it could not perform at the time it accepted payment, that the Bank was aware of this fraudulent conduct, and that the Bank therefore received Bowl-Mor's deposit impressed with a constructive trust in plaintiff's favor. The district court rejected plaintiff's view of the evidence, concluding instead that the Bank was a holder in due course * * * and was therefore entitled to take the item in question free of all personal defenses. Bowling Green, Inc., etc. v. State Street Bank and Trust Co., 307 F.Supp. 648 (D.Mass.1969).

* * *

Plaintiff's first objection arises from a technical failure of proof. The district court found that plaintiff had endorsed the item in question to Bowl-Mor, but there was no evidence that Bowl-Mor supplied its own endorsement before depositing the item in the Bank. Thus we cannot tell whether the Bank is a holder within the meaning of § 1–201(20), which defines holder as one who takes an instrument endorsed to him, or to bearer, or in blank. But, argues plaintiff, once it is shown that a defense to an instrument exists, the Bank has the burden of showing that it is in all respects a holder in due course. This failure of proof, in plaintiff's eyes, is fatal to the Bank's case.

We readily agree with plaintiff that the Bank has the burden of establishing its status in all respects. UCC § 3–307(3), on which plaintiff relies to establish the defendant's burden, seems addressed primarily to cases in which a holder seeks to enforce an instrument, but Massachusetts courts have indicated that the policy of § 3–307(3) applies whenever a party invokes the rights of a holder in due course either offensively or defensively. Cf. Elbar Realty Inc. v. City Bank & Trust Co., 342 Mass. 262, 267–268, 173 N.E.2d 256 (1961). The issue, however, is not whether the Bank bears the burden of proof, but whether it must establish that it took the item in question by endorsement in order to meet its burden. We think not. The evidence in this case indicates that the Bank's transferor, Bowl-Mor, was a holder. Under UCC § 3–201(a), transfer of an instrument vests in the transferee all the rights of the transferor. As the Official Comment to § 3–201 indicates, one who is not a holder must first establish the transaction by which he acquired the instrument before enforcing it, but the Bank has met this burden here.

We doubt, moreover, whether the concept of "holder" as defined in § 1–201(20) applies with full force to Article 4. Article 4 establishes a comprehensive scheme for simplifying and expediting bank collections. Its provisions govern the more general rules of Article 3 wherever inconsistent. UCC § 4–102(1). As part of this expediting process, Article 4 recognizes the common bank practice of accepting unendorsed checks for deposit. * * * § 4–201(1) provides that the lack of an endorsement shall not affect the bank's status as agent for collection, and § 4–205(1) authorizes the collecting bank to supply the missing endorsements as a matter of course. In practice, banks comply with § 4–205 by stamping the item "deposited to the account of the named payee" or some similar formula. * * * We doubt whether the bank's status should turn on proof of whether a clerk employed the appropriate stamp, and we hesitate to penalize a bank which accepted unendorsed checks for deposit in reliance on the Code, at least when, as here, the customer himself clearly satisfies the definition of "holder". Section 4–209 does provide that a bank must comply "with the requirements of section 3–302 on what constitutes a holder in due course," but we think this language refers to the enumerated requirements of good faith and lack of notice rather than to the status of holder, a status which § 3–302 assumes rather than requires. We therefore hold that a bank which takes an item for collection from a customer who was himself a holder need not establish that it took the item by negotiation in order to satisfy § 4–209.

* * *

This brings us to plaintiff's final argument, that the Bank gave value only to the extent of the $5,024.85 overdraft, and thus cannot be a holder in due course with respect to the remaining $10,047.54 which the Bank credited against Bowl-Mor's loan account. Our consideration of this argument is confined by the narrow scope of the district court's findings. The Bank may well have given value under § 4–208(1)(a) when it credited the balance of Bowl-Mor's checking account against its outstanding indebtedness. See Banco Espanol de Credito v. State Street Bank & Trust Co., 409 F.2d 711 (1st Cir. 1969). But by that time the Bank knew of Bowl-Mor's petition for reorganization, additional information which the district court did not consider in finding that the Bank acted in good faith and without notice at the time it received the item. We must therefore decide whether the Bank gave value for the additional $10,047.54 at the time the item was deposited.[5]

Resolution of this issue depends on the proper interpretation of § 4–209, which provides that a collecting bank has given value to the extent that it has acquired a "security interest" in an item. In plaintiff's view, a collecting bank can satisfy § 4–209 only by extending credit against an item in compliance with § 4–208(1). The district court, on the other hand, adopted the view that a security interest is a security interest, however acquired. The court then found that defendant and Bowl-Mor had entered a security agreement which gave defendant a floating lien on Bowl-Mor's chattel paper. Since the item in question was part of the proceeds of a Bowl-Mor contract, the court concluded that defendant had given value for the full $15,306.00 at the time it received the deposit.[a]

With this conclusion we agree. Section 1–201(37) defines "security interest" as an interest in personal property which secures payment or performance of an obligation. There is no indication in § 4–209 that the term is used in a more narrow or specialized sense. Moreover, as the official comment to § 4–209 observes, this provision is in accord with prior law and with § 3–303, both of which provide that a holder gives value when he accepts an instrument as security for an antecedent debt. Reynolds v. Park Trust Co., 245 Mass. 440, 444–445, 139 N.E. 785 (1923). Finally, we note that if one of the Bank's prior loans to Bowl-Mor had been made in the expectation that this particular instrument would be deposited, the terms of § 4–208(1)(c) would have been literally satisfied. We do not think the case is signifi-

---

5. Defendant suggests that we can avoid the analytical problems of § 4–209 by simply holding that the Bank's inchoate right to set off Bowl-Mor's outstanding indebtedness against deposits, as they were made constituted a giving of value. See Wood v. Boylston National Bank, 129 Mass. 358 (1880). There are, however, some pitfalls in this theory. First, under prior law a secured creditor could not exercise its right of set-off without first showing that its security was inadequate. Forastiere v. Springfield Institution for Savings, 303 Mass. 101, 104, 20 N.E.2d 950 (1939). Second, although the Uniform Commercial Code forswears any intent to change a banker's right of set-off, § 4–201 does change the presumption that a bank owns items deposited with it. This presumption played a role under prior law in assessing the bank's rights against uncollected commercial paper. Compare Wood v. Boylston National

Bank, supra, with Boston-Continental National Bank v. Hub Fruit Co., 285 Mass. 187, 190, 189 N.E. 89 (1934) and American Barrel Co. v. Commissioner of Banks, 290 Mass. 174, 179-181, 195 N.E. 335 (1935).

a. [Eds.] The bank secured its loan to Bowl-Mor by a security interest in Bowl-Mor's installment sale contracts (defined as chattel paper by § 9–105(1)(b)). Its security interest applied not only to the chattel paper but also to any proceeds of the chattel paper. § 9–306. Bowling Green's check to Bowl-Mor, since it was in payment of the first installment of its sales contract, was proceeds. Under § 9–306 and § 9–203 the bank automatically obtained a security interest in this check as soon as Bowl-Mor obtained "rights" in the check, which in this case was when Bowl-Mor received the check.

cantly different when the Bank advances credit on the strength of a continuing flow of items of this kind. We therefore conclude that the Bank gave value for the full $15,306.00 at the time it accepted the deposit.

We see no discrepancy between this result and the realities of commercial life. Each party, of course, chose to do business with an eventually irresponsible third party. The Bank, though perhaps unwise in prolonging its hopes for a prospering customer, nevertheless protected itself through security arrangements as far as possible without hobbling each deposit and withdrawal. Plaintiff, on the other hand, not only placed its initial faith in Bowl-Mor, but later became aware that Bowl-Mor was having difficulties in meeting its payroll. It seems not too unjust that this vestige of caveat emptor survives.

Affirmed.

NOTES

1. The conclusion in *Bowling Green* that a depositary bank could become a holder in due course of a check which did not bear the indorsement of the depositor was very controversial and was not supported by the text of Article 3 and Article 4 then in effect. Some courts refused to follow *Bowling Green*. But the 1990 Official Text of Article 4 follows *Bowling Green* in this regard. Section 4–205 states that a depositary bank receiving a check for collection becomes a holder when it receives the check if the customer was then a holder regardless of whether the check is indorsed by the customer. It goes on to state that the bank becomes a holder in due course if it satisfies the other requirements of § 3–302.

2. In footnote 5 of *Bowling Green* the court's reference to "the Bank's inchoate right to set off" is apparently meant to apply to the banker's lien. It is clear that a banker's lien is not a security interest under § 4–210, but Comment 1 to that section states that "Subsection (a) does not derogate from the banker's general common law lien or right of set-off against indebtedness owing in deposit accounts." The Comment to § 4–211 states that that section is in accord with the prior law (NIL § 27) and with § 3–303. NIL § 27 states: "Where the holder has a lien on the instrument, arising either from contract or by implication of law, he is deemed a holder for value to the extent of his lien." Section 3–303(a)(2) states that an instrument is transferred for value if the transferee acquires a security interest or other lien in the instrument other than a lien obtained by judicial proceeding. Assuming that the Bowl-Mor loan was due at the time the check was deposited, there is abundant authority, including Wood v. Boylston National Bank, 129 Mass. 358 (1880), cited by the court, which supports the defendant's argument that it acquired a lien in the

check when it was deposited. But the Massachusetts courts seem to severely restrict the banker's lien by their reading of the special deposit rule, which is a qualification on a bank's ability to obtain a lien. This qualification states that the banker's lien does not apply to items deposited for a special purpose. Jones on Liens § 251 (3d ed. 1914). Two examples illustrate the doctrine. In Bank of the United States v. Macalester, 9 Pa. 475 (1849), the obligor on interest coupons payable to bearer deposited funds with Bank, which as its agent was to use the funds to pay holders of the coupons who presented them for payment. At the time of the deposit the obligor on the coupons was indebted to Bank. Instead of paying the coupons Bank asserted a lien on the deposited funds to pay the debt owing to it. The court held that because the funds were deposited for a special purpose Bank could not assert a lien against them. In Rockland Trust Co. v. South Shore National Bank, 366 Mass. 74, 314 N.E.2d 438 (1974), the court stated that "it seems at least doubtful" that a depositary bank could assert a lien against a certified check deposited to the account of its customer for the purpose of having the funds represented by the check wired to a third party to whom its customer was indebted. But the Massachusetts courts have also applied the special deposit rule to checks deposited for collection with the effect that a depositary bank acting as agent of its customer to collect the check cannot claim any beneficial interest in the check. Under this reading of the rule the qualification apparently destroys the banker's lien in most of the cases to which it has historically been applied, and the bank is limited to a right of setoff after the check is paid. See Boston-Continental National Bank v. Hub Fruit Co., 285 Mass. 187, 189 N.E. 89 (1934).

3. Acquisition of a lien by a depositary bank does not depend upon the bank's making any accounting entries to "apply" the check to the outstanding debt. See Maryland Casualty Co. v. National Bank of Germantown & Trust Co., 320 Pa. 129, 182 A. 362 (1936). By contrast § 4–210(a)(1) states that the bank gets a security interest in the deposited check at the time that credit given for it is "applied." In *Bowling Green* the court indicates that this refers to the time when Bowl-Mor's deposit account, which had been credited with the amount of the check, was charged $10,047.54 in reduction of the loan. Suppose a check payable to Customer was indorsed by Customer to Depositary Bank and delivered to one of its officers in reply to a demand by Depositary Bank to immediately cover an overdraft. Thereafter, but before the check was deposited to Customer's account the drawer of the check told the officer handling the transaction that the check was issued without consideration. At what time was "credit given for the item * * * applied"? § 4–210(a)(1). At what time did Depositary Bank take the instrument "as payment of, or as security for, an antecedent claim"? § 3–303(a)(3). At

what time did Depositary Bank acquire a "lien in the instrument other than a lien obtained by judicial proceeding?"   § 3–303(a)(2). Peoria Savings & Loan Association v. Jefferson Trust & Savings Bank of Peoria, 81 Ill.2d 461, 43 Ill.Dec. 712, 410 N.E.2d 845 (1980).

c. ANTECEDENT CLAIMS AND SECURITY INTERESTS IN GOODS

The depositary bank in *Bowling Green* was able to assert rights in the deposited check as a holder in due course because its Article 9 security interest in the check securing an antecedent debt satisfied the taking-for-value requirement.   Thus, without giving any new value and without showing any detrimental reliance, it was able to profit from its customer's fraud against Bowling Green.   An analogous problem is raised in the case of goods.   Negotiability is provided by § 2–403(1) and value is provided, as in *Bowling Green*, by an antecedent debt and an Article 9 security interest.   We have already seen an example, Swets Motor Sales, Inc. v. Pruisner, p. 56.

Chapter 7

LIABILITY OF PARTIES TO NEGOTIABLE INSTRUMENTS

A. LIABILITY OF DRAWER AND DRAWEE

The promissory note is the most simple kind of negotiable instrument. The person primarily obliged to pay is the maker who has expressly agreed to do so. The draft is a more complex form of instrument. The drawer orders the drawee to pay an amount of money to the payee, but nobody has expressly agreed to make the payment. A draft normally arises out of a pre-existing creditor-debtor relationship between the drawer and the drawee. For example, a seller ships goods to a buyer who is located in a distant market. The contract of sale provides for payment of the price of the goods by a draft drawn by the seller on the buyer or the buyer's bank acting on behalf of the buyer. The seller draws a draft ordering the drawee to pay to the order of a named payee a sum of money equal to the price of the goods. The named payee may be the seller's bank which buys the draft from the seller for the face amount less a discount to compensate the bank for its services. In that case, the draft is delivered to the bank, which then becomes its holder. The draft is then "presented" to the drawee for payment. "Presentment" is defined in § 3–501(a). In this case, presentment is simply a demand made on the drawee to pay. Subsection (b) of § 3–501 states rules regarding the place, time, and manner of presentment. In our example, presentment might be made by the bank named as payee of the draft, but often the draft will be negotiated to another bank located near the buyer and that bank will present the draft to the drawee for payment. When the draft is paid the buyer has discharged the obligation to the seller to pay the price of the goods.

The most common example of a draft is the ordinary check which is a draft drawn on a bank and payable on demand. Payment of checks is also normally based on a creditor-debtor relationship. A check is drawn by a customer of a bank who has a checking account in the bank; the credit balance in the account represents a debt of the bank to the customer. When the bank pays the check, the bank's debt to the customer is reduced by the amount of the check.

Since the drawee of a draft has made no promise in the instrument to pay the payee or other holder, the holder has no action on the instrument against the drawee to enforce payment.

§ 3–408. Sometimes the drawee will obligate itself, by a letter of credit or other separate contract, to pay a draft. In that case failure by the drawee to pay the draft may result in liability to the holder for breach of the letter of credit (§ 5–114(1) and § 5–115(1)), but there is no liability based on an obligation created by the draft. In the absence of a separate contract of the drawee such as a letter of credit, payment by the drawee will normally depend upon the drawee's obligation to the drawer arising from an express or implied contract between them. For example, in opening a checking account for a customer, the bank incurs an obligation to the customer to pay properly payable checks drawn on the account. Failure to pay a properly payable check may result in liability to the customer for wrongful dishonor (§ 4–402), but the holder of the check has no cause of action against the drawee bank. Before codification of negotiable instruments law by the NIL in the late 19th century a minority of states took the view that a check created a direct liability on the part of the drawee bank to the holder. The theory was that a check amounted to an equitable assignment of the drawer's funds on deposit, but NIL § 189 took the majority view that the check is not itself an assignment. Article 3 follows the NIL in that respect.

Although a draft, by its stated terms, is simply an order of the drawer to the drawee to pay, it is also an obligation of the drawer to pay the draft if the draft is dishonored. § 3–414(b). "Dishonor" occurs if the drawee fails to make timely payment when the draft is presented for payment. Dishonor of ordinary checks and drafts is defined in § 3–502(b) and (e). The drawer of a draft other than a check can avoid liability under § 3–414(b) if the signature of the drawer is accompanied by words which disclaim liability such as "without recourse." § 3–414(e). Disclaimer of the drawer's liability is normally limited to documentary drafts. Comment 5 to § 3–414. With respect to checks, disclaimer is not effective. § 3–414(e). A relatively unimportant limitation on drawer's liability is provided by § 3–414(f). This provision is explained in Comment 6 to § 3–414.

Section 3–408 states that "the drawee is not liable on the instrument until the drawee accepts it." Section 3–409(a) defines "acceptance" as "the drawee's signed agreement to pay a draft as presented." The acceptance "must be written on the draft and may consist of the drawee's signature alone." A drawee that accepts a draft is known as the "acceptor" and is obliged to the holder to pay the draft. § 3–413(a). To better understand the concept of acceptance it is appropriate to distinguish between two types of drafts. The most common type of draft is the demand draft or "sight draft." It contemplates that the amount of the draft will be paid by the drawee upon presentation or "on sight." A draft which does not specify a time of payment is payable on demand. § 3–108(a). A check is the most common example of a demand draft. Another type of draft, called a "time draft" does not contemplate immediate payment by the drawee. For example, suppose the draft reads as follows: "Pay $1,000 to the order of Jane Doe sixty days after presentment of this draft." Here, two steps are contemplated. Jane Doe, or some subsequent holder, will initially present the draft to the drawee to start the running of the 60 days, and when that period of time has passed a second presentment will be made for payment. The first presentment is known as a "presentment for acceptance." Its purpose is to allow the holder to know whether the drawee is agreeable to honoring the draft. Agreement of the drawee is manifested by acceptance, i.e., the drawee's signing of the draft with or without the addition of the word "accepted" or other words indicating an intention to accept. The date of acceptance is normally included but is not required. § 3–409(a) and (c). The drawer's acceptance is equivalent to a promise to pay the amount of the draft to the holder. Thus, the obligation of an acceptor is like that of the maker of a note.

Another example of an accepted draft is the certified check. If the payee of an ordinary check wants assurance of payment, one way of getting it is to insist that the drawer obtain the acceptance of the drawee bank before the check is taken by the payee. This is done by the drawee bank's signing the check in much the same way as described in the case of a time draft. Only the terminology differs. The bank's signature is called "certification" but it is identical to acceptance. § 3–409(d). Certification is normally obtained by the drawer before delivery of the check to the payee, but in unusual cases the holder of an uncertified check may prefer to obtain the drawee bank's agreement to pay rather than payment itself. This can be done by asking the drawee bank to certify the check. The drawee of a check may certify it as a courtesy to the drawer or to the holder, but is not obliged to do so. Nor is refusal to certify a dishonor of the check. § 3–409(d). Because certification of a check is treated by the bank as the equivalent of payment insofar as the drawer is concerned, the account of the drawer will be debited in the amount of the check at the time of certification. The effect of certification is to transform the check, which originally represented an order to pay of the drawer, into a promise of the drawee to pay the amount of the check to its holder. This transformation is reflected in § 3–414(c) which states that acceptance of a draft by a bank discharges the drawer's obligation to pay the draft.

B. LIABILITY OF INDORSER

In Chapter 6 we examined the function of an indorsement in the negotiation of an instrument. Indorsement also has the additional function of causing the indorser to incur liability on the instrument. The obligation of the indorser, stated in § 3–415(a), is to pay the instrument if the instrument is dishonored, but indorser's liability may be avoided by appropriate words accompanying the signature which disclaim liability. The most commonly used words indicating disclaimer are "without recourse." § 3–415(b).

Drafts

The obligation of the indorser to pay an instrument arises upon its dishonor. With respect to unaccepted drafts, dishonor usually requires presentment for payment and a failure of the drawee to pay. § 3–502(b)(1) through (3). With respect to some time drafts, dishonor requires presentment for acceptance and failure of the drawee to accept. § 3–502(b)(4). In some cases, dishonor can occur without presentment. § 3–502(e) and § 3–504(a).

The obligation of an indorser of an unaccepted draft is subject to discharge in two situations. First, if the draft is a check and collection of the check is not initiated within 30 days of the indorsement, the indorser is discharged. § 3–415(e). Second, discharge can occur as the result of a failure to give timely notice of dishonor to the indorser. § 3–415(c) and § 3–503(a). The manner and time for giving notice are stated in § 3–503(b) and (c). Notice of dishonor need not be given if it is excused. § 3–504(b). Delay in giving notice may also be excused in some cases. § 3–504(c).

Indorser's liability with respect to checks has very limited importance because most checks are deposited by the payee with a depositary bank for collection. The depositary bank gives the depositor provisional credit for the check. Under § 4–214(a), if the check is dishonored, the depositary bank may revoke the credit or otherwise obtain refund from the depositor. Normally, the depositary bank will use this remedy rather than the remedy provided by § 3–415(a).

If a draft is accepted by a bank after the draft is indorsed, the indorser is discharged. § 3–415(d). The rule is similar to § 3–414(c) with respect to the liability of a drawer. Thus, with respect to an accepted draft, an indorser has liability under § 3–415(a) only if the indorsement is made after the acceptance or if the acceptor is not a bank. Rules with respect to dishonor of accepted drafts are stated in § 3–502(d).

Notes

Dishonor of a note payable at a definite time does not normally require presentment unless the note is payable at or through a bank. § 3–502(a)(2) and (3). In the case of notes that do not require presentment, indorser's liability under § 3–415(a) arises automatically if the note is not paid when due. If a note is payable on demand, is payable at or through a bank, or the terms of the note require presentment, dishonor requires presentment and a failure to pay by the maker. But the requirements in § 3–502(a) with respect to presentment can be waived. § 3–504(a). Notice of dishonor required by § 3–503(a) also can be waived, and waiver of presentment is also waiver of notice of dishonor. § 3–504(b). Since most promissory note forms contain a clause waiving presentment and notice of dishonor, these formalities have little importance with respect to indorser liability in note cases.

C. LIABILITY OF TRANSFEROR

If goods are sold the law gives to the buyer the benefit of certain warranties of the seller that are implied by reason of the sale and which apply unless they are disclaimed in the contract between the parties. For example, the seller warrants that the buyer is receiving good title to the goods and, if the seller is a merchant, that the goods are fit for the ordinary purposes for which such goods are used. § 2–312(1) and § 2–314. If an instrument is sold the law gives to the buyer the benefit of implied warranties that are comparable to sale of goods warranties, but which are expressed in terms appropriate to what the buyer is buying—a right to receive payment from the person obliged to pay the instrument. These warranties are known as "transfer warranties" and are stated in § 3–416(a).

Two of the transfer warranties relate to the authenticity of the instrument; the transferor warrants that all signatures are authentic and authorized and the instrument has not been altered. § 3–416(a)(2) and (3). The other three warranties relate to the enforceability of the instrument. Under § 3–416(a)(1) there is a warranty that the transferor is a person entitled to enforce the instrument. If the transferor is a person entitled to enforce the instrument, transfer will give the transferee that right. § 3–203(b). The § 3–416(a)(1) warranty, in practice, serves as a warranty that there are no unauthorized or missing indorsements that prevent the transferor from giving to the transferee the right to enforce the instrument. Under § 3–416(a)(4) there is a warranty that the right to enforce the instrument is not subject to defenses that can be asserted against the transferor. Finally, there is a warranty of no knowledge of bankruptcy or other insolvency proceedings initiated against the person obliged to pay the instrument. § 3–416(a)(5).

The transfer warranties are of very limited importance because in most cases the transferor is also an indorser and, as such, guarantees payment of the instrument. § 3–415(a). In those cases the transfer warranties are redundant because the guarantee of payment gives greater rights to the transferee than do the warranties. Thus, the transfer warranties are important only in cases in which the transfer is made without indorsement or there is an indorsement without recourse. If the payee of a note indorsed the note without recourse, the transferee is assured of receiving an authentic and enforceable instrument but takes the risk that the maker will be unwilling or unable to pay the note.

D. CASHIER'S CHECKS AND TELLER'S CHECKS

1. USE IN PAYMENT OF OBLIGATIONS

In some transactions a creditor is unwilling to take the personal check of the debtor in payment of the obligation owed to the creditor. Instead, the creditor may insist on delivery by the debtor of the obligation of a bank as payment. The debtor can comply by delivering a cashier's check, a teller's check, or a check of the debtor that has been certified by the drawee. We have already discussed the certified check. Many banks have discontinued the practice of certifying checks. Cashier's checks and teller's checks have become the principal means of allowing a debtor to pay a debt with a bank obligation.

A cashier's check is a rather strange instrument. It is always issued by a bank and is in the form of an ordinary check, except that the drawer and the drawee are the same bank. Thus, Bank A orders itself to pay a sum of money to the payee stated in the instrument. One can justly argue that an order to oneself to pay money is fundamentally different from an order by one person to another person to pay money. In fact, the original Article 3, which did not specifically deal with cashier's checks, supports that argument in § 3–118(a) which states: "A draft drawn on the drawer is effective as a note." An order to oneself to pay money was given effect as a promise to pay money. The approach of revised Article 3 is somewhat different. Section 3–104(f) follows the universal banking practice of referring to a cashier's check as a check. This practice is also reflected in legislation other than Articles 3 and 4. Section 3–103(a)(6) defines "order" as a "written instruction to pay money" and artificially states that the "instruction may be addressed to anyone, including the person giving the instruction." Thus, a cashier's check is an order and, under § 3–104(e) and (f), is a draft and a check. The purpose of the artificiality in the definition of "order" was to allow references to drafts and checks in Article 3 to include cashier's checks. But the liability of the "issuer" (§ 3–105(c)) of a cashier's check is not stated in § 3–414(b) which applies to drawers of drafts. § 3–414(a). Rather, the liability of the issuer of a cashier's check is found in § 3–412 and is identical to the obligation of the maker of a note.

A teller's check, like a cashier's check, is always issued by a bank. The difference between the two is that a cashier's check is drawn on the issuing bank while a teller's check typically is drawn on another bank. In some cases a teller's check is drawn on a nonbank but is payable at or through a bank. § 3–104(h). The issuer of a teller's check is obliged to pay the check as drawer of the check. § 3–414(b). If a teller's check is issued by Bank A and the check is drawn on Bank B, presentment for payment of the check is made to Bank B, the drawee. As in the case of the drawee of an ordinary check, Bank B as drawee of a teller's check has no obligation to the payee to pay the check. § 3–408. If the check is dishonored, the remedy of the payee is against Bank A. Thus, a teller's check represents an obligation of the bank that issues the check, not of the bank on which it is drawn.

PROBLEMS

1. Buyer wants to buy goods from Seller. Seller insists that Buyer pay for the goods by a check issued by a bank. Buyer purchases a cashier's check issued by Bank A. Bank A issues the check either to the order of Buyer or to the order of Seller. In either case Bank A delivers the check to Buyer, who becomes the owner of the check. If the check is payable to Buyer when issued, Buyer will also become the holder of the check. If the check is payable to Seller, Buyer is the "remitter" of the check rather than its holder. § 3–103(a)(11). In either case, Buyer can negotiate the check to Seller. If the check is payable to Buyer, negotiation requires the indorsement of Buyer and delivery to Seller. If the check is payable to Seller, negotiation occurs by delivery alone. § 3–201.

On April 1, Seller delivers the goods to Buyer immediately after the check is negotiated to Seller. The check is deposited in Seller's account in Seller's bank. On April 2, the check is presented for payment and is dishonored because Bank A suspended payments on that day. § 4–104(a)(12). The dishonored check is returned by Bank A to Seller's bank and then to Seller.

If the cashier's check received by Seller was payable to the order of Buyer when issued, what cause of action does Seller have against Buyer (a) on the dishonored check, and (b) on the obligation of Buyer to pay the price of the goods delivered to Buyer? § 2–607(1) and § 3–310(a).

If the cashier's check received by Seller was payable to the order of Seller when issued, what cause of action does Seller have against Buyer?

2. The facts are the same as in Problem 1, except as follows: The check was not a cashier's check. Rather, it was a teller's check issued by Bank A and drawn on Bank B. The check when issued was payable to the order of Seller. On April 2, the check

was presented for payment to Bank B which refused payment because Bank A suspended payments on that day. The dishonored check was returned by Bank B to Seller's bank which then returned the check to Seller.

What cause of action does Seller have against Bank A because of dishonor of the check? What cause of action does Seller have against Bank B because of dishonor of the check? Does Seller have any cause of action against Buyer?

3. The facts are the same as in Problem 1 except as follows: Buyer did not purchase a cashier's check to pay for the goods. Rather, Buyer paid for the goods by delivery of an uncertified personal check of Buyer drawn on Bank A to the order of Seller. The check was dishonored by Bank A and returned by Bank A to Seller's bank which then returned the check to Seller.

What cause of action does Seller have against Buyer (a) on the dishonored check, and (b) on the obligation of Buyer to pay the price of the goods delivered to Buyer? § 3–310(b)(1) and (3).

2. PAYMENT WITH NOTICE OF ADVERSE CLAIM

Suppose a buyer pays for goods by delivering the buyer's uncertified personal check to the seller. Shortly after the goods are delivered, the buyer examines them and decides that they are unsatisfactory. The buyer seeks to return the goods to the seller and obtain return of the check. The seller denies that the goods are defective and refuses to return the buyer's check. Or, suppose there is a fraudulent sale. The seller took the buyer's check after promising to deliver the goods, but the seller had no intention of carrying out the promise. No goods were ever delivered to the buyer. In either of these two cases the best remedy of the buyer is to prevent the drawee of the check from paying the check. Without that remedy the buyer has the burden of bringing an action against the seller. If the buyer can prevent payment of the check, it is the seller who has the burden of bringing an action. The buyer can prevent payment of an uncertified check of the buyer if the buyer can act very quickly. The check issued by the buyer to the seller functions as an order by the buyer to the buyer's bank to pay money to the seller. Section 4–403 allows the buyer to countermand that order by what is referred to as a "stop-payment order," which is simply an instruction to the bank not to pay the check. A stop-payment order may be given orally or in writing and must describe the check with reasonable certainty so that the bank can identify the check. The bank is obliged to carry out the order if it is received in time to allow the bank a reasonable opportunity to act on the order before the check is paid. § 4–403(a). Failure to carry out the order can give rise to an action for damages. § 4–403(c).

The remedy provided by § 4–403 is not available, however, if the buyer pays for the goods with a certified check, cashier's check, or teller's check. Section 4–403 applies to an "item [check] drawn on the customer's [buyer's] account." What are the rights of the buyer under § 4–403 if a certified check is delivered to the seller? A certified check, in form, is drawn on the customer's account, but it is not treated that way under § 4–403(a). The right of a customer to stop payment of a check is conditioned upon receipt by the bank of a stop-payment order "before any action by the bank with respect to the item described in Section 4–303." One of the actions referred to in § 4–303 is payment of the check. § 4–303(a)(2). Another is certification. § 4–303(a)(1). So far as the rights and obligations of the drawer are concerned, certification of a check is treated as the equivalent of payment. When the check is certified it is treated as an obligation of the certifying bank rather than an item drawn on the drawer's account. Thus, if the buyer delivers a certified check to the seller, no right to stop payment of the check ever arises.

If the buyer delivered a cashier's check or teller's check to the seller, the analysis under § 4–403 is somewhat different. A cashier's check or teller's check is not drawn on the buyer's account even though the buyer may have bought the check from the buyer's bank which obtained payment for it by debiting the buyer's account. Section 4–403 allows the buyer to stop payment of a check of the buyer, but does not allow the buyer to stop payment of a check issued by the buyer's bank. Comment 4 to § 4–403. Section 4–403 does not apply at all to a cashier's check because the obligation of the issuer is the same as the obligation of the issuer of a note. § 3–412. There is no instruction by one person to another that can be countermanded. Section 4–403 does apply to a teller's check. The issuer of a teller's check is like the drawer of an ordinary check. The bank issuing the teller's check draws the check on the account of the issuer in the drawee bank. The issuer is a customer of the drawee bank. § 4–104(a)(5). Thus, under § 4–403, the issuer of the teller's check has a right to stop payment by the drawee bank. But that right belongs only to the issuer of the check; the buyer has no right to stop payment.

The rights of a buyer who has paid a seller with a cashier's check and who either has been defrauded or has received defective goods are considered in the following problem.

PROBLEM

Seller agreed to sell goods to Buyer but insisted on immediate payment by means of a cashier's check. Buyer had an account in Bank. At the request of Buyer, Bank issued a cashier's check payable to the order of Seller and delivered it to Buyer. Bank debited the account of Buyer in the amount of the cashier's check.

Buyer delivered the check to Seller, but Seller failed to deliver the promised goods stating that they would be delivered as soon as they became available. Buyer stated that Seller had promised immediate delivery and demanded return of the check. Seller refused.

a. Immediately before Buyer delivered the check to Seller, was Buyer the owner of the check? At that time was Buyer a "person entitled to enforce" the check? § 3–301. If Buyer had not delivered the check to Seller, would Buyer be entitled to return the check to Bank and obtain refund from Bank of the amount Buyer paid Bank? § 1–103.

b. After Seller refused to return the check, did Buyer have a claim to the check that could be asserted against Seller? § 3–306, § 3–202(b), § 3–201(a), and Comment 2 to § 3–201. If Buyer had a claim to the check, could that claim be asserted against a holder in due course to whom Seller negotiated the check? § 3–306.

c. After Seller refused to return the check, Buyer asked Bank to refuse payment of the check. Buyer informed Bank of all of the facts with respect to the negotiation of the check to Seller and asserted that Seller had deceived Buyer in order to obtain possession of the check. Buyer demanded that Bank return the money that Buyer paid for the check. Does Bank have to return the money it received from Buyer for the check? If Seller presents the check for payment, does Bank satisfy its obligations with respect to the check by paying Seller? § 3–602. If Seller presents the check for payment, may Bank refuse payment on the ground that Buyer has a claim to the check that is enforceable against Seller? § 3–305(c) (first sentence) and Comment 4 to § 3–305. If Seller presents the check for payment and Bank refuses payment, what rights does Seller have against Bank? § 3–412 and § 3–411. If Bank tells Buyer that it intends to pay the check when it is presented for payment, what can Buyer do to prevent Bank from paying? § 3–305(c), § 3–602(b)(1), and § 3–411(c)(iv).

3. LOST INSTRUMENTS

We have seen that the person obliged to pay an instrument can obtain discharge by paying the holder even if some other person has a claim to the instrument. The discharge can be asserted against anyone other than a person with rights of a holder in due course who took the instrument without notice of the discharge. § 3–601(b). If the instrument is surrendered when payment is made, there is no risk that the instrument will be negotiated to a holder in due course. But we have also seen that in some cases the person entitled to enforce the instrument is not in possession of the instrument. § 3–301. Although payment to a person entitled to enforce who does not have possession results in discharge (§ 3–602(a)), there is the possibility that the instrument is in existence and has or will come into the possession of a holder in due course. Section 3–309 deals with enforcement of lost instruments. Suppose the payee indorses the instrument in blank and then loses it. The payee can enforce the instrument, but § 3–309(b) requires the court to find that the person required to pay the instrument is "adequately protected against loss that might occur by reason of a claim by another person to enforce the instrument." The predecessor of § 3–309 is § 3–804 of the original Article 3 which provided that "the court may require security indemnifying the defendant against loss by reason of further claims on the instrument." The quoted language in § 3–804 was not uniformly adopted. Some states, including New York, changed the language in their versions of Article 3.

Since § 3–309 deals with enforcement, it can be used only by a person entitled to enforce under § 3–301. Although § 3–309 and its predecessor, former § 3–804, apply to any instrument, most lost instrument problems arise with respect to cashier's checks, teller's checks, and certified checks. Section 3–312, which has no predecessor, applies only to these bank obligations and can be used as an alternative to § 3–309. But in some cases a person with rights under § 3–312 does not have rights under § 3–309 because the person is not a person entitled to enforce the instrument. In that category are remitters of cashier's checks or teller's checks and drawers of certified checks who cannot enforce the lost check but who can use § 3–312 to obtain refund from the bank that issued or certified the check.

Diaz, which follows, was decided under the New York version of § 3–804 of the original Article 3. It involved loss of a certified check by the payee of the check.

DIAZ v. MANUFACTURERS HANOVER TRUST CO.

New York Supreme Court, Queens County, Special Term, 1977.
92 Misc.2d 802, 401 N.Y.S.2d 952.

MARTIN RODELL, JUSTICE.

The petitioner moves by order to show cause to require the respondent Manufacturers Hanover Trust Company to pay the sum of $37,000 or in the alternative to require the respondent Al Newman to issue a new negotiable instrument to her in the same amount.

The facts are uncontroverted. The petitioner posted the sum of $37,000 as security for a bond in behalf of a defendant in a criminal proceeding. Said security was posted with the respondent Newman, a licensed bail bondsman.

The aforementioned criminal action was concluded on July 20, 1977. Subsequently, the petitioner made demand upon the respondent Newman for the sum of $37,000, which she had heretofore posted with him. On August 4, 1977 the respondent Newman dutifully delivered to the petitioner two certified checks, in the amounts of $12,000 and $25,000, drawn on the respondent Manufacturers Hanover Trust Company. Shortly thereafter, the petitioner lost, misplaced, or was criminally relieved of the said certified checks and has to this date been unable to locate them.

The petitioner notified the respondent Newman, who, in turn, requested that the respondent Manufacturers Hanover Trust Co. stop payment. To this date, the checks have not been presented to Manufacturers Hanover Trust Co. for payment.

The petitioner also contacted an unnamed officer of the respondent Manufacturers Hanover Trust Co., who informed her that the bank would not honor any replacement checks issued by the respondent Newman unless an indemnity bond was posted in twice the amount of the original checks. The petitioner avers that this is an onerous and unjust burden; justifiably so, as it would require the posting of $74,000 as security.

* * * When a bank certifies a check, it accepts that check and has the obligation to pay the amount for which it is drawn. * * * The bank in certifying a check obligates itself to an innocent holder in due course to pay the amount for which the check is drawn. Thus, the respondent Manufacturers Hanover Trust Co., through its act of certification, assumed liability on the instruments.

> The owner of an instrument which is lost, whether by destruction, theft or otherwise, may maintain an action in his own name and recover from any party liable thereon upon due proof of his ownership, the facts which prevent his production of the instrument and its terms. The court shall require security, in an amount fixed by the court not less than twice the amount allegedly unpaid on the instrument, indemnifying the defendant, his heirs, personal representatives, successors and assigns against loss, including costs and expenses, by reason of further claims on the instrument, but this provision does not apply where an action is prosecuted or defended by the state or by a public officer in its behalf. L.1962, c. 553; amended L.1963, c. 1003, § 9, eff. Sept. 27, 1964 (Uniform Commercial Code, § 3–804.)

While it is clear that the petitioner has the right to recover the amount of the checks upon sufficient proof that in fact the checks did at one time exist, were payable to her and cannot be produced, the issue to be decided is presented to this court as follows:

May the court order payment on a lost negotiable instrument without requiring the payee to post security as required in Uniform Commercial Code, § 3–804? In 487 Clinton Avenue v. Chase Manhattan Bank, 63 Misc.2d 715, 313 N.Y.S.2d 445 (1970, Supreme Court, Kings County), the payee of a certified check was robbed of same at gun point and offered to pay the proceeds into an account controlled by the certifying bank. The court held that it had discretion to fix the security and that the security offered by the plaintiff was adequate.

The court notes that no appeal has been taken from the above decision, and thus no Appellate Court guidance is available. However, the Supreme Court in New York County in Guizani v. Manufacturers Hanover Trust, N.Y.L.J. October 12, 1971, p. 2, col. 5, held that under New York's version of this section (Uniform Commercial Code, § 3–804), the furnishing of the security is mandatory and not discretionary.

The section, as drawn by the drafters of the Uniform Commercial Code, and found in the Official Text and Official Commentaries, made the requirement for security discretionary with the court by the use of the word *"may."* The Official Commentaries to the Uniform Commercial Code state as follows:

> "There may be cases in which so much time has elapsed, or there is so little possible doubt as to the destruction of the instrument and its ownership that there is no good reason to require the security."

The court, in 487 Clinton Avenue v. Chase Manhattan Bank, supra, predicated its decision on the above reasoning. However, the New York version of section 3–804 of the Uniform Commercial Code pointedly changed the word "may" to "shall," and the Legislature in 1964 further amended this section to fix the amount of security to be not less than twice the amount allegedly unpaid on the instrument. * * * Thus, our Legislature appears to have considered the matter and amended the statute to make the furnishing of security not only mandatory but has also set the minimal amount at not less than twice the amount allegedly unpaid on the instrument.

* * *

The New York Commission Commentaries on section 3–804 of the Uniform Commercial Code leave little doubt that the express purpose of the Legislature was to make the furnishing of security mandatory rather than discretionary and thus conform to section 333 of the old Civil Practice Act.

* * *

If the court is to have the authority to determine the amount of security to be furnished, it would seem on the basis of the legislative history of this section that the change must come from the Legislature.

The court notes additionally that this section, as enacted by our Legislature, while being most positive in regard to the requirement of security and the amount thereof, fails to set any limit whatsoever as to the amount of time the security shall remain posted. The problem of the longevity of a certified check no doubt rendered the Legislature unable to fix a time limit. There being no legislative scheme to either limit the life of a certified check or the duration of time for which a bond must be posted, an unfortunate gap exists into which the petitioner's prayer must fall. It is the opinion of this court that further revision of this section of the Uniform Commercial Code is mandated, or in the alternative, legislation dealing with the valid life of certified checks must be enacted. Simple justice cries out for remedial legislation at the next session of the Legislature. The petitioner is being deprived of her life savings; the bank receives no benefit from the funds which are necessarily frozen. Under the present posture of the law, the funds will remain in that condition until the end of time or it escheats to the state, whichever comes first.

In light of the above, the court is constrained to reject the petitioner's application for recovery without posting of security as required by section 3–804 of the Uniform Commercial Code.

* * *

PROBLEMS

Section 3–312 was drafted in response to the hardship suffered by people like Diaz who have the misfortune to lose a cashier's, teller's, or certified check or to have such a check stolen from them. How does § 3–312 resolve the following problems? Comment 4 to § 3–312.

Claimant lives in New York and has her life savings amounting to almost $100,000, in First Bank. She decides to retire and move to Miami Beach to be near her sister. In anticipation of the move she obtained a cashier's check, dated January 2, from First Bank for $90,000 payable to her order. Her deposit account was immediately debited for $90,000.

1. Thief stole Claimant's purse on January 5 and it contained the cashier's check. The check was not indorsed by Claimant. She immediately called First Bank and asked that payment be stopped. An employee explained to her that if she would come in and sign a form asserting a claim to the check she could get her money back 90 days after the date of the check, but if she wanted her money immediately she would have to provide a bond to protect the bank. § 3–309. Having no resources to obtain a bond, Claimant went to First Bank on January 6 and signed a form asserting her rights under § 3–312(b). Included in the form was a declaration of loss complying with § 3–312(a)(3). Thief forged Claimant's signature as an indorsement of the cashier's check and deposited the check in his account in Second Bank on January 8. The check was promptly presented to First Bank for payment. First Bank paid the check. Thief withdrew the proceeds of the check from his account in Second Bank and absconded. Ninety days after the date of the check, Claimant demanded payment of

$90,000 from First Bank. What are Claimant's rights against First Bank if it refuses to pay? If First Bank pays, what are its rights against Second Bank?

2. Change the facts in Problem 1. When First Bank issued the check to Claimant, she indorsed the check by writing her name on the back. She then mailed the check to her sister in Miami Beach who had agreed to deposit it in her account until Claimant could arrive and open her own account. The check was stolen from the mail by Thief who deposited it in his account in Second Bank. By January 10, Claimant realized that something had happened to the check. On that date she went to First Bank and requested that payment be stopped. She was given the same information that was given in Problem 1 and on January 10 executed the necessary form to claim her rights under § 3–312(b). On January 11 Second Bank presented the check to First Bank for payment. First Bank paid the check. Ninety days after the date of the check, Claimant sought $90,000 from First Bank and it refused to pay. What are Claimant's rights against First Bank?

3. Change the facts in Problem 2 in one respect. The check was deposited by Thief in Second Bank on May 10. Second Bank promptly presented the check to First Bank for payment. At the time the check was presented for payment First Bank had already paid $90,000 to Claimant because 90 days had elapsed since the date of the check. First Bank dishonored the check. What are Second Bank's rights against First Bank and Claimant?

E. ACCOMMODATION PARTIES

1. LIABILITY OF ACCOMMODATION PARTY AND RIGHTS AGAINST ACCOMMODATED PARTY

A creditor taking the promissory note of a debtor who is not a good credit risk may require that a third party act as guarantor of the debtor's obligation to pay the note. Sometimes this guaranty is expressly stated. In many cases, however, a person who intends to act as guarantor does not expressly state that intention and signs the note as co-maker or indorser. For example, Son wants to buy equipment from Dealer for use in Son's business venture. Dealer is willing to sell to Son on credit only if Mother signs the note as co-maker along with Son. Two people who sign a note as co-makers are jointly and severally liable to pay the note. § 3–412 and § 3–116(a). Thus, if the note is not paid at the due date, Dealer as holder can enforce payment for the full amount against either Son or Mother or both. If two people are jointly and severally liable to pay an obligation and one of the obligors pays the entire amount, the normal rule, in the absence of a contrary agreement between the two obligors, is that the burden is shared equally by the two obligors. This principle of equal sharing is expressed as a right of the obligor who pays the obligation to receive "contribution" from the other obligor. § 3–116(b). The contribution rule is based on the assumption that the joint obligation was incurred for the joint benefit of the two obligors and that each should contribute equally in the payment of the obligation. But this assumption is not true if Mother did not have any property interest either in Son's business venture or in the equipment for which the note was given. There is a suretyship relationship between Son and Mother. Generically, Mother is referred to as the "surety" and Son is referred to as the "principal" or "principal debtor." In Article 3, the terminology is different. Mother is the "accommodation party," Son is the "accommodated party," and the note is signed by Mother "for accommodation." § 3–419(a).

Mother, as accommodation party, has certain rights against Son. If Son doesn't pay the note when due and Mother has to pay, it is only fair that she be entitled to recover from Son the full amount that she paid. He got the full benefit of the transaction that gave rise to the note and therefore should have to bear the full burden. Otherwise, Son would be unjustly enriched at the expense of Mother. Instead of having the normal right of contribution from a co-obligor, Mother has a right of "reimbursement" for the amount she paid and has subrogation rights as well. By subrogation she succeeds to the rights that Dealer had against Son on the note. § 3–419(e). When she pays the note she can require its surrender by Dealer (§ 3–501(b)(2)) and becomes the person entitled to enforce the note. § 3–301. Thus, if a note is secured by a security interest in collateral, the accommodation party who pays the note succeeds to the rights of the creditor with respect to the security interest (§ 9–504(5)) and is entitled to a formal transfer of the note and security interest. Reimann v. Hybertsen, 275 Or. 235, 550 P.2d 436 (1976).

If Son pays the note when due, Son has no right of contribution against Mother because she did not benefit from the transaction. § 3–419(e) and § 3–116(b).

Any type of instrument can be signed for accommodation and an accommodation party could sign as maker, drawer, acceptor, or indorser, but in the typical case the instrument is a note and the accommodation party signs either as maker or indorser. We have examined the function of indorsement in the negotiation of an instrument and that is its primary function, but an indorsement can also be made for the purpose of incurring liability on the instrument. § 3–204(a). In most cases, the negotiation and liability purposes coincide, but in some cases only one is present. For example, if an instrument is payable to an identified person, negotiation requires indorsement by the holder. § 3–201(b). But the holder can negotiate the instrument without incurring liability as an indorser by indorsing without recourse. § 3–415(b). The purpose of the indorsement is negotiation, not liability. An indorsement for accommodation is the converse. Because it is not made by the holder of the instrument, it has no negotiation function and is referred to in § 3–205(d) as an "anomalous indorsement." Its only purpose is to impose liability on the indorser.

The predecessor to § 3–419 is § 3–415 of the original Article 3. It is discussed in the following case.

FITHIAN v. JAMAR

Court of Appeals of Maryland, 1979.
286 Md. 161, 410 A.2d 569.

COLE, JUDGE. The dispute in this case involves the rights and liabilities of co-makers of a note in a suit among themselves, where none of the disputants is a holder of the note. We granted certiorari to consider two questions, which simply stated are:

　　1.　Whether a co-maker of a note was also an accommodation maker of the note and thus not liable to the party accommodated;

　　2.　Whether the agreement of one co-maker to assume another co-maker's obligation on a note constitutes a defense to the latter when sued for contribution by the former.

In 1967 Walter Fithian (Walter) and Richard Jamar (Richard), who were employed as printers at Baltimore Business Forms, decided to form a partnership to carry on their own printing business. They applied to the People's Bank of Chestertown, Maryland (Bank) for an $11,000 business loan to enable them to purchase some equipment. The Bank agreed to lend the money to Walter and Richard only if Walter's wife, Connie, Richard's wife, Janet, and Walter's parents, Walter William (Bill) and Mildred Fithian would co-sign the note. The Executive Vice-President of the Bank explained that the additional signatures were required to make the Bank more secure. The note, which authorized confession of judgment in the event of default, was signed on its face in the bottom right-hand corner by these six parties. The monies loaned were deposited in Walter and Richard's business checking account and were used to purchase printing equipment.

By 1969, Walter and Richard were encountering business problems. They spoke with Frank Hogans (Hogans) and Gerald Bos (Bos) (who were interested in joining the business) about forming a corporation to be called J–F Printing Co., Inc. and refinancing the note so that it (the note) could become a corporate rather than an individual obligation. The business continued to falter and on March 23, 1972 Walter, Richard, Hogans and Bos met and entered into a written agreement in their individual capacities whereby Richard was to take over management and ownership of the business in exchange for his assumption of liability for the company's outstanding obligations, one of which was the note in question in this case. The agreement also provided that should Richard default in the performance of those obligations, Walter, Hogans, and Bos would have the right to terminate the agreement and resume ownership of the business.

Pursuant to the agreement Richard assumed control of the business but was unable to make any further payments on the note. Consequently, the Executive Vice-President of the Bank requested that Bill and Mildred Fithian pay the note in full. They did and the Bank assigned the note to them for whatever disposition they might choose. Bill demanded that Richard indemnify him for the total amount Bill paid on the note.

Receiving no satisfaction from Richard, Bill and Mildred sought judicial relief. On November 10, 1976, a confessed judgment against Richard and Janet of $8,953.95, the balance on the note paid by Bill and Mildred, with interest from January 18, 1974 * * * was entered in the Circuit Court for Kent County. Richard and Janet filed a motion to vacate the judgment, which the circuit court granted and ordered a hearing on the merits. Prior to trial, Richard and Janet filed a third party claim against Walter and Connie averring that as co-makers of the note, Walter and Connie were liable to Richard and Janet for any judgment that Bill and Mildred might recover against Richard and Janet. Walter and Connie counterclaimed contending that the agreement barred Richard's recovery.

The matter was brought to trial on August 25, 1977 before the circuit court, sitting without a jury. The court found that the J–F Printing Company, Inc. was never a de jure corporation and that those who attempted to act under that name were merely acting in their individual capacities; that the March 23, 1972 agreement was not material to the determination of the case; that Bill and Mildred were accommodation makers for Richard, Janet, Walter and Connie and were entitled to collect from any one of the four.

Final judgment was entered on September 6, 1977 for Bill and Mildred against Richard and Janet in the amount of $8,953.95, the principal sum due, plus $2,288.95, representing interest from January 18, 1974 to August 25, 1977. The court * * * entered a judgment for Richard and Janet on Walter and Connie's counterclaim. In the third party claim of Richard and Janet against Walter and Connie, judgment was entered for Richard and Janet in the amount of $5,621.45, fifty percent of the total judgment. * * *

In an unreported per curiam decision * * *, the Court of Special Appeals affirmed the circuit court's finding that Connie Fithian was a co-maker of the note, and not an accommodation party. The Court of Special Appeals also affirmed the trial court's finding that the March, 1972 agreement was not material to the case because it was "a private agreement between only two (2) of the six (6) makers of the note."

Walter and Connie requested review of these rulings in this Court, and we granted their petition for certiorari on June 21, 1978 to consider the two questions presented: whether Connie Fithian was an accommodation maker of the note and thus not liable to the party accommodated; and whether the March, 1972 agreement constitutes a defense to Richard and Janet's third party claim against Walter and Connie.

Our disposition of the questioned rulings requires us to reverse and remand. The error which occurred in the court below was caused in part by a failure to fully analyze the individual rights and obligations of Connie, Walter, Janet and Richard. Therefore, in the discussion which follows, in addition to examining the two questions presented, we will clarify the resulting rights and obligations of these parties.

Richard v. Connie

Since there is no dispute that Connie signed the note, the answer to the first question depends on her purpose in doing so. This is made clear by * * * § 3–415(1) of the Uniform Commercial Code which provides that an accommodation party is "one who signs the instrument in any capacity for the purpose of lending his name to another party to it." The undisputed evidence as presented by the Executive Vice-President of the Bank was to the effect that the wives' signatures were required before the Bank would make the loan to Walter and Richard. Such practices are common among lending institutions which recognize that

> [o]ne with money to lend, goods to sell or services to render may have doubts about a prospective debtor's ability to pay. In such cases he is likely to demand more assurance than the debtor's bare promise of payment. The prospective creditor can reduce his risk by requiring some sort of security. One form of security is the Article 9 security interest in the debtor's goods. Another type of security takes the form of joining a third person on the debtor's obligation. [J. White and R. Summers, Uniform Commercial Code § 13–12, at 425 (1972)].

It is readily apparent, therefore, that Connie lent her name to facilitate the loan transaction. As such she lent her name to two parties to the instrument, Richard and Walter, to enable them to receive a *joint* loan for the purchase of equipment for their printing business, thereby giving the Bank the added assurance of having another party to the obligation. Connie signed as an accommodation party as to both Walter and Richard.

Nor is there any merit in the argument advanced by Richard that Connie must be either a co-maker or an accommodation party, that she cannot be both. The actual language of § 3–415(1) indicates that an accommodation party also signs in a particular capacity, as maker, acceptor or indorser of an instrument. The Official Comment 1 to § 3–415 explains that

> [s]ubsection (1) recognizes that an accommodation party is always a surety (which includes a guarantor), and it is his only distinguishing feature. He differs from other sureties only in that his liability is on the instrument and he is a surety for another party to it. His obligation is therefore determined by the capacity in which he signs. An accommodation maker or acceptor is bound on the instrument without any resort to his principal, while an accommodation indorser may be liable only after presentment, notice of dishonor and protest.

Moreover, § 3–415(2) refers specifically to the liability of an accommodation party "in the capacity in which he has signed." It follows, therefore, that the fact that Connie was a co-maker of the note does not preclude her from also being an accommodation party.

Section 3–415(5) states that "[a]n accommodation party is not liable to the party accommodated"; thus, Connie is not liable to Richard. Our predecessors, prior to Maryland's adoption of the Uniform Commercial Code, explained the reasons for this proposition in Crothers v. National Bank, 158 Md. 587, 593, 149 A. 270, 273 (1930):

> Since the accommodating party lends his credit by request to the party accommodated upon the assumption that the latter will discharge the debt when due, it is an implied term of this agreement that the party accommodated cannot acquire any right of action against the accommodating party.

Richard contends, however, that Connie intended to accommodate only her husband, Walter. Even if there were evidence to this effect (and there is none), the subjective intent of a co-maker of a note is of little weight when objective facts and circumstances unambiguously demonstrate the capacity in which the note was signed. ＊ ＊ ＊ It is clear to us that the signatures of both wives were required to effect this joint business venture and thus Connie's signature was as much an accommodation to Richard as it was to Walter. We hold that Connie was an accommodation maker and that she cannot be liable to Richard, the party accommodated. The Court of Special Appeals erroneously held to the contrary.

Janet v. Connie

The preceding discussion of Connie's status demonstrates that each of the four parties, Walter, Connie, Richard, and Janet, has certain rights and obligations with respect to this note which are not affected by his or her marital status. The court below erred in not fully analyzing these separate rights and obligations. It follows that our finding that Connie has no liability to Richard in no way changes any obligation she may have to Janet. Janet, as well as Connie, is a co-accommodation maker on this note.

The question is therefore whether one co-accommodation maker who pays more than her proportionate share of the debt has a right of contribution against another co-accommodation maker. The Uniform Commercial Code contains no provision expressly dealing with the right of an accommodation party to contribution from another accommodation party. However, § 1–103 of the Code does provide that the principles of the common law remain applicable "[u]nless displaced by the particular provisions" of the Code.

That an accommodation maker has a right of contribution from a co-accommodation maker is a settled principle of the law. The Restatement of Security provides

> A surety who in the performance of his own obligation discharges more than his proportionate share of the principal's duty is entitled to contribution from a co-surety. [Restatement of Security § 149 (1941)].

* * *

This Court has not addressed this question in regard to a note controlled by the U.C.C. Our research revealed only one case which directly confronted the effect of the U.C.C. on the common law rule. The court stated that the U.C.C. does not change the rule of suretyship law permitting contribution by one surety from a co-surety. McLochlin v. Miller, 139 Ind.App. 443, 217 N.E.2d 50 (1966).

Accordingly Janet has a right of contribution against Connie. But this right to contribution is an inchoate claim which does not ripen into being unless and until Janet pays more than her proportionate share to Bill and Mildred. * * * Judgment can be entered on behalf of Janet against Connie, but it must be fashioned so that it may not be enforced until Janet proves she actually paid more than her proportionate share to Bill and Mildred.[1] * * *

---

1. A surety who is called upon to pay more than his proportionate share of the debt has a right of contribution from his co-sureties in an amount not to exceed each co-surety's proportionate share of the debt. * * * Here the note was signed by four sureties (Bill, Mildred, Connie and Janet); Janet's proportionate share of indebtedness to her co-sureties is 25% of the debt.

Richard v. Walter

[Omitted is the portion of the opinion in which the court held that Richard's agreement in 1972 to assume all liabilities of the printing business, including the note, precluded any right of contribution that Richard would otherwise have against Walter, his joint obligor on the note.]

Janet v. Walter

That the 1972 agreement serves as a defense by Walter against Richard in no way serves to insulate Walter against Janet. Janet's status as an accommodation maker is unaffected by the agreement. As an accommodation maker, Janet has a right to look to any principal, including Walter for any amounts she actually pays. * * * Janet's status as Richard's wife does not affect her status as an accommodation maker. She is entitled to judgment from either principal when she actually pays any amount of the debt.

In summary, Richard is not entitled to judgment against Walter because of the agreement. Rather, Walter is entitled to indemnification from Richard for any amount Walter is forced to pay. Richard is not entitled to judgment against Connie because an accommodation party is not liable to the party accommodated. Janet is entitled to contribution from her co-surety, Connie, the judgment being unenforceable unless and until Janet proves she actually has paid more than her proportionate share of the debt to Bill and Mildred. Similarly, Janet as a surety is entitled to judgment against Walter as a principal for any amount of the debt for which Janet proves payment.[3]

NOTE

In footnote 3 the court states that it does not decide whether Bill and Mildred were entitled to recover the full amount of the debt from Janet. How much were Bill and Mildred entitled to recover from Janet?

PROBLEM

X owned 50% of the capital stock of Corporation and was its President. Y and Z each owned 25%. Corporation needed money for working capital and borrowed it from Bank which insisted as a condition to the loan that X sign the note because of the precari-

---

3. Whether Bill and Mildred were entitled to judgment in the full amount of the debt against Janet we do not decide because Janet did not appeal from that judgment.

ous financial condition of Corporation. The note was signed as
follows:

> Corporation
> By X, President
> X, individually

The loan, which is unsecured, was made by crediting the
entire principal amount to Corporation's account with Bank and
was used entirely for corporate purposes. Corporation has defaulted on the loan. After Corporation's default on the loan to
Bank, X paid Bank the entire unpaid balance amounting to
$10,000. Is X an accommodation party? Is X entitled to reim-
bursement from Corporation for the $10,000 paid to Bank or are
X's rights limited to a claim for contribution? Would X's rights be
any different if X owned 100% of the stock of Corporation rather
than 50%?

2. SURETYSHIP DEFENSES

A surety, in addition to having rights against the principal
debtor, also has certain rights which can be asserted against the
creditor seeking enforcement of the surety's obligation to pay the
debt. These rights are usually referred to as "suretyship defenses." Suretyship defenses relate to changes in the obligation of
the principal debtor without the consent of the surety. For
example, a surety guarantees performance of the principal debtor
as buyer under a contract of sale of coal to be supplied on credit by
a seller. The seller and the principal debtor agree to amend the
contract so that it refers to fuel oil rather than coal. The surety
didn't agree to the amendment. If the principal debtor fails to
pay for fuel oil purchased under the amended contract and the
seller demands payment, the surety has a complete defense. The
surety's obligation related to a contract of the principal debtor to
buy coal not fuel oil. The seller and the principal debtor cannot
impose a new contract on the surety. Restatement, Security
§ 128(b). But in some cases it cannot be said that the creditor and
the principal debtor have attempted to impose an entirely new
contract on the surety. There might be only some modification of
the contract. In those cases the existence of a defense may be
justified only if the modification causes loss to the surety. A few
examples illustrate the problem. The principal debtor borrows
money from a lender. The debt is payable with interest and is
secured by a security interest in personal property of the principal
debtor. After the suretyship relationship arises, the lender agrees
with the principal debtor to an amendment of the debt obligation
as follows: (1) the amendment changes the interest rate; or (2) it
extends the due date of the debt; or (3) it releases some of the
collateral that secures the debt; or (4) it releases the principal
debtor from any personal obligation to pay the debt. In each of

these cases, if the surety does not agree to the change it may be unfair to allow the lender to enforce the surety's obligation to pay if, at the time the change was made, the lender had knowledge of the suretyship relationship. The suretyship defenses are intended to protect the surety by providing that in some cases a change in the terms of the debt may result in a total or partial discharge of the surety.

The suretyship defenses with respect to negotiable instruments are stated in § 3–605. These defenses are not identical to suretyship defenses that may apply under the general law of suretyship with respect to obligations other than negotiable instruments. Section 3–605 gives defenses to accommodation parties and to indorsers whether or not they are accommodation parties. Subsection (f) of § 3–605 gives a defense to a co-maker of a secured note in some cases even if the co-maker is not an accommodation party.

PROBLEM

In each of the following cases Corporation borrowed money from Bank and the proceeds of the loan were paid to Corporation and used solely in the conduct of the business of Corporation. Corporation has three stockholders, Doe, Roe, and Poe, each of whom owns one-third of the stock. Doe and Roe manage the business of Corporation. Poe is a passive investor who takes no part in managing Corporation. The loan was made to Corporation by Bank in exchange for a negotiable note payable to the order of Bank and signed by Corporation as maker. Doe and Roe signed on behalf of Corporation as its authorized officers. Poe also signed the note as co-maker at the request of Bank.

Case # 1

Assume the following facts. The note was not secured by a security interest. $50,000 was owed on the note when it became due. At that time Doe and Roe informed Bank that Corporation was unable to pay the full amount. They also informed Bank that if Bank initiated any proceedings to collect the note, Corporation would file in bankruptcy. Doe and Roe explained that they wanted to avoid bankruptcy and were willing to settle the obligation of Corporation on the note by paying a part of the amount owed. Bank and Corporation then signed an agreement providing for payment by Corporation to Bank of $20,000 in full satisfaction of Corporation's obligation on the note. The payment was made and Bank executed a release of all rights of Bank against Corporation on the note. Poe did not consent to this transaction. Bank then demanded that Poe pay the remaining $30,000 due on the note.

If Poe pays $30,000 to Bank, what rights does Poe have against Corporation? § 3–419(e) and § 3–604(a). If Poe refuses to pay Bank, is Bank entitled to recover from Poe the amount due on the note? § 3–419(b), § 3–412, § 3–605(b), Comment 3 to § 3–605.

Case # 2

Assume the following facts: The note was secured by a perfected security interest in collateral owned by Corporation. The collateral consisted of two pieces of equipment (Machine # 1 and Machine # 2) used in the business of Corporation. On behalf of Corporation, Doe and Roe asked Bank to release its security interest in Machine #2 and to permit Corporation to sell Machine # 2 for cash. They explained to Bank that they intended to use the proceeds of the sale to buy a more modern piece of equipment which would be substituted for Machine # 2 as collateral for the loan. Bank agreed. Poe did not consent to the release of the security interest by Bank or to the sale of Machine #2. Corporation made the sale for $40,000 cash, but the $40,000 was not used to buy substitute equipment. Rather, it was used to pay various debts of Corporation. No substitute for Machine # 2 was ever acquired by Corporation. Later, Corporation filed in bankruptcy. At that time $50,000 was owed on the note and Machine # 1 had a net resale value of $30,000. Corporation is insolvent and no money will be available for payment of unsecured claims in the bankruptcy. Bank demanded that Poe pay the $50,000 due on the note.

If Poe pays $50,000 to Bank and then files a claim in the bankruptcy, how much will Poe receive in the bankruptcy? § 3–419(e) and § 9–504(5). If Poe refuses to pay Bank and Bank brings an action against Poe to enforce the note, how much is Bank entitled to recover from Poe? § 3–419(b), § 3–412, § 3–605(e) and (g), § 9–306(2), Comment 6 to § 3–605. How much is Bank entitled to recover from Poe if the note included a clause as follows: "All signers of the note are principals and not accommodation parties, guarantors, or other sureties?" § 3–605(i) and Comments 2 and 8 to § 3–605.

Case # 3

Assume the following facts: The note was not secured by a security interest. The note had a stated due date which was one year after the date it was issued. Shortly before the due date, Doe and Roe informed Bank that Corporation did not have sufficient cash to pay the note on the due date. They also stated that if Bank initiated any proceedings to collect the note, Corporation would file in bankruptcy. Doe and Roe asked Bank to extend the due date of the note. Corporation and Bank then signed an agreement under which the due date of the note was extended for a period of two years in return for an agreement by Corporation to pay interest during the two-year period at a rate higher than the rate stated in the note. Poe did not consent to the agreement between Bank and Corporation. About a year after this agreement was signed Corporation filed a petition in bankruptcy. No money will be available for payment of unsecured claims in bankruptcy. At the time of the bankruptcy the note was unpaid. Bank demanded payment from Poe.

Does Poe have any defense against Bank? § 3–605(c), § 3–605(d), and Comments 4 and 5 to § 3–605.

F. SIGNATURES BY REPRESENTATIVES

A person is not liable on an instrument unless the instrument is signed personally by that person or by a representative who is authorized to sign for that person. § 3–401(a). Whether a representative is authorized to sign for a represented person is determined by general principles of the law of agency. § 3–402(a). Consider this case: Employer, an individual, has a checking account in Bank which is used to pay obligations incurred in Employer's business. Employer follows the practice of personally signing all checks, except that Employer authorizes Employee to sign Employer's name to checks during extended absences of Employer. Bank has paid all checks drawn on Employer's account whether Employer's name was written in Employer's handwriting or that of Employee. Employer never objected to the payment by Bank of any check on which Employer's name was written by Employee. On one occasion Employer was about to leave town and instructed Employee to pay all invoices arriving during Employer's absence except invoices of John Doe. In violation of these instructions Employee writes a check on Employer's account to John Doe in payment of a bill that Doe submitted. Employee's act of signing Employer's name to that particular check is not authorized by Employer in the sense that Employer never assented to it, but Employer nevertheless may be bound by the signature. The question of whether the signature is binding on Employer is determined by the law of agency. In our example, the probable result under agency law is that Employer is bound because Employee, although lacking actual authority to sign the Doe check, had apparent authority to do so because Employee had general authority to sign checks. In that event, under § 3–401(a) and § 3–402(a), the signature by Employee is effective as the authorized signature of Employer.

Signatures by agents on behalf of principals occur most often with respect to the obligations of organizations such as corporations whose signatures are made by its officers or employees. Two problems arise. First, there is the question of whether the corporation is bound by the signature of the officer or employee. Second, there is the question of whether the officer or employee also becomes a party to the instrument by signing it on behalf of the principal. If it is clear that an agent is signing on behalf of a named principal, only the principal is bound. But sometimes it is not clear whether the agent's signature is in behalf of the principal or whether it is made to impose liability on the officer as an accommodation party.

The problem of ambiguous signatures by representatives is governed by § 3–402(b) and (c). The following case considered the problem under § 3–403(2) of the original Article 3.

WEATHER–RITE, INC. v. SOUTHDALE PRO–BOWL, INC.

Supreme Court of Minnesota, 1974.
301 Minn. 346, 222 N.W.2d 789.

KELLY, JUSTICE. Plaintiff, Weather-Rite, Inc., brought this action as payee on a promissory note given by Southdale Pro-Bowl, Inc., against defendant Frank Buetel, an officer of Southdale whom plaintiff alleges is an individual endorser of the note. The trial court, over plaintiff's continuing objection, admitted parol evidence concerning the execution of the note and its endorsements, and concluded that defendant had endorsed the note as an officer and agent of Southdale and not in his individual capacity. Plaintiff appeals from an order denying a motion for a new trial. We affirm.

The note in question was a preprinted form. On the maker's signature line was the typewritten name of the corporate debtor, "Southdale Pro-Bowl, Inc." On the line below, one of its officers, John Dorek, signed his name and representative capacity, "President." On the third line, defendant's signature, "Frank Buetel," appears without indication of agency status.[1] The signatures of these men also appear on the reverse side of the note: "John H. Dorek, Pres." and "Frank Buetel."

1. The significant issue raised by this appeal is whether parol evidence was properly admitted in the court below. The controlling statute, UCC § 3–403(2), provides:

"An authorized representative who signs his own name to an instrument

(a) is personally obligated if the instrument neither names the person represented nor shows that the representative signed in a representative capacity;

(b) except as otherwise established between the immediate parties, is personally obligated if the instrument names the person represented but does not show that the representative signed in a representative capacity, or if the instrument

---

1. Plaintiff concedes that Buetel signed the note as a maker in his capacity as an officer of Southdale Pro-Bowl, Inc.

does not name the person represented but does show that the representative signed in a representative capacity."

Plaintiff contends that, since neither the defendant's representative capacity nor the principal on whose behalf defendant allegedly acted is shown in the endorsement, parol evidence of agency status should have been excluded. A further argument is made that the Minnesota case law is in accord with the code. This court in Giltner v. Quirk, 131 Minn. 472, 155 N.W. 760 (1915), did hold that evidence of parol contemporaneous agreement to vary the effect of an endorsement of a promissory note is inadmissible. However, in *Giltner* this court noted that there were exceptions to that rule.

Defendant argues that this situation should be an exception to the parol evidence rule applicable to the immediate parties, as provided for in UCC § 3–403(2)(b).

If plaintiff were a holder in due course of the note in question, we would have no difficulty in agreeing that parol evidence would be inadmissible under UCC § 3–403(2)(a). But where only the immediate parties are involved, the issue is less clear. There are few decisions, none of them identical to this case. One of the closest is Central Trust Co. v. J. Gottermeier Development, 65 Misc.2d 676, 677, 319 N.Y.S.2d 25, 26 (1971). The facts and holding of that case are briefly summarized in the following excerpts from the decision:

> "Plaintiff is the holder of a note * * * payable to its order * * * made by the defendant corporation and signed by John B. Gottermeier as its president. On the reverse side of the note the signature of 'John B. Gottermeier' appears under a printed guarantee agreement. * * *

> "John B. Gottermeier claims that his endorsement was made in his capacity as president of the defendant corporation and not as an individual, that he is not personally obligated on the note, and that parol evidence is admissible on the trial to prove the foregoing. Neither the name of the corporation, which he claims he represented, nor the nature of the representative capacity, in which he claims he acted, appears on the portion of the instrument which bears his indorsement. Under these facts, he is personally obligated by reason of his indorsement of the note, and parol evidence is inadmissible to prove that he indorsed the note in a representative capacity."

While this may be a sound position, there is a critical distinction between the facts of that case and ours. The presence on the reverse side of the note of the signature, "John H. Dorek, Pres.," shows at least a possibility that the immediate parties understood that defendant, too, was signing in a representative capacity. Since this dispute is restricted to the immediate parties, the endorsement, ambiguous when viewed in its complete context,

should be clarified by parol evidence of the circumstances surrounding its execution.[2] To this end, the trial court was correct in
overruling plaintiff's objection to the admission of parol evidence.

   2. The issue of sufficiency of the evidence to support the trial
court's finding that defendant endorsed the note as a corporate
officer rather than individually requires a brief statement of the
facts. The note in question had its genesis in a contract between
Weather-Rite and Southdale for installation of air-conditioning
equipment at the latter's bowling alley. In payment for the
completed work, a promissory note dated April 9, 1969, and
payable in six installments, was executed in favor of plaintiff in
the principal amount of $6,039. On April 21, 1969, a corporate
officer of plaintiff met with defendant and obtained his signature
below that of Dorek on both the front and back of the note.
According to testimony at the trial, defendant signed twice in one
continuous act after the plaintiff's officer said, "we need your
signature on here as an officer of the corporation." While there
was some testimony to the contrary, we cannot interfere with the
trial court's findings where the evidence, taken as a whole, furnishes substantial support for them. 1B Dunnell, Dig. (3 ed.)
§ 411. Such is the case with the trial court's finding that defendant executed the endorsement as an officer and agent of
Southdale Pro-Bowl, Inc., and not in an individual capacity.

   Affirmed.

NOTES

   1. Section 3–402(b) of Revised Article 3 is substantially different from § 3–403(2) of the pre–1990 Code which was involved in
Weather–Rite. In *Weather–Rite*, Buetel was allowed to introduce
evidence that his apparent personal indorsement was in fact an
indorsement by Southdale made by Buetel as a representative of
Southdale. The basis of the court's conclusion was that Buetel's
signature was ambiguous. But was it in fact ambiguous? An
indorsement by the maker of a note serves no purpose whatsoever.
If Buetel was asked to sign the note on the reverse side where
indorsements normally appear and Buetel's name was not accompanied by the name of Southdale, would it be reasonable for

   2. This position has the support of
the Permanent Editorial Board for the
Uniform Commercial Code. The board
filed a brief as amicus curiae in this
case, and came to the following conclusion:

   "In the present case, the form of
the note itself raises doubt. If the
payee wanted the individual liability
of the two officers of Southdale, why
did it accept the indorsement: 'John
H. Dorek, Pres.'? On the other hand,

if Buetel thought he was signing only
as an officer of Southdale, why did he
not add to his signatures something
to show he was vice president? Anyone looking at the present note will
have at least some shadow of doubt
cross his mind, and since the plaintiff
is the payee, all of the parties should
be allowed to tell their stories. There
is a factual question which should be
resolved by a jury, or a judge sitting
without a jury."

anyone to suppose that the signature might be an indorsement by Southdale of the note? In concluding that Buetel's signature was ambiguous the court was influenced by the fact that Dorek also signed on the reverse side of the note and identified himself as a representative by using the word "Pres." Suppose Dorek had not signed on the reverse side of the note. Would this have changed the result in *Weather–Rite?* Would the presence or absence of Dorek's signature affect the result in *Weather–Rite* if the case were decided under § 3–402(b) of Revised Article 3? Comment 2 to § 3–402. If the signature by Buetel on the reverse side of the note does not make sense as an intended indorsement by Southdale, can it be explained as anything other than a signature intended to make Buetel personally liable? Analysis based on an assumption of rational and informed behavior by Buetel may not produce the right result. The officer of Weather–Rite who obtained Buetel's signature may not have understood its significance or may have been seeking personal liability of Buetel without making full disclosure about the significance of the signature. It may be that the court in *Weather–Rite* believed that Buetel in signing his name to the note was unaware of the precise legal effect of his signature and that he should not be held to a liability that Weather–Rite had not openly bargained for. According to the court, "defendant signed twice in one continuous act after plaintiff's officer said, 'we need your signature on here as an officer of the corporation'." Revised Article 3 takes the view that the representative should always be allowed to prove the intent of the parties at the time the signature was made if the person asserting liability of the representative is an immediate party to the note.

2. American, a corporation, owed Disneyland $93,000 on open account. Disneyland insisted that the indebtedness be evidenced by ten promissory notes which it prepared. The notes did not mention American. Schwartz, the president of American, signed his name to the notes without adding any other words. Thus, there was no indication that he was signing in a representative capacity. Schwartz by affidavit stated that he, acting on behalf of American, and Disneyland agreed that the notes were to be obligations of American. Schwartz also swore that he mistakenly signed the notes thinking that he was carrying out this agreement. Disneyland by affidavit stated that when Schwartz executed the notes by simply signing his name to them it "elected to treat the executed Notes as a counter offer which it accepted" and to treat the notes as a guaranty by Schwartz of American's indebtedness. American paid four of the notes and then defaulted. In an action by Disneyland against Schwartz as maker of the notes it was held that under the original § 3–403(2), as a matter of law, Schwartz was personally liable. The court dismissed Schwartz's counterclaim for reformation of the notes to substitute

American for Schwartz as maker of the notes. Schwartz v. Disneyland Vista Records, 383 So.2d 1117 (Fla.App.1980). On similar facts, the Washington Supreme Court was more sympathetic to the defendant's plight and allowed reformation. St. Regis Paper Co. v. Wicklund, 93 Wn.2d 497, 610 P.2d 903 (1980). How would these cases be decided under Revised Article 3? § 3–402(b) and § 3–117.

  3. In Griffin v. Ellinger, 538 S.W.2d 97 (Tex.1976), the following facts were presented. Griffin was president of Greenway Bldg. Co., Inc. and was authorized to draw checks on the corporate bank account on behalf of Greenway. Greenway was indebted to Ellinger for labor and materials supplied by Ellinger to Greenway on a construction project. Griffin wrote three checks to Ellinger in payment of the debt. Each check was drawn on Greenway's bank account and Greenway's name and address was conspicuously printed on the heading of the check. However, Greenway's name was not printed above the signature line of the check. Griffin signed his name on the signature line without addition of any words indicating his status as president or other representative of Greenway. The bank on which the checks were drawn refused payment because there were insufficient funds in Greenway's account to cover the amount of the checks. Ellinger then brought an action against Griffin to recover the amount of the checks. The theory of the action was that Griffin was personally liable as drawer of the checks. Griffin argued that each check showed conclusively on its face that Griffin was signing in a representative capacity only and that Greenway rather than Griffin was the drawer. The court held Griffin personally liable as drawer. The court stated:

>   The first question is whether the draft shows on its face that Griffin signed in a representative capacity only. Although the draft clearly names the person represented, it does not show that Griffin signed only in his capacity as president of Greenway. Griffin contends, however, that considering the instrument as a whole, and taking into account the normal business usage of personalized checks, it should be apparent from the instrument itself that Griffin signed only as an authorized agent of Greenway. We disagree. We recognize that it is unusual to demand the individual obligation of a corporate officer on checks drawn on the corporate account, and that the more usual way of obtaining the personal obligation of an officer on such a check would be by endorsement. Business practice and usage are proper factors to be considered in construing the particular instrument under consideration. We also recognize that an instrument may disclose on its face that a signature was executed only in a representative capacity even though the particular office or position of the signer is not disclosed thereon. Pollin v. Mindy Manufactur-

ing Co., 211 Pa.Super. 87, 236 A.2d 542 (1967), cited by petitioner, is such a case. In *Pollin,* the plaintiff, a holder in due course of checks drawn on a corporate account, sued the signer of the checks, an agent of the corporation, asserting his personal liability as drawer. The checks, issued to pay employees of the corporation, were stamped with the name of the company and the designation "Payroll Checks"; the company name was also printed above the two signature lines in the lower right-hand corner. The defendant had signed under this printed name without designating his office or capacity. The court held, nevertheless, that the instrument considered as a whole showed that the signer was signing only in a representative capacity:

> In the present instance the checks clearly showed that they were payable from a special account set up by the corporate defendant for the purpose of paying its employees. This information disclosed by the instrument itself would refute any contention that the appellant intended to make the instrument his own order on the named bank to pay money to the payee.

236 A.2d at 545.

Unlike the checks in *Pollin,* we can find nothing on the face of the checks in the present case to show that Griffin intended to sign only in a representative capacity. Petitioner points out that each check is stamped by a "check protector," which imprinted not only the amount of the draft but also the company's name. Although the stamp clearly reveals the name of the principal, it does not aid petitioner because it gives no information as to the capacity in which *he* signed the instrument.

How would *Griffin* be decided under Revised Article 3? § 3–402(c) and Comment 3 to § 3–402.

G. ACCORD AND SATISFACTION

COUNTY FIRE DOOR CORP. v. C.F. WOODING CO.

Supreme Court of Connecticut, 1987.
202 Conn. 277, 520 A.2d 1028.

PETERS, CHIEF JUSTICE.

The principal issue in this appeal is whether the Uniform Commercial Code modifies the common law of accord and satisfaction so that a creditor can now effectively reserve his rights against a debtor while cashing a check that the debtor has

explicitly tendered in full satisfaction of an unliquidated debt.
* * *

The trial court's articulation and the exhibits at trial establish the following facts. On November 17, 1981, the defendant ordered a number of metal doors and door frames from the plaintiff. The plaintiff undertook responsibility for delivery of the goods to the worksite. Alleging that the plaintiff's delay in delivery of the doors and frames had caused additional installation expenses, the defendant back charged the plaintiff an amount of $2180. The defendant informed the plaintiff that, on the basis of this back charge, and other payments and credits not at issue, the remaining balance due the plaintiff was $416.88. The plaintiff responded by denying the validity of this back charge. According to the plaintiff, the balance due on its account was $2618.88. The defendant immediately replied, in writing, that it would stand by its position on the validity of the back charge and the accuracy of its calculation of the amount owed to the plaintiff.

The defendant thereafter, on January 10, 1983, sent the plaintiff the check that is at the heart of the present controversy. The check was in the amount of $416.88. It bore two legends. On its face was the notation:

" 'Final payment
Upjohn Project
Purchase Order # 3302 dated 11/17/81.' "

On the reverse side, the check stated: "By its endorsement, the payee accepts this check in full satisfaction of all claims against the C.F. Wooding Co. arising out of or relating to the Upjohn Project under Purchase Order # 3302, dated 11/17/81." The plaintiff did not advise the defendant directly that it planned to cash this check under protest. Instead, the plaintiff crossed out the conditional language on the reverse side of the check and added the following: "This check is accepted under protest and with full reservation of rights to collect the unpaid balance for which this check is offered in settlement." The plaintiff then indorsed and deposited the check in its account.

The defendant made no further payments to the plaintiff and the plaintiff brought the present action to recover the remaining amount to which it claimed it was entitled. The trial court rendered judgment for the plaintiff on two grounds. The court agreed with the plaintiff that the enactment of § 1–207 had deprived debtors generally of the power unilaterally to enforce the terms of a conditional tender of a check to their creditors. Furthermore, in the specific circumstances of this case, the court concluded that the plaintiff could rightfully treat the defendant's offer of an accord as if it had been a payment on account, because the amount of the tender had been no more than the amount the defendant itself had calculated to be due and owing to the plaintiff. For these reasons, the court awarded the plaintiff $2100 as the unpaid balance of the account.

The defendant's appeal does not contest the monetary calculation used by the court in arriving at the amount of the judgment against the defendant, but maintains instead that the trial court erred because the plaintiff's cause of action was foreclosed as a matter of law. The defendant maintains that, when the plaintiff knowingly cashed a check explicitly tendered in full satisfaction of an unliquidated debt, the plaintiff became bound by the terms of settlement that the check contained. The defendant's argument takes issue with both aspects of the contrary ruling of the trial court. First, the defendant claims that the plaintiff's action of cashing this check constituted an acceptance of its offer, including its terms of settlement, despite the plaintiff's reliance on § 1–207 for authority to substitute words of protest for words of satisfaction. Second, the defendant claims that the amount that it tendered the plaintiff constituted a valid offer of an accord and satisfaction because the underlying debt was unliquidated in amount. We agree with both of the defendant's claims. We will, however, take them up in reverse order, because we would not reach the statutory issue if the defendant had failed to establish its common law defense to the plaintiff's cause of action.

I

When there is a good faith dispute about the existence of a debt or about the amount that is owed, the common law authorizes the debtor and the creditor to negotiate a contract of accord to settle the outstanding claim. Such a contract is often initiated by the debtor, who offers an accord by tendering a check as "payment in full" or "in full satisfaction." If the creditor knowingly cashes such a check, or otherwise exercises full dominion over it, the creditor is deemed to have assented to the offer of accord. Upon acceptance of the offer of accord, the creditor's receipt of the promised payment discharges the underlying debt and bars any further claim relating thereto, if the contract of accord is supported by consideration. * * *

A contract of accord and satisfaction is sufficiently supported by consideration if it settles a monetary claim that is unliquidated in amount. This court has had numerous occasions to decide whether, in the context of accord and satisfaction, a claim is unliquidated when the debtor tenders payment in an amount that does not exceed that to which the creditor is concededly entitled. "Where it is admitted that one of two specific sums is due, but there is a dispute as to which is the proper amount, the demand is regarded as unliquidated, within the meaning of that term as applied to the subject of accord and satisfaction * * *. Where the claim is unliquidated any sum, given and received in settlement of the dispute, is a sufficient consideration." Hanley Co. v. American Cement Co., 108 Conn. 469, 473, 143 A. 566 (1928); * * *

Application of these settled principles to the facts of this case establishes, as the defendant maintains, that the parties entered into a valid contract of accord and satisfaction. The defendant offered in good faith to settle an unliquidated debt by tendering, in full satisfaction, the payment of an amount less than that demanded by the plaintiff. Under the common law, the plaintiff could not simultaneously cash such a check and disown the condition on which it had been tendered. * * * Having received the promised payment, the plaintiff discharged the defendant from any further obligation on this account, unless the enactment of § 1–207 of the Uniform Commercial Code has changed this result.

II

The principal dispute between the parties is what meaning to ascribe to § 1–207 when it states that "[a] party who with explicit reservation of rights * * * assents to performance in a manner * * * offered by the other party does not thereby prejudice the rights reserved. Such words as 'without prejudice,' 'under protest' or the like are sufficient." The plaintiff contends, as the trial court concluded, that this section gave the plaintiff the authority to cash the defendant's check "under protest" while reserving the right to pursue the remainder of its underlying claim against the defendant at a later time. The defendant maintains that the statutory reference to "performance" contemplates something other than the part payment of an unliquidated debt. We noted in Kelly v. Kowalsky, 186 Conn. at 622 and n. 3, 442 A.2d 1355, that there was considerable disagreement in the cases and the scholarly commentaries about the scope of the transactions governed by § 1–207, but did not then undertake to resolve this disagreement. We now decide that § 1–207 does not displace the common law of accord and satisfaction and that the trial court erred in so concluding.

Because § 1–207 is part of the Uniform Commercial Code, it is important to reconcile its provisions with those found in other articles of the code. * * *

Two likely candidates for such a reconciliation are the provisions of article 3, dealing generally with the law of negotiable instruments, including checks * * * and the provisions of article 2, dealing generally with contracts for the sale of goods. * * *

Article 3 provides little support for reading § 1–207 to permit a creditor unilaterally to change the terms of a check tendered in full satisfaction of an unliquidated debt. As the parties have noted, § 3–112(1)(f) preserves the negotiability of a check that includes "a term * * * providing that the payee by indorsing or cashing it acknowledges full satisfaction of an obligation of the drawer." There is no such validation, anywhere in article 3, for a term on a check that negates a condition that a drawer has incorporated in a negotiable instrument. On the contrary, § 3–407 takes a dim view of the unauthorized alteration of an instrument. Under § 3–407(1) "[a]ny alteration of an instrument is material which changes the contract of *any* party thereto in *any* respect * * *." (Emphasis added.) The effect of the material alteration of a completed instrument is either to discharge the liability, on the instrument, of "any party whose contract is thereby changed," or to continue the enforceability of the instrument "according to its original tenor." § 3–407(2) and (3). According to this section, the plaintiff's conduct in substituting words of protest for words of satisfaction would have put the plaintiff at risk of discharging the defendant entirely, if such conduct were deemed to have been fraudulent. § 3–407(2)(a). Even without a finding of fraud, however, the most for which the plaintiff could hope, under article 3, was to enforce the instrument "in full satisfaction," because that was "its original tenor." This result is supported by § 3–802(1)(b), which provides that, presumptively, the taking of a negotiable instrument suspends the underlying obligation "until the instrument is due," and that "discharge of the underlying obligor on the instrument also discharges him on the obligation." Under § 3–603(1), a drawer is discharged from liability on an instrument "to the extent of his payment or satisfaction."

The impact of these various article 3 rules is clear. Because the check tendered by the defendant was only enforceable "according to its original tenor," the plaintiff, by receiving "payment or satisfaction," discharged the defendant not only on the instrument but also on the underlying obligation. See J. White & R. Summers, Uniform Commercial Code (2d Ed.1980) pp. 603–604 n. 57. To read § 1–207 to validate the plaintiff's conduct in this case would, therefore, fly in the face of the relevant provisions of article 3, which signal the continued vitality of the common law principles of accord and satisfaction.

Although § 1–207 does not fit easily within the principles of article 3 that govern checks, the section has a close and harmonious connection with article 2. Article 2 regulates ongoing conduct relating to performance of contracts for the sale of goods. That article recurrently draws inferences from acquiescence in, or objection to, the performance tendered by one of the contracting parties. A course of performance "accepted or acquiesced in without objection" is relevant to a determination of the meaning of a contract of sale. § 2–208(1). Between merchants, proposals for additional terms will be added to a contract of sale unless there is a timely "notification of objection." § 2–207(2)(c). A buyer who is confronted by a defective tender of goods must make a seasonable objection or lose his right of rejection. §§ 2–602(1), 2–605, 2–606(1), 2–607(2); * * * In an instalment sale, a party aggrieved by nonconformity or default that substantially impairs the value of the contract as a whole will nonetheless have reinstated the contract "if he accepts a nonconforming instalment without seasonably notifying of cancellation * * *." § 2–612(3). A contract whose performance has become impracticable requires the buyer, after notification by the seller, to offer reasonable alternatives for the modification or the termination of the affected contract; the buyer's failure to respond, within a reasonable period of time, causes the sales contract to lapse. § 2–616(1) and (2). In these and other related circumstances, article 2 urges the contracting parties to engage in a continuing dialogue about what will constitute acceptable performance of their sales contract. See generally J. White & R. Summers, supra, §§ 3–1 through 3–9. It is entirely consistent with this article 2 policy to provide, as does § 1–207, a statutory methodology for the effective communication of objections. See J. McDonnell, "Purposive Interpretation of the Uniform Commercial Code: Some Implications for Jurisprudence," 126 U.Pa.L.Rev. 795, 828 (1978).

From the vantage point of article 2, it is apparent that § 1–207 contemplates a reservation of rights about some aspect of a possibly nonconforming tender of goods or services or payment in a situation where the aggrieved party may prefer not to terminate the underlying contract as a whole. * * * A. Rosenthal, "Discord and Satisfaction: Section 1–207 of the Uniform Commercial Code," 78 Colum.L.Rev. 48, 63 (1978). Indeed, the Official Comment to § 1–207 itself explains that the section supports ongoing contractual relations by providing "machinery for the continuation of performance along the lines contemplated by the contract despite a pending dispute." See W.D. Hawkland, "The Effect of U.C.C. § 1–207 on the Doctrine of Accord and Satisfaction by Conditional Check," 74 Com.L.J. 329, 331 (1969). It is significant, furthermore, that the text of § 1–207 recurrently refers to "performance," for "performance" is a central aspect of the sales transactions governed by article 2. By contrast, article 3 instruments, which promise or order the payment of money, are not characteristically described as being performed by anyone. The contracts encapsulated in various forms of negotiable instruments instead envisage conduct of negotiation or transfer, indorsement or guaranty, payment or acceptance, and honor or dishonor. See, e.g., §§ 3–201, 3–413, 3–414, 3–416, 3–418; see generally J. White & R. Summers, supra, §§ 13–6 through 13–10, 13–12. We conclude, therefore, that, in circumstances like the present, when performance of a sales contract has come to an end, § 1–207 was not intended to empower a seller, as payee of a negotiable instrument, to alter that instrument by adding words of protest to a check tendered by a buyer on condition that it be accepted in full satisfaction of an unliquidated debt.

Our conclusion is supported by the emerging majority of cases in other jurisdictions. While the case law was divided five years ago, when we postponed resolution of the controversy about the meaning of § 1–207; Kelly v. Kowalsky, supra, 186 Conn. at 621–22, 442 A.2d 1355; it is now the view of the substantial majority of courts that have addressed the issue that § 1–207 does not overrule the common law of accord and satisfaction. * * * The majority finds support as well in much of the recent scholarly commentary. See 2 Restatement (Second), Contracts (1981) § 281, comment d; R. Anderson, Uniform Commercial Code (1984) § 3–408–56; W. Grosse & E. Goggin, supra, 546; W.D. Hawkland, supra, 331; J. McDonnell, supra, 824–28; A. Rosenthal, supra, 61; contra, J. Calamari & J. Perillo, Contracts (2d Ed.1977) § 5–16; J. White & R. Summers, supra, § 13–21.

Both under prevailing common law principles, and under the Uniform Commercial Code, the parties in this case negotiated a contract of accord whose satisfaction discharged the defendant from any further monetary obligation to the plaintiff. The plaintiff might have avoided this result by returning the defendant's check uncashed, but could not simultaneously disregard the condition on which the check was tendered and deposit its proceeds in the plaintiff's bank account.

There is error, the judgment is set aside and the case is remanded with direction to render judgment for the defendant.

NOTES

1. Revised Article 3 deals with accord and satisfaction in § 3–311. At the time Revised Article 3 was promulgated, § 1–207 was also amended by adding a new subsection (2) as follows:

> (2) Subsection (1) does not apply to accord and satisfaction.

A new Comment 3 to § 1–207 was also added.

2. Effectuating an accord and satisfaction of a disputed claim by a "full satisfaction" legend on a check is a cheap and fast way in which to settle a claim. Section 3–311(a) and (b) provide that, as a general rule, if the legend on the check is conspicuous and the claim is subject to a bona fide dispute, the claimant cannot obtain payment of the check without agreeing to the accord and satisfaction. If the claimant wishes to avoid settlement for the amount of the check, it must not cash the check. As Comment 1 to § 3–311 points out, accord and satisfaction by use of notations on checks is useful to consumers in disputes about the quality of goods or services purchased, but it is also commonly employed by insurance companies to settle claims of insured parties. Section 3–311(c)(1)

addresses a problem encountered by organizations like large retailers and other high volume recipients of checks who find it
burdensome and wasteful to conduct a visual search of tens of
thousands of checks to see if a handful contain a proposed accord
and satisfaction legend. This provision allows such an organization to notify its customers to send any communications concerning disputed debts, including checks containing full satisfaction
legends, to a specified address at which these checks and other
communications can be examined and decisions made with respect
to whether to accept them as settlement of claims. This allows
the retailer to rapidly process other checks without examination
to detect accord and satisfaction language. Section 3–311(c)(2) is
an alternative to § 3–311(c)(1) which is also designed to prevent an
inadvertent accord and satisfaction. It is explained in Comment 6
to § 3–311.

Chapter 8

PAYMENT SYSTEMS

A. CHECK COLLECTION

---

1. TIME CHECK IS PAID BY PAYOR BANK

---

a. THE MIDNIGHT DEADLINE

Article 4 governs the rights and obligations of banks and their customers with respect to the collection of checks by the banking system, but the Federal Reserve Board has always played a very important role in check collection. This role has been expanded by Regulation CC, 12 C.F.R. § 229, issued pursuant to the Expedited Funds Availability Act of 1987, 12 U.S.C. § 4001 et seq. We discuss the impact of Regulation CC on pp. 656–660.

The next two cases in this book discuss the issue of when, under Article 4, the bank on which a check is drawn is deemed to have paid the check. This issue is presented in its most simple form if the payee of a check takes it to the drawee bank and asks for payment in cash over the counter. The check is paid when the bank gives cash equal to the amount of the check to the payee. § 4–215(a)(1). But that case is not at all typical. Very few checks are paid in cash. Almost all checks are deposited to a bank account of the holder of the check. To understand how Article 4 applies to checks deposited in a bank it is necessary to understand the concept of settlement in Article 4. § 4–104(a)(11) and § 4–213. Typically, in the check-collection process, each bank that takes a check pays for it at, or shortly after, the time that the check is taken. Article 4 uses the terms "settlement" and "settle" to refer to this act of paying for the check. But to say that a bank has settled or paid for a check is not the same as saying that the bank has paid the check. The bank on which a check is drawn is referred to in Article 4 as the payor bank. § 4–105(3). The payor bank can pay the check, but any other bank giving value for the check may be buying the check but is not paying it. And even in the case of the payor bank there is a distinction between the bank's settling for the check and paying the check. For example, suppose the payee of a check deposits it to the payee's account in Bank A. The drawer of the check also has an account in Bank A

623

and the check is drawn on that account. In this case, Bank A is both the depositary bank with respect to the check and the payor bank. § 4–105(2) and (3). Bankers refer to this kind of check as an "on us" item. At or shortly after the time Bank A receives the check from the payee, Bank A will credit the account of the payee for the amount of the check. By making that credit Bank A settles for the check. § 4–104(a)(11) and § 4–213(a)(2)(iii). This settlement, however, is provisional in nature because Bank A has the right to revoke it under certain circumstances. At the time Bank A settles with the payee for the check, it usually does not know whether, as the payor bank, it should pay the check. For example, suppose the balance in the drawer's account in Bank A is not sufficient to cover the amount of the check. Bank A has no obligation to the payee of the check to pay the check (§ 3–408) and, if Bank A is not assured of reimbursement from the drawer of the check, Bank A normally would refuse to pay the check. Under Article 4, Bank A is given a time-limited right to revoke or recover the payment that it made to the payee when the payee's account was credited. § 4–301(a). The prescribed technique for accomplishing this result is to return the check to the payee and to debit ("charge-back") the payee's account in the amount of the check. As payor bank, Bank A "pays the check" if and when it has not exercised its right to recover a provisional payment that it has made and the right of recovery no longer exists. § 4–215(a)(3) and § 4–301(a). This practice of pay-first-take-back-later is in effect because it is operationally efficient. Since payor banks have reason to refuse payment with respect to only a tiny percentage of the vast number of checks that are processed each day for payment, it is sensible to pay for all checks as they are received ("settlement") and to deal later with the small number of checks that turn out to be bad by revoking the settlement and returning the checks.

A similar analysis applies with respect to the more common case in which the depositary bank is not also the payor bank. In that case the depositary bank is a collecting bank that acts as agent of the holder to obtain payment of the check. § 4–105(5). The depositary bank will either present the check directly to the payor bank or it will negotiate the check to an intermediary bank which acts as a collecting bank to obtain payment of the check. § 4–105(4) and (5). The intermediary bank is likely to be a Federal Reserve Bank and often there is more than one intermediary bank. Each collecting bank will give provisional settlement to the bank from which the check is received. The last collecting bank will present the check for payment to the payor bank which will give provisional settlement to the presenting bank. In transactions between banks settlement is normally made by a credit to the Federal Reserve account of the bank receiving the settlement. The payor bank may refuse payment of the check by returning it to the presenting bank and recovering the amount of the check from that bank. § 4–301(a). In turn the presenting bank and each collecting bank may return the check to the bank from which it received the check and recover the provisional payment. § 4–214(a). As discussed on pp. 656–660, Regulation CC requires payor and collecting banks to expedite the return of checks and authorizes them to return checks directly to the depositary bank or to any bank that has agreed to handle the checks for expeditious return to the depositary bank. Any bank returning the check may obtain the amount of the check from the bank to which the check is transferred. When the depositary bank receives the returned check it may recover the provisional payment given to the holder from whom it took the check for collection. § 4–214(a).

Blake, which follows, describes in more detail the time-limited right that Article 4 gives to a payor bank to return a check and recover any provisional settlement given for the check or to avoid liability to pay the check under § 4–302.

BLAKE v. WOODFORD BANK & TRUST CO.

Court of Appeals of Kentucky, 1977.
555 S.W.2d 589.

PARK, JUDGE.

This case involves the liability of * * * Woodford Bank and Trust Company on two checks drawn on the Woodford Bank and Trust Company and payable to the order of * * * Wayne Blake. Following a trial without a jury, the Woodford Circuit Court found that the bank was excused from meeting its "midnight deadline" with respect to the two checks. Blake appeals from the judgment of the circuit court dismissing his complaint. The bank cross-appeals from that portion of the circuit court's opinion relating to the extent of the bank's liability on the two checks if it should be determined that the bank was not excused from meeting its midnight deadline.

BASIC FACTS

The basic facts are not in dispute. On December 6, 1973, Blake deposited a check in the amount of $16,449.84 to his account at the Morristown Bank, of Morristown, Ohio. This check was payable to Blake's order and was drawn on the K & K Farm Account at the Woodford Bank and Trust Company. The check was dated December 3, 1973.

On December 19, 1973, Blake deposited a second check in the amount of $11,200.00 to his account in the Morristown Bank. The second check was also drawn on the K & K Farm Account at the Woodford Bank and Trust Company and made payable to Blake's order. The second check was dated December 17, 1973.

When Blake deposited the second check on December 19, he was informed by the Morristown Bank that the first check had been dishonored and returned because of insufficient funds. Blake instructed the Morristown Bank to re-present the first check along with the second check. Blake was a cattle trader, and the two checks represented the purchase price for cattle sold by Blake to James Knight who maintained the K & K Farm Account. Blake testified that he had been doing business with Knight for several years. On other occasions, checks had been returned for insufficient funds but had been paid when re-presented.

The two checks were forwarded for collection through the Cincinnati Branch of the Federal Reserve Bank of Cleveland. From the Federal Reserve Bank, the two checks were delivered to the Woodford Bank and Trust Company by means of the Purolator Courier Corp. The checks arrived at the Woodford Bank and Trust Company on Monday, December 24, 1973, shortly before the opening of the bank for business. The next day, Christmas, was not a banking day. The two checks were returned by the Woodford Bank and Trust Company to the Cincinnati Branch of the Federal Reserve Bank by means of Purolator on Thursday, December 27, 1973.

The two checks were received by the bank on Monday, December 24. The next banking day was Wednesday, December 26. Thus, the bank's "midnight deadline" was midnight on Wednesday, December 26. § 4–104(1)(h) [Revised § 4–104(a)(10)]. As the bank retained the two checks beyond its midnight deadline, Blake asserts that the bank is "accountable" for the amount of the two checks under § 4–302(1)(a) [Revised § 4–302(a)(1)].

HISTORY OF PAYOR BANK'S LIABILITY FOR RETAINING CHECK

Under the Uniform Negotiable Instruments Law a payor bank was not liable to the holder of a check drawn on the bank until the bank had accepted or certified the check. * * * Because of the payor bank's basic nonliability on a check, it was essential that some time limit be placed upon the right of the payor bank to dishonor a check when presented for payment. If a payor bank could hold a check indefinitely without incurring liability, the entire process of collection and payment of checks would be intolerably slow. To avoid this problem, a majority of courts construing § 136 and § 137 of the Uniform Negotiable Instruments Law held that a payor bank was deemed to have accepted a check if it held the check for 24 hours after the check was presented for payment. * * * Thus, in a majority of jurisdictions, the payor bank had only 24 hours to determine whether to pay a check or return it. However, in Kentucky and a few other jurisdictions, the courts held that § 136 and § 137 of the Uniform

Negotiable Instruments Law applied only to checks which were presented for acceptance. * * * Consequently, the payor bank would be liable on the check only if it held the check "for an unreasonable length of time" and could thus be deemed to have converted the check.

In order to bring uniformity to the check collection process, the Bank Collection Code was proposed by the American Bankers' Association. The Bank Collection Code was adopted by Kentucky in 1930. Under § 3 of the Bank Collection Code, a payor bank could give provisional credit when a check was received, and the credit could be revoked at any time before the end of that business day. The payor bank became liable on the check if it retained the item beyond the end of the business day received. * * *

Banks had only a few hours to determine whether a check should be returned because of insufficient funds. Banks were required to "dribble post checks" by sorting and sending the checks to the appropriate bookkeepers as the checks were received. This led to an uneven workload during the course of a business day. At times, the bookkeeping personnel might have nothing to do while at other times they would be required to process a very large number of checks in a very short time. * * * Because of the increasingly large number of checks processed each day and the shortage of qualified bank personnel during World War II, it became impossible for banks to determine whether a check was "good" in only 24 hours. The banks were forced to resort to the procedure of "paying" for a check on the day it was presented without posting it to the customer's account until the following day. See First National Bank of Elwood v. Universal C.I.T. Credit Corporation, 132 Ind.App. 353, 170 N.E.2d 238, at 244 (1960). To meet this situation, the American Banking Association proposed a Model Deferred Posting Statute. * * *

Under the Model Deferred Posting Statute, a payor bank could give provisional credit for a check on the business day it was received, and the credit could be revoked at any time before midnight of the bank's next business day following receipt. A provisional credit was revoked "by returning the item, or if the item is held for protest or at the time is lost or is not in the possession of the bank, by giving written notice of dishonor, nonpayment, or revocation; provided that such item or notice is dispatched in the mails or by other expeditious means not later than midnight of the bank's next business day after the item was received." * * * If the payor bank failed to take advantage of the provisions of the deferred posting statute by revoking the provisional credit and returning the check within the time and in the manner provided by the act, the payor bank was deemed to have paid the check and was liable thereon to the holder. * * *

The Model Deferred Posting Statute was the basis for the provisions of the Uniform Commercial Code. Under § 4–301(1) [Revised § 4–301(a)] of the Uniform Commercial Code (UCC), a payor bank may revoke a provisional "settlement" if it does so before its "midnight deadline" which is midnight of the next banking day following the banking day on which it received the check. Under the Model Deferred Posting Statute, the payor bank's liability for failing to meet its midnight deadline was to be inferred rather than being spelled out in the statute. Under UCC § 4–302, the payor bank's liability for missing its midnight deadline is explicit. If the payor bank misses its midnight deadline, the bank is "accountable" for the face amount of the check.

* * *

Like the Model Deferred Posting Statute, the Uniform Commercial Code seeks to decrease, rather than increase, the risk of liability to payor banks. By permitting deferred posting, the Uniform Commercial Code extends the time within which a payor bank must determine whether it will pay a check drawn on the bank. Unlike the Bank Collection Code or the Uniform Negotiable Instruments Law as construed by most courts, the Uniform Commercial Code does not require the payor bank to act on the day of receipt or within 24 hours of receipt of a check. The payor bank is granted until midnight of the next business day following the business day on which it received the check.

EXCUSE FOR FAILING TO MEET MIDNIGHT DEADLINE

UCC § 4–108(2) [Revised § 4–109(b)] provides:

"Delay by a * * * payor bank beyond time limits prescribed or permitted by this Act * * * is excused if caused by interruption of communications facilities, suspension of payments by another bank, war, emergency conditions or other circumstances beyond the control of the bank provided it exercises such diligence as the circumstances require."

The circuit court found that the bank's failure to return the two checks by its midnight deadline was excused under the provisions of UCC § 4–108.

The circuit court dictated its findings of fact into the record:

"From all of the evidence that was presented in this case, it would appear that there was no intentional action on the part of the bank to hold these checks beyond the normal course of business as an accommodation to its customer. In fact, the uncontroverted testimony of the bank officers was to the contrary. To say that the bank failed, through certain procedures, to return the checks by the midnight deadline does not, in the mind of this Court, imply or establish an intentional act on the part of the bank.

*   *   *   *   *   *   *   *   *

"In this instance we have the Christmas Holiday, which caused in the bank, as in all businesses, certain emergency and overloaded situations. This is not unique to the banking industry; but is true of virtually every business in a christian society, in which the holiday of Christmas is observed as the major holiday of the year. Special considerations are always given to employees as well as customers of these banking institutions.

" *   *   * On the Christmas Holiday, two machines were broken down for periods of time during this critical day in question. There was an absence of a regular bookkeeper."

Under CR 52.01, these findings of fact cannot be set aside by this court unless they are clearly erroneous. The foregoing findings are supported by the record, and are not questioned by Blake on the appeal.

After making findings of fact, the circuit court dictated the following conclusions into the record:

" *   *   * The entire cumulative effect of what happened would constitute diligence on the part of the bank, as circumstances required.

"It is the opinion of the Court and it is the Finding of the Court that the circumstances described by the banking officers, the standards of banking care, as described by expert witnesses, would bring the bank within 4–108(2), and the Court therefore, finds as a fact that there were circumstances here beyond the control of the bank, and that it exercised such diligence as those circumstances required."

When the circuit court concluded "that there were circumstances here beyond the control of the bank, and that it exercised such diligence as those circumstances required," the circuit court was doing no more than repeating the words of the statute. This court must determine whether the circuit court's findings of fact support these conclusions.

Before turning to the facts presented in this case, it is appropriate to discuss the only two cases involving the application of UCC § 4–108 to a payor bank's midnight deadline. In Sun River Cattle Co. v. Miners Bank of Montana, 164 Mont. 237, 521 P.2d 679 (1974), the payor bank utilized a computer in the adjacent town of Great Falls to process its checks. The checks were picked up at the Miners Bank by an armored car between 5:00 p.m. and 6:00 p.m. on the date of receipt. The checks would normally reach the computer center at Great Falls around 10:30 p.m. Ordinarily the checks would have been processed by 11:30 p.m., returned to the Miners Bank by 8:00 a.m. the next morning. The checks in question were received by the Miners Bank on May 11. On that day, the armored car broke down, and the checks did not reach the computer center at Great Falls until 1:30 a.m. the next morning, May 12. On that morning, the computer malfunctioned and the checks were not returned to the Miners Bank until 2:30 p.m. on May 12. There was no testimony as to what actually happened to the checks after they were received by the Miners Bank on the afternoon of May 12, but the Miners Bank failed to return the checks by midnight of May 12. The trial court held that the failure of the Miners Bank to meet its midnight deadline was excused by the provisions of UCC § 4–108(2). The Montana Supreme Court reversed, holding that the Miners Bank had failed to show the degree of diligence required under the circumstances. The Montana court pointed out that the Miners Bank had more than the normal interest in the activities in the account upon which the checks were drawn, and that due diligence could not be shown merely by following ordinary operating procedures.

In Port City State Bank v. American National Bank, 486 F.2d 196 (10th Cir.1973), the payor bank, American National, was changing from machine posting to computer processing of its checks commencing Monday, December 1, 1969. Two checks were in dispute. The first check arrived at American National on Friday, November 28, 1969. As Monday was the next banking day, the midnight deadline for the first check was December 1. The second check arrived on Tuesday, December 2, 1969, and the midnight deadline for that check was Wednesday, December 3. American National's new computer developed a "memory error" which rendered it unusable at 10:00 a.m. on December 1, the first day of computer operations. The computer manufacturer assured the bank that repairs would not take "too long." Unfortunately repairs and testing were not completed until the early hours of Tuesday, December 2. In the meantime, American National attempted to utilize an identical computer in a bank some two and a half hours away. Processing commenced at the other bank at 11:30 p.m. on December 1, and continued through the night. Although work proceeded to the point of "capturing" all of the items on discs, the backup computer was required by its owner, and the American National personnel returned to the bank to complete the printing of the trial balances. Another memory error developed in the new computer which again rendered the computer unusable. No further use could be made of American National's computer until a new memory module was installed on Thursday, December 4. The trial court held that the computer breakdown constituted a condition beyond the control of American National and that the bank had exercised due diligence. On appeal, the United States Court of Appeals affirmed, holding that the findings of the district court were not clearly erroneous.

* * *

The basic facts found by the circuit court can be summarized as follows: a) the bank had no intention of holding the checks beyond the midnight deadline in order to accommodate its customer; b) there was an increased volume of checks to be handled by reason of the Christmas Holiday; c) two posting machines were broken down for a period of time on December 26; d) one regular bookkeeper was absent because of illness. Standing alone, the bank's intention not to favor its customer by retaining an item beyond the midnight deadline would not justify the application of § 4–108(2). The application of the exemption statute necessarily will turn upon the findings relating to heavy volume, machine breakdown, and absence of a bookkeeper.

The bank's president testified that 4,200 to 4,600 checks were processed on a normal day. Because the bank was closed for Christmas on Tuesday, the bank was required to process 6,995 checks on December 26. The bank had four posting machines. On the morning of December 26, two of the machines were temporarily inoperable. One of the machines required two and one half hours to repair. The second machine was repaired in one and one half hours. As the bank had four bookkeepers, the machine breakdown required the bookkeepers to take turns using the posting machines for a time in the morning. One of the four bookkeepers who regularly operated the posting machines was absent because of illness on December 26. This bookkeeper was replaced by the head bookkeeper who had experience on the posting machines, although he was not as proficient as a regular posting machine operator.

Because of the cumulative effect of the heavy volume, machine breakdown and absence of a regular bookkeeper, the bank claims it was unable to process the two checks in time to deliver them to the courier from Purolator for return to the Federal Reserve Bank on December 26. As the bank's president testified:

> "Because we couldn't get them ready for the Purolator carrier to pick them up by 4:00 and we tried to get all our work down there to him by 4:00, for him to pick up and these two checks were still being processed in our bookkeeping department and it was impossible for those to get into returns for that day."

* * *

The increased volume of items to be processed the day after Christmas was clearly foreseeable. The breakdown of the posting machines was not an unusual occurrence, although it was unusual to have two machines broken down at the same time. In any event, it should have been foreseeable to the responsible officers of the bank that the bookkeepers would be delayed in completing posting of the checks on December 26. Nevertheless, the undisputed evidence establishes that no arrangements of any kind were made for return of "bad" items which might be discovered by the bookkeepers after the departure of the Purolator courier. The two checks in question were in fact determined by Mrs. Stratton to be "bad" on December 26. The checks were not returned because the regular employee responsible for handling "bad" checks had left for the day, and Mrs. Stratton had no instructions to cover the situation.

Even though the bank missed returning the two checks by the Purolator courier, it was still possible for the bank to have returned the checks by its midnight deadline. Under UCC § 4–301(4)(b) [Revised § 4–301(d)(2)] an item is returned when it is "sent" to the bank's transferor, in this case the Federal Reserve Bank. Under UCC § 1–201(38) an item is "sent" when it is deposited in the mail. 1 R. Anderson, Uniform Commercial Code § 1–201 pp. 118–119 (2d ed. 1970). Thus, the bank could have returned the two checks before the midnight deadline by the simple procedure of depositing the two checks in the mail, properly addressed to the Cincinnati branch of the Federal Reserve Bank.

This court concludes that circumstances beyond the control of the bank did not prevent it from returning the two checks in question before its midnight deadline on December 26. The circumstances causing delay in the bookkeeping department were foreseeable. On December 26, the bank actually discovered that the checks were "bad," but the responsible employees and officers had left the bank without leaving any instructions to the bookkeepers. The circuit court erred in holding that the bank was excused under § 4–108 from meeting its midnight deadline. The facts found by the circuit court do not support its conclusion that the circumstances in the case were beyond the control of the bank.

RE–PRESENTMENT OF CHECK PREVIOUSLY DISHONORED BY NONPAYMENT

On its cross-appeal, the bank argues that the circuit court erred in holding that there was no difference in the status of the two checks. The bank makes the argument that it is not liable on the first check which had previously been dishonored by nonpayment. Blake received notice of dishonor when the first check was returned because of insufficient funds. The bank claims that it was under no further duty to meet the midnight deadline when the check was re-presented for payment.

The bank relies upon the decision of the Kansas Supreme Court in Leaderbrand v. Central State Bank, 202 Kan. 450, 450 P.2d 1 (1969). A check drawn on the Central State Bank was presented for payment on two occasions over the counter. On both occasions, the holder of the check was advised orally that there were not sufficient funds in the account to honor the check. Later, the holder deposited the check in his own account at the

First State Bank. The First State Bank did not send the check through regular bank collection channels, but rather mailed the check directly to the Central State Bank for purposes of collection. The check arrived at the Central State Bank on March 21 or March 22, and the check was not returned by the Central State Bank to the First State Bank until April 5. The Kansas Supreme Court held that there was no liability under § 4–302 of UCC for a check which had previously been dishonored when presented for payment.

Relying on the provisions of UCC § 3–511(4), the Kansas Supreme Court held that "any notice of dishonor" was excused when a check had been "dishonored by nonacceptance" and was later re-presented for payment. The Kansas Supreme Court specifically held that § 3–511(4) [See Revised § 3–502(f)] applied to a check which was dishonored when presented for payment, stating:

> "While the language of 84–3–511(4), supra—'Where a draft has been dishonored by nonacceptance'—does not refer to a dishonor by nonpayment, we think reference to the dishonor of a 'draft' 'by nonacceptance' would, a fortiori, include the dishonor of a check by nonpayment."

The Kansas Supreme Court concluded that a payor bank was excused from giving any further notice of dishonor when a previously dishonored check was re-presented for payment and there were still insufficient funds in the drawer's account to cover the check.

* * *

The decision of the Kansas Supreme Court in the *Leaderbrand* case has been criticized. As UCC § 3–511(4) applies by its terms to a "draft" which has been "dishonored by nonacceptance," most of the criticism has been directed to the Kansas court's application of § 3–511(4) to a check which had been dishonored by nonpayment. As stated in B. Clark and A. Squillante, The Law of Bank Deposits, Collections and Credit Cards at 71–72 (1970):

> "Use of this section to excuse retention under § 4–302 seems questionable, since the draftsmen are saying nothing more than dishonor by nonacceptance excuses notice of dishonor by nonpayment. If a time draft is not accepted, it is a useless act to present it for payment. On the other hand, sending a check through a second or third time often yields results, since the depositor may have had time to make a deposit to his account. It is presumably for this reason that the Code draftsmen limited the excuse rule of § 3–511(4) to 'nonacceptance' of 'drafts' and did not by express language indicate 'nonpayment' of 'checks.' "

See also Note, Uniform Commercial Code—Nonapplicability of Payor Banks "Midnight Deadline" to Re-Presented Checks, 18 Kan.L.Rev. 679 (1970).

Two courts have refused to follow the *Leaderbrand* decision. In Wiley, Tate and Irby v. Peoples Bank and Trust Company, 438 F.2d 513 (5th Cir.1971), the United States Court of Appeals for the Fifth Circuit held:

> "We disagree with *Leaderbrand* and hold § 3–511(4) inapplicable here. Acceptance applies only to time items. It has nothing to do with demand items."

In Sun River Cattle Co. v. Miners Bank of Montana, supra, the Montana Supreme Court rejected the *Leaderbrand* decision and followed the decision of the United States Court of Appeals in the *Wiley, Tate and Irby* case. The Montana Supreme Court held that § 3–511(4) of the UCC was inapplicable to checks payable on demand.

* * *

A practical reason also exists for rejecting the *Leaderbrand* decision. In 1972, approximately 25 billion checks passed through the bank collection process. The Federal Reserve Banks handled 8 billion checks that year. * * * An earlier study indicated that only one half of one percent of all checks were dishonored when first presented for payment. Of those initially dishonored, approximately one half were paid upon re-presentment. F. Leary, Check Handling Under Article Four of the Uniform Commercial Code, 49 Marq.L.Rev. 331, 333, n. 7 (1965). A significant number of previously dishonored checks are paid upon re-presentment in the regular course of the check collection process. Such checks are often presented through intermediate collecting banks, such as the Federal Reserve Bank in this case. Each collecting bank will have made a provisional settlement with its transferor, and, in turn, received a provisional settlement from the bank to which it forwarded the check. In this way, a series of provisional settlements are made as the check proceeds through the bank collection process.

Under UCC § 4–213(2) [Revised § 4–215(c)], final payment of a check "firms up" all of the provisional settlements made in the collection process. Under subsection (1)(d) of UCC § 4–213 [Revised § 4–215(a)(3)], a payor bank makes final payment of a check when it fails to revoke a provisional settlement "in the time and manner permitted by statute, clearing house rule or agreement." As to items not presented over the counter or by local clearing house, this means that a payor bank is deemed to have made final payment of a check when it fails to revoke a provisional settlement by its midnight deadline. See UCC § 4–213, Official Code Comment 6 [Comment 7 to Revised § 4–215]. In his article on check handling, Leary has described § 4–213 as the "zinger" section: "when provisional credit given by the payor bank becomes firm then—'zing'—all prior provisional credits are instantaneously made firm." Leary, op.cit., at 361. If a payor bank was not required to meet its midnight deadline with respect to previously dishonored items, then none of the other banks involved in the collection process could safely assume that the check had been paid. Consider the problems of the depository bank. It must permit its customer to withdraw the amount of the credit given for the check when provisional settlements have become final by payment and the bank has had "a reasonable time" to learn that the settlement is final. See UCC § 4–213(4)(a) [Revised § 4–215(e)(1)]. The depository bank will rarely receive notice that an item has been paid. In actual practice, the depository bank will utilize availability schedules to compute when it should receive the check if it is to be returned unpaid. Leary, op.cit., at 345–346. If a payor bank is not bound by its midnight deadline as to previously dishonored items, then there is no way for the depository bank to know whether a previously dishonored item has been paid upon re-presentment except by direct communication with the payor bank. Such a procedure would impose an unnecessary burden upon the check collection process.

This court concludes that the circuit court was correct in holding that there was no difference in the status of the two checks.

*   *   *

b. PROCESS OF POSTING CHECKS BY PAYOR BANK

Merrill Lynch, which follows, describes the process followed by a payor bank in deciding whether to pay a check presented to it for payment. The result in the case turned on an analysis of § 4–109 and § 4–213(1)(c) of the pre–1990 Article 4. Both of these provisions were eliminated in Revised Article 4. Section 4–213(1) (c) provided that a payor bank paid a check when the bank completed the process of posting the check to the account of the drawer of the check. Section 4–109 defined "process of posting." Revised § 4–215 is the successor to the pre–1990 § 4–213. A different result would have been reached in *Merrill Lynch* if Revised Article 4 had been in effect at the time.

MERRILL LYNCH, PIERCE, FENNER & SMITH, INC. v. DEVON BANK

United States Court of Appeals, Seventh Circuit, 1987.
832 F.2d 1005.

EASTERBROOK, CIRCUIT JUDGE.

Manus, Inc., gave the Los Angeles office of Merrill Lynch, Pierce, Fenner & Smith, Inc., a check for $647,250 payable to Merrill Lynch's order. The check was drawn on Devon Bank in Chicago. Merrill Lynch immediately deposited the check with Crocker National Bank in Los Angeles; a clearing house presented the check to Devon for payment at 9:30 a.m. on Wednesday, August 1, 1979. The clearing house and Devon provisionally settled for the check immediately. Under § 4–301(1) [Revised § 4–301(a)] of the Uniform Commercial Code, Devon had to decide no later than midnight of the next banking day whether to make final payment. Devon gave notice of dishonor at 4:22 p.m. on August 3. If this is too late, Devon is liable on the check even though Manus cannot cover the instrument. The district court thought the dishonor timely, 654 F.Supp. 506 (N.D.Ill.1987), and granted summary judgment to Devon in this diversity litigation.

I

The initial question is whether Devon gave notice of dishonor before the deadline on midnight of the "banking day" after it received the instrument. Under § 4–104(1)(c) [Revised § 4–104(a)(3)] of the UCC, a " 'banking day' means that part of any day on which a bank is open to the public for carrying on substantially all of its banking functions". On Wednesday, August 1, 1979, Devon's lobby was closed to the public. It offered services, essentially limited to deposits and withdrawals, at a walk-up window. No one could open an account or arrange for a loan; so far as the record reveals, no one could draw down a line of credit previously arranged. Merrill Lynch observes that on Wednesdays Devon processed checks and made inter-bank loans, but neither these nor related activities made it "open to the public" for "substantially all of its banking functions".

Devon is an Illinois bank, and a "bank" in Illinois is "any person doing a banking business whether subject to the laws of this or any other jurisdiction." Ill.Rev.Stat. ch. 17 ¶ 302 (1986). So a person doing a "banking business" but not subject to anyone's laws is not a "bank", but the statute does not illuminate on "banking business". Perhaps the statute uses a circular definition because the elements of banking are not particularly obscure. Making loans is a necessary part of "banking"; consider the definition of a "bank" in the Bank Holding Company Act, the only federal statute defining the term: "an institution * * * which both (i) accepts demand deposits or deposits that the depositor may withdraw by check or similar means for payment to third parties or others; and (ii) is engaged in the business of making commercial loans." 12 U.S.C. § 1841(c)(1)(B) (1987) * * * Banks are financial intermediaries, facilitating transactions between those who want to lend and those who want to borrow. * * * Devon, which was open to the public for only the deposit side of the banking business on August 1, 1979, was not open for "substantially all" of the services of a bank. Its services on August 1 were less extensive than those offered by a "nonbank bank" for purposes of the Bank Holding Company Act. Devon's walk-up window may have been a "branch bank", for both state and federal law define branches as places where deposits are received *or* money lent. 12 U.S.C. § 36(f); Ill.Rev.Stat. ch. 17 ¶ 302 (1986). One of these is not "substantially all" of the *bank's* functions, however. The district court properly resolved this question by summary judgment. It would unacceptably disrupt commercial relations to put to a jury, case-by-case, the question whether a given day was a "banking day". Billions of dollars in transactions must be processed by every midnight deadline, and everyone has an interest in having this time defined with precision. The record supplies enough information to make decision possible. Devon's midnight deadline was 11:59 p.m. on Friday, August 3, 1979.

II

The midnight deadline is only the outside limit, however. Section 4–301(1) allows a bank to return an item if it acts "before it has made final payment (subsection (1) of Section 4–213) *and* before its midnight deadline" (emphasis added). Section 4–213(1) says that a settlement becomes final "when the bank has done any of the following, whichever happens first". The only subsection we need consider is § 4–213(1)(c), which provides that payment becomes final when the bank has "completed the process of posting the item to the indicated account of the drawer, maker, or other person to be charged therewith". Section 4–109 defines the process of posting, to which we return after stating some undisputed facts.

Manus, the maker of the check, had a subsidiary, Cash Reserve Management, Inc. Cash Management maintained an account in Boston. Manus gave its check to Merrill Lynch on July 26; on July 27 Manus deposited in Devon a check for an identical sum of which Cash Management was the maker. Devon promptly submitted that check for payment. Devon places a "hold" of three or four business days on uncollected funds. The Manus check was presented for payment on August 1, the fourth business day (the fifth if Devon counted Saturday, July 28).

When Devon receives a bundle of checks from its clearing house, its computers tally the checks to ensure that the clearing house has debited Devon the correct amount. During the evening, reader/sorter machines read the account code on each check and compute the balance in each active account; a computer compares the balance and activity information with information the bank maintains to facilitate the decision whether to pay checks. The computer prepares, by the morning of the next business day, several reports for the bank's staff. One report lists checks that have caused overdrafts in the account; another report lists checks that are subject to stop payment orders; a third report lists accounts in which uncollected funds are essential to cover the latest checks; there are more. The morning of the second business day, Devon returns most of the checks that appear on these lists—though its staff may elect to pay some of them. The bookkeeping department stamps checks "paid" and photographs them. Devon then examines the signatures on substantial checks. If the signature appears genuine (or if the bank elects not to examine the signature), Devon places the check in the customer's file. This process usually is completed in the afternoon.

Manus's check was processed in the ordinary course. The account contained about $1.2 million, more than enough to cover the check. About $650,000 of this represented the Cash Management check deposited on July 27. Devon's computer treated these as "collected" funds because the check had been deposited four or more business days ago. The uncollected funds reports of August 1 and 2 do not flag the Manus check. Devon verified the signature and placed the Manus check in the file during the afternoon of August 2. There it remained until 4:10 p.m. on August 3, when Continental Illinois National Bank told Devon by telephone that Cash Management's bank in Boston had dishonored the check of July 27. At 4:22 p.m. Devon gave telephonic notice of dishonor of the Manus check. Crocker Bank resubmitted the Manus check, which was dishonored a second time; Manus was placed in receivership on August 28.

Merrill Lynch, which prefers collecting from a solvent Devon Bank to standing in line as one of Manus's creditors, maintains that Devon "completed the process of posting the item" within the meaning of § 4–213(1)(c) during the afternoon of August 2, when it placed the check in the file. Devon had carried out all the steps in its ordinary process and planned to do nothing further. The process was free from operational error; no steps had been omitted, no judgmental blunders made along the way. Devon replies that it does not intentionally pay checks written against uncollected funds, to which Merrill Lynch responds that Devon made a business judgment to pay checks written against instruments that had been on deposit for four business days. Devon applied that rule to Manus's check, and the belated return of the item may show that four days was too short but does not undermine the conclusion that "the process of posting" had come to an end.

The district court sided with Devon, 654 F.Supp. at 509–10, relying on § 4–109, which provides:

> The "process of posting" means the usual procedure followed by a payor bank in determining to pay an item and in recording the payment including one or more of the following or other steps as determined by the bank:
>
> (a) verification of any signature;
>
> (b) ascertaining that sufficient funds are available;
>
> (c) affixing a "paid" or other stamp;

(d) entering a charge or entry to a customer's account;

(e) correcting or reversing an entry or erroneous action with respect to the item.

Devon completed its ordinary steps, including each of (a) through (d), but the court concluded that § 4–109(e) gives a bank the privilege to dishonor a check until the midnight deadline. To return the item is to "reverse" the entry. As the court put it, "Devon's returning the check * * * demonstrated that the posting process was not completed" (654 F.Supp. at 510).

This reading of § 4–109(e) rips § 4–213(1)(c) out of the Uniform Commercial Code. Section 4–301(1) sets the midnight deadline as the last instant at which a check may be returned; § 4–213(1) lists four events that terminate the return privilege sooner. If the return of an item establishes that the "process of posting" was not completed, then § 4–213(1)(c) is meaningless. It is not beyond belief that statutes contain meaningless provisions, but a court should treat statutory words as dross only when there is no alternative. The Uniform Commercial Code is an uncommonly well drafted statute, with links among its provisions. Section 4–213(1) is there for a reason—to expedite the final settlement on checks, so that banks such as Devon Bank may make funds available to customers faster. The "midnight deadline", and "deferred posting" in general, is a concession to the flux of paper with which any bank must contend. See Official Comment 1 to § 4–301. Section 4–213(1)(c) provides that final payment should not take any longer than the bank actually requires to process each item. That function would be defeated if the bank could reverse any posting under § 4–109(e) until the midnight deadline.

Perhaps § 4–213(1)(c) causes more trouble than it is worth. It potentially calls for a case-by-case inquiry into the details of posting; a bank may defeat its function by dragging out its normal processes so that they consume the entire period allotted by § 4–301(1); the drawee's bank cannot rely on § 4–213(1)(c) to credit a customer's account, because it does not know how long the drawer's bank takes to post any given item. Considerations of this sort led the UCC's Permanent Editorial Board, now at work on a Uniform New Payments Code, to propose the repeal of § 4–213(1)(c). * * * Until the Board makes a final revision in the model UCC and states delete § 4–213(1)(c)—if that should occur—our job is to enforce the statute.

That § 4–213(1)(c) has meaning is reinforced by Official Example 3 to § 4–109:

A payor bank receives in the mail on Monday an item drawn upon it. The item is sorted and otherwise processed on Monday and during Monday night is provisionally recorded on tape by an electronic computer as charged to the customer's account. On Tuesday a clerk examines the signature of the

item and makes other checks to determine finally whether the
item should be paid. If the clerk determines the signature is
valid and makes a decision to pay and all processing of this
item is complete, e.g., at 12 noon on Tuesday, the "process of
posting" is completed at that time. If, however, the clerk
determines that the signature is not valid or that the item
should not be paid for some other reason, the item is returned
to the presenting bank and in the regular Tuesday night run
of the computer the debit to the customer's account for the
item is reversed or an offsetting credit entry is made. In this
case * * * there has been no determination to pay the item,
no completion of the process of posting and no payment of the
item.

This puts the "payment" of the check at the completion of the
bank's ordinary process, whatever that process may be. The
check that passes the bank's internal controls and is posted to the
account is "paid". None of the official comments suggests that a
check that has been accurately handled in accordance with the
bank's ordinary procedure nonetheless may be dishonored any
time before the midnight deadline.

Doubtless we must give § 4–109(e) meaning, just as we must
leave some function for § 4–213(1)(c). The Supreme Court of
Wisconsin thought the language of § 4–109(e) so "plain" that it
overrode § 4–213(1)(c). West Side Bank v. Marine National Exchange Bank, 37 Wis.2d 661, 669–72, 155 N.W.2d 587 (1968). That
court read the language with this emphasis: "correcting or *reversing an entry* or erroneous action with respect to the item." The
"reversing an entry" language, the court thought, allowed the
bank to dishonor a check at any time before the midnight deadline, whether or not the processing had been completed without
error. This reading is inconsistent with the official comments to
§ 4–109 and any plausible reason for making payment final on
posting. As a result, the courts that have addressed the problem
since 1968 have rejected West Side. Nelson v. Platte Valley State
Bank & Trust Co., 805 F.2d 332 (8th Cir.1986); North Carolina
National Bank v. South Carolina National Bank, 449 F.Supp. 616,
620 (D.S.C.1976); H. Schultz & Sons, Inc. v. Bank of Suffolk
County, 439 F.Supp. 1137 (E.D.N.Y.1977); R. Hoag v. Valley National Bank, 147 Ariz. 137, 708 P.2d 1328 (1985). Students of the
subject likewise disagree with the reading of § 4–109(e) proposed
by *West Side,* although they are not entirely in accord on the
meaning the section should take. * * * We think it likely that
the Supreme Court of Illinois would follow *Nelson* and *Schultz*
rather than *West Side.*

Section 4–109(e) does not simply say that a bank may reverse
an entry; the full text of the section says that it may correct or
reverse an entry or erroneous action. It is not possible to divorce

the "reversing an entry" language from the words immediately before and after. If we group the words this way—"(correcting or reversing) an (entry or erroneous action)"—the statute makes sense. The bank may correct (alter) or reverse (set aside completely) an entry that should not have been made or an "erroneous action" that does not involve an "entry". This reading leaves a role for both § 4–109(e) and § 4–213(1)(c), and it also makes sense of the official comment to § 4–109, which states that when the bank's ordinary process is completed before the midnight deadline, the check has been paid.

Nelson, Schultz, and the commentators on the payments process have stressed that the decision to pay a check has both mechanical and judgmental components. The examination of the signature and the determination that an account has sufficient funds are mechanical; the decision whether to permit an overdraft in the account is judgmental. Section 4–109 allows a bank to follow its *ordinary* processes for dealing with both of these. There is nothing magical about putting the instrument in the customer's file. Suppose, for example, the bank mechanically puts all checks in customers' files and then makes random spot checks to verify signatures; that an item with a forged signature had to be pulled from the file to be returned would not prevent its dishonor. Or suppose the bank verifies signatures and puts the checks (stamped "paid") in customers' files before examining the computer printouts for stop payment orders. Again it would not be important that the bank had to remove the stopped check from the customer's file. The alternative—holding all checks in stasis until each of the bank's steps had been completed—would delay "final payment" for the checks as a group even longer, contrary to the purpose of § 4–213(1)(c). *West Side* may have been a case of this sort; if it was, we do not question its result even though its language was unduly broad. But none of this assists Devon. Its process—as Devon defines its process—had been completed by the afternoon of August 2. All of the check-specific steps, mechanical and judgmental, had been finished to the Bank's satisfaction. The system functioned as it was supposed to. True, Devon may wish that it had told its computer to assume that checks take five rather than four business days to clear, but regret over a managerial judgment in the design of the check processing system is not a reason to dishonor a check after it has been posted to the account and finally paid.

*   *   *

III

Devon makes one last argument. Merrill Lynch sued Crocker Bank, claiming that it dallied in informing Merrill Lynch of the dishonor of the Manus check. The complaint in that suit states that had Merrill Lynch received timely notice of the dishonor, it could have obtained good funds from Manus to cover the check before Manus entered bankruptcy. Devon says that this is an "admission" that Devon's actions did not injure Merrill Lynch. Nonsense. Merrill Lynch had to mitigate any damages it suffered, and its pleading in the California case says that had it known of the problem, it could have mitigated. But it did not know, and therefore could not take the necessary steps. Whatever rights Devon may have against Crocker Bank, this pleading is hardly a reason why Merrill Lynch should lose.

Reversed.

2. RIGHT OF COLLECTING BANK TO REVOKE SETTLEMENT ON DISHONORED CHECK

We saw in the preceding section that a payor bank may inadvertently pay a check by failing to return the check within its midnight deadline. A collecting bank, including a depositary bank, is also subject to a midnight deadline in the case of return of a dishonored check to the bank. If a check forwarded to the payor bank is not paid, the depositary bank may revoke the provisional credit that it gave to its customer with respect to the check. § 4–214(a). But the depositary bank is required to either return the check to its customer or give notice of dishonor to the customer before the bank's midnight deadline. *Appliance Buyers*, which follows, discusses the consequences of failure of the depositary bank to act within the deadline. The case was decided under pre–1990 § 4–212(1), the predecessor of Revised § 4–214(a). Revised § 4–214(a) resolves the ambiguity in the former § 4–212(1) and speaks directly to the issue presented in *Appliance Buyers*.

APPLIANCE BUYERS CREDIT CORP. v. PROSPECT NATIONAL BANK
United States Court of Appeals, Seventh Circuit, 1983.
708 F.2d 290.

COFFEY, CIRCUIT JUDGE.

This is an appeal from the district court's dismissal of the plaintiff's claim under section 4–212 of the Uniform Commercial Code on the grounds that the plaintiff failed to establish its damages. Affirmed.

The Appliance Buyers Credit Corporation, a Delaware corporation with its principal place of business in Michigan, is a finance company that provides wholesale "floor-plan financing" to appliance dealers.[1] The corporation makes monthly inspections of participating dealers' inventory to determine whether the dealers are current in their finance payments to Appliance Buyers. Dur-

---

1. As a "floor-plan financier," Appliance Buyers finances the inventory of various appliance dealers and main-tains a security interest in the merchandise so financed.

ing one of Appliance Buyers' monthly inspections of the Nevius Appliance & Furniture inventory it was determined that Nevius had failed to report the sale of certain merchandise to Appliance Buyers and owed $65,736.78. Immediately following the inspection on October 17, 1979 Nevius gave a check to the Appliance Buyers Credit Corporation representative in the amount of $55,736.78 and delivered a $10,000 check to the corporation the next day, October 18, 1979; both checks were drawn on the Corn Belt Bank of Bloomington, Illinois. Appliance Buyers Credit Corporation deposited these two checks on October 18, 1979 with the Prospect National Bank, and Prospect National credited Appliance Buyers' account with a provisional credit. Prospect National processed these two checks through the Chicago Federal Reserve Bank who in turn forwarded the checks to the drawee bank, the Corn Belt Bank of Bloomington. On October 22, 1979, the Corn Belt Bank dishonored the checks due to insufficient funds (NSF) and notified the Federal Reserve Bank of the dishonor by telephone that day. On the day following, October 23, 1979, the Federal Reserve Bank of Chicago notified Prospect National Bank of the dishonor, by telephone, and returned the dishonored checks to the Prospect National Bank by mail. Prospect National, upon receipt of the NSF checks on October 29, 1979, immediately revoked the provisional credit given to the Appliance Buyers' account and notified Appliance Buyers of the dishonor that same day (October 29th). Appliance Buyers received the dishonored checks through the regular mail on the day following, October 30, 1979, and on the next day, October 31, Nevius Appliance & Furniture filed a voluntary petition for bankruptcy. Appliance Buyers then brought suit to recover the $65,736.78.

The district court dismissed the plaintiff's claim under section 4–202[2] of the Uniform Commercial Code initially finding that Prospect National Bank was negligent in failing to notify the Appliance Buyers Credit Corporation of the dishonor of Nevius' checks by the October 24th midnight deadline, the day it received a telephone notification of the checks' dishonor. 505 F.Supp. 163. However, notwithstanding the fact that Prospect National was negligent in notifying Appliance Buyers of the dishonor, in its order the district court also found that Appliance Buyers failed to establish its damages and therefore was not entitled to recover:

2. Uniform Commercial Code § 4–202 reads, in pertinent part:

"(1) A collecting bank must use ordinary care in

*   *   *   *   *

(b) sending notice of dishonor or non-payment * * * after learning that the item has not been paid or accepted, as the case may be; and

*   *   *   *   *

(2) A collecting bank taking proper action before its midnight deadline following receipt of an item, notice or payment acts seasonably; taking proper action within a reasonably longer time may be seasonable but the bank has the burden of so establishing."

"Because the plaintiff has not demonstrated that it had a reasonable chance to collect all or part of the amount of the checks, the amount plaintiff was actually damaged, if any, as a result of the bank's failure to exercise ordinary care in notification is pure speculation. The court will not indulge in such speculation. [Appliance Buyers] has not produced any evidence that if it had known of the dishonor on October 24, 1979, it might have had a reasonable chance to collect any part of the money represented by the checks that it can't recover in the bankruptcy proceeding. Because the court is unable to determine what an appropriate award of damages would be in this case, if any, none can be awarded." (Footnote and citations omitted).

The district court denied the Appliance Buyers Credit Corporation's motion to modify the above quoted court order regarding the corporation's failure to prove its damages:

"The court is not convinced, however, that § 4–212 gives a depositor a complete and automatic windfall if the bank is late in notification of dishonor of deposited and provisionally-credited items, when it is not proved that such lateness made any financial difference to the depositor, or, if so, within reasonable limits, how much difference it made. The court is not willing to adjudicate such an inconsistency of consequences between two sections of the Uniform Commercial Code dealing with the same subject, especially in a case where plaintiff took large checks it had substantial reason to suspect might 'bounce,' and now seeks thereby to saddle its bank with liability thereon after its debtor's bankruptcy."

The plaintiff (Appliance Buyers Credit Corp.) appealed.

Appliance Buyers does not "seek review * * * of the trial court's dismissal of [its] section 4–202 claim," recognizing that "the trier of fact's weighing of the evidence is not an appropriate subject for appellate review in this case." Because there is no challenge to the district court's application of section 4–202, the question in this case is one of first impression: is a bank strictly liable as the plaintiff contends for the face value of a check under section 4–212 of the Uniform Commercial Code if, after failing to give the depositor timely notice of the check's dishonor, the bank charges back the depositor's account?

Appliance Buyers Credit Corp. asserts that section 4–212 makes a bank liable for the face value of a check when the bank breaches its duty to give a depositor timely notice of the check's dishonor, as under section 4–212 timely notice of dishonor is a precondition to the bank's right to charge-back. While it is clear that the drafters of section 4–212 of the Uniform Commercial Code intended to condition a bank's right to charge-back upon the giving of timely notice of dishonor, section 4–212 fails to set forth language holding a bank "accountable" for the face value of a dishonored check if and when the bank fails to give timely notice of dishonor.

Uniform Commercial Code § 4–212 provides:

"(1) If a collecting bank has made provisional settlement with its customer for an item and itself fails by reason of dishonor, suspension of payments by a bank or otherwise to receive a settlement for the item which is or becomes final, the bank may revoke the settlement given by it, charge back the amount of any credit given for the item to its customer's account or obtain refund from its customer whether or not it is able to return the items if by its midnight deadline or within a longer reasonable time after it learns the facts it returns the item or sends notification of the facts. These rights to revoke, charge back and obtain refund terminate if and when a settlement for the item received by the bank is or becomes final (subsection (3) of section 4–211 and subsections (2) and (3) of section 4–213)."

A reading of section 4–212 reveals that while the section conditions a bank's right to "charge-back" on a timely notice of dishonor, it is silent on the measure of damages a depositor can recover, if any, when the bank breaches its duty of giving a timely notice of dishonor and still charges back the provisionally credited check. In its brief, Appliance Buyers contends that the bank should be held strictly liable for the face value of the dishonored check and for any other damages arising out of the bank's improper charge-back. The plaintiff has failed to supply the court and we have been unable to find any legal support either in the Uniform Commercial Code or case law for Appliance Buyers' unique contention that banks should be held strictly liable for the face value of dishonored checks under section 4–212. For example, certain sections of the Uniform Commercial Code such as 4–302(a), 4–213(1)(d) [Revised § 4–215(a)(3)] and 4–213(3) [Revised § 4–215(d)] do impose liability on a bank for the face value of items in given situations, but we have found no similar obligation under section 4–212. The specific language of sections 4–302(a), 4–213(1)(d) and 4–213(3) holds the bank "accountable for the amount of" the item in question. Cases construing these sections hold that the term "accountable" is "the operative term * * * which imposes liability for the face amount of a check * * *." Colorado National Bank v. First National Bank & Trust Co., 459 F.Supp. 1366, 1372 (W.D.Mich.1978). Section 4–212 does not contain the "operative term" holding a bank "accountable" for the face value of a check if the bank improperly charges back the amount of a provisional credit against the depositor's account. It is obvious that if the drafters of the Uniform Commercial Code had intended to make a bank liable for the face value of a check under section

4–212, they would have held the bank "accountable" in specific language for the face amount of the check as they have under other Code sections. Because section 4–212 does not contain any language holding a bank "accountable" for the face value of a dishonored check, nor has our independent research uncovered any case law holding a bank "accountable" under section 4–212, we hold that the drafters of section 4–212 did not intend to impose absolute liability on a bank if the bank charged back a dishonored check against the depositor's account after failing to give the depositor timely notice of the check's dishonor.

Because section 4–212 is silent concerning a depositor's measure of damages arising out of an improper charge-back, we will examine the Code and case law to determine the proper standard to be applied when deciding what Appliance Buyers must establish in order to recover under section 4–212. Section 4–103(5) [Revised § 4–103(e)], the general damages section of the Uniform Commercial Code, provides:

> "The measure of damages for failure to exercise ordinary care in handling an item is the amount of the item reduced by an amount which could not have been realized by the use of ordinary care, and where there is bad faith it includes other damages, if any, suffered by the party as a proximate consequence."

The official comment to section 4–103 states that "[w]hen it is established that some part or all of the item could not have been collected even by the use of ordinary care the recovery is reduced by the amount which would have been in any event uncollectible." In applying this standard to the instant dispute, the district court ruled that there was serious question as to whether Appliance Buyers could have recovered any of the disputed $65,736.78 even if it had received timely notice of the checks' dishonor, as Nevius Appliance was in severe financial difficulty during the period in question and filed for bankruptcy just nine days after the checks were dishonored. Indeed, the district court found that the "fact of bankruptcy within two weeks of issuance of the first check and other evidence concerning Nevius' [insolvency] during the relevant period * * * raise serious doubt that [Appliance Buyers] could have collected any part of the amount of the checks, even if notified of the checks' dishonor in timely fashion." When evidence at trial demonstrated that "some or all of the item could not have been collected" had Appliance Buyers received timely notice of dishonor, the district court found that under section 4–103 the burden was on Appliance Buyers to establish "that it had a reasonable chance of collecting something on the checks, before any award of damages caused by [Prospect National's] negligence could be made." We hold the district court was correct in placing the burden on Appliance Buyers to establish their damages and in dismissing the corporation's claim on the grounds that Appliance Buyers failed to prove to the court's satisfaction that they would have been able to recover any funds from Nevius had they in fact received timely notice from the bank.

A depositor bears the burden of establishing its actual damages under section 4–103 in order to recover damages arising out of the negligence of a bank for failing to give a timely notice under other sections of the Code. See generally Marcoux v. Van Wyk, 572 F.2d 651 (8th Cir.1978); Whalen & Sons Grain Co. v. Missouri Delta Bank, 496 F.Supp. 211 (E.D.Mo.1980); and Bank of Wyandotte v. Woodrow, 394 F.Supp. 550 (W.D.Mo.1975). It is the Appliance Buyers' position that the bank's failure to give timely notice of dishonor has caused their difficulty in proving damages since Nevius' business records do not reveal whether Appliance Buyers could have recovered a measure of damages from Nevius Appliance by repossessing those items in which Appliance Buyers had a security interest. Thus, under the plaintiff's analysis, the bank must prove the amount Appliance Buyers could not have collected even had the bank given timely notice of dishonor and if it is unable to meet this burden, Prospect National should be held liable for the face value of the checks. However, Appliance Buyers has failed to cite any sections of the Code or case law that do in fact shift the burden of proof from the depositor to the bank to prove the extent of a depositor's loss.

*   *   *

The district court in its decision noted that when Appliance Buyers accepted Nevius' checks, Appliance Buyers "had substantial reason to suspect [the checks] might 'bounce' * * *." Indeed, testimony was presented at trial that a representative of Appliance Buyers was told by Ken Nevius that he (Nevius) was unsure whether "we have enough money to cover this check." Moreover, one of Appliance Buyers' employees testified that although Nevius Appliance had agreed to make weekly payments on its account to Appliance Buyers, Nevius had not done so in the last month and a half prior to the time they issued the two NSF checks in question. Now, Appliance Buyers is attempting to shift the loss, caused by their own lax financial policy, to Prospect National Bank. Finance companies such as Appliance Buyers Credit Corporation have the obligation to actively police the floor plans of participating dealers and to ensure that dealers are current in their payments. When a finance company fails to develop a sound financial policy and allows dealers to fall behind in their payments, the finance company must bear the burden if the dealers fail to pay their bills when due. It is apparent from the record that having failed in its duty to protect its investments by keeping tighter reins on Nevius' account, absent proof that Prospect National Bank's untimely notice actually damaged the corporation, Appliance Buyers cannot now shift the responsibility for their own negligence to the bank.

We agree with and affirm the district court's decision and hold that in order for the plaintiff in this case to recover for damages arising out of Prospect National Bank's alleged failure to give timely notice of dishonor as required by section 4–212 of the Uniform Commercial Code, the burden is on the depositor (Appliance Buyers) to establish that Prospect National failed to give timely notice, and the amount of damage Appliance Buyers actually suffered as a result of Prospect National's untimely notice.

[The dissenting opinion of Judge Cudahy is omitted.]

PROBLEM

Customer was the payee of a $5,000 check drawn on Payor Bank. On April 1, Customer deposited the check in Depositary Bank. When it received the check, Depositary Bank credited $5,000 to Customer's account but neglected to immediately forward the check to Payor Bank for payment. Depositary Bank's teller who received the check inadvertently dropped the check into a desk drawer where it remained until it was discovered about two months later. At the time Depositary Bank received the check on April 1 and for a period of 45 days thereafter there was more than $5,000 in the account of the drawer of the check in Payor Bank. When the check was discovered by Depositary Bank, it was forwarded for payment to Payor Bank, but it was returned to Depositary Bank because there were insufficient funds in the drawer's account to cover the amount of the check. On the same day that Depositary Bank learned of the dishonor, it informed Customer of the dishonor and made a debit of $5,000 to Customer's account. Was Depositary Bank entitled to make the debit to Customer's account? § 4–214(a). Does Customer have any cause of action against Depositary Bank? § 4–202(a) and (b); § 4–104(a)(10); § 4–103(a) and (e).

3. ENCODING OF CHECKS

In order to permit electronic processing of checks for presentment for payment, almost all checks in use today are preprinted with a row of numerals and symbols along the bottom of the check that can be read by machines that process the checks for payment. This machine-readable printing is referred to as Magnetic Ink Character Recognition (MICR) encoding. The preprinted MICR encoding identifies the payor bank, the Federal Reserve district in which the bank is located, the Federal Reserve Bank or branch that serves the payor bank, the number of the check, and the number of the account at the payor bank on which the check is drawn. When the check is deposited, either the depositary bank or the next collecting bank that has encoding equipment will add to the MICR line numerals that indicate the amount of the check. In some cases the encoding of the amount of the check will be done by the payee of the check before the check is deposited in the depositary bank. This can occur if the payee is a person receiving a very large volume of checks that are processed in processing centers operated by the payee. Examples of such payees are public utilities, insurance companies, and large retailers.

Most checks that have been encoded with the amount of the check will be processed by automated equipment by the payor bank and by collecting banks on the basis of the encoded information without any examination of the check by a human being. What happens if a check is payable in the amount of $123.45 but the person encoding the amount of the check erroneously encodes the amount as $12,345? The misencoding does not change the amount of the check. There has been no alteration of the check. But if the check is read only by machines on the basis of the encoded amount, the bank that processes the check will treat it as a check in the amount of $12,345. If the payor bank pays the check, it has paid out the encoded amount to the presenting bank but will be entitled to debit the account of the drawer of the check only for the actual amount of the check. Or, the payor bank might wrongfully dishonor the check because the balance in the drawer's account, although large enough to cover the actual amount of the check, is not enough to cover the encoded amount. Before the 1990 revision, Article 4 did not address the problem of misencoding because MICR encoding did not exist when Article 4 was drafted. The case that follows discusses how losses caused by misencoding were allocated under the pre–1990 Article 4. Consider how that case would have been decided if Revised § 4–209 had been in effect.

FIRST NATIONAL BANK OF BOSTON v. FIDELITY BANK

United States District Court, E.D. Pennsylvania, 1989.
724 F.Supp. 1168, aff'd without opinion, 908 F.2d 962 (3d Cir.1990).

FULLAM, CHIEF JUDGE.

This dispute between two banks over a mis-handled check transaction requires the court to explore some of the consequences which automation has visited upon the respective legal liabilities of banks under Article 4 of the Uniform Commercial Code, which was enacted before the advent of computerized check-processing.

*   *   *

The parties have stipulated the facts pertinent to their dispute. Plaintiff is the First National Bank of Boston (hereinafter "Boston"). The defendant is Fidelity Bank, National Association, successor to Industrial Valley Bank (hereinafter "Fidelity"). On or about September 22, 1986, one of defendant's customers, New

York City Shoes ("NYC") issued a check in the amount of $100,000, to the Maxwell Shoe Company ("Maxwell"). The check was drawn on one of NYC's accounts at Fidelity in Philadelphia. Maxwell, a New England concern, deposited the check in its account at Boston, which credited Maxwell's account with the face amount of the check, and then proceeded to process the check through the Federal Reserve system. The check was properly encoded by Boston, and duly presented to Fidelity for payment. But NYC's account did not contain sufficient funds to cover the check, and Fidelity therefore returned the check to Boston for "non-sufficient funds".

Boston did not charge Maxwell's account because of the uncollectability of the check, but instead, at Maxwell's request, undertook to re-present the check to Fidelity. In order to re-process the check, Boston attached a "tape skirt" to the bottom of the check, and thereon re-encoded the check so that it could be processed through the Federal Reserve system. Unfortunately, however, Boston's encoder made an error, and encoded the amount of the check as $10,000, rather than $100,000. The computers which processed the check were, of course, unaware of the error and unable to appreciate it. When the check arrived at Fidelity, it was charged against NYC's account in the amount of $10,000, and that sum was duly forwarded to Boston. At that point, the error surfaced.

Boston made demand on Fidelity for the $90,000 difference between the face amount of the check and the amount which Fidelity had paid. * * * At no time between September 22, 1986 and November 21, 1986, when NYC's account was closed, did NYC's account contain sufficient collected funds to cover Maxwell's $100,000 check, or the balance remaining after the initial payment of $10,000.

Because of the unusual nature of several transactions in NYC's account—a large number of checks drawn against uncollected funds, and a large number of deposits which later proved to be uncollectible—the account had come to the attention of Fidelity's Security Division in July of 1986. As a result of the investigation, Mr. Donald Ebner, vice-president in charge of security at Fidelity, decided to end Fidelity's banking relationship with NYC. By agreement, all of NYC's accounts at Fidelity were closed, as of the end of business on November 21, 1986.

At the start of business the next banking day, November 24, 1986, Mr. Ebner had in his possession, ready for delivery to NYC, a check representing the combined balances of all of NYC's accounts which had just been closed—a total of $101,383.61. That same morning, Mr. Ebner received from Fidelity's Adjustment Department the adjustment request which had been resubmitted by Boston, seeking the $90,000 balance on the Maxwell check.

NYC, however, refused to permit Fidelity to use funds from any of its other accounts to make good the Maxwell check; and, since the account on which the check had originally been drawn was insufficient to cover it, Mr. Ebner rejected the adjustment request, and delivered to NYC the $101,383.61 check closing out its various accounts.

After this final rejection of Boston's adjustment request, Boston attempted to collect the $90,000 from NYC. An agreement was reached for NYC to pay off the balance in installments. NYC paid a total of $40,000 on account, but then defaulted and, on July 7, 1987, filed for bankruptcy.

* * *

As the foregoing recital demonstrates, the court is presented with two separate but related sets of questions. The first is the liability of Fidelity as payor bank, for having paid only $10,000 when the check was in the amount of $100,000, and the effect of Boston's encoding error on that liability. The second area of inquiry centers upon Fidelity's handling of the adjustment request, and its payout to NYC notwithstanding its awareness of Fidelity's adjustment request.

I.

* * *

Section 4–213(1) of the UCC provides:

" * * * An item is finally paid by a payor bank when the bank has done any of the following, whichever happens first:

*   *   *   *   *   *   *   *   *

"(c) Completed the process of posting the item to the indicated account of the drawer, maker or other person to be charged therewith * * *

*   *   *   *   *   *   *   *   *

"Upon final payment under subparagraphs (b), (c) or (d), the payor bank shall be accountable for the amount of the item."

Boston's argument is straightforward: Fidelity did post the check against NYC's account on October 3, 1986, and is therefore, under the plain language of the statute, accountable to Boston "for the amount of the item". The fact that Fidelity listed the item in the wrong amount is irrelevant, since it is undisputed that Fidelity "completed the process of posting the item to the indicated account of the drawer" on October 3, 1986.

The defendant, on the other hand, argues that, for purposes of § 4–213(1) the "amount of the item" for which the payor bank must account should be the encoded amount of the check, rather than its actual face amount. Alternatively, the defendant contends that equitable principles mandate rejection of plaintiff's claims.

Both parties find support for their respective positions in Georgia R.R. Bank & Trust Co. v. First National Bank & Trust Co. of Augusta, 139 Ga.App. 683, 229 S.E.2d 482 (1976), aff'd per curiam, 238 Ga. 693, 235 S.E.2d 1 (1977). The facts of that case are strikingly similar to the present case: plaintiff bank erroneously encoded a $25,000 check as a $2500 check. The defendant, the payor bank, charged the drawer's account in the lesser amount, and remitted that sum to plaintiff. The error was not discovered for several weeks, by which time the cancelled check had already been returned to the maker. When plaintiff made demand upon the defendant, the defendant brought the error to the maker's attention, but the latter refused to allow the defendant to charge his account with the additional $22,500. The Georgia court held, without extended discussion, that the defendant was liable to the plaintiff for the face amount of the check, pursuant to UCC § 4–213(1), and also pursuant to the "midnight deadline" provisions of § 4–302. The court reasoned that the defendant had made "final payment" by charging the maker's account, albeit in the wrong amount, and that it was therefore liable as payor for the full amount of the check; and that, alternatively, it had retained the check beyond the midnight deadline without "completely settling for it".

Although the actual holding of the *Georgia R.R. Bank & Trust Co.* case plainly supports plaintiff's arguments, one part of the court's explanation for its decision suggests that the true rationale for the decision is one which vindicates defendant's position in the present case: the court made much of the fact that, at all times, the maker's account contained more than sufficient funds to honor the check in its full amount. The court stated:

> "We are not here concerned with a situation wherein the drawee cannot recover from the drawer the amount of the deficiency. In such a situation, there would possibly exist a defense or counterclaim in favor of the drawee bank against the collecting bank which had under-encoded the check. See J. Clarke, *Mechanized Check Collection,* supra at 1004. The record in the present case shows that the drawer's account contained sufficient funds, as of the date payment was demanded by plaintiff, to cover the deficiency. 229 S.E.2d at p. 484.

It thus appears that, to the extent liability is sought to be imposed under the "final payment" rule of § 4–213(1), the Georgia court might well sustain an equitable defense where plaintiff's encoding error caused the payor bank to suffer a loss which it could not avoid by charging its customer's account. Recognition of such equitable defenses is more problematical when liability is sought to be imposed under the "midnight deadline" provisions of § 4–302. With due deference to the views of the Georgia courts, however, I am not persuaded that § 4–302 has any application in these circumstances. The whole purpose of the "midnight deadline" rule is to promptly remove uncertainties concerning the collectability of a check, and to enable depositary and collecting banks to rely upon the payor's silence as an unconditional assurance of collectability. If the payor bank acts before the deadline, it seems to me, § 4–302 is no longer implicated.

Like the Georgia court, however, I reject the argument that the "amount of the item" for § 4–213(1) purposes is the encoded amount, rather than the face amount, of the check. Stated that broadly, the argument is manifestly unacceptable, for if the encoded amount were greater than the face amount of the check, the error would produce a windfall for the collecting bank, and patently unjustifiable increases in the potential liability of the payor bank, the maker, or both. Any such rule would have chaotic repercussions, and would be totally inconsistent with the scheme of the UCC.

A more narrowly stated rule—that the "amount of the item" for purposes of § 4–213(1) is the face amount of the check or the encoded amount, whichever is less—is merely another way of stating what I conceive to be the true thrust of defendant's argument in this case, namely, that as between the encoding bank and all other banks in the collecting process, including the payor bank, the encoder is estopped from claiming more than the encoded amount of the check. Framing the argument in terms of estoppel is, I believe, preferable, in that it avoids the problems inherent in trying to ascribe different meanings to the same words in various parts of the UCC.

Section 1–103 of the UCC preserves equitable principles and common-law tort law, except where inconsistent with specific UCC provisions. Most of the decided cases have arisen under the "midnight deadline" provisions of § 4–302, which mandates automatic liability for missing the acceptance deadline "in the absence of a valid defense such as breach of a presentment warranty, settlement effected, or the like." In Bank Leumi Trust Co. v. Bank of Mid–Jersey, 499 F.Supp. 1022 (D.N.J.), aff'd without opinion, 659 F.2d 1065 (3d Cir.1981), it was held that the quoted language precludes assertion of an equitable defense based upon mis-encoding, where the payor bank failed to act before the deadline. In Chrysler Credit Corp. v. First National Bank & Trust Co., 746 F.2d 200 (3d Cir.1984), however, the Court of Appeals expressly declined to consider whether the defense of equitable estoppel could be asserted in a "midnight deadline" case, because the evidence in that case did not adequately support the asserted defense. The court made clear that, at the very least, the facts giving rise to the claimed estoppel would have to be such as to have been a cause of the payor's failure to meet the "midnight deadline".

Whether or not equitable defenses are available in "midnight deadline" cases, I am satisfied that such defenses are not precluded under § 4–302. That appears to be the view of most commentators. * * * The proposed ALI/NCCUSL revisions to Article 4 (specifically, revised § 4–209) would explicitly provide that an encoding bank warrants the accuracy of encoded amounts, and is liable for any resulting loss; this on the theory that the encoding bank is the party best able to avoid the loss. * * *

In my view, most, if not all, of the reported decisions can readily be harmonized with the existence of the right of the payor bank to hold the encoding bank liable for any under-encoding error, if this equitable right is considered in conjunction with the obligation to mitigate damages. That is, the payor bank has the corollary obligation of attempting to avoid loss altogether, by recourse to the account of the maker of the check. If the maker's account, when the check is correctly presented, is insufficient to cover the item, the payor bank has a claim against the encoding bank, which it can offset against any claim made by the encoding bank under § 4–213(1).

I therefore conclude that Fidelity may not be held liable to plaintiff under § 4–213(1) of the UCC, the "final payment" rule.

II.

Plaintiff's alternative claim that the defendant is liable * * * for permitting NYC to close out its accounts without honoring the check in question, is readily disposed of. At no time during the entire period did the account on which the check was drawn contain sufficient collected funds to cover the correct amount of the check (or, more particularly, the $90,000 balance due on that check). * * *

It is true that, by the time Fidelity released $101,383.61 to NYC on November 24, 1986, it was fully aware of plaintiff's adjustment request and the circumstances which occasioned it. But when NYC insisted upon receiving the entire balance from all of its accounts, Fidelity was obliged to comply. The underlying check, and plaintiff's adjustment request, established no basis for a charge against any account but the one upon which the check was drawn; and that account was insufficient. In the circumstances, Fidelity had no legal right to freeze NYC's other accounts, and certainly had no obligation to do so.

For all of the foregoing reasons, judgment will be entered in favor of the defendant.

4. ELECTRONIC PRESENTMENT

With respect to collection of checks by a depositary bank, the present system depends upon transportation of the check through the banking system from the depositary bank to the payor bank. More than one billion checks a week are processed by the banking system; the transportation of this volume of paper to the payor bank is very expensive and delays payment. In recent years the banking system has been seeking ways to reduce the need for the transportation of checks and is moving toward a process in which most checks will be retained by the depositary bank for destruction after a relatively short period of time. Under that process, presentment for payment of a check will be made to the payor bank by electronic transmittal of essential information describing the check rather than delivery of the check. After the check is destroyed, an image of the check will be stored electronically so that a copy of the check can be produced if needed at some later time.

Although, under the present system, the check itself is normally transported to the payor bank, we have seen that most checks are not examined by anybody in the payor bank's process of payment. In most cases the check serves only as the carrier of the electronic encoding on the MICR line which is read by the automated machinery of the payor bank. Use of the check itself to convey the information contained on the MICR line is both inefficient and unnecessary. It is technologically feasible to provide this information to the payor bank by electronic transmission. Eventually, electronic presentment of checks will be the norm and Revised Articles 3 and 4 reflect that fact.

With respect to collection of checks, presentment is simply a demand made to the drawee to pay the check. § 3–501(a). The demand may be made by an electronic communication. § 3–501(b)(1). But Revised Article 3 follows the pre–1990 law in preserving the right of the drawee to demand exhibition of the check and its surrender as a condition to payment. § 3–501(b)(2). This right of the drawee to require exhibition and surrender of the check is subject, however, to rules stated in Article 4 and may be waived by the drawee by agreement. Section 4–110 permits electronic presentment by means of a "presentment notice" which is defined as "transmission of an image of an item or information describing the item." The presentment notice is in lieu of delivery of the check itself. Presentment under § 4–110 requires an "agreement for electronic presentment" which provides for the presentment notice. The quoted term includes not only an agreement between the drawee and the presenting bank, but also a clearing-house rule or Federal Reserve regulation or operating circular providing for electronic presentment. Thus, Article 4 leaves the mechanics of electronic presentment to be developed by the banking industry pursuant to inter-bank agreements or by the Federal Reserve pursuant to its regulatory authority.

Electronic presentment raises a number of problems. The payor bank will not be able to examine the signature of the drawer to detect a possible forgery, but this problem exists under current practice as well, because most checks are not examined for forgery. Under the current practice, payor banks look at the drawer's signature only on some checks such as, for example, those in large dollar amounts. This practice could continue under a regime of electronic presentment by a requirement that certain checks be excluded from electronic presentment. Or, presentment of some checks might be made by transmitting an image of the check rather than information describing the check to allow examination of the drawer's signature.

The agreement for electronic presentment would also have to provide for retention and destruction of the check in order to protect the drawer of the check against further negotiation of the check. Under present practice many payor banks return all cancelled checks to the drawer after the checks are paid. This will not be possible with respect to checks paid pursuant to electronic presentment. But this practice of returning checks to the drawer has become less prevalent in recent years. Many banks, through the technique of differential pricing, have induced customers to opt for checking-account plans in which cancelled checks are not returned and instead the customer is given a statement describing the checks paid. Under electronic presentment the payor bank would be able to obtain, at the request of a customer, a copy of any check paid for the customer's account for which the customer may have a particular need. The agreement for electronic presentment would provide for electronic storage of copies of checks presented electronically and would impose a duty on the storing bank to provide a copy of a check on request of the payor bank. § 4–406(a) and (b).

5. FUNDS AVAILABILITY AND REGULATION CC

Suppose Father living in Sacramento, California, mails a check for $1,000, drawn on First Bank in Sacramento, to Daughter, attending school in College Town, New York, 80 miles from New York City. The check arrives on Monday morning. Daughter takes it to Second Bank's College Town branch and deposits it in her account. On Monday night the check is driven by a courier to Second Bank's central check processing center in New York City and is run through a reader-sorter machine. On Tuesday morning it is taken to the New York Fed where it goes through another reader-sorter and is sent by air courier on Tuesday night to the San Francisco Fed where it arrives early Wednesday morning. There it goes through a reader-sorter machine, and on Wednesday afternoon is driven by a courier to First Bank in Sacramento. By early Thursday morning the check has been posted by automation to Father's account which was then debited. When Daughter deposited the check in Second Bank she asked when she could withdraw her money; she was told it would be available for her in two weeks. She needed the money earlier and called Father to describe her plight. He was irritated to learn that although the banking system had withdrawn the amount of the check from his account on Thursday morning, Daughter would not be able to withdraw the funds until eleven days later.

Second Bank's action in placing a two week "hold" period on Daughter's check was thought necessary to protect itself from the possibility that the check would not be paid by First Bank, owing to insufficient funds in the account, entry of a stop-payment order or other reasons. Relatively long hold periods were necessary because of the slow and inefficient system banks use for returning checks that have been dishonored. Second Bank will not learn whether the check has been dishonored until the unpaid check is physically returned to it. The forward collection of the check in this case from College Town to Sacramento was fairly prompt because the MICR line enabled the collecting banks to utilize an automated system for sorting checks and directing them to the banks on which they are drawn. But there is no automated system for the return of checks. Each must be processed manually by clerks who must attempt to return the check to the proper bank by deciphering the sometimes unintelligible indorsements on the back of the check. Moreover, before institution of the reforms discussed below, the system of provisional credits made it desirable to send the check back through the same chain of banks as in the forward collection of the check. Thus, had First Bank dishonored the check which arrived there after that bank's 2:00 p.m. cutoff hour on Wednesday, it could have waited until its Friday night midnight deadline to send the check back to the San Francisco Fed. That bank would probably need a second banking day after the banking day of receipt for the manual processing of the check. The same is true for the New York Fed. Although the check would probably be returned by truck and air courier services, returning banks could slow the process down even more by mailing the returns back. One study found that although the forward collection process for checks averaged 1.6 days, the return averaged 5.2 days. Clark & Clark, Regulation CC Funds Availability and Check Collection 1–4 (1988).

Banks met the growing chorus of customer complaints about what seemed to be excessive hold periods by justifying their actions as necessary to protect them from bad check losses. But in the 1980s several states passed laws limiting hold periods, and in 1987 Congress enacted the Expedited Funds Availability Act of

1987, 12 U.S.C. § 4001 et seq. The Board of Governors of the Federal Reserve System implemented this statute by promulgating Regulation CC in 1988, 12 C.F.R. 229. Subpart B of Regulation CC prescribes mandatory availability schedules. Next day availability is required for deposits for which a hold period is not needed to protect the depositary bank from risk. Examples are cashier's checks, certified checks, teller's checks, wire transfer payments, "on us" items, Treasury and state and local government checks. § 229.10. For local checks the funds must be made available to the depositor not later than the second day after the banking day of deposit. § 229.12(b). For nonlocal checks funds must be made available not later than the fifth business day following the banking day of deposit. § 229.12(c). But a depositor is allowed to withdraw up to $100 on the next banking day after deposit of either local or nonlocal checks. § 229.10(c). Section 229.13 sets out exceptions to these mandatory availability schedules with respect to new accounts, large deposits, redeposited checks, repeated overdrafts, and cases in which there is reasonable cause to doubt collectibility. Anecdotal evidence from the first years of experience under Regulation CC indicates that the operational difficulties of dealing with the multiple availability schedules have led banks to permit next day availability on a large portion of their deposits.

To allow the banking system to meet the funds availability standards set by Regulation CC without exposing depositary banks to excessive bad check losses, it was necessary to expedite the return system. Subpart C of Regulation CC sets out a sweeping revision of the law of check collection and return in order to speed the return of dishonored checks, thereby preempting portions of Article 4. As two commentors put it:

> In biblical terms, the genesis of Regulation CC might be stated as follows: The slow check return process begat risks perceived as unacceptable by depositary banks in allowing customers to draw on uncollected funds. This perception of risk begat extended blanket holds. Extended blanket holds begat consumer agitation. Consumer agitation begat state legislative initiatives focusing on mandatory expedited availability. State legislative initiatives begat congressional response in the form of the EFAA. The EFAA begat Regulation CC. Regulation CC begat an entirely new check collection code to speed the return process. And all of this is certain to beget confusion and litigation.

Clark & Clark, supra, 1–10.

In the early stages of the revision of Article 4, before the EFAA had been passed, the drafters had proposed several provisions designed to speed the return of dishonored checks. These provisions included: facilitating direct return of dishonored checks to depositary banks; reducing the number of returned checks by extending the payor bank's midnight deadline for checks under $100 (thus giving the drawer time to put enough money in the account to pay the check); requiring compliance with uniform indorsement standards governing the content and placement of bank indorsements; commencing the running of the midnight deadline for return from the time of delivery of checks to central bank processing centers; and imposing on payor banks the duty to give prompt notice of the nonpayment of items of $2,500 or more. Regulation CC preempted all these provisions except the extension of the midnight deadline for small checks which was not included in Regulation CC and dropped from Article 4 because of the belief that it would slow the collection of checks; hence, all these provisions were deleted from Article 4.

But Regulation CC went far beyond these modest steps. In sections 229.30 and 229.31, it authorizes a payor or returning bank to return a check directly to the depositary bank or to any returning bank agreeing to handle the returned check for expeditious return to the depositary bank, regardless of whether the returning bank had handled the check for forward collection. The contemplation was that the banks most likely to agree to handle a returning check expeditiously were the regional Federal Reserve Banks. The consequences of allowing a check presented by one bank to be returned by the payor bank to a different bank undermined the usual methods of interbank settlements. Under these methods, the payor bank gives the presenting bank a provisional settlement which it revokes when it returns the dishonored check to that bank. If the payor bank returns the check to a bank that was not the presenting bank, the payor bank cannot obtain settlement for the returned check by revoking the settlement with the presenting bank. Rather, it must recover settlement from the bank to which it returned the check. But in order to give banks incentive to make expeditious returns, even if the payor bank does return the dishonored check to the presenting bank, section 229.31(c) forbids a payor bank to obtain settlement for the check by charging back against a credit it had previously given the presenting bank. The payor bank cannot recover settlement from a bank to which it has returned a check until the check has reached the returning bank, as though in forward collection. In harmony with these two provisions, section 229.36(d) provides that all settlements between banks for the forward collection of checks are final when made.

The interbank settlement provisions of Article 4 are stated in terms of provisional settlements. § 4–201(1). Bank credit given by a settling payor or collecting bank is provisional in the sense that it can be revoked upon return of the item. The Fed's decision in Regulation CC to make all settlements final meant that now the conceptual approach of Article 4 to interbank settlements differed from that of Regulation CC, though, at least with respect to the issues addressed by Article 4, there is little functional difference between the two laws. The fact that under Regulation CC any credit given for a check is final rather than provisional was not intended by the drafters of Regulation CC to limit the right of a payor or collecting bank to return a check and recover the amount of the check from the bank to which it was returned. After stating that settlement under Regulation CC is final rather than provisional, the commentary to section 229.36(d) of Regulation CC explains: "Settlement by a paying bank is not considered to be final payment for the purposes of U.C.C. [§ 4–215(a)], because a paying bank has the right to recover settlement from a returning or depositary bank to which it returns a check under this subpart." Appendix Commentary, 53 Fed.Reg. 19, 486 (1988).

Today the law of check collection and return is found in Regulation CC as well as in Article 4, to the extent that its provisions are not preempted by Regulation CC. Consideration in the revision of Article 4 was given to redrafting Article 4 in order to make it compatible with Regulation CC. This approach was rejected because of the likelihood that Regulation CC will continue to evolve, leaving inconsistencies between Article 4 and Regulation CC.

B. WHOLESALE WIRE TRANSFERS

1. THE BASIC TRANSACTION COVERED BY ARTICLE 4A

Article 4A of the UCC was approved in 1989 by the National Conference of Commissioners on Uniform State Laws and the American Law Institute and has been enacted in a majority of the states. The primary focus of Article 4A is a type of payment usually referred to as a "wholesale wire transfer." Most transactions governed by Article 4A are between business or financial institutions. The dollar volume of payments made by wire transfer is far greater than the dollar volume of payments by check, credit card, and all other means.

The transaction governed by Article 4A is referred to in the statute as a "funds transfer" (§ 4A–104(a)) and comprises the series of transactions by which a person called the "originator" (§ 4A–104(c)) makes payment to a person called the "beneficiary" (§ 4A–103(a)(2)). The funds transfer is made by one or more "payment orders" (§ 4A–103(a)) beginning with that of the originator. A payment order is always given directly to a bank and it instructs the bank to pay money to the beneficiary or to cause (by means of a payment order) another bank to make the payment. In a large percentage of cases, payment orders are transmitted electronically, and this is the derivation of the term "wire transfer," but a payment order can also be given in writing or orally. Payment to the beneficiary is normally made by credit to an account of the beneficiary in the "beneficiary's bank" (§ 4A–103(a) (3)). The terms "payment order" and "funds transfer" determine the scope of Article 4A and they are discussed in detail in the Comment to § 4A–104.

Rights and obligations under Article 4A arise as the result of "acceptance" (§ 4A–209) of a payment order by the bank to which the order is sent. That bank is called the "receiving bank." § 4A–103(a)(4). A receiving bank is not required to carry out a funds transfer for its customer, the "sender" (§ 4A–103(a)(5)) of the payment order, unless it has agreed to do so. Substantial risk is involved in funds transfers and a bank may not be willing to give this service to all its customers, and may not be willing to offer it to any customer unless certain safeguards against loss such as security procedures are in effect. Moreover, funds transfers often involve the giving of credit by the receiving bank to the customer, and that also is based on agreement. These considerations are reflected in Article 4A by the principle that, in the absence of a contrary agreement, a receiving bank does not incur liability with respect to a payment order until it accepts it. In the case of a payment order sent to a receiving bank other than the beneficiary's bank, acceptance occurs when the receiving bank "executes" the payment order of the sender by sending a payment order to some other bank intended to carry out the payment order received by the receiving bank. § 4A–209(a) and § 4A–301(a). In the case of a payment order sent to the beneficiary's bank, acceptance usually occurs when the bank receives payment of the sender's payment order or when the bank pays the beneficiary or notifies the beneficiary of receipt of the payment order. § 4A–209(b)(1) and (2). When a payment order is accepted, the sender of the order is obliged to pay the amount of the order to the receiving bank. § 4A–402(b) and (c). If a payment order is accepted by the beneficiary's bank, that bank is obliged to pay the amount of the order to the beneficiary. § 4A–404(a). Acceptance by the beneficiary's bank also means that the funds transfer has been completed; payment by the originator of the funds transfer to the beneficiary occurs when the acceptance occurs. § 4A–406(a). Thus, under Article 4A, if a funds transfer is made to pay an obligation, the obligation is paid by the originator at the time the beneficiary's bank incurs an obligation to pay the beneficiary and in the amount of the payment order accepted by that bank. § 4A–406(b).

BANQUE WORMS v. BANKAMERICA INTERNATIONAL

New York Court of Appeals, 1991.
77 N.Y.2d 362, 568 N.Y.S.2d 541, 570 N.E.2d 189.

ALEXANDER, JUDGE.

On April 10, 1989, Security Pacific International Bank (Security Pacific), a Federally chartered banking corporation with offices in New York City, mistakenly wired $1,974,267.97 on behalf of Spedley Securities (Spedley), an Australian corporation, into the account of Banque Worms, a French Bank, maintained with BankAmerica International (BankAmerica), another Federally chartered bank with New York offices. Initially intending to make payment on its debt to Banque Worms under a revolving credit agreement, Spedley instructed Security Pacific, which routinely effected wire transfers for Spedley, to electronically transfer funds from Security Pacific to Banque Worms' account at BankAmerica.

A few hours after directing this wire transfer, Spedley, by a second telex, directed Security Pacific to stop payment to Banque Worms and to make payment instead to National Westminster Bank USA (Natwest USA) for the same amount. At the time Security Pacific received the telexes, Spedley had a credit balance of only $84,500 in its account at Security Pacific, but later that morning, Security Pacific received additional funds sufficient to cover the transaction and then began to execute the transaction. However, in mistaken disregard of Spedley's second telex canceling the wire transfer to Banque Worms, Security Pacific transferred the funds into Banque Worms' account at BankAmerica. The funds were credited to the account after Banque Worms was notified through the Clearing House Interbank Payment System (CHIPS) that the funds had been received. That afternoon, Security Pacific executed Spedley's second payment order and transferred $1,974,267.97 to Natwest USA. Spedley's account at Security Pacific was debited twice to record both wire transfers thus producing an overdraft.

Meanwhile, at Security Pacific's request made prior to the transfer to Natwest USA, BankAmerica agreed to return the funds mistakenly transferred, provided Security Pacific furnished a United States Council on International Banking, Inc. (CIB) indemnity. The indemnity was furnished and the funds returned to Security Pacific on the following day. Banque Worms, however, refused BankAmerica's request that it consent to its account being debited to reflect the return of the funds. Consequently BankAmerica called upon Security Pacific to perform pursuant to the CIB indemnity and return the funds. Security Pacific's attempt to obtain funds from Spedley to cover this indemnity was unavailing because by that time, Spedley had entered into involuntary liquidation.

Banque Worms brought suit against BankAmerica in the United States District Court for the Southern District of New York seeking to compel BankAmerica to recredit $1,974,267.97 to Banque Worms' account. BankAmerica instituted a third-party action against Security Pacific for return of the funds, and Security Pacific counterclaimed against Banque Worms seeking a declaration that neither Banque Worms nor BankAmerica were entitled to the $1,974,267.97. Eventually, for reasons not here pertinent, Security Pacific returned the funds to BankAmerica, BankAmerica recredited Banque Worms' account and was voluntarily dismissed from the case leaving only Banque Worms and Security Pacific as the sole contestants seeking entitlement to the $1,974,267.97.

On their respective motion and cross motion for summary judgment, the District Court, applying the "discharge for value" rule, granted judgment for Banque Worms. Security Pacific appealed to the United States Court of Appeals for the Second Circuit, arguing that New York neither recognized nor applied the "discharge for value" rule in situations such as this; that the controlling rule under New York law was the "mistake of fact" rule pursuant to which, in order to be entitled to retain the mistakenly transferred funds, Banque Worms was required to demonstrate detrimental reliance. The case is before us upon a certified question from the Second Circuit * * * inquiring "[w]hether in this case, where a concededly mistaken wire transfer by [Security Pacific] was made to [Banque Worms], a creditor of Spedley, New York would apply the 'Discharge for Value' rule as set forth at section 14 of the Restatement of Restitution or, in the alternative, whether in this case New York would apply the rule that holds that money paid under a mistake may be recovered, unless the payment has caused such a change in the position of the receiving party that it would be unjust to require the party to refund."

For the reasons that follow, we conclude that, under the circumstances of this case, the "discharge for value" rule should be applied, thus entitling Banque Worms to retain the funds mistakenly transferred without the necessity of demonstrating detrimental reliance.

I

A

In the area of restitution, New York has long recognized the rule that "if A pays money to B upon the erroneous assumption of the former that he is indebted to the latter, an action may be maintained for its recovery. The reason for the rule is obvious.

Since A was mistaken in the assumption that he was indebted to B, the latter is not entitled to retain the money acquired by the mistake of the former, even though the mistake is the result of negligence." (Ball v. Shepard, 202 N.Y. 247, 253, 95 N.E. 719.) This rule has been applied where the cause of action has been denominated as one for money had and received * * * for unjust enrichment or restitution * * * or upon a theory of quasi contract * * *. Where, however, the receiving party has changed its position to its detriment in reliance upon the mistake so that requiring that it refund the money paid would be "unfair," recovery has been denied * * *.

This rule has evolved into the "mistake of fact" doctrine, in which detrimental reliance is a requisite factor, and which provides that "money paid under a mistake of fact may be recovered back, however negligent the party paying may have been in making the mistake, unless the payment has caused such a change in the position of the other party that it would be unjust to require him to refund." (National Bank v. National Mechanics' Banking Assn., 55 N.Y. 211, 213; see also, Hathaway v. County of Delaware, 185 N.Y. 368, 78 N.E. 153; Mayer v. Mayor of City of N.Y., 63 N.Y. 455, 457 ["general rule that money paid under a mistake of material fact may be recovered back * * * is subject to the qualification that the payment cannot be recalled when the position of the party receiving it has been changed in consequence of the payment, and it would be inequitable to allow a recovery."].)

The Restatement of Restitution, on the other hand, has established the "discharge for value" rule which provides that "[a] creditor of another or one having a lien on another's property who has received from a third person any benefit in discharge of the debt or lien, is under no duty to make restitution therefor, although the discharge was given by mistake of the transferor as to his interests or duties, if the transferee made no misrepresentation and did not have notice of the transferor's mistake" (Restatement of Restitution § 14[1]).

The question as to which of these divergent rules New York will apply to electronic fund transfers divides the parties and prompts the certified question from the Second Circuit. Security Pacific argues that New York has rejected the "discharge for value" rule and has required that detrimental reliance under the "mistake of fact" rule be demonstrated in all cases other than where the mistake was induced by fraud. Banque Worms, on the other hand, invokes the "discharge for value" rule, arguing that because it is a creditor of Spedley and had no knowledge that the wire transfer was erroneous, it is entitled to keep the funds. It points out, as indicated by the official comment to section 14(1) of the Restatement of Restitution, that the "discharge for value" rule is simply a "specific application of the underlying principle of bona fide purchase" set forth in section 13 of the Restatement (Restatement of Restitution § 14, *comment a*).

* * *

Indeed one may find, as does Banque Worms, language in a myriad of cases that arguably lends support to the proposition that New York, long ago, embraced the "discharge for value" rule * * *.

On the other hand, cases can also be cited where the language employed supports the contrary view—that New York not only eschews the "discharge for value" rule, as Security Pacific argues, but also embraces exclusively the detrimental reliance rule-mistake of fact doctrine * * *. These cases for the most part, however, present issues involving more traditional aspects of mistake and restitution, and do not satisfactorily address the unique problems presented by electronic funds transfer technology.

While courts have attempted in wire transfer cases to employ, by analogy, the rules of the more traditional areas of law, such as contract law, the law of negotiable instruments and the special relations between banks, these areas are governed by principles codified in articles 3 and 4 of the Uniform Commercial Code. Various commentators found these efforts ineffective and inadequate to deal with the problems presented (see, Official Comment to UCC 4A–102 * * *). As pointed out by the Official Comment to article 4A, "attempts to define rights and obligations in funds transfers by general principles or by analogy to rights and obligations in negotiable instruments law or the law of check collection have not been satisfactory" * * *. Consequently, it was concluded, as the Prefatory Note to the new article 4A of the UCC approved by the National Conference of Commissioners on Uniform State Law and the American Law Institute observes, that a new article was needed because "[t]here is no comprehensive body of law that defines the rights and obligations that arise from wire transfers." * * *

B

Electronic funds transfers have become the preferred method utilized by businesses and financial institutions to effect payments and transfers of a substantial volume of funds. These transfers, commonly referred to as wholesale wire transfers, differ from other payment methods in a number of significant respects, a fact which accounts in large measure for their popularity. Funds are moved faster and more efficiently than by traditional payment instruments, such as checks. The transfers are completed at a relatively low cost, which does not vary widely depending on the amount of the transfer, because the price charged reflects primarily the cost of the mechanical aspects of the funds transfer (Prefatory Note to UCC art. 4A). Most transfers are completed within one day and can cost as little as $10 to carry out a multimillion dollar transaction ∗ ∗ ∗. The popularity of wholesale wire transfers is evidenced by the fact that nearly $1 trillion in transactions occur each day, averaging $5 million per transfer and on peak days, this figure often approaches $2 trillion ∗ ∗ ∗.

Wholesale wire transfers are generally made over the two principal wire payment systems: the Federal Reserve Wire Transfer Network (Fedwire) and the CHIPS.[2] The CHIPS network handles 95% of the international transfers made in dollars, transferring an average of $750 billion per day ∗ ∗ ∗. These funds are transferred through participating banks located in New York because all of the banks belonging to the CHIPS network must maintain a regulated presence in New York. As a result, this State is considered the national and international center for wholesale wire transfers.

The low cost of electronic funds transfers is an important factor in the system's popularity and this is so even though banks executing wire transfers often risk significant liability as a result of losses occasioned by mistakes and errors, the most common of which involve the payment of funds to the wrong beneficiary or in an incorrect amount ∗ ∗ ∗. Thus, a major policy issue facing the drafters of UCC article 4A was determining how the risk of loss might best be allocated, while preserving a unique price structure. In order to prevent or minimize losses, the industry had adopted and employed various security procedures designed to prevent losses[3] such as the use of codes, identifying words or numbers, call-back procedures and limits on payment amounts or beneficiaries that may be paid.

As indicated above, it was the consensus among various commentators that existing rules of law did not adequately address the problems presented by these wholesale electronic funds transfers. Thus, the National Conference of Commissioners on Uniform State Laws (NCCUSL) and the American Law Institute (ALI) undertook to develop a body of unique principles of law that would address every aspect of the electronic funds transfer process and define the rights and liabilities of all parties involved in such transfers (Prefatory Note to UCC art. 4A, *op. cit.*). After extensive investigation and debate and through a number of drafts, in 1989,

2. CHIPS is owned and operated by the New York Clearing House Association and the Federal Reserve Bank owns and operates Fedwire, the largest American wire transfer network.

3. The Official Comment to UCC 4A–201 as drafted by the American Law Institute and National Conference of Commissioners on Uniform State Laws states that "it is standard practice to use security procedures that are designed to assure the authenticity of the message ∗ ∗ ∗ [and] to detect error in the content of messages. ∗ ∗ ∗ The question of whether loss that may result from the transmission of a spurious or erroneous payment order will be borne by the receiving bank or the sender or purported sender is affected by whether a security procedure was or was not in effect and whether there was or was not compliance with the procedure." ∗ ∗ ∗

both the NCCUSL and the ALI approved a new article 4A of the Uniform Commercial Code * * *. In 1990, the New York State Legislature adopted the new article 4A and incorporated it into the New York Uniform Commercial Code (N.Y. UCC art. 4–A).[4] Although the new statute, which became effective January 1, 1991, may not be applied retroactively to resolve the issues presented by this litigation, the statute's legislative history and the history of article 4A of the Uniform Commercial Code from which it is derived and the policy considerations addressed by this legislation, can appropriately inform our decision and serve as persuasive authority in aid of the resolution of the issue presented in this case * * *.

II

Both the NCCUSL and ALI drafters of article 4A and the New York Legislature sought to achieve a number of important policy goals through enactment of this article. National uniformity in the treatment of electronic funds transfers is an important goal, as are speed, efficiency, certainty (i.e., to enable participants in fund transfers to have better understanding of their rights and liabilities), and finality. Establishing finality in electronic fund wire transactions was considered a singularly important policy goal * * *. Payments made by electronic funds transfers in compliance with the provisions of article 4A are to be the equivalent of cash payments, irrevocable except to the extent provided for in article 4A (see, Assn of Bar of City of NY, Committee on Banking Law, Report on proposed New York UCC art. 4–A; see also, Delbrueck & Co. v. Manufacturers Hanover Trust Co., 609 F.2d 1047, 1049–1051 [2d Cir.] [once an electronic fund transfer is completed and the funds released, the transaction is final and irrevocable under the CHIPS system]).

This concern for finality in business transactions has long been a significant policy consideration in this State. In a different but pertinent context, we observed in Hatch v. Fourth Natl. Bank, 147 N.Y. 184, 192, 41 N.E. 403 that "to permit in every case of the payment of a debt an inquiry as to the source from which the debtor derived the money, and a recovery if shown to have been dishonestly acquired, would disorganize all business operations and entail an amount of risk and uncertainty which no enterprise could bear".

A consequence of this concern has been the adoption of a rule which precludes recovery from a third person, who as the result of

---

4. The new article 4A will regulate funds transfers other than consumer transactions governed by the Federal Electronic Fund Transfer Act of 1978 (15 USC § 1693 et seq.). It will not apply to consumer transactions such as check payments or credit card payments for the Federal EFTA will continue to govern these transactions. If any part of a fund transfer is covered by the EFTA, the entire funds transfer will be excluded from article 4A.

the mistake of one or both of the parties to an original transaction receives payment by one of them in good faith in the ordinary course of business and for a valuable consideration (see, Ball v. Shepard, 202 N.Y. 247, 95 N.E. 719, supra). This rule is grounded in "considerations of public policy and convenience for the protection and encouragement of trade and commerce by guarding the security and certainty of business transactions, since to hold otherwise would obviously introduce confusion and danger into all commercial dealings" (44 N.Y.Jur., Payment, § 107; see also, Southwick v. First Natl. Bank, 84 N.Y. 420). We have previously held that from these considerations, "[t]he law wisely * * * adjudges that the possession of money vests the title in the holder as to third persons dealing with him and receiving it in due course of business and in good faith upon a valid consideration." (Stephens v. Board of Educ., 79 N.Y. 183, 187–188.)

The "discharge for value" rule is consistent with and furthers the policy goal of finality in business transactions and may appropriately be applied in respect to electronic funds transfers. When a beneficiary receives money to which it is entitled and has no knowledge that the money was erroneously wired, the beneficiary should not have to wonder whether it may retain the funds; rather, such a beneficiary should be able to consider the transfer of funds as a final and complete transaction, not subject to revocation.

We believe such an application accords with the legislative intent and furthers the policy considerations underlying article 4–A of the New York Uniform Commercial Code. Although no provision of article 4–A calls, in express terms, for the application of the "discharge for value" rule, the statutory scheme and the language of various pertinent sections, as amplified by the Official Comments to the UCC, support our conclusion that the "discharge for value" rule should be applied in the circumstances here presented.

Subject to certain exceptions not here relevant, § 4A–209(b)(1) provides that a beneficiary's bank accepts a payment order when the bank pays the beneficiary by crediting the beneficiary's account and notifying the beneficiary of the right to withdraw the credit. When a payment order has been accepted by the beneficiary's bank, cancellation or amendment of that payment order is not effective unless, for example, the order was issued because of a mistake of the sender resulting in a duplicate payment order or an order that directs payment to a beneficiary not entitled to receive the funds. § 4A–211(c)(2)(i) and (ii). Where a duplicate payment order is erroneously executed or the payment order is issued to a beneficiary different from the beneficiary intended by the sender, the receiving bank in either case is entitled to recover the erroneously paid amount from the beneficiary "to the extent allowed by the law governing mistake and restitution". § 4A–303(a) and (c).

More specifically, § 4A–303(c) instructs that "[i]f a receiving bank executes the payment order of the sender by issuing a payment order to a beneficiary different from the beneficiary of the sender's order and the funds transfer is completed on the basis of that error, the sender ∗ ∗ ∗ [is] not obliged to pay the payment order[ ]. The issuer of the erroneous order is entitled to recover from the beneficiary ∗ ∗ ∗ to the extent allowed by the law governing mistake and restitution." Official Comment 1 to § 4A–303 from which the identical New York statute is derived, explains that although section 4A–402(c) obligates the sender to pay the [payment] order to the beneficiary's bank if that bank has accepted the payment order, section 4A–303 takes precedence and "states the liability of the sender and the rights of the receiving bank in various cases of erroneous execution".

Thus, as in the example discussed in comment 2 [to § 4A–303], where the originator's bank mistakenly directs payment of $2,000,000 to the beneficiary's bank but payment of only $1,000,000 was directed by the originator, the originator's bank is obligated to pay the $2,000,000 if the beneficiary's bank has accepted the payment, although the originator need only pay its bank the $1,000,000 ordered. The originator's bank ordinarily would be entitled to recover the excess payment from the beneficiary. The comment points out, however, that "if Originator owed $2,000,000 to Beneficiary and Beneficiary received the extra $1,000,000 in good faith in discharge of the debt, Beneficiary may be allowed to keep it. In this case Originator's Bank has paid an obligation of Originator and under the law of restitution ∗ ∗ ∗ Originator's Bank would be subrogated to Beneficiary's rights against Originator on the obligation paid by Originator's Bank".

A further example discussed in comment 3 of the Official Comment is of a duplicate payment order erroneously made, which transfers a second $1,000,000 payment to beneficiary's bank and beneficiary's bank accepts the payment. Although the originator's bank is only entitled to receive $1,000,000 from the originator, it must pay $2,000,000 to beneficiary's bank and would be relegated to a remedy the same as "that of a receiving bank that executes by issuing an order in an amount greater than the sender's order. It may recover the overpayment from Beneficiary to the extent allowed by the law governing mistake and restitution and in a proper case ∗ ∗ ∗ may have subrogation rights if it is not entitled to recover from Beneficiary".

∗　∗　∗

Application of the "discharge for value" rule to the circumstances presented here is particularly appropriate. The undisputed facts demonstrate that Security Pacific executed Spedley's initial order directing payment to Banque Worms notwithstanding having already received a cancellation of that order. The District Court also found that the second transfer to Natwest USA was executed despite the fact that Spedley's account did not have sufficient funds to cover this second transfer. Moreover, it appears that, as a creditor of Spedley, Banque Worms was a beneficiary entitled to the funds who made no "misrepresentation and did not have notice of the transferor's mistake."

Accordingly, we conclude, in answer to the certified question, that the "discharge for value" rule as set forth at section 14 of the Restatement of Restitution, should be applied in the circumstances in this case.

* * *

2. FAILURE OF RECEIVING BANK TO PROPERLY EXECUTE PAYMENT ORDER

In *Evra*, the case that follows, Hyman–Michaels issued a payment order to Continental (Chicago) to pay a sum of money to an account in Banque de Paris in Geneva. Continental (Chicago) executed the order by issuing a payment order to Continental (London) and debited the account of Hyman–Michaels in the amount of the order. Continental (London) executed that payment order of Continental (Chicago) by issuing a payment order to Swiss Bank in Geneva. Swiss Bank was supposed to issue a payment order to Banque de Paris to complete the funds transfer, but failed to do so. As a result of the failure to complete the wire transfer, Hyman–Michaels suffered a loss. *Evra*, which was decided before Article 4A was drafted, discusses the issue of whether, under general common-law principles, Hyman–Michaels was entitled to any recovery from either Continental (Chicago) or Swiss Bank.

Consider how *Evra* would have been decided if Article 4A had been in effect. Under Article 4A Hyman–Michaels is the originator of the funds transfer, Continental (Chicago) is the originator's bank, and Continental (London) and Swiss Bank are both "intermediary banks" (§ 4A–104(b)). Each of the three banks is also a receiving bank with respect to the payment order it received. The duty of a receiving bank with respect to a payment order that it receives is stated in § 4A–212. The duty of a receiving bank in executing a payment order is stated in § 4A–302. The extent of liability of a receiving bank for late or improper execution or for failure to execute a payment order is stated in § 4A–305. The right of the originator or other sender of a payment order to refund of amounts paid by them if the funds transfer is not completed is stated in § 4A–402(c) and (d).

EVRA CORP. v. SWISS BANK CORP.

United States Court of Appeals, Seventh Circuit, 1982.
673 F.2d 951.

POSNER, CIRCUIT JUDGE.

The question—one of first impression—in this diversity case is the extent of a bank's liability for failure to make a transfer of funds when requested by wire to do so. The essential facts are undisputed. In 1972 Hyman-Michaels Company, a large Chicago dealer in scrap metal, entered into a two-year contract to supply steel scrap to a Brazilian corporation. Hyman-Michaels chartered a ship, the *Pandora,* to carry the scrap to Brazil. The charter was for one year, with an option to extend the charter for a second year; specified a fixed daily rate of pay for the hire of the ship during both the initial and the option period, payable semi-monthly "in advance"; and provided that if payment was not made on time the *Pandora*'s owner could cancel the charter. Payment was to be made by deposit to the owner's account in the Banque de Paris et des Pays-Bas (Suisse) in Geneva, Switzerland.

The usual method by which Hyman-Michaels, in Chicago, got the payments to the Banque de Paris in Geneva was to request the Continental Illinois National Bank and Trust Company of Chicago, where it had an account, to make a wire transfer of funds. Continental would debit Hyman-Michaels' account by the amount of the payment and then send a telex to its London office for retransmission to its correspondent bank in Geneva—Swiss Bank Corporation—asking Swiss Bank to deposit this amount in the Banque de Paris account of the *Pandora*'s owner. The transaction was completed by the crediting of Swiss Bank's account at Continental by the same amount.

When Hyman-Michaels chartered the *Pandora* in June 1972, market charter rates were very low, and it was these rates that were fixed in the charter for its entire term—two years if Hyman-Michaels exercised its option. Shortly after the agreement was signed, however, charter rates began to climb and by October 1972 they were much higher than they had been in June. The *Pandora*'s owners were eager to get out of the charter if they could. At the end of October they thought they had found a way, for the payment that was due in the Banque de Paris on October 26 had not arrived by October 30, and on that day the *Pandora*'s owner notified Hyman-Michaels that it was canceling the charter because of the breach of the payment term. Hyman-Michaels had mailed a check for the October 26 installment to the Banque de Paris rather than use the wire-transfer method of payment. It had done this in order to have the use of its money for the period that it would take the check to clear, about two weeks. But the check had not been mailed in Chicago until October 25 and of course did not reach Geneva on the twenty-sixth.

When Hyman-Michaels received notification that the charter was being canceled it immediately wired payment to the Banque de Paris, but the *Pandora*'s owner refused to accept it and insisted that the charter was indeed canceled. The matter was referred to arbitration in accordance with the charter. On December 5, 1972, the arbitration panel ruled in favor of Hyman-Michaels. The panel noted that previous arbitration panels had "shown varying degrees of latitude to Charterers"; "In all cases, a pattern of obligation on Owners' part to protest, complain, or warn of intended withdrawal was expressed as an essential prerequisite to withdrawal, in spite of the clear wording of the operative clause. No such advance notice was given by Owners of M/V Pandora." One of the three members of the panel dissented; he thought the *Pandora*'s owner was entitled to cancel.

Hyman-Michaels went back to making the charter payments by wire transfer. On the morning of April 25, 1973, it telephoned Continental Bank and requested it to transfer $27,000 to the Banque de Paris account of the *Pandora*'s owner in payment for the charter hire period from April 27 to May 11, 1973. Since the charter provided for payment "in advance," this payment arguably was due by the close of business on April 26. The requested telex went out to Continental's London office on the afternoon of April 25, which was nighttime in England. Early the next morning a telex operator in Continental's London office dialed, as Continental's Chicago office had instructed him to do, Swiss Bank's general telex number, which rings in the bank's cable department. But that number was busy, and after trying unsuccessfully for an hour to engage it the Continental telex operator dialed another number, that of a machine in Swiss Bank's foreign exchange department which he had used in the past when the general number was engaged. We know this machine received the telexed message because it signaled the sending machine at both the beginning and end of the transmission that the telex was being received. Yet Swiss Bank failed to comply with the payment order, and no transfer of funds was made to the account of the *Pandora*'s owner in the Banque de Paris.

No one knows exactly what went wrong. One possibility is that the receiving telex machine had simply run out of paper, in which event it would not print the message although it had received it. Another is that whoever took the message out of the machine after it was printed failed to deliver it to the banking department. Unlike the machine in the cable department that the Continental telex operator had originally tried to reach, the machines in the foreign exchange department were operated by junior foreign exchange dealers rather than by professional telex operators, although Swiss Bank knew that messages intended for other departments were sometimes diverted to the telex machines in the foreign exchange department.

At 8:30 a.m. the next day, April 27, Hyman-Michaels in Chicago received a telex from the *Pandora*'s owner stating that the charter was canceled because payment for the April 27–May 11 charter period had not been made. Hyman-Michaels called over to Continental and told them to keep trying to effect payment through Swiss Bank even if the *Pandora*'s owner rejected it. This instruction was confirmed in a letter to Continental dated April 28, in which Hyman-Michaels stated: "please instruct your London branch to advise their correspondents to persist in attempting to make this payment. This should be done even in the face of a rejection on the part of Banque de Paris to receive this payment. It is paramount that in order to strengthen our position in an arbitration that these funds continue to be readily available." Hyman-Michaels did not attempt to wire the money directly to the Banque de Paris as it had done on the occasion of its previous default. Days passed while the missing telex message was hunted unsuccessfully. Finally Swiss Bank suggested to Continental that it retransmit the telex message to the machine in the cable department and this was done on May 1. The next day Swiss Bank attempted to deposit the $27,000 in the account of the *Pandora*'s owner at the Banque de Paris but the payment was refused.

Again the arbitrators were convened and rendered a decision. In it they ruled that Hyman-Michaels had been "blameless" up until the morning of April 27, when it first learned that the Banque de Paris had not received payment on April 26, but that "being faced with this situation," Hyman-Michaels had "failed to do everything in [its] power to remedy it. The action taken was immediate but did not prove to be adequate, in that [Continental] Bank and its correspondent required some 5/6 days to trace and effect the lost instruction to remit. [Hyman-Michaels] could have ordered an immediate duplicate payment—or even sent a Banker's check by hand or special messengers, so that the funds could have reached owner's Bank, not later than April 28th." By failing to do any of these things Hyman-Michaels had "created the opening" that the *Pandora*'s owner was seeking in order to be able to cancel the charter. It had "acted imprudently." The arbitration panel concluded, reluctantly but unanimously, that this time the *Pandora*'s owner was entitled to cancel the agreement. The arbitration decision was confirmed by a federal district court in New York.

Hyman-Michaels then brought this diversity action against Swiss Bank, seeking to recover its expenses in the second arbitration proceeding plus the profits that it lost because of the cancellation of the charter. The contract by which Hyman-Michaels had agreed to ship scrap steel to Brazil had been terminated by the buyer in March 1973 and Hyman-Michaels had promptly subchartered the *Pandora* at market rates, which by April 1973 were double the rates fixed in the charter. Its lost profits are based on the difference between the charter and subcharter rates.

Swiss Bank impleaded Continental Bank as a third-party defendant, asking that if it should be ordered to pay Hyman-Michaels, then Continental should be ordered to indemnify it. Continental filed a cross-claim against Hyman-Michaels seeking to shift back to Hyman-Michaels the cost of any judgment that Swiss Bank might obtain against it, on the ground that any errors by Continental were caused by Hyman-Michaels' negligence. Hyman-Michaels in turn counterclaimed against Continental, alleging that Continental had both been negligent and broken its contract with Hyman-Michaels in failing to effect payment on April 26, and was therefore liable to Hyman-Michaels along with Swiss Bank.

The case was tried to a district judge without a jury. In his decision, 522 F.Supp. 820 (N.D.Ill.1981), he first ruled that the substantive law applicable to Hyman-Michaels' claim against Swiss Bank was that of Illinois, rather than Switzerland as urged by Swiss Bank, and that Swiss Bank had been negligent and under Illinois law was liable to Hyman-Michaels for $2.1 million in damages. This figure was made up of about $16,000 in arbitration expenses and the rest in lost profits on the subcharter of the *Pandora*. The judge also ruled that Swiss Bank was not entitled to indemnification from Continental Bank, which made Continental's cross-claim moot; and lastly he dismissed Hyman-Michaels' counterclaim against Continental on the ground that Continental had not breached any duty to Hyman-Michaels. The case comes to us on Swiss Bank's appeal from the judgment in favor of Hyman-Michaels and from the dismissal of Swiss Bank's claim against Continental Bank, and on Hyman-Michaels' appeal from the dismissal of its counterclaim against Continental Bank.

Logically the first question we should address is choice of law. The parties seem agreed that if Swiss law applies, Hyman-Michaels has no claim against Swiss Bank, because under Swiss law a bank cannot be held liable to someone with whom it is not in privity of contract and there was no contract between Swiss Bank and Hyman-Michaels. Illinois does not have such a privity requirement. But this creates a conflict of laws only if Hyman-Michaels has a good claim against Swiss Bank under Illinois law; if it does not, then our result must be the same regardless of which law applies. Because we are more certain that Hyman-Michaels cannot recover against Swiss Bank under Illinois law than we are that Swiss rather than Illinois law applies to this case under Illinois choice-of-law principles (which we must apply in a diversity suit tried in Illinois, see Klaxon Co. v. Stentor Elec. Mfg. Co., 313 U.S. 487, 496–97, 61 S.Ct. 1020, 1021–22, 85 L.Ed. 1477 (1941)), we shall avoid the choice-of-law question and discuss Swiss Bank's liability to Hyman-Michaels under Illinois law without deciding—for, to repeat, it would make no difference to the outcome—whether it really is Illinois law or Swiss law that governs.

When a bank fails to make a requested transfer of funds, this can cause two kinds of loss. First, the funds themselves or interest on them may be lost, and of course the fee paid for the transfer, having bought nothing, becomes a loss item. These are "direct" (sometimes called "general") damages. Hyman-Michaels is not seeking any direct damages in this case and apparently sustained none. It did not lose any part of the $27,000; although its account with Continental Bank was debited by this amount prematurely, it was not an interest-bearing account so Hyman-Michaels lost no interest; and Hyman-Michaels paid no fee either to Continental or to Swiss Bank for the aborted transfer. A second type of loss, which either the payor or the payee may suffer, is a dislocation in one's business triggered by the failure to pay. Swiss Bank's failure to transfer funds to the Banque de Paris when requested to do so by Continental Bank set off a chain reaction which resulted in an arbitration proceeding that was costly to Hyman-Michaels and in the cancellation of a highly profitable contract. It is those costs and lost profits—"consequential" or, as they are sometimes called, "special" damages—that Hyman-Michaels seeks in this lawsuit, and recovered below. It is conceded that if Hyman-Michaels was entitled to consequential damages, the district court measured them correctly. The only issue is whether it was entitled to consequential damages.

If a bank loses a check, its liability is governed by Article 4 of the Uniform Commercial Code, which precludes consequential damages unless the bank is acting in bad faith. See Ill.Rev.Stat. ch. 26, § 4–103(5). If Article 4 applies to this transaction, Hyman-Michaels cannot recover the damages that it seeks, because Swiss Bank was not acting in bad faith. Maybe the language of Article 4 could be stretched to include electronic fund transfers, see section 4–102(2), but they were not in the contemplation of the draftsmen. For purposes of this case we shall assume, as the Second Circuit held in Delbrueck & Co. v. Manufacturers Hanover Trust Co., 609 F.2d 1047, 1051 (2d Cir.1979), that Article 4 is inapplicable, and apply common law principles instead.

Hadley v. Baxendale, 9 Ex. 341, 156 Eng.Rep. 145 (1854), is the leading common law case on liability for consequential damages caused by failure or delay in carrying out a commercial undertaking. The engine shaft in plaintiffs' corn mill had broken and they hired the defendants, a common carrier, to transport the shaft to the manufacturer, who was to make a new one using the broken shaft as a model. The carrier failed to deliver the shaft within the time promised. With the engine shaft out of service the mill was shut down. The plaintiffs sued the defendants for the lost profits of the mill during the additional period that it was shut down because of the defendants' breach of their promise. The court held that the lost profits were not a proper item of damages, because "in the great multitude of cases of millers sending off broken shafts to third persons by a carrier under ordinary circumstances, such consequences [the stoppage of the mill and resulting loss of profits] would not, in all probability, have occurred; and these special circumstances were here never communicated by the plaintiffs to the defendants." 9 Ex. at 356, 156 Eng.Rep. at 151.

The rule of Hadley v. Baxendale—that consequential damages will not be awarded unless the defendant was put on notice of the special circumstances giving rise to them—has been applied in many Illinois cases, and *Hadley* cited approvingly. See, e.g., Underground Constr. Co. v. Sanitary Dist. of Chicago, 367 Ill. 360, 369, 11 N.E.2d 361, 365 (1937); Western Union Tel. Co. v. Martin, 9 Ill.App. 587, 591–93 (1882); Siegel v. Western Union Tel. Co., 312 Ill.App. 86, 92–93, 37 N.E.2d 868, 871 (1941); Spangler v. Holthusen, 61 Ill.App.3d 74, 80–82, 18 Ill.Dec. 840, 378 N.E.2d 304, 309–10 (1978). In *Siegel*, the plaintiff had delivered $200 to Western Union with instructions to transmit it to a friend of the plaintiff's. The money was to be bet (legally) on a horse, but this was not disclosed in the instructions. Western Union misdirected the money order and it did not reach the friend until several hours after the race had taken place. The horse that the plaintiff had intended to bet on won and would have paid $1650 on the plaintiff's $200 bet if the bet had been placed. He sued Western Union for his $1450 lost profit, but the court held that under the rule of Hadley v. Baxendale Western Union was not liable, because it "had no notice or knowledge of the purpose for which the money was being transmitted." 312 Ill.App. at 93, 37 N.E.2d at 871.

The present case is similar, though Swiss Bank knew more than Western Union knew in *Siegel*; it knew or should have known, from Continental Bank's previous telexes, that Hyman-Michaels was paying the Pandora Shipping Company for the hire of a motor vessel named *Pandora*. But it did not know when payment was due, what the terms of the charter were, or that they had turned out to be extremely favorable to Hyman-Michaels. And it did not know that Hyman-Michaels knew the *Pandora*'s owner would try to cancel the charter, and probably would succeed, if Hyman-Michaels was ever again late in making payment, or that despite this peril Hyman-Michaels would not try to pay until the last possible moment and in the event of a delay in transmission would not do everything in its power to minimize the consequences of the delay. Electronic funds transfers are not so unusual as to automatically place a bank on notice of extraordinary consequences if such a transfer goes awry. Swiss Bank did not have enough information to infer that if it lost a $27,000 payment order it would face a liability in excess of $2 million. * * *

It is true that in both *Hadley* and *Siegel* there was a contract between the parties and here there was none. We cannot be certain that the Illinois courts would apply the principles of those cases outside of the contract area. * * *The district judge found that Swiss Bank had been negligent in losing Continental Bank's telex message and it can be argued that Swiss Bank should therefore be liable for a broader set of consequences than if it had only broken a contract. But *Siegel* implicitly rejects this distinction. Western Union had not merely broken its contract to deliver the plaintiff's money order; it had "negligently misdirected" the money order. "The company's negligence is conceded." 312 Ill.App. at 88, 91, 37 N.E.2d at 869, 871. Yet it was not liable for the consequences.

Siegel, we conclude, is authority for holding that Swiss Bank is not liable for the consequences of negligently failing to transfer Hyman-Michaels' funds to Banque de Paris; reason for such a holding is found in the animating principle of Hadley v. Baxendale, which is that the costs of the untoward consequence of a course of dealings should be borne by that party who was able to avert the consequence at least cost and failed to do so. In *Hadley* the untoward consequence was the shutting down of the mill. The carrier could have avoided it by delivering the engine shaft on time. But the mill owners, as the court noted, could have avoided it simply by having a spare shaft. 9 Ex. at 355–56, 156 Eng.Rep. at 151. Prudence required that they have a spare shaft anyway, since a replacement could not be obtained at once even if there was no undue delay in carting the broken shaft to and the replacement shaft from the manufacturer. The court refused to imply a duty on the part of the carrier to guarantee the mill owners against the consequences of their own lack of prudence, though of course if the parties had stipulated for such a guarantee the court would have enforced it. The notice requirement of Hadley v. Baxendale is designed to assure that such an improbable guarantee really is intended.

This case is much the same, though it arises in a tort rather than a contract setting. Hyman-Michaels showed a lack of prudence throughout. It was imprudent for it to mail in Chicago a letter that unless received the next day in Geneva would put Hyman-Michaels in breach of a contract that was very profitable to it and that the other party to the contract had every interest in canceling. It was imprudent thereafter for Hyman-Michaels, having narrowly avoided cancellation and having (in the words of its appeal brief in this court) been "put . . . on notice that the payment provision of the Charter would be strictly enforced thereafter," to wait till arguably the last day before payment was due to instruct its bank to transfer the necessary funds overseas. And it was imprudent in the last degree for Hyman-Michaels, when it received notice of cancellation on the last possible day payment was due, to fail to pull out all the stops to get payment to the Banque de Paris on that day, and instead to dither while Continental and Swiss Bank wasted five days looking for the lost telex message. Judging from the obvious reluctance with which the arbitration panel finally decided to allow the *Pandora*'s owner to cancel the charter, it might have made all the difference if Hyman-Michaels had gotten payment to the Banque de Paris by April 27 or even by Monday, April 30, rather than allowed things to slide until May 2.

This is not to condone the sloppy handling of incoming telex messages in Swiss Bank's foreign department. But Hyman-Michaels is a sophisticated business enterprise. It knew or should have known that even the Swiss are not infallible; that messages sometimes get lost or delayed in transit among three banks, two of them located 5000 miles apart, even when all the banks are using reasonable care; and that therefore it should take its own precautions against the consequences—best known to itself—of a mishap that might not be due to anyone's negligence.

We are not the first to remark the affinity between the rule of Hadley v. Baxendale and the doctrine, which is one of tort as well as contract law and is a settled part of the common law of Illinois, of avoidable consequences. See Dobbs, Handbook on the Law of Remedies 831 (1973); cf. Benton v. J.A. Fay & Co., 64 Ill. 417 (1872). If you are hurt in an automobile accident and unreasonably fail to seek medical treatment, the injurer, even if negligent, will not be held liable for the aggravation of the injury due to your own unreasonable behavior after the accident. See, e.g., Slater v. Chicago Transit Auth., 5 Ill.App.2d 181, 185, 125 N.E.2d 289, 291 (1955). If in addition you failed to fasten your seat belt, you may be barred from collecting the tort damages that would have been prevented if you had done so. See, e.g., Mount v. McClellan, 91 Ill. App.2d 1, 5, 234 N.E.2d 329, 331 (1968). Hyman-Michaels' behavior in steering close to the wind prior to April 27 was like not fastening one's seat belt; its failure on April 27 to wire a duplicate payment immediately after disaster struck was like refusing to seek medical attention after a serious accident. The seat-belt cases show that the doctrine of avoidable consequences applies whether the tort victim acts imprudently before or after the tort is committed. See Prosser, Handbook of the Law of Torts 424 (4th ed. 1971). Hyman-Michaels did both.

The rule of Hadley v. Baxendale links up with tort concepts in another way. The rule is sometimes stated in the form that only foreseeable damages are recoverable in a breach of contract action. E.g., Restatement (Second) of Contracts § 351 (1979). So expressed, it corresponds to the tort principle that limits liability to the foreseeable consequence of the defendant's carelessness. * * * The amount of care that a person ought to take is a function of the probability and magnitude of the harm that may occur if he does not take care. * * * If he does not know what that probability and magnitude are, he cannot determine how much care to take. That would be Swiss Bank's dilemma if it were liable for consequential damages from failing to carry out payment orders in timely fashion. To estimate the extent of its probable liability in order to know how many and how elaborate fail-safe features to install in its telex rooms or how much insurance to buy against the inevitable failures, Swiss Bank would have to collect reams of information about firms that are not even its regular customers. It had no banking relationship with Hyman-Michaels. It did not know or have reason to know how at once precious and fragile Hyman-Michaels' contract with the *Pandora*'s owner was. These were circumstances too remote from Swiss Bank's practical range of knowledge to have affected its decisions as to who should man the telex machines in the foreign department or whether it should have more intelligent machines or should install more machines in the cable department, any more than the falling of a platform scale because a conductor jostled a passenger who was carrying fireworks was a prospect that could have influenced the amount of care taken by the Long Island Railroad. See Palsgraf v. Long Island R.R., 248 N.Y. 339, 162 N.E. 99 (1928); cf. Ney v. Yellow Cab Co., 2 Ill.2d 74, 80–84, 117 N.E.2d 74, 78–80 (1954).

In short, Swiss Bank was not required in the absence of a contractual undertaking to take precautions or insure against a harm that it could not measure but that was known with precision to Hyman-Michaels, which could by the exercise of common prudence have averted it completely. As Chief Judge Cardozo (the author of *Palsgraf*) remarked in discussing the application of Hadley v. Baxendale to the liability of telegraph companies for errors in transmission, "The sender can protect himself by insurance in one form or another if the risk of nondelivery or error appears to be too great. * * * The company, if it takes out insurance for itself, can do no more than guess at the loss to be avoided." Kerr S.S. Co. v. Radio Corp. of America, 245 N.Y. 284, 291–92, 157 N.E. 140, 142 (1927).

* * *

The legal principles that we have said are applicable to this case were not applied below. Although the district judge's opinion is not entirely clear, he apparently thought the rule of Hadley v. Baxendale inapplicable and the imprudence of Hyman-Michaels irrelevant. See 522 F.Supp. at 833. He did state that the damages to Hyman-Michaels were foreseeable because "a major international bank" should know that a failure to act promptly on a telexed request to transfer funds could cause substantial damage; but *Siegel*—and for that matter [other cases discussed in omitted portion of opinion]—make clear that that kind of general foreseeability, which is present in virtually every case, does not justify an award of consequential damages.

We could remand for new findings based on the proper legal standard, but it is unnecessary to do so. The undisputed facts, recited in this opinion, show as a matter of law that Hyman-Michaels is not entitled to recover consequential damages from Swiss Bank.

Since Hyman-Michaels' complaint against Swiss Bank must be dismissed, Swiss Bank's third-party complaint against Continental Bank and Continental Bank's cross-claim against Hyman-Michaels are moot. That leaves only Hyman-Michaels' counterclaim against Continental Bank still to be considered.

* * *

On the merits, we agree with the district judge that Hyman-Michaels did not prove its case. Continental did not break any contract with Hyman-Michaels. All it undertook to do on April 25 was to transmit a telex message to Swiss Bank, and it did so. All it undertook to do on April 27, by the evidence of Hyman-Michaels' own confirming letter, was to advise its correspondent—that is, Swiss Bank—to "persist in attempting to make * * * payment," and it did so advise its correspondent. Nor was Continental negligent on either occasion. Its telex operator had used the machine in Swiss Bank's foreign department before, for the same purpose and without incident; he had no reason to expect a mishap. And Continental used due care in assisting Swiss Bank in the latter's vain hunt for the missing telex. The district court's findings on these issues were skimpy but the facts are clear and a remand is unnecessary.

No other issues need be decided. The judgment in favor of Hyman-Michaels against Swiss Bank is reversed with directions to enter judgment for Swiss Bank. The judgment in favor of Continental Bank on Swiss Bank's third-party complaint is vacated with instructions to dismiss that complaint as moot. The judgment dismissing Continental's cross-claim against Hyman-Michaels as moot, and the judgment in favor of Continental on Hyman-Michaels' counterclaim, are affirmed. The costs of the appeals shall be borne by Hyman-Michaels (EVRA Corporation).

3. FRAUDULENT PAYMENT ORDERS

A wire transfer is a very efficient method of payment. Very large amounts can be transferred in a very short time at very low cost. But this great efficiency also provides a highly efficient method for the theft of money. The thief might steal funds in a bank account by fraudulently inducing either the bank or the owner of the account to make a wire transfer of the funds to an account controlled by the thief in some other bank. For example, the thief might electronically transmit to the bank a payment order purporting to be that of the owner of the account. If the bank is unaware that its customer did not send the order, the fraud can succeed. If the bank executes the fraudulent payment order, it has transferred funds on behalf of the customer without authority of the customer to do so. Who takes the loss? Has the thief stolen funds of the customer or funds of the bank? Under Article 4A a receiving bank that executes a payment order is not acting as the agent of the sender. § 4A–212. But if the bank executes an order that it believes to be the order of its customer but which in fact was issued by a person not authorized to act for its customer, should the law of agency determine whether the customer is bound by the unauthorized payment order issued in its name? If agency law applies, the customer is not bound by the unauthorized order, the bank has no authority to debit the customer's account and the bank takes the loss. But the law of agency is not very useful in determining whether the risk of loss with respect to an unauthorized payment order transmitted electronically should fall upon the receiving bank's customer, the purported sender of the fraudulent payment order, or the receiving bank that accepted it. The agency doctrines of actual, implied, and apparent authority grew out of cases in which the person purporting to be the agent and the third party acting in reliance on the acts of the purported agent have some personal contact with each other. These doctrines do not work well in cases in which a commercial transaction normally is carried out in the name of a principal by a person who is anonymous and who has no direct contact with the third person. In the case of electronic transmission of a payment order, the receiving bank is acting on the basis of a message that appears on a computer screen. There is no way of determining the identity or authority of the person who caused the message to be sent. The receiving bank is not relying on the authority of any particular person to act for its customer. Instead, the receiving bank relies on a security procedure pursuant to which the authenticity of the message can be "tested" by various devices such as identification codes or other security information in the control of the customer designed to provide certainty that the message is that of the customer identified in the payment order as its sender.

In the wire transfer business, the concept of "authorized" is different from the concept found in agency law. A payment order is treated as the order of the person in whose name it is issued if it is properly tested pursuant to a security procedure and the order passes the test. Risk of loss rules regarding unauthorized payment orders with respect to which verification pursuant to a security procedure is in effect are stated in § 4A–202 and § 4A–

203. The general rule is that a payment order is effective as the order of the customer, whether or not authorized, if the security procedure is commercially reasonable and the receiving bank proves that it accepted the order in good faith after verifying the order in compliance with the security procedure. There are certain exceptions and qualifications to this rule that are explained in the Comment to § 4A–203. The general rule is based on the assumption that losses due to unauthorized payment orders can best be avoided by the use of commercially reasonable security procedures, and that the use of such procedures should be encouraged. If a commercially reasonable security procedure is not in effect or if the bank fails to comply with a commercially reasonable procedure, ordinary rules of agency apply with the effect that, if the payment order was not authorized by the customer, the receiving bank acts at its peril in accepting the order.

The Article 4A rules are designed to protect both the customer and the receiving bank. A receiving bank needs to be able to rely on objective criteria to determine whether it can safely act on a payment order. Employees of that bank can be trained to "test" a payment order according to the various steps specified in the security procedure. The bank is responsible for the acts of these employees. The interests of the customer are protected by providing an incentive to a receiving bank to make available to the customer a security procedure that is commercially reasonable. Prudent banking practice may require that security procedures be utilized with respect to virtually all payment orders, except for those in which personal contact between the customer and the bank eliminates the possibility of an unauthorized order. The burden of making available commercially reasonable security procedures is imposed on receiving banks because generally they determine what security procedures can be used and are in the best position to evaluate the efficacy of procedures offered to customers to combat fraud. The burden on the customer is to supervise its employees to assure compliance with the security procedure, to safeguard confidential security information, and to restrict access to transmitting facilities so that the security procedure cannot be breached.

In the example that we have just examined, the dispute is between a bank customer, the purported originator of a funds transfer, and the originator's bank that executed the unauthorized order. *Bradford Trust,* the case that follows, raises a different issue and a more complex type of fraud. Bradford, as agent for a mutual fund, sent a payment order to State Street, which in turn sent a payment order to Texas American, the beneficiary's bank. Bradford issued its payment order to carry out instructions given by an impostor who impersonated Rochefort, a customer of the mutual fund, who owned the funds that Bradford's payment order was intended to transfer. Bradford conceded that it was not entitled to reimbursement from either the mutual fund or Rochefort. Rather, Bradford was attempting to shift the loss to Texas American, the beneficiary's bank. The fraud in *Bradford Trust* was made possible because the identity of the beneficiary of the fraudulent payment order was disguised. The beneficiary was described in the payment order by a name which identified one person, Rochefort, and a bank account number that identified another person, Colonial. The beneficiary's bank paid Colonial rather than Rochefort. *Bradford Trust* was decided before Article 4A was drafted and the court used principles of fault based on negligence to allocate the loss. Article 4A follows a different approach. If the case had arisen under Article 4A, § 4A–207(b)(1), (c), and (d) would have governed. Under Article 4A, would Bradford have been entitled to recover the payment from either Texas American or Colonial? Comment 2 to § 4A–207.

BRADFORD TRUST CO. v. TEXAS AMERICAN BANK

United States Court of Appeals, Fifth Circuit, 1986.
790 F.2d 407.

W. Eugene Davis, Circuit Judge:

This diversity case presents the question of who should bear the loss flowing from a fraudulently induced $800,000 wire transfer. We must choose between the institution that honored the forged order of its customer to wire funds and the bank to whom the funds were wired which did not credit the account as directed. On cross-motions for summary judgment the district court applied the Texas comparative negligence statute * * * and apportioned the loss equally between the two parties. Both parties appeal and argue that the other party should bear the entire loss. We decline to apply comparative negligence principles and reverse the judgment of the district court. We conclude that the initial bank that honored the forged order must bear the entire loss.

I.

In an ingenious scheme, two con artists, using aliases of Hank and Dave Friedman, arranged to buy rare coins and gold bullion from Colonial Coins, Inc. (Colonial) in Houston for $800,000. The impostors informed Colonial that they would wire funds from their bank in Boston to Colonial's account at Texas American Bank— Houston N.A. (Texas American) to pay for the coins. Colonial agreed and gave the Friedmans its account number at Texas American.

The impostors next sent a forged letter and stock power to Bradford Trust Company (Bradford), the agent for a mutual fund, directing the liquidation of $800,000 from the mutual fund account of Frank Rochefort. The forged order also instructed Bradford to wire the $800,000 from this account to Colonial's account in Texas American in Houston. Bradford, without following internal procedures recently instituted because of a similar scam,[3] ordered its correspondent bank, State Street Bank of Boston (State Street) to wire the funds to Texas American. The text of the transfer included the number of Colonial's account at Texas American, but stated that it was for the account of Frank S. Rochefort.[4] When the funds were received, Texas American notified Colonial that the funds had been deposited into Colonial's account. With this assurance, Colonial released the coins to the impostors.

Bradford became aware of the scam when an astonished Rochefort received notice of the withdrawal and informed Bradford that he had not authorized it. Bradford reinstated Rochefort's account and demanded that Texas American and Colonial reimburse it. Texas American and Colonial refused and this lawsuit followed. Bradford compromised its claim against Colonial, which was dismissed from the litigation. The district court, on summary judgment, applied the Texas comparative negligence statute and divided the loss equally between Bradford and Texas American. Bradford appeals, contending that Texas American should bear the entire loss because its negligence in failing to follow Bradford's order to deposit the funds in Rochefort's account was the primary cause of the loss. Texas American cross-appeals, arguing that Bradford should suffer the entire loss because Bradford dealt with the impostor, honored the forged order to pay and hence was in the best position to prevent the loss.

II.

A.

The district court, having no well-defined body of law that clearly applied to resolve the dispute in this case, relied on the Texas comparative negligence statute as authority to divide the damages between the parties. * * *

Although we feel the same equitable tug the district court undoubtedly felt to apply comparative negligence principles, we are persuaded that it would be a mistake to do so in this commercial case.

The comparative negligence statute expressly extends to actions "to recover damages for negligence resulting in *death or*

3. In April of 1980, Bradford was the victim of a similar fraudulent scheme. As a result, new security procedures were instituted. For transactions over $100,000, the new procedures required thorough review of the documents, shareholder confirmation when the shareholder instructed Bradford to wire the money to a person or to an address other than that on record, and approval by senior management.

4. The wire transfer stated: "State Street Bos/Michealpiemont MCMT 5207 X 6386 Southern Hou/A/O/Frank S. Rochnefort, Jr. Acct. * 057 141." (Note that Rochefort was misspelled.)

injury to persons or property * * *." * * * This language clearly extends comparative negligence principles to cases of physical harm to persons and property; whether this statute was intended to apply to other types of damage is doubtful. Although it is not inconceivable that a Texas court would interpret property broadly enough to include a loss such as that at issue here, we are persuaded that a federal diversity court should not adopt such a questionable interpretation. This is particularly true where, as here, neither party to the appeal urges us to apply comparative negligence principles.

We are also influenced by our recognition that in commercial disputes between seasoned bankers and other businessmen, certainty of result is more important than in traditional tort litigation. In commercial relationships known risks can be priced or shifted to others; if disputes arise, a bright line rule results in faster, easier settlements. The principal reason for a comparative negligence rule in physical harm cases—avoiding the harsh distributional results of precluding the recovery of the slightly negligent plaintiff who has suffered a devastating loss—has considerably less force in the commercial banking world. Prosser and Keeton on The Law of Torts, § 67, p. 469 (5th ed. 1984).

B.

Having decided that the Texas comparative negligence statute does not apply to this case, we widen our search for Texas law that does apply. Unfortunately, we have found no direct authority that resolves the question. * * * Other courts faced with resolving controversies relating to wire transfers have applied the UCC by analogy. * * * Because of the close analogy between allocation of fraud losses in negotiable instruments and wire transfers we look to both Texas court decisions before Texas adopted the UCC and the UCC for guidance. Two factors emerge from these sources that are helpful in analyzing the question of who should bear the loss in this case: 1) which party was in the best position to avoid the loss; and 2) which solution promotes the policy of finality in commercial transactions?

The first factor, which party is in the best position to avoid the loss, is a principal reason underlying a number of loss allocation calls in the UCC. For example, it provides the essential reason for requiring the drawee bank to bear the loss if it pays on the drawer's forged signature. * * * This is because the bank, which can verify its customer's signature, is in the best position to discover the forgery and avoid the loss. Similarly, if an endorsement on an instrument is forged, the loss is ordinarily placed on the party in the collection chain who accepted the instrument from the forger. * * * Again, the UCC recognizes that the party dealing directly with the forger has an opportunity to verify

the endorser's identity and is in the best position to avoid the loss.
Indeed, the common thread running through the impostor cases is
to "throw the loss resulting from dealing with an impostor on the
person who dealt with the impostor, and presumably, had the best
opportunity to take precautions that would have detected the
fraud, rather than on a subsequent holder, who had no similar
opportunity." Fair Park National Bank v. Southwestern Investment Co., 541 S.W.2d 266, 269–70 (Tex.Civ.App.1976).

Bradford dealt directly with the impostor. It received the
forged order directing the liquidation of Rochefort's account. If
Bradford had followed procedures it had in place that called for
verification of the customer's order, the loss would not have
occurred. Instead of following those procedures and verifying
Rochefort's order, Bradford set the fraudulent scheme into motion
by liquidating Rochefort's account and wiring the funds to Texas
American. Although Texas American should have recognized the
discrepancy between the account number and the name of the
owner of the account to whom the wire directed the funds be
credited, we are persuaded that Texas American's fault was secondary to that of Bradford's. It is far from certain that the loss
would have been prevented even if Texas American had noticed
the discrepancy between the account number and the holder of the
account and had called this discrepancy to Bradford's attention.
To conclude that this action by Texas American would have
avoided the loss requires us to assume that such a call to Bradford
would have caused Bradford to contact Rochefort and verify his
order. On the other hand, it is certain that if Bradford had called
Rochefort to verify his purported order to transfer funds to Colonial this scheme would have been discovered and no loss would have
been suffered.

*   *   *

For the reasons set forth above, we are persuaded that Bradford, by honoring the forged order to transmit Rochefort's funds
after dealing directly with the impostor, was in the best position to
avoid the loss.

*   *   *

C.

Bradford urges us to find that Texas American's failure to
follow Bradford's instructions in the wire transfer was the primary, overriding cause of the loss. Bradford argues that its earlier
negligence in accepting the forged order of Rochefort to pay would
have been inconsequential had Texas American handled the transfer with due care and in accordance with ordinary standards and
practices of the banking industry. We agree with Bradford that
Texas American was negligent in failing to notice the discrepancy
between the account number and the name of the owner of the
account to which the funds were to be credited. Even if allocation

of the loss depended entirely upon a determination of which party was more at fault, however, this would not alter our decision to lay the loss at Bradford's feet. We are persuaded that Bradford's act in honoring the forged authorization without following its own internal procedures to verify the genuineness of the request was the primary cause of the loss. The fault of Texas American failing to note the discrepancy between the account number and the name of the owner of the account to whom the money was to be credited was less grave than that of Bradford.

    *   *   * For the reasons stated above, despite the negligence of Texas American, we conclude that Bradford must bear the loss. Accordingly, the judgment of the district court is reversed and the action is remanded to the district court for entry of judgment in favor of Texas American and against Bradford.

C.   CREDIT CARDS

---

1.   INTRODUCTION

    Credit cards fall into two broad categories. In the first category are credit cards issued by a merchant as a means of identifying customers who have charge accounts with the merchant. They are particularly convenient for merchants who have numerous retail outlets located over a large geographical area. These cards originally could be used to make purchases only from the merchant that issued the card, but in some cases use of the card to purchase from a limited number of other merchants is also permitted. Included in this first category are cards issued by oil companies for use at affiliated or independently owned service stations that sell products of the company that issued the card. The most important characteristic of this category of credit card is that the primary purpose of the issuer is to facilitate sales of goods or services of the issuer.

    A second category comprises credit cards issued by financial institutions that provide short-term credit, usually unsecured, to cardholders to allow them to make purchases from a multitude of merchants and other sellers of goods and services who are not related to the issuer of the card. Prominent examples of the second category are the Visa card, MasterCard, and the American Express card. This category of credit card has emerged as an important substitute for cash or a personal check in paying for goods or services. A merchant who accepts this type of credit card as the payment mechanism is party to a preexisting arrangement either directly with the issuer of the card or with an interbank system to which the issuer belongs, such as Visa or MasterCard. Pursuant to this arrangement the merchant can obtain payment from the issuer for purchases made by use of the card. In a face-to-face purchase, the cardholder signs a credit card slip indicating the amount of the purchase and bearing an imprint, taken by use of the card, of the name and account number of the cardholder. The merchant is faced with several risks in taking a credit card. First, the person using the card may not be a person authorized to use the card. Second, the card may have been revoked by the issuer. One common reason for revocation is a report to the issuer that the card has been lost or stolen. Third, the amount of credit given by the issuer to the cardholder may not be sufficient to cover the amount of the purchase. The merchant can normally avoid the last two risks. At the time a purchase is to be made, the merchant can determine, through telephonic or electronic access to a computer center having a record of the card, whether the card is valid and whether the charge is within the cardholder's line of credit. Through this process the merchant obtains approval of the charge before the purchase is made and has assurance of receiving payment in accordance with the arrangement to which the issuer and merchant are parties. Normally the merchant receives the amount of the charge less a discount to compensate the issuer for financing the purchase. The issuer obtains this compensation by obtaining payment of the full amount of the charge from the cardholder. Thus, the credit risk of nonpayment by the cardholder is taken by the issuer. The issuer normally sends a monthly statement of charges to the cardholder. Under most plans, the cardholder has the option of paying the full amount by a specified date without an interest charge or of making payment in installments with an interest charge. A newspaper report indicates that about three quarters of credit cardholders maintain an unpaid balance in their accounts. The typical unpaid balance on credit card accounts was reported to be $2,474. Wall Street Journal, p. A1, col. 6, Dec. 26, 1991.

Rights and obligations between the issuer of the credit card and the cardholder are governed by the contract between the parties under which the card is issued to the cardholder, but this contract is subject to regulation of the issuer-cardholder relationship by some state statutes and by federal law, found in various provisions of the Consumer Credit Protection Act.

2. FRAUDULENT USE OF LOST OR STOLEN CREDIT CARDS

---

a. ALLOCATION OF LOSS UNDER COMMON LAW

In *Sears,* the case that follows, the court discusses common-law principles for allocation of loss when a lost credit card is fraudulently used to charge purchases of goods to the cardholder's account. *Sears* is one of the most favorable decisions to the issuer of the credit card, but many other courts, on one theory or another, imposed the loss on the issuer of the card. After the *Sears* case was decided liability of the cardholder for unauthorized use of the card was limited by Federal statute.

SEARS, ROEBUCK & CO. v. DUKE

Supreme Court of Texas, 1969.
441 S.W.2d 521.

REAVLEY, JUSTICE. Sears, Roebuck and Co. sued Waldo Duke for the price of merchandise sold to an impostor using the Sears credit card issued to Duke. The purchases were made within two weeks following Duke's loss of the card, and two weeks before either he or Sears had knowledge of its loss. After the jury absolved both parties of negligence, the trial court entered judgment for Sears. The Court of Civil Appeals ordered a new trial on the ground that Sears failed to offer sufficient proof of the exercise of care, on the occasion of each sale, to ascertain the identity of the credit card user. 433 S.W.2d 919. We hold that the Court of Civil Appeals imposed an incorrect duty on Sears, that Sears was entitled to rely upon the card alone as identification unless circumstances presented cause for further inquiry; and we remand the case to that court for reconsideration of points before it.

Duke and his wife lived in Lubbock, Texas and did business with the Sears store located there. In 1960 he signed a "Sears Revolving Charge Account Agreement" which began as follows:

"In consideration of your selling merchandise to me on Sears revolving Charge Account, I agree to the following regarding all purchases made by me or on my Sears revolving Charge Account identification * * * "

Two credit cards were issued with the account number and the name, Waldo N. Duke, on the front of the cards. There is no question raised at any point in this record but that the credit cards were the Sears "identification" to which the credit agreement refers. No additional terms of agreement appear on the back of the card, but there is a statement saying that the card is the property of Sears and its loss or theft should be reported. Mrs. Duke signed as "authorized purchaser" and used one of the cards. The second card, unsigned, was carried by Duke with a number of other credit cards.

Duke was in New York on a business trip during the week of December 12, 1965, and he left his credit cards in a suitcase in his hotel room. Apparently the thief took the Sears card and a Sinclair Refining Company card, made a note of Duke's home address and signed "Waldo N. Duke" in his own handwriting on the Sears card. Presumably the card was taken December 13, and over $1,200 in merchandise was purchased in various Sears stores in the New York area within the following two weeks. On

January 12, 1966, the credit department of the Sears store in Lubbock received notice of the unusual number of charges on the Duke account, and an inquiry was made to Mr. and Mrs. Duke. It was then that all of the parties first realized that the card was missing.

Duke has taken the position that he is not liable for the unauthorized use of his credit card, or for sales made by Sears to a stranger. There is no basis here for tort liability against Duke. The evidence clearly supports the findings of the jury to the effect that Duke was not negligent in the loss of his card or in the failure to report the loss to Sears. The jury has found that Duke was not negligent in failing to sign his card, and no point in that connection is presented to us. The question then is his contractual obligation, and this turns upon the construction of the words of the credit agreement set forth above. By that agreement Duke did more than promise to pay for merchandise he purchased. He promised to pay for "all purchases made on my Sears revolving Charge Account identification." The meaning we give to these words is that Duke will pay for *all* sales made by Sears to a purchaser identifying himself by the use of the credit card, which was issued by Sears upon receipt of the executed credit agreement.

Duke says that his obligation does not cover the sale to a person who is not in fact authorized to use the card or to make a purchase on Duke's credit. But this is precisely the purpose of this card: to satisfy the question of identity and of authorization. It is the reason why Duke was called upon to sign an agreement to pay not only for his purchases from Sears but for those made on the issued identification as well.

Duke further argues that if Sears wanted the agreement to have so drastic an effect as to bind him to pay for unauthorized purchases, Sears should have expressly so stated on either the agreement or the credit cards. We believe this to be the meaning of the agreement, and we do not regard this result to be so surprising in this credit card age. When Duke himself made a purchase and presented his credit card, he would not expect to be questioned. He should not expect the disguised thief to be.

The convenience of the credit card to both issuer and holder presents both with attendant risks. In general, and subject to contrary agreement by the parties, the one who can best control the risk should assume it. Thus, the issuer who puts a card into the mail without prior agreement with its intended holder should assume the larger part of the risk of improper use. After a holder accepts the card or agrees to pay for purchases made through its use, the risk of misuse is his unless and until he notifies the issuer otherwise. The holder can destroy his card if he feels that this is too great a burden. But if he is to carry it about, he must guard it as he does his currency if he is to avoid the expense of use by an impostor. If it is lost or stolen, by notifying the issuer, the holder shifts the risk of misuse back to the one who created the device. Texaco, Inc. v. Goldstein, 34 Misc.2d 751, 229 N.Y.S.2d 51 (N.Y. Mun.Ct.) aff'd 39 Misc.2d 552, 241 N.Y.S.2d 495 (App.Div., 1962).

The issuer of the card, or the seller of the goods, cannot ignore suspicious circumstances when selling to an impostor. The holder's liability has its limitations whether it be said that the issuer cannot avoid liability for his own negligence, or that the promise of the holder should be construed as being conditional upon the merchant's fulfillment of his obligation. See Comment: The Tripartite Credit Card Transaction: The Legal Infant, 48 Calif.L.R. 459, 483 (1960). In Gulf Refining Co. v. Williams Roofing Co., 208 Ark. 362, 186 S.W.2d 790, 158 A.L.R. 754 (1945), the holder of the card had printed "GOOD FOR TRUCK ONLY" on the face of the credit card. It was held that the seller was required to observe the limitation. In an often cited Oregon case, the address on the credit card of the holder was shown to be in Oregon, while Idaho license plates were on the car used by the impostor when the purchases were made. This was held to raise a fact question as to the seller's care. Union Oil Co. of California v. Lull, 220 Or. 412, 349 P.2d 243 (1960).

The cases differ as to the nature of the issuer-seller's duty of care, and as to the burden of proof. We hold that the seller need not demand more identification than the credit card as a matter of normal procedure. This is the function of the credit card, and it should be considered satisfactory evidence of identity of the holder or authorized user, unless the appearances or circumstances would raise a question in the mind of a reasonable seller. Proof that the seller did fail to use ordinary care in this respect is a defense to the liability of the holder of the card, and the burden of proof should be placed upon him.

The Court of Civil Appeals has ruled that the jury finding in favor of Sears, as to its care in ascertaining the identity and authority of the persons using the credit card, was not supported by sufficient evidence. However, that court has incorrectly placed the burden of proof upon Sears and has further enlarged the burden on Sears by holding that it could not discharge its duty of care by accepting the credit card as the only proof of identity. The judgment must therefore be reversed. We are unable to render judgment here in favor of Sears by holding, as Sears urges, that there was no evidence of its lack of care. Many purchases were made in the same stores, and one New York area store inquired of the Lubbock store as to Duke's credit standing in connection with one large purchase without any question being raised about the irregularity. The case must be remanded to the Court of Civil Appeals for reconsideration of the points of factual insufficiency to support the jury finding, which is a matter solely within that court's jurisdiction.

The judgment is reversed and the cause is remanded to the Court of Civil Appeals for further proceedings consistent with this opinion.

b. LIMITATION OF LIABILITY OF CARDHOLDER FOR UNAUTHORIZED USE

In 1970 Congress enacted legislation banning the practice of some issuers of acquiring cardholders by issuing credit cards to people who did not request them. Consumer Credit Protection Act ("CCPA") § 132, 15 U.S.C. § 1642. At the same time Congress severely limited the amount of liability of a cardholder for unauthorized use of a credit card. That legislation, in amended form, is CCPA § 133, 15 U.S.C. § 1643. This limitation applies to any credit card whether used for consumer or business purposes. CCPA § 135, 15 U.S.C. § 1645.

WALKER BANK & TRUST CO. v. JONES
Supreme Court of Utah, 1983.
672 P.2d 73.

Hall, Chief Justice:

At issue in these consolidated cases is the liability of defendants to plaintiff Walker Bank for expenses allegedly incurred by defendants' separated spouses upon credit card accounts established by the plaintiff bank in the names of the defendants. Defendants appeal from adverse summary judgment orders on the grounds that their rights under the Federal Truth in Lending Act [1] were violated.

A. Defendant Betty Jones

In 1977, Defendant Jones established VISA and Master Charge accounts with plaintiff Walker Bank (hereinafter "Bank"). Upon her request, credit cards were issued on those accounts to herself and her husband in each of their names.

On or about November 11, 1977, defendant Jones informed the Bank, by two separate letters, that she would no longer honor charges made by her husband on the two accounts, whereupon the Bank immediately revoked both accounts and requested the return of the credit cards.[2] Despite numerous notices of revocation and requests for surrender of the cards, both defendant Jones and her husband retained their cards and continued to make charges against the accounts.

1. 15 U.S.C. §§ 1601, et seq.

2. By the terms of the credit card account agreement, an account can be closed by returning to the Bank all outstanding credit cards.

It was not until March 9, 1978, that defendant Jones finally relinquished her credit cards to the Bank, and then only after a persuasive visit to her place of employment by a Bank employee. At the time she surrendered her cards, the balance owing on the combined accounts (VISA and Master Charge) was $2,685.70. Her refusal to pay this balance prompted the Bank's institution of this suit to recover the same.

B. Defendant Gloria Harlan

In July, 1979, defendant Harlan, who was prior to that time a VISA cardholder at plaintiff Bank, requested that her husband, John Harlan, be added to the account as an authorized user. The Bank honored this request and issued a card to Mr. Harlan. Shortly thereafter, at some point between July and the end of 1979, the Harlans separated and defendant (Mrs.) Harlan informed the Bank by letter that she either wanted the account closed or wanted the Bank to deny further extensions of credit to her husband.

Notwithstanding the explicit requirement in the account agreement that all outstanding credit cards be returned to the Bank in order to close the account, defendant Harlan did not tender either her card or her husband's at the time she made the aforementioned request. As to her card, she informed the Bank that she could not return it because it had been destroyed in the Bank's automated teller. Notwithstanding, however, she returned the card to the Bank some three months later (March, 1980).

In the interim period, i.e., after defendant's correspondence with the Bank regarding the exclusion of her husband from her account and prior to the relinquishment of her card, several charges were made (purportedly by Mr. Harlan) on the account for which the Bank now seeks recovery. The Bank has sued only Mrs. Harlan, as owner of the account.

Defendants' sole contention on appeal is that the Federal Truth in Lending Act (hereinafter "TILA") limits their liability, for the unauthorized use of the credit cards by their husbands, to a maximum of $50. The specific section of the Act upon which this contention rests is 15 U.S.C. § 1643. In pertinent part, it reads thus:

> (a) A cardholder shall be liable for the unauthorized use of a credit card only if the card is an accepted credit card, the liability is not in excess of $50.00 * * * and the unauthorized use occurs before the cardholder has notified the issuer that an unauthorized use of the credit card has occurred or may occur as the result of loss, theft, or otherwise.
>
>   * * *
>
> (d) Except as provided in this section, a cardholder incurs no liability from the unauthorized use of a credit card.

The Bank's rejoinder is that § 1643 does not apply, inasmuch as defendants' husbands' use of the credit cards was at no time "unauthorized use" within the meaning of the statute. Whether such use was "unauthorized," as that term is contemplated by the statute, is the pivotal question in this case.

The term "unauthorized use" is defined in 15 U.S.C. § 1602(o) (1974) as:

> [U]se of a credit card by a person other than the cardholder who does not have actual, implied, or apparent authority for such use and from which the cardholder receives no benefit.

A "cardholder" is described in 15 U.S.C. § 1602(m) as:

> [A]ny person to whom a credit card is issued or any person who has agreed with the card-issuer to pay obligations arising from the issuance of a credit card to another person.

Defendants contend that they alone occupied the status of "cardholder," by reason of their request to the bank that credit cards be issued to their husbands and their assumption of liability therefor. Accordingly, they maintain that their husbands were no more than authorized users of defendants' accounts.

Defendants further aver that the effect of their notification to the Bank stating that they would no longer be responsible for charges made against their accounts by their husbands was to render any subsequent use (by their husbands) of the cards unauthorized. This notification, defendants maintain, was all that was necessary to revoke the authority they had once created in their husbands and thereby invoke the § 1643 limitations on cardholder liability.

The Bank's position is that unauthorized use within the meaning of § 1643 is precisely what the statutory definition (§ 1602(o) supra) says it is, to wit: "[U]se * * * by a person * * * who does not have actual, implied, or apparent authority * * *," and that notification to the card issuer has no bearing whatsoever on whether the use is unauthorized, so as to entitle a cardholder to the statutory limitation of liability. We agree with this position.

Where § 1643 governs, the liability of the cardholder for unauthorized charges is limited to $50 regardless of any notification to the card issuer. Notification, if given prior to the unauthorized charges, serves only to eliminate the $50 liability and not, as defendants argue, to render a use unauthorized. Unless and until the unauthorized nature of the use has been established, the notification provision, as well as the statute itself, is irrelevant and ineffectual.

The language of the statute defining unauthorized use (§ 1602(o) supra) is clear and unambiguous. It excludes from the category of unauthorized users, any person who has "actual, implied, or apparent authority."

The Bank maintains that defendants' husbands clearly had "apparent" authority to use the cards, inasmuch as their signatures were the same as the signatures on the cards, and their names, the same as those imprinted upon the cards. Accordingly, it contends that no unauthorized use was made of the cards, and that defendants therefore cannot invoke the limitations on liability provided by the TILA.

Again, we find the Bank's position to be meritorious. Apparent authority exists:

> [W]here a person has created such an appearance of things that it causes a third party reasonably and prudently to believe that a second party has the power to act on behalf of the first person * * *.[5]

As previously pointed out, at defendants' request their husbands were issued cards bearing the husbands' own names and signatures. These cards were, therefore, a representation to the merchants (third parties) to whom they were presented that defendants' husbands (second parties—card-bearers) were authorized to make charges upon the defendants' (first parties—cardholders) accounts. This apparent authority conferred upon defendants' husbands by reason of the credit cards thus precluded the application of the TILA.

In view of our determination that the TILA has no application to the present case, we hold that liability for defendants' husbands' use of the cards is governed by their contracts with the Bank. The contractual agreements between defendants and the Bank provided clearly and unequivocally that *all* cards issued upon the accounts be returned to the Bank in order to terminate defendants' liability. Accordingly, defendants' refusal to relinquish either their cards or their husbands', at the time they notified the Bank that they no longer accepted liability for their husbands' charges, justified the Bank's disregard of that notification and refusal to terminate defendants' liability at that time.

The dissent expresses concern that the decision of the Court imposes an unreasonable burden on the cardholder. We disagree because in our opinion justice is better served by placing the responsibility for the credit escapades of an errant spouse (or son, daughter, mother, father, etc.) on the cardholder rather than the Bank. The cardholder is not left powerless to protect against misuse of the card. He or she need only surrender the cards and close the account, just as the defendants in the instant case were requested by the Bank to do.

5. Wynn v. McMahon Ford Co., Mo. App., 414 S.W.2d 330, 336 (1967).

Affirmed.   No costs awarded.

OAKS, J., and J. ROBERT BULLOCK, DISTRICT JUDGE, concur.

DURHAM, JUSTICE (dissenting):

I dissent from the majority opinion because I believe that the federal statute and the specific cardholder agreements in question relieve the defendants of liability for the unauthorized use of their credit cards by their spouses.

The pertinent portions of § 1643 of the Federal Truth in Lending Act (hereafter "TILA") are set forth in the majority opinion.   See 15 U.S.C.A. § 1643 (1982).   Section 1643(a) of the TILA limits a cardholder's liability to a maximum of $50 for any unauthorized use of a credit card which occurs *before* the cardholder has notified the card issuer of the possibility of any unauthorized use.   More importantly, however, § 1643(d) relieves a cardholder of "all" liability for any unauthorized use which occurs *after* the cardholder has notified the card issuer of the possibility of an unauthorized use.   The cardholder agreements in the present case contain provisions which implement, and are virtually identical to, § 1643:

> Unauthorized Use.   Cardholder is responsible for all authorized transactions made and credit extended by use of Cardholder's [credit card], regardless of credit limits and the party using them.   Cardholder may be liable for the unauthorized use of the cards where the cards are used by a person other than the Cardholder who does not have actual, implied or apparent authority for such use and from which the Cardholder receives no benefit.   However, *Cardholder will not be liable for the unauthorized use of a [credit card] which occurs after written or oral notice of the loss, theft or possible unauthorized use is given* either verbally at any office of Bank or in writing * * *.   Liability for unauthorized use shall in no event exceed $50.00 on each account established.

(Emphasis added.)   Thus, as recognized by the majority opinion, the resolution of this case focuses on whether the defendants' husbands' use of the defendants' credit cards constitutes an "unauthorized use" within the meaning of the statute and the cardholder agreements.

The term "unauthorized use" is defined as follows:

> "[U]nauthorized use" * * * means use of a credit card by a person * * * who does not have actual, implied, or apparent authority for such use and from which the cardholder receives no benefit.

15 U.S.C.A. § 1602(*o*) (1982).   Thus, the pivotal issue in this case is whether the defendants' notification to the Bank was sufficient to revoke the defendants' husbands' "actual, implied, or apparent authority" to use the credit cards, thereby rendering the hus-

bands' use unauthorized. The majority opinion responds in the negative by contending that the defendants' husbands were clothed with apparent authority because they carried credit cards imprinted with the husbands' names and bearing the husbands' signatures. The majority opinion holds that, despite notification to the Bank by the defendants that all authority has been expressly revoked, this apparent authority continues to exist until the defendants obtain the cards from their estranged husbands and return them to the Bank. I disagree with that holding for three reasons.

First, the result of the majority opinion runs counter to the purpose of § 1643 of the TILA, which has been described as follows:

> The federal credit card statute reflects a policy decision that it is preferable for the issuer to bear fraud losses arising from credit card use.

> * * * [I]ssuers are in a better position to control the occurrence of these losses. They not only select the merchants who may accept the card and the holders who may use it, but also design the security systems for card distribution, user identification, and loss notification. Hence, *the statutory choice of issuer liability assures that the problem of credit card loss is the responsibility of the party most likely to take efficient steps in its resolution.*

Weistart, Consumer Protection in the Credit Card Industry: Federal Legislative Controls, 70 Mich.L.Rev. 1475, 1509–10 (1972) (citations omitted) (emphasis added). Cf. First National Bank of Mobile v. Roddenberry, 701 F.2d 927 (11th Cir.1983) (stating that, by issuing a credit card, a bank assumes the risk of nonpayment and that only the bank can decide when and if credit will be revoked). Under the present circumstances, I acknowledge that the burden or risk of liability should initially fall on the cardholder because use of the credit card by a spouse is, and remains, authorized until notice is given to the card issuer that the authority to use the credit card is revoked. However, once the cardholder notifies the card issuer of the revocation of that authority, it is clear that the card issuer is in the best position to protect itself, the cardholder and third parties. The card issuer can protect both itself and the cardholder by refusing to pay any charges on the account, and it can protect third parties by listing the credit card in the regional warning bulletins. See Weistart, supra; Standard Oil Co. v. State Neon Co., 120 Ga.App. 660, 171 S.E.2d 777 (1969). The issuer need only terminate the existing account, transfer all existing charges to a new number, and issue a new card to the cardholder.

In circumstances similar to the present case, the Supreme Court of New York stated:

It is interesting to note, parenthetically, that under the provisions above quoted, defendant [cardholder] would not be liable for purchases made after notice of loss or theft of the card and if he was in fact unable to obtain the card from his estranged wife, the result was not greatly different. Indeed the plaintiff's [card issuer's] situation was no worse than in the case of a loss of theft but probably considerably better since it knew the whereabouts of the card and of the holder.

Socony Mobil Oil Co. v. Greif, 10 A.D.2d 522, 197 N.Y.S.2d 522, 523–24 (1960) (decided prior to the enactment of § 1643 of the TILA and based on the language of the particular cardholder agreement). Thus, in conformance with the purpose of § 1643 of the TILA, the better holding in this case, as a policy matter, is that, after notification to the card issuer, the cardholder should be relieved of all liability for the unauthorized use of the credit card by an estranged spouse.

Second, the language of § 1643 and the law of agency require that the defendants be relieved of liability. As the majority opinion recognizes, state law determines the question of whether the defendants' husbands are clothed with "apparent authority." See, e.g., FRB Letter of July 23, 1974, No. 822, by J. Kluckman, Chief, Truth-in-Lending Section (excerpted in Consumer Credit Guide (CCH) ¶ 31,144 (October 8, 1974)). Under Utah law, a husband or wife may terminate an agency created in the spouse in the same manner as any other agency. See U.C.A., 1953, § 30–2–8. The majority opinion holds that the defendants' husbands' use was authorized because the husbands had "apparent authority." This is apparently a reference to the relationship between the husband and third-party merchants who rely on the husband's possession of a credit card with his name and matching signature on it. It cannot refer to the existence of apparent authority vis-a-vis the Bank, because the Bank has been *expressly notified* of the revocation of all authority. I fail to see why the existence of "apparent authority" as to third-party merchants should govern the liability of a cardholder whose spouse "steals" a card in the context of marital difficulties, any more than it would govern in the case of a cardholder whose card is stolen before delivery and bears a "matching signature" forged thereon by a thief.

It is well recognized that apparent authority exists only to the extent that the *principal* represents to a third person that another is one's agent. See, e.g., Restatement (Second) of Agency § 8 & comments (1958). In the present case, with respect to the Bank, the husbands' authority, actual, implied and apparent, was specifically terminated by the defendants (the principals) when the Bank was notified that the husbands' authority to use the defendants' credit cards was revoked. See, e.g., id. §§ 124A, 125 & 130. Thus, after notification, the husbands' use was unauthorized and both

§ 1643 and the provisions of the cardholder agreements relieved the defendants of all liability for charges incurred by their husbands subsequent to that notification. See, e.g., In re Shell Oil Co., 95 F.T.C. 357 (1980); Socony Mobil Oil Co. v. Greif, supra. Accord Neiman–Marcus Co. v. Viser, La., 140 So.2d 762 (1962).

In the *Shell Oil* case, supra, several cardholders petitioned the Federal Trade Commission (hereafter "FTC"), which is vested with authority to enforce both the Federal Trade Commission Act and the TILA, for relief from certain practices of the Shell Oil Co. which were allegedly in violation of those Acts. Shell Oil Co. issued credit cards to cardholders to enable them to purchase goods and services at Shell's service stations. Some cardholders authorized third persons to use their credit cards. In certain instances, several cardholders notified Shell Oil Co. that such previously authorized users were no longer authorized. Shell Oil Co. responded by informing the cardholders that they would remain liable for charges incurred by the third persons until the credit cards used by the third persons were returned. The FTC ordered Shell Oil Co. to forthwith cease and desist from:

1. *Failing to limit the liability of a cardholder* for use of a credit card by a third person, in those cases where such third person has been given authorization by the cardholder to use such credit card, *to the amount* of money, property, labor, or services *obtained by use prior to notification* ∗ ∗ ∗ by the cardholder that such use is no longer authorized ∗ ∗ ∗ [and]

2. Informing a cardholder that [the card issuer] considers the cardholder liable for use of a credit card by a third person which occurs after the cardholder notifies [the card issuer] that such use is no longer authorized.

In re Shell Oil Co., supra, at 359–60 (emphasis added). Thus, under § 1643 as interpreted by the FTC in the *Shell Oil* case, the defendants' liability in the present case is limited to the charges incurred by their husbands prior to notification.

The majority opinion sanctions the Bank's refusal to terminate the defendants' liability based on the majority opinion's interpretation that the cardholder agreements require "clearly and unequivocally that *all* cards issued upon the accounts be returned to the Bank in order to terminate defendants' liability." To the contrary, the cardholder agreements do not mandate the return of the credit cards as a condition precedent to termination of *liability*. The cardholder agreements provide that "Cardholder may terminate this *Agreement* at any time by returning the cards issued under this Agreement to the Bank." (Emphasis added.) This provision deals with termination of the "account," not termination of liability for unauthorized use. In fact, like § 1643, the relevant portions of the cardholder agreements, quoted above, provide specifically that the cardholder is not liable for charges incurred *after* notice of the possible unauthorized use is given to the Bank. Contrary to the majority opinion's suggestion, there are no provisions in the cardholder agreements that require the return of the credit cards to the Bank as a prerequisite to relieving the defendants of "liability" for the unauthorized use of their credit cards.

Finally, the majority opinion ignores the impracticality of imposing the burden on a cardholder of obtaining a credit card from an estranged spouse in order to return it to the Bank. It is unrealistic to think that estranged spouses will be cooperative. Moreover, it is extremely unwise to arm one spouse with a weapon which permits virtually unlimited spending at the expense of the other. As is illustrated by the facts of these cases, where the whereabouts of the unauthorized spouse are unknown, the cardholder may be powerless to acquire possession of his or her card and return it to the Bank, which, according to the majority opinion, is the only way to limit liability. One result of the majority opinion will surely be to encourage the "theft" by divorcing spouses of credit cards they were authorized to use during the marriage and the liberal use of those cards at the other spouse's expense.

In conclusion, I dissent from the majority opinion because (1) it runs counter to the language and purpose of § 1643 of the TILA and the language of the cardholder agreements, (2) it violates principles of the law of agency, and (3) it imposes an unreasonable burden on cardholder spouses and sets the stage for abusive use of credit cards by estranged spouses. I believe that § 1643 of the TILA and the provisions of the cardholder agreements relieve the defendants from liability for the unauthorized charges incurred by their husbands subsequent to the notification given to the Bank.

HOWE, J., concurs in the dissenting opinion of DURHAM, J.

NOTE

1. The meaning of the term "unauthorized use" in CCPA § 103(*o*), 15 U.S.C. § 1602, was also at issue in Martin v. American Express, Inc., 361 So.2d 597 (Ala.Civ.App.1978). In that case Martin, the cardholder, authorized a business associate, McBride, to use the credit card but McBride was not authorized to make charges in excess of $500. McBride made charges of over $5,000 and Martin refused to pay. Martin argued that all charges by McBride beyond $500 constituted "unauthorized use" within the meaning of the Federal statute and that Martin's liability with respect to the unauthorized use was limited to $50. Under the statute, use is unauthorized if the use is "by a person who does not have actual, implied or apparent authority for such use." It seems clear that mere possession by McBride of a credit card

bearing the name of Martin did not give McBride apparent authority to make any charge on the card. Although McBride may not have had any apparent authority to use the card, he had actual authority to use the card to make charges up to $500 but no actual authority, express or implied, to use it above that amount. Is it reasonable that Congress intended this type of unauthorized use to be subject to the $50 limitation? The definition of "unauthorized use" is not very helpful. The court in *Martin* refused to apply the $50 limitation and held Martin liable for the entire amount charged by McBride. This result seems right as a matter of policy and is probably what Congress intended, but the court's rationale seems shaky: "McBride was actually authorized by Martin to use the latter's card. Martin admitted this fact. And the authority to use it, if not actual, remained apparent even after McBride ignored Martin's directions by charging over $500 to Martin's credit card account." 361 So.2d at 600.

3. ASSERTION AGAINST ISSUER BY CARDHOLDER OF DEFENSES ARISING FROM TRANSACTION IN WHICH CREDIT CARD USED

In Chapter 6, with respect to a promissory note issued by a consumer to obtain goods or services, we saw that various doctrines of case law or provisions of statutory or administrative law have been used to allow the consumer to assert against a financial institution that holds the note defenses that the consumer has against the seller of the goods or services. If a consumer uses a bank credit card to buy goods and the goods are either never delivered or are defective, should the cardholder be allowed to refuse to pay the issuer of the credit card to the extent that the cardholder would have been excused from paying the seller of the goods if the sale had been a credit sale by the seller? This question was hotly debated at the state level in the late 1960s. Financial institutions that were issuers of credit cards argued that they had only the most tenuous relationship with retailers honoring their cards, and should not be subjected to claims and defenses arising out of sales made pursuant to their cards. The card issuer, it was contended, should be no more involved in the sale transaction financed by a credit card than should a drawee bank in a sale paid for by a check drawn on the bank. Moreover, would not subjecting card issuers to sales defenses ultimately restrict the acceptability of credit cards by retailers? The concern of the retailer was that the card issuer would insist on a right to charge back against the retailer debts as to which the cardholder raised claims or defenses. Would a retailer in Maine feel secure in honoring a credit card presented by a cardholder who lives in California knowing that if the cardholder claims the goods are defective the retailer may end up with an unsecured claim against the debtor three thousand miles away?

In 1974 Congress enacted an amendment to the Consumer Credit Protection Act stating rights and obligations of the cardholder and the issuer of the credit card with respect to the correction of a billing error that the cardholder believes have been made in the billing statement received from the issuer. The statement of these rights and obligations now appears, in amended form, in CCPA § 161, 15 U.S.C. § 1666. "Billing error" is defined in CCPA § 161(b) and includes reflection on the statement of an extension of credit not made by the cardholder and reflection on the statement of goods or services not accepted by the cardholder or not delivered to the cardholder in accordance with the agreement made at the time of the sales transaction. The 1974 legislation covered a number of other aspects of the issuer-cardholder relationship in CCPA §§ 162–170, 15 U.S.C. §§ 1666a–1666i. CCPA § 170, 15 U.S.C. § 1666i, addressed the issue of the extent to which the cardholder can assert, as a defense to the obligation to pay the issuer, claims and defenses of the cardholder arising from the transaction in which the credit card was used. That section is discussed in the case that follows.

IZRAELEWITZ v. MANUFACTURERS HANOVER TRUST CO.

Civil Court, City of New York, Kings County, 1983.
120 Misc.2d 125, 465 N.Y.S.2d 486.

Ira B. Harkavy, Judge.

As the texture of the American economy evolves from paper to plastic, the disgruntled customer is spewing its wrath upon the purveyor of the plastic rather than upon the merchant.

Plaintiff George Izraelewitz commenced this action to compel the Defendant bank Manufacturers Hanover Trust Company to credit his Mastercharge account in the amount of $290.00 plus finance charges. The disputed charge, posted to Plaintiff's account on July 16, 1981, is for electronic diagrams purchased by Plaintiff via telephone from Don Britton Enterprises, a Hawaii-based mail order business.

On September 9, 1981 Plaintiff advised Defendant bank, Manufacturers Hanover Trust Company (Trust Company), that the diagrams had been unsuitable for his needs and provided Defendant with a UPS receipt indicating that the purchased merchandise had been returned to Don Britton. Defendant's Customer Service Department credited Plaintiff's account and waived finance charges on the item. Trust Company subsequently proceeded to charge back the item to the merchant. The merchant refused the charge back through The 1st Hawaii Bank, and advised Defendant bank of their strict "No Refund" policy. Don Britton also indicated that Plaintiff, during the course of conversation, had admitted that he was aware of this policy. On April 1,

1982 Defendant advised Plaintiff that his account would be redebited for the full amount. At two later dates, Plaintiff advised Trust Company of said dispute, denied knowledge of the "No Refund" policy and stated that the goods had been returned. The Trust Company once again credited Plaintiff's account and attempted to collect from Don Britton. The charge back was again refused and Plaintiff's account was subsequently redebited.

Bank credit agreements generally provide that a cardholder is obligated to pay the bank regardless of any dispute which may exist respecting the merchandise. An exception to this rule arises under a provision in the Truth in Lending Law which allows claimants whose transactions exceed $50.00 and who have made a good faith attempt to obtain satisfactory resolution of the problem, to assert claims and defenses arising out of the credit card transaction, if the place of the initial transaction is in the same state or within 100 miles of the cardholder. Consumer Credit Protection Act, 15 U.S.C.A. § 1666i.

It would appear that Plaintiff is precluded from asserting any claims or defenses since Britton's location exceeds the geographical limitation. This assumption is deceiving. Under Truth in Lending the question of where the transaction occurred (e.g. as in mail order cases) is to be determined under state or other applicable law. Truth in Lending, 12 CFR, § 226.12(c). Furthermore, any state law permitting customers to assert claims and defenses against the card issuer would not be preempted, regardless of whether the place of the transaction was at issue. In effect, these federal laws are viewed as bare minimal standards.

In Lincoln First Bank, N.A. v. Carlson, 103 Misc.2d 467, 426 N.Y.S.2d 433 (1980), the court found that:

> "(T)he statement that a card issuer is subject to all defenses if a transaction occurred less than 100 miles from the cardholder's address, does not automatically presume a cardholder to give up all his defenses should the transaction take place at a distance of greater than 100 miles from the mailing address." Id. at 436.

The facts at bar do not warrant a similar finding. Whereas in *Lincoln,* supra, the cardholder's defense arose due to an alleged failure of the card issuer itself to comply with statutory rules, the Defendant herein is blameless. The geographical limitation serves to protect banks from consumers who may expose them to unlimited liability through dealings with merchants in faraway states where it is difficult to monitor a merchant's behavior. These circumstances do not lend the persuasion needed to cast-off this benefit.

Considering, arguendo, that under the Truth in Lending Act, Plaintiff was able to assert claims and defenses from the original transaction, any claims or defenses he chose to assert would only be as good as and no better than his claim against the merchant. Accordingly, Plaintiff's claim against the merchant must be scrutinized to ascertain whether it is of good faith and substantial merit. A consumer cannot assert every miniscule dispute he may have with a merchant as an excuse not to pay an issuer who has already paid the merchant.

The crux of Plaintiff's claim, apparently, is that he returned the diagrams purportedly unaware of merchant's "No Refund" policy. The merchant contends that Plaintiff admitted that he knew of the policy and nonetheless used deceptive means to return the plans; in that they were sent without a name so they would be accepted; were not delivered to an employee of the company; were not in the original box; and showed evidence of having been xeroxed.

"No Refund" policies, per se, are not unconscionable or offensive to public policy in any manner. Truth in Lending Law "(n)either requires refunds for returns nor does it prohibit refunds in kind." Truth in Lending Regulations, 12 CFR, § 226.12(e). Bank-merchant agreements, however, usually do contain a requirement that the merchant establish a fair policy for exchange and return of merchandise.

To establish the fairness in Don Britton's policy, the strength of the reasons behind the policy and the measures taken to inform the consumer of it must necessarily be considered. Don Britton's rationale for its policy is compelling. It contends that printing is a very small part of its business, which is selling original designs, and "once a customer has seen the designs he possesses what we have to sell." Britton's policy is clearly written in its catalog directly on the page which explains how to order merchandise. To compensate for not having a refund policy, which would be impractical considering the nature of the product, Britton offers well-advertised backup plans with free engineering assistance and an exchange procedure, as well, if original plans are beyond the customer's capabilities. The Plaintiff could have availed himself of any of these alternatives which are all presumably still open to him.

On the instant facts, as between Plaintiff and the Defendant bank, Plaintiff remains liable for the disputed debt, as he has not shown adequate cause to hold otherwise.

Judgment for Defendant dismissing the complaint.

D. CONSUMER ELECTRONIC FUND TRANSFERS

We have seen that wholesale wire transfers have become a dominant method of transferring funds between business or financial institutions. The use of electronics to make payments to or by consumers is also becoming an increasingly important substitute for the check. Electronic communication has also become an important substitute for communication face-to-face or by mail in making transfers between a bank and its customer with respect to the customer's account in the bank.

In 1974 Congress established the National Commission on Electronic Fund Transfers to study the use of electronics with respect to consumer transactions as a prelude to federal regulation of the practice. The Commission's Final Report was submitted in 1977. The Electronic Fund Transfer Act was enacted in November 1978 and most of its provisions went into effect eighteen months after enactment. The statute, which is Title IX of the Consumer Credit Protection Act, 15 U.S.C. §§ 1693–1693r, provides for administrative regulation by the Board of Governors of the Federal Reserve System to carry out the purposes of the statute. CCPA § 904, 15 U.S.C. § 1693c. The Board has issued Federal Reserve Regulation E, 12 C.F.R. § 205, to carry out this mandate. Regulation E is amended from time to time to deal with issues arising under the Act. The Federal Reserve also issues official commentary to Regulation E to address in detail specific problems faced by the institutions that are subject to the Act. There is very little litigation with respect to the Act and the courts have played only a minor role in interpreting the Act. The principal consumer electronic fund transfer systems are very briefly described below.

1. **Point-of-sale (POS) systems.** The buyer pays for goods or services by using a plastic coded card, called an access or debit card, inserted in a computer terminal on the merchant's premises which is linked to the merchant's bank and to the buyer's bank, usually by means of an interbank network. The access card contains machine readable identification of the buyer's bank account. When the card is inserted into the computer terminal, the amount of the transaction and the buyer's personal identification number (PIN) are also entered into the terminal. The result is that the buyer's account is debited and the merchant's account is credited in that amount at the same time. For a variety of reasons POS systems were slow in obtaining widespread acceptance after they were first introduced, but in recent years they have become increasingly popular and are emerging as an important alternative to the check or credit card as a means of payment for goods or services. These systems provide great convenience to the consumer and they allow the merchant to obtain immediate and irrevocable payment at the time of the sale.

2. **Automated teller machine (ATM).** The most popular system governed by the Act is the ubiquitous ATM system. Terminals are located in places convenient to customers and are available for use most of the hours of the day. The customer can use an access card and a PIN to make deposits to and withdrawals

from the customer's account in a bank or other financial institution. The cost of human teller-handled deposits and withdrawals is far less than the cost of deposits and withdrawals made by ATM.

3. **Payment made by automated clearing houses (ACH).** ACH payments are particularly important with respect to recurring payments to the consumer such as those with respect to salary, pension benefits, insurance company annuities and the like. For example, an employee having a bank account can authorize the employer to deposit the employee's salary directly into the employee's account by means of electronic communication of the relevant payment information. The employer's bank transmits the information to an automated clearing house which processes it and in turn transmits the information to the employee's bank which makes payment to the employee by crediting the employee's account. ACH payments may also be made by a consumer to pay recurring bills such as mortgage payments or insurance premiums. The consumer authorizes the consumer's bank to debit the consumer's account and to make payments to the creditor as they become due by an ACH transfer to the creditor's bank for the account of the creditor.

4. **Telephone bill payment.** The customer may call the bank or other financial institution and direct that institution to pay designated creditors. This type of payment is feasible when the customer has recurring debts with the creditor and many other customers are paying the same creditor through the same bank. Examples are payments to a local public utility or a large retail store. Payment to the creditor is made by the bank by a single payment on behalf of many customers. The payment is deposited directly to the bank account of the creditor and, by means of electronically transmitted information, the creditor is given a list of the customers and the amount paid by each.

5. **Consumer wire services.** Western Union wires cash anywhere in the United States, but the recipient must go to a Western Union office to receive the money. Fees vary with the amount sent. In 1991 senders were charged $22 to send $200, with $5 added if a credit card is used; use of a credit card allows senders to direct the funds transfer by telephone. The fee to send $500 was $40 or $45 if a credit card is used. American Express performs a similar function by sending "moneygrams." Los Angeles Times, Sept. 30, 1991, p. D5, col. 5, is the source of information about fees.

Chapter 9

FRAUD, FORGERY, AND ALTERATION

A. FORGERY

---

1. ALLOCATION OF LOSS BETWEEN CUSTOMER AND PAYOR BANK WITH RESPECT TO CHECKS BEARING FORGERY

---

a. INTRODUCTION

Suppose Customer has a checking account in Payor Bank. Thief steals Customer's checkbook, writes a check payable to Payee, and signs Customer's name to the check as drawer. Because Thief was not authorized to sign Customer's name to the check the signature is ineffective as the signature of Customer unless some provision of Article 3 or Article 4 makes it effective. § 3–403(a). Since Customer did not sign the check and did not authorize Thief to sign the check, Customer is not liable on the check. § 3–401(a). The check, however, is not a nullity. Although it is not Customer's check, Article 3 treats it as Thief's check even though Thief signed it by using Customer's name. § 3–403(a) and § 3–401(b). Checks like the check in this example, i.e. a check bearing a forged drawer's signature, are known as "forged checks." Such checks sometimes are transferred for value and paid by the drawee bank. Rights of a holder with respect to such checks can be acquired by persons who take them.

A more common type of forgery can be illustrated by the following example. Customer writes a check to the order of Payee, signs it as drawer, and mails it to Payee. Thief steals the check from Payee, indorses the check by signing Payee's name on the back of the check, and obtains payment of the check from Payor Bank. The check in this example is not a forged check because Customer's signature was not forged. Rather, the infirmity of the check is that it bears a "forged indorsement." Under § 3–403(a) and § 3–401 the signature by Thief is ineffective as the indorsement of Payee. Since Payee did not indorse the check, Thief cannot negotiate the check and nobody can obtain rights as a holder unless some provision of Article 3 otherwise provides. § 3–201(b) and § 3–109(b).

707

What are the rights of Customer and Payor Bank toward each other if Payor Bank pays the forged check in the first example or the check bearing the forged indorsement in the second example? Under § 4–401(a) a payor bank "may charge against the account of a customer an item that is properly payable from the account" and, to be properly payable, the check must be "authorized by the customer." Thus, in the case of the forged check, the normal rule is that Payor Bank may not debit Customer's account and is not entitled to reimbursement from Customer. The risk of loss falls on Payor Bank even though it may not have had any way of discovering the forgery.

The result is the same in the case of the check bearing the forged indorsement. By the terms of the check Payor Bank was ordered by Customer to pay the check to the order of Payee. Since Payee did not receive payment and did not order payment to anybody else, Payor Bank did not comply with the terms of the check. Since Payor Bank did not pay a holder or other person entitled to receive payment, it has no right to reimbursement from Customer.

The normal rule protecting Customer from loss from forgery is changed in some cases by other provisions of Article 3 or Article 4. Two of the most important provisions that may allow Payor Bank to shift the forgery loss to Customer are § 3–406(a), discussed in *Thompson Maple Products*, p. 709, and § 4–406, discussed in *Rhode Island Hospital*, p. 714.

b. NEGLIGENCE OF CUSTOMER CONTRIBUTING TO FORGERY

With respect to payment by a payor bank of a forged check or a check bearing a forged indorsement, if the bank can prove a failure by the customer to exercise ordinary care that substantially contributed to the making of the forged signature, the customer is precluded from asserting the forgery. § 3–406(a). "Ordinary care" is defined in § 3–103(a)(7). The leading case on the meaning of the words "substantially contributes to * * * the making of a forged signature" in § 3–406(a) is *Thompson Maple Products*, the case that follows. Comment 2 to § 3–406 discusses the meaning of the quoted words. In the absence of proof of negligence by the bank contributing to the loss, the effect of the preclusion is to give to the bank a right to reimbursement from the customer for the amount paid on the check. Under the original § 3–406, discussed in *Thompson Maple Products*, the preclusion against the customer did not occur if the bank was negligent in paying the check. This result is changed by Revised § 3–406. Negligence by the bank does not prevent the preclusion from arising but, under subsection (b), the loss from the forgery can be apportioned between the negligent customer and the negligent bank.

THOMPSON MAPLE PRODUCTS, INC. v. CITIZENS NATIONAL BANK

Superior Court of Pennsylvania, 1967.
211 Pa.Super. 42, 234 A.2d 32.

HOFFMAN, JUDGE:

*   *   *

The plaintiff [Thompson Maple Products] is a small, closely-held corporation, principally engaged in the manufacture of bowling pin "blanks" from maple logs. Some knowledge of its operations from 1959 to 1962 is essential to an understanding of this litigation.

The plaintiff purchased logs from timber owners in the vicinity of its mill. Since these timber owners rarely had facilities for hauling logs, such transportation was furnished by a few local truckers, including Emery Albers.

At the mill site, newly delivered logs were "scaled" by mill personnel, to determine their quantity and grade. The employee on duty noted this information, together with the name of the owner of the logs, as furnished by the hauler, on duplicate "scaling slips."

In theory, the copy of the scaling slip was to be given to the hauler, and the original was to be retained by the mill employee until transmitted by him directly to the company's bookkeeper. This ideal procedure, however, was rarely followed. Instead, in a great many instances, the mill employee simply gave both slips to the hauler for delivery to the company office. Office personnel then prepared checks in payment for the logs, naming as payee the owner indicated on the scaling slips. Blank sets of slips were readily accessible on the company premises.

Sometime prior to February, 1959, Emery Albers conceived the scheme which led to the forgeries at issue here. Albers was an independent log hauler who for many years had transported logs to the company mill. For a brief period in 1952, he had been employed by the plaintiff, and he was a trusted friend of the Thompson family. After procuring blank sets of scaling slips, Albers filled them in to show substantial, wholly fictitious deliveries of logs, together with the names of local timber owners as suppliers. He then delivered the slips to the company bookkeeper, who prepared checks payable to the purported owners. Finally, he volunteered to deliver the checks to the owners. The bookkeeper customarily entrusted the checks to him for that purpose.

Albers then forged the payee's signature and either cashed the checks or deposited them to his account at the defendant bank, where he was well known. *   *   *

In 1963, when the forgeries were uncovered, Albers confessed and was imprisoned. The plaintiff then instituted this suit against the drawee bank, asserting that the bank had breached its contract of deposit by paying the checks over forged endorsements. * * *

The trial court determined that the plaintiff's own negligent activities had materially contributed to the unauthorized endorsements, and it therefore dismissed the substantial part of plaintiff's claim. We affirm the action of the trial court.

Both parties agree that, as between the payor bank and its customer, ordinarily the bank must bear the loss occasioned by the forgery of a payee's endorsement.

* * *

The trial court concluded, however, that the plaintiff-drawer, by virtue of its conduct, could not avail itself of that rule, citing § 3–406 of the Code: "Any person who by his negligence substantially contributes to * * * the making of an unauthorized signature is precluded from asserting the * * * lack of authority against * * * a drawee or other payor who pays the instrument in good faith and in accordance with the reasonable commercial standards of the drawee's or payor's business." * * *

Before this Court, the plaintiff Company argues strenuously that this language is a mere restatement of pre-Code law in Pennsylvania. Under those earlier cases, it is argued, the term "precluded" is equivalent to "estopped," and negligence which will work an estoppel is only such as "directly and proximately affects the conduct of the bank in passing the forgery * * *." See, e.g., Coffin v. Fidelity–Philadelphia Trust Company, 374 Pa. 378, 393, 97 A.2d 857, 39 A.L.R.2d 625 (1953); Land Title Bank and Trust Company v. Cheltenham National Bank, 362 Pa. 30, 66 A.2d 768 (1949). The plaintiff further asserts that those decisions hold that "negligence in the conduct of the drawer's business," such as appears on this record, cannot serve to work an estoppel.

Even if that was the law in this Commonwealth prior to the passage of the Commercial Code, it is not the law today. The language of the new Act is determinative in all cases arising after its passage. This controversy must be decided, therefore, by construction of the statute and application of the negligence doctrine as it appears in § 3–406 of the Code. * * *

Had the legislature intended simply to continue the strict estoppel doctrine of the pre-Code cases, it could have employed the term "precluded," without qualification, as in § 23 of the old Negotiable Instruments Law, 56 P.S. § 28 (repealed). However, it chose to modify that doctrine in § 3–406, by specifying that negligence which "*substantially contributes to * * * the making of an unauthorized signature * * *.*" will preclude the drawer from asserting a forgery. [emphasis supplied]. The Code has thus abandoned the language of the older cases (negligence which "directly and proximately affects the conduct of the bank in passing the forgery") and shortened the chain of causation which the defendant bank must establish. "[N]o attempt is made," according to the Official Comment to § 3–406, "to specify what is negligence, and the question is one for the court or jury on the facts of the particular case."

In the instant case, the trial court could readily have concluded that plaintiff's business affairs were conducted in so negligent a fashion as to have "substantially contributed" to the Albers forgeries, within the meaning of § 3–406.

Thus, the record shows that pads of plaintiff's blank logging slips were left in areas near the mill which were readily accessible to any of the haulers. Moreover, on at least two occasions, Albers was given whole pads of these blank logging slips to use as he chose. Mrs. Vinora Curtis, an employee of the plaintiff, testified:

"Q. Did you ever give any of these logging slips to Mr. Albers or any pads of these slips to Mr. Albers?

"A. Yes.

*   *   *   *   *   *   *   *   *

"Q. What was the reason for giving [a pad of the slips] to him, Mrs. Curtis?

"A. Well, he came up and said he needed it for [scaling] the logs, so I gave it to him."

Mrs. Amy Thompson, who also served as a bookkeeper for the plaintiff, testified:

"Q. As a matter of fact, you gave Mr. Albers the pack of your logging slips, did you not?

"A. Yes, I did once.

"Q. Do you remember what you gave them to him for?

"A. I don't right offhand, but it seems to me he said he was going out to look for some logs or timber or something and he needed them to mark some figures on * * *.

"Q. Well, if he was going to use them for scratch pads, why didn't you give him a scratch pad that you had in the office?

"A. That's what I should have done."

In addition, the plaintiff's printed scaling slips were not consecutively numbered. Unauthorized use of the slips, therefore, could easily go undetected. Thus, Mr. Nelson Thompson testified:

"Q. Mr. Thompson, were your slips you gave these haulers numbered?

"A. No, they were not.

"Q. They are now, aren't they?

"A. Yes.

"Q. Had you used numbered logging slips, this would have prevented anybody getting logging slips out of the ordinary channel of business and using it to defraud you?

"A. Yes.

Moreover, in 1960, when the company became concerned about the possible unauthorized use of its scaling slips, it required its own personnel to initial the slips when a new shipment of logs was scaled. However, this protective measure was largely ignored in practice. Mrs. Amy Thompson testified:

"Q. And later on in the course of your business, if you remember Mr. Thompson said he wanted the logging slips initialed by one of the so-called authorized people?

"A. Yes.

"Q. [D]idn't you really not pay too much attention to them at all?

"A. Well, I know we didn't send them back to be sure they were initialed. We might have noticed it but we didn't send them back to the mill.

"Q. In other words, if they came to you uninitialed, you might have noticed it but didn't do anything about it.

"A. Didn't do anything about it."

The principal default of the plaintiff, however, was its failure to use reasonable diligence in insuring honesty from its log haulers including Emery Albers. For many years, the haulers were permitted to deliver both the original and the duplicate of the scaling slip to the company office, and the company tolerated this practice. These slips supplied the bookkeeper with the payees' names for the checks she was to draw in payment for log deliveries. Only by having the company at all times retain possession of the original slip could the plaintiff have assured that no disbursements were made except for logs received, and that the proper amounts were paid to the proper persons. The practice tolerated by the plaintiff effectively removed the only immediate safeguard in the entire procedure against dishonesty on the part of the haulers.

Finally, of course, the company regularly entrusted the completed checks to the haulers for delivery to the named payees, without any explicit authorization from the latter to do so.

While none of these practices, in isolation, might be sufficient to charge the plaintiff with negligence within the meaning of § 3–406, the company's course of conduct, viewed in its entirety, is surely sufficient to support the trial judge's determination that it substantially contributed to the making of the unauthorized signatures.[6] In his words, that conduct was "no different than had the plaintiff simply given Albers a series of checks signed in blank for his unlimited, unrestricted use."

* * *

Judgment affirmed.

WATKINS, J., dissents.

c. FAILURE OF CUSTOMER TO REPORT FORGERY

In a large percentage of cases involving forged checks, the malefactor forges a series of checks on the same account over a considerable period of time. Forgery with respect to a single check is much more likely to involve a forged indorsement rather than a forgery of the drawer's signature. Typically, repeated forged check cases involve a dishonest employee of the person whose signature is forged. Usually the employee has access to the employer's checkbook and often has duties related to bookkeeping. In the case of repeated forgeries the later forgeries could have been easily prevented if the person whose signature was forged had detected the earlier forgeries. Such detection is relatively easy because in most cases the payor bank, after paying a check, returns the cancelled check to the customer on whose account the check was drawn. The customer should be able to determine whether a check written on the customer's account is a forgery. On the other hand it is very difficult for the payor bank to detect forgery. Since it is easy for the customer to detect a forgery, § 4–406 imposes a duty on the customer to report forged checks to the bank. Failure of the customer to comply with this duty can, in some cases, result in a shifting of the loss from the bank to the customer.

Although § 3–406 applies to checks bearing a forged indorsement as well as forged checks, § 4–406 does not apply to forged indorsements. Both sections also apply to altered checks which are discussed later in this chapter. The 1990 Revision of Article 4 made substantial changes to the original § 4–406. *Rhode Island Hospital,* the case that follows, discusses the original provision. Original § 4–406(2)(b) and (3), discussed by the court, were substantially amended and now appear as § 4–406(d)(2) and (e). Section 3–103(a)(7) ("ordinary care") was added.

---

6. In this connection, the trial court also noted that the plaintiff at all times prior to the commencement of this litigation failed to keep an accurate inventory account. It could not therefore verify, at any given point in time, that it actually possessed the logs which it had paid for.

RHODE ISLAND HOSPITAL TRUST NATIONAL BANK v. ZAPATA CORP.

United States Court of Appeals, First Circuit, 1988.
848 F.2d 291.

BREYER, CIRCUIT JUDGE.

The issue that this appeal presents is whether Zapata Corporation has shown that the system used by Rhode Island Hospital Trust National Bank for detecting forged checks—a system used by a majority of American banks—lacks the "ordinary care" that a bank must exercise under the Uniform Commercial Code § 4–406(3) * * *. The question arises out of the following district court determinations, all of which are adequately supported by the record and by Rhode Island law.

1. In early 1985, a Zapata employee stole some blank checks from Zapata. She wrote a large number of forged checks, almost all in amounts of $150 to $800 each, on Zapata's accounts at Rhode Island Hospital Trust National Bank. The Bank, from March through July 1985, received and paid them.

2. Bank statements that the Bank regularly sent Zapata first began to reflect the forged checks in early April 1985. Zapata failed to examine its statements closely until July 1985, when it found the forgeries. It immediately notified the Bank, which then stopped clearing the checks. The Bank had already processed and paid forged checks totaling $109,247.16.

3. The Bank will (and legally must) reimburse Zapata in respect to all checks it cleared before April 25, 1985 (or for at least two weeks after Zapata received the statement that reflected the forgeries). * * *.

4. In respect to checks cleared on and after April 25, the Bank need not reimburse Zapata because Zapata failed to "exercise reasonable care and promptness to examine the [bank] statement." U.C.C. § 4–406(1) (1977).

The question before us is whether this last-mentioned conclusion is correct or whether Zapata can recover for the post-April 24 checks on the theory that, even if it was negligent, so was the Bank.

To understand the question, one must examine U.C.C. § 4–406 * * *. Ordinarily a bank must reimburse an innocent customer for forgeries that it honors, * * * but § 4–406 makes an important exception to the liability rule. The exception operates in respect to a series of forged checks, and it applies once a customer has had a chance to catch the forgeries by examining his bank statements and notifying the bank but has failed to do so.

The statute, in relevant part, reads as follows:

(1) *When a bank sends to its customer a statement of account* accompanied by items paid in good faith in support of the debit entries or holds the statement and items pursuant to a request or instructions of its customer or otherwise in a reasonable manner makes the statement and items available to the customer, *the customer must exercise reasonable care and promptness to examine the statement* and items *to discover his unauthorized signature* or any alteration on an item *and must notify the bank promptly* after discovery thereof.

(2) *If the bank establishes that the customer failed* with respect to an item *to comply with* the duties imposed on the customer by *subsection (1) the customer is precluded from asserting against the bank*

    (a) *His unauthorized signature* or any alteration on the item if the bank also establishes that it suffered a loss by reason of such failure; *and*

    (b) *An unauthorized signature or alteration by the same wrongdoer on any other item paid in good faith by the bank after the* first item and *statement was available to the customer for a reasonable period not exceeding fourteen (14) calendar days* and before the bank receives notification from the customer of any such unauthorized signature or alteration.

§ 4–406(1)–(2) (emphasis added).

The statute goes on to specify an important exception to the exception. It says:

(3) The preclusion under subsection (2) does not apply if the customer establishes lack of ordinary care on the part of the bank in paying the item(s).

§ 4–406(3). Zapata's specific claim, on this appeal, is that it falls within this "exception to the exception"—that the bank's treatment of the post-April 24 checks lacked "ordinary care."

Zapata says as a preliminary matter, that the district court failed to make a finding on this "ordinary care" question. We do not think that is so. * * *

Whether or not the district court made an explicit finding, however, we should, and do, affirm the district court's judgment in the bank's favor. Our examination of the statute reveals that the statute places the burden of proof on Zapata. Our examination of the record reveals that Zapata failed to shoulder that burden; and, given the record, no reasonable person could find the contrary.

    a. The statute places the burden of proof on Zapata. It says that strict bank liability terminates fourteen days after the customer receives the bank's statement unless "*the customer estab-*

lishes lack of ordinary care." § 4–406(3) (emphasis added); see, e.g., Vending Chattanooga, Inc. v. American National Bank & Trust Co., 730 S.W.2d 624, 628 (Tenn.1987). And, the U.C.C. commentary makes clear that the statute means what it says. The commentators explain the purpose of the statutory section as follows:

> One of the most serious consequences of failure of the customer * * * [to examine his statement and notify the bank promptly of an unauthorized signature] * * * is the opportunity presented to the wrongdoer to repeat his misdeeds. Conversely, one of the best ways to keep down losses in this type of situation is for the customer to promptly examine his statement and notify the bank * * * so that the bank will be alerted to stop paying further items.

U.C.C. § 4–406 comment 3. The Commentary goes on to say:

> [E]ven if the bank succeeds in establishing that the customer has failed to exercise ordinary care, if in turn the customer succeeds in establishing that the bank failed to exercise ordinary care in paying the items[,] the preclusion rule does not apply. *This distribution of the burden of establishing between the customer and the bank provides reasonable equality of treatment and requires each person asserting the negligence to establish such negligence rather than requiring either person to establish that his entire course of conduct constituted ordinary care.*

Id. comment 4 (emphasis added).

b. The record convinces us that Zapata failed to carry its burden of establishing "lack of ordinary care" on the part of the Bank. First, the Bank described its ordinary practices as follows: The Bank examines all signatures on checks for more than $1,000. It examines signatures on checks between $100 and $1,000 (those at issue here) if it has reason to suspect a problem, e.g., if a customer has warned it of a possible forgery or if the check was drawn on an account with insufficient funds. It examines the signatures of a randomly chosen one percent of all other checks between $100 and $1,000. But, it does not examine the signatures on other checks between $100 and $1,000. Through expert testimony, the Bank also established that most other banks in the nation follow this practice and that banking industry experts recommend it. Indeed, Trust National Bank's practices are conservative in this regard, as most banks set $2500 or more, not $1,000, as the limit beneath which they will not examine each signature.

This testimony made out a *prima facie* case of "ordinary care." U.C.C. § 4–103(3) ("[a]ction or nonaction * * * consistent with * * * a general banking usage not disapproved by this [Article or] chapter, prima facie constitutes the exercise of ordinary care") ∗ ∗ ∗. Of course, Zapata might still try to show that the entire industry's practice is unreasonable, that it reflects lack of "ordinary care." The T.J. Hooper, 60 F.2d 737, 740 (2d Cir.), cert. denied, 287 U.S. 662, 53 S.Ct. 220, 77 L.Ed. 571 (1932). In doing so, however, "the *prima facie* rule does ∗ ∗ ∗ impose on the party contesting the standards to establish that they are *unreasonable, arbitrary,* or *unfair.*" U.C.C. § 4–103 comment 4 (emphasis added).

Second, both bank officials and industry experts pointed out that this industry practice, in general and in the particular case of the Trust National Bank, saved considerable expense, compared with the Bank's pre–1981 practice of examining each check by hand. To be specific, the change saved the Bank about $125,000 annually. Zapata accepts this testimony as accurate.

Third, both a Bank official and an industry expert testified that changing from an "individual signature examination" system to the new "bulk-filing" system led to *no* significant increase in the number of forgeries that went undetected. Philip Schlernitzauer, a Bank vice-president and the officer in charge of the Zapata account, testified that under the prior "individual signature examination" system, some forgeries still slipped through. The Bank's loss was about $10,000 to $15,000 per year. He also determined through a feasibility study that by implementing a "bulk-filing" system in which 99 percent of checks under $1,000 were not individually screened, the loss would remain between $10,000 and $15,000. Dr. Lipis, an executive vice-president of a large consulting firm to the financial industry, testified that among its purposes was the following:

> Well, it improves the ability to return checks back to customers more correctly, simply that the checks do not get misplaced when they are handled; generally [it] can improve the morale within th[e] bank because ∗ ∗ ∗ the signature verification is very tedious, very difficult, and not a function that is liked by anybody who does it. In addition, *it does not impact the amount of forgeries that are produced at the bank.*

Rec.App. 179 (emphasis added).

Zapata points to *no* testimony or other evidence tending to contradict these assertions. An industry-wide practice that saves money without significantly increasing the number of forged checks that the banks erroneously pay is a practice that reflects at least "ordinary care." Cf. *Vending Chattanooga,* 730 S.W.2d at 628–29 (weighing economic feasibility and business practice into definition of "ordinary care" or "reasonable commercial standards").

Fourth, even if one assumes, contrary to this uncontradicted evidence, that the new system meant *some* increase in the number of undetected forged checks, Zapata still could not prevail, for it presented *no* evidence tending to show any such increased loss unreasonable in light of the costs that the new practice would save. Instead, it relied simply upon the assertion that costs saved the bank are irrelevant. But, that is not so, for what is reasonable or unreasonable insofar as "ordinary care" or "due care" or "negligence" (and the like) are concerned is often a matter of costs of prevention compared with correlative risks of loss. See *Vending Chattanooga*, 730 S.W.2d at 628–29; United States v. Carroll Towing Co., 159 F.2d 169, 173 (2d Cir.1947) (Hand, J.) ("duty" defined by calculating probability of injury times gravity of harm to determine "burden of precaution" that is warranted). One does not, for example, coat the base of the Grand Canyon with soft plastic nets to catch those who might fall in, or build cars like armored tanks to reduce injuries in accidents even though the technology exists. * * *

As Zapata contends, there are several cases that hold or imply that "ordinary care" necessarily implies individualized scrutiny of every check. But, several of those cases are old, decided in different technological circumstances and before the U.C.C. * * *

The U.C.C. intends technological change to make a difference, a fact which its *prima facie* equation of "ordinary care" and "general banking usage" implies, see § 4–103(3), and which its commentators made explicit. See U.C.C. § 4–103 comment 1 ("[i]n view of the technical complexity of the field of bank collections, the enormous number of items handled by banks, * * * and the possibility of developing improved methods of collection to speed the process, it would be unwise to freeze present methods of operation by mandatory statutory rules"); *see also Vending Chattanooga*, 730 S.W.2d at 628 ("ordinary care" cannot "require the bank to hire such a large number of skilled handwriting experts so as to be economically not feasible, * * * [not] commercially reasonable").

We have found a few, more modern cases that arguably support Zapata's view, but they involve practices more obviously unreasonable than those presented here. See, e.g., Hanover Insurance Cos. v. Brotherhood State Bank, 482 F.Supp. 501 (D.Kan. 1979) (no ordinary care where *no* examination of *any size* checks, conspicuous forgeries); *Perley*, 170 Conn. at 702–03, 368 A.2d at 155 (no ordinary care where *no* authentication of endorsements of *any size* checks); Indiana National Corp. v. Faco, Inc., 400 N.E.2d 202 (Ind.App.1980) (checks *without signatures* paid, 30 check copies lost); *Medford Irrigation District*, supra (same where *no* examination of any checks under $5,000). And, in any event, we believe Rhode Island would follow the more significant body of modern case law suggesting analysis along the lines we have undertaken. * * *

For these reasons, the judgment of the district court is
Affirmed.

NOTES

1.   There has been some disagreement in the courts on the
question of what constitutes reasonable promptness by the customer in discovering an unauthorized signature and in notifying the
bank when the wrongdoer is the person designated by the customer to check the monthly statement.   Under § 1–201(27) the customer would seem to be bound by the information supplied by the
bank when that information reaches the customer's employee who
is authorized to receive it and act on it.   Under the law of agency,
if that employee fails to notify the bank of the forgery the
customer should be bound by the employee's conduct regardless of
whether the employee's failure to notify is due to negligence or is
the deliberate act of the employee to cover up the employee's
wrongdoing.   The issue should not be whether the customer was
negligent in the procedure chosen for reviewing the bank statements if the employee receiving and acting on the statements was
the designated agent of the customer for that purpose.   See
Seavey, Notice Through An Agent, 65 U. of Pa.L.Rev. 1, 7–8 (1916).

2.   In Pine Bluff National Bank v. Kesterson, 257 Ark. 813,
520 S.W.2d 253 (1975), the bank paid checks of a trust bearing the
signatures of two trustees.   There were three trustees of the trust
and the agreement with the bank required the signatures of all
three on checks.   The court held that the authorized signature of
the trust was comprised of the signature of all three trustees;
therefore, the bank paid checks bearing an unauthorized signature
of the trust and § 4–406 applied.   Wolfe v. University National
Bank, 270 Md. 70, 310 A.2d 558 (1973), represents a contrary view.
In that case the customer, a partnership, agreed with its bank that
all checks drawn on the partnership account had to be signed by
two of the three partners.   The bank paid out on 37 checks signed
by only one partner.   Customer brought suit nearly two years
after the last check in issue was written, and the bank claimed the
one-year limitation in former § 4–406(4) (now § 4–406(f)) barred
the action.   The court disagreed stating: "UCC § 4–406 is inapplicable here because it is only concerned with unauthorized signatures and alterations.   An 'unauthorized signature' 'means one
made without actual, implied or apparent authority and includes a
forgery,' UCC § 1–201(43) * * * The signatures of the * * *
[the partners who signed] were not forged, not made without
authority, nor did they constitute an alteration of any kind." 310
A.2d at 560.   The court saw the infirmity not as the presence of an
unauthorized signature but the absence of a second authorized
signature.

This split of authority has been resolved by Revised Article 3 in favor of the view stated in *Pine Bluff.* § 3–403(b) and § 4–104(c) ("unauthorized signature").

PROBLEM

Corporation has a checking account in Bank. The agreement with respect to the account states that Bank may pay a check drawn on Corporation's account only if the check is signed by both the president and the treasurer of Corporation. The treasurer fraudulently wrote three checks on Corporation's account payable to the order of the treasurer. Each check bore two signatures on behalf of Corporation. One was that of the treasurer. The other purported to be that of the president of Corporation, but in fact it was a forgery made by the treasurer.

1. The first check, in the amount of $1,000, was paid by Bank on January 2 by automated equipment without any human examination of the check. The cancelled check was returned to Corporation on January 4.

2. The second check, in the amount of $2,000, was paid by Bank on February 20 by automated equipment without any human examination of the check. The cancelled check was returned to Corporation on March 3.

3. The third check, in the amount of $5,000, was paid by Bank on February 28. Before the check was paid an employee of Bank examined the check but failed to detect the forgery of the president's signature. The cancelled check was returned to Corporation on March 3.

Under the established procedures of Bank, checks presented for payment in amounts less than $2,500 were not examined by anybody before payment. All checks paid by Bank were returned to Corporation each month along with Corporation's monthly statement of account.

The fraud by the treasurer was discovered by Corporation in June. The treasurer, who is insolvent, used the proceeds of the three checks to pay gambling debts. Corporation notified Bank of the forged checks on June 7, promptly after discovery of the fraud. Corporation demanded that Bank restore to Corporation's account the $8,000 debited to the account as a result of payment of the checks.

With respect to each of the checks, state your opinion whether, under § 4–406, Corporation is entitled to recover from Bank.

2. RIGHT OF PAYOR BANK TO RECOVER MISTAKEN PAYMENT OF CHECK

---

a. FORGED CHECKS

The law of mistake and restitution recognizes the general principle that a person who confers a benefit upon another person because of a mistake is entitled to restitution from the person receiving the benefit. For example, a shopkeeper receives a $10 bill from a customer in payment of goods purchased by the customer for a price of $8. The shopkeeper, who has an obligation to give the customer $2 change, gives the customer $12 because of a mistaken belief that the customer had paid with a $20 bill. The shopkeeper is entitled to get back the $10 paid by mistake. Restatement of Restitution § 19.

Mistake can also occur when money is paid for a negotiable instrument either by a person who buys the instrument or by a person such as a payor bank who pays the instrument. The law of mistake and restitution applies to negotiable instrument cases, but special rules apply in some cases. The mistake cases fall into various categories and most of the cases involve payment or acceptance of a check or other draft by the drawee. The principal categories involve forged checks, checks bearing a forged indorsement, altered checks, checks on which the drawer has stopped payment, and checks drawn on an account with insufficient funds to cover the check.

The seminal case in this area is Price v. Neal, 3 Burr. 1354, 97 Eng.Rep. 871 (1762), which involved two forged bills of exchange drawn on Price and indorsed to Neal, a bona fide purchaser for value. Price paid Neal on the first bill and then accepted the second bill which was subsequently purchased by Neal. After Price paid the second bill he learned that the signature of the drawer of the bills had been forged. Price sued Neal to get his money back. Lord Mansfield, in deciding in favor of the defendant, stated:

> It is an action upon the case, for money had and received to the plaintiff's use. In which action, the plaintiff can not recover the money, unless it be against conscience in the defendant, to retain it: and great liberality is always allowed, in this sort of action.

> But it can never be thought unconscientious in the defendant, to retain this money, when he has once received it upon a bill of exchange indorsed to him for a fair and valuable consideration, which he had bona fide paid, without the least priority or suspicion of any forgery.

Here was no fraud: no wrong. It was incumbent upon the plaintiff, to be satisfied "that the bill drawn upon him was the drawer's hand," before he accepted or paid it: but it was not incumbent upon the defendant, to inquire into it. Here was notice given by the defendant to the plaintiff of a bill drawn upon him: and he sends his servant to pay it and take it up. The other bill he actually accepts; after which acceptance, the defendant innocently and bona fide discounts it. The plaintiff lies by, for a considerable time after he has paid these bills; and then found out "that they were forged:" and the forger comes to be hanged. He made no objection to them, at the time of paying them. Whatever neglect there was, was on his side. The defendant had actual encouragement from the plaintiff himself, for negotiating the second bill, from the plaintiff's having without any scruple or hesitation paid the first: and he paid the whole value, bona fide. It is a misfortune which has happened without the defendant's fault or neglect. If there was no neglect in the plaintiff, yet there is no reason to throw off the loss from one innocent man upon another innocent man: but, in this case, if there was any fault or negligence in any one, it certainly was in the plaintiff, and not in the defendant.

Payment or acceptance by the drawee of a forged check or other draft is addressed in § 3–418(a) and (c) and § 3–417(a)(3). Under these provisions the rule of Price v. Neal is preserved. Section 4–208(a)(3) is identical in effect to § 3–417(a)(3) and applies specifically to warranties made in the bank-collection process to a payor bank with respect to an Article 4 "draft" (§ 4–104(a)(7)) which includes a check.

PROBLEMS

1. Nieman introduced himself to Altman, a diamond merchant, as a buyer for J.W. Mays, a corporation. Nieman then selected some diamonds to be purchased by J.W. Mays. Altman put the diamonds into a sealed envelope and set them aside for Nieman. Altman retained possession of the envelope containing the diamonds. A few days later Altman received a letter from Nieman confirming the purchase by J.W. Mays of the diamonds. Enclosed was a check for $22,000 to the order of Altman. The check was drawn on the account of J.W. Mays in City Bank in full payment of the diamonds. Altman deposited the check in Altman's account in Trade Bank and Trade Bank presented the check to City Bank for payment. A few days later Nieman appeared to pick up the diamonds. Altman called Trade Bank and asked whether the $22,000 check had been paid. When Altman was told that the check had been paid by City Bank, Altman delivered the diamonds to Nieman. Later, City Bank learned that the signature

of J.W. Mays on the check was forged and demanded that Altman repay the $22,000 received in payment of the check. Altman refused to repay.

What warranty did Altman make to City Bank when the $22,000 check was presented for payment? § 3–417(a)(3). Did Altman breach that warranty? Did Altman take the check in good faith and for value? Did Altman in good faith change position in reliance on the payment by City Bank? Is City Bank entitled to recover the $22,000 payment from Altman? § 3–418(a) and (c). Would your answers to the last two questions be different if Altman had not called Trade Bank to verify that the check had been paid before he released the diamonds to Nieman?

This problem is based on the facts of First National City Bank v. Altman, 3 U.C.C.Rep. 815 (N.Y.Sup.Ct., N.Y.Co.1966).

2. Buyer drew a check on the account of Doe in Payor Bank and forged Doe's signature as drawer of the check. The check was payable to the order of Buyer. Buyer bought an automobile from Dealer and offered to negotiate the check to Dealer as a down payment of the price of the automobile. Dealer refused to take the check unless it was certified by Payor Bank. Buyer took the check to Payor Bank and obtained certification of the check. Buyer then negotiated the check to Dealer and received delivery of the automobile. The next day, while still in possession of the check, Dealer learned from a credit reporting agency that Buyer had a criminal record that included arrests for forgery. Dealer then took the check to Payor Bank and demanded payment without disclosing the information about Buyer's criminal record. Payor Bank paid Dealer the amount of the check. Ten days later Payor Bank discovered the forgery and demanded that Dealer repay the money received in payment of the check. Dealer refused to repay.

What warranty did Dealer make to Payor Bank when the check was presented for payment? Does § 3–417(a) apply? Does § 3–417(d) apply? Was there any breach of warranty by Dealer? Is Payor Bank entitled to recover from Dealer the amount paid on the check? § 3–418(a) and (c). Does Payor Bank have any cause of action against Buyer? § 3–417(a)(3) and Comment 4 to § 3–417.

Suppose Dealer, at the time the check was presented for payment, told Payor Bank about Buyer's criminal record. Payor Bank called Doe and was informed that the check was a forgery. Payor Bank refused to pay Dealer. Is Dealer entitled to payment? § 3–413(a).

b. FORGED INDORSEMENT

PROBLEM

Drawer drew a check to the order of Payee. The check was stolen from Payee by Thief who signed Payee's name to the check as a blank indorsement. Thief then delivered the check to Faith, who purchased for value, in good faith and without notice that the indorsement was forged. Faith deposited the check with Depositary Bank which presented the check and received payment from Payor Bank. Depositary Bank credited Faith's account and the credit was withdrawn. Payee then notified Drawer of the theft. Drawer notified Payor Bank but was told that the check had already been paid. Is Payor Bank entitled to recover the amount of the check from Depositary Bank or Faith? § 3–417(a)(1), § 4–208(a)(1), and Comments 2 and 3 to § 3–417. If Depositary Bank has to pay, is Depositary Bank entitled to recover from Faith? § 3–416(a)(1) and (2). Is the result in this case consistent with Price v. Neal?

NOTE

The preceding Problem is discussed by Judge Goldberg in Perini Corp. v. First National Bank of Habersham County, 553 F.2d 398, 403–406 (5th Cir. 1977):

A. The Code Framework

Perpetuating a distinction introduced into the legal annals by Lord Mansfield in the eighteenth century, the Code accords separate treatment to forged drawer signatures (hereinafter "forged checks") and forged indorsements. In general, the drawee bank is strictly liable to its customer drawer for payment of either a forged check or a check containing a forged indorsement. In the case of a forged indorsement, the drawee generally may pass liability back through the collection chain to the party who took from the forger and, of course, to the forger himself if available. In the case of a forged check, however, liability generally rests with the drawee. The patchwork of provisions from which this general allocation of liability emerges merits more detailed description.

1. Forged Indorsements

A check bearing a forged indorsement, included in the § 1–201(43) definition of unauthorized signatures,[6] is not

---

6. Section 1–201(43) provides:

"Unauthorized" signature or indorsement means one made without actual, implied or apparent authority and includes a forgery.

"properly payable." J. White and R. Summers, Uniform Commercial Code 559 (1972).[7] Regardless of the care exercised, a drawee bank is with few exceptions liable to its drawer customer for payment of such a check. * * *

Upon recrediting the drawer's account after payment over a forged indorsement, the drawee will seek redress against prior parties in the collection chain through an action for breach of the statutory warranty of good title. Each person who obtains payment of a check from the drawee and each prior transferor warrants to the party who in good faith pays the check that he has good title to the instrument. * * * A forged indorsement is ineffective to pass title * * *. The drawee may therefore bring a breach of warranty action against a person who presented a check bearing a forged indorsement. These warranty actions will continue up the collection chain to the party who took from the forger or to the forger himself.

Additionally, payment of a check bearing a forged indorsement constitutes conversion * * *. This conversion action at least provides the check's "true owner," the payee or indorsee from whom it was stolen and whose name was falsely indorsed, direct relief from the drawee. * * * Without the conversion action the true owner would have to seek payment from the drawer, who might be overcautious and unaware of his right to force the drawee to recredit his account for any payment over a forged indorsement.

The danger created by forged indorsements is that the party designated by the instrument as entitled to its proceeds will appear with a claim to those proceeds after payment has been made to the malefactor. The statutory actions for improper payment, conversion, and breach of warranty of good title combine, however, inartfully, to safeguard the drawer against double liability and to assure the payee of payment.

---

7. A check drawn to the order of the payee, i.e., an order instrument, may not be negotiated without the payee's indorsement. * * * The unauthorized indorsement by the forger does not operate as the true payee's signature. See § 3–404(1), which provides that "any unauthorized signature is wholly inoperative as that of the person whose name is signed unless he ratifies it or is precluded from denying it." A forged indorsement check therefore lacks the payee's indorsement and, without that necessary indorsement, may not be negotiated. * * * Negotiation is necessary to confer holder status on a check's transferee. Id. Accordingly, the transferee of a forged indorsement check does not become a holder. Only a holder or the holder's agent may properly present the check for payment. * * * Thus the UCC reaffirms the general pre-Code rule that a drawee may not charge its drawer customer's accounts for payment of an order instrument bearing a forged indorsement. * * *

It may be assumed for purposes of this introductory sketch that the analysis described for forged indorsement checks equally applies to checks drawn to a principal and indorsed by an ostensible agent with no showing of representative capacity. Considerations unique to the representative capacity problem are developed more fully in Part III infra.

The loss falls on the party who took the check from the forger, or on the forger himself.

2. Forged Checks

As opposed to diverting an intended payment to someone other than the intended recipient, forged checks present the problem of depleting the ostensible drawer's funds when he had intended no payment. The Code's treatment of forged checks, however, begins in the same place as its treatment of forged indorsements. The forgery does not operate as the ostensible drawer's signature. * * * Payment consequently is not to the ostensible drawer's order and violates the drawee bank's strict duty to charge its customer's account only for properly payable items. * * *

The Code's analysis of forged check liability not only begins with the drawee, however; it also generally ends there. The drawee's payment of a forged check is final in favor of a holder in due course or one who has relied on the payment in good faith. § 3–418. This final payment rule codifies and attempts to clarify the rule of Price v. Neal, 3 Burr. 1354 (K.B.1762), "under which a drawee who accepts or pays an instrument on which the signature of the drawer is forged is bound on his acceptance and cannot recover back his payment." * * * Prior parties in the collection chain who meet the prerequisites set out in § 3–418 will be immunized by its final payment rule from any liability for negligence in dealing with the forged check.

The above scheme allocating forgery losses among the various parties to the check collection process operates without regard to fault. The drawee's duty to charge its customer's account only for "properly payable" items and the warranty of title given by prior parties in the chain of transfer impose standards of strict liability.

Fault does occupy a secondary role in the UCC treatment of forgery losses. One whose negligence substantially contributes to the making of an unauthorized signature cannot assert the invalidity of that signature against a holder in due course or a drawee who without negligence pays the check. § 3–406. Thus the drawee can pass the loss back to a drawer or forward to a prior party in the collection chain whose negligence substantially contributed to a forgery. The complaining party's negligence will not, however, bar otherwise available recovery against a party, including a drawee, who is also negligent. Id. Additionally, while nothing in the Code precludes a bank and its customer from modifying the forgery loss rules by contract, the bank cannot enforce an agreement permitting it to act in violation of reasonable commercial standards. § 4–103(1).

B. The Code Policy: Incompletely Greasing the Commercial Wheels

In sum, the Code, while allowing for some modification on the basis of fault or agreement, sets up a system of strict liability rules allocating loss according to the type of forgery. The system uneasily rests on two policy bases. First, it incorporates an at least partially outmoded notion of the relative positions of drawee banks and prior parties in the collection chain with respect to detecting different types of forgeries. Second, it incompletely serves the notion that commerce will be facilitated by bringing to the swiftest practicable conclusion the processing of a check transaction.

As mentioned, the separate treatment given forged checks and forged indorsements harkens back to the eighteenth century decision of the King's Bench in Price v. Neal. That decision left forged check liability on the drawee on the view that, as against other parties in the line of transfer, the drawee stood in the best position to recognize the signature of the drawer, its customer. The corollary principle for forged indorsements is that the person who takes the check from the forger—frequently, as here, the depositary bank—is in the best position to detect the bogus indorsement.

Reaffirming Price v. Neal in the final payment rule of § 3–418, the Code drafters recognized that the case's appraisal of relative opportunity to scrutinize drawer signatures was somewhat unrealistic in a nation where banks may handle some 60 million checks daily.[9] The contemporary pace of commerce has eroded the five senses used by bankers in the face-to-face era of Price versus Neal; little remains save the sensory activity of punching keys. While the drafters thus concluded that Price v. Neal had been drained of all its personality, they nevertheless insisted that its conclusion survives. The drafters noted that modern groundwork for the final payment rule could be found in the

---

9. For a discussion of the volume of checks processed and the resultant interplay between the law of forgery losses and bankers' perceptions of the forgery problem, see Murray, Price v. Neal in the Electronic Age: An Empirical Survey, 87 Banking L.J. 686 (1970). We note the commentator's interesting observation that many banks do not record separately losses from forged checks and forged indorsements, contrary to the implicit assumption in the final payment rule that the two types of losses represent security breakdowns in different functions of a bank—accepting checks for deposit to its customers accounts and paying checks drawn by its customers—which might call for different protective measures.

On the other hand, the author does suggest specific measures for protecting banks against forged check losses. The possibility remains that the separate allocation of strict liability for forged check and forged indorsement losses may act as some incentive for the development of those precautionary measures that consistent with the press of business will most effectively reduce the risk of loss from either type of forgery.

less fictional rationalization ＊ ＊ ＊ that it is highly desirable to end the transaction on an instrument when it is paid rather than reopen and upset a series of commercial transactions at a later date when the forgery is discovered.

§ 3–418, Comment 1. In recognition of the frenetic commerce of our time, the thrust of the UCC here and elsewhere is for speed and facility at some expense to exact checks and balances.

Leaving forged check liability on the drawee may serve well this finality policy. That policy, however, does not itself justify separate treatment for forged checks and indorsements. The concern that commercial transactions be swiftly brought to rest applies with equal force to both varieties of wrongdoing. See White and Summers, supra, at 522–23; Comment, Allocation of Losses From Check Forgeries Under the Law of Negotiable Instruments and the Uniform Commercial Code, 62 Yale L.J. 417, 459–60 (1953).

While finality viewed alone calls for equal treatment of forged checks and forged indorsements, one might still maintain that forged indorsements merit separate rules. The modern demands of commerce have as the drafters recognized, deprived drawees of any superior opportunity to detect forged drawer's signatures. Only a concern for finality therefore justifies placing forged check losses on drawee banks.

Such simple expedients as requiring identification, however, may still permit transferees of checks to provide a significant protection against forged indorsements that drawees cannot. To insure such protective measures are taken, it may be sensible to override the finality policy and to place forged indorsement losses on the depositary bank or other party who takes from the forger. ＊ ＊ ＊

c. OVERDRAFTS

If a payor bank pays a check that is forged or which bears a forged indorsement, it is clear that the bank paid the check by mistake. No bank would knowingly pay such a check because the check is not properly payable and the payor bank is not entitled to charge the account of the drawer. The payment of a check drawn on an account in which there are insufficient funds to cover the check is different. Under § 4–401(a) such a check is properly payable and the drawer's account can be charged. Thus, it may not be clear at the time of payment whether the payor bank paid by mistake or intended to grant credit to the drawer. Intentional payment of checks that create overdrafts is very common. There is some authority denying a payor bank any right of restitution in overdraft cases, but most courts follow Restatement of Restitution

§ 29 which recognizes a limited right of restitution in such cases. In Revised Article 3, overdraft cases are governed by § 3–418(b) which gives to the payor bank a right to recover "to the extent permitted by the law governing mistake and restitution." But § 3–418(b) is subject to § 3–418(c). No right of restitution may be asserted against a person who took the check in good faith and for value or who in good faith changed position in reliance on payment of the check.

National Savings, which follows, discusses the issue under common law and § 3–418 of the original Article 3.

NATIONAL SAVINGS & TRUST CO. v. PARK CORP.

United States Court of Appeals, Sixth Circuit, 1983.
722 F.2d 1303, cert. denied, 466 U.S. 939, 104 S.Ct. 1916, 80 L.Ed.2d 464
(1984).

BOYCE F. MARTIN, JR., CIRCUIT JUDGE.

In this diversity action, National Savings and Trust challenges the summary denial of its claim for restitution of $74,737.25 it mistakenly paid to Park Corporation on a bad check.

On January 8, 1980, Park Corporation contracted to sell some used mining equipment to DAI International Investment Corporation. The sales agent for the transaction was Garland Caribbean Corporation. As part of its down payment, DAI gave Garland a check for $75,000 drawn on its account with the plaintiff, National Savings and Trust Company. On January 16, Garland called National Savings to determine if DAI had sufficient funds in its account to cover this check. The bank said DAI did not. That same day, Garland endorsed the check over to Park Corporation. Park Corporation then sent the check to National Savings "for collection."

On January 22, Garland once again called the bank to determine if DAI had sufficient funds in its account to cover the check. Once again, the bank said DAI did not.[1] Moreover, on this occasion, the banking employee who received the inquiry went to the bank's "platform officer" and notified him not to accept any DAI checks drawn on insufficient funds. Unfortunately for the bank, the platform officer only saw checks arriving through normal banking channels and not those coming in "for collection."

DAI's check arrived at the bank that same day. However, the employee who normally processed "for collection" checks was scheduled to work in another department that day. Prior to her departure, she did manage to open the incoming mail, including the DAI check. Her supervisor then volunteered to help out by taking the DAI check to the wire room for payment. Neither

---

[1] There is no evidence Park was ever aware of Garland's phone conversations with the bank.

employee followed the bank's standard procedure and checked DAI's account to ensure that it held sufficient funds to cover the check. Each assumed that the other had done so. As a result, the check was paid even though DAI had only $263.75 in its account.

On January 28, 1980, after discovering its mistake, National Savings asked Park Corporation to return the $75,000. Park refused and National Savings subsequently brought this lawsuit. On motion for summary judgment by the defendant, the court found for Park on the grounds that National Savings had made an improvident extension of credit and that the bank was in a better position to know the true facts and to guard against mistakes. We disagree.

The basic law of restitution in Ohio, the state whose law controls, is summarized in Firestone Rubber & Tire Co. v. Central Nat'l Bank of Cleveland, 159 Ohio St. 423, 112 N.E.2d 636 (1953). The *Firestone* case held that money paid to another by mistake is recoverable unless the other person has changed his position in reliance on the payment. This rule applies even if the mistake was the result of negligence.

Park Corporation attempts to circumvent the holding in *Firestone* by arguing that banks are not protected by normal restitutionary principles when they pay an insufficient funds (NSF) check. There is some support for this position. See, e.g., Spokane & Eastern Trust Co. v. Huff, 63 Wash. 225, 115 P. 80 (1911); 7 Zollman, *The Law of Banks and Banking* § 5062 (1936). Nonetheless, this rule has not been universally applied, see, e.g., Manufacturers Trust Co. v. Diamond, 17 Misc.2d 909, 186 N.Y.S.2d 917, 919 (1959), and Park has not cited, nor have we been able to find, any Ohio cases adopting this rule. Moreover, it is questionable whether such a doctrine, if ever in existence, would survive the subsequent enactment of the Uniform Commercial Code in Ohio and the particular provisions applicable to the facts of the present case.

Park Corporation next argues that *Firestone* does not control because National Savings' payment was not a mistake but rather a knowing extension of credit. Park relies heavily on the New Jersey case of Demos v. Lyons, 151 N.J.Super. 489, 376 A.2d 1352 (Law Div.1977). The factual circumstances of *Demos,* however, are quite distinct from the present case. In *Demos,* the bank actually examined the customer's account, realized the customer had insufficient funds to cover the check, yet paid the check anyway. The bank did not want to embarrass its customer and it hoped that he had made a late deposit to cover the check which would appear on the next day's balance sheet. No such deposit was ever made. In our case, National Savings never intended to make good on an NSF check. The platform officer had been notified not to pay out on DAI's check. The "for collection" employees were operating under standing orders to check balances before paying a check and never to pay on an NSF check. Despite all these precautions, the check was paid. At no time, however, did the employees making the payment decision know that DAI's account had insufficient funds to cover the check.

[Omitted is the part of the opinion in which the court holds that the case is governed by § 3–418.]

Park Corporation next contends that, even if section 3–418 controls, it is both a holder in due course and one who has changed its position in reliance on National Saving's payment and therefore should be allowed to retain the $75,000. We find no support in the record for either proposition. On the holder in due course issue, Park does not qualify because it did not give value for the check. It was still in possession of the machinery it had contracted to sell to DAI. Although it had promised to deliver the equipment to DAI, such an executory promise does not constitute value. U.C.C. § 3–303, Comment 3. Park Corporation is, of course, no longer required to carry out its promise because DAI has breached its agreement to pay.

As for detrimental reliance, Park contends that it paid $37,500 as a commission to Garland Corporation on the assumption that DAI's check was good. However, Park did not pay Garland until February 13, 1980, two weeks after National Savings had informed Park that it had paid the DAI check by mistake and that it wanted Park to return the money. Section 3–418 only makes payment by the bank final in favor of someone who has "*in good faith* changed his position in reliance on the payment." Once aware of the insufficiency in funds, Park could not have "in good faith" paid Garland $37,500 in reliance on that check. Park also alleges it paid rent for storing the equipment and painted the equipment in reliance on the payment. There is no evidence to support these allegations.

Accordingly, the decision of the district court is reversed.

3. CONVERSION ACTIONS REGARDING CHECKS BEARING FORGED INDORSEMENT

a. ACTION BY PAYEE

(i) INTRODUCTION

In a common type of forged-indorsement case the check is stolen by an employee of the payee. The check is an ordinary check mailed to the payee by the drawer in payment of an obligation owed to the payee. The check is received by the payee when the mail delivery is made and the payee becomes a holder of the check at that time. Suppose the check is stolen by an employee of the payee who works as a clerk in the payee's mailroom. The employee forges the payee's name as an indorsement of the check, and obtains payment from the drawee bank. How does the theft of the check and its collection affect the payee's rights with respect to the check and the obligation of the drawer to the payee that the check was intended to pay? Under § 3–310(b) the obligation for which the check was received becomes "suspended" at the time the payee receives the check. In the hands of the payee the check represents a right to receive money which is a property right of the payee. This property right is provisionally substituted for the right of the payee to enforce the obligation for which the check was received. If the payee receives payment of the check, the obligation for which the check was received is discharged to the extent of the payment. § 3–310(b)(1). If the payee presents the check for payment and the check is dishonored, the payee has a cause of action against the drawer of the check either on the check (§ 3–414(b)) or on the obligation for which the check was received. § 3–310(b)(3).

What rights does the payee have if the check is stolen from the payee and the thief obtains payment from the drawee? Under § 3–310(b)(1) "payment * * * of the check" results in discharge of the obligation for which a check was taken, but under § 3–602(a), the check is not paid unless payment is made to a person entitled to enforce the check. Payment to the thief or a transferee of the thief does not result in payment of the check and the obligation of the drawer on the check is not discharged. The payee of the check remains the owner of the check and the person entitled to enforce it. § 3–301 and § 3–309. The drawee's payment to a person not entitled to enforce the check does not affect the payee's rights in the check. The payee, however, does not have a right to enforce the obligation for which the check was received. That obligation remains suspended under § 3–310(b) because neither dishonor nor payment of the check has occurred. Under the last sentence of § 3–310(b)(4), the payee of a stolen check who is not in possession of the check, has rights against the drawer only on the check. § 3–309, § 3–414, and Comment 4 to § 3–310. Thus, the payee has the burden of asserting rights with respect to the stolen check, and there are several possible courses of action available to the payee against third parties as well as the drawer.

Although the payee from whom a check has been stolen has no right to obtain a substitute check from the drawer, sometimes the drawer will issue such a check. In the case in which payment with respect to the stolen check has not yet been made by the drawee, the drawee can be informed of the theft and payment to the thief may be avoided. If payment by the drawee has already been made, the drawer can insist that the drawee recredit the drawer's account because payment to the thief did not entitle the drawee to debit the drawer's account. § 4–401. If the drawer refuses to issue a replacement check, the payee has a remedy against the drawer on the check, but that remedy may not be convenient. § 3–309. Often a forged indorsement case involves thefts of many checks from one payee by the same thief. Actions against the various drawers of the stolen checks may not be feasible. An action against the person who took the checks from the thief is usually a better remedy.

In the hands of the payee, a check is property and, if that property is stolen, the rules of conversion applying to personal property also apply to the check. Thus, the payee of the stolen check has an action in conversion against the thief for the amount of the check. But the law of conversion also allows an action to be brought against "innocent converters," i.e. persons who exercise dominion over stolen property without knowledge that it was stolen. Thus, if a thief sells stolen goods to a good faith purchaser for value, the owner has an action against the BFP as well. A stolen check bearing the forged indorsement of the payee can be turned into money by selling it to a depositary bank or other purchaser for cash, by depositing it to the thief's bank account for bank credit that can subsequently be withdrawn, or by presenting the check for payment to the drawee bank. Each of these takers of the check is a potential defendant. The common law was clear that a conversion action could be brought by the payee against the person who bought the check. The common law cases were divided on the issue of whether the drawee bank was liable in conversion if it paid a stolen check bearing a forged indorsement, but most courts held that a conversion action was available and that view was adopted by original Article 3. Revised Article 3 states the current rules regarding conversion in § 3–420.

(ii) POSSESSION OF CHECK BY PAYEE

Barclay's Bank, which follows, discusses the conversion remedy of the payee of a stolen check and the necessity of possession by the payee. The issue which is the focus of this case is now specifically addressed in § 3–420(a).

STATE OF NEW YORK v. BARCLAY'S BANK OF NEW YORK

Court of Appeals of New York, 1990.
76 N.Y.2d 533, 563 N.E.2d 11.

HANCOCK, JUDGE.

In the absence of actual or constructive possession of a check, does the named payee have a right of action against the depositary bank which has paid out the proceeds over a forged indorsement?

This is the question presented in plaintiff's appeal from a dismissal of its action to recover the amounts of several checks drawn by taxpayers to the order of various State taxing authorities. The checks were never delivered to plaintiff; the taxpayers' dishonest accountant misappropriated them, and deposited them in his own account at Banker's Trust Company of Hudson Valley, N.A.[1] For reasons stated hereafter, we hold that plaintiff has no right of action and accordingly affirm the order granting summary judgment to defendant.

The case stems from the activities of Richard Caliendo, an accountant. Caliendo prepared tax returns for various clients. To satisfy their tax liability, the clients issued checks payable to various State taxing entities, and gave them to Caliendo. Between 1977 and 1979, he forged indorsements on these checks, deposited them in his own account with defendant, and subsequently withdrew the proceeds. In November 1980—shortly after the scheme was uncovered—Caliendo died when the plane he was piloting crashed. The State never received the checks. In 1983, after learning of these events, the State commenced this action seeking to recover the aggregate face amount of the checks.

Supreme Court denied defendant's motion to dismiss the complaint and its subsequent motion for summary judgment, concluding that the payee's possession of the checks was not essential to its action against the depositary bank. On appeal, the Appellate Division reversed and dismissed the complaint. It held that requiring "delivery, either actual or constructive, [as] an indispensable prerequisite for" a conversion action under UCC 3–419(1)(c) is consistent with the view of most authorities and supported by practical considerations (State of New York v. Barclays Bank, 151 A.D.2d 19, 21–24, 546 N.Y.S.2d 479). We agree.[2]

II

It has long been held that a check has no valid inception until delivery * * *. Further, a payee must have actual or constructive possession of a negotiable instrument in order to attain the status of a holder (see, UCC 1–201[20]) and to have an interest in

1. Defendant Barclays Bank of New York, N.A. is a successor to Bankers Trust Company. Henceforth, "defendant" will refer to Barclays and Bankers Trust as one entity.

2. Plaintiff's complaint is framed as one for money had and received. Supreme Court in denying defendant's dismissal motion under CPLR 3211(a)(7), however, treated the action as one in contract, alone, or in both contract and conversion. Although, in its brief, plaintiff now appears to view the action primarily as one for money had and received or quasi contract, it cites cases and authorities pertaining to a conversion action under UCC 3–419(1)(c), and the Appellate Division apparently viewed it as such. For purposes of resolving the legal question before us—the effect of lack of delivery of the checks—it makes no difference whether plaintiff's action is under UCC 3–419(1)(c) or under some common-law theory. The result is the same (see, part III, infra). We accordingly discuss the authorities as being applicable to both the statutory and common-law theories.

it. These are established principles of negotiable instruments law
* * *.

Permitting a payee who has never had possession to maintain
an action against the depositary bank would be inconsistent with
these principles. It would have the effect of enforcing rights that
do not exist. For this reason, most courts and commentators have
concluded that either actual or constructive delivery to the payee
is a necessary prerequisite to a conversion action * * *.

Significant practical considerations support this conclusion.
Where a payee has never possessed the check, it is more likely
that the forged indorsement resulted from the drawer's negligence, an issue which could not be readily contested in an action
between the payee and the depositary bank * * *. Moreover, as
noted by the Appellate Division, the payee is not left without a
remedy, inasmuch as it can sue on the underlying obligation
* * *.

Henderson v. Lincoln Rochester Trust Co., 303 N.Y. 27, 100
N.E.2d 117, on which plaintiff relies, does not support its argument in this respect. There, in concluding that the payee could
maintain an action either in contract or conversion, the court did
not reach the issue of nondelivery of the check. Other cases cited
by plaintiff are readily distinguished. They involve situations
where the plaintiff, unlike the State here, had received constructive possession of the check through delivery to the payee's agent,
to a copayee, or to a coindorsee (see, e.g., Lund's, Inc. v. Chemical
Bank, 870 F.2d 840 [2d Cir.] [delivery to coindorsees]; [3] United
States v. Bankers Trust Co., 17 UCC Rep.Serv. 136 [E.D.N.Y.1975]
[delivery to copayee]; Burks Drywall v. Washington Bank & Trust
Co., 110 Ill.App.3d 569, 66 Ill.Dec. 222, 442 N.E.2d 648 [1982]
[delivery to copayee or agent]; Thornton & Co. v. Gwinnett Bank
& Trust Co., 151 Ga.App. 641, 260 S.E.2d 765 [1979] [delivery to
agent]).

Plaintiff maintains, however, citing language in *Burks Drywall,* 66 Ill.Dec. at 226, 442 N.E.2d, supra, at 652 and *Thornton,*
260 S.E.2d, supra, at 767, that, based solely on its status as named
payee and intended beneficiary of the checks, it has a sufficient
interest to bring a conversion action under UCC 3–419(1)(c) or a
common-law action for money had and received. We believe such
a rule would be contrary to the underlying theory of the UCC and,
to the extent that the cases cited by plaintiff suggest it, we decline
to follow them.

3. *Lund's* involved three checks, two
of which were indorsed and delivered to
coindorsees of plaintiff, thus, giving
plaintiff sufficient possession to maintain a conversion action with respect to
those checks under UCC 3–419(1)(c). A
third check indorsed solely to Lund's
Inc. was determined on remand not to
have been constructively delivered to
plaintiff Lund. As to that check, the
action was dismissed in reliance upon
the Appellate Division's decision in this
case (see, Lund v. Chemical Bank, 1990
WL 17711 [S.D.N.Y.]).

* * *

Nor are we persuaded by plaintiff's suggestion that permitting a suit * * * by a payee not-in-possession would promote judicial economy and avoid circuity of action. On the contrary, relegating such a payee to a suit against the drawer on the underlying obligation would give full effect to the UCC's loss allocation scheme by furthering the aim of placing ultimate responsibility on the party at fault through an orderly process in which each defendant in the transactional chain may interpose the defenses available to it * * *. And requiring a payee-not-in-possession to sue the drawer on the underlying claim would actually avoid circuity of action in some instances—for example, where the drawer's suit against the drawee bank is barred by valid defenses (see, UCC 3–406, 4–406) or where the drawer has an effective defense against the payee's claim. This concern has particular pertinence here where—as the Appellate Division observed (151 A.D.2d, at 20, 546 N.Y.S.2d 479)—it is contended that some of the checks were for inflated or nonexistent tax liabilities for which the drawers-taxpayers would have valid defenses against the State. In such cases, permitting a payee-not-in-possession to sue the depositary bank at the other end of the transactional chain would only produce unnecessary litigation. Accordingly, we agree with the Appellate Division that the rule requiring actual or constructive possession by a payee as a prerequisite for a suit against the depositary bank is preferable * * * and we adopt it.

III

Plaintiff contends, nevertheless, that even if possession is a prerequisite to a cause of action by a named payee against a depositary bank, it should prevail because the drawers' delivery of the checks to Caliendo constituted constructive delivery to the State. It is a general rule that putting a check in the hands of the drawer's own agent for purpose of delivery to the payee does not constitute delivery to the payee * * *; this is so because the drawer has control of the agent and the check is revocable and ineffective until the agent delivers it * * *. Here, of course, Caliendo had no agency or other relationship with the State which might have imputed his possession of the checks to it. Indeed, the State does not contend that it knew of Caliendo's dealings with the drawers or even of the checks' existence. Thus, applying these general rules, the State's claim must fail.

Wolfin v. Security Bank, (170 App.Div. 519, 156 N.Y.S. 474, affd. 218 N.Y. 709, 113 N.E. 1068), relied on by plaintiff, is not to the contrary. There, the drawer of the check gave it to the named payee with instructions that it be indorsed and delivered to plaintiff. Unlike the case at bar—where the checks were never delivered to the payee but remained in the hands of the drawers' accountant and agent—in *Wolfin* the drawer retained no control after the check was delivered to the named payee as a fully negotiable instrument * * *.

Finally, contrary to plaintiff's contentions, it cannot recover under a theory of unjust enrichment or quasi contract. It is true that, in creating a statutory right to bring a conversion action for payment over a forged indorsement * * * at the time of the Uniform Commercial Code's enactment, the Legislature did not intend to abrogate the payee's pre-Code common-law rights to sue in assumpsit, for money had and received or unjust enrichment * * *. This does not help plaintiff, however.

The theory of an action in quasi contract "rests upon the equitable principle that a person shall not be *allowed to enrich himself unjustly at the expense of another.* * * * It is an obligation which the law creates, in the absence of any agreement, when and because the acts of the parties or others have placed in the possession of one person money, or its equivalent, under such circumstances that in equity and good conscience he ought not to retain it" (Miller v. Schloss, 218 N.Y. 400, 407, 113 N.E. 337 [emphasis added]; *see,* Restatement of Restitution § 1, at 12–15). The general rule is that "the plaintiff *must have suffered a loss* and an action not based upon loss is not restitutionary." (Restatement of Restitution § 128, comment f, at 531 [emphasis added]). On this point, plaintiff's action in quasi contract, like its action for conversion * * *, must fail. The checks were never actually or constructively delivered to plaintiff. It, therefore, never acquired a property interest in them and cannot be said to have suffered a loss.

The order of the Appellate Division should, accordingly, be affirmed, with costs.

(iii) LIABILITY OF DEPOSITARY BANK AS AGENT FOR COLLECTION

When a check is transferred to a depositary bank by its customer, the bank sometimes purchases the check from the customer by giving cash for it or by giving the customer a credit to the customer's account immediately available for withdrawal as of right. More commonly the depositary bank doesn't buy the check. Rather, it takes the check as agent of the customer to obtain payment of the check from the payor bank and pays the proceeds of the check to the customer after the check is paid. This distinction can have some importance in Article 3 because the status of the depositary bank as a holder in due course may depend upon whether it had given value for the check at the time the check was presented for payment. But in Article 4 the depositary bank is normally treated as an agent for collection whether or not the bank gave value to the customer for the check. § 4–201(a).

Under original Article 3 the law was clear that a person that cashed a check stolen from the payee could be held liable in conversion to the payee. But the question of whether a depositary bank that took a stolen check as an agent for collection was also liable was made unclear by a highly controversial provision of that statute, § 3–419(3). That issue is discussed in *Denn,* the case that follows. The result in *Denn* is reversed in Revised Article 3 by § 3–420(c).

DENN v. FIRST STATE BANK

Supreme Court of Minnesota, 1982.
316 N.W.2d 532.

Wahl, Justice.

This appeal raises the issue of whether a depositary bank [1] which collected and paid out on two checks bearing forged indorsements is absolved from liability to the payee of the checks under UCC § 3–419(3) when it acted in good faith and in accordance with reasonable commercial standards. We hold that it is.

The facts are straightforward. Plaintiff Edward Denn, the sole shareholder of Advance Foam of Minnesota, brought an action against the First State Bank of Spring Lake Park (Spring Lake) and Northfield National Bank (Northfield) for conversion of two checks paid over a forged indorsement. Both checks were drawn on Northfield by Blesener Roofing and Insulation and were issued to Advance Foam. The first check, dated July 7, 1978, was in the amount of $5,004.67. The second check, dated August 5, 1978, was in the amount of $2,468.38.

Dennis Carlson, a former employee of Advance Foam, deposited the checks to an account which he had opened at Spring Lake on March 29, 1978. He and his wife were joint owners of that account, which was titled "Dennis Carlson/Advanced Foam Account." Carlson indorsed the checks "Advanced Foam/Dennis Carlson" before depositing them.

Spring Lake gave Carlson provisional credit and then presented the checks to drawee Northfield, which paid them. Once Northfield had paid the checks, Spring Lake allowed Carlson to withdraw the money from the account. On September 5, 1978, Denn executed an Affidavit of Forgery in which he stated that he

---

1. The Uniform Commercial Code provides these definitions: "(a) 'Depositary bank' means the first bank to which an item is transferred for collection even though it is also the payor bank; • • • (d) 'collecting bank' means any bank handling the item for collection except the payor bank." UCC § 4–105. Under the facts of this case, the First State Bank of Spring Lake Park is both a depositary bank and a collecting bank. Northfield National Bank, the drawee (or payor) bank, is neither a collecting nor a depositary bank.

had not received the proceeds of the checks in question, but the affidavit reached Northfield too late to prevent payment.

After Denn brought his conversion action against the two banks, Spring Lake cross-claimed against Northfield on the ground of failure to comply with proper banking procedures and initiated a third-party complaint against Carlson. Plaintiff then also asserted a claim against Carlson, and Northfield cross-claimed against Spring Lake, alleging that Spring Lake had breached the presentment warranties imposed on a collecting bank by § 4–207(1)(a) [now § 4–208(a)(1)]. The trial court granted Northfield's motion for summary judgment on its cross-claim against Spring Lake, after which Denn dismissed without prejudice his cause of action against Northfield.

The court submitted the remaining issues to a jury which found that (1) Spring Lake had acted in accordance with reasonable commercial standards in accepting for deposit the two checks in question, (2) Denn and Carlson were not business partners, (3) Carlson did not have the authority to indorse and deposit the two checks, (4) the check proceeds were not used in furtherance of the Denn business, (5) Denn had been negligent in the use of his corporate name, and (6) Denn's negligence did not contribute to the making of the indorsement at issue.

The court found Carlson liable to Denn in the amount of the forged checks and denied Denn's claim against Spring Lake. The court held, in effect, that UCC § 3–419(3) absolves from liability in conversion a depositary bank which acts in good faith and in accordance with reasonable commercial standards. Since the depositary bank is ultimately liable on the presentment warranties of § 4–207(1)(a), the effect of the trial court's decision is to require the rightful payee of a check to bring his conversion action against the drawee bank, which will then proceed against the depositary bank. Denn appeals from the trial court's decision in this regard and argues that he should be allowed to collect directly from Spring Lake, the depositary bank.

Appellant's position would be unassailable at common law. A payee was allowed to bring his conversion suit directly against the depositary bank. Moler v. State Bank of Bigelow, 176 Minn. 449, 223 N.W. 780 (1929). The depositary bank was liable to the true owner of the check because the first party to take from a forger was ultimately liable on his indorsement. F. Kessler, Forged Instruments, 47 Yale L.J. 863 (1938). In Minnesota, this result obtained prior to the adoption of the U.C.C. whether the bank cashed the check or gave the forger provisional credit. Rosacker v. Commercial State Bank, 191 Minn. 553, 254 N.W. 824 (1934).

The Minnesota legislature adopted the Uniform Commercial Code (U.C.C.) in 1965. Although the Code contemplates actions in conversion, there is no provision which expressly governs suits by a payee against a depositary bank. Spring Lake does not claim that the U.C.C. prohibits Denn from bringing this action. It does claim, however, to be absolved from liability to Denn by UCC § 3–419(3), which provides:

> Subject to the provisions of this Act concerning restrictive indorsements a representative, including a depositary or collecting bank, who has in good faith and in accordance with the reasonable commercial standards applicable to the business of such representative dealt with an instrument or its proceeds on behalf of one who was not the true owner is not liable in conversion or otherwise to the true owner beyond the amount of any proceeds remaining in his hands.

Spring Lake claims it is free of liability to Denn because it (1) was acting in a representative capacity, (2) was acting in good faith and in accordance with reasonable commercial standards, and (3) did not retain any "proceeds" of the forged instruments.

There is considerable controversy among the courts and legal commentators over the question of when a bank is acting in a representative capacity. The Code itself defines a representative simply as "an agent, an officer of a corporation or association, and a trustee, executor or administrator of an estate, or any other person empowered to act for another." UCC § 1–201(35). At common law such an agent is "liable in conversion when he disposes of goods for his principal, even though the agent has acted in good faith and no longer exercises control over the converted goods." Cooper v. Union Bank: California Protects the True Owner Against a Forged Indorsement Despite Uniform Commercial Code Section 3–419(3), 25 Hastings L.J. 715, 719 (1974) (hereinafter *California Protects*). There was a common-law exemption from such liability, however, for a broker who dealt with stolen negotiable bonds on behalf of his principal. Id.; First National Bank v. Goldberg, 340 Pa. 337, 17 A.2d 377 (1941).

Did the Code drafters intend merely to codify the existing exemption for brokers, or did they intend also to exempt from liability depositary and collecting banks dealing with order instruments in the normal check collection process? To resolve this question we turn to the history of U.C.C. § 3–419(3) and its comments.

The "representative exception" was first included in the May 1949 draft, which stated that "A representative who in good faith has dealt with an instrument or its proceeds is not liable for conversion even though his principal was not the owner of the instrument." Payee v. Depositary Bank: What is the UCC Defense to Handling Checks Bearing Forged Indorsements? 45 U.Colo.L.Rev. 281, 308 (1974) (quoting ALI & National Conference of Commissioners on Uniform State Laws, Uniform Commercial Code § 3–427 (May 1949 Draft)). Under "Purposes of Section," the drafters went on to state that the intent of the section is "to adopt the rule of decisions which have held that a *broker* who *sells* a negotiable instrument for his principal * * * is not liable for conversion of the instrument." Id. at 309 (citing Official Comment) (emphasis added). It is quite likely that the drafters of the 1949 version of the Code meant to exempt from liability only those brokers who had been exempt at common law.

However, in 1951 the drafters added to section 3–419(3) the phrase "including a depositary or collecting bank." Id. The fact that this crucial phrase was added to the Code and was not part of the original version supports the idea that the 1951 drafters intended specifically to exempt depositary and collecting banks from liability. In 1952, the drafters added Comment 5, which also included a reference to depositary banks. Id. Comment 5 states:

> Subsection (3), which is new, is intended to adopt the rule of decisions which has held that a representative such as a broker or depositary bank, who deals with a negotiable instrument for his principal in good faith is not liable to the true owner for conversion of the instrument or otherwise, except that he may be compelled to turn over to the true owner the instrument itself or any proceeds of the instrument remaining in his hands.

UCC § 3–419. The fact that the phrase "such as a broker or *depositary bank*" is used to describe representative strongly suggests that the drafters intended to expand the scope of the common-law exception for brokers.[4]

Comment 6 to section 3–419(3) further supports the idea that the drafters intended to offer defenses to a depositary bank which took from a forger. Comment 6 states:

> The provisions of this section are not intended to eliminate any liability on warranties of presentment and transfer (Section 3–417). Thus a collecting bank might be liable to a drawee bank which had been subject to liability under this section, even though the collecting bank might not be liable directly to the owner of the instrument.

Id. Since, at common law, a collecting bank which took from a forger would have been liable to the true payee, the suggestion here that such a bank "might not be liable" implies that the bank

4. At least one commentator believes that the bankers, who presumably urged the addition of the phrase "including a depositary or collecting bank," intended to relieve such banks from liability only when they were acting in the capacity of a broker:

Unfortunately, the drafters of the Code did not leave this provision in a separate action where it belongs. When it was incorporated as a subsec-

tion under Section 3–419, its meaning was inevitably intermingled with the notion of handling checks bearing forged indorsements. It is probable that the drafters never foresaw the way in which its meaning would get expanded.

Payee v. Depositary Bank: What is the UCC Defense to Handling Checks Bearing Forged Indorsements?, 45 U.Colo.L. Rev. 281, 311 (1974).

now has some defenses by which it may absolve itself from its common-law liability.

Several courts have interpreted "representative" not to include a depositary or collecting bank. The Pennsylvania Court of Common Pleas, in Ervin v. Dauphin Deposit Trust Co., 84 Dauph. 280, 38 Pa.D. & C.2d 473, 3 U.C.C.Rep. 311 (1965), reasoned that the legislature could not have intended to exempt collecting and depositary banks from their common-law liability to the true payee because such an exception would lead to an unreasonable result. Id. at 287, 38 Pa.D. & C.2d at 483, 3 U.C.C.Rep. at 318–19. It would seem to limit the liability of the collecting bank "in the face of other sections of the code which place the ultimate liability on the check cashing bank when the payee's name is forged * * * because of the check cashing bank's warranties on the indorsements." Id. at 287, 38 Pa.D. & C.2d at 483, 3 U.C.C.Rep. at 319.

The California Supreme Court has reached the same results primarily because of the absence of Code comment on such a major change from the common law: "Had such substantial and controversial deviation from prior law been intended, moreover, it could be expected that the official commentary to section 3419 would have so stated and would have included extensive explanation of the reasons for the change." Cooper v. Union Bank, 9 Cal. 3d 371, 382, 107 Cal.Rptr. 1, 9–10, 507 P.2d 609, 617 (1973). Similarly, the District Court of the Northern District of Texas has concluded simply that section 3–419(3) does not contemplate the normal check collection process. Tubin v. Rabin, 389 F.Supp. 787 (N.D.Tex.1974).

The arguments of the *Ervin* and *Cooper* courts are persuasive, but we are compelled to reach an opposite conclusion. We can ignore neither the plain language of the statute which expressly includes depositary and collecting banks in its description of representatives nor the comments which appear to exclude such banks from liability.

Professor Stanley V. Kinyon, in his comment to the Minnesota version of the Code, noted that UCC § 3–419(3) applies to collecting banks and went on to distinguish *Moler* from *Rosacker*. The *Moler* decision "is *not* within the rule of this subsection and will not be changed" because the bank acted as a purchaser in cashing the check and not as a representative or collecting bank. UCC § 3–419(3) (1966), p. 468 (emphasis in original). However, the *Rosacker* decision would be changed by the U.C.C. because the bank, acting in a representative capacity, credited the forger's account and permitted withdrawals from it. Id. at 469. Appellant offers us no authority for ignoring this comment, which the legislature has left in its original form since its adoption.

Professor Allan Farnsworth's analysis parallels that of Kinyon: "The depositary bank would be liable under the Code if it cashed checks, but it would not be liable if it took them for collection and gave a provisional credit. If it cashed them, then it is not a representative, but is purchasing the checks." Farnsworth & Leary, U.C.C. Brief No. 10: Forgery and Alteration of Checks, 14 Prac.Law, No. 3, 75, 79 (1968).

The facts of this case are similar to those of *Rosacker*. In allowing Carlson to deposit the Advance Foam checks in his account and then presenting the checks to Northfield for payment, Spring Lake was acting as Carlson's representative. Spring Lake is, therefore, absolved of liability to Denn unless it has failed to act in good faith and in accordance with reasonable commercial standards or has retained any proceeds of the checks.

The trial court found on the jury's special verdict that Spring Lake had acted in good faith and in accordance with reasonable commercial standards. Denn did not contest testimony to this effect at trial. Rather, he urges this court, as a matter of law, to find, as did the Court of Appeals of Washington, that a bank is not acting in accordance with reasonable commercial standards when it accepts for deposit to a personal account checks which are payable to a corporation. Von Gohren v. Pacific National Bank, 8 Wash.App. 245, 505 P.2d 467 (1973). This we decline to do absent proof that the bank would know either that these checks were payable to a corporation or that Carlson was depositing them in an individual account. Denn has failed to show that the facts of this case fall within the *Von Gohren* rule.

The California Supreme Court rested its decision in the *Cooper* case on the theory that, even though the depositary bank had paid over money to the forger, it had not turned over the "proceeds" of the checks. With reference to the law of constructive trusts, which allows a claimant to trace funds which are rightfully his, the court concludes that "the banks retain the proceeds of the instruments even though amounts set forth in the instruments, in the banks' own money, were remitted to [the forger]." 9 Cal.3d at 379, 107 Cal.Rptr. at 7, 507 P.2d at 615.

The Florida Court of Appeals, faced with this "proceeds" rationale in Jackson Vitrified China Co. v. People's American Bank, 388 So.2d 1059 (Fla.Dist.Ct.App.1980), could find no evidence that the drafters of the Code intended such a strained construction. Nor can we. "To the extent that a distinction is drawn regarding the time of payment vis à vis the time of collection, such a distinction is artificial; to the extent that no distinction is made, the provision is rendered nugatory." Id. at 1061.

Furthermore, it is the law of this state that, when the depositary bank had disbursed the amount it had received from the drawee bank, it had "paid out the entire proceeds of the check." Soderlin v. Marquette National Bank, 214 Minn. 408, 412, 8 N.W.2d 331, 332 (1943). Minnesota thus favors the less mechanistic "balance sheet" view of proceeds, with the result in this case that, because Spring Lake has paid out the total amount to the forger, it no longer holds proceeds of the checks and is not liable to Denn.

There are strong policy arguments in Denn's favor. It is judicially efficient to allow the true payee to proceed directly against a collecting bank. The collecting bank will bear the ultimate loss in most cases. If the payee must sue the drawee bank, the drawee bank will sue the collecting bank on the warranties of UCC § 4–207 as Northfield did in this case. Therefore, "a suit by the owner-payee against the depositary bank avoids an additional suit and thus resolves the entire dispute in a more economical manner." J. White & R. Summers, Uniform Commercial Code 590 (2d ed. 1980). Collecting banks are also more convenient defendants. While the forged checks may be drawn on several different banks, the forger often cashes or deposits them all at the same bank, or at banks in the same geographical area. Both the payee and the judicial system suffer when the payee is required to sue the drawee banks in a number of jurisdictions to recover on a forged indorsement. The Michigan Court of Appeals relied on this policy consideration when it held that "3–419(3) provides no defense for the collecting bank in a suit by the true owner of the instrument in this type of fact situation." Sheriff-Goslin Co. v. Cawood, 91 Mich.App. 204, 210, 283 N.W.2d 691, 694 (1979). The court was concerned about the number of suits that would result if it did not allow a payee's direct action against a depositary bank.

We reluctantly conclude, however, that to deny a collecting bank the defenses of UCC § 3–419(3) in Denn's case is to ignore the clear intent of our legislature. As the Florida Court of Appeals so well stated, where the choice is "between following what appears to be bad law, or 'adapting' that law to what we perceive to be commercial reality, * * * [o]ur role commands adherence to lawful legislative decree." *Jackson,* 388 So.2d at 1063. The authority for changing the plain meaning of [UCC §] 3–419(3) lies with the Minnesota legislature. Although the people of Minnesota would benefit by a change which would hold a depositary bank directly liable to the true payee of a check which it has paid over a forged indorsement, we hold that UCC § 3–419(3), as it was passed by the legislature in 1965, provides defenses which absolve the depositary bank of such liability.

Affirmed.

(iv) FORGERY BY ENTRUSTED EMPLOYEE OF PAYEE

The following scenario is a summary of some of the facts, somewhat modified, of Cooper v. Union Bank, 9 Cal.3d 371, 107 Cal.Rptr. 1, 507 P.2d 609 (1973):

> Stell, a lawyer, was retained by Ruff to represent her in connection with her insolvency and litigation brought against her by several creditors. She informed Stell that her financial difficulties were primarily due to gambling losses she had sustained. A short time later Stell hired Ruff as a secretary and bookkeeper. Ruff's duties included posting the amounts of checks received by Stell to the proper accounts in Stell's accounting records and to reconcile the monthly bank statement of deposits and withdrawals with respect to Stell's checking account with Stell's accounting records. Over a period of a year and a half Ruff stole 29 checks payable to Stell that were received in the mail and she forged Stell's indorsement to these checks. Most of these checks were cashed over the counter at Depositary Bank at which both Stell and Ruff had checking accounts. A few of the checks were deposited to Ruff's account in Depositary Bank. Stell was well known to the tellers at the bank as a customer of the bank and Ruff was well known as Stell's secretary. It was the policy of Depositary Bank to allow checks payable to known customers to be cashed over the counter by the customer or the customer's secretary. The forgeries by Ruff were so well done that only a handwriting expert could have detected them.

> Stell exercised practically no supervision over Ruff, never reviewed the books that she kept, and never checked the bank reconciliation of deposits to Stell's checking account.

> Stell brought an action in conversion against Depositary Bank with respect to the 29 checks that were transferred by Ruff to that bank. Assume that Revised Article 3 governs the case.

Under the second sentence of § 3–420(a), Depositary Bank is liable to Stell as a converter of the 29 checks that Ruff transferred to it if (1) Depositary Bank did not become the holder of the checks as a result of the transfer, i.e. the transfer was not a negotiation, and (2) Ruff was not a person entitled to enforce the checks when she transferred them to Depositary Bank, i.e. she was not a holder at the time of the transfer. Both of these elements depend upon whether the forgery by Ruff of Stell's signature was effective as Stell's indorsement in spite of the fact that it was a forgery. Section 3–405 addresses this issue.

Section 3–405 applies to this case if a "fraudulent indorsement" (§ 3–405(a)(2)) was made by Ruff, and Ruff was entrusted by Stell, her employer, with "responsibility" (§ 3–405(a)(3)) with respect to the checks that she transferred to Depositary Bank. Under the first sentence of § 3–405(b), is the indorsement by Ruff effective as the indorsement of Stell? The first and last paragraphs of Comment 1 to § 3–405 address this issue. The Ruff–Stell scenario should be compared with Case #1, Case #3, and Case #4 of Comment 3 to § 3–405. If Stell is not entitled to recover from Depositary Bank as a converter of the 29 checks because of the first sentence of § 3–405(b), is Stell entitled to any recovery against Depositary Bank based on the last sentence of § 3–405(b)? Under that sentence is there any difference in result with respect to the checks cashed over the counter and the checks deposited to Ruff's account?

b. ACTION BY DRAWER

Forged indorsement cases usually involve a theft of the check from the payee, but sometimes the theft of the check occurs before the check is received by the payee. *Barclay's Bank,* p. 733, is such a case. In *Stone & Webster,* which follows, an employee of the drawer of several checks stole the checks from the drawer before the checks could be mailed to the payee. The stolen checks were intended to pay debts of the drawer to the payee. We saw in *Barclay's Bank* that in such a case the payee has no legal claim with respect to the checks because the payee never received them. How does the act of the thief affect the payee? The theft of the check and payment by the drawee to the thief do not change payee's rights with respect to the debt for which the check was written. The payee never became the owner of the check and the drawer's debt to the payee remains unpaid. § 3–310 does not apply. The drawer of the stolen check has a continuing obligation to pay the debt for which the check was issued and thus is obliged to issue a replacement check to the payee. The drawer normally will not suffer any loss with respect to a check bearing a forged indorsement if the drawer is free of negligence contributing to the theft and forgery. § 3–406. The payor bank's payment with respect to the stolen check does not give it a right to debit the drawer's account. The drawer is entitled to have the account credited for the amount of the payment. This remedy of the drawer is clear and convenient since in most cases the drawer's account will be in a local bank. Nevertheless, there have been a number of cases in which the drawer, instead of suing the payor bank, sued the depositary bank. Such a suit might be brought in the uncommon case in which the depositary bank is a local bank and the payor bank is out of state, or the drawer may simply be reluctant to sue the payor bank with which the drawer has a favorable business relationship.

The issue in these cases is whether the drawer of a check stolen from the drawer has a property right in the check that can be asserted in a conversion action. The authority on the issue was divided under original Article 3. The view expressed in *Stone & Webster* was adopted by Revised Article 3 in § 3–420(a).

STONE & WEBSTER ENGINEERING CORP. v. FIRST NATIONAL BANK & TRUST CO.

Supreme Judicial Court of Massachusetts, 1962.
345 Mass. 1, 184 N.E.2d 358.

WILKINS, CHIEF JUSTICE. In this action of contract or tort in four counts for the same cause of action a demurrer to the declaration was sustained, and the plaintiff, described in the writ as having a usual place of business in Boston, appealed. G.L. (Ter. Ed.) c. 231, § 96. The questions argued concern the rights of the drawer against a collecting bank which "cashed" checks for an individual who had forged the payee's indorsement on the checks, which were never delivered to the payee.

In the first count, which is in contract, the plaintiff alleges that between January 1, 1960, and May 15, 1960, it was indebted at various times to Westinghouse Electric Corporation (Westinghouse) for goods and services furnished to it by Westinghouse; that in order to pay the indebtedness the plaintiff drew three checks within that period on its checking account in The First National Bank of Boston (First National) payable to Westinghouse in the total amount of $64,755.44; that before delivery of the checks to Westinghouse an employee of the plaintiff in possession of the checks forged the indorsement of Westinghouse and presented the checks to the defendant; that the defendant "cashed" the checks and delivered the proceeds to the plaintiff's employee who devoted the proceeds to his own use; that the defendant forwarded the checks to First National and received from First National the full amounts thereof; and that First National charged the account of the plaintiff with the full amounts of the checks and has refused to recredit the plaintiff's checking account; wherefore the defendant owes the plaintiff $64,755.44 with interest.

Count 2, also in contract, is on an account annexed for money owed, namely $64,755.44, the proceeds of checks of the plaintiff "cashed" by the defendant on forged indorsements between January 1, 1960, and May 15, 1960.

Counts 3 and 4 in tort are respectively for conversion of the checks and for negligence in "cashing" the checks with forged indorsements.

By order, copies of the three checks were filed in court. The checks are respectively dated at Rowe in this Commonwealth on January 5, March 8, and May 9, 1960. Their respective amounts are $36,982.86, $10,416.58 and $17,355. They are payable to the order of "Westinghouse Electric Corporation, 10 High Street, Boston." The first two checks are indorsed in typewriting, "For Deposit Only: Westinghouse Electric Corporation By: Mr. O. D. Costine, Treasury Representative" followed by an ink signature "O. D. Costine." The Third check is indorsed in typewriting, "Westinghouse Electric Corporation By: [Sgd.] O. D. Costine Treasury Representative." All three checks also bear the indorsement by rubber stamp, "Pay to the order of any bank, banker or trust co. prior indorsements guaranteed * * * [date] [1] The First National Bank & Trust Co. Greenfield, Mass."

The demurrer, in so far as it has been argued, is to each count for failure to state a cause of action.

* * *

1. Count 1, the plaintiff contends, is for money had and received. We shall so regard it. "An action for money had and received lies to recover money which should not in justice be retained by the defendant, and which in equity and good conscience should be paid to the plaintiff." Cobb v. Library Bureau, 268 Mass. 311, 316, 167 N.E. 765, 767; Adams v. First Nat. Bank, 321 Mass. 693, 694, 75 N.E.2d 502; Trafton v. Custeau, 338 Mass. 305, 308, 155 N.E.2d 159.

The defendant has no money in its hands which belongs to the plaintiff. The latter had no right in the proceeds of its own check payable to Westinghouse. Not being a holder or an agent for a holder, it could not have presented the check to the drawee for payment. * * * See Uniform Commercial Code § 3–419, comment 2: "A negotiable instrument is the property of the holder." See also Restatement 2d: Torts, Tent. draft no. 3, 1958, § 241A. The plaintiff contends that "First National paid or credited the proceeds of the checks to the defendant and charged the account of the plaintiff, and consequently, the plaintiff was deprived of a credit, and the defendant received funds or a credit which 'in equity and good conscience' belonged to the plaintiff."

In our opinion this argument is a non sequitur. The plaintiff as a depositor in First National was merely in a contractual relationship of creditor and debtor. * * * The amounts the defendant received from First National to cover the checks "cashed" were the bank's funds and not the plaintiff's. The Uniform Commercial Code does not purport to change the relationship. * * * Section 3–409(1) provides: "A check or other draft does not of itself operate as an assignment of any funds in the hands of the drawee available for its payment, and the drawee is not liable on the instrument until he accepts it." * * *

---

1. The respective dates are January 13, March 9, and May 11, 1960. Each check bears the stamped indorsement of the Federal Reserve Bank of Boston and on its face the paid stamp of The First National Bank of Boston.

Whether the plaintiff was rightfully deprived of a credit is a matter between it and the drawee, First National.

If we treat the first count as seeking to base a cause of action for money had and received upon a waiver of the tort of conversion—a matter which it is not clear is argued—the result will be the same. In this aspect the question presented is whether a drawer has a right of action for conversion against a collecting bank which handles its checks in the bank collection process. Unless there be such a right, there is no tort which can be waived.

The plaintiff relies upon the Uniform Commercial Code § 3–419, which provides, "(1) An instrument is converted when * * * (c) it is paid on a forged indorsement." This, however, could not apply to the defendant, which is not a "payor bank," defined in the Code, § 4–105(b), as "a bank by which an item is payable as drawn or accepted." * * *

A conversion provision of the Uniform Commercial Code which might have some bearing on this case is § 3–419(3).[3] This section implicitly recognizes that, subject to defences, including the one stated in it, a collecting bank, defined in the Code, § 4–105(d), may be liable in conversion. In the case at bar the forged indorsements were "wholly inoperative" as the signatures of the payee, Code §§ 3–404(1), 1–201(43), and equally so both as to the restrictive indorsements for deposits, see § 3–205(c), and as to the indorsement in blank, see § 3–204(2). When the forger transferred the checks to the collecting bank, no negotiation under § 3–202(1) occurred, because there was lacking the necessary indorsement of the payee. For the same reason, the collecting bank could not become a "holder" as defined in § 1–201(20), and so could not become a holder in due course under § 3–302(1). Accordingly, we assume that the collecting bank may be liable in conversion to a proper party, subject to defences, including that in § 3–419(3). See A. Blum Jr.'s Sons v. Whipple, 194 Mass. 253, 255, 80 N.E. 501, 13 L.R.A.,N.S., 211. But there is no explicit provision in the Code purporting to determine to whom the collecting bank may be liable, and consequently, the drawer's right to enforce such a liability must be found elsewhere. Therefore, we conclude that the case must be decided on our own law, which, on the issue we are discussing, has been left untouched by the Uniform Commercial Code in any specific section.

In this Commonwealth there are two cases (decided in 1913 and 1914) the results in which embrace a ruling that there was a

3. "Subject to the provisions of this chapter concerning restrictive indorsements a representative, including a depositary or collecting bank, who has in good faith and in accordance with the reasonable commercial standards applicable to the business of such representative dealt with an instrument or its proceeds on behalf of one who was not the true owner is not liable in conversion or otherwise to the true owner beyond the amount of any proceeds remaining in his hands." See Code §§ 1–201(35); 4–201(1).

conversion, but in neither was the question discussed and, for aught that appears, in each the ruling seems to have been assumed without conscious appreciation of the issue here considered. Franklin Sav. Bank v. International Trust Co., 215 Mass. 231, 102 N.E. 363; Quincy Mut. Fire Ins. Co. v. International Trust Co., 217 Mass. 370, 140 N.E. 845, L.R.A.1915B, 725. * * *

The authorities are hopelessly divided. We think that the preferable view is that there is no right of action. * * *

We state what appears to us to be the proper analysis. Had the checks been delivered to the payee Westinghouse, the defendant might have been liable for conversion to the payee. The checks, if delivered, in the hands of the payee would have been valuable property which could have been transferred for value or presented for payment; and, had a check been dishonored, the payee would have had a right of recourse against the drawer on the instrument under § 3–413(2). Here the plaintiff drawer of the checks, which were never delivered to the payee * * *, had no valuable rights in them. Since, as we have seen, it did not have the right of a payee or subsequent holder to present them to the drawee for payment, the value of its rights was limited to the physical paper on which they were written, and was not measured by their payable amounts. * * *

The enactment of the Uniform Commercial Code opens the road for the adoption of what seems the preferable view. An action by the drawer against the collecting bank might have some theoretical appeal as avoiding circuity of action. * * * It would have been in the interest of speedy and complete justice had the case been tried with the action by the drawer against the drawee and with an action by the drawee against the collecting bank. * * * So one might ask: If the drawee is liable to the drawer and the collecting bank is liable to the drawee, why not let the drawer sue the collecting bank direct? We believe that the answer lies in the applicable defences set up in the Code.[4]

The drawer can insist that the drawee recredit his account with the amount of any unauthorized payment. Such was our common law. * * * This is, in effect, retained by the Code §§ 4–401(1),[5] 4–406(4). But the drawee has defences based upon the drawer's substantial negligence, if "contributing," or upon his duty to discover and report unauthorized signatures and alterations. §§ 3–406, 4–406. As to unauthorized indorsements, see § 4–406(4).[6] Then, if the drawee has a valid defence which it

4. Cases where a payee has acquired rights in an instrument may stand on a different footing.

5. "As against its customer, a bank may charge against his account any item which is otherwise properly payable from that account * * *."

6. "Without regard to care or lack of care of either the customer or the bank a customer who does not within one year from the time the statement and items are made available to the customer (subsection [1]) discover and report his unauthorized signature or any alteration on the face or back of the item or

waives or fails upon request to assert, the drawee may not assert against the collecting bank or other prior party presenting or transferring the check a claim which is based on the forged indorsement. § 4–406(5).[7] * * * If the drawee recredits the drawer's account and is not precluded by § 4–406(5), it may claim against the presenting bank on the relevant warranties in §§ 3–417 and 4–207, and each transferee has rights against his transferor under those sections.

If the drawer's rights are limited to requiring the drawee to recredit his account, the drawee will have the defences noted above and perhaps others; and the collecting bank or banks will have the defences in § 4–207(4) [8] and § 4–406(5), and perhaps others. If the drawer is allowed in the present case to sue the collecting bank, the assertion of the defences, for all practical purposes, would be difficult. The possibilities of such a result would tend to compel resort to litigation in every case involving a forgery of commercial paper. It is a result to be avoided.

[The court sustained demurrers to all plaintiff's counts.]

4. IMPOSTORS AND FICTITIOUS PAYEES

In some cases in which a forged indorsement is alleged, it may not be clear whether there is a forged indorsement because it is not clear to whom the instrument is payable. In identifying the person to whom the instrument is payable, the starting point is § 3–110.

Suppose Jane Doe writes a check to the order of Richard Roe. Under § 3–110(a) the intent of Doe determines to whom the check is payable. There may be many people in the world named Richard Roe, but only the Richard Roe intended by Doe is the payee of the check. If the check gets into the hands of a different Richard Roe, an indorsement by that Richard Roe is ineffective as an indorsement of the payee of the check.

Change the facts. Suppose Doe made a mistake in writing the check. Intending to issue a check to a person that she thinks is Richard Roe, she writes that name as the payee of the check. In fact the name of the person to whom she intended to issue the check is Peter Poe and Poe has never used the name Richard Roe.

does not within three years from that time discover and report any unauthorized indorsement is precluded from asserting against the bank such unauthorized signature or indorsement or such alteration."

7. "If under this section a payor bank has a valid defense against a claim of a customer upon or resulting from payment of an item and waives or fails upon request to assert the defense the [drawee] may not assert against

* * * [a] collecting bank or other prior party presenting or transferring the item a claim based upon the unauthorized signature or alteration giving rise to the customer's claim."

8. "Unless a claim for breach of warranty under this section is made within a reasonable time after the person claiming learns of the breach, the person liable is discharged to the extent of any loss caused by the delay in making claim."

If Doe delivers the check to Poe, Poe becomes the holder of the check even though the check states that it is payable to Richard Roe. An indorsement by Poe is effective because Poe is the payee of the check. Poe may indorse by signing either the name on the check or Poe's name. § 3–110(a) and § 3–204(d).

The rules stated in § 3–110(a) apply to the issuer of a negotiable instrument in determining to whom the instrument is initially payable and the same rules apply in determining to whom an instrument is subsequently made payable by a holder making a special indorsement. § 3–205(a). Thus, if Jane Doe is the payee of the check rather than the drawer and she indorses the check with the indorsement "Pay to Richard Roe," the person to whom the check becomes payable is determined by Doe's intent according to the rules in § 3–110.

Section 3–110 is also important with respect to forged checks. Suppose Thief steals Jane Doe's checkbook and forges her name to a check on her bank account. The check is made payable to Richard Roe. Although Thief's act of signing Doe's name to the check is ineffective as the signature of Doe, the signature is effective as Thief's signature. § 3–403(a). Under § 3–110(a), it is the intention of Thief, the drawer of the check, that determines to whom the check is payable.

An organization such as a corporation must act through human agents in the drawing of checks and the organization normally identifies officers who are authorized to sign checks in behalf of the organization. Often, the organization requires that its checks be signed by more than one authorized officer. Under § 3–110(a) the intent of the authorized officer or officers signing in behalf of the organization determines to whom the check is payable. But in many cases, checks of organizations do not bear any manually-made signature in behalf of the organization. Rather, the check is produced by a check-writing machine and the signature of the drawer is a printed or facsimile signature. The terms of the check, including the name of the payee, are determined by information entered into the computer that controls the check-writing machine. The person providing the information usually is an authorized employee acting in good faith in behalf of the organization, but sometimes the person providing the information is acting fraudulently and might be either an employee authorized to operate the machine or a wholly unauthorized person. In all of these cases the intention of the person supplying the information determines to whom the check is payable. § 3–110(b).

People engaged in fraud usually try to mask the fraud. For example, an employee authorized to operate a corporation's check-writing machine wants to steal money by obtaining payment of checks produced by the machine. Instead of causing the machine to produce checks payable to the employee, the employee causes the machine to produce checks payable to a different payee. The payee named on the check may be an imaginary person, a so-called "fictitious payee," or the check may name as payee a real person who is not intended to have any interest in the check. In either case, the intent of the dishonest employee is to produce a check for the employee's benefit that the employee can turn into cash after indorsing it by signing the name of the payee indicated on the check. In either case, to whom is the check payable? Is the indorsement by the employee an effective indorsement or a forgery? These cases are governed by § 3–404(b) which validates the indorsement and allows the check to be negotiated by the employee.

Although § 3–110(a) states that the intent of the person writing the check determines to whom the check is payable, in some cases it is not possible to clearly identify the payee that way. These cases involve issuance of checks to impostors. *Cohen*, which follows, is an impostor case decided under the NIL which left the issue to be decided by common-law analysis. In *Cohen* the court was divided on the question of the intent of the person signing the check and the case illustrates the futility of trying to decide intent when no clear intent exists. *Cohen* is unusual in that it involved the intent of the maker of a special indorsement rather than the intent of the drawer of the check, but the analysis is the same in either case. Indeed, the court treats the case as though it were a drawer case. Under Revised Article 3 the impostor problem is addressed in § 3–404(a). Because that provision refers only to instruments "issued" (§ 3–105(a)) to an impostor, it would not directly govern a case such as *Cohen*, but the principles stated in § 3–404(a) should apply by analogy to a check indorsed or negotiated to an impostor. If those principles are applied to the facts of *Cohen*, would the result be that of the majority or the minority opinion?

COHEN v. LINCOLN SAVINGS BANK OF BROOKLYN

Court of Appeals of New York, 1937.
275 N.Y. 399, 10 N.E.2d 457.

The city of New York made an award in a condemnation proceeding to Harry Wolter. William L. Abrams, an attorney who also apparently dealt in condemnation awards, met Samuel Goldberg, the plaintiff's husband, and offered to sell him a condemnation award at a discount. Later Goldberg and Abrams agreed upon the price to be paid for the award and Goldberg referred Abrams to his attorney, Irving Feinstein, who would search the record title, attend to the legal details, and fix a date for closing.

The plaintiff gave her husband, Goldberg, full authority as her agent to handle the matter. Goldberg, who had known Abrams for some time, relied upon him for the regularity of the transaction and relied upon his own attorney, Feinstein, in the matter of the title. Feinstein and Goldberg met Abrams at his office to close the transaction. Attorney Albert Kurtz, who was supposed to represent the owner of the award, was also present, and was dealt with as the attorney for an impostor called Harry Wolter, who appeared at the office and was introduced as Harry Wolter. Goldberg testified that he believed him to be the person from whom he purchased the award. Goldberg had in his possession a check issued by the defendant Lincoln Savings Bank for $4,500, and drawn on Irving Trust Company, payable to the order of plaintiff, a depositor, who had indorsed it in blank and delivered it to her husband, Goldberg. He handed the check to Abrams with instructions to deliver it to Attorney Kurtz or his client.

Goldberg saw Abrams write over the blank indorsement of plaintiff, "pay to the order of Harry Wolter." At the same time he delivered to Abrams another check for an assignment of an interest in the award to a third party. That check is not involved in this action.

Goldberg testified that he gave the two checks to Abrams to deliver to Attorney Kurtz or his client. The man who represented himself as Harry Wolter was an impostor. His true name was Dennis. He executed and acknowledged an assignment of the award in the name of Harry Wolter and it was delivered to plaintiff's attorney. He indorsed the check in the name of Harry Wolter and transferred it to the defendant Jacoby, who became an innocent holder for value. The check was presented in due course to the Irving Trust Company, the drawee, and paid. The defendant Lincoln Savings Bank, the drawer, charged the amount against the account of the plaintiff, the payee.

This action is to recover from the Lincoln Savings Bank the amount of the check upon the ground that the indorsement was a forgery and, therefore, that the charge of the amount against the plaintiff's account should be canceled. The other parties were interpleaded and judgment over sought against them.

The assignment of the award was stricken from the records as it was a forgery. If this judgment is affirmed, the loss will fall upon the appellant Jacoby, an innocent holder for value, as judgment over has been recovered by each of the other defendants. If the indorsement of the name "Harry Wolter" on the check made by the impostor Dennis was a forgery, the loss must be borne by the appellant Jacoby, as he was the person who accepted the check from Dennis, the impostor, and thereafter transferred it.[*]

LEHMAN, JUDGE.

The Negotiable Instruments Law (Consol.Laws, c. 38) provides (section 42): "Where a signature is forged or made without author-

[*] [Editors' Note. The statement of facts is taken from the dissenting opinion of Judge Hubbs.]

ity of the person whose signature it purports to be, it is wholly inoperative, and no right to retain the instrument, or to give a discharge therefor, or to enforce payment thereof against any party thereto, can be acquired through or under such signature, unless the party, against whom it is sought to enforce such right, is precluded from setting up the forgery or want of authority." In considering the effect of an indorsement made by one who falsely impersonates a payee named in a negotiable instrument, the courts have usually treated the statutory provision as a restatement of the common law and, at least, so far as concerns the problem as presented in this case, no distinction need be drawn.

We have said recently: "In determining whether there was a forgery the true test is whether or not the indorsement of the name of the payee was made by the person who was intended by the drawer to be the payee. If such person indorsed, there is no forgery." Halsey v. Bank of New York & Trust Co., 270 N.Y. 134, 138, 200 N.E. 671, 673. We apply that test here. It is indeed the test which is almost universally applied in determining whether there has been a forgery. * * *

Where a person has been induced by fraud to draw a check to the order of an existing person, whose name and identity has been fraudulently assumed by another, and to deliver the check to the impostor, it has been held by most courts that an indorsement by the impostor is not a forgery and the bank upon which it is drawn may pay it upon such indorsement. "This result may be reached in several ways, none of which is without difficulty." See McKeehan, The Negotiable Instruments Law, 41 American Law Register (N.S.) 499, 503, reprinted in Brannan's Negotiable Instruments Law (2d Ed.) pp. 220, 247, 248. In that article the author says: "As a matter of fact, the courts base their decision on the first ground, namely, that the bank has merely carried out the drawer's intent. * * * The reasoning is briefly this: A man's name is the verbal designation by which he is known, but the man's visible presence affords a surer means of identification. C. was deceived as to the man he was dealing with, but he dealth with and intended to deal with the visible man who stood before him, identified by sight and hearing. Thinking that this man's name was B., he drew the check to B.'s order intending thereby to designate the person standing before him; so the bank has simply paid the money to the person for whom it was intended." * * *

An academic legal problem may be greatly simplified by excluding, in its formulation, all facts which might introduce conflicting considerations to be weighed in the balance in reaching a sound conclusion. Legal problems, as presented in actual litigation, are seldom free from such complications. The rule that the payee of the check is the particular person who was intended by the drawer to be the payee can hardly be questioned. The name by which he is designated is merely the tag by which the intended person may be identified. A person, though bearing that name, if not the person intended, has no title to the check and cannot indorse or transfer title to it. * * * When an instrument is made "payable to the order of a fictitious or nonexisting person, and such fact was known to the person making it so payable," the instrument is payable to bearer. Negotiable Instruments Law, § 28, subd. 3. Even before the Negotiable Instruments Law was adopted, a bill payable to a fictitious payee was payable to bearer without being indorsed by the maker or the person to whom it was delivered. * * *

Every valid instrument which is not payable to bearer must be payable to a determinate payee and, where it appears that the maker intended a particular person to be the payee, the payee so intended, even though designated by a wrong name and even though he induced the maker to deal with him through fraudulent misrepresentation as to his responsibility, character, or name, is the real payee and can by indorsement transfer title to the instrument. "Although one may be deceived as to the name of the man with whom he is dealing, if he dealt with and intended to deal with the visible person before him the check may properly be indorsed by the impostor." Halsey v. Bank of New York & Trust Co., supra, 270 N.Y. 134, at page 139, 200 N.E. 671, 673.

Thus, if we assume the premises of the problem as formulated by the author of the article, viz., that the maker of a check, though "deceived as to the man he was dealing with," yet "intended to deal with the visible man who stood before him, identified by sight and hearing," and if, "thinking that this man's name was B., he drew the check to B.'s order intending thereby to designate the person standing before him," then there can be little, if any, room for disagreement with the conclusion, generally accepted by courts and academic writers, that a drawee bank which pays the check upon the indorsement of the person intended to be the designated payee "has simply paid the money to the person for whom it was intended."

* * *

It has been said that "In these fraudulent impersonation cases, the maker or drawer of the instrument may be said to have a double intent. First, he intends to make the instrument payable to the person before him or to the person writing at the other end of the line, in case the negotiation is by correspondence. Second, he intends to make the instrument payable to the person whom he believes the stranger to be. * * *

Perhaps, in truth, both intents are so inseparable that the choice of one intent rather than the other is purely arbitrary—an example of rationalization, perhaps unconscious, to reach a desired result. * * * Nevertheless an examination of the cases in other jurisdictions can leave no doubt that, as Brannan points out, in most jurisdictions it has been held that "the first is the controlling intent" * * * though a minority sustain the view that the latter intent is controlling. * * * We do not attempt in this opinion to analyze these cases in detail. In none are the facts exactly similar to those presented in the case under consideration. It is sufficient to point out that even in those cases which apply the so-called "majority rule" there was proof of an antecedent fraud by which a stranger induced a person to deal with him by masquerading as another and the negotiable instrument was made payable to the impostor as a result of the antecedent fraud and the negotiations induced thereby; and it appeared that the instrument was delivered to consummate the dealings with the stranger and with intent that it should be paid to him, though that intent may have been coupled with a second intent of the drawee "to make the instrument payable to the person whom he believes the stranger to be." It was the finding of this first intent which has dictated the conclusion in every case where a bank has been exonerated of fault in the payment of a negotiable instrument to a person not named in the instrument.

* * *

In every case in this court where the loss has been imposed upon the drawer there has been proof of dealings between the drawer and another person who deceived the drawer as to his name and identity and there has been a finding that the drawer delivered the instrument to the impostor as the consummation of such dealings or negotiations and with intent that the instrument should be paid to the person with whom such dealings were previously had, even though that person was designated by a name he did not bear. * * * No person can become a "holder for value" of a negotiable instrument by transfer from a person not named therein and who has no title thereto or authority to transfer it. A person who pays value for an instrument takes the risk that the person named therein as payee is not the person designated and intended as payee, at least where the party to the instrument against whom a right thereunder is asserted has not by act or default contributed to the deception. He may protect himself against such risk by requiring sufficient identification or guaranty by others upon whom reliance can be placed. The drawer of an instrument payable to a named payee is under no duty to assure himself that the person to whom it is delivered is the payee so named or is entitled to receive it in his behalf. Though Goldberg erroneously believed that the visible person was in fact Harry Wolter, the person entitled to the check as consideration for the promised assignment of the award, reasonable care did not require that he determine it. He and Abrams were justified in delivering to him the check made out to Harry Wolter in reliance on the fact that the check could not be transferred except by Harry Wolter, the named payee, or paid except upon an order made by him. * * * That may be true, indeed, even where there is some doubt in the mind of the drawer whether the person to whom the check is delivered may not be masquerading as the named payee. * * *

Unless the evidence in this case dictates the inference that Goldberg or Abrams had the actual intent that the visible person, though masquerading as Wolter, should receive payment of the check, there can be no ground for reversing the judgment.

We have pointed out at the beginning of the opinion that the negotiations for the purchase of the award were conducted by Goldberg entirely with Abrams. The plaintiff and Goldberg, her representative, had no dealings or communications of any kind with the impostor or indeed with the owner of the property until the moment that the impostor came into the room, and even thereafter, so far as appears, their only dealing with him was through their agent to hand him the check indorsed to the order of Harry Wolter. The absence of all prior dealings differentiates this case from every case which has been cited to sustain the contentions of the appellants. The premises fall upon which the conclusion in those cases rested that the drawer must bear the loss. Here there was no antecedent fraud by which the drawer was induced to enter into a transaction with the impostor. At the time when Goldberg left the office knowing that the checks were payable only to the order of Harry Wolter, the assignment had not been executed, delivered, or examined. The impostor did not deceive "by misrepresenting his responsibility or character." He deceived by inducing Goldberg and Abrams to believe that he was Harry Wolter, who, as they thought, was assigning an award which he owned, and thus he succeeded in appropriating what was intended for another.

* * *

The judgment should be affirmed, with costs.

HUBBS, JUDGE (dissenting).

* * *

If an impostor deceives a drawer of a negotiable instrument as to identity by posing as another, and the instrument is delivered to and indorsed by him in the name of the person whom he fraudulently represents himself to be, his indorsement is not a forgery and a subsequent innocent holder for value may enforce it against the maker. The same principle applies under the facts in this case. * * *

The underlying basic principles which have induced a great majority of courts to adopt that rule are the business necessity of keeping commercial paper negotiable; the fact that the maker delivers the instrument to the person intended, although deceived as to the actual identity of that person * * *; the fact that a

maker has the opportunity of ascertaining the true identity of a
person to whom the instrument is delivered, while a purchaser for
value of the instrument may know the signature of the drawer
and rely upon it but cannot in the ordinary course of business
know to whom the maker intended to deliver the instrument; and
finally that where one of two innocent persons must suffer a loss
that loss should fall upon the one who was at fault in the first
instance and made the loss possible * * *.

Only one inference can be drawn from the undisputed facts
here involved. No one present knew the true Harry Wolter.
Dennis, the impostor, was introduced as Harry Wolter and Goldberg testified that he believed him to be the owner of the award
and that he was present with his attorney, Kurtz, to close the
transfer of the award. He also testified as follows: "Q. Did you
give the two checks to Abrams to deliver to Kurtz or his client?
A. Yes."

The only client Kurtz had, so far as Goldberg knew, was the
impostor introduced as Harry Wolter. Goldberg's instructions,
according to his testimony, were to deliver the check to Kurtz or
his client. His client, according to the testimony, was the impostor. True it is that at one time in his testimony Goldberg stated
that he instructed Abrams to "assign the checks to the proper
owner," but he also testified that he believed the impostor to be
the person from whom he purchased the award, and, therefore,
the owner. It is perfectly clear that Goldberg believed the impostor to be the true Harry Wolter, the owner of the award, and that
he intended the check to be delivered to him upon his executing
and delivering an assignment of the award. The impostor, at the
same time, executed and delivered an assignment of the award in
the name of Harry Wolter and it was accepted by the attorney for
the plaintiff and the check was delivered as Goldberg instructed
and intended it should be. Goldberg determined for himself the
identity of the person to whom he instructed the check to be
delivered and plaintiff is bound by his act. In those circumstances, the indorsement of the check by the impostor was not a
forgery and there can be no recovery in this action. This is not a
case where a purchaser has negotiated with the owner for the
purchase of property and by fraud was induced to deliver a check
to an impostor representing himself to be the owner. Here the
purchaser did not know the true Harry Wolter, the owner, and
had never communicated with him. The only person known as
Harry Wolter was the impostor to whom Goldberg gave instructions that the check should be delivered.

While it is unfortunate that the plaintiff must suffer the loss
caused by the fraud, it would be equally unfortunate if the
innocent purchaser for value of the check should be required to
bear the loss when he was entirely free from fault.

The judgment should be reversed, with costs, and the complaint dismissed.

LOUGHRAN, FINCH, and RIPPEY, JJ., concur with LEHMAN, J.

HUBBS, J., dissents in opinion in which CRANE, C.J., concurs.

O'BRIEN, J., takes no part.

Judgment affirmed.

PROBLEM

Dowager is a wealthy widow who frequently makes large gifts to charitable institutions. She has a checking account in Centerville Bank. Faith has been employed by Dowager for many years as a housekeeper and companion. Faith has a younger brother who is a ne'r do well with an addiction to illegal betting on the outcome of sports events. He told Faith that he had been making bets on credit with a bookie reputed to be a violent criminal and owed him $21,000 which had to be paid within 30 days. He told Faith that he had no money and feared for his life if the debt was not paid. Faith earns very little and had no available funds, but she agreed to help.

Faith travelled to Metropolis, a large city several hundred miles from Centerville, and called upon the manager of a branch of Metropolis Bank. She introduced herself as Priscilla Prim, the owner of Prim Academy, a school for girls located in a city in an adjoining state. There is such a school but Faith had no connection with it. She explained to the bank manager that she planned to open a second campus of Prim Academy in Metropolis and needed a checking account in a local bank. An account was then opened in Metropolis Bank in the name of Prim Academy and Priscilla Prim was designated as the person authorized to act with respect to the account. Faith gave the bank manager an unindorsed check for $25,000 payable to the order of Prim Academy and asked that it be deposited to the Prim Academy account. The bank manager followed Faith's instructions. The check was drawn on the account of Dowager in Centerville Bank. Faith had written the check and forged Dowager's signature after taking a blank check from Dowager's checkbook which Faith found in a drawer in Dowager's desk. A few days later Metropolis Bank presented the check for payment and received $25,000 from Centerville Bank. Before the payment was made an employee of Centerville Bank examined the check and approved it for payment. Faith's forgery of Dowager's signature was not detected because it was skillfully done and appeared to be genuine.

Two weeks later Faith returned to Metropolis Bank. She identified herself to a teller as Priscilla Prim and requested that the bank issue a cashier's check for $21,000 to the order of Prim Academy. The check was issued and delivered to Faith. As payment for issuance of the cashier's check, Metropolis Bank debited $21,000 to the Prim Academy account in that bank. No checks on the Prim Academy account were ever written.

Faith indorsed the cashier's check "Prim Academy by Priscilla Prim" and gave the check to her brother. He delivered it to the bookie. A few days later Metropolis Bank paid the cashier's check.

When Dowager received her monthly statement of account from Centerville Bank she found the forged check among the checks paid by the bank that month. She immediately informed Centerville Bank of the forgery and demanded that the bank restore $25,000 to her account. The bank complied with her demand and then brought an action against Metropolis Bank.

1. Is Centerville Bank entitled to recover from Metropolis Bank on the basis that Faith forged Dowager's signature on the check? § 3–418 and § 3–417(a)(3).

2. Is Centerville Bank entitled to recover from Metropolis Bank on the basis that the signature of Prim Academy as an indorsement of the check was not authorized? § 3–417(a)(1), § 3–110, § 3–404, Case #5 of Comment 2 to § 3–404, and Comment 3 to § 3–404.

5. PAYROLL PADDING

We have seen that the payee of a check can be denied an action in conversion with respect to the check if a fraudulent indorsement of the check is made by an employee of the payee entrusted with responsibility with respect to the check. § 3–405(a)(2)(i) and (3); § 3–405(b) and the last paragraph of Comment 1 to § 3–405. Sometimes the employee who commits fraud is an entrusted employee of the drawer rather than the payee of the check. Those cases are governed by § 3–405 as well. § 3–405(a)(2)(ii).

Merrill Lynch, which follows, is an example of the kind of case to which § 3–405(a)(2)(ii) relates. *Merrill Lynch* was decided under § 3–405(1)(c) of original Article 3. Although § 3–405(a)(2)(ii) and (3), read in conjunction with § 3–405(b), applies to all of the cases covered by § 3–405(1)(c) of original Article 3, the Revised Article 3 provisions are broader in scope and will, in some cases, produce results different from those under original Article 3. See the second paragraph of Comment 1 and Comment 2 to § 3–405. The scope of § 3–405 is illustrated by the hypothetical cases discussed in Comment 3 to § 3–405.

MERRILL LYNCH, PIERCE, FENNER & SMITH
v. CHEMICAL BANK

Court of Appeals of New York, 1982.
57 N.Y.2d 439, 456 N.Y.S.2d 742, 442 N.E.2d 1253.

FUCHSBERG, JUDGE.

This appeal requires us to explore the extent to which, if at all, immunity from liability accorded a drawee bank by section 3–405 (subd. [1], par. [c]) of the Uniform Commercial Code may be limited by the drawee's negligence in paying checks over forged indorsements.

The section at issue, commonly referred to in commercial circles as either the "fictitious payee" or "padded payroll" rule, provides: "An indorsement by any person in the name of a named payee is effective if * * * an agent or employee of the maker or drawer has supplied him with the name of the payee intending the latter to have no such interest".

The factual context in which the case is here is undisputed. The defendant, Chemical Bank, unaware that the indorsements of the payees' names were forged, routinely paid 13 checks drawn by the plaintiff, Merrill Lynch, on its Chemical account in the aggregate sum of $115,180. The forgeries were occasioned by chicanery of a Merrill Lynch accounts payable employee who, by presenting his employer's New York check issuing department with false invoices which ostensibly represented obligations due its suppliers, caused checks to be issued to the order of these supposed creditors. The malefactor or accomplices then indorsed the names of the payees and, in face of the fact that New York addresses appeared below the payees' names, caused the checks to be deposited in California and Ohio bank accounts in names other than those to whose order they had been drawn. Seven of the checks were presented to Chemical by the Federal Reserve Bank (FRB) as collecting bank and the remainder by the depositary banks themselves. In due course, Chemical charged its Merrill Lynch account.

This suit, instituted by Merrill Lynch to recover the amount so debited, was brought on three theories. As set out in its complaint, the first was that "Chemical acted negligently and contrary to normal and accepted banking practices, breached its duty of good faith and failed to exercise ordinary care". Particularizing, it added that Chemical should have been alerted to the irregular nature of the checks because "the purported indorsements of the corporate payees were handwritten, and in many instances illegible", were indorsed "in blank, rather than for deposit only" and bore "second indorsements of unrelated persons or entities." Reiterating the allegations of the first count, the second sounded in breach of contract and the third in conversion. In its answer, Chemical relied, among other affirmative defenses, on what, in the circumstances of this case, it took to be the exculpatory effect of section 3–405.

At the same time, Chemical, by way of a third-party summons and complaint, impleaded FRB essentially on the rationale that, if Merrill Lynch recovered, Chemical, in turn, should be made whole by FRB, which, as a collecting bank, would then have to be found in breach of its warranty of good title (Uniform Commercial Code, § 4–207). FRB countered with a motion for summary judgment, premised on the position that, under section 3–405, "endorsement of the checks in the name of the payee thereof was sufficient and effective to transfer title to the instrument". On the same ground, Chemical thereupon cross-moved for partial summary judgment dismissing Merrill Lynch's complaint * * *. Special Term denied both motions.

On appeal, the Appellate Division unanimously modified Special Term's order, on the law, by granting the motion directed to Chemical's third-party case against FRB. In so deciding, the court agreed that, under section 3–405 of the Uniform Commercial Code, the forged indorsements were effective to transfer title to the checks. However, as to Chemical's cross motion against Merrill Lynch, the court, by a vote of 3 to 2, found that section 3–405 was "not available to defendant to avoid liability for its own negligence" (82 A.D.2d 772, 773, 440 N.Y.S.2d 643); on this view, it affirmed, thus relegating the issue of Chemical's negligence to trial.

On the present appeal, which brings up for review Chemical's motion against Merrill Lynch only, the appellant in the main presses the point that its alleged negligence in disregarding irregularities in the indorsements may not deprive it of the benefits of section 3–405 of the Uniform Commercial Code and, in the alternative, that, in any event, it was not negligent because it was under no obligation to inspect the indorsements, a duty which, it insists, was the responsibility of FRB and the depositary banks alone. Echoing the dissent of Presiding Justice Murphy and Justice Silverman at the Appellate Division, Chemical also advances the pragmatic argument that a contrary reading of the statute would impose what, at least for large commercial banks, would constitute an unrealistically onerous and expensive burden of inspecting an "immense volume of checks", all the more so since these checks must be "processed and paid or alternatively, returned or dishonored by midnight of the following business day" (see David Graubart, Inc. v. Bank Leumi Trust Co. of N.Y., 48 N.Y.2d 554, 557–558, 423 N.Y.S.2d 899, 399 N.E.2d 930). Merrill Lynch, on the other hand, choosing to interpret our decision in Underpinning & Foundation Constructors v. Chase Manhattan Bank, N.A., 46 N.Y.2d 459, 414 N.Y.S.2d 298, 386 N.E.2d 1319 as supportive of its stance, continues to contend that section 3–405 of the Uniform Commercial Code will not absolve a banking institution, be it a depositary, drawee or collecting bank, from liability for its own negligence.

For the ensuing reasons, we believe that, under the circumstances of this case, Chemical's motion for partial summary judgment should have been granted.

Our analysis may well begin with the observation that section 3–405 (subd. [1], par. [c]) bespeaks an exception to the general rule governing the responsibility of a bank to its customers. For it is basic that ordinarily a drawee bank may not debit its customer's account when it pays a check over a forged indorsement. This is because the underlying relationship between a bank and its depositor is the contractual one of debtor and creditor * * * implicit in which is the understanding that the bank will pay out its customer's funds only in accordance with the latter's instructions * * *. Thus, absent contrary instruction or legislative exception, when a drawer issues a check in the name of a particular payee, the drawee bank is to apply funds from the drawer's account to its payment only upon receiving the payee's authorized indorsement. In this perspective, a forged indorsement, since it is an unauthorized signature (Uniform Commercial Code, § 1–201, subd. [43]), in and by itself would be "wholly inoperative" (Uniform Commercial Code, § 3–404, subd. [1]).

It follows that, in the typical case in which payment is made on a check that is not properly payable (see Uniform Commercial Code, § 4–401, subd. [1]), the payment is deemed to have been made solely from the funds of the drawee bank rather than from those of its depositor. But, when the conditions which section 3–405 contemplates prevail, the indorsement, though forged, is still effective, and the instrument then must be treated as "both a valuable instrument and a valid instruction to the drawee to honor the check and debit the drawer's account accordingly" (Underpinning & Foundation Constructors v. Chase Manhattan Bank, N.A., supra, at p. 465, 414 N.Y.S.2d 298, 386 N.E.2d 1319).

This departure from the general rule is explained by section 3–405's Official Comment 4, which advises, "The principle followed is that the loss should fall upon the employer as a risk of his business enterprise rather than upon the subsequent holder or drawee. The reasons are that the employer is normally in a better position to prevent such forgeries by reasonable care in the selection or supervision of his employees, or, if he is not, is at least in a better position to cover the loss by fidelity insurance; and that the cost of such insurance is properly an expense of his business rather than of the business of the holder or drawee".

Since the assumptions instinct in this rationalization are hardly indisputable, it is no surprise that the rule it supports represents a conscious choice between the traditional one, which, as we have seen, was more protective of the bank's customer, and the one in the code, which, as some commentators have bluntly acknowledged, was "a banker's provision intended to narrow the liability of banks and broaden the responsibility of their customers" (White & Summers, Uniform Commercial Code, § 16–8, p. 639). Thus, whatever, in the abstract, may have been the equities of the respective contentions of the competing commercial camps, there can be little doubt but that the outcome, so far as the adoption of section 3–405 of the Uniform Commercial Code is concerned, was calculated to shift the balance in favor of the bank "in situations in which the drawer's own employee has perpetrated the fraud or committed the crime giving rise to the loss" (1 Hawkland, A Transactional Guide to the Uniform Commercial Code, pp. 391–394).

That this represents contemporary legislative thinking is clear from the way in which the statutory scheme evolved. Long before section 3–405 of the Uniform Commercial Code came into being, subdivision 3 of section 28 of the former Negotiable Instruments Law already provided that a check is "payable to bearer * * * [w]hen it is payable to the order of a fictitious or non-existing person, and such fact was known to the person making it so payable". Carrying this language to its logical limits, one then might have thought that, because an instrument forged by an employee was to be treated as bearer paper, the fact of forgery had been rendered irrelevant to its negotiability.

Nevertheless, most courts, reluctant to read the statute this broadly, applied it only when the faithless employee made or drew the check himself, but not, as in the case before us now, when he had merely furnished the payee's name to the employer, for then the falsity presumably would not be "known to the person making it so payable" (Hawkland, op. cit.). This narrow interpretation apparently fell short of the drafters' intention because the reaction, first, in 1960, was to amend section 28 of the Negotiable Instruments Law to make it explicit that knowledge to the malefactor who furnished the name was sufficient (Britton, Handbook of the Law of Bills and Notes, § 149, pp. 433–437). And, secondly, by the adoption of section 3–405 of the Uniform Commercial Code, the bearer fiction device was replaced by the more forthright effective indorsement concept (see Official Comment 1 to § 3–405 * * *).

The special scrutiny this legislative course demanded also highlights the fact that section 3–405's failure to delineate a standard of care, to which a bank itself must adhere if it is to advantage itself of this section, was no oversight. In contrast are sections 3–406 and 4–406 of the Uniform Commercial Code, which, along with section 3–405's "padded payroll" provision, deal with defenses which may be available to a drawee bank in forged indorsement cases.

For instance, subdivision (2) of section 4–406, which otherwise precludes a customer from asserting a claim which might have been averted but for its neglect in examining "the [bank] statement and items to discover his unauthorized signature or any alteration on an item" (subd. [1]), makes preclusion inapropos when "the customer establishes lack of ordinary care on the part of the bank in paying the item" (subd. [3]). And, similarly, section 3–406, which puts the onus for a forgery on a customer who "substantially contributes to a material alteration of the instrument or to the making of an unauthorized signature", still requires the bank to have paid the instrument "in good faith and in accordance with the reasonable commercial standards of the drawee's or payor's business".

It is fair to conclude, therefore, that, unlike cases which fall within the foregoing sections, a drawee bank's mere failure to use ordinary care in the handling of a check whose forgery has brought it within the embrace of section 3–405 (subd. [1], par. [c]) will not subject it to liability (White & Summers, Uniform Commercial Code, § 16–8, p. 639).[3]

This is not to say that, if a check is "tainted in *some other way* which would put the drawee on notice, and which would make its payment unauthorized" (Underpinning & Foundation Constructors v. Chase Manhattan Bank, N.A., 46 N.Y.2d 459, 466, 414 N.Y.S.2d 298, 386 N.E.2d 1319, *supra;* emphasis supplied), a drawee bank may yet not be liable. For instance, a drawee bank surely is not immunized by section 3–405 when it acts dishonestly. In short, "a basis for liability *independent* of any liability which might be created by payment over a forged instrument alone" may very well survive (Underpinning & Foundation Constructors v. Chase Manhattan Bank, N.A., supra, at p. 469, 414 N.Y.S.2d 298, 386 N.E.2d 1319; emphasis supplied).

In contrast, without more, in the present case, it is at once clear that the irregularities on which Merrill Lynch here focuses were part and parcel of the forgeries themselves and, as the dissenters at the Appellate Division observed, "could not possibly have alerted the bank to the fact that the checks were tainted, indeed it would have been most remarkable if the drawee bank had even noticed them". (82 A.D.2d 772, 774, 440 N.Y.S.2d 643, supra.)

3. Because of the manifest advantages of uniformity in the law of bills and notes, we observe that other courts which have considered the matter have arrived at the same conclusion (see, e.g., Prudential Ins. Co. of Amer. v. Marine Nat. Exch. Bank of Milwaukee, 371 F.Supp. 1002; Kraftsman Container Corp. v. United Counties Trust Co., 169 N.J.Super. 488, 404 A.2d 1288; Fair Park Nat. Bank v. Southwestern Inv. Co., 541 S.W.2d 266 [Tex.]; General Acc. Fire & Life Assur. Corp. v. Citizens Fid. Bank & Trust Co., 519 S.W.2d 817 [Ky.]; Western Cas. & Sur. Co. v. Citizens Bank of Las Cruces, 33 UCC Rep. 1018).

* * *

Accordingly, the order of the Appellate Division, insofar as appealed from, should be reversed, with costs, and defendant Chemical's motion for partial summary judgment granted. The certified question should be answered in the negative.

COOKE, CHIEF JUDGE (concurring).

To permit a drawee bank to avoid liability for paying a check on a forged indorsement by asserting the "fictitious payee" rule, when the bank itself may have acted negligently in paying the check, is a harsh result. Inasmuch as section 3–405 of the Uniform Commercial Code does not include any requirement that a bank act with ordinary care, however, I am constrained to concur in the majority's result.

* * *

The absence of a standard of care in section 3–405 must be deemed an intentional omission by the Legislature in light of its ability to include such language when it desires, as manifested by sections 3–406 and 4–406. This court should not require ordinary care by the drawee when the Legislature has declined to do so * * *. Instead, section 3–405 should be amended to preclude its invocation by a drawee or other transferee who has failed to exercise due care * * *.

JASEN, GABRIELLI, JONES and MEYER, JJ., concur with FUCHS-BERG, J.

COOKE, C.J., concurs in a separate opinion in which WACHTLER, J., concurs.

B. ALTERATION

---

1. COMPLETE INSTRUMENTS

"Alteration," defined in § 3–407(a), refers to a change that purports to modify the obligation of a party to an instrument if the change is unauthorized. Thus, if the payee raises the amount of a check without the consent of the drawer the check has been altered. But if the payee's act is authorized by the drawer before any other person becomes obligated on the check, the check has not been altered; the change is treated as a change made by the drawer.

The definition of alteration is very broad. It includes fraudulent changes as well as changes made in good faith. For example, the holder of a note changes the due date of the note because the holder believes in good faith that the original due date was erroneous. Even if the holder was mistaken, the alteration is not fraudulent. Under the second sentence of § 3–407(b) the non-fraudulent alteration is ineffective to modify the obligation of the maker and the note is enforceable according to its original terms. Non-fraudulent alteration is described in the first paragraph of Comment 1 to § 3–407.

The concept of alteration can apply to incomplete instruments described in § 3–115 as well as complete instruments, but the effect of alteration is not the same in each case. A discussion of alteration of incomplete instruments starts on p. 773.

Fraudulent alteration is the principal focus of § 3–407 and can be illustrated by the following hypothetical case:

> An authorized employee of Drawer, a large corporation, signed and delivered a typewritten check for $10 payable to the order of Payee. Without Drawer's consent Payee raised the amount of the check to $10,000 by adding a comma and three zeroes after the figure "10" and the word "thousand" after the word "ten." Payee deposited the check in Payee's account with Depositary Bank and the bank obtained $10,000 from Drawee in payment of the check. Drawee then debited Drawer's account in the same amount. Payee withdrew the $10,000 that had been credited to Payee's account in Depositary Bank with respect to the check. When Drawer learned that Drawee had debited $10,000 to Drawer's account with respect to the check, Drawer notified Drawee of the alteration.

Who takes the loss in the hypothetical case? The liability of the drawer with respect to a check is based on the terms of the order to pay made by the person against whom the drawer's liability is asserted. Liability on an altered check can be compared to liability on a forged check. In the absence of fault, the person whose signature as drawer is forged has no liability on the check because the order to pay on which liability is asserted was not made by that person. In the case of the check in the hypothetical case, Drawer can reasonably be held liable with respect to the order to pay $10 because that order was made by Drawer, but in the absence of fault by Drawer it is not reasonable to hold Drawer liable with respect to the raised amount because Drawer did not order payment of that amount.

How is this analysis reflected in § 3–407? In the hypothetical case, to what extent is Drawee entitled to debit Drawer's account with respect to the check? § 3–407(c). If Drawee had dishonored the check, to what extent would Depositary Bank have had a right to recover from Drawer? § 3–414(b) and § 3–407(c). What is the significance of the first sentence of § 3–407(b) which states that "a party whose obligation is affected by the alteration" is discharged? Comment 1 (second paragraph) to § 3–407. If Drawee pays the check but is not entitled to full reimbursement from Drawer, what remedy does it have against Depositary Bank? § 3–417(a)(2) and (b). If Depositary Bank is liable to Drawee, what recourse does Depositary Bank have against Payee? § 3–416(a)(3) and (b).

Suppose, in the hypothetical case, that the employee who wrote the check in behalf of Drawer left blank spaces in the amount lines on the check allowing Payee to raise the amount of the check without leaving any easily detectable evidence that the check had been altered. How does this additional fact affect your answers to the questions asked in the preceding paragraph? § 3–406.

2. CERTIFIED CHECKS

The liability of a bank that certifies an altered check has long troubled the courts. The common law view that a bank which certified an altered check was liable on the check only as originally drawn was justified in Marine National Bank v. National City Bank, 59 N.Y. 67, 17 Am.Rep. 305 (1874) as follows:

> That an acceptor of a bill of exchange by acceptance only admits the genuineness of the signature of the drawer, and does not admit the genuineness of the indorsements, whether of the drawee of the same bill, or of any other person whose name appears upon it, or any other part of the bill, is elementary and sustained by an unbroken current of authority. (Story on Bills, §§ 262, 263, and cases cited in notes.) Judge Story says the reason usually assigned is, that when the bill is presented for acceptance the acceptor looks to the handwriting of the drawer with which he is presumed to be acquainted, and he affirms its genuineness by giving credit to the bill, by his acceptance in favor of the legal holder thereof. But the acceptor cannot be presumed to have any such knowledge of the other facts upon which the rights of the holder may depend. In analogy to this, courts have held that the certificate only holds the bank for the truth of the facts presumed to be within its own knowledge, viz., the genuineness of the signature of the drawer and the state of his account. Moneys paid upon checks and drafts which have been forgeries, either in the body of the instrument or in the indorsements, or in any respect, except the name of the drawer, have uniformly been held recoverable as for money paid by mistake, and expressly upon the ground that payment, as an admission of the genuineness of the instrument, was the same as an acceptance, and only operated as an admission of the signature of the drawer. 59 N.Y. at 76–77.

However, two leading cases, National City Bank v. National Bank of the Republic, 300 Ill. 103, 132 N.E. 832 (1921), and Wells Fargo Bank & Union Trust Co. v. Bank of Italy, 214 Cal. 156, 4

P.2d 781 (1931), interpreted the NIL as changing the common law rule and as binding a certifying bank to the terms of the instrument at the time of certification. After the California and Illinois decisions banks adopted the practice of qualifying their certifications: "payable as originally drawn." Under the UCC, what is the liability of a bank that certifies an altered check? Does it make any difference whether the bank qualifies the certification as stated in the quoted language? § 3–413(a).

PROBLEM

Payee receives a check in the amount of $10 drawn on Payor Bank. Payee raises the amount of the check to $10,000 and obtains certification of the check from Payor Bank. Is there a breach of warranty by Payee when certification is obtained? § 3–417(a)(2).

Payee negotiates the certified check to Holder who takes as a holder in due course. Holder presents the certified check to Payor Bank and is paid $10,000. Is there a breach of warranty by Holder when payment is obtained? Does § 3–417(a)(2) apply? Does § 3–417(d) apply? Is Payor Bank entitled to recover from Payee for breach of warranty? § 3–417(a)(2) and (b); Comment 4 to § 3–417.

Suppose that Payor Bank refused to pay Holder when the certified check was presented for payment. Is Payor Bank obliged to pay? § 3–413(a). What is the effect of the penultimate sentence of § 3–417(b)? Is Holder subject to the defense? § 3–305(b) and the first paragraph to Comment 2 to § 3–305.

BROWER v. FRANKLIN NATIONAL BANK

United States District Court, S.D. New York, 1970.
311 F.Supp. 675.

WYATT, DISTRICT JUDGE. This is a motion by defendant Franklin National Bank, a successor in interest to the Federation Bank & Trust Company (the Bank) for summary judgment in its favor (Fed.R.Civ.P. 56(b)). For reasons to be given, the motion must be denied.

* * *

The complaint, filed May 27, 1968, avers that in July 1967 one Anthony Ricci maintained a checking account at the Bank's branch on Williamsbridge Road in the Bronx; that on July 12, 1967 Anthony drew two checks on the Bank in the amounts of $8 and $10 payable to the plaintiff Frederick J. Brower (Frederick) and procured the Bank's certification of those checks; that Anthony subsequently raised the checks from $8 to $28,600 and from $10 to $10,000 and delivered them to Frederick in payment for real property in New Jersey; that the Bank refused to honor the checks because they had been "raised"; that the Bank was negligent in certifying the checks, among other things, because when certified they contained blank spaces and could easily be raised. Frederick claims damages of $75,000.

It may be noted that the complaint purports to plead a claim based on negligence of the Bank in certifying the checks under circumstances which made it easy to raise them thereafter and thus to cause them to be passed off to plaintiff in their altered form. The claim ought to be treated, however, as in legal theory based on the Bank's certifications but governed by New York Uniform Commercial Code § 3–406: "Any person who by his negligence substantially contributes to a material alteration of the instrument * * * is precluded from asserting the alteration * * * against a holder in due course * * *." It may be noted that plaintiff does not sue simply for the amounts of the two checks as raised, $38,600, but rather for $75,000 averring other damages, such as dishonor of his own checks, impairment of "credit standing", etc.

* * *

Apart from damages, there is no dispute as to any material fact. The facts are as follows:

On July 12, 1967, Anthony presented two checks, numbered 139 and 140, to the Bank for certification. "Every item" (apparently the date, payee's name, drawer's name and the amount) in both checks was filled out. Number 139 was in the amount of $10; number 140 in the amount of $8. Both were payable to "Mr. F. Brower." The checks were certified by the Assistant Manager of the Bank. The certification stamp does not show the amount for which the checks were certified.

Check number 139 was raised after certification apparently by Anthony from $10 to $10,000 and deposited by Frederick in the Plainfield Trust State National Bank, Plainfield, New Jersey. Check number 140 was likewise raised after certification from $8 to $28,600 and deposited in the National Bank of New Jersey, bearing the endorsements of "Mr. F. Brower" and "Edward A. Ryan." Both checks were presented to the Bank on July 19, 1967 and were returned unpaid, because the checks had been altered as to amount. Neither check has been paid and this action was commenced to secure payment.

Before adoption of the Uniform Commercial Code (U.C.C.) effective in 1964, the law of New York appears to have been clear that a bank certifying a check was not liable on its certification for an altered amount of the check, whether alteration took place after or before certification. * * *

Under the U.C.C. this rule is changed and the certifying bank is liable on its certification where the alteration was *before* certification. The engagement in certifying is now to pay the check "according to its tenor at the time of his engagement". U.C.C. § 3–413(1). If alteration (raising) occurs *after* certification, the certifying bank is not bound by its certification to pay the instrument as raised.

As to *negligence,* at common law it was believed, on the authority of Young v. Grote, 4 Bing. 253 (1827), that a *drawer* who negligently drew a check in such a way as to make it easy to raise the check was responsible to a drawee who paid the raised check in good faith.

It was sought in a leading English case to extend this rule to the acceptor. Just as here, a check was drawn for 500 with spaces left so that it could be raised to 3,500. As originally drawn, it was presented and certified (accepted); thereafter it was raised to 3,500 as planned and negotiated to a holder in due course. It was said as against the acceptor that the acceptance was negligent because the check was in such form that alteration (raising) was made easy and was a likely result. The House of Lords refused to sanction an action against an acceptor for negligence because there is no duty on an acceptor to take precautions against a possible alteration. Scholfield v. Earl of Londesborough, (1896) A.C. 514.

The plain words of the Uniform Commercial Code § 3–406 seem clearly to change the old rule and to authorize this action. "Any person who by his negligence substantially contributes to a material alteration of the instrument * * * is precluded from asserting the alteration * * * against a holder in due course * * *." U.C.C. § 3–406.

The certifying bank would certainly seem to be included in the words "any person." Under the averments of the complaint, plaintiff should be given an opportunity to show at trial that he is "a holder in due course."

Plaintiff therefore is entitled to a trial of the issues (a) whether or not he is "a holder in due course", and if he is such a holder, (b) whether defendant was or was not guilty of negligence when it certified these checks and if it was negligent (c) whether or not such negligence substantially contributed to the raising of the checks.

There are lower court decisions in New York which reach a contrary result. Sam Goody, Inc. v. Franklin Nat. Bank, 57 Misc. 2d 193, 291 N.Y.S.2d 429 (Sup.Ct.Nassau Cty.1968); Wallach Sons, Inc. v. Bankers Trust Co., 307 N.Y.S.2d 297 (Civ.Ct.New York Cty. 1970). After carefully reading the opinions in these two cases and with great deference to the two distinguished judges who wrote them, I cannot accept their result and feel that the Court of Appeals of New York would not reach their result.

It is, of course, true that the plaintiff is here in form suing in tort whereas his claim is more properly on the certification. The effect of negligence and its substantial contribution to the raising, if proved, is not to give rise to a tort claim but to preclude the Bank "from asserting the alteration." The Bank would not appear to be liable in any event for more than the amount of the checks as altered. See Official Comment 5, McKinney's U.C.C. § 3–406, page 263. However, the form of pleading adopted by plaintiff would not justify dismissing his action.

The motion is denied.

NOTE

How would *Brower* be decided under Revised Article 3? § 3–413(b).

PROBLEMS

1. Thief stole a check payable to Payee and had it certified. Thief then wrote Payee's name on the back as an indorsement and transferred the check to Depositary Bank that paid value in good faith without notice of the forged indorsement. Depositary Bank obtained payment of the check from Drawee Bank. Drawee Bank then discovered the forged indorsement. What are the rights of Drawee Bank against Depositary Bank? § 3–417(d) and § 3–301.

2. John Smithson stole a check payable to John Smith and altered the check by adding "son" to the end of "Smith." Smithson then obtained certification of the check and indorsed it to Depositary Bank that paid value in good faith without notice of the alteration. Depositary Bank obtained payment of the check from Drawee Bank. Drawee Bank then discovered the alteration. What are the rights of Drawee Bank against Depositary Bank? § 3–413(a)(i). Was there a breach of warranty by Depositary Bank when it obtained payment of the check? § 3–417(d). Who was the payee of the check when Smithson obtained certification?

3. INCOMPLETE INSTRUMENTS

Assume that A is indebted to B but is not sure of the precise amount of the debt. In payment of the debt A sends to B a check payable to B, leaving the amount of the check blank. A instructs B to complete the check by filling in the amount of the debt. If the amount of the debt is $10 and B fills in the check for that amount there is no difficulty in enforcing the check against A. The intent of A has been carried out by B's completion of the check. The result is the same as if A had personally completed the check. When the check was received by B the check was an "incomplete instrument" defined in § 3–115(a). Because the amount of the check was not stated, the check was not a negotiable instrument under § 3–104 and the last sentence of § 3–115(b) applies. If B completes the check by writing in $10 as its amount, the check becomes an instrument under § 3–104 and the last sentence of § 3–115(b) states that the check can be enforced as completed. There is no alteration.

But if B fills in $10,000 rather than $10, the act of B is not authorized by A. Under § 3–115(c) there is an alteration of the incomplete instrument and § 3–407 applies. The case is analogous to the hypothetical case on p. 768 in which a check payable in the amount of $10 was altered by changing the amount to $10,000. In each case the drawer intended a check in the amount of $10 and in each case the payee raised the intended amount to $10,000.

Suppose B deposited the altered check to B's account in Depositary Bank and the bank obtained $10,000 from Drawee Bank in payment of the check. Drawee Bank then debited A's account in the same amount. B withdrew the $10,000 that had been credited to B's account in Depositary Bank with respect to the check. When A learned that Drawee Bank had debited $10,000 to A's account with respect to the check, A notified Drawee Bank of the alteration. Who takes the loss in this case? To what extent is Drawee Bank entitled to debit A's account with respect to the check? § 3–407(c). If Drawee Bank had dishonored the check, to what extent would Depositary Bank have had a right to recover from A? § 3–414(b) and § 3–407(c).

Compare the results in this case with the results in the hypothetical case on p. 768. Why are the results different? Is there any relationship between § 3–406 and § 3–407(c) as it applies to fraudulent completion of incomplete instruments?

C. FRAUDULENT MISENCODING OF CHECKS

In Chapter 8 there is a description of the way in which checks are encoded with preprinted machine-readable numerals and symbols which allow presentment of the checks for payment by automated processing. We examined the consequences of mistake by the depositary bank when it encodes the check by adding to the preprinted MICR line numerals and symbols that indicate the amount of the check. Such mistakes are inevitable. Unfortunately it is also inevitable that somebody will find in the MICR line an opportunity to steal money.

USF & G, the case that follows, involved the preprinted part of the MICR line that identifies the payor bank, the Federal Reserve district in which the bank is located, and the Federal Reserve Bank or branch that serves the payor bank. On the basis of this encoded information, sorting machines of the depositary bank and other collecting banks will determine the route that the check will take to get to the payor bank. Since the routing of the check is determined by the MICR encoding, there is an opportunity to commit fraud by depositing a counterfeit check, drawn on a nonexistent account, that is reprinted with MICR encoding designed to cause confusion and delay in the presentment of the check for payment.

UNITED STATES FIDELITY & GUARANTY CO. v. FEDERAL RESERVE BANK OF NEW YORK

United States District Court, Southern District of New York, 1985.
620 F.Supp. 361, aff'd, 786 F.2d 77 (2d Cir.1986).

HAIGHT, DISTRICT JUDGE:

Plaintiff Union Trust Company of Maryland ("Union Trust") and its insurer, United States Fidelity and Guaranty Company, brought this action to recover damages caused by a clever check fraud perpetrated upon Union Trust by a nonparty. Following denial of its motion to dismiss, in an opinion reported at 590 F.Supp. 486 (hereafter cited as *"USF & G I"*), defendant Federal Reserve Bank of New York ("New York Fed") impleaded third-party defendants State Bank of Albany ("Albany State"), Philadelphia National Bank ("PNB"), and First Pennsylvania Bank ("First Penn"). Soon after filing of the third-party complaint, plaintiffs amended their complaint to assert claims against Albany State. It was unnecessary for them to assert claims against the remaining third-party defendants because the Court accepted for transfer and consolidation a suit which plaintiffs had previously filed against those two Pennsylvania banks in the Eastern District of Pennsylvania, United States Fidelity and Guaranty Co. v. Philadelphia National Bank, No. 83–1304 (E.D.Pa.).

* * *

I.

As described more fully in *USF & G I,* 590 F.Supp. at 489–91, Union Trust was fraudulently induced to permit a depositor to withdraw funds against a worthless check. In April 1980, a man who called himself Marvin Goldstein established a checking account with Union Trust. Soon after, he deposited a check for over $880,000 in the account. The account upon which the check purported to be drawn did not exist, but a clever manipulation of the numerals on the face of the check caused it to be routed among a number of New York and Pennsylvania banks before being returned to Union Trust as uncollectible. In the meantime, Union Trust had permitted Goldstein to withdraw a substantial amount of cash from his account, having assumed from the lapse of time that the check had been paid.[2] The foregoing information was pleaded in the original complaint, and discovery has con-

---

2. As explained in *USF & G I,* 590 F.Supp. at 489, familiarity with which is assumed throughout this decision, this would ordinarily have been an entirely legitimate assumption; indeed, it is an assumption made thousands of times daily by every bank in the nation without adverse consequences.

firmed its accuracy. The interesting details unearthed in discovery primarily concern not the behavior of the defendant banks in routing the bogus check but that of Union Trust's employees in accepting it and releasing funds against it. A summary of that new information follows.

On April 16, 1980, Goldstein walked into a Baltimore branch of Union Trust. He told the branch manager, John Gemmill, that he and his father were precious metals dealers and that he planned to establish a Baltimore office of his father's New York business, Goldstein Precious Metals and Stones. In preparation, he sought to open a checking account with Union Trust in the name of the business. In opening the account, Goldstein produced one piece of personal identification, a New Jersey driver's license, and a New York certificate of business proprietorship, and supplied a New York bank reference. Gemmill recorded this and other information on a "New Account Information Form." Goldstein opened the new account with a cash deposit of $15,000.

Gemmill then turned the new account form over to assistant branch manager John Clement with instructions to prepare two signature cards. Clement did so, but he unaccountably neglected to transcribe the bank reference from the new account form to the signature cards. The form and one card were then sent to central Union Trust files, while one card was retained at the local branch.

One week later, Goldstein returned to the branch and withdrew $14,000 from his account, reducing his balance to $1,000. Little was heard from him until May 6, when he deposited a check for $880,000 at a second Union Trust branch located a few blocks from the branch with which he had opened the account. Deposit of such a large check ordinarily triggers self-protective internal alerts at a bank, and Union Trust was no exception. Tellers who received for deposit checks over $100,000 were supposed to notify the branch manager, according to written Union Trust procedural guidelines. The manager was then to decide whether a "hold" should be placed on the check—that is, whether the depositor should be denied access to the deposited funds for an extended period of time in order to permit the bank to confirm the collectibility of the check. In the absence of such a hold, funds ordinarily become available to the depositor within one to two days of deposit of the check. The teller who accepted Goldstein's check, however, neither notified bank officers of the large deposit nor placed a hold on it.

The teller, however, was merely the bank's first line of defense against fraud. During the next few days, Gemmill, the branch manager, was reviewing a document known as a "balance fluctuation report," designed to alert bank officers to unusually large balance changes in the accounts under their supervision. The leap in the Goldstein Precious Metals account balance from one thousand to nearly a million dollars naturally caught his attention, and he decided to investigate. Gemmill first requested, or had Clement request, credit reports on the Goldstein business from two national credit reporting services. Both services reported that they had no record of Goldstein Precious Metals and Stones. Upon receiving this information, Gemmill had Clement retrieve the Goldstein signature card in order to pursue the credit references which would ordinarily be listed on it. Because Clement had neglected to transfer the reference from the account form, however, the signature card was no help, and neither bank employee pursued this further.[3]

Wisely, Gemmill instructed Clement to look into the $880,000 check. The check was drawn on an account at First Penn of a company called Metropolitan Investment Corporation. On instructions from Clement, an employee of Union Trust's credit department called officials at First Penn and was told that no such account existed. First Penn had no banking relationship with Metropolitan Investment Corporation. This information was relayed to Clement, who told Gemmill. All of the foregoing occurred on or before Friday, May 9, within four days of the check's May 6 deposit.

According to his deposition testimony, Gemmill, who was leaving for vacation on May 9, told Clement to report to senior bank officers any activity in the Goldstein account, perhaps recognizing that the First Penn report made it unlikely that the Goldstein check would be honored. Clement remembers no such instructions. Either way, no other action was taken at that time to prevent Goldstein from withdrawing funds against the check.

On Monday, May 12, Gemmill was temporarily replaced by another bank officer. The next day, Goldstein telephoned Clement to ask instructions for making a "wire transfer" of funds, that is, for arranging the automatic transfer of funds from his account to an account in another bank. When Goldstein arrived at the branch to arrange for the transfer, he presented Clement with a bottle of expensive champagne. They discussed arrangements for the transfer, and Clement told him that the bank could only wire "collected" balances, that is, could only wire funds from the check after a sufficient time had passed to permit the bank to conclude that the check had been paid.[4] Apparently Goldstein was willing to wait. No further action was taken on Tuesday.

---

3. According to an affidavit filed by New York Fed, the New York bank reference, if contacted, would have reported no history of dealings with the Goldstein company.

4. As explained in *USF & G I*, 590 F.Supp. at 489, banks are never actually notified when a check which has been deposited with them is paid by, or "clears," the payor bank. Instead, they are only told if it fails to clear. Therefore, before releasing funds against a suspect check, banks commonly hold the check for the number of days which experience has taught them will be required for the check to reach the payor bank and for that bank to inform them if the check is uncollectable. If no word arrives in this time, it is assumed that the check has been paid.

Two days later, on Thursday, May 15, seven business days after deposit of the check, Goldstein returned and sought both to effect a wire transfer of $660,000 and to withdraw $95,000 in cash. The wire transfer was to be made to the account of a Maryland coin dealer. Apparently concluding that sufficient time had passed, Clement undertook to make the wire transfer. His first step was to check the Union Trust computer to find out whether sufficient funds were available in Goldstein's account to satisfy the transfer request. Because this act was crucial to the success of the fraud, it must be examined in some detail.

As explained in note 4, supra, banks are never notified when checks deposited with them are paid by the payor bank. The large volume of checks in the banking system would make any such notification system expensive and unwieldy. If payment is refused, however, the payor bank must notify the depositary bank of the refusal within roughly twenty-four hours of its receipt of the check. See N.Y.U.C.C. § 4–302. In order to protect themselves against uncollectible checks, banks commonly guess at the amount of time the check is likely to spend in the collection system before reaching the payor bank and place a hold on the deposited check for at least that amount of time. Union Trust's computer was charged with keeping track of such holds.

The Union Trust computer apparently registered two types of holds. When a check was deposited into a checking account such as Goldstein's, the Union Trust computer automatically placed a one- or two-day hold on the deposited check. These holds were keyed to the Federal Reserve clearing system. Member banks of the Federal Reserve system keep accounts with their local Federal Reserve bank. See *USF & G I*, 590 F.Supp. at 490 n. 7. One of the functions of these accounts is to permit the Reserve bank to credit and debit member banks for checks cleared through the Reserve bank. Banks are ordinarily not given immediate credit for or access to the funds represented by checks such as that deposited with Union Trust by Goldstein. In other words, regardless of whether a depository bank gives its depositor immediate access to the funds represented by a deposited check, the Federal Reserve will not, in most instances, give the bank immediate credit for the check in the account which the bank maintains with the Reserve bank. Instead, the Reserve bank credits the check to a one- or two-day deferred account, equivalent to placing a hold on the check, with the length of the deferral depending primarily upon the distance the check must travel to reach the payor bank. Once the deferral period elapses, the Reserve bank grants the depositary bank a provisional credit for the amount of the check.

In reality, however, checks frequently do not clear in the one- or two-day time period allotted for this purpose by the Federal Reserve. The provisional status of the credit given by the Reserve bank signifies that although a credit has been given to the account of the depositary bank, no corresponding debit has been made in the account of the payor bank. Once the payor bank receives the check, it must notify the Reserve bank within twenty-four hours whether it will honor the check. If the Reserve bank is notified that the check has been honored, it debits the account of the payor bank and removes the provisional status of the credit given the depositary bank.

The Union Trust computer automatically placed the equivalent of a hold on all deposited checks corresponding to the length of the deferral imposed by the Federal Reserve. The duration of Reserve system deferrals were never intended, however, to estimate or correspond precisely to the actual clearing time of a check. On the contrary, they intentionally underestimate this time. For that reason, as suggested above, banks frequently place their own extended hold on checks which are not likely to clear within one or two days. This prevents the depositor from withdrawing funds until the bank has satisfied itself that no word of dishonor has arrived or, in theory, will arrive. Such holds could also be recorded on the Union Trust computer, but they were not imposed automatically.

As noted above, no such hold was placed on the Goldstein check. The only hold in the Union Trust computer was a two-day Federal Reserve hold, which expired several days before May 15. Therefore, when Clement checked, he found no hold on the Goldstein funds. This, of course, did not indicate that the Goldstein check had been paid. It simply indicated that whatever precautions Union Trust had taken against premature withdrawal had expired, and the check had not been returned. Clement called the bookkeeping department of the bank, which confirmed that no hold was in effect—in other words, that, according to the bank's computer, the funds from the check were available for withdrawal.

Apparently misunderstanding the nature of the information supplied by the computer, Clement, according to his deposition testimony, concluded from his computerized inquiry not only that all holds had expired but that the check had actually cleared. Although he was aware of the First Penn report that no account existed against which the check could possibly have been drawn, he concluded that the report must have been incorrect. Without checking once again with First Penn, he authorized the wire transfer and the cash withdrawal.

Goldstein picked up the cash in person on May 15. The wire transfer was made to the bank of the Maryland coin dealer the same day. The dealer, however, had insufficient coins on hand to satisfy Goldstein's order. The dealer gave Goldstein the coins available on May 15; the remainder were delivered to him in mid-afternoon the following day. Goldstein thereafter disappeared with the cash and coins.

At about the same time Goldstein was receiving his coins on May 16, a Union Trust Vice President was informed that First Penn was returning the $880,000 check. Only later was it discovered that the Goldstein check was a fraud. The numbers printed in magnetic ink at the bottom of the check and the routing number, printed in ordinary ink in the top right hand corner, did not match, a circumstance which caused the check to be routed to several banks over several days before arriving at First Penn. It is now possible to describe the circumstances surrounding the routing of the check in more detail.

Union Trust's central check processing facility attempted to computer-process the check on May 6, the day of deposit. This machine rejected the check because the magnetic ink character recognition number ("MICR number") was not printed in magnetic ink and was the wrong size, necessitating hand processing.[8] At that time all of Union Trust's non-local checks which required hand processing were sent to PNB for processing and collection. The Goldstein check was accordingly dispatched to PNB in the early morning of May 7; because of its great value, it was sent by courier.

Based on the check's routing number, it was sent by PNB to a New York Fed processing center in Utica, New York, for forwarding to Albany State. Albany State received the check on the morning of May 9 and returned it to the Utica center of New York Fed, stamped "Sent in Error," on May 12. The next day the Utica center sent the check to New York Fed's New York City office.

Despite irregularities in the check described as "glaring" by a New York Fed chief of operations, that office failed to detect the fraudulent nature of the check. Instead, on May 14, New York Fed sent the check to the Federal Reserve Bank of Philadelphia. A document accompanying the check indicated that New York Fed intended the check to be presented for collection to First Penn rather than returned to PNB as an unpaid item.[10] The Philadel-

---

8. It is interesting to note that Goldstein's technique of printing an improper MICR number has been used in other types of fraud. According to published reports, the scheme which resulted in the well-publicized May, 1985, conviction for fraud of the brokerage firm of E.F. Hutton & Co. also used improperly printed checks. Hutton had checks printed with incorrect MICR numbers to foil its banks' computer-aided check-processing machines, thereby lengthening the time needed for processing the checks and increasing Hutton's "float," or amount of funds on deposit by checks which have not yet been collected from the payor bank. Hutton deposited the flawed checks drawn on its own accounts at various banks in its accounts at other banks. Until the checks were paid by the former banks, Hutton received payment for use of the funds by both banks at once. The longer the time required to process the check, the greater the "double" payments Hutton received. This was where the incorrect MICR numbers came in handy. See Bleakley, How Hutton Scheme Worked, N.Y. Times, May 17, 1985, at D4, cols. 2–4.

10. Because both PNB, to which the check would have been returned, and First Penn, to which it was sent for collection, are in the same Federal Reserve district, it was impossible to determine on the facts pleaded in the complaint whether New York Fed had

phia Reserve bank presented the check to First Penn at 9:00 a.m. on the same day it received it, May 14. At this time, it must be remembered, Goldstein had not yet been permitted to withdraw any funds against the check by Union Trust.

If First Penn was going to dishonor the Goldstein check, it was required by the U.C.C. to notify PNB of this fact by midnight of May 15. It did not. Instead, processing of the check was not completed until 9:45 a.m. on the morning of May 16, when First Penn finally notified PNB of the dishonor. At this point it was still not too late to recover the fraudulently gained funds, for the second shipment of gold coins had not yet been made to Goldstein. Quick action might have caught him. Quick action, however, was not forthcoming. PNB did not pass word of the dishonor to Union Trust until mid-afternoon of May 16, too late to prevent Goldstein from slipping away. He has never been located.

II.

Albany State and the three defendant banks all move for summary judgment on plaintiffs' claims. Each is in a somewhat different factual posture, and each accordingly raises somewhat different legal issues. Overhanging all of the arguments, however, is the issue of the effect of Union Trust's behavior in its dealings with Goldstein. It cannot be contended that Union Trust's behavior was anything but reckless. Gemmill opened an account with a man who presented only one form of personal identification, an out-of-state driver's license. Whether or not this alone was poor commercial practice, it placed particular importance on the bank reference which he provided, for the reference was Union Trust's only independent means of confirming Goldstein's identity. Yet Clement left the reference off the signature card, and neither man made an effort to track it down when it was needed. In addition, the teller who accepted the check for deposit did so without presenting it to a branch manager, in breach of bank regulations.[12] This failure was particularly serious, for it deprived the banking system of its one opportunity for the check to be examined by an experienced professional who was unhurried by time pressures and simultaneously had access to information about the depositor. The most astounding act of carelessness, however, was the bank's release of funds against a check which it had been told was drawn on a non-existent account. Such an act was more than mere negligence, for it entailed acting in the face

returned the check or sent it for collection. See *USF & G I*, 590 F.Supp. at 497. It now seems clear, based on discovered materials, that New York Fed did not return the item but sent it for collection.

12. In retrospect, the teller's failure to place a hold on the check, while poor practice, was of less consequence. Union Trust's standard, and apparently proper, hold for a check drawn on a Pennsylvania bank was five to six days. Since Goldstein withdrew funds on the seventh day, the hold would not have prevented execution of his scheme.

of a known and obvious risk. Viewed in its entirety, Union Trust's conduct was breathtakingly foolhardy; nay, commercially suicidal.[13]

New York Fed argues, with backing from Albany State, that such almost incomprehensible conduct should act as a bar to any recovery based on the dramatically lesser negligence of other banks in the check's chain of collection.

A.

In understanding this claim, it is helpful to review the basis of New York Fed's alleged liability. Section 4–202(1) of the U.C.C. imposes upon all banks which handle checks sent for collection a duty of ordinary care both in forwarding checks for collection and in returning checks deemed uncollectible. Care must be exercised both in the promptness of action and in the choice of action. Timing is handled by the "midnight deadline" rule; banks exercise care in the timing of an action by responding, generally, before midnight of the business day following the day on which the check is received. N.Y.U.C.C. §§ 4–104 and 4–202(2). The proper choice of action cannot be so easily codified and is governed by a general rule of reasonableness borrowed from tort law. *USF & G I*, 590 F.Supp. at 491–92. This is the duty New York Fed is accused of failing to satisfy.

At the time of *USF & G I*, the lack of discovery made it impossible to define precisely New York Fed's alleged breach of care, since its exact actions were then unknown. It now appears that plaintiffs' claim is twofold: that New York Fed should have, in the exercise of ordinary care, either 1) recognized the risk of fraud inherent in the check and sent it for return to PNB rather than collection from First Penn or 2) recognized that the routing of the check to Albany State caused a significant risk that Union Trust would release funds before the check cleared and sent wire notice to Union Trust or PNB that the check had taken the long route to First Penn. See *USF & G I*, 590 F.Supp. at 494–99. Union Trust argues that these actions would have permitted it either to prevent the fraud or to catch Goldstein before he absconded with the cash and coins.

It is by no means a foregone conclusion that New York Fed's failure to take these actions, given the realities of modern check processing, was negligent. *USF & G I*, 590 F.Supp. at 499. On

13. This is not the whole of the bank's carelessness. First, discovery revealed that after being rejected by the automatic sorting machinery the check was examined by a Union Trust supervisor, but this supervisor failed to detect the "glaring" facial irregularities in the check and instead forwarded it to PNB. Second, Clement's wire transfer of $660,000 exceeded the amount of money he was authorized by bank regulations to transfer. Third, several of Goldstein's actions known to Clement labelled him as "shady," including his transparent attempt at a bribe and his request that the money be wired to a coin dealer, who presumably would convert the funds into highly liquid assets.

the other hand, as discussed above, Union Trust's recklessness was gross and obvious. New York Fed argues, on several grounds, that the tenuous nature of its alleged negligence should not serve as a basis for recovery in the face of Union Trust's conduct.

The primary difficulty with defendant's theory is that it is not expressly sanctioned by the UCC. Plaintiffs' suit is for violation of a duty imposed in the first instance by the UCC, and it is to that body of law which resort must first be had to determine the rights and liabilities of the parties. Although the UCC in some specific circumstances apportions liability on the basis of relative fault—most notably in the law of forged signatures and endorsements, see, generally, Five Towns College v. Citibank, N.A., 108 A.D.2d 420, 489 N.Y.S.2d 338, 342–43 (1985), it incorporates no general rule of comparative or contributory negligence. In the area with which we are concerned, check collection, the Code imposes upon collecting banks a duty of due care and subjects them to "but for" liability for violations of the duty. N.Y.U.C.C. §§ 4–103(5) and 4–202(1); Northpark National Bank v. Bankers Trust Co., 572 F.Supp. 524, 531 (S.D.N.Y.1983) (hereafter "*Northpark*"). There is no express requirement that the plaintiff demonstrate its own due care as a prerequisite to recovery, nor is there any mention of comparative negligence.[14] There is simply no mention of the effect, if any, of a plaintiff's negligence on its recovery under § 4–202(1).

The question cannot be permitted to end there, however. Article 4 of the Code, governing check collection, was developed in the 1950s, prior to the advent of large scale fraud upon the check collection system. See *Northpark,* 572 F.Supp. at 533. The rules of liability which govern the allocation of losses arising from check transit were not—could not have been—designed with such fraud in mind. In these circumstances, to adhere blindly to the limitations imposed by those rules, if to do so would violate the policies which the UCC otherwise seeks to promote, would be unwise and unjust. Nor does the Code demand such adherence. As Judge Knapp noted in his seminal *Northpark* decision, "the history of the UCC makes it abundantly clear that, especially in the context of those provisions which impose a duty of care, the Code's watchword is 'flexibility.'" 572 F.Supp. at 533. I do not, therefore, find the lack of a rule of contributory or comparative negligence in Article 4 to be an insuperable barrier to defendants' claim that such a rule should be imposed. Rather, the decision turns upon whether to do so would, on the one hand, be consistent with the aims of § 4–202(1) and Article 4 as a whole and, on the

14. The latter is not surprising. The UCC predated the widespread acceptance of comparative negligence of the 1970s. More important, the concept of comparative negligence is anathema to a code which had as a primary aim the fostering of swift resolution of disputes through the clear delineation of commercial liabilities. See Perini Corp. v. First National Bank of Habersham County, 553 F.2d 398, 405 (5th Cir.1977).

other, would promote the policies which animate the rules of liability found elsewhere in the Code.

B.

In making its claim, New York Fed argues primarily by analogy to tort law. Because, the argument goes, the ordinary care standard of § 4–202(1) is borrowed from tort law, tort principles of comparative or contributory negligence should apply. As plaintiffs point out, however, this is not a tort case. The standard of care, though reliant on a concept borrowed from tort law, is imposed by the UCC. In allegedly violating § 4–202(1), defendants did not breach a duty imposed by tort law; they breached a duty imposed by statute, the UCC. It is the policies served by the UCC, therefore, rather than those served by tort law, which must determine whether plaintiff's negligence should affect its recovery under § 4–202(1). Because, as discussed below, the aims of tort law are not identical with those of the UCC, I decline to borrow the tort rule.

Tort law is designed primarily to apportion loss. Because it is typically imposed upon lay parties with little or no appreciation of its finer points, only secondarily can it hope to guide behavior so as to minimize harm. Rather, it most often becomes relevant only after the fact; the courts are asked to decide who must bear or respond for a loss previously incurred, and to what degree. As such, its guiding principle is fairness. In tort law courts have equated fairness with fault. The rule of comparative negligence is a perfect expression of this principle.

The UCC, however, was designed to facilitate commerce primarily by guiding and making predictable the consequences of behavior. It is imposed primarily upon a comparatively sophisticated group, businessmen and bankers, who look to its provisions to direct their business transactions. This is not to overlook its loss allocation function. Rules designed to guide behavior are inevitably turned against those who fail to follow them, and even the most carefully planned transactions may end in dispute. This function, however, is secondary to the creation of a system of rules to bring order and predictability to commercial transactions.

Interestingly, this fact is forcefully demonstrated by a series of provisions in the Code which were designed, unlike the bulk of the Code, to distribute loss. Several provisions of Article 3 determine which party must bear loss which results from the use of a forged signature or endorsement on a negotiable instrument. Tort law would ordinarily distribute such a loss on the basis of fault: that party or parties whose carelessness resulted in the forgery would bear the consequences of it. The UCC, however, for the most part does not look at actual fault.[15]   Instead, it places responsibility on the party which ordinarily would be in the best position to prevent the loss.[16]   See *Northpark,* supra, 572 F.Supp. at 535 and n. 26; Underpinning & Foundation Constructors, Inc. v. Chase Manhattan Bank, N.A., 46 N.Y.2d 459, 468, 414 N.Y.S.2d 298, 302, 386 N.E.2d 1319 (1979).   Such a result accomplishes two purposes: first, it increases the efficiency and fraud-resistance of the banking system by placing upon those best able to guard against it the responsibility for preventing fraud,[17] and, second, it speeds the resolution of disputes by establishing clear rules of liability which do not depend heavily upon the specific facts of individual instances of fraud.   See Perini Corp. v. First National Bank, 553 F.2d 398, 405–06 (5th Cir.1977) (describing this policy as promoting "finality").   Therefore, while the purpose of these rules is, as with tort law, to apportion loss, they are guided not by the policy which guides tort loss apportionment—fairness in the circumstances—but by the policies which shape the UCC—the promotion of efficient and predictable commerce.

Because tort law and the UCC are designed to serve different ends, I find it inappropriate to borrow a rule of comparative or contributory negligence from tort law for use in the UCC.   Nevertheless, the question remains open whether such a rule should be implied from within the UCC itself.

C.

The policies which underlie the UCC were explored above.   As relevant here, they were usefully summed up by Judge Knapp in *Northpark:* "[i]f there is a policy implicit in the UCC's rules for the allocation of losses due to fraud, it is surely that the loss be placed on the party in the best position to prevent it."   572 F.Supp. at 535.   See similarly, Leigh Co. v. Bank of New York, 617 F.Supp. 147 (S.D.N.Y.1985), at 151.   These rules are most elaborately developed in connection with the law of forged endorsements and signatures.   Liabilities for forgeries are assigned in the first instance without regard to fault.   Instead, as noted above, the

---

15.   The exception, discussed infra, is UCC § 3–406.

16.   In most cases, loss falls on the forger's immediate transferee.   N.Y. U.C.C. §§ 3–417(2)(a), 4–207(2)(a), 3–414(1), and 4–212(1).   However, when a check is paid over a forged signature, loss is placed upon the drawee bank, which in theory could have checked its client's signature.   N.Y.U.C.C. § 3–417, comment 3.   See generally, *Northpark,* supra, 572 F.Supp. at 535 n. 26.

17.   Because such parties are generally commercial banks, they are presumed to be aware of the UCC's rules of liability and to take precautions to guard against forgeries.   The rule of absolute liability regardless of fault would, one would think, tend to increase their efforts at protecting against forgeries, since to avoid liability they would be forced to guard against not only their own carelessness but the carelessness and deviousness of others.   In theory, by placing this burden upon the shoulders of those best able to guard against fraud the UCC achieves such fraud resistance in the most efficient manner.

drafters placed liability upon the party which they determined would typically be best situated to prevent a particular type of forgery.

Creation of this type of rule is essentially a legislative task, outside the scope of the proper exercise of judicial power. Even assuming that courts are competent to determine which party most commonly can prevent a particular type of forgery, the decision whether to assign liability to that party in all circumstances, without regard to fault, is best left to the legislature. This is particularly true where, as here, the legislature has already undertaken to create a complex network of laws in the area. For that reason, I rejected in *USF & G I* New York Fed's request that I create such a rule, on grounds of public policy, assigning strict liability for MICR fraud to depositary banks. 590 F.Supp. at 500 and n. 23.

Nor is it particularly clear that depositary banks are best situated in all, or even most, cases to detect MICR fraud. If such fraud is carried out with more sophistication than demonstrated by Goldstein, the deposit and collection of funds may escape the notice of even a careful bank. In such cases, the bank best situated to detect the fraud might be the first bank to refuse payment, Albany State in this case. That bank would be the first with concrete knowledge that the check is flawed.[18] On the other hand, the fraud could not be confirmed until the check has been examined by the purported payor. Which of these banks should be assigned liability under all circumstances, if any of them should, is a choice I declined and decline to make.

If such legislative assignments of strict liability comprised the whole of the UCC's system for distributing loss due to forgeries, it might properly be concluded that the concept of contributory or comparative negligence had no role to play within the UCC. However, all rules governing liability for forged signatures are

18. It appears that the first banks in the collection chain, Union Trust, PNB, and New York Fed here, would not automatically be suspicious of a check bearing a routing number inconsistent with its listed name of the payor bank. According to the deposition testimony of a Union Trust employee, such checks may be intentionally and properly circulated. They are used, when one bank maintains an account at a second bank. Union Trust, in fact, participated in such an arrangement. On these checks, Union Trust's routing number appeared in the upper right corner of the checks, and the checks were drawn on an account held by Union Trust, but the name of a second bank, Union Trust's customer bank which maintained the account at Union Trust, appeared where one would otherwise have expected Union Trust's name. The employee called such checks "due-from" checks.

The Goldstein check, of course, had other irregularities which might have attracted attention: the MICR numbers were neither in magnetic ink nor of the proper size and style, and they were nonsensical. The discrepancy between the Albany State and First Penn designations alone, however, would not automatically have suggested fraud to a collecting bank.

subject to the following provision, which incorporate what is, in effect, a rule of contributory negligence:

> Any person who by his negligence substantially contributes to a material alteration of the instrument or to the making of an unauthorized signature is precluded from asserting the alteration or lack of authority against a holder in due course or against a drawee or other payor who pays the instrument in good faith and in accordance with the reasonable commercial standards of the drawee's or payor's business.

N.Y.U.C.C. § 3–406.[19]

Section 3–406 is consistent with the remainder of the Code. It places a burden of due care on a person well situated to prevent a forgery: the drawer of the check. Drawers are forced to draw their checks so as to prevent alterations and to safeguard their blank checks so as to prevent their falling into unauthorized hands.[20]

While § 3–406 does not directly apply to the case at bar, I am persuaded that it is appropriate to apply its spirit by analogy to apportionment of loss due to MICR fraud. The depositary bank, like the drawer of the check, is well situated to protect the system against MICR fraud. The depositary bank has an opportunity to examine the check free of the time pressures which prevent collecting banks from giving checks more than a cursory glance. Perhaps more important, the depositary bank is in the unique position of being able to examine both the depositor and the check. No other bank in the collecting chain can examine the depositor, a crucial disadvantage given the seeming difficulty of detecting this type of fraud.

In many cases examination of the depositor and check might well reveal nothing unusual or alarming,[21] in which event the collecting banks will be obliged, to avoid liability, to demonstrate their compliance with § 4–202. As this case proves, however, a careful examination of either depositor or check, or both, might well reveal the fraud and protect the banking system. Because the depositary bank is uniquely situated to perform such an examination, it is entirely consistent with the policies served by the UCC to place upon it the duty to do so. Conversely, to refuse to imply such a duty would be equally inconsistent with those policies. It would permit the individual or entity in the best

---

19. A more complex and specific provision, N.Y.U.C.C. § 4–406, establishes non-exclusive circumstances which constitute *per se* negligence by checking account customers who are victims of forged signatures.

20. According to the Code, "[t]he most obvious case is that of the drawer who makes use of a signature stamp or other automatic signing device and is negligent in looking after it." N.Y. U.C.C. § 3–406, comment 7. Again, this shows the commercial orientation of the Code; businessmen are warned to watch those with access to signing machines.

21. See note 18, supra.

position, at least in those circumstances, to prevent the fraud to evade any duty to do so. Not only would such an approach be inefficient, it could well be, as this case demonstrates, entirely unjust.

Moreover, because only the depositary bank possesses this ability to examine both the depositor and the check, it is appropriate to place upon it the initial burden of care. In the banking system, the depositary bank is the first line of defense against MICR fraud, and the most efficient point at which to take precautions against it. It may properly be prevented from holding other banks liable if it has not adequately fulfilled this role.[22]

I hold that a depositary bank which is a victim of MICR fraud may be precluded from recovering damages from collecting banks under UCC § 4–202(1) if those banks can demonstrate that the negligence of the depositary bank played a substantial role in the success of the fraud.[23] I have no hesitation in holding that, for the reasons stated previously, it has been demonstrated as a matter of law that the recklessness of Union Trust played a substantial— nay, indispensable—role in the success of this fraud. I grant summary judgment in favor of defendants Albany State, New York Fed, and PNB.

---

22. To this extent, this imposed rule differs from § 3–406, which requires an otherwise liable bank seeking to evade liability to demonstrate not only the drawer's lack of due care but its own exercise of due care. The rules of liability of which § 3–406 is a part are quite different, however, from § 4–202. "Otherwise liable" banks are not liable, as is the case with banks liable under § 4–202, because of their negligence. They are strictly liable. It is arguably appropriate to require them to demonstrate their own exercise of care before evading the severe standard of strict liability. Further, drawers, who may be made liable under § 3–406, stand on a much different footing than the banks which would be liable. They are generally individuals and corporations, and the forgeries are presumably carried out without their awareness. Because of this, they do not possess the tools to protect against fraud—for example, the chance to ask a customer for identification or to check a signature card— which the strictly liable banks do. Indeed, it is these tools to protect against forgery which the UCC uses to justify holding those particular banks liable.

See *Northpark,* supra, 572 F.Supp. at n. 26.

By contrast, depositary banks under § 4–202(1) differ from the collecting banks in their ability not only to examine the check but the depositor. They thus have advantage over the collecting banks. It is therefore appropriate to place liability on their shoulders should they fail to exercise due care, even if the collecting banks have also failed to do so.

23. It might be contended that application of comparative negligence would be more fair. The UCC, however, contains no provision for comparative negligence. See *Northpark,* supra, 572 F.Supp. at n. 28. Even in New York the legislature has left the UCC's all-or-nothing rules alone while statutorily adopting comparative negligence in other areas. See N.Y.Civ.P.L.R. § 1411. Contributory negligence serves the UCC's aims of efficiency and finality by definitively assigning liability. See note 14, infra. It would be improper to impose the more tort-oriented comparative negligence in the absence of legislative approval of such a step.

III.

First Penn stands on a somewhat different footing, since it is alleged to be liable not under § 4–202(1) but § 4–302. Section 4–302 makes a payor bank which fails to return a dishonored check within its midnight deadline liable for resulting damages. It has been repeatedly recognized, however, that § 4–302 does not shift the burden of loss to a payor bank which misses its deadline if the payee was already aware when presenting the check that it would not be accepted or paid except by mistake. See N.Y.U.C.C. § 3–511(2)(b); Bank Leumi Trust Co. v. Bally's Park Place, 528 F.Supp. 349 (S.D.N.Y.1981); Leaderbrand v. Central State Bank of Wichita, 202 Kan. 450, 450 P.2d 1, 9 (1969); cf. Continental National Bank v. Sanders, 581 S.W.2d 293, 296 (Tex.Civ.App.1979). Although Union Trust did not know that the Goldstein check would not be paid when it forwarded the check for collection, it learned long before releasing funds to Goldstein that First Penn had no account from which to pay the check. The same policy reasons which preclude recovery under § 4–302 by those who forward checks which they have reason to know are uncollectible also argue in favor of precluding Union Trust from recovering. It had reason to know of the uncollectibility of Goldstein's check. Therefore, it can and should be estopped from claiming that at the time it suffered the loss it was not aware that First Penn would refuse the check.

To hold otherwise would be inequitable to First Penn. First Penn informed Union Trust that it had no account relationship with the purported drawer of the check. It should not now be held liable because Union Trust chose to ignore that information and subsequently release funds against the check.

Also relevant is National Savings and Trust Co. v. Park Corp., 722 F.2d 1303, 1304 (6th Cir.1983), cert. denied, 466 U.S. 939, 104 S.Ct. 1916, 80 L.Ed.2d 464 (1984), in which it was held that a bank may recover funds paid by mistake on a bad check unless the plaintiff has changed its position in reliance on the payment. Because Union Trust had been informed before allowing Goldstein to withdraw funds that First Penn would not pay the check, Union Trust may be estopped from claiming that it permitted withdrawal in reliance on First Penn's deemed payment at the expiration of its midnight deadline. Under both lines of authority, First Penn is entitled to summary judgment on plaintiffs' claims.

IV.

For the reasons stated above, all defendants are entitled to summary judgment on plaintiffs' claims. The third-party claims are therefore moot. The Clerk is directed to dismiss both complaints with prejudice.

NOTE

In *USF & G* the fraud was crudely done and the conduct of the depositary bank was ludicrously deficient. However, as Judge Haight pointed out, "If such fraud is carried out with more sophistication than demonstrated by Goldstein the deposit and collection of funds may escape the notice of even a careful bank." 683. Which bank would be liable in a case in which the depositary bank is not negligent? The MICR fraud cases are exhaustively discussed in Leary & Fry, MICR Fraud: A Systems Approach to Foiling the Felon's Fun, 40 U. of Miami L.Rev. 737 (1986). The authors conclude: "By a proper interpretation of U.C.C. section 4–202(1)(e), liability would be placed on the bank diverting the return from the normal route back to the depositary bank. The diverting bank, by its own actions, will have actual knowledge that the transit from depositary bank to one bank, thought to be a payor bank, and back has been delayed by transit to the second bank for payment and back. This places the burden for giving notice of delay on the first bank to have actual knowledge of the delay." Id. at 765. How would this test be applied in *USF & G* had the depositary bank not been negligent?

D. RESTRICTIVE INDORSEMENTS

Indorsement of an instrument may serve several purposes, but most commonly an indorsement is made in order to negotiate the instrument. § 3–204(a). The form of the indorsement can affect rights with respect to the instrument if it is stolen and collected or transferred to a third party. If a check indorsed in blank by the holder is stolen, the thief may negotiate the check to a transferee who may obtain rights as a holder in due course. If the stolen check was payable to an identified person and the payee made a special indorsement or did not indorse the check at all, the thief cannot negotiate the check and nobody taking through the thief can become a person entitled to enforce the check. Thus, the rights of a person taking a stolen check may depend upon whether an indorsement by the holder was made and whether the indorsement was special or in blank. The rights of the taker, however, can also depend upon whether the holder made a "restrictive indorsement" governed by § 3–206.

The purpose of a restrictive indorsement is to restrict payment of the instrument. That restriction can be expressed as part of a special indorsement or an indorsement in blank. For example, an indorsement of a check consisting solely of the signature of the holder under the words "for deposit only" is a blank indorsement because it does not identify a person to whom it makes the check payable, and is a restrictive indorsement because it indicates that the check is to be deposited to an account. This restrictive indorsement is governed by § 3–206(c). Comment 3 to § 3–206. An indorsement "Pay to John Doe in trust for Jane Doe" is a special indorsement because it identifies John Doe as the person to whom the check is payable, and is a restrictive indorsement because it indicates that the proceeds of the check are to be paid for the benefit of Jane Doe. This restrictive indorsement is governed by § 3–206(d). Comment 4 to § 3–206.

Some attempts to restrict payment of an instrument by an indorser are nullified by § 3–206. An indorsement "Pay to John Doe only" is ineffective to prohibit payment to any other holder. In spite of the indorsement John Doe may indorse the instrument to another person and that person may become entitled to enforce the instrument. § 3–206(a). An indorsement that attempts to prohibit payment unless a stated condition is satisfied is also ineffective to restrict payment. § 3–206(b). Invalid restrictions are discussed in Comment 2 to § 3–206.

PROBLEMS

1. Peter, the payee of a check for $10,000 drawn on Payor Bank, indorsed and mailed the check to Bank # 1 where he had an account. When the check arrived at Bank # 1, Thief stole the check and wrote Thief's name under Peter's indorsement. Thief then deposited the check to Thief's account in Bank # 2. Bank # 2 presented the check to Payor Bank and Payor Bank paid the check. Thief then withdrew the $10,000 that had been credited to Thief's account in Bank # 2 with respect to the check.

What are Peter's rights against Bank # 2 and Payor Bank if Peter's indorsement had been as follows:

Case # 1

    For deposit only

    Peter

Case # 2

    Pay to Bank # 1 for Account No. 1234321

    Peter

Case # 3

    Peter

    For deposit only

2. Peter, the payee of a check for $10,000 drawn on Payor Bank, gave the check to Faith, the legal guardian of Ward, her elderly father who had become legally incompetent. Peter told Faith that the check was a contribution to defray Ward's nursing home expenses. Before giving the check to Faith, Peter indorsed the check as follows:

Pay to Faith as Guardian for Ward
Peter

Faith indorsed the check by signing her name under Peter's indorsement and deposited the check to her personal account in Depositary Bank. Faith also had a fiduciary account as guardian for Ward in the same bank. Pursuant to her instructions, Depositary Bank credited Faith's personal account $10,000 and obtained payment of the check from Payor Bank. Faith subsequently withdrew the $10,000 that had been credited to her personal account by writing checks on the account for her personal expenses.

Suit on behalf of Ward has been brought against Faith for breach of trust and against Depositary Bank and Payor Bank. Faith is insolvent and has no funds. What is the liability of Depositary Bank and Payor Bank?

Chapter 10

THE BANK–CUSTOMER RELATIONSHIP

A. INTRODUCTION

A customer with a checking account in a bank has a contractual relationship with the bank that is governed by Part 4 of Article 4. If the bank pays a check written on the customer's account, § 4–401(a) allows the bank to charge the customer's account only if the check is "properly payable," that is if the customer has authorized the payment and it violates no agreement between the customer and the bank. Thus a bank cannot charge a customer's account if the customer's signature is forged, but may charge the account even though the charge creates an overdraft. Of course, the bank does not have to pay an overdraft unless it has agreed to do so. § 4–402(a). Agreements by banks to pay overdrafts up to specified limits are common. If a bank fails to pay a check that is properly payable and covered by funds in the customer's account, the bank has wrongfully dishonored the check under § 4–402(a) and may be liable in damages under § 4–402(b). A customer has the right for any reason or no reason to order a bank to stop payment of checks on the customer's account or to close the account, and if the bank fails to do so it may be liable for the loss caused by its failure. § 4–403. However, a bank is not liable for dishonoring a check presented more than six months after its date. § 4–404.

The provisions of Article 4 are only one source of rules on the bank-customer relationship. Federal statutes and Federal Reserve regulations are another source. The Expedited Funds Availability Act and Regulation CC expressly override the UCC. Regulation J does so as well. Still another source is provided by § 4–103(a) under which the "effect of the provisions" of Article 4 may be varied by bank-customer agreements; it is customary for banks to have some form of deposit agreement with their customers. Thus § 4–103(a) restates and even enlarges upon the "freedom of contract" principle embodied in § 1–102. Comment 1 to § 4–103 says, "This section, therefore, permits within wide limits variation of the effect of provisions of the Article by agreement." Since deposit agreements have aspects of contracts of adhesion, a continuing matter of dispute between banks and their customers is what are the "wide limits" the comment speaks of. To what extent may the deposit contract take from customers rights expressly given by Article 4 or legitimize acts of a bank that might otherwise be improper? Comment 2 to § 1–102 says, "The meaning of

793

the statute itself must be found in its text, including its definitions, and in appropriate extrinsic aids; it cannot be varied by agreement. * * * But an agreement can change the legal consequences which would otherwise flow from the provisions of the Act."

The only limitation found in Article 4 on the freedom of the parties to vary the provisions of Article 4 is the statement in § 4–103(1) that "the parties to the agreement cannot disclaim a bank's responsibility for its lack of good faith or failure to exercise ordinary care or limit the measure of damages for the lack or failure." We will see in Perdue v. Crocker National Bank, p. 818, that courts may also police the terms of deposit agreements by invoking the doctrine of unconscionability. Another issue in the bank-customer relationship is whether a bank bears an obligation to its customer of good faith and fair dealing. See Copesky v. Superior Court, p. 826.

PROBLEM

Husband (H) and Wife (W) have a joint checking account in Bank. Their deposit agreement with Bank provides among other matters: (1) that either party may write checks on the account, may stop payment of any check drawn on the account, or may close the account, and (2) that Bank may pay an overdraft drawn by either party, the account may be debited for the overdraft, and either party is liable for the amount of the overdraft without respect to whether that party signed the check or benefited from the overdraft. H wrote a check which Bank paid that overdrew the account. W did not know of the overdraft and she did not benefit in any way from the proceeds of the overdraft. H is insolvent and Bank seeks to hold W liable for the amount of the overdraft. May it do so? § 4–401(b) and § 4–103(a). White & Summers, Uniform Commercial Code § 18–2 (3d ed. 1988); Clark, Law of Bank Deposits, Collections and Credit Cards ¶ 2.09 (3d ed. 1990).

B. STOP PAYMENT ORDERS

HUGHES v. MARINE MIDLAND BANK

City Court of Rochester, Civil Branch, Monroe County, 1985.
127 Misc.2d 209, 484 N.Y.S.2d 1000.

JOHN MANNING REGAN, JUDGE.

There are no controverted questions of fact between the parties to this action in respect to any material issue. Accordingly, this motion for summary judgment presents solely a question of law, and this Court should, and will, proceed to judgment.
* * *

Plaintiffs, Dr. and Mrs. Frederick Hughes are depositors in the defendant, Marine Midland's bank. They have transacted banking with the defendant at its office on East Avenue in Rochester, New York, for some years.

In February, 1983, the plaintiffs were on vacation in Sarasota, Florida. In Sarasota, they leased a resort cottage from Diane Barth, a real estate agent. Ms. Barth insisted, prior to granting possession of the cottage, that the plaintiffs pay the full month's rental of the property in the sum of $1,470.00. Mrs. Hughes tendered her personal check, dated February 1, 1983, for the sum of $1,470.00 to Ms. Barth in compliance with her preconditions. The check was drawn on defendant bank's East Avenue, Rochester, New York, office from the Hughes' personal joint account. Ms. Barth deposited the check in the First Presidential Savings & Loan of Sarasota the very next day, February 2, 1983, for collection.

On February 4, 1983, a Friday, Dr. Hughes telephoned the defendant bank and spoke with Gail Stevens, a bank employee whose duties as an operations supervisor included the processing of telephoned stop payment orders. Dr. Hughes told Ms. Stevens the correct account number, the correct name of the payee, the correct date of the check, and the correct amount of money for which the check was drawn. He did not give her the correct check number, however, describing the number as 292 instead of 280.

Moreover, Dr. Hughes amplified his stop payment telephone call with his reasons for stopping payment. He advised that the payee, Ms. Barth, had misrepresented the quality of the accommodations for which the check had been delivered to her, whereupon Ms. Stevens duly recorded "misrepresentation" as the reason for the stop order.

This telephone call was placed at 8:55 a.m. on Friday, the 4th day of February, 1983. On Monday, February 7, 1983, the Barth check was posted as a debit to the Hughes' account, and the full sum of $1,470.00 was deducted.

In reliance on the conversation with Ms. Stevens, Dr. Hughes notified Ms. Barth that he and his wife were leaving the premises. After contentious arguments had ended, the Hughes paid Ms. Barth the sum of $350.00 later that same Friday afternoon, February 4, 1983, in full settlement of all claims between them.

The bank sent the Hughes a form for written confirmation of the stop-payment order and Dr. Hughes returned it, duly signed, to the bank on February 18, 1983. On February 22, 1983, the bank mailed the plaintiffs their monthly statement which showed the $1,470.00 deduction for the Barth check on February 7, 1983. When they received the statement some three days later, they learned, for the first time, that the bank had not honored their stop-payment order.

The Hughes' cause of action asserts that the bank is liable to them for this loss of $1,470.00 under the provisions of Article 4, Section 4–403 of the Uniform Commercial Code, which reads as follows:

"(1) A customer may by order to his bank stop payment of any item payable for his account but the order must be received at such time and in such manner as to afford the bank a reasonable opportunity to act on it prior to any action by the bank with respect to the item described in Section 4–303.

(2) An oral order is binding upon the bank only for fourteen calendar days unless confirmed in writing within that period. A written order is effective for only six months unless renewed in writing.

(3) The burden of establishing the fact and amount of loss resulting from the payment of an item contrary to a binding stop payment order is on the customer."

The bank's Answer does not contain a general denial. It selects certain allegations in the Complaint for specific denials upon information and belief. However, the affidavits and documentary proof have convincingly established the above facts.

In addition, the Answer pleads four affirmative defenses— failure to state a cause of action, contributory negligence, a defense labeled "the complaint is subject to rebuttal by documentary evidence", and forum non conveniens (C.P.L.R. § 327).

The bank's principal defenses to plaintiffs' assertion of liability is that the bank's actions did not cause the loss, but, rather, the plaintiffs' error did, for when plaintiffs gave Ms. Stevens the wrong check number, the bank's computer correctly reported that check number 292 had *not* been negotiated, and thereafter payment of check number 292 was, in fact, stopped. But, of course, payment of check number 280 was not stopped.

The bank has also pleaded a novel procedural defense. They have urged this Court to forego jurisdiction under C.P.L.R. § 327, *forum non conveniens,* on the grounds that because this Court has no *in personam* jurisdiction over Diane Barth, a resident of Sarasota, Florida, the plaintiffs should be relegated to a Florida forum. Furthermore, the defendant points out that, under the Florida Uniform Commercial Code, Article 4, § 674.4, 4–403(1) requires stop-payment orders to describe the check "with certainty", and that supplying the wrong check number is fatal. Finally, they argue that this case has more significant contacts with Florida and involves interpretations of a Florida realty contract, questions as to which this New York forum has neither jurisdiction nor competence to decide.

I

THE PLAINTIFFS' CAUSE OF ACTION
UNDER UCC 4–403

Since Dr. Hughes and his wife are residents of New York, and they live in Monroe County, and since the defendant bank owns and operates a branch bank in Rochester, on East Avenue, and since the banking contract between these parties was made in Rochester, and the debtor-creditor relationship it created is to be performed in Rochester, New York law will govern the legal incidents of that debtor-creditor relationship and will determine whatever liability the bank may have. U.C.C. § 1–105(1); § 4–102(2); Auten v. Auten, 308 N.Y. 155, 124 N.E.2d 99 (1954).

Because the bank received the stop payment order in plenty of time to act on it,[3] the only flaw in the plaintiffs' case is the error they made in providing Ms. Stevens with an incorrect check number. Ms. Stevens' affidavit states that the bank's central computer in Syracuse, New York, "can be directed to identify: (1) a specific check by number; (2) all checks for a specific amount; (3) a specific check having a stated number and amount." Ms. Piper, a bank employee who actually works at the computer center in Syracuse, and whose affidavit states that the center processes almost a million items a day, reports that any stop payment order can be processed in any of three ways: "(1) by check number and dollar amount (2) by check number, or (3) by dollar amount."

From these circumstances, it is evident that the bank's intraoffice memorandum, which Ms. Stevens made from her conversation with Dr. Hughes over the telephone on February 4, 1983, contained enough information—the account number, and the amount of the check—to process the stop payment order at the computer center in Syracuse.

The legal question then becomes whether these facts meet the standards of legal sufficiency set out in U.C.C. § 4–403(1) which are that: "the order must be received at such time and in such manner as to afford the bank a reasonable opportunity to act." The case law is not easily reconciled. In Mitchell v. Security Bank, 85 Misc. 360, 147 N.Y.S. 470 (App.Term 1st Dept. 1914) a wrong date, and a single digit error in the amount of the check was held insufficient. Yet in Thomas v. Marine Midland Tinkers Natl. Bank, 86 Misc.2d 284, 287, 381 N.Y.S.2d 797 (Civ.Ct.N.Y.Co.

---

3. A full banking day, a full weekend, and a portion of the next banking day elapsed before payment. This is time enough to act as a matter of law. Dunbar v. First National Bank, 63 A.D.2d 755, 404 N.Y.S.2d 722 (3rd Dept. 1978). See also Chute v. Bank One of Akron, 10 Ohio App.3d 122, 460 N.E.2d 720 (1983).

1976), a digit error in the check number was deemed "trivial and insignificant", and the check description held to be adequate.

In view of the *Thomas* decision in 1976, and recognizing the capabilities of modern computers to respond to programmed software, the Court concludes that New York banks have had ample time to design software to identify and stop payment on checks from a specific account simply by account number and dollar amount. In fact, Ms. Piper's affidavit admits that Marine's computers now have that capability. Accordingly, in the interests of commercial stability and predictability, and in furtherance of the doctrine of *stare decisis*,[4] this Court will follow the rule in *Thomas* and hold that the information provided met the statutory standards of reasonable accuracy, and did therefore provide a reasonable opportunity for the bank to act.

Subdivision (3) of § 4–403 of the U.C.C. puts the burden of establishing the fact and amount of loss occurring upon payment over a valid stop order on the customer. At first glance, most would infer that this loss would always be equal to the face amount of the check, and that deducting that face sum from the customer's account would establish that sum as "the amount of the loss". For example, the Complaint in this case makes that assumption and demands judgment for $1,470.00, the sum defendant deducted from the account.

Prior to enactment of the U.C.C., this was the law in New York. Unless a customer ratified, and adopted as correct, the bank's wrongful payment over a valid stop order, the bank was liable for the full sum deducted from a customer's account. Chase Natl. Bank v. Battat, 297 N.Y. 185, 78 N.E.2d 465 (1948). Moreover, the Court specifically held in *Battat* that the validity or invalidity of the underlying transaction was *no defense* to the customer's cause of action:

> "*In the absence of ratification the bank [is] liable to the depositor,* as [a bank cannot] justify paying out the depositor's money without authority by showing *that the recipient* [payee] *was justly entitled to it.*" 297 N.Y. at p. 190, 78 N.E.2d 465. Citing American Defense Society v. Sherman National Bank, 225 N.Y. 506, 122 N.E. 695 (1919).

In post-Code cases in New York, particularly in Thomas v. Marine Midland, supra, and, obliquely, in Sunshine v. Bankers Trust Co., 34 N.Y.2d 404, 358 N.Y.S.2d 113, 314 N.E.2d 860 (1974), that issue has become muddled.[5]

---

4. Other state courts have agreed with the decision in *Thomas*. See Parr v. Security National Bank, 680 P.2d 648, 38 U.C.C. Reporting Service 275 (1984) reporting a Court of Appeals case from Oklahoma, which held that a digit error in the check number did not vitiate the sufficiency of the stop order.

5. Under the official comments to U.C.C. § 4–407, at McKinney's Consolidated Laws of N.Y., Book 62½, at page 631, the author informs us that the code

Thomas regards the problem as a conflict between § 4–403(3) and § 4–407 (the subrogation provisions) and holds, under the authority of *Sunshine,* that the plaintiff must prove, as part of his case, that the underlying transaction caused a loss so long as the bank's answer raises that issue; and the bank adduces some evidence of that fact. Much of this rationale is dicta, however, because the bank in *Thomas* did not plead, nor prove, any affirmative defense as to non-loss. See 86 Misc.2d at page 291, 381 N.Y.S.2d 797.

In the instant case, the bank has pleaded forum non conveniens both as a procedural and affirmative defense. In its affidavits and briefs, it has argued that the underlying transaction with Barth raises factual questions about whether the plaintiffs truly sustained a loss, and, if so, what the amount of that loss was.

This Court agrees with the bank to this extent: if the underlying transaction is part of the plaintiff's case—as *Thomas* says it is—then the bank has raised a factual issue in this case, and summary judgment should be denied. However, *Thomas* cannot bind this Court in the face of both common sense and the holding of the Court of Appeals in both *American Defense Society* and the *Battat* cases. *Sunshine* did not overrule either *American Defense Society,* or *Battat,* explicitly or implicitly, and, moreover, unequivocally, *Sunshine* still held that: "a stop-payment order need not be supported by a sound legal basis". See 34 N.Y.2d at p. 413, footnote 5, 358 N.Y.S.2d 113, 314 N.E.2d 860.

Therefore, in this Court's judgment, *Battat* is still good law in New York; and a bank may not defend a U.C.C. § 4–403 violation by pleading that the payee of the check, which was the subject of a valid stop order, was justly entitled to the money. Further, the payee, Ms. Barth's, entitlements, if any, are not a part of the plaintiffs' *prima facie* case. This Court now holds that the plaintiffs meet their burden to prove loss both under the common law, and under the code, if they show that the bank has paid out from the depositor's account a sum of money over a valid stop order, and the loss, both *prima facie,* and at trial, is that sum so paid out.[6]

drafters were aware that a routine defense to a valid stop order action was that the underlying debt was due in any event. While this defense was available in some states, it was *not in New York.* See Chase Natl. v. Battat, supra. The New York Annotations in McKinney's Consolidated Laws of N.Y., Book 62½, U.C.C. § 4–403, at page 613, meekly suggest that subdivision (3) of U.C.C. § 4–403 appears to be "contra" the rule, but they cite no authority for that interpretation, and this court can find none. Certainly, the language itself creates no categorical imperative for such an interpretation.

6. The Court must here acknowledge that decisions in other states, particularly Florida, are to the contrary. See Southeast First National Bank v. Atlantic Telec, Inc., 389 So.2d 1032 (Fla. App.1980), which follows the rules set out in Thomas v. Marine Midland Bank.

Contrary judicial interpretations of U.C.C. § 4–403, subdivision (3) are the rule, however, not the exception; and

Common sense precludes involving banking institutions in litigation among their customers and those with whom their customers deal. The bank's contract obligations with their customers are separate and distinct from the commercial transactions which the customers may have with others. In granting subrogation rights to any bank which has sustained a loss due to a wrongful payment over a valid stop order, the Legislature in U.C.C. § 4–407, gave a method of mitigating such losses, if a bank chose to exercise such rights. The analogy to an insurance subrogation—where the carrier must pay the insured upon the event of loss—is apposite and comparable. The carrier can sue the guilty party—and it frequently does; but that option bears no relationship to the carrier's duty to pay its insured under its insurance contract on a proper proof of loss.[7] Here the debtor-creditor contract between the Hughes and the bank governs the bank's liability. The bank's subrogation rights, after it has experienced a liability for its breach of that debtor-creditor contract, are irrelevant.

Sunshine is not contrary to this holding. That case holds that regardless of whether the underlying transaction between the bank's customer and a third party is valid or invalid, and regardless of whether the *depositor* himself has sustained a loss, subroga-

Florida and New York are merely examples.

* * *

Georgia courts have ruled that the underlying transaction between a depositor and a third party is wholly irrelevant in a U.C.C. § 4–403 action between the bank and its depositor based on an improper payment over a valid stop order. See Whitmire v. Woodbury, 154 Ga.App. 159, 267 S.E.2d 783 (1980).

Massachusetts courts, on the contrary, have espoused the rule enunciated in Thomas v. Marine Midland Bank, supra. See Siegel v. Northeast Merchants Nat'l Bank, 386 Mass. 672, 437 N.E.2d 218 (1982), which allows the bank to introduce proof of the underlying transaction on the question of plaintiff's damages.

This Court's decision, in the instant case, does not stem from any animadversions to North Carolina, Massachusetts, or Florida courts. The predicates for the instant holding are two-fold: (1) *Battat, American Defense Society,* and *Sunshine,* all eschew involvement with the underlying transaction either as part of plaintiff's damages, or as an affirmative defense, and all three cases bind this Court; and (2) absolutely

nothing in the official comments to U.C.C. § 4–403, nor in the language of subdivision (3), itself, constrains so bizarre and cumbersome an interpretation.

Finally, the law of damages has always been to *confine* economic losses, not expand them. The direct damages from the breach of the depositor's contract is the sum wrongfully deducted. The underlying transaction introduces, at least, the issue of consequential damages. Opening that issue may expand a bank's liability beyond immediate reckoning, and allow plaintiffs to prove that wrongful payment of the stopped item caused a whole series of events far more damaging, financially, than the amount paid out. Excursions of this kind are at war with the conservative history of commercial law and the law of contracts generally.

7. While large banks may be self-insurers, many smaller banks insure themselves against both forgeries and collection losses. In those cases, the insurance subrogation process is more than an analogy, it is a fact, as the carrier who pays eventually winds up as the subrogee under § 4–407.

tion (the equitable transfer of legal rights from one person to another) occurs when the bank has sustained a loss.

If the underlying transaction were an ingredient of the § 4–403 claim, then the § 4–403 action would subsume the underlying transaction and subdivisions (b) and (c) of § 4–407, the subrogation statute, would become superfluous since the underlying transaction would always be litigated in the § 4–403 suit, because the parties in the underlying transaction would be necessary (C.P.L.R. § 1001) to any depositor's *prima facie* case. The effect of any such rule would be to merge these statutes into a single cause of action.

Sunshine (34 N.Y.2d 404, 358 N.Y.S.2d 113, 314 N.E.2d 860, supra), however, recognizes separate causes of action: One by the customer against the bank under § 4–403, and one by the bank, as subrogee, against the payee under § 4–407(c). In footnote 5 on page 413 of 34 N.Y.2d, 358 N.Y.S.2d 113, 314 N.E.2d 860, the Court of Appeals candidly admits that the finality of the trial court's order precluded their consideration of the cause of action under subdivision (b) of § 4–407 against the depositor-maker, but their implication is that such a cause of action, as that statute gives, does exist.

Moreover, the cases contain two persuasive reasons for recognizing this sequential separateness of these causes of action: (1) The "innocent" party who has issued a timely stop-payment order is entitled to the use of his funds pending the determination of his legal obligations in the underlying transaction; and (2) the cost of prosecuting the suit on the underlying transaction may exceed the maximum possible recovery, and it may never be brought. In such event, the bank must bear the loss as a cost of doing business. See 34 N.Y.2d at page 413, footnote 5, 358 N.Y.S.2d 113, 314 N.E.2d 860.

This Court understands that this holding allows a depositor-plaintiff possibly to become a third-party defendant in his own § 4–403 action. In such an action, the defendant bank can, and sometimes surely will, prosecute its subrogation claims under U.C.C. § 4–407(b) and (c) in a third-party suit against both its depositor and the person with whom the depositor has had an underlying transaction. But that possible procedural posture should not, and does not, affect or alter the substantive legal relationships among all these parties, nor ought it to confuse and merge the sequential separateness of the causes of action each of these statutes has created.

II

THE BANK'S AFFIRMATIVE DEFENSES

The affirmative defenses of failure to state a cause of action, contributory negligence and "rebuttal by documentary evidence" are all dismissed on the law and the findings of fact set out above.

The affirmative defense of *forum non conveniens* deserves comment. If U.C.C. § 4–403, subparagraph (3), did impose upon a plaintiff the duty to prove that the underlying transactions had, in fact and law, caused him a loss, then in this case Diane Barth would become a necessary party. C.P.L.R. § 1001. In such an eventuality, subparagraph (b) of C.P.L.R. § 1001 [8] and C.P.L.R. § 327 as well, would practically combine to compel a dismissal without prejudice.

However, since subdivision (3) of U.C.C. § 4–403 does not require that proof of the underlying transaction's validity be adduced in the plaintiff's case, and since both *Battat* and *American Defense Society,* decisions of our Court of Appeals foreclose these questions as affirmative defenses to the bank, New York is the appropriate forum to decide the substantive legal issues between the parties to this action in respect to their depository contract and its mutual obligations.

For the same reasons, it is clear that this determination will have no *res judicata* effect whatsoever, either for or against the bank, or Dr. Hughes, or their assignees, or subrogees, in respect to the underlying transaction between Dr. Hughes and Ms. Barth, in direct, or in subrogation actions under subparagraphs (b) and (c) of U.C.C. § 4–407.

The order in this action should contain, in addition to the itemizations of the affidavits and pleadings submitted on the motion, a decretal paragraph specifically keeping open *all* issues pertaining to the underlying transaction, in order to eliminate any possible misunderstanding by any Florida court which may have occasion to hear that case that this New York judgment does not preclude any of the issues any party may wish to plead in respect to that underlying transaction litigation.

8. " * * * If jurisdiction over him can be obtained and only by his consent or appearance, the court, when justice requires, may allow the action to proceed without his being made a party. In determining whether to allow the action to proceed, the court shall consider * * * 2. the prejudice which may accrue from the nonjoinder to the defendant or to the person not joined * * * 5. whether an effective judgment may be rendered in the absence of the person who is not joined." C.P.L.R. 1001(b).

III

ORDER AND JUDGMENT

In view of the foregoing, the Court grants the plaintiffs' motion for Summary Judgment, and directs entry of a judgment for plaintiffs in the sum of $1,470.00, with interest at 9% from February 7, 1983, together with the costs and disbursements of this action.

NOTES

1. Would the decision in *Hughes* be affected by a clause in the bank's deposit agreement stating: "In order to stop payment on a check, you must inform the bank of the exact amount of the item, the number of the check, and your account number; otherwise our computer may not catch the stop order. Unless this is done the bank will not be responsible for any loss resulting from its failure to stop payment"? Clark, The Law of Bank Deposits, Collections and Credit Cards ¶ 2.09[2][d]. Is this clause valid under § 4–103(a) as determining "the standards by which the bank's responsibility is to be measured" or is it invalid as an attempt to disclaim the bank's responsibility for its "failure to use ordinary care"? Comment 1 to § 4–403.

2. In *Hughes* Judge Regan acknowledges that there are a number of cases that disagree with his analysis on the question of whether the customer must prove loss on the underlying contract as a part of the cause of action under § 4–403. *Hughes* may not have even represented the law of New York. Siegel v. New England Merchants National Bank, 386 Mass. 672, 437 N.E.2d 218 (1982) states the contrary view.

Siegel did not involve a stop order. Rather, the payor bank paid a postdated check before the date of the check. Under original Article 3 a demand instrument such as a check did not become payable before its date. Thus, in *Siegel*, the payor bank could not debit the drawer's account with respect to the postdated check because the check was not properly payable. In *Siegel*, the court assimilated improper payment of a postdated check to payment in violation of a valid stop order and analyzed the case as though it involved a stop order governed by § 4–403. The drawer, Siegel, drew a check to the order of Peters for $20,000 and the bank paid the check two months before the date on the check and charged Siegel's account. Siegel brought suit based on the wrongful debit. The bank asserted by subrogation the rights of Peters, who received the $20,000 paid by the bank, and impleaded Peters but he was in bankruptcy. The trial court awarded $20,000 to Siegel. In reversing, the Supreme Judicial Court of Massachusetts stated:

We begin with § 4–401(1), which governs bookkeeping between depositor and bank. A bank may charge any "properly payable" item against its depositor's account. Implicitly, the bank may not charge items, such as post-dated checks, that are not properly payable. If the charge is unauthorized, it follows that the depositor has a valid claim to the amount of the charge by virtue of the account itself. * * *

As the bank points out, the depositor's realization of this claim may produce unjust enrichment. Even when an item is not properly payable, due to prematurity or a stop payment order, the bank's payment may discharge a legal obligation of the depositor, or create a right in the depositor's favor against the payee. * * * If the depositor were permitted to retain such benefits, and recover the amount of the check as well, he would profit at the bank's expense. Therefore, § 4–407 provides that upon payment, the bank is "subrogated" to any rights prior holders may have had against the drawer-depositor, on either the check or the initial underlying transaction, and to any rights the drawer may have against the payee or other holders.[5] * * *

Thus, the code fixes the rights of the bank and the depositor by a two part adjustment. The depositor has a claim against the bank for the amount improperly debited from its account, and the bank has a claim against the depositor based on subrogation to the rights of the payee and other holders. The bank may assert its subrogation rights defensively when its depositor brings an action for wrongful debit. * * *

Here, the bank asserted a subrogation claim based on the rights of Peters, the payee.[6] Neither party, however, introduced evidence concerning Peters's rights against Siegel.[7] A

5. * * *

At the time a bank asserts subrogation rights, the check will of course have been paid, and prior holders will have no rights against the drawer. * * * Therefore, we understand § 4–407 to refer to rights existing prior to the payment.

6. The bank waived all claims based on the rights of the collecting banks.

7. The trial judge did find that the transaction between Peters and Siegel arose out of Siegel's sale of a shopping mall to Peters, and Peters's subsequent default on payments due Siegel on notes, and that Siegel and Peters had agreed to the post-dating of the check. He also found that Peters had "made no payment to [Siegel] since he received the check, either as payment on the

notes or as a repayment of the $20,000 extended by the check." The bank objects to these findings on the ground that there is no evidence in the record to support them. The bank appears to be correct on this point. In any event, the judge's findings, while they tend to suggest that the transaction was a loan, do not clearly establish either that Peters was entitled to receive the money on November 14, or that Siegel had a right to cancel the transaction before the check became due. It should be noted that the mere circumstance that the transaction was a loan, and that the loan had since proved uncollectible, would not necessarily mean that the bank's premature payment had caused the depositor a loss. If the payee was unconditionally entitled to receive the loan, the risk that he would not repay it question then arises as to what matters each party was obligated to prove in order to prevail.

Section 4–403(3) of the code provides that when the problem is one of improper payment over a stop order, the "burden of establishing the fact and amount of loss * * * is on the customer." * * * Here, of course, the bank's liability is for premature payment rather than for payment over a stop order. Nevertheless, these two forms of improper payment have in common the problem of unjust enrichment, and we believe that § 4–403(3) is a source of useful analogy.

The rule of § 4–403(3), that a depositor must prove his loss, may at first seem at odds with our earlier conclusion that § 4–401(1) provides the depositor with a claim against the bank in the amount of the check, leaving the bank with recourse through subrogation under § 4–407. See Mitchell v. Republic Bank & Trust Co., 35 N.C.App. 101, 104, 239 S.E.2d 867 (1978); Thomas v. Marine Midland Tinkers Nat'l Bank, 86 Misc.2d 284, 288–289, 381 N.Y.S.2d 797 (N.Y.Sup.Ct.1976); J. White & R. Summers, supra at 684–691. We believe, however, that § 4–403(3) was intended to operate within the process of credit and subrogation established by §§ 4–401(1) and 4–407. See § 4–403, comment 8. When a bank pays an item improperly, the depositor loses his ability to exercise any right he had to withhold payment of the check. His "loss," in other words, is equivalent to his rights and defenses against the parties to whose rights the bank is subrogated—the other party to the initial transaction and other holders of the instrument. Section 4–403(3) simply protects the bank against the need to prove events familiar to the depositor, and far removed from the bank, before it can realize its subrogation rights. The depositor, who participated in the initial transaction, knows whether the payee was entitled to eventual payment and whether any defenses arose. Therefore, § 4–403(3) requires that he, rather than the bank, prove these matters. * * *

This view of the three relevant sections of the code suggests a fair allocation of the burden of proof. The bank, which has departed from authorized bookkeeping, must acknowledge a credit to the depositor's account. It must then assert its subrogation rights, and in doing so must identify the status of the parties in whose place it claims. If the bank's subrogation claims are based on the check, this would entail

was a risk the depositor assumed in making the loan, and was not increased by the bank's action. Section 4–407, by extending the bank's subrogation to rights on the instrument as well as to rights on the transaction, makes clear that the depositor could not recover in this situation. Thus, to defeat the bank's subrogation rights the depositor must establish a condition on the right to cash the check, an element of fraud, or some other defense good against the payee as a holder of the instrument.

proof that the third party subrogor was a holder, or perhaps a holder in due course. This responsibility falls reasonably upon the bank, because it has received the check from the most recent holder and is in at least as good a position as the depositor to trace its history.

The depositor must then prove any facts that might demonstrate a loss. He must establish defenses good against a holder or holder in due course, as the case may be. See UCC §§ 3–305, 3–306. If the initial transaction is at issue, he must prove either that he did not incur a liability to the other party, or that he has a defense to liability. Thus the bank, if it asserts rights based on the transaction, need not make out a claim on the part of its subrogor against the depositor. Responsibility in this area rests entirely with the depositor, who participated in the transaction and is aware of its details. Further, the depositor must establish any consequential loss.[8]

PROBLEMS

1. Suppose Bank induces its customer to sign a stop payment form containing the following clause: "In requesting you to stop payment of this or any other item, the undersigned agrees to hold you harmless for all expenses and costs incurred by you on account of refusing payment of said item, and further agrees not to hold you liable on account of payment contrary to this request if same occurs through inadvertence, accident or oversight, or if by reason of such payment other items drawn by the undersigned are returned insufficient." Is this clause, or any part of it, enforceable? § 4–103(a) and § 4–403. Opinion of Attorney General of Connecticut, 25 U.C.C.Rep. 238 (1978).

2. In view of the fact that the customer has an absolute right to stop payment by complying with § 4–403, is the drawee bank entitled to impose a charge for processing a stop payment order? Opinions of Attorney General of Michigan, 30 U.C.C.Rep. 1626 (1981); 33 U.C.C. Rep. 1445 (1981). If a typical charge for a stop order is $6, could a bank legally impose a $60 charge for a stop order?

---

8. Several courts have harmonized § 4–403(3) with §§ 4–404(1) and 4–407 in terms of shifting burdens of production and persuasion. "Simply because a bank pays a check over a stop payment order does not entitle the customer to recover damages against the bank, but it does establish a *prima facie* case for the customer. The bank must present evidence to show absence of loss, or the right of the payee of the check to receive payment. Then the customer must sustain the ultimate burden to show why there was a defense to payment of the item." Southeast First Nat'l Bank v. Atlantic Telec, Inc., 389 So.2d 1032, 1033 (Fla.Dist.Ct.App.1980). Mitchell v. Republic Bank & Trust Co., 35 N.C.App. 101, 104, 289 S.E.2d 867 (1978). Thomas v. Marine Midland Tinkers Nat'l Bank, 86 Misc.2d 284, 290–291, 381 N.Y.S.2d 797 (N.Y.Sup.Ct. 1976). Although our analysis will often have the same result as that of the cited cases, it may in some cases give greater force to § 4–403(3).

NOTE: POSTDATED CHECKS

A luxury that manual processing of checks allowed customers was the postdated check. The customer could hold off an impatient creditor by writing a check for the debt and could control the time of payment by postdating the check. The customer could be confident that the check would not be paid before its date because a bank clerk would examine the check for date before payment by the bank. Under original Article 3 and pre-1990 Article 4 the check was not properly payable until the date of the check, and the bank could not charge the customer's account until that time. But when automated processing of checks became universal in the 1960s, there was no visual examination of the vast majority of checks. Checks were paid or dishonored on the basis of the balance in the account and the machine-readable information on the MICR line. Since there is no space on that line for the date of the check, the usual result is that the check is paid or dishonored without regard to its date. A bank prematurely paying a postdated check that depleted the customer's account balance could be liable for wrongfully dishonoring subsequent checks that would have been paid had the postdated check not been paid. A bank might seek protection against this liability by a clause in the bank-customer agreement allowing payment of any check at the time of presentment regardless of the date of the check. To the extent such a clause was enforceable, it deprived the customer of the ability to rely on postdating.

Section 4–401(c) offers a compromise that allows customers to utilize postdating while protecting banks from potential liability for failure to examine each check for its date. Under this provision the bank can pay all checks at the time of presentment unless it has received a notice of postdating from the customer. This allows the bank time to order its computer to identify the described check when it is presented so that its date may be examined before a decision to pay is made. Banks charge a fee for processing notices of postdating just as they charge for stop-payment orders.

C. CUSTOMER'S DEATH, INCAPACITY, OR BANKRUPTCY

The bank's authority to pay a check of a customer may be revoked by the express direction of the customer, as in the case of a stop payment order, but it may also be revoked by operation of law as in the case of the death, adjudication of incompetency or bankruptcy of the customer. The risk to the bank in making unauthorized payment in these cases is similar to that involved in the case of stop payment orders. Section 4–405(a) deals specifically with the bank's authority in the case of death or incapacity and § 4–405(b) gives to the bank additional authority in the case of death. On the latter point see Comments 2 and 3 to § 4–405.

The authority of the bank to act in the case of the bankruptcy of the customer is not dealt with by the UCC because the question is governed by federal rather than state law. Under Bankruptcy Code § 541(a) the property of the bankrupt (including bank accounts) passes to the estate in bankruptcy when the bankruptcy case is commenced. Thus, after bankruptcy any payment by the bank would be a payment of funds owned by the bankruptcy estate rather than by the bankrupt customer. Authority to dispose of property of the bankruptcy estate rests with the trustee in bankruptcy, and in the case of a Chapter 7 bankruptcy, this means that the bankrupt has no right to dispose of assets of the estate. But, under Bankruptcy Code § 542(c) a bank, until it has actual notice or actual knowledge of the bankruptcy of its customer, may continue to pay checks of the customer. The latter provision codifies the result of Bank of Marin v. England, 385 U.S. 99, 87 S.Ct. 274, 17 L.Ed.2d 197 (1966), which recognized the same right of the bank under the previous statute, the Bankruptcy Act of 1898.

D. WRONGFUL DISHONOR

LOUCKS v. ALBUQUERQUE NATIONAL BANK
Supreme Court of New Mexico, 1966.
76 N.M. 735, 418 P.2d 191.

LA FEL E. OMAN, JUDGE, COURT OF APPEALS.

The plaintiffs-appellants, Richard A. Loucks and Del Martinez, hereinafter referred to as plaintiffs, Mr. Loucks and Mr. Martinez, respectively, were partners engaged in a business at Albuquerque, New Mexico, under the partnership name of L & M Paint and Body Shop.

By their complaint they sought both compensatory and punitive damages on behalf of the partnership, on behalf of Mr. Loucks, and on behalf of Mr. Martinez against the defendants-appellees, Albuquerque National Bank and W. J. Kopp, hereinafter referred to as defendants, the bank, and Mr. Kopp, respectively.

Prior to March 15, 1962 Mr. Martinez had operated a business at Albuquerque, New Mexico, under the name of Del's Paint and Body Shop. He did his banking with defendant bank and he dealt with Mr. Kopp, a vice-president of the bank.

On February 8, 1962 Mr. Martinez borrowed $500 from the bank, which he deposited with the bank in the account of Del's

Paint and Body Shop. He executed an installment note payable to the bank evidencing this indebtedness.

On March 15, 1962 the plaintiffs formed a partnership in the name of L & M Paint and Body Shop. On that date they opened a checking account with the bank in the name of L & M Paint and Body Shop and deposited $620 therein. The signatures of both Mr. Loucks and Mr. Martinez were required to draw money from this account. The balance in the account of Del's Paint and Body Shop as of this time was $2.67. This was drawn from this account by a cashier's check and deposited in the account of L & M Paint & Body Shop on April 18, 1962.

Two payments of $50.00 each were made on Mr. Martinez' note of February 8, 1962, or on notes given as a renewal thereof. These payments were made by checks drawn by plaintiffs on the account of L & M Paint and Body Shop. The checks were payable to the order of the bank and were dated June 29, 1962 and August 28, 1962. A subsequent installment note was executed by Mr. Martinez on October 17, 1962 in the principal amount of $462 payable to the order of the bank. This was given as a replacement or renewal of the prior notes which started with the note of February 8, 1962.

Mr. Martinez became delinquent in his payments on this note of October 17, 1962 and the bank sued him in a Justice of the Peace court to recover the delinquency.

As of March 14, 1963 Mr. Martinez was still indebted to the bank on this note in the amount of $402, and on that date, Mr. Kopp, on behalf of the bank, wrote L & M Paint and Body Shop advising that its account had been charged with $402 representing the balance due "on Del Martinez installment note," and the indebtedness was referred to in the letter as the "indebtedness of Mr. Del Martinez."

The charge of $402 against the account of L & M Paint and Body Shop was actually made on March 15, 1963, which was a Friday.

Although Mr. Martinez at one time testified he telephoned Mr. Kopp on either Friday or the following Monday about this charge, when he was questioned more closely he admitted he discussed the matter with Mr. Kopp by telephone on Friday. Mr. Loucks testified that as he recalled, it was on Monday. Both plaintiffs went to the bank on Monday, March 18, and talked with Mr. Kopp. They both told Mr. Kopp that the indebtedness represented by the note was the personal indebtedness of Mr. Martinez and was not a partnership obligation. Mr. Loucks explained that they had some outstanding checks against the partnership account. Mr. Kopp refused to return the money to the partnership account. There was evidence of some unpleasantness in the conversation. The partnership account, in which there was then a balance of only $3.66, was thereupon closed by the plaintiffs.

The bank refused to honor nine, and possibly ten, checks drawn on the account and dated between the dates of March 8 and 16, inclusive.

The checks dated prior to March 15 total $89.14, and those dated March 15 and 16 total $121.68. These figures do not include the tenth check to which some reference was made, but which was not offered into evidence and the amount of which does not appear in the record.

The case came on for trial before the court and a jury. The court submitted the case to the jury upon the question of whether or not the defendants wrongfully made the charge in the amount of $402 against the account of L & M Paint and Body Shop. The allegations of the complaint concerning punitive damages and compensatory damages, other than the amount of $402 allegedly wrongfully charged by the defendants against the partnership account, were dismissed by the court before the case was submitted to the jury. The jury returned a verdict for the plaintiffs in the amount of $402.

The plaintiffs have appealed and assert error on the part of the trial court in taking from the jury the questions of (1) punitive damages, (2) damages to business reputation and credit, (3) damages for personal injuries allegedly sustained by Mr. Loucks, and (4) in disallowing certain costs claimed by plaintiffs.

* * *

The plaintiffs, as partners, sought recovery on behalf of the partnership of $402 allegedly wrongfully charged against the partnership account. This question was submitted to the jury, was decided in favor of the partnership, and against the defendants, and no appeal has been taken from the judgment entered on the verdict. They also sought recovery on behalf of the partnership of $5,000 for alleged damages to its credit, good reputation, and business standing in the community, $1,800 for its alleged loss of income, and $14,404 as punitive damages.

Each partner also sought recovery of $5,000 for alleged damages to his personal credit, good reputation and business standing. Mr. Martinez sought punitive damages individually in the amount of $10,000, and Mr. Loucks sought punitive damages individually in the amount of $60,000. Mr. Loucks also sought $25,000 by way of damages he allegedly sustained by reason of an ulcer which resulted from the wrongful acts of the defendants.

The parties have argued the case in their respective briefs and in their oral arguments upon the theory that the questions here involved, except for Point IV, which deals with the disallowance by the trial court of some claimed costs, are questions of the damages which can properly be claimed as a result of a wrongful dishonor by a bank of checks drawn by a customer or depositor on the bank, and of the sufficiency of the evidence offered by plaintiffs to support their claims for damages.

Both sides quote UCC § 4–402. * * *

It would appear that the first question to be resolved is that of the person, or persons, to whom a bank must respond in damages for a wrongful dishonor. Here, the account was a partnership account, and if there was in fact a wrongful dishonor of any checks, such were partnership checks.

We have adopted the Uniform Commercial Code in New Mexico. In UCC § 4–402 it is clearly stated that a bank "is liable to its customer." In UCC § 4–104(1)(e), entitled "Definitions and index of definitions" it is stated that:

"(1) In this article unless the context otherwise requires

"(e) 'Customer' means any person having an account with a bank or for whom a bank has agreed to collect items and includes a bank carrying an account with another bank; * * *"

This requires us to determine who is a "person" within the contemplation of this definition. Under part II, article I of the Uniform Commercial Code, entitled "General Definitions and Principles of Interpretation," we find the term "person" defined in § 1–201(30) as follows: " 'Person' includes an individual or an organization * * *."

Subsection (28) of the same section expressly includes a "partnership" as one of the legal or commercial entities embraced by the term "organization."

It would seem that logically the "customer" in this case to whom the bank was required to respond in damages for any wrongful dishonor was the partnership. The Uniform Commercial Code expressly regards a partnership as a legal entity. This is consistent with the ordinary mercantile conception of a partnership. * * *

The Uniform Partnership Act, which has been adopted in New Mexico and appears as chapter 66, article I, N.M.S.A.1953, recognizes that a partnership has a separate legal entity for at least some purposes. * * *

Suits may be brought in New Mexico by or against the partnership as such. * * * A partnership is a distinct legal entity to the extent that it may sue or be sued in the partnership name. National Surety Co. v. George E. Breece Lumber Co., 60 F.2d 847 (10th Cir. 1932).

* * *

The relationship, in connection with which the wrongful conduct of the bank arose, was the relationship between the bank and the partnership. The partnership was the customer, and any damages arising from the dishonor belonged to the partnership and not to the partners individually.

The damages claimed by Mr. Loucks as a result of the ulcer, which allegedly resulted from the wrongful acts of the defendants, are not consequential damages proximately caused by the wrongful dishonor as contemplated by § 4–402. In support of his right to recover for such claimed damages he relies upon the cases of Jones v. Citizens Bank of Clovis, 58 N.M. 48, 265 P.2d 366 and Weaver v. Bank of America Nat. Trust & Sav. Ass'n., 59 Cal.2d 428, 30 Cal.Rptr. 4, 380 P.2d 644. The California and New Mexico courts construed identical statutes in these cases. The New Mexico statute appeared as § 48–10–5, N.M.S.A.1953. This statute was repealed when the Uniform Commercial Code was adopted in 1961.

Assuming we were to hold that the decisions in those cases have not been affected by the repeal of the particular statutory provisions involved and the adoption of the Uniform Commercial Code, we are still compelled by our reasoning to reach the same result, because the plaintiffs in those cases were the depositor in the California case and the administratrix of the estate of the deceased depositor in the New Mexico case. In the present case, Mr. Loucks was not a depositor, as provided in the prior statute, nor a customer, as provided in our present statute. No duty was owed to him personally by reason of the debtor-creditor relationship between the bank and the partnership.

It is fundamental that compensatory damages are not recoverable unless they proximately result from some violation of a legally-recognized right of the person seeking the damages, whether such be a right in contract or tort. * * *

Insofar as the damage questions are concerned, we must still consider the claims for damages to the partnership. As above stated, the claim on behalf of the partnership for the recovery of the $402 was concluded by judgment for plaintiffs in this amount. This leaves (1) the claim of $5,000 for alleged damage to credit, reputation and business standing, (2) the claim of $1,800 for alleged loss of income, and (3) the claim of $14,404 as punitive damages.

The question with which we are first confronted is that of whether or not the customer, whose checks are wrongfully dishonored, may recover damages merely because of the wrongful dishonor. We understand the provisions of UCC § 4–402 to limit the damages to those proximately caused by the wrongful dishonor, and such includes any consequential damages so proximately caused. If the dishonor occurs through mistake, the damages are limited to actual damages proved.

It is pointed out in the comments to this section of the Uniform Commercial Code that:

" *   *   *

"This section rejects decisions which have held that where the dishonored item has been drawn by a merchant, trader or fiduciary he is defamed in his business, trade or profession by a reflection on his credit and hence that substantial damages may be awarded on the basis of defamation 'per se' without proof that damage has occurred. *   *   *" Uniform Commercial Code, § 4–402, Comment 3.

If we can say as a matter of law that the dishonor here occurred through mistake, then the damages would be limited to the "actual damages proved." Even if we are able to agree, as contended by defendants in their answer brief, that the defendants acted under a mistake of fact in " *   *   * that Mr. Kopp acting on behalf of the bank thought that the money was invested in the partnership and could be traced directly from Mr. Martinez to the L & M Paint and Body Shop," still defendants cannot rely on such mistake after both Mr. Martinez and Mr. Loucks informed them on March 15 and 18 that this was a personal obligation of Mr. Martinez and that the partnership had outstanding checks. At least it then became a question for the jury to decide whether or not defendants had wrongfully dishonored the checks through mistake.

The problem then resolves itself into whether or not the evidence offered and received, together with any evidence properly offered and improperly excluded, was sufficient to establish a question as to whether the partnership credit and reputation were proximately damaged by the wrongful dishonors. There was evidence that ten checks were dishonored, that one parts dealer thereafter refused to accept a partnership check and Mr. Loucks was required to go to the bank, cash the check, and then take the cash to the parts dealer in order to get the parts; that some persons who had previously accepted the partership checks now refused to accept them; that other places of business denied the partnership credit after the dishonors; and that a salesman, who had sold the partnership a map and for which he was paid by one of the dishonored checks, came to the partnership's place of business, and ripped the map off the wall because he had been given "a bad check for it."

This evidence was sufficient to raise a question of fact to be determined by the jury as to whether or not the partnership's credit had been damaged as a proximate result of the dishonors. This question should have been submitted to the jury.

Damages recoverable for injuries to credit as a result of a wrongful dishonor are more than mere nominal damages and are referred to as " * * * compensatory, general, substantial, moderate, or temperate, damages as would be fair and reasonable compensation for the injury which he [the depositor] must have sustained, but not harsh or inordinate damages. * * *" 5A Michie, Banks and Banking, § 243 at 576.

What are reasonable and temperate damages varies according to the circumstances of each case and the general extent to which it may be presumed the credit of the depositor would be injured. * * * The amount of such damages is to be determined by the sound discretion and dispassionate judgment of the jury. * * *

The next item of damages claimed on behalf of the partnership, which was taken from the jury, was the claim for loss of income in the amount of $1,800 allegedly sustained by the partnership as a result of the illness and disability of Mr. Loucks by reason of his ulcer. We are of the opinion that the trial court properly dismissed this claim for the announced reason that no substantial evidence was offered to support the claim, and for the further reason that the partnership had no legally-enforceable right to recover for personal injuries inflicted upon a partner.

Even if we were to assume that a tortious act had been committed by defendants which proximately resulted in the ulcer and the consequent personal injuries and disabilities of Mr. Loucks, the right to recover for such would be in him. An action for damages resulting from a tort can only be sustained by the person directly injured thereby, and not by one claiming to have suffered collateral or resulting injuries. * * *

As was stated by Mr. Justice Holmes in Robins Dry Dock & Repair Co. v. Flint, 275 U.S. 303, 48 S.Ct. 134, 72 L.Ed. 290:

> " * * * no authority need be cited to show that, as a general rule, at least, a tort to the person or property of one man does not make the tort-feasor liable to another merely because the injured person was under a contract with that other, unknown to the doer of the wrong. * * * The law does not spread its protection so far."

The last question of damages concerns the claim for punitive damages. The trial court dismissed this claim for the reason that he was convinced there was no evidence of willful or wanton conduct on the part of defendants. Punitive or exemplary damages may be awarded only when the conduct of the wrongdoer may be said to be maliciously intentional, fraudulent, oppressive, or committed recklessly or with a wanton disregard of the plaintiffs' rights. * * *

Malice as a basis for punitive damages means the intentional doing of a wrongful act without just cause or excuse. This means that the defendant not only intended to do the act which is ascertained to be wrongful, but that he knew it was wrong when he did it. * * *

Although, as expressed above, we are of the opinion that there was a jury question as to whether defendants acted under a mistake of fact in dishonoring the checks, we do not feel that the unpleasant or intemperate remark or two claimed to have been made by Mr. Kopp, and his conduct, described by Mr. Martinez as having "run us out of the bank more or less," are sufficient upon which an award of punitive damages could properly have been made. Thus, the trial court was correct in taking this claim from the jury.

* * *

It follows from what has been said that this cause must be reversed and remanded for a new trial solely upon the questions of whether or not the partnership credit was damaged as a proximate result of the dishonors, and, if so, the amount of such damages.

NOTES

1. *"Liable to its customer."* Since *Loucks*, interesting developments have taken place on the issue of who can recover for damages incurred from a wrongful dishonor of the check of a corporate customer. Obviously the corporation cannot suffer emotional distress or acquire ulcers resulting from the bank's mistake, much less the personal embarrassment and social ostracism stemming from being jailed for writing a check that was wrongfully dishonored. But in a closely held corporation these damages may well be sustained by the individuals who own and operate the business. In an era in which plaintiffs are successfully seeking more adequate awards for their injuries, it comes as no surprise that courts are finding ways of reading the term "customer" more flexibly or finding alternative bases for liability. In Kendall Yacht Corp. v. United California Bank, 50 Cal.App.3d 949, 123 Cal. Rptr. 848 (1975), Corporation was the depositor and Laurence and Linda Kendall were officers and prospective shareholders who personally guaranteed Corporation's debts to Bank. Corporation never issued stock and "it was, in effect, nothing but a transparent shell, having no viability as a separate and distinct legal entity." 123 Cal.Rptr. at 853. The court held that the Kendalls were "customers" within the meaning of § 4–402. "Thus it was entirely foreseeable that the dishonoring of the Corporation's check would reflect directly on the personal credit and reputation of the Kendalls and that they would suffer the adverse personal consequences which resulted when the Bank reneged on its commitments." 123 Cal.Rptr. at 853. The court allowed recovery by the Kendalls of damages for emotional distress under § 4–402.

Parrett v. Platte Valley State Bank & Trust Co., 236 Neb. 139, 459 N.W.2d 371 (1990), goes beyond *Kendall Yacht*. Parrett was the principal shareholder and president of the corporate customer. He personally participated in the business relationship between the corporate customer and the bank and entered into a personal guaranty for the corporation's obligations to the bank. When the bank wrongfully dishonored the corporate customer's check, Parrett was charged with felony theft and went to trial on the charge; at trial the charge was dismissed. Parrett sued for wrongful dishonor under § 4–402. The lower court sustained the bank's demurrer on the ground that Parrett was not the customer. The Supreme Court of Nebraska, relying on *Kendall Yacht*, reversed and said:

> As reflected by Parrett's petition, the parties' business relationship, which included Parrett's personal guaranty for P & P Machinery's obligations to the bank, was such that it was foreseeable that dishonoring the corporation's check would reflect directly on Parrett. This is borne out by the fact that a criminal charge based on the dishonored check was brought against Parrett, but was dismissed during Parrett's trial. Since the consequences of the wrongful dishonor fell upon Parrett, it would elevate form over substance to say that he was not the bank's "customer" within the meaning of § 4–402. This is not to say that in every case a corporate officer has a wrongful dishonor action against the depository bank on which the corporation's check has been drawn and later dishonored. However, in view of the facts of this case alleged in Parrett's petition, Parrett has a cause of action against the bank.

459 N.W.2d at 378. Although the majority opinion in *Parrett* purported to rely on *Kendall Yacht*, the dissent pointed out that the key factor in that case was that the corporation was not a separate legal entity; the decision was based on veil-piercing. But in *Parrett* the corporate customer was clearly a separate legal entity and had always been treated as such by the bank.

Another line of decisions has held fast to the view expressed in *Loucks* that only the corporate customer can proceed under § 4–402. See, e.g., Farmers Bank v. Sinwellan Corp., 367 A.2d 180 (Del.1976) (president of corporate customer denied right to sue under § 4–402 for damages resulting from a criminal action brought against him because of the dishonor). An approach to allowing insiders to recover in cases in which corporate checks have been dishonored even in jurisdictions taking the *Sinwellan* point of view is to contend that § 4–402 does not displace any cause of action that such an insider may have had against the bank at common law. § 1–103 and Comment 5 to § 4–402.

2. *Damages*. The common law rule was stated in 2 Morse, Banks and Banking 1007–1008 (6th ed., Voorhees, 1928): "[T]he better authority seems to be, that, even if * * * actual loss or injury is not shown, yet more than nominal damages shall be given. It can hardly be possible that a customer's check can be wrongfully refused payment without some impeachment of his credit, which must in fact be an actual injury, though he cannot from the nature of the case furnish independent distinct proof thereof. It is as in cases of libel and slander, which description of suit, indeed, it closely resembles, inasmuch as it is a practical slur upon the plaintiff's credit and repute in the business world. Special damage may be shown, if the plaintiff be able; but, if he be not able, the jury may nevertheless give such [temperate] damages as they conceive to be a reasonable compensation for that indefinite mischief which such an act must be assumed to have inflicted, according to the ordinary course of human events." At the behest of the American Bankers Association a number of states enacted a version of the following: "No bank shall be liable to a depositor because of the nonpayment through mistake or error, and without malice, of a check which should have been paid unless the depositor shall allege and prove actual damage by reason of such nonpayment and in such event the liability shall not exceed the amount of damage so proved." Cal.Civ.Code § 3320 (repealed).

The original version of what is now § 4–402(b) read: "A payor bank is liable to its customer for damages proximately caused by the wrongful dishonor of an item. When the dishonor occurs through mistake liability is limited to actual damages proved. If so proximately caused and proved damages may include damages for an arrest or prosecution of the customer or other consequential damages. Whether any consequential damages are proximately caused by the wrongful dishonor is a question of fact to be determined in each case." Comment 1 to § 4–402 contains a critique of this language and discusses the changes made in the revision.

Section 4–402(b) provides very broadly that a bank is liable for any damages proximately caused by a wrongful dishonor. Comment 1 to § 4–402 vaguely describes a customer's right to sue as a "statutory cause of action." The principal damages issue has been whether aggrieved customers can recover for emotional distress. Certainly a wrongful dishonor can proximately cause emotional distress and this type of damage is within the limitation in the second sentence of § 4–402(b) that the damages must be "actual." Although courts show their concern about the potential for abuse present in allowing damages for emotional distress, a number of courts have awarded customers damages for emotional distress in wrongful dishonor cases. The precedents are collected and discussed in Buckley v. Trenton Saving Fund Society, 111 N.J. 355,

544 A.2d 857 (1988). In that case the court held that the facts did not justify recovery for mental anguish and said:

> To some extent, slight emotional distress arising from the occasional dishonor of a check is one of the regrettable aggravations of living in today's society. See *Restatement,* [(Second) of Torts], § 436A comment b. Accordingly, we are reluctant to allow compensation for the intentional infliction of emotional distress when a bank wrongfully dishonors a check unless the bank's conduct is intentional, as well as reckless or outrageous, and the distress is severe or results in bodily injury. See *Hume,* 428 A.2d 966; *Restatement,* [(Second) of Torts], § 46. When those conditions are met, a customer should be compensated for the emotional distress that is caused by the wrongful dishonor of a check.

544 A.2d at 864. Comment 1 to § 4–402 points out in its last sentence that whether punitive damages are appropriate depends, under § 1–106, on non–UCC state law. The matter is discussed in *Buckley.*

E. UNCONSCIONABILITY AND GOOD FAITH AND FAIR DEALING

Courts have used the doctrines of unconscionability and good faith to police bank-customer agreements. Examples of this are found in *Perdue,* the following case, and in Best v. United States National Bank, Note 2 on p. 826. In the quest for legal alchemy— the transforming of a breach of contract into a tort yielding punitive damages—customers have contended that the special relationship between banks and their customers is a "quasi fiduciary" relationship which justifies tort damages if a breach of the implied covenant of good faith and fair dealing can be shown on the part of the bank. This issue is discussed in Copesky v. Superior Court, p. 826.

PERDUE v. CROCKER NATIONAL BANK

Supreme Court of California, 1985.
38 Cal.3d 913, 216 Cal.Rptr. 345, 702 P.2d 503.

BROUSSARD, JUSTICE.

Plaintiff filed this class action to challenge the validity of charges imposed by defendant Crocker National Bank for the processing of checks drawn on accounts without sufficient funds. (The parties refer to such checks as NSF checks and to the handling charge as an NSF charge.) He appeals from a judgment of the trial court entered after that court sustained defendant's general demurrer without leave to amend.

On July 3, 1978, plaintiff filed suit on behalf of all persons with checking accounts at defendant bank and a subclass of customers who have paid NSF charges to the bank. The complaint first alleges a contract under which the bank furnishes checking service in return for a maintenance charge. It then asserts that "It is the practice of defendants to impose and collect a unilaterally set charge for processing checks presented against plaintiffs' accounts when such accounts do not contain sufficient funds to cover the amount of the check." "Defendants have at various times unilaterally increased the NSF charge to an amount the defendants deemed appropriate, without reference to any criteria, and defendants imposed and collected the said increased amount without any explanation or justification by defendants to plaintiffs." At the time of filing of the suit, the charge was $6 for each NSF check, whether the check was honored or returned unpaid, even though "the actual cost incurred by the defendants in processing an NSF check is approximately $0.30."

The bank requires each depositor to sign a signature card which it uses "to determine and verify the authenticity of endorsements on checks". In extremely small (6 point) type, the signature card states that the undersigned depositors "agree with Crocker National Bank and with each other that * * * this account and all deposits therein shall be * * * subject to all applicable laws, to the Bank's present and future rules, regulations, practices and charges, and to its right of setoff for the obligations of any of us." The card does not identify the amount of the charge for NSF checks, and the bank does not furnish the depositor with a copy of the applicable bank rules and regulations.

On the basis of these allegations, plaintiff asserts * * * causes of action: (1) for a judicial declaration that the bank's signature card is not a contract authorizing NSF charges [and] (2) for a judicial declaration that such charges are oppressive and unconscionable * * *.

I. *Plaintiff's first cause of action: whether the signature card is a contract authorizing NSF charges.*

The complaint alleges that "The signature card prepared by the defendants does not identify the amount of any charge to be paid by the plaintiffs for processing NSF checks and is not an agreement for such payment. The card does not constitute mutual assent to NSF charges in any particular sum or at all and accordingly is not a contract conferring authority to do the acts complained of herein." "Based upon the language of the signature card, the plaintiffs believed and expected that the signature card was intended as a handwriting example for purposes of identification and verification only." Plaintiff therefore seeks a judicial declaration "as to whether the signature card is a valid or enforceable contract and * * * a lawful basis for the imposition of the NSF charge."

The cases unanimously agree that a signature card such as the Crocker Bank card at issue here is a contract. "The bank is authorized to honor withdrawals from an account on the signatures authorized by the signature card, which serves as a contract between the depositor and the bank for the handling of the account."

* * *

Plaintiff does not seriously dispute this proposition. His complaint alleges that the depositors "agreed to pay [the bank's] maintenance charge * * *" in return for checking privileges, and one could infer that they agreed to do so by affixing their signatures to the card. Complaints filed by plaintiff in an earlier action stated expressly that the signature card was a contract.

Plaintiff argues, however, that even if a signature card is a contract to establish a checking account, it is not a contract authorizing NSF charges. He contends that the contract is illusory because it permits the bank to set and change the NSF charges at its discretion, and without assent from the customer except such as may be inferred from the fact that the customer does not cancel his account after the bank posts notice of its rates.[6]

Plaintiff relies on the rule that "[a]n agreement that provides that the price to be paid, or other performance to be rendered, shall be left to the will and discretion of one of the parties is not enforceable." (Automatic Vending Co. v. Wisdom (1960) 182 Cal. App.2d 354, 357, 6 Cal.Rptr. 31.) That rule, however, applies only if the total discretion granted one party renders the contract lacking in consideration. (See ibid.) If there are reciprocal promises, as in the present case, the fact that the contract permits one party to set or change the price charged for goods or services does not render the contract illusory. Thus in Cal. Lettuce Growers v. Union Sugar Co. (1955) 45 Cal.2d 474, 289 P.2d 785, the court upheld a contract permitting the buyer of sugar beets to set the price to be paid. The buyer did not have arbitrary power, the court explained, because "where a contract confers on one party a discretionary power affecting the rights of the other, a duty is imposed to exercise that discretion in good faith and in accordance with fair dealing." * * * Likewise, "a contracting party's discretionary power to vary the price or other performance does not render the agreement illusory if the party's *actual* exercise of that power is reasonable."

* * *

We conclude that plaintiff here is not entitled to a judicial declaration that the bank's signature card is not a contract authorizing NSF charges. To the contrary, we hold as a matter of law that the card is a contract authorizing the bank to impose such

---

6. Financial Code section 865.4, subdivision (b)(1) requires a bank to give customers 15 days' notice of any change in charges imposed on bank accounts.

charges, subject to the bank's duty of good faith and fair dealing in setting or varying such charges. Plaintiff may, upon remand of this case, amend his complaint to seek a judicial declaration determining whether the charges actually set by the bank are consonant with that duty.

II. *Plaintiff's second cause of action: whether the bank's NSF charges are oppressive, unreasonable, or unconscionable.*

Plaintiff's second cause of action alleges that the signature card is drafted by defendant bank which enjoys a superior bargaining position by reason of its greater economic power, knowledge, experience and resources. Depositors have no alternative but to acquiesce in the relationship as offered by defendant or to accept a similar arrangement with another bank. The complaint alleges that the card is vague and uncertain, that it is unclear whether it is intended as an identification card or a contract, that it imposes no obligation upon the bank, and permits the bank to alter or terminate the relationship at any time.[8] It then asserts that "The disparity between the actual cost to defendants and the amount charged by defendants for processing an NSF check unreasonably and oppressively imposes excessive and unfair liability upon plaintiffs." Plaintiff seeks a declaratory judgment to determine the rights and duties of the parties.

Plaintiff's allegations point to the conclusion that the signature card, if it is a contract, is one of adhesion. The term contract of adhesion "signifies a standardized contract, which, imposed and drafted by the party of superior bargaining strength, relegates to the subscribing party only the opportunity to adhere to the contract or reject it." (Neal v. State Farm Ins. Co. (1961) 188 Cal. App.2d 690, 694, 10 Cal.Rptr. 781 * * * The signature card, drafted by the bank and offered to the customer without negotiation, is a classic example of a contract of adhesion; the bank concedes as much.

In Graham v. Scissor–Tail, Inc., 28 Cal.3d 807, 171 Cal.Rptr. 604, 623 P.2d 165, we observed that "To describe a contract as adhesive in character is not to indicate its legal effect * * *. [A] contract of adhesion is fully enforceable according to its terms [citations] unless certain other factors are present which, under established legal rules—legislative or judicial—operate to render it otherwise." (Pp. 819–820, 171 Cal.Rptr. 604, 623 P.2d 165, fn. omitted.) "Generally speaking," we explained, "there are two judicially imposed limitations on the enforcement of adhesion contracts or provisions thereof. The first is that such a contract or provision which does not fall within the reasonable expectations of the weaker or 'adhering' party will not be enforced against him.

8. The depositor also has the right to terminate the relationship at any time, but lacks the right asserted by the bank to alter the relationship without terminating it.

[Citations.] The second—a principle of equity applicable to all contracts generally—is that a contract or provision, even if consistent with the reasonable expectations of the parties, will be denied enforcement if, considered in its context, it is unduly oppressive or 'unconscionable.' " (P. 820, 171 Cal.Rptr. 604, 623 P.2d 165, fns. omitted.)

In 1979, the Legislature enacted Civil Code section 1670.5, which codified the established doctrine that a court can refuse to enforce an unconscionable provision in a contract. Section 1670.5 reads as follows: "(a) If the court as a matter of law finds the contract or any clause of the contract to have been unconscionable at the time it was made the court may refuse to enforce the contract, or it may enforce the remainder of the contract without the unconscionable clause, or it may so limit the application of any unconscionable clause as to avoid any unconscionable result. [¶] (b) When it is claimed or appears to the court that the contract or any clause thereof may be unconscionable the parties shall be afforded a reasonable opportunity to present evidence as to its commercial setting, purpose, and effect to aid the court in making the determination."

In construing this section, we cannot go so far as plaintiff, who contends that even a conclusory allegation of unconscionability requires an evidentiary hearing. We do view the section, however, as legislative recognition that a claim of unconscionability often cannot be determined merely by examining the face of the contract, but will require inquiry into its setting, purpose, and effect.

Plaintiff bases his claim of unconscionability on the alleged 2,000 percent differential between the NSF charge of $6 and the alleged cost to the bank of $0.30.[11] The parties have cited numerous cases on whether the price of an item can be so excessive as to be unconscionable. The cited cases are from other jurisdictions, often from trial courts or intermediate appellate courts, and none is truly authoritative on the issue. Taken together, however, they provide a useful guide to analysis of the claim that a price is so excessive as to be unconscionable.

To begin with, it is clear that the price term, like any other term in a contract, may be unconscionable. * * * Allegations that the price exceeds cost or fair value, standing alone, do not state a cause of action. * * * Instead, plaintiff's case will turn

---

11. The bank's briefs claim the alleged $0.30 cost is too low and plaintiff's briefs admit that a higher figure, but still $1 or less, might be more accurate. We do not, however, find in plaintiff's briefs a sufficiently clear concession to enable us to depart from the general principle that, in reviewing a judgment after the sustaining of a general demurrer without leave to amend, we must assume the truth of all material factual allegations in the complaint. (Alcorn v. Anbro Engineering, Inc., supra, 2 Cal.3d 493, 496, 86 Cal.Rptr. 88, 468 P.2d 216.)

upon further allegations and proof setting forth the circumstances of the transaction.

The courts look to the basis and justification for the price (cf. A & M Produce Co. v. FMC Corp., supra, 135 Cal.App.3d 473, 487, 186 Cal.Rptr. 114), including "the price actually being paid by * * * other similarly situated consumers in a similar transaction." (Bennett v. Behring Corp., supra, 466 F.Supp. 689, 697, italics omitted.) The cases, however, do not support defendant's contention that a price equal to the market price cannot be held unconscionable. While it is unlikely that a court would find a price set by a freely competitive market to be unconscionable (see Bradford v. Plains Cotton Cooperative Assn. (10th Cir.1976) 539 F.2d 1249, 1255 [cotton futures]), the market price set by an oligopoly should not be immune from scrutiny. Thus courts consider not only the market price, but also the cost of the goods or services to the seller (Frostifresh Corporation v. Reynoso (N.Y. Dist.Ct.1966) 52 Misc.2d 26, 274 N.Y.S.2d 757; Toker v. Westerman (1970) 113 N.J.Super. 452, 274 A.2d 78), the inconvenience imposed on the seller (see Merrel v. Research & Data, Inc., supra, 589 P.2d 120, 123), and the true value of the product or service (American Home Improvements, Inc. v. MacIver (1964) 105 N.H. 435, 201 A.2d 886, 889).

In addition to the price justification, decisions examine what Justice Weiner in *A & M Produce* called the "procedural aspects" of unconscionability. (See *A & M Produce Co.,* supra, 135 Cal.App. 3d at p. 489, 186 Cal.Rptr. 114.) Cases may turn on the absence of meaningful choice (Patterson v. Walker–Thomas Furniture Co., supra, 277 A.2d 111, 113 and cases there cited), the lack of sophistication of the buyer (compare Geldermann & Co., Inc. v. Lane Processing, Inc. (8th Cir.1975) 527 F.2d 571, 576 [relief denied to sophisticated investor] with Frostifresh Corporation v. Reynoso, supra, 274 N.Y.S.2d 757 [relief granted to unsophisticated buyers]) and the presence of deceptive practices by the seller (ibid.; Vom Lehn v. Astor Art Galleries, Ltd., supra, 380 N.Y.S.2d 532).

Applying this analysis to our review of the complaint at hand, we cannot endorse defendant's argument that the $6 charge is so obviously reasonable that no inquiry into its basis or justification is necessary.[12] In 1978 $6 for processing NSF checks may not

---

12. In Jacobs v. Citibank, N.A. (1984) 61 N.Y.2d 869, 474 N.Y.S.2d 464, 462 N.E.2d 1182, the New York Court of Appeals upheld a summary judgment for defendant bank in a suit attacking NSF check charges. In rejecting the claim that such charges were unconscionable, the court said that "[p]laintiffs have failed to show that they were deprived of a meaningful choice of banks with which they could do business and that the terms of these agreements with defendant were unreasonably favorable to the bank." (P. 872, 474 N.Y.S.2d 464, 462 N.E.2d 1182.)

While the New York court ruled on a motion for summary judgment, we rule upon a demurrer, and look only to plaintiff's allegations, not to the proof he had advanced to support those alle-

seem exorbitant,[13] but price alone is not a reliable guide. Small charges applied to a large volume of transactions may yield a sizeable sum. The complaint asserts that the cost of processing NSF checks is only $0.30 per check, which means that a $6 charge would produce a 2,000 percent profit; even at the higher cost estimate of $1 a check mentioned in plaintiff's petition for hearing, the profit is 600 percent.[14] Such profit percentages may not be automatically unconscionable, but they indicate the need for further inquiry.[15]

Other aspects of the transaction confirm plaintiff's right to a factual hearing. Defendant presents the depositor with a document which serves at least in part as a handwriting exemplar, and whose contractual character is not obvious. The contractual language appears in print so small that many could not read it. State law may impose obligations on the bank (e.g., the duty to honor a check when the account has sufficient funds (Allen v. Bank of America, supra, 58 Cal.App.2d 124, 127, 136 P.2d 345)), but so far as the signature card drafted by the bank is concerned, the bank has all the rights and the depositor all the duties. The signature card provides that the depositor will be bound by the bank's rules, regulations, practices and charges, but the bank does not furnish the depositor with a copy of the relevant documents. The bank reserves the power to change its practices and fees at any time, subject only to the notice requirements of state law.

In short, the bank structured a totally one-sided transaction. The absence of equality of bargaining power, open negotiation, full disclosure, and a contract which fairly sets out the rights and duties of each party demonstrates that the transaction lacks those checks and balances which would inhibit the charging of unconscionable fees. In such a setting, plaintiff's charge that the bank's NSF fee is exorbitant, yielding a profit far in excess of cost, cannot

gations. Plaintiff here has alleged that the charges imposed by defendant bank were excessive, and that similar arrangements would be imposed by other banks. Such allegations, which we must assume to be true, distinguish the New York decision.

13. Defendant cites Merrel v. Research & Data, Inc., supra, 589 P.2d 120, which held a $5 fee imposed by merchants for NSF checks was a "modest" amount (p. 123) and not unconscionable. NSF checks pose a substantial inconvenience to a seller, who has been deceived into an involuntary extension of credit to a customer whose credit standing may not be very good. A bank, however, is not deceived. It checks the balance of the account, and may reject any overdraft. A fee reasonable to compensate the merchant for

the cost, inconvenience, and risk of an NSF check may be excessive if exacted by a bank.

14. The complaint does not state the market price for the service of processing NSF checks, although one might infer it is similar to defendant's price since plaintiff alleges that if he did not contract with defendant, he would be "forced to accept a similar arrangement with other banks." The complaint does not set a figure for the "fair" or "true" value or worth of the service.

15. We observe that the bank charges the same fee whether it honors or rejects an NSF check. The fee, consequently, cannot be intended as compensation for the credit risk arising from paying such a check, or for the interest on the amount loaned.

be dismissed on demurrer.   Under Civil Code section 1670.5, the parties should be afforded a reasonable opportunity to present evidence as to the commercial setting, purpose, and effect of the signature card and the NSF charge in order to determine whether that charge is unconscionable.

* * *

NOTES

1.   The court reached the decision in *Perdue* in the face of a regulation promulgated by the Comptroller of the Currency stating:

"(b) Establishment of deposit account service charges, and the amounts thereof, is a business decision to be made by each bank according to sound banking judgment and federal standards of safety and soundness.   In establishing deposit account service charges, the bank may consider, but is not limited to considering: [¶] (1) Costs incurred by the bank, plus a profit margin, in providing the service; [¶] (2) The deterrence of misuse by customers of banking services; [¶] (3) The enhancement of the competitive position of the bank in accord with the bank's marketing strategy; [¶] (4) Maintenance of the safety and soundness of the institution.

"(c) A national bank may establish any deposit account service charge pursuant to paragraphs (a) and (b) of this section notwithstanding any state laws which prohibit the charge assessed or limit or restrict the amount of that charge. Such state laws are preempted by the comprehensive federal statutory scheme governing the deposit-taking function of national banks."

216 Cal.Rptr. at 360.   The court stated:

We conclude that the Comptroller's assertion that state laws regulating service charges are preempted by a "comprehensive federal statutory scheme governing the deposit-taking function of national banks" (12 C.F.R. § 7.8000) is not a reasonable interpretation of the controlling statutes.   It is not an attempt to interpret the language of the statute, fill in the gaps in the statutory coverage, or to explain how the Comptroller will exercise his discretion.   Instead, the regulation, insofar as it claims federal preemption, represents legislation of far-reaching character and effect, of a type never considered by Congress, which would radically alter the respective roles of the states and the Comptroller in the regulation of bank-depositor contracts.   Such legislation cannot be enacted in the guise of statutory interpretation.

216 Cal.Rptr. at 365.

2. In Best v. United States National Bank, 739 P.2d 554 (Ore. 1987), customers brought a class action against the bank challenging the validity of the bank's service charge for processing NSF checks. The customers had signed an "account agreement" when opening their account which stated: "This account is subject to Bank service charges existing at any time." The parties agreed that "service charges" in the agreement included NSF fees. The practice of the bank's employees was not to inform customers of the existence or amount of NSF fees and these fees were not specifically set out in the agreement. Between 1973 and 1979, the bank increased its NSF fee from $3 to $5; these amounts were similar to fees charged by other banks. In their suit the customers contended the fees were unconscionable and were in breach of the bank's obligation of good faith. The court sustained the lower courts summary judgment in favor of the bank on the unconscionability claim but reversed on the good faith claim. The court concluded that if a party has a contractual right to specify a price term, as the bank had here, the obligation of good faith imposes on the bank the duty to set the price within the reasonable expectations of the customer. But the court inferred that the reasonable expectations of the customer in this case were that the NSF fee would not exceed an amount covering check processing costs, an allowance for overhead costs, and the bank's ordinary profit margin. Since there was evidence that the bank's NSF fees greatly exceeded this amount, the court further inferred that the bank's intent was to use the fee to discourage its customers from writing NSF checks. Because there were genuine issues of fact with respect to the good faith claim, the trial court erred in granting the bank summary judgment on that claim.

COPESKY v. SUPERIOR COURT

Court of Appeal, Fourth District, 1991.
229 Cal.App.3d 678, 280 Cal.Rptr. 338.

FROEHLICH, ASSOCIATE JUSTICE.

This petition seeks review of the sustaining without leave to amend of a demurrer to one cause of action of petitioner's complaint. The cause so terminated was entitled, and is properly characterized as, "Breach of the Implied Covenant of Good Faith and Fair Dealing." By means of this cause of action the petitioner sought to recover tort damages because of the real party in interest bank's wrongful cashing of checks drawn without proper signature. The allegations of the complaint were obviously drawn so as to bring the action within the rationale of this court's decision in Commercial Cotton Co. v. United California Bank (1985) 163 Cal.App.3d 511, 209 Cal.Rptr. 551 (hereinafter *Commercial Cotton*). In argument before the superior court, counsel for petitioner contended the case was controlled by *Commercial Cot-*

ton, and indeed that his case was "a mirror image of *Commercial Cotton.*"

The trial court responded "*Commercial Cotton* is flat out wrong * * *. I don't think our appellate court is going to uphold the decision they took in *Commercial Cotton* bank in 1985. I don't think they would do that in this case." The principal category of argument in the petitioner's brief is entitled "The sole issue is whether *Commercial Cotton* remains viable." While this pithy characterization of the issue is perhaps more abbreviated than would become an appellate court, it accurately goes right to the point.

*   *   *

1. *Factual and Procedural Background*

Petitioner is an individual doing business as Torrey Pines Chiropractic Clinic. Petitioner maintained an ordinary commercial checking account with real party in interest bank. Checks from the account were authorized upon the signature only of petitioner or his wife. Over a period of some 18 months, from March 1987 through September 1988, a number of checks with forged signatures were presented to the bank; all checks were in denominations under $1,000. The forgeries were accomplished by petitioner's bookkeeper, using his signature stamp. Petitioner's failure to discover the forgeries over the period of 18 months was the result of the absence of his wife from the business for that period of time, the wife being the person who customarily supervised the bookkeeper's activities. The total of improperly withdrawn funds was $32,913.

The bank was negligent in cashing the checks by failing to require identification from the bookkeeper when the checks were presented, and also by accepting checks executed with a signature stamp rather than manual signature. Petitioner alleged that the checks constituted obvious forgeries which the bank reasonably should have noted. When petitioner reported the forgeries to the bank it refused to redeposit the lost funds, asserting a one-year statute of limitations on petitioner's claim as well as the contention that the bank had not been negligent in failing to discover the forgeries. Each of these defenses, petitioner contends, was without merit and constituted "stonewalling."

In addition to stating causes of action for breach of the contractual terms of the deposit agreement and for negligence, petitioner stated a "textbook" cause of action for "breach of the implied covenant of good faith and fair dealing." [2] The principal allegations of this cause of action are as follows:

---

2. As can be seen from our review of Wallis v. Superior Court (1984) 160 Cal. App.3d 1109, footnote 7, 207 Cal.Rptr. 123, the pleading tracks the several "factors" identified in *Wallis* which give rise to the "special relationship" affording relief in tort for breach of the implied covenant of good faith and fair

Petitioner and the bank, in entering upon the contract were in inherently unequal bargaining positions and the bank dictated the terms of the contract;

Petitioner's motivation for entering into the agreement was strictly nonprofit and was to secure "peace of mind, security and protection of * * * funds;"

Ordinary contract damages would be inadequate;

Petitioner was particularly vulnerable because his funds were placed at the disposal of the bank, and a "special quasi-fiduciary relationship existed between [petitioner] and [bank]" which resulted in a duty of good faith and fair dealing;

This duty was breached when the bank refused to recredit the account but instead interposed "stonewalling" defenses without any reasonable belief in their validity;

This intentionally tortious action on the bank's part warrants the imposition of punitive damages.

A general demurrer was interposed only as to the "breach of the implied covenant" cause of action. As noted above, the demurrer was sustained without leave to amend, the court concluding that as a matter of law the bank-depositor contractual status revealed by the pleadings could not give rise to a relationship between the parties sufficient to support the tort cause of action for breach of the implied covenant.

2. Revisitation of Commercial Cotton

Since everyone involved in this case (the court below and all counsel) agree that its disposition depends upon the continued viability of the rule in *Commercial Cotton*, we are perhaps well advised at the outset to summarize that case. *Commercial Cotton* was decided by a unanimous panel of this court in 1985. As asserted by counsel for petitioner, the facts of *Commercial Cotton* bear considerable similarity to the facts of this case. The plaintiff, a commercial enterprise, maintained an ordinary checking account with defendant bank. Some of the plaintiff's blank checks were lost, and the loss was reported to the bank. Later one of the checks was presented to the bank with forged signatures, and paid. When the loss was discovered some time later by the depositor, demand for repayment was made. The bank refused to cover the loss, relying upon the defense of the one-year statute of limitations as well as a claim of comparative negligence. (Id., 163 Cal.App.3d at p. 514, 209 Cal.Rptr. 551.)

dealing. As such, the pleading is an excellent example of a statement of conclusions of law rather than allegations of fact, and no doubt would have been subject to a special demurrer. (See 4 Witkin, Cal.Procedure (3d ed. 1985) Pleading § 332, pp. 381–383.) However, the attack on the complaint was by way of general demurrer, and both we and the trial judge therefore have passed over the rather obvious attempt to fit the individual facts of this case into a convenient mold of existing case precedent.

Unlike our case, *Commercial Cotton* went to trial, and the presentation to the appellate court was by way of ordinary appeal from a jury verdict in favor of the plaintiff. The portion of the appeal of interest to us is that which dealt with the breach of the covenant of good faith and fair dealing. The trial court permitted this claim to be presented to the jury, and the jury awarded $100,000 in punitive damages based thereon.

In its review of the factual background of the case, our court was particularly impressed with the shallow nature of the defenses asserted by the bank. Some eleven days before the final letter of denial from the bank's general counsel, the Supreme Court in Sun 'N Sand, Inc. v. United California Bank (1978) 21 Cal.3d 671, 699, 148 Cal.Rptr. 329, 582 P.2d 920 had specifically ruled that the three-year statute of limitations, rather than the one-year statute, was applicable for a claim such as that of *Commercial Cotton.*

Our court found it "inexplicable that [the bank's] general counsel could have been unaware of the Supreme Court's holding affecting the bank for which he was general counsel at the time he wrote the * * * letter." (*Commercial Cotton,* 163 Cal.App.3d at p. 515, 209 Cal.Rptr. 551.) Our court also found the contention of contributory negligence on the part of the depositor to be spurious, since whatever negligence was involved in failing promptly to note the forged check when it was returned to the depositor had no causal relationship to its original negligent cashing. It is fair to say, therefore, that our court regarded the bank's refusal to reimburse its depositor and its continued assertions of spurious defenses, right through a jury trial and to appeal, as an example of the most egregious of "stonewalling" tactics. Although not mentioned in the opinion, the fact that the dispute involved a mere $4,000 adds practical argument to the conclusion that the bank's position was completely unreasonable.

In its discussion of the tort of breach of the covenant of good faith and fair dealing, the *Commercial Cotton* court acknowledged the contention that the tort existed, outside the insurance context, only as to parties in a "special relationship." It cited Egan v. Mutual of Omaha Ins. Co. (1979) 24 Cal.3d 809, 820, 169 Cal.Rptr. 691, 620 P.2d 141 (hereinafter *Egan*) for the proposition that this relationship (at least in the insurance context) is characterized by "elements of public interest, adhesion, and fiduciary responsibility." (*Commercial Cotton,* 163 Cal.App.3d at p. 516, 209 Cal.Rptr. 551.) It was noted that in the then very recent Seaman's Direct Buying Service, Inc. v. Standard Oil Co. (1984) 36 Cal.3d 752, 206 Cal.Rptr. 354, 686 P.2d 1158 (hereinafter *Seaman's*), the Supreme Court had found it unnecessary to determine how far, if at all, the doctrine should extend to ordinary commercial contracts.

The court then ventured into what the Supreme Court had identified as uncharted seas, and found that the assertion by the bank of spurious defenses to the claim was an "unjustifiable, stonewalling effort to prevent an innocent depositor from recovering money," and constituted evidence adequate to support a jury finding of tortious breach of the covenant. (*Commercial Cotton*, 163 Cal.App.3d at p. 516, 209 Cal.Rptr. 551.)

The court reached the conclusion that the tort in question, originating in insurance relationships, could be applied in a banking context because "banking and insurance have much in common, both being highly regulated industries performing vital public services substantially affecting the public welfare." (*Commercial Cotton* at p. 516, 209 Cal.Rptr. 551.) The court then went on to publish the famous quote, much discussed and disputed thereafter, that "The relationship of bank to depositor is at least quasi-fiduciary." This statement rounded out the three findings posited in the *Egan* formula for imposition of the special duty: (1) elements of public interest, (2) adhesion contractual relationship, and (3) fiduciary responsibility.

Our digest of the rule of *Commercial Cotton* might be stated as follows: The ordinary relationship between commercial bank and its depositor is such as to impose upon the bank a duty, derived from the obligation of good faith and fair dealing implied in all contracts, to refrain from intentional breaches of contract and from interjection of spurious and bad faith defenses to contract claims, which duty if breached will give rise to an action in tort with attendant entitlement to punitive damages.

3. *Evolution of the Tort of Breach of the Obligation of Good Faith and Fair Dealing*

(a) Early Development in Insurance and Wrongful Termination Cases

In order to weigh the current value of the rule of *Commercial Cotton* we are required to review the history and evolution of the tort therein described. We do so briefly, recognizing that this is a field several times previously plowed by other jurists and by academics (some of which are cited hereunder) and hence neither merits nor requires extended comment here.

The existence of implied covenants of good faith and fair dealing in all contracts has long been the law. As stated in Universal Sales Corp. v. Cal. etc. Mfg. Co. (1942) 20 Cal.2d 751, 771, 128 P.2d 665: "In every contract there is an implied covenant that neither party shall do anything which will have the effect of destroying or injuring the right of the other party to receive the fruits of the contract, which means that in every contract there exists an implied covenant of good faith and fair dealing."

Reliance upon the covenant to support damages in excess of ordinary contract damages first arose in the insurance context. Initially supporting damages in excess of policy limits for wrongful refusal to settle a claim (Comunale v. Traders & General Ins. Co. (1958) 50 Cal.2d 654, 328 P.2d 198; Crisci v. Security Ins. Co. (1967) 66 Cal.2d 425, 58 Cal.Rptr. 13, 426 P.2d 173), the concept was later expanded to embrace general tort damages for bad faith refusal to pay a claim (Gruenberg v. Aetna Ins. Co. (1973) 9 Cal.3d 566, 575, 108 Cal.Rptr. 480, 510 P.2d 1032). The rationale for imposing tort liability in the insurance context was explained and justified in *Egan.* Emphasized were the nonprofit objectives of the insured in seeking protection and peace of mind (id., 24 Cal.3d at p. 819, 169 Cal.Rptr. 691, 620 P.2d 141), that insurance companies provided vital services quasi-public in nature (id. at p. 820, 169 Cal.Rptr. 691, 620 P.2d 141) and that the insurance relationship had a fiduciary quality (*ibid.*).

The other arena in which recovery in tort for breach of the covenant of good faith and fair dealing was sanctioned, pre-*Seaman's,* was that of employment termination. Cleary v. American Airlines, Inc. (1980) 111 Cal.App.3d 443, 168 Cal.Rptr. 722 is a clear statement of the proposition that an implied covenant of continued employment can be found in certain otherwise undefined employment circumstances, and that a breach of this covenant by a discharge without cause can give rise to tort damages. (Id. at pp. 454–456, 168 Cal.Rptr. 722.)

* * *

[The court discusses Foley v. Interactive Data Corp., 47 Cal.3d 654, 254 Cal.Rptr. 211 (1988), in which the Supreme Court redirected the law of good faith and fair dealing in holding that there was no special relationship in employment contracts comparable to that in the insurance context. Eds.]

The most directly applicable current authority is Price v. Wells Fargo Bank (1989) 213 Cal.App.3d 465, 261 Cal.Rptr. 735 (hereinafter *Price*). In that case an action was brought against the bank by a commercial borrower, who complained that the bank's refusal to extend the terms of loans caused forced liquidation of assets and financial loss. One of the principal causes of action (dismissed on summary judgment by the trial court) was an action in tort for breach of the implied covenant, brought specifically in reliance upon the authority of *Commercial Cotton.* The court rejected the decision and reasoning of *Commercial Cotton,* declined seriously to attempt application of the *Wallis* factors to the case, and held rather simply that no contractual implication can be made in a bank's lending contract which precludes it from foreclosing in accordance with the terms of the contract. Referring to *Foley,* the *Price* court stated that "The impact of the *Foley* decision cannot be assessed with certainty [but] [t]he decision surely precludes the sort of loose extension of tort recovery, based on 'quasi-fiduciary' relationship, sanctioned in [*Commercial Cotton*] * * *." (*Price*, 213 Cal.App.3d at p. 478, 261 Cal.Rptr. 735.)

Coming finally to the facts of our case: We must conclude that the application of the *Wallis* five points do not indicate a "special relationship," and hence an action in tort by the depositor cannot be stated for simple breach of the deposit contract. Looking to the *Wallis* criteria, we believe that a commercial entity and a bank are not ordinarily in inherently unequal bargaining positions. There is nothing in these pleadings, nor is there any aspect of common banking transactions, which suggests to us that banks in general are, or this bank in particular was, in a superior bargaining position. Banks in our society are commonly most competitive. That the bank offers a standard product certainly cannot make its bargaining position "unequal."

Referring to the second *Wallis* criterion, the motivation for entering into the contract, we can conceive of very few contracts which are more profit-oriented than the commercial bank account of a chiropractor. Obviously one chooses a bank in which to deposit his money in part because of the apparent security of the institution; this does not mean, however, that the motivation for the transaction is "peace of mind" in the sense that such motivation inheres in an insurance contract.[13]

The third *Wallis* factor relates to damages. It is true that damages to be recovered for suing a bank for cashing a forged check may be inadequate. This is not because of anything special about banks or commercial deposits, however. The problem with suing banks is the same problem that besets the typical judicial remedy for all commercial breaches. Unless one has included an attorney fee clause in the contract, recovery of the fees and practical costs of litigation is not possible. No one, therefore, involved in commercial litigation these days can be made completely whole. *Wallis* was not talking about this defect in our jurisprudential system—it had to do instead with the peculiar loss associated with denial of payment of insurance proceeds or, as in *Wallis*, the peremptory interruption of monthly termination payments to an aged retired employee.

---

13. We follow, here, the line of reasoning developed in *Foley* 47 Cal.3d at pages 692–693, 254 Cal.Rptr. 211, 765 P.2d 373. The employment relation was distinguished from the insurance relation by noting the unique economic dilemma faced by the insured whose insurer refuses in bad faith to pay policy benefits. The insured has lost the very benefit for which he contracted, and is not in a position to seek alternative relief from competitors. The employee, however, has not bargained for any similar type of "protection," and the breach of the employment contract causes damages essentially similar to those resulting from breaches of other kinds of contractual agreements—such as the refusal to honor a contract for the supply of goods vital to a small dealer's business. We conclude that the breach of a banker's agreement with its depositor similarly results in damage typical to all commercial contracts.

The fourth and fifth *Wallis* criteria identify special vulnerability of one party of which the other party is aware. One can posit unusual banking arrangements whereby minors or other dependent people specifically inform the bank of their complete dependence upon the liquidity of their bank account, in which case these criteria might be satisfied. The ordinary bank checking account is not, however, of this nature. We note in this case that the account was so fluid its owners did not notice the theft of some $32,000 for over a period of 18 months. Anyone who has lost money because of breach of a commercial obligation is going to consider himself damaged, and the continuing state of loss causes such person to experience a certain feeling of vulnerability. As with the damage issue, however, this is a problem common to all commercial transactions, not different in the typical bank-depositor transaction, and certainly not the sort of vulnerability envisaged by the *Wallis* criteria.

We should refer also to the specific factors cited in *Commercial Cotton* as promotive of treating the banking industry the same as the insurance industry in terms of the implied covenant tort applicability. The *Commercial Cotton* court did not utilize the *Wallis* factors, but instead relied upon those factors stated in *Egan* and *Seaman's:* public interest, adhesion, and fiduciary responsibility. We have discounted, above, the concept that the deposit contract is an adhesion contract. We have serious doubts that the status of banking as an industry important to the public welfare should have an effect upon the issue before us. As noted in Comment, Fiduciary Controversy: Injection of Fiduciary Principles Into the Bank–Depositor and Bank–Borrower Relationship (1987) 20 Loyola L.A.L.Rev. 816–817, "The concept of 'affected with the public interest' can be applied to common carriers, theaters, restaurants, inns/motels, food retailers, garbage collectors, doctors and landlords. The list is virtually endless. Therefore, it would be absurd to single out banks as having a 'special relationship' with its customers merely because banking is 'affected with the public interest.' " (Fns. omitted.)

Of most concern, however, is the statement made in *Commercial Cotton*, 163 Cal.App.3d at page 516, 209 Cal.Rptr. 551 that "[t]he relationship of bank to [its] depositor is at least quasi-fiduciary." This statement is severely criticized in *Price*, 213 Cal. App.3d at page 476, 261 Cal.Rptr. 735, and its assertion countered by the citation of well-established authority for the proposition that the relationship between a bank and its depositor is *not* a fiduciary relationship, but that of debtor-creditor. (Morse v. Crocker National Bank (1983) 142 Cal.App.3d 228, 232, 190 Cal. Rptr. 839; Downey v. Humphreys (1951) 102 Cal.App.2d 323, 332, 227 P.2d 484, and a case contemporaneous with Commercial Cotton: Lawrence v. Bank of America (1985) 163 Cal.App.3d 431, 209 Cal.Rptr. 541.) We note that the statement in *Commercial*

Cotton was made without benefit of citation of authority. Presuming that the court was aware of Morse v. Crocker National Bank, supra, Downey v. Humphreys, supra, and other authorities which had established the bank-depositor relationship as merely debtor-creditor, and that the *Commercial Cotton* court did *not* purport to classify the relationship actually as "fiduciary," we are led to a search for what might have been meant by the phrase "quasi-fiduciary." In Garner, A Dictionary of Modern Legal Usage (1987, Oxford Univ. Press) page 457, "quasi" is defined as "seeming or seemingly; in the nature of; nearly," and its use demeaned by a quote from Corbin on Contracts (1963 ed.) section 19, pages 45–46 that "the term *quasi* is introduced as a weasel word that sucks all the meaning of the word that follows it." (Italics in original.)

We conclude both from the manner of use and the omission of any citation that when the court in *Commercial Cotton* used "quasi-fiduciary" it intended *not* to question prior authority establishing that banks in ordinary deposit relationships are not fiduciaries, but sought only a shorthand phrase to describe attributes in the relationship which are similar to *some* of the attributes of a true fiduciary relationship. The court was, simply, grappling with the criteria described in *Egan* and *Seaman's* (elements of public interest, adhesion and fiduciary responsibility) for establishing "special relationship," and noting that some contractual features of a banking relationship establish elements of reliance and trust which "seem like" or are "in the nature of" (to refer to our dictionary definition) obligations resulting from a true fiduciary relationship.

In light of the reasoning of *Foley,* we are convinced *Commercial Cotton*'s characterization of a bank-depositor relationship as quasi-fiduciary is now inappropriate. While some aspects of that relationship may resemble aspects of the insurer-insured relationship, there are equally marked differences between those relationships. Since appending the quasi-fiduciary label to the ordinary bank-depositor relationship runs counter to both pre- and post-*Commercial Cotton* authority, and such a label provides no analytical framework against which to evaluate (after *Foley*) the propriety of extending tort remedies for contractual breaches, we no longer approve the denomination of the ordinary bank-depositor relationship as quasi-fiduciary in character.

Conclusion and Disposition

It is thus our conclusion that banks, in general and in this case, are not fiduciaries for their depositors; and that the bank-depositor relationship is not a "special relationship" under the *Wallis* test, or any other test, such as to give rise to tort damages when an implied contractual covenant of good faith is broken. We are therefore forced to acknowledge that our decision in *Commercial Cotton,* while in its time seemingly in harmony with the direction of the Supreme Court, turned out, after *Foley,* to be misdirected. We acknowledge the accuracy of *Price,* and Careau & Co. v. Security Pacific Business Credit, Inc., supra, 222 Cal.App. 3d 1371, 272 Cal.Rptr. 387 in their characterization of the ordinary bank-customer relationship as *not* a special relationship giving rise to tort remedies when the bank unreasonably, and even in bad faith, denies liability on a contract or interposes spurious defenses. The third cause of action in this case, therefore, was defective and the trial court was correct in sustaining the general demurrer to it. The petition is denied. Real party in interest is entitled to costs. (Union Trust Co. v. Superior Court (1939) 13 Cal.2d 541, 543, 90 P.2d 582.)

Part III

SALES

Chapter 11

CONTRACT FORMATION AND MODIFICATION

A. THE BATTLE OF THE FORMS

Suppose Seller sent Buyer a letter soliciting orders for widgets at $10 apiece. No terms of sale were stated. Buyer sends Seller an order form ordering 1,000 widgets at the $10 price. Buyer's form stated that delivery was to be made within 30 days of Seller's acceptance of the order and that payment was to be made within 90 days of delivery. By return mail Seller sent its form which stated, "We confirm sale to you of 1,000 widgets at a price of $10 each. Terms of sale are as follows: Delivery within 30 days after the date of this confirmation. Payment within 10 days of delivery."

Have Seller and Buyer made a contract of sale? If a contract has been made, what are its terms?

Under traditional common-law analysis no contract of sale was made when Seller sent its confirmation to Buyer because Seller did not accept Buyer's offer. Seller's confirmation agreed with Buyer's offer as to price, amount, and time of delivery, but it disagreed with respect to time of payment. Under the traditional common-law "mirror image rule" an acceptance is not effective to form a contract unless it agrees with all of the terms of the offer. Thus, Seller's confirmation is treated as a rejection of Buyer's offer and as a counteroffer to Buyer. There are two effects of this rule. Unless Buyer accepts the counteroffer there is no contract and neither party is obliged to perform. The second effect occurs if the parties perform in spite of the difference in the terms of sale stated by each party. Suppose Buyer does not object to Seller's variance of the terms of Buyer's offer, Seller delivers the widgets, and Buyer accepts them. Buyer's acceptance of the goods is treated as an acceptance of Seller's counteroffer and a contract results. The terms of the contract are the terms of Seller's counteroffer. In this kind of case terms of sale other than price, quantity and description of goods, are often contained in boiler-

836

plate provisions in the forms that the buyer and seller use. Negotiations between the buyer and seller are usually carried out by nonlawyers and they may not be aware of conflicts in the forms being used. If performance gives rise to a contract, the party using the last form is favored.

The mirror image rule is changed by § 2–207. The purpose of this provision is to allow the formation of a contract in spite of discrepancies between the terms stated by the buyer and the terms stated by the seller. This section also states rules that are intended to allow a court to determine the terms of the resulting contract.

As the quotation from *Daitom* starting on page 841 demonstrates, the courts have had great difficulty in applying § 2–207. That case, as well as *Idaho Power* and *Diamond*, p. 844, all involve sellers who attempted to limit warranty liability in their forms and buyers who used forms under which warranty liability would not be limited. In *Idaho Power* the seller's form prevailed. In *Daitom* and *Diamond* the seller's form did not prevail. *Idaho Power* and *Diamond* were decided by the same Court of Appeals. Can the differences in result be justified as a matter of policy?

IDAHO POWER CO. v. WESTINGHOUSE ELECTRIC CORP.

United States Court of Appeals, Ninth Circuit, 1979.
596 F.2d 924.

EUGENE A. WRIGHT, CIRCUIT JUDGE:

We affirm the dismissal by summary judgment of Idaho Power Company's damage suit against Westinghouse Electric. The action alleged that Westinghouse was liable on theories of warranty, negligence, and strict liability for damages caused by a defective voltage regulator which it manufactured and sold to Idaho Power.

On appeal, Idaho Power argues that (1) the district court erred in concluding that limitations of liability in the Westinghouse sales form were part of the contract between the parties, and that (2) even if they were part of the contract, Westinghouse could not disclaim strict liability.

FACTS

On January 12, 1973, Idaho Power sent an inquiry to Westinghouse asking its price for a three-phase voltage regulator. Westinghouse responded on January 25 with a price quotation which provided that it was subject to the terms and conditions on the back of the form.

The terms limited Westinghouse's liability, providing that it would not be liable "for special, indirect, incidental, or consequential damages," and that its liability, "whether in contract, in tort, under any warranty, or otherwise, * * * shall not exceed the price of the product or part on which such liability is based."

The form also limited the contract by this language:

> The above terms, together with those set forth or referred to on the face of this quotation and such others as may be accepted by Westinghouse in writing, constitute the entire agreement for the sale of the product.

Idaho Power responded with a purchase order describing the regulator and referring to Westinghouse's price quotation. Idaho Power's order form provided, "acceptance of this order shall be deemed to constitute an agreement upon the part of the seller to the conditions named hereon and supersedes all previous agreements." Although it contained additional terms regarding shipping charges, it did not limit Westinghouse's liability.

Idaho Power received and installed the regulator in June, 1974. The equipment allegedly failed on July 31, causing a fire which damaged it and other machinery.

Westinghouse repaired the regulator at its expense, but Idaho Power sought $21,241.52 for other damages on theories of negligence, breach of implied and express warranty, and strict liability in tort. The summary judgment of dismissal was based on the liability limitations in Westinghouse's sales form.

DISCUSSION

Idaho Power concedes that Westinghouse's price quotation and sales form was an offer. It argues, however, that its purchase order was not an effective acceptance. It contends, alternatively, that if the order constituted acceptance, the liability limitations were not a part of the resulting contract. Finally, it argues that the disclaimer, if a part of the contract, was not an effective defense to its strict liability action.

Acceptance.

This issue is controlled by U.C.C. § 2–207(1).

* * *

Idaho Power contends first that this provision is inapplicable because its purchase order was not a "seasonable expression of acceptance or a written confirmation." It points to the printed language in its order form, which purported to restrict the agreement to its terms.

Under common law, its purchase order would have failed as an acceptance since it varied from the offer's terms. 1 Williston,

The Law of Contracts § 73 (3d ed. 1957). Section 2–207, however, rejects the "mirror image" rule, and converts a common law counteroffer into an acceptance even though it states additional or different terms. * * *

The Official Comments to § 2–207 state:

2. Under this Article a proposed deal which in commercial understanding has in fact been closed is recognized as a contract. Therefore, any additional matter contained * * * in the writing intended to close the deal * * * falls within subsection (2) and must be regarded as a proposal for an added term * * *.

Here, Idaho Power's order referred to and accepted the price quoted in Westinghouse's offer. It requested shipment within the time limits specified by Westinghouse. No other correspondence ensued and the regulator was shipped and installed accordingly. In commercial transactions such an order, especially when followed by performance, would normally be understood to have closed the deal between the parties. Consequently, it was a "seasonable expression of acceptance," even though it contained the additional terms.

Idaho Power next attempts to invoke the proviso to § 2–207(1), arguing that, if its purchase order constituted acceptance, it was "expressly made conditional on assent" to additional terms. We disagree.

The proviso has been construed narrowly. The court in *Dorton v. Collins & Aikman Corp.*, 453 F.2d 1161, 1168 (6th Cir. 1972), held that it was intended to apply "only to an acceptance which clearly reveals that the offeree is unwilling to proceed with the transaction unless he is assured of the offeror's assent to the additional or different terms therein." It concluded that an acceptance " 'subject to all of the terms and conditions on the face and reverse side hereof, * * * all of which are accepted by the [offeror],' " was not "expressly made conditional on assent" within the meaning of § 207. Id. at 1167–68. * * *

Idaho Power relies upon similar language to demonstrate that acceptance, if any, was conditional on assent. Its purchase order form states: "Acceptance of this order shall be deemed to constitute an agreement to the conditions named hereon and supersedes all previous agreements."

By this language, Idaho Power attempted to alter the terms of the offer. As in *Dorton,* however, the language used does not clearly reveal that Idaho Power was "unwilling to proceed with the transaction unless * * * assured of [Westinghouse's] assent to the additional or different terms." Consequently, the proviso in § 207(1) does not apply.

The Terms of the Contract.

Idaho Power also contends that even if the purchase order was an effective acceptance under § 2–207(1), the disclaimer in Westinghouse's form is not part of the contract. It relies on Southern Idaho Pipe & Steel v. Cal-Cut Pipe & Supply, Inc., 98 Idaho 495, 567 P.2d 1246 (1977), dismissed, 434 U.S. 1056, 98 S.Ct. 1225, 55 L.Ed.2d 757 (1978).

In *Southern Idaho Pipe,* the court held that when a contract is formed under § 2–207 by documents with conflicting terms, those terms cancel out, leaving the court to supply the contested term. It reasoned that under such circumstances the offeror's terms should not be conclusive simply because its document was sent first. Id., 567 P.2d at 1253–55. The court then omitted from the contract terms which provided different delivery dates.

Here, Idaho Power's form did not contest Westinghouse's disclaimer. It merely purported to "supersede all previous agreements." At best, the term conflicted with Westinghouse's integration clause. We conclude that it did not nullify the disclaimer.

Because the disclaimer in the Westinghouse offer was part of the contract, the district court did not err in granting summary judgment of Idaho Power's actions based on negligence or warranty. * * *

NOTE

In *Idaho Power* the buyer's purchase order was silent on the question of damages for failure of the seller to provide conforming goods, but if the contract had been determined by the terms of the buyer's purchase order the result would have been that the seller's disclaimer would not have been given effect. If the buyer's purchase order purported to state the terms of the sale, is it true that the order "did not contest Westinghouse's disclaimer?" Would the result have been different if the buyer's purchase order had contained the following clause:

> If the goods covered by this purchase order fail in any respect to conform to the contract the seller shall be liable for any loss to the buyer resulting from the nonconformity including incidental and consequential damages. Any attempt by the seller to avoid or limit liability for incidental or consequential damages shall be null and void.

Consider Daitom, Inc. v. Pennwalt Corp., 741 F.2d 1569 (10th Cir. 1984), in which the court discussed various ways in which § 2–207 can be read.

In *Daitom* the seller made a formal proposal to sell equipment to the buyer. The proposal contained a warranty under which the seller agreed to repair or replace any part of the equipment that failed because of a defect in material or workmanship if the failure occurred within one year after the date of delivery. All other express and implied warranties were disclaimed. The buyer's purchase order in response to the seller's offer also contained terms and conditions among which was an unlimited seller's warranty that the goods were merchantable and free of defects. The equipment was delivered to the buyer, but was not installed in the buyer's plant until 13 months after the delivery. A few days after installation the buyer informed the seller that the equipment did not perform properly. Suit was brought by the buyer after the seller's failure to correct alleged defects in the equipment. The complaint alleged breach of warranty. The district court held that the seller's warranty was determined by the terms of the seller's written proposal and granted summary judgment to the seller on the ground that the buyer's warranty claim was barred because the failure of the equipment occurred more than one year after it was delivered. In reversing the district court, Judge Doyle stated:

> The difficulty in determining the effect of different terms in the acceptance is the imprecision of drafting evident in § 2–207. The language of the provision is silent on how different terms in the acceptance are to be treated once a contract is formed pursuant to § 2–207(1). That section provides that a contract may be formed by exchanged writings despite the existence of additional or different terms in the acceptance. Therefore, an offeree's response is treated as an acceptance while it may differ substantially from the offer. This section of the provision, then, reformed the mirror-image rule; that common law legal formality that prohibited the formation of a contract if the exchanged writings of offer and acceptance differed in any term.

[handwritten margin note: 207(2) goes only to "addi. tional" terms]

> Once a contract is recognized pursuant to § 2–207(1), 2–207(2) provides the standard for determining if the additional terms stated in the acceptance become a part of the contract. Between merchants, such *additional* terms become part of the resulting contract *unless* 1) the offer expressly limited acceptance to its terms, 2) the additional terms materially alter the contract obligations, or 3) the offeror gives notice of his or her objection to the additional terms within a reasonable time. Should any one of these three possibilities occur, the *additional* terms are treated merely as proposals for incorporation in the contract and absent assent by the offeror the terms of the offer control. In any event, the existence of the additional terms does not prevent a contract from being formed.

> Section 2–207(2) is silent on the treatment of terms stated in the acceptance that are *different*, rather than merely additional, from those stated in the offer. It is unclear whether "different" terms in the acceptance are intended to

be included under the aegis of "additional" terms in § 2–207(2) and, therefore, fail to become part of the agreement if they materially alter the contract. Comment 3 suggests just such an inclusion.[7] However, Comment 6 suggests that different terms in exchanged writings must be assumed to constitute mutual objections by each party to the other's conflicting terms and result in a mutual "knockout" of both parties' conflicting terms; the missing terms to be supplied by the U.C.C.'s "gap-filler" provisions.[8] At least one commentator, in support of this view, has suggested that the drafting history of the provision indicates that the word "different" was intentionally deleted from the final draft of § 2–207(2) to preclude its treatment under that subsection.[9] The plain language, comments, and drafting history of the provision, therefore, provide little helpful guidance in resolving the disagreement over the treatment of different terms pursuant to § 2–207.

Despite all this, the cases and commentators have suggested three possible approaches. The first of these is to treat "different" terms as included under the aegis of "additional" terms in § 2–207(2). Consequently, different terms in the acceptance would never become part of the contract, because, by definition, they would materially alter the contract (i.e., the offeror's terms). Several courts have adopted this approach. * * *

The second approach, which leads to the same result as the first, is that the offeror's terms control because the offeree's different terms merely fall out; § 2–207(2) cannot rescue the different terms since that subsection applies only to *additional* terms. Under this approach, Comment 6 (apparently supporting a mutual rather than a single term knockout) is not applicable because it refers only to conflicting terms in confirmation forms following oral agreement, not conflicting terms in the writings that form the agreement. This approach is supported by Professor Summers. J.J. White & R.S.

---

7. Comment 3 states (emphasis added):

Whether or not *additional or different* terms will become part of the agreement depends upon the provision of subsection (2).

It must be remembered that even official comments to enacted statutory text do not have the force of law and are only guidance in the interpretation of that text. In re Bristol Associates, Inc., 505 F.2d 1056 (3rd Cir.1974) (while the comments to the Pennsylvania U.C.C. are not binding, the Pennsylvania Supreme Court gives substantial weight to the comments as evidencing application of the Code).

8. Comment 6 states, in part:

Where clauses on confirming forms sent by both parties conflict each party must be assumed to object to a clause of the other conflicting with one on the confirmation sent by himself * * *. The contract then consists of the terms expressly agreed to, terms on which the confirmations agree, and terms supplied by the Act, including subsection (2).

9. See D.G. Baird & R. Weisberg, Rules, Standards, and the Battle of the Forms: A Reassessment of § 2–207, 68 Va.L.R. 1217, 1240, n. 61.

Summers, Uniform Commercial Code, § 1–2, at 29 (2d ed. 1980).

The third, and preferable approach, which is commonly called the "knock-out" rule, is that the conflicting terms cancel one another. Under this view the offeree's form is treated only as an acceptance of the terms in the offeror's form which did not conflict. The ultimate contract, then, includes those non-conflicting terms and any other terms supplied by the U.C.C., including terms incorporated by course of performance (§ 2–208), course of dealing (§ 1–205), usage of trade (§ 1–205), and other "gap fillers" or "off-the-rack" terms (e.g., implied warranty of fitness for particular purpose, § 2–315). As stated previously, this approach finds some support in Comment 6. Professor White supports this approach as the most fair and consistent with the purposes of § 2–207. White & Summers, supra, at 29. Further, several courts have adopted or recognized the approach. * * *

We are of the opinion that this is the more reasonable approach, particularly when dealing with a case such as this where from the beginning the offeror's specified period of limitations would expire before the equipment was even installed. The approaches other than the "knock-out" approach would be inequitable and unjust because they invited the very kind of treatment which the defendant attempted to provide.

* * *

This particular approach and result are supported persuasively by the underlying rationale and purpose behind the adoption of § 2–207. As stated previously, that provision was drafted to reform the infamous common law mirror-image rule and associated last-shot doctrine that enshrined the fortuitous positions of senders of forms and accorded undue advantages based on such fortuitous positions. * * * To refuse to adopt the "knock-out" rule and instead adopt one of the remaining two approaches would serve to re-enshrine the undue advantages derived solely from the fortuitous positions of when a party sent a form. * * * This is because either approach other than the knock-out rule for different terms results in the offeror and his or her terms always prevailing solely because he or she sent the first form. Professor Summers argues that this advantage is not wholly unearned, because the offeree has an opportunity to review the offer, identify the conflicting terms and make his or her acceptance conditional. * * * While it is laudable for business persons to read the fine print and boilerplate provisions in exchanged forms, there is nothing in § 2–207 mandating such careful consideration. The provision seems drafted with a recognition of the reality that merchants seldom review exchanged forms with the scrutiny of lawyers. The "knock-out" rule is there-

fore the best approach. Even if a term eliminated by operation of the "knock-out" rule is reintroduced by operation of
the U.C.C.'s gap-filler provisions, such a result does not indicate a weakness of the approach. On the contrary, at least
the reintroduced term has the merit of being a term that the
U.C.C. draftpersons regarded as fair.

In *Diamond*, the case that follows, the parties were aware of
the differences between the forms used by the buyer and seller.
Does the rationale espoused by Judge Doyle in *Daitom* apply
equally to such a case?

DIAMOND FRUIT GROWERS, INC. v. KRACK CORP.

United States Court of Appeals, Ninth Circuit, 1986.
794 F.2d 1440.

WIGGINS, CIRCUIT JUDGE:

* * *

Krack is a manufacturer of cooling units that contain steel
tubing it purchases from outside suppliers. Metal–Matic is one of
Krack's tubing suppliers. At the time this dispute arose, Metal–
Matic had been supplying tubing to Krack for about ten years.
The parties followed the same course of dealing during the entire
ten years. At the beginning of each year, Krack sent a blanket
purchase order to Metal–Matic stating how much tubing Krack
would need for the year. Then, throughout the year as Krack
needed tubing, it sent release purchase orders to Metal–Matic
requesting that tubing be shipped. Metal–Matic responded to
Krack's release purchase orders by sending Krack an acknowledgment form and then shipping the tubing.[1]

Metal–Matic's acknowledgment form disclaimed all liability
for consequential damages and limited Metal–Matic's liability for
defects in the tubing to refund of the purchase price or replacement or repair of the tubing. As one would expect, these terms
were not contained in Krack's purchase order. The following
statement was printed on Metal–Matic's form: "Metal–Matic,
Inc.'s acceptance of purchaser's offer or its offer to purchaser is
hereby expressly made conditional to purchaser's acceptance of
the terms and provisions of the acknowledgment form." This
statement and the disclaimer of liability were on the back of the
acknowledgment form. However, printed at the bottom of the
front of the form in bold-face capitals was the following statement:

1. The blanket purchase order apparently did no more than establish
Krack's willingness to purchase an
amount of tubing during the year. The
parties' conduct indicates that they intended to establish their contract based
on Krack's release purchase orders and
Metal–Matic's acknowledgments sent in
response to those purchase orders.

"SEE REVERSE SIDE FOR TERMS AND CONDITIONS OF SALE."

On at least one occasion during the ten-year relationship between Metal–Matic and Krack, Allen Zver, Krack's purchasing manager, discussed the limitation of warranty and disclaimer of liability terms contained in Metal–Matic's acknowledgment form with Robert Van Krevelen, Executive Vice President of Metal–Matic. Zver told Van Krevelen that Krack objected to the terms and tried to convince him to change them, but Van Krevelen refused to do so. After the discussions, Krack continued to accept and pay for tubing from Metal–Matic.

In February 1981, Krack sold one of its cooling units to Diamond Fruit Growers, Inc. (Diamond) in Oregon, and in September 1981, Diamond installed the unit in a controlled-atmosphere warehouse. In January 1982, the unit began leaking ammonia from a cooling coil made of steel tubing.

After Diamond discovered that ammonia was leaking into the warehouse, Joseph Smith, the engineer who had been responsible for building Diamond's controlled-atmosphere warehouses, was called in to find the source of the leak. Smith testified that he found a pinhole leak in the cooling coil of the Krack cooling unit.
* * *

Diamond sued Krack to recover the loss in value of fruit that it was forced to remove from the storage room as a result of the leak. Krack in turn brought a third-party complaint against Metal–Matic * * * seeking contribution or indemnity in the event it was held liable to Diamond. At the close of the evidence * * * Metal–Matic * * * moved for a directed verdict on the third party complaint. * * * The court denied Metal–Matic's motion.

The jury returned a verdict in favor of Diamond against Krack. It then found that Krack was entitled to contribution from Metal–Matic for thirty percent of Diamond's damages. Metal–Matic moved for judgment n.o.v. The court denied that motion and entered judgment on the jury verdict.

Metal–Matic * * * contends that as part of its contract with Krack, it disclaimed all liability for consequential damages and specifically limited its liability for defects in the tubing to refund of the purchase price or replacement or repair of the tubing.
* * *

If the contract between Metal–Matic and Krack contains Metal–Matic's disclaimer of liability, Metal–Matic is not liable to indemnify Krack for part of Diamond's damages. Therefore, the principal issue before us on this appeal is whether Metal–Matic's disclaimer of liability became part of the contract between these parties.

Relying on Uniform Commercial Code (U.C.C.) § 2–207, * * * Krack argues that Metal–Matic's disclaimer did not become part of the contract. Metal–Matic, on the other hand, argues that section 2–207 is inapplicable to this case because the parties discussed the disclaimer, and Krack assented to it.

Krack is correct in its assertion that section 2–207 applies to this case. * * * In this case, Krack and Metal–Matic exchanged purchase order and acknowledgment forms that contained different or additional terms. This, then, is a typical section 2–207 situation. The fact that the parties discussed the terms of their contract after they exchanged their forms does not put this case outside section 2–207. * * *

Generally, section 2–207(1) "converts a common law counteroffer into an acceptance even though it states additional or different terms." *Idaho Power,* 596 F.2d at 926 * * *. The only requirement under section 2–207(1) is that the responding form contain a definite and seasonable expression of acceptance. The terms of the responding form that correspond to the offer constitute the contract. Under section 2–207(2), the additional terms of the responding form become proposals for additions to the contract. Between merchants the additional terms become part of the contract unless the offer is specifically limited to its terms, the offeror objects to the additional terms, or the additional terms materially alter the terms of the offer. * * *

However, section 2–207(1) is subject to a proviso. If a definite and seasonable expression of acceptance expressly conditions acceptance on the offeror's assent to additional or different terms contained therein, the parties' differing forms do not result in a contract unless the offeror assents to the additional terms. * * * If the offeror assents, the parties have a contract and the additional terms are a part of that contract. If, however, the offeror does not assent, but the parties proceed with the transaction as if they have a contract, their performance results in formation of a contract. U.C.C. § 2–207(3). In that case, the terms of the contract are those on which the parties' forms agree plus any terms supplied by the U.C.C. * * *

In this case, Metal–Matic expressly conditioned its acceptance on Krack's assent to the additional terms contained in Metal–Matic's acknowledgment form. That form tracks the language of the section 2–207(1) proviso, stating that "Metal–Matic, Inc.'s acceptance * * * is hereby *expressly made conditional* to purchaser's acceptance of the terms and provisions of the acknowledgment form." * * * Therefore, we must determine whether Krack assented to Metal–Matic's limitation of liability term.

Metal–Matic argues that Krack did assent to the limitation of liability term. This argument is based on the discussions between Zver for Krack and Van Krevelen for Metal–Matic. Some time during the ten-year relationship between the companies, these two men discussed Krack's objections to the warranty and liability limitation terms in Metal–Matic's acknowledgment form. Krack attempted to persuade Metal–Matic to change its form, but Metal–Matic refused to do so. After the discussions, the companies continued to do business as in the past. Metal–Matic contends that Krack assented to the limitation of liability term when it continued to accept and pay for tubing after Metal–Matic insisted that the contract contain its terms.

To address Metal–Matic's argument, we must determine what constitutes assent to additional or different terms for purposes of section 2–207(1). The parties have not directed us to any cases that analyze this question and our research has revealed none. We therefore look to the language and structure of section 2–207 and to the purposes behind that section to determine the correct standard.

One of the principles underlying section 2–207 is neutrality. If possible, the section should be interpreted so as to give neither party to a contract an advantage simply because it happened to send the first or in some cases the last form. * * * Section 2–207 accomplishes this result in part by doing away with the common law's "last shot" rule. * * * At common law, the offeree/counterofferor gets all of its terms simply because it fired the last shot in the exchange of forms. Section 2–207(3) does away with this result by giving neither party the terms it attempted to impose unilaterally on the other. * * * Instead, all of the terms on which the parties' forms do not agree drop out, and the U.C.C. supplies the missing terms.

Generally, this result is fair because both parties are responsible for the ambiguity in their contract. The parties could have negotiated a contract and agreed on its terms, but for whatever reason, they failed to do so. Therefore, neither party should get its terms. * * * However, as White and Summers point out, resort to section 2–207(3) will often work to the disadvantage of the seller because he will "wish to undertake less responsibility for the quality of his goods than the Code imposes or else wish to limit his damages liability more narrowly than would the Code." J. White & R. Summers, § 1–2 at 34. Nevertheless, White and Summers recommend that section 2–207(3) be applied in such cases. Id. We agree. Application of section 2–207(3) is more equitable than giving one party its terms simply because it sent the last form. Further, the terms imposed by the code are presumably equitable and consistent with public policy because they are statutorily imposed. * * *

With these general principles in mind, we turn now to Metal–Matic's argument that Krack assented to the disclaimer when it continued to accept and pay for tubing once Metal–Matic indicated that it was willing to sell tubing only if its warranty and liability terms were part of the contract. Metal–Matic's argument is appealing. Sound policy supports permitting a seller to control the terms on which it will sell its products, especially in a case in which the seller has indicated both in writing and orally that those are the only terms on which it is willing to sell the product. Nevertheless, we reject Metal–Matic's argument because we find that these considerations are outweighed by the public policy reflected by Oregon's enactment of the U.C.C.

If we were to accept Metal–Matic's argument, we would reinstate to some extent the common law's last shot rule. To illustrate, assume that the parties in this case had sent the same forms but in the reverse order and that Krack's form contained terms stating that Metal–Matic is liable for all consequential damages and conditioning acceptance on Metal–Matic's assent to Krack's terms. Assume also that Metal–Matic objected to Krack's terms but Krack refused to change them and that the parties continued with their transaction anyway. If we applied Metal–Matic's argument in that case, we would find that Krack's term was part of the contract because Metal–Matic continued to ship tubing to Krack after Krack reaffirmed that it would purchase tubing only if Metal–Matic were fully liable for consequential damages. Thus, the result would turn on which party sent the last form, and would therefore be inconsistent with section 2–207's purpose of doing away with the last shot rule.

That result is avoided by requiring a specific and unequivocal expression of assent on the part of the offeror when the offeree conditions its acceptance on assent to additional or different terms. If the offeror does not give specific and unequivocal assent but the parties act as if they have a contract, the provisions of section 2–207(3) apply to fill in the terms of the contract. Application of section 2–207(3) is appropriate in that situation because by going ahead with the transaction without resolving their dispute, both parties are responsible for introducing ambiguity into the contract. Further, in a case such as this one, requiring the seller to assume more liability than it intends is not altogether inappropriate. The seller is most responsible for the ambiguity because it inserts a term in its form that requires assent to additional terms and then does not enforce that requirement. If the seller truly does not want to be bound unless the buyer assents to its terms, it can protect itself by not shipping until it obtains that assent.
* * *

We hold that because Krack's conduct did not indicate unequivocally that Krack intended to assent to Metal–Matic's terms, that conduct did not amount to the assent contemplated by section 2–207(1). * * *

B. STATUTE OF FRAUDS

1. THE GENERAL RULE

MONETTI v. ANCHOR HOCKING CORP.

United States Court of Appeals, Seventh Circuit, 1991.
931 F.2d 1178.

POSNER, CIRCUIT JUDGE.

This is a diversity suit for breach of contract; the parties agree that Illinois law governs the substantive issues. The district judge dismissed the suit, on the defendant's motion for summary judgment, as barred by the statute of frauds, and also refused to allow the plaintiffs to amend their complaint to add a claim of promissory estoppel. The appeal, which challenges both rulings, presents difficult and important questions concerning both the general Illinois statute of frauds, Ill.Rev.Stat. ch. 59, ¶ 1, and the statute of frauds in the Uniform Commercial Code, UCC § 2–201, adopted by Illinois in Ill.Rev.Stat. ch. 26, ¶ 2–201.

The plaintiffs are Monetti, an Italian firm that makes decorative plastic trays and related products for the food service industry, and a wholly owned subsidiary, Melform U.S.A., which Monetti set up in 1981 to market its products in the U.S. In 1984, Monetti began negotiations with a father-and-son team, the Schneiders, importers of food service products, to grant the Schneiders the exclusive right to distribute Monetti's products in the United States and in connection with this grant to turn over to them Melform's tangible and intangible assets. While these negotiations were proceeding, the Schneiders sold their importing firm to Anchor Hocking, the defendant, and their firm became a division of Anchor Hocking, though—at first—the Schneiders remained in charge. In the fall of 1984, the younger Schneider, who was handling the negotiations with Monetti for his father and himself, sent Monetti a telex requesting preparation of an agreement "formalizing our [i.e., Anchor Hocking's] exclusive for the United States." In response, Monetti terminated all of Melform's distributors and informed all of Melform's customers that Anchor would become the exclusive U.S. distributor of Monetti products on December 31, 1984.

On December 18, the parties met, apparently for the purpose of making a final agreement. Monetti—which incidentally was not represented by counsel at the meeting—submitted a draft the principal provisions of which were that Anchor Hocking would be the exclusive distributor of Monetti products in the U.S., the contract would last for ten years, and during each of these years Anchor Hocking would make specified minimum purchases of Monetti products, adding up to $27 million over the entire period. No one from Anchor Hocking signed this or any other draft of the agreement. However, the record contains a memo, apparently prepared for use at the December 18 meeting, entitled "Topics of Discussion With Monetti." The memo's first heading is "Exclusive Agreement—Attachment # 1"—a reference to an attached draft which is identical to the Monetti draft except for two additional, minor paragraphs added in handwriting. Under the heading appears the notation "Agree" beside each of the principal paragraphs of the agreement, with one exception: beside the first paragraph, the provision for exclusivity, the notation is "We want Canada" (i.e., exclusive distribution rights in Canada as well as in the U.S.). On the bottom of the left-hand side of the last page appears the legend "SS/mh"—indicating that the younger Schneider (Steve Schneider) had dictated the memo to a secretary.

Shortly after the December 18 meeting, Monetti—which had already, remember, terminated Melform's distributors and informed Melform's customers that Anchor Hocking would be the exclusive distributor of Monetti products in the United States as of the last day of 1984—turned over to Anchor Hocking all of Melform's inventory, records, and other physical assets, together with Melform's trade secrets and know-how.

Several months later, in May 1985, Anchor Hocking abruptly fired the Schneiders. Concerned about the possible implications of this démarche for its relationship with Anchor Hocking, Monetti requested a meeting between the parties, and it was held on May 19. Reviewing the events up to and including that meeting, a memo dated June 12, 1985, from Raymond Davis, marketing director of Anchor Hocking's food services division, to the law department of Anchor Hocking, states that "In the middle to latter part of 1984 Irwin Schneider and his company were negotiating an agreement with [Monetti and Melform] to obtain exclusive distribution rights on Melform's plastic tray product line in the United States"; "later, this distribution agreement was expanded to also include Canada, the Caribbean and Central and South America"; there had been many meetings between the parties, including the meeting of May 19 (at which Davis had been present); "Exhibit A (attached) represents the summary agreement that was reached in the meeting. You will notice that I have added some handwritten changes which I believe represents more clearly our current position regarding the agreement * * *. Now that we have had our 'New Management' [i.e., the management team that had replaced the Schneiders] meeting with Monetti, both parties would like to have a written and signed agreement to guide this new relationship." Exhibit A to the Davis memo is identical to Attachment # 1 to Steve Schneider's memo, except that it contains the handwritten changes to which the Davis memo refers. Shortly after this memo was written, the parties' relationship began to deteriorate, and eventually Monetti sued for breach of contract.

Illinois' general statute of frauds forbids a suit upon an agreement that is not to be performed within a year "unless the promise or agreement upon which such action shall be brought, or some memorandum or note thereof, shall be in writing, and signed by the party to be charged therewith, or some other person thereunto by him lawfully authorized." The statute of frauds in Article 2 of the Uniform Commercial Code makes a contract for the sale of goods worth at least $500 unenforceable "unless there is some writing sufficient to indicate that a contract for sale has been made between the parties and signed by the party against whom enforcement is sought or by his authorized agent or broker." The differences between these formulations are subtle but important. The Illinois statute requires that the writing "express the substance of the contract with reasonable certainty." Frazer v. Howe, 106 Ill. 564, 574 (1883) * * * The UCC statute of frauds does not require that the writing contain the terms of the contract. Ill.Code Comment 1 to UCC § 2–201. In fact it requires no more than written corroboration of the alleged oral contract. Even if there is no such signed document, the contract may still be valid "with respect to goods * * * which have been received and accepted." § 2–201(3)(c). This provision may appear to narrow the statute of frauds still further, but if anything it curtails a traditional exception, and one applicable to Illinois' general statute: the exception for partial performance * * *. The Uniform Commercial Code does not treat partial delivery by the party seeking to enforce an oral contract as a partial performance of the *entire* contract, allowing him to enforce the contract with respect to the undelivered goods.

Let us postpone the question of partial performance for a moment and focus on whether there was a signed document of the sort that the statutes of frauds require. The judge, over Monetti's objection, refused to admit oral evidence on this question. He was right to refuse. The use of oral evidence to get round the requirement of a writing would be bootstrapping, would sap the statute of frauds of most of its force, and is therefore forbidden. Western Metals Co. v. Hartman Co., 303 Ill. 479, 485, 135 N.E. 744, 746 (1922); R.S. Bennett & Co. v. Economy Mechanical Industries, Inc., 606 F.2d 182, 186 n. 4 (7th Cir.1979); Bazak International Corp. v. Mast Industries, Inc., 73 N.Y.2d 113, 117–18, 538 N.Y.S.2d 503, 505, 535 N.E.2d 633, 635 (1989). The Hip Pocket, Inc. v. Levi Strauss & Co., 144 Ga.App. 792, 793, 242 S.E.2d 305, 306 (1978), is *contra,* but does not discuss the question and is, we think, wrong; while Impossible Electronic Techniques, Inc. v. Wackenhut Protective Systems, Inc., 669 F.2d 1026, 1034 (5th Cir.1982), on which

Monetti also relies, is distinguishable from our case because there the writing was first held to satisfy the statute of frauds and only then was oral evidence admitted to clear up a detail, albeit a vital one—the identity of one of the parties!

Although we have cited cases from different jurisdictions, the question whether oral evidence is admissible to show that an ambiguous document satisfies the requirements of the statute of frauds is ultimately one of state law. So far as we have been able to discover, the question is uniformly assumed to be substantive rather than procedural for purposes of determining, in accordance with the *Erie* doctrine, whether state or federal law applies, though direct authority on the question is sparse. * * * We think the assumption is well founded, although the point is not crucial in this case because neither party questions the applicability of Illinois law. It is true that a statute of frauds is procedural in form and that its main proximate goal is evidentiary; it is largely based on distrust of the ability of juries to determine the truth of testimony that there was or was not a contract. 2 E. Allan Farnsworth, Farnsworth on Contracts § 6.1, at p. 85 (1990). But it is usually and we think correctly regarded as a part of contract law, not of general procedural law. * * * It is designed to make the contractual process cheaper and more certain by encouraging the parties to contracts to memorialize their agreement. The end of the statute of frauds thus is substantive (albeit the means is procedural), which makes essential aspects of the administration of the statute, such as the admissibility of oral evidence to disambiguate an ambiguous document that is contended to satisfy the statute of frauds, a matter of primary concern to the states rather than to the federal government. So Illinois law applies to the issue; and *Western Metals* indicates that Illinois courts would not allow oral evidence to be used to enable a vague document to satisfy the statute of frauds.

Because oral evidence was inadmissible on the question whether the documents meet the requirements of the statutes of frauds, it was proper for the judge to resolve it on motion for summary judgment. The parties agree that, if this was proper, our review is plenary. This does not follow, however, from the documentary character of the issue, Anderson v. City of Bessemer City, 470 U.S. 564, 105 S.Ct. 1504, 84 L.Ed.2d 518 (1985), as the parties may believe. But in view of the parties' agreement concerning the proper scope of our review, we need not resolve the matter, beyond noting that there is authority * * * for regarding the issue as one of law, not fact—and if it is an issue of law, then our review is indeed plenary.

We have two documents (really, two pairs of documents) to consider. The first is Steve Schneider's "Topics for Discussion" memo with its "Attachment # 1." Since "signed" in statute-of-frauds land is a term of art, meaning executed or adopted by the defendant, * * * Schneider's typed initials are sufficient. The larger objection is that the memo was written before the contract—any contract—was made. The memo indicates that Schneider (an authorized representative of the defendant) agrees to the principal provisions in the draft agreement prepared by Monetti, but not to all the provisions; further negotiations are envisaged. There was no contract when the memo was prepared and signed, though it is fair to infer from the memo that a contract much like the draft attached to it would be agreed upon—if Monetti agreed to Anchor Hocking's demand for Canada, as Monetti concedes (and the Davis memo states) it did.

Can a memo that precedes the actual formation of the contract ever constitute the writing required by the statute of frauds? Under the Uniform Commercial Code, why not? Its statute of frauds does not require that any contracts "be in writing." All that is required is a document that provides solid evidence of the existence of a contract; the contract itself can be oral. Three cases should be distinguished. In the first, the precontractual writing is merely one party's offer. We have held, interpreting Illinois' version of the Uniform Commercial Code, that an offer won't do. * * * Otherwise there would be an acute danger that a party whose offer had been rejected would nevertheless try to use it as the basis for a suit. The second case is that of notes made in preparation for a negotiating session, and this is another plausible case for holding the statute unsatisfied, lest a breakdown of contract negotiations become the launching pad for a suit on an alleged oral contract. Third is the case—arguably this case— where the precontractual writing—the Schneider memo and the attachment to it—indicates the promisor's (Anchor Hocking's) acceptance of the promisee's (Monetti's) offer; the case, in other words, where all the essential terms are stated in the writing and the only problem is that the writing was prepared before the contract became final. The only difficulty with holding that such a writing satisfies the statute of frauds is the use of the perfect tense by the draftsmen of the Uniform Commercial Code: the writing must be sufficient to demonstrate that "a contract for sale *has been made* * * *. The 'futuristic' nature of the writing disqualifies it." Micromedia v. Automated Broadcast Controls, 799 F.2d 230, 234 (5th Cir.1986) (emphasis in original); see also American Web Press, Inc. v. Harris Corp., 596 F.Supp. 1089, 1093 (D.Colo.1983). Yet under a general statute of frauds, "it is well settled that a memorandum satisfying the Statute may be made before the contract is concluded." Farrow v. Cahill, 663 F.2d 201, 209 (D.C.Cir.1980) (footnote omitted). And while merely because the UCC's draftsmen relaxed one requirement of the statute of frauds—that there be a writing containing all the essential terms of the contract—doesn't exclude the possibility that they wanted to stiffen another, by excluding writings made before the contract itself was made, the choice of tenses is weak evidence. No doubt they had in mind, as the typical case to be governed by section 2–201, a deal made over the phone and evidenced by a confirmation slip. They may not have foreseen a case like the present, or provided for it. The distinction between what is assumed and what is prescribed is critical in interpretation generally.

In both of the decisions that we cited for the narrow interpretation, the judges' concern was with our first two classes of case; and judicial language, like other language, should be read in context. *Micromedia* involved an offer; in *American Web*, negotiations were continuing. We agree with Professor Farnsworth that in appropriate circumstances a memorandum made before the contract is formed can satisfy the statute of frauds, 2 Farnsworth on Contracts, supra, § 6.7, at p. 132 and n. 16, including the UCC statute of frauds. This case illustrates why a rule of strict temporal priority is unnecessary to secure the purposes of the statute of frauds. Farnsworth goes further. He would allow a written *offer* to satisfy the statute, provided of course that there is oral evidence it was accepted. Id., n. 16. We needn't decide in this case how far we would go with him, and therefore needn't reexamine *Bennett*.

Nor need we decide whether the first memo (Schneider's) can be linked with the second (Davis's)—probably not, since they don't refer to each other, * * *—to constitute a post-contract writing and eliminate the issue just discussed. For, shortly after the Schneider memo was prepared, Monetti gave dramatic evidence of the existence of a contract by turning over its entire distribution operation in the United States to Anchor Hocking. (In fact it had started to do this even earlier.) Monetti was hardly likely to do that without a contract—without in fact a contract requiring Anchor Hocking to purchase a minimum of $27 million worth of Monetti's products over the next ten years, for that was a provision to which Schneider in the memo had indicated agreement, and it is the only form of compensation to Monetti for abandoning its distribution business that the various drafts make reference to and apparently the only one the parties ever discussed.

This partial performance took the contract out of the general Illinois statute of frauds. Unilateral performance is pretty solid evidence that there really was a contract—for why else would the party have performed unilaterally? Almost the whole purpose of contracts is to protect the party who performs first from being taken advantage of by the other party, so if a party performs first there is some basis for inferring that he had a contract. The inference of contract from partial performance is especially powerful in a case such as this, since while the nonenforcement of an oral contract leaves the parties free to pursue their noncontractual remedies, such as a suit for quantum meruit (a form of restitution), * * * once Monetti turned over its trade secrets and other intangible assets to Anchor Hocking it had no way of recovering these things. (Of course, Monetti may just have been foolish.) The partial-performance exception to the statute of frauds is often explained (and its boundaries fixed accordingly) as necessary to protect the reliance of the performing party, so that if he can be made whole by restitution the oral contract will not be enforced. This is the Illinois rationale * * * and it is not limited to Illinois. * * * It supports enforcement of the oral contract in this case.

This discussion assumes, however, that the contract is governed by the general Illinois statute of frauds rather than, as the district judge believed, by the UCC's statute of frauds (or in addition to it—for both might apply, as we shall see), with its arguably narrower exception for partial performance. The UCC statute of frauds at issue in this case appears in Article 2, the sale of goods article of the Code, and, naturally therefore, is expressly limited to contracts for the sale of goods. That is a type of transaction in which a partial-performance exception to a writing requirement would make no sense if the seller were seeking payment for more than the goods he had actually delivered. Suppose A delivers 1,000 widgets to B, and later sues B for breach of an alleged oral contract for 100,000 widgets and argues that the statute of frauds is not a bar because he performed his part of the contract in part. In such a case partial performance just is not indicative of the existence of an oral contract for any quantity greater than that already delivered, so it is no surprise that the statute of frauds provides that an oral contract cannot be enforced in a quantity greater than that received and accepted by the buyer. § 2–201(3)(c); cf. § 2–201(1). The present case is different. The partial performance here consisted not of a delivery of goods alleged to be part of a larger order but the turning over of an entire business. *That* kind of partial performance *is* evidence of an oral contract and also shows that this is not the pure sale of goods to which the UCC's statute of frauds was intended to apply.

This is not to say that the *contract* is outside the Uniform Commercial Code. It is a contract for the sale of goods plus a contract for the sale of distribution rights and of the assets associated with those rights. Courts forced to classify a mixed contract of this sort ask, somewhat unhelpfully perhaps, what the predominant purpose of the contract is. Yorke v. B.F. Goodrich Co., 130 Ill.App.3d 220, 223, 85 Ill.Dec. 606, 608, 474 N.E.2d 20, 22 (1985), and cases cited there. And, no doubt, they would classify this contract as one for the sale of goods, therefore governed by the UCC, because the $27 million in sales contemplated by the contract (if there was a contract, as we are assuming) swamped the goodwill and other intangibles associated with Melform's very

new, very small operation. Distributorship agreements, such as
this one was in part, and even sales of businesses as going
concerns, are frequently though not always classified as UCC
contracts under the predominant-purpose test. * * *

We may assume that the UCC applies to this contract; but
must *all* of the UCC apply? We have difficulty seeing why. It is
not a matter of holding the contract partly enforceable and partly
unenforceable, a measure disapproved in Distribu–Dor, Inc. v.
Karadanis, 11 Cal.App.3d 463, 468, 90 Cal.Rptr. 231, 234 (1970).
Because of the contract's mixed character, the UCC statute of
frauds doesn't make a nice fit; it's designed for a pure sale of
goods. The general statute works better. The fact that Article 2,
which we have been loosely referring to as the sale of goods
article, in fact applies not to the sale of goods as such but rather to
"transactions in goods," § 2–102, while its statute of frauds is
limited to "contract[s] for the sale of goods," § 2–201(1), could be
thought to imply that the statute of frauds does not cover every
transaction that is otherwise within the scope of Article 2. 2
Farnsworth on Contracts, supra, § 6.6, at p. 126 and n. 5. Perhaps the contract in this case is better described as a transaction
in goods than as a contract for the sale of goods, since so much
more than a mere sale of goods was contemplated.

Another possibility is to interpret the UCC statute of frauds
flexibly (an approach endorsed in Meyer v. Logue, 100 Ill.App.3d
1039, 1044–46, 56 Ill.Dec. 707, 710–12, 427 N.E.2d 1253, 1256–58
(1981)) in consideration of the special circumstances of the class of
cases represented by this case, so that it does make a smooth fit.
There is precedent for doing this. When the partial performance
is not the delivery of some of the goods but part payment for all
the goods, most courts will enforce oral contracts under the UCC.
* * * Such cases do not present the danger at which the limitation on using partial performance to take the entire contract
outside of the statute of frauds was aimed, that of the seller's
unilaterally altering the quantity ordered by the buyer, although
they could be thought to present the analogous danger of the
seller's unilaterally altering the price the buyer had agreed to
pay—by claiming that full payment was actually part payment.
This case, at all events, presents no dangers of the sort the
provision in question was designed to eliminate. The semantic
lever for the interpretation we are proposing is that the UCC does
not abolish the partial-performance exception. It merely limits
the use of partial delivery as a ground for insisting on the full
delivery allegedly required by the oral contract. That is not what
Monetti is trying to do.

We need not pursue these interesting questions about the
applicability and scope of the UCC statute of frauds any further in
this case, because our result would be unchanged no matter how

they were answered. For we have said nothing yet about the second writing in the case, the Davis memorandum of June 12. It was a writing on Anchor Hocking's letterhead, so satisfied the writing and signature requirements of the UCC statute of frauds, and it was a writing sufficient to evidence the existence of the contract upon which Anchor Hocking is being sued. It is true that "Exhibit A" does not contain all the terms of the contract; it makes no reference to the handing over of Melform's assets. But, especially taken together with the Davis memo itself (and we are permitted to connect them provided that the connections are "apparent from a comparison of the writings themselves," Western Metals Co. v. Hartman Co., supra, 303 Ill. at 483, 135 N.E. at 746, and they are, since the Davis memo refers explicitly to Exhibit A), Exhibit A is powerful evidence that there was a contract and that its terms were as Monetti represents. Remember that the UCC's statute of frauds does not require that the contract be in writing, but only that there be a sufficient memorandum to indicate that there really was a contract. The Davis memorandum fits this requirement to a t. So even if the partial-performance doctrine is not available to Monetti, the UCC's statute of frauds was satisfied. And since the general Illinois statute was satisfied as well, we need not decide whether, since the contract in this case both was (we are assuming) within the UCC *and* could not be performed within one year, it had to satisfy both statutes of frauds. 2 Farnsworth on Contracts, supra, § 6.2, at pp. 90–91.

Our conclusion that Monetti's suit for breach of contract is not barred by the statute(s) of frauds makes the district judge's second ruling, refusing to allow Monetti to add a claim for promissory estoppel, academic. The only reason Monetti wanted to add the claim was as a backstop should it lose on the statute of frauds. In light of our decision today, he does not need a backstop.

Can promissory estoppel be used to avoid the limitations that the statute of frauds places on the enforcement of oral promises? It can be argued that a party to a contract for the sale of goods should not be allowed to get around the statute of frauds merely by alleging promissory estoppel and using partial performance to establish the necessary reliance in circumstances in which the requirements for the exception in the statute of frauds for partial performance would for one reason or another not be satisfied. It can further be argued that since promissory estoppel unlike equitable estoppel is a method of establishing contractual liability, the statute of frauds should be no less applicable than if the contract were supported by consideration or a seal rather than by promissory estoppel. * * * On the other side it can be argued that promissory estoppel is deliberately open-ended, and should therefore remain available to overcome, in appropriate cases, possible rigidities in the statute of frauds. * * * Consistent with this

counterargument, we held in R.S. Bennett & Co. v. Economy
Mechanical Industries, Inc., supra, 606 F.2d at 187–89, that Illinois' version of the UCC statute of frauds was inapplicable to
promissory estoppel cases. * * * See also 2 Farnsworth on
Contracts, supra, § 6.12, at p. 185 n. 26. We have been having
second thoughts lately. Goldstick v. ICM Realty, 788 F.2d 456,
464–66 (7th Cir.1986); Evans v. Fluor Distribution Cos., 799 F.2d
364, 367–68 (7th Cir.1986). But as in *Goldstick* and *Evans,* so in
this case, we need not and do not decide whether *Bennett* was an
accurate forecast of Illinois law. Not only is the issue moot in
view of our decision that the statute of frauds does not bar Monetti
from enforcing the contract, but *Bennett* was not a case in which
the plaintiff was using promissory estoppel to avoid the UCC's
provision disallowing a defense to the statute of frauds for partial
performance consisting of the delivery of some but not all of the
quantity allegedly contracted for orally. It is in such a case that
the "end run" character of promissory estoppel appears most
strongly; yet we need not and do not decide whether the appearance is so strong as to preclude resort to promissory estoppel.

Reversed and Remanded.

NOTE

The general rule, stated in § 2–201(1), which requires a signed
writing is subject to exceptions stated in subsections (2) and (3).
Under subsection (3)(b) an oral agreement is enforceable "if the
party against whom enforcement is sought admits in his pleading,
testimony or otherwise in court that a contract for sale was
made." Suppose an action is brought on an oral agreement that is
unenforceable under § 2–201(1). The defendant is asked on the
witness stand or in a deposition proceeding whether the oral
agreement was made. If the defendant, constrained by penalty of
perjury, admits the agreement, the oral agreement becomes enforceable under § 2–201(3)(b). Suppose the defendant, to avoid
this result, answers the complaint by admitting the alleged oral
agreement while asserting that it is unenforceable because § 2–
201(1) is not satisfied. Under § 2–201(3)(b), does the admission by
the defendant make the oral agreement enforceable? Can the
defendant avoid § 3–201(3)(b) by simply demurring to the complaint or making a motion to dismiss based on § 3–201(1) without
either admitting or denying the existence of the oral agreement?
These issues have been discussed in several cases.

In Simmons Oil Corp. v. Bulk Sales Corp., 498 F.Supp. 457
(D.N.J.1980), the plaintiff's complaint specifically referred to an
"oral sales contract." The defendant made a motion to dismiss on
the ground that the alleged contract was not enforceable under
§ 2–201. The plaintiff argued that the defendant should be required to raise its statute of frauds defense by answer to the

complaint rather than by a motion to dismiss "on the chance it will admit the existence of the alleged contract, thereby removing the statute as a bar under subsection 2–201(3)(b)." Judge Lacey dismissed this argument as follows: "This contention is without merit. Such a result would vitiate the statute." But the seller's argument has been accepted by some other courts. The following is taken from Garrison v. Piatt, 113 Ga.App. 94, 147 S.E.2d 374 (1966):

> While, under the law as it stood prior to the adoption of the Commercial Code, a party sued upon a parol contract for the sale of goods within the statute of frauds * * * could admit the contract and at the same time insist upon the benefit of the statute * * *; yet, since the adoption of the Uniform Commercial Code * * * such a contract, if otherwise valid, is enforceable "if the party against whom enforcement is sought admits in his pleading, testimony or otherwise in court that a contract for sale was made, * * *" as to the quantity of the goods admitted. UCC § 2–201(3)(b). Under the statute as it now stands, as to the sale of goods of the value of $500 or more, the party charged cannot admit the fact of the contract in the manner provided and at the same time claim the benefit of the statute of frauds. It is the intent of this change in the statute of frauds, that if, after the petition or cross action is filed, the person charged admits the contract in the case thus pending, the statute of frauds as a defense shall not be available to the party charged; but on the contrary the case thus made shall be determined on the merits without reference to the statute of frauds. This provision was designed to prevent the statute of frauds itself from becoming an aid to fraud, by prohibiting one claiming the benefit of the statute who admits in the case the oral contract sued upon. Since a contract, which is within the statute at the time of filing the petition or cross action, can become enforceable by admissions *only* in the case itself by the party charged, rather than admissions made outside the case prior to the filing of the petition or cross action,—it would, therefore, be contrary to the intention and purpose of the statutory change to permit the sustaining of a demurrer to a petition or cross action upon such a contract based on the ground that such petition or cross action shows upon its face that the contract is within the statute of frauds when it may become enforceable by acts occurring after the petition or cross action is filed. If a demurrer on this ground should be sustained to the petition, the plaintiff is denied his opportunity of determining on a trial whether the making of the contract would be admitted and thus made enforceable for the first time. By these changes in the statute of frauds, it is clearly the intent of the legislature that the enforceability of a contract, which

on its face may be within the statute, is tested by the answer, testimony or plea of the party charged, and not merely by the allegations in the petition or cross action brought to enforce the contract. It follows, therefore, that a petition upon such a contract which is valid in other respects is not demurrable because it shows on its face that it is within the statute of frauds; this for the reason that the demurrer admits the facts pleaded (for the purpose of the demurrer only) and the demurrer, thus admitting the contract, is ineffective to set up the benefit of the statute of frauds.

When California enacted the UCC it deleted § 2–201(3)(b), thus continuing previous law which allowed a defendant to raise a statute of frauds defense by demurrer. One reason for the deletion was expressed as follows: " * * * [§ 2–201(3)(b)] would reward a defendant's perjured denial. If a defendant denies the existence of the oral contract, no matter how strong the proof he is lying, the contract remains unenforceable. The same contract would be enforceable against a defendant who truthfully admitted an oral contract had been made." The Uniform Commercial Code, A Special Report by the California State Bar Committee on the Commercial Code, 37 Calif. State Bar Journal 142 (1962). In 1988 § 2–201(3)(b) was restored to the California UCC.

2. ESTOPPEL

WARDER & LEE ELEVATOR, INC. v. BRITTEN

Supreme Court of Iowa, 1979.
274 N.W.2d 339.

McCORMICK, JUSTICE.

The question in this action for breach of an oral contract to sell grain is whether the trial court erred in holding defendant's statute of frauds defense under the Uniform Commercial Code was defeated by promissory estoppel. We affirm the trial court.

* * *

Plaintiff Warder & Lee Elevator, Inc., operates a grain elevator in the town of Webster. The corporation president, Francis Lee, managed the elevator for many years until he suffered a slight stroke in November 1974. He was succeeded as manager by his son James who had been an elevator employee since 1964. The Lees were the only witnesses at trial.

We recite the evidence in the light most favorable to the judgment. Francis Lee was alone in the elevator office on July 4, 1974. Defendant John W. Britten, a farmer in the area, came to the office during the morning with a friend. The elevator had purchased Britten's grain for years, and he and Lee were well acquainted. At Britten's request Lee quoted him the price the elevator would pay for new-crop corn and soybeans for fall delivery based on market prices of the prior day.

Britten offered to sell and Lee agreed for the elevator to purchase from Britten 4000 bushels of corn at $2.60 per bushel and 2000 bushels of beans at $5.70 per bushel for October-November delivery.

The elevator did not at that time require a seller to sign a memorandum or other writing to show the agreement. Instead, the only writing consisted of notes showing the terms of sale made by Lee for internal bookkeeping purposes. All of the elevator's prior purchases from Britten had been upon oral agreement, and Britten had kept his promises on each occasion. In fact, no seller had previously refused to perform an oral agreement with the elevator.

It was the custom of the elevator not to speculate in grain but to act essentially as a broker. Thus on July 5, 1974, the elevator sold the same quantities of corn and beans as were involved in the Britten purchase for fall delivery to terminal elevators at Muscatine for a few cents more per bushel.

Grain prices increased substantially during July. On July 29, 1974, Britten called Francis Lee and said he wished to "call the deal off". Lee told him: "You cannot call it off. We sold this grain, and we expect delivery this fall." Britten said he would not deliver the grain.

In an effort to mitigate its loss and to enable it to meet its commitment to sell the grain, the elevator purchased appropriate quantities of new-crop corn and beans from other farmers on and shortly after July 29.

In August 1974, James Lee met Britten on a street in Webster. Britten initiated a conversation in which he said he would not fulfill his agreement and offered $500 in settlement. Although counsel for Britten objected to the admissibility of the evidence at trial, the objection was untimely and no motion to strike was made. Lee rejected the offer. He told Britten the elevator had sold the grain and expected him to perform under his contract.

Britten sold his 1974 crop elsewhere.

The elevator brought this action against Britten for breach of the oral agreement, seeking as damages the loss it sustained in covering its delivery obligation under the July 5 contracts by which it sold the quantity of grain purchased from Britten. See § 2–712. That loss was $6478.34, which was the amount, plus interest, for which the trial court entered judgment.

Britten offered no evidence at trial. He relied solely on the statute of frauds in § 2–201. The elevator urged promissory estoppel in bar of the defense.

The statute of frauds applicable to the sale of crops is § 2–201. Under this statute an oral contract for the sale of goods for a price of $500 or more is unenforceable, with certain stated exceptions. The elevator does not contend any of those exceptions is applicable. Promissory estoppel is not among them.

Authority for use of promissory estoppel to defeat the statute of frauds, if it exists, must be found under § 1–103. It provides:

> Unless displaced by the particular provisions of this chapter, the principles of law and equity, including the law merchant and the law relative to capacity to contract, principal and agent, estoppel, fraud, misrepresentation, duress, coercion, mistake, bankruptcy, or other validating or invalidating cause shall supplement its provisions.

We have not had occasion to decide whether the provisions of § 2–201 displace the doctrine of estoppel which would otherwise be available in accordance with § 1–103. However, other courts which have considered the question have held the doctrine is available. Several of those decisions involved grain sales in circumstances analogous to those in the present case. * * *

When other courts have refused to apply the doctrine they have done so because of a different view of the doctrine of promissory estoppel rather than because of any perceived statutory bar to its use. * * *

We have long recognized promissory estoppel as a means of defeating the general statute of frauds * * *. We see nothing in § 2–201 which purports to require a different rule under the Uniform Commercial Code.

The listing of exceptions to the statute of frauds in § 2–201 is plainly definitional. The provision does not purport to eliminate equitable and legal principles traditionally applicable in contract actions. Therefore it does not affect the viability of defenses to application of the rule of evidence which it defines. See White and Summers, Handbook of the Law Under the Uniform Commercial Code § 2–6 at 59 (1972) ("There is every reason to believe these remain good law, post-Code.").

If § 2–201 were construed as displacing principles otherwise preserved in § 1–103, it would mean that an oral contract coming within its terms would be unenforceable despite fraud, deceit, misrepresentation, dishonesty or any other form of unconscionable conduct by the party relying upon the statute. No court has taken such an extreme position. Nor would we be justified in doing so. Despite differences relating to the availability of an estoppel defense, courts uniformly hold "that the Statute of

Frauds, having been enacted for the purpose of preventing fraud, shall not be made the instrument of shielding, protecting, or aiding the party who relies upon it in the perpetration of a fraud or in the consummation of a fraudulent scheme." 3 Williston on Contracts § 553A at 796 (Third Ed. Jaeger, 1960). The estoppel defense, preserved on the same basis as the fraud defense by § 1–103, developed from this principle. "The Statute was designed as the weapon of the written law to prevent frauds; the doctrine of estoppel is that of the unwritten law to prevent a like evil." Id. at 797–798.

We have found no reported decision in any jurisdiction holding that the statute of frauds in the Uniform Commercial Code, defined as it is in § 2–201, displaces principles preserved in § 1–103. We do not believe that our legislature intended for it to do so.

We hold that the provisions of § 2–201 do not displace the doctrine of estoppel in relation to the sale of goods in Iowa.

We recently discussed the elements of promissory estoppel in Merrifield v. Troutner, 269 N.W.2d 136, 137 (Iowa 1978). Those elements are (1) a clear and definite oral agreement, (2) proof that the party urging the doctrine acted to his detriment in relying on the agreement, and (3) finding that the equities support enforcement of the agreement.

* * *

The issue is whether one has acted to his detriment in reliance upon the promise of another, and it is immaterial whether that promise was unilateral or bilateral. * * *

Specific circumstances which justify use of the doctrine as a means of avoiding a statute of frauds defense are now expressed in Restatement (Second) of Contracts § 217A (Tent.Draft 1–7, 1973), as follows:

(1) A promise which the promisor should reasonably expect to induce action or forbearance on the part of the promisee or a third person and which does induce the action or forbearance is enforceable notwithstanding the Statute of Frauds if injustice can be avoided only by enforcement of the promise. The remedy granted for breach is to be limited as justice requires.

(2) In determining whether injustice can be avoided only by enforcement of the promise, the following circumstances are significant:

(a) the availability and adequacy of other remedies, particularly cancellation and restitution;

(b) the definite and substantial character of the action or forbearance in relation to the remedy sought;

(c) the extent to which the action or forbearance corroborates evidence of the making and terms of the promise, or the making and terms are otherwise established by clear and convincing evidence;

(d) the reasonableness of the action or forbearance;

(e) the extent to which the action or forbearance was foreseeable by the promisor.

This section complements Restatement (Second) of Contracts § 90, the predecessor of which we previously approved. * * * We now approve and adopt the standard in § 217A.*

* * *

In order to obtain the benefit of the doctrine of promissory estoppel to defeat a statute of frauds defense, the promisee must show more than the nonperformance of an oral contract. * * * Under § 217A the defense cannot be overcome, when it is otherwise applicable, unless the promisee proves (1) the promisor should reasonably have expected the agreement to induce action or forbearance, (2) such action or forbearance was induced, and (3) enforcement is necessary to prevent injustice.

In determining whether injustice can be avoided only by enforcement of the promise, the circumstances listed in § 217A(2) must be considered. In this manner, § 217A provides a means of deciding whether the equities support enforcement of the agreement.

We must now decide whether the trial court erred in applying the doctrine of promissory estoppel in this case.

Britten contends the elevator should not have the benefit of the doctrine because it did not * * * prove he knew it would rely on the oral agreement.

* * * We * * * believe substantial evidence supports the inference he expected or reasonably should have expected the agreement to induce action by the elevator. It was not necessary for the elevator to prove he actually knew it would rely on his promise. He should have known his prior dealings with the elevator gave the elevator manager every reason to believe he would keep his word. Furthermore, it is reasonable to believe that a farmer who sells grain regularly to country elevators knows they may immediately sell the grain which they purchase. In this case, Britten expressed no surprise when the elevator refused to allow him to rescind because of its sales in reliance on the agreement. Instead he sought to buy his way out of the transaction.

We conclude that the elements of promissory estoppel were supported by substantial evidence. In keeping with the standard in Restatement § 217A, we hold that injustice could be avoided only by enforcement of Britten's promise. The trial court did not

---

* Editors' Note: This section is now Restatement, Second, Contracts, § 139.

err in holding the agreement was enforceable despite the statute of frauds defense.

Affirmed.

All Justices concur except REYNOLDSON, C.J., and ALLBEE, J., who dissent.

REYNOLDSON, CHIEF JUSTICE (dissenting).

I respectfully dissent. The contract in issue falls squarely within the language and intent of the statute of frauds, § 2–201. The majority opinion, in my view, misapprehends and misapplies our rules relating to promissory estoppel. Further, the facts in this case do not bring it within the new principles pioneered in this decision.

* * *

The lead sentence in § 2–201 now provides:

> Except as otherwise provided *in this section* a contract for the sale of goods for the price of five hundred dollars or more is not enforceable by way of action or defense unless there is some writing sufficient to indicate that a contract for sale has been made between the parties and signed by the party against whom enforcement is sought or by his authorized agent or broker.

(Emphasis provided.) * * *

With exceptions to the statute of frauds now specifically limited by the terms of the statute to those enumerated in its provisions, the majority's claim that promissory estoppel may be engrafted as simply another exception by virtue of § 1–103 loses viability. § 1–103 permits application of other legal principles, including estoppel, "unless displaced by the particular provisions of this chapter." Plainly, the limiting language of § 2–201 constitutes such a displacement. Had the legislature intended the concepts of §§ 90 and 217A of the tentative draft of the Restatement (Second) of Contracts to serve as an exception to its statute of frauds, it would have incorporated them as an exception in the act.

Displacing § 1–103 with the exceptions in § 2–201 does not render ineffectual the common-law principles contained in the former. First, they supplement other sections of the UCC except those, like § 2–201, which provide otherwise. Second, the victim of fraud who has no legal remedy because § 2–201 prevents proof of the oral contract is not left out in the cold. The equitable remedy of restitution is not dependent upon proof of a contract. The basic elements of equitable estoppel and fraud are (1) intentional misrepresentation, (2) innocent, reasonable and foreseeable reliance, and (3) injury. * * * Nor is a contract enforced in those situations. Recovery is based on the injury suffered in the course of reliance. As we stated in [Grefe v. Ross], the liability is predicated on the fraud, not on any contract. 231 N.W.2d at 868. With these remedies available, the statute of frauds gives a fraudulent party little protection.

The limiting language of § 2–201 at least ought to displace a doctrine which would gut the legislative intent of the statute. Distilled to its essence, § 217A, as interpreted by the majority, provides that if one contracting party should know the other contracting party will rely on the contract and injustice will result if the oral contract is not enforced, the statute of frauds will be ignored. It is a rare case when either promisor in a bilateral contract does not rely on the contract. * * * Any party to a contract should realize such reliance occurs. Most situations in which such an oral contract is breached result in injustice.

But the § 2–201 statute of frauds obviously is designed to suffer these injustices in isolated oral contract cases in favor of the general public policy to reduce fraud and perjury, curtail litigation and controversy, and encourage written contracts in sales of goods for a price of $500 or more. It is significant that by trial time the plaintiff corporation in the case at bar was using written sales contracts with its customers.

Adopting §§ 90 and 217A as an unwritten exception to § 2–201 will not only encourage oral contracts, it will bring a massive infusion of litigation to our overloaded courts. Trial courts will be compelled to determine, on an *ad hoc* basis, whether there was a contract, whether the promisor could "reasonably expect" the other party to rely on it, whether reasonable action or forbearance resulted, whether "justice requires" a remedy, and otherwise engage in the delicate balancing maneuvers mandated by § 217A(2).

* * *

Many courts have declined to create an additional exception based on promissory estoppel. They continue, as I am convinced we should, to view promissory estoppel as a doctrine of equity which provides only a means of enforcing unilateral promises, not a method of proving bilateral contracts. * * *

I agree that new § 217A (aided by revised § 90 as it is interpreted under the tentative draft) moots these problems and blends unilateral and bilateral promises, but that is why I would not adopt them. The tentative draft has essentially created a concept which is indistinguishable from promissory estoppel and applies it to bilateral contract proof problems.

The effect of promissory estoppel on § 2–201 under the majority opinion is devastating. If the statute is to be repealed the policy decision should be left with the legislature.

Finally, it should be noted the facts in this case would not warrant application of § 217A of the Restatement Tentative Draft.

Imposition of § 217A would require proof the defendant seller in this case "should reasonably expect" that the plaintiff corporation would promptly resell the grain. There is no evidence in the transcript in this case to show defendant either knew this was plaintiff's practice or that it was a custom in the industry.

Majority seeks to supply this crucial missing proof by asserting "it is reasonable to believe a farmer who sells grain regularly to country elevators knows they may immediately sell the grain which they purchase."

Majority seems to be judicially noting not only what defendant knew about elevator operations but also the sales practices in a private industry. I doubt these matters qualify for judicial notice as being within common knowledge or capable of certain verification. * * * Plaintiff corporation's operating officer did not assume defendant had this knowledge. He felt compelled to tell defendant the grain had been resold. This, of course, was long after the event and had no bearing on whether defendant should have "reasonably expect[ed]" such action.

*   *   *

NOTES

1. The dissenting judge in *Warder & Lee* made the following statement: "* * * the victim of fraud who has no legal remedy because § 2–201 prevents proof of the oral contract is not left out in the cold. The equitable remedy of restitution is not dependent upon proof of a contract." He also indicates that the fraud, rather than the contract, is the basis of the recovery. Does a remedy based on restitution or fraud help a buyer in a case such as *Warder & Lee?* Restatement, Second, Contracts § 375 states as follows:

> A party who would otherwise have a claim in restitution under a contract is not barred from restitution for the reason that the contract is unenforceable by him because of the Statute of Frauds unless the Statute provides otherwise or its purpose would be frustrated by allowing restitution.

The remedy of restitution is based on unjust enrichment. The typical case to which § 375 applies is that in which one party to the unenforceable contract confers a benefit on the other party by partially performing the contract or by making expenditures in reliance on the contract which benefit the other party. In either case, the contract cannot be enforced against the party receiving the benefit, but if that party refuses to honor the contract it must pay for the value of the benefit conferred. This remedy, however, has no application to a case such as *Warder & Lee.* The buyer in that case suffered a loss because of the seller's refusal to honor the oral contract but it did not confer any benefit on the seller.

Although a seller that repudiates a contract unenforceable under § 2–201 could be held liable to the other party on a fraud theory in unusual cases, recovery by the buyer for fraud in a typical case such as *Warder & Lee* is not likely. If the seller had not intended to honor the promise to sell when it was made, and if the promise was made to induce the buyer to act in reliance, as for example the making of some payment to the seller or a third party, the seller could be held liable in a deceit action for the buyer's reliance damages. Restatement, Second, Torts § 525 and § 530. Although in some cases tort damages might be the same as breach of contract damages, the oral contract is not being enforced. Rather, recovery is based on the injury to the buyer suffered in reliance on the seller's deceit. But in most cases of failure to perform an unenforceable contract there is no deceit involved. In *Warder & Lee* the seller undoubtedly intended to perform when he made the oral contract. He decided not to perform only when the rising market made performance disadvantageous. There was a breach of the promise to sell but there was no deceit.

2. Some courts, when presented with facts similar to those in *Warder & Lee,* will enforce the oral contract on the basis of equitable estoppel, a doctrine related to promissory estoppel but grounded on different principles. Northwest Potato Sales, Inc. v. Beck, 208 Mont. 310, 678 P.2d 1138 (1984), is an example. The facts were similar to those of *Warder & Lee.* * * * The court held that the seller was estopped to rely on the statute of frauds. The buyer (McCullough), and the repudiating seller (Beck), had done business with each other over a period of years, they were neighbors and their past dealings were such as to lull the seller into believing that he could rely on the buyer's oral promise. The court stated:

> This Court has never held that the absence of a signature to a contract otherwise binding is absolutely fatal to a contract for the sale of personal property. We recognized this principle most recently in Cargill Inc. v. Wilson (1975), 166 Mont. 346, 532 P.2d 988, where the defense was that the seller had not agreed to the contract because he had not signed the contract, even though his name had been signed to the contract by the grain dealer, with the seller's acquiescence. Although we recognized that the requirement of some writing is important to evidence the agreement, we held strict adherence to the signature requirement is not necessary where the "relationship and course of dealings between the parties justifies one party's belief that the other has consented to the written statement of contract, even though he had not signed it." 532 P.2d at 990. If the necessary relationship and course of dealings is established, we held that:

" * * * the contract may be enforced. The beneficial purposes of the statute of frauds are preserved—the dangers of mistake or fraud are averted—and the ends of justice are served." *Cargill,* supra, 532 P.2d at 990.

Although the facts of *Cargill* are not directly analogous to the factual situation here, the case clearly recognizes that lack of a signature to a contract for the sale of goods is not indispensable to the enforcement of a contract otherwise binding. And that is the situation here. But here we rely on the principles of estoppel in holding that Beck cannot be permitted to rely on the statute of frauds where his active and passive conduct in the transaction led McCullough to detrimentally rely on the belief that he had a contract.

*   *   *

This Court has recognized equitable estoppel, promissory estoppel, and estoppel by silence. * * *

Although we base our decision on estoppel by silence, we cannot deny that the facts may fit elements of estoppel also appropriate to equitable estoppel. This is so, because as is so often the case in any branch of the law, each form of estoppel does not fall into a neatly packaged and exclusive category. Rather, the forms of estoppel also blend with each other. For example, here there was not only a duty to speak imposed on Beck because of his relationship to McCullough and his knowledge that McCullough was relying on a belief that a contract existed, there was also active conduct by Beck that can only be interpreted as constituting an intent to mislead McCullough into thinking that Beck would honor the July 17th contract.

This Court set out the rule of estoppel by silence in Sherlock v. Greaves (1938), 106 Mont. 206, 76 P.2d 87, where we stated:

> "To constitute an estoppel by silence or acquiescence, it must appear that the party to be estopped was bound in equity and good conscience to speak, and that the party claiming estoppel relied upon the acquiescence and was misled thereby to change his position to his prejudice. [citing authority] Mere silence cannot work an estoppel. To be effective for this purpose, the person to be estopped must have had an intent to mislead or a willingness that another would be deceived; and the other must have been misled by the silence." Sherlock v. Greaves, supra, 106 Mont. at 217, 76 P.2d at 91.

The general situation is that Beck and McCullough knew each other well for many years, they had many dealings with each other over the years, and they had three previous potato seed sales where the same procedure was followed. Based on

past experience, Beck knew that McCullough had most probably committed the 10,000 cwt of Beck potatoes to Washington
"table-stock" farmers, and Beck testified that he assumed
such was the case in this transaction. Beck further testified
that from July 17, 1980, until the end of November, 1980,
McCullough at all times believed that he had a contract with
Beck. And yet if Beck did subjectively believe that he had no
contract with McCullough, he admitted he did nothing to
inform McCullough of his position until the end of November.
If Beck believed he had no contract with McCullough, he was
clearly bound in equity and good conscience to tell McCullough at his earliest opportunity that he believed he had no
contract. But Beck was silent.

However, the situation that existed after Beck received
the July 17th contract in the mail, involves more than mere
silence. Between July 17th and the end of November, McCullough testified that both Beck and Beck's wife told him on
more than one occasion that the contract would be signed and
sent to McCullough. Although Mrs. Beck denied the substance of these conversations with McCullough by stating that
she could not recall the details of the calls, McCullough's
testimony about his conversations with Charles Beck stands
unrefuted. Further, on two occasions Beck told McCullough
that his banker was concerned that he had not made a good
deal but that he (Beck) was unconcerned because he was
running the operation, not the banker. One of these occasions was in October when McCullough stopped at the Beck
place on his way from Townsend, Montana to the state of
Washington. This testimony also stands unrefuted. * * *
All of this is clear evidence that Beck, by his active as well as
passive conduct, led McCullough to believe that he had a
contract with Beck.

The uncontradicted evidence is that McCullough clearly
relied to his detriment on the belief, fostered by Beck's active
and passive conduct, that he had a contract with Beck. It was
not until the end of November, when the market price for
seed potatoes was up to $9.00 per cwt, that Beck first told
McCullough that a misunderstanding had occurred, that he
had never agreed to the contract, and that in any event he
had not signed the contract. When McCullough learned of
Beck's decision, in order to cover his commitment to Washington "table-stock" farmers for 10,000 cwt of Beck's seed potato
crop, McCullough was forced to borrow an additional $45,000
at interest to purchase the potato seeds at the existing higher
market price of $9.00 per cwt.

Finally, although Beck now makes an issue of not having
signed the July 17th contract, he did not hesitate in selling his

1980 seed potato crops to others on the basis of unwritten, unsigned contracts. The only difference was that Beck sold his crops for the then existing market price of approximately $9.00 per cwt rather than the $4.50 per cwt he would have obtained had he honored the July 17th contract with McCullough.

These facts establish an estoppel by silence as a matter of law.

3. THE MERCHANT'S EXCEPTION

BAZAK INTERNATIONAL CORP. v. MAST INDUSTRIES, INC.

Court of Appeals of New York, 1989.
73 N.Y.2d 113, 538 N.Y.S.2d 503, 535 N.E.2d 633.

KAYE, JUDGE.

This dispute between textile merchants concerning an alleged oral agreement to sell fabric centers on the "merchant's exception" to the Statute of Frauds (UCC 2–201[2]). We conclude that annotated purchase order forms signed by the buyer, sent to the seller and retained without objection, fall within the merchant's exception, satisfying the statutory requirement of a writing even without the seller's signature. It was therefore error to dismiss the buyer's breach of contract action on Statute of Frauds grounds, and deny it any opportunity to prove that the alleged agreement had indeed been made.

For purposes of this dismissal motion, we accept the facts as stated by plaintiff buyer (Bazak International). On April 22, 1987 Karen Fedorko, marketing director of defendant seller (Mast Industries), met with Tuvia Feldman, plaintiff's president, at Feldman's office. Fedorko offered to sell Feldman certain textiles that Mast was closing out, and the two negotiated all the terms of an oral agreement except price. At a meeting the following day, Fedorko and Feldman agreed on a price of $103,330. Fedorko told Feldman that Bazak would receive written invoices for the goods the next day and that the textiles would be delivered shortly. When no invoices arrived, Feldman contacted Fedorko, who assured him that everything was in order and that the invoices were on the way. However, on April 30, 1987, Fedorko had Feldman come to the New York City offices of Mast's parent company where, following Fedorko's instructions, Feldman sent five purchase orders by telecopier to Mast's Massachusetts office. That same day Feldman received written confirmation of Mast's receipt of the orders. Mast made no objection to the terms set forth in the telecopied purchase orders, but never delivered the textiles despite Bazak's demands.

Bazak then filed a complaint alleging breach of contract * * * which Mast moved to dismiss for failure to state a cause of action * * *. Mast contended that the only writings alleged in the complaint—the purchase orders sent by Bazak to Mast, and Mast's confirmation of receipt of the purchase orders—were insufficient under UCC 2–201 to satisfy the Statute of Frauds. * * *

Supreme Court denied the motion to dismiss, but the Appellate Division reversed, 140 A.D.2d 211, 528 N.Y.S.2d 62, holding that the breach of contract claim was barred by the Statute of Frauds * * *. The focal issue before us on Bazak's appeal from that order is whether the disputed documents qualified as confirmatory writings within the "merchant's exception" to the Statute of Frauds (UCC 2–201[2]). We conclude that they did, and therefore reverse the Appellate Division order.

At the heart of the dispute are two issues involving the telecopied purchase orders. *First,* the parties disagree as to the standard for determining whether the purchase orders are confirmatory documents: Mast asserts that there is a presumption against application of UCC 2–201(2)—if the memorandum on its face is such that a reasonable merchant could reasonably conclude that it was not a confirmation, then the claim is barred as a matter of law by the Statute of Frauds. Bazak, on the other hand, argues for a less restrictive standard—that is, a requirement only that the writings afford a belief that the alleged oral contract rests on a real transaction, a requirement Bazak contends that it has met. *Second,* the parties disagree as to the application of the governing standard to this complaint. Bazak contends that the purchase orders were sent in confirmation of the agreement already reached, and that there is sufficient support for that interpretation in the documents themselves; Mast argues that on their face, the purchase orders are no more than offers to enter into an agreement, and thus inadequate to satisfy the Statute of Frauds.

As to both issues, we are essentially in agreement with Bazak, and therefore reverse the order dismissing its complaint.

* * *

Description of the Writings

A total of five printed purchase order forms, all of them on Bazak's letterhead, were telecopies by Feldman to Mast from the offices of Mast's parent company. The first four are individual orders for various quantities of different types of fabric, while the fifth summarizes the orders and states the total price. All are dated April 23, 1987—the date of the alleged oral contract. On each form, are the handwritten words "As prisented [*sic*] by Karen Fedorko." At the bottom of each form are several lines of small type reading: "All claims must be made within 5 days after receipt of goods. No allowances or returns after goods are cut. This is only an offer and not a contract unless accepted in writing by the seller, and subject to prior sale." Each form concludes with two signature lines, one for "BAZAK INTERNATIONAL CORP." and one for "CUSTOMERS ACCEPTANCE." Each form is signed by Bazak, but the space for "CUSTOMERS ACCEPTANCE" remains blank.

An interoffice memorandum confirms that the purchase orders were telecopied to Mast's Massachusetts office from the premises of Mast's parent company on April 30, 1987.

The Writings as Confirmations of a Contract

* * *

Undisputedly, the alleged oral contract in this case was for the sale of more than $500 worth of goods, and the only writings were not signed by Mast, against whom enforcement is sought. Bazak claims, however, that the orders fall under the merchant's exception to the signature requirement contained in UCC 2–201(2): "Between merchants if within a reasonable time a writing in confirmation of the contract and sufficient against the sender is received and the party receiving it has reason to know its contents, it satisfies the requirements of subsection (1) against such party unless written notice of objection to its contents is given within 10 days after it is received." Bazak contends that the purchase orders are writings in confirmation of the oral agreement reached between Fedorko and Feldman, and that having failed to object to their contents Mast cannot now assert the Statute of Frauds defense.

At the outset, we are called upon to define the standard to be applied in determining whether a document can be construed as a confirmatory writing under UCC 2–201(2): are explicit words of confirmation necessary? Should there be a presumption against application of the section? Relying on a New Jersey case, Trilco Term. v. Prebilt Corp., 167 N.J.Super. 449, 400 A.2d 1237, affd. without opn. 174 N.J.Super. 24, 415 A.2d 356, and a subsequent Federal case applying (Trilco, Norminjil Sportswear Corp. v. TG & Y Stores Co., 644 F.Supp. 1 [S.D.N.Y.]), Mast argues that confirmatory language is necessary, and that an exacting standard should be imposed.

The cases cited by Mast do stand for the proposition that a writing offered as confirmatory in satisfaction of UCC 2–201(2) is insufficient unless it explicitly alerts the recipient to the fact that it is intended to confirm a previous agreement. In *Trilco* (supra), the lower court stated its belief that as a policy matter, a more stringent test was appropriate under UCC 2–201(2) than that applied under UCC 2–201(1) to determine if a writing was "sufficient to indicate that a contract for sale has been made", because under the merchant's exception, a party could be bound by a writing it had not signed. The Federal District Court in *Norminjil* (supra) found this reasoning persuasive in what it perceived to be the absence of any New York case law on the point.

We disagree. Cases dealing with the sufficiency of a confirmatory writing between merchants are hardly legion, but this is not the first time any New York court has interpreted the confirmatory writing requirement. In (B & R Textile Corp. v. Domino Textiles, 77 A.D.2d 539, 430 N.Y.S.2d 89), the Appellate Division found that an invoice specifying the parties to the sale, the goods, prices and quantities involved, and the terms of payment constituted a writing in confirmation of an oral contract. Moreover, although the Appellate Division did not articulate the standard it had applied in reaching that result, there was no mention of any express language of confirmation in the invoice, suggesting that a more liberal test was employed.

But even writing on a clean slate, we reject the exacting standard proposed by *Trilco* and *Norminjil* as inconsistent with the letter and spirit of the relevant UCC sales provisions.

UCC 2–201(1) requires that the writing be "sufficient to indicate" a contract, while UCC 2–201(2) calls for a writing "in confirmation of the contract." We see no reason for importing a more stringent requirement of explicitness to the latter section, and holding merchants engaged in business dealings to a higher standard of precision in their word choices. The official comment describes UCC 2–201(1) as simply requiring "that the writing afford a basis for believing that the offered oral evidence rests on a real transaction." As Karl Llewellyn, a principal drafter of UCC 2–201, explained to the New York Law Revision Commission: "What the section does * * * is to require some objective guaranty, other than word of mouth, that there really has been some deal." (1954 Report of N.Y.Law Rev.Commn., at 119.) We hold that the same standard applies under UCC 2–201(1) and 2–201(2), noting that this conclusion accords with the majority of courts and commentators that have considered the issue * * *.

Special merchant rules are sprinkled throughout article 2 of the Uniform Commercial Code, distinguishing the obligations of business people from others (see, UCC 2–103[1][b]; 2–205, 2–207[2]; 2–209[2]; 2–312[3]; 2–314[1]; 2–327[1][c]; 2–402[2]; 2–403[2]; 2–509[3]; 2–603[1]; 2–605[1][b]; and 2–609[2]). Among the suggested motivations was to state clear, sensible rules better adjusted to the reality of what commercial transactions were (or should be), thereby promoting predictable, dependable, decent business practices * * *. Section 2–201(2) recognized the common practice among merchants, particularly small businesses, to enter into oral sales agreements later confirmed in writing by one of the parties. Absent such a provision, only the party receiving the confirmatory writing could invoke the Statute of Frauds, giving that party the option of enforcing the contract or not, depending on how advantageous the transaction proved to be. UCC 2–201(2) was intended to address that inequity; it encourages the sending of confirmatory writings by removing the unfairness to the sender. * * *

In imposing a requirement that the writing explicitly state that it is sent in confirmation, the understandable concern of the New Jersey court in *Trilco* was that the effect of UCC 2–201(2) was "to bind a merchant to a writing that he did not sign" (167 N.J. Super., at 455, 400 A.2d, at 1240, supra), and thus to create a new potential unfairness: a merchant might unilaterally create a binding contract simply by dispatching unsolicited purchase orders, thus unfairly disadvantaging the recipient. Consequently, the court perceived it was necessary to require that the writing contain explicit language of confirmation or reference to the prior agreement, so the recipient could know that the sender was asserting the existence of a contract, and hence had a "meaningful opportunity" to exercise the right of objection found in UCC 2–201(2) (id., at 454, 400 A.2d, at 1240). This argument is not without merit. However, in our view it overlooks other protections provided by UCC 2–201.

A confirmatory writing does not satisfy the requirements of UCC 2–201(2) unless it is "sufficient against the sender." This alone provides some protection against abuse, for the sending merchant itself runs the risk of being held to a contract. Moreover, while we hold that explicit words of confirmation are not required, the writing still must satisfy the test articulated in UCC 2–201(1) that it be "sufficient to indicate that a contract for sale has been made". A purchase order, standing alone, is unlikely to meet this test. On the other hand, if the writing contains additional evidence that it is based upon a prior agreement, then as a policy matter it is not unfair to require the recipient to make written objection where there is an intent to disavow it. True, a rule requiring explicit confirmatory language or an express reference to the prior agreement could be applied mechanically and would afford the broadest possible protection to recipients of unsolicited orders. But that rigidity and breadth also could work unnecessary injustice and be unresponsive to the realities of business practice, which was a likely motivation for the merchant's exception in the first instance. Indeed, such a rule would reintroduce the very unfairness addressed by the reform, for the sending merchant still would be bound by the writing while the recipient could ignore it or enforce it at will (*see*, Comment, The Merchant's Exception to the Uniform Commercial Code's Statute of Frauds, 32 Villanova L.Rev. 133, 165–173 [1987]).

Finally, as additional protection against abuse and inequity, we note that the consequence of a failure to give timely written notice of objection to a confirmatory writing is only to remove the bar of the Statute of Frauds. The burden of proving that a contract was indeed made remains with the plaintiff, as does the burden of proving the terms of the contract. By the same token, the defendant remains free to urge that no contract was made, or that it differed from the one claimed by plaintiff (UCC 2–201, official comment 3). Thus, UCC 2–201(2) neither binds the receiving merchant to an agreement it has not made nor delivers an undeserved triumph to the sending merchant. It does no more than permit the sender to proceed with an attempt to prove its allegations.

We therefore conclude that, in determining whether writings are confirmatory documents within UCC 2–201(2), neither explicit words of confirmation nor express references to the prior agreement are required, and the writings are sufficient so long as they afford a basis for believing that they reflect a real transaction between the parties.

It remains for us to apply this standard to the facts and determine whether the documents in issue satisfy the requirements of UCC 2–201(2).

Of the various requirements of UCC 2–201(2), four are not in controversy. There is no dispute that both parties are merchants, that the writing was sent within a reasonable time after the alleged agreement, that it was received by someone with reason to know of its contents, and that no written objection was made. If the writings can be construed as confirming the alleged oral agreement, they are sufficient under UCC 2–201(1) against Bazak—the sender—since Bazak signed them. Thus, the open question is whether, applying the governing standard, the documents here were sufficient to indicate the existence of a prior agreement.

Cases considering whether writings containing the words "order" or "purchase order" could satisfy the "confirmatory" requirement of UCC 2–201(2) fall into two categories. In some, the writings on their face contemplated only a future agreement, and they were held insufficient to overcome the Statute of Frauds defense * * *; in others, there was language clearly indicating that a contract had already been made, and the writings were deemed sufficient * * *. The writings here do not fit neatly into either group. However, taken as a whole, there is sufficient evidence that the writings rest on a real transaction, and therefore satisfy the Statute of Frauds.

We first address Mast's contention—apparently decisive in the Appellate Division—that the small print at the foot of the forms to the effect that they are "ONLY AN OFFER AND NOT A CONTRACT UNLESS ACCEPTED IN WRITING BY THE SELLER" must be given literal effect and precludes the possibility that the writings were confirmatory of an

agreement. While an express disclaimer generally would suffice
to disqualify a memorandum as confirmatory of an oral agreement
* * * it is plain from the face of these documents that the
printed matter was entirely irrelevant to the dealings between
these parties. The forms themselves bespeak their purpose: to
record a sale by Bazak as seller, not a purchase by Bazak as buyer.
The language regarding claims, allowances and returns are clearly
all referable to a transaction in which Bazak was the seller, as is
the signature line for Bazak. Read literally, these forms would
not even have allowed for Mast's signature; the line for "CUSTOM-
ERS ACCEPTANCE" is obviously inapplicable—Bazak, not Mast, was
the customer. In short, though Mast is free to argue at trial that
different inferences should be drawn, the forms indicate that
Bazak simply used its seller's documents to record its confirmation
of the alleged contract, and that the small print at the bottom of
the page was no part of that communication.

The handwritten notations on the purchase order forms provide a basis for believing that the documents were in furtherance
of a previous agreement. The terms set forth are highly specific;
precise quantities, descriptions, prices per unit and payment terms
are stated. The documents refer to an earlier presentation by
defendant's agent Karen Fedorko. The date April 23, 1987 is
written on the forms and the date April 30 on the transmission,
indicating reference to a transaction that took place a week before
they were sent. Finally, Mast itself relayed Bazak's forms. The
telecopier transmittal sheet shows that the forms were sent to
Mast by defendant's own parent company in New York, using its
facilities—obviously suggesting that the forms were not merely
unsolicited purchase orders from Bazak, but that their content
reflected an agreement that had been reached between the parties.

While no one of these factors would be sufficient under UCC
2–201(2), considered together they adequately indicate confirmation of a preexisting agreement so as to permit Bazak to go
forward and prove its allegations.

Finally on this issue, addressing the dissent, it is apparent
that a philosophical difference divides the court. The plain implication of the dissent is that express confirmatory language is
needed because "ambiguous" confirmatory writings unfairly burden receiving merchants. The majority, by contrast, perceives
that the Code intended to place such a burden on the receiving
merchant because there is less unfairness in requiring it to disavow than in denying the sending merchant who has failed to use
any magic words an opportunity to prove the existence of a
contract. A merchant bent on fraud, of course, can easily send
documents containing express confirmation of a nonexistent oral
contract, so it is difficult to see how our reading of the statute
"weakens" its protection against fraud * * *. The protection

consists of requiring a writing that provides a basis for belief that
it rests on a real transaction—no more, no less. If the writing is
sufficient to indicate the existence of a contract, it is also sufficient
at the pleading stage to support an inference that the receiving
merchant knew full well what it was.

* * *

ALEXANDER, JUDGE, dissenting.

In my view, the purchase orders at issue here, which describe
themselves as offers and do not otherwise indicate the existence of
a completed agreement are not "sufficient against the sender"
(UCC 2–201[2]) because they fail to "indicate that a contract for
sale has been made between the parties" (UCC 2–201[1]). Consequently they are not confirmatory memoranda sufficient to satisfy
the Statute of Frauds and plaintiff's contract cause of action was
properly dismissed. * * *

The majority concludes that the merchant's exception of UCC
2–201(2) does not require that writings contain express confirmatory language * * * and that writings satisfy both UCC 2–201(1)
and (2) when they are "sufficient to indicate that a contract for
sale has been made between the parties" (UCC 2–201[1]) and are
therefore "sufficient against the sender" (UCC 2–201[2]). In my
view, however, it is unnecessary to reach the question of whether
UCC 2–201(2) requires that writings "in confirmation of the contract" contain express confirmatory language because Bazak's
purchase orders do not satisfy UCC 2–201(1). As the only proper
inference to be drawn from the plain language of the purchase
orders is that they are offers, the majority's determination that
they evidence a completed contract is nothing more than speculation. These purchase orders expressly state that they are offers,
and even if this plain language can be disregarded, the remaining
language of the orders is ambiguous at best. By holding that the
requirements of UCC 2–201 are satisfied by these writings, the
majority undermines the very protections the statute was intended to afford.

* * *

The official comment explains that a writing sufficiently "indicate[s] that a contract for sale has been made" (UCC 2–201[1])
when it "afford[s] a basis for believing that the offered oral
evidence rests on a real transaction" (UCC 2–201, official comment
1). While the majority correctly articulates this standard, it
misapplies this standard by holding that these writings, which are
at best ambiguous, satisfy the statute.

* * *

Here, the majority's conclusion that there is sufficient evidence that Bazak's purchase orders evidence a completed contract
is refuted by the writings themselves. As indicated earlier, the
writings are at best ambiguous, allowing for equally probable

inferences that the parties either engaged only in negotiations or entered a contract. They do not demonstrate that the existence of a contract is more probable than not ＊   ＊   ＊ and therefore cannot satisfy the statute. Indeed, in view of this manifest ambiguity, a finding that these purchase orders "indicate that a contract for sale has been made" would require resort to the extraneous evidence of the practices and intentions of the parties offered by Bazak. Consideration of such evidence outside the terms of the documents themselves, however, is clearly precluded by the Statute of Frauds (UCC 2–201).

The purchase orders, by their own terms, are only offers. Each form states "THIS IN [*sic*] ONLY AN OFFER AND NOT A CONTRACT UNLESS ACCEPTED IN WRITING BY THE SELLER". The plain import of this language, in this action where defendant was a seller, was that defendant would not be bound unless it signed the form. The majority attempts to avoid the import of this plain language, urging that it should be disregarded because this printed statement is on a form plaintiff usually used when acting as a seller and thus is meaningless in this alleged transaction where plaintiff was acting as a buyer ＊   ＊   ＊. Significantly, plaintiff, who prepared the documents, never indicated on any of the forms that this disclaimer should be disregarded and, fully aware of the existence of the disclaimer, signed each form on the line provided beneath it. Moreover, the fact that plaintiff usually used these forms in its capacity as a seller is not properly considered in evaluating the sufficiency of the documents on their face ＊   ＊   ＊.

Even if the "offer" language properly could be disregarded, the purchase orders nevertheless are ambiguous and therefore insufficient to "indicate that a contract for sale has been made" (UCC 2–201[1]). Four of the purchase orders merely list quantities of goods and prices, with the additional notation "as prisented [*sic*] by Karen Fedorko". This reference to a presentation by defendant's employee is simply that—there is no indication that an agreement was reached at that presentation. Additionally, the list of goods and prices, as well as the totals contained in the fifth purchase order similarly provide no basis for inferring that a contract was made before the orders were drafted. They do not list delivery terms or other special requirements of the seller which might indicate that an agreement had been reached ＊   ＊   ＊. The fact that the purchase orders were transmitted from defendant's home office, while possibly unusual, sheds no light on whether the parties had reached an agreement. Thus, nothing in the purchase orders reasonably leads to the conclusion that the existence of a completed contract is more probable than not.

Finally, the majority's holding that these purchase orders satisfy UCC 2–201(1) and (2) substantially weakens the statute's protection against fraud. To assert the Statute of Frauds defense,

merchants will be required to promptly respond to writings which
provide no notice that the sender believes that they have a
contract and which may in fact indicate to the contrary: that the
sender has submitted an offer. Such a rule unfairly burdens the
receiving merchants and effectively negates the very purpose and
intent of UCC 2–201(2): to put both the sending merchant and the
receiving merchant on equal footing.

* * *

NOTE

The majority opinion states that "special merchant rules are
sprinkled throughout Article 2 of the Uniform Commercial Code,
distinguishing the obligations of business people from others
* * *." It goes on to cite 13 provisions of Article 2 in which a
special rule applicable to merchants is stated. Thus, the definition of "merchant" in § 2–104(1) is a key provision of Article 2.
The term is used in many different contexts and the question of
whether a person is or is not a merchant may depend upon the
context in which the issue arises. Under § 2–104(1) a person is
deemed to be a merchant for the purposes of the transaction
involved if either of two tests is satisfied. First, if the person
"deals" in the goods involved, the person is a merchant. The
quoted term is not defined in the UCC and its precise meaning is
not clear but, in Article 2, it primarily refers to a person engaged
in the business of buying or selling goods of the kind involved in
the transaction. The definition also applies to Article 2A which
applies to leases of goods. Second, a person is deemed to be a
merchant if the person "by his occupation holds himself out as
having knowledge or skill peculiar to the practices or goods
involved in the transaction * * *." This aspect of the definition
is very broad and a person may be deemed to be a merchant or not
depending upon the particular section of Article 2 that is involved
in the dispute.

Comment 2 to § 2–104 discusses the flexible nature of the
definition of "merchant" and the way in which it is read broadly
or narrowly in different contexts.

C. MODIFICATION

WISCONSIN KNIFE WORKS v. NATIONAL METAL CRAFTERS

United States Court of Appeals, Seventh Circuit, 1986.
781 F.2d 1280.

POSNER, CIRCUIT JUDGE.

* * *

We come, then, to the merits of the appeal. Wisconsin Knife Works, having some unused manufacturing capacity, decided to try to manufacture spade bits for sale to its parent, Black & Decker, a large producer of tools, including drills. A spade bit is made out of a chunk of metal called a spade bit blank; and Wisconsin Knife Works had to find a source of supply for these blanks. National Metal Crafters was eager to be that source. After some negotiating, Wisconsin Knife Works sent National Metal Crafters a series of purchase orders on the back of each of which was printed, "Acceptance of this Order, either by acknowledgment or performance, constitutes an unqualified agreement to the following." A list of "Conditions of Purchase" follows, of which the first is, "No modification of this contract, shall be binding upon Buyer [Wisconsin Knife Works] unless made in writing and signed by Buyer's authorized representative. Buyer shall have the right to make changes in the Order by a notice, in writing, to Seller." There were six purchase orders in all, each with the identical conditions. National Metal Crafters acknowledged the first two orders (which had been placed on August 21, 1981) by letters that said, "Please accept this as our acknowledgment covering the above subject order," followed by a list of delivery dates. The purchase orders had left those dates blank. Wisconsin Knife Works filled them in, after receiving the acknowledgments, with the dates that National Metal Crafters had supplied in the acknowledgments. There were no written acknowledgments of the last four orders (placed several weeks later, on September 10, 1981). Wisconsin Knife Works wrote in the delivery dates that National Metal Crafters orally supplied after receiving purchase orders in which the space for the date of delivery had again been left blank.

Delivery was due in October and November 1981. National Metal Crafters missed the deadlines. But Wisconsin Knife Works did not immediately declare a breach, cancel the contract, or seek damages for late delivery. Indeed, on July 1, 1982, it issued a new batch of purchase orders (later rescinded). By December 1982 National Metal Crafters was producing spade bit blanks for Wisconsin Knife Works under the original set of purchase orders in adequate quantities, though this was more than a year after the delivery dates in the orders. But on January 13, 1983, Wisconsin Knife Works notified National Metal Crafters that the contract was terminated. By that date only 144,000 of the more than 281,000 spade bit blanks that Wisconsin Knife Works had ordered in the six purchase orders had been delivered.

Wisconsin Knife Works brought this breach of contract suit, charging that National Metal Crafters had violated the terms of delivery in the contract that was formed by the acceptance of the six purchase orders. National Metal Crafters replied that the delivery dates had not been intended as firm dates. It also counterclaimed for damages for (among other things) the breach of an alleged oral agreement by Wisconsin Knife Works to pay the expenses of maintaining machinery used by National Metal Crafters to fulfill the contract. The parties later stipulated that the amount of these damages was $30,000.

The judge ruled that there had been a contract but left to the jury to decide whether the contract had been modified and, if so, whether the modified contract had been broken. The jury found that the contract had been modified and not broken. Judgment was entered dismissing Wisconsin Knife Works' suit and awarding National Metal Crafters $30,000 on its counterclaim. Wisconsin Knife Works has appealed from the dismissal of its suit. The appeal papers do not discuss the counterclaim, and the effect on it of our remanding the case for further proceedings on Wisconsin Knife Works' claim will have to be resolved on remand.

The principal issue is the effect of the provision in the purchase orders that forbids the contract to be modified other than by a writing signed by an authorized representative of the buyer. The theory on which the judge sent the issue of modification to the jury was that the contract could be modified orally or by conduct as well as by a signed writing. National Metal Crafters had presented evidence that Wisconsin Knife Works had accepted late delivery of the spade bit blanks and had cancelled the contract not because of the delays in delivery but because it could not produce spade bits at a price acceptable to Black & Decker.

Section 2–209(2) of the Uniform Commercial Code provides that "a signed agreement which excludes modification or rescission except by a signed writing cannot be otherwise modified or rescinded, but except as between merchants such a requirement on a form supplied by the merchant must be separately signed by the other party." The meaning of this provision and its proviso is not crystalline and there is little pertinent case law. One might think that an agreement to exclude modification except by a signed writing must be signed in any event by the party against whom the requirement is sought to be enforced, that is, by National Metal Crafters, rather than by the party imposing the requirement. But if so the force of the proviso ("but except as between merchants * * *") becomes unclear, for it contemplates that between merchants no separate signature by the party sought to be bound by the requirement is necessary. A possible reconciliation, though not one we need embrace in order to decide this case, is to read the statute to require a separate signing or initialing of the clause forbidding oral modifications, as well as of the contract in which the clause appears. There was no such signature here; but it doesn't matter; this was a contract "between merchants." Although in ordinary language a manufacturer is not a merchant, "between merchants" is a term of art in the Uniform Commercial

Code. It means between commercially sophisticated parties (see UCC § 2–104(1); White & Summers, Handbook of the Law Under the Uniform Commercial Code 345 (2d ed. 1980)), which these were.

Of course there must still be a "signed agreement" containing the clause forbidding modification other than by a signed writing, but there was that (see definition of "agreement" and of "signed" in UCC §§ 1–201(3), (39)). National Metal Crafters' signed acknowledgments of the first two purchase orders signified its assent to the printed conditions and naturally and reasonably led Wisconsin Knife Works to believe that National Metal Crafters meant also to assent to the same conditions should they appear in any subsequent purchase orders that it accepted. Those subsequent orders were accepted, forming new contracts on the same conditions as the old, by performance—that is, by National Metal Crafters' beginning the manufacture of the spade bit blanks called for by the orders. See UCC § 2–207(3). So there was an agreement, signed by National Metal Crafters, covering all the purchase orders. The fact that the delivery dates were not on the purchase orders when received by National Metal Crafters is nothing of which it may complain; it was given *carte blanche* to set those dates.

When National Metal Crafters had difficulty complying with the original specifications for the spade bit blanks, Wisconsin Knife Works modified them; and National Metal Crafters argues that the engineering drawings containing those modifications are the written modification that section 2–209(2), if applicable, calls for. In fact these particular modifications seem to fall within the clause of the contract that allows the buyer (Wisconsin Knife Works) to modify the specifications by notice. The context of this clause makes clear that such notice is not the written modification to which the previous sentence refers. But in any event there was no modification of the delivery dates. The "pert charts" which National Metal Crafters supplied Wisconsin Knife Works, and which showed new target dates for delivery, do not purport to modify the contract and were not signed by Wisconsin Knife Works.

We conclude that the clause forbidding modifications other than in writing was valid and applicable and that the jury should not have been allowed to consider whether the contract had been modified in some other way. This may, however, have been a harmless error. Section 2–209(4) of the Uniform Commercial Code provides that an "attempt at modification" which does not satisfy a contractual requirement that modifications be in writing nevertheless "can operate as a waiver." Although in instructing the jury on modification the judge did not use the word "waiver," maybe he gave the substance of a waiver instruction and maybe therefore the jury found waiver but called it modification. Here is the relevant instruction:

> Did the parties modify the contract? The defendant bears the burden of proof on this one. You shall answer this question yes only if you are convinced to a reasonable certainty that the parties modified the contract.
>
> If you determine that the defendant had performed in a manner different from the strict obligations imposed on it by the contract, and the plaintiff by conduct or other means of expression induced a reasonable belief by the defendant that strict enforcement was not insisted upon, but that the modified performance was satisfactory and acceptable as equivalent, then you may conclude that the parties have assented to a modification of the original terms of the contract and that the parties have agreed that the different mode of performance will satisfy the obligations imposed on the parties by the contract.

To determine whether this was in substance an instruction on waiver we shall have to consider the background of section 2–209, the Code provision on modification and waiver.

Because the performance of the parties to a contract is typically not simultaneous, one party may find himself at the mercy of the other unless the law of contracts protects him. Indeed, the most important thing which that law does is to facilitate exchanges that are not simultaneous by preventing either party from taking advantage of the vulnerabilities to which sequential performance may give rise. If A contracts to build a highly idiosyncratic gazebo for B, payment due on completion, and when A completes the gazebo B refuses to pay, A may be in a bind—since the resale value of the gazebo may be much less than A's cost—except for his right to sue B for the price. Even then, a right to sue for breach of contract, being costly to enforce, is not a completely adequate remedy. B might therefore go to A and say, "If you don't reduce your price I'll refuse to pay and put you to the expense of suit"; and A might knuckle under. If such modifications are allowed, people in B's position will find it harder to make such contracts in the future, and everyone will be worse off.

The common law dealt with this problem by refusing to enforce modifications unsupported by fresh consideration. See, e.g., Alaska Packers' Ass'n v. Domenico, 117 Fed. 99 (9th Cir.1902), discussed in Selmer Co. v. Blakeslee-Midwest Co., 704 F.2d 924, 927 (7th Cir.1983). Thus in the hypothetical case just put B could not have enforced A's promise to accept a lower price. But this solution is at once overinclusive and underinclusive—the former because most modifications are not coercive and should be enforceable whether or not there is fresh consideration, the latter because, since common law courts inquire only into the existence and not the adequacy of consideration, a requirement of fresh consideration has little bite. B might give A a peppercorn, a kitten, or a robe in exchange for A's agreeing to reduce the contract price, and then the modification would be enforceable and A could no longer sue for the original price. See White & Summers, supra, at 47; Farnsworth, Contracts 271–78 (1982).

The draftsmen of the Uniform Commercial Code took a fresh approach, by making modifications enforceable even if not supported by consideration (see section 2–209(1)) and looking to the doctrines of duress and bad faith for the main protection against exploitive or opportunistic attempts at modification, as in our hypothetical case. See UCC § 2–209, official comment 2. But they did another thing as well. In section 2–209(2) they allowed the parties to exclude oral modifications. National Metal Crafters argues that two subsections later they took back this grant of power by allowing an unwritten modification to operate as a waiver.

The common law did not enforce agreements such as section 2–209(2) authorizes. The "reasoning" was that the parties were always free to agree orally to cancel their contract and the clause forbidding modifications not in writing would disappear with the rest of the contract when it was cancelled. "The most ironclad written contract can always be cut into by the acetylene torch of parol modification supported by adequate proof." Wagner v. Graziano Construction Co., 390 Pa. 445, 448, 136 A.2d 82, 83–84 (1957). This is not reasoning; it is a conclusion disguised as a metaphor. It may have reflected a fear that such clauses, buried in the fine print of form contracts, were traps for the unwary; a sense that they were unnecessary because only modifications supported by consideration were enforceable; and a disinclination to allow parties in effect to extend the reach of the Statute of Frauds, which requires only some types of contract to be in writing. But the framers of the Uniform Commercial Code, as part and parcel of rejecting the requirement of consideration for modifications, must have rejected the traditional view; must have believed that the protection which the doctrines of duress and bad faith give against extortionate modifications might need reinforcement—if not from a requirement of consideration, which had proved ineffective, then from a grant of power to include a clause requiring modifications to be in writing and signed. An equally important point is that with consideration no longer required for modification, it was natural to give the parties some means of providing a substitute for the cautionary and evidentiary function that the requirement of consideration provides; and the means chosen was to allow them to exclude oral modifications.

If section 2–209(4), which as we said provides that an attempted modification which does not comply with subsection (2) can nevertheless operate as a "waiver," is interpreted so broadly that *any* oral modification is effective as a waiver notwithstanding section 2–209(2), both provisions become superfluous and we are back in the common law—only with not even a requirement of consideration to reduce the likelihood of fabricated or unintended oral modifications. [A conceivable but unsatisfactory way around this result is to distinguish between a modification that substitutes a new term for an old, and a waiver, which merely removes an old term.] On this interpretation National Metal Crafters could not enforce an oral term of the allegedly modified contract but could be excused from one of the written terms. This would take care of a case such as *Alaska Packers,* where seamen attempted to enforce a contract modification that raised their wages, but would not take care of the functionally identical case where seamen sought to collect the agreed-on wages without doing the agreed-on work. Whether the party claiming modification is seeking to impose an onerous new term on the other party or to wriggle out of an onerous term that the original contract imposed on it is a distinction without a difference. We can see that in this case. National Metal Crafters, while claiming that Wisconsin Knife Works broke their contract as orally modified to extend the delivery date, is not seeking damages for that breach. But this is small comfort to Wisconsin Knife Works, which thought it had a binding contract with fixed delivery dates. Whether called modification or waiver, what National Metal Crafters is seeking to do is to nullify a key term other than by a signed writing. If it can get away with this merely by testimony about an oral modification, section 2–209(2) becomes very nearly a dead letter.

The path of reconciliation with subsection (4) is found by attending to the precise wording of (4). It does not say that an attempted modification "is" a waiver; it says that "it can operate as a waiver." It does not say in what circumstances it can operate as a waiver; but if an attempted modification is effective as a waiver only if there is reliance, then both sections 2–209(2) and 2–209(4) can be given effect. Reliance, if reasonably induced and reasonable in extent, is a common substitute for consideration in making a promise legally enforceable, in part because it adds something in the way of credibility to the mere say-so of one party. The main purpose of forbidding oral modifications is to prevent the promisor from fabricating a modification that will let him escape his obligations under the contract; and the danger of successful fabrication is less if the promisor has actually incurred a cost, has relied. There is of course a danger of bootstrapping—of incurring a cost in order to make the case for a modification. But it is a risky course and is therefore less likely to be attempted than merely testifying to a conversation; it makes one put one's money where one's mouth is.

We find support for our proposed reconciliation of subsections (2) and (4) in the secondary literature. See Eisler, Oral Modification of Sales Contracts Under the Uniform Commercial Code: The Statute of Frauds Problem, 58 Wash.U.L.Q. 277, 298–302 (1980); Farnsworth, supra, at 476–77; 6 Corbin on Contracts 211 (1962). It is true that 2 Anderson on the Uniform Commercial Code § 2–209:42 (3d ed. 1982), opines that reliance is not necessary for an attempted modification to operate as a waiver, but he does not explain his conclusion or provide any reason or authority to support it. This provision was quoted along with other material from Anderson in Double-E Sportswear Corp. v. Girard Trust Bank, 488 F.2d 292, 295 (3d Cir.1973), but there was no issue of reliance in that case. 2 Hawkland, Uniform Commercial Code Series § 2–209:05, at p. 138 (1985), remarks, "if clear factual evidence other than mere parol points to that conclusion [that an oral agreement was made altering a term of the contract], a waiver may be found. In the normal case, however, courts should be careful not to allow the protective features of sections 2–209(2) and (3) to be nullified by contested parol evidence." (Footnote omitted.) The instruction given by the judge in this case did not comply with this test, but in any event we think a requirement of reliance is clearer than a requirement of "clear factual evidence other than mere parol."

Our approach is not inconsistent with section 2–209(5), which allows a waiver to be withdrawn while the contract is executory, provided there is no "material change of position in reliance on the waiver." Granted, in (5) there can be no tincture of reliance; the whole point of the section is that a waiver may be withdrawn unless there is reliance. But the section has a different domain from section 2–209(4). It is not limited to attempted modifications invalid under subsections (2) or (3); it applies, for example, to an express written and signed waiver, provided only that the contract is still executory. Suppose that while the contract is still executory the buyer writes the seller a signed letter waiving some term in the contract and then, the next day, before the seller has relied, retracts it in writing; we have no reason to think that such a retraction would not satisfy section 2–209(5), though this is not an issue we need definitively resolve today. In any event we are not suggesting that "waiver" means different things in (4) and (5); it means the same thing; but the *effect* of an attempted modification as a waiver under (4) depends in part on (2), which (4) (but not (5)) qualifies. Waiver and estoppel (which requires reliance to be effective) are frequently bracketed. See, e.g., Chemetron Corp. v. McLouth Steel Corp., 522 F.2d 469, 472–73 (7th Cir.1975); Hirsch Rolling Mill Co. v. Milwaukee & Fox River Valley Ry., 165 Wis. 220, 161 N.W. 741 (1917).

The statute could be clearer; but the draftsmen were making a big break with the common law in subsections (1) and (2), and

naturally failed to foresee all the ramifications of the break.
* * *

We know that the draftsmen of section 2–209 wanted to make it possible for parties to exclude oral modifications. They did not just want to give "modification" another name—"waiver." Our interpretation gives effect to this purpose. It is also consistent with though not compelled by the case law. There are no Wisconsin cases on point. Cases from other jurisdictions are diverse in outlook. Some take a very hard line against allowing an oral waiver to undo a clause forbidding oral modification. See, e.g., South Hampton Co. v. Stinnes Corp., 733 F.2d 1108, 1117–18 (5th Cir.1984) (Texas law); U.S. Fibres, Inc. v. Proctor & Schwartz, Inc., 358 F.Supp. 449, 460 (E.D.Mich.1972), aff'd, 509 F.2d 1043 (6th Cir. 1975) (Pennsylvania law). Others allow oral waivers to override such clauses, but in most of these cases it is clear that the party claiming waiver had relied to his detriment. * * *

Missing from the jury instruction on "modification" in this case is any reference to reliance, that is, to the incurring of costs by National Metal Crafters in reasonable reliance on assurances by Wisconsin Knife Works that late delivery would be acceptable. And although there is evidence of such reliance, it naturally was not a focus of the case, since the issue was cast as one of completed (not attempted) modification, which does not require reliance to be enforceable. National Metal Crafters must have incurred expenses in producing spade bit blanks after the original delivery dates, but whether these were *reliance* expenses is a separate question. Maybe National Metal Crafters would have continued to manufacture spade bit blanks anyway, in the hope of selling them to someone else. It may be significant that the stipulated counterclaim damages seem limited to the damages from the breach of a separate oral agreement regarding the maintenance of equipment used by National Metal Crafters in fulfilling the contract. The question of reliance cannot be considered so open and shut as to justify our concluding that the judge would have had to direct a verdict for National Metal Crafters, the party with the burden of proof on the issue. Nor, indeed, does National Metal Crafters argue that reliance was shown as a matter of law.

* * *

Reversed and remanded.

EASTERBROOK, CIRCUIT JUDGE, dissenting.

The majority demonstrates that the clause of the contract requiring all modifications to be in writing is enforceable against National Metal Crafters. There was no modification by a "signed writing." Yet § 2–209(4) of the Uniform Commercial Code, which Wisconsin has adopted, provides that "an attempt at modification" that is ineffective because of a modification-only-in-writing clause "can operate as a waiver." The majority holds that no "attempt at modification" may be a "waiver" within the meaning of § 2–209(4) unless the party seeking to enforce the waiver has relied to its detriment. I do not think that detrimental reliance is an essential element of waiver under § 2–209(4).

"Waiver" is not a term the UCC defines. At common law "waiver" means an intentional relinquishment of a known right. A person may relinquish a right by engaging in conduct inconsistent with the right or by a verbal or written declaration. I do not know of any branch of the law—common, statutory, or constitutional—in which a renunciation of a legal entitlement is effective only if the other party relies to his detriment. True, the law of "consideration" imposed something like a reliance rule; payment of a pine nut (the peppercorn of nouvelle cuisine) is a tiny bit of detriment, and often the law of consideration is expressed in terms of detriment. But § 2–209(1) of the UCC provides that consideration is unnecessary to make a modification effective. The introduction of a reliance requirement into a body of law from which the doctrine of consideration has been excised is novel.

* * *

Not all novel things are wrong, although legal novelties, like biological mutations, usually die out quickly. This novelty encounters an obstacle within § 2–209. Section 2–209(5) states that a person who "has made a waiver affecting an executory portion of the contract may retract the waiver" on reasonable notice "unless the retraction would be unjust in view of a material change of position in reliance on the waiver." Section 2–209 therefore treats "waiver" and "reliance" as different. Under § 2–209(4) a waiver may be effective; under § 2–209(5) a waiver may be effective *prospectively* only if there was also detrimental reliance.

The majority tries to reconcile the two subsections by stating that they have different domains. Section 2–209(4) deals with oral waivers, while § 2–209(5) "is not limited to attempted modifications invalid under subsections (2) or (3); it applies, for example, to express written waivers, provided only that the contract is executory." This distinction implies that subsection (4) applies to a subset of the subjects of subsection (5). Things are the other way around. Subsection (4) says that an attempt at modification may be a "waiver," and subsection (5) qualifies the effectiveness of "waivers" in the absence of reliance. See comment 4 to § 2–209. The two have the same domain—all attempts at modification, be they oral, written, or implied from conduct, that do not satisfy the Statute of Frauds, § 2–209(3), or a "signed writing" requirement of a clause permitted under § 2–209(2). The majority suggests that § 2–209(5) also applies to signed waivers, but this gets things backward. A "signed writing" is binding as a modification under § 2–209(2) without the need for "waiver." Section 2–209(1) lifts the requirement of consideration, so a signed pledge not to enforce a term of a contract may not be revoked under § 2–209(5) unless the pledge reserves the power of revocation. Because "waiver" is some subset of failed efforts to modify, it cannot be right to treat a successful effort to modify (a signed writing) as a "waiver" governed by subsection (5).

"Waiver" therefore ought to mean the same in subsections (4) and (5). Unsuccessful attempts at modification may be waivers under § 2–209(4). Then § 2–209(5) deals with a subset of these "waivers," the subset that affects the executory portion of the contract. Waivers affecting executory provisions are enforceable or not depending on reliance. We know from the language and structure of § 2–209 that there is a difference between waivers that affect the executory portions of contracts and waivers that do not. Under the majority's reading, however, there is no difference. No waiver is effective without detrimental reliance. It is as if the majority has eliminated § 2–209(4) from the UCC and rewritten § 2–209(5) to begin: "A party who has made [an ineffectual attempt at modification] affecting [any] portion of the contract may retract * * *."

                                   *   *   *

The majority makes reliance an ingredient of waiver not because the structure of the UCC demands this reading, but because it believes that otherwise the UCC would not deal adequately with the threat of opportunistic conduct. The drafters of the UCC chose to deal with opportunism not through a strict reading of waiver, however, but through a statutory requirement of commercial good faith. See § 2–103 and comment 2 to § 2–209. The modification-only-in-writing clause has nothing to do with opportunism. A person who has his contracting partner over a barrel, and therefore is able to obtain a concession, can get the concession in writing. The writing will be the least of his worries. In almost all of the famous cases of modification the parties reduced the new agreement to writing.

A modification-only-in-writing clause may permit the parties to strengthen the requirement of commercial good faith against the careless opportunist, but its principal function is to make it easier for business to protect their agreement against casual subsequent remarks and manufactured assertions of alteration. It strengthens the Statute of Frauds. Even so, the Code does not allow the clause to be air-tight. Comment 4 to § 2–209 states: "Subsection (4) is intended, despite the provisions of subsections (2) and (3), to prevent contractual provisions excluding modification except by a signed writing from limiting in other respects the legal effect of the parties' actual later conduct. The effect of such conduct as a waiver is further regulated in subsection (5)." In other words, the UCC made modification-only-in-writing clauses effective for the first time, but the drafters meant to leave loopholes. The majority's observation that waiver under § 2–209(4) could nullify some benefits of clauses permitted under § 2–209(2) is true, but it is not a reason for adding novel elements to "waiver." It might be sensible to treat claims of oral waiver with suspicion and insist on waiver by course of performance—for example, accepting belated deliveries without protest, or issuing new orders (or changing the specifications of old orders) while existing ones are in default. Waiver implied from performance is less prone to manipulation. This method of protecting modification-only-in-writing clauses gives waiver the same meaning throughout the statute, but it does not help Wisconsin Knife, for the claim of waiver here is largely based on the course of performance.

The reading I give to waiver also affords substantial effect to modification-only-in-writing clauses. To see this, consider three characterizations of the dealings between Wisconsin Knife Works and National Metal Crafters. The first, which Wisconsin Knife Works presses on us, is that there was no modification and no "attempt at modification" within the meaning of § 2–209(4). National Metal Crafters promised to deliver the blanks in the fall of 1981. When it fell behind, Wisconsin Knife Works had to decide whether to give up on National Metal Crafters (and collect any damages to which it may have been entitled) or ask National Metal Crafters to keep trying. National Metal Crafters may have been slow, but it had a head start on anyone else Wisconsin Knife Works might have asked to make the blanks. Wisconsin Knife Works wanted both to preserve its rights and to minimize its damages, and it did not surrender its legal remedies by trying to mitigate. It was entitled to throw up its hands in January 1983 and collect damages from National Metal Crafters for nonperformance.

The second characterization is that when National Metal Crafters ran into trouble producing on schedule, National Metal Crafters and Wisconsin Knife Works discussed the problem and agreed that National Metal Crafters could have more time in order to get the job done right. On this story, Wisconsin Knife Works valued a high quality product and a successful business relation more than it valued its legal right to prompt performance. Perhaps Wisconsin Knife Works did not even want performance so soon, for it was not ready to turn the blanks into spade bits and did not want blanks piling up in warehouses. So Wisconsin Knife Works told National Metal Crafters to take the time to do it right. On my view this would be a waiver under § 2–209(4). When National Metal Crafters took more time than Wisconsin Knife Works could stomach, Wisconsin Knife Works announced that too much is enough, and it retracted the waiver. Section 2–209(5) allowed it to do just this unless National Metal Crafters had relied to its detriment on Wisconsin Knife Works's words and conduct. Having retracted the waiver, Wisconsin Knife Works could declare National Metal Crafters in breach—but because the waiver excused National Metal Crafters's performance until January 1983, Wisconsin Knife Works could not collect damages for delay. The parties would simply walk away from the contract. * * *

The third characterization is the one National Metal Crafters presses here. National Metal Crafters tells us that the purchase orders never were the "real" contract. Instead Wisconsin Knife Works and National Metal Crafters embarked on joint operations to find a new way to make spade bits. The purchase orders were parts of a larger joint venture, which did not have formal terms. As the parties went along they modified their understandings and accommodated each other's needs. The latest modification occurred when National Metal Crafters gave Wisconsin Knife Works a "pert chart" indicating realistic dates for quantity shipments, and people at Wisconsin Knife Works said that these dates and quantities were acceptable. The dates ran into April 1983. This implies that when Wisconsin Knife Works declared the relationship at an end in January 1983, it breached the contract (as modified), and National Metal Crafters is entitled to damages—at a minimum profits lost on blanks scheduled for delivery through April 1983, perhaps even profits National Metal Crafters anticipated through continuation of this relationship for a longer run.

Section 2–209(2) puts this third position out of court. The third story would be a thoroughgoing reshaping of the obligations, which could not occur unless reflected in a "signed writing." The "pert chart" is not such a writing because Wisconsin Knife Works, the party sought to be bound, did not sign it. The discussions could be at most "an attempt at modification" under § 2–209(4), and therefore could be a waiver. Under § 2–209(5) Wisconsin Knife Works could rescind its waiver prospectively unless that "would be unjust in view of a material change of position in reliance on the waiver"—here, for example, proof that National Metal Crafters had already manufactured the blanks scheduled for delivery in April 1983, or had bought equipment with no alternative use. National Metal Crafters has not argued that it had the sort of reliance that would enable it to enforce the executory portion of any modification, and therefore Wisconsin Knife Works was entitled to cancel the contract and walk away in January 1983 free from liability save for goods furnished or expenses incurred in reliance before January 1983. This treatment of § 2–209(5) solves, for the most part, the problem of fabricated claims of modification. "Attempts at modification" generally are not enforceable prospectively—and if there is commercial bad faith (that is, opportunistic conduct), they are not enforceable at all. There is no serious remaining problem to which a reliance element in the definition of waiver is a solution.

Because § 2–209(2) and (5) eliminate National Metal Crafters's principal position, we are left with the first two—either

Wisconsin Knife Works stood on its entitlement to timely delivery but stuck with National Metal Crafters to mitigate damages, or Wisconsin Knife Works waived the requirement of timely delivery but in January 1983 rescinded the waiver. The jury's finding that Wisconsin Knife Works and National Metal Crafters "modified" their contract, though an answer to a legally erroneous question, resolves this dispute. Wisconsin Knife Works vigorously argued at trial that at all times it stood on its rights but went along with delayed delivery as a second-best solution. The jury's finding that Wisconsin Knife Works and National Metal Crafters modified their contract—in the words of the instruction, that Wisconsin Knife Works "by conduct or other means of expression induced a reasonable belief by [National Metal Crafters] that strict enforcement was not insisted upon, but that the modified performance was satisfactory and acceptable as equivalent"—necessarily rejects Wisconsin Knife Works's version of events. The evidence was sufficient to permit the jury to reject this version. We are left with "an attempt at modification" that may operate as a waiver, which Wisconsin Knife Works may and did revoke. * * *

A requirement of reliance will not make a difference very often—certainly not in this case. Any waiver that is more than a condonation of an existing default will induce some reliance. The buyer who asks a seller of fungible goods to defer delivery induces reliance even though the waiver of timely delivery will not affect the production of the goods. When the goods have a custom design, as the spade bit blanks do, some reliance is close to a certainty. I doubt that National Metal Crafters would have produced the same goods in the same quantity but for a belief that Wisconsin Knife Works wanted to have them. A change of position in reliance on the frequent discussions is all the majority requires. Summary judgment cannot be far away. Still, it is better not to ask unnecessary questions even when the questions have ready answers.

Chapter 12

ACCEPTANCE AND REJECTION OF GOODS AND CONTRACT CANCELLATION

A. INTRODUCTION

---

1. ACCEPTANCE

The UCC distinguishes between the buyer's act of "receiving" and the buyer's act of "accepting" the goods that are the subject of a sale. "Receipt" of goods is defined by § 2–103(1)(c) as taking physical possession of them. "Acceptance" of goods, defined by § 2–606, does not refer to any physical taking. Although receipt of goods and their acceptance by the buyer will most often occur together, acceptance can occur without actual receipt of the goods, and a buyer can receive goods without accepting them. Acceptance refers to a manifestation by the buyer of willingness to take the goods as performance of the seller's obligation sufficient to allow the seller to demand performance of the buyer's obligation. Section 2–607(1) provides that the buyer must pay at the contract rate for any goods accepted. This is the most important result of acceptance. A buyer who refuses to accept the goods, i.e., who rejects them, may be liable for breach of contract if the rejection was wrongful and the seller has suffered a resulting loss, but is not necessarily liable to pay the price of the goods. A buyer that accepts is liable to pay the price of the goods regardless of whether the performance of the seller is in breach of the contract. Although acceptance of goods obligates the buyer to pay for them at the contract rate it does not prevent the buyer from recovering from the seller damages for any loss suffered as a result of any breach of contract by the seller. § 2–714. Under § 2–717, a buyer that complies with that section may also deduct from the price any damages for breach of contract by the seller. Another result of acceptance is its effect on the burden of proving breach of contract. If goods are rejected by the buyer the burden of proving breach of contract rests on the seller, i.e., the seller must prove that goods conforming to the contract were properly tendered to the buyer and that the buyer wrongfully rejected them. § 2–503 and § 2–507. If goods are accepted by the buyer the burden of proving breach of contract shifts to the buyer, i.e., the buyer must prove that the goods delivered did not conform to the contract or that the seller's performance was otherwise in breach of the contract. § 2–607(4). What are the reasons for thus shifting the burden of proof?

Read § 2–606. You will note that acceptance can occur in three ways: (1) by an affirmative statement or other act by the buyer that signifies to the seller that the goods are acceptable; (2) by a failure of the buyer to reject the goods; and (3) by acts of the buyer in reference to the goods that are inconsistent with rejection, i.e., inconsistent with treating the goods as still belonging to the seller. The question of when a buyer will be held to have accepted goods is considered in the cases which follow.

2. REJECTION AND REVOCATION OF ACCEPTANCE

The UCC introduced into the law of sales a novel concept: "revocation of acceptance." This concept is related to but is not identical to the common law notion of "rescission." Read § 2–608. This section, in subsections (1) and (2), sets forth the conditions under which a buyer's acceptance of goods may be revoked and in subsection (3) states the legal effect of revocation. Under subsection (3) a buyer that has effectively revoked acceptance is put in the same position as a buyer that has rejected the goods. There are, however, some hidden complexities in this seemingly simple statement. A buyer can always reject goods if the rejection is timely and the notice required by § 2–602(1) is given. The rejection, however, may be rightful or it may be wrongful. If it is wrongful the buyer may be liable for breach of contract, but is not liable as an acceptor of goods. Revocation of acceptance, on the other hand, may not be wholly within the power of the buyer. An acceptance, once made, can be revoked only if the conditions stated in § 2–608 are met. Section 2–608 states that the buyer "may" revoke only if the goods do not conform to the contract. It is not clear whether "may" means "is permitted to" or "is able to" but Comment 2 to § 2–608 apparently adopts the latter interpretation. It states that revocation is "possible" only if the conditions of the section are met. Akron Brick & Block Co. v. Moniz Engineering Co., Inc., 365 Mass. 92, 310 N.E.2d 128 (1974), supports this view. If this interpretation is correct a revocation, if it complies with § 2–608 is rightful, and if it does not comply is not effective. This interpretation, however, is not free from doubt because the UCC in several places refers to revocation that is "wrongful" or "justified." See for example, § 2–401(4), § 2–703 and § 2–709(3). The conditions under which acceptance can be revoked and the conditions under which goods can be rightfully rejected should be compared. Section 2–601 states that the buyer may reject the goods "if the goods or the tender of delivery fail in any respect to conform to the contract." This is the UCC restatement of the so-called "perfect tender rule." In effect it states that the buyer may rightfully reject the goods if the performance by the seller does not conform perfectly to the performance promised in the contract. We will see in the cases that follow, that in many situations the buyer does not get the benefit of this rule, either because of some exception to the rule, for example § 2–612, or because as a practical matter the buyer is not able to exercise the right of rejection provided by the UCC. Section 2–601 is also subject to § 2–719 which allows modification by agreement of the buyer's remedies. After reading the cases that follow you should consider to what extent § 2–601 states an important right of the buyer. What are the differences between the conditions under which the buyer can rightfully reject the goods and the conditions under which the buyer can revoke an acceptance?

3. CURE

The UCC introduced another novel concept to the law of sales: "cure" by the seller. We have seen that § 2–601 allows the buyer to reject goods tendered by the seller if the goods or the tender fails in any respect to conform to the contract. Although the buyer may, in cases subject to the rule of § 2–601, rightfully reject goods even for a very minor nonconformity in the goods or the tender by the seller, the harshness of the rule is mitigated by § 2–508 which in effect gives the seller a second chance. If the conditions of § 2–508 are met the seller may "cure" a nonconforming tender by making another conforming tender. What are the reasons for this rule? If goods do not conform perfectly to the contract but the nonconformity either does not materially affect their value or can be corrected by the seller, under what circumstances is the buyer likely to accept or reject? What are the economic effects of a rule that requires a seller to take back from the buyer goods that are nonconforming but which can be made to conform? The cases that follow consider the right of the seller to cure a nonconforming tender that has been rejected by the buyer. They also consider the extent to which failure by the seller to cure a non-conformity in accepted goods affects the ability of the buyer to revoke the acceptance. § 2–608. Finally we will examine the special rule for installment contracts concerning the buyer's ability to rightfully reject nonconforming individual installments of the goods and to treat the seller as in breach of the entire contract because of that nonconformity. The seller's ability and willingness to cure defects are major components in determining the rights of the buyer. § 2–612.

B. BUYER'S RIGHTS ON TENDER
OR DELIVERY OF NONCONFORMING GOODS

---

1. ACCEPTANCE OR TIMELY REJECTION?

LA VILLA FAIR v. LEWIS CARPET MILLS, INC.
Supreme Court of Kansas, 1976.
219 Kan. 395, 548 P.2d 825.

MILLER, JUSTICE. This is an action for rescission of a portion of a contract for the purchase of carpet and for the recovery of the purchase price, interest thereon, incidental damages and loss of profit. Plaintiff (the purchaser) is a wholesaler and retailer of carpet and other furnishings specializing in apartment projects and commercial buildings. It is a Kansas corporation and its principal place of business is Lawrence, Kansas. Defendant is a carpet manufacturer, incorporated in Georgia with its principal place of business in Cartersville, Georgia.

The * * * plaintiff placed an order for the purchase of approximately 12,000 square yards of carpet, which order was accepted by the defendant by letter dated May 29, 1967. The carpet ordered, described as * * * 25 oz. face weight * * *, was to be delivered on defendant's truck to either Kansas City, Missouri, or Lawrence, Kansas * * *. Prior to the shipment in question eleven smaller deliveries were made from defendant's mill to plaintiff between July 24, 1967 and August 24, 1967. All conformed to the specifications and were accepted and paid for without incident.

The carpet which gave rise to this action is twenty-one of the forty-five rolls shipped by the defendant to the plaintiff on April 26, 1968. These rolls averaged about 180 square yards each. Due to a construction strike in Kansas City in the spring of 1968, the plaintiff's purchaser, Stanley Christopher Investment Company of Lawrence, an apartment builder, was not ready to receive the carpet. Plaintiff therefore arranged with the defendant to have the defendant transport and deliver the carpet to Wagner Cartage Company, Kansas City, Missouri, for storage in their bonded warehouse until Christopher was in a position to make use of it. * * *

By January 2, 1969, Christopher Investment Company, plaintiff's purchaser, had collapsed financially and had been taken over by its financier, James B. Nutter Company. Nutter was aware of Christopher's intention to purchase carpet from the plaintiff. It was also aware that the carpet was stored in the bonded ware-

house. Both Christopher and Nutter paid part of the storage
charges. Nutter gave the plaintiff assurances that it would honor
the Christopher contract, and would pay for the carpet as soon as
it was cut and laid at the apartment project site. On or about
January 2, 1969, Nutter indicated to the plaintiff that it was ready
to receive the carpet. Plaintiff therefore arranged for the carpet
to be moved from Wagner Cartage to Lay-Rite Carpet Company,
which company was employed by Nutter to cut the carpet and to
install it in the apartment complex. Employees of Lay-Rite inspected several rolls of the carpet, but were unable to find 23 feet
of carpet that matched so as to lay carpet in one display apartment. Lay-Rite informed Nutter, who also inspected the carpet.
Nutter rejected the carpet and refused to pay to the plaintiff the
purchase price of $10,791.10. Plaintiff then informed the defen-
dant that it, too, rejected the carpet. After the exchange of some
correspondence, this action was filed August 1, 1969. In its
supplemental memorandum opinion filed September 10, 1973, the
trial court found in favor of the plaintiff in the amount of
$11,805.44 plus the costs of the action, less a $202 judgment in
favor of the defendant against the plaintiff. The court directed
that judgment be entered against the defendant after applying
funds on hand from the court-ordered sale of the carpet on
November 17, 1971 (amounting to $2,944) and the $202 judgment
in favor of the defendant. It is from that judgment of $8,659.44
plus costs that the defendant appeals.

* * *

Defendant's brief is divided into four parts, with each part
having several divisions, but when boiled down the defendant's
theory of the case is this: that plaintiff's argument is based upon
the unsupported assumption that since the carpet was undisputedly nonconforming when it was removed from the warehouse, the
carpet must have been nonconforming when it was delivered; that
there is no direct evidence that the carpet did not conform to the
contract specifications at the time of delivery to the warehouse,
and thus it must be deemed to have presumptively conformed to
the contract; but that even if all that the plaintiff says is true,
plaintiff's action was unreasonable and amounted to commercial
bad faith in that it failed to make a timely inspection of the
carpet, thereby effectively depriving the defendant of any opportunity to invoke its statutory right to cure the nonconformity.

[Omitted is the portion of the opinion in which the court
concluded that the carpet was nonconforming when it was delivered.]

Having disposed of the nonconformity issue, it is now necessary to turn to what, by stipulation, was supposed to be the sole
issue on appeal. That is: Notwithstanding the carpet's noncon-

formity, was plaintiff's rejection, or revocation of its acceptance of the same, timely?

Appellant relies heavily on *Cervitor Kitchens v. Chapman,* 7 Wash.App. 520, 500 P.2d 783, in support of its position that plaintiff's delayed inspection was unreasonable as a matter of law. That case sets forth the rule to be applied to determine whether the question of rejection within a reasonable time is one of fact or of law:

> "If the facts are disputed, the question of what is a reasonable time is for the trier of the fact. * * *
>
> "If the facts are undisputed concerning the duration of the time for inspection, the question of whether the goods were retained for an unreasonable time becomes one for the court to decide. * * *" (pp. 522, 523, 500 P.2d p. 785.)
> * * *

Defendant contends that a failure by plaintiff to inspect is only justified where such inspection is wholly impracticable, not just inconvenient or time-consuming and thus it argues that the plaintiff had a reasonable opportunity to inspect and that its failure to do so amounts to acceptance under UCC § 2–606. *Cervitor,* supra, 7 Wash.App. at p. 524, 500 P.2d 783.

Cervitor was a case in which a plumbing contractor, Chapman, was working on the construction of a college dormitory. Chapman purchased from Cervitor Kitchens, Inc., a merchandising business, four kitchen units to be installed in a dormitory. On May 4, 1967, Chapman received from Cervitor four kitchen units enclosed in shipping crates or cartons. Chapman did not inspect the units on delivery, although Chapman's manager was present when the units arrived and noticed some minor exterior shipping damage on two of the crates. The units remained in their shipping crates and were stored in a separate room at the dormitory then under construction. No inspection was made of the units until shortly before installation on or about August 5, 1967. A few days later Chapman notified the engineer that the units had been installed. Somewhat later the engineer informed Chapman that the units were of poor quality and did not comply with specifications. Chapman in turn notified Cervitor that the units did not comply with the specifications and would be rejected. Chapman shipped the units to Cervitor, who refused them. They were later sold for storage charges. The sole question in *Cervitor* was whether Chapman was deemed to have accepted the four kitchen units because of his failure to inspect and reject them for a period of approximately three months after delivery and because of his installation of the units without prior inspection and rejection. Cervitor contended that Chapman waited too long to inspect and reject the units, and his installation of the

units without inspection further precluded him from rejecting
them. The Washington Court of Appeals, with one dissent,
agreed with both contentions. Not noted in defendant's brief,
however, is the Washington Supreme Court's reversal of the
intermediate appellate court as to Cervitor's first point, that is,
that Chapman's inspection was not timely. The Washington
Supreme Court in Cervitor Kitchens, Inc. v. Chapman [*Cervitor
II*], 82 Wash.2d 673, 513 P.2d 25, stated:

> "* * * We * * * cannot agree with the Court of
> Appeals that, as a matter of law, the 3-month time delay in
> failing to inspect and accept or reject the goods constituted an
> acceptance." (p. 676, 513 P.2d p. 26.)

The dissent in the appeals court decision had noted that
there was evidence to indicate that suppliers that deal in
commercial fixtures such as these units recognize that their
merchandise will frequently be stored on job sites and that
when delivery is made, the purchasers may not be ready to
install the units immediately. *Cervitor* I, supra, p. 526, 513
P.2d 25. The supreme court's opinion also noted this testimony
and concluded that the trial court's finding that the units were
timely inspected was supported by substantial competent evidence in the record. *Cervitor* II, supra, p. 678, 513 P.2d 25.
The supreme court did, however, affirm the appeals court's
ruling that Chapman's *installation* of the units without inspection after over 3 months' delay was inconsistent with the
seller's ownership as a matter of law and amounted to acceptance where the deficiencies claimed were readily apparent
upon inspection after the units were taken from the crates and
before installation. *Cervitor* II, supra, p. 676, 513 P.2d 25.

Applying *Cervitor* II to the facts of this case it would seem
that it cannot be said that plaintiff's nine-month delay in
inspecting and accepting or rejecting the carpet is itself an
acceptance as a matter of law, but rather should be left to the
trier of fact. As in *Cervitor* II there was evidence in the
instant case that the defendant was aware that plaintiff's
purchaser was not ready to use the goods it shipped (because of
the construction strike) and that it was aware that the goods
were to be shipped to a warehouse for storage. There was also
evidence that no set time for inspection exists but that the
industry practice is not to inspect until a purchaser is found
and is ready to use the goods. There was further evidence that
the carpet, when received in a large order such as this one, is
stacked until ready for use rather than unrolled for inspection
of concealed defects. Under all the evidence the carpet was
timely and reasonably inspected and the trial court's finding to
that effect is supported by substantial competent evidence.

There is a further question, however, whether or not the acts of the carpet installer for plaintiff's purchaser, Lay-Rite, were so inconsistent with the seller's ownership as to amount to the exercise of ownership and dominion by the plaintiff thereby constituting acceptance.

Once again applying *Cervitor* II to the facts of this case, it would appear that the actions of the installer for plaintiff's purchaser were not inconsistent with seller's ownership and could not be said to amount to acceptance as a matter of law. In *Cervitor* there was no evidence that installation of the units was necessary to enable a proper inspection to take place, particularly where the deficiencies complained of were readily apparent upon inspection after the units were taken from the crates and before installation. In the instant case there would appear to be evidence that it was necessary to unroll and cut into three or four rolls of carpet in order to determine that the carpet was extensively patched, was delaminated in places, that it varied in width and in hue, and that it was not 25 oz. face weight. That is analogous to the uncrating of the units in *Cervitor*. After unrolling three or four rolls of carpet it became obvious that the carpet was defective since Lay-Rite could not find 23 feet in several hundred feet of carpet that would match for installation in a "show" apartment. Had Lay-Rite installed the carpet in the "show" apartment or other apartments before rejecting it, *Cervitor* II might be in point. Here, however, the deficiencies complained of were readily apparent upon inspection after the carpet was unrolled, and rejection preceded installation. It cannot be said that the unrolling and cutting of the carpet in an attempt to match portions for installation was inconsistent with the seller's ownership as a matter of law so as to constitute an acceptance of the carpet.

Defendant contends that because of plaintiff's unreasonable and untimely conduct, it was deprived of its statutory right to cure under UCC § 2–508(1). The fact is that the contract made no provision for a time for performance, and since it could not therefore have expired by the time of plaintiff's rejection, defendant could have offered to cure at that time. It did not. Defendant's cry that it was deprived of this opportunity has a somewhat hollow ring. Additionally, defendant claims it was deprived of sufficiently prompt notice of damage to be able to invoke its right of inspection, right to ascertain the facts, and right to preserve evidence under UCC § 2–515. Defendant did have two inspections of the carpet, and it was not prejudiced in this regard.

* * *

The judgment is affirmed.

NOTE: TIME FOR REJECTION

The following is taken from Societe Nouvelle Vaskene v.
Lehman Saunders, Ltd., 14 U.C.C.Rep. 692 (N.Y.Sup.Ct., N.Y.Co.
Spec.Term 1974):

It is conceded, at least for purposes of this application,
that there is a bona fide dispute as to whether plaintiff
warranted that the wearing apparel manufactured by it in
France and shipped to defendants in New York pursuant to
the latter's order would be properly sized for the American
market and whether it complied with such warranty.

Essentially, plaintiff's position is that, even assuming, ad
arguendo, such warranty had been made and breached, it is
nevertheless entitled to recover the agreed price of the goods
by reason of defendants' failure to timely reject same and to
seasonably notify it of the alleged breach.

Defendants admit that most of the goods were received by
them in the "latter part of August 1970" and that the balance
was received in the "latter part of October 1970." It is
further admitted that they put size numbers and price tags on
all of the apparel in question and placed then on their sales
floor sometime in the middle of November, 1970, when their
new store opened for business. In addition, defendants concede that they first realized that the garments were faultily
sized when they "were unpacked for preparation to be placed
on the sales floor"—i.e., presumably, sometime in early November, 1970, at the latest, and that their first complaint to
plaintiff regarding this problem was by their letter dated Dec.
7, 1970.

In addition to the foregoing, it also appears to be substantially undisputed that the goods were seasonal in nature, that
some items were sold prior to defendants' letter of complaint
and offer to return (which plaintiff rejected by letter dated
Jan. 6, 1971), that a substantial number of items were sold in
November and December 1970 and in January, 1971, and that
the balance were removed from the sales floor in February,
1971 and ultimately sold to a jobber at a greatly reduced price
in March 1972.

In the indicated circumstances, the court is of the opinion
that defendants' purported rejection of the goods, and notification to plaintiff of the alleged breach must, as a matter of law,
be regarded as untimely. Under UCC § 2–602(1), notice of
rejection of goods must be given to the seller within a reasonable time after their delivery or tender and, if no such notice is
given and the buyer has had a reasonable opportunity for
inspection, they are deemed to have been accepted (UCC § 2–
606[1][b]). In actions between merchants based upon facts

substantially similar to those here presented, it has been held that a delay of fifty days in inspecting the goods and discovering defects which were, as here, apparent on examination was unreasonable and bars any defense predicated thereon. (Lamport Company, Inc. v. Fisher Bookbinding Co., Inc., 277 App.Div. 870). Similarly, in Milz & Cie v. Bloomfield, 146 Misc. 649, it was held that silent retention of the goods for thirty-six days after delivery and for three weeks after examination had disclosed their condition constituted an acceptance under the predecessor of UCC § 2–606.

In Wakerman Leather Co. v. Irvin B. Foster Sportswear Co., 34 A.D.2d 594, 308 N.Y.S.2d 103 (1970), the court affirmed the finding by the trial court that considering the usage and custom of the leather trade the buyer accepted leather delivered by the seller because it did not make a timely rejection. The court stated:

> Additionally, there was a notation on respondent's invoices requiring all claims to be made within five days from the receipt of the goods, testimony that the trade custom was to require claims to be made in from five to ten days, and further testimony that skins were usually inspected immediately upon receipt. This supports the findings that ten days was a reasonable time within which to return the skins and that appellant had had a reasonable time within which to inspect them.

2. RIGHTS OF REJECTING BUYER IN POSSESSION OF GOODS

ASKCO ENGINEERING CORP. v. MOBIL CHEMICAL CORP.

Court of Civil Appeals of Texas, 1976.
535 S.W.2d 893.

COLEMAN, CHIEF JUSTICE. This is a suit on a sworn account by Askco Engineering Corporation (Askco) against Mobil Chemical Corporation (Mobil) to recover the agreed purchase price of 276,317 pounds of scrap plastic. Mobil denied the account and alleged that it had accepted 110,212 pounds of the material and had rightfully rejected the balance. Prior to the institution of the suit Mobil had tendered a payment for the material which it had accepted and had returned the balance to Askco. Askco declined to accept the tendered payment and refused to receive the returned material. Mobil filed a counterclaim for the cost of warehousing, freight, loading and unloading expense and disposal charges. The case was tried to the court without a jury and judgment was rendered in favor of Askco in the amount of $21,510.28, the sum previously tendered by Mobil, less the sum of

$14,079.65, found to be due to Mobil from Askco on the counter-claim. Prior to the trial Mobil had impleaded Mr. San Sew Tsai, and alleged that he was the actual owner of most of the material in controversy. The court's judgment was in favor of Askco and San Sew Tsai jointly and severally. Askco brings this appeal. The judgment is affirmed.

* * *

The evidence fully supports a finding that Askco expressly warranted the material purchased by Mobil to be low density polyethylene film, and that the material shipped to Mobil and received by them did not conform to the warranty.

* * *

UCC § 2–602 provides that nonconforming goods must be rejected within a reasonable time after their delivery. It further provides that if the buyer has before rejection taken physical possession of goods he is under a duty after rejection to hold them with reasonable care at the seller's disposition for a time sufficient to permit the seller to remove them. UCC § 2–604 provides that if the seller gives no instructions within a reasonable time after notification of rejection the buyer may store the rejected goods for the seller's account or reship them to him or resell them for the seller's account. Mobil elected to and did reship the goods to Askco, and on failure of Askco to accept such goods incurred additional expense in storing and testing the goods, and thereby acquired a security interest in the goods. UCC § 2–711. Mobil unsuccessfully attempted to sell the goods and incurred additional expense in disposing of them. There is no merit in appellants' contention that the trial court erred in finding that Mobil rightfully rejected 166,105 pounds of the merchandise in question.

UCC § 2–602, in paragraph (2)(a) provides that after rejection any exercise of ownership by the buyer with respect to any commercial unit is wrongful as against the seller. There is evidence that the material could not be identified as low density polyethylene by visual or manual inspection. At the time Mobil rejected 166,000 pounds of the merchandise it knew that it was unable to reprocess the material and had identified a small amount of the material as being cellophane. Prior to the rejection of the material Mobil received a letter from Askco in which Mr. Birdsall stated:

> "* * * Most of this was low density polyethylene with some laminate material with various interlayers (some nylon and polypropylene) * * *"

After Askco was notified that the goods were being rejected Mobil held the goods for a reasonable time for instructions from Askco. When no instructions were received Mobil elected to reship the goods to Askco as authorized by UCC § 2–604. There is no specific provision in the Code governing the action to be taken where returned goods are not accepted by the seller. Mobil elected to store the goods for the seller's benefit for a period of one year. After that period the goods were carted off and buried. There is evidence that at that time the goods had no value.

This course of conduct on the part of Mobil does not constitute an exercise of ownership by the buyer within the meaning of [UCC § 2–602]. After Askco refused to accept the returned goods, spectrographic tests made by Mobil identified some of the rejected material as being low density polyethylene which would conform to the contract. In view of the difficulty of identifying the various types of chemical compounds in the large mass of materials, Mobil was not required to "cull out" the conforming goods. Simmons Cohn & Co. v. Weil, 244 S.W. 562 (Tex.Civ.App.—Beaumont 1922, no writ hist.). Nor was Mobil required to again tender the goods to Askco. Seley v. Parker, 45 S.W. 1026 (Tex.Civ.App.1898, no writ history). The goods were worthless and Mobil could reasonably believe that Askco would again refuse to accept them. 67 Amer.Jur.2d, § 771.

C. REVOCATION OF ACCEPTANCE

ERLING v. HOMERA, INC.
Supreme Court of North Dakota, 1980.
298 N.W.2d 478.

ERICKSTAD, CHIEF JUSTICE. Defendant, Homera, Inc., appeals from a judgment which allowed the plaintiffs, Mr. and Mrs. William Erling, to revoke their acceptance of a mobile home and required Homera and the co-defendant, Jerry Carlson, to return the plaintiffs' purchase price. The case was tried to the court without a jury. The judgment allowing revocation is affirmed, but the determination of set off is remanded with directions.

In August of 1976, the Erlings purchased a mobile home from Jerry Carlson, who was doing business as J & J Trailer Sales in Jamestown, North Dakota. The home had been manufactured by Homera, a Minnesota corporation. The purchase price was $13,936. That fall, the Erlings noticed what they believed to be leakage along the inside of the mobile home. They notified Carlson. Moisture was noticed again in March of 1977. In addition, the Erlings noticed that the siding was warping and that the windows collected water when it rained, which then ran into the interior of the trailer. In response to the window complaint, Homera flew an employee into Jamestown, where the trailer was located, to examine the problem, but no repair was attempted. Erling then made the repairs to the windows himself and Homera reimbursed him for his time and for the materials. In response to the moisture problem, Carlson cool-sealed the roof twice in the spring of 1977. In addition, Mr. Erling also cool-sealed the roof.

Moisture was again noticed in the fall of 1977, which at various times required that pots and pans be placed to catch the dripping water. In December of 1977, the moisture was finally diagnosed as being condensation which was forming on the inside of the roof which would alternately freeze and melt with the varying temperatures of the spring and fall. At the request of Homera, a humidity gauge was placed in the home over the winter of 1977–78. This revealed no excessively high humidity in the home. The problem was believed to be due to inadequate air space above the insulation. In an attempt to correct this problem, a wind-powered ventilator was installed at Homera's expense in February of 1978, but this still did not solve the moisture problem.

The problem with the siding was referred by Homera to Masonite Corporation, the manufacturer of the siding. Masonite agreed to replace several panels of the warped siding if the moisture problem was corrected. The moisture problem persisted, even after installation of the wind-powered ventilator. The Erlings gave notice of revocation in April of 1978. In their notice of revocation, the Erlings offered the return of the mobile home upon receiving shipping instructions. They also demanded their entire purchase price plus interest at six percent. Suit was filed in June of 1978. The Erlings refused further attempts at repair by Homera. A court trial was held November 7, 1979, to determine the issue of revocation of acceptance. After trial, the court allowed the revocation of acceptance and ordered the return of the Erlings' purchase price of $13,936 without interest. It was apparently thought that the value of the use of the home and interest on the purchase price would offset each other.

Homera appeals on four grounds:

1. The finding that the appellees' mobile home was defectively designed is not supported by the evidence.

2. The condition of the appellees' mobile home did not substantially impair its value.

3. The district judge should have set off the fair and reasonable value of the appellees' use from the judgment awarding return of the purchase price.

4. The plaintiffs waived the right to rescind the contract by continuing to make full use of the mobile home.

UCC § 2–608 provides for revocation of acceptance. The relevant part of this section requires a non-conformity which substantially impairs the value to the buyer. Homera's first contention is that the finding that the mobile home was defective or non-conforming is not supported by the evidence.

I. NON–CONFORMITY OF TRAILER

[Omitted is the part of the opinion in which the court affirms the finding of non-conformity of the trailer.]

II. SUBSTANTIALLY IMPAIRED VALUE
TO THE BUYER

Homera's second contention is that the condition did not substantially impair the mobile home's value. UCC § 2–608 provides that the buyer may revoke when the product's non-conformity "substantially impairs its value to him." This is a factual determination to be made by the trier of fact. * * *

Homera argues that the determination of substantial impairment is a legal conclusion. It relies on Durfee v. Rod Baxter Imports, Inc., 262 N.W.2d 349 (Minn.1977). Minnesota appears to be among a minority of jurisdictions which deem substantial impairment to be a conclusion of law. We believe that the better view is that substantial impairment is a question of fact for the trier of fact. * * *

In this case, the Erlings purchased their trailer home as their sole residence. The record shows that the defects in the home were not discoverable prior to their acceptance of the home. These defects were not cured by the seller. Mr. Erling had to repair the windows himself. He was reimbursed, however, for his labor and materials. The siding panels became so warped that Masonite Corporation agreed to replace at least three of the panels if the moisture problem was remedied. After one and one-half years of complaints and attempts to correct the problem, there was still condensation which, on occasions in the spring and fall, required placing pots and pans to catch dripping water. Considering this was a new mobile home, this must have been very aggravating. Under these circumstances, we cannot say that the trial court's determination that the value of the mobile home to the Erlings was substantially impaired was a clearly erroneous finding.

Homera also contends that it should have been allowed to make further efforts to repair the defect. After notice of revocation was given to Homera and Carlson, the Erlings refused to permit further efforts to correct the problem. Specifically, they refused the installation of an electrically-powered ventilator. Homera admitted that it could not guarantee that the ventilator would solve the moisture problem. The offer to install the electrically-powered ventilator came after one and one-half years of dissatisfaction on the part of the Erlings, after only minimal attempts on behalf of Homera and others to remedy the problem, and not until after notice of revocation.

A seller does not have an unlimited amount of time to cure the defects. Jorgensen v. Pressnall, 274 Or. 285, 545 P.2d 1382, 1385 (1976). Therefore, the refusal by the Erlings to allow any further attempts at repair after their revocation was not improper.

III. WAIVER OF RIGHT TO REVOKE

Homera also alleges that the Erlings waived their right to revoke their acceptance by continuing to make full use of the mobile home. The Erlings use of the home prior to the notice of revocation was proper. UCC § 2–608(1). Their acceptance was without notice of the defects in the trailer because such defects were not easily discoverable. UCC § 2–608(1)(b). The Erlings continuing use prior to the revocation was in reliance on the seller's assurances that the defects would be corrected. Id.

After notice of revocation, the Erlings continued to use the mobile home as their residence. Subsection 3 of UCC § 2–608 provides:

> "3. A buyer who so revokes has the same rights *and duties* with regard to the goods involved as if he had rejected them." [Emphasis added.]

UCC § 2–602 sets out the requirements of a rightful rejection:

> "2. Subject to the provisions of the two following sections on rejected goods (sections 2–603 and 2–604),
>
>> a. after rejection any exercise of ownership by the buyer with respect to any commercial unit is wrongful as against the seller; * * *"

UCC § 2–604 provides that "if the seller gives no instructions within a reasonable time after notification of rejection [revocation], the buyer may store the rejected goods for the seller's account."

In this case, neither Homera nor Carlson gave the Erlings instructions concerning retaking of the home after receiving notice of revocation. Therefore, the Erlings were entitled to retain possession of the home. UCC § 2–604.

In addition, UCC § 2–711 gives the buyers a security interest in goods upon a justifiable revocation of acceptance of such goods. Living in the trailer home was the Erlings' most reasonable method of protecting their security interest in the home. Jorgensen v. Pressnall, supra, 545 P.2d at 1386.

In this case, Carlson testified that the home was in very good condition and was maintained in as good a condition as could be expected during the Erlings' continued possession. Under the circumstances, the continued possession of the mobile home by the Erlings was not wrongful.

IV. SET OFF FOR REASONABLE VALUE OF USE

Homera's final assertion is that the trial court should have allowed a set off against the judgment for a refund of the purchase price for the reasonable value of the Erlings' use of the mobile home. As we have earlier commented, the trial court apparently thought the value of the use of the premises and the value of the interest were equal, but no evidence was received upon which such a finding could be based.

Though the value of the home to the Erlings was substantially impaired, they have lived in it since it was purchased. The home has an ascertainable use value which should be determined and set off against the Erlings' purchase price. * * *

UCC § 1–103 provides that other principles of law and equity are applicable unless specifically displaced by provisions of the Uniform Commercial Code sections of the North Dakota Century Code. The official Code comments to Section 2–608, U.C.C. * * * indicate that the drafters intended to allow a buyer to both revoke acceptance and recover damages for breach. UCC § 2–608 does not use the term rescission; rather, it uses revocation of acceptance to prevent confusion. * * * Therefore, the sections of the North Dakota Century Code relating to rescission are applicable except where the Code specifically provides otherwise. Two sections on rescission are applicable. They are Sections 9–09–04(2), and 32–04–23, N.D.C.C., which provide:

> "9–09–04. *Rules governing rescission.*—Rescission, when not effected by consent or pursuant to sections 9–08–08 and 9–08–09, can be accomplished only by the use, on the part of the party rescinding, of reasonable diligence to comply with the following rules:

> * * *

> 2. He must restore to the other party everything of value which he has received from him under the contract or must offer to restore the same upon condition that such party shall do likewise, unless the latter is unable or positively refuses to do so."

> "32–04–23. *Compensation may be required.*—On adjudging the rescission of a contract, the court may require the party to whom such relief is granted to make any compensation to the other which justice may require."

As there was no evidence supporting the trial judge's award of set off of interest on the purchase price against the value of the use of the home, we remand for determination of the reasonable value of use of the home from the time of purchase to date of hearing on remand. The value of this use less interest at the rate of six percent per annum on the purchase price to the date of

hearing on remand should be set off against the purchase price.
The Erlings asked for interest at the rate of six percent per annum
in their notice of rescission (revocation of acceptance) and this is
consistent with Section 47–14–05, N.D.C.C.

The judgment of revocation is affirmed, but the case is remanded for the taking of additional testimony and for amendment
of judgment consistent with this opinion.

NOTE: USE OF GOODS BY BUYER REJECTING OR REVOKING ACCEPTANCE

Section 2–606(1)(c) may cause difficulty in cases in which the
buyer cannot easily return the rejected goods to the seller. For
example, in Garfinkel v. Lehman Floor Covering Co., 60 Misc.2d
72, 302 N.Y.S.2d 167 (1969), carpeting was installed in Buyer's
home. Buyer noticed unsightly pressure bands on the carpeting.
When the defect was not corrected Buyer notified Seller that he
was rejecting the carpeting and demanded that Seller remove it.
Seller failed to remove it. In allowing Buyer to recover the price
paid the court stated:

> The merchandise is substantially defective and the plain-
> tiff is entitled to have the purchase price refunded unless he
> has in some way prejudiced that right by retaining the carpet
> which is still on his floor and in use.

* * *

Section 2–602 of the Uniform Commercial Code provides
that the buyer, if he has possession of the goods, is under a
duty after rejection to "hold them with reasonable care at the
seller's disposition for a time sufficient to permit the seller to
remove them; but the buyer has no further obligations with
regard to goods rightfully rejected." It follows that the plaintiff was then permitted to retain the goods at his home
awaiting removal by the seller and had no further obligation
if the rejection was within a reasonable time and he had
notified the seller.

The court finds as a fact that the rejection was justified;
that it was made within a reasonable time and that proper
notification was given to the seller.

The need for this provision of the Uniform Commercial
Code has been apparent in this court for some time. Many
cases were brought where a merchant delivered defective
merchandise, bulky in character, expensive to transport and
store. He then left the defective merchandise and refused to
remove it. This placed the consumer in a dilemma. If the
consumer removes and returns the goods, it is an expensive
proposition. He is out of pocket money, in addition to the loss
of his purchase price, in exchange for the gamble of recover-

ing some of it by court action. On the other hand, if he retains the merchandise in his home, he loses the right to rescind the contract and his purchase money is gone. In return he has to seek the right to damage for which he will need expensive expert testimony.

It is the opinion of the court that one of the beneficial purposes intended by the new commercial code was to put the burden on the merchant where the goods are defective and he is given proper notice of the defect. He delivered the goods and it is fair that he should remove them or let them remain at his peril.

A number of cases, like *Erling*, have involved mobile homes. The courts have been favorable to the buyer who has made a substantial down payment and who has no practical alternative to remaining in the home when the seller refuses to return the down payment. Some courts have seized on the buyer's duty under § 2–602(2)(b) to hold the goods "for a time sufficient to permit the seller to remove them." The rationale is that occupation by the buyer of the rejected mobile home for a reasonable period was simply a way of preserving the goods for the seller, not an exercise of ownership by the buyer. Minsel v. El Rancho Mobile Home Center, Inc., 32 Mich.App. 10, 188 N.W.2d 9 (1971). Others are in agreement with the rationale in *Erling*. But acts inconsistent with mere caretaking such as, for example, remodeling or changing the heating unit may constitute acceptance of the goods. Bowen v. Young, 507 S.W.2d 600 (Tex.Civ.App.1974).

A similar problem is raised by § 2–608(2) which provides that revocation of acceptance must occur "before any substantial change in condition of the goods which is not caused by their own defects." Many cases have allowed revocation of acceptance after the goods declined substantially in value because they were used for extensive periods. Most involved defective automobiles or mobile homes that the seller refused to repair or that the seller after repeated attempts was unable to repair. An example is Conte v. Dwan Lincoln-Mercury, Inc., 172 Conn. 112, 374 A.2d 144 (1976), in which the buyer used the car for 14 months. Revocation of acceptance was allowed and the buyer was not required to pay for use of the car. Similar results were reached in Dopieralla v. Arkansas Louisiana Gas Co., 255 Ark. 150, 499 S.W.2d 610 (1973) (air conditioner used for 40 months) and Fablok Mills, Inc. v. Cocker Machine & Foundry Co., 125 N.J.Super. 251, 310 A.2d 491 (1973) (knitting machines used for more than two years while the seller attempted to repair). In some cases the courts have adopted an approach similar to that taken in *Erling* of requiring the revoking buyer to compensate the seller for the use of the goods.

ZABRISKIE CHEVROLET, INC. v. SMITH

Superior Court of New Jersey Law Division, 1968.
99 N.J.Super. 441, 240 A.2d 195.

DOAN, J.D.C. (temporarily assigned). On February 2, 1967 defendant signed a form purchase order for a new 1966 Chevrolet Biscayne Sedan which was represented to him to be a brand-new car that would operate perfectly. On that occasion he paid plaintiff $124 by way of deposit. On February 9, 1967 defendant tendered plaintiff his check for $2069.50 representing the balance of the purchase price ($2064) and $5.50 for license and transfer fees. Delivery was made to defendant's wife during the early evening hours of Friday, February 10, 1967, at which time she was handed the keys and the factory package of printed material, including the manual and the manufacturer-dealer's warranty, none of which she or her husband ever read before or after the sale was made, nor were the details thereof specifically explained to or agreed to by defendant. While en route to her home, about 2½ miles away, and after having gone about 7/10 of a mile from the showroom, the car stalled at a traffic light, stalled again within another 15 feet and again thereafter each time the vehicle was required to stop. When about half-way home the car could not be driven in "drive" gear at all, and defendant's wife was obliged to then propel the vehicle in "low-low" gear at a rate of about five to ten miles per hour, its then maximum speed. In great distress, defendant's wife was fearful of completing the journey to her home and called her husband, who thereupon drove the car in "low-low" gear about seven blocks to his home. Defendant, considerably upset by this turn of events, thereupon immediately called his bank (which was open this Friday evening), stopped payment on the check and called plaintiff to notify them that they had sold him a "lemon," that he had stopped payment on the check and that the sale was cancelled. The next day plaintiff sent a wrecker to defendant's home, brought the vehicle to its repair shop and after inspection determined that the transmission was defective.

Plaintiff's expert testified that the car would not move, that there was no power in the transmission and in that condition the car could not move. Plaintiff replaced the transmission with another one removed from a vehicle then on plaintiff's showroom floor, notifying defendant thereafter of what had been done. Defendant refused to take delivery of the vehicle as repaired and reasserted his cancellation of the sale. Plaintiff has since kept the vehicle in storage at his place of business. Within a short period following these occurrences plaintiff and defendant began negotiations for a new 1967 Chevrolet, but these fell through when plaintiff insisted that a new deal could only be made by giving defendant credit for the previously ordered 1966 Chevrolet. This defendant refused to do because he considered the prior transaction as cancelled.

* * *

Plaintiff urges that defendant accepted the vehicle and therefore under UCC § 2–607(1) is bound to complete payment for it. Defendant asserts that he never accepted the vehicle and therefore under the Code properly rejected it; further, that even if there had been acceptance he was justified under the Code in revoking the same. Defendant supports this claim by urging that what was delivered to him was not what he bargained for, i.e., a new car with factory new parts, which would operate perfectly as represented and, therefore, the Code remedies of rejection and revocation of acceptance were available to him. These remedies have their basis in breach of contract and failure of consideration although they are also viewed as arising out of breach of warranty. The essential ingredient which determines which of these two remedies is brought into play is a determination, *in limine*, whether there had been an "acceptance" of the goods by the buyer. Thus, the primary inquiry is whether the defendant had "accepted" the automobile prior to the return thereof to the plaintiff.

UCC § 2–606(1) states in pertinent part: [Quotation omitted.]

* * *

It is clear that a buyer does not accept goods until he has had a "reasonable opportunity to inspect." Defendant sought to purchase a new car. He assumed what every new car buyer has a right to assume and, indeed, has been led to assume by the high powered advertising techniques of the auto industry—that his new car, with the exception of very minor adjustments, would be mechanically new and factory-furnished, operate perfectly, and be free of substantial defects. The vehicle delivered to defendant did not measure up to these representations. Plaintiff contends that defendant had "reasonable opportunity to inspect" by the privilege to take the car for a typical "spin around the block" before signing the purchase order. If by this contention plaintiff equates a spin around the block with "reasonable opportunity to inspect", the contention is illusory and unrealistic. To the layman, the complicated mechanisms of today's automobiles are a complete mystery. To have the automobile inspected by someone with sufficient expertise to disassemble the vehicle in order to discover latent defects before the contract is signed, is assuredly impossible and highly impractical. * * * Consequently, the first few miles of driving become even more significant to the excited new car buyer. This is the buyer's first reasonable opportunity to enjoy his new vehicle to see if it conforms to what it was represented to be and whether he is getting what he bargained for. How long the buyer may drive the new car under the guise of inspection of new goods is not an issue in the present case. It is clear that defendant discovered the nonconformity within $7/10$ of a mile and minutes after leaving plaintiff's showroom. Certainly this was well within the ambit of "reasonable opportunity to inspect." That the vehicle was grievously defective when it left plaintiff's possession is a compelling conclusion, as is the conclusion that in a legal sense defendant never accepted the vehicle.

Nor could the dealer under such circumstances require acceptance. Cf. Code Comment 2 (subsection 2) to UCC § 2–106:

"It is in general intended to continue the policy of requiring exact performance by the seller of his obligations as a condition to his right to require acceptance. * * *"

Even if defendant had accepted the automobile tendered, he had a right to revoke under UCC § 2–608. * * *

The New Jersey Study Comment to UCC § 2–608 reads:

"3. Subsection 2–608(1) permits revocation of acceptance only where there has been a non-conformity which substantially impairs the value of the lot or commercial unit which was accepted. No similar restriction is placed on the buyer's rights to rescind under section 69 of the [Uniform Sales Act]. Under the [Uniform Sales Act], however, the courts have not allowed rescission for a trivial breach of warranty. Therefore, the U.C.C. requirement of substantial impairment does not differ radically from the decisions under the [Uniform Sales Act]. See, in this connection, Miller & Sons Bakery Co. v. Selikowitz, 4 N.J.Super. 97, 66 A.2d 441 (1949) ('The *right to rescind*, however, is an extreme one and does not arise from every breach. * * * The general rule is that rescission will not be permitted for a slight or casual breach of contract, but only for such breaches as are *so substantial* * * * *as to defeat the objective of the parties* * * *')." * * *

Nor did plaintiff have reasonable grounds to believe that a new automobile which could not even be driven a bare few miles to the buyer's residence would be acceptable. The dealer is in an entirely different position from the layman. The dealer with his staff of expert mechanics and modern equipment knows or should know of substantial defects in the new automobile which it sells. There was offered into evidence the dealer's inspection and adjustment schedule containing over 70 alleged items that plaintiff caused to be inspected, including the transmission. According to that schedule the automobile in question had been checked by the seller for the satisfaction of the buyer, and such inspection included a road test. The fact that the automobile underwent a tortured operation for about 2½ miles from the showroom to defendant's residence demonstrates the inherent serious deficiencies in this vehicle which were present when the so-called inspection was made by plaintiff, and hence plaintiff was aware (or should have been) that the vehicle did not conform to the bargain the parties had made, and plaintiff had no reasonable right to expect that the vehicle in that condition would be accepted.

There having been no acceptance, the next issue presented is whether defendant properly rejected under the Code. That he cancelled the sale and rejected the vehicle almost concomitantly with the discovery of the failure of his bargain is clear from the evidence. UCC § 2–601 delineates the buyer's rights following non-conforming delivery.

* * *

There was no evidence at the trial concerning any "custom or usage," although plaintiff in its brief argued that it is the usage of the automobile trade that a buyer accept a new automobile, although containing defects of manufacture, if such defects can be and are seasonably cured by the seller. Perhaps this represents prevailing views in the automobile industry which have, over the years, served to blanket injustices and inequities committed upon buyers who demurred in the light of the unequal positions of strength between the parties. The spirit of the *Henningsen* opinion [32 N.J. 358, 161 A.2d 69 (1960)] contemplated these conditions which cried out for correction. In the present case we are not dealing with a situation such as was present in Adams v. Tramontin Motor Sales, 42 N.J.Super. 313, 126 A.2d 358 (App.Div.1956). In that case, brought for breach of implied warranty of merchantability, the court held that minor defects, such as adjustment of the motor, tightening of loose elements, fixing of locks and dome light, and a correction of rumbling noise, were not remarkable defects, and therefore there was no breach. Here the breach was substantial. The new car was practically inoperable and endowed with a defective transmission. This was a "remarkable defect" and justified rejection by the buyer.

Lastly, plaintiff urges that under UCC § 2–508 it had a right to cure the nonconforming delivery.

* * *

The New Jersey Study Comment to UCC § 2–508 reads:

"3. Subsection 2–508(2) has been applauded as a rule aimed at ending 'forced breaches.' See, Hawkland, Sales and Bulk Sales Under the Uniform Commercial Code, 120–122 (1958). * * *

Section 2–508 prevents the buyer from forcing the seller to breach by making a surprise rejection of the goods because of some minor non-conformity at a time at which the seller cannot cure the deficiency within the time for performance."

* * *

It is clear that in the instant case there was no "forced breach" on the part of the buyer, for he almost immediately began to negotiate for another automobile. The inquiry is as to what is intended by "cure," as used in the Code. This statute makes no attempt to define or specify what a "cure" shall consist of. It would appear, then, that each case must be controlled by its own facts. The "cure" intended under the cited section of the Code does not, in the court's opinion, contemplate the tender of a new vehicle with a substituted transmission, not from the factory and of unknown lineage from another vehicle in plaintiff's possession. It was not the intention of the Legislature that the right to "cure" is a limitless one to be controlled only by the will of the seller. A "cure" which endeavors by substitution to tender a chattel not within the agreement or contemplation of the parties is invalid.

For a majority of people the purchase of a new car is a major investment, rationalized by the peace of mind that flows from its dependability and safety. Once their faith is shaken, the vehicle loses not only its real value in their eyes, but becomes an instrument whose integrity is substantially impaired and whose operation is fraught with apprehension. The attempted cure in the present case was ineffective.

Accordingly, and pursuant to UCC § 2–711, judgment is rendered on the main case in favor of defendant. On the counterclaim judgment is rendered in favor of defendant and against plaintiff in the sum of $124, being the amount of the deposit, there being no further proof of damages.

Defendant shall, as part of this judgment, execute for plaintiff, on demand, such documents as are necessary to again vest title to the vehicle in plaintiff.

NOTE: REJECTION OR REVOCATION OF ACCEPTANCE?

In Rozmus v. Thompson's Lincoln-Mercury Co., 209 Pa.Super. 120, 224 A.2d 782 (1966), Buyer took delivery of a new automobile and drove it to his house. On the way "he noticed smoke coming from the exhaust and that the car made a loud, banging and thumping sound." Buyer returned the car to Seller for correction of the defect. Buyer called for the car the next day, and after determining in a test drive that the noise persisted, immediately returned the car to Seller and demanded a new car or return of his down payment. When his demands were not met he left without taking the new car with him. Although the defect was corrected in a few minutes by tightening two loose engine mounting bolts that had caused a misalignment of the drive shaft, Buyer never returned for the car. The court stated: "There is no doubt that the plaintiff accepted this new automobile. He executed the conditional sales contract which provided that he acknowledged the acceptance of the Mercury in good order, and he drove it from the showroom to his home. * * * § 2–606 * * * provides that acceptance takes force when the buyer either signifies his acceptance to the seller or does an act inconsistent with the seller's ownership."

Would the court that decided *Zabriskie* have held under the facts of *Rozmus* that the buyer could rightfully reject the car? § 2–601. If we assume that the buyer rejected rightfully, would the buyer have been required to accept a tender of the car by the seller after the car was repaired by tightening the loose bolts? § 2–508. Is there any difference in result if it is held that the buyer accepted the car initially? Could the buyer in *Rozmus* have revoked the acceptance because of the defect? Note that § 2–608(1)(b) contemplates a situation in which a defect cannot easily be detected by a superficial pre-delivery inspection such as was made in *Zabriskie*. A person buying goods in sealed containers, as for example cans of peas, has a right to inspect the goods before accepting them, but what is the meaning of the right to inspect in a case of this kind? If the right of inspection means simply the right to look at the labels on the cans it is a right which gives to the buyer no more than the seller's warranty has already given. The buyer cannot determine at the time of acceptance whether the goods are those bargained for. Sometimes inspection can be made by taking a sample of the goods, for example by opening a certain number of cans taken at random from those delivered. In other cases this might not be possible, as for example when the number of sealed units delivered is very small or where each unit is relatively costly. Suppose a buyer takes delivery of goods in sealed containers and later discovers upon opening the containers that the goods don't conform. As a matter of policy is it better to treat the case as one of rejection or of revocation of acceptance?

D. CONTRACTUAL LIMITATIONS ON RIGHT OF REJECTION

1. EFFECT OF WARRANTY

Suppose a new car is sold with the following warranty:

Dealer warrants each new motor vehicle sold by Dealer to be free from defects in material and workmanship under normal use and service. Dealer's obligation under this warranty is limited to making good any part or parts thereof which shall, within ninety days after delivery of such vehicle to the original purchaser or before such vehicle has been driven 4,000 miles, whichever event shall first occur, be returned to Dealer at Dealer's place of business and which Dealer's examination shall disclose to its satisfaction to have been defective. This warranty is expressly in lieu of all other warranties, express or implied.

Buyer takes delivery of the car without having had the opportunity to test drive it. Assume that a court would hold that the taking of delivery under these circumstances does not constitute acceptance. While driving the car home Buyer discovers (a) the defect involved in *Rozmus*, p. 916, or (b) the defect involved in *Zabriskie*, p. 912. Could Buyer rightfully reject the car in case (a)? In case (b)? Does the car "fail in any respect to conform to the contract"? § 2–601. Does rightful rejection depend upon repairability? Does Dealer agree to sell a car free of defects or merely a car whose defects can be repaired? If the quoted clause is effective to limit Buyer's right of rejection under § 2–601, then § 2–508 is not relevant because it applies only to a case of rejection for a nonconformity. If the clause is not given any effect, § 2–601 and § 2–508 control. Does it make any difference if the clause is given effect or not?

2. OBLIGATION TO PAY PRICE BEFORE INSPECTION

Section 2–606(1)(a) and (b) require as a prerequisite to acceptance reasonable opportunity to inspect the goods. Although acceptance of the goods gives to the seller the right to receive payment of the contract price (§ 2–607(1)) acceptance is not a prerequisite to the buyer's obligation to pay the price. § 2–512. The parties may, and commonly do, provide in the sales contract that payment be made for the goods before delivery or at the time of delivery before inspection. Section 2–513 states the buyer's rights regarding inspection of goods and in subsection (1) gives to the buyer a right to inspect before acceptance or payment.

Suppose Seller advertises in a magazine the sale of stereo equipment and provides an order form that a prospective buyer can use to order the goods. Buyer fills in and mails the order form to Seller. The form provides that the stereo equipment will be sent C.O.D. A sealed package identified as containing the stereo equipment ordered from Seller is tendered to Buyer by Seller's agent and demand is made for payment of the price. Buyer refuses to pay unless allowed to see what is in the package. Seller's agent refuses to deliver on Buyer's terms. Is Buyer's refusal to pay a breach of contract? Is Seller's refusal to deliver a breach of contract? Suppose the order form had said nothing about payment. Would Buyer's refusal to pay be a breach of contract? Would Seller's refusal to deliver be a breach of contract? § 2–513.

E. BUYER'S DUTIES CONCERNING REJECTED GOODS

In the preceding section we have seen that a Buyer that uses rejected goods or deals with them in a way that is inconsistent with Seller's ownership runs the risk that those acts may be held to be an acceptance of the goods. On the other hand, Buyer may be allowed, or may be under a duty, to exercise control over the goods in order to protect the interests of Seller. For example, Buyer may ship, store or sell under § 2–604 and may be required to sell the rejected goods under § 2–603. Thus in any case in which Buyer is exercising control over the goods it is necessary to determine (1) whether Buyer's acts are for the purpose of protecting some interest of Buyer such as a security interest (§ 2–711(3)), (2) whether, if that is not the case, the acts of Buyer are contrary to the rights of Seller (§ 2–602(2)(a) and § 2–606(1)(c)), or (3) whether the acts of Buyer are necessary and sufficient to carry out a duty to Seller (§ 2–602(2)(b) and § 2–603). The cases in the preceding section and those that follow illustrate the fine line that sometimes must be drawn.

BORGES v. MAGIC VALLEY FOODS, INC.

Supreme Court of Idaho, 1980.
101 Idaho 494, 616 P.2d 273.

SHEPARD, JUSTICE. This is an appeal from a judgment following a jury verdict which awarded plaintiffs-respondents Borges and G & B Land and Cattle Company $12,832.00 for potatoes received by defendant-appellant Magic West pursuant to a contract with respondents. We affirm.

In 1975, respondents grew and harvested approximately 45,000 c.w.t. of potatoes, which were stored in a cellar near Buhl, Idaho. Magic West inspected those potatoes and, although their inspection indicated that some contained a "hollow heart" defect, Magic West agreed to purchase them for $3.80 per c.w.t. "Hollow heart" indicates a vacant space in the middle of the potato. The purchase contract provided that "if internal problems develop making these potatoes unfit for fresh pack shipping, this contract becomes null and void." It was agreed that the cost of transporting the potatoes from the storage cellar to the processing plant would be borne by Magic West. Examination of the potatoes by State inspectors would occur at the plant to determine that the number of potatoes affected by the hollow heart defect did not exceed the limit prescribed for shipping under the fresh pack grade.

The potatoes were transported to the processing plant, where more than 30,000 c.w.t. were processed and shipped under the fresh pack grade. In March, 1976, State inspectors declared the remaining 4,838.77 c.w.t. of potatoes unfit for the fresh pack grade because of the increased incidence of hollow heart condition. On March 31, 1976, the parties met to discuss the problem of the remaining potatoes and it was apparently agreed that Magic West should attempt to blend them with other potatoes of a higher grade in the hope that such a blend would meet fresh pack grade standards. That experiment failed and Magic West, without notifying the respondents, processed the remaining 4,838.77 c.w.t. of potatoes into flakes and sold them for $1.25 per c.w.t. The evidence in the record disclosed that the remaining potatoes could not be removed from the processing plant without destroying at least one-third of the potatoes.

Respondents demanded the contract price of $3.80 per c.w.t. for the potatoes sold as flakes. Magic West refused, and instead offered to pay $1.25 per c.w.t. This action resulted. The jury returned a general verdict to the respondents of $12,832.00 [2] and the trial court also awarded $6,975.00 as and for attorney fees and costs to the respondents.

Magic West's basic contention is that the 4,838.77 c.w.t. of potatoes were clearly defective and that they were never accepted. It is claimed that when Magic West processed the potatoes into flakes and sold them for $1.25 per c.w.t., they were only following respondents' instructions.

The potatoes in the instant case were clearly movable at the time they were identified in the contract, UCC § 2–105(1), and, hence, were "goods" within the purview of the Idaho Uniform Commercial Code * * * and the dispute is governed by the provisions of the Uniform Commercial Code.

It is clear and undisputed that Magic West had the responsibility of transporting the potatoes from the storage cellar to the processing plant and that State inspection would occur at the plant. It is also clear that the 4,838.77 c.w.t. of potatoes, unable to make the fresh pack grade, did not conform to the contract and gave Magic West the right of rejection. UCC § 2–601(a). Also, it is not disputed that when Magic West determined that the potatoes would not meet fresh pack grade, Magic West so notified the respondents and met with them to determine what disposition should be made of the potatoes. The record is unclear as to precisely what was decided at that March 31, 1976 meeting, but respondents apparently approved of Magic West's proposal to blend the defective potatoes with those with higher quality in an attempt to meet the fresh pack grade. However, it is clear that no agreement on price was reached at that meeting.

A buyer must pay the contract rate for any goods accepted. UCC § 2–607(1). Generally, a buyer is deemed to have accepted defective goods when, knowing of the defect, he resells the goods

---

2. Both parties agreed that the jury had apparently awarded respondents the full contract price of $3.80 per c.w.t. for the potatoes in dispute. If no deductions were made, a jury award of $3.80 per c.w.t. would have resulted in a jury verdict of $18,387.32 [$3.80 x 4838.77].

Obviously, some deductions were made although they are not apparent from the record and were not explained or challenged by counsel. For purposes of this appeal, we assume, as counsel do, that the jury awarded $3.80 per c.w.t. for the potatoes in dispute.

without notifying the seller. See White & Summers, Uniform Commercial Code, § 8–2 (2d ed. 1980); 67 Am.Jur.2d Sales (1973). A buyer accepts goods whenever he does any act inconsistent with the seller's ownership. UCC § 2–606(1)(c). Respondents assert that Magic West's processing of the remaining potatoes into flakes and the subsequent sale constituted acts inconsistent with the respondents' ownership.

Magic West argues, however, that their processing of the potatoes into flakes and their subsequent sale did not constitute an acceptance, but rather was a permissible resale under the provisions of either UCC § 2–603(1) or § 2–604.

*   *   *

We note that both UCC § 2–603(1) and § 2–604 were given in their entirety as instructions to the jury. We find it unclear from the record whether the respondents had agents or a place of business at the "market of rejection." Also, the duty to resell under UCC § 2–603(1) is triggered by an absence of instructions from a seller. Here, given the state of the record and its lack of clarity and the conflicting evidence, the jury could have reasonably found that the respondents did instruct Magic West to attempt to blend the potatoes, but did not instruct them to process the potatoes into flakes. While UCC § 2–604 allows a buyer an option to resell rejected goods if the seller gives no instructions within a reasonable time after the notification of rejection, the jury could have reasonably found that respondents' instructions were only to blend the potatoes in hope of accomplishing fresh pack grade and that Magic West's processing of the potatoes into flakes and subsequent resale thereof was a precipitate action taken before the lapse of a reasonable time within which respondents could give further instructions.

In addition, even if a reasonable time had elapsed, thus permitting Magic West to resell the potatoes, the jury properly could have concluded that processing of the potatoes by Magic West was an acceptance rather than a resale. There was no evidence presented either of an attempt to resell the potatoes in the bins to an independent third party, or of the value of the potatoes in the bins, less damage caused by removal, should it have been effected. Absent any evidence that the $1.25 per c.w.t. offered by Magic West was the highest value obtainable for the potatoes, Magic West's use of the potatoes in the ordinary course of its own business (presumably for profit) was an act inconsistent with the seller's ownership, and constituted an acceptance of the goods. UCC § 2–606(1)(c).

The jury was adequately and correctly instructed regarding the provisions of UCC § 2–603(1) and § 2–604 which constituted Magic West's theory of its duty or option of resale because of an absence of instructions from respondents. The jury was at liberty to reject Magic West's theory of defense based on substantial, albeit conflicting, evidence that Magic West's resale of the potatoes after processing them into flakes constituted an acceptance and Magic West was hence liable for the full contract price.

We have examined appellants' remaining assignments of error and find them to be without merit.

Affirmed.

SULLIVANS ISLAND SEAFOOD CO. v. ISLAND SEAFOOD CO.

District Court of Appeal of Florida, First District, 1980.
390 So.2d 113.

BOOTH, JUDGE. This cause is before us on appeal and cross-appeal from final judgment in a cause tried to the court without a jury. Appellee was the seller, and appellant the buyer, of some 44,370 pounds of shrimp. The trial court found appellee's tender of the shrimp to be nonconforming under UCC § 2–601; that appellant rightfully and timely inspected and rejected the shrimp with proper notice; and that appellee gave no instructions to appellant as to the disposition of the tendered shrimp after notice of their rejection. These findings are essentially undisputed. The issue here is the damage awarded in the amount of $29,755.04 plus costs, an award challenged by both sides.

The trial court's order is, in pertinent part, as follows:

8. Plaintiff stored the shrimp at its expense in Mobile and eventually reshipped them and sold them piecemeal over a period of time extending from 1977 to mid 1978, recovering in the range of $80,000 to $90,000 as resale proceeds.

9. Some 30 days after plaintiff's rejection, while the tendered shrimp were warehoused in Mobile, Alabama, one Albert King, a seafood merchant, inspected the shrimp and made a good faith offer to buy the tendered lot at a price of $.30 per pound less than plaintiff's purchase price. Plaintiff declined this offer.

10. The decision not to accept King's offer was made at plaintiff's peril.

11. Plaintiff is entitled to recover the difference between the offered price and the purchase price, plus sales commission and incidental expenses incurred in the storage and inspection of said shrimp up to the time of Mr. King's offer, plus interest where appropriate as set out in the addendum hereto.

By addendum to the final judgment, the court computed the damages as follows:

Price Difference:

$.30 lb. x 44,370 lbs.	$13,311.00
Commission:	10,537.77
Storage:	194.02
Inspection:	747.15
Interest:	4,965.10
Total:	$29,755.04

Thus, the trial court determined that appellant should have sold the shrimp to Albert King, whom the record shows discussed the purchase of the entire lot. The record also shows that appellant and King were between "20 and 30 cents per pound apart" on price. Apparently, the trial judge computed damages based on the assumption that appellant was asking its full purchase price, $118,688.70, and that the potential buyer, King, was offering between 20 and 30 cents a pound less than *that* amount. The record, however, does not reveal what price King was willing to pay; and, in fact, the evidence falls short of showing that an offer to purchase at any price was made.

Findings number nine and eleven of the trial court's order, supra, based as they are on a supposed offer by King, are, accordingly, set aside. Also set aside is the trial court's finding number ten that the failure to sell to King was at appellant's "peril." What is required under UCC § 2–603 is a showing of lack of good faith on the part of the buyer such as appellant in failing to make a salvage sale of the nonconforming merchandise. The question is whether there was a good faith exercise of reasonable business judgment in an effort to mitigate damages. Appellant here cannot be held to have acted at its peril under this standard, and the record is devoid of evidence showing a lack of good faith.

Accordingly, the judgment below is affirmed in part and reversed in part, and the cause is remanded for computation of damages in accordance herewith.

F. INSTALLMENT CONTRACTS

1. INTRODUCTION

Section 2–307 provides that in the absence of contrary agreement or circumstances indicating a contrary intent, Seller is obliged to tender all the goods called for by the contract of sale in a single delivery. In other words Buyer is not obliged to accept partial performance by Seller unless it has agreed, explicitly or implicitly, to accept Seller's performance in installments. The Comments to § 2–307 give illustrations of the kind of circumstances that allow installment deliveries in the absence of express agreement. These so-called installment contracts are very common and are the subject of special treatment in the UCC. If a contract qualifies as an installment contract there are various consequences: (a) Buyer cannot reject a delivery simply because it does not include all of the goods covered by the contract; (b) Seller can demand payment of the price for goods delivered, if price can be apportioned, even if all goods have not yet been delivered; and (c) Buyer's right to reject the goods is governed by the special rule of § 2–612 rather than the rule of § 2–601. In this regard compare § 2–601, § 2–612(2) and § 2–608(1). The following material considers some of the problems peculiar to installment contracts.

2. CANCELLATION BY BUYER

GRAULICH CATERER, INC. v. HANS HOLTERBOSCH, INC.

Superior Court of New Jersey, Appellate Division, 1968.
101 N.J.Super. 61, 243 A.2d 253.

The opinion of the court was delivered by FOLEY, J.A.D.

* * *

Contact between the litigants sprung from the turmoil surrounding the preparations for the opening of the 1964 New York World's Fair. Holterbosch, an American importer and distributor of Lowenbrau beer, was granted the franchise to operate the Lowenbrau Pavilion at the Fair. Final approval of this award was given on or about January 15, 1964 and contemplated an April 15, 1964 opening. This was the last major pavilion awarded, making time essential in all of defendant's considerations.

In aid of this enterprise defendant engaged a metropolitan-based industrial design consultant, Becker & Becker Associates, to formulate a feasible production plan for serving the required beer and, as a desired adjunct, platters of German food. As stated by defendant, the goal of both Lowenbrau and Holterbosch was the "quality concept of merchandising."

The Raytheon Corporation, knowing the Becker firm's privy role and eager to market their microwave concept of cooking, suggested plaintiff's name to Becker as one able to discharge the culinary requirements of the Lowenbrau Pavilion. Thus approached by Becker, plaintiff on March 10, 1964 entered into preliminary negotiations with the consultant regarding the feasibility of the Raytheon microwave cooking concept as related to the superior quality of food desired by defendant. Briefly, microwave preparation depends upon platters of food prepared and frozen at a central commissary and stored at the place of distribution and/ or consumption. Receiving an order for food, the vendor places the frozen, nearly "done" food platter into a Raytheon microwave oven which "reconstitutes" the frozen food to the desired degree of "doneness." The unit then may be served to the customer. The direct microwave primarily heats, but also serves as a minimal cooking agent bringing the platter to the desired temperature and "doneness" simultaneously. The entire process of reconstitution is completed in a matter of seconds or minutes, depending on the nature and state of the stored units.

At the March 10, 1964 meeting Becker and another employee of the planning firm reviewed with approval ten general food samples submitted by Graulich. Defendant Holterbosch did not personally attend this initial meeting. Informed of defendant's needs, plaintiff redesigned the samples and presented eight platters at a second meeting held on March 17, 1964. This was attended by two Becker employees, Holterbosch, a chef from a German-based steamship company, Graulich and an employee of plaintiff corporation.

Defendant was impressed by six of the samples, recalling at trial that "the food was good, the quality was obvious. It was well prepared." From this date defendant was committed to the microwave concept of satisfying his desire to complement the Lowenbrau beer with an appropriate German cuisine of high quality.

The samples presented and approved on March 17, 1964 were prepared in the Graulich commissary at Port Elizabeth, New Jersey, by plaintiff's employees and were presented to defendant at the Raytheon office in New York City. The operation was agreed upon, with the initial delivery set for April 15, 1964. Daily preparation was to be based on the orders transmitted by defendant to plaintiff's commissary, with daily delivery of the orders made between midnight and 8 A.M. Consumption, theoretically, was to be on the day of delivery. Although the number of units was to fluctuate in relation to the many variables of the operation, the figure of 1,000,000 units was used in estimating the tentative demand for the initial year. Service of the food was to be made on specially designed and colored plastic platters which were required by defendant.

* * *

Returning to the chronology of events, plaintiff, after purchasing its component materials, established a production line commissary at the Jamaica City, Long Island, plant of Met Provisions, where the operation was to be supervised by plaintiff's personnel. This change of commissary site was made in an effort to comply with the Fair requirements of union labor and federal food inspection. A Long Island commissary had the additional delivery advantage of neighboring the Fair. Met also directly supplied plaintiff's raw food product for this venture, as it had, indirectly, through a New Jersey distributor for enterprises in the past.

Plaintiff's production of deliverable product awaited only defendant's order.

The delayed and muddled opening of the Fair brought the parties into daily, and at times even hourly, contact. Postponements followed premature orders until a firm order for April 23, 1964 was placed by Mr. Leigh, an employee of Becker & Becker. Upon delivery the members of defendant's organization were stunned by the product and complained immediately that the tendered units did not, in any way, match the contract samples. Rejecting this 955-unit installment as unacceptable, defendant described the food as "bland," unpresentable, tasteless and "just wasn't the type of food that we could sell." Notwithstanding this low grade delivery, defendant, obligated to the Fair to serve food and committed in theory to the Raytheon ovens, conferred with the equally dissatisfied plaintiff in seeking to improve the quality standard of the product to the point where it would be acceptable. Plaintiff's effort to improve the quality of the units was aided by Becker and defendant's pavilion personnel manager, Mueller, as well as the special foods chef from the "VIP" section of defendant's exhibit.

The second delivery, made on April 25, 1964, was likewise unacceptable. Of the 2520 units delivered, between 500 to 700 were distributed among the employees and patrons of the exhibit for a fast reaction. The complaints in response to the food were many and varied. Defendant, describing the sources of unfavorable comment, stated that the sauerbraten was dry and the gravy, pasty and unpalatably "gooey," surrounded rather than enveloped the meat. The knockwurst platter suffered similarly, being dry and comparing unfavorably with the standards established by the samples. Generally, defendant complained that the food was simply not "German food" and as such was unacceptable for the Lowenbrau Pavilion.

Following the failure of the second delivery Holterbosch claimed that plaintiff took no further curative measures, while plaintiff protested that defendant was "not available" following the second and last delivery of April 25, 1964. Graulich stated that he was told through Becker that plaintiff's food would be unsuitable for the Lowenbrau Pavilion. Becker, affirming the nonconformity of the deliveries, denied terminating the relationship and insisted that such an act was beyond his authority as an agent.

Hellmuch Laufer, defendant's pavilion factotum, affirmed hearing Graulich verbally acknowledge Holterbosch's complaints. Laufer agreed that the second delivery was qualitatively no different than the first, stressing that plaintiff's efforts to cure the unpalatable food failed. This witness, joined by Mueller and the "VIP" chef, converted the microwave cooking area into a conventional kitchen using pot burners to successfuly prepare the food served for the duration of the Fair.

* * *

Giving due regard to the original trier's opportunity to observe the demeanor and to judge the credibility of the witnesses, we find as a matter of fact that the deliveries of April 23 and 25, 1964 did not conform to the samples originally presented and approved. Since warranties of sample and description are characterized as "express warranties," the "whole of the goods shall conform to the sample or model." UCC § 2–313(1)(c). The "goods" to "conform" to the sample or model must be "in accordance with the obligations under the contract" UCC § 2–106(2); here, to comply with the standards established by the March 17 taste-test of the samples. Any distinguishing language would be controlled by the sample as presented on March 17. Additionally, the implied warranty of fitness for purpose attaches to contracts of this type, where, as here, they are not specifically excluded. A breach of these warranties triggers a buyer's rights following seller's breach as catalogued in UCC § 2–711. These remedies include, but are not limited to, cancellation [UCC § 2–711(1), § 2–106(4)] "if the breach goes to the whole of the contract." UCC § 2–612(3).

UCC § 2–612 discloses the rights of the parties to installment contracts.

* * *

Here, Holterbosch had the right to reject any installment that was nonconforming, provided that the nonconformity substantially impaired the value of that installment and could not be cured. UCC § 2–612(2). "Cure," novel to New Jersey's jurisprudence, permits the seller to cure a defective tender through repair, replacement or price allowance if he reasonably notifies the buyer of his curative intention and, in effecting the cure, makes a timely conforming delivery. UCC § 2–508(1).

The effect of the installment contract section, UCC § 2–612(2), is to extend the time for cure past the contract delivery date for that nonconforming installment, provided the nonconformity does not "substantially [impair] the value of that installment" and can be cured. We find that Holterbosch was justified in rejecting Graulich's tender of the April 23 initial installment since the nonconformity of the tendered goods with the accepted sample was incurable, and thus substantially impaired the value of that installment.

Replacing considerations of anticipatory repudiation and the material injury with the test of substantial impairment, UCC § 2–612 adopts a more restrictive seller-oriented approach favoring "the continuance of the contract in the absence of an overt

cancellation." See Comment to UCC § 2–612 par. 6; also New
Jersey Study Comment, par. 2; Hawkland, supra, c. 3, c(3), p. 116.
To allow an aggrieved party to cancel an installment contract,
UCC § 2–612(3) requires (1) the breach be of the whole contract
which occurs when the nonconformity of "one or more installments substantially impairs the value of the whole contract;" and
(2) that seasonable notification of cancellation has been given if
the buyer has accepted a non-conforming installment.

What amounts to substantial impairment presents a question
of fact. Analyzing this factual question, the New Jersey commentators counsel that the test as to whether the nonconformity in
any given installment justifies cancelling the entire contract depends on whether the nonconformity substantially impairs the
value of the whole contract, and not on whether it indicates an
intent or likelihood that the future deliveries also will be defective. Continuing, the Comment relates the intent underlying a
breach to insecurity and those sections of the Code providing
buyer with adequate assurance of performance, § 2–609, and anticipatory repudiation, § 2–610. More practical in its treatment of
"substantial impairment," the official Comment states that "substantial impairment of the value of an installment can turn not
only on the quality of the goods but also on such factors as time,
quantity, assortment and the like. It must be judged in terms of
the normal or specifically known purposes of the contract." Comment to § 2–612, par. 4; also, Hawkland, supra, at p. 117.

At the Lowenbrau Pavilion on April 23, 1964 plaintiff Graulich, timely noticed of the nonconforming initial tender, gave
assurance that future tenders would be cured to match the original samples. Unequivocally committed to the microwave kitchen
method, defendant lent plaintiff three members from its staff in
aid of this adjustment. Since plaintiff was given the opportunity
to cure, there is no need to touch upon the substantiality of the
initial nonconforming installment.

The second installment tender was as unsatisfactory as the
first. The meat was dry, the gravy "gooey" and the complaints
abundant. After the nonconforming second delivery it became
apparent that eleventh-hour efforts attempting to rework and
adjust the platters failed. Translating this into legal parlance,
there was a nonconforming tender of the initial installment on a
contract for the sale of goods; upon tender the buyer Holterbosch
notified the seller Graulich of the nonconformity and unacceptable
nature of the platters tendered; the failure of the cure assured by
plaintiff, seller, was evidenced by a subsequently defective nonconforming delivery. The second unacceptable delivery and the failure of plaintiff's additional curative efforts left defendant in a
position for one week without food. Time was critical. Plaintiff
knew that platters of maximum quality were required on a daily

installment basis.   Because of defendant's immediate need for quality food and plaintiff's failure to cure, we find that the nonconformity of the second delivery, projected upon the circumstances of this case, "substantially impair[ed] the value of the whole contract [and resulted in] a breach of the whole." UCC § 2–612(3).   If the breach goes to the whole contract the buyer may cancel the whole contract.   UCC § 2–711(1).   Accordingly we find that Holterbosch was justified in cancelling the installment agreement signed on April 1, 1964.

Since defendant's counterclaim was withdrawn it is unnecessary to treat of the right retained by a cancelling party to press any remedy for breach of the whole contract.   UCC § 2–106(4).

Judgment in favor of defendant for the reasons herein stated.

NOTE

The court in *Graulich* states that the right of Holterbosch to cancel the contract because of breach by Graulich depended upon "whether the nonconformity substantially impairs the value of the whole contract, and not on whether it indicates an intent or likelihood that the future deliveries also will be defective."   Do you agree?   Could Holterbosch have rightfully cancelled because of the nonconformity of the first installment?   If after the second installment Graulich had been able to demonstrate conclusively that the causes of the nonconformity of the first two installments would no longer be operative as to future installments could Holterbosch have rightfully cancelled?

3. CANCELLATION BY SELLER

FLOOD v. M. P. CLARK, INC.
United States District Court, E.D. Pennsylvania, 1970.
319 F.Supp. 1043.

WOOD, DISTRICT JUDGE.

FINDINGS OF FACT

1. Plaintiff, David A. Flood, is the Trustee in Bankruptcy of the Estate of Taylor's Potato Chip Company, Inc., whose address is Bellefonte, Pennsylvania.

2. Defendant, M. P. Clark, Inc., is a corporation located at 226 N. Decatur Street, Strasburg, Pennsylvania.   At the time of the transactions involved, defendant was licensed under the Perishable Agricultural Commodities Act, 1930, § 1 et seq., 7 U.S.C. § 499a et seq.

3. On or about August 23, 1963, a written contract was entered into between [Taylor's Potato Chip Company] and M. P. Clark, Inc., which provided that Clark agreed to sell and Taylor's agreed to buy approximately one trailer load of potatoes every ten days for a period of one year beginning May 1, 1964. The contract further provided that all potatoes would be of chipping quality and delivered at Bellefonte, Pennsylvania, at a price of $3.00 per 100 lbs.   *   *   *

8. The first delivery under the contract was made on May 6, 1964 of 175 100 lb. bags of potatoes for which Taylor's Potato Chip Company, Inc., paid $700.00 on or about June 9, 1964. The second delivery under the contract was made on May 12, 1964 of 380 100 lb. bags of potatoes for which Taylor's paid $1,520.00 on or about June 26, 1964.

9. From May 26, 1964, until September 14, 1964, M. P. Clark delivered to Taylor's 2,988 100 lb. bags of potatoes, the total cost of which was $11,802.00. Taylor's paid Clark $10,000.00 on October 14, 1964, and the balance was paid on December 3, 1964.

10. On or about September 15, 1964, M. P. Clark notified Richard Taylor that no further deliveries would be forthcoming until payment for past deliveries was made.

11. On or about October 14, 1964, M. P. Clark agreed to make further deliveries to Taylor's on a c.o.d. basis. A delivery was made on October 20, 1964, of 390 100 lb. bags of potatoes for which Taylor's paid $1,170.00. No further deliveries were made until Taylor's paid the balance due on past deliveries.

12. Clark made deliveries of potatoes to Taylor's on a c.o.d. basis on December 3, 1964, December 16, 1964, December 30, 1964, and January 19, 1965.

13. Clark refused to make any further deliveries to Taylor's after January 19, 1965.

14. After Clark's refusal to make further deliveries, Taylor's purchased 1,433½ 100 lb. bags of potatoes from E. K. Bare & Sons. 375 of the bags were purchased at $5.80 per 100 lbs. The remainder were purchased at $6.00 per 100 lbs.

15. Taylor's made an overpayment of $3,393 on 3,393 100 lb. bags of potatoes purchased from Clark for one dollar over the contract price. This overpayment is still owing to Taylor's.

DISCUSSION

This case arises on appeal by M. P. Clark, Inc., (hereinafter Clark) from a reparation order of the Secretary of Agriculture under the Perishable Agricultural Commodities Act, 1930 § 1 et seq., 7 U.S.C. § 499a et seq. The Secretary found that Clark breached its duty to sell and deliver potatoes to Taylor's Potato

Chip Company, Inc., (hereinafter Taylor) pursuant to a contract of sale between the parties.

There are two separate time periods during which deliveries were not made. The first period is from September 14, 1964, to December 3, 1964.[1] The Secretary concluded that Clark was justified in refusing to make deliveries during that time as Taylor owed $11,800.00 for past deliveries despite the contract provision that payment be made upon presentation of invoices. Taylor's contention is that Clark's refusal to deliver was a breach of the contract as, by its course of performance in accepting prior payments made after the presentation of invoices, Clark waived its right to object to such payments. U.C.C. § 2–208. However, even were we to conclude that Clark waived the right to demand payment upon presentation of invoices, we cannot conclude that it waived the right to payment within a reasonable time. The evidence is clear that as soon as the president of Clark became aware of the extent of the amount owed by Taylor, he immediately contacted the latter and demanded payment before he would tender further deliveries. We agree with the Secretary that he was within his rights in doing so.

The second time period during which deliveries were not made was from January 19, 1965 until the contract's termination date, April 30, 1965. The testimony is in conflict here as to whether Clark refused to make deliveries or whether Taylor merely refused to request them. The Secretary found that from the weight of the evidence Clark refused to make any deliveries after January 19, 1965, and thereby breached the contract. Such a finding is *prima facie* correct. Wesco Foods Co. v. De Mase, 194 F.2d 918 (3rd Cir. 1952). We find nothing in the evidence before us to overturn this finding. Clark suggests that Taylor purchased potatoes from other suppliers during this time because it could purchase on credit, whereas it could only purchase from Clark on a c.o.d. basis.[2] However, we cannot believe that Taylor would pay $6.00 per 100 pounds of potatoes instead of the contract price of $3.00 per hundred pounds for the sole purpose of buying on credit.

Clark also contends that Taylor's failure to pay for deliveries from June 26, 1964 to October 14, 1964 substantially impaired the value of the entire contract and therefore constituted a breach of the entire contract. U.C.C. § 2–612(3). Consequently, Clark argues, it had the right to cancel the contract with respect to future deliveries. U.C.C. § 2–703. It is clear, however, that Clark did not cancel the contract at this time, but rather agreed to continue dealing with Taylor provided the dealing was on a c.o.d. basis. There is no evidence as to any act on Taylor's part after the resumption of dealing between the parties which would give rise

1. Only one delivery was made during this time, a delivery of 390 100 lb. bags on October 20.

2. After Taylor paid Clark the $11,800.00 debt, the parties resumed dealings, but only on a c.o.d. basis.

to the right of cancellation by Clark. Therefore we agree with the Secretary that Clark's failure to deliver potatoes to Taylor from January 19, 1965 to April 30, 1965, constituted a breach of the contract.

* * *

NOTE

The seller in *Flood* argued that the failure of the buyer to pay was a breach of the entire contract which gave the seller a right to cancel. The court replied by stating that in fact the seller didn't cancel but agreed to continue deliveries on a C.O.D. basis. Could the seller have cancelled? What should the seller have done? Consider § 2–609 and § 2–610 and the cases that follow.

CHERWELL–RALLI, INC. v. RYTMAN GRAIN CO.

Supreme Court of Connecticut, 1980.
180 Conn. 714, 433 A.2d 984.

PETERS, JUSTICE. This case involves a dispute about which of the parties to an oral instalment contract was the first to be in breach. The plaintiff, Cherwell-Ralli, Inc., sued the defendant, Rytman Grain Co., Inc., for the nonpayment of moneys due and owing for accepted deliveries of products known as Cherco Meal and C-R-T Meal. The defendant, conceding its indebtedness, counterclaimed for damages arising out of the plaintiff's refusal to deliver remaining instalments under the contract. The trial court, Bordon, J., trial referee, having found all issues for the plaintiff, rendered judgment accordingly, and the defendant appealed.

The trial court's unchallenged finding of fact establishes the following: The parties, on July 26, 1974, entered into an instalment contract for the sale of Cherco Meal and C-R-T Meal on the basis of a memorandum executed by the Getkin Brokerage House. As modified, the contract called for shipments according to weekly instructions from the buyer, with payments to be made within ten days after delivery. Almost immediately the buyer was behind in its payments, and these arrearages were often quite substantial. The seller repeatedly called these arrearages to the buyer's attention but continued to make all shipments as requested by the buyer from July 29, 1974 to April 23, 1975.

By April 15, 1975, the buyer had become concerned that the seller might not complete performance of the contract, because the seller's plant might close and because the market price of the goods had come significantly to exceed the contract price. In a telephonic conversation between the buyer's president and the seller's president on that day, the buyer was assured by the seller that deliveries would continue if the buyer would make the payments for which it was obligated. Thereupon, the buyer sent the seller a check in the amount of $9825.60 to cover shipments through March 31, 1975.

Several days later, on April 23, 1975, the buyer stopped payment on this check because he was told by a truck driver, not employed by the seller, that this shipment would be his last load. The trial court found that this was not a valid reason for stoppage of payment. Upon inquiry by the seller, the buyer restated his earlier concerns about future deliveries. Two letters, both dated April 28, 1975, describe the impasse between the parties: the seller again demanded payment, and the buyer, for the first time in writing, demanded adequate assurance of further deliveries. The buyer's demand for assurance was reiterated in its direct reply to the seller's demand for payment. The buyer, however, made no further payments, either to replace the stopped check or otherwise to pay for the nineteen accepted shipments for which balances were outstanding. The seller made no further deliveries after April 23, 1975, when it heard about the stopped check; the buyer never made specific requests for shipments after that date. Inability to deliver the goods forced the seller to close its plant, on May 2, 1975, because of stockpiling of excess material.

The trial court concluded, on the basis of these facts, that the party in breach was the buyer and not the seller. The court concluded that the seller was entitled to recover the final balance of $21,013.60, which both parties agreed to be due and owing. It concluded that the buyer could not prevail on its counterclaim because it had no reasonable grounds to doubt performance from the seller and had in fact received reasonable assurances. Further, the buyer had presented no reasonably accurate evidence to establish the damages it might have sustained because of the seller's failure to deliver.

The buyer on this appeal challenges first the conclusion that the buyer's failure to pay "substantially impaired the value of the whole contract," so as to constitute "a breach of the whole contract," as is required by the applicable law governing instalment contracts. UCC § 2–612(3). What constitutes impairment of the value of the whole contract is a question of fact; Graulich Caterer, Inc. v. Holterbosch, Inc., 101 N.J.Super. 61, 75, 243 A.2d 253 (1968); Holiday Mfg. Co. v. B.A.S.F. Systems, Inc., 380 F.Supp. 1096, 1102 (D.Neb.1974). The record below amply sustains the trial court's conclusion in this regard, particularly in light of the undenied and uncured stoppage of a check given to comply with the buyer's promise to reduce significantly the amount of its outstanding arrearages. See Frigiking, Inc. v. Century Tire & Sales Co., 452 F.Supp. 935, 938 (N.D.Tex.1978).

The buyer argues that the seller in an instalment contract may never terminate a contract, despite repeated default in payment by the buyer, without first invoking the insecurity methodology of UCC § 2–609. That is not the law. If there is reasonable doubt about whether the buyer's default is substantial, the seller may be well advised to temporize by suspending further performance until it can ascertain whether the buyer is able to offer adequate assurance of future payments. Kunian v. Development Corporation of America, 165 Conn. 300, 312, 334 A.2d 427 (1973); Dangerfield v. Markel, 252 N.W.2d 184, 192–93 (N.D.1977). But if the buyer's conduct is sufficiently egregious, such conduct will, in and of itself, constitute substantial impairment of the value of the whole contract and a present breach of the contract as a whole. An aggrieved seller is expressly permitted, by UCC § 2–703(f), upon breach of a contract as a whole, to cancel the remainder of the contract "with respect to the whole undelivered balance." See Frigiking, Inc. v. Century Tire & Sales Co., supra. Nor is the seller's remedy to cancel waived, as the buyer argues, by a law suit seeking recovery for payments due. While § 2–612(3) states that a contract is reinstated if the seller "brings an action with respect *only* to past instalments" (emphasis added), it is clear in this case that the seller intended, as the buyer well knew, to bring this contract to an end because of the buyer's breach.

The buyer's attack on the court's conclusions with respect to its counterclaim is equally unavailing. The buyer's principal argument is that the seller was obligated, on pain of default, to provide assurance of its further performance. The right to such assurance is premised on reasonable grounds for insecurity. Whether a buyer has reasonable grounds to be insecure is a question of fact. AMF, Inc. v. McDonald's Corporation, 536 F.2d 1167, 1170 (7th Cir. 1976). The trial court concluded that in this case the buyer's insecurity was not reasonable and we agree. A party to a sales contract may not suspend performance of its own for which it has "already received the agreed return." At all times, the buyer had received all of the goods which it had ordered. The buyer could not rely on its own nonpayments as a basis for its own insecurity. The presidents of the parties had exchanged adequate verbal assurances only eight days before the buyer itself again delayed its own performance on the basis of information that was facially unreliable. Contrary to the buyer's argument, subsequent events proved the buyer's fears to be incorrect, since the seller's plant closed due to a surplus rather than due to a shortage of materials. Finally, it is fatal to the buyer's appeal that neither its oral argument nor its brief addressed its failure to substantiate, with probative evidence, the damages it alleged to be attributable to the seller's nondeliveries.

There is no error.

4. ASSURANCE OF PERFORMANCE

In addition to the Comments to § 2–609 a number of cases have illustrated the way in which the assurance of due performance fits into the law. In Copylease Corp. of America v. Memorex Corp., 403 F.Supp. 625 (S.D.N.Y.1975), in the course of a dispute between a manufacturer and a distributor of the manufacturer's goods, concerning the terms of their contract, the general manager of the manufacturer expressed his annoyance with the distributor's "continuous threats, harassments, threats of lawsuits" and stated that he "didn't want to continue the business under the present * * * relationship." The general counsel of the manufacturer expressed his opinion that there existed an "unworkable business agreement" which did not represent "any mutually acceptable basis for doing business" and that there was a "substantial question" about the validity of the contract between the manufacturer and the distributor. The court held that these statements gave the distributor reasonable grounds for insecurity concerning the manufacturer's performance under the contract and could demand assurances of performance.

An example of insecurity based on doubts about the seller's ability to meet contract performance specifications is Creusot-Loire International, Inc. v. Coppus Engineering Corp., 585 F.Supp. 45 (S.D.N.Y. 1983). Plaintiff purchased five burners from Defendant for installation in an ammonia plant in Yugoslavia. Defendant expressly warranted that the burners were capable of continuous operation using heavy fuel oil with combustion air preheated to 260°C. The term of the warranty was one year from the start-up of the plant but not exceeding three years from the date of shipment of the burners. Plaintiff paid the $175,000 purchase price and the burners were shipped to Yugoslavia in November 1979. The scheduled start-up date for the plant was in 1981, but for unstated reasons start-up was delayed until the end of 1983. Defendant sold similar burners which were installed in an ammonia plant in Sri Lanka. In early 1981 Plaintiff discovered that the burners installed in the Sri Lankan plant failed to operate properly in that they overheated when operated with heavy fuel oil. Plaintiff wrote to Defendant expressing its concern that the burners would not perform satisfactorily in the Yugoslavian plant. About six months later Defendant suggested modifications to the burners to be made at Plaintiff's expense to ensure satisfactory performance. Plaintiff answered by demanding proof that the burners would satisfy the contract specifications. Defendant answered that it had no experience with operating burners under conditions like those at the Yugoslavian plant and suggested that the contract specifications be modified to provide for a different type of fuel and a different preheat temperature. In fact, the contract specifications for the burners used in Sri Lanka were less

rigorous than those for the Yugoslavian burners and the operating
conditions at the two plants were similar. Defendant did not
disclose that similar modifications made with respect to the Sri
Lankan burners proved unsuccessful. Plaintiff demanded that
Defendant take back the burners and refund the purchase price.
When Defendant refused Plaintiff stated that it would accept the
burners if Defendant extended the term of its warranty because of
the delay in the start-up date of the Yugoslavian plant and if
Defendant would provide a letter of credit to guarantee repayment
of the purchase price if the burners failed to perform satisfactorily. Defendant refused. In the action brought by Plaintiff for
refund of the purchase price and incidental damages the court
stated, 585 F.Supp at 49–50:

> Turning to defendant's claim that plaintiff's request for
> assurances was unreasonable, the Court notes that defen-
> dant promised to do more than just deliver the burners.
> The contract plainly states that defendant was obligated to
> provide burners which would operate under certain condi-
> tions. The present record establishes that plaintiff was
> justified in seeking assurances that the burners were able
> to meet the Yugoslavian operating specifications. As Offi-
> cial Comment 3 to U.C.C. § 2–609 recognizes, a buyer of
> precision parts has reasonable grounds for insecurity "if he
> discovers that his seller is making defective deliveries of
> such parts to other buyers with similar needs." As stated
> previously, defendant's own documents indicate that the
> burners delivered to Sri Lanka did not conform to specifica-
> tions; thus plaintiff was justified in seeking assurances
> from defendant. * * *
>
> With respect to defendant's claim that the assurances
> sought by plaintiff were unreasonable, the Court initially
> observes that after being asked for technical assurances in
> February, defendant did not respond until September;
> thereby heightening plaintiff's suspicions. * * * Fur-
> ther, the Court finds that the assurances later sought by
> plaintiff—an extension of contractual guarantee and the
> posting of a letter of credit—were not unreasonable in light
> of the circumstances. First, plaintiff's contention that its
> demand for a letter of credit comported with accepted
> international business practice is not seriously contested.
> Second, the record demonstrates that defendant's stalling
> and lack of candor forced plaintiff to request security in
> the form of a letter of credit and an extension of the
> warranty. Third, while it understands that defendant bar-
> gained for a contract that included a limited warranty, in
> view of the strategy adopted to meet plaintiff's demand for
> assurances, the Court concludes that plaintiff's request to
> extend its warranty also was reasonable. Thus, defen-

dant's failure to provide any assurances save its statement that the burners would work if installed, constitutes a repudiation of the contract. U.C.C. § 2–609(4).

Pittsburgh-Des Moines Steel Co. v. Brookhaven Manor Water Co., 532 F.2d 572 (7th Cir. 1976), provides an example of the inapplicability of § 2–609. There PDM agreed to construct a water tank for Brookhaven at a price of $175,000. PDM's original proposal for payment of the price—60% at the time of receipt of materials by PDM, 30% on erection of the tank, and 10% after testing of the tank—was rejected by Brookhaven, and the parties finally agreed in November 1968 to payment of the entire price only after the tank was completed, erected and tested. The district manager of PDM had been told by a third party that Brookhaven had obtained a loan to buy the tank. This information was incorrect; Brookhaven had negotiated for a loan but the negotiations had been dropped. PDM early in 1969 then demanded as a condition to its performance either that Brookhaven escrow funds to pay for the tank or that Brookhaven's president personally guarantee the contract. The court stated:

> We, of course, would not deprive PDM of resort to § 2–609 if there had been a demonstration that reasonable grounds for insecurity had arisen. The proof in that respect was lacking. The comptroller and supervisor of PDM's credit department testified that he had access to all of the credit information that the company had regarding Brookhaven, that he had reviewed that information, and that he was unaware of any change in the financial condition of Brookhaven between November of 1968 and the end of 1969. Finally, we note that despite the professed subjective questioning in April as to whether PDM might be paid, the credit manager as early as January had said that the job would be held in abeyance until arrangements had been made for escrowing and a month after the questioning, the questioning officer had offered to proceed with construction in exchange for an interest in Brookhaven, an unlikely course if Brookhaven were financially in a questionable condition. There was also testimony with the same inference that PDM was not fearful of Brookhaven's financial stability or ability to pay in connection with PDM lending to Brookhaven the amount involved at an interest rate of $9\frac{1}{2}\%$ which rate was then unacceptable to Brookhaven. If the buyer was unable to pay for the performance of the contract, it is difficult to see that it was better able to pay a promissory note. We do not fault Brookhaven for its rejection of various proposals advanced by PDM each of which amounted to a rewriting of the contract in the absence of a proper § 2–609 basis. The fact, if it were a

fact, that Brookhaven may not have had a large amount of cash lying in the bank in a checking account, not an unusual situation for a real estate developer, does not support the belief that it, as a company with substantial assets, would fail to meet its obligations as they fell due. Section 2–609 is a protective device when reasonable grounds for insecurity arise; it is not a pen for rewriting a contract in the absence of those reasonable grounds having arisen, particularly when the proposed rewriting involves the very factors which had been waived by the one now attempting to wield the pen. The situation is made no more persuasive for PDM when it is recalled that that company was the original scrivener.

G. CANCELLATION OF CONTRACT BECAUSE OF BREACH OF SEPARATE CONTRACT BETWEEN SAME PARTIES

NATIONAL FARMERS ORGANIZATION v. BARTLETT & CO., GRAIN

United States Court of Appeals, Eighth Circuit, 1977.
560 F.2d 1350.

VAN OOSTERHOUT, SENIOR CIRCUIT JUDGE. This is a diversity action brought by the National Farmers Organization (hereinafter Seller) against Bartlett and Company, Grain (hereinafter Buyer) to recover an alleged balance due, in the stipulated amount of $18,441.62, on the price of grain sold and delivered under four of a series of fourteen contracts between the parties. The Buyer admits that the $18,441.62 was withheld from the total payment otherwise due but claims by way of setoff that the stated sum was properly withheld as damages due it by virtue of the Seller's alleged breach or anticipatory repudiation of all fourteen contracts. The pertinent facts were largely stipulated, and the cause was tried to the district court sitting without a jury. The court, agreeing with the Buyer that the Seller had breached or anticipatorily repudiated all fourteen contracts, rendered judgment for the Buyer. We affirm.

I.

Prior to January 30, 1973, the parties had entered into forty-five contracts for the sale of grain. Of these contracts, thirty-one were performed in full by both parties and are not in issue. The remaining fourteen, which are the subject of this lawsuit, are summarized in the following table.

Table 1.

Contract Number	Date of Execution (all 1972)	Quantity (bushels)	Price (per bu.)	Delivery Dates
22868	Aug. 5	40,000	$1.80	Dec. 1972
996	Aug. 7	5,000	1.68	Aug. 7–Sept. 22, 1972
1338	Sept. 6	3,400	1.97	Feb.–Mar., 1973
1366	Sept. 11	10,000	1.96	Jan. 15–Mar. 15, 1973
1371	Sept. 11	12,000	1.96	Jan. 15–Mar. 15, 1973
1380	Sept. 11	5,400	1.99	Jan. 15–Mar. 15, 1973
1389	Sept. 12	20,000	1.98	Dec. 1972
1400	Sept. 13	750	2.035	Jan. 15–Mar. 15, 1973
1425	Sept. 16	5,500	1.86	June–Aug., 1973
1575	Oct. 12	10,000	1.87	June–Aug., 1973
7415	Oct. 17	30,000	1.155	Oct.–Dec., 1972
1729	Nov. 13	15,000	1.87	June–Aug., 1973
1824	Nov. 29	13,000	2.26	Dec. 1972
1845	Dec. 4	2,700	2.34	Jan. 1973

Contract No. 7415 was for the sale of corn; each of the others was for the sale of wheat.

The controversy over the above contracts began in December 1972. As of December 1, the only contract on which the delivery date had passed was No. 996; although the September 22 last delivery date had long since expired, 1672 of the 5,000 bushels called for under the contract remained undelivered. Deliveries were due in December on Nos. 22868, 1389, 7415 and 1824. At the end of the month, none of the 40,000 bushels had been delivered on No. 22868, 16,480 of the 20,000 bushels had been delivered on No. 1389, 19,364 of the 30,000 bushels had been delivered on No. 7415, and 8,125 of the 13,000 bushels had been delivered on No. 1824. Additional deliveries on these four contracts, although late, were tendered and accepted in January 1973; by the end of January, 31,725 of 40,000 bushels remained undelivered on No. 22868, 397 of 20,000 bushels remained undelivered on No. 1389, 8,049 of 30,000 bushels remained undelivered on No. 7415, and 648 of 13,000 bushels remained undelivered on No. 1824. In addition, none of the 2,700 bushels due in January under No. 1845 were delivered. The eight contracts not mentioned above in this paragraph had last delivery dates subsequent to January 31, 1973. No deliveries were ever made on any of these contracts, except that 3,943 of 12,000 bushels due no later than March 15 under No. 1371 were delivered in January. On several occasions during the month of January, prior to January 26, the Buyer had given notice to the Seller that the Seller had not completed delivery on certain contracts by the delivery dates designated in the contracts.

Beginning early in December 1972 and continuing throughout January 1973 the Buyer "was retaining some of the purchase price of grain actually delivered as protection against realized or potential loss caused by failure on the [Seller's] part to perform all contracts not yet fully performed."[1] On several occasions during December and January the Seller made verbal demands for the purchase price of grain already delivered.

On or about January 26, 1973, the Seller notified the Buyer that the Seller "was not going to deliver any grain to [Buyer] on any of the 14 outstanding contracts between the parties unless and until [Buyer] paid [Seller] a substantial amount of money due on deliveries already made as of that date on contracts Nos. 22868, 1371, 1389 and 1824." The Seller did in fact suspend performance on all fourteen contracts as of January 27. Thereafter, no grain was ever tendered under any of the contracts.

It is the above communication which the Buyer elected to treat as an anticipatory repudiation of the contracts not yet due. On January 30, the Buyer sent the Seller the following telegram (punctuation supplied in part):

> AS OF TODAY'S MARKET CLOSE WE ARE BRINGING ALL OUTSTANDING CONTRACTS WE HAVE WITH YOUR OFFICE TO CURRENT MARKET PRICE, NAMELY, OUR CONTRACTS 996, 1338, 1366, 1371, 1380, 1425, 1575, 1729, AND 22868. SETTLEMENT WILL BE FORTHCOMING.

On or about January 30–31, the Buyer mailed a debit memo and two credit memos to the Seller. The numerical accuracy of the figures used and calculations made in these memos is stipulated. These memos reflect a balance due the Seller for deliveries made under contracts Nos. 22868, 1371, 1389, and 1824 of $72,894.89 and a balance due the Seller for deliveries made under contract No. 7415 of $1,919.50, for a total balance due of $74,814.39.

The same credit and debit memos claimed setoffs on thirteen of the fourteen contracts, in each case by virtue of the Seller's past breach or alleged anticipatory repudiation of the particular contract. The claimed setoffs were as follows:

---

1. Stipulation 34. The precise import of this stipulation is disputed. The Seller maintains the Buyer withheld payment as protection against the anticipated failure on the Seller's part to deliver grain as contracted for in all fourteen contracts. The Buyer appears to maintain that the payments, which were withheld on contracts Nos. 22868, 1371, 1389 and 1824, were only withheld to cover past losses on Nos. 22868, 996, 1389 and 1845. Although we think the Seller's interpretation of the stipulation more nearly accords with the words used, under the view we ultimately take of the case the reasons for the Buyer's withholding payment are irrelevant.

Table 2.

Contract No.	Undelivered Quantity (bushels)	Difference in Market and Contract Prices (see note 3, supra)	Claimed Setoff
22868	31,732	$ .785	$24,909.62
996	1,673	.67	1,154.37
1338	3,400	.40	1,360.00
1366	10,000	.41	4,100.00
1371	8,057	.41	3,303.37
1380	5,400	.38	2,052.00
1389	405	.39	157.95
1400	750	.335	251.25
1425	5,500	.25	1,375.00
1575	10,000	.24	2,400.00
7415	8,770	.125	1,096.25
1729	15,000	.24	3,600.00
1845	2,700	.03	81.00
			Total $45,840.81

———

The Buyer, deducting the claimed setoff of $45,840.81 from the net balance due of $74,814.39, sent the Seller a check dated February 9 for the $28,973.58 difference. The check was subsequently paid.

The Seller, one day after receiving the January 30 telegram, informed the Buyer that, while it consented to cancellation of contracts Nos. 22868 and 996, it did not recognize and would not agree to cancellation of contracts for future delivery. It is now stipulated that the claimed setoffs shown in Table 2 were proper as to all contracts with last delivery dates of January 31, or earlier, *viz.*, Nos. 22868, 996, 1389, 1845 and 7415. Accordingly, at issue herein is the propriety of claimed setoffs, totaling $18,441.62, on those contracts having last delivery dates subsequent to January 31, *viz.*, Nos. 1338, 1366, 1371, 1380, 1400, 1425, 1575 and 1729. The resolution of this issue turns on the question whether the Seller's January 26 communication constituted an anticipatory repudiation of these contracts.

Before turning to the legal issue presented, we mention one additional fact not expressly stipulated or expressly found by the district court. It is quite clear from the stipulations that as of January 26 a very substantial sum, over and above the amount of damages by then sustained by the Buyer as a consequence of the Seller's past defaults, was due the Seller for deliveries already made under contracts Nos. 22868, 1371, 1389 and 1824,[7] and a very substantial portion of that sum was not only due but past due.[8]

II.

The question tendered to us for decision—whether the Seller's communication of January 26 constituted an anticipatory repudiation of the contracts on which performance was not yet due—is a difficult and close one. Ultimately, its resolution is governed by Section 2–610 of the Uniform Commercial Code and the common law. However, as the parties readily concede, neither the Code language nor the case law of any jurisdiction provides a definitive answer.

Before examining the tendered question directly, we find it useful for the purpose of comparison to consider what the Seller clearly could have done on January 26 under Uniform Commercial Code § 2–609 and what it clearly could not have done on January 26 under Uniform Commercial Code § 2–612.

Uniform Commercial Code § 2–609(1) provides in part: "When reasonable grounds for insecurity arise with respect to the performance of either party the other may in writing demand adequate assurance of due performance and until he receives such assurance may if commercially reasonable suspend any performance for which he has not already received the agreed return." Comment 3 to this section states in part:

> Under commercial standards and in accord with commercial practice, a ground for insecurity need not arise from or be directly related to the contract in question.

* * *

7. At least $65,877.77 was due on the four contracts as of January 26. This figure represents the $72,894.89 due on January 30–31 less the contract price of certain deliveries made on Nos. 22868 and 1389 on January 27. The total damages sustained by the Buyer on Nos. 22868, 996, 1389, 7415 and 1845 (assuming the Buyer could claim a breach on No. 1845 on January 26) are stipulated at $27,399.19 (from Table 2). The difference between $65,877.77 and $27,399.19, which is $38,478.58, thus represents roughly the amount due on January 26 over and above past losses sustained by the Buyer. While a number of downward adjustments should undoubtedly be made to this figure, the adjustments would not alter the conclusion stated in the test.

8. The four contracts had payment terms as follows: No. 22868—"each Tuesday and Friday"; No. 1371—"Cash on Delivery"; No. 1389—"Defer Payments until January 2, 1973"; No. 1824—"Daily upon delivery by noon of the following business day". Deliveries on No. 1389 subsequent to January 2 would be governed by Uniform Commercial Code § 2–310, providing that unless otherwise agreed payment is due on delivery. Thus, in each case prompt payment was part of the contract. The Seller concedes that payment within five days was acceptable to it. Even if we assume ten days, payment for all deliveries prior to January 16 would be past due on January 26. Slightly more than $5000 worth of grain was delivered on the four contracts between January 16 and 26. All other sums due on the four contracts on January 26 were past due.

Thus a buyer who falls behind in "his account" with the seller, even though the items involved have to do with separate and legally distinct contracts, impairs the seller's expectation of due performance.

The example just cited conforms precisely to the facts before us. Plainly, the Seller could have availed itself of a Section 2–609 remedy on January 26. Equally plainly, however, it did not do so.[9]

Uniform Commercial Code § 2–612(3) provides in part: "Whenever nonconformity or default with respect to one or more installments substantially impairs the value of the whole contract there is a breach of the whole." Comment 6 to this section states in part:

> Whether the non-conformity in any given installment justifies cancellation as to the future depends [on] * * * whether the non-conformity substantially impairs the value of the whole contract. If only the seller's security in regard to future installments is impaired he has the right to demand adequate assurances of proper future performance but has not an immediate right to cancel the entire contract.

Although the Buyer was on January 26 substantially behind on payment on some of the contracts, in none of the contracts was time of the essence, and there is no indication that the Buyer's ability to pay was impaired. With respect to those contracts on which payments had not been withheld, at least,[10] the value of each such contract was plainly not substantially impaired as a whole on January 26, and the Seller plainly could not have cancelled those contracts on that date. Equally plainly, however, the Seller did not purport to cancel any of the contracts.[11]

---

9. The Seller so concedes. For two reasons, the concession is a proper one. First, the communication of January 26 was not in writing. Second, the communication did not seek assurance of performance on the future contracts, it sought actual part performance on the contracts on which payment was past due.

The Buyer, we note, has also conceded that it never pursued a remedy under Section 2–609.

10. It is doubtful that the Seller could have cancelled even those contracts on which payments had been withheld. See Laredo Hides Co. v. H & H Meat Products Co., 513 S.W.2d 210 (Tex.Civ.App.1974); Gulf Chem. & Metal. Corp. v. Sylvan Chem. Corp., 122 N.J.Super. 499, 300 A.2d 878 (Law Div.), affirmed, 126 N.J.Super. 261, 314 A.2d 73 (App.Div.1973); Ellis Mfg. Co. v.

Brant, 480 S.W.2d 301 (Tex.Civ.App. 1972).

11. The communication of January 26 was to the effect that deliveries would be withheld or suspended until the Seller received a substantial payment for past deliveries. Ignoring for the moment the complicating and ultimately decisive factor that the present case involves not one but a number of installment contracts, we point out that the distinction between renouncing a contract altogether and suspending performance until past-due counter-performance is received is a well-recognized one: Generally, but not quite always, the seller will be privileged to suspend the succeeding delivery until the previous instalment has been paid for. * * *

A buyer is not justified in refusing to pay an instalment for the mere reason

With the above comments in mind, we turn to the controlling issue under Uniform Commercial Code § 2–610. The district court, acknowledging that the issue was a close one, concluded that the Seller anticipatorily repudiated the contracts with last delivery dates subsequent to January 31 when on January 26 it notified the Buyer that no grain would be delivered under any of the contracts unless and until the Buyer made a substantial payment for deliveries already made under contracts Nos. 22868, 1371, 1389 and 1824. The court reasoned:

> Plaintiff's imposition on January 26 of a condition precedent that defendant perform under various independent contracts clearly amounted to a statement of intention not to perform except on conditions which went beyond each of [the contracts not yet due]. * * * A party to a contract may not refuse performance simply because the other party has breached a separate contract between them. Northwest Lumber Sales, Inc. v. Continental Forest Products, Inc., 261 Or. 480, 495 P.2d 744 (1972).

Uniform Commercial Code § 2–610 provides in part: "When either party repudiates the contract with respect to a performance not yet due the loss of which will substantially impair the value of the contract to the other, the aggrieved party may * * * (b) resort to any remedy for breach * * *." The Code does not articulate what constitutes an anticipatory repudiation. Comment 2 to Section 2–610, however, offers the following guidance:

> It is not necessary for repudiation that performance be made literally and utterly impossible. Repudiation can result from action which reasonably indicates a rejection of the continuing obligation. * * * Under the language of this section, a demand by one or both parties for more than the contract calls for in the way of counter-performance is not in itself a repudiation nor does it invalidate a plain expression of desire for future performance. However, when under a fair reading it amounts to a statement of intention not to perform except on conditions which go beyond the contract, it becomes a repudiation.

It is the last sentence of this Comment which is of foremost concern to us. The communication of January 26, fairly read, amounts to a statement of intention not to perform future contracts except on conditions which go beyond those contracts.

that he fears that the seller will fail to make future deliveries. Such a refusal, with accompanying factors, will justify the refusal to make further deliveries. It has been held in such a case, however, that the seller was not justified in renouncing the contract. Such a decision is correct if the actual risk of non-payment is not increased and if further

performance by the seller is not thereby made more difficult. Note also, that a seller may be justified in holding up further deliveries until paid, without being justified in renouncing the contract.

3A A. Corbin, Contracts § 690 at 254 and 256 (1960) (footnotes omitted).

Under the language of the Comment, therefore, the communication was indeed an anticipatory repudiation of the future contracts.

As a general rule, the principle embraced in the Comment's last sentence is unremarkable, unquestionably sound and in any event binding upon us by virtue of its acceptance by the Supreme Court of Missouri in Miran Investment Co. v. Medical West Bldg. Corp., 414 S.W.2d 297, 302–03 (Mo.1967) (refusal to perform except on execution of personal guarantee not required under contract held a repudiation). See also Pittsburgh-Des Moines Steel Co. v. Brookhaven Manor Water Co., 532 F.2d 572 (7th Cir. 1976) (applying Illinois law) (refusal to perform except on execution of personal guarantee or escrowing of payment not required under contract held a repudiation); Westinghouse Elec. Corp. v. CX Processing Labs., 523 F.2d 668 (9th Cir. 1975) (applying Washington law) (refusal to deliver except at price higher than contract price held a repudiation).[12]

The general rule is not subject to variance when the stated condition derives from a separate contract or contracts—regardless of the validity of the repudiator's claim under the separate contract or contracts. It is well established that the breach of one contract does not justify the aggrieved party in refusing to perform another separate and distinct contract. 3A A. Corbin, Contracts § 696 (1960); Annotation, 27 A.L.R. 1157 (1923) and cases there cited.

The decision cited by the district court, Northwest Lumber Sales, Inc., v. Continental Forest Products, Inc., 261 Or. 480, 495 P.2d 744 (1972), illustrates the separate contracts rule perhaps as well as any. In that case the plaintiff seller had separately contracted for a delivery of pine lumber and a delivery of 2 x 4 studs to the defendant buyer. After the pine lumber had been delivered and allegedly after payment therefor had become thirty days past due, the seller informed the buyer that it would not deliver the studs. The Supreme Court of Oregon, assuming that payment for the pine lumber had been wrongfully withheld, held: "[n]either the Uniform Commercial Code nor general contract law gives either party to a contract the right to refuse performance because the other has breached a separate contract between them." 495 P.2d at 749. Judgment was accordingly rendered for the buyer on its claimed setoff.

12. Professor Corbin is in accord:

If one party to a contract, either wilfully or by mistake, demands of the other a performance to which he has no right under the contract and states definitively that, unless his demand is complied with, he will not render his promised performance, an anticipatory breach has been committed. Such a breach is conditional in character, it is true; but the condition is a performance to which the repudiator has no right.

4 A. Corbin, Contracts § 973 at 910 (1951) (footnote omitted).

On the basis of the authorities cited above, we believe that the *Northwest Lumber Sales* decision was correct and that the Missouri Supreme Court, if confronted with the issue, would agree with the Oregon Supreme Court. Moreover, although the facts before us do present a closer question, we think the Missouri Supreme Court would apply the same principle here.

We may concede to the Seller that the general rule could occasionally dictate a result which for commercial reasons would be unacceptable. Perhaps in such a case the Missouri Supreme Court would decline to apply the rule. The Seller makes an argument of some merit in that regard. Two facts stand out. First, under even the Buyer's interpretation of stipulation 34, see note 1, supra, the Buyer was withholding payment on some contracts to cover losses on other contracts. Under Uniform Commercial Code § 2–717 it was not privileged to do so. See Jurek v. Thompson, 241 N.W.2d 788 (Minn.1976). Second, the Seller's communication of January 26, unlike the communication in *Northwest Lumber Sales*, did not purport to be an outright cancellation or renouncement of any obligation under any of the contracts. See note 11, supra. These two facts lend some credence to the Seller's contention that the January 26 communication was a justified one under the circumstances.

On the other hand, as noted previously, time was not of the essence under the contracts, and there is no indication that the Buyer's ability to pay was impaired. Measures short of suspending delivery on all contracts could have preserved the Seller's contractual right to payment. Moreover, as we have concluded above, a Section 2–609 remedy was specifically available but not used. Despite the Buyer's wrongful withholding of payment on contracts not in default, the separate identities of the various contracts were unquestionably preserved, as all deliveries and payments were separately accounted for throughout the pertinent time period. In addition the Seller, having failed to deliver 1672 bushels of wheat on contract No. 996 by the September 22 last delivery date, was the first breaching party on any of the contracts. Finally, no grain was in fact tendered under any of the contracts after January 27, even though a substantial payment was received and accepted shortly after February 9.

Taking all of the above-mentioned facts into account, we agree with the view of the district court that the Supreme Court of Missouri would find an anticipatory repudiation here. At the very least, the district court's conclusion on this question of state law in a diversity case is entitled to great deference and should be sustained. Howard v. Green, 555 F.2d 178, 182 (8th Cir. 1977).

The judgment appealed from is affirmed.

Chapter 13

WARRANTY

A. INTRODUCTION

In this chapter we will examine how the goods that are the subject of a sale are defined and the responsibility of the seller if the goods do not conform. In the UCC these matters are dealt with through various warranties that the seller makes to the buyer. These warranties can arise from specific conduct or representations that the seller makes to the buyer or they may be imposed on the seller by operation of law. We are dealing with the problem of providing remedies to a disappointed buyer who expected one thing from the seller but in fact received something else. Warranties define what the seller has agreed to sell and what the buyer has agreed to buy. Thus warranties depend upon the agreement, but agreement, defined by § 1–201(3), is not limited to the formal writing that the seller and the buyer may have signed. It may also include elements of the bargain that are implied because of a common unstated understanding that the law specifically recognizes or which can be found in trade usage or the conduct of the parties themselves.

If the parties agree to a sale of sweaters made of "100% virgin wool" that description is covered by § 2–313 and is known as an express warranty. If the seller delivers goods that are not sweaters made of 100% virgin wool there is a breach of warranty by the seller. But some warranties are not expressed. Rather, they are implied because it can reasonably be assumed that the parties would have expressed them if they had thought about the matter. For example, the buyer would normally assume, consciously or unconsciously, that when the sweaters are delivered by the seller the buyer will receive good title to them. A sale of goods is defined in § 2–106 as "the passing of title from the seller to the buyer for a price." Although a sale means that the seller's title is passed to the buyer, if the seller had no title at all or if the seller's title was defective the buyer may not get title to the goods or may get a title that is clouded. On the assumption that a buyer would not normally agree to that result, the law imposes on the seller a warranty that the title conveyed "shall be good and its transfer rightful." § 2–312(1)(a).

There may be other implied warranties. Suppose that the seller of the sweaters is a manufacturer and the buyer is a wholesaler that intends to resell to retailers. Section 2–314(1) implies a warranty by the seller that the sweaters are "merchantable." This very important warranty has an imprecise meaning and has been applied to a wide range of cases. But in our example, one thing that it means is that the buyer is entitled to sweaters that will "pass without objection in the trade under the contract description." § 2–314(2)(a). One aspect of this warranty is similar to the express warranty. Designations such as "100% virgin wool" have meanings that are commonly accepted by merchants who deal in goods to which the designation refers. If the sweaters produced by the seller would not be resalable as "100% virgin wool" garments they are not merchantable. In this respect the warranty of merchantability adds little to the express warranty. But the merchantability warranty has a broader reach. For example, if the dyeing of the sweaters resulted in color that was not uniform or was faded and this defect would cause the sweaters to be unacceptable to retailers, the buyer need not accept them. Thus, the merchantability warranty imposes some minimal standard of quality in cases in which the agreement does not specifically cover quality. This warranty might also cover matters that do not relate to quality but which make the goods unacceptable. For example, sweaters that are otherwise good merchandise, might be unsalable to retailers if they do not contain customary labels regarding size, fiber content or country of origin. § 2–314(2)(e).

The warranty of merchantability can also be described as a "general suitability" warranty. Goods are bought for use or resale and the buyer is entitled to receive goods that are "fit for the ordinary purposes for which such goods are used." § 2–314(2)(c). For example, if a customer buys meat in a food store the customer is entitled to revoke acceptance if it turns out that the meat was inedible because of spoilage. Sometimes goods are fit for the ordinary purposes for which they are sold, but may not be fit for the special needs of the particular buyer. For example, a machine for shearing metal sheets may be suitable for all metals except a few. If the buyer tells the seller that a machine is needed to shear sheets of a particular metal and the seller's machine is not suitable for that metal there may be a breach of the warranty of fitness for a particular purpose of the buyer which is described in § 2–315.

Since warranties are based on an assumption about the normal expectations of the parties, they may not reflect the intention of the parties in abnormal situations. A warranty is a guaranty by the seller that the warranted fact is true. A seller would not normally be concerned about a warranty of good title or description of the goods to be sold because in most cases the seller would have no doubt about those matters. But that is not always the case. In a contract for the sale of a painting by Rembrandt, there may be reasonable doubt about whether the painting is authentic or about the ownership of the painting. The seller takes the risk of authenticity or title if warranties apply, and the seller may not be willing to assume that risk. Or, to take another example, in a sale of a machine intended to perform some function for the buyer, the seller may not be willing to guarantee that the machine will perform the function as intended. To allow shifting of the risk of loss from the seller to the buyer in cases of this kind, warranties can be excluded or disclaimed under § 2–312(2) and § 2–316, or damages for breach of warranty may be limited under § 2–719(3).

We have analyzed warranty in terms of a disappointed buyer. The typical case is that of a buyer who received goods that were worth less than the goods bargained for, or which were not suitable for the buyer's purpose. The buyer's loss is typically an economic loss measured by the difference in value of the goods delivered and those bargained for, or by expenses incurred or profits lost because of the unsuitability of the goods. But in some cases that is not true. Suppose the child of the buyer or some other child is injured while playing with a toy purchased by the buyer and that the injury was caused by a defect in the toy that made it unsafe. Suppose also that the seller of the toy advertised it as being safe for children. The question of liability can be analyzed in terms of warranty, i.e., that the statement of the seller in its advertisements was an express warranty that the toy was safe, or that there was a breach of the warranty of merchantability because the unsafe toy was unfit for the ordinary purposes for which toys are used. But who is the beneficiary of the warranty? In this case the person injured was somebody other than the buyer. The buyer may or may not have an economic loss. Does the injured child have a warranty cause of action? Policies of tort law may be more germane to this kind of problem, and it is not surprising to find that there has grown up a tort doctrine of strict liability for defective products that parallels warranty liability. Warranty law was first used in this kind of situation because it was frequently difficult or impossible to impose liability on the seller based on negligence. The law of warranty thus served as a stopgap until a doctrine of strict liability in tort was fashioned from warranty law. Paradoxically the tort doctrine of strict liability can also be adapted to economic loss situations that were the traditional province of warranty or contract law. To the extent that warranty liability and strict tort liability may differ with respect to such things as disclaimers, privity, limitations of action, and contributory fault, the courts have created a difficult task of deciding the proper province of each body of law.

B. EXPRESS WARRANTY

SESSA v. RIEGLE

United States District Court, E.D. Pennsylvania, 1977.
427 F.Supp. 760.

HANNUM, DISTRICT JUDGE. This civil action was instituted by the buyer of a standardbred race horse against the seller, to recover for breach of express warranties, an implied warranty of merchantability and an implied warranty of fitness for particular purpose. * * *

FINDINGS OF FACT

1. Plaintiff, Joseph Sessa, Jr. (Sessa) is a citizen of Pennsylvania.

2. Defendants Gene Riegle (Riegle), Mrs. Gene Riegle and Mrs. John A. Frantz are citizens of Ohio.

3. The amount in controversy exceeds the sum of $10,000, exclusive of interest and costs.

4. Sessa is employed as a beer distributor in Philadelphia, and as an avocation owns and races standardbred horses. In connection with his avocation, Sessa has bought, sold, valued, selected and generally dealt in standardbreds at various locations in the Eastern United States.

5. Riegle buys, sells, owns, trains, drives and deals in and with standardbred horses and engages in racing competition at various harness tracks in Ohio, Illinois and other parts of the country.

6. Sessa became interested in purchasing a standardbred race horse named Tarport Conaway owned by defendants, Mrs. Gene Riegle and Mrs. John A. Frantz after hearing about the horse and his record in February and March of 1973 from one Robert J. Maloney. Maloney had seen the horse at Riegle's farm in Greenville, Ohio.

7. At all times herein relevant, Riegle acted for himself and as agent for Mrs. Riegle and Mrs. Frantz in connection with the sale of Tarport Conaway.

8. Based on what Robert J. Maloney had told him, on March 9, 1973, Sessa sent Maloney to Riegle's place of business in Greenville, Ohio as his agent to effect the purchase of Tarport Conaway. Maloney carried Sessa's check for the $25,000. purchase price to be delivered to Riegle if the sale was consummated.

9. Sessa also instructed his son, Richard Sessa, to obtain a veterinarian to go to Ohio to examine the horse. When he failed

to do so, Sessa sent Maloney, a personal friend and knowledgeable horseman, to Ohio to complete the sale alone.

10. Sessa was relying chiefly on Maloney's judgment and evaluation in purchasing Tarport Conaway.

11. Maloney arrived in Ohio on Friday, March 9, 1973. On Saturday, March 10, 1973 he examined and jogged Tarport Conaway. His examination was not restricted in any way.

12. Maloney then telephoned Sessa from Riegle's house. He reported that he had jogged Tarport Conaway and "liked him."

13. Maloney then gave the telephone to Riegle who spoke to Sessa. In a short conversation he told Sessa that Sessa would like the horse, that he was a good one and that he was sound. They also discussed arrangements for transportation of the horse and the manner in which he could best be driven. Sessa indicated that he would send a van for transportation. Riegle then gave the phone back to Maloney.

14. After a brief conversation, the telephone call ended.

15. At some point just prior to or after the telephone call, Maloney delivered Sessa's check for the $25,000. purchase price to Riegle.

16. Later in the day, Sessa called Riegle to report that he was unable to obtain a van to ship the horse.

17. Riegle agreed to obtain a van on Sessa's behalf.

18. Tarport Conaway remained in Riegle's custody until March 23, 1973. During this interval he received proper care.

19. On March 23, 1973, Riegle placed the horse in the hands of an ICC approved carrier for shipment to plaintiff at Freehold Raceway in Freehold, New Jersey.

20. At 4:30 A.M., on March 24, 1973 Tarport Conaway arrived at Freehold Raceway.

21. At 8:00 A.M., that morning, Tarport Conaway was examined by Dr. S. P. Dey, D.V.M., and was found to have tendinitis (swelling of the tendons) in both front legs.

22. The cause of the tendinitis was not determined, however, it could have been caused by incidents during shipping.

23. After learning of the tendinitis, Sessa called Riegle, asked him to take the horse back and return the purchase price.

24. Riegle could not believe there was anything wrong with Tarport Conaway and said he would come to Freehold to examine the horse.

25. On March 26, 1973 Riegle came to Freehold Raceway accompanied by Maloney to see Tarport Conaway.

26. It was apparent to both men that the horse was being kept in unclean physical surroundings.

27. By March 26, 1973, Tarport Conaway had recovered from tendinitis. When jogged by Richard Sessa for Riegle and Maloney, the horse jogged normally.

28. Expert medical testimony did not establish that the tendinitis was present on or before March 23, 1973.

29. Subsequently, on March 29, 1973, Tarport Conaway went lame in his hind legs while being jogged on the track at Freehold Raceway.

30. This lameness resulted from "intermittent claudication," a condition created by the stoppage of the flow of blood through the arteries.

31. Intermittent claudication is a result of a thrombosis or blockage of the arteries supplying fresh blood to an area.

32. The intermittent claudication in Tarport Conaway resulted from a thrombosis of the left and right iliac arteries which provide the main blood supply to the hind limbs.

33. None of the medical experts who testified was able to identify the cause of the thrombosis in Tarport Conaway. One main known cause of a thrombosis in a horse's artery is the invasion of and attachment to the arterial walls of the third-stage larvae of the strongylus vulgaris worm, causing an irritation against which the horse reacts by deposition of fibrous tissue in an attempt to wall off the internal parasite. The fibrous tissue builds up inside the artery and ultimately forms a blockage.

There are, however, other known causes for thrombosis in a horse's artery. In addition, a thrombosis can arise without known cause.

34. Expert medical testimony did not establish that the thrombosis was present in Tarport Conaway on or before March 23, 1973.

35. On March 29, 1973, after receiving the report from Dr. Dey that Tarport Conaway had intermittent claudication in the hind limbs, Sessa again called Riegle and asked him to take the horse back and return the purchase money.

36. This Riegle refused to do.

37. There is no immediate cure for thrombosis of the iliac arteries in a horse. The disease is treatable by time and rest.

38. In general, a horse afflicted with a thrombosis of the iliac arteries is unable to race to the potential shown prior to the affliction.

39. In order to treat Tarport Conaway, Sessa sent him to a farm near Dover, Delaware to be turned out for one year.

40. After one year, the horse was put in training for five months but did not race.

41. Tarport Conaway was again turned out, first at Linden Creek Farm near Pittsburgh and then at Green Valley Training Center in Maryland.

42. Tarport Conaway was put back into training in March of 1975.

43. Between June 6, 1975 and December 29, 1975, the date of trial, Tarport Conaway raced 13 times, winning 3 races and earning a total of $1306.00.

44. Between March 24, 1973, the date of Tarport Conaway's arrival at Freehold, through December 29, 1975, the date of trial, Sessa incurred necessary expenses for the horse's transportation, maintenance, training and veterinary care in the amount of $9073.00.

45. Because of his excellent blood lines and early racing record, Tarport Conaway may have substantial value for breeding purposes.

DISCUSSION

* * *

On March 10, 1973, the day of the sale of Tarport Conaway, Sessa and Riegle had a telephone conversation during which the horse was discussed in general terms. Arrangements were made for transportation, and Riegle gave Sessa some instructions for driving Tarport Conaway based on Riegle's experience with him. Sessa contends that certain statements made by Riegle during that conversation constitute express warranties on which Riegle is liable in this action. The most important of these is Riegle's alleged statement that, "the horse is sound," or words to that effect.[1]

In deciding whether statements by a seller constitute express warranties, the Court must look to U.C.C. § 2–313 which presents three fundamental issues. First, the Court must determine whether the seller's statement constitutes an "affirmation of fact or promise" or "description of the goods" under § 2–313(1)(a) or (b) or whether it is rather "merely the seller's opinion or commendation of the goods" under § 2–313(2). Second, assuming the Court finds the language used susceptible to creation of a warranty, it must then be determined whether the statement was "part of the basis of the bargain." If it was, an express warranty exists and, as

---

1. Sessa also cites the statement,

"Tarport Conaway can leave like a deer, take a forward position, and if you brush him from the head of the stretch home, he would just jog home in preferred company every week."

as an express warranty. However, this statement is instruction on driving based on Riegle's experience and constitutes merely an opinion, not an express warranty. Sessa cites other statements as express warranties. However, the credible evidence does not establish that these statements were in fact made.

the third issue, the Court must determine whether the warranty was breached.

With respect to the first issue, the Court finds that in the circumstances of this case, words to the effect that "The horse is sound" spoken during the telephone conversation between Sessa and Riegle constitute an opinion or commendation rather than express warranty. This determination is a question for the trier of fact.[3] * * * There is nothing talismanic or thaumaturgic about the use of the word "sound." Whether use of that language constitutes warranty, or mere opinion or commendation depends on the circumstances of the sale and the type of goods sold. While § 2–313 makes it clear that no specific words need be used and no specific intent need be present, not every statement by a seller is an express warranty.

Several older Pennsylvania cases dealing with horse sales show that similar statements as to soundness are not always similarly treated under warranty law. In Wilkinson v. Stettler, 46 Pa.Super. 407 (1911), the statement that a horse "was solid and sound and would work any place" was held not to constitute an express warranty. This result was followed in Walker v. Kirk, 72 Pa.Super. 534 (1919) which considered the statement, "This mare is sound and all right and a good worker double." *Walker* was decided after the passage of § 12 of the Uniform Sales Act, the precursor of U.C.C. § 2–313 and thus presumably rests on the standard there established. The Official Comments to U.C.C. § 2–313 indicate that no changes in the law of warranties under Uniform Sales Act § 12 were intended.

However, in Flood v. Yeager, 52 Pa.Super. 637 (1912) an express warranty was found where the plaintiff informed the defendant that, "he did not know anything at all about a horse and that he did not want * * * the defendant to make a mean deal with him; whereupon the defendant said that the horse was solid and sound; that he would guarantee him to be solid and sound" 52 Pa.Super. at 638. While all three of these cases are premised partly on the now displaced rule that specific intent to warrant is a necessary concomitant of an express warranty, they do show that statements of the same tenor receive varying treatment depending on the surrounding circumstances.

The results in these cases are all consistent with custom among horse traders as alluded to by Gene Riegle.[6] He testified that it is "not a common thing" to guarantee a horse, that he has

3. The Court is aware that in Norton v. Lindsay, 350 F.2d 46 (10th Cir. 1965), statements as to a horse's soundness were held to be express warranties. However, the facts are sufficiently difficult in the case at bar to warrant an opposite finding.

6. U.C.C. § 1–205(3) permits the Court to consider usage of trade in determining the content of the agreement between Sessa and Riegle.

never guaranteed a horse unless he had an "understanding" with the buyer and that he did not guarantee Tarport Conaway. In other words, because horses are fragile creatures, susceptible to myriad maladies, detectable and undetectable, only where there is an "understanding"[8] that an ignorant buyer, is relying totally on a knowledgeable seller not "to make a mean deal," are statements as to soundness taken to be anything more than the seller's opinion or commendation.

The facts suggest no special "understanding" between Sessa and Riegle. Sessa was a knowledgeable buyer, having been involved with standardbreds for some years. Also, Sessa sent Maloney, an even more knowledgeable horseman, as his agent to inspect the horse.

Also militating against the finding of express warranty is the nature of the conversation between Sessa and Riegle. It seemed largely collateral to the sale rather than an essential part of it. Although Sessa testified that Riegle's "personal guarantee" given during the conversation was the quintessence of the sale, the credible evidence suggests otherwise. While on the telephone, Riegle made statements to the effect that "the horse is a good one" and "you will like him." These bland statements are obviously opinion or commendation, and the statement, "The horse is sound," falling within their penumbra takes on their character as such.

Under all the facts and circumstances of this case, it is clear to the Court that Riegle's statements were not of such a character as to give rise to express warranties under § 2–313(1) but were opinion or commendation under § 2–313(2).

Even assuming that Riegle's statements could be express warranties, it is not clear that they were "part of the basis of the bargain", the second requisite of § 2–313. This is essentially a reliance requirement and is inextricably intertwined with the initial determination as to whether given language may constitute an express warranty since affirmations, promises and descriptions tend to become part of the basis of the bargain. It was the intention of the drafters of the U.C.C. not to require a strong showing of reliance. In fact, they envisioned that all statements of the seller became part of the basis of the bargain unless clear affirmative proof is shown to the contrary. See Official Comments 3 and 8 to U.C.C. § 2–313.

It is Sessa's contention that his conversation with Riegle was the principal factor inducing him to enter the bargain. He would have the Court believe that Maloney was merely a messenger to deliver the check. The evidence shows, however, that Sessa was relying primarily on Maloney to advise him in connection with the

---

8. As in Flood v. Yeager, supra, for example.

sale. Maloney testified that he had talked to Sessa about the horse on several occasions and expressed the opinion that he was convinced "beyond the shadow of a doubt" that he was a good buy. With respect to his authority to buy the horse he testified

"Well, Mr. Sessa said he had enough confidence and faith in me and my integrity and honesty that I, what I did say about the horse, I was representing the horse as he is or as he was, and that if the horse, in my estimation, was that type of a horse and at that given price, the fixed price of $25,000. he would buy the horse."

When, at the airport, Maloney protested that he did not want to accept full responsibility to go to Ohio alone, Sessa told him "* * * I take your word. I—I trust your judgment and I trust your—your honesty, that if this horse, is right, everything will be all right." In Ohio, Maloney examined the horse, jogged him and reported to Sessa over the telephone that he "liked him."

The Court believes that Maloney's opinion was the principal, if not the only, factor which motivated Sessa to purchase the horse. The conversation with Riegle played a negligible role in his decision.

Even assuming that an express warranty was made, for plaintiff to recover, the issue of whether there had been a breach of the warranty must be resolved in his favor. In connection with this determination, it must first be determined who bears the burden of proof. U.C.C. § 2–607(4) places the burden of proof of breach of warranty on the buyer (here the plaintiff) with respect to any goods "accepted." If the goods were not "accepted," the seller would have the burden of showing that they conform to the contract. Thus, incidence of the burden of proof here depends on whether Sessa "accepted" the horse within the meaning of the U.C.C. U.C.C. § 2–606 defines acceptance. Under § 2–606(1)(a), Sessa accepted Tarport Conaway through his agent Maloney on March 10, 1973. At that time, Maloney was permitted unlimited inspection and both Sessa and Maloney indicated that Sessa would take the horse. Sessa contends that there has been no acceptance and that the telephone calls after the horse was shipped (Findings of fact 23 and 35) constitute effective rejection. However, U.C.C. § 2–607 provides that "Acceptance of goods by the buyer precludes rejection of the goods accepted". Since Sessa could not make an effective rejection, the burden of proof of the breach of warranty rests on him as the buyer.

This conclusion is not changed by the fact that the horse was not shipped until March 23, 1973. On March 10, 1973, Riegle tendered delivery of the horse in accordance with U.C.C. § 2–503 by putting and holding him at Sessa's disposal. Testimony shows that the parties' initial understanding was that transportation of the horse was to be Sessa's responsibility. However, when Sessa was unable to get a van, Riegle was authorized to arrange for one.

Consequently, the contract of sale authorized Riegle to ship the goods, but did not require delivery at a particular destination.

While not relevant to incidence of the burden of proof, the delay in shipment does shift the relevant date for determining breach of warranty. U.C.C. § 2–509 provides that the risk of loss shifts to the buyer when the seller delivers the goods to the carrier. In this case, Riegle delivered the goods to the carrier on March 23, 1973 for shipment to Freehold, New Jersey. Thus, any defects which existed on that date would breach the warranty, but any which arose thereafter would not. Miron v. Yonkers Raceway, Inc., 400 F.2d 112 (2d Cir. 1968); Strauss v. West, 100 R.I. 388, 216 A.2d 366 (1966).

The issue for the Court therefore becomes whether plaintiff sustained his burden of proving that defects in Tarport Conaway existed on March 23, 1973. Two separate defects are alleged:

1. That the horse had tendinitis.

2. That the horse had a thrombosis of the iliac artery causing intermittent claudication.

First, with respect to the tendinitis, Sessa clearly did not carry the burden. The Riegles testified that the horse received proper care between March 10 and March 23, 1973 and was put on the van in sound condition. Further, the expert testimony conceded that injury on the van could have caused the tendinitis. See also Strauss v. West, supra. The evidence produced by plaintiff which is alleged to indicate treatment for tendinitis before March 23 (scarff on the horse's legs) was shown to be equally consistent with normal leg care for a race horse. Moreover, even if the tendinitis had pre-existed March 23, it cleared up in a few days and the horse's legs returned to normal. It was not a substantial defect and would not give rise to a breach of warranty.

The alleged thrombosis of the iliac artery poses a much more complex problem. There is no question that Tarport Conaway had a thrombosis of the iliac arteries after March 23, 1973, but no evidence conclusively establishes the cause. Experts testified that the main known cause of thrombosis in horses is invasion of the blood vessel wall by third stage larvae of the strongylus vulgaris worm, but that there are other known and unknown causes. Although the experts testified that *if* the thrombosis was caused by strongyle larvae, it would have been present before March 23, 1973 because of the progressive nature of this affliction, no expert could testify to a reasonable medical certainty that Tarport Conaway's thrombosis was so caused. Some of the circumstances tend to show that it was not so caused.

First, there was undisputed testimony that Tarport Conaway was regularly wormed. According to this testimony, all horses have worms to some degree. They ingest the worm eggs, which have been spread by the feces of other horses, on grass and other foods. The worms hatch and go through their life cycle inside the horse during which they lay eggs which pass out in feces. Regular worming significantly reduces the worm population in a horse and renders it unlikely that worms would cause a thrombosis. In addition, none of the veterinary examinations showed the presence of strongylus vulgaris larvae.

Second, no early symptoms of intermittent claudication were observed. Tarport Conaway's regular veterinarian before the sale testified that he saw him jog almost every Thursday up to the time of sale and observed no early symptoms such as holding the hind leg out to the side after jogging, coldness or lack of pulsation.

For these reasons, the Court believes that plaintiff failed to carry the burden of proof by a preponderance of the evidence that any warranties which might have been made were breached. Pennsylvania law demands that the burden of proof be met with more than conjecture. * * * There must be evidence sufficient to convince the finder of fact that plaintiff's contention is more likely true than not. The evidence in this case fails to convince the Court that it is more likely than not that the thrombosis in Tarport Conaway was caused by strongylus vulgaris worms. It is equally consistent with the evidence that it arose from another known cause or an unknown cause.

For the foregoing reasons, plaintiff cannot recover on the basis of express warranties.

* * *

[The court's discussion of plaintiff's claims under § 2–314 and § 2–315 is omitted.]

NOTE: AFFIRMATION OF FACT OR MERE OPINION OR COMMENDATION

1. Not all statements by the seller concerning the goods are warranties. Under § 2–313 the statement must be a description of the goods or an affirmation of fact or a promise that relates to the goods, and the statement must become part of the basis of the bargain. Comment 3 indicates that "affirmations of fact" (and presumably "promises") made by the seller about the goods during a bargain are regarded as part of the description of the goods. Thus, the express warranty tells us what it is that is the subject of the sale. But § 2–313 goes on to say that "an affirmation merely of the value of the goods or a statement purporting to be merely the seller's opinion or commendation of the goods does not create a warranty." Thus, if the seller merely "commends" the automobile that is being sold by describing it as "in tip-top condition" the subject of sale is an automobile, not an automobile in tip-top condition. Does this limitation reflect a belief that buyers do not pay any

attention to commendations or opinions of sellers? Is there any basis for such a belief? In Hauter v. Zogarts, 14 Cal.3d 104, 120 Cal.Rptr. 681, 534 P.2d 377 (1975), it was held that the statement "Completely Safe Ball Will Not Hit Player" on the carton containing the seller's golf training device was an express warranty. The court stated "The assertion that the [device] is completely safe, that the ball will not hit the player, does not indicate the seller's subjective opinion about the merits of his product but rather factually describes an important characteristic of the product." Could a similar statement have been made about the seller's statement in *Sessa* that the horse was "sound"? Aren't both expressions of an opinion by seller? Does it help very much in analyzing the proper scope of warranty liability to call a statement an "affirmation of fact" or an "opinion or commendation?" Is the statement that a mobile home will "last a lifetime" a statement merely of the seller's opinion (Performance Motors, Inc. v. Allen, 280 N.C. 385, 186 S.E.2d 161 (1972)) (Held: not a warranty), while a statement that panels for greenhouses "won't turn black or discolor * * * even after years of exposure" is an affirmation of fact (General Supply & Equipment Co., Inc. v. Phillips, 490 S.W.2d 913 (Tex.Civ.App.1972)) (Held: warranty)?

2. Seller and Buyer negotiated a sale of machine tools to be used in the manufacture of widgets by Buyer. Seller told Buyer that the machine tools were as durable and accurate as those of X, a manufacturer well known for the quality of its products. Seller's tools, though usable, are of relatively poor quality. Compared to the tools of X they need to be replaced more often, and they cause a higher percentage of widgets to be rejected because imperfectly made. Buyer incurred substantial production losses because of the poor performance of the tools. Would the question of Seller's liability for breach of express warranty be influenced by the fact that the price of its tools was only slightly lower than X's price? Should Buyer recover if Seller's price was one half that of X's price? Does the price have anything to do with whether Seller's statement is a mere opinion or an affirmation of fact? In deciding the question of whether Seller made an express warranty should it make any difference whether the statement was in writing? Would it make any difference if the statement was made in a letter soliciting the order, or if it was written on the purchase order at the request of Buyer? In the case of a commercial buyer should the law be interpreted restrictively or expansively with respect to characterizing oral statements as warranties? Would it make any difference if the quality of Seller's tools could be determined by Buyer by a relatively simple testing procedure, or if the quality could be determined only after using the tools for an extended period under actual production conditions?

NOTE: BASIS OF THE BARGAIN

1. In determining whether a seller's statement is an express warranty it may be necessary to look not only to the seller's conduct but also to the conduct of the buyer, because a statement can become an express warranty only if it is "part of the basis of the bargain." In the words of Comment 1 to § 2–313 the warranty rests "on 'dickered' aspects of the individual bargain." Assume the sale of a stereo radio receiver and amplifier sold for $800. Before buying it Buyer listened to it and was completely satisfied with the sound quality. Seller's sales literature stated that the stereo set met certain detailed technical specifications. Buyer looked at this literature, but because of ignorance about the technical terms used did not understand the significance of the statements made. A stereo set meeting the specifications stated by Seller was worth at least $800. Seller's product was far inferior to the specifications stated. Stereo sets comparable in quality to that of Seller were readily obtainable for less than $500. Were the statements made in Seller's sales literature part of the basis of the bargain and therefore an express warranty? Comment 3 to § 2–313 makes it clear that no particular reliance by Buyer is necessary. Comment 4 to § 2–313 states "the whole purpose of the law of warranty is to determine what it is that seller has in essence agreed to sell." Is this the same standard as "basis of the bargain"? Compare pre-code law exemplified by Section 12 of the Uniform Sales Act which provided that "Any affirmation of fact or any promise by the seller relating to the goods is an express warranty if the natural tendency of such affirmation or promise is to induce the buyer to purchase the goods, and if the buyer purchases the goods relying thereon."

2. Buyer purchased an electrical appliance contained in a sealed box in which there was a descriptive pamphlet which contained statements concerning the performance capabilities of the appliance. Buyer was not aware that the box contained the pamphlet. Do Seller's statements in the pamphlet constitute an express warranty? Section 2–209(1) provides that an agreement modifying a contract needs no consideration to be binding. Comment 7 to § 2–313 suggests that § 2–209 can make warranties of post-sale statements of the seller "as when the buyer when taking delivery asks and receives an additional assurance." Are the statements in the pamphlet an "agreement" under § 1–201(3) and § 2–209? In Winston Industries, Inc. v. Stuyvesant Insurance Co., Inc., 55 Ala.App. 525, 317 So.2d 493 (1975), a buyer bought a mobile home from a retailer and testified that he received no written warranty concerning the home. It was the practice of the defendant manufacturer to deliver to its dealers a standard written warranty with each home delivered. The dealer apparently neglected to deliver the warranty to the buyer. The court held

that the manufacturer was bound by its usual written warranty. It is usually held that § 2–209 does not permit a seller to disclaim a warranty previously given (for example, the implied warranty of merchantability) by a post-sale delivery of a document such as a warranty booklet or owner's manual in which a disclaimer clause is included. The disclaimer to be effective requires an agreement by the buyer, and mere acceptance of the document containing the disclaimer does not constitute an agreement by the buyer. White & Summers, Uniform Commercial Code 502–504 (3d ed. 1988). Does the same reasoning apply when the seller's statement does not attempt to take away rights of the buyer but rather purports to add to them? Note the first sentence of Comment 4 to § 2–313.

3. Buyer bought a motor from Seller. During negotiation of the sale Buyer asked Seller how often the motor needed to be lubricated. Seller stated "every 100 hours." After Buyer used the motor for 90 hours it overheated and was extensively damaged. The motor should have been lubricated every 50 hours. Does Buyer have a cause of action for breach of express warranty? This problem may not involve injury because Buyer received less than the consideration bargained for. Whether the machine needed to be lubricated every 50 hours or every 100 hours may have no appreciable effect on the value of the machine and may not have played any part in Buyer's decision to buy. The injury is simply the result of Buyer's reliance on the erroneous instructions of Seller. If Seller made the statement knowing it was false, or if the statement was made negligently, liability may be found on common tort theories. Is there any basis for liability on a warranty theory? In Texsun Feed Yards, Inc. v. Ralston Purina Co., 447 F.2d 660 (5th Cir. 1971), the court allowed recovery on a warranty theory for loss due to erroneous instructions. It suggested that if a seller has strict liability for statements made about the quality of the product sold, the seller should also have strict liability for statements concerning use of the product if reliance by the buyer results in loss.

C. THE WARRANTIES OF MERCHANTABILITY AND FITNESS FOR A PARTICULAR PURPOSE

BETHLEHEM STEEL CORP. v. CHICAGO EASTERN CORP.

United States Court of Appeals, Seventh Circuit, 1988.
863 F.2d 508.

FLAUM, CIRCUIT JUDGE.

* * *

Chicago Eastern is in the business of building circular grain storage tanks for its customers located throughout the United

States. In May 1976, Chicago Eastern purchased corrugated sheet
steel from Bethlehem ("the first purchase"). This steel was used
as wall sheets in some of the tanks constructed by Chicago
Eastern. The tanks subsequently developed fractures and Chicago
Eastern was forced to incur substantial expenses to replace the
fractured steel. Chicago Eastern attributed the fractures to defects in Bethlehem's steel and attempted to communicate the
problem to Bethlehem. This proved unsuccessful. In November
1979, Chicago Eastern proceeded to order more steel from Bethlehem, but instead of sending Bethlehem a check, Chicago Eastern
mailed a "debit memo" offsetting the purchase price by the
amount of the alleged damages it incurred in repairing the defective grain bins for its customers ("the second purchase").

Bethlehem filed suit in federal district court seeking to collect
payment for the second shipment. The amended complaint alleged that Chicago Eastern had breached the parties' contract
* * *. Chicago Eastern counterclaimed, alleging * * * breach
of both an implied warranty of merchantability and an implied
warranty of fitness for a particular purpose ("the implied warranty claims"). The dispute was tried to a jury. After Chicago
Eastern had presented its evidence, the district court granted
Bethlehem's motion for a directed verdict on Chicago Eastern's
merchantability claim. On September 26, 1986, the jury rendered
a verdict in favor of Bethlehem for $23,749.30. The jury found
against * * * Chicago Eastern on its particular purpose warranty claim.

* * * Chicago Eastern argues that the district court erred
in granting Bethlehem's motion for a directed verdict on Chicago
Eastern's claim that Bethlehem breached the implied warranty of
merchantability applicable to the first purchase. * * * [An]
issue on appeal is whether the district court properly granted
Bethlehem's motion for a directed verdict on Chicago Eastern's
claim that Bethlehem breached the implied warranty of
merchantability applicable to the steel acquired in the first purchase. Bethlehem's motion was made after Chicago Eastern concluded presenting its evidence relating to its implied warranty
claims. * * *

Under Illinois law, if the seller of goods is a merchant of goods
of the kind being sold, a warranty that the goods are "merchantable" is implied into a contract for their sale as a matter of law,
unless otherwise expressly excluded or modified. * * * UCC §§
2–314(1) and 2–316. Chicago Eastern and Bethlehem agree that
the first purchase included an implied warranty that the steel sold
by Bethlehem would be "merchantable." * * * UCC § 2–314(2)
(c) states that goods must be "fit for the ordinary purposes for
which such goods are used." Chicago Eastern contends that it
introduced evidence at trial from which a reasonable juror could

conclude that the steel acquired from Bethlehem in the first purchase failed to satisfy [this requirement] and that the district court therefore erred in granting Bethlehem's motion for a directed verdict.

Prior to trial, Bethlehem and Chicago Eastern stipulated to a number of facts. The parties agreed that Chicago Eastern submitted an order for steel sheets to be manufactured by Bethlehem and that confirmation of the first purchase was memorialized on two Chicago Eastern purchase orders. The first purchase order, dated February 4, 1976, states that Chicago Eastern ordered sheet steel of a type designated by the American Society of Testing Materials (ASTM) as "446 Grade C." The second confirmation, a supplement to the first confirmation, did not use the ASTM designation; rather it specified a certain chemical composition and maximum yield strength: ".14–.20 carbon yield to 40,000 PSI after roll forming."

Chicago Eastern acknowledges that it received steel that complied with the requirements necessary to qualify as ASTM 446 Grade C and the requirements specified in the second purchase order. Chicago Eastern also acknowledged at oral argument that the steel would pass without objection in the trade under the contract description. It argues, however, that the steel was not merchantable because the steel was subjected to a renitrogenization process—a process not traditionally used with steel of this designation. Under this process, the nitrogen content of the steel was substantially increased. This increased the yield strength of the steel, but also made the steel more brittle and more susceptible to fracturing upon sudden impact. In other words, Chicago Eastern admits that the steel it received from Bethlehem did indeed possess the properties necessary to comply with the ASTM designation it ordered, but argues that the steel also possessed additional properties as a result of the renitrogenization process that made the steel unmerchantable. In the procedural posture of this case, the specific inquiry is whether Chicago Eastern introduced evidence from which a reasonable juror could conclude that steel which admittedly was ASTM 446 Grade C steel, was also * * * not "fit for the ordinary purposes for which such goods are used."

Chicago Eastern points to the testimony of its expert, Professor David W. Levinson, as evidence introduced at trial from which a reasonable juror could conclude that the steel acquired from Bethlehem in the first purchase was not merchantable. Levinson testified that although there was no specific prohibition against using the renitrogenization process in the production of ASTM 446 Grade C steel, the amount of nitrogen was 25 to 50 times higher than the level found in typical steel of this designation and that this amount of nitrogen "is added to very few steels." He further testified that this amount of nitrogen increased the yield strength of the steel, but also raised the "transition temperature" of the steel. Levinson explained that the transition temperature is the temperature below which fractures in a steel are substantially brittle and above which they are substantially ductile. This distinction is important because steel above the transition temperature stretches before it fractures. More pressure is therefore required to cause a ductile fracture than a brittle fracture.

Levinson testified that after examining samples of the fractured steel from the grain bins that it was his opinion that the fractures were brittle and not ductile. He also noted that tests conducted by third parties indicated that the transition temperature of the fractured steel was substantially higher because of the renitrogenization process than it otherwise would have been. Chicago Eastern's direct examination of Levinson culminated with his agreement that the renitrogenized steel was unsuitable "for use as a wall sheet in a grain tank which could be erected anywhere in the United States." Chicago Eastern contends that this was evidence which indicated that the steel acquired from Bethlehem * * * was not fit for the ordinary purposes for which such steel is used. In Chicago Eastern's view, Levinson's testimony provided sufficient evidence that the Bethlehem steel was not merchantable and therefore the warranty of merchantability issue should have been presented to the jury.

Even viewing the evidence presented at trial in the light most favorable to Chicago Eastern, we hold that no reasonable juror could conclude that the steel acquired from Bethlehem was not merchantable. All the evidence introduced by Chicago Eastern, including Levinson's testimony, was directed towards showing that the steel acquired in the first purchase was unfit for use as wall sheets in grain storage bins. Merchantability, however, does not look only at the particular use to which the buyer puts the goods. * * * It is therefore appropriate to analyze the transaction from the selling merchant's perspective. Bethlehem is in the business of selling unfinished steel products, including ASTM 446 Grade C steel. Chicago Eastern was required to show the ordinary purposes for which this type of steel is used and that the renitrogenization made the steel acquired from Bethlehem unfit for these purposes. This Chicago Eastern did not do.

Chicago Eastern has not pointed to any evidence presented at trial on the ordinary uses of this type of steel or how the renitrogenization affected these uses, nor has Chicago Eastern directed us to any place in the record where it introduced evidence showing that use as wall sheets in grain bins was in fact an ordinary use of this type of steel. * * * Levinson's testimony indicated that the nitrogen increased the transition temperature and made the steel more brittle, but that it also increased the yield strength of the steel. The steel was therefore not defective in the typical warranty of merchantability sense because the nitrogen that allegedly made the product defective by making the steel too brittle also had the seemingly desirable effect of making the steel stronger. It seems possible that different uses of steel require a different balancing of the apparent trade-off between strength and brittleness. We do not hold that steel subjected to this process is merchantable under the ASTM 446 Grade C description, rather we hold only that Chicago Eastern failed to offer evidence that it was not. Chicago Eastern was required to introduce evidence that the brittleness of the steel, regardless of the improved strength, made this steel unfit for the ordinary uses of ASTM 446 Grade C steel; no such evidence was introduced.[9]

In addition to its merchantability claim, Chicago Eastern alleged that the steel acquired from Bethlehem in the first purchase violated an implied warranty of fitness for a particular purpose ("the particular purpose warranty") which Chicago Eastern claims was applicable to the sale. Unless otherwise modified, the particular purpose warranty arises when a seller knows or has reason to know: (1) the particular use for which the acquired goods are to be put, and (2) that the buyer is relying on the seller's skill and judgment to select the appropriate product for the task. UCC § 2–315 Bethlehem stipulated that it knew or had reason to know that the steel sold to Chicago Eastern would be used as wall sheets in the construction of grain storage bins. Bethlehem argued at trial, however, that (1) it did not know that Chicago Eastern was relying on Bethlehem's skill and judgment to select the appropriate steel, and (2) that Chicago Eastern did not in fact rely on Bethlehem. The jury returned a verdict in favor of Bethlehem.

Chicago Eastern challenges the jury's verdict on the ground that it was induced by an improper jury instruction. In addition to setting forth the elements necessary to establish the existence of a particular purpose warranty and a breach thereof, the district court instructed the jury that:

> If a buyer has taken upon himself the responsibility of furnishing technical specifications, you may find that he is not relying on the seller's skill or judgment and no implied warranty of fitness for a particular purpose exists. Whether or not the buyer furnished technical specifications is for you to decide.[10]

9. Indeed, Chicago Eastern conceded at oral argument that the steel it acquired would pass without objection under the contract description of ASTM 446 Grade C steel. Although this designation does not speak to brittleness or provide for a particular level of nitrogen, if the steel was in fact too brittle to be used for ordinary purposes it is difficult to understand how it would pass without objection in the trade.

10. The complete jury instructions on the issue of implied warranty of fitness for a particular purpose were as follows:

Chicago Eastern apparently acknowledges that the instruction "states a proposition of law that is correct in the abstract," but argues that it was inappropriate in this case. Chicago Eastern claims that the "technical specifications" instruction foreclosed inquiry into whether or not Chicago Eastern relied on Bethlehem and whether Bethlehem knew or should have known of this reliance. In Chicago Eastern's view, once this jury instruction was given the issue was resolved in Bethlehem's favor because it was undisputed that Chicago Eastern ordered and received ASTM 446 Grade C steel.

* * *

When a buyer orders a product, the extent of the description of the product can vary broadly. At one extreme is the situation where the buyer does not describe the product itself at all; rather the buyer describes what the product must do and allows the seller to determine the appropriate product to accomplish the task. This is the paradigm case where the particular purpose warranty arises. The seller knows the buyer is relying on the seller to select the best product to do the job; the risk of loss is therefore allocated to the seller. At the other extreme is the situation where the buyer describes each detail of both the product and the manufacturing process used to produce it. In this situation the buyer is relying on its own expertise, not the seller's. The buyer therefore appropriately bears the risk of loss when the product is manufactured in accordance with the buyer's direction, but the product does not function as anticipated; a particular purpose warranty does not arise.

In this case, the parties agree that Chicago Eastern ordered the steel acquired in the first purchase by an industry trade name, ASTM 446 Grade C. The Uniform Commercial Code * * * modified prior law. Previously, a particular purpose warranty did not arise when the buyer ordered goods using the product's trade name. This rule was changed by the Uniform Commercial Code

For CEC to succeed on its claim that Bethlehem breached the implied warranty of fitness for a particular purpose, CEC must prove by a preponderance of the evidence each of the following four elements: One, the seller, Bethlehem must have reason to know the buyer's, CEC's, particular purpose. The seller must have reason to know the buyer is relying on the seller's skill or judgment to furnish appropriate goods. That was the second. The third, buyer must, in fact, rely upon the seller's skill or judgment. And four, buyer's damages, if any, must be caused by the unsuitability of the goods furnished by the seller.

If you find from your consideration of all the evidence that each of these four elements has been proved, then your verdict should be for CEC. But if on the other hand you find from your consideration of all the evidence that any one of these four elements has not been proved, then your verdict should be for Bethlehem.

If a buyer has taken upon himself the responsibility of furnishing technical specifications, you may find that he is not relying on the seller's skill or judgment, and no implied warranty of fitness for a particular purpose exists. Whether or not the buyer furnished technical specifications is for you to determine.

and now a buyer who orders goods by a trade name is not automatically precluded from bringing a particular purpose warranty claim. Designating a product by its trade name "is only one of the facts to be considered on the question of whether the buyer actually relied on the seller, ✳ ✳ ✳ it is not of itself decisive of the issue." UCC § 2–315 Comment 5. Even under the Code, however, if the buyer does in fact furnish detailed technical specifications such that the buyer has not relied on the seller, then no particular purpose warranty arises.

The district court's "detailed technical specifications" instruction merely described that situation where the buyer has specified with such detail that no reliance has in fact occurred. To determine whether a product order amounted to a technical specification, the jury would examine the detail provided in the order and the context in which the order was placed, including the comparative knowledge of the parties. In other words, the jury would look at substantially the same factors traditionally used to determine whether the buyer relied on the seller.

The thrust of Chicago Eastern's argument is that the jury was not permitted to exercise independent judgment on the issue of reliance. The jury instruction, however, did not state that ASTM 446 Grade C was a technical specification; this issue was specifically left for the jury to resolve. Chicago Eastern argued at trial, as it does to us on appeal, that the ASTM designation only specified certain properties of the steel it acquired from Bethlehem, not all the essential properties, and it therefore relied on Bethlehem to provide steel that could be used in the wall of grain bins. We decline to assume that the jury did not follow the instruction to independently reflect on this issue. We hold that the jury instructions, when read as a whole, conveyed to the jury the correct message.

✳ ✳ ✳ The decision of the district court is AFFIRMED.

NOTES

1. Section 2–314, which defines the warranty of merchantability, characterizes it as a warranty that is implied in the contract of sale. From an examination of § 2–314(2), however, it is apparent that there is a considerable overlap between what is treated as an express warranty under § 2–313 and what is treated as an implied warranty under § 2–314. In a contract for the sale of "Grade A medium size eggs" the seller has made an express warranty that the goods delivered will be "Grade A medium size eggs." Section 2–314 tells us that the seller has also made an implied warranty that the goods delivered will "pass without objection in the trade" under the name "Grade A medium size eggs." If the contract designation has a well established definition that includes quality, the implied warranty may not add anything

to the express warranty. But the contract designation may be ambiguous as to quality. Gardiner v. Gray, 4 Camp. 144, 171 Eng. Rep. 46 (1815), involved a contract for the sale of 12 bags of "waste silk." The seller delivered goods which fit the description "waste silk" but they were of such low quality that they were not salable under that denomination. The buyer refused delivery. Lord Ellenborough in construing what the seller was obliged to deliver stated:

> I am of the opinion, however, that under such circumstances, the purchaser has a right to expect a saleable article answering the description in the contract. Without any particular warranty, this is an implied term in every such contract. Where there is no opportunity to inspect the commodity, the maxim of *caveat emptor* does not apply. He cannot without a warranty insist that it shall be of any particular quality or fineness, but the intention of both parties must be taken to be, that it shall be saleable in the market under the denomination mentioned in the contract between them. The purchaser cannot be supposed to buy goods to lay them on a dunghill. The question then is, whether the commodity purchased by the plaintiff be of such a quality as can be reasonably brought into the market to be sold as *waste silk?* The witnesses describe it as unfit for the purposes of waste silk, and of such quality that it cannot be sold under that denomination.

Lord Ellenborough's statement of the warranty, which can be found with some modification in § 2–314(2)(a) and (c), adds the requirement of a certain minimum quality in those cases in which the contract of sale does not describe the goods in terms of quality.

2. Trade usage can also be used to define minimum quality. Seller sold a quantity of steel to Buyer. The contract did not specify quality. The steel cracked when it was later welded into railroad cars because its carbon content was too low. Seller did not know to what use Buyer was to put the steel. If Seller's steel, although too low in carbon to suit Buyer's needs, can be used for some purposes for which steel is commonly used does it meet the standard of § 2–314(2)(c)? In Ambassador Steel Co. v. Ewald Steel Co., 33 Mich.App. 495, 190 N.W.2d 275 (1971), Buyer was allowed to recover upon proof of a usage in the steel trade that in the absence of a particular specification of quality, a contract for the delivery of steel meant steel of "commercial quality," i.e., of a carbon content between 1010 and 1020. Suppose Seller delivered 100 pieces of steel, all with a carbon content of 1010, the minimum carbon content allowable. Was there a breach of warranty? Section 2–314(2)(b) applies to fungible goods that are defined in § 1–201(17). Does § 2–314(2)(b) apply to a case like *Ambassador Steel?* See Comment 7 to § 2–314. Is it possible to give subsection (b) independent effect, i.e., if fungible goods pass the test of subsection (a) do they also have to pass the test of subsection (b)?

Or is subsection (b) simply meant to be a particular illustration of subsection (a)?

3. The warranty of merchantability arises only if the seller is a "merchant" with respect to goods of the kind sold in the transaction. § 2–314(1). "Merchant" is defined in § 2–104. Consider the following cases:

a. Seller is a brewer of beer. A byproduct of the manufacture of beer is carbon dioxide which is then used in the making of canned beer. Seller produces more carbon dioxide than it uses in its canning operations. It makes a contract with Buyer to sell to it all of this excess carbon dioxide. Over a period of several months Seller delivered about 350 tons of carbon dioxide at a total price of about $3,500. Is Seller a merchant with respect to carbon dioxide? Rock Creek Ginger Ale Co., Inc. v. Thermice Corp., 352 F.Supp. 522 (D.D.C.1971).

b. Seller, a sawmill operator, sold an extra saw that had been used in Seller's sawmill operations to Buyer who is also a sawmill operator. Is Seller a merchant with respect to the saw? Siemen v. Alden, 34 Ill.App.3d 961, 341 N.E.2d 713 (1975). Does the fact that Seller had never before sold a saw necessarily mean that Seller is not a merchant? Comment 3 to § 2–314 states: "A person making an isolated sale of goods is not a 'merchant' within the meaning of the full scope of this section and, thus, no warranty of merchantability would apply." Under § 2–104 is there any basis for this statement?

NOTE: WARRANTY OF FITNESS FOR PARTICULAR PURPOSE

We have previously discussed cases in which the seller gives the buyer erroneous instructions concerning the proper use of the goods. If the buyer misuses the goods by following the seller's instructions, economic loss can occur. Some courts have allowed recovery by the buyer on a breach of warranty theory. The gravamen of these cases is that the seller's statements about use of the goods caused detrimental reliance by the buyer and consequential loss. Under these cases warranty liability is not restricted to claims based on receipt of goods that are defective or of a quality lower than that bargained for. This distinction between warranty liability that is based on the quality of the goods delivered and warranty liability that is based on conduct of the seller relating to use of the goods is made most clearly in the warranty of fitness for a particular purpose which is defined by § 2–315.

Consider the following cases:

Case # 1. Buyer was a manufacturer of air-conditioners and furnaces. Previously it had painted metal component parts for its products with a spray system. It decided to change over to an electroplating-type process for painting. Seller contracted to provide paint for use in the new system and supervised installation of the system. Component parts painted by operation of the system with Seller's paint often emerged with blotches and streaks. As a result repainting was required and Buyer suffered economic loss. Buyer alleged that the cause of the difficulty was Seller's paint. Seller maintained that the difficulty was caused by a faulty pretreatment of the component parts by Buyer before painting. The court upheld a finding by the jury that Seller's paint was not suitable for the particular purpose of Buyer and held Seller liable for breach of warranty under § 2–315. Singer Co. v. E.I. du Pont de Nemours & Co., 579 F.2d 433 (8th Cir.1978).

Case # 2. Patient went to Doctor for treatment of an infection. Doctor prescribed an antibiotic that was effective for combating many infections, but not one of the type that Patient had. Patient had the prescription filled at a drug store. This case is not covered by the UCC because it is not a sale of goods by Doctor. § 2–102.

In Case # 2, if Patient suffered injury as a result of taking the wrong medicine Doctor is liable only if Patient proves that Doctor was negligent. In Case # 1 Buyer had a cause of action against Seller regardless of any negligence by Seller. What is the difference between the two cases? A physician is paid for advice but is not required to guarantee its accuracy. The only obligation is to use due care and a minimum level of competence in giving it. A seller of goods is paid for the goods that are supplied, but if the seller chooses to give advice concerning the suitability of those goods the advice is given, in the normal case, without further compensation. But if § 2–315 applies the seller is a guarantor of the accuracy of that advice. Why?

LEWIS v. MOBIL OIL CORP.

United States Court of Appeals, Eighth Circuit, 1971.
438 F.2d 500.

GIBSON, CIRCUIT JUDGE. In this diversity case the defendant appeals from a judgment entered on a jury verdict in favor of the plaintiff in the amount of $89,250 for damages alleged to be caused by use of defendant's oil.

Plaintiff Lewis has been doing business as a sawmill operator in Cove, Arkansas, since 1956. In 1963, in order to meet competition, Lewis decided to convert his power equipment to hydraulic equipment. He purchased a hydraulic system in May 1963, from a competitor who was installing a new system. The used system was in good operating condition at the time Lewis purchased it. It was stored at his plant until November 1964, while a new mill building was being built, at which time it was installed. Following the installation, Lewis requested from Frank Rowe, a local

Mobil oil dealer, the proper hydraulic fluid to operate his machinery. The prior owner of the hydraulic system had used Pacemaker oil supplied by Cities Service, but plaintiff had been a customer of Mobil's for many years and desired to continue with Mobil. Rowe said he didn't know what the proper lubricant for Lewis' machinery was, but would find out. The only information given to Rowe by Lewis was that the machinery was operated by a gear-type pump; Rowe did not request any further information. He apparently contacted a Mobil representative for a recommendation, though this is not entirely clear, and sold plaintiff a product known as Ambrex 810. This is a straight mineral oil with no chemical additives.

Within a few days after operation of the new equipment commenced, plaintiff began experiencing difficulty with its operation. The oil changed color, foamed over, and got hot. The oil was changed a number of times, with no improvement. By late April 1965, approximately six months after operations with the equipment had begun, the system broke down, and a complete new system was installed. The cause of the breakdown was undetermined, but apparently by this time there was some suspicion of the oil being used. Plaintiff Lewis requested Rowe to be sure he was supplying the right kind of oil. Ambrex 810 continued to be supplied.

From April 1965 until April 1967, plaintiff continued to have trouble with the system, principally with the pumps which supplied the pressure. Six new pumps were required during this period, as they continally broke down. During this period, the kind of pump used was a Commercial pump which was specified by the designer of the hydraulic system. The filtration of oil for this pump was by means of a metal strainer, which was cleaned daily by the plaintiff in accordance with the instruction given with the equipment.

In April 1967, the plaintiff changed the brand of pump from a Commercial to a Tyrone pump. The Tyrone pump, instead of using the metal strainer filtration alone, used a disposable filter element in addition. Ambrex 810 oil was also recommended by Mobil and used with this pump, which completely broke down three weeks later. At this point, plaintiff was visited for the first time by a representative of Mobil Oil Corporation, as well as a representative of the Tyrone pump manufacturer.

On the occasion of this visit, May 9, 1967, plaintiff's system was completely flushed and cleaned, a new Tyrone pump installed, and on the pump manufacturer's and Mobil's representative's recommendation, a new oil was used [1] which contained certain

1. Upon recommendation of Mobil, plaintiff used Mobil's DTE 23 and Del Vac Special after the second Tyrone was installed on May 9, 1967, until July 25, 1967, when plaintiff changed to Pacemaker XD–15. All of the above oils contained certain chemical additives for anti-wear, anti-oxidation and anti-foaming.

chemical additives, principally a "defoamant." Following these changes, plaintiff's system worked satisfactorily up until the time of trial, some two and one-half years later.

Briefly stated, plaintiff's theory of his case is that Mobil supplied him with an oil which was warranted fit for use in his hydraulic system, that the oil was not suitable for such use because it did not contain certain additives, and that it was the improper oil which caused the mechanical breakdowns, with consequent loss to his business. The defendant contends that there was no warranty of fitness, that the breakdowns were caused not by the oil but by improper filtration, and that in any event there can be no recovery of loss of profits in this case.

I. THE EXISTENCE OF WARRANTIES

Defendant maintains that there was no warranty of fitness in this case, that at most there was only a warranty of merchantability and that there was no proof of breach of this warranty, since there was no proof that Ambrex 810 is unfit for use in hydraulic systems generally. * * *

When the first Tyrone pump was installed in April 1967, Rowe referred the request for a proper oil recommendation to Ted Klock, a Mobil engineer. Klock recommended Ambrex 810. When this pump failed a few weeks later, Klock visited the Lewis plant to inspect the equipment. The system was flushed out completely and the oil was changed to DTE–23 and Del Vac Special containing several additives. After this, no further trouble was experienced.

This evidence adequately establishes an implied warranty of fitness.

* * *

Under UCC § 2–315, there are two requirements for an implied warranty of fitness: (1) that the seller have "reason to know" of the use for which the goods are purchased, and (2) that the buyer relies on the seller's expertise in supplying the proper product. Both of these requirements are amply met by the proof in this case. Lewis' testimony, as confirmed by that of Rowe and Klock, shows that the oil was purchased specifically for his hydraulic system, not for just a hydraulic system in general, and that Mobil certainly knew of this specific purpose. It is also clear that Lewis was relying on Mobil to supply him with the proper oil for the system, since at the time of his purchases, he made clear that he didn't know what kind was necessary.

Mobil contends that there was no warranty of fitness for use in his particular system because he didn't specify that he needed an oil with additives, and alternatively that he didn't give them enough information for them to determine that an additive oil was required. However, it seems that the circumstances of this case come directly within that situation described in the first comment to this provision of the Uniform Commercial Code:

> "1. Whether or not this warranty arises in any individual case is basically a question of fact to be determined by the circumstances of the contracting. Under this section the buyer need not bring home to the seller *actual knowledge of the particular purpose* for which the goods are intended or of his reliance on the seller's skill and judgment, if the circumstances are such that the seller has reason to realize the purpose intended or that the reliance exists." * * *

Here Lewis made it clear that the oil was purchased for his system, that he didn't know what oil should be used, and that he was relying on Mobil to supply the proper product. If any further information was needed, it was incumbent upon Mobil to get it before making its recommendation. That it could have easily gotten the necessary information is evidenced by the fact that after plaintiff's continuing complaints, Mobil's engineer visited the plant, and, upon inspection, changed the recommendation that had previously been made.

* * *

II. BREACH OF WARRANTY AS THE CAUSE OF PLAINTIFF'S DAMAGE

The primary controversy in this case is whether the damage done to the plaintiff's hydraulic system was caused by the defendant's breach of warranty in failing to provide a proper oil. This issue primarily presents a question of the sufficiency of the evidence to support the jury's verdict that the cause of the plaintiff's damage was the use of Ambrex 810 and that Ambrex 810 was an improper oil for his system. * * *

Plaintiff's theory was that the damage was caused by pump cavitation induced by the failure of the oil to expurgate air bubbles quickly enough from its body, and that this characteristic of the oil could have been prevented by the addition of proper additives, principally a defoamant additive, but also anti-wear, anti-oxidation, and anti-rust additives.

Pump cavitation occurs when air bubbles in the body of the oil are sucked into the pump along with the hydraulic fluid. The moving parts within the pump have very small tolerances and must be kept lubricated at all times by the hydraulic fluid. Due to the exceedingly high pressures within the pump, when there are air bubbles in the fluid, they become compressed into larger bubbles and at some point interfere with the lubricating qualities of the oil, permitting the metal parts of the pump to come in contact. When this contact occurs, small metal pieces flake off and get into the fluid, which then disperses these metal contaminants throughout the system. These metal particles can in turn be responsible for causing other problems in the system which would result in the introduction of atmospheric contamination— i.e., dirt—into the system. As the metal particles, plus the other contamination, are circulated throughout the system by means of the hydraulic fluid and returned to the pump intake, serious damage is caused to the pump which cannot tolerate these contaminants.

According to the plaintiff's theory, this process can be prevented by the addition of an anti-fomant additive in the oil which aids it in expurgating air quickly so that air bubbles are not sucked into the pump in the first place.

Defendant's theory of the cause of damage was that plaintiff failed to maintain his equipment properly, failed to have a proper filtration system, and failed to flush the system after pump failures. Defendant also contested plaintiff's allegations that a defoamant additive in the oil would prevent damage from pump cavitation.

*   *   *

The above description of the theory of cavitation was testified to in substance by plaintiff's expert witness Edwards. This witness also testified that it was his opinion that plaintiff's trouble with his system was caused by pump cavitation, and the cavitation damage was caused by the use of Ambrex 810. It was his further opinion that Ambrex 810 caused pump cavitation because of its failure to have suitable additives which could have prevented this damage and that Ambrex 810 was unsuitable for use in equipment of this type. *   *   *

Another expert witness for the plaintiff also testified that a non-additive oil such as Ambrex 810 was unsuitable for use in plaintiff's equipment and that an additive oil was necessary. The manufacturer of plaintiff's equipment testified similarly. The jury was also entitled to consider the fact that when a Mobil engineer actually visited plaintiff's mill and saw the equipment, he changed his oil recommendation to one containing additives. Further circumstantial evidence that the oil was the cause of the problems was the fact that once the system was flushed and additive oil was used, the system thereupon functioned satisfactorily.

Against the foregoing evidence, the defendant presented the following evidence. First, two expert witnesses testified that, using new samples of oil, Ambrex 810 performed as well as or better than an additive oil on certain standard laboratory tests of foam dissipation and air release qualities. Plaintiff's expert witness testified in rebuttal that such tests were not indicative of how the two oils would perform in actual operation, because once they had actually been "worked" the non-additive oil (Ambrex 810) underwent certain chemical changes which would affect these qualities, while the chemicals in the additive oil would counteract these changes so as not to affect the qualities so much.

* * *

The defendant contended that the cause of the plaintiff's trouble was his failure to have an adequate filtration process on his equipment to clean the oil. Some of the defense witnesses testified that metal strainers were not sufficient and that paper filters were necessary. The evidence on this point is somewhat unsatisfactory, because no attempt was made by the defense to make distinctions between the kinds of pumps used by the plaintiff. Plaintiff admits that as to the Tyrone pumps which were used in the later stages of operation, paper filters were required by the manufacturer, but it is uncontested that they were used on these pumps. The system originally operated with Commercial pumps. The manufacturer of that equipment testified that with these pumps only metal strainers were used, not paper filters, and that he had installed many systems which worked satisfactorily under these circumstances so long as the proper oil was used. While the evidence on this issue is conflicting, we think the jury was entitled to conclude, as it obviously did, that inadequate filtration was not the cause of plaintiff's trouble.

* * *

We conclude that there was adequate evidence to sustain the jury's verdict that plaintiff's damage was caused by the breach of warranty.

III. DAMAGES

[We omit the portion of the opinion in which the court held that Mobil was liable for lost profits caused by the breach of warranty during the 2½ years that Lewis used Ambrex 810.]

D. WARRANTIES IN FINANCE LEASES OF GOODS

Under the common law, commercial sellers of goods were subject to implied warranties of quality with respect to the goods sold. This common-law doctrine is now reflected in § 2–314 and § 2–315. But sellers are not the only providers of goods in commercial transactions. Use of goods can also be obtained under leases or short-term rentals. The common law also recognized implied warranties of quality similar to § 2–314 and § 2–315 in commercial transactions in which the provider of the goods was a lessor or short-term renter of the goods. Article 2A follows this common-law development in § 2A–212 which states a warranty of merchantability and § 2A–213 which states a warranty of fitness for particular purpose with respect to a lease of goods. "Lease" is defined very broadly in § 2A–103(1)(j) to mean "a transfer of the right to possession and use of goods for a term in return for consideration * * *." The word "term" is not defined, but the

Comment to § 2A–102 states that Article 2A "governs transactions as diverse as the lease of a hand tool to an individual for a
few hours and the leveraged lease of a complex line of industrial
equipment to a multi-national organization for a number of
years."

Like the common-law warranties, § 2A–212 and § 2A–213 are
intended to apply to transactions in which the lessor is the person
providing the goods for use—a person similar to a seller of goods.
But in some cases, a transaction will involve a lessor who is not a
provider of goods but rather a financer of what is in essence, if not
legal form, a sale of goods by a seller to the person described in the
transaction as the lessee. For example, User needs equipment to
be used for a period of years in the enterprise carried on by User.
Supplier is a seller of equipment of the type desired by User.
User is unable or unwilling to buy the equipment for cash.
Rather, User wants to pay for the use of the equipment by
monthly payments. Supplier, however, wants to receive full payment of the price immediately. Financer is willing to provide the
funds which will accommodate the requirements of User and
Supplier. To carry out that end a three-party transaction will
result, but its form may differ. One form is that of an Article 9
secured transaction which can be structured in various ways.
Take two cases.

> Case # 1. Financer lends money to User who uses the
> money to buy the equipment from Supplier. As security for
> the loan, which is repayable by User in installments, User
> grants a security interest in the equipment to Financer.

> Case # 2. User buys the equipment from Supplier on
> credit under an installment sale contract and grants Supplier
> a security interest in the equipment. Supplier immediately
> sells the installment sale contract to Financer for an amount
> equal to the cash price of the equipment.

Essentially the same result is obtained in Case # 1 and Case # 2.
In either case no implied warranties of quality are made by
Financer to User and warranties by Supplier to User with respect
to the equipment are governed by Article 2.

An Article 9 security interest can take many forms including
a "lease * * * intended as security." § 9–102(2). In the hypothetical case discussed in the preceding paragraph, a third way of
accommodating the requirements of User and Supplier is as follows:

> Case # 3. At the request of User, Financer buys the
> equipment from Supplier and, at the request of Financer,
> Supplier delivers the equipment to User. Contemporaneously
> User and Financer enter into an agreement providing for the
> lease of the equipment by Financer to User. Rent is payable
> monthly over a period of years.

In analyzing Case # 3, the first issue is to determine whether the agreement between User and Financer is a "lease intended as security." If it is, the interest of Financer in the equipment, i.e. legal title, becomes a security interest in equipment of which User is deemed to be the owner. The rights and obligations of User and Financer with respect to the equipment are governed by Article 9. Whether the lease was intended as security is determined by the complex tests stated in the second and third paragraphs of § 1–201(37) which defines "security interest." If it is determined that a security interest has been created, Article 2A does not apply because the agreement between User and Financer is not recognized as a lease. The transaction is treated as a sale of equipment by Supplier for the benefit of User in which the price of the goods was paid by Financer. Warranty liability of Supplier is determined by Article 2.

If the analysis of Case # 3 under § 1–201(37) results in a determination that a security interest was not created, the agreement between User and Financer is a lease of goods and Article 2A rather than Article 9 governs the rights and obligations of User and Financer with respect to the equipment. However, Article 2A recognizes that Financer is a special kind of lessor. In the typical case Financer is not a provider of goods similar to a seller. Financer normally would know little or nothing about the equipment, and may not even have seen it. Usually the sole function of Financer in the transaction is to provide the money necessary to allow User to obtain use of the equipment. The lease between User and Financer is known in Article 2A as a "finance lease" if the requirements of § 2A–103(1)(g) are satisfied. If the lease qualifies as a finance lease, Financer is not a warrantor under § 2A–212 or § 2A–213. Instead, § 2A–209 applies and User becomes the beneficiary of the promises and warranties of Supplier to Financer under the contract of sale of the equipment. The requirements of the four subparagraphs of § 2A–103(1)(g)(iii) are designed to assure that the lessee is given sufficient information to get the benefit of § 2A–209. If Financer fails to comply with § 2A–103(1)(g), Financer has the burden of implied warranties to User to the extent stated in § 2A–212 and § 2A–213. Finance leases are discussed in detail in Comment (g) to § 2A–103 and they can also arise in some cases that are different from Case # 3.

E. CONTRACTUAL LIMITATIONS ON WARRANTIES

---

1. FORMAL REQUIREMENTS

Under the UCC sales warranties arise from the bargain of the buyer and seller. The bargain may provide for warranties or it may negate them. An implied warranty must be specifically negated or disclaimed if the parties to the sale do not want it to apply. With respect to an express warranty it is perhaps a contradiction in terms to speak of disclaiming the warranty since it is not reasonable to hold that the seller has made a promise and disclaimed it in the same contract. As a practical matter, however, we have seen that some statements of the seller are ambiguous and might or might not be held to be warranties. An employee of the seller may have made representations about the goods to the buyer without the authorization of the seller, or the statements made might be classifiable as either enforceable promises or unenforceable puffing. A formal disclaimer in the formal sales agreement in this context may serve the purpose of defining the basis of the bargain. An illustrative provision is as follows:

> This instrument constitutes the entire agreement between the parties, superseding all previous communications, oral or written, and no changes, amendments or additions hereto will be recognized unless in writing signed by both the seller and the buyer. It is expressly agreed that no representations or warranties, express or implied, have been or are made by the seller except as stated herein, and the seller makes no warranty, express or implied, as to the merchantability of the goods purchased hereunder or to their fitness for the buyer's purposes.

Whether this provision is effective in disclaiming prior statements made to the buyer that would otherwise qualify as express warranties depends upon the effect given to the parol evidence rule stated in § 2–202. Evidence of a prior warranty not repeated in the formal sales agreement contradicts the statement in that agreement that no representations or warranties had been made. But in order for § 2–202 to be given effect a court would have to find that the formal sales agreement was in fact intended by the buyer and the seller to be the final and exclusive statement of their understanding. If the buyer signs the formal sales agreement without reading it, will the disclaimer be given effect? What can the seller do to ensure that the provision will be given effect?

Sometimes a warranty is not disclaimed but the formal sales agreement provides that the warranty will be limited or modified. For example, it may be provided that the warranty on a new automobile expires one year after purchase or when the automobile has been driven 10,000 miles, whichever shall occur first.

Once a warranty has been made the UCC provides to the buyer certain remedies (§ 1–201(34)) in the event of breach. Examples are § 2–601, § 2–608 and § 2–711. Damages for breach with respect to accepted goods are provided for in § 2–714. A remedy provided by the UCC may be very onerous and a seller may be unwilling to assume the burden imposed by the statute.

Suppose a farmer purchases seeds for $100. The seeds fail to produce the crop they should have produced. The lost crop value is $10,000. A seller whose profit on the seeds is only a few dollars may be willing to risk losing the price of the seeds if they turn out to be defective, but may not be willing to bear the risk of paying for crop losses. The parties to the sales contract may decide on whom the risk of various losses shall fall; if they agree that the maximum liability of the seller shall be equal to the price of the seeds, they have not negated or disclaimed the warranty of quality of the seeds, but they have limited the buyer's remedy for breach of that warranty. Disclaimers and modifications are governed by § 2–316. Limitations on the buyer's remedies are governed by § 2–719. Disclaimers and limitations on remedy are both subject to § 2–302 regarding unconscionable contracts.

If the parties have bargained about disclaimers or limitations on remedy the task of the court is simply to find what it is that the parties have agreed to, and to carry out their bargain subject to any limitations that § 2–302 might impose. In most cases, however, the parties do not bargain about these matters. Rather, a provision purporting to disclaim warranty or limit liability is inserted by the seller in some document or other writing given to the buyer, sometimes for signature and sometimes not. For example, the provision may be in the sales contract itself, in the owner's manual or warranty book, or on the package in which the goods are sold. In this kind of situation an agreement by the seller and buyer can only be found if we assume that purchase by the buyer is tantamount to acceptance of the conditions of sale stated by the seller. Here there are two questions to be considered: (1) Has the seller adequately informed the buyer that the disclaimer or limitation exists? and (2) Even if the buyer has been adequately informed is it reasonable to allow the seller to obtain the advantage of the disclaimer or limitation in this manner?

Express Warranties

Seller advertised for sale at auction "4,200 pairs of pants." At the sale the lawyer representing Seller announced "[Seller] is not making any representation that that is exactly how many there are. The pants are being sold as is as you see them right there, the pants that you see in those cartons." The pants were contained in 62 sealed cartons labeled as containing 60 pairs each. The cartons were so arranged in a restricted space that it was not apparent to anybody that there were 62 rather than 70 cartons and thus only 3,720 pairs of pants. Buyer's bid of $8,000 was accepted and Buyer paid by check. Later, Buyer discovered the discrepancy in quantity and stopped payment on the check. Seller argued that Buyer was required to pay $8,000 because any express warranty as to quantity was disclaimed. Was the disclaimer effective? Comment 1 to § 2–316. In re Duty Free Shops Corp., 17 B.R. 274 (Bkrtcy. Fla.1982).

Implied Warranties of Merchantability and Fitness for Particular Purpose

Under § 2–316(2) the implied warranty of merchantability can be excluded or modified orally while "any implied warranty of fitness" can be excluded or modified only in writing. Comments 3 and 4 to § 2–316 shed no light on the reason for this provision. Section 2–316(2) also provides that to exclude the implied warranty of merchantability the language must "mention merchantability." Suppose the disclaimer states "there is no implied warranty that the goods are fit for their ordinary purposes," or that it states "the seller does not make any warranties express or implied of whatever nature and shall not be liable in any way for loss resulting from inferior quality, defect or unsuitability of the goods." Has the warranty of merchantability been disclaimed? If the disclaimer clearly states that the seller does not intend to be bound by any implied warranty, is there an effective disclaimer of the implied warranty of merchantabililty under § 2–316(3)(a)? In Michigan Mutual Liability Insurance Co. v. Fruehauf Corp., 63 Mich.App. 109, 234 N.W.2d 424 (1975) the court held that a clause stating "Lessor has made no warranties, express or implied, with respect to the equipment" was not effective to disclaim the implied warranty of merchantability because merchantability was not specifically mentioned.

CATE v. DOVER CORP.

Supreme Court of Texas, 1990.
790 S.W.2d 559.

DOGGETT, JUSTICE.

We consider the enforceability of a disclaimer of implied warranties. The trial court upheld the disclaimer and granted summary judgment in favor of Dover Corporation. The court of appeals affirmed. 776 S.W.2d 680. We reverse the judgment of the court of appeals and remand this cause to the trial court for further proceedings consistent with this opinion.

In September 1984, Edward Cate, doing business as Cate's Transmission Service, purchased from Beech Tire Mart three lifts manufactured and designed by Dover Corporation to elevate vehicles for maintenance. Despite repairs made by Beech and Dover, the lifts never functioned properly. Dover contends that Cate's subsequent claim against it for breach of the implied warranty of merchantability is barred by a disclaimer contained within a written, express warranty.

[The written warranty is reproduced on the following page.]

YOU CAN TAKE ROTARY'S NEW 5·YEAR WARRANTY AND TEAR IT APART.

And, when you're through, it'll be just as solid as the No. 1 lift company in America. Rotary. Not so with some of the other companies. They may offer you a multi-year warranty, too. But you're likely to discover it's limited to parts only.

And, hidden in all the mumbo-jumbo, you may find out—too late—that their beautifully worded "warranty" doesn't even cover major components...like power units. So what you really have is a great warranty that covers almost nothing.

We at Rotary are proud of the surface lift products we manufacture. And we don't have to "play it safe" when it comes to guaranteeing them. Here's what our new 5-year warranty says:

WARRANTY

All Rotary Surface Mounted Lifts are guaranteed to the original owner for five years from invoice date. Rotary Lift Division here after is known as "The Company". The Company shall replace for the full five years those parts returned to the factory which prove upon inspection by the Company to be defective. The Company shall pay for reasonable costs of transportation and labor for replacement of said parts for the first 12 months only. Purchaser will bear costs of transportation and labor for parts returned after the first year and the remainder of this warranty. This warranty shall not apply unless the product is installed, used and maintained in accordance with the Company's specifications as set forth in the Company's installation, operation and maintenance instructions.

This warranty does not cover normal maintenance or adjustments, damage or malfunction caused by improper handling, installation, abuse, misuse, negligence or carelessness of operation.

This warranty is exclusive and is in lieu of all other warranties expressed or implied including any implied warranty of merchantability or any implied warranty of fitness for a particular purpose, which implied warranties are hereby expressly excluded.

The remedies described are exclusive and in no event shall the Company be liable for special, consequential or incidental damages for the breach of or delay in performance of the warranty.

This warranty shall be governed by the State of Indiana, and shall be subject to the exclusive jurisdiction of the Court of the State of Indiana in the County of Jefferson.

American made

Rotary ®

Exhibit A

This warranty is set forth on a separate page headed in blue half inch block print, with the heading: "YOU CAN TAKE ROTARY'S NEW 5–YEAR WARRANTY AND TEAR IT APART." The statement is followed by bold black type stating, "And, when you are through, it'll be just as solid as the No. 1 lift company in America. Rotary." The text of the warranty itself is in black type, contained within double blue lines, and appears under the blue three-eighths inch block print heading "WARRANTY." The disclaimer of implied warranties, although contained in a separate paragraph within the warranty text, is in the same typeface, size, and color as the remainder of the text.

An implied warranty of merchantability arises in a contract for the sale of goods unless expressly excluded or modified by conspicuous language. § 2–314(1), § 2–316(2). Whether a particular disclaimer is conspicuous is a question of law to be determined by the following definition:

> A term or clause is conspicuous when it is so written that a reasonable person against whom it is to operate ought to have noticed it. A printed heading in capitals (as: NON–NEGOTI-ABLE BILL OF LADING) is conspicuous. Language in a body of a form is conspicuous if it is larger or of other contrasting type or color. But in a telegram, any stated term is conspicuous.

§ 1–210(10). Further explanation is provided by comment 10 thereto:

> This [section] is intended to indicate some of the methods of making a term attention-calling. But the test is whether attention can reasonably be expected to be called to it.

In interpreting this language, Dover argues that a lesser standard of conspicuousness should apply to a disclaimer made to a merchant, such as Cate. Admittedly, an ambiguity is created by the requirement that disclaimer language be conspicuous to "a reasonable person *against whom it is to operate.*" Comment 10, however, clearly contemplated an objective standard, stating the test as "whether attention can reasonably be expected to be called to it."

We then turn to an application of an objective standard of conspicuousness to Dover's warranty. The top forty percent of the written warranty is devoted to extolling its virtues. The warranty itself, contained within double blue lines, is then set out in five paragraphs in normal black type under the heading "WARRAN-TY." Nothing distinguishes the third paragraph, which contains the exclusionary language. It is printed in the same typeface, size and color as the rest of the warranty text. Although the warranty in its entirety may be considered conspicuous, the disclaimer is hidden among attention-getting language purporting to grant the best warranty available.[1]

Dover cites Ellmer v. Delaware Mini–Computer Systems, Inc., 665 S.W.2d 158 (Tex.App.—Dallas 1983, no writ), as authority for imposing a subjective standard of conspicuousness. In finding a disclaimer conspicuous, that court did look to the circumstances surrounding the transaction. That particular language, however, was in bold print, unlike the language under review here. Nor did that court give consideration to the effect of comment 10. Nevertheless, to the extent that *Ellmer* may be read as imposing a subjective standard, we disapprove it.

Although this is a case of first impression in Texas, the facts here parallel those reviewed in other states. In Massey–Ferguson, Inc. v. Utley, 439 S.W.2d 57, 59 (Ky.Ct.App.1969), a disclaimer hidden under the heading "WARRANTY and AGREEMENT" was found not to be conspicuous:

> It is true that the *heading* was in large, bold-face type, but there was nothing to suggest that an exclusion was being made; on the contrary, the words of the heading indicated a *making* of warranties rather than a *disclaimer.*

(Emphasis in original.) Similarly, in Hartman v. Jensen's, Inc., 277 S.C. 501, 289 S.E.2d 648 (1982), the court found that placing a disclaimer under the bold heading "Terms of Warranty" failed to alert the consumer to the fact that an exclusion was intended.[3] Dover's disclaimer similarly fails to attract the attention of a reasonable person and is not conspicuous.

1. Justice Grant's dissent in the court of appeals correctly characterizes the warranty as follows:

> Dover has cleverly buried the disclaimer provision within language that strongly suggests a warranty that greatly benefits the consumer. The bold print language suggests that warranties were included rather than excluded.

> * * *

776 S.W.2d at 685.

3. See also Mack Trucks of Arkansas, Inc. v. Jet Asphalt & Rock Co., 246 Ark. 101, 437 S.W.2d 459 (1969) (disclaimer contained within warranty text under headings "Vehicle Warranty" and "Supplement to Mack Standard Warranty applicable to Mack Diesel Engines" held not conspicuous in part because neither title suggests the exclusion or modification of an implied warranty); Blankenship v. Northtown Ford, Inc., 95 Ill.App.3d 303, 50 Ill.Dec. 850, 420 N.E.2d 167 (1981) (the heading "Factory Warranty" is misleading, and a disclaimer which follows a misleading heading cannot be deemed to comply with the UCC); Seibel v. Layne & Bowler, Inc., 56 Or.App. 387, 641 P.2d 668, rev. denied, 293 Or. 190, 648 P.2d 852 (1982) (disclaimer held not conspicuous when only the paragraph heading "Warranty" stood out and suggested the making of the warranties, not their exclusion); Dorman v. International Harvester Co., 46 Cal.App.3d 11, 120 Cal.Rptr. 516 (2d Dist.1975) (inconspicuous disclaimer provision lacked a heading such as "DISCLAIMER OF WARRANTIES" which would adequately call the exclusionary language to the attention of the buyer); Richards v. Goerg Boat & Motors, Inc., 179 Ind.App. 102, 384 N.E.2d 1084 (3d Dist.1979) (disclaimer language contained within warranty text held ineffective); B. Clark & C. Smith, The Law of Product Warranties ¶ 8.03[2] (1984) ("disclaimer paragraph should be conspicuously captioned as a "DISCLAIMER OF WARRANTIES," or the paragraph should at least capitalize all words relating to the disclaimer").

*   *   *

Dover argues that even an inconspicuous disclaimer should be given effect because Cate had actual knowledge of it at the time of the purchase. Because the object of the conspicuousness requirement is to protect the buyer from surprise and an unknowing waiver of his or her rights, inconspicuous language is immaterial when the buyer has actual knowledge of the disclaimer. This knowledge can result from the buyer's prior dealings with the seller, or by the seller specifically bringing the inconspicuous waiver to the buyer's attention. The Code appears to recognize that actual knowledge of the disclaimer overrides the question of conspicuousness. For example, § 2–316(2) does not mandate a written disclaimer of the implied warranty of merchantability but clearly provides that an oral disclaimer may be effective. Similarly, § 2–316(3)(c) allows an implied warranty to be excluded or modified by methods other than a conspicuous writing: course of dealing, course of performance, or usage of trade. When the buyer is not surprised by the disclaimer, insisting on compliance with the conspicuousness requirement serves no purpose. * * * The extent of a buyer's knowledge of a disclaimer of the implied warranty of merchantability is thus clearly relevant to a determination of its enforceability. * * * The seller has the burden of proving the buyer's actual knowledge of the disclaimer.

As this is a summary judgment case, the issue on appeal is whether Dover met its burden by establishing that there exists no genuine issue of material fact thereby entitling it to judgment as a matter of law. * * * All doubts as to the existence of a genuine issue of material fact are resolved against the movant, and we must view the evidence in the light most favorable to the Petitioner. * * * In support of its claim that Cate had actual knowledge of the disclaimer, Dover relies on Cate's deposition testimony, as follows:

Q: Do you know, or do you remember what kinds of warranties you received when you bought the lifts?

A: I may be wrong, but I think it was a five year warranty.

Q: What was your understanding of that warranty?

A: Any problems would be taken care of within the five year period.

Q: Do you know if that warranty was from Beech Equipment, or from Dover?

A: I believe it was from Dover.

Q: Did you receive any written documentation in regard to that warranty?

A: Yes, ma'am.

Although it is clear that Cate understood the warranty to extend for only five years, it is not clear that he understood any other limitations or exclusions. Merely providing a buyer a copy of documents containing an inconspicuous disclaimer does not establish actual knowledge. Dover has failed to establish that as a matter of law Cate had actual knowledge of the disclaimer.

We hold that, to be enforceable, a written disclaimer of the implied warranty of merchantability made in connection with a sale of goods must be conspicuous to a reasonable person. We further hold that such a disclaimer contained in text undistinguished in typeface, size or color within a form purporting to grant a warranty is not conspicuous, and is unenforceable unless the buyer has actual knowledge of the disclaimer. For the reasons stated herein, we reverse the judgment of the court of appeals and remand to the trial court for further proceedings consistent with this opinion.

SPEARS, JUSTICE, concurring.

Although I concur in the court's opinion, I write separately to declare that the time has come for the legislature to consider the realities of the marketplace and prohibit all disclaimers of the implied warranties of merchantability and fitness.

These implied warranties, created by common-law courts long before the adoption of the U.C.C., developed to protect purchasers from losses suffered because of "the frustration of their expectations about the worth, efficacy, or desirability" of a product. W. Keeton, Prosser and Keeton on The Law of Torts § 95A (5th ed. 1984). Implication of these warranties into every goods contract, without regard to the parties' actual assent to their terms, served "to police, to prevent, and to remedy" unfair consumer transactions. Llewellyn, On Warranty of Quality, and Society, 39 Colum. L.Rev. 699, 699 (1936). * * * These implied warranties also serve other important purposes: they create incentives to produce and market higher quality products; they discourage shoddy workmanship and unethical trade practices; and they place responsibility on those who profit from the sale of goods, have the greatest control over the products, and are better able to bear the risk of loss. Section 2–316 however, subverts all of these purposes by giving sellers almost unlimited license to disclaim implied warranties.

We live in an age when sellers of goods "saturate the marketplace and all of our senses" with the most extraordinary claims about the worth of their products. * * * Yet, the same sellers under the *carte blanche* granted them by section 2–316 of the U.C.C. refuse to guarantee and indeed expressly disclaim that their products are merchantable or even fit for their intended purposes. * * *

By establishing specific "requirements" for disclaimers, § 2–316 ostensibly "seeks to protect a buyer from unexpected and unbargained language of disclaimer." Comment 1. In reality, however, section 2–316 completely undermines implied warranties. Implicitly, section 2–316 adopts the position that disclaimers should be enforced because society benefits when parties to a contract are allowed to set *all* the terms of their agreement. The problem with this position, and with section 2–316 generally, is two-fold: it ignores the fact that governmental implication of protective terms into private contracts is commonplace (e.g. the *implied* warranties of merchantability and fitness); and, more importantly, it rests on the faulty premise that contractual disclaimers are generally freely bargained for elements of a contract.

Freedom of contract arguments generally, and section 2–316 specifically, presuppose and are based on "the image of individuals meeting in the marketplace" on equal ground to negotiate the terms of a contract. Rakoff, Contracts of Adhesion: An Essay in Reconstruction, 96 Harv.L.Rev. 1174, 1216 (1983). At one time, this image may have accurately reflected marketplace realities. However, the last half of the twentieth century has witnessed "the rise of the corporation" and, increasingly, the displacement of physical persons as sellers in consumer and commercial contracts. Phillips, Unconscionability and Article 2 Implied Warranty Disclaimers, 62 Chi.–Kent L.Rev. 199, 239 (1985). This development has led to innumerable situations in which consumers deal from an unequal bargaining position, the most prominent example being the ubiquitous standard form contract which is now used by most sellers of goods and which invariably contains an implied warranty disclaimer.

*   *   *

The great majority of buyers never read an implied warranty disclaimer found in a standard form contract. Even when implied warranty disclaimers are read, their legal significance is not generally understood. Such disclaimers include unfamiliar terminology (e.g. "implied warranty of merchantability"), and comprehending their legal effect requires one not only to understand what substantive rights are involved, but also to grasp that these rights have been lost via the disclaimer. * * * Finally, even if a buyer reads and understands an implied warranty disclaimer, chances are he will be without power to either strike these terms or "shop around" for better ones. If the buyer attempts the former, he will likely run into an employee who is unauthorized to alter the form contract; if he attempts the latter, he will likely confront a competitor who offers substantially the same form terms. * * * In short, the "marketplace reality" suggests that freedom of contract in the sale of goods is actually nonexistent; a buyer today can either take the contract with the disclaimer attached or leave it and go without the good.

Increasingly, the courts and legislatures of other states have acted to ameliorate or to avoid entirely the harsh consequences wrought by section 2–316. Several courts have refused to enforce disclaimers, on public policy grounds, unless the disclaimer sets forth the particular qualities and characteristics of fitness being waived, is clearly brought to the buyer's attention and is expressly agreed to by the buyer. * * *

A number of other courts have found even conspicuous disclaimers to be unconscionable under section 2–302 of the U.C.C., despite the disclaimer's compliance with § 2–316. * * * See generally Phillips, Unconscionability and Article 2 Implied Warranty Disclaimers, 62 Chi.–Kent L.Rev. 199, 262–63 (1985) (arguing that § 2–302 should be aggressively applied to invalidate disclaimers of implied warranties, and concluding that such disclaimers should be "per se unconscionable" in consumer cases).

Several states have gone even further by enacting protective legislation which forbids implied warranty disclaimers or by repealing section 2–316 of the Code. * * *

Finally, the federal Magnuson–Moss Warranty Act places severe limits on the seller's ability to disclaim implied warranties in the sale of consumer goods. 15 U.S.C. § 2301–12 (1982). The Act's most important clause essentially provides that *if* a seller gives a written express warranty, he cannot disclaim the implied warranties. Id. § 2308(a). The Act effectively prohibits the common practice of a seller boldly announcing an express warranty of limited value and then disclaiming the more valuable implied warranties, leaving the consumer with a delusive remedy at best.

* * *

The realities of the modern marketplace demand that the legislature prohibit implied warranty disclaimers by repealing section 2–316 of the U.C.C. Without such action, Texas courts will be forced to rely on "covert tools", such as the unconscionability provision in section 2–302 or the "conspicuous" requirement in section 2–316, to reach a just and fair result in disclaimer suits. When these tools are used, guidance, predictability and consistency in the law is sacrificed, while limited judicial resources are spent policing unjust bargains that could have been avoided. Were it up to the judicial branch, the courts could declare such disclaimers void as against public policy. If the legislature has the interests of Texas citizens at heart, it will repeal section 2–316 because, no matter how conspicuous, such disclaimers are abusive of consumers.

MAUZY, J., joins in this concurring opinion.

RAY, JUSTICE, concurring and dissenting.

I concur in that portion of the court's opinion requiring that a written disclaimer of the implied warranty of merchantability must be conspicuous to a reasonable person. I write separately, however, to take issue with the court's immediate erosion of that standard by permitting a showing of actual knowledge of the disclaimer to override a lack of conspicuousness.

The statute, on its face, provides for no actual knowledge exception. There is no room for judicial crafting of those omitted by the legislature. I would hold that the extent of a buyer's knowledge of a disclaimer is irrelevant to a determination of its enforceability under § 2–316(2) of the UCC.

The effect of actual knowledge is subject to debate among leading commentators on commercial law. The purpose of the objective standard of conspicuousness adopted by the court today reflects the view that "the drafters intended a rigid adherence to the conspicuousness requirement in order to avoid arguments concerning what the parties said about the warranties at the time of the sale." J. White and R. Summers, Uniform Commercial Code § 12–5 (2d ed. 1980). An absolute rule that an inconspicuous disclaimer is invalid, despite the buyer's actual knowledge, encourages sellers to make their disclaimers conspicuous, thereby reducing the need for courts to evaluate swearing matches as to actual awareness in particular cases. * * * Today's decision condemns our courts to a parade of such cases.

NOTES

1. Maritime Air Service, Ltd., while it was the lessee of a helicopter leased by Fairchild Industries, purchased the helicopter from Fairchild pursuant to a purchase option contained in the lease. The purchase was made under a printed purchase agreement form supplied by Fairchild which contained the following typewritten provision:

"It is specifically understood and agreed by the parties that the Aircraft is sold in an 'As is' condition. Seller makes no representation or warranties express or implied whatsoever except Warranty of Title. * * *"

Maritime brought an action against Fairchild alleging breach of the implied warranties of merchantability and fitness for particular purpose. Fairchild defended on the ground that these warranties were effectively disclaimed by the provision quoted above. Assume that the quoted provision is not "conspicuous" within the meaning of § 1–201(10). Were the implied warranties effectively disclaimed? Compare subsections (2) and (3) of § 2–316. Fairchild Industries v. Maritime Air Service, Ltd., 274 Md. 181, 333 A.2d 313 (1975).

2. A contract of sale of manufacturing equipment contained the following printed provisions:

"LIABILITY CLAUSE: The Company's liability hereunder shall be subject to the following:

"General:

"1. The Company warrants the machine against defects in materials or workmanship, but makes no other warranties, express or implied (except as set forth under 'Patent') unless the word 'guarantee' is used. Warranties of merchantability or of fitness for a particular purpose or arising from a course of dealing or usage of trade, are specifically excluded. The Purchaser agrees that any affirmations of fact, description of the machine or sample or model machine herein referred to, whether or not the same relate to production or capability of the machine to perform, are not the basis of this contract, unless the word 'guarantee' is used in connection therewith, in which case the same shall be express warranties."

In the typewritten portion of the sales contract under the heading PERFORMANCE was the statement "in view of the variables affecting the capacity of the machine, no guarantee can be extended" and the statement "The [Seller's] standard warranty outlined later in this contract does apply." In United States Fibres, Inc. v. Proctor & Schwartz, Inc., 509 F.2d 1043 (6th Cir. 1975) the court held that the implied warranty of merchantability was effectively disclaimed. The heading under which the disclaimer clause appeared was conspicuous. The court rejected the argument that as a matter of law a disclaimer is not conspicuous if type of the same size and color is used in the text. The court relied on the Comment to § 1–201(10) which indicates that that section merely indicates some of the methods of drawing attention to a statement. The test is whether attention can reasonably be expected to be called to the statement. The court stated that in this case the buyer was put on notice of the limited warranty of the seller, that the buyer in fact was familiar with the printed portions of the contract and that there was no surprise. The court emphasized that the buyer knew that the manufacturing equipment was untried and experimental and could not reasonably expect it to be fully warranted.

2. UNCONSCIONABILITY

HENNINGSEN v. BLOOMFIELD MOTORS, INC.

Supreme Court of New Jersey, 1960.
32 N.J. 358, 161 A.2d 69.

FRANCIS, J. * * * The complaint was predicated upon breach of express and implied warranties and upon negligence. At the trial the negligence counts were dismissed by the court and the cause was submitted to the jury for determination solely on the issues of implied warranty of merchantability. Verdicts were returned against both defendants and in favor of the plaintiffs. Defendants appealed and plaintiffs cross-appealed from the dismissal of their negligence claim. The matter was certified by this court prior to consideration in the Appellate Division.

The facts are not complicated, but a general outline of them is necessary to an understanding of the case.

On May 7, 1955 Mr. and Mrs. Henningsen visited the place of business of Bloomfield Motors, Inc., an authorized De Soto and Plymouth dealer, to look at a Plymouth. They wanted to buy a car and were considering a Ford or a Chevrolet as well as a Plymouth. They were shown a Plymouth which appealed to them and the purchase followed. The record indicates that Mr. Henningsen intended the car as a Mother's Day gift to his wife. He said the intention was communicated to the dealer. When the purchase order or contract was prepared and presented, the husband executed it alone. His wife did not join as a party.

The purchase order was a printed form of one page. On the front it contained blanks to be filled in with a description of the automobile to be sold, the various accessories to be included, and the details of the financing. The particular car selected was described as a 1955 Plymouth, Plaza "6", Club Sedan. The type used in the printed parts of the form became smaller in size, different in style, and less readable toward the bottom where the line for the purchaser's signature was placed. The smallest type on the page appears in the two paragraphs, one of two and one-quarter lines and the second of one and one-half lines, on which great stress is laid by the defense in the case. These two paragraphs are the least legible and the most difficult to read in the instrument, but they are most important in the evaluation of the rights of the contesting parties. They do not attract attention and there is nothing about the format which would draw the reader's eye to them. In fact, a studied and concentrated effort would have to be made to read them. De-emphasis seems the motive rather than emphasis. More particularly, most of the printing in the body of the order appears to be 12 point block type, and easy to read. In the short paragraphs under discussion, however, the type appears to be six point script and the print is solid, that is, the lines are very close together.

The two paragraphs are:

"The front and back of this Order comprise the entire agreement affecting this purchase and no other agreement or understanding of any nature concerning same has been made or entered into, or will be recognized. I hereby certify that no credit has been extended to me for the purchase of this motor vehicle except as appears in writing on the face of this agreement.

"I have read the matter printed on the back hereof and agree to it as a part of this order the same as if it were printed above my signature. I certify that I am 21 years of age, or older, and hereby acknowledge receipt of a copy of this order."

* * *

The testimony of Claus Henningsen justifies the conclusion that he did not read the two fine print paragraphs referring to the back of the purchase contract. And it is uncontradicted that no one made any reference to them, or called them to his attention. With respect to the matter appearing on the back, it is likewise uncontradicted that he did not read it and that no one called it to his attention.

The reverse side of the contract contains 8½ inches of fine print. It is not as small, however, as the two critical paragraphs described above. The page is headed "Conditions" and contains ten separate paragraphs consisting of 65 lines in all. The paragraphs do not have headnotes or margin notes denoting their particular subject, as in the case of the "Owner Service Certificate" to be referred to later. In the seventh paragraph, about two-thirds of the way down the page, the warranty, which is the focal point of the case, is set forth. It is as follows:

"7. It is expressly agreed that there are no warranties, express or implied, *made* by either the dealer or the manufacturer on the motor vehicle, chassis, or parts furnished hereunder except as follows.

" 'The manufacturer warrants each new motor vehicle (including original equipment placed thereon by the manufacturer except tires), chassis or parts manufactured by it to be free from defects in material or workmanship under normal use and service. Its obligation under this warranty being limited to making good at its factory any part or parts thereof which shall, within ninety (90) days after delivery of such vehicle *to the original purchaser* or before such vehicle has been driven 4,000 miles, whichever event shall first occur, be returned to it with transportation charges prepaid and which its examination shall disclose to its satisfaction to have been thus defective; *this warranty being expressly in lieu of all other warranties expressed or implied, and all other obligations or liabilities on its part,* and it neither assumes nor authorizes any other person to assume for it any other liability in connection with the sale of its vehicles. * * *.' "
(Emphasis ours.)

After the contract had been executed, plaintiffs were told the car had to be serviced and that it would be ready in two days. According to the dealer's president, a number of cars were on hand at the time; they had come in from the factory about three or four weeks earlier and at least some of them, including the one selected by the Henningsens, were kept in the back of the shop for display purposes. When sold, plaintiffs' vehicle was not "a serviced car, ready to go." The testimony shows that Chrysler Corporation sends from the factory to the dealer a "New Car Preparation Service Guide" with each new automobile. The guide contains detailed instructions as to what has to be done to prepare the car for delivery. The dealer is told to "Use this form as a guide to inspect and prepare this new Plymouth for delivery." It specifies 66 separate items to be checked, tested, tightened or adjusted in the course of the servicing, but dismantling the vehicle or checking all of its internal parts is not prescribed. The guide also calls for delivery of the Owner Service Certificate with the car.

This Certificate, which at least by inference is authorized by Chrysler, was in the car when released to Claus Henningsen on May 9, 1955. It was not made part of the purchase contract, nor was it shown to him prior to the consummation of that agreement. The only reference to it therein is that the dealer "agrees to promptly peform and fulfill all terms and conditions of the owner service policy." The Certificate contains a warranty entitled "Automobile Manufacturers Association Uniform Warranty." The provisions thereof are the same as those set forth on the reverse side of the purchase order, except that an additional paragraph is added by which the dealer extends that warranty to the purchaser in the same manner as if the word "Dealer" appeared instead of the word "Manufacturer."

The new Plymouth was turned over to the Henningsens on May 9, 1955. No proof was adduced by the dealer to show precisely what was done in the way of mechanical or road testing beyond testimony that the manufacturer's instructions were probably followed. Mr. Henningsen drove it from the dealer's place of business in Bloomfield to their home in Keansburg. On the trip nothing unusual appeared in the way in which it operated. Thereafter, it was used for short trips on paved streets about the town. It had no servicing and no mishaps of any kind before the event of May 19. That day, Mrs. Henningsen drove to Asbury Park. On the way down and in returning the car performed in normal fashion until the accident occurred. She was proceeding north on Route 36 in Highlands, New Jersey, at 20–22 miles per hour. The highway was paved and smooth, and contained two lanes for northbound travel. She was riding in the right-hand lane. Suddenly she heard a loud noise "from the bottom, by the hood." It "felt as if something cracked." The steering wheel spun in her hands; the car veered sharply to the right and crashed into a highway sign and a brick wall. No other vehicle was in any way involved. A bus operator driving in the left-hand lane testified that he observed plaintiffs' car approaching in normal fashion in the opposite direction; "all of a sudden [it] veered at 90 degrees * * * and right into this wall." As a result of the impact, the front of the car was so badly damaged that it was impossible to determine if any of the parts of the steering wheel mechanism or workmanship or assembly were defective or improper prior to the accident. The condition was such that the collision insurance carrier, after inspection, declared the vehicle a total loss. It had 468 miles on the speedometer at the time.

The insurance carrier's inspector and appraiser of damaged cars, with 11 years of experience, advanced the opinion, based on the history and his examination, that something definitely went "wrong from the steering wheel down to the front wheels" and that the untoward happening must have been due to mechanical defect or failure; "something down there had to drop off or break loose to cause the car" to act in the manner described.

As has been indicated, the trial court felt that the proof was not sufficient to make out a *prima facie* case as to the negligence of either the manufacturer or the dealer. The case was given to the jury, therefore, solely on the warranty theory, with results favorable to the plaintiffs against both defendants. * * *

[The treatment of the existence of a warranty and the abolition of privity is omitted.]

II.

The Effect of the Disclaimer and Limitation of Liability Clauses on the Implied Warranty of Merchantability.

Judicial notice may be taken of the fact that automobile manufacturers, including Chrysler Corporation, undertake large scale advertising programs over television, radio, in newspapers, magazines and all media of communication in order to persuade the public to buy their products. As has been observed above, a number of jurisdictions, conscious of modern marketing practices, have declared that when a manufacturer engages in advertising in order to bring his goods and their quality to the attention of the public and thus to create consumer demand, the representations made constitute an express warranty running directly to a buyer who purchases in reliance thereon. The fact that the sale is consummated with an independent dealer does not obviate the warranty. * * *

In view of the cases in various jurisdictions suggesting the conclusion which we have now reached with respect to the implied warranty of merchantability, it becomes apparent that manufacturers who enter into promotional activities to stimulate consumer buying may incur warranty obligations of either or both the express or implied character. These developments in the law inevitably suggest the inference that the form of express warranty made part of the Hennigsen purchase contract was devised for general use in the automobile industry as a possible means of avoiding the consequences of the growing judicial acceptance of the thesis that the described express or implied warranties run directly to the consumer.

In the light of these matters, what effect should be given to the express warranty in question which seeks to limit the manufacturer's liability to replacement of defective parts, and which disclaims all other warranties, express or implied? In assessing its significance we must keep in mind the general principle that, in the absence of fraud, one who does not choose to read a contract before signing it, cannot later relieve himself of its burdens. Fivey v. Pennsylvania R.R. Co., 67 N.J.L. 627, 52 A. 472 (E. & A.1902). And in applying that principle, the basic tenet of freedom of competent parties to contract is a factor of importance. But in the framework of modern commercial life and business practices, such rules cannot be applied on a strict, doctrinal basis. The conflicting interests of the buyer and seller must be evaluated realistically and justly, giving due weight to the social policy evinced by the Uniform Sales Act, the progressive decisions of the courts engaged in administering it, the mass production methods of manufacture and distribution to the public, and the bargaining position occupied by the ordinary consumer in such an economy. This history of the law shows that legal doctrines, as first expounded, often prove to be inadequate under the impact of later experience. In such case, the need for justice has stimulated the necessary qualifications or adjustments. * * *

In these times, an automobile is almost as much a servant of convenience for the ordinary person as a household utensil. For a multitude of other persons it is a necessity. Crowded highways and filled parking lots are a commonplace of our existence. There is no need to look any farther than the daily newspaper to be convinced that when an automobile is defective, it has great potentiality for harm.

* * *

What influence should these circumstances have on the restrictive effect of Chrysler's express warranty in the framework of the purchase contract? As we have said, warranties originated in the law to safeguard the buyer and not to limit the liability of the seller or manufacturer. It seems obvious in this instance that the motive was to avoid the warranty obligations which are normally incidental to such sales. The language gave little and withdrew much. In return for the delusive remedy of replacement of defective parts at the factory, the buyer is said to have accepted the exclusion of the maker's liability for personal injuries arising from the breach of the warranty, and to have agreed to the elimination of any other express or implied warranty. An instinctively felt sense of justice cries out against such a sharp bargain. But does the doctrine that a person is bound by his signed agreement, in the absence of fraud, stand in the way of any relief?

In the modern consideration of problems such as this, Corbin suggests that practically all judges are "chancellors" and cannot fail to be influenced by any equitable doctrines that are available. And he opines that "there is sufficient flexibility in the concepts of fraud, duress, misrepresentation and undue influence, not to mention differences in economic bargaining power" to enable the courts to avoid enforcement of unconscionable provisions in long printed standardized contracts. 1 Corbin on Contracts (1950) § 128, p. 188. Freedom of contract is not such an immutable doctrine as to admit of no qualification in the area in which we are concerned.

* * *

The traditional contract is the result of free bargaining of parties who are brought together by the play of the market, and who meet each other on a footing of approximate economic equality. In such a society there is no danger that freedom of contract will be a threat to the social order as a whole. But in present-day commercial life the standardized mass contract has appeared. It is used primarily by enterprises with strong bargaining power and position. "The weaker party, in need of the goods or services, is frequently not in a position to shop around for better terms, either because the author of the standard contract has a monopoly (nature or artificial) or because all competitors use the same clauses. His contractual intention is but a subjection more or less voluntary to terms dictated by the stronger party, terms whose consequences are often understood in a vague way, if at all." Kessler, "Contracts of Adhesion—Some Thoughts About Freedom of Contract," 43 Colum.L.Rev. 629, 632 (1943); Ehrenzweig, "Adhesion Contracts in the Conflict of Laws," 53 Colum.L.Rev. 1072, 1075, 1089 (1953). Such standardized contracts have been described as those in which one predominant party will dictate its law to an undetermined multiple rather than to an individual. They are said to resemble a law rather than a meeting of the minds. Siegelman v. Cunard White Star, 221 F.2d 189, 206 (2 Cir. 1955).

Vold, in the recent revision of his Law of Sales (2d ed. 1959) at page 447, wrote of this type of contract and its effect upon the ordinary buyer:

"In recent times the marketing process has been getting more highly organized than ever before. Business units have been expanding on a scale never before known. The standardized contract with its broad disclaimer clauses is drawn by legal advisers of sellers widely organized in trade associations. It is encountered on every hand. Extreme inequality of bargaining between buyer and seller in this respect is now often conspicuous. Many buyers no longer have any real choice in the matter. They must often accept what they can get through accompanied by broad disclaimers. The terms of these disclaimers deprive them of all substantial protection with regard to the quality of the goods. In effect, this is by force of contract between very unequal parties. It throws the risk of defective articles on the most dependent party. He has the least individual power to avoid the presence of defects. He also has the least individual ability to bear their disastrous consequences."

The warranty before us is a standardized form designed for mass use. It is imposed upon the automobile consumer. He takes it or leaves it, and he must take it to buy an automobile. No bargaining is engaged in with respect to it. In fact, the dealer through whom it comes to the buyer is without authority to alter it; his function is ministerial—simply to deliver it. The form warranty is not only standard with Chrysler but, as mentioned above, it is the uniform warranty of the Automobile Manufacturers Association. Members of the Association are: General Motors, Inc., Ford, Chrysler, Studebaker-Packard, American Motors, (Rambler), Willys Motors, Checker Motors Corp., and International Harvester Company. Automobile Facts and Figures (1958 Ed., Automobile Manufacturers Association) 69. Of these companies, the "Big Three" (General Motors, Ford, and Chrysler) represented 93.5% of the passenger-car production for 1958 and the independents 6.5%. Standard & Poor (Industrial Surveys, Autos, Basic Analysis, June 25, 1959) 4109. And for the same year the "Big Three" had 86.72% of the total passenger vehicle registrations. Automotive News, 1959 Almanac (Slocum Publishing Co., Inc.) p. 25.

The gross inequality of bargaining position occupied by the consumer in the automobile industry is thus apparent. There is no competition among the car makers in the area of the express warranty. Where can the buyer go to negotiate for better protection? Such control and limitation of his remedies are inimical to the public welfare and, at the very least, call for great care by the courts to avoid injustice through application of strict common-law principles of freedom of contract. Because there is no competition among the motor vehicle manufacturers with respect to the scope of protection guaranteed to the buyer, there is no incentive on their part to stimulate good will in that field of public relations. Thus, there is lacking a factor existing in more competitive fields, one which tends to guarantee the safe construction of the article sold. Since all competitors operate in the same way, the urge to be careful is not so pressing. See "Warranties of Kind and Quality," 57 Yale L.J. 1389, 1400 (1948).

Although the courts, with few exceptions, have been most sensitive to problems presented by contracts resulting from gross disparity in buyer-seller bargaining positions, they have not articulated a general principle condemning, as opposed to public policy, the imposition on the buyer of a skeleton warranty as a means of limiting the responsibility of the manufacturer. They have endeavored thus far to avoid a drastic departure from age-old tenets of freedom of contract by adopting doctrines of strict construction, and notice and knowledgeable absent by the buyer to the attempted exculpation of the seller. 1 Corbin, supra, 337; 2 Harper & James, supra, 1590; Prosser, "Warranty of Merchantable Quality," 27 Minn.L.Rev. 117, 159 (1932). Accordingly to be found in the cases are statements that disclaimers and the consequent limitation of liability will not be given effect if "unfairly procured" * * * if not brought to the buyer's attention and he was not made understandingly aware of it * * * or if not clear and explicit.

* * *

It is undisputed that the president of the dealer with whom Henningsen dealt did not specifically call attention to the warranty on the back of the purchase order. The form and the arrangement of its face, as described above, certainly would cause the minds of reasonable men to differ as to whether notice of a yielding of basic rights stemming from the relationship with the manufacturer was adequately given. The words "warranty" or "limited warranty" did not even appear in the fine print above the place for signature, and a jury might well find that the type of print itself was such as to promote lack of attention rather than sharp scrutiny. The inference from the facts is that Chrysler placed the method of communicating its warranty to the purchaser in the hands of the dealer. If either one or both of them wished to make certain that Henningsen became aware of that agreement and its purported implications, neither the form of the document nor the method of expressing the precise nature of the obligation intended to be assumed would have presented any difficulty.

But there is more than this. Assuming that a jury might find that the fine print referred to reasonably served the objective of directing a buyer's attention to the warranty on the reverse side, and, therefore, that he should be charged with awareness of its language, can it be said that an ordinary layman would realize what he was relinquishing in return for what he was being granted? Under the law, breach of warranty against defective parts or workmanship which caused personal injuries would entitle a buyer to damages even if due care were used in the manufacturing process. Because of the great potential for harm if the vehicle was defective, that right is the most important and fundamental one arising from the relationship. Difficulties so frequently encountered in establishing negligence in manufacture in the ordinary case make this manifest. 2 Harper & James, supra, §§ 28.14, 28.15; Prosser, supra, 506. Any ordinary layman of reasonable intelligence, looking at the phraseology, might well conclude that Chrysler was agreeing to replace defective parts and perhaps replace anything that went wrong because of defective workmanship during the first 90 days or 4,000 miles of operation, but that he would not be entitled to a new car. It is not unreasonable to believe that the entire scheme being conveyed was a proposed remedy for physical deficiencies in the car. *In the context* of this warranty, only the abandonment of all sense of justice would permit us to hold that, as a matter of law, the phrase "its obligation under this warranty being limited to making good at its factory any part or parts thereof" signifies to an ordinary reasonable person that he is relinquishing any personal injury claim that might flow from the use of a defective automobile. Such claims are nowhere mentioned. The draftsmanship is reflective of the care and skill of the Automobile Manufacturers Association in undertaking to avoid warranty obligations without drawing too much attention to its effort in that regard. No one can doubt that if the will to do so were present, the ability to inform the buying public of the intention to disclaim liability for injury claims arising from breach of warranty would present no problem.

In this connection, attention is drawn to the Plymouth Owner Certificate mentioned earlier. Obviously, Chrysler is aware of it because the New Car Preparation Service Guide sent from the factory to the dealer directs that it be given to the purchaser. That certificate contains a paragraph called "Explanation of Warranty." Its entire tenor relates to replacement of defective parts. There is nothing about it to stimulate the idea that the intention of the warranty is to exclude personal injury claims.

* * *

The task of the judiciary is to administer the spirit as well as the letter of the law. On issues such as the present one, part of that burden is to protect the ordinary man against the loss of important rights through what, in effect, is the unilateral act of the manufacturer. The status of the automobile industry is unique. Manufacturers are few in number and strong in bargaining position. In the matter of warranties on the sale of their products, the Automotive Manufacturers Association has enabled them to present a united front. From the standpoint of the purchaser, there can be no arms length negotiating on the subject. Because his capacity for bargaining is so grossly unequal, the inexorable conclusion which follows is that he is not permitted to bargain at all. He must take or leave the automobile on the warranty terms dictated by the maker. He cannot turn to a competitor for better security.

Public policy is a term not easily defined. Its significance varies as the habits and needs of a people may vary. It is not static and the field of application is an ever increasing one. A contract, or a particular provision therein, valid in one era may be wholly opposed to the public policy of another. See Collopy v.

Newark Eye & Ear Infirmary, 27 N.J. 29, 39, 141 A.2d 276 (1958). Courts keep in mind the principle that the best interests of society demand that persons should not be unnecessarily restricted in their freedom to contract. But they do not hesitate to declare void as against public policy contractual provisions which clearly tend to the injury of the public in some way. Hodnick v. Fidelity Trust Co., 96 Ind.App. 342, 183 N.E. 488 (App.Ct.1932).

Public policy at a given time finds expression in the Constitution, the statutory law and in judicial decisions. In the area of sale of goods, the legislative will has imposed an implied warranty of merchantability as a general incident of sale of an automobile by description. The warranty does not depend upon the affirmative intention of the parties. It is a child of the law; it annexes itself to the contract because of the very nature of the transaction. Minneapolis Steel & Machinery Co. v. Casey Land Agency, 51 N.D. 832, 201 N.W. 172 (Sup.Ct.1924). The judicial process has recognized a right to recover damages for personal injuries arising from a breach of that warranty. The disclaimer of the implied warranty and exclusion of all obligations except those specifically assumed by the express warranty signify a studied effort to frustrate that protection. True, the Sales Act authorizes agreements between buyer and seller qualifying the warranty obligations. But quite obviously the Legislature contemplated lawful stipulations (which are determined by the circumstances of a particular case) arrived at freely by parties of relatively equal bargaining strength. The lawmakers did not authorize the automobile manufacturer to use its grossly disproportionate bargaining power to relieve itself from liability and to impose on the ordinary buyer, who in effect has no real freedom of choice, the grave danger of injury to himself and others that attends the sale of such a dangerous instrumentality as a defectively made automobile. In the framework of this case, illuminated as it is by the facts and the many decisions noted, we are of the opinion that Chrysler's attempted disclaimer of an implied warranty of merchantability and of the obligations arising therefrom is so inimical to the public good as to compel an adjudication of its invalidity. See 57 Yale L.J., supra, at pp. 1400–1404; proposed Uniform Commercial Code, 1958 Official Text, § 202. (U.C.C. 2–302 ed.)

The trial court sent the case to the jury against Chrysler on the theory that the evidence would support a finding of breach of an implied warranty of merchantability. In fact, at one point in his charge he seemed to say that as a matter of law such a warranty existed. He also told them that:

> "A provision in a purchase order for an automobile that an express warranty shall exclude all implied warranties will not be given effect so as to defeat an implied warranty that the machine shall be fit for the purposes for which it was

intended unless its inclusion in the contract was fairly procured or obtained."

Thereafter, the court charged that when the car was sold a warranty arose that it was reasonably suited for ordinary use, and that if they found that it was defective and "not reasonably suited for ordinary driving" liability would exist "provided * * * you find there was an implied warranty and a breach thereof." The reasonable inference to be drawn from the whole context is that a preliminary finding against the binding effect of the disclaimer would have to be made, i.e., that the disclaimer was not "fairly procured," before an implied warranty could be deemed to exist. Even assuming that the duty to make such a finding was not as explicit as it should have been, in view of our holding that the disclaimer is void as a matter of law, the charge was more favorable to the defendant than the law required it to be. The verdict in favor of the plaintiffs and against Chrysler Corporation establishes that the jury found that the disclaimer was not fairly obtained. Thus, this defendant cannot claim to have been prejudiced by a jury finding on an aspect of the case which the court should have disposed of as a matter of law.

MARTIN v. JOSEPH HARRIS CO., INC.

United States Court of Appeals, Sixth Circuit, 1985.
767 F.2d 296.

MILBURN, CIRCUIT JUDGE.

The defendant, Joseph Harris Co., Inc., brings this appeal following the district court's granting the plaintiffs' motion for a judgment not withstanding the verdict and a second trial in plaintiffs' action for damages as a result of defective seeds. Because we hold that the district court was correct in holding that, under the facts of this case, the disclaimer of warranty and limitation of remedy clause used by the defendant was unconscionable under Michigan law, and because we further hold that the district court properly held that the implied warranty of merchantability was breached as a matter of law, we affirm.

I.

Plaintiffs Duane Martin and Robert Rick ("Martin and Rick") were commercial farmers in Michigan. In August of 1972, Martin and Rick placed independent orders for cabbage seed with the defendant, Joseph Harris Co., Inc. ("Harris Seed"), a national producer and distributor of seed. Plaintiffs had been customers of Harris Seed for several years and, as in earlier transactions, the order form supplied by Harris Seed included a clause disclaiming the implied warranty of merchantability and limiting buyers' remedies to the purchase price of the seed.[1] A similar clause was also used by Harris Seed's competitors for the same purpose. Neither of the plaintiffs read the clause nor did the salesman make any attempt either to point it out or to explain its purpose.

Three to four months after placing their orders, plaintiffs received Harris Seed's 1973 Commercial Vegetable Growers Catalog. Included in the lower right-hand corner of one page of the catalog was a notification that Harris Seed would no longer "hot water" treat cabbage seed. Hot water treatment had successfully been used since 1947 to eradicate a fungus known as *phoma lingam* or "black leg," a seed borne disease that causes affected plants to rot before maturing.[2]

Plaintiffs planted their cabbage crop in April and May of 1973, using, among other seed, that supplied by Harris Seed. In mid-July, Harris Seed notified plaintiffs that the seed lot used to fill plaintiffs' order was infected with black leg. Although plaintiffs attempted to minimize the effect of the disease, large portions of their cabbage crops were destroyed. However, in marketing their smaller than usual crop, both plaintiffs made a profit equal to or higher than previous years. This unusual profit margin was due to the rise in market price for cabbage in 1973, which in turn was affected in part by the fact that the 1973 black leg epidemic reduced the amount of available cabbage.

On August 5, 1975, plaintiffs brought this action. After a hearing on the enforceability of the disclaimer of warranty and limitation of liability clause, the district court ruled that the clause was unconscionable and, therefore, unenforceable. A jury was impaneled to try plaintiffs' legal liability theories of negligence and breach of implied warranty. Following a six-day trial the jury returned a verdict against plaintiffs on both theories; however, the district court granted the plaintiffs' motion for a j.n.o.v. on the implied warranty issue. A second jury impaneled to hear the issue of damages returned verdicts in favor of Martin in the amount of Thirty-six Thousand ($36,000.00) Dollars and in

---

1. The disclaimer of warranties and exclusion of remedies clause, which was printed in the order form, seed catalogs and on the seed packages, appeared as follows:

NOTICE TO BUYER: Joseph Harris Company, Inc. warrants that seeds and plants it sells conform to the label descriptions as required by Federal and State seed laws. IT MAKES NO OTHER WARRANTIES, EXPRESS OR IMPLIED, OF MERCHANTABILITY, FITNESS FOR PURPOSE, OR OTHERWISE, AND IN ANY EVENT ITS LIABILITY FOR BREACH OF ANY WAR-

RANTY OR CONTRACT WITH RESPECT TO SUCH SEEDS OR PLANTS IS LIMITED TO THE PURCHASE PRICE OF SUCH SEEDS OR PLANTS.

No question has been raised as to whether this clause complies with the requirements of U.C.C. § 2–316.

2. According to testimony at trial, the only black leg epidemic between 1947 and 1973 was in 1966, and was traced to cabbage seed imported from Australia. The 1947 and the 1973 black leg was traced to State of Washington produced cabbage seed.

favor of Rick in the amount of Sixteen Thousand ($16,000.00) Dollars.

II.

Our review of the district court's rulings in this diversity case is controlled by the State of Michigan's version of the Uniform Commercial Code * * *. As we have often stated, "[w]hen this court is reviewing a district judge's interpretation of state law, we give 'considerable weight' to the interpretation of the judge." Bagwell v. Canal Insurance Co., 663 F.2d 710, 712 (6th Cir.1981). Accordingly, "if a federal district judge has reached a permissible conclusion upon a question of local law, the Court of Appeals should not reverse even though it may think the law should be otherwise." Insurance Co. of North America v. Federated Mutual Insurance Co., 518 F.2d 101, 106 n. 3 (6th Cir.1975) (quoting Rudd-Melikian, Inc. v. Merritt, 282 F.2d 924, 929 (6th Cir.1960)).

The first issue raised by Harris Seed is whether the district court erred in holding the disclaimer and limitation clause unconscionable under U.C.C. § 2–302. The question of the unconscionability of a contract clause is one of law for the court to decide in light of "its commercial setting, purpose and effect." U.C.C. § 2–302. Since the Code does not define unconscionability, the district court reviewed case law to aid it in its resolution of this question.

A threshold problem in this context is whether under Michigan law warranty disclaimers which comply with U.C.C. § 2–316 are limited by U.C.C. § 2–302. In holding Harris Seed's disclaimer clause unconscionable under the facts of this case, the district court implicitly held that U.C.C. § 2–302 is a limitation on U.C.C. § 2–316. Harris Seed argues that by enacting § 2–316 the Michigan Legislature "unequivocally [authorized the] exclusion or modification of the implied warranty of merchantability by disclaimer." We have been presented with no Michigan cases resolving this issue; however, a number of arguments support the district court's conclusion that § 2–316 is not insulated from review under § 2–302. First, § 2–302 provides that "any clause" of a contract may be found unconscionable. Similarly, "section 2–316 does not state expressly that all disclaimers meeting its requirements are immune from general policing provisions like section 2–302. * * *" J. White & R. Summers, Handbook of the Law Under the Uniform Commercial Code, § 12–11, at 476 (2d Ed.1980). Had the drafters of the Uniform Commercial Code or the Michigan Legislature chosen to limit the application of § 2–302, language expressly so stating could easily have been included. Furthermore, as pointed out by Professors White and Summers:

Comment 1 [to § 2–302] lists and describes ten cases which are presumably intended to illustrate the underlying basis of the section: In seven of those cases disclaimers of warranty were denied full effect. It is difficult to reconcile the intent on the part of the draftsman to immunize disclaimers from the effect of 2–302 with the fact that they used cases in which courts struck down disclaimers to illustrate the concept of unconscionability.

Id. (footnotes omitted). Therefore, because this issue is unsettled under Michigan law and according the district court's conclusion "considerable weight," we hold that the district court correctly relied upon § 2–302 as a limitation on § 2–316.

We next turn to a more troublesome subissue; viz., whether within the special facts of this case the disclaimer and exclusionary clause was unconscionable under Michigan law. As has often been stated, commercial contracts will rarely be found unconscionable, see, e.g., A & M Produce Co. v. FMC Corp., 135 Cal.App.3d 473, 186 Cal.Rptr. 114 (1982), Stanley A. Klopp, Inc. v. John Deere Co., 510 F.Supp. 807, 810 (E.D.Pa.1981), aff'd, 676 F.2d 688 (3rd Cir.1982),[4] because in the commercial setting the relationship is between business parties and is not so one-sided as to give one party the bargaining power to impose unconscionable terms on the other party.

In making its determination of unconscionability, the district court relied upon Allen v. Michigan Bell Telephone, 18 Mich.App. 632, 171 N.W.2d 689 (1969).[5] In *Allen* an insurance agent contracted with Michigan Bell Telephone Company to place advertisements in the classified telephone directory. When the advertisements were not included, he brought an action for damages. To

---

4. It is unclear whether the contract at issue is a commercial contract. As noted by the district court, some courts have held farmers and ranchers are not merchants. See, e.g., Fear Ranches, Inc. v. Berry, 470 F.2d 905 (10th Cir. 1972); Cook Grains, Inc. v. Fallis, 239 Ark. 962, 395 S.W.2d 555 (1965). Other courts have taken the opposite position and held farmers are merchants. See, e.g., Campbell v. Yokel, 20 Ill.App.2d 702, 313 N.E.2d 628 (1974); Nelson v. Union Equity Co-Operative Exchange, 548 S.W.2d 352 (Tex.1977). Although these cases deal with the definition of "merchant" in § 2–104 for purposes of application to § 2–201(2) (the "between merchants" exception to the statute of frauds), the inquiry is relevant here for purposes of determining whether the transaction at issue occurred in a true "commercial setting," where unconscionability is rarely found. However, since we hold that, even if considered a

"commercial setting," the clause at issue was unconscionable under the facts of this case, we do not reach the issue.

5. Although it may be, as Harris Seed argues, that the criticisms of *Allen* by courts, see, e.g., Robinson Insurance & Real Estate, Inc. v. Southwestern Bell, 366 F.Supp. 307 (W.D.Ark.1973), and commentators, see J. White & R. Summers, Handbook of the Law Under the Uniform Commercial Code, § 4–9, at 172 (2d Ed.1980) are well founded, the Michigan Appellate Court's holding is nevertheless an appropriate guide to our inquiry in the present case. Cf. Simpson v. Jefferson Standard Life Insurance Co., 465 F.2d 1320, 1323 (6th Cir.1972) ("[d]ecisions of intermediate state courts must be followed by the federal courts unless there is reason to believe they would not be followed by the state's highest court.").

defend the action, Michigan Bell Telephone Company relied on a limitation of remedies clause which, if upheld, would have limited the plaintiff's recovery to the contract price. In refusing to uphold the limitation, the Michigan court stated "the principle of freedom to contract does not carry a license to insert any provision in an agreement which a party deems advantageous." Id. at 691–92. Rather, the court stated that:

> [i]mplicit in the principle of freedom of contract is the concept that at the time of contracting each party has a realistic alternative to acceptance of the terms offered. Where goods and services can only be obtained from one source (or several sources on non-competitive terms) the choices of one who desires to purchase are limited to acceptance of the terms offered or doing without. Depending on the nature of the goods or services and the purchaser's needs, doing without may or may not be a realistic alternative. Where it is not, one who successfully exacts agreement to an unreasonable term cannot insist on the court's enforcing it on the ground that it was "freely" entered into, when it was not. * * *
>
> There are then two inquiries in a case such as this: (1) what is the relative bargaining power of the parties, their relative economic strength, the alternative sources of supply, in a word, what are their options?; (2) is the challenged term substantively reasonable?

Id. at 692.

With reference to the test announced in *Allen,* Harris Seed argues that the relative bargaining power of the parties is not a proper consideration under § 2–302. This is an issue on which courts and commentators have taken varying approaches. Compare, e.g., Phillips Machinery Co. v. LeBlond, Inc., 494 F.Supp. 318 (N.D.Okla.1980) (no requirement of equality of bargaining power, but rather must be some element of deception or substantive unfairness) and Majors v. Kalo Laboratories, Inc., 407 F.Supp. 20, 23 (M.D.Ala.1975) ("[T]he Official Comment to § 2–302 suggests that [consideration of bargaining power] would be inappropriate.") with Kerr-McGee Corp. v. Northern Utilities, Inc., 673 F.2d 323, 329 (10th Cir.1982) (relative considerations include whether "there was a gross inequality of bargaining power.") and J. White & R. Summers, supra, § 12–11, at 477 ("[o]ne can argue that when a seller has such a strong bargaining position that he can impose a perfectly drafted disclaimer, which operates to deprive the buyer of virtually all protection that a law would otherwise provide, and he refuses to bargain at all concerning its scope, then that clause has become 'oppressive' and so 'one-sided' as to be unconscionable."). We agree with the district court that relative bargaining power is an appropriate consideration in determining unconscionability under the Michigan Uniform Commercial Code.

Other closely related factors suggested by the Michigan court in *Allen* for determining the presence of procedural unconscionability are the relative economic strength of the parties and the alternative sources of supply. With reference to the relative economic strength of the parties, we note that Harris Seed is a large national producer and distributor of seed, dealing here with independent, relatively small farmers. As to alternative sources of supply, the farmers were faced with a situation where all seed distributors placed disclaimers and exclusionary clauses in their contracts. Thus, this presents a situation where "goods [could] only be obtained from * * * several sources on non-competitive terms * * * and doing without [was] not a realistic alternative." *Allen,* supra, 171 N.W.2d at 692.[6]

Another pertinent factor considered by the district court in its unconscionability finding was that Harris Seed's salesman did not make Martin and Rick, who were uncounseled laymen, aware of the fact that the clauses in question altered significant statutory rights. Such a disclosure is an important consideration under Michigan law. Mallory v. Conida Warehouses, Inc., 134 Mich.App. 28, 350 N.W.2d 825, 827 (1984); cf. Johnson v. Mobil Oil Corp., 415 F.Supp. 264, 269 (E.D.Mich.1976) ("[b]efore a contracting party with * * * immense bargaining power * * * may limit its liability vis-a-vis an uncounseled layman * * * it has an affirmative duty to obtain the voluntary knowing assent of the other party.").

Furthermore, although the terms of the 1972 sale appeared to be the same as in previous years (unknown to Martin and Rick), Harris Seed decided to discontinue the hot water treatment of its cabbage seed, a standard practice for the previous twenty-six years. This decision by Harris Seed was one which had far-reaching consequences to the purchasers of its cabbage seed. As noted above, hot water treatment had been successful in preventing black leg in Washington State produced cabbage seed since 1947, and although Martin and Rick were unaware of the potential effects of black leg, or indeed even what black leg was, Harris Seed had considerable expertise in such matters.

Another important consideration is the fact that the presence of black leg in cabbage seed creates a *latent* defect. Although in many cases the fact that a latent defect is present seems to be dispositive, see Majors v. Kalo Laboratories, Inc., 407 F.Supp. 20 (M.D.Ala.1975); Corneli Seed Company v. Ferguson, 64 So.2d 162 (Fla.1953), we note only that it is important to the disposition of this case.

6. Harris Seed argued before the district court that the plaintiffs did not have to grow cabbage. However, we agree with the district court that, in light of the facts of this case, doing without would be an unrealistic alternative.

Significantly, in the present case not only was the defect latent, but it was also one which was within the control of Harris Seed to prevent. Even if Martin and Rick had been apprised of and understood the significance of Harris Seed's decision to discontinue hot water treatment, they would have been unable to detect the presence of the disease in the seed until their crop had developed into young plants. If Harris Seed were permitted to rely on the disclaimer and limitation clause to avoid liability under the facts of this case, the farmers who had no notice of, ability to detect, or control over the presence of the black leg could lose their livelihood. On the other hand, Harris Seed which had the knowledge, expertise and means to prevent the disease would only lose a few hundred dollars. Given the unique facts of this case, and giving "considerable weight" to the district court's decision that Michigan law would not permit the disclaimer and limitation clause to be enforced under such circumstances, we affirm the district court's finding of unconscionability.

* * *

NOTE

Suppose in *Martin* that the seller had conspicuously printed on the order form, seed catalog and seed package (1) a clear and accurate description of black leg disease and its economic consequences, (2) a statement that the cabbage seed had not been treated against the disease, (3) that the seller did not know whether the cabbage seed was infected with the disease, and (4) that the seller did not guarantee that the seed was not infected with the disease. If all other facts in *Martin* are unchanged should the court's conclusion be altered?

PROBLEM

Buyer was killed in an automobile accident caused by blowout of a tire on the vehicle in which Buyer was riding. Suit was brought by the administrator of Buyer's estate against Uniroyal, the manufacturer of the tire for breach of the following express warranty:

"The new U.S. Royal Master tire wraparound tread and pin stripe (1/2 inch) whitewall design is of such quality and reliability that U.S. Rubber Tire Company makes the following Guarantee:

"LIFETIME—Every such U.S. Royal Master tire of our manufacture, bearing our name and serial number, other than "seconds," is guaranteed to be free from defects in workmanship and material for the life of the original tread without limit as to time or mileage.

"ROAD HAZARD—In addition, every such U.S. Royal Master tire, when used in normal passenger car service, is guaranteed during the life of the original tread against blowouts, cuts, bruises, and similar injury rendering the tire unserviceable. Tires which are punctured or abused, by being run flat, improperly aligned, balanced, or inflated, cut by chains or obstructions on vehicle, damaged by fire, collision or vandalism, or by other means, and 'seconds' are not subject to the road hazard provision of this Guarantee.

"If our examination shows that such a U.S. Royal Master tire is eligible for adjustment under either the Lifetime or Road Hazard provision of this Guarantee, we will repair it or provide a new U.S. Royal Master tire at a fractional price computed on percentage of wear of original tread depth and then current U.S. suggested exchange price as follows: [There follow a rate chart and several additional paragraphs not relevant here.]

"This Guarantee does not cover consequential damage, and the liability of the manufacturer is limited to repairing or replacing the tire in accordance with the stipulations contained in this guarantee. No other guarantee or warranty, express or implied, is made."

Various advertisements of Uniroyal were also introduced into evidence. Included in these advertisements were the following statements:

"If it only saves your life once, it's a bargain."

"It could pay off some day. The day you hit a pothole at 70 miles an hour. The day you sweep around a tricky, rain-slicked curve. The day it's 90 degrees in the shade and you have to go 600 miles in a hurry. The day you pick up a nail and it's three in the morning."

"You're getting a brute of a carcass that's so strong, you can practically forget about blowouts."

Assume that the evidence supports a finding that the tire was not defective. Is there a breach of express warranty? Is the italicized portion of the warranty effective to limit Uniroyal's liability to repair or replacement of the tire? See § 2–719. See Collins v. Uniroyal, Inc., 64 N.J. 260, 315 A.2d 16 (1974).

3. FAILURE OF ESSENTIAL PURPOSE OF EXCLUSIVE REMEDY

MILGARD TEMPERING, INC. v. SELAS CORP. OF AMERICA

United States Court of Appeals, Ninth Circuit, 1990.
902 F.2d 703.

CYNTHIA HOLCOMB HALL, CIRCUIT JUDGE.

This appeal marks the end of nearly seven years of litigation over a "sure fire" glass tempering furnace purchased over ten years ago. The seller, Selas Corporation of America ("Selas") appeals the judgment of the district court awarding the buyer, Milgard Tempering, Inc. ("Milgard"), damages resulting from its failure to repair serious defects in the furnace.

*   *   *

Milgard Manufacturing, Inc. ("Milgard Manufacturing") cuts and installs glass for use in residential construction. On June 11, 1979, it entered into a carefully-negotiated contract with appellant Selas to purchase a horizontal batch tempering furnace. With Selas' consent, Milgard Manufacturing assigned the contract to appellee Milgard.

Under the contract, Selas agreed to design and manufacture the furnace for $1.45 million. Its design was complex, and in Selas' eyes, experimental. However, Selas marketed it as a working piece of equipment. The contract provided a $50,000 bonus if Selas delivered all the major components before January 31, 1980. It also provided a penalty of $5,000 per week (not to exceed a total of $25,000) for every week of late delivery after March 31, 1980. Selas failed to meet either deadline, having completed delivery of major components in November, 1982.

Selas agreed to assemble the furnace at Milgard's plant and to assist in a "debugging period" that both parties expected would end June or July 1980. The contract also required Selas, in a series of preacceptance tests, to demonstrate that the furnace was capable of achieving designated yield and cycle rates.[2] Section 28.5 of the contract limited Selas' liability for breach of warranty to repair or replacement of the furnace and barred liability for consequential damages. The parties modified the contract and agreed to forego the preacceptance tests and instead place the furnace in commercial production in July, 1980, thus making glass available for the "debugging" process.

---

    2. "Yield rate" refers to the percentage of saleable glass tempered in a given batch. "Cycle rate" refers to the speed at which glass of a particular size and thickness is tempered.

By January, 1982, Selas continued work on the furnace, but failed to achieve yield and cycle rates that substantially conformed with the contract specifications. Milgard then filed suit against Selas for breach of contract.

In March, 1982, the parties, without counsel, attempted to enter into a contractual agreement to settle the dispute. Under the proposed agreement, Selas would take over the tempering operation for 60 days to demonstrate the furnace's ability to achieve a 90% yield rate. It would also pay any operating losses Milgard incurred during that period. Then, if Milgard operated the furnace for six months without incident, Selas would "fine-tune" the furnace to achieve a 95% rate. Selas did the work and paid Milgard's operating losses.

Milgard then dismissed the suit without prejudice. However, during the six-month period, the furnace failed to perform to the specifications of either the contract or the attempted settlement agreement.

Milgard initiated a second lawsuit on March 4, 1983, alleging breach of contract and breach of warranty. On June 29, 1984, Judge Tanner in the district court granted summary judgment in favor of Selas. He found that the cap on consequential damages was a conscionable allocation of risk between sophisticated parties and therefore enforceable. He further held that the parties had reached an accord and satisfaction in March, 1982. The court awarded Selas the balance of the purchase price minus the delivery bonus. * * *

This court, in Milgard Tempering, Inc. v. Selas Corp. of America, 761 F.2d 553 (9th Cir.1985) [hereinafter *Milgard I*], reversed and remanded for trial. We held that the enforceability of the consequential damages limitation not only depended upon the conscionability of the provision when drafted, but upon the circumstances surrounding Selas' breach and inability to repair. Because these circumstances were disputed, we found summary judgment inappropriate. * * * We further noted that serious factual disputes surrounding the alleged accord and satisfaction required trial of that issue as well. * * *

On remand, after a five-week bench trial, Judge Bryan in the district court found that the furnace had never lived up to the specifications in the contract. He held that the limited repair remedy failed of its essential purpose and that Selas' default was sufficiently severe to expunge the cap on consequential damages. He awarded Milgard $1,076,268 in net damages. * * *

Selas appeals the judgment * * *. We affirm.

Selas first argues that the district court erred in ruling that the limited repair remedy failed of its "essential purpose" and that such failure lifted the contractual cap on consequential damages.

Section 28.5 of the contract limited Milgard's remedies in the event of breach of warranty to repair or replacement of the defective equipment. Such limitations on a party's remedies are permitted by Washington's version of the U.C.C., § 2–719(1)(a).

An exclusive or limited remedy, however, must be viewed against the background of § 2–719(2), which provides: "Where circumstances cause an exclusive or limited remedy to fail of its essential purpose, remedy may be had as provided in this Title." This section requires a court to examine the contract in general and the remedy provision in particular to determine what the remedy's essential purpose is and whether it has failed.

A limited repair remedy serves two main purposes. First, it serves to shield the seller from liability during her attempt to make the goods conform. Second, it ensures that the buyer will receive goods conforming to the contract specifications within a reasonable period of time. * * *

A contractual provision limiting the remedy to repair or replacement of defective parts fails of its essential purpose within the meaning of § 2–719(2) if the breaching manufacturer or seller is unable to make the repairs within a reasonable time period. * * *

It is not necessary to show negligence or bad faith on the part of the seller, for the detriment to the buyer is the same whether the seller's unsuccessful efforts were diligent, dilatory, or negligent. * * *

The district court in this case found that the furnace had never lived up to the specifications of the contract. Moreover, the court found that the few successful improvements were not made within a reasonable period of time, taking over two and one-half years. We agree that under these circumstances, the unreasonable delay and ultimate failure in repair made the repair remedy ineffective; thus, the remedy failed of its essential purpose.

Washington courts have not addressed the issue of whether failure of a limited repair remedy may serve to invalidate a consequential damages exclusion. Therefore, it is our responsibility to determine how the state's supreme court would resolve it. In undertaking this task, we may draw upon recognized legal sources including statutes, treatises, restatements, and published opinions. Molsbergen v. United States, 757 F.2d 1016, 1020 (9th Cir.), cert. denied, 473 U.S. 934, 106 S.Ct. 30, 87 L.Ed.2d 706 (1985). We may also look to "well-reasoned decisions from other jurisdictions." Takahashi v. Loomis Armored Car Serv., 625 F.2d 314, 316 (9th Cir.1980). We review the district court's construction of Washington law de novo. * * *

We begin our analysis with Fiorito Bros., Inc. v. Fruehauf Corp., 747 F.2d 1309, 1314–15 (9th Cir.1984). In that case, we held that under Washington law, the failure of a repair remedy does not automatically remove a cap on consequential damages. We predicted that Washington courts would take a case-by-case approach and examine the contract provisions to determine whether the exclusive remedy and damage exclusions are either "separable elements of risk allocation" or "inseparable parts of a unitary package of risk-allocation." Id. at 1315 (quoting district court).

If the exclusions are inseparable, we reasoned, a court's analysis should track the Official Comments to § 2–719(2), which explain that the subsection "relates to contractual arrangements which become oppressive by change of circumstances * * *." 747 F.2d at 1315. We then affirmed the district court's ruling that the seller's arbitrary and unreasonable refusal to live up to the limited repair clause "rendered the damages limitation clause oppressive and invalid." Id.

Fiorito relied heavily on this circuit's analysis of California U.C.C. § 2–719(2) in *Wilson,* 587 F.2d 1363. *Wilson* involved a contract between commercially sophisticated parties for a tunnel boring machine. The contract contained both a limited repair clause and a cap on consequential damages. After concluding that the repair remedy failed of its essential purpose within § 2–719(2), this court held that the bar to consequential damages remained enforceable. We explained:

> Parties of relatively equal bargaining power negotiated an allocation of their risks of loss. Consequential damages were assigned to the buyer, Wilson. The machine was a complex piece of equipment designed for the buyer's purposes. The seller Smith did not ignore his obligation to repair; he simply was unable to perform it. This is not enough to require that the seller absorb losses the buyer plainly agreed to bear. Risk shifting is socially expensive and should not be undertaken in the absence of a good reason. An even better reason is required when to so shift is contrary to a contract freely negotiated. *The default of the seller is not so total and fundamental as to require that its consequential damage limitation be expunged from the contract.*

Id. at 1375 (emphasis added). However this court in *Wilson* quickly pointed out that its holding was limited to the facts and was in no way intended to state that consequential damages caps always survive failure of limited repair remedies. Id. at 1375–76.

The district court in the instant case found Selas' default "fundamental, but not total." Nonetheless, it found the breach sufficiently fundamental to remove the cap on consequential damages. Selas claims that the court misunderstood the legal standard and that consequential damages may be allowed only when the seller's breach is both total and fundamental.[7]

We agree that the district court's characterization of the case law was flawed.[8] However, the analysis it employed was not. This court has found nothing magical about the phrase "total and fundamental default" in relation to U.C.C. § 2–719(2). In *Fiorito* we eschewed such wooden analysis, leaving "[e]ach case [to] stand on its own facts." Id., 747 F.2d at 1314 (quoting *Wilson*, 587 F.2d at 1376). We further expressed our distaste for talismanic analysis in *Milgard I*, finding t'.e "oppressive circumstances" analysis utilized by *Fiorito* and the [§ 2–719] Comments and the "total and fundamental" default analysis in *Wilson* in accord with each other. 761 F.2d at 556.

The task before the district court was to examine the remedy provisions and determine whether Selas' default caused a loss which was not part of the bargained-for allocation of risk. * * * This was the analysis that the district court actually employed.

We agree with the district court's decision to lift the cap on consequential damages. Milgard did not agree to pay $1.45 million in order to participate in a science experiment. It agreed to purchase what Selas represented as a cutting-edge glass furnace that would accommodate its needs after two months of debugging. Selas' inability to effect repair despite 2.5 years of intense, albeit injudicious,[9] effort caused Milgard losses not part of the bargained-for allocation of risk. Therefore, the cap on consequential damages is unenforceable.

* * *

For these reasons, the judgment of the district court is AF-FIRMED.

NOTE

The following quotation is taken from White & Summers, Uniform Commercial Code 526–528 (3d ed. 1988).

7. Selas does not challenge the court's finding that the limited repair remedy and the consequential damages limitation were part of a single risk-allocation package.

8. In his March 24 Oral Ruling, the district judge noted that while Wilson and RRX Indus. v. Lab–Con, Inc., 772 F.2d 543, 547 (9th Cir.1985), referred to "total and fundamental breach," *Fiorito* and *Milgard I* referred to consequential damages limitations becoming "oppressive by change of circumstances." He felt this circuit had developed two slightly different tests, the former being more stringent. * * *

9. Selas exacerbated the repair problem by not providing a qualified process engineer during the initial debugging period and stubbornly refusing to replace the unproven ircon transfer system with more reliable methods that were available. We therefore agree with the district court's conclusion that "Selas did not make a completely open and honest effort to bring the furnace into compliance with the contract requirements." Finding 88. However, as noted earlier, the question of Selas' good faith is not dispositive of this appeal.

There is now a deep division among the courts on the question whether consequential damages under section 2–715 are recoverable when a limited warranty has failed of its essential purpose and a separate contractual provision excludes liability for consequential economic loss. Many courts * * * emphasize the broad language of 2–719(2) and Comment 1 and allow recovery of consequential damages despite the exclusion. The Fourth Circuit has recently reached this result in a novel way. In Waters v. Massey–Ferguson, Inc. [775 F.2d 587 (4th Cir.1985)], a defective tractor prevented the plaintiff from timely planting his soybean crop and he was allowed to recover his lost profits despite a contractual exclusion of consequential damages. The court reasoned that since the express warranty assumed a successful repair effort, the 2–719(3) exclusion referred only to losses incurred by the buyer before the repair was effectuated. Because the parties premised the warranty provisions on certain repair, the damage exclusion only referred to consequential loss pending repair. Once repair became impossible, the limitation no longer applied.

A leading case on the other side is American Electric Power Co. v. Westinghouse Elec. Corp. [418 F.Supp. 435 (S.D. N.Y.1976)], where the court gave effect to a limitation of liability clause despite the failure of a repair or replace provision covering a $12 million generator. The court found "no reason to disturb the consensual allocation of business risk" embodied in a commercial agreement that was "painstakingly negotiated between industrial giants." In addition, the court was persuaded by the fact that this was not a case where the failure to repair left the plaintiff without a "minimum adequate remedy" because the contract provided for a damage recovery that was distinct from the limited warranty. Given this, the two provisions (i.e., the repair warranty and the exclusion of consequential damages) were deemed to be independent and the failure of the limited warranty under section 2–719(2) did not affect an exclusion under section 2–719(3) so long as that exclusion was not unconscionable.

In general we favor the American Electric Power line of cases. Those cases seem most true to the Code's general notion that the parties should be free to contract as they please. When the state intervenes to allocate the risk of consequential loss, we think it more likely that the loss will fall on the party who cannot avoid it at the lowest cost. This is particularly true when a knowledgeable buyer is using an expensive machine in a business setting. It is the buyer who operates the machine, adjusts it, and understands the consequences of its failure. Sometimes flaws in such machines are inherent and attributable to the seller's faulty design or manufacture. But the fault may also lie in buyer neglect, in inadequate training and supervision of the operators or even in intentional use in ways forbidden by the seller. Believing the parties to know their own interests best, we would leave the risk allocation to the parties.

Although the consumer purchaser usually makes a more sympathetic case for court intervention, we are disposed to apply American Electric in such cases as well. Of course, where the consequential damages consist of personal injury or property damage, the buyer plaintiff can recover in tort without regard to a 2–719 limitation. Where it consists of more conventional economic loss, the consumer may still be able to avoid the loss at the lowest cost.

F. PRIVITY

MORROW v. NEW MOON HOMES, INC.

Supreme Court of Alaska, 1976.
548 P.2d 279.

RABINOWITZ, CHIEF JUSTICE. This appeal raises questions concerning personal jurisdiction over, and the liability of, a nonresident manufacturer of a defective mobile home that was purchased in Alaska from a resident seller.

In October of 1969, Joseph R. and Nikki Morrow bought a mobile home from Golden Heart Mobile Homes, a Fairbanks retailer of mobile homes. A plaque on the side of the mobile home disclosed that the home had been manufactured in Oregon by New Moon Homes, Inc. The Morrows made a down payment of $1,800, taking out a loan for the balance of the purchase price from the First National Bank of Fairbanks. The loan amount of $10,546.49 plus interest of 9 percent per year, was to be repaid by the Morrows in 72 monthly installments of $190.13 each.

At the time of the purchase, the Morrows inspected the mobile home and noticed that the carpeting had not been laid and that several windows were broken. Roy Miller, Golden Heart's salesman, assured them that these problems would be corrected and later made good his assurances. Miller also told the Morrows that the mobile home was a "good trailer", " * * * as warm as * * * any other trailer." After the sale, Miller moved the Morrows' mobile home to Lakeview Terrace, set it up on the space the Morrows had rented, and made sure that the utilities were connected. Then the troubles started.

On the first night that the mobile home's furnace was in use, the motor went out and had to be replaced. The electric furnace installed by the manufacturer had been removed by someone who had replaced the original with an oil furnace. The furnace vent did not fit, and consequently the "stove pipe" vibrated when the furnace was running. Subsequent events showed the furnace malfunction was not the primary problem with the mobile home.

About four days after the mobile home had been set up, the Morrows noticed that the doors did not close all the way and that the windows were cracked. The bathtub leaked water into the middle bedroom. In March of 1970 when the snow on the roof began to melt, the roof leaked. Water came in through gaps between the ceiling and the wall panels, as well as along the bottom of the wallboard. A short circuit developed in the electrical system; the lights flickered at various times. When it rained, water came out of the light fixture in the hallway. Other problems with the mobile home included the following: the interior walls did not fit together at the corners; the paneling came off the walls; the windows and doors were out of square; the door frames on the bedroom doors fell off and the closet doors would not slide properly; the curtains had glue on them; and the finish came off the kitchen cabinet doors.

Despite all these problems, the Morrows continued to live in the mobile home and make the loan payments. Golden Heart Mobile Homes was notified many times of the difficulties the Morrows were having with their mobile home. Roy Miller, the Golden Heart salesman with whom the Morrows had dealt, did put some caulking around the bathtub, but otherwise he was of little assistance. Finally, sometime before April 1, 1970, Nikki Morrow informed Miller that if Golden Heart did not fix the mobile home the Morrows wanted to return it. Miller said the Morrows would "[h]ave to take it up with the bank." Subsequently, Golden Heart went out of business.

The First National Bank of Fairbanks was more sensitive to the Morrows' plight. Upon being informed by the Morrows that they intended to make no further payments on the mobile home, bank personnel went out and inspected the home several times. In addition, on May 27, 1970, the bank wrote to New Moon Homes, Inc. in Silverton, Oregon. Its letter informed New Moon of the problems the Morrows were having with their New Moon mobile home and asked whether New Moon expected to send a representative to Fairbanks since Golden Heart, the dealer, was no longer in business. Apparently, New Moon did not respond to the bank's letter.

A short time later the Morrows' counsel wrote a letter to New Moon Homes notifying New Moon that the Morrows intended to hold the company liable for damages for breach of implied warranties. About a month later the Morrows separated, with Nikki Morrow continuing to live in the mobile home. She continued to make payments to First National because she "couldn't afford

Alaskan rents." Nikki Morrow eventually moved out of the mobile home but made no effort to sell or rent it because she considered it "not fit to live in." In October of 1971 the Morrows filed this action against both New Moon Homes and Golden Heart Mobile Homes, alleging that defendants had breached implied warranties of merchantability and fitness for particular purpose in manufacturing and selling an improperly constructed mobile home.

* * *

The superior court granted the Morrows a default judgment against Golden Heart, but dismissed their claim against New Moon "for both failure of jurisdiction and failure of privity of contract." The Morrows then appealed from that portion of the superior court's judgment which dismissed their claim against New Moon.

The heart of this appeal concerns the remedies which are available to a remote purchaser against the manufacturer of defective goods for direct economic loss. The superior court held that the Morrows had no legal claim against New Moon because they were not in privity of contract with New Moon. The first argument advanced here by the Morrows amounts to an end run around the requirement of privity. The Morrows contend that their complaint asserted a theory of strict liability in tort. They further argue that they should have prevailed irrespective of any lack of privity of contract between New Moon and themselves, because lack of privity of contract is not a defense to a strict tort liability claim. It is true that in Bachner v. Pearson, 479 P.2d 319 (Alaska 1970), we held:

> that implied warranty and strict products liability are sufficiently similar to require that a complaint worded in terms of the former theory should be deemed to raise a claim under the latter theory.

Thus, although the Morrows' complaint sounded in breach of implied warranties, it also raised a strict liability claim if such a claim is legally cognizable against New Moon.

In Clary v. Fifth Avenue Chrysler Center, Inc., 454 P.2d 244 (Alaska 1969), Alaska adopted the Greenman v. Yuba Power Products, Inc.,[4] rule of strict products liability, which provides that

> [a] manufacturer is strictly liable in tort when an article he places on the market, knowing that it is to be used without inspection for defects, proves to have a defect that causes injury to a human being.[5]

---

4. 59 Cal.2d 57, 27 Cal.Rptr. 697, 377 P.2d 897 (1962).

5. 454 P.2d at 247, quoting Greenman v. Yuba Power Products, Inc., 59 Cal.2d 57, 27 Cal.Rptr. 697, 700, 377 P.2d 897, 900 (1962).

By its terms the *Greenman* formulation applies only when the defective product causes personal injury. Since the Morrows did not sustain any personal injuries which were caused by the defects in their mobile home, strict liability is seemingly unavailable to them in the instant case. However, the Morrows argue that strict liability should nonetheless apply in the situation where a consumer sues a manufacturer solely for economic loss attributable to the manufacturer's defective product. This precise contention presents a question of first impression in Alaska.

The issue whether strict liability in tort should extend to economic loss has prompted no small amount of discussion in legal journals. The two leading judicial opinions are probably Santor v. A and M Karagheusian, Inc., 44 N.J. 52, 207 A.2d 305 (1965), and Seely v. White Motor Co., 63 Cal.2d 9, 45 Cal.Rptr. 17, 403 P.2d 145 (1965). In the former case, Santor purchased from a retailer certain carpeting manufactured and advertised by Karagheusian. Almost immediately after the carpet was laid, Santor noticed an unusual line in it. As the pile wore down, the line became worse and two additional lines appeared. Since the retailer had gone out of business, Santor sued the manufacturer for damages for breach of the implied warranty of merchantability. In a unanimous decision, the Supreme Court of New Jersey held that the plaintiff, as the ultimate purchaser of defective carpeting, could maintain an action against the manufacturer on either of two theories, breach of implied warranty of reasonable fitness or strict liability in tort. Privity of contract was not necessary in order to pursue either theory, although damages were limited to loss of value of the carpeting. Although the opinion emphasized the widespread advertising carried on by Karagheusian, the *Santor* court made clear that "strict liability in tort is not conditioned upon advertising to promote sales."

> [W]hen the manufacturer presents his goods to the public for sale he accompanies them with a representation that they are suitable and safe for the intended use. * * * [S]uch a representation must be regarded as implicit in their presence on the market. * * * The obligation of the manufacturer thus becomes what in justice it ought to be—an enterprise liability, and one which should not depend on the intricacies of the law of sales. The purpose of such liability is to insure that the cost of injuries or damage, either to the goods sold or to other property, resulting from defective products, is borne by the makers of the products who put them in the channels of trade, rather than by the injured or damaged persons who ordinarily are powerless to protect themselves.

Barely four months after *Santor* came down, its strict liability holding was rejected by the Supreme Court of California in Seely v. White Motor Co., supra. Seely purchased a truck manufactured by White Motor Co. for use in his heavy duty hauling business. Upon taking possession of the truck, Seely found that it bounced violently. This "galloping" continued for 11 months until the truck's brakes failed and the truck overturned, sustaining in excess of $5,000 in damages. Seely was not injured in the incident.

Seely sued White Motor Co. seeking damages for the cost of repairing the truck and for both the money paid on the purchase price and the profits lost in his business because he was unable to make normal use of the truck. The Supreme Court of California affirmed the trial court's award of damages in the amount of the payments made plus lost profits, on the grounds that White Motor Co. had breached an express warranty to Seely, the ultimate purchaser. The majority opinion, written by Chief Justice Traynor, condemned in broad *dicta Santor's* application of strict liability principles to a case involving only economic loss:

> The distinction that the law has drawn between tort recovery for physical injuries and warranty recovery for economic loss is not arbitrary and does not rest on the "luck" of one plaintiff in having an accident causing physical injury. The distinction rests, rather, on an understanding of the nature of the responsibility a manufacturer must undertake in distributing his products. He can appropriately be held liable for physical injuries caused by defects by requiring his goods to match a standard of safety defined in terms of conditions that create unreasonable risks of harm. He cannot be held for the level of performance of his products in the consumer's business unless he agrees that the product was designed to meet the consumer's demands. A consumer should not be charged at the will of the manufacturer with bearing the risk of physical injury when he buys a product on the market. He can, however, be fairly charged with the risk that the product will not match his economic expectations unless the manufacturer agrees that it will.[9]

Seely appears to enjoy the support of the vast majority of the other courts which have considered the question whether strict liability in tort should extend to instances of economic loss.[10] We

9. 45 Cal.Rptr. at 23, 403 P.2d at 151.

10. See, e.g., Bright v. Goodyear Tire & Rubber Co., 463 F.2d 240 (9th Cir. 1972) (buyer of an automobile allegedly having defective tires could not sue under California law the tire manufacturer in strict liability because the buyer did not allege he had suffered physical injury); Eli Lilly & Co. v. Casey, 472 S.W.2d 598 (Tex.Civ.App.1971) (buyer of weed control chemical may not sue the manufacturer on a strict liability theo-ry to recover damages for economic loss); Melody Home Mfg. Co. v. Morrison, 455 S.W.2d 825 (Tex.Civ.App.1970) (purchaser of house trailer cannot hold manufacturer strictly liable in tort where only injury was economic loss); Rhodes Pharmacal Co. v. Continental Can Co., 72 Ill.App.2d 362, 219 N.E.2d 726 (1966) (damages for leaking aerosol cans could not be recovered from the manufacturer of the cans on the basis of strict liability, but held that case could proceed on theory of breach of

also prefer the result in *Seely,* although our reasoning differs slightly in emphasis from that of the *Seely* court. Under the Uniform Commercial Code the manufacturer is given the right to avail himself of certain affirmative defenses which can minimize his liability for a purely economic loss. Specifically, the manufacturer has the opportunity, pursuant to UCC § 2–316 to disclaim liability and under UCC § 2–719 to limit the consumer's remedies, although the Code further provides that such disclaimers and limitations cannot be so oppressive as to be unconscionable and thus violate UCC § 2–302. In addition, the manufacturer is entitled to reasonably prompt notice from the consumer of the claimed breach of warranties, pursuant to UCC § 2–607(3)(a).

In our view, recognition of a doctrine of strict liability in tort for economic loss would seriously jeopardize the continued viability of these rights. The economically injured consumer would have a theory of redress not envisioned by our legislature when it enacted the U.C.C., since this strict liability remedy would be completely unrestrained by disclaimer, liability limitation and notice provisions. Further, manufacturers could no longer look to the Uniform Commercial Code provisions to provide a predictable definition of potential liability for direct economic loss. In short, adoption of the doctrine of strict liability for economic loss would be contrary to the legislature's intent when it authorized the aforementioned remedy limitations and risk allocation provisions of Article II of the Code. To extend strict tort liability to reach the Morrows' case would in effect be an assumption of legislative prerogative on our part and would vitiate clearly articulated statutory rights. This we decline to do. Thus, we hold that the theory of strict liability in tort which we recognized in *Clary* does not extend to the consumer who suffers only economic loss because of defective goods.

The principal theory of liability advocated by the Morrows at trial was that New Moon had breached statutory warranties which arose by operation of law with the manufacture and distribution of this mobile home. Specifically, the Morrows rely upon § 2–314 and § 2–315 of the Uniform Commercial Code as enacted in Alaska. The former section provides for an implied warrant of "merchantability" in the sale of goods governed by the Code; the

implied warranty of fitness); Price v. Gatlin, 241 Or. 315, 405 P.2d 502 (1965) (wholesaler could not be held liable to the buyer on a strict liability theory for economic loss). * * *

Only one case follows the Santor decision, Cova v. Harley Davidson Motor Co., 26 Mich.App. 602, 182 N.W.2d 800 (1970). Notwithstanding lack of privity, other courts have permitted suits against the manufacturer of a product, based on a misrepresentation theory, where the product has been widely advertised and the buyer relied on the advertising. See, e.g., Ford Motor Co. v. Lonon, 217 Tenn. 400, 398 S.W.2d 240 (1966); Randy Knitwear, Inc. v. American Cyanamid Co., 11 N.Y.2d 5, 226 N.Y.S.2d 363, 181 N.E.2d 399 (1962). The misrepresentation theory has no application here because the Morrows have made no showing that they were aware of, or relied on, advertising by New Moon.

latter establishes an implied warranty that the goods are fit for the particular purpose for which they were purchased. The superior court was of the view that these Code warranties operated only for the benefit of those purchasing directly from a manufacturer or seller. Since the Morrows were not in privity of contract with New Moon, the superior court concluded that a warranty theory based on UCC § 2–314 and UCC § 2–315 could not serve as a basis for liability.

There is little question that the Code applies to the distribution of mobile homes. New Moon qualifies as a "merchant" within the meaning of the relevant section, UCC § 2–104 and mobile homes, being highly movable, are "goods" as defined in UCC § 2–105. Further, in George v. Willman, 379 P.2d 103 (Alaska 1963), we held that the implied warranty of merchantable quality established by the Code's predecessor, the Uniform Sales Act, was fully applicable to the sale of mobile homes. The result is no different under UCC § 2–314 and UCC § 2–315.

It is equally clear that in this jurisdiction the Morrows, as immediate purchasers, can recover against their seller for breach of the Code's implied warranties. Indeed, this was the theory upon which the default judgment against Golden Heart Mobile Homes was predicated. The critical question in this case is whether the Morrows, as remote purchasers, can invoke the warranties attributable to the manufacturer which arose when New Moon passed title of the mobile home to the next party in the chain of distribution. In other words, do the implied warranties of merchantability and fitness run from a manufacturer only to those with whom the manufacturer is in privity of contract?

Although sometimes criticized, the distinction between horizontal and vertical privity is significant in this case. The issue of horizontal privity raises the question whether persons other than the buyer of defective goods can recover from the buyer's immediate seller on a warranty theory. The question of vertical privity is whether parties in the distributive chain prior to the immediate seller can be held liable to the ultimate purchaser for loss caused by the defective product. The Code addresses the matter of horizontal privity in UCC § 2–318, extending the claim for relief in warranty to any " * * * person who is in the family or household of his buyer or who is a guest in his home if it is reasonable to expect that the person may use, consume, or be affected by the goods * * *." With regard to vertical privity, the Code is totally silent and strictly neutral, as Official Comment 3 to UCC § 2–318 makes eminently clear. The Code leaves to the courts the question of the extent to which vertical privity of contract will or will not be required.

This court has never previously confronted the question whether a requirement of privity of contract will preclude a purchaser from recovering against the original manufacturer on a theory of implied warranties. As mentioned previously, we expressly held in Clary v. Fifth Avenue Chrysler Center, Inc., 454 P.2d 244 (Alaska 1969), that a manufacturer is strictly liable in tort for personal injuries attributable to his defective goods. In approving a theory based on strict liability in tort, we stressed the efficacy, simplicity, and comprehensiveness of that theory. Appellees in *Clary* had urged this court to limit the consumer's source of redress to possible application of the statutory provisions governing sales warranties, particularly UCC § 2–314. This we declined to do. As we have noted, under the statutory scheme an injured consumer is required to give notice of the defect to the warrantor within a relatively short period of time, and potential liability may be circumscribed by express disclaimers from the manufacturer. The *Clary* court was concerned that such provisions might operate as a trap for the unwary, and it expressed a preference for a tort theory more solicitous of the needs of the consumer in the modern, prepackaged, mass merchandised market place. However, this preference was never intended to imply that reliance on the statutory warranty provisions was not available as an alternative vehicle for relief. There is nothing incompatible in affording parallel consumer remedies sounding in tort and in contract, and several jurisdictions which have adopted strict liability in tort also make available an implied warranty theory without regard to privity of contract.

The dispute here is whether the requirement of vertical privity of contract should be abolished in Alaska. This battle has already been waged in many jurisdictions, and the results are well known: the citadel of privity has largely toppled. The course of this modern development is familiar history and we need not recount it at length here. Contrived "exceptions" which paid deference to the hoary doctrine of privity while obviating its unjust results have given away in more recent years to an open frontal assault. The initial attack came in Spence v. Three Rivers Builders & Masonry Supply, Inc., 353 Mich. 120, 90 N.W.2d 873 (1958), but the leading case probably remains Henningsen v. Bloomfield Motors, Inc., 32 N.J. 358, 161 A.2d 69 (1960), in which the New Jersey Supreme Court held liable for personal injuries and property damages both the manufacturer of an automobile and the dealer who sold the vehicle. The rationale for the widespread abolition of the requirement of privity stems from the structure and operation of the free market economy in contemporary society; it was succinctly summed up not long ago by the Supreme Court of Pennsylvania: [31]

31. Kassab v. Central Soya, 432 Pa. 217, 246 A.2d 848, 853 (1968) (footnote omitted).

Courts and scholars alike have recognized that the typical consumer does not deal at arms length with the party whose product he buys. Rather, he buys from a retail merchant who is usually little more than an economic conduit. It is not the merchant who has defectively manufactured the product. Nor is it usually the merchant who advertises the product on such a large scale as to attract consumers. We have in our society literally scores of large, financially responsible manufacturers who place their wares in the stream of commerce not only with the realization, but with the avowed purpose, that these goods will find their way into the hands of the consumer. Only the consumer will use these products; and only the consumer will be injured by them should they prove defective.

The policy considerations which dictate the abolition of privity are largely those which also warranted imposing strict tort liability on the manufacturer: the consumer's inability to protect himself adequately from defectively manufactured goods, the implied assurance of the maker when he puts his goods on the market that they are safe, and the superior risk bearing ability of the manufacturer. In addition, limiting a consumer under the Code to an implied warranty action against his immediate seller in those instances when the product defect is attributable to the manufacturer would effectively promote circularity of litigation and waste of judicial resources. Therefore, we decide that a manufacturer may be held liable for a breach of the implied warranties of UCC § 2–314 and UCC § 2–315 without regard to privity of contract between the manufacturer and the consumer.

The more difficult question before this court is whether we should extend this abolition of privity to embrace not only warranty actions for personal injuries and property damage but also those for economic loss. Contemporary courts have been more reticent to discard the privity requirement and to permit recovery in warranty by a remote consumer for purely economic losses. In considering this issue we note that economic loss may be categorized into direct economic loss and consequential economic loss, a distinction maintained in the Code's structure of damage remedies. One commentator has summarized the distinction:

> Direct economic loss may be said to encompass damage based on insufficient product value; thus, direct economic loss may be "out of pocket"—the difference in value between what is given and received—or "loss of bargain"—the difference between the value of what is received and its value as represented. Direct economic loss also may be measured by costs of replacement and repair. Consequential economic loss in-

cludes all indirect loss, such as loss of profits resulting from inability to make use of the defective product.[35]

The claim of the Morrows in this case is one for direct economic loss.

A number of courts recently confronting this issue have declined to overturn the privity requirement in warranty actions for economic loss. One principal factor seems to be that these courts simply do not find the social and economic reasons which justify extending enterprise liability to the victims of personal injury or property damage equally compelling in the case of a disappointed buyer suffering "only" economic loss.[37] There is an apparent fear that economic losses may be of a far greater magnitude in value than personal injuries, and being somehow less foreseeable these losses would be less insurable, undermining the risk spreading theory of enterprise liability.

Several of the courts which have recently considered this aspect of the privity issue have found those arguments unpersuasive. We are in agreement and hold that there is no satisfactory justification for a remedial scheme which extends the warranty action to a consumer suffering personal injury or property damage but denies similar relief to the consumer "fortunate" enough to suffer only direct economic loss. Justice Peter's separate opinion in Seely v. White Motor Co., 63 Cal.2d 9, 45 Cal.Rptr. 17, 24, 403 P.2d 145, 152 (1965), persuasively establishes that the cleavage between economic loss and other types of harm is a false one, that each species of harm can constitute the "overwhelming misfortune" in one's life which warrants judicial redress. The Supreme Court of New Jersey is also in complete agreement with this view:

> From the standpoint of principle, we perceive no sound reason why the implication of reasonable fitness should be attached to the transaction and be actionable against the manufacturer where the defectively made product has caused personal injury and not actionable when inadequate manufacture has put a worthless article in the hands of an innocent

---

35. Note, Economic Loss in Products Liability Jurisprudence, 66 Colum.L. Rev. 917, 918 (1966).

37. See e.g., State ex rel. Western Seed Prod. Corp. v. Campbell, 250 Or. 262, 442 P.2d 215 (1968) and Price v. Gatlin, 241 Or. 315, 405 P.2d 502 (1965). In the latter case Justice Holman tried to elucidate the distinction in a concurring opinion at 504:

In establishing liability in personal injury cases courts have been motivated to overlook any necessity for privity because the hazard to life and health is usually a personal disaster of major proportions to the individual both physically and financially and something of minor importance to the manufacturer or wholesaler against which they can protect themselves by a distribution of risk through the price of the article sold. There has not been the same social necessity to motivate the recovery for strict economic losses where the damaged person's health, and therefore his basic earning capacity, has remained unimpaired.

See also Seely v. White Motor Co., 63 Cal.2d 9, 45 Cal.Rptr. 17, 23, 403 P.2d 145, 151 (1965).

purchaser who has paid the required price for it. In such situations considerations of justice require a court to interest itself in originating causes and to apply the principle of implied warranty on that basis, rather than to test its application by whether personal injury or simply loss of bargain resulted in the breach of the warranty. True, the rule of implied warranty had its gestative stirrings because of the greater appeal of the personal injury claim. But, once in existence, the field of operation of the remedy should not be fenced in by such a factor.[40]

The fear that if the implied warranty action is extended to direct economic loss, manufacturers will be subjected to liability for damages of unknown and unlimited scope would seem unfounded. The manufacturer may possibly delimit the scope of his potential liability by use of a disclaimer in compliance with UCC § 2–316 or by resort to the limitations authorized in UCC § 2–719. These statutory rights not only preclude extending the theory of strict liability in tort, supra, but also make highly appropriate this extension of the theory of implied warranties. Further, by expanding warranty rights to redress this form of harm, we preserve " * * * the well developed notion that the law of contract should control actions for purely economic losses and that the law of tort should control actions for personal injuries." [41] We therefore hold that a manufacturer can be held liable for direct economic loss attributable to a breach of his implied warranties, without regard to privity of contract between the manufacturer and the ultimate purchaser.[42] It was therefore error for the trial court to dismiss the Morrows' action against New Moon for want of privity.

Our decision today preserves the statutory rights of the manufacturer to define his potential liability to the ultimate consumer, by means of express disclaimers and limitations, while protecting the legitimate expectation of the consumer that goods distributed on a wide scale by the use of conduit retailers are fit for their intended use. The manufacturer's rights are not, of course, unfettered. Disclaimers and limitations must comport with the rele-

40. Santor v. A & M Karagheusian, Inc., 44 N.J. 52, 60, 207 A.2d 305, 309 (1965). See also Lang v. General Motors Corp., 136 N.W.2d 805 (N.D.1965); Note, Economic Loss in Products Liability Jurisprudence, 66 Colum.L.Rev. 917, 964 (1966).

41. Comment, The Vexing Problem of Purely Economic Loss in Products Liability: An Injury in Search of a Remedy, 4 Seton Hall L.Rev. 145, 175 (1972).

42. We recognize that the arguments against the abolition of privity are more compelling when the injury alleged is damages of a consequential nature many times the value of the manufacturer's product. See, e.g., Note, Economic Loss in Products Liability Jurisprudence, 66 Colum.L.Rev. 917, 965–66 (1965). We do not speak today to the issue of consequential economic loss, other than to note that UCC § 2–715 governs the recovery of such damages and requires, among other things, that said damages must have been foreseeable by the manufacturer. Adams v. J.I. Case Co., 125 Ill.App.2d 388, 261 N.E.2d 1 (1970).

vant statutory prerequisites and cannot be so oppressive as to be unconscionable within the meaning of UCC § 2–302. On the other hand, under the Code the consumer has a number of responsibilities if he is to enjoy the right of action we recognize today, not the least of which is that he must give notice of the breach of warranty to the manufacturer pursuant to UCC § 2–607(3)(a). The warranty action brought under the Code must be brought within the statute of limitations period prescribed in UCC § 2–725. If the action is for breach of the implied warranty of fitness for particular purpose, created by UCC § 2–315, the consumer must establish that the warrantor had reason to know the particular purpose for which the goods were required and that the consumer relied on the seller's skill or judgment to select or furnish suitable goods. In the case of litigation against a remote manufacturer, it would appear that often it will be quite difficult to establish this element of actual or constructive knowledge essential to this particular warranty.

In the case at bar the trial judge failed to enter written findings of fact, as are required by Alaska Rule of Civil Procedure 52. We cannot determine from the record whether the Morrows would have prevailed on a theory of breach of implied warranties had the trial court not erred in raising the barrier of privity. Trial was had over two years ago. We are therefore of the opinion that, if the dismissal for want of jurisdiction was also erroneous, a new trial is warranted at which the Morrows will have the opportunity to assert their warranty theories free from the confines of privity.

* * *

NOTE: METHOD OF MERCHANDISING

Modern merchandising affects fundamentally the nature of warranties and the way in which they are given. When a person buys a product at a retail store which is advertised by its manufacturer, what is the "basis of the bargain," and by whom is it determined? On this point the court in Lang v. General Motors Corp., 136 N.W.2d 805 (N.D.1965) stated,

It is perfectly clear * * * that where a sale is made under a trade name and where the manufacturer has conducted a national advertising campaign and sales are accomplished through local dealers, the demand for such products is created by the advertising of the manufacturer. The purpose of the advertising conducted by such manufacturer is to cultivate the ultimate consumer. Thus, where the article sold as a new article is defectively manufactured, the interests of the ultimate consumers can be protected only by eliminating the requirement of privity between the manufacturer and his dealers and the expected ultimate consumer. It would be unreasonable to hold that, if a buyer purchases, for example, a "Ford" or "Chevrolet" or "Cadillac" or "Chrysler" or any other make of automobile, no implied warranty of merchantable quality can be asserted by the purchaser against the manufacturer even though the particular car delivered as a new automobile is in such bad condition and so defective in materials or construction that it cannot be operated at all and is wholly useless or unsatisfactory for the ordinary purposes which such automobile is designed to serve.

Accordingly, under modern marketing conditions, when a manufacturer puts a new truck-tractor or other new product into the stream of trade and promotes its sale to the public, an implied warranty that it is reasonably fit and suitable for use, as such, accompanies such new vehicle into the hands of the ultimate buyer. Absence of privity between the manufacturer and buyer is immaterial.

In merchandising like that described in *Lang* express warranties are often specifically made by the manufacturer directly to the consumer. Representations of the manufacturer are meant to and do influence the decision of the consumer to purchase. The manufacturer may exercise considerable control over the price of the goods to the consumer and over other terms of sale. To hold the manufacturer liable for economic loss to the consumer for breach of express warranties or for the implied warranty of merchantability in this context is perfectly consistent with the purpose of warranty law to protect the expectations of the buyer that are fairly described by the bargain the buyer makes.

Much of modern merchandising is like that described in *Lang*. But a large part of merchandising is not done that way. Suppose Consumer bought a machine from Seller that was defective and unmerchantable and that Consumer suffered economic loss as a result. Assume that unmerchantability was caused by a defective component of the machine that was manufactured by Supplier who sold it to Seller. Or, assume that Seller is a mass merchandiser such as Sears or Montgomery-Ward which sold the defective machine under its own advertised trade name or brand, but the machine was manufactured by Supplier to Seller's specifications. In either case assume that Seller did not disclose to its customers that Supplier had any connection with the goods sold by Seller. Should Consumer be able to hold Supplier liable for breach of a warranty of merchantability concerning the component or the machine that it manufactured?

NOTE: NOTICE OF BREACH

Section 2–607(3)(a) provides that a buyer who has accepted goods "must within a reasonable time after he discovers or should have discovered any breach notify the seller of breach or be barred from any remedy." By virtue of this provision an action for breach of warranty can be maintained only if the required notice of breach has been given, and if the notice was timely.

Why is notice of breach required? Eastern Air Lines, Inc. v. McDonnell Douglas Corp., 532 F.2d 957 (5th Cir. 1976), dealt with the question of whether a buyer had to give notice to the seller that delays in delivery were a breach of contract. The court, applying the California UCC, stated:

> Even though § 2–607, by its very terms, governs 'any breach,' the trial court found the notice requirement to be inapplicable to delivery delays because a seller necessarily has knowledge of this sort of contract violation * * * the District Judge concluded that notice is useless where a breach is apparent to both parties. The trial court apparently was of the view that the sole function of § 2–607 is to inform the seller of hidden defects in his performance. Under this approach, the only purpose of notice is to provide the seller with an opportunity to remedy an otherwise unknown nonconforming tender. * * *
>
> Section 2–607's origins, however, reveal that it has a much broader function. The Code's notice requirement was derived from decisional law in California and several other states which sought to ameliorate the harsh common law rule that acceptance of goods by the buyer waived any and all of his remedies. * * * This approach was codified under § 49 of the Uniform Sales Act. * * *
>
> As Professor Williston, the author of the Sales Act, has noted, § 49 continued the common law rule treating a seller's tender of goods as an offer of them in full satisfaction. 3 S. Williston, Contracts § 714 (rev. ed. 1961). The buyer, though, was permitted to accept the offer without waiving any claims if he gave the seller prompt notice to this effect. * * * This approach reconciled the desire to give finality to transactions in which goods were accepted with the need to accommodate a buyer who, for business reasons, had to accept the tendered goods despite unsatisfactory performance by the seller. * * * Pre-UCC decisions in California and elsewhere, therefore, recognized that the primary purpose of notice is to inform the seller that, even though his tender has been accepted by the buyer, his performance is nonetheless considered a breach of contract. * * *
>
> Under § 49 it was irrelevant whether a seller had actual knowledge of a nonconforming tender. Instead, the critical question was whether the seller had been informed that the buyer considered him to be in breach. Consequently, in Professor Williston's words, 'the section is applicable not only to defects in quality but to breach of any promise or warranty, as for instance, *delaying time.*' 5 Williston on Contracts § 714 at

409 (3d ed. 1961) (emphasis supplied). Pre-UCC decisions, therefore, applied the notice requirement in delivery delay cases.
* * *

As the drafters of Article 2 acknowledge, § 2–607 continues the basic policies underlying § 49 of the Uniform Sales Act. Indeed, the notice requirement developed in pre-UCC cases is entirely consistent with the Article 2 goals of encouraging compromise and prompting good faith in commercial relations. As Comment 4 to § 2–607 indicates, the purpose of notice is not merely to inform the seller that his tender is nonconforming, but to open the way for settlement through negotiation between the parties. In the words of the California Supreme Court, 'the sound commercial rule' codified in § 2–607 also requires that a seller be reasonably protected against stale claims arising out of transactions which a buyer has led him to believe were closed. * * * Early warning permits the seller to investigate the claim while the facts are fresh, avoid the defect in the future, minimize his damages, or perhaps assert a timely claim of his own against third parties. * * *

Given these undeniable purposes, it is not enough under § 2–607 that a seller has knowledge of the facts constituting a nonconforming tender; he must also be informed that the buyer considers him to be in breach of the contract. The Code's notice requirement, then, is applicable to delivery delays as well as other breaches.

In cases involving dispute between "merchants" the courts tend to apply the notice requirement rigorously. In A. C. Carpenter, Inc. v. Boyer Potato Chips, 7 U.C.C.Rep. 493 (U.S.Dept.Agr. 1969), defective potatoes were delivered to Buyer on March 27. On April 2 Buyer discovered the defect and, on April 4 wrote to Seller who received the letter April 8. The potatoes were "dumped" on April 6. Held, notice not timely. The court stated:

The requirement that notice be given within a reasonable time is important, especially when the alleged breach concerns perishables. The purpose of the rule, as stated in the comment to the UCC, is to defeat commercial bad faith. If the seller is notified of a breach within a reasonable time he has opportunity to ascertain for himself the nature and extent of the breach by taking advantage of UCC § 2–515 which gives either party upon reasonable notification to the other, the right to inspect, test and sample the goods or have a third party perform similar functions for the purpose of ascertaining the facts and preserving evidence.

No particular form of notice is required. See Comment 4 to § 2–607. Oral notices are sufficient. Suppose Buyer sends seller a letter containing a proper notice but Seller does not receive it. Has Buyer "notified" Seller? § 1–201(26).

Actions to recover damages for personal injuries or injuries to property caused by a defect in goods sold by a seller can be brought under a warranty theory or in tort to impose strict liability for defective products. If the action is brought on a warranty theory, § 2–607(3)(a) applies. There is no comparable notice requirement if the action is in tort. The wording of § 2–607(3)(a) assumes a dispute between a buyer-plaintiff and a defendant from whom the goods were purchased. But the courts have allowed plaintiffs injured by defective goods to recover from a seller of the goods despite the fact that the plaintiff did not purchase the goods from the defendant or did not purchase the goods at all. The three alternative versions of § 2–318 reflect various limitations on defining the protected class of plaintiffs. It has proved difficult to apply the notice requirement to what are essentially tort injury claims brought under a warranty theory when there was no contract between the plaintiff and the defendant. The noncontract cases are simply not dealt with by § 2–607. Comment 5 to § 2–607 is a rather feeble attempt to bridge this void in the statute.

In warranty-based personal injury cases in which the plaintiff is not a buyer of the goods some courts have held that no notice is required. An example is Johnson v. Clemco Industries, 368 So.2d 509 (Ala.1979). The Alabama Supreme Court reasoned as follows: § 2–318 (Alternative B) gives to a nonbuyer plaintiff the protection of warranties covering defective goods that cause personal injury; the notice requirement of § 2–607(3)(a) specifically applies to "the buyer" and there is no other provision for anyone other than the buyer to give notice; it follows, therefore, that notice by a nonbuyer is not required by the UCC. The court refused to follow Comment 5 to § 2–607 which suggests the contrary.

In warranty-based personal injury cases in which the plaintiff was a buyer but did not purchase directly from the defendant the courts have often reduced the notice requirement to a meaningless formality. In Pritchard v. Liggett & Myers Tobacco Co., 295 F.2d 292 (3d Cir.1961), the plaintiff brought an action for breach of warranty under the Uniform Sales Act against a manufacturer of cigarettes alleging that his smoking of cigarettes from 1921 to 1953 caused lung cancer. In October 1954 the plaintiff's lawyer sent a notice to the defendant stating only that the plaintiff "elected to treat an injury he received as a result of smoking Chesterfield cigarettes as a breach of warranty on the part of Liggett & Myers Tobacco Co." The plaintiff's lung had been removed in December 1953. Sales Act § 49 contained a notice provision that is substantially the same as § 2–607(3)(a). The court held that the notice was adequate, stating that factors to be considered were the plaintiff's situation and whether the defendant had been prejudiced by the delay. In Palmer v. A.H. Robins Co., Inc., 684 P.2d 187 (Colo.1984), the plaintiff was fitted with an intrauterine contraceptive device by her gynecologist. The device was purchased from the defendant by the gynecologist. The plaintiff subsequently became pregnant and suffered a septic abortion caused by the intrauterine device. The Colorado Supreme Court relied on previous authority to the effect that a buyer was required to give notice of the breach of warranty only to that buyer's "immediate seller." That notice was sufficient to bind any remote seller. Because the gynecologist included the cost of the device in his fee for inserting the device he was the "immediate seller" to the plaintiff. When the gynecologist diagnosed the septic abortion as having been caused by the device he had notice of the breach of warranty. The court noted that any failure to give notice to the defendant did not prejudice the defendant in any way. Some courts hold that the bringing of the lawsuit is itself notice of the breach of warranty that will satisfy § 2–607(3)(a). In Maybank v. S.S. Kresge Co., 302 N.C. 129, 273 S.E.2d 681 (1981), the plaintiff was injured by a camera flash cube that exploded in her face while she was taking a picture. No notice of breach of warranty was given until suit was filed three years after the injury occurred. The court held that the three-year delay was not unreasonable as a matter of law and left the question to the jury. "While three years might conceivably be a per se unreasonable delay in a commercial context, differing considerations applicable in retail situations may mean that a delay of three years by a consumer in giving notice to a retail seller is within the bounds of a reasonable time." The court noted a lack of evidence that the defendant was prejudiced by the delay. Both the flashcube that exploded and the carton in which it was purchased were available as evidence.

Where a delay in giving notice can prejudice the seller the courts are more likely to disallow the plaintiff's claim. In San Antonio v. Warwick Club Ginger Ale Co., 104 R.I. 700, 248 A.2d 778 (1968), the plaintiff alleged that she bought a bottle of soda water and that she incurred a serious injury when the bottle broke in her hand when she tried to open it. Written notice was given to the bottler about four months after the accident, and "informal" notice was given to the retailer one year after the accident. The broken bottle had already been thrown away. The court held, as a matter of law, that notice to the retailer was not sufficient. The question of adequacy of the notice to the bottler was not presented in the case.

G. RELATIONSHIP BETWEEN WARRANTY AND TORT

EAST RIVER STEAMSHIP CORP. v. TRANSAMERICA DELAVAL, INC.

Supreme Court of the United States, 1986.
476 U.S. 858, 106 S.Ct. 2295, 90 L.Ed.2d 865.

JUSTICE BLACKMUN delivered the opinion of the Court.

In this admiralty case, we must decide whether a cause of action in tort is stated when a defective product purchased in a commercial transaction malfunctions, injuring only the product itself and causing purely economic loss. The case requires us to consider preliminarily whether admiralty law, which already recognizes a general theory of liability for negligence, also incorporates principles of products liability, including strict liability. Then, charting a course between products liability and contract law, we must determine whether injury to a product itself is the kind of harm that should be protected by products liability or left entirely to the law of contracts.

I

In 1969, Seatrain Shipbuilding Corp. (Shipbuilding), a wholly owned subsidiary of Seatrain Lines, Inc. (Seatrain), announced it would build the four oil-transporting supertankers in issue—the T.T. Stuyvesant, T.T. Williamsburgh, T.T. Brooklyn, and T.T. Bay Ridge. Each tanker was constructed pursuant to a contract in which a separate wholly owned subsidiary of Seatrain engaged Shipbuilding. Shipbuilding in turn contracted with respondent, now known as Transamerica Delaval, Inc. (Delaval), to design, manufacture, and supervise the installation of turbines (costing $1.4 million each) that would be the main propulsion units for the 225,000-ton, $125 million, ibid., supertankers. When each ship was completed, its title was transferred from the contracting subsidiary to a trust company (as trustee for an owner), which in turn chartered the ship to one of the petitioners, also subsidiaries of Seatrain. Queensway Tankers, Inc., chartered the Stuyvesant; Kingsway Tankers, Inc., chartered the Williamsburgh; East River Steamship Corp. chartered the Brooklyn; and Richmond Tankers, Inc., chartered the Bay Ridge. Each petitioner operated under a bareboat charter, by which it took full control of the ship for 20 or 22 years as though it owned it, with the obligation afterwards to return the ship to the real owner. See G. Gilmore and C. Black, Admiralty §§ 4-1, 4-22 (2d ed. 1975). Each charterer assumed responsibility for the cost of any repairs to the ships.

The Stuyvesant sailed on its maiden voyage in late July 1977. On December 11 of that year, as the ship was about to enter the Port of Valdez, Alaska, steam began to escape from the casing of the high-pressure turbine. That problem was temporarily resolved by repairs, but before long, while the ship was encountering a severe storm in the Gulf of Alaska, the high-pressure turbine malfunctioned. The ship, though lacking its normal power, was able to continue on its journey to Panama and then San Francisco. In January 1978, an examination of the high-pressure turbine revealed that the first-stage steam reversing ring virtually had disintegrated and had caused additional damage to other parts of the turbine. The damaged part was replaced with a part from the Bay Ridge, which was then under construction. In April 1978, the ship again was repaired, this time with a part from the Brooklyn. Finally, in August, the ship was permanently and satisfactorily repaired with a ring newly designed and manufactured by Delaval.

The Brooklyn and the Williamsburgh were put into service in late 1973 and late 1974, respectively. In 1978, as a result of the Stuyvesant's problems, they were inspected while in port. Those inspections revealed similar turbine damage. Temporary repairs were made, and newly designed parts were installed as permanent repairs that summer.

When the Bay Ridge was completed in early 1979, it contained the newly designed parts and thus never experienced the high-pressure turbine problems that plagued the other three ships. Nonetheless, the complaint appears to claim damages as a result of deterioration of the Bay Ridge's ring that was installed in the Stuyvesant while the Bay Ridge was under construction. In addition, the Bay Ridge experienced a unique problem. In 1980, when the ship was on its maiden voyage, the engine began to vibrate with a frequency that increased even after speed was reduced. It turned out that the astern guardian valve, located between the high-pressure and low-pressure turbines, had been installed backwards. Because of that error, steam entered the low-pressure turbine and damaged it. After repairs, the Bay Ridge resumed its travels.

II

The charterers' second amended complaint, filed in the United States District Court for the District of New Jersey, invokes admiralty jurisdiction. It contains five counts alleging tortious conduct on the part of respondent Delaval and seeks $3.03 million in damages for the cost of repairing the ships and for income lost while the ships were out of service. The first four counts, read liberally, allege that Delaval is strictly liable for the design defects in the high-pressure turbines of the Stuyvesant, the Williamsburgh, the Brooklyn, and the Bay Ridge, respectively. The fifth count alleges that Delaval, as part of the manufacturing process, negligently supervised the installation of the astern guardian valve on the Bay Ridge. The initial complaint also had listed Seatrain and Shipbuilding as plaintiffs and had alleged breach of contract and warranty as well as tort claims. But after Delaval interposed a statute of limitations defense, the complaint was amended and the charterers alone brought the suit in tort. The nonrenewed claims were dismissed with prejudice by the District Court. Delaval then moved for summary judgment, contending that the charterers' actions were not cognizable in tort.

The District Court granted summary judgment for Delaval, and the Court of Appeals for the Third Circuit, sitting en banc, affirmed. East River S.S. Corp. v. Delaval Turbine, Inc., 752 F.2d 903 (1985). The Court of Appeals held that damage solely to a defective product is actionable in tort if the defect creates an unreasonable risk of harm to persons or property other than the product itself, and harm materializes. Disappointments over the product's quality, on the other hand, are protected by warranty law. Id., at 908, 909–910. The charterers were dissatisfied with product quality: the defects involved gradual and unnoticed deterioration of the turbines' component parts, and the only risk created was that the turbines would operate at a lower capacity. Id., at 909. See Pennsylvania Glass Sand Corp. v. Caterpillar Tractor Co., 652 F.2d 1165, 1169–1170 (CA3 1981). Therefore, neither the negligence nor the strict liability claims were cognizable.

Judge Garth concurred on "grounds somewhat different," 752 F.2d, at 910, and Judge Becker, joined by Judge Higginbotham, concurred in part and dissented in part. Id., at 913. Although Judge Garth agreed with the majority's analysis on the merits, he found no strict liability claim presented because the charterers had failed to allege unreasonable danger or demonstrable injury.

Judge Becker largely agreed with the majority's approach, but would permit recovery for a "near miss," where the risk existed but no calamity occurred. He felt that the first count, concerning the Stuyvesant, stated a cause of action in tort. The exposure of the ship to a severe storm when the ship was unable to operate at full power due to the defective part created an unreasonable risk of harm.

We granted certiorari to resolve a conflict among the Courts of Appeals sitting in admiralty.

III

* * *

B

The torts alleged ＊ ＊ ＊ clearly fall within the admiralty jurisdiction.

＊ ＊ ＊

C

With admiralty jurisdiction comes the application of substantive admiralty law. ＊ ＊ ＊ Absent a relevant statute, the general maritime law, as developed by the judiciary, applies. ＊ ＊ ＊ Drawn from state [2] and federal sources, the general maritime law is an amalgam of traditional common-law rules, modifications of those rules, and newly created rules. ＊ ＊ ＊ This Court has developed a body of maritime tort principles, ＊ ＊ ＊ and is now asked to incorporate products-liability concepts, long a part of the common law of torts, into the general maritime law.

＊ ＊ ＊

The Courts of Appeals sitting in admiralty overwhelmingly have adopted concepts of products liability, based both on negligence, Sieracki v. Seas Shipping Co., 149 F.2d 98, 99–100 (CA3 1945), aff'd on other grounds, 328 U.S. 85, 66 S.Ct. 872, 90 L.Ed. 1099 (1946), and on strict liability, Pan-Alaska Fisheries, Inc. v. Marine Constr. & Design Co., 565 F.2d 1129, 1135 (CA9 1977) (adopting Restatement (Second) of Torts § 402A (1965)). Indeed, the Court of Appeals for the Third Circuit previously had stated that the question whether principles of strict products liability are part of maritime law "is no longer seriously contested." Ocean Barge Transport Co. v. Hess Oil Virgin Islands Corp., 726 F.2d 121, 123 (CA3 1984) (citing cases).

We join the Courts of Appeals in recognizing products liability, including strict liability, as part of the general maritime law. This Court's precedents relating to injuries of maritime workers long have pointed in that direction. See Seas Shipping Co. v. Sieracki, 328 U.S. 85, 94, 66 S.Ct. 872, 877, 90 L.Ed. 1099 (1946) (strict liability for unseaworthiness); Italia Societa per Azioni di Navigazione v. Oregon Stevedoring Co., 376 U.S. 315, 322, 84 S.Ct. 748, 752, 11 L.Ed.2d 732 (1964) (strict liability for breach of implied warranty of workmanlike service). The Court's rationale in those cases—that strict liability should be imposed on the party best able to protect persons from hazardous equipment—is equally applicable when the claims are based on products liability. Com-

2. The charterers do not ask us to defer to the law of New Jersey, the forum State. Nor is application of state-law principles required here. New Jersey lacks any "pressing and significant" interest in the tort action. See Kossick v. United Fruit Co., 365 U.S. 731, 739, 81 S.Ct. 886, 892, 6 L.Ed. 2d 56 (1961). In any event, reliance on state law would not help the charterers' case, since it mandates the same conclusion reached by the District Court and the Court of Appeals: that Delaval had no tort duty to the charterers. See Spring Motors Distributors, Inc. v. Ford Motor Co., 98 N.J. 555, 579, 489 A.2d 660, 672 (1985).

pare *Sieracki,* 328 U.S., at 93–94, 66 S.Ct., at 876–877, with Escola v. Coca Cola Bottling Co., 24 Cal.2d 453, 462, 150 P.2d 436, 441 (1944) (concurring opinion). And to the extent that products actions are based on negligence, they are grounded in principles already incorporated into the general maritime law. See Kermarec v. Compagnie Generale Transatlantique, 358 U.S., at 632, 79 S.Ct., at 410. Our incorporation of products liability into maritime law, however, is only the threshold determination to the main issue in this case.

IV

Products liability grew out of a public policy judgment that people need more protection from dangerous products than is afforded by the law of warranty. See Seely v. White Motor Co., 63 Cal.2d 9, 15, 45 Cal.Rptr. 17, 21, 403 P.2d 145, 149 (1965). It is clear, however, that if this development were allowed to progress too far, contract law would drown in a sea of tort. See G. Gilmore, The Death of Contract 87–94 (1974). We must determine whether a commercial product injuring itself is the kind of harm against which public policy requires manufacturers to protect, independent of any contractual obligation.

A

The paradigmatic products-liability action is one where a product "reasonably certain to place life and limb in peril," distributed without reinspection, causes bodily injury. See, e.g., MacPherson v. Buick Motor Co., 217 N.Y. 382, 389, 111 N.E. 1050, 1051, 1053 (1916). The manufacturer is liable whether or not it is negligent because "public policy demands that responsibility be fixed wherever it will most effectively reduce the hazards to life and health inherent in defective products that reach the market." Escola v. Coca Cola Bottling Co., 24 Cal.2d, at 462, 150 P.2d, at 441 (concurring opinion).

For similar reasons of safety, the manufacturer's duty of care was broadened to include protection against property damage. See Marsh Wood Products Co. v. Babcock & Wilcox Co., 207 Wis. 209, 226, 240 N.W. 392, 399 (1932); Genesee County Patrons Fire Relief Assn. v. L. Sonneborn Sons, Inc., 263 N.Y. 463, 469–473, 189 N.E. 551, 553–555 (1934). Such damage is considered so akin to personal injury that the two are treated alike. See Seely v. White Motor Co., 63 Cal.2d, at 19, 45 Cal.Rptr., at 24, 403 P.2d, at 152.

In the traditional "property damage" cases, the defective product damages other property. In this case, there was no damage to "other" property. Rather, the first, second, and third counts allege that each supertanker's defectively designed turbine components damaged only the turbine itself. Since each turbine was supplied by Delaval as an integrated package, each is properly regarded as a single unit. "Since all but the very simplest of machines have component parts, [a contrary] holding would require a finding of 'property damage' in virtually every case where a product damages itself. Such a holding would eliminate the distinction between warranty and strict products liability." Northern Power & Engineering Corp. v. Caterpillar Tractor Co., 623 P.2d 324, 330 (Alaska 1981). The fifth count also alleges injury to the product itself. Before the high-pressure and low-pressure turbines could become an operational propulsion system, they were connected to piping and valves under the supervision of Delaval personnel. Delaval's supervisory obligations were part of its manufacturing agreement. The fifth count thus can best be read to allege that Delaval's negligent manufacture of the propulsion system—by allowing the installation in reverse of the astern guardian valve—damaged the propulsion system. Cf. Lewis v. Timco, Inc., 736 F.2d 163, 165–166 (CA5 1984). Obviously, damage to a product itself has certain attributes of a products-liability claim. But the injury suffered—the failure of the product to function properly—is the essence of a warranty action, through which a contracting party can seek to recoup the benefit of its bargain.

B

The intriguing question whether injury to a product itself may be brought in tort has spawned a variety of answers.[3] At one end of the spectrum, the case that created the majority land-based approach, Seely v. White Motor Co., 63 Cal.2d 9, 45 Cal.Rptr. 17, 403 P.2d 145 (1965) (defective truck), held that preserving a proper role for the law of warranty precludes imposing tort liability if a defective product causes purely monetary harm. See also Jones & Laughlin Steel Corp. v. Johns-Manville Sales Corp., 626 F.2d 280, 287 and n. 13 (CA3 1980) (citing cases).

At the other end of the spectrum is the minority land-based approach, whose progenitor, Santor v. A and M Karagheusian, Inc., 44 N.J. 52, 66–67, 207 A.2d 305, 312–313 (1965) (marred carpeting), held that a manufacturer's duty to make nondefective products encompassed injury to the product itself, whether or not the defect created an unreasonable risk of harm.[4] See also La-

---

3. The question is not answered by the Restatement (Second) of Torts §§ 395 and 402A (1965), or by the Uniform Commercial Code, see Wade, Is Section 402A of the Second Restatement of Torts Preempted by the UCC and Therefore Unconstitutional?, 42 Tenn.L.Rev. 123 (1974).

* * *

4. Interestingly, the New Jersey and California Supreme Courts have each taken what appears to be a step in the direction of the other since *Santor* and *Seely*. In Spring Motors Distributors, Inc. v. Ford Motor Co., 98 N.J., at 579, 489 A.2d, at 672, the New Jersey court rejected *Santor* in the commercial context. And in J'Aire Corp. v. Gregory, 24 Cal.3d 799, 157 Cal.Rptr. 407, 598 P.2d 60 (1979), the California court recognized a cause of action for negligent interference with prospective economic advantage.

Crosse v. Schubert, 72 Wis.2d 38, 44–45, 240 N.W.2d 124, 127–128 (1976). The courts adopting this approach, including the majority of the Courts of Appeals sitting in admiralty that have considered the issue,[5] e.g., Emerson G.M. Diesel, Inc. v. Alaskan Enterprise, 732 F.2d 1468 (CA9 1984), find that the safety and insurance rationales behind strict liability apply equally where the losses are purely economic. These courts reject the *Seely* approach because they find it arbitrary that economic losses are recoverable if a plaintiff suffers bodily injury or property damage, but not if a product injures itself. They also find no inherent difference between economic loss and personal injury or property damage, because all are proximately caused by the defendant's conduct. Further, they believe recovery for economic loss would not lead to unlimited liability because they think a manufacturer can predict and insure against product failure. See Emerson G.M. Diesel, Inc. v. Alaskan Enterprise, 732 F.2d, at 1474.

Between the two poles fall a number of cases that would permit a products-liability action under certain circumstances when a product injures only itself. These cases attempt to differentiate between "the disappointed users * * * and the endangered ones," Russell v. Ford Motor Co., 281 Or. 587, 595, 575 P.2d 1383, 1387 (1978), and permit only the latter to sue in tort. The determination has been said to turn on the nature of the defect, the type of risk, and the manner in which the injury arose. See Pennsylvania Glass Sand Corp. v. Caterpillar Tractor Co., 652 F.2d 1165, 1173 (CA3 1981) (relied on by the Court of Appeals in this case). The Alaska Supreme Court allows a tort action if the defective product creates a situation potentially dangerous to persons or other property, and loss occurs as a proximate result of that danger and under dangerous circumstances. Northern Power & Engineering Corp. v. Caterpillar Tractor Co., 623 P.2d 324, 329 (1981).

We find the intermediate and minority land-based positions unsatisfactory. The intermediate positions, which essentially turn on the degree of risk, are too indeterminate to enable manufacturers easily to structure their business behavior. Nor do we find persuasive a distinction that rests on the manner in which the product is injured. We realize that the damage may be qualitative, occurring through gradual deterioration or internal breakage. Or it may be calamitous. Compare Morrow v. New Moon Homes, Inc., 548 P.2d 279 (Alaska 1976), with Cloud v. Kit Mfg. Co., 563 P.2d 248, 251 (Alaska 1977). But either way, since by definition no person or other property is damaged, the resulting

5. Most of the admiralty cases concerned fishing vessels. See Emerson G.M. Diesel, Inc., v. Alaskan Enterprise, 732 F.2d 1468, 1472 (CA9 1984) (relying on solicitude for fishermen as a reason for a more protective approach). Delaval concedes that the courts, see Carbone v. Ursich, 209 F.2d 178, 182 (CA9 1953), and Congress, see 46 U.S.C. § 533, at times have provided special protection for fishermen. This case involves no fishermen.

loss is purely economic. Even when the harm to the product itself occurs through an abrupt, accident-like event, the resulting loss due to repair costs, decreased value, and lost profits is essentially the failure of the purchaser to receive the benefit of its bargain— traditionally the core concern of contract law. See E. Farnsworth, Contracts § 12.8, pp. 839–840 (1982).

We also decline to adopt the minority land-based view espoused by *Santor* and *Emerson*. Such cases raise legitimate questions about the theories behind restricting products liability, but we believe that the countervailing arguments are more powerful. The minority view fails to account for the need to keep products liability and contract law in separate spheres and to maintain a realistic limitation on damages.

C

Exercising traditional discretion in admiralty, see Pope & Talbot, Inc. v. Hawn, 346 U.S. 406, 409, 74 S.Ct. 202, 204, 98 L.Ed. 143 (1953), we adopt an approach similar to *Seely* and hold that a manufacturer in a commercial relationship has no duty under either a negligence or strict products-liability theory to prevent a product from injuring itself.

"The distinction that the law has drawn between tort recovery for physical injuries and warranty recovery for economic loss is not arbitrary and does not rest on the 'luck' of one plaintiff in having an accident causing physical injury. The distinction rests, rather, on an understanding of the nature of the responsibility a manufacturer must undertake in distributing his products." Seely v. White Motor Co., 63 Cal.2d, at 18, 45 Cal.Rptr., at 23, 403 P.2d, at 151. When a product injures only itself the reasons for imposing a tort duty are weak and those for leaving the party to its contractual remedies are strong.

The tort concern with safety is reduced when an injury is only to the product itself. When a person is injured, the "cost of an injury and the loss of time or health may be an overwhelming misfortune," and one the person is not prepared to meet. Escola v. Coca Cola Bottling Co., 24 Cal.2d, at 462, 150 P.2d, at 441 (concurring opinion). In contrast, when a product injures itself, the commercial user stands to lose the value of the product, risks the displeasure of its customers who find that the product does not meet their needs, or, as in this case, experiences increased costs in performing a service. Losses like these can be insured. See 10A Couch on Insurance §§ 42:385–42:401, 42:414–417 (2d ed. 1982); 7 Benedict on Admiralty, Form No. 1.16–7 (7th ed. 1985); 5A Appleman, Insurance Law and Practice § 3252 (1970). Society need not presume that a customer needs special protection. The increased cost to the public that would result from holding a manufacturer liable in tort for injury to the product itself is not justified. Cf. United States v. Carroll Towing Co., 159 F.2d 169, 173 (CA2 1947).

Damage to a product itself is most naturally understood as a warranty claim. Such damage means simply that the product has not met the customer's expectations, or, in other words, that the customer has received "insufficient product value." See J. White and R. Summers, Uniform Commercial Code 406 (2d ed. 1980). The maintenance of product value and quality is precisely the purpose of express and implied warranties.[7] See UCC § 2–313 (express warranty), § 2–314 (implied warranty of merchantability), and § 2–315 (warranty of fitness for a particular purpose). Therefore, a claim of a nonworking product can be brought as a breach-of-warranty action. Or, if the customer prefers, it can reject the product or revoke its acceptance and sue for breach of contract. See UCC §§ 2–601, 2–608, 2–612.

Contract law, and the law of warranty in particular, is well suited to commercial controversies of the sort involved in this case because the parties may set the terms of their own agreements.[8] The manufacturer can restrict its liability, within limits, by disclaiming warranties or limiting remedies. See UCC §§ 2–316, 2–719. In exchange, the purchaser pays less for the product. Since a commercial situation generally does not involve large disparities in bargaining power, cf. Henningsen v. Bloomfield Motors, Inc., 32 N.J. 358, 161 A.2d 69 (1960), we see no reason to intrude into the parties' allocation of the risk.

While giving recognition to the manufacturer's bargain, warranty law sufficiently protects the purchaser by allowing it to obtain the benefit of its bargain. See J. White and R. Summers, supra, ch. 10. The expectation damages available in warranty for purely economic loss give a plaintiff the full benefit of its bargain by compensating for foregone business opportunities. See Fuller and Perdue, The Reliance Interest in Contract Damages: 1, 46

---

7. If the charterers' claims were brought as breach-of-warranty actions, they would not be within the admiralty jurisdiction. Since contracts relating to the construction of or supply of materials to a ship are not within the admiralty jurisdiction, see Thames Towboat Co. v. The Schooner "Francis McDonald", 254 U.S. 242, 243, 41 S.Ct. 65, 66, 65 L.Ed. 245 (1920); Kossick v. United Fruit Co., 365 U.S. 731, 735, 81 S.Ct. 886, 889, 6 L.Ed.2d 56 (1961), neither are warranty claims grounded in such contracts. See 1 Benedict, Admiralty § 188, p. 11–36 (7th ed. 1985). State law would govern the actions. See North Pacific S.S. Co. v. Hall Brothers Marine Railway & Shipbuilding Co., 249 U.S. 119, 127, 39 S.Ct. 221, 223, 63 L.Ed. 510 (1919). In particular the Uni-form Commercial Code, which has been adopted by 49 States, would apply.

8. We recognize, of course, that warranty and products liability are not static bodies of law and may overlap. In certain situations, for example, the privity requirement of warranty has been discarded. E.g., Henningsen v. Bloomfield Motors, Inc., 32 N.J. 358, 380–384, 161 A.2d 69, 81–84 (1960). In other circumstances, a manufacturer may be able to disclaim strict tort liability. See, e.g., Keystone Aeronautics Corp. v. R.J. Enstrom Corp., 499 F.2d 146, 149 (CA3 1974). Nonetheless, the main currents of tort law run in different directions from those of contract and warranty, and the latter seem to us far more appropriate for commercial disputes of the kind involved here.

Yale L.J. 52, 60–63 (1936); R. Posner, Economic Analysis of Law
§ 4.8 (3d ed. 1986). Recovery on a warranty theory would give the
charterers their repair costs and lost profits, and would place
them in the position they would have been in had the turbines
functioned properly.[9] See Hawkins v. McGee, 84 N.H. 114, 146 A.
641 (1929). Thus, both the nature of the injury and the resulting
damages indicate it is more natural to think of injury to a product
itself in terms of warranty.

A warranty action also has a built-in limitation on liability,
whereas a tort action could subject the manufacturer to damages
of an indefinite amount. The limitation in a contract action
comes from the agreement of the parties and the requirement that
consequential damages, such as lost profits, be a foreseeable result
of the breach. See Hadley v. Baxendale, 9 Ex. 341, 156 Eng.Rep.
145 (1854). In a warranty action where the loss is purely economic, the limitation derives from the requirements of foreseeability
and of privity, which is still generally enforced for such claims in a
commercial setting. See UCC § 2–715; J. White and R. Summers,
Uniform Commercial Code 389, 396, 406–410 (2d ed. 1980).

In products-liability law, where there is a duty to the public
generally, foreseeability is an inadequate brake. Cf. Petitions of
Kinsman Transit Co., 388 F.2d 821 (CA2 1968). See also Perlman,
Interference with Contract and Other Economic Expectancies: A
Clash of Tort and Contract Doctrine, 49 U.Chi.L.Rev. 61, 71–72
(1982). Permitting recovery for all foreseeable claims for purely
economic loss could make a manufacturer liable for vast sums. It
would be difficult for a manufacturer to take into account the
expectations of persons downstream who may encounter its product. In this case, for example, if the charterers—already one step
removed from the transaction—were permitted to recover their
economic losses, then the companies that subchartered the ships
might claim their economic losses from the delays, and the charterers' customers also might claim their economic losses, and so
on. "The law does not spread its protection so far." Robins Dry
Dock & Repair Co. v. Flint, 275 U.S. 303, 309, 48 S.Ct. 134, 135, 72
L.Ed. 290 (1927).

And to the extent that courts try to limit purely economic
damages in tort, they do so by relying on a far murkier line, one
that negates the charterers' contention that permitting such recovery under a products-liability theory enables admiralty courts

---

9. In contrast, tort damages generally compensate the plaintiff for loss and
return him to the position he occupied
before the injury. Cf. Sullivan v.
O'Connor, 363 Mass. 579, 584–586, 588,
n. 6, 296 N.E.2d 183, 187–188, 189, n. 6
(1973); Prosser, The Borderland of Tort
and Contract, in Selected Topics on the
Law of Torts 380, 424–427 (Thomas M.
Cooley Lectures, Fourth Series 1953).
Tort damages are analogous to reliance
damages, which are awarded in contract when there is particular difficulty
in measuring the expectation interest.
See, e.g., Security Store & Mfg. Co. v.
American Railways Express Co., 227
Mo.App. 175, 51 S.W.2d 572 (1932).

to avoid difficult linedrawing. Cf. Ultramares Corp. v. Touche, 255 N.Y. 170, 174 N.E. 441 (1931); State ex rel. Guste v. M/V Testbank, 752 F.2d 1019, 1046–1052 (CA5 1985) (en banc) (dissenting opinion), cert. pending, No. 84–1808.

D

For the first three counts, the defective turbine components allegedly injured only the turbines themselves. Therefore, a strict products-liability theory of recovery is unavailable to the charterers. Any warranty claims would be subject to Delaval's limitation, both in time and scope, of its warranty liability. The record indicates that Seatrain and Delaval reached a settlement agreement. We were informed that these charterers could not have asserted the warranty claims. Even so, the charterers should be left to the terms of their bargains, which explicitly allocated the cost of repairs.

In the charterers' agreements with the owners, the charterers took the ships in "as is" condition, after inspection, and assumed full responsibility for them, including responsibility for maintenance and repairs and for obtaining certain forms of insurance. In a separate agreement between each charterer and Seatrain, Seatrain agreed to guarantee certain payments and covenants by each charterer to the owner. The contractual responsibilities thus were clearly laid out. There is no reason to extricate the parties from their bargain.

Similarly, in the fifth count, alleging the reverse installation of the astern guardian valve, the only harm was to the propulsion system itself rather than to persons or other property. Even assuming that Delaval's supervision was negligent, as we must on this summary judgment motion, Delaval owed no duty under a products-liability theory based on negligence to avoid causing purely economic loss. Cf. Flintkote Co. v. Dravo Corp., 678 F.2d 942 (CA11 1982); S.M. Wilson & Co. v. Smith International, Inc., 587 F.2d 1363 (CA9 1978). Thus, whether stated in negligence or strict liability, no products-liability claim lies in admiralty when the only injury claimed is economic loss.

While we hold that the fourth count should have been dismissed, we affirm the entry of judgment for Delaval.

H. STATUTE OF LIMITATIONS

---

1. PERSONAL INJURY

DAVIDSON LUMBER SALES, INC. v. BONNEVILLE INVESTMENT, INC.

Supreme Court of Utah, 1990.
794 P.2d 11.

STEWART, JUSTICE:

* * *

I. FACTS

Bonneville designed and constructed a laminated wood beam and, on April 29, 1976, sold it to Davidson Lumber. Approximately two months after the sale, Davidson sold the beam to Quality Construction. The beam was eventually installed by Abrams Construction Co. in a building in Las Vegas, Nevada. The owner of the building leased the building to Thrifty Corporation for the operation of a drugstore.

On October 20, 1978, the roof of the building collapsed, causing property damage in excess of $80,000 to Thrifty's drugstore and its contents. On May 21, 1979, Thrifty filed suit in California against several parties, including Davidson. Against Davidson, Thrifty's lawsuit alleged claims for relief based on strict liability in tort, breach of implied warranties of merchantability and fitness for a particular purpose, and negligence. The suit sought damages for the loss of inventory, fixtures, and equipment, for lost profits, and for the costs of repair, salvage, and cleanup. Thrifty did not seek damages for replacement of the beam, since the building belonged to the lessor.

On February 18, 1981, Davidson filed a cross-claim against Bonneville in the California action, but it was dismissed July 28, 1982, because of lack of personal jurisdiction over Bonneville. On August 4, 1982, Davidson sent a letter to Sproul as president of Bonneville, asking Bonneville to defend the California suit against Davidson, but Bonneville declined to defend. On November 16, 1983, Davidson settled Thrifty's claims for $45,000.

Prior to the settlement, on July 26, 1983, Davidson filed the instant action in Salt Lake County against Bonneville and Sproul. Davidson alleged claims against Bonneville for negligence in the construction and design of the wood beam, breach of the implied warranties of merchantability and fitness for a particular purpose, indemnity, and contribution. * * * Davidson's suit against

Bonneville and Sproul was filed more than seven years after Davidson purchased the beam from Bonneville.

Bonneville and Sproul moved for summary judgment on the ground that Davidson's claims were barred by the statutes of limitation in Utah Code Ann. § 78–12–23(2) and § 78–12–25(2) (1987). That motion was denied. Bonneville and Sproul again moved for summary judgment against Davidson on the ground that Davidson's claims were barred by the Uniform Commercial Code's ("U.C.C.") statute of limitations found in § 2–725. The trial court ruled that § 2–725, if constitutional, would bar the action under Perry v. Pioneer Wholesale Supply Co., 681 P.2d 214 (Utah 1984), but that § 2–725 was unconstitutional under Berry v. Beech Aircraft Corp., 717 P.2d 670 (Utah 1985). The court therefore denied defendants' motion for summary judgment. We granted a petition for an interlocutory appeal.

Defendants contend that the four-year limitations period in § 2–725 controls this case under *Perry* and requires a reversal of the trial court's denial of their motion for summary judgment against Davidson. Davidson counters with two arguments. First, Davidson contends that § 2–725 was designed only to bar U.C.C. contract claims and not the types of claims asserted in this case. Second, Davidson argues that, even if it is wrong on the first point, Berry v. Beech Aircraft Corp., makes application of the statute of repose in § 2–725 unconstitutional in this case. Berry v. Beech Aircraft Corp., held that a products liability statute of repose was unconstitutional under the open courts provision of the Utah Constitution. Utah Const. art. I, § 11. We need not, however, reach the question of whether § 2–725 would be unconstitutional on the facts of this case under Berry v. Beech Aircraft Corp. unless and until we first decide that § 2–725 is applicable to this case.

II.　THE SCOPE OF U.C.C. § 2–725

The first question is whether the trial court erred in holding that § 2–725 applies to Davidson's claims against Bonneville and Sproul. ＊ ＊ ＊

A.　*Perry v. Pioneer Wholesale Supply Co.*

At first blush, Perry v. Pioneer Wholesale Supply Co., 681 P.2d 214 (Utah 1984), seems to require the conclusion that the four-year statute of repose in § 2–725 governs this case. That case held that § 2–725 applies to indemnity actions which grow out of an underlying U.C.C. contract or warranty action. *Perry* is, however, distinguishable. In *Perry,* the manufacturer sold defective doors to Pioneer, a wholesale supply company, who in turn sold them to Perry, a subcontractor. Perry installed the doors as part of its subcontract on a building project. The general contractor rejected the doors and covered by purchasing replacement doors.

The general contractor then sued Perry, and Perry filed a third-party complaint against the wholesaler and the manufacturer for breach of warranty.

The general contractor's action against Perry was based on delivery of nonconforming goods and sought only a contract measure of damages based on the delivery of defective doors. This Court held that § 2–725 governed Perry's third-party complaint and that Perry had four years from the tender of delivery of defective goods to bring its action against the wholesaler and the manufacturer for breach of warranty.[3] *Perry,* 681 P.2d at 217. The Court stated that the "limitation period specified in the Uniform Commercial Code conflicts with the general limitations rule for indemnity actions * * *. By its terms, this provision [§ 2–725] appears to override the general rule regarding indemnity actions." *Perry,* 681 P.2d at 218.

In the present case, the trial court applied *Perry* and held that Davidson's indemnity claims were barred by § 2–725. The trial court then held that provision unconstitutional as applied.

Davidson's action against Bonneville and Sproul grew out of a prior lawsuit in which Thrifty Corporation sued Davidson. Thrifty, however, was not the purchaser of the beam; rather, it was the lessee of the premises where the beam was installed. Thrifty sued for the damages that the collapse of the beam caused to its personal property and its business. Thus, the damages it sought were not for breach of contract or breach of a U.C.C. warranty, but for the commission of a tort.

The issue in this case is whether § 2–725 applies only to actions for economic or breach of contract damages or whether it also applies to tort actions.

B. Application of § 2–725

The U.C.C. limitations period for breach of contract and warranty cases is four years from the date of the breach of contract or four years from the tender of delivery for a breach of warranty. § 2–725.

* * *

1. Negligence claims

Since § 2–725 applies only to "an action for breach of any contract for sale," it does not apply to tort actions and does not, therefore, apply to any of Davidson's claims for relief insofar as they are claims based on tort. In short, it does not apply to Davidson's claims against Bonneville and Sproul that are based on negligence. Since contribution in this context is also a tort

---

3. The Court in *Perry* assumed that the third-party action was in fact an indemnity action. 681 P.2d at 217.

concept, it is likewise not subject to § 2–725. *See* Utah Code Ann. § 78–27–40 (1987).

2. Warranty claims

Whether § 2–725 applies to a breach of warranty action should be decided by the nature of the action and not by the pleading labels chosen. * * * Whether Davidson's claims for breach of the implied warranties of merchantability and fitness for a particular purpose are actions for "breach of any contract of sale" within the meaning of that term in § 2–725 or are tort actions is the issue we must now address. It is here that terminology tends to become slippery and legal concepts blurred.

The term "implied warranty" is used in at least two different ways in modern legal parlance. It has been used to denote a contract-type action, and it has also been used to denote a tort-type action. Each action has its own history and set of rules which governs its application.

The U.C.C., as initially written, used the term "warranty" to mean a contract-based action. * * *

The term "warranty" has also been used, however, in tort law to have a meaning that is synonymous with strict liability. * * * The U.C.C. was drafted before the judicial revolution giving rise to the expansion of strict liability had really occurred, and hence the Code failed to take that development into account. * * * Tort actions, whether called breach of warranty or strict liability actions, developed outside the confines of the U.C.C. and evolved into somewhat broader actions than those that developed under the U.C.C.; nevertheless, there is some overlap.

The common law development of strict product liability law led to the drafting of § 402A of the Restatement (Second) of Torts (1965), which is entitled "Special liability of seller of product for physical harm to user or consumer" and specifies that in certain circumstances "[o]ne who sells any product in a defective condition unreasonably dangerous to the user or consumer or to his property is subject to liability for physical harm therefore caused to the ultimate user or consumer, or to his property * * *." The comments to § 402A state the intent of the rule and explain the different history of tort and contract "warranty" actions:

> In order for the rule stated in this Section to apply, it is not necessary that the ultimate user or consumer have acquired the property directly from the seller, although the rule applies equally if he does so * * *. The liability stated is one in tort, and does not require any contractual relation, or privity of contract, between the plaintiff and the defendant.

Id., comment 1. Comment m states:

> A number of courts, seeking a theoretical basis for the liability, have resorted to a "warranty," either running with

the goods sold, by analogy to covenants running with the land, or made directly to the consumer without contract. In some instances, this theory has proved to be an unfortunate one. Although warranty was in its origin a matter of tort liability, and it is generally agreed that a tort action will still lie for its breach, it has become so identified in practice with a contract of sale between the plaintiff and the defendant that the warranty theory has become something of an obstacle to the recognition of the strict liability where there is no such contract. There is nothing in this Section which would prevent any court from treating the rule stated as a matter of "warranty" to the user or consumer. But if this is done, *it should be recognized and understood that the "warranty" is a very different kind of warranty from those usually found in the sale of goods, and that it is not subject to the various contract rules which have grown up to surround such sales.*

  * * * The rule stated in this Section is not governed by the provisions of the Uniform Sales Act, or those of the Uniform Commercial Code, as to warranties; and it is not affected by limitations on the scope and content of warranties * * *.

(Emphasis added.) There is, however, a similarity between strict tort liability and liability under the U.C.C. on implied warranties. Each type of liability can give rise to damages for both personal injuries and for personal property damage. Thus, U.C.C. § 2–715(2) defines "consequential damages," which may arise from a seller's breach of warranty, to include personal injury damages, as well as property damages. Nevertheless, under this provision, recovery for personal injury and property damage is dependent on a breach of warranty arising in connection with the sale of a product pursuant to a U.C.C. contract of sale.

Given the somewhat parallel development and history of strict liability law and U.C.C. warranties and the occasional tendency to use the term "warranty" to designate both contract and tort actions, it is not surprising that the courts have not been altogether uniform as to what actions § 2–725 controls. * * * In general, three different positions have been taken by the courts with respect to whether § 2–725 applies to actions for personal injuries and damages to property arising from a defective product. * * *

The first position, which is said to be the majority view, applies § 2–725 to "all actions for breach of warrant[y], regardless of whether the plaintiff seeks personal injury damages or economic and contractual damages." *Wieser,* 596 F.Supp. at 1475. See Reid v. Volkswagen of America, Inc., 512 F.2d 1294, 1297 (6th Cir. 1975); *Johnson,* 420 A.2d at 157. Under this view, it makes no difference whether the warranty action is an action in contract or tort.

A second view holds that the type of damages sought in an action determines whether the statute of limitations in § 2–725 applies. Actions for personal injury damages or tortious injury to personal property are governed by general, non-U.C.C. limitations periods, while actions for economic or breach of contract damages are governed by § 2–725. * * *

A third view applies § 2–725 only when there is privity between the parties. * * *

In our view, the language of § 2–725 and the expressed intent of the drafters of the U.C.C. support the view that § 2–725 applies only to actions in which economic or breach of contract damages are sought. We hold that § 2–725 does not apply to an action for personal injury or personal property damage, unless the latter is recoverable as consequential damages for breach of a contract or sales warranty. Our view is, therefore, similar to the second view stated above. See Heavner v. Uniroyal, Inc., 63 N.J. 130, 305 A.2d 412 (1973).

Section 2–725 was always intended to have an application consistent with the overall purposes and objectives of the U.C.C. It is plainly focused on economic and contractual damages. The Official Comment to § 2–725 emphasizes that it applies only to disputes of a "commercial" and "contractual" nature arising under a sales contract:

> **Purposes:** To introduce a uniform statute of limitations for *sales contracts,* thus eliminating the jurisdictional variations and providing needed relief for concerns doing business on a nationwide scale whose *contracts* have heretofore been governed by several different periods of limitation depending upon the state in which the transaction occurred. This Article takes sales contracts out of the general law limiting the time for commencing *contractual* actions and selects a four year period as the most appropriate to modern *business practice.* This is within the normal *commercial* record keeping period.

* * *

One scholar explained this limited policy behind the scope of the limitations period in § 2–725:

> Section 2–725 sets the period for limitation of action at four years from the time the breach of warranty occurs. The breach occurs "when tender of delivery is made." This is obviously based entirely on the concept that the product is not in accordance with expectations so the buyer has been damaged and has a cause of action at the moment the article is tendered to him. It completely fails to provide appropriate relief in the case of personal injury, where the cause of action

arises only when the injury occurs. If the injured party is not the buyer, the statute of limitations may well have run before he even has a cause of action. The drafters were clearly not thinking of personal injury cases in this section, and if it applies to them the unjust result carries overtones of unconstitutionality. The courts have uniformly felt that they must be resourceful to find a way around such an "unbelievable" result. The usual method is to find that the provision is not intended to apply to tort actions.

Wade, Tort Liability for Products Causing Physical Injury and Article 2 of the U.C.C., 48 Mo.L.Rev. 1, 9–10 (1983) (footnotes omitted). In short, § 2–725 was not intended to govern tort actions for injuries to persons or to personal property, and this is so even though a U.C.C. warranty action may now be maintained for personal injury, independent of a contract of sale, under § 2–318.

* * *

Except for § 2–318, the language of the U.C.C. warranty provisions presuppose bargaining by parties in privity of contract. The contractual nature of § 2–725 is emphasized by the language in subsection (1) that the parties to the contract may reduce the limitations period: "By the original agreement the parties may reduce the period of limitation to not less than one year but may not extend it." Indeed, the contracting parties may even bargain as to the scope of the warranties and whether consequential damages may even be allowed. See § 2–316, § 2–719(3). But see § 2–318. Tort "warranties" are not subject to such modifications. See *Heavner,* 63 N.J. at 155, 305 A.2d at 425–26.

C. Conclusion

Bonneville sold the beam to Davidson on April 29, 1976, and Davidson sold it to Quality Construction on June 24, 1976. Quality Construction installed the beam in a building owned by the landlord of the original plaintiff, Thrifty Corporation. It was Thrifty's personal property that was damaged when the roof collapsed. This suit was filed on July 26, 1983, more than seven years after Bonneville sold and delivered the beam to Davidson. As shown above, § 2–725 applies only to U.C.C. contract and U.C.C. warranty actions (except a warranty action under § 2–318) and to indemnity actions that grow out of such warranty actions. It follows that § 2–725 does not apply to Davidson's indemnity actions where the underlying action was not for a breach of a U.C.C. contract or warranty.

In sum, § 2–725 does not govern any of Davidson's claims against Bonneville or Sproul, whether based on negligence, breach of warranty, contribution, or indemnity.

III. APPLICABLE STATUTE OF LIMITATIONS

We turn next to the general statutes of limitation to determine what the controlling limitations periods are for the actions alleged. What is really involved in this case is the assertion of a right of indemnification, even though the plaintiff has rather liberally invoked other claims for relief in addition.

Except for an indemnity action growing out of a U.C.C. action for the sale of goods, see Perry v. Pioneer Wholesale Supply Co., 681 P.2d 214 (Utah 1984), it makes no difference what the underlying claim is that gives rise to an action for indemnity. A common-law indemnity action is based on a theory of quasi-contract or contract implied in law and is generally held to be governed by the statute of limitations applicable to actions on implied contracts. A common-law indemnity action is, therefore, wholly distinct from the underlying action which gave rise to the right of indemnity. One commentator has stated:

> An action on an implied contract of indemnity is wholly independent as a cause of action from the transaction or situation which gave rise to the right of indemnity. Although the right to indemnity may arise out of a tort, the action to enforce the right usually is not governed by the statute relating to the tort. Similarly, a right of indemnity which arises out of an express contract to pay money or perform some other act generally is not governed by the statute of limitations applicable to an action upon an express contract, where such statute is distinct from the statute governing actions upon implied contracts.

Annotation, What Statute of Limitations Covers Action for Indemnity, 57 A.L.R.3d 833, § 3 (1974). It is generally held that a contract statute of limitations, and specifically the statute that governs implied-in-fact contracts, applies to an action for common-law indemnity. * * *

Section 78–12–25(1) provides a four-year statute of limitations for "an action on a contract, obligation or liability not founded on an instrument in writing." This provision, according to the authorities above-stated, governs the indemnity action in this case.

A common-law indemnity action does not arise when the underlying damage occurs; rather, it runs from the time of the payment of the underlying claim or the payment of a judgment or a settlement.

* * *

The general policy in Utah is that statutes of limitations commence to run when the cause of action accrues. * * *

All Davidson's claims for relief were subject to the four-year statute of limitations in § 78–12–25. They arose when payment was made on the underlying settlement agreement on November 16, 1983. Davidson's claims were filed July 26, 1983, long before the four-year period allowed by § 78–12–25 ran and are not therefore barred.

2. WARRANTY OF FUTURE PERFORMANCE

SAFEWAY STORES, INC. v. CERTAINTEED CORP.

Supreme Court of Texas, 1986.
710 S.W.2d 544.

McGee, Justice.

* * * Safeway Stores sued Certainteed Corporation and Certainteed Products Corporation for alleged breach of express and implied warranties in connection with roofing material affixed to Safeway's warehouse roof. The trial court granted an instructed verdict for Certainteed because Safeway failed to prosecute its claim within the statute of limitations. The court of appeals affirmed the trial court's judgment. 687 S.W.2d 22. We must decide whether Certainteed's express and implied warranties explicitly extend to future performance under UCC § 2–725(2) so that Safeway's cause of action did not accrue until discovery of the breach.

* * *

In 1970, Safeway Stores contracted with Herman Smith & Company to build a warehouse. Herman Smith subcontracted with Gunn & Briggs to install a roof. The original plans and specifications called for a "20–year bonded type built-up roof." Gunn & Briggs contacted Certainteed to supply roofing material. Certainteed advertised that its "Dual 80" two-ply roof was "bondable up to 20 years." The Safeway/Herman Smith contract was amended to include the "Dual 80" roof and construction of the roof was completed in 1970.

Safeway first experienced leaks in the roof in 1977. Nine years after the roof was completed, in 1979, Safeway filed this action against Certainteed alleging breach of express and implied warranties. The trial court granted an instructed verdict for Certainteed.

Safeway appealed. The court of appeals affirmed the trial court's judgment, holding that Certainteed's advertisement did not create a warranty that explicitly extended to future performance. Thus, Safeway's action was barred by the four-year statute of limitations as suit was brought nine years after the roof was "delivered." * * *

Safeway contends that Certainteed's implied and express warranties covering its roofing material fall under the exception to

UCC § 2–725(2). It argues that the warranties explicitly extended to future performance; therefore, the four-year statute of limitations should not begin to run until discovery of the breach, i.e., the roof started leaking.

* * * The language of the statute clearly states that a cause of action in breach of warranty arising from a contractual relationship accrues at the time of delivery, not at the time of discovery. This occurs "regardless of the aggrieved party's lack of knowledge of the breach" unless the exception applies. * * *

It is clear that a buyer and a seller can freely negotiate to extend liability into the future; that is why specific allowance was made for warranties "explicitly" extending to future performance. *Black Clawson Co.,* 587 F.2d at 820. Then, the warranty cause of action does not accrue until discovery of the breach. * * *

Implied warranties relate to the condition, kind, characteristics, suitability, etc. of sold goods at the time of sale; thus, the statute of limitations on implied warranties runs from the date of sale. * * * The drafters of the Uniform Commercial Code intended to reserve the benefits of an extended warranty to those who explicitly bargained for them. * * * Therefore, only *express* warranties may explicitly extend to future performance. * * * The universal rule in other jurisdictions is that an implied warranty does not fall under the exception in the Code because, by its very nature, it cannot explicitly extend to future performance. * * *

Some courts have stated in *dicta* that an implied warranty may be extended to future performance. * * * We are not persuaded by this dicta. The Code's attempt to establish uniformity among the various jurisdictions suggests that we adhere to an interpretation consistent with the clear majority rule.

* * *

Express warranties that meet the "explicitness" exception of UCC § 2–725(2) may extend to future performance. Courts construe the exception narrowly, with the emphasis on the term "explicitly." * * *

Certainteed represented that its "Dual 80" roof was "bondable up to 20 years." This roof was specifically added to the construction contract and affixed to Safeway's warehouse roof. A representation as to the description of the goods which becomes a basis of the bargain that the goods shall conform to the description is an express warranty. * * *

A fact question exists whether Certainteed's express warranty extends to future performance. In Certainteed's bill of exceptions, Robert A. George and an expert witness, E.T. Schreiber, were asked: "In the roofing industry, what is the meaning of the words '20–year bonded type roof,' insofar as the life-expectancy of the roof is concerned?" The formal bill reflects that both witnesses would have answered in substance, "It means a roof which will last at least 20 years before it has to be removed and replaced." Thus, it is not conclusively established that Certainteed's express warranty meant only that the roofing materials were of such a quality that a 20–year bond could have been obtained at the time the goods were tendered.

A case very similar to this cause is Little Rock School District of Pulaski County v. Celotex Corp., 264 Ark. 757, 574 S.W.2d 669 (1978) (in banc). There, the school district sued Celotex, a roofing manufacturer, for breach of implied and express warranties in connection with roofing material affixed to a new school facility. Celotex represented its product to be a "two-ply 20–year roof," "bonded for up to 20 years," which contained a 20–year bond to cover defects caused by normal wear and tear. The trial court directed a verdict for Celotex on the basis that the warranty claims were not brought within the 4–year statute of limitations under UCC § 2–275. The Supreme Court of Arkansas affirmed the trial court judgment barring the implied warranty claim, but reversed on the express warranty claims holding that a fact issue was raised by Celotex's representations whether the warranty explicitly extended to future performance. Id., 574 S.W.2d at 675.

We hold that Safeway's implied warranty claim is barred by UCC § 2–725. We hold that a fact issue exists whether Certainteed's express warranties that its roof was "bondable up to 20 years" is an explicit reference to future performance. We reverse the court of appeals' judgment insofar as it holds that there is no evidence of breach of express warranty between Safeway and Certainteed and remand the cause to the trial court for determination on the express warranty claim.

*   *   *

WALLACE, JUSTICE, dissenting.

I respectfully dissent. The contractual provision that a roof is "bondable up to 20 years," by its nature, means *capable* of being bonded for a period of up to 20 years. In other words, the product is made of such quality that a surety is willing to issue a 20 year bond, as opposed to a ten year bond for lesser quality materials or a 30 year bond for higher quality materials. The surety bond itself is what protects the purchaser against repairs or defects in the roof. *   *   * It would be logically inconsistent for a seller to represent on the one hand that the purchaser could obtain a repair bond and at the same time guarantee the product against repairs and defects. See Little Rock School District of Pulaski County v. Celotex, 264 Ark. 757, 574 S.W.2d 669, 675 (1978) (Smith, J., dissenting).

Furthermore, even if this term could be construed as an express warranty, what it expresses is clearly confined to a specific point in time: i.e., the time the roof is completed. To say, as the majority does, that "bondable up to 20 years" may be construed as an explicit reference to future performance is tantamount to saying that the purchaser of the roof could approach a surety at any time and obtain a bond for 20 years into the future. The majority makes the term "bondable" synonymous with "bonded" and, in doing so, defies the plain meaning of the term and reforms the manner in which it is used in the construction industry.

I would hold that Certainteed made no express warranty to Safeway that the roof would last for 20 years and, accordingly, affirm the judgment of the court of appeals.

I. NON–CODE REMEDIES FOR BREACH OF WARRANTY

1. MAGNUSON–MOSS WARRANTY ACT

Although the UCC was drafted long before the consumer movement, courts were usually able to use Code provisions to reach a result fair to consumers in product warranty cases. Nevertheless, the public perception of the consumer product warranties was that they gave little protection to buyers and excluded much liability of sellers. Congressman Moss summed up this impression: "It is all but fraud when a guarantee declares in large print that the manufacturer is giving protection to the buyer and in the fine print attempts to take away common-law buyer protection."[1] The early 70s were probably the high-water mark of the consumer movement, and legislative activity at both state and federal levels was intense in the area of consumer product warranties.

In 1975 the Magnuson-Moss Warranty—Federal Trade Commission Act[2] was enacted by Congress. It provides that a seller making a written warranty (narrowly defined in the Act) to a consumer must fully disclose the terms of the warranty; moreover, the warranty must meet certain prescribed standards. In any case in which a written warranty is given, the seller cannot disclaim implied warranties of quality. An innovative informal dispute resolution mechanism is authorized. Consumers are encouraged to assert their remedies under the act by being allowed to recover costs and expenses, including attorneys' fees, in cases in which they prevail. The FTC was given regulatory authority.

---

1. Quoted in Eddy, Effects of the Magnuson-Moss Act upon Consumer Product Warranties, 55 No.Car.L.Rev. 835, 856 (1977).

2. 15 U.S.C. § 2301 et seq.

SKELTON v. GENERAL MOTORS CORP.

United States Court of Appeals, Seventh Circuit, 1981.
660 F.2d 311.

CUDAHY, CIRCUIT JUDGE.   Section 110(d) of Title I of the Magnuson-Moss Warranty-Federal Trade Commission Improvements Act ("Magnuson-Moss" or the "Act") creates a federal private cause of action for consumers damaged by the failure of a warrantor "to comply with any obligation under * * * a written warranty." 15 U.S.C. § 2310(d)(1) (1976). The issue on this interlocutory appeal is whether a "written warranty" actionable under § 110(d) is limited to the particular promises, undertakings or affirmations of fact expressly defined as "written warranties" by Congress in the Act. The district court held that § 110(d) provides a federal cause of action not merely for breach of a "written warranty" as defined in the Act but also for breach of "all written promises presented in connection with the sale of a formally warranted product." 500 F.Supp. 1181, 1190 (N.D.Ill.1980). We reverse.

I.

Plaintiffs, purchasers of automobiles manufactured by defendant General Motors Corporation ("GM"), brought this action as a nationwide class action on behalf of all purchasers of GM automobiles manufactured from 1976 through 1979. In Count I of their amended complaint, plaintiffs allege that GM, through its "brochures, manuals, consumer advertising and other forms of communications to the public generally and to members of plaintiffs' class specifically," warranted and represented that 1976 through 1979 GM automobiles contained THM 350 (M38) transmissions, or "transmissions of similar quality and performance * * * and that [such transmissions] would meet a specified level of performance." Plaintiffs charge in Count I that, contrary to these warranties and representations, GM substituted inferior THM 200 (M29) transmissions for THM 350 (M38) transmissions in GM automobiles manufactured from 1976 through 1979. This undisclosed substitution is alleged to constitute a violation of written and implied warranties under § 110(d) of Magnuson-Moss. In Count II, plaintiffs claim that the substitution is actionable as a "deceptive warranty" under § 110(c)(2) of the Act, 15 U.S.C. § 2310(c)(2) (1976).

General Motors moved to dismiss both counts of plaintiffs' complaint for failure to state a claim upon which relief could be granted. On October 1, 1980, the district court granted this motion with respect to the "implied warranty" portion of Count I and the "deceptive warranty" claim in Count II, but denied GM's motion to dismiss the "written warranty" claim on Count I. 500

F.Supp. 1181 (N.D.Ill.1980). GM's interlocutory appeal from the district court's refusal to dismiss the "written warranty" claim was certified by the district court on October 31, 1980 and accepted by this court on December 4, 1980. Plaintiffs did not take timely interlocutory appeals from the district court's determinations against them with respect to the "implied warranty" and "deceptive warranty" claims.

II.

Magnuson-Moss is, in the main, a remedial statute designed to protect consumers from deceptive warranty practices. Its draftsmen believed that consumer product warranties often were too complex to be understood, too varied to allow meaningful comparisons and too restricted to provide meaningful warranty protection. See S.Rep.No.93–151, 93d Cong., 1st Sess. 6–8 (1973); H.R.Rep.No. 93–1107, 93d Cong., 2d Sess. 22–29, reprinted in [1974] U.S.Code Cong. & Ad.News 7702, 7705–11.[2] The Act's draftsmen sought to remedy these perceived ills by imposing extensive disclosure requirements and minimum content standards on particular types of written consumer product warranties. And, to promote enforcement of these warranties, the draftsmen devised a detailed remedial apparatus, which includes optional informal dispute settlement procedures as well as private and governmental judicial actions.

Although Magnuson-Moss does not require any manufacturer or seller to extend a warranty with its product, any "written warranty" offered with a consumer product is subject to the Act's regulatory requirements. The term "written warranty" is defined "for purposes of [the Act]" in § 101(6) which reads:

(6) The term written warranty means—

(A) any written affirmation of fact or written promise made in connection with the sale of a consumer product by a supplier to a buyer which relates to the nature of the material or workmanship and affirms or promises that such material or workmanship is defect free or will meet a specified level of performance over a specified period of time, or

(B) any undertaking in writing in connection with the sale by a supplier of a consumer product to refund, repair, replace, or take other remedial action with respect to such product in

2. The Report of the House Committee on Interstate and Foreign Commerce states a particular concern that appeared recurrently in legislative discussions of the Act:

[T]he paper with the filigree border bearing the bold caption 'Warranty' or 'Guarantee' was often of no greater worth than the paper it was printed on. Indeed, in many cases where a warranty or guarantee was ostensibly given the old saying applied 'The bold print giveth and the fine print taketh away.' For the paper operated to take away from the consumer the implied warranties of merchantibility and fitness arising by operation of law leaving little in its stead.

H.R.Rep. No. 93–1107, 93d Cong., 2d Sess. 13, reprinted in [1974] U.S.Code Cong. & Ad.News 7706.

the event that such product fails to meet the specifications set forth in the undertaking.

which written affirmation, promise, or undertaking becomes part of the basis of the bargain between a supplier and a buyer for purposes other than resale of such product.

15 U.S.C. § 2301(6) (1976).

Sections 102 through 109 of the Act set forth the content and disclosure rules applicable to all "written warranties." Section 102 provides that "any warrantor warranting a consumer product to a consumer by means of a written warranty shall, to the extent required by the rules of the [Federal Trade] Commission, fully and conspicuously disclose in simple and readily understood language the terms and conditions of such warranty." 15 U.S.C. § 2302(a) (1976). Pursuant to this provision, the FTC has, by regulation, required that warrantors make detailed disclosures of information necessary to allow consumers to understand and enforce written warranties.[4] The FTC regulations also require, pursuant to § 102(b), that sellers of consumer products with written warranties make available to the consumer the text of such warranties prior to sale. 16 C.F.R. § 702.3 (1980).

Under § 103, warrantors must conspicuously designate written warranties as either "full" or "limited." If a warranty is designated as "full," § 104 provides that the warrantor must (1) remedy defects or malfunctions without charge and within a reasonable period of time; (2) make no limitation on the duration of any implied warranty on the product; (3) provide for no exclusion of limitation of consequential damages unless conspicuously stated, and (4) refund or replace the product if, after a reasonable number of attempted repairs, the supplier fails to remedy defects or malfunctions. 15 U.S.C. § 2304 (1976).

An additional obligation placed on suppliers extending written warranties is found in § 108, which provides that such suppliers may not disclaim, modify or limit the duration of implied warranties to a period shorter than the "duration of a written warranty of reasonable duration." 15 U.S.C. § 2308 (1976).

Section 110(d) creates a private cause of action for breach of "written warranty," subject to the requirements that: (1) the consumer must have an individual claim of at least $25; (2) the total amount in controversy must equal or exceed $50,000; and (3) if brought as a class action, the complaint must name at least one hundred plaintiffs. 15 U.S.C. § 2310(d)(3) (1976). Section 110 also makes any failure to comply with the requirements of the Act a violation of § 5(a)(1) of the Federal Trade Commission Act (15 U.S.C. § 45(a)(1) (1976)), and empowers the FTC and the Attorney General to seek injunctive relief against (1) failure to comply with

---

4. [Ed. note: The court quotes 16 C.F.R. § 701.3(a).]

any obligation under the Act, and (2) written warranties which may be "deceptive" to a reasonable individual. 15 U.S.C. § 2310(c) (1976).

III.

The scope of the private action for breach of "written warranty" created by § 110(d) is the issue presented to us for resolution.[7] Section 110(d) provides in part that:

> [A] consumer who is damaged by the failure of a supplier, warrantor, or service contractor to comply with any obligation under this title, or a written warranty, implied warranty, or service contract, may bring suit for damages and other legal and equitable relief [in any state court of competent jurisdiction or in any appropriate federal district court].

15 U.S.C. § 2310(d)(1) (1976).

The district court properly rejected plaintiffs' argument that the Act's draftsmen intended in § 110(d) to create a federal private cause of action for breach of all written express warran-

---

7. Plaintiffs' complaint alleged that GM had warranted that its automobiles contained THM 350 (M38) transmissions, or "transmissions of similar quality and performance * * * and that [such transmissions] would meet a specified level of performance." The district court concluded that such a warranty did not fall within the § 101(6) definition of "written warranty," because it did not affirm that the transmission would "meet a specified level of performance *over a specified period of time.*" 15 U.S.C. § 2301(6) (1976) (emphasis added). See 500 F.Supp. at 1185–86. This conclusion is consistent with the FTC's interpretation of § 101(6), which is set forth in its regulations at 16 C.F.R. § 700.3(a) (1980):

> The Act imposes specific duties and liabilities on suppliers who offer written warranties on consumer products. Certain representations, such as energy efficiency ratings for electrical appliances, care labeling of wearing apparel, and other product information disclosures may be express warranties under the Uniform Commercial Code. However, these disclosures alone are not written warranties under this Act. Section 101(6) provides that a written affirmation of fact or a written promise of a specified level of performance must relate to a specified period of time in order to be considered a "written warranty." A product information disclosure with-

out a specified time period to which the disclosure relates is therefore not a written warranty.

The district court noted that, by this reading of § 101(6), a representation that a "transmission would perform like a THM 350 transmission for the life of the transmission" would constitute a "written warranty," while the representation that a "transmission would perform like a THM 350 transmission" does not. The arbitrariness of this distinction is apparent, but a certain amount of arbitrariness is inevitable whenever a bright line must be drawn. And the need for a clearly circumscribed definition in the statutory scheme before us is apparent since, to comply with the Act's obligations, manufacturers and suppliers must know in advance exactly which representations are subject to those obligations. Moreover, it is quite plausible that the Act's draftsmen defined "written warranty" in § 101(6) so as to exclude general descriptions of consumer products or their components from the reach of the Act, since it would be excessively cumbersome to impose the Act's disclosure rules on every advertisement containing a description of a product or its components. On this appeal, plaintiffs do not challenge the district court's conclusion that the warranties described in their complaint are not within the § 101(6) definition. 500 F.Supp. at 1185–86.

ties. None of the legislative history offered by plaintiffs in this record provides the clear evidence of Congressional intent necessary to overcome the "familiar principle governing the interpretation of statutes * * * that if a statutory definition of a word is given, that definition must prevail, regardless of what other meaning may be attributable to the word." Evans v. Int'l Typographical Union, 76 F.Supp. 881, 887 (S.D.Ind.1948). Indeed, we are less than confident that it is possible to distill any unambiguous Congressional intent from the Act's legislative history. As the district court noted:

> [A review of the Act's legislative history] is the legal equivalent of an archaeological dig. Various consumer warranty bills were pending before the House and Senate for four years, during which each body defined, discarded, reintroduced and redefined concepts which in some fashion or another are related to the enacted legislation. Some provisions of the Act are vestigial reminders of concepts buried but not totally forgotten during the ongoing legislative process. Both proponents and opponents of an expansive interpretation have cited compelling, to them, legislative history only dimly related to the language which finally emerged as law.

500 F.Supp. at 1184.

In support of their argument that § 110(d) created a federal private cause of action for breach of all written express warranties, plaintiffs rely heavily on the fact that the version of § 110 passed by the Senate and submitted to Conference had both defined "express warranty" and created a cause of action for breach of any express or implied warranty. But the Conference rejected the Senate approach, and the version of § 110 enacted into law was adopted substantially verbatim from the House bill, which had neither defined "express warranty" nor provided a cause of action for its breach. The House version of the Act created instead a cause of action for failure to comply with "any obligation under [the Act], or under a warranty or service contract (as defined in section 10(10) and (11))." The Conference Committee modified this language by substituting for the word "warranty," the term "written warranty," which the Conference Committee had newly defined in § 101(6).

It is also significant to note that the limitations imposed on federal jurisdiction by the Senate version of § 110, which plaintiffs view as expansive, were actually stricter than those imposed by the House bill. The Senate bill did not create a cause of action cognizable in federal court for breach of express warranties; instead, it apparently operated only to provide for recovery of attorneys' fees by consumers who prevailed in actions for breach of express warranties in *state court*. And, because it incorporated the $10,000 amount in controversy requirement of 28 U.S.C. § 1331 (1976), few, if any, actions could have been brought in federal court under the Senate version of the Act. As the Report of the Senate Committee on Commerce explained:

> Subsection (b) authorizes any "consumer" * * * to sue for breach of warranty or service contract in an appropriate district court, but any such suit shall be subject to the jurisdictional requirements of section 1331 of title 28 of the United States Code. In effect, this means a person or at this time a class of persons must show individual damages of ten thousand dollars or more in order to bring suit in a Federal court.
>
> But any 'consumer' damaged by the failure of a supplier to comply with any obligations assumed under an express or implied warranty or service contract subject to this title—i.e. a warranty in writing, a service contract in writing, an express warranty * * * or implied warranties—may sue in any State or District of Columbia court of competent jurisdiction. Thus, for the most part, the Federal rights created by title I of this bill will be enforced in State rather than Federal courts.

S.Rep.No. 93–151, 93rd Cong., 1st Sess. 23 (1973).[15] Thus, although the Senate bill defined "express warranty" and in some manner created a federal claim for breach of such warranties, it limited the jurisdiction of *federal courts* to actions alleging breach of "written warranties," as that term was defined in § 101 of the Act.

Therefore, in arguing that § 110(d) provides consumers with a claim actionable in federal court for breach of any written express warranty, plaintiffs argue for a construction of § 110(d) that was not contemplated by either the House or the Senate.[16] It is

15. In contrast to the Senate version of § 110, the federal jurisdictional provision of the House bill, which was adopted by the Conference, required only that each individual claim be greter than $25, although the amount in controversy in the aggregate must exceed $50,000. In addition, if the action is brought as a class action, at least 100 plaintiffs must be named. 15 U.S.C. § 2310(d)(3) (1976). The House Report stated that the purpose of these jurisdictional requirements "is to avoid trivial or insignificant actions being brought as class actions in the federal courts." H.R.Rep. No. 93–1107, 93d Cong., 2d Sess., reprinted in [1974], U.S.Code Cong. and Ad.News 7724. Absent these requirements, actions could have been brought in federal court under the Act without regard to the amount in controversy. See 28 U.S.C. § 1337 (1976); Novosel v. Northway Motor Car Corp., 460 F.Supp. 541 (N.D.N.Y.1978). Thus, the federal jurisdictional requirements of the Act, although less severe than those initially adopted by the Senate, evince an intent to limit the private remedy in federal court.

16. The single legislative statement cited by plaintiffs which bears directly on the issue before us is found in a single paragraph of the House Conference Report:

Remedies for breach of express warranties not in writing

The Senate bill afforded reasonable attorney's fees to a consumer who successfully sued for the breach of an express oral warranty. The House amendment did not provide reasonable attorney's fees in that situation. The conferees adopted the House approach, but stated that they would reexamine the issue if oral express warranties became more prevalent.

Joint Explanatory Statements of the Committee of Conference, S.Conf.Rep. No. 93–1408 and H.R.Conf.Rep. 93–1606, 93rd Cong., 2d Sess., reprinted in [1974 U.S.Code Cong. and Ad.News 7755, 7758.

inconceivable that, by deleting any reference to "express warranty" from the Act, and by providing instead a cause of action for breach of "written warranty" (which the Conference Committee had newly defined in § 101(6)), the Committee could have meant to create a private remedy actionable in federal court for breach of all written express warranties, when neither the Senate nor the House had so provided.

In sum, there is simply no substantial evidence in the legislative history that Congress intended to create a broad federal cause of action for breach of written express warranties. Rather, it appears that the draftsmen of § 110(d) intended to adopt the House approach, which was to create a federal private cause of action for consumers injured by the violation of (1) any obligation under the Act, (2) any warranty subject to the extensive regulatory requirements of the Act, or (3) any implied warranty—the deceptive and unconscionable limitation of which was a major focus of the Act's regulatory provisions.

IV.

Although the district court properly declined to adopt plaintiffs' interpretation of § 110(d), it also rejected GM's argument that the only written warranties actionable under § 110(d) are those promises, representations or undertakings defined as "written warranties" in § 101(6). In its view:

> Congress * * * indicated that although the Magnuson-Moss Act only regulates transactions involving written warranties as the term is narrowly defined in § 101(6), once a consumer is involved in such a transaction there is a policy of providing federal remedies beyond the four corners of the formal warranty.

Plaintiffs argue that this language indicates that "there was no intention of the Conference Committee to restrict the range of written representations actionable under Section 110(d)(1)." We disagree. The negative inference urged by plaintiffs is simply too attenuated to provide the clear evidence of contrary intent necessary to override the specific language of the statute. See Zychinski v. Commissioner, 506 F.2d 637, 639 (8th Cir. 1974), cert. denied, 421 U.S. 999, 95 S.Ct. 2397, 44 L.Ed.2d 666 (1975); Luckman v. Commissioner, 418 F.2d 381, 387 (7th Cir. 1969).

Moreover, this paragraph must be read in light of the fact that neither the Senate nor the House versions of § 110(d) had provided that all written express warranties would be actionable in federal court. The Senate bill had provided for recovery of attorneys' fees by consumers who prevailed in *state court* actions for breach of any express or implied warranty. The House bill, as the Conference Report correctly stated, did not provide attorneys' fees in actions for breach of oral express warranties. See note 11, supra. It would also have been correct for the Report to note that the House bill had created a federal cause of action and provided attorneys' fees only for consumers damaged by breach of those warranties defined in § 101(10) of the bill. Id. But the failure of the Report to so note does not support the conclusion that the Conference Committee, in adopting the House approach, intended to do something that neither the House nor the Senate had contemplated, i.e., create a cause of action cognizable in federal court for breach of any written express warranty.

500 F.Supp. at 1191. Thus, the district court concluded that, whenever a manufacturer elects to extend a "written warranty" to a consumer, "[o]ther written promises presented in connection with the same transaction should also be enforceable as part of the 'written warranty.'" 500 F.Supp. at 1190.

The district court's determination that "written warranty" in § 110(d) means something more than it was defined to mean in § 101(6) has two aspects. First, the court found that the "Act itself suggests several different possible meanings of the phrase 'written warranty'" and is therefore ambiguous. 500 F.Supp. at 1187. Second, because of this ambiguity, the district court looked to the purposes of the Act, as derived from its legislative history, and concluded that § 110(d) should be construed to provide "a remedy for all written promises presented in connection with the sale of a formally warranted product." 500 F.Supp. at 1190.

We believe that the three ambiguities identified by the district court, which we shall consider individually, are not sufficiently real or substantial to warrant rejection of the definition of "written warranty" provided by Congress in the Act. Moreover, as already discussed, we do not find in the Act's legislative history a clear Congressional intention that the term "written warranty" was meant to have different meanings in different sections of the Act. See Part III, supra. And, if anything is apparent from the statutory scheme, it is the importance of providing a clear, carefully circumscribed meaning to the term "written warranty." See note 7, supra.

One ambiguity in the use of the term "written warranty" which was identified by the district court appears in § 103(b). That subsection provides that the Act's content and disclosure requirements "shall not apply to statements or representations which are similar to expressions of general policy concerning consumer satisfaction and which are not subject to any specific limitations." 15 U.S.C. § 2303(b) (1976). The district court concluded that this provision would be "unnecessary" if the § 101(6) definition was intended to apply throughout the Act, presumably because, in the view of the district court, the generalized representations described in § 103(b) could never fall within the § 101(6) definition and were therefore statements or representations of a sort other than those defined in § 101(6). We cannot accept this supposition, however, because it is possible to construe these generalized representations to fit within the § 101(6) definition in some cases. For example, a written statement that "your money will be refunded if you are not completely satisfied" might be deemed to constitute an "undertaking in writing in connection with the sale by a supplier of a consumer product to refund * * * in the event that such product fails to meet the specifications set forth in the undertaking," i.e., complete satisfaction. 15

U.S.C. § 2301(6)(B) (1976). Section 103(b) may quite plausibly have been included in the Act precisely to foreclose such interpretations.

A second ambiguity identified by the district court concerns § 110(c)(2)(B), which provides that a "deceptive warranty" includes a "written warranty created by the use of such terms as 'guaranty' or 'warranty,' if the terms and conditions of such warranty so limit its scope and application as to deceive a reasonable individual." 15 U.S.C. § 2310(c)(2)(B) (1976). The district court concluded that this "apparently" means that "a written warranty can be 'created' by the use or misuse of the words 'guaranty' or 'warranty,' even if the document using these terms does not include representations which constitute warranties under § 101(6)." 500 F.Supp. at 1187–88. Although the district court offers a sensible reading of § 110(c)(2)(B), its interpretation is not by any means required by the language of that section, and the interpretation is without support in the legislative history. The deceptive warranty provision was taken largely verbatim from the House version of the Act, which defined "deceptive warranty" to mean, *inter alia,* "a warranty (as so defined [in section 101(10)]) created by the use of such terms as 'guaranty' or 'warranty' * * *" Thus, while the draftsmen's diction may have been suspect (insofar as they used the phrase "created by the use of" instead of "including" or "containing"), it appears most plausible that they intended for the term "deceptive warranty" to mean a written warranty *as defined in § 101(6),* which contains such terms as "guaranty" or "warranty," if the warranty's terms and conditions "so limit its scope and application as to deceive a reasonable individual." 15 U.S.C. § 2310(d) (1976). See also C. Reitz, Consumer Protection Under the Magnuson-Moss Warranty Act 77 (1978).

The district court also found an inconsistency between the § 101(6) definition of "written warranty" as a particular type of promise, affirmation or undertaking, and § 102, which "authorizes the Federal Trade Commission to promulgate rules requiring 'inclusion *in the written warranty*' of various explanations of the rights of the consumer, including such statements as a 'brief, general description of the legal remedies available to the consumer.' " 500 F.Supp. at 1187 (emphasis in original). From this, the district court concluded that "in the written warranty" suggests that "[a] written warranty is not just a particular type of 'promise' or 'affirmation' but a type of document or written contract as well." Id. In its brief on appeal, GM similarly stated that a " 'written warranty' can be both a particular type of written promise or affirmation *and* the document incorporating it."

The text of a "written warranty" must, in the nature of things, be written *on* something. And, to this extent, a written warranty as defined in § 101(6) might be described as a written document. But there is nothing in the scheme of the statute to suggest that the Act was intended to apply to any promises, affirmations or undertakings other than those defined as written warranties in § 101(6). And we ought not to take a leap of faith to a documentary definition allegedly suggested by the seemingly inapt phrasing of § 102. As already noted, it is apparent from the statutory scheme that "written warranty" should be accorded a single, precise meaning. Moreover, we are constrained by sensible rules of statutory construction to interpret the phrase "written warranty" in § 102, as in the other sections of the statute, to be consistent with the clear meaning given to it by § 101(6).   *   *   *

There is no clear evidence that Congress intended for written warranty in § 102 to mean something different than the definition it ascribed to the term in § 101(6), and we consequently presume that Congress intended for "written warranty" to have the same meaning in both sections. We therefore decline to accept the position that "written warranty" means both a particular class of representations and some undefined "document" containing those representations. It is more appropriate to read the inconsistent phrase "inclusion *in* the written warranty" [emphasis supplied] to mean "inclusion *with* the written warranty" or "inclusion in *the document containing* the written warranty."

The term "written warranty" serves a central function in the Act of identifying the particular representations that are subject to the Act's disclosure and content requirements. Because of the function it serves, it is important that the term have a single, precise meaning. The § 101(6) definition provides that unambiguous meaning, and that definition is used (all things considered) with commendable aptness by the draftsmen in the forty-odd appearances of the term "written warranty" in every section of the Act. We cannot agree that syntactical slips such as the use of the preposition "in" in § 102, create ambiguities in the statutory scheme of sufficient weight to justify discarding the meticulously worded definition of "written warranty" in § 101(6) in favor of an undefined "document," or "pile of written documents," as urged by the district court. See 500 F.Supp. at 1190.

In sum, we are constrained to interpret "written warranty" in § 110(d) in accordance with the definition of "written warranty" provided by Congress in § 101(6).

Reversed.

HARLINGTON WOOD, JR., CIRCUIT JUDGE, dissenting. This is a close case of statutory interpretation, but I respectfully dissent from the majority's conclusion that the Act must be so strictly and rigidly read as to exclude coverage of the alleged transmission substitution by General Motors.

Judge Moran, in the trial court, carefully pondered the arguments and concluded that the act was broader than General Motors argued, but not so broad as plaintiffs' urged. I generally agree with his interpretation.

As Judge Moran noted, 500 F.Supp. at 1184, he was not the first one to have some difficulty interpreting the Act. Others before him have characterized it as serving as no exemplar of legislative clarity. I would, therefore, not begin and end by viewing the Act's definition provisions in such isolation as to conclude that the beneficial consumer protection purposes of the Act are thereby completely limited. Were this a criminal statute, I might be bound to resolve the question in favor of General Motors, but it is not.

This Act needs some limited judicial first aid in order to be able to accomplish its remedial purposes. Therefore, I would interpret the Act to mean that those written documents of General Motors which made specific representations of substance about the product, not just advertising ballyhoo, and which were introduced by General Motors into the transaction became, as a practical matter, inferentially incorporated into the written warranty. The written warranty would then more fully deserve its gold filigree frame.

PROBLEM

Dealer sold Buyer a Mercury Marquis, manufactured by the Ford Motor Corporation, for $8,000. There were repeated problems with engine hesitation and stalling which continued without interruption despite Dealer's repeated attempts to repair the vehicle. Finally, some three months after the sale, Ford's zone service manager inspected the car and told Buyer that there was nothing wrong with the car and that Buyer would "have to live with this one."

Dealer's contract with Buyer contained the following language:

Dealer hereby expressly disclaims all warranties, either expressed or implied, including any implied warranty of merchantability or fitness for a particular purpose, and neither assumes nor authorizes another person to assume for it any liability in connection with the sale of the vehicle.

On the back of the contract were these terms:

7. It is expressly agreed that there are no warranties, express or implied, made by either the selling dealer or the manufacturer on the motor vehicle, chassis or parts furnished hereunder except, in the case of a new motor vehicle the warranty expressly given to the purchaser upon the delivery of such motor vehicle or chassis.

The selling dealer also agrees to promptly perform and fulfill all terms and conditions of the owner service policy.

Ford furnished the following warranty which Dealer passed on to Buyer at the time of the sale:

LIMITED WARRANTY (12 MONTHS OR 12,000 MILES/ 19,312 KILOMETRES) 1978 NEW CAR AND LIGHT TRUCK

Ford warrants for its 1978 model cars and light trucks that the Selling Dealer will repair or replace free any parts, except tires, found under normal use in the U.S. or Canada to be defective in factory materials or workmanship within the earlier of 12 months or 12,000 miles/19,312 km from either first use or retail delivery. All we require is that you properly operate and maintain your vehicle and that you return for warranty service to your Selling Dealer or any Ford or Lincoln-Mercury Dealer if you are traveling, have moved a long distance or need emergency repairs. Warranty repairs will be made with Ford Authorized Service or Remanufactured Parts. THERE IS NO OTHER EXPRESS WARRANTY ON THIS VEHICLE.

The warranty also provided:

TO THE EXTENT ALLOWED BY LAW:

1. ANY IMPLIED WARRANTY OF MERCHANTABILITY OR FITNESS IS LIMITED TO THE 12 MONTH OR 12,000–MILE/19,312–KM DURATION OF THIS WRITTEN WARRANTY.

2. NEITHER FORD NOR THE SELLING DEALER SHALL HAVE ANY RESPONSIBILITY FOR LOSS OF USE OF THE VEHICLE, LOSS OF TIME, INCONVENIENCE, COMMERCIAL LOSS OR CONSEQUENTIAL DAMAGES.

Buyer wants to return the automobile and get refund of the purchase price. Assume Buyer can prove that the vehicle was substantially impaired and that Dealer and Ford were either unable or unwilling to repair it. Consider Buyer's rights under the UCC and under Magnuson-Moss.

1. Can Buyer get the desired relief under § 104(a)(4) against Dealer? Against Ford? § 101(10), § 103, and § 110(d)(1) and (f).

2. Can Buyer get the desired relief under UCC § 2–608 and § 2–711 against Dealer? Against Ford? § 101(7), § 108, § 110(d)(1) and § 110(f). If so is Buyer entitled to attorneys' fees? § 110(d)(2).

3. Had there been consequential damages in this case, would either Dealer or Ford be liable for them? § 104(a)(3).

4. In what court may Buyer bring the action? § 110(d)(1).

This problem is based on Ventura v. Ford Motor Corp., 180 N.J.Super. 45, 433 A.2d 801 (1981).

NOTES

1. The court in *Skelton* states that Magnuson-Moss does not require a seller to extend a warranty. In fact, if the seller does not make a "written warranty" or give a "service contract," the statute does not apply to the sale. Given the power of a seller to disclaim implied warranties under the UCC, we find that the two national laws governing warranties, taken together, allow sellers to avoid any warranty liability to buyers if they wish. Apparently Congress's major concern in Magnuson-Moss was to assure a consumer who is given a warranty that the warranty will be effective.

2. Professor Curtis R. Reitz has commented on the function of labeling warranties as "full" or "limited" as follows:

> Congress obviously expected that marketplace forces would lead some warrantors to seek the benefit of persuading consumers to buy their products by the sales punch of the offer of a "full" warranty. This expectation is based on the somewhat unlikely assumption that consumers generally would become familiar with the differences between a "full" warranty and a "limited" warranty and would use that knowledge as a significant element in product choice.

> An FTC study, surveying the marketplace in 1982, concluded generally that no radical changes in consumer knowledge and attitudes about warranties had taken place since the Magnuson–Moss Warranty Act had taken effect. On the difference between a "full" and "limited" warranty, consumers were asked whether the title "means much" and whether a consumer has to read the warranty's terms to find out what is covered and for how long. A reported 62.5 per cent of the respondents agreed strongly and an additional 28.4 per cent agreed somewhat that the title does not mean much and that the terms must be read.

> When over 90 per cent of consumers declare that the key word in a *written warranty's* title does not "mean much," manufacturers and retailers have little incentive to seek consumer's favor by offering "full" warranties. Casual observation of the marketplace indicates that "full" warranties are relatively rare and, where found at all, are likely to accompany lower priced consumer goods.

Reitz, Consumer Product Warranties Under Federal and State Laws 22–23 (2d ed. 1987) hereinafter cited as *Reitz.*

3. Sellers commonly limit the duration of their express undertaking to repair or replace defective goods. Sellers making written warranties under Magnuson-Moss cannot disclaim implied warranties arising under the UCC. § 108(a). If the written war-

ranty is a limited warranty the duration of the implied warranty can be limited. § 108(b). If it is a full warranty no limitation can be made. § 104(a)(2). Thus the warranty of merchantability is preserved. Consider the warranties in Problem on p. 1064. Suppose Buyer had discovered after driving the car for one week after purchase (1) that the dashboard clock did not operate, or (2) that because of a defect in the transmission the car could not be driven at all. Suppose in each case that the defect was curable by replacing the defective clock or transmission. In each case: Was there a breach of the warranty of merchantability? If there was what was Buyer's remedy? Does Buyer get any remedy under the merchantability remedy that is not provided by Ford's express warranty to repair or replace? Ford disclaimed "responsibility for loss of use of the vehicle, loss of time, inconvenience, commercial loss or consequential damages." If this limitation of liability for breach of warranty is effective what does the warranty of merchantability add to Buyer's rights? Is the limitation effective? Suppose, for example, that Buyer was without a car for three days while Ford replaced the transmission. As a result Buyer lost wages for one day and incurred expenses in renting a substitute car. § 104(a)(3) and UCC § 2–715.

4. One of the shortcomings of the legal system with respect to consumer product warranties was the difficulty consumers experienced in asserting their rights. Magnuson-Moss took a major step toward improving the consumer's position in this respect by allowing the recovery from the warrantor of the expenses of litigation, including attorneys' fees. In addition § 110(a) authorized the establishment by warrantors of informal dispute procedures. The FTC regulations on these procedures are found in 16 C.F.R. Part 703. Industry response to these procedures is summarized by Professor Reitz as follows:

> Warrantors did not rush to accept the statutory invitation to set up informal dispute settlement mechanisms. Before 1982, only two warrantors established mechanisms under Rule 703. More recently, additional mechanisms have been set up by automobile manufacturers. According to the FTC, almost all new car manufacturers now participate in a Rule 703 mechanism, and some mechanisms have been set up in the housing industry. Outside of these industries, no warrantors have elected to use a mechanism. It is not clear, however, whether the mechanisms in operation comply fully with Part 703. The FTC has not been rigorously examining mechanisms to determine that they are in compliance.

Reitz, pp. 100–101.

2. STATE "LEMON LAWS"

Since the adoption of Magnuson-Moss many states have adopted "lemon laws" which give remedies to buyers of new motor vehicles if the warranties under which they are sold are not honored. Professor Reitz reports that more than half of the states have adopted such laws. See *Reitz*, pp. 235–241, for a discussion of these laws. Lemon laws vary as to coverage. All apply to automobiles, but other vehicles such as trucks, motorcycles and motor homes are covered by some of the statutes. There is also some variation in the remedy afforded to the buyer, but they follow a typical pattern and provide a remedy similar to that of § 104(a)(1) and (4) of Magnuson-Moss. These laws impose a duty on the manufacturer to repair the vehicle if the buyer (or a transferee) reports a nonconformity within a statutory warranty period. The warranty period is usually defined as the period specified in the warranty or a period, typically one year, after the first delivery of the vehicle. Nonconformity is usually defined to refer to defects that substantially impair the utility, value or safety of the vehicle. If the nonconformity is not cured after "a reasonable number of attempts" the usual remedy is return of the defective vehicle and replacement with a new vehicle or refund of the purchase price. Under some laws the option of either refund or replacement is given to the customer. In others the option is given to the manufacturer. The remedy applies regardless of whether the warranty was designated as "limited" or "full" under Magnuson-Moss. A customer who obtains refund or a new vehicle is required to pay for the reasonable value of the use of the defective vehicle. Most of the laws do not specify how this value is to be determined. Typically, the laws create a presumption that the customer is entitled to refund or replacement if the same defect has not been cured after four attempts or if the vehicle has been out of service due to the repair process for 30 days or more.

J. SCOPE OF THE UCC

NEWMARK v. GIMBEL'S INC.
Supreme Court of New Jersey, 1969.
54 N.J. 585, 258 A.2d 697.

FRANCIS, J. This appeal involves the liability of a beauty parlor operator for injury to a patron's hair and scalp allegedly resulting from a product used in the giving of a permanent wave. The action was predicated upon charges of negligence and breach of express and implied warranty. Trial was had before the county district court and a jury. At the close of the proof, the court ruled as a matter of law that the warranty theory of liability was not maintainable because in giving a permanent wave a beauty parlor is engaged in rendering a service and not a sale; hence responsibility for injurious results could arise only from negligence. Consequently the court dismissed the warranty counts and submitted the issue of negligence for the jury's determination. Upon the return of a verdict for defendants, plaintiffs appealed. The Appellate Division reversed holding that a fact issue existed requiring jury decision as to whether there was an implied warranty of fitness of the lotion applied to Mrs. Newmark's hair and scalp for the purpose of producing the permanent wave.[1] Newmark v. Gimbel's Inc., 102 N.J.Super. 279, 246 A.2d 11 (App.Div.1968). Thereafter we granted defendants' petition for certification. 53 N.J. 62, 247 A.2d 886 (1968).

In dismissing the cause of action based on warranty, the trial court expressed the view that the transaction with Mrs. Newmark was not a sale within the contemplation of the Uniform Commercial Code, § 2–106(1), but rather an agreement for the rendition of services. Therefore, it was not accompanied by any warranty of fitness of products used in rendering the services, and the liability of the beauty parlor was limited to the claim of negligence. Having in mind the nature of a permanent wave operation, we find that the distinction between a sale and a rendition of services is a highly artificial one. If the permanent wave lotion were sold to Mrs. Newmark by defendants for home consumption or application or to enable her to give herself the permanent wave, unquestionably an implied warranty of fitness for that purpose would have been an integral incident of the sale. Basically defendants argue that if, in addition to recommending the use of a lotion or other product and supplying it for use, they applied it, such fact (the application) would have the effect of lessening their liability to the patron by eliminating warranty and by limiting their responsibility to the issue of negligence. There is no just reason why it should. On the contrary by taking on the administration of the product in addition to recommending and supplying it, they might increase the scope of their liability, if the method of administration were improper (a result not suggested on this appeal because the jury found no negligence).

The transaction, in our judgment, is a hybrid partaking of incidents of a sale and a service. It is really partly the rendering of service, and partly the supplying of goods for a consideration. Accordingly, we agree with the Appellate Division that an implied warranty of fitness of the products used in giving the permanent wave exists with no less force than it would have in the case of a simple sale. Newmark v. Gimbel's Inc., supra, at 285–286, 246 A.2d 11; Watson v. Buckley, 1 All.E.R. 174 (K.B.D.1940). Obvi-

1. The Appellate Division found no factual basis for the claim of express warranty. The trial evidence furnishes reasonable support for that finding and we accept it as dispositive of that aspect of the case.

ously in permanent wave operations the product is taken into consideration in fixing the price of the service. The no-separate-charge argument puts excessive emphasis on form and down-grades the overall substance of the transaction. If the beauty parlor operator bought and applied the permanent wave solution to her own hair and suffered injury thereby, her action in warranty or strict liability in tort (Santor v. A. & M. Karagheusian, Inc., 44 N.J. 52, 64–65, 207 A.2d 305, 16 A.L.R.3d 670 (1965)) against the manufacturer-seller of the product clearly would be maintainable because the basic transaction would have arisen from a conventional type of sale. It does not accord with logic to deny a similar right to a patron against the beauty parlor operator or the manufacturer when the purchase and sale were made in anticipation of and for the purpose of use of the product on the patron who would be charged for its use. Common sense demands that such patron be deemed a consumer as to both manufacturer and beauty parlor operator.

A beauty parlor operator in soliciting patronage assures the public that he or she possesses adequate knowledge and skill to do the things and to apply the solution necessary to produce the permanent wave in the hair of the customer. When a patron responds to the solicitation she does so confident that any product used in the shop has come from a reliable origin and can be trusted not to injure her. She places herself in the hands of the operator relying upon his or her expertise both in the selection of the products to be used on her and in the method of using them. The ministrations and the products employed on her are under the control and selection of the operator; the patron is a mere passive recipient.

The oft quoted statement that in the modern commercial world the liability of a manufacturer or a retail seller of a product should not be made to depend strictly upon the intricacies of the law of sales is most pertinent here. Santor v. A. & M. Karagheusian, Inc., supra, 44 N.J. at 65, 207 A.2d 305; Henningsen v. Bloomfield Motors, Inc., 32 N.J. 358, 384, 161 A.2d 69, 75 A.L.R.2d 1 (1960). It was not the intention of the framers of the Uniform Commercial Code to limit the birth of implied warranties to transactions which technically meet its definition of a sale. The comment to § 2–313 makes this clear by saying:

> "Although this section is limited in its scope and direct purpose to warranties made by the seller to the buyer as part of a contract for sale, the warranty sections of this Article are not designed in any way to disturb those lines of case law growth which have recognized that warranties need not be confined either to sales contracts or to the direct parties to such a contract. They may arise in other appropriate circumstances such as in the case of bailments for hire, whether such

bailment is itself the main contract or is merely a supplying of containers under a contract for the sale of their contents. * * *." (Comment 2, p. 190).

This Court has already said there is no sound reason for restricting implied warranties of fitness to conventional sales of goods. Cintrone v. Hertz Truck Leasing, 45 N.J. 434, 446, 212 A.2d 769 (1965); Schipper v. Levitt & Sons, Inc., 44 N.J. 70, 207 A.2d 314 (1965); and see § 2–314(1) treating as a sale the serving of food for value by a restaurateur for consumption on or off the premises, and subjecting the transaction to an implied warranty of fitness; Farnsworth, "Implied Warranties of Quality in Non-Sales Cases," 57 Colum.L.Rev. 653, 662–669 (1957). It seems to us that the policy reasons for imposing warranty liability in the case of ordinary sales are equally applicable to a commercial transaction such as that existing in this case between a beauty parlor operator and a patron. Although the policy reasons which generate the responsibility are essentially the same, practical administration suggests that the principle of liability be expressed in terms of strict liability in tort thus enabling it to be applied in practice unconfined by the narrow conceptualism associated with the technical niceties of sales and implied warranties. (This seems to be the overall import of the Appellate Division statement that the "core" question is whether "warranty principles" permit a recovery in this kind of case.) One, who in the regular course of a business sells or applies a product (in the sense of the sales-service hybrid transaction involved in the present case) which is in such a dangerously defective condition as to cause physical harm to the consumer-patron, is liable for the harm. Consumption in this connection includes all ultimate uses for which the product is intended. 2 Restatement, Torts 2d, § 402A, p. 347 (1965) adopts this view. Obviously the ultimate use of the Helene Curtis permanent wave solution intended by both manufacturer and beauty parlor operator was its application to the hair of a patron. And as Comment 1 to the Restatement section says "the customer in a beauty shop to whose hair a permanent wave solution is applied by the shop is a consumer." 2 Restatement, supra, at p. 354.

Defendants claim that to hold them to strict liability would be contrary to Magrine v. Krasnica, 94 N.J.Super. 228, 227 A.2d 539 (Cty.Ct.1967), aff'd sub nom. Magrine v. Spector, 100 N.J.Super. 223, 241 A.2d 637 (App.Div.1968), aff'd 53 N.J. 259, 250 A.2d 129 (1969). We cannot agree. Magrine, a patient of the defendant-dentist, was injured when a hypodermic needle being used, concededly with due care, to administer a local anesthetic broke off in his gum or jaw. The parties agreed that the break resulted from a latent defect in the needle. It was held that the strict liability in tort doctrine was not applicable to the professional man, such as a dentist, because the essence of the relationship with his patient was the furnishing of professional skill and services. We accepted the view that a dentist's bill for services should be considered as representing pay for that alone. The use of instruments, or the administration of medicines or the providing of medicines for the patient's home consumption cannot give the ministrations the cast of a commercial transaction. Accordingly the liability of the dentist in cases involving the ordinary relationship of doctor and patient must be tested by principles of negligence, i.e., lack of due care and not by application of the doctrine of strict liability in tort.

Defendants suggest that there is no doctrinal basis for distinguishing the services rendered by a beauty parlor operator from those rendered by a dentist or a doctor, and that consequently the liability of all three should be tested by the same principles. On the contrary there is a vast difference in the relationships. The beautician is engaged in a commercial enterprise; the dentist and doctor in a profession. The former caters publicly not to a need but to a form of aesthetic convenience or luxury, involving the rendition of non-professional services and the application of products for which a charge is made. The dentist or doctor does not and cannot advertise for patients; the demand for his services stems from a felt necessity of the patient. In response to such a call the doctor, and to a somewhat lesser degree the dentist, exercises his best judgment in diagnosing the patient's ailment or disability, prescribing the sometimes furnishing medicines or other methods of treatment which he believes, and in some measure hopes, will relieve or cure the condition. His performance is not mechanical or routine because each patient requires individual study and formulation of an informed judgment as to the physical or mental disability or condition presented, and the course of treatment needed. Neither medicine nor dentistry is an exact science; there is no implied warranty of cure or relief. There is no representation of infallibility and such professional men should not be held to such a degree of perfection. There is no guaranty that the diagnosis is correct. Such men are not producers or sellers of property in any reasonably acceptable sense of the term. In a primary sense they furnish services in the form of an opinion of the patient's condition based upon their experienced analysis of the objective and subjective complaints, and in the form of recommended and, at times, personally administered medicines and treatment. Compare, Gagne v. Bertran, 43 Cal.2d 481, 275 P.2d 15 (1954). Practitioners of such callings, licensed by the State to practice after years of study and preparation, must be deemed to have a special and essential role in our society, that of studying our physical and mental ills and ways to alleviate or cure them, and that of applying their knowledge, empirical judgment and skill in an effort to diagnose and then to relieve or to cure the ailment of a particular patient. Thus their paramount function— the essence of their function—ought to be regarded as the furnishing of opinions and services. Their unique status and the rendition of these *sui generis* services bear such a necessary and intimate relationship to public health and welfare that their obligation ought to be grounded and expressed in a duty to exercise reasonable competence and care toward their patients. In our judgment, the nature of the services, the utility of and the need for them, involving as they do, the health and even survival of many people, are so important to the general welfare as to outweigh in the policy scale any need for the imposition on dentists and doctors of the rules of strict liability in tort.

The judgment of the Appellate Division is affirmed for the reasons stated, and the cause is remanded for a new trial.

PROBLEMS

1. Dentist extracts all of Patient's teeth and then fits Patient with a set of false teeth. If it turns out that the false teeth are unsatisfactory because they are badly fitted to Patient's mouth, does Patient have a cause of action for breach of warranty against Dentist? Would Patient have a cause of action against Dentist for breach of warranty if the trouble with the false teeth is not the way they fit but the fact that they became badly discolored because of a defect in the material of which they were made? In the latter case, would Patient have a cause of action for breach of warranty against the manufacturer of the teeth?

2. Patient went to Doctor complaining of an illness. Doctor prescribed a brand-named pill which is the proper medication for Patient's illness. Patient had the prescription filled by Pharmacist. Because of an error by the manufacturer of the medicine all pills produced on a certain date contained a foreign substance capable of causing grave physical harm to anybody using them. The pills purchased by Patient were part of this lot. Patient used the pills and became very ill. Does patient have a cause of action for breach of warranty against Doctor? Against Pharmacist? Suppose that Doctor did not give Patient a prescription for the pills but instead provided the pills themselves. Would Patient have a cause of action against Doctor for breach of warranty if Patient became ill after using the pills? Would it make any difference whether or not Doctor made a separate charge for the pills?

3. Plaintiff bought from Defendant custom-made metal braces to be used as supports in a construction project. One of the braces used by Plaintiff collapsed when a welded joint separated due to a defect in the metal used in the welding. The defective metal was purchased by Defendant from a supplier and Defendant was not negligent in the manufacture of the braces. If Defendant is in the business of manufacturing braces is Defendant liable under § 2–314? Suppose Plaintiff owned a brace that needed to be

repaired because of a separated joint. Defendant who is a professional welder carefully welded the joint. Because the metal used in the welding was defective the welded joint separated and caused the brace to collapse when Plaintiff used it. Is Defendant liable to Plaintiff under § 2–314?

ADVENT SYSTEMS LIMITED v. UNISYS CORP.
United States Court of Appeals, Third Circuit, 1991.
925 F.2d 670.

WEIS, CIRCUIT JUDGE.

* * *

Plaintiff, Advent Systems Limited, is engaged primarily in the production of software for computers. As a result of its research and development efforts, by 1986 the company had developed an electronic document management system (EDMS), a process for transforming engineering drawings and similar documents into a computer data base.

Unisys Corporation manufactures a variety of computers. As a result of information gained by its wholly-owned United Kingdom subsidiary during 1986, Unisys decided to market the document management system in the United States. In June 1987 Advent and Unisys signed two documents, one labeled "Heads of Agreement" (in British parlance "an outline of agreement") and, the other "Distribution Agreement."

In these documents, Advent agreed to provide the software and hardware making up the document systems to be sold by Unisys in the United States. Advent was obligated to provide sales and marketing material and manpower as well as technical personnel to work with Unisys employees in building and installing the document systems. The agreement was to continue for two years, subject to automatic renewal or termination on notice.

During the summer of 1987, Unisys attempted to sell the document system to Arco, a large oil company, but was unsuccessful. Nevertheless, progress on the sales and training programs in the United States was satisfactory, and negotiations for a contract between Unisys (UK) and Advent were underway.

The relationship, however, soon came to an end. Unisys, in the throes of restructuring, decided it would be better served by developing its own document system and in December 1987 told Advent their arrangement had ended. Unisys also advised its UK subsidiary of those developments and, as a result, negotiations there were terminated.

Advent filed a complaint in the district court alleging, *inter alia,* breach of contract * * *. The district court ruled at pretrial that the Uniform Commercial Code did not apply because although goods were to be sold, the services aspect of the contract predominated.

* * *

On appeal * * * Unisys contends that the relationship between it and Advent was one for the sale of goods and hence subject to the terms of statute of frauds in the Uniform Commercial Code. Because the agreements lacked an express provision on quantity, Unisys insists that the statute of frauds bans enforcement.

* * *

The district court ruled that as a matter of law the arrangement between the two parties was not within the Uniform Commercial Code and, consequently, the statute of frauds was not applicable. As the district court appraised the transaction, provisions for services outweighed those for products and, consequently, the arrangement was not predominantly one for the sale of goods.

In the "Heads of Agreement" Advent and Unisys purported to enter into a "joint business collaboration." Advent was to modify its software and hardware interfaces to run initially on equipment not manufactured by Unisys but eventually on Unisys hardware. It was Advent's responsibility to purchase the necessary hardware. "[I]n so far as Advent has successfully completed [some of the processing] of software and hardware interfaces," Unisys promised to reimburse Advent to the extent of $150,000 derived from a "surcharge" on products purchased.

Advent agreed to provide twelve manweeks of marketing manpower, but with Unisys bearing certain expenses. Advent also undertook to furnish an experienced systems builder to work with Unisys personnel at Advent's prevailing rates, and to provide sales and support training for Unisys staff as well as its customers.

The Distribution Agreement begins with the statement, "Unisys desires to purchase, and Advent desires to sell, on a non-exclusive basis, certain of Advent hardware products and software licenses for resale worldwide." Following a heading "Subject Matter of Sales," appears this sentence, "(a) Advent agrees to sell hardware and license software to Unisys, and Unisys agrees to buy from Advent the products listed in Schedule A." Schedule A lists twenty products, such as computer cards, plotters, imagers, scanners and designer systems.

Advent was to invoice Unisys for each product purchased upon shipment, but to issue separate invoices for maintenance fees. The cost of the "support services" was set at 3% "per annum of the prevailing Advent user list price of each software module for which Unisys is receiving revenue from a customer." Services included field technical bulletins, enhancement and maintenance releases, telephone consultation, and software patches, among others. At no charge to Unisys, Advent was to provide

publications such as installation manuals, servicing and adjustment manuals, diagnostic operation and test procedures, sales
materials, product brochures and similar items. In turn, Unisys
was to "employ resources in performing marketing efforts" and
develop "the technical ability to be thoroughly familiar" with the
products.

In support of the district court's ruling that the U.C.C. did not
apply, Advent contends that the agreement's requirement of furnishing services did not come within the Code. Moreover, the
argument continues, the "software" referred to in the agreement
as a "product" was not a "good" but intellectual property outside
the ambit of the Uniform Commercial Code.

Because software was a major portion of the "products" described in the agreement, this matter requires some discussion.
Computer systems consist of "hardware" and "software." Hardware is the computer machinery, its electronic circuitry and
peripheral items such as keyboards, readers, scanners and printers. Software is a more elusive concept. Generally speaking,
"software" refers to the medium that stores input and output data
as well as computer programs. The medium includes hard disks,
floppy disks, and magnetic tapes.

In simplistic terms, programs are codes prepared by a
programmer that instruct the computer to perform certain functions. When the program is transposed onto a medium compatible
with the computer's needs, it becomes software. * * *

The increasing frequency of computer products as subjects of
commercial litigation has led to controversy over whether
software is a "good" or intellectual property. The Code does not
specifically mention software.

In the absence of express legislative guidance, courts interpret
the Code in light of commercial and technological developments.
The Code is designed "[t]o simplify, clarify and modernize the law
governing commercial transactions" and "[t]o permit the continued expansion of commercial practices." UCC § 1–102. As Comment 1 makes clear:

"This Act is drawn to provide flexibility so that, since it is
intended to be a semi-permanent piece of legislation, it will
provide its own machinery for expansion of commercial practices. It is intended to make it possible for the law embodied
in this Act to be developed by the courts in the light of
unforeseen and new circumstances and practices."

The Code "applies to transactions in goods." * * * Goods
are defined as "all things (including specially manufactured goods)
which are moveable at the time of the identification for sale."
§ 2–105(1). The Pennsylvania courts have recognized that
" 'goods' has a very extensive meaning" under the U.C.C. Duffee

v. Judson, 251 Pa.Super. 406, 380 A.2d 843, 846 (1977); see also Lobianco v. Property Protection, Inc., 292 Pa.Super. 346, 437 A.2d 417 (1981) ("goods" under U.C.C. embraces every species of property other than real estate, choses in action, or investment securities.).

Our Court has addressed computer package sales in other cases, but has not been required to consider whether the U.C.C. applied to software per se. See Chatlos Systems, Inc. v. National Cash Register Corp., 635 F.2d 1081 (3d Cir.1980) (parties conceded that furnishing the plaintiff with hardware, software and associated services was governed by the U.C.C.); see also Carl Beasley Ford, Inc. v. Burroughs Corporation, 361 F.Supp. 325 (E.D.Pa.1973) (U.C.C. applied without discussion), aff'd 493 F.2d 1400 (3d Cir. 1974). Other Courts of Appeals have also discussed transactions of this nature. RRX Industries, Inc. v. Lab–Con, Inc., 772 F.2d 543 (9th Cir.1985) (goods aspects of transaction predominated in a sale of a software system); Triangle Underwriters, Inc. v. Honeywell, Inc., 604 F.2d 737, 742–43 (2d Cir.1979) (in sale of computer hardware, software, and customized software goods aspects predominated; services were incidental).

Computer programs are the product of an intellectual process, but once implanted in a medium are widely distributed to computer owners. An analogy can be drawn to a compact disc recording of an orchestral rendition. The music is produced by the artistry of musicians and in itself is not a "good," but when transferred to a laser-readable disc becomes a readily merchantable commodity. Similarly, when a professor delivers a lecture, it is not a good, but, when transcribed as a book, it becomes a good.

That a computer program may be copy-rightable as intellectual property does not alter the fact that once in the form of a floppy disc or other medium, the program is tangible, moveable and available in the marketplace. The fact that some programs may be tailored for specific purposes need not alter their status as "goods" because the Code definition includes "specially manufactured goods."

The topic has stimulated academic commentary [2] with the majority espousing the view that software fits within the definition of a "good" in the U.C.C.

2. Among the articles and notes that have reviewed extant caselaw are: Boss & Woodward, Scope of the Uniform Commercial Code; Survey of Computer Contracting Cases, 43 Bus.Law. 1513 (1988); Owen, The Application of Article 2 of the Uniform Commercial Code To Computer Contracts, 14 N.Kentucky L.Rev. 277 (1987); Rodau, Computer Software: Does Article 2 of the Uniform Commercial Code Apply, 35 Emory L.J. 853 (1986); Holmes, Application of Article Two of the Uniform Commercial Code to Computer System Acquisitions, 9 Rutgers Computer & Technology L.J. 1 (1982); Note, Computer Software As A Good Under the Uniform Commercial Code: Taking a Byte Out of the Intangibility Myth, 65 B.U.L.Rev. 129 (1985); Note, Computer Programs as Goods Under the U.C.C., 77 Mich.L.Rev. 1149 (1979).

Applying the U.C.C. to computer software transactions offers substantial benefits to litigants and the courts. The Code offers a uniform body of law on a wide range of questions likely to arise in computer software disputes: implied warranties, consequential damages, disclaimers of liability, the statute of limitations, to name a few.

The importance of software to the commercial world and the advantages to be gained by the uniformity inherent in the U.C.C. are strong policy arguments favoring inclusion. The contrary arguments are not persuasive, and we hold that software is a "good" within the definition in the Code.

The relationship at issue here is a typical mixed goods and services arrangement. The services are not substantially different from those generally accompanying package sales of computer systems consisting of hardware and software. * * *

Although determining the applicability of the U.C.C. to a contract by examining the predominance of goods or services has been criticized, we see no reason to depart from that practice here. As we pointed out in De Filippo v. Ford Motor Co., 516 F.2d 1313, 1323 (3d Cir.), cert. denied, 423 U.S. 912, 96 S.Ct. 216, 46 L.Ed.2d 141 (1975), segregating goods from non-goods and insisting "that the Statute of Frauds apply only to a portion of the contract, would be to make the contract divisible and impossible of performance within the intention of the parties."

We consider the purpose or essence of the contract. Comparing the relative costs of the materials supplied with the costs of the labor may be helpful in this analysis, but not dispositive. * * *

In this case the contract's main objective was to transfer "products." The specific provisions for training of Unisys personnel by Advent were but a small part of the parties' contemplated relationship.

The compensation structure of the agreement also focuses on "goods." The projected sales figures introduced during the trial demonstrate that in the contemplation of the parties the sale of goods clearly predominated. The payment provision of $150,000 for developmental work which Advent had previously completed, was to be made through individual purchases of software and hardware rather than through the fees for services and is further evidence that the intellectual work was to be subsumed into tangible items for sale.

We are persuaded that the transaction at issue here was within the scope of the Uniform Commercial Code and, therefore, the judgment in favor of the plaintiff must be reversed.

* * *

K. WARRANTY OF TITLE

JEFFERSON v. JONES

Court of Appeals of Maryland, 1979.
286 Md.App. 544, 408 A.2d 1036.

DIGGES, JUDGE. In the present case, we are called upon to decide an issue arising under the Maryland Uniform Commercial Code that this Court has not before had occasion to consider—whether a purchaser of goods must prove that a third party has a superior or paramount title to those goods in order to substantiate a claim that a seller's warranty of title as established by section 2–312 has been breached?

The genesis of this dispute was the sale of a Honda motorcycle by appellee Lawrence V. Jones to appellant Thomas N. Jefferson in July, 1975. At the time of sale, although the appellant received immediate possession of the cycle, the seller retained the title certificate as security for the unpaid portion of the agreed purchase price. Upon the receipt of the balance due, Jones executed an assignment of the certificate to Jefferson, which was then reissued in the new owner's name by the Maryland Motor Vehicle Administration. Approximately two years later, while Jefferson was having the motorcycle repaired at a garage in the District of Columbia, he was asked by the D.C. police, for reasons not apparent in the record, to prove his entitlement to the vehicle. In an effort to establish his ownership, Jefferson produced his title certificate, but when the identification number listed on it (CB450E1009012) did not correspond to the one embossed on the frame of the vehicle (CB4501010009), the police became suspicious and seized the motorcycle. Following the denial of his demand that possession of the motorcycle be relinquished to him, Jefferson instituted an action in the Superior Court of the District of Columbia against the police in replevin and for conversion. Before trial, the matter was settled and the motorcycle was returned to Jefferson. He then asked Jones to indemnify him for the legal expenses which he had incurred in retrieving the vehicle, and when Jones refused, the appellant filed the present breach of warranty action.

In deciding in favor of the appellee, the District Court (Fisher, J.) made the following factual and legal rulings:

> [T]itle to the motorcycle in question is in the plaintiff, * * * it has been in the plaintiff since the day the title was delivered to him and * * * recorded by an Officer of the State Government by the issuance of a registration card and a certificate of title. * * * [T]he history of the title * * * shows that there has been no change, [and that] nobody in

> authority has made a claim against that title. * * * *There
> has been no superior or paramount title shown, hence, I feel I
> have no alternative under the circumstances [but] to grant a
> judgment in favor of the defendant * * *. [(emphasis add-
> ed).]*

Jefferson appealed this ruling to the Circuit Court for Prince
George's County (Woods, J.), which, with one minor exception,
affirmed Judge Fisher's findings of fact and his interpretation of
the relevant law. We granted certiorari, and now explain why we
disagree with the two earlier court interpretations of section 2–312
in this action as requiring the buyer to prove superior or paramount title in a third party before a breach of the warranty of
title is established.

Section 2–312 of the Maryland Uniform Commercial Code sets
forth the warranty of title, relevant here, that is inherent in every
sale of goods in this State: * * * Of primary concern in this case
is the requirement imposed upon the seller by subsection (1)(a)
that a good title be rightfully transferred. In analyzing its meaning we mention that the term "good title" is not one of art with a
fixed significance in the law of property, R. Nordstrom, Handbook
of the Law of Sales § 58, at 185 (1970), nor is it in any way defined
by the provisions of the Commercial Law Article. Consequently,
as is so often the case with legislative enactments, we must resort
to the principles of statutory construction if we are to understand
the obligation which section 2–312 establishes.

Although we are directed by § 1–102 to construe the Uniform
Commercial Code in a manner which "make[s] uniform the law
among the various [states]" adopting it, we nonetheless utilize, in
interpreting the Code, the same principles of statutory construction that we would apply in determining the meaning of any other
legislative enactment. * * * These well settled principles require ascertainment of the legislative intent, and if, as is the case
here, construction becomes necessary because the terminology
chosen is not clear, then we must consider not only the significance of the literal language used, but the effect of our proposed
reading in light of the legislative purpose sought to be accomplished. * * * Unlike most state statutory enactments, the
U.C.C. is accompanied by a useful aid for determining the purpose
of its provisions—the official comments of the Code's draftsmen.
While these comments are not controlling authority and may not
be used to vary the plain language of the statute * * * they are
an excellent place to begin a search for the legislature's intent
when it adopted the Code. * * * A perusal of [comment 1]
reveals that the purpose of section 2–312 is to provide for a
"buyer's basic needs in respect to a title * * *." A seller
accomplishes this objective whenever he transfers to his purchaser
"a good, clean title * * * in a rightful manner *so that [the buyer]*

will not be exposed to a lawsuit in order to protect it." Id. (emphasis added). Thus, in the absence of any indication, express or otherwise, that the General Assembly intended anything to the contrary, we hold, in accord with the above quoted comments, that the U.C.C.'s warranty of title requirement is to protect a vendee from legal claims which may arise concerning his ownership of the purchased goods. Accord, * * * American Container Corp. v. Hanley Trucking Corp., 111 N.J.Super. 322, 268 A.2d 313, 317–18 (1970). The type or nature, however, of a third party's claim of title or right to possession giving rise to a breach of the warranty is not further delineated by the statute. Consequently, we will now proceed to determine the nature of the claims which the legislature intended should have the protection of the warranty of title provided for in section 2–312.

The intermediate appellate and trial court's answer to this query was that a breach of section 2–312(1)(a) occurs only when a purchaser establishes the existence of a "superior or paramount" title in a third party. These rulings are in accord with the showing that was required at common law before a breach of the implied warranty of title could be found. * * * However, it is our view that the legislature intended, in accord with the design of the drafters that the Code's warranty of title would provide a buyer with greater protection than its common law counterpart. Our determination in this regard here is amply supported by the statement in the comments that "[d]isturbance of quiet possession, * * * [which at common law required interference by a holder of a superior or paramount title before a breach was declared * * *] is one way, *among many,* in which the breach of the warranty of title may be established." § 2–312, comment 1 (emphasis added). Again, finding nothing to the contrary, we therefore conclude that the General Assembly intended that section 2–312's protection, unless waived by the purchaser, applies to third party claims of title no matter whether eventually determined to be inferior or superior to the buyer's ownership. This conclusion is also in accord with the decisions of those courts in our sister states which have had an opportunity to address this warranty, as well as the authors of leading treatises discussing this provision of the Code. See * * * American Container Corp. v. Hanley Trucking Corp., supra, 268 A.2d at 317–18; Trial v. McCoy, 553 S.W.2d 199, 200–01 (Tex.Civ.App.1977) * * *. Because of their factual similarity to the case now under consideration, we will examine two of these decisions further. In American Container Corp. v. Hanley Trucking Corp., supra, the New Jersey Superior Court considered the question of whether the seizure of a motor vehicle by the police as stolen property due to an irregularity in the vehicle's identification numbers constituted a breach of section 2–312's provisions. Although the evidence arguably established that the vehicle was in fact stolen, the court held this factor to be an irrelevant consideration, id. at 317, ruling that:

> The purchaser of goods warranted as to title has a right to rely on the fact that he will not be required, at some later time, to enter into a contest over the validity of his ownership. The mere casting of a substantial shadow over his title, regardless of the ultimate outcome, is sufficient to violate a warranty of good title. [Id. at 318.]

The Texas Court of Appeals dealt with a similar situation in Trial v. McCoy, supra. There, an antique pistol purchased by McCoy from Trial was seized by the police as stolen and turned over to a third party claimant. The buyer sued the seller for breach of the warranty of title, but at the ensuing trial, failed to establish that the gun which he purchased had earlier been stolen from another; instead, the buyer produced testimony only tending to show that the gun was taken from his possession by police under a colorable claim of authority and never returned to him. Id. at 200–01. As stated by the Texas court: "If there is a duty to prove that the gun was stolen for breach of warranty of title, then Appellee's [(the buyer)] failure to do so would require a reversal of the summary judgment. We are of the opinion, however, that the proof made was sufficient under Section 2.312." Id. at 201.

Our holding here, that proof of a superior title is not necessary, does not mean, however, that all claims, no matter how unfounded, which may be made against the buyer's title should result in a breach of the warranty. "Good title" is "usually taken to mean that the title which the seller gives to the buyer is 'free from reasonable doubt, that is, not only a valid title in fact, but [also] one that can again be sold to a reasonable purchaser or mortgaged to a person of reasonable prudence.' " 2 A. Squillante & J. Fonseca, Williston on Sales § 16–5, at 423 (quoting from Langford v. Berry, 68 Ga.App. 193, 22 S.E.2d 349, 351 (1942)). As such, "there is some point at which [a] third party's claim against the goods becomes so attenuated that we should not regard it as an interference against which the seller has warranted." J. White & R. Summers, Uniform Commercial Code § 9–11, at 901 (1972). All that a purchaser should expect from a seller of property is that he be protected from colorable claims against his title and not from all claims. Spurious title claims can be made by anyone at any time. The need for a limitation on the type of claim which will constitute a breach of the warranty was aptly stated by Judge Smith in his opinion for this Court in Schlosser v. Creamer, 263 Md. 583, 284 A.2d 220 (1971), as he discussed the analogous area of marketable title in real property law:

> In today's world there is no shortage of individuals willing to litigate on virtually any subject without regard to the soundness of the propositions advanced and, therefore, without

> regard to the possibility of success. In our affluent society some are blessed with sufficient worldly goods to finance such litigation. Others litigate at the expense of the public treasury * * *. It no doubt was a recognition of human contentiousness that led the courts to speak of reasonable doubt as to marketability and not just as to the possibility of litigation. [Id. at 592–93, 284 A.2d at 225.]

* * * Thus, before a third party's claim against the title of another will result in a breach of the warranty of title, the claim must be colorable, nonspurious and of such a nature as to produce a reasonable doubt as to the title's validity. * * *

Whether a given claim relating to title is sufficient to establish a breach of the warranty under section 2–312 is a mixed question of law and fact. A claimed breach may be based on evidence that is free from dispute and concerning which reasonable minds could not differ as to whether the alleged claim affecting title to the goods is spurious, thus creating a matter of law for determination by the court. On the other hand, if there exists a factual dispute, or an issue relating to the nature of the claim is generated on which reasonable minds may differ, resolution of the matter then rests with the trier of fact. When analyzing the legal questions presented, a court, in our opinion, may profitably draw upon the principles which this Court has developed over the years for deciding whether title to real property is marketable. * * * Decisions of this Court, stretching back for over 100 years, have discussed the reasonable doubt concept in this regard as it pertains to real property. * * * The criteria which have developed essentially require a determination of whether the claim is of such a substantial nature that it may reasonably subject the buyer to serious litigation. * * * While such a standard may be considered vague, it is one which courts have successfully applied for many years. Furthermore, the public policy considerations underlying this standard concerning marketability of title to realty are similar to those which section 2–312 was designed to foster in the sales of personalty—to balance the needs of the purchaser concerning title with the litigious nature of our society and the seller's needs for a limit to his liability. * * *

When we examine the facts of the case now before us, in the light of the legal standard just mentioned, we conclude that, as a matter of law, there exists a warranty of title that has been breached here. An undisputed aspect of possessing good title is that a purchaser be "enable[d] * * * to hold the [property] in peace and, if he wishes to sell it, to be reasonably certain that no flaw will appear to disturb its market value." New Freedom Corp. v. Brown, 260 Md. 383, 389, 272 A.2d 401, 404 (1971). Whenever the title to personal property is evidenced by a document which is an aid to proving ownership, as is true in the case of motor vehicles, see Md. Code (1977), Transportation Art., § 13–101.1, any substantial defect in that document necessarily creates a reasonable doubt as to that ownership. A certificate of title, which, with limited exceptions, all owners of motor vehicles must have in this State * * * is prima facie evidence of ownership. * * * To be valid, such a certificate must include, among other things, the vehicle's identification number * * * and while the owner of the vehicle may prove his title by means other than the certificate, * * * any seller of a motor vehicle who executes, as required by section 13–112(a) of the Transportation Article, an assignment of the vehicle's certificate of title that contains identifying information that is different from that on the vehicle itself, knows or should know that problems concerning the buyer's ownership would arise. Without a valid title certificate, the owner of a vehicle cannot register, drive or sell it * * * and if problems do arise, as in this case, the seller is responsible for any damages caused. In other words, a breach of the warranty of title occurs whenever a seller of a motor vehicle fails to provide his purchaser with adequate proof of ownership because of the reasonable doubts which faulty documentation raise as to the validity of the buyer's title. * * *

In conclusion, we hold that the warranty of title provided by section 2–312 of the Commercial Law Article does not require proof of a superior title in a third party in order to establish a breach of its provisions, but only a colorable claim or one that is not spurious. Furthermore, we find that in the situation presented here, the appellee, as a matter of law, breached the title warranty, and accordingly, a verdict should be entered in favor of appellant Thomas N. Jefferson.

NOTE

The court indicates that the warranty of title protects the buyer only "from colorable claims against his title and not from all claims." Suppose a third party brought an action against the buyer in the mistaken belief that the goods held by the buyer belonged to the third party. The buyer immediately notified the seller of the action and demanded that the seller defend it. The seller refused. The buyer allowed the third party to take a default judgment. § 2–607(5)(a). If the buyer complied with the notice requirements of that section, would the seller be precluded from asserting that the third party did not have title if the buyer subsequently brings an action for breach of warranty of title? Is the buyer required to defend the action? What is the effect of a statute such as Federal Rules of Civil Procedure, Rule 14(a) (At anytime after commencement of the action a defending party, as a third-party plaintiff, may cause a summons and complaint to be served upon a person not a party to the action who is or may be liable to the third-party plaintiff for all or part of the plaintiff's claim against the third-party plaintiff. * * *)?

ITOH v. KIMI SALES, LTD.
New York Civil Court, Queens County, 1973.
74 Misc.2d 402, 345 N.Y.S.2d 416.

CHARLES H. COHEN, JUDGE. On or about May 15, 1970 plaintiff purchased from Kimi Sales, Ltd. ("Kimi"), the defendant and third party plaintiff, for the sum of $2,173.00, a certain automobile which turned out to have been stolen and was picked up by the police from plaintiff on May 29, 1972. Kimi had purchased this automobile at a public auction conducted by Lander, the third party defendant, who was a licensed auctioneer.

Plaintiff sues Kimi for damages of $2,692.79 consisting of $2,173.00, the purchase price of the automobile paid in May of 1970; $493.63, paid by plaintiff for additions and improvements to the automobile; and $26.16, paid by plaintiff for the hiring of an automobile to enable him and his family to return home when the police picked up the stolen automobile while they were driving away from home. In addition, plaintiff asks for punitive damages of $2,500.00 as a consequence of anguish, shame and embarrassment suffered when the police picked up this automobile. Kimi brings a third party action against Lander asking that whatever damages are awarded against it be awarded to it against Lander.

No question is raised concerning the fact that on or about May 15, 1970 plaintiff purchased this stolen automobile from Kimi for $2,173.00. It is also unquestioned that when the automobile was purchased by plaintiff, Kimi, in a "Used Car Guarantee", stated that "Title to this car is guaranteed free and clear of all previous liens and encumbrances".

Kimi claims that it believed that Lander had good title to the automobile, and that it checked the visible apparent identification number with the police and was told that the automobile was not stolen. (Apparently, the true identification number had been changed). Even accepting Kimi's claim as true, it is still liable to plaintiff for breach of warranty of title, both express, by virtue of the Guarantee, and implied, by virtue of Uniform Commercial Code Sec. 2–312. * * *

As far as damages are concerned, there are triable issues of fact concerning all items claimed except with respect to the purchase price paid which, if a proper item of damage, could be awarded on this motion for summary judgment. There is a question, however, as to whether this latter item is a proper item of damage. In cases specifically involving breach of warranty of title of an automobile, there have been varying results. In John St. Auto Wrecking v. Motors Insurance Co., 56 Misc.2d 232, 288 N.Y.S.2d 281, the purchase price paid was regarded as a proper item of damage. In Spillane v. Liberty Mutual Insurance Co., 65 Misc.2d 290, 317 N.Y.S.2d 203, aff'd 68 Misc.2d 783, 327 N.Y.S.2d 701, it was also allowed as an item of damage although without any discussion. Yet in Wilson v. Manhasset Ford, Inc., 27 Misc.2d 154, 209 N.Y.S.2d 210, the Court awarded as damages, again without discussion, the fair and reasonable value of the stolen automobile at the time it was surrendered.

The Court of Appeals in Menzel v. List, 24 N.Y.2d 91, 298 N.Y.S.2d 979, 246 N.E.2d 742, in a case involving a stolen painting which had appreciated in value after it was purchased, has resolved this question. After carefully considering possible measures of damage arising out of a cause of action for breach of warranty of title, it concluded that the proper measure of damages was the value of the painting at the time the injured party was required to return it, and not the purchase price. That the value of a stolen item may have depreciated in value—as may be the case with automobiles generally (although not necesarily as in the case of, for example, antiques)—would not require a different measure of damages. The object is to reflect what the buyer has "actually lost" and * * * award " * * * to him only the loss which has directly and naturally resulted, in the ordinary course of events, from the seller's breach of warranty." Menzel v. List, 24 N.Y.2d 91, 98, 298 N.Y.S.2d 979, 983, 246 N.E.2d 742, 746, supra. This language was undoubtedly based upon former Personal Property Law Sec. 150(6) which read "The measure of damages for breach of warranty is the loss directly and naturally resulting, in the ordinary course of events, from the breach of warranty". While this language has been rewritten in the presently applicable statute, UCC Secs. 2-714 and 2-715, the result, in a case involving breach of warranty of title, is the same. * * *

As stated in Comment 2 to § 2-714, "Subsection (2) describes the usual, standard and reasonable method of ascertaining damages in the case of breach of warranty, but it is not intended as an exclusive measure." It recognizes the possibility of a different measure where "special circumstances show proximate damages of a different amount" and subsection (3) allows "In a proper case any incidental and consequential damages * * *". A case involving breach of warranty of title, where stolen tangible property is taken away from the buyer at some time after the purchase, is one where there are special circumstances so that the measure of damages should be the value of such property when it is taken away. In this way, the buyer will recover what he has "actually lost". He will get the benefit of any appreciation in value, as occurred Menzel v. List (24 N.Y.2d 91, 298 N.Y.S.2d 979, 246 N.E.2d 742, supra), including items of value he may have added to the stolen property—as claimed by plaintiff; and, on the other hand, he will not be unduly enriched by depreciation in the value of the property, from the use of which he benefitted until it was taken from him—as claimed by Kimi. In addition, plaintiff may seek to recover for incidental and consequential damages (UCC Secs. 2–714(3) and 2–715) which may include expenses for hiring an automobile (and, perhaps, punitive damages regarding which the Court is not now expressing an opinion as to whether this is recoverable at all. See Walker v. Sheldon, 10 N.Y.2d 401, 223 N.Y.S.2d 488, 179 N.E.2d 497).

Since all of the items of damage to which plaintiff may be entitled involve triable issues of fact, the Court, while granting plaintiff's motion for summary judgment against Kimi, directs that there be an assessment of damages after which judgment shall be entered in favor of plaintiff against defendant for the amount of damages determined upon such assessment. CPLR 3212(c).

* * *

NOTE

Although *Itoh* states the proper measure of damages for breach of warranty of title some cases without detailed discussion have applied § 2–714(2) without regard to the unless clause. For example, in Murdock v. Godwin, 154 Ga.App. 824, 269 S.E.2d 905 (1980), Buyer bought a used car from Seller in April 1974. In February 1977 the car was seized by the police as stolen goods. Buyer had paid $2,884 for the car but he testified that in order to buy the car he borrowed $3,000 from a bank to which he repaid $3,652 including the finance charge. There was also testimony that the fair market value of the automobile at the time of purchase was as high as $3,688. A jury award of $3,652 compensatory damages was affirmed by the court which stated that the proper measure of damages was the difference between the actual value of the automobile at the time of delivery and the value the automobile would have had if the title had been as warranted. Applying this standard the court stated: "As the automobile was shown by the evidence to have been stolen and defendant had no authority to sell it to plaintiff, the actual value of the automobile at the time of delivery (and acceptance) to the plaintiff * * * was absolutely zero. The value the automobile would have had, if the title had been as warranted and represented, could have been its purchase price or the bargain which the plaintiff would have received." The court held that the jury's verdict was within the range of the testimony. It refused to allow as a setoff any amount for the value of Buyer's use of the automobile. Is the court correct in stating that the value of the automobile to Buyer was zero if in fact Buyer was able to use the car for nearly three years?

PROBLEM

Seller sold an automobile to Buyer for $3,000 which Buyer paid in cash. After using the automobile for one year Buyer was informed by Owner that the automobile was the property of Owner. Assuming that Owner's claim is valid, what damages is Buyer entitled to receive from Seller in each of the following cases?

1. Owner retook possession of the automobile from Buyer and made no other claim against Buyer.

2. Owner brought an action against Buyer and recovered damages for conversion.

Assume in each case that $3,000 was the fair market value of the automobile when Buyer bought it from Seller and that $2,000 was the fair market value when Owner claimed the automobile from Buyer. Does § 2–714 help you solve this problem?

Chapter 14

GOOD FAITH PURCHASE AND DOCUMENTS OF TITLE

A. GOOD FAITH PURCHASE

---

1. GOODS

Under the holder-in-due-course doctrine, a person who purchases a negotiable instrument from a thief can, under some circumstances, acquire title to the instrument free of the claim of the owner from whom the instrument was stolen. § 3–306. There is no comparable common-law doctrine applicable to goods. At common law a person without legal title to goods cannot convey legal title to anybody. There is, however, a common-law doctrine that allows a person with an imperfect title to goods to convey good title to a bona fide purchaser for value. For example, if X, through fraudulent representations, induced Y to transfer title of goods to X, traditional legal analysis was that X had legal title to the goods, but Y had a right recognized in equity to rescind the transaction and revest title in Y. X's imperfect legal title is referred to as "voidable title." But if X sold the goods to a bona fide purchaser for value having no notice of Y's claim, the BFP got good title free of Y's claim. The transaction of sale between X and the BFP resulted in passage of the legal title to the BFP. Since in equity there was no basis for choosing between Y and BFP, two innocent parties, BFP's legal title was left undisturbed. Y had rights only against X. The common-law doctrine is illustrated by Phelps v. McQuade which follows. *Phelps* demonstrates that the common-law rule is easy to state but difficult to apply. Section 2–403(1) is a codification of the common-law rule with some amplification.

a. VOIDABLE TITLE

PHELPS v. McQUADE

Court of Appeals of New York, 1917.
220 N.Y. 232, 115 N.E. 441, 1918B, L.R.A. 973.

ANDREWS, J. One Walter J. Gwynne falsely represented to the appellants that he was Baldwin J. Gwynne, a man of financial responsibility, residing at Cleveland, Ohio. Relying upon the truth of this statement the appellants delivered to him upon credit a quantity of jewelry. Gwynne in turn sold it to the respondent, who bought it without notice, express or implied, of any defect in title, and for value. Learning of the deception practiced upon them, the appellants began an action in replevin to recover the goods.

The only question before us is whether under such circumstances, the vendor of personal property does or does not retain title thereto after he has parted with possession thereof.

The learned Appellate Division rested their decision upon the definition of common-law larceny, holding that where such larceny had been committed the thief acquired no title by his crime; where it had not, at least a voidable title passed. We agree with that statement of the law. But we should prefer to define the rule in another form. Where the vendor of personal property intends to sell his goods to the person with whom he deals, then title passes, even though he be deceived as to that person's identity or responsibility. Otherwise it does not. It is purely a question of the vendor's intention.

The fact that the vendor deals with the person personally rather than by letter is immaterial, except in so far as it bears upon the question of intent.

Where the transaction is a personal one, the seller intends to transfer title to a person of credit, and he supposes the one standing before him to be that person. He is deceived. But in spite of that fact his primary intention is to sell his goods to the person with whom he negotiates.

Where the transaction is by letter the vendor intends to deal with the person whose name is signed to the letter. He knows no one else. He supposes he is dealing with no one else. And while in both cases other facts may be shown that would alter the rule, yet in their absence, in the first, title passes; in the second, it does not. Two cases that illustrate the distinction are Edmunds v. Merchants' Despatch Transportation Company, 135 Mass. 283, and Cundy v. Lindsay, 3 App.Cas. 463.

In Edmunds v. Merchants' Transportation Company a swindler, representing himself to be one Edward Pape, personally bought goods of the plaintiff on credit. The court held that the title passed. "The minds of the parties met and agreed upon all the terms of the sale, the thing sold, the price and time of payment, the person selling and the person buying. The fact that the seller was induced to sell by fraud of the buyer made the sale voidable, but not void. He could not have supposed that he was selling to any other person; his intention was to sell to the person present, and identified by sight and hearing; it does not defeat the sale because the buyer assumed a false name, or practiced any other deceit to induce the vendor to sell."

* * *

In Cundy v. Lindsay one Blenkarn, signing himself Blenkiron & Co., bought goods by letter of Lindsay & Co. The latter shipped the goods to Blenkiron & Co. They knew of the firm of Blenkiron & Son; believed the letter came from that firm and that the goods were shipped to it. Blenkiron & Son were the persons with whom Lindsay & Co., intended to deal and supposed they were dealing. Under those circumstances it was held that, although Blenkarn obtained possession of the goods, he never acquired title thereto.

* * *

Another class of cases such as Hentz v. Miller, 94 N.Y. 64, and Consumers' Ice Company of Buffalo v. Webster, Son & Co., 32 App. Div. 592, 53 N.Y.S. 56, illustrate the rule under different circumstances. In them, persons falsely stating that they are the agents or representatives of others fraudulently obtained possession of goods under a pretense of sale to such others. There is no intention on the part of the vendor to sell to the pretended agent or representative and no title passes.

In indictments for larceny, before the definition of that crime was changed by statute, this question of the passing of title was material; and, therefore, discussions as to whether an indictment or conviction could be sustained were relevant in cases where the question was whether or not the title had in fact passed. But in cases of each class the intention of the person having title to the goods and delivering them to another was the ultimate matter to be decided. And although it might be said in the one class of cases that where title did not pass there was no larceny, and in the other that where there was larceny the title did not pass, yet in both the test to be applied was this same intention on the part of the owner of the property.

The judgment of the Appellate Division must be affirmed, with costs.

NOTES

1. In Rogers v. Dutton, 182 Mass. 187, 65 N.E. 56 (1902), a man who identified himself as Simmons fraudulently represented to Seller that he was Buyer's agent and that Buyer wanted to purchase some hay. Induced by these misrepresentations, Seller agreed to sell Buyer the hay and delivered it to Buyer's place of business. Simmons told Buyer that the hay belonged to Simmons. Simmons sold it to Buyer, received payment, and absconded. Seller was allowed to recover the hay. Holmes, C. J., stated: "It is evident on these facts that there was no sale and that plaintiff never parted with his title." 182 Mass. at 188–189, 65 N.E. at 56. In *Rogers* there was a misrepresentation of authority to act for Buyer but no impersonation. Suppose Buyer had an authorized agent named Simmons, that Seller was aware of that fact, and

that an impostor represented to Seller that he was Simmons. If all the other facts in *Rogers* were the same, should the result be different?

2. How would § 2–403 apply to the face-to-face impersonation in *Phelps*, the impersonation by letter referred to in *Phelps*, and the misrepresentation of agency in *Rogers*?

3. The third sentence of § 2–403(1) provides that when goods have been delivered under a "transaction of purchase" the purchaser has the power to transfer good title to a good faith purchaser for value in four cases: deception as to identity, receipt of a bad check, cash sale, and fraudulent delivery. Was the use of the quoted phrase a drafting error which might frustrate the purpose of the third sentence? That is, if a jurisdiction's pre-Code case law is that of *Phelps*, has the property been delivered to the defrauder pursuant to a "transaction of purchase" if the seller did not intend to pass title? See the definition of "purchase" in § 1–201(32).

b. ENTRUSTING

Article 2 codifies the common-law doctrine of good faith purchase in § 2–403(1), but it goes beyond that doctrine by introducing the concept of "entrusting to a merchant" which may allow a buyer to acquire good title to goods from a seller who had no title whatsoever. This concept is stated in § 2–403(2) and (3).

CANTERRA PETROLEUM, INC. v. WESTERN DRILLING & MINING SUPPLY

Supreme Court of North Dakota, 1987.
418 N.W.2d 267.

ERICKSTAD, CHIEF JUSTICE.

*   *   *

This multi-party litigation arises out of various transactions involving a certain quantity of oilfield pipe. The pipe was originally owned by Mitchell Energy Corporation ["Mitchell"]. In late 1981, Mitchell entrusted the pipe to Port Pipe Terminal, Inc. ["Port Pipe"] for storage.

Through paper transactions, two high-ranking employees of Port Pipe succeeded in fraudulently transferring apparent ownership of the pipe to Pharoah, Inc. ["Pharoah"], a "dummy" corporation which they had created to facilitate the fraudulent sale of merchandise stored at Port Pipe's facilities. On March 3, 1982, Pharoah sold the pipe owned by Mitchell to Nickel Supply Company, Inc. ["Nickel"]. On that same date, Nickel sold the pipe to Yamin Oil Supply ["Yamin"]. Five days later Yamin sold the pipe to NorthStar. On March 23, 1982, NorthStar sold it to Western, which a few days later sold it to Canterra Petroleum, Inc. ["Canterra"].

All of these intervening transactions, culminating in the sale to Canterra, were paper transactions only. The pipe never left Port Pipe's storage facility in Houston, Texas, until Canterra had it delivered to Getter Trucking in Dickinson sometime after its purchase in March 1982. The pipe remained stored at Getter Trucking until December 1983, when Canterra relinquished the pipe to Mitchell upon being informed by law enforcement agencies that the pipe was owned by Mitchell.

Canterra sued Western for breach of warranty of title seeking damages of $201,014.39, the price Canterra had paid for the pipe, plus interest. Western commenced a third-party action against NorthStar for breach of warranty of title, and NorthStar commenced a fourth-party action against Yamin.

Canterra moved for and received summary judgment against Western. Western then moved for summary judgment on its third-party claim against NorthStar. The court granted summary judgment to Western, awarding $228,245.72 in damages and interest. NorthStar has appealed from the judgment.

NorthStar contends that it did not breach the warranty of title, and that it presented sufficient evidence to demonstrate that material issues of fact remain to be resolved on the issue of title. * * * NorthStar contends that this case falls within the entrustment provision of * * * U.C.C. § 2-403:

> "2. Any entrusting of possession of goods to a merchant who deals in goods of that kind gives him power to transfer all rights of the entruster to a buyer in ordinary course of business."

In essence, this statute contains three elements: (1) an entrustment of goods, (2) to a merchant who deals in goods of the kind, (3) followed by a sale to a buyer in the ordinary course of business. * * * If all three elements are present, the rights of the entruster are transferred to the buyer in ordinary course of business. NorthStar argues that Mitchell entrusted the pipe to Port Pipe, a merchant who dealt in pipe, and that through Pharoah the pipe was sold to Nickel, a buyer in the ordinary course of business.

The trial court held that, based upon the affidavits presented, there was no factual dispute as to Port Pipe's status and that, as a matter of law, Port Pipe was merely a storage facility and not a merchant which dealt in pipe. * * *

The determination whether a party to a transaction is a "merchant" under the Uniform Commercial Code is a question of fact. * * *

Western contends that there is no dispute as to the facts regarding this issue, and that the court correctly determined as a matter of law that Port Pipe is a storage facility and not a merchant dealing in pipe. Western relies primarily upon the affidavits of Bradley Beers, an assistant district attorney in Texas who prosecuted the two employees responsible for diverting materials stored at Port Pipe's facilities, and Janet Chisholm, former president of Port Pipe. These affidavits state in conclusory terms that Port Pipe was not a "merchant" dealing in oilfield pipe. Chisholm's affidavit, however, goes on to state that "Port Pipe * * * did sell small quantities of pipe from time to time, to clear odd lots, or to sell that pipe remaining after a substantial portion of a lot was sold."

The entrustment statute requires that goods be entrusted to a "merchant who deals in goods of that kind." * * * U.C.C. § 2–403. The requirement that the party "deals in goods" has been construed to mean one who is engaged regularly in selling goods of the kind. * * *

The conclusory statements contained in the affidavits of Beers and Chisholm that Port Pipe was not a merchant which dealt in oilfield pipe are not dispositive of the issue. * * *

The relevant factual inquiry is whether Port Pipe was regularly engaged in selling pipe. The party opposing summary judgment, in this case NorthStar, is entitled to all favorable inferences which can reasonably be drawn from the evidence. * * * Viewing Chisholm's affidavit in the light most favorable to NorthStar, we conclude that it does raise an inference that Port Pipe regularly sold pipe. Chisholm admits that Port Pipe did sell pipe "from time to time." It will be for the factfinder, after presentation of further evidence regarding the frequency and quantity of Port Pipe's sales of pipe, to determine whether Port Pipe regularly engaged in the sale of pipe and therefore was a merchant which dealt in pipe.

* * *

Western also contends that, even if a fact question remains unresolved regarding Port Pipe's merchant status, summary judgment is nevertheless appropriate. Western asserts that the entrustment doctrine of Section 2–403(2) applies only when the merchant who has been entrusted with the goods sells them in the ordinary course of business. Western contends that the doctrine does not apply where the goods are fraudulently transferred to a dummy corporation by employees of the entrustee and subsequently sold through the dummy corporation to a buyer in the ordinary course of business.

This is a troublesome issue, with neither party directing our attention to a case precisely on point. Both sides have, however, cited cases involving somewhat similar circumstances.

Western relies primarily upon * * * Olin Corp. v. Cargo Carriers, Inc., 673 S.W.2d 211 (Tex.Ct.App.1984).

* * *

In *Olin,* Olin had entrusted fertilizer for storage at the warehouse of Cargo Carriers. The superintendent of Cargo Carriers' warehouse, Jerry Dollar, entered into a scheme with Charles Flowers to sell some of Olin's fertilizer. Flowers would represent himself as the owner of the fertilizer, and Dollar would use his authority to release the fertilizer to the buyer. Several loads of fertilizer were sold in this manner to Ragsdale. When Olin sued Dollar, Flowers, Cargo Carriers, and Ragsdale for the misappropriated fertilizer, Ragsdale sought the protection of Section 2–403, U.C.C. The court held that the statute was inapplicable to Ragsdale because (1) his seller, Flowers, had no title,[2] (2) Olin never entrusted the fertilizer to Flowers, and (3) Flowers was not a merchant who dealt in the sale of fertilizer. *Olin,* supra, 673 S.W.2d at 216. These circumstances are materially distinguishable from the instant case. Flowers, Ragsdale's seller, was not an employee of Cargo Carriers but an outside party. Of even more significance is the court's finding that Flowers was not a merchant. Under those circumstances, the entrustment doctrine of Section 2–403, U.C.C., was inapplicable.

This case is readily distinguishable * * *. In *Olin,* the court's holding was based upon the intervention of Flowers, who was not a merchant and was a party unrelated to either the entruster or the entrustee. In this case, however, there is no intervention by an unrelated party. The intervention was by two high-ranking employees of Port Pipe, the entrustee, who allegedly sold the pipe through their dummy corporation, Pharoah, to a buyer in the ordinary course of business.

We believe this case to be more closely analogous to Standard Leasing Corp. v. Missouri Rock Co., 693 S.W.2d 232 (Mo.Ct.App. 1985). In that case, Standard Leasing had entrusted two trucks to Herco for repair. Herco was a corporation in the business of leasing, selling, and repairing construction equipment. Herco's president, Robert Herring, transferred the trucks to Superior, a sham corporation created by Herring to fraudulently dispose of assets held by Herco. The trucks were sold by Superior to Dean, who in turn sold them to Missouri Rock. Standard Leasing sued Missouri Rock for replevin and conversion, and Missouri Rock claimed title under the entrustment doctrine. The court, in sustaining a jury verdict for Missouri Rock, held that the fraudulent transfer of the trucks from the entrustee, Herco, to a sham corporation controlled by Herco's president did not render the

---

2. We are not certain why Flowers's lack of title was important. The entrustment statute *presupposes* that the seller to the buyer in ordinary course of business has no title to convey. If the seller had title, the buyer would not need the protection afforded by the statute, which allows the title of the entruster to pass to the buyer. Thus, in the classic entrustment example, when an owner entrusts goods to a merchant for repair and the merchant sells them to a buyer in the ordinary course of business, the merchant has no title but the title of the entruster passes to the buyer by operation of the statute.

entrustment doctrine inapplicable. The court focused upon the underlying policies of Section 2–403:

"Our conclusion is consistent with the policy of § 2–403(2) to increase the marketability of goods. See, Padgett, Uniform Commercial Code Section 2–403(2): The Authority of a Bailee to Convey Title, 21 U.Fla.L.Rev. 241, at 251 (1968–69). Section 2–403(2) places a greater burden on bailors than previous uniform commercial statutory enactments to exercise discretion in entrusting their goods to bailees. Id. In our case, both plaintiffs and defendants are innocent victims of fraudulent schemers. But under UCC 2–403(2) Standard took the risk that its bailee might set up a sham corporation to aid it in its unlawful transfer of Standard's property. Where one of two innocent parties must suffer a loss occasioned by a third person, the person who enabled the acts of the wrongdoer must suffer the loss." *Standard Leasing,* supra, 693 S.W.2d at 237.

This rationale has also been expressed in 3 Anderson, Uniform Commercial Code § 2–403:4 (3d ed. 1983) (quoting Sacks v. State, 172 Ind.App. 185, 360 N.E.2d 21 (1977)):

" 'Section 2–403 was intended to determine the priorities between two innocent parties: (1) the original owner who parts with his goods through fraudulent conduct of another and (2) an innocent third party who gives value for the goods to the perpetrator of the fraud without knowledge of the fraud. By favoring the innocent third party, the Uniform Commercial Code endeavors to promote the flow of commerce by placing the burden of ascertaining and preventing fraudulent transactions on the one in the best position to prevent them, the original seller.' "

We believe this policy also supports application of the entrustment doctrine to a situation where employees of the entrustee transfer the entrusted goods to their sham corporation, which in turn sells the goods to a buyer in the ordinary course of business. As between the two innocent parties in this case [Mitchell, which entrusted the pipe to Port Pipe, and Nickel, which bought the pipe in the ordinary course of business from Pharoah], the policy of the Code places the risk of the entrustee's employees fraudulently diverting and selling the goods upon the entruster, Mitchell, which had the opportunity to select its entrustee. Applying the doctrine to this case, Nickel would acquire the title of the entruster, Mitchell, and title would have passed on to the subsequent purchasers of the pipe.[3]

3. This scenario presupposes, of course, that Port Pipe was a merchant. As previously noted, that determination will be for the finder of fact at trial. If it is found that Port Pipe was not a merchant, U.C.C. § 2–403 is inapplicable, and Mitchell retained title to the pipe.

We conclude that the trial court erred in holding that, as a matter of law, Port Pipe was not a "merchant" under UCC § 2–403(2) and that the entrustment doctrine was therefore inapplicable. Material issues of fact remain which require resolution upon trial.

* * *

NOTE

Is the analysis in *Canterra* consistent with the language and policy of § 2–403(2)? In *Canterra*, Mitchell entrusted the pipe to Port Pipe. If Port Pipe is a merchant of pipe, § 2–403(2) applies and Port Pipe obtains "power to transfer all rights of the entruster to a buyer in ordinary course of business." Section 2–403(2) is meant to apply to cases in which the merchant to whom goods are entrusted sells the goods to a buyer in ordinary course. But in *Canterra*, Port Pipe did not sell the goods to anybody. Rather, "two high-ranking employees of Port Pipe succeeded in fraudulently transferring apparent ownership" of the pipe to Pharoah, a dummy corporation created by the employees. The court does not explain how this "transfer" occurred, but we do know that the pipe remained in the possession of Port Pipe. The court apparently reads the statute to apply not only to a sale by the merchant to whom the goods are entrusted, but also to a sale by an employee of the merchant. But even under that reading, to divest Mitchell of its title it is necessary to find that the employees sold to a buyer in ordinary course. The first purchaser of the pipe was Nickel but it bought from Pharoah. To divest Mitchell's title it is necessary to equate Pharoah and the employees who controlled it. But more is required. Pharoah couldn't give title to Nickel unless Nickel was a buyer in ordinary course. Nickel may have been a bona fide purchaser, but it apparently was not a buyer in ordinary course. As a dummy corporation created for the purpose of carrying out the fraud, Pharoah would not appear to be a "person in the business of selling" pipe as required by § 1–201(9). There may have been entrustment to a merchant and a buyer in ordinary course may have eventually purchased the pipe, but that alone is not enough to divest Mitchell of title.

Although not addressed by the parties, the "shelter" principle governs subsequent transactions after entrusted goods have been sold and title transferred to a buyer in ordinary course of business. The rule is explained in 3 Anderson, Uniform Commercial Code § 2–403:59 (3d ed. 1983):

"The sale by the entrustee makes a definitive transfer of the entruster's title. Hence, not only the immediate buyer from the entrustee but all successive transferees of the goods hold the title of the entruster. That is, once a buyer acquires title by virtue of UCC § 2–403, subsequent purchasers from him benefit by his title without regard to whether they themselves would qualify as buyers in ordinary course of business."

PROBLEM

Consider the following cases:

Case # 1. Thief stole a diamond watch from Owner and sold it to Jeweler for $2,000.

Case # 2. Owner delivered a diamond watch to Jeweler for the purpose of having certain alterations made to it.

Case # 3. Owner delivered a diamond watch to Jeweler on the following terms: Jeweler was to exhibit it for sale at a price of $5,000; in the event that Jeweler found a purchaser no sale was to be made without Owner's prior consent; and, in the event of sale, Jeweler was to remit the proceeds of sale, less a 25% commission to Owner.

In each case assume the following: Jeweler is engaged in the business of buying, selling, and repairing jewelry and watches, both new and used. Jeweler sold Owner's watch for $3,000 cash to Faith, an ordinary retail customer who bought in good faith without any notice of Owner's rights in the watch. Owner had no prior knowledge of the sale and did not consent to it. Jeweler failed to remit any part of the proceeds of sale to Owner and is insolvent.

What are the rights of Faith under § 2–403(2) and (3) in each case if Owner brings an action for conversion against Faith? Section 2–403 represents a balancing of the interests of Owner and Faith, each of whom may be the victim of the dishonesty of Jeweler. How is the balancing done in each case? Are the equities the same in each case?

2. DOCUMENTS OF TITLE

Article 7 of the UCC is concerned with documents of title which are divided into two categories: bills of lading and warehouse receipts. A document of title arises out of a transaction in which goods are delivered to a commercial bailee. In the case of a bill of lading, defined in § 1–201(6), the bailee is "a person engaged in the business of transporting or forwarding goods" and is referred to as the carrier. In the case of a warehouse receipt, defined in § 1–201(45), the bailee is "a person engaged in the business of storing goods for hire" and is referred to as the warehouseman. § 7–102(h). A document of title is both an acknowledgment of receipt of the goods by the bailee and a statement of the terms of the bailment contract.

Documents of title can be either negotiable or nonnegotiable, and negotiability is determined by the form of the document. § 7–104(1)(a) and (2). The process by which a negotiable document of title is negotiated is described in § 7–501(1), (2), and (3) and that process is similar to that with respect to negotiable instruments.

Negotiation refers to a transfer of the document resulting in the transferee's becoming the holder of the document and can be illustrated by some examples.

If the document calls for delivery of the goods "to bearer," any person in possession of the document is the holder and is entitled to receive delivery of the goods. § 1–201(20) and § 7–403(1) and (4). Suppose a bearer document is issued by the bailee and is delivered to Doe. Doe can negotiate the document to Roe by simply delivering the document to Roe who becomes its holder. § 7–501(2)(a). Or Doe can deliver the document to Roe after indorsing the document by signing it and naming Roe as indorsee. In that case the goods covered by the document are deliverable to Roe and further negotiation of the document requires Roe's indorsement. § 7–501(3).

If the original terms of the document call for delivery of the goods to the order of Doe, negotiation requires the indorsement of Doe. § 7–501(1). Doe's indorsement can name Roe as indorsee as in the previous example, or the indorsement can be "in blank" which means it is simply Doe's signature without designation of an indorsee. In the latter case the document becomes "bearer" paper and further negotiation of the document can be made by delivery alone.

Section 7–501(4) defines when a document is "duly negotiated" and § 7–502(1) states the rights of a holder to whom a document is duly negotiated. Under § 7–502(1) a holder to whom a document is duly negotiated obtains title to the document, title to the goods, and the right to receive the goods from the bailee. Thus, a holder without title to either the document or the goods may be able to transfer good title to both to a holder to whom the document is duly negotiated. But in some cases due negotiation does not give the transferee good title to the goods because rights under § 7–502(1) are subject to important limitations stated in § 7–503(1). These limitations are illustrated in the Problems that follow.

Negotiability with respect to documents of title borrows some elements from the law applicable to negotiable instruments and some elements from the law applicable to goods. The Problems that follow illustrate that fact.

PROBLEMS

1. O, a cotton producer, stored cotton in Public Warehouse which issued to O a warehouse receipt providing that the cotton was deliverable to the bearer of the warehouse receipt. X, an employee of O, stole the warehouse receipt from O and sold and delivered it to Y, a cotton merchant who knew that the warehouse receipt had been stolen. Y then sold and delivered the warehouse receipt to BFP, another cotton merchant who purchased in good faith and without notice that the document was not the property

of Y. O later learned all the facts and brought an action against BFP to recover the warehouse receipt and against Public Warehouse for delivery of the cotton represented by the warehouse receipt. Decide the merits of the two actions brought by O. § 7–104(1)(a); § 7–501(2)(a); § 7–501(4); § 1–201(25); § 1–201(20); § 7–502(1) and (2); § 7–403(1) and (4).

2. O, a cotton producer, stored cotton in Public Warehouse which issued to O a warehouse receipt in bearer form. X, an employee of O, stole the warehouse receipt from O and sold and delivered it to Y, a cotton merchant who knew that the warehouse receipt had been stolen. Y then obtained delivery of the cotton from Public Warehouse upon presentation and surrender of the warehouse receipt. Y then sold the cotton to BFP, a cotton merchant who purchased in good faith without any notice of O's claim to the cotton. O, upon learning the facts, brought an action against BFP for conversion of the cotton. Decide the merits of the action. Read the sections cited in Problem 1.

3. O, a cotton producer, was the owner of cotton that was being transported in O's truck to O's customer. X, a hijacker, stole O's truck and the cotton that it contained. X delivered the cotton to Public Warehouse which issued to X a warehouse receipt in bearer form. X sold and delivered the warehouse receipt to Y, a cotton merchant who knew that the warehouse receipt was stolen. Y then sold and delivered the warehouse receipt to BFP, another cotton merchant who purchased in good faith and without notice that the document was not the property of Y. BFP then obtained delivery of the cotton from Public Warehouse upon presentation and surrender of the warehouse receipt. O later learned all of the facts and brought an action against BFP and Public Warehouse for conversion of the cotton. Decide the merits of the two actions brought by O. In addition to the sections cited in Problem 1, read § 7–503(1)(a) and (b); § 7–404. Suppose Public Warehouse had not yet delivered the cotton to anyone. If both O and BFP demand delivery, to whom is Public Warehouse required to deliver? What should Public Warehouse do to protect itself? § 7–603.

4. O, a cotton producer, was the owner of cotton. O, not having any space on its premises to store the cotton, asked Y, a cotton merchant, for permission to store the cotton on Y's premises for a few days while O found a buyer for it. Y agreed and the cotton was delivered to Y. Y received no consideration for storing O's cotton and was not engaged in the business of storing goods for hire. Assume the following two alternative fact situations:

> (a) Y, without O's permission or knowledge, sold the cotton to BFP, a cotton merchant who bought the cotton in good faith believing that it was the property of Y.

(b) Y, without O's permission or knowledge, delivered the cotton to Public Warehouse which issued to Y a warehouse receipt in bearer form. Y then sold and delivered the warehouse receipt to BFP, a cotton merchant, who bought in good faith and without notice of O's claim to the cotton. BFP then obtained delivery of the cotton from Public Warehouse upon presentation and surrender of the warehouse receipt.

In each case O, upon learning the facts, brought an action against BFP for conversion of the cotton. Decide the merits of the actions. In addition to the sections cited in Problems 1 and 3, read § 2–403(2).

B. BILLS OF LADING

1. USE OF NEGOTIABLE BILLS OF LADING IN DOCUMENTARY SALES

The UCC sets a pattern of inspection-acceptance-payment for a typical sale of goods. Upon acceptance Buyer is obliged to pay the price (§ 2–607) but acceptance presupposes an opportunity by Buyer to inspect the goods (§ 2–606). Thus, unless Seller agrees to give Buyer credit, delivery and acceptance of the goods and payment for the goods take place contemporaneously. In a face-to-face transaction Buyer is protected by the ability to reject the goods if inspection discloses that they are not as warranted, and Seller, who still has possession of the rejected goods, is adequately protected by the ability to dispose of the goods. However, where Buyer and Seller are physically remote from each other, different considerations apply. Buyer's power to reject the goods, whether exercised rightfully or wrongfully, while serving to protect the Buyer's interests can be damaging to the interests of Seller. Seller may be unable to dispose of rejected goods in a distant market in which Seller is not adequately represented. We have seen that § 2–603 deals with this problem by placing on Buyer certain duties with respect to rejected goods, but Seller has no assurances that these duties will be carried out. And, it may be small solace to unpaid Seller to have a cause of action against Buyer for breach of contract for Buyer's failure to perform duties imposed by the UCC. Seller, in some cases, may be willing to give Buyer credit and simply ship the goods. In many cases, however, particularly those involving international sales, Seller may not be willing to take the risk that the goods will be rejected and not paid for when delivered. If Seller has sufficient bargaining power Seller can demand payment prior to shipment, but in that case, Buyer is left to the mercy of Seller. Since Buyer has no assurance of ever getting the goods Buyer may be unwilling to accept these terms. A method of protecting the interests of both Buyer and Seller in this kind of case is provided by the documentary sale.

The documentary sale involves the use of a bill of lading and a sight draft, and usually a third document, a letter of credit. We saw previously that a bill of lading can be either nonnegotiable (a "straight bill") or negotiable (an "order bill" or "bearer bill"). A straight bill acknowledges instructions from the shipper or consignor to deliver the goods to a named consignee at a specified destination. The shipper under a straight bill, however, has control of the goods through the ability to change the destination or the consignee at any time before delivery; the carrier will normally follow those instructions regardless of who has possession of the bill of lading. § 7–303(1)(b). A negotiable bill in this respect is different. Under a negotiable bill the goods are to be delivered only to the holder of the bill of lading and only upon its surrender. § 7–403(1), (3) and (4). Thus, the shipper that retains possession of an order bill has maximum control of the goods, but all control over the goods is lost when the bill is delivered to Buyer. § 7–303(1)(a). A negotiable bill of lading thus represents the right to receive the goods. Because the goods are represented by a negotiable bill, it can be used as a device for giving a security interest in the goods. Possession of a negotiable bill by the holder is for these purposes tantamount to possession of the goods. If Seller ships the goods to Buyer but has a bill of lading issued to Seller's order, the goods represented by the bill of lading in effect become collateral for the obligation of Buyer under the sales contract to pay the price of the goods. A shipment made in this manner is known as a shipment under reservation. § 2–505(1)(a).

The second document used in a documentary sale is the sight draft. A sight draft is an order by the drawer of the draft to the drawee of the draft to pay, on presentation of the draft to the drawee ("on sight"), a stated sum of money to the order of a named payee. In the case of a documentary sale the drawer is Seller, the drawee is Buyer or Buyer's bank, and the payee is usually Seller, or a bank or other financial institution that either is acting as Seller's collecting agent or is acting in its own behalf as purchaser of the draft from Seller.

The object of a documentary sale is to assure Seller of payment for the goods before they arrive at their destination, and to assure Buyer that at the time of payment for the goods Buyer will have effective control of the goods. To carry out these objectives, a negotiable bill of lading is used. Although details of the transaction may vary, the following conforms to the basic pattern of a documentary sale: Seller ships the goods to Buyer and takes from the carrier an order bill of lading. Seller takes the order bill of lading, to which is attached a sight draft for the amount owed by Buyer for the goods, to Seller's bank. The bank is directed to present the draft to Buyer for payment, and upon payment to simultaneously deliver the order bill of lading. Since Buyer is in a distant place the presentation of the draft and the exchange of the bill of lading for the amount of the draft is made by a correspondent bank in Buyer's city that acts as agent of Seller's bank. Or in some cases, Seller may send the documents directly to Seller's agent in Buyer's city. The proceeds of the draft are remitted through the chain of agents to Seller. Sometimes Seller's bank purchases or "discounts" the draft at the outset and takes the order bill of lading as security for payment of the draft. In that event Seller is paid immediately for the goods and the proceeds of the draft when paid by Buyer are paid to Seller's bank.

Although possession of the order bill of lading assures Buyer of control of the goods, this type of exchange denies to Buyer the right to inspect the goods before payment of the price. At the time the exchange is made the goods normally will not have arrived at their destination. Buyer can look only to the often inadequate description of the goods in the bill of lading as assurance that the goods will be those bargained for.

Although this type of exchange assures Seller of payment for the goods before giving up control of them, it does not guarantee that Buyer in fact will pay the draft when presented. Buyer may not pay either because financially unable to pay, or because Buyer is repudiating the contract. If Buyer doesn't pay, Seller will have to find some other destination for the goods that are at that point in transit to Buyer. A third document, the irrevocable letter of credit, can be used to eliminate this risk. The irrevocable letter of credit, used in a variety of commercial transactions, is usually used in documentary sales involving overseas shipments where the consequences to Seller of nonpayment by Buyer are particularly onerous. The irrevocable letter of credit, in this context, is a document usually issued by a bank ("the issuer") at the request of Buyer ("the customer") in which the issuer undertakes to honor drafts of Seller ("the beneficiary") when those drafts are presented in accordance with conditions stated in the letter of credit, including the presentation of described bills of lading. § 5–103(1)(a). Because the irrevocable letter of credit is for the benefit of the beneficiary, once it has been delivered to the beneficiary or the beneficiary has been advised of its issuance it can't be revoked without the consent of the beneficiary. § 5–106(1) and (2). The letter of credit represents an obligation of the issuer independent of the underlying transaction between the beneficiary and the customer, and if the draft is presented in accordance with the terms of the credit with all supporting documents the issuer must honor it. § 5–114(1). In that case Buyer cannot prevent payment by the issuer even if Seller is in breach of the underlying contract. If the documents appear on their face to comply with the credit the only remedy of Buyer is to enjoin the issuer from paying, but the injunction can be granted only in case of fraud in the transaction, forged documents, or other defect not apparent on the face of the documents. § 5–114(2)(b).

Bills of lading are regulated by many federal and state statutes. State law is found primarily in Article 7 of the UCC but that article has limited application. Section 7–103 makes Article 7 subject to "any [applicable] treaty or statute of the United States, regulatory statute of this State or tariff, classification or regulation filed or issued pursuant thereto." Federal law plays a dominant role in the regulation of bills of lading. The Federal Bills of Lading Act, 49 U.S.C. §§ 81–124, applies to carriages of goods by a common carrier from any state to a foreign country or to another state, or from any state that passes through a foreign country or another state. Coverage of Article 7 is thus limited to carriages of goods in which the goods never leave the state of origin and to shipments of goods from a foreign country to any state. In the latter case, however, if an ocean bill of lading is involved the Carriage of Goods by Sea Act, 46 U.S.C. §§ 1300–15, and the Harter Act, 46 U.S.C. §§ 190–195, apply. With respect to the liability of the carrier for loss or damage to the goods the Carmack Amendment to the Interstate Commerce Act, 49 U.S.C. § 20, applies to interstate shipments. There are numerous other federal and state statutes, as well as regulations of the Interstate Commerce Commission, that may apply to a particular case involving rights under a bill of lading.

Thus, the rights and obligations of parties to a bill of lading are in the majority of cases decided by federal law, principally the Bills of Lading Act. That Act is in most respects consistent with Article 7 and is almost identical to the Uniform Bills of Lading Act which was the applicable state law in a majority of the states before adoption of Article 7.

BANQUE de DEPOTS v. FERROLIGAS

Court of Appeal of Louisiana, Fourth Circuit, 1990.
569 So.2d 40.

LOBRANO, JUDGE.

* * *

Banque de Depots, a Swiss bank, (Bank) instituted these proceedings against Bozel Mineracao E Ferroligas (Bozel) in the Thirty Fourth Judicial District seeking a money judgment asserting numerous allegations that Bozel fraudulently misused and/or misapplied the Bank's funds. The Bank asserts that Bozel is a foreign corporation existing under the laws of Brazil, is not licensed to do business in Louisiana, and has no designated agent for service of process. Pursuant to the provisions of Code of Civil Procedure Article 3541(5), the Bank sought and obtained a nonresident writ of attachment wherein 1,300 metric tons of calcium silicon were seized. The calcium silicon was shipped by Bozel from Rio de Janerio to the port of New Orleans for transit to three purchasers, none of whom are located in Louisiana, or do business here. The order of seizure was signed on May 14, 1990, and the property was seized the same day at the facilities of Chalmette Slip in Arabi, Louisiana.

On May 25, 1990 Bozel filed a motion to dissolve the writ of attachment asserting three errors, namely that the verified petition was deficient, that Bozel was not the owner of the goods, and that the cargo was subject to bills of lading and thus UCC § 7–602 prevented their seizure.

* * *

The trial court dismissed Bozel's rule to dissolve the attachment and issued extensive reasons. Bozel seeks relief from this court.

Initially, we note that the only issue for our determination is whether the writ of attachment should be dissolved. * * *

The cargo seized was in transit to three non-Louisiana purchasers. Forty percent (455 metric tons) of the total shipment, represented by bills of lading nos. 71–80, was sold to Picklands Mather Sales Company in Cleveland, Ohio (the Pickland cargo). The remainder of the cargo, represented by bills of lading nos. 70 and 81–94, was sold to Lakeside Metals and Petrochemicals of Geneva, Switzerland, with its ultimate destination to Odermath (USA), and Shieldalloy Metallurgical Corporation (the Lakeside cargo).

The record is clear that the entirety of the cargo was shipped under negotiable bearer bills of lading. With respect to the Pickland cargo, Bozel's bank in Brazil forwarded the bills of lading, and other documentation, to Society National Bank for collection from Pickland. The Lakeside cargo was handled in a similar manner. Payment for that cargo was by letters of credit issued by Banque Bruxelles Lambert. Neither purchaser paid for its cargo prior to the issuance of the attachment, although the record is unclear as to whether all of the Lakeside bills of lading were in the possession of the collecting bank.[1]

For the following reasons we hold that the trial court was in error and that the attachment was erroneously issued. We grant the relief sought, and dissolve the writ of seizure.

Most of the argument between the parties concerns the ownership of the cargo when it reached the dock in Chalmette. Bozel asserts that once the cargo was placed on the ship in Brazil title passed to the purchasers. In support they refer to numerous articles of Article 2 of the U.C.C. with respect to the shipping

1. The forwarding bank is Bozel's bank in Brazil. The collecting banks are the recipients of the delivery documentation.

instructions designated as "F.O.B." and "C.I.F." [2] They further argue that title to the cargo follows the bills of lading, and once those were transferred to the collecting entities, they (Bozel) were no longer the owner of the cargo.

The Bank asserts that ownership must be determined under Louisiana law, and since Article 2 of the U.C.C. has not been adopted in this state, arguments with respect to shipping instructions, i.e. the designations "F.O.B." and "C.I.F.", lack merit. They further urge that only bills of lading which are "duly negotiated" transfer ownership of the goods, citing UCC § 7–502. They contend that the bills of lading may have been transferred to collecting agencies, but they were not "duly negotiated" as contemplated by section 7–502 since there was no value given prior to the attachment, citing UCC § 7–501(4).

We agree that Louisiana law governs the ownership of the cargo when it reached Chalmette. Article 2 of the U.C.C. has not been adopted in Louisiana, hence the courts must look to the Civil Code in determining the ownership of movables. However, with respect to movables shipped under a negotiable bill of lading, * * * we deem UCC § 7–602 to be controlling in the instant case.

* * * By adopting UCC § 7–602 Louisiana law makes it clear that irrespective of who may be deemed the owner of the property, if it is shipped pursuant to a negotiable bill of lading, no seizure can be effected unless the document is surrendered to the carrier (depositary) or impounded by a court (i.e. its negotiation enjoined).

The Bank argues, however, that UCC § 7–602 is inapplicable because its intent is to protect the bailee (depositary) from competing claims, rather than shielding a debtor's property from seizure, citing the U.C.C. comment to the statute. They further argue that, even if the statute is applicable, on May 18, 1990 and June 1, 1990, after the attachment issued, they instituted proceedings in Switzerland and Ohio, respectively, to enjoin negotiation of the documents.

The holder of a duly negotiated bill of lading acquires title to the document and title to the goods described therein. UCC § 7–502. It is clear that once a carrier has issued a negotiable bill of lading for goods being placed in commerce, the intent of the law is to protect those who subsequently become holders through "due negotiation." * * * Part and parcel of that intent is the protection afforded the depositary in relinquishing possession of the goods to the holder of the document. Thus, although goods in the

---

2. The Picklands cargo was shipped "C.I.F." meaning "Cost Insurance and Freight." The Lakeside cargo was shipped "F.O.B. Rio de Janeiro" meaning "Free on Board in Rio de Janeiro." Under both situations, Bozel argues that responsibility for the cargo and its ownership pass to the purchasers once the cargo is loaded on the carrier.

possession of a depositary may have been seized, if the document's negotiation has not been enjoined or the document is not in its possession, UCC § 7–602 permits the depositary to surrender the goods to the duly negotiated holder. The law protects that holder from acquiring goods that are subject to a seizure. Any other conclusion would lead to the absurd result of requiring the holder, prior to his purchase of the bill of lading, to check every jurisdiction through which the goods passed to determine if it has been seized by judicial process. This would defeat the purpose of our commercial laws.

The record is clear that on May 14, 1990, the date of the seizure, the negotiable bills of lading were outstanding. They were not in the hands of the carrier and their negotiation had not been enjoined. As discussed supra, the validity of the attachment must be determined as of the date it was issued. The Bank cannot cure this defect by seeking to impound the bills of lading after it obtained the seizure. To hold otherwise would create an impossible contradiction in our commercial laws since the "seized" goods would still be subject to the legal effects of the unimpaired "due negotiation" of the corresponding bills of lading. The legal "capture" of the bills of lading is a prerequisite to the seizure of the goods.

* * * Accordingly, we reverse the trial court and make Bozel's rule absolute. We order that the writ of attachment be dissolved.

2. NONNEGOTIABLE BILLS OF LADING

CLOCK v. MISSOURI–KANSAS–TEXAS RAILROAD CO.

United States District Court, E.D.Missouri, 1976.
407 F.Supp. 448.

NANGLE, DISTRICT JUDGE. Plaintiff Gerald Clock brought this action to recover the cost of goods which were allegedly converted by defendant Missouri-Kansas-Texas Railroad Company. By amended complaint, plaintiff added Stanley L. Crawford as defendant. Plaintiff also alleges that defendant Railroad breached its obligation to deliver the goods. Prior to the filing of plaintiff's amended complaint, defendant Railroad filed a third-party complaint against Crawford, alleging that if the Railroad should be liable to plaintiff, third-party defendant would be liable to the Railroad to the extent of the liability to plaintiff. Crawford now being a defendant in this action, defendant Railroad's complaint is in fact a cross-claim and will be treated as such.

* * *

On January 14, 1975, Crawford sold two carloads of bulk ammonium nitrate fertilizer to Buford Cunningham and received two checks in payment therefor. On the same date, the goods were placed in the care and custody of defendant Railroad for shipment from Oklahoma to Eaton Agricultural Center in Indiana. Defendant Railroad issued bills of lading to cover the goods.

* * *

At the time of sale, Crawford knew that Cunningham was going to sell the goods to a third party. Soon after the sale to Cunningham, Cunningham did sell the goods to plaintiff for $30,195.12. At the time of this sale, plaintiff had no knowledge of any infirmities in title, or right to possession, by Cunningham.

On January 23, 1975, the bank notified Crawford that there were insufficient funds in Cunningham's account to cover the checks. Accordingly, they were returned to Crawford.

The goods were still in transit at this point. Crawford instructed the Railroad to hold the railroad cars containing the goods until further instructions from him. Defendant Railroad complied.

On February 3, 1975, Crawford certified to defendant Railroad that he was the true owner of the goods and he issued a reconsignment order on the goods, instructing that they be sent to Farmers Union Coop, instead of Eaton Agricultural Center. Defendant Railroad complied with these instructions.

Plaintiff furnished replacement goods to Eaton Agricultural Center of a like quantity and value, and acquired the right, title and interest of Eaton Agricultural Center to the goods, by reason of an assignment by Eaton Agricultural Center executed on February 10, 1975.

* * *

The bills of lading involved herein are straight bills of lading. 49 U.S.C.A. §§ 82, 86. It is clear that "[a] straight bill can not be negotiated free from existing equities * * *". 49 U.S.C.A. § 109. While not negotiable, straight bills are transferable. The transferee stands in the shoes of the transferor, acquiring no additional rights over those held by the transferor. * * *

A carrier may deliver goods to "a person lawfully entitled to the possession of the goods" or to the consignee. 49 U.S.C.A. § 89. The question for determination therefore is whether Crawford was lawfully entitled to possession of the goods. While it is true that title passes to a buyer when the seller completes his performance under the contract, UCC § 2–401, it is equally true that

> where the buyer * * * fails to make a payment due * * * the aggrieved seller may
>
> (a) withholding delivery of such goods;
>
> (b) stop delivery by any bailee * * * ;

* * *

(d) resell and recover damages * * *;

* * *

(f) cancel. UCC § 2–703.

It is the Court's conclusion, therefore, that upon the failure of the checks presented by Cunningham to Crawford, Crawford was "lawfully entitled to the possession of the goods." Plaintiff, as transferee of a straight bill of lading, can not have any greater rights than did Cunningham, and can not have the status of a bona fide purchaser for value. Since Crawford was entitled to possession of the goods, defendant Railroad can not be liable for delivering the goods in accordance with Crawford's instructions. 49 U.S.C.A. § 89. * * *

The applicable provisions of the Commercial Code provide that

(1) Unless the bill of lading otherwise provides, the carrier may deliver the goods to a person or destination other than that stated in the bill or may otherwise dispose of the goods on instructions from

(b) the consignor on a nonnegotiable bill notwithstanding contrary instructions from the consignee * * *. UCC § 7–303.

Under the facts established herein, Crawford was the consignor, as Crawford was "the person from whom the goods have been received for shipment." UCC § 7–102(c). Since the bills of lading were nonnegotiable, and defendant Railroad delivered the goods pursuant to the instructions of the consignor, there can be no liability. See Comments, UCC §§ 7–303 and 7–504(3).

Under 49 U.S.C.A. § 112, the authority of the shipper to stop shipment in transit and redirect it is well established. * * * The same right is recognized in the Commercial Code. See UCC §§ 2–703 and 2–705. Accordingly there can be no recovery by plaintiff against Crawford.

Plaintiff has claimed that both the Railroad and Crawford converted the shipments in question to their own use. Conversion has been defined as " * * * an *unauthorized* assumption and exercise of the right of ownership over the personal property of another to the exclusion of the owners' right". Carson Union May Stern Co. v. Pennsylvania Railroad Co., 421 S.W.2d 540 (Mo.App. 1967) [emphasis in the original]. Having concluded that Crawford was lawfully entitled to possession of the goods, it is clear that recovery for conversion will not lie.

The cases cited by plaintiff are inapposite as they involve a bona fide purchaser for value. Under the authority of 49 U.S.C.A.

§ 81 et seq., there can not be such status where one is a transferee under a straight bill of lading. North American Van Lines, Inc. v. Heller, 371 F.2d 629 (5th Cir. 1967) is equally unavailing since the Court concludes that Crawford was lawfully entitled to possession.

Accordingly, judgment will be for defendants Railroad and Crawford. Since plaintiff will not recover any damages from defendant Railroad, judgment will be for defendant Crawford on the Railroad's cross-claim.

NOTES

1. In *Clock,* when Crawford gave his reconsignment order to Railroad he certified that he was "the true owner of the goods." If we assume that the contract of sale was a shipment contract, who had title to the goods at the time of the reconsignment order? § 2–401(2). Did the right of Crawford to reconsign the goods depend on who had title to the goods at that time? Did the right of Crawford to reconsign the goods depend on who had possession of the bill of lading? § 2–703 and § 2–705. Suppose Crawford wrongfully reconsigned the goods, i.e., assume that the checks of Cunningham had not been returned for insufficient funds. Would Railroad have been liable to Clock, who was the transferee of the bill of lading from Cunningham? § 7–303(1). Would Crawford have been liable to Clock? § 7–504(1). Would Farmers Union Coop, which received the goods on reconsignment, have been liable to Clock? § 7–504(3).

2. How would you have answered the questions asked in Note 1 if, at the time of receipt of Cunningham's checks, Crawford had delivered to Cunningham a negotiable bill of lading to the order of Cunningham rather than a nonnegotiable bill?

C. WAREHOUSE RECEIPTS

---

1. LIABILITY OF WAREHOUSEMAN FOR LOSS OF IDENTIFIED GOODS

I.C.C. METALS, INC. v. MUNICIPAL WAREHOUSE CO.

Court of Appeals of New York, 1980.
50 N.Y.2d 657, 431 N.Y.S.2d 372, 409 N.E.2d 849.

GABRIELLI, JUDGE. At issue on this appeal is whether a warehouse which provides no adequate explanation for its failure to return stored property upon a proper demand is entitled to the benefit of a contractual limitation upon its liability. For the reasons discussed below, we conclude that proof of delivery of the stored property to the warehouse and its failure to return that property upon proper demand suffices to establish a prima facie case of conversion and thereby renders inapplicable the liability-limiting provision, unless the warehouse comes forward with evidence sufficient to prove that its failure to return the property is not the result of its conversion of that property to its own use. If the warehouse does proffer such evidence and is able to persuade the trier of facts of the truth of its explanation, then the limitation of liability will be given effect and the bailor will be required to prove the warehouse to be at fault if it is to recover even those limited damages allowed by the provision.

The facts relevant to this appeal are undisputed and may be simply stated. In the autumn of 1974, plaintiff, an international metals trader, delivered three separate lots of an industrial metal called indium to defendant commercial warehouse for safekeeping. The parties have stipulated that the three lots of indium, which had an aggregate weight of some 845 pounds, were worth $100,000. When the metal was delivered to defendant, it supplied plaintiff with warehouse receipts for each lot. Printed on the back of each receipt were the terms and conditions of the bailment, as proposed by defendant. Section 11 of those terms and conditions provided as follows: "Limitation of Liability—Sec. 11. The Liability of the warehouseman as to all articles and items listed on the face of this warehouse receipt is limited to the actual value of each article and item, but the total liability of the warehouseman shall not exceed in any event for damage to any or all the items or articles listed on this warehouse receipt the sum of fifty ($50.00) dollars; provided, however, that such liability may, on written request of the bailor at the time of signing this warehouse receipt or within twenty (20) days after receipt of this warehouse receipt, be increased on part or all of the articles and items hereunder, in which event, increased rates shall be charged based upon such increased valuation, but the warehouseman's maximum liability shall in no event exceed the actual value of any or all of the articles and items in question. In no case shall the liability be extended to include any loss of profit".[1] Plaintiff did not request any increase in defendant's contractual liability, nor did it inform defendant of the value of the metal.

For almost two years, defendant billed plaintiff for storage of each of the three lots by means of monthly invoices that specifically identified the stored metal, and plaintiff duly paid each invoice. Finally, in May of 1976, plaintiff requested the return of one of the three lots of indium. At that point defendant for the first time informed plaintiff that it was unable to locate any of the indium. Plaintiff then commenced this action in conversion, seeking to recover the full value of the indium. In response, defendant

---

1. In light of our disposition of the main issue presented by this case we need not and accordingly do not determine whether this limitation applies to loss of bailed property as well as damage to that property.

contended that the metal had been stolen through no fault of defendant's and that, at any rate, section 11 of the terms printed on each warehouse receipt limited plaintiff's potential recovery to a maximum of $50 per lot of indium.

Special Term granted summary judgment to plaintiff for the full value of the indium. The court found that plaintiff had made out a prima facie case of conversion by proffering undisputed proof that the indium had been delivered to defendant and that defendant had failed to return it upon a proper demand. As to defendant's contention that the metal had been stolen, the court concluded that this allegation was completely speculative and that defendant had failed to raise any question of fact sufficient to warrant a trial on the issue. Finally, Special Term held that the contractual limitation upon defendant's liability was inapplicable to an action in conversion. The Appellate Division, 67 A.D.2d 640, 412 N.Y.S.2d 531, affirmed the judgment in favor of plaintiff and we granted defendant leave to appeal to this court. We now affirm the order appealed from.

Absent an agreement to the contrary, a warehouse is not an insurer of goods and may not be held liable for any injury to or loss of stored property not due to some fault upon its part (Uniform Commercial Code, § 7–204, subd. [1]). As a bailee, however, a warehouse is required both to exercise reasonable care so as to prevent loss of or damage to the property * * * and, a fortiori, to refrain from itself converting materials left in its care * * *. If a warehouse does not convert the goods to its own use and does exercise reasonable care, it may not be held liable for any loss of or damage to the property unless it specifically agrees to accept a higher burden. If, however, the property is lost or damaged as a result of negligence upon the part of the warehouse, it will be liable in negligence. Similarly, should a warehouse actually convert stored property to its own use, it will be liable in conversion. Hence, a warehouse which fails to redeliver goods to the person entitled to their return upon a proper demand, may be liable for either negligence or conversion, depending upon the circumstances * * *.

A warehouse unable to return bailed property either because it has lost the property as a result of its negligence or because it has converted the property will be liable for the full value of the goods at the time of the loss or conversion * * * unless the parties have agreed to limit the warehouse's potential liability. It has long been the law in this State that a warehouse, like a common carrier, may limit its liability for loss of or damage to stored goods even if the injury or loss is the result of the warehouse's negligence, so long as it provides the bailor with an opportunity to increase that potential liability by payment of a higher storage fee * * *. If the warehouse converts the goods, however, strong policy considerations bar enforcement of any such limitation upon its liability * * *. This rule, which has now been codified in subdivision (2) of section 7–204 of the Uniform Commercial Code, is premised on the distinction between an intentional and an unintentional tort. Although public policy will in many situations countenance voluntary prior limitations upon that liability which the law would otherwise impose upon one who acts carelessly * * * such prior limitations may not properly be applied so as to diminish one's liability for injuries resulting from an affirmative and intentional act of misconduct * * *. Any other rule would encourage wrongdoing by allowing the converter to retain the difference between the value of the converted property and the limited amount of liability provided in the agreement of storage. That result would be absurd. To avoid such an anomaly, the law provides that when a warehouse converts bailed property, it thereby ceases to function as a warehouse and thus loses its entitlement to the protections afforded by the agreement of storage * * *. In short, although the merely careless bailee remains a bailee and is entitled to whatever limitations of liability the bailor has agreed to, the converter forsakes his status as bailee completely and accordingly forfeits the protections of such limitations. Hence, in the instant case, whether defendant is entitled to the benefit of the liability-limiting provision of the warehouse receipt turns upon whether plaintiff has proven conversion or merely negligence.

Plaintiff has proffered uncontroverted proof of delivery of the indium to defendant, of a proper demand for its return, and of defendant's failure to honor that demand. Defendant has failed to make a sufficient showing in support of its suggested explanation of the loss to defeat plaintiff's motion for summary judgment. Its unsupported claim that the metal was stolen does not suffice to raise any issue of fact on this point.[3] Upon this record, it is

---

3. The explanation proffered by the warehouse in such a case must be supported by sufficient evidence and cannot be merely the product of speculation and conjecture. "The explanation must show with reasonable certainty how the loss occurred, as, by theft or fire * * * It is not enough to show that defendant-bailee used reasonable care in its system of custody if mysterious disappearance is the only 'explanation' given" * * *. In the instant case, defendant offered proof of the following facts in support of its claim that the indium had been stolen: "(1) the storage of the indium in three different locations in two different buildings, and the absence of any indication in [defendant] Municipal's records that the indium was moved, negate the possibility of misdelivery; (2) the storage of the indi-

um without special precautions, because [plaintiff] ICC failed to advise Municipal of its true value, supports the likelihood of theft; (3) the form of the indium (small bars) would have facilitated removal without detection; (4) a recently discharged employee was experienced in 'weighing and sampling' and thus presumably was aware of the value of indium; (5) there was a series of alarms, any one of which could have been caused by a theft; (6) Municipal promptly reported the loss to the police; and (7) ICC reported the loss to its insurers as a theft and continued to employ Municipal's services, thus negating any suspicion that Municipal had misappropriated the indium or had been grossly negligent in its care." Viewed most favorably to defendant, this evidence would indicate at most that theft

beyond cavil that plaintiff would be entitled to judgment had it elected to sue defendant in negligence * * *. We now hold that such a record also suffices to sustain plaintiff's action in conversion, thereby rendering inapplicable the contractual limitation upon defendant's liability.[4]

The rule requiring a warehouse to come forward with an explanation for its failure to return bailed goods or be cast in damages in negligence is based upon practical necessity. As is noted above, a warehouse may only be held liable for loss of or damage to bailed goods if the loss or damage is due to the negligence of the warehouse or if the warehouse has converted the property. Hence, in order to recover damages for lost or damaged goods, a bailor must prove either that the warehouse was negligent or that it converted the goods. Since bailed property is in the possession of and under the sole control of the warehouse at the time of injury or loss, however, it is the warehouse which is in the best, if not the only, position to explain the loss of or damage to the property. Indeed, such information normally will be exclusively in the possession of the warehouse and will not be readily accessible to the bailor. Because of this, the law properly refuses to allow a warehouse, which has undertaken for a fee to securely store goods belonging to another, to avoid liability by simply pleading ignorance of the fate of the stored merchandise. To allow the warehouse to so easily escape its responsibilities would be to place the bailor in an untenable position and would serve to encourage both dishonesty and carelessness. Clearly, the temptation to convert stored property would be significantly increased could the warehouse then avoid all civil liability by simply denying all knowledge of the circumstances of the loss and placing upon the bailor the well nigh impossible burden of determining and proving what happened to his property while it was hidden from sight in the depths of the defendant's warehouse. Similarly, such a rule would reward those warehouses with the least efficient inventory control procedures, since they would be most able to

by a third party was one possible explanation for the defendant's failure to redeliver the indium to plaintiff. This is simply insufficient, since the warehouse is required to show not merely what might conceivably have happened to the goods, but rather what actually happened to the goods. Defendant proved only that theft was possible, and presented no proof of an actual theft. Hence, the proffered explanation was inadequate as a matter of law.

4. We emphasize at this point that we do not suggest by our holding in this case that proof of negligence will support a recovery in conversion. Rather, our holding is limited to those situations in which the warehouse fails to provide an adequate explanation for its failure to return stored goods. If the warehouse comes forward with an explanation supported by evidentiary proof in admissible form, the plaintiff will then be required to prove that the loss was due to either negligence or conversion, depending on the circumstances. For plaintiff to recover in conversion after the warehouse has established a prima facie explanation for its failure to deliver, the trier of facts must find all the traditional elements of conversion.

honestly plead ignorance of the fate of goods entrusted to their care.

To prevent such absurd results, the law has long placed upon the warehouse the burden of advancing an adequate explanation of the reasons for its failure to properly return stored property * * *. This does not mean that the warehouse is required to prove that it acted properly, nor does this doctrine shift the burden of proof to the warehouse. Rather, the warehouse must come forward and explain the circumstances of the loss of or damage to the bailed goods upon pain of being held liable for negligence. If the warehouse does provide an explanation for the loss or damage, the plaintiff then must prove that the warehouse was at fault if he is to recover * * *. A few illustrations of this principle may be of some assistance. Where the warehouse simply refuses to return bailed property upon a legitimate demand and does not advance any explanation for that refusal, the plaintiff will be entitled to recover without more. Similarly, where the warehouse does suggest an explanation for the loss but is unable to proffer sufficient evidentiary support for that explanation to create a question of fact, as in this case, the plaintiff will be entitled to recover without more. Where, however, the warehouse proffers sufficient evidence supporting its explanation to create a question of fact, the jury must be instructed that if it believes that explanation, the plaintiff must be denied any recovery unless he has proven that the warehouse was at fault (Uniform Commercial Code, § 7–403, subd. [1], par. [b]). In other words, if the jury is persuaded that the goods were accidentally mislaid or destroyed in a fire or accident or stolen by a third party, the plaintiff cannot recover unless he has proven that the loss or the fire or the accident or the theft were the proximate result of either a purposive act or a negligent commission or omission by the warehouse.

Although it has long been settled that this is the rule in an action in negligence, there has been considerable inconsistency and uncertainty as to the application of this principle to an action in conversion. Thus, although we have on occasion declared that a bailor establishes a prima facie case of conversion by simply proving delivery to the bailee and an unexplained failure to return the stored goods upon demand * * * we have at other times indicated that something more is needed to maintain an action in conversion and that a plaintiff will be required to provide positive evidence of an intentional act by the warehouse inconsistent with the plaintiff's interest in the property * * *. We deem it unnecessary to engage in an extended discussion of each of the precedents in this area, for they appear essentially irreconcilable. Rather, we have decided to take this opportunity to re-examine the matter and to determine the most appropriate resolution of this controversy.

We now conclude that there exists no sound reason to apply a different rule to the two types of action where, as here, the bailee comes forward with insufficient proof of its explanation for the loss of the bailed goods. The same policy considerations which prevent a warehouse from avoiding liability in negligence by a declaration of ignorance appear equally applicable to an action in conversion. Indeed, as a practical matter, a bailor will be even less able to prove conversion by a warehouse than he would negligence, since a warehouseman who actually converts stored property will generally strive mightily to prevent knowledge of his malfeasance from coming to light. The possibility of fraud is obvious, for a dishonest warehouseman might well be encouraged to convert bailed property if he could then obtain the benefit of a contractual limitation of liability by the simple expedient of professing ignorance as to the fate of the goods. The rule requiring a warehouse to explain the loss of or damage to the goods lest it be held liable would be severely undermined could a warehouse avoid the bulk of potential liability in such a case by means of a contractual provision.

We note, moreover, that the requirement that a warehouse provide an explanation for loss of property entrusted to it is certainly not overly harsh, nor does it impose a heavy burden upon the warehouse. The warehouse must only offer proof of what actually happened to the goods and need not show that it was free from fault, for once the warehouse makes the initial required showing, the burden of proving the warehouse to be at fault will fall squarely upon the plaintiff. No greater duty of care is created by this rule, nor does it establish any sort of strict liability. Certainly a warehouse may reasonably be required to keep track of goods entrusted to it and to supply an accurate explanation of any loss to the bailor.

Finally, where a warehouse does not explain the cause of the loss, it would appear as reasonable to assume that this profession of ignorance is due to the fact that the warehouse has converted the goods as to presume that it is due to the fact that the warehouse has been negligent. Indeed, one who commits an intentional wrong is more likely to attempt to cover his tracks than one who has been at most negligent, especially in light of the disparity in potential liability created by the insertion of a limitation of liability clause. For all these reasons, we conclude that plaintiff was entitled to summary judgment in its action in conversion. Quite simply, plaintiff proved delivery of the indium to defendant warehouse and defendant's subsequent failure to return the metal, whereas defendant has not come forward with adequate evidentiary proof in admissible form to support its suggested explanation of that failure. That being so, the limitation on liability was inapplicable, and plaintiff was entitled to recover the actual value of the missing indium.

Accordingly, the order appealed from should be affirmed, with costs.

JASEN, JUDGE (dissenting).   My disagreement with the majority stems from their conclusion that plaintiff is entitled to summary judgment on the theory of conversion absent any proof whatsoever that defendant converted the indium metal to its own use or the use of another.   The plaintiff bailor having failed to demonstrate in an evidentiary manner an intentional act by the defendant bailee which worked to deprive the plaintiff of its property, the defendant should not be held liable for the conversion of the stored property.

* * *

Conversion is viewed as requiring "an intentional exercise of dominion or control over a chattel which so seriously interferes with the right of another to control it that the actor may justly be required to pay the other the full value of the chattel." (Restatement, Torts 2d, § 222A * * *.)   Thus, one who does not intentionally exercise dominion or control over property is not liable for conversion, even though his act or omission may be said to constitute negligence.   As was stated in Magnin v. Dinsmore, 70 N.Y. 410, 417: "A conversion implies a wrongful act, a misdelivery, a wrongful disposition, or withholding of the property.   A mere nondelivery will not constitute a conversion, nor will a refusal to deliver, on demand, if the goods have been lost through negligence, or have been stolen." * * *

While proof of delivery to a bailee, of a demand for the property's return, and of a failure of the bailee to return the goods establishes a prima facie case of negligence, these items of proof do not, in my opinion, constitute a prima facie case of conversion. The majority, obviously recognizing this fact, resorts to a newly created presumption of conversion in order to sustain the judgment rendered plaintiff below.   Such legal reasoning is unwarranted.

First, I would consider the law in this commercial area well settled and in accordance with the basic principle that a cause of action sounding in conversion will not be maintainable absent proof of intentional wrongdoing by the bailee. * * * Here, plaintiff has presented no proof whatsoever of an intentional wrongdoing by defendant, and the majority's conclusion that this "record * * * suffices to sustain plaintiff's action in conversion" flies in the face of this established rule that an action for conversion requires an evidentiary showing that defendant bailee *intentionally* acted in a manner so as to deprive plaintiff of its property.

Second, I take issue with the policy reasons cited by the majority to support their obliteration of the distinction between negligence and conversion—that the bailee is in the better position to explain what happened to the goods and, thus, should be required to come forth with such explanation; and that instances of fraud would proliferate if a bailee could merely profess ignorance as to the goods' disappearance and, then, claim as a sanctuary the contractual limitation of liability. While I would agree that a bailee should keep track of goods entrusted to it and that a bailee is in a better position than the bailor to explain what happened to the goods, it does not follow that its failure to produce the stored goods upon demand should serve as the vehicle to thrust upon the bailee the burden traditionally placed upon a plaintiff bailor when suing in conversion to demonstrate an intentional act by the defendant bailee which worked to deprive that plaintiff of its property. As a matter of public policy, I believe the burden of proving a wrongful act such as conversion should remain upon the party claiming it, rather than the one accused of the wrongdoing.

There is simply no rational reason, under the guise of policy considerations, to shift the burden of coming forward with evidence of what "actually happened" [4] to the goods when a cause of action is framed in conversion. If the bailor is seeking to circumvent the contractual limitation on damages, agreed upon by the parties as a condition of the bailment, the bailor should be put to the task of demonstrating that the bailee converted the goods to its own use or the use of another. To hold otherwise is to permit the bailor to have its cake and eat it too. This is so because the bailor, as in this case, need not declare the full value of the goods and, as a result, is required to pay only a *de minimus* bailment fee, rather than a fee based on actual value; yet, upon loss of the goods, it may seek compensation for their full value even though it was never disclosed to the bailee.

This, it seems to me, is fundamentally unfair, especially when one considers that plaintiff voluntarily signed as a condition of bailment a contractual limitation of liability ($50) as to each article and item stored, although the true value of the three lots of indium was $100,000. The limitation of liability and the actual value of the stored property were known to plaintiff, and yet it chose not to avail itself of the opportunity to declare the full value of the goods to insure that it would be made whole in case of loss. Plaintiff had only to be candid about the true value of the goods

---

4. The majority stesses that their holding is limited to only requiring a warehouseman to establish, in the first instance, "a prima facie explanation for its failure to deliver" the goods [footnote 4]. However, I derive little solace from this qualification, inasmuch as a bailee "is required to show not merely what might conceivably have happened to the goods, but rather what *actually* happened to the goods" [footnote 3] [emphasis added]. Since we are concerned with cases involving unexplained losses, the majority opinion sanctions, for all practical purposes, the imposition of full liability for the value of the goods stored whenever the bailee is unable to deliver the stored goods or explain "what actually happened to the goods." This, I suggest, is an onerous burden upon the warehouseman.

entrusted to defendant and pay a storage rate commensurate with the risk in order to protect itself from any and all loss, whether such loss be precipitated by fraud, conversion, negligence, or otherwise. Having not exercised this option and, thus, having paid a much lower storage fee than what would have been charged had the bailee known the true value of the goods and been responsible for the same, the bailor should be held to the terms of the bailment absent an affirmative evidentiary showing of intentional wrongdoing by the bailee. In this commercial setting, dealing as we are with sophisticated businessmen, we should not reach out and relieve the plaintiff of its failure to protect itself contractually. I can only read the majority's opinion as doing violence to the law, without rhyme or reason.

For the above-stated reasons, I would reverse the order of the Appellate Division and grant summary judgment to defendant.

COOKE, C.J., and JONES, WACHTLER, FUCHSBERG and MEYER, JJ., concur with GABRIELLI, J.

JASEN, J., dissents and votes to reverse in a separate opinion.

Order affirmed.

2. COMMERCIAL USES OF WAREHOUSE RECEIPTS

DOLAN, GOOD FAITH PURCHASE AND WAREHOUSE RECEIPTS: THOUGHTS ON THE INTERPLAY OF ARTICLES 2, 7, AND 9 OF THE UCC
30 Hast.L.J. 1, 2–3 (1978).

Functions of the Warehouse Receipt

Historically, documents of title such as warehouse receipts facilitated the practice of storing and transporting commodities. More recently, the receipt has taken on significant marketing and financing features.

The Marketing Function

For some purchasers, delivery is not an essential part of the purchase transaction. Grain dealers, for example, frequently purchase from producers and sell to industry consumers without moving the grain from the elevators to which the producers delivered it for drying and storing after harvest. Customarily these buyers and sellers effect such transfers by negotiable warehouse receipts. The producer obtains the receipt, which describes the grain according to industry standards; the grain dealer then purchases the receipt and transfers it, perhaps through a series of buyers, to a buyer who desires to ship or otherwise take possession of the grain. This last purchaser then surrenders the receipt to the elevator and takes delivery. The result is that the parties have achieved the marketing of the grain without incurring unnecessary transportation expenses.

Similarly, in the cotton industry a producer will deliver cotton to a gin for processing and storing. The gin will issue a negotiable receipt for the cotton with a sample attached. Brokers then display the samples to buyers who may be located in markets distant from the gin. Upon receipt of a satisfactory offer, the broker forwards the receipt with a draft through banking channels. When the purchaser honors the draft the bank delivers the receipt; the purchaser, unless he desires to resell the cotton without taking possesssion, will surrender the receipt to the gin and take delivery of the goods. Again, the receipt simplifies the marketing process and saves transportation costs.

The Financing Function

In transactions similar to the foregoing illustrations, market conditions or production schedules may force a buyer to hold a commodity. During that interval the buyer owns a valuable asset but cannot utilize it and, therefore, may seek to borrow against it. Lenders will grant credit on the security of the stored commodity by taking the negotiable warehouse receipt. When the borrower finds a buyer for the commodity or is prepared to use it in its own production process, the borrower will pay off the loan, obtain the receipt from the creditor and surrender the receipt to the warehouse against delivery of the goods.

Some borrowers use nonnegotiable receipts in connection with inventory financing. This form of inventory loan satisfies a lender's policing requirements in situations in which the lender fears his collateral may disappear quickly. The borrower delivers the inventory to a "field warehouse," usually a part of the borrower's premises controlled by an independent, field-warehouse company. The warehouse then issues nonnegotiable receipts to the lender. When the borrower needs inventory to fill customer orders, he will satisfy a portion of the loan; the lender in turn will issue delivery orders to the field warehouse, which will then release part of the inventory to the borrower.

These models illustrate typical patterns through which business people employ warehouse receipts to save transaction costs and to achieve liquidity. The models also forecast the potential conflicts in these commodity paper transactions. With respect to each purchase, for example, there is the classic tension between the purchaser, on the one hand, and the seller's secured lender, on the other. Conflicts between purchasers and lenders claiming an interest in the same goods may also arise because some sellers will enter into a contract of sale with more than one buyer or grant a security interest to more than one lender.

3. WAREHOUSE RECEIPTS FOR FUNGIBLE GOODS

Suppose Farmer delivers 1,000 units of grain to Warehouse Co. for storage in a grain elevator that Warehouse operates. The grain will lose its identity by being added to the mass of similar grain in the grain elevator. The grain in this case is referred to as "fungible goods." § 1–201(17). How do we characterize the transaction if Warehouse issues to Farmer a warehouse receipt for the grain? Conceptually the transaction does not have the normal characteristics of a bailment because Farmer is not entitled to get back the same grain that Farmer deposited. If the transaction is not a bailment, how is it analyzed? We could say that Farmer transferred title to the grain to Warehouse and, in return, Farmer received the obligation of Warehouse to pay on demand the economic equivalent of the deposited grain measured at the time of demand. Thus, if Farmer deposited 1,000 units of grain Farmer is entitled on demand to receive from Warehouse 1,000 units of similar grain or its then market value if Warehouse does not have the grain to deliver. Whether the transaction is characterized in this way or as a bailment is not important so long as Warehouse is solvent. In either case Warehouse is required to deliver grain to Farmer, or if it has no grain to deliver, its value. Characterization of the transaction is important, however, in the case of insolvency of Warehouse.

If Farmer gave up title to the grain in exchange for a claim against Warehouse, Farmer is only an unsecured creditor of Warehouse which is now an insolvent debtor. Grain owned by Warehouse is an asset available for payment of all creditors of Warehouse. If the transaction is treated as a bailment, Farmer has an ownership interest in the grain held by Warehouse for Farmer at the time of the insolvency proceeding. In that case Farmer is asserting a claim to Farmer's grain rather than a creditor's claim against Warehouse.

Section 7–207 deals with this issue. Under the first sentence of subsection (2) Farmer is an owner of the grain held by Warehouse, as a tenant in common with other "persons entitled" to the grain. The extent of Farmer's right to the grain is affected by the question of "overissue" addressed in § 7–402 and the last sentence of § 7–207(2).

Sometimes a warehouseman will fraudulently or mistakenly issue a warehouse receipt for goods which were never deposited in the warehouse. Assume that that occurred with respect to a negotiable warehouse receipt covering goods specifically identified in the receipt rather than fungible goods. The warehouse receipt was then duly negotiated to a bank as collateral for a loan. § 7–

501. In the event of default by the debtor the bank's expectation is that it can, under § 7–502 and § 7–403(1), obtain possession of the goods represented by the receipt and use the goods as a source of payment of the debt. But since the warehouse receipt does not in fact represent any goods deposited with the warehouseman, all that the bank has is a claim for damages against the warehouseman. § 7–203. If the warehouseman becomes insolvent the bank's collateral is reduced to an unsecured claim against the warehouseman that may have no value. How is the case changed if the warehouse receipt did not purport to represent specifically identified goods, but rather fungible goods like grain?

Let us return to our original hypothetical case. Assume that originally there was no grain on deposit in the grain elevator of Warehouse. Then, Farmer A and Farmer B each deposited 3,000 units of grain. Warehouse commingled the grain and issued negotiable warehouse receipts for 3,000 units to each of them. Farmer A and Farmer B became tenants in common of the 6,000 units in the grain elevator. § 7–207(2), first sentence. Warehouse then fraudulently issued a negotiable warehouse receipt for 3,000 units of grain to Farmer C who deposited no grain. The receipt purported to give to Farmer C common tenancy ownership rights in grain held by Warehouse. But since the only grain held by Warehouse is that deposited by Farmer A and Farmer B, the receipt issued to Farmer C was an overissue. Warehouse held 6,000 units of grain and issued receipts covering 9,000 units. The normal rule, applicable to goods other than fungible goods, is that if two warehouse receipts have been issued for the same goods the second receipt is not effective to confer any rights to the goods. § 7–402. The issuer is liable for damages caused by the overissue (§ 7–203) but the holder of the second receipt gets no ownership right to the goods. But Article 7 applies a different rule to commingled fungible goods. If Farmer C duly negotiates the warehouse receipt to Bank as collateral for a loan, the apparent result under the second sentence of § 7–207(2) is that Bank acquires common tenancy ownership rights equal to those of Farmer A and Farmer B even though no deposit of grain was made with respect to Bank's warehouse receipt. Before Farmer C duly negotiated the warehouse receipt to Bank, Farmer A and Farmer B owned 3,000 units each. After that event they and Bank each owned 2,000 units. The last sentence of § 7–207(2) is a change from pre-Code law. 1 Hawkland, Transactional Guide to the UCC 367 (1964).

Thus, persons entitled under warehouse receipts (§ 7–403(4)) with respect to commingled grain have ownership rights in the commingled mass but they bear the risk that their interest in the commingled grain may be reduced as the result of overissued receipts that are duly negotiated. This risk is similar to the risk that they take with respect to fraudulent sales by the warehouse-

man of commingled grain which is not owned by the warehouseman. Frequently, the warehouseman is in the business of buying
and selling grain for its own account as well as storing grain for
others. In that case, some of the grain in the elevator is owned by
the warehouseman and some of the grain is owned by holders of
warehouse receipts. If the warehouseman sells and delivers some
of the latter grain to a person who is a buyer in ordinary course of
business (§ 1–201(9)), that person gets good title to the grain and
defeats any ownership claim of the defrauded holders. § 7–205.
The rationale of § 7–205 is similar to that of § 2–403(2).

Branch, the case that follows, involved the rights of a bank
which took as collateral for a loan fraudulently issued negotiable
warehouse receipts which purported to represent grain deposited
in the warehouse, but which in fact were issued without any
deposit having been made.

BRANCH BANKING & TRUST CO. v. GILL

Supreme Court of North Carolina, 1977.
293 N.C. 164, 237 S.E.2d 21.

[Woodcock was the manager of Farmers Grain Elevator at
Warsaw ("Elevator"), a public warehouse, and was also Secretary-
Treasurer of Southeastern Farmers Grain Association, Inc.
("Southeastern"), which was engaged in the business of buying and
selling grain. All warehouse receipts issued by Elevator bore
Woodcock's signature. The plaintiff, Branch Banking & Trust Co.
("Bank") loaned money to Southeastern under an agreement
which provided that warehouse receipts representing stored grain
would be pledged as security for the loans. Bank was aware that
Woodcock was employed by both Elevator and Southeastern.
Southeastern pledged to Bank 13 negotiable warehouse receipts
(numbered 974–986) issued by Elevator as collateral for loans
totalling $314,354.38. The 13 warehouse receipts were fraudulent-
ly issued by Woodcock. They did not represent any grain deposited by Southeastern with Elevator.]

SHARP, CHIEF JUSTICE. In our earlier opinion in this case we
held: (1) that the Bank did not take the 13 fraudulent warehouse
receipts (Nos. 974–986) by "due negotiation" and thus did not
acquire the rights specified in UCC § 7–502; (2) that "nothing else
appearing" the Bank was merely a transferee of the negotiable
warehouse receipts and thus acquired no greater rights or title
than its transferor, Southeastern; * * *

Our prior holding that the Bank did not take the 13 receipts
through "due negotiation" is clearly correct.

* * *

By their terms, the grain the 13 warehouse receipts purportedly represented was to be delivered to Southeastern or to its
order. These receipts, therefore, were negotiable documents of

title.   UCC § 1–201(15), UCC § 7–102(1)(e), UCC § 7–104(1)(a).
These receipts, however, were not indorsed by Southeastern at the
time they were delivered to the Bank.   Neither Woodcock, the
secretary-treasurer, nor any other officer of Southeastern ever
signed the receipts.   Upon Bank's request for its indorsement,
Southeastern's bookkeeper, Mrs. Carlton, stamped the name
"Southeastern Farmers Grain Association, Inc." on the reverse
side of the receipts.

As we said in our former opinion, "[T]he affixing of the
payee's (or subsequent holder's) name upon the reverse side of a
negotiable document of title by rubber stamp is a valid indorsement, if done by a person authorized to indorse for the payee and
with intent thereby to indorse.   *   *   *   However, the Superior
Court found that Mrs. Carlton, who stamped the name of Southeastern upon the reverse side of these receipts, had neither the
authority nor the intent thereby to indorse them in the name of
Southeastern.   The evidence supports these findings and would
support no contrary finding."   *   *   *   Since the receipts were not
properly indorsed to the Bank, they were not negotiated to it.   The
Bank, therefore, not having acquired the receipts through "due
negotiation," did not acquire the rights provided in UCC § 7–502.

Under UCC § 7–506 the Bank could compel Southeastern to
supply the lacking indorsement to the 13 receipts.   However, the
transfer "becomes a negotiation only as of the time the indorsement is supplied."   Since the Bank was specifically informed of
the fraud surrounding the issuance of the receipts on the evening
of 7 May 1970 any subsequent indorsement by Southeastern would
be ineffective to make the Bank "a holder to whom a negotiable
document of title [was] duly negotiated."   UCC § 7–501(4).

Thus, because of the lack of proper negotiation, the Bank
became a mere transferee of the 13 warehouse receipts.   The
status of such a transferee is fixed by UCC § 7–504(1) which
provides: "A transferee of a document, whether negotiable or
nonnegotiable, to whom the document has been delivered but not
duly negotiated, acquires the title and rights which his transferor
had or had actual authority to convey."   Here Southeastern, the
Bank's transferor, had no title by way of the fraudulent receipts to
any grain held by Elevator, and it had no rights against Elevator.
Woodcock, acting for and on behalf of Southeastern, had fraudulently procured the issuance of these receipts to Southeastern
without the deposit of any grain.   Then, as Southeastern's manager, he had pledged them to Bank in substitution of 16 previously
issued receipts purportedly representing corn deposited in Elevator.   However, at least six of these represented no grain at the
time they were issued, and between the warehouse examiner's
inspections of 10 February 1970 and May 1970,—without requiring
the surrender of any receipts—Elevator had delivered to or for the

account of Southeastern nearly 113,000 bushels of grain more than Southeastern allegedly had in storage there. Thus, Elevator had no obligation to deliver any grain to Southeastern, and it did not become obligated to Bank merely because Southeastern transferred the receipts.

*   *   *

The purpose of UCC § 7–203 is to protect specified parties to or purchasers of warehouse receipts by imposing liability upon the warehouseman when either he or his agent fraudulently or mistakenly issues receipts (negotiable or nonnegotiable) for misdescribed or nonexistent goods. This section, coupled with the definition of issuer (UCC § 7–102(1)(g)), clearly places upon the warehouseman the risk that his agent may fraudulently or mistakenly issue improper receipts. The theory of the law is that the warehouseman, being in the best position to prevent the issuance of mistaken or fraudulent receipts, should be obligated to do so; that such receipts are a risk and cost of the business enterprise which the issuer is best able to absorb. *   *   *

In the Comment to UCC § 7–203 it is said: "The issuer is liable on documents issued by an agent, contrary to instructions of his principal, without receiving goods. No disclaimer of the latter liability is permitted." *Issuer* is defined by UCC § 7–102 as "a bailee who issues a document. *   *   * Issuer includes any person for whom an agent or employee purports to act in issuing a document if the agent or employee has real or apparent authority to issue documents, notwithstanding that the issuer received no goods or that the goods were misdescribed or that in any other respect the agent or employee violated his instructions." Under these provisions Elevator would clearly be liable to the Bank on the 13 fraudulent receipts issued by its agent Woodcock *provided* the Bank could carry its burden of affirmatively proving that it came within the protection of UCC § 7–203.

*   *   *

We now consider whether the Bank qualifies for this protection. At the outset of our discussion we note that UCC § 7–203 contains no requirement that the purchaser take negotiable documents through "due negotiation" before he can recover from the issuer. (Compare this section with the analogous U.C.C. provision covering bills of lading, which provides protection to "a consignee of a nonnegotiable bill who has given value in good faith or a holder to whom a negotiable bill has been duly negotiated relying in either case upon the description *   *   *." UCC § 7–301(1).) Of course, had the Bank met all the requirements of due negotiation it also would have met the requirements of UCC § 7–203.

To be entitled to recover under UCC § 7–203 a claimant has the burden of proving that he (1) is a party to or *purchaser of a document of title* other than a bill of lading; (2) *gave value* for the document; (3) took the document in *good faith;* (4) *relied* to his detriment upon the description of the goods in the document; and (5) took *without notice* that the goods were misdescribed or were never received by the issuer. Many of these terms are defined in Article 1 of the U.C.C., and those definitions are also made applicable to Article 7.

Under UCC § 1–201(33) and UCC § 1–201(32) Bank acquired the 13 negotiable warehouse receipts by purchase. Further, when Bank surrendered to Southeastern its old notes and the 16 receipts securing them, taking in return the new notes secured by the 13 receipts, it gave "value." Under UCC § 1–201(44) a person, *inter alia,* gives "value" for rights if he acquires them "(b) as security for or in total or partial satisfaction of a pre-existing claim; or (d) generally, in return for any consideration sufficient to support a simple contract." It now remains to determine whether Bank, at the time it relinquished the 16 old receipts in return for the 13 receipts, was acting (1) without notice that no goods had been received by the issuer for the 13 receipts, (2) in good faith, and (3) in reliance upon the descriptions in the receipts.

The trial court, after making detailed findings as to facts known to Bank at the time it accepted the 13 receipts, found and concluded the ultimate fact that "the plaintiff Bank did not receive warehouse receipts numbered 974 through 986 in good faith without notice of claims and defenses." This finding, although stated in the negative in order to use the precise language of UCC § 7–501(4), is equivalent to a positive finding that Bank took the 13 receipts with notice that they were spurious. On the same findings the judge also concluded that plaintiff did not come into court with "clean hands." This finding likewise is equivalent in import and meaning to a finding that Bank did not take the 13 receipts in good faith. * * * Upon these findings he held that plaintiff had no cause of action either at law or in equity based on the 13 receipts against either the State Warehouse Superintendent or against the State Treasurer as custodian of the State Indemnity and Guaranty Fund. We must, therefore, determine whether these findings are supported by competent evidence.

Upon our reconsideration of this case we have concluded (1) that the record evidence fully supports the trial judge's findings that Bank did not take the receipts in good faith and without notice that they had been fraudulently issued and (2) that his findings compel his conclusions of law.

[The court's review of the evidence on the issue of good faith is omitted.]

The Code was not designed to permit those dealing in the commercial world to obtain rights by an absence of inquiry under circumstances amounting to an intentional closing of the eyes and mind to defects in or defenses to the transaction. * * * Nor did the General Assembly, when, by G.S. 106–435, it created the State Indemnifying and Guaranty Fund to safeguard the State Warehouse System and to make its receipts acceptable as collateral, intend that it should encourage individuals or financial institutions to engage in transactions from which they would otherwise have recoiled. On the contrary, the fund was created to protect those parties to or purchasers of warehouse receipts who, acting in good faith and without reason to know that the goods described thereon are misdescribed or nonexistent, suffer loss through their acceptance or purchase of the receipt.

The case comes down to this: Plaintiff Bank based its right to recover on the 13 fraudulent warehouse receipts numbered 974–986 for which Elevator received no grain. Its action, if any, was under UCC § 7–203. Therefore, if plaintiff could prove it acquired the receipts in good faith and without notice of the fraud, it was entitled to recover; otherwise, not. The trier of facts, upon sufficient evidence, found that plaintiff did not acquire the receipts in good faith and without notice.

The judgment of the trial court is therefore affirmed as to all defendants and our former decision as reported in 286 N.C. 342, 211 S.E.2d 327 (1975) is withdrawn.

Affirmed.

PROBLEM

Smith is manager of Grain Elevator, a public warehouse which also engages in the business of buying and selling grain. Grain Elevator stores in one common mass both the grain which it owns and the grain deposited by farmers for which it issues warehouse receipts. Smith is authorized to issue warehouse receipts on behalf of Grain Elevator. Smith is also President of Grain Corporation which is engaged in the business of buying and selling grain.

During a six-month period the following transactions occurred: 100 farmers each deposited with Grain Elevator 1,000 units of grain for which Grain Elevator issued negotiable warehouse receipts; Grain Elevator stored in its elevator 10,000 units of grain which it owned; and Grain Elevator sold 40,000 units of grain to various buyers in ordinary course of business. No other withdrawals of grain were made during the period. At the end of the period there were 70,000 units of grain in the elevator and there were outstanding negotiable warehouse receipts covering 100,000 units of grain. At that time Smith, acting on behalf of Grain Elevator, fraudulently issued a negotiable warehouse receipt to Grain Corporation for 20,000 units of grain. No grain was deposited by Grain Corporation. Grain Corporation then negotiated this warehouse receipt to Bank as collateral for a loan made contemporaneously. Bank acted in good faith and had no knowledge of the circumstances surrounding the issuance of the warehouse receipt. It believed that the warehouse receipt represented grain deposited with Grain Elevator by Grain Corporation.

Both Grain Elevator and Grain Corporation are now insolvent. Grain Elevator has in storage the same 70,000 units of grain on hand at the end of the six-month period. There are outstanding warehouse receipts covering 100,000 units of grain deposited by the 100 farmers and 20,000 units covered by the warehouse receipt held by Bank. Bank's loan to Grain Corporation remains unpaid.

Assume that in the insolvency proceedings any person who can prove ownership of the grain in the possession of Grain Elevator is entitled to take delivery free of the claims of the creditors of Grain Elevator.

1. What rights do the 100 farmers have against the customers of Grain Elevator who purchased the 40,000 units of grain during the six-month period? Should it make any difference that some of the farmers deposited grain before the sale of the 40,000 units to buyers in ordinary course while other farmers deposited grain after the sale?

2. What rights do the 100 farmers and Bank have to the grain held by Grain Elevator?

Chapter 15

RISK OF LOSS

_____

A. INTRODUCTION

After a buyer and seller have entered into a contract for the sale of goods, the goods are sometimes lost, destroyed, or damaged without fault of either party to the contract. The loss may occur either before or after the goods are delivered to the buyer. The problem is to decide which party must bear the loss. If the buyer bears the risk of loss the buyer must pay for the goods according to the contract in spite of the fact that it has received or will receive damaged goods or no goods at all. If the seller bears the risk of loss the seller, because it has not given to the buyer goods conforming to the contract, is not entitled to payment and may itself be in breach of contract. The person bearing the risk of loss, to recoup the loss, must proceed against any person who might be liable for causing the loss or against any insurer of the loss.

Under the Uniform Sales Act risk of loss fell on the person who held legal title to the goods at the time of the loss. This approach was abandoned in the UCC which sets forth, in § 2–509 and § 2–510, rules that determine on whom the risk shall fall in various cases. Section 2–509 governs cases in which at the time of loss neither party to the sales contract was in breach and § 2–510 governs cases in which either the buyer or the seller was in breach. The UCC rules are designed in large part to place the risk of loss on the person who is in the best position to carry on any claim procedure against a person responsible to pay the loss— usually an insurance company. Section § 2–401 states rules for determining who has legal title to the goods. This section should be examined along with § 2–509.

Section 2–509 covers three classes of cases: (1) those in which the contract contemplates shipment of the goods from the seller to the buyer by a carrier; (2) those in which the contract relates to goods held by a bailee; and (3) those in which the contract contemplates delivery of the goods by the seller to the buyer without shipment.

B. CONTRACTS CONTEMPLATING SHIPMENT OF GOODS

Suppose Seller, in Los Angeles, and Buyer, in New York, make a contract for a sale of oranges. The contract describes the oranges and states the price, but is silent on the question of how possession of the oranges is to be transferred from Seller to Buyer. Suppose Seller put the oranges in the possession of a railroad company with orders to deliver the oranges to Buyer in New York upon payment by Buyer of the transportation charges. During transit the oranges were destroyed when the train in which they were being transported was derailed. If we assume that Seller delivered to the carrier oranges that conformed to the contract, is Buyer obliged to pay the contract price?

Who owned the oranges at the time the loss occurred? § 2–401(2), § 2–308(a), § 2–311(2), § 2–503(2) and Comment 5, § 2–504. Examine § 2–509(1)(a) and (b). Was Seller required or authorized to ship the oranges? If you conclude that Seller was authorized to ship the oranges, was Seller authorized to require payment of the transportation charges by Buyer? How would the rights of the parties have been changed if the contract had provided for shipment of the oranges F.O.B. Los Angeles, or if it had provided for shipment F.O.B. New York? § 2–319(1). What effect do shipment terms have on the risk of loss under § 2–509(1)? Consider the following case.

EBERHARD MANUFACTURING CO. v. BROWN

Michigan Court of Appeals, 1975.
61 Mich.App. 268, 232 N.W.2d 378.

J. H. GILLIS, PRESIDING JUDGE. Plaintiff brought action to recover for the price of goods sold and delivered to defendant pursuant to a distributorship agreement. Defendant counterclaimed for damages for breach of the agreement. The matter was tried in the 48th District Court and the judge, sitting without a jury, gave judgment for defendant on his counterclaim in the amount of $6,315.82.

Plaintiff appealed to the circuit court, which affirmed the district court judgment. Application for leave to appeal was denied in this Court. Subsequently the Supreme Court granted leave to appeal and remanded the cause to this Court.

Plaintiff has made five assignments of error. Only two of these require discussion. First, the plaintiff alleges that the court erred in giving defendant a credit of $559.03 for goods which were apparently lost in transit.

At trial, the plaintiff introduced evidence that the goods were sold to defendant F.O.B. plaintiff's factory, and the goods were placed by plaintiff on board a common carrier with instructions to deliver to defendant. This evidence was not controverted by any evidence of defendant's. It is plaintiff's contention that the risk of loss passed to defendant buyer when the goods were put on board the carrier.

On appeal both parties point to UCC § 2–509(1) as controlling. Plaintiff, however, cites subsection (a) and defendant subsection (b). Subsection (a) states the rule where the contract is a "shipment" contract, in which case risk of loss passes to the buyer where the goods are duly delivered to the carrier; subsection (b) states the rule where a contract is a "destination" contract, in which case risk of loss passes to the buyer when the goods are duly tendered at the destination.

An agreement of the parties would control as to who has the risk of loss. UCC § 2–509(4), UCC § 1–102(3); (Official UCC Comment 3); UCC § 2–303. * * *

The parties here did not expressly agree on who was to bear the risk of loss. The contract contained no F.O.B. term. See UCC § 2–319. There was testimony by plaintiff that its goods are sold F.O.B. place of shipment, plaintiff's factory. That testimony might be evidence of a usage of trade. See UCC § 1–205. It was not proof that the parties had agreed, expressly or in fact, as to who had the risk of loss.

Under Article 2 of the Uniform Commercial Code, the "shipment" contract is regarded as the normal one and the "destination" contract as the variant type. The seller is not obligated to deliver at a named destination and bear the concurrent risk of loss until arrival, unless he has specifically agreed so to deliver or the commercial understanding of the terms used by the parties contemplates such delivery. UCC § 2–503 (Official UCC Comment 5). Thus a contract which contains neither an F.O.B. term nor any other term explicitly allocating loss is a shipment contract.

Defendant argues that since the goods were to be shipped to defendant's place of business in Birmingham, the contract required plaintiff to deliver the goods "at a particular destination." See UCC § 2–509(1)(b). Defendant's position is that "ship to" substitutes for and is equivalent to an F.O.B. term, namely F.O.B. place of destination. But that argument is persuasively refuted by the response that a "ship to" address must be supplied in any case in which carriage is contemplated. Thus a "ship to" term has no significance in determining whether a contract is a shipment or destination contract for risk of loss purposes.

Other buyers have occasionally argued that the "ship to" term made the contract into a destination contract. Courts have properly rejected this argument. * * *

Since the presumption of a shipment contract controls in this case, the trial court should not have given defendant the $559.03 credit for the lost shipment.

* * *

C. SALES OF GOODS IN THE POSSESSION OF
THE SELLER OR IN THE POSSESSION
OF A BAILEE

A sale is defined in § 2–106 as consisting of "the passing of title from the seller to the buyer for a price." Usually this passage of title (§ 2–401) is accompanied by a delivery of the goods by the seller to the buyer. The most common example is the retail sale in which the goods are handed over to the buyer at the seller's place of business. Sometimes, the goods are delivered by the seller to the buyer at the buyer's place of business or residence. In dealing with the question of when risk of loss passes when a sale of this type is contemplated, § 2–509(3) states one rule for sellers that fit the definition of "merchant" (§ 2–104(1)) and another rule for non-merchant sellers. What is the policy basis for this distinction? Comment 3 to § 2–509. Merchant status affects the rights and obligations of a party to a sales contract in a number of different contexts. Comment 2 to § 2–104 explains how a person can be considered a merchant for some purposes under the UCC and not for others. The rules of § 2–509(3) involve two defined terms: "receipt" of goods (§ 2–103(1)(c)) and "tender of delivery" of goods (§ 2–503(1)). The rules of § 2–509 are subject to any contrary agreement of the parties. § 2–303.

Sometimes the sale is of goods that are not in the seller's possession. For example, at the time of sale the goods might be in the possession of a commercial bailee such as a warehouseman or a common carrier. In this kind of case the sale consists only of passage of title to the goods. There is no accompanying delivery of the goods, but normally the sale is accompanied by some act by the seller or the bailee that puts the buyer in a position to get possession of the goods. This type of sale is covered by § 2–509(2), which is discussed in *Jason's Foods*, which follows.

Although subsections (2) and (3) of § 2–509 are meant to deal with two types of sales that in most cases are easily differentiated, sometimes it is not easy to decide which of the two subsections controls. *Caudle*, on p. 1137, illustrates the problem.

JASON'S FOODS, INC. v. PETER ECKRICH
& SONS, INC.

United States Court of Appeals, Seventh Circuit, 1985.
774 F.2d 214.

POSNER, CIRCUIT JUDGE.

* * * Section 2–509(2) of the Uniform Commercial Code as adopted in Illinois (whose law, the parties agree, governs this diversity suit) provides that where "goods are held by a bailee to be delivered without being moved, the risk of loss passes to the buyer * * * (b) on acknowledgment by the bailee of the buyer's

right to possession of the goods." * * * We must decide whether acknowledgment to the *seller* complies with the statute. There are no reported cases on the question, either in Illinois or elsewhere. Three commentators have opined that acknowledgment must be to the buyer, but without discussion. See Nordstrom, Handbook of the Law of Sales 404–05 (1970); Howard, Allocation of Risk of Loss Under the UCC: A Transactional Evaluation of Sections 2–509 and 2–510, 15 UCC L.J. 334, 347 n. 42 (1983); Comment, Risk of Loss Under Section 2509 of the California Uniform Commercial Code, 20 UCLA L.Rev. 1352, 1358 n. 30 (1973). There is a hint of the same position, again without explanation, in Latty, Sales and Title and the Proposed Code, 16 Law & Contemp.Prob. 3, 14 (1951); Note, Risk of Loss Under the Uniform Commercial Code, 7 Ind.L.Rev. 711, 726 (1974), and Note, Commercial Transactions: Risk of Loss: What Does the Code Mean by Bailee?, 21 Okla.L.Rev. 310 (1968). The defendant submitted in the district court an affidavit from a professor of commercial law at Ohio State University (Professor Clovis), who also concluded, also without elaboration, that acknowledgment must be to the buyer. * * *

On or about December 30, 1982, Jason's Foods contracted to sell 38,000 pounds of "St. Louis style" pork ribs to Peter Eckrich & Sons, delivery to be effected by a transfer of the ribs from Jason's' account in an independent warehouse to Eckrich's account in the same warehouse—which is to say, without the ribs actually being moved. In its confirmation of the deal, Jason's notified Eckrich that the transfer in storage would be made between January 10 and January 14. On January 13 Jason's phoned the warehouse and requested that the ribs be transferred to Eckrich's account. A clerk at the warehouse noted the transfer on its books immediately but did not mail a warehouse receipt until January 17 or January 18, and it was not till Eckrich received the receipt on January 24 that it knew the transfer had taken place. But on January 17 the ribs had been destroyed by a fire at the warehouse. Jason's sued Eckrich for the price. If the risk of loss passed on January 13 when the ribs were transferred to Eckrich's account, or at least before the fire, Jason's is entitled to recover the contract price; otherwise not. The district judge ruled that the risk of loss did not pass by then and therefore granted summary judgment for Eckrich.

Jason's argues that when the warehouse transferred the ribs to Eckrich's account, Jason's lost all rights over the ribs, and it should not bear the risk of loss of goods it did not own or have any right to control. Eckrich owned them and Eckrich's insurance covered any ribs that it owned; Jason's had no insurance and anyway, Jason's argues, it could not insure what it no longer owned. (The warehouse would be liable for the fire damage only if negligent. Cf. Refrigeration Sales Co. v. Mitchell-Jackson, Inc.,

770 F.2d 98 (7th Cir.1985).) Finally, Jason's points out that the draftsmen of the Uniform Commercial Code were careful and deliberate. Both subsections (a) and (c) of section 2–509(2)—the subsections that surround the "acknowledgment" provision at issue in this case—provide that the risk of loss passes to the buyer on or after "his receipt" of a document of title (negotiable in (a), nonnegotiable in (c)). If the draftsmen had meant that the acknowledgment of the buyer's right to possession of the goods—the acknowledgment that is subsection (b)'s substitute for a document of title—must be to the buyer, they would have said so.

Eckrich argues with great vigor that it cannot be made to bear the loss of goods that it does not know it owns. But that is not so *outré* a circumstance as it may sound. If you obtain property by inheritance, you are quite likely to own it before you know you own it. And Eckrich's position involves a comparable paradox: that Jason's continued to bear the risk of loss of goods that it knew it no longer owned. So the case cannot be decided by reference to what the parties knew or did not know; and neither can it be decided, despite Jason's' urgings, on the basis of which party could have insured against the loss. Both could have. Jason's had sufficient interest in the ribs until the risk of loss shifted to Eckrich to insure the ribs until then. You do not have to own goods to insure them; it is enough that you will suffer a loss if they are lost or damaged, * * * as of course Jason's would if the risk of loss remained on it after it parted with title. * * * Section 2–509(2) separates title from risk of loss. Title to the ribs passed to Eckrich when the warehouse made the transfer on its books from Jason's' account to Eckrich's, but the risk of loss did not pass until the transfer was "acknowledged."

Thus, as is usually the case, insurability cannot be used to guide the assignment of liability. (The costs of insurance might sometimes be usable for this purpose, as we shall see, but not in this case.) Since whoever will be liable for the loss can insure against it, the court must determine who is liable before knowing who can insure, rather than vice versa. If acknowledgment to the seller is enough to place the risk of loss on the buyer, then Eckrich should have bought insurance against any losses that occurred afterward. If acknowledgment to the buyer is necessary (we need not decide whether acknowledgment to a third party may ever suffice), Jason's should have bought insurance against any losses occurring until then.

The suggestion that the acknowledgment contemplated by subsection (b) can be to the seller seems very strange. What purpose would it serve? When Jason's called up the warehouse and directed that the transfer be made, it did not add: and by the way, acknowledge to me when you make the transfer. Jason's assumed, correctly, that the transfer was being made forthwith;

and in fact there is no suggestion that the warehouse clerk ever "acknowledged" the transfer to Jason's. If the draftsmen of subsection (b) had meant the risk of loss to pass when the transfer was made, one would think they would have said so, and not complicated life by requiring "acknowledgment."

A related section of the Uniform Commercial Code, section 2–503(4)(a), makes acknowledgment by the bailee (the warehouse here) a method of tendering goods that are sold without being physically moved; but, like section 2–509(2)(b), it does not indicate to whom acknowledgment must be made. The official comments on this section, however, indicate that it was not intended to change the corresponding section of the Uniform Sales Act, section 43(3). See UCC comment 6 to § 2–503. And section 43(3) had expressly required acknowledgment to the buyer. * * * Rules on tender have, it is true, a different function from rules on risk of loss; they determine at what point the seller has completed the performance of his side of the bargain. He may have completed performance, but if the goods are still in transit the risk of loss does not shift until the buyer receives them, if the seller is a merchant. See UCC § 2–509(3) and UCC comment 3 to section 2–509. In the case of warehouse transfers, however, the draftsmen apparently wanted risk of loss to conform to the rules for tender. For comment 4 to section 2–509 states that "where the agreement provides for delivery of the goods as between the buyer and seller without removal from the physical possession of a bailee, the provisions on manner of tender of delivery apply on the point of transfer of risk." And those provisions as we have said apparently require (in the case where no document of title passes) acknowledgment to the buyer. The acknowledgment need not, by the way, be in writing, so far as we are aware. Jason's could have instructed the warehouse to call Eckrich when the transfer was complete on the warehouse's books. * * * That is why Jason's' case is not utterly demolished by the fact that the document of title—that is, the warehouse receipt—was not received by Eckrich till after the fire. Acknowledgment in a less formal manner is authorized; indeed, section 509(2)(b) would have no function if the only authorized form of acknowledgment were by document of title, whether negotiable or nonnegotiable.

The second sentence of comment 4 to section 509 is also suggestive: "Due delivery of a negotiable document of title covering the goods or acknowledgment by the bailee that he holds for the buyer completes the 'delivery' and passes the risk." The reference to a document of title is to subsections (a) and (c); and in both of those cases, of course, the tender involves notice to the buyer. It would be surprising if the alternative of acknowledgment did not.

All this may seem a rather dry textual analysis, remote from the purposes of the Uniform Commercial Code, so let us shift now to the plane of policy. The Code sought to create a set of standard contract terms that would reflect in the generality of cases the preferences of contracting parties at the time of contract. One such preference is for assignments of liability—or, what amounts to the same thing, assignments of the risk of loss—that create incentives to minimize the adverse consequences of untoward events such as (in this case) a warehouse fire. There are two ways of minimizing such consequences. One is to make them less painful by insuring against them. Insurance does not prevent a loss—it merely spreads it—but in doing so it reduces (for those who are risk averse) the disutility of the loss. So if one of the contracting parties can insure at lower cost than the other, this is an argument for placing the risk of loss on him, to give him an incentive to do so. But that as we have seen is not a factor in this case; either party could have insured (or have paid the warehouse to assume strict liability for loss or destruction of the goods, in which event the warehouse would have insured them), and so far as the record shows at equal cost.

The other method of minimizing the consequences of an unanticipated loss is through prevention of the loss. If one party is in a better position than the other to prevent it, this is a reason for placing the risk of loss on him, to give him an incentive to prevent it. It would be a reason for placing liability on a seller who still had possession of the goods, even though title had passed. But between the moment of transfer of title by Jason's and the moment of receipt of the warehouse receipt by Eckrich, neither party to the sale had effective control over the ribs. They were in a kind of limbo, until (to continue the Dantesque image) abruptly propelled into a hotter region. With Jason's having relinquished title and Eckrich not yet aware that it had acquired it, neither party had an effective power of control.

But this is not an argument for holding that the risk of loss shifted at the moment of transfer; it is just an argument for regarding the parties' positions as symmetrical from the standpoint of ability either to prevent or to shift losses. In such a case we have little to assist us besides the language of subsection (b) and its surrounding subsections and the UCC comments; but these materials do point pretty clearly to the conclusion that the risk of loss did not pass at the moment of transfer.

When did it pass? Does "acknowledgment" mean receipt, as in the surrounding subsections of 2–509(2), or mailing? Since the evidence was in conflict over whether the acknowledgment was mailed on January 17 (and at what hour), which was the day of the fire, or on January 18, this could be an important question— but in another case. Jason's waived it. The only theory it tendered to the district court, or briefed and argued in this court, was that the risk of loss passed either on January 13, when the transfer of title was made on the books of the warehouse, or at the latest on January 14, because Eckrich knew the ribs would be transferred at the warehouse sometime between January 10 and 14. We have discussed the immateriality of the passage of title on January 13; we add that the alternative argument, that Eckrich knew by January 14 that it owned the ribs, exaggerates what Eckrich knew. By the close of business on January 14 Eckrich had a well-founded expectation that the ribs had been transferred to its account; but considering the many slips that are possible between cup and lips, we do not think that this expectation should fix the point at which the risk shifts. If you were told by an automobile dealer from whom you bought a car that the car would be delivered on January 14, you would not take out insurance effective that day, without waiting for the actual delivery.

Finally, Jason's' argument from trade custom or usage is unavailing. The method of transfer that the parties used was indeed customary but there was no custom or usage on when the risk of loss passed to the buyer.

Affirmed.

NOTE

Judge Posner states that "title to the ribs passed to Eckrich when the warehouse made the transfer on its books from Jason's' account to Eckrich's * * *." That occurred on January 13. A warehouse receipt was mailed to Eckrich on January 17 or 18 and the receipt was received on January 24. Section 2–401(2) and (3) state rules to determine when title passed. How do those provisions apply in *Jason's Foods?*

CAUDLE v. SHERRARD MOTOR CO.

Court of Civil Appeals of Texas, 1975.
525 S.W.2d 238.

AKIN, JUSTICE. The question on this appeal is whether the risk of loss of a house trailer had passed from the seller, Sherrard Motor Company, to the buyer, Caudle, under UCC § 2–509 before the house trailer was stolen from the seller's premises.

The relevant facts are undisputed. On February 10, 1972, plaintiff Sherrard Motor Company and defendant John Caudle entered into a contract for the purchase of a house trailer. It provided for a cash down payment of $2,685 and a balance of $4,005 in the form of a note payable to Sherrard. This contract was assigned with recourse to the Citizens National Bank of Denison, Texas, by Sherrard on the date executed. While Sherrard was making the trailer ready for the defendant, Caudle received a telephone call from his business office advising that he should return immediately to Dallas. Since the trailer was not ready, Caudle told Sherrard that he would return later to Denison and take possession of the trailer. Before Caudle returned and sometime between February 12 and 14, 1972, the house trailer was stolen from plaintiff's place of business. Upon learning of the theft, Caudle stopped payment on the check he had given Sherrard as down payment for the trailer. Sherrard then sued Caudle on the contract of sale for the contract price.

In answer to special issues, the jury found that a contract had been entered into between the parties; that Caudle breached the contract; and that Sherrard sustained no damage as a result of the breach by Caudle. The trial court, upon motion by Sherrard, entered a judgment *non obstante veredicto* in Sherrard's favor in the sum of $6,285.70. Caudle appeals from this judgment.

Caudle argues that the trial court erred in failing to grant Caudle's motion for an instructed verdict because there is no evidence that the contract was breached by Caudle. We agree. We hold that the contract failed as a matter of law for want of consideration since the trailer was stolen *before* the risk of loss under UCC § 2–509 had passed to Caudle. We, therefore, reverse and render the judgment of the trial court.

In making this determination, we were presented with three principal questions. First, had the risk of loss passed to the buyer, Caudle, before the trailer was stolen, because the trailer was held by a bailee, Sherrard, to be delivered without being moved pursuant to UCC § 2–509(2)? Secondly, did the contract provide that the risk of loss passed to Caudle when the contract was signed by the parties under UCC § 2–509(4)? Thirdly, had the risk of loss remained with the merchant-seller, Sherrard, because the trailer was stolen before the purchaser, Caudle, had taken actual physical possession of the goods pursuant to UCC § 2–509(3)? We answer questions one and two in the negative and question three in the affirmative.

It is plaintiff's contention that the risk of loss had passed to the defendant before the trailer's disappearance under UCC § 2–509(2)(b), which provides:

> Where the goods are held by a bailee to be delivered without being moved, the risk of loss passes to the buyer

> * * *

> (b) on acknowledgement by the bailee of the buyer's right to possession of the goods.

Plaintiff contends that it was acting as a bailee while the trailer remained on its premises and that by executing the contract, it had acknowledged the defendant's right to possession of the trailer. Plaintiff further argues that because it did not agree to deliver the trailer to Caudle in Dallas, the trailer was to be delivered to Caudle "without being moved." These arguments, however, erroneously assume that the plaintiff is a bailee under the Code. It is apparent that the drafters of the Code contemplated a common law commercial bailee, such as a warehouseman, when using the term "bailee" in UCC § 2–509(2). Certain analogies in the Code compel this conclusion. For example, a bailee is defined in UCC § 7–102(1)(A) as a person "who by a warehouse receipt, bill of lading or other document of title acknowledges possession of goods and *contracts to deliver them."* [Emphasis added.] UCC § 2–509(2)(a) speaks of goods held by a bailee to be delivered to the buyer on the buyer's receipt of a negotiable document of title and UCC § 2–509(2)(c) speaks of the buyer's receipt of a non-negotiable document of title. A document of title "includes bill of lading, dock warrant, dock receipt, warehouse receipt * * *. To be a document of title a document must purport to be issued by or addressed to a bailee and purport to cover goods in the bailee's possession * * *." UCC § 1–201(15). A bill of lading is defined as "a document evidencing the receipt of goods for shipment issued by a person *engaged in the business* of transporting or forwarding goods * * *." UCC § 1–201(6) [Emphasis added.] Similarly, a warehouse receipt is defined as "a receipt issued by a person *engaged in the business* of storing goods for hire." UCC § 1–201(45) [Emphasis added.] Implicit in this language is the concept that the party who issues these documents and acknowledges the buyer's right to possession of the goods be in the business of storing goods for hire—a commercial bailee. This is not true here. We conclude, therefore, that the plaintiff was not a bailee under the Code. Hence, UCC § 2–509(2) does not control the determination of whether the risk of loss had passed to the defendant.

Plaintiff contends further that if UCC § 2–509(2) is inapplicable then the risk of loss passed to the defendant pursuant to UCC § 2–509(4). This section provides that a buyer and seller may specifically enter into a contract contrary to the other provisions of UCC § 2–509. Plaintiff argues that such a contrary agreement was made because the terms of the contract for the sale of the trailer provided that the risk of loss passed to the defendant when the contract was signed by the parties.

The pertinent clause of the sales contract states:

> No transfer, renewal, extension or assignment of this agreement or any interest hereunder, and no loss, damage or destruction of said motor vehicle shall release buyer from his obligation hereunder.

We hold that this language is insufficient to constitute a "contrary agreement" between the parties pursuant to UCC § 2–509(4). A contract which shifts the risk of loss to the buyer before he receives the merchandise is so unusual that a seller who desires to achieve this result must clearly communicate his intent to the buyer. Hayward v. Postma, 31 Mich.App. 720, 188 N.W.2d 31, 33 (1971); Comment, Risk of Loss Under Section 2509 of the California Uniform Commercial Code, 20 U.C.L.A.L.Rev. 1352, 1362 (1973). This clause was apparently intended to fix responsibility for loss *after the defendant had taken possession* of the trailer. This interpretation is consistent with other provisions of the contract. For example, the contract provides that the "buyer shall keep said motor vehicle in good order and repair * * *." It would indeed be difficult for the buyer to honor this responsibility without having acquired actual possession of the trailer. It is also apparent that the provisions of the contract were drafted for the benefit of a third party—the bank or other lending institution to which the contract would be sold. The contract was assigned to the Citizens National Bank of Denison, Texas with recourse on Sherrard. Furthermore, since risk of loss is not specifically mentioned in the contract, we cannot say that an agreement to the contrary may be inferred from reading the document as a whole. We, therefore, conclude that it was not the intention of the parties to transfer risk of loss of the trailer *prior to delivery of possession to the buyer*. To hold otherwise would be to set a trap for the unwary. If parties intend to shift the burden of the risk of loss from the seller to the buyer before delivery of the goods, then such must be done in clear and unequivocal language.

It is defendant's contention that pursuant to UCC § 2–509(3) the risk of loss remained with the plaintiff because he had not taken actual physical possession of the trailer. We agree. That section provides,

> In any case not within Subsection (1) or (2), the risk of loss passes to the buyer on his receipt of the goods if the seller is a merchant; otherwise the risk of loss passes to the buyer on tender of delivery.

To determine if this section applies, the following questions must be resolved: (1) was the plaintiff a merchant? and (2) did the defendant receive the trailer? The plaintiff is a merchant under Article 2 of the Code as it "deals in goods of the kind * * * involved in the transaction * * *." UCC § 2–104(1). The language "receipt of the goods" is defined in the Code as "taking physical possession of them." UCC § 2–103(1)(c). It is undisputed that the defendant never took physical possession of the trailer; therefore, he had not received the goods. Accordingly, we hold that the risk of loss did not pass to the buyer before the trailer was stolen. It follows therefore, that no breach of contract occurred.

Our holding is in accordance with the underlying principles of UCC § 2–509 dealing with risk of loss. Under the Uniform Commercial Code, the risk of loss is no longer determined arbitrarily by which party had title to the goods at the time of the loss. Instead, as the drafters of the Code state: "The underlying theory of these sections on risk of loss is the adoption of the contractual approach * * *." Uniform Commercial Code, § 2–509, Comment 1. For example, under UCC § 2–509(1)(a) and (b), the risk of loss depends on whether the goods are shipped by a carrier pursuant to a "destination" or "shipment" *contract.* In addition, UCC § 2–509(4) provides that the buyer and seller are free to adjust by contract their rights and risks contrary to the other provisions of UCC § 2–509. Subject to the placement of a contractual approach at the analytic center of risk of loss problems is the policy that a party who had control over the handling of goods should bear their loss. For example, under UCC § 2–509(1)(a) and (b), the seller must bear the risk of loss until the goods reach the *control* of the carrier, if it is a "shipment" contract, or the buyer, if it is a "destination" contract. Strong policy reasons support this approach. The party in control is in the best position to handle properly the goods, to contract for shipment with a reliable carrier, and to insure the goods.[4] This theory is particularly applicable when the buyer is not a merchant and is unfamiliar with the problems of handling the goods.

Illustrative of these principles is the decision of Ellis v. Bell Aerospace Corp., 315 F.Supp. 221 (D.Or.1970), where the vendee purchased a helicopter from the defendant-vendor, and authorized him to store the helicopter with a bailee. The helicopter was later flown back to the vendor's factory where the plaintiff was to be instructed in its operation. During this instruction, the aircraft crashed. The court concluded that the vendor could not transfer risk of loss to the buyer until the buyer had actually received the merchandise, even though the buyer had paid the full price and had been notified that the goods were at his disposal. The fact that the helicopter had been held by a bailee with the consent of the buyer was not sufficient to bring the contract under Uniform Commercial Code, § 2–509(2), because the helicopter remained under the practical control of the vendor. The court further observed that a merchant who is to make delivery at his own place of business continues to maintain control over the goods and can be expected to carry insurance to protect his interest in them. On the other hand, the buyer has no control over the goods and may not have had the foresight to obtain insurance on the undelivered merchandise. Id. at 224. See also Baumgold Bros. v. Allan M. Fox Co., 375 F.Supp. 807 (N.D.Ohio 1973).

Accordingly, this cause is reversed and rendered.

---

4. Uniform Commercial Code, § 2–509, Comment 3 states:

The underlying theory of this rule is that a merchant who is to make physical delivery at his own place continues meanwhile to control the goods and can be expected to insure his interest in them. The buyer, on the other hand, has no control of the goods and it is extremely unlikely that he will carry insurance on goods not yet in his possession.

PROBLEMS

1.   Seller is engaged in two businesses at the same location. It sells boats and leases winter dead storage space in the boat yard.   In November Buyer ordered a boat from Seller.   It was agreed that when the boat was delivered by the manufacturer to Seller the boat would be placed in Seller's boat yard for winter storage.   When the boat arrived Buyer paid Seller the price of the boat and Seller delivered to Buyer a bill of sale as evidence of the sale.   In addition Buyer paid Seller the normal charge for storage space in Seller's boat yard.   In March the boat was destroyed by fire while stored in Seller's boat yard.   Who had the risk of loss? Is this case distinguishable from *Caudle*?

2.   On May 1 Seller sold to Buyer a boat that at the time was being stored with X who operated a boat yard where boats were stored for a fee.   Immediately after the sale Seller informed X that the boat had been sold to Buyer and that Buyer would pick up the boat within a few days.   On May 2 Buyer informed X that the boat would be taken away the next day.   X agreed.   On the night of May 2 the boat was destroyed by fire while stored in X's boat yard.   Who had the risk of loss—Buyer or Seller?   Does the result depend upon whether Seller is or is not a merchant? Compare Whately v. Tetrault, 29 Mass.App.Dec. 112 (1964).

D.   RISK OF LOSS WHEN ONE PARTY IN BREACH OF CONTRACT

PROBLEM

Buyer, in Massachusetts, by telephone ordered pocket calculators from Seller, in New York City.   Seller normally shipped its goods to customers by United Parcel, but at the time of Buyer's order United Parcel could not be used because its employees were on strike.   Seller agreed to the sale if Buyer prepaid the price. Buyer sent Seller a letter enclosing a check for the purchase price of $2,700 and a second check (blank as to amount) "to cover postage."   Buyer authorized Seller to use the second check to a maximum amount of $50.   Seller mailed the calculators to Buyer by fourth class mail in two cartons with labels that clearly indicated their contents.   Each carton was insured by Seller for a value of $200.   The cost of postage and insurance was $9.98.   To insure the parcels for their full value of $2,700 postage and insurance would have been $16.26.   Buyer received only one of the cartons.   The value of the lost carton was $1,600.   There is no evidence concerning what happened to the lost carton.   At the time of the loss who had title to the carton?   § 2–401.   At that time who had the risk of loss?   § 2–509(1) and (4), § 2–510 and § 2–504. This problem is based on La Casse v. Blaustein, 93 Misc.2d 572, 403 N.Y.S.2d 440 (1978).

MULTIPLASTICS, INC. v. ARCH INDUSTRIES, INC.

Supreme Court of Connecticut, 1974.
166 Conn. 280, 348 A.2d 618.

BOGDANSKI, ASSOCIATE JUSTICE. The plaintiff, Multiplastics, Inc., brought this action to recover damages from the defendant, Arch Industries, Inc., for the breach of a contract to purchase 40,000 pounds of plastic pellets. From a judgment rendered for the plaintiff, the defendant has appealed to this court.

The facts may be summarized as follows: The plaintiff, a manufacturer of plastic resin pellets, agreed with the defendant on June 30, 1971, to manufacture and deliver 40,000 pounds of brown polystyrene plastic pellets for nineteen cents a pound. The pellets were specially made for the defendant, who agreed to accept delivery at the rate of 1000 pounds per day after completion of production. The defendant's confirming order contained the notation "make and hold for release. Confirmation." The plaintiff produced the order of pellets within two weeks and requested release orders from the defendant. The defendant refused to issue the release orders, citing labor difficulties and its vacation schedule. On August 18, 1971, the plaintiff sent the defendant the following letter: "Against P.O. 0946, we produced 40,000 lbs. of brown high impact styrene, and you have issued no releases. You indicated to us that you would be using 1,000 lbs. of each per day. We have warehoused these products for more than forty days, as we agreed to do. However, we cannot warehouse these products indefinitely, and request that you send us shipping instructions. We have done everything we agreed to do." After August 18, 1971, the plaintiff made numerous telephone calls to the defendant to seek payment and delivery instructions. In response, beginning August 20, 1971, the defendant agreed to issue release orders but in fact never did.

On September 22, 1971, the plaintiff's plant, containing the pellets manufactured for the defendant, was destroyed by fire. The plaintiff's fire insurance did not cover the loss of the pellets. The plaintiff brought this action against the defendant to recover the contract price.

The trial court concluded that the plaintiff made a valid tender of delivery by its letter of August 18, 1971, and by its subsequent requests for delivery instructions; that the defendant repudiated and breached the contract by refusing to accept delivery on August 20, 1971; that the period from August 20, 1971, to September 22, 1971, was not a commercially unreasonable time for the plaintiff to treat the risk of loss as resting on the defendant under UCC § 2–510(3), and that the plaintiff was entitled to recover the contract price plus interest.

* * * The defendant contends that UCC § 2–510 is not applicable because its failure to issue delivery instructions did not constitute either a repudiation or a breach of the agreement. The defendant also argues that even if UCC § 2–510 were applicable, the period from August 20, 1971, to September 22, 1971, was not a commercially reasonable period of time within which to treat the risk of loss as resting on the buyer. The defendant does not claim that the destroyed pellets were not "conforming goods already identified to the contract for sale," as required by UCC § 2–510(3), nor does it protest the computation of damages. With regard to recovery of the price of goods and incidental damages, see UCC § 2–709(1)(a).

The trial court's conclusion that the defendant was in breach is supported by its finding that the defendant agreed to accept delivery of the pellets at the rate of 1000 pounds per day after completion of production. The defendant argues that since the confirming order instructed the defendant to "make and hold for release," the contract did not specify an exact delivery date. This argument fails, however, because nothing in the finding suggests that the notation in the confirming order was part of the agreement between the parties. Since, as the trial court found, the plaintiff made a proper tender of delivery, beginning with its letter of August 18, 1971, the plaintiff was entitled to acceptance of the goods and to payment according to the contract. UCC § 2–507(1), UCC § 2–307.

* * *

The remaining question is whether, under UCC § 2–510(3), the period of time from August 20, 1971, the date of the breach, to September 22, 1971, the date of the fire, was a "commercially reasonable" period within which to treat the risk of loss as resting on the buyer. The trial court concluded that it was "not, on the facts in this case, a commercially unreasonable time," which we take to mean that it was a commercially reasonable period. The time limitation in UCC § 2–510(3) is designed to enable the seller to obtain the additional requisite insurance coverage. * * * The trial court's conclusion is tested by the finding. * * * Although the finding is not detailed, it supports the conclusion that August 20 to September 22 was a commercially reasonable period within which to place the risk of loss on the defendant. As already stated, the trial court found that the defendant repeatedly agreed to transmit delivery instructions and that the pellets were specially made to fill the defendant's order. Under those circumstances, it was reasonable for the plaintiff to believe that the goods would soon be taken off its hands and so to forego procuring the needed insurance.

We consider it advisable to discuss one additional matter. The trial court concluded that "title" passed to the defendant, and the defendant attacks the conclusion on this appeal. The issue is immaterial to this case. UCC § 2–401 states: "Each provision of this article with regard to the rights, obligations and remedies of the seller, the buyer, purchasers or other third parties applies irrespective of title to the goods except where the provision refers to such title." As one student of the Uniform Commercial Code has written: "The single most important innovation of Article 2 of the Uniform Commercial Code is its restatement of * * * the parties' responsibilities in terms of operative facts rather than legal conclusions; where pre-Code law looked to 'title' for the definition of rights and remedies, the Code looks to demonstrable realities such as custody, control and professional expertise. This shift in approach is central to the whole philosophy of Article 2. It means that disputes, as they arise, can focus, as does all of the modern law of contracts, upon actual provable circumstances, rather than upon a metaphysical concept of elastic and endlessly fluid dimensions." Peters, "Remedies for Breach of Contracts Relating to the Sale of Goods Under the Uniform Commercial Code: A Roadmap for Article Two," 73 Yale L.J. 199, 201.

There is no error.

JAKOWSKI v. CAROLE CHEVROLET, INC.

Superior Court of New Jersey, 1981.
180 N.J.Super. 122, 433 A.2d 841.

NEWMAN, J. S. C. Plaintiff seeks summary judgment on count I of the complaint alleging breach of a new car sales contract by defendant Carole Chevrolet, Inc.

The essential facts are not in dispute. On March 8, 1980 plaintiff Jakowski (hereinafter "buyer") entered into a contract of sale with defendant Carole Chevrolet, Inc. (hereinafter "seller"), calling for the purchase of one new 1980 Chevrolet Camaro. The parties also agreed that the car would be undercoated and that its finish would have a polymer coating. While there is some disagreement as to exactly when the buyer ordered the coatings, it is undisputed that prior to delivery the seller agreed to deliver the car with the coatings applied. Likewise, it is undisputed that the car in question was delivered to the buyer without the required coatings on May 19, 1980.

The next day, May 20, 1980, the seller contacted the buyer and informed him that the car delivered to him lacked the coatings in question and seller instructed buyer to return the car so that the coatings could be applied. On May 22, 1980 the buyer returned the auto to the seller for application of the coatings. Sometime during the evening of May 22 or the morning of May 23 the car was stolen from the seller's premises and it was never recovered. Seller has refused to either provide a replacement auto to buyer or to refund the purchase price. Buyer remains accountable on the loan, provided through GMAC, for the purchase of the car.

The narrow question thus presented is upon whom, as between buyer and seller, this loss should fall. In U.C.C. terminology, on May 22, 1980 which party bore the risk of the car's loss.

Seller argues that the risk of loss passed to the buyer upon his recipt of the auto. This is consistent with U.C.C. § 2–509(3) pursuant to which the risk of loss passes to the buyer upon his receipt of the goods. Section 2–509(4), however, expressly provides that the general rules of § 2–509 are subject to the more specific provisions of § 2–510 which deals with the effect of breach upon risk of loss.

Buyer relies upon § 2–510(1) which provides:

Where a tender or delivery of goods so fails to conform to the contract as to give a right of rejection the risk of their loss remains on the seller until cure or acceptance.

Application of this section to the instant facts requires that three questions be answered. First, did the car "so fail to conform" as to give this buyer a right to reject it? If so, did the buyer "accept" the car despite the nonconformity? Finally, did the seller cure the defect prior to the theft of the auto?

The first question must be answered in the affirmative. The contract provided that the car would be delivered with undercoating and a polymer finish, and it is undisputed that it was delivered without these coatings. The goods were thus clearly nonconforming and, despite seller's assertion to the contrary, the degree of their nonconformity is irrelevant in assessing the buyer's concomitant right to reject them.

* * *

The language of § 2–510(1), "so fails to conform," is misleading in this respect: no particular quantum of nonconformity is required where a single delivery is contemplated. The allusion is to § 2–612 which substitutes a rule of substantial compliance where, *and only where*, an installment deal is contemplated. White & Summers, Uniform Commercial Code (2 ed. 1980), § 5.5 at 187–188.

Secondly, did buyer "accept" the auto by taking possession of it? This question was presented in Zabriskie Chevrolet, Inc. v. Smith, 99 N.J.Super. 441, 240 A.2d 195 (Law Div.1968). In *Zabriskie* it was held that the mere taking of possession by the purchaser is not equivalent to acceptance. Before he can be held to have accepted, a buyer must be afforded a "reasonable opportunity to inspect" the goods. UCC § 2–606.

Seller's actions in this matter preclude analysis in conventional "acceptance" terms. Buyer had no opportunity, indeed no reason, to reject, given seller's own communication to buyer shortly after delivery, to the effect that the goods did not conform and that the seller was exercising its right to cure said nonconformity. See UCC § 2–508 (seller's right to cure). This communication, in effect an acknowledgement of nonconformity, obviated the need for a formal rejection on buyer's part, if, indeed, § 2–510(1) imposes such an obligation. Put another way, it precluded the buyer from rejecting the car. Consistent with this analysis, I find as a matter of law that there was no acceptance by buyer of this nonconforming auto.

As to the final question of whether the seller effected a cure, there is no evidence—in fact defendant does not even contend—that cure was ever effected.

Given the undisputed facts, the operation of § 2–510(1) is inescapable. The goods failed to conform, the buyer never accepted them and the defect was never cured. Accordingly, the risk of loss remained on the seller and judgment is granted for plaintiff.

A further note on the law is in order. It is possible to conjure up a host of hypotheticals leading to seemingly perverse results under § 2–510. The section has been the subject of some scholarly criticism. See e.g., White & Summers, supra, § 5.5 at 187. Williston, "The Law of Sales in the Proposed Uniform Commercial Code," 63 Harv.L.Rev. 561, 583 (1950).

The fact is, however, that those courts considering it have had little difficulty in applying it as written. See, e.g., United Airlines, Inc. v. Conductron Corp., 69 Ill.App.3d 847, 26 Ill.Dec. 344, 387 N.E.2d 1272 (Ill.App.1979) (flight trainer destroyed in fire after delivery to buyer); Southland Mobile Home v. Chyrchel, 255 Ark. 366, 500 S.W.2d 778 (Sup.Ct.1973) (mobile home detroyed in fire after delivery to buyer); Graybar Elec. Co. v. Shook, 283 N.C. 213, 195 S.E.2d 514 (Sup.Ct.1973) (nonconforming cable stolen while in buyer's possession); Wilke v. Cummins Diesel Eng'g, Inc., 252 Md. 611, 250 A.2d 886 (Ct.App.1969) (engine block frozen while in buyer's possession).

The rule is simple enough: under UCC § 2–510(1) where goods fail to conform to the contract of sale the risk of loss remains on the seller until the buyer accepts the goods or until the seller cures the defect. Such was the result in the aforecited cases, even though in all of them the goods were still in the *buyer's* possession at the time of their destruction.

For present purposes it is adequate to hold simply that where a seller obtains possession of the goods in an effort to cure defects in them so as to comply with his end of the bargain, he is under a contractual duty to redeliver them to the buyer. In failing to do so, he has breached the contract.

Pursuant to UCC § 2–711 buyer is entitled to a refund of so much of the purchase price as has been paid to seller. Included in the cost of the automobile are the finance charges incurred by the buyer, who secured financing from GMAC pursuant to a retail installment sales contract entered into with the seller. There is no dispute about including these charges in the purchase cost, and the buyer, as of March 30, 1981, indicated the total amount due on any judgment to be $9,398.75. However, since this case was first heard some additional time has passed and a current pay-off figure should be obtained for inclusion in this judgment.

PROBLEMS

1. The court in *Jakowski,* relying on *Zabriskie,* p. 912, held that Buyer had not accepted the automobile at the time the loss occurred. It then applied § 2–510(1). Do Buyer's rights depend upon whether or not he had insurance against theft of the automobile? Assume that Buyer had insurance and that he had recovered the price of the car from his insurer. What rights would the insurer have had against Seller? § 2–711(1) and § 1–103.

2. Assume, on the same facts as *Jakowski,* that a court relying on *Rozmus,* discussed in Note, p. 916, holds that Buyer had accepted the automobile when it was delivered to him. How does this change Buyer's rights? In answering this question consider the following cases:

Case # 1. Seller delivered goods to Buyer C.O.D. Buyer paid for the goods without inspecting them because no opportunity to inspect was given. A short time later Buyer inspected the goods and determined that they did not conform to the contract. Buyer immediately notified Seller that the goods were rejected. § 2–513(3) and § 2–512(2). A few days later, while the goods were still in the possession of Buyer, the goods were destroyed by fire without Buyer's fault. Assume that the rejection was rightful and effective and that Buyer's insurance covered the goods. What are Buyer's rights under § 2–510(1) and § 2–711(1) against Seller? If Buyer did not assert rights against Seller but instead recovered from its insurance company what rights does the insurance company have against Seller? § 1–103.

Case # 2. Seller delivered goods to Buyer who accepted and paid for them. A short time later Buyer discovered that the goods did not conform to the contract. The nonconformity was not apparent when Buyer inspected at the time the goods were delivered. Buyer immediately notified Seller of revocation of acceptance because of the nonconformity. Assume that the revocation was effective under § 2–608(1) and (2). A few days later while the goods were still in the possession of Buyer, the goods were destroyed by fire without Buyer's fault.

Buyer's insurance covered the goods. Does Buyer have any rights against Seller under § 2–510(1) and § 2–711(1)? Does § 2–510(2) apply to this case? What is the effect of § 2–608(3)?

Case # 3. The facts are the same as in Case # 2 except that (1) the goods were destroyed before Buyer discovered the nonconformity; (2) Buyer notified Seller of revocation of acceptance after the goods were destroyed; and (3) Buyer was not insured against the loss. Was revocation of acceptance effective? § 2–608(2). Does § 2–510(2) apply to this case? What is the significance of that provision's concluding phrase "from the beginning?"

Chapter 16

REMEDIES FOR BREACH OF CONTRACT

————

A. BUYER'S REMEDIES

————

1. REPUDIATION BY SELLER OR NONACCEPTANCE BY BUYER

————

a. DAMAGES MEASURED BY COVER PURCHASE OR MARKET PRICE

Section 2–711(1) states two rights of the buyer if the seller repudiates or fails to deliver or the buyer rightfully rejects or revokes acceptance: the buyer may "cover" and get damages under § 2–712 or may recover damages under § 2–713. A buyer that does not cover is necessarily limited to damages under § 2–713. A buyer that covers can use § 2–712, but in that case is the buyer limited to damages based on cover? Does the buyer have the option of proceeding under § 2–713? Section § 2–712(3) indicates that the buyer does not have a duty to cover. Comment 3 to § 2–712 indicates that the buyer is free to cover or not; although a failure to cover may affect the buyer's right to consequential damages under § 2–715 that could have been avoided by cover. But Comment 5 to § 2–713 states that the remedy provided by that section "applies only when and to the extent that the buyer has not covered." In most cases it is not important whether a buyer who covers claims damages under one or the other of the sections. If cover is made at the time of breach by a purchase of standard goods in the open market the measure of damages under either section will be the same. In fact, in many cases a cover purchase can be looked on as the best evidence of market price. But in some cases the two sections may produce different results. Section § 2–713 takes market price "at the time when the buyer learned of the breach." Under § 2–712 the cover purchase, which must be made "without unreasonable delay," may not have been made at the time specified in § 2–713. Particularly difficult problems are presented by cases of anticipatory repudiation by the seller, i.e., repudiation before the time the seller's performance is due.

WILSON v. HAYS

Court of Civil Appeals of Texas, 1976.
544 S.W.2d 833.

JAMES, JUSTICE. This is a suit by the buyer against the seller for breach of an oral contract to sell and deliver used bricks. Trial was had to a jury, which rendered a verdict favorable to the Plaintiff buyer, pursuant to which verdict the trial court entered judgment. We affirm in part and reverse and render in part.

Plaintiff-Appellee W. D. Hays was in the business of buying and selling used building materials. Defendant-Appellant Bobby Wilson doing business as Wilson Salvage Co. was in the business of wrecking or demolishing buildings. In March 1972, Defendant Wilson was in the process of wrecking some buildings in Midland, Texas. Plaintiff Hays became interested in buying the used, uncleaned brick from Defendant Wilson's demolition work. Whereupon, Hays and Wilson entered into an oral agreement whereby Wilson agreed to sell and deliver 600,000 used uncleaned bricks to Hays at a price of one cent per brick, and Hays agreed to buy said bricks at said price. Hays paid Wilson $6,000 in advance. Wilson delivered the uncleaned brick to a designated area where Hays had people hired to clean and stack the brick. Wilson delivered a lesser number of brick than 600,000 thereby precipitating this suit.

Plaintiff-Appellee Hays brought this suit for the return of the proportionate part of the purchase price paid for the bricks he did not get, plus damages. In answer to special issues the jury found:

* * *

(6) That Bobby Wilson did not deliver 600,000 uncleaned bricks to Hays (but)

(6A) delivered only 400,000 bricks to Hays;

(7) The market value of used bricks in Midland, Texas in April 1972, was five cents per brick;

(8) Hays suffered lost profits in the amount of $6250 by virtue of the failure of Bobby Wilson to deliver to Hays at least 600,000 bricks;

(9) That Hays saved $2605 in expenses in consequence of the failure of Bobby Wilson to deliver to him (Hays) at least 600,000 bricks.

Pursuant to the jury verdict, the trial court entered judgment in favor of Plaintiff Hays against Defendant Bobby Wilson in the amount of $13,645, plus accrued interest at 6% per annum from and after May 15, 1972, up to Jan. 27, 1976, same being the date of the trial court's judgment, plus interest at 9% per annum from and after the date of said judgment. From this judgment, Defendant Wilson appeals.

* * *

By Appellant's remaining three points, he challenges the $13,645 judgment upon the ground, among other things, that there is no evidence to support the jury's findings in answer to Special Issues No. 8 (lost profits) and No. 9 (expenses). We sustain these points of error insofar as they assert no evidence to support the jury's findings concerning lost profits less expenses, and in all other respects we overrule such points.

Plaintiff-Appellee Hays's remedies and measures of damages as a buyer of goods in the case at bar are governed by Sections 2–711, 2–712, 2–713, and 2–715 of the UCC.

* * *

Let us analyze the verdict and judgment in the light of the foregoing statutory provisions. In the first place, it is established that Plaintiff Hays paid $6000 for 600,000 used brick at the rate of one cent per brick, whereas he received only 400,000 brick. Therefore he paid $2000 for 200,000 brick that he never got, and he is thereby entitled to recover $2000 under Section 2–711 for "recovering so much of the price as has been paid."

Next, under Section 2–713, he is entitled to damages for "nondelivery or repudiation," and here his measure of damages is the difference between the market price and the contract price. The contract price of the 200,000 brick not delivered is established at $2000. The market price at the appropriate time and place of the undelivered brick was five cents per brick or $10,000. This jury finding of market value (five cents per brick) although challenged by Appellant for legal and factual insufficiency, is amply supported by the evidence and is well within the range of probative testimony. Therefore under Section 2–713 and appropriate jury findings, Plaintiff is entitled to $8000 damages (or $10,000 market price less $2000 contract price) for non-delivery.

Now we come to the problem of "consequential damages * * * less expenses saved in consequence of the seller's breach" as mentioned in Section 2–713 and which damages are provided for in Section 2–715. As stated, the jury found Hays sustained lost profits of $6250 (Special Issue No. 8) and saved $2605 expenses (No. 9), thereby suffering a lost profits net of $3645, which last-named amount was included in the $13,645 judgment total. This $3645 lost profits amount has no support in the evidence. Under Section 2–715, "consequential damages" includes "any loss * * * which could not reasonably be prevented by cover or otherwise." There is no evidence in the record whatever that Plaintiff Hays at any time made any effort to cover or in any other manner attempt to prevent or mitigate a loss resulting from the Defendant Wilson's non-delivery of the 200,000 brick in question. In the absence of such a showing these consequential damages are unauthorized under Section 2–715. The burden of proving the extent of loss incurred by way of consequential damage is on the buyer. * * * This being so, we are of the opinion that there is no evidence to support these jury findings concerning consequential damages, and that the trial court's judgment insofar as it awarded Plaintiff Hays $3645 lost profits is improper and this amount should be deleted from said judgment.

As stated before, the judgment is proper and should be affirmed for the amount of $10,000, same being composed of $2000 paid by Plaintiff for which he received no bricks plus $8000 damages for non-delivery.

We therefore affirm in part and reverse and render in part the trial court's judgment as follows: Plaintiff-Appellee Hays is hereby awarded judgment against Defendant-Appellant Wilson in the amount of $10,000, plus interest at six percent per annum from and after May 15, 1972 up until January 27, 1976, the date of entry of the trial court's judgment, together with interest from the date of the trial court's judgment upon the amount then due at the rate of nine percent per annum until paid.

Costs of the trial court and of this appeal are taxed one-half each to Appellant and Appellee.

Affirmed in Part and Reversed and Rendered in Part.

NOTES

1. M. K. Metals, Inc. v. Container Recovery Corp., 645 F.2d 583 (8th Cir. 1981), involved a contract for the sale by CRC of scrap beverage containers to M. K. Metals which CRC repudiated. With respect to the issue of damages the court stated:

> The last instruction to which M. K. Metals objects involved damages. The trial court instructed the jury that "* * * the measure of damages for defendant's failure to sell bi-metal beverage containers to plaintiff is the lost profits you believe the plaintiff suffered as a consequence of the breach by defendant." The damages instruction offered by M. K. Metals but refused by the district court stated:
>
> > If you find the issues in favor of the plaintiff and are thereafter determining what sum if any to award the plaintiff, you are instructed that the measure of damages for defendant's failure to sell bi-metal beverage containers to plaintiff is the difference between the market price at the time plaintiff learned of the breach and the contract price together with any incidental and consequential damages, including any lost profits claimed by plaintiff, less

any expenses saved in consequence of the breach by defendant.

With the exception of the "lost profits" clause, the refused instruction basically follows § 2–713 of the U.C.C. which is entitled "Buyer's damages for nondelivery or repudiation." * * * Recently, this court noted that Missouri law allows the recovery of lost profits caused by the breach if the evidence is sufficient for estimating their amount with reasonable certainty. Vigano v. Wylain, Inc., 633 F.2d 522, 528 (8th Cir. 1980).

M. K. Metals argues that the district court erred in refusing to instruct the jury that the measure of damages was the difference between market and contract price *plus* lost profits. While this argument at first appears to have merit based on §§ 2–713 and 2–715 of the U.C.C., the record does not support appellant's contentions.

M. K. Metals' evidence concerning damages was introduced through the testimony of Ray Plummer. Mr. Plummer's calculations of lost profits were based on the difference between the cost per ton of scrap metal at the alleged *contract* price and the resale price per ton M. K. Metals was receiving for a ton of processed metal (minus such items as freight costs and processing costs). Because Mr. Plummer's calculations were based on contract price rather than market price (which was considerably higher), his estimate of lost profits, in fact, already included the difference between contract price and market price.

Under § 2–715(2)(a) of the U.C.C. proof of such consequential damages as lost profits may require additional proof by the buyer of foreseeability and opportunity to cover. See comments 2, 3 and 6 to Section 2–715. While it may be preferable to treat the difference between contract and market price as a separate item of damages, appellant's evidence lumped that amount into its calculations of "lost profits." The district court was understandably worried that to allow damages on both of appellant's theories would amount to double recovery. Based on appellant's evidence of "lost profits," we find no error in the district court limiting damages to that amount.

To illustrate its point the court quoted the following from White and Summers, Uniform Commercial Code 394, n. 91 (2d ed. 1980):

In granting a buyer lost profits because he is unable to resell a product, a court must be careful not to overcompensate him. Assume for example, that a buyer sues wholesaler for nondelivery of a shipment of fiberglass skiis under section 2–713. He might ask for the market-contract differential (assume it is $10,000–$8,000) plus consequential damages which are lost resale profits. If he could resell the shipment of skiis at $15,000 but he cannot cover, his lost profits will be $7,000 ($15,000–$8,000). Should a court allow a recovery of $9,000 (the market-contract differential plus lost profits)? First, 2–715(2)(a) requires cover if it is at all reasonable, and that principle would eliminate lost profits in most cases. Secondly, in the unusual case where cover is impossible the court should award only $7,000 since that amount will put the wholesaler in the same position he would have been in if the manufacturer had sent the skiis. If the court gives the buyer the market-contract differential of $2,000 under 2–713, then the "loss resulting" from the wholesaler's inability to resell under 2–715(2)(a) is only $5,000.

2. Comment 2 to § 2–712 states that the definition of cover includes "goods not identical with those involved but commercially usable as reasonable substitutes under the circumstances of the particular case." Consider this case. Buyer needed a large computer capable of performing certain specified tasks and invited several manufacturers to submit bids. Seller, a newcomer to the computer field, was in the process of developing a computer that it characterized as "a truly revolutionary system utilizing all of the latest technical advances." Seller's offer to sell it for $230,000 was accepted by Buyer. Seller was unable to develop a satisfactory computer and repudiated the contract. Buyer purchased for $410,000 an IBM computer that is capable of performing the same tasks specified in the invitation for bids. A computer of a third manufacturer capable of performing the same tasks was also available for $350,000. Buyer testified that the IBM computer was chosen over the less expensive computer because of superior quality control which it believed would reduce maintenance costs. What, if any, damages are recoverable under § 2–712? This hypothetical case is based on United States v. Wegematic Corp., 360 F.2d 674 (2d Cir. 1966), but facts have been added which might have changed the result reached in that case. Compare Valley Die Cast Corp. v. A.C.W. Inc., 25 Mich.App. 321, 181 N.W.2d 303 (1970), in which Buyer purchased a "pressure" car wash system which it subsequently rejected because it did not wash cars clean. Buyer purchased in substitution a more expensive "brush" car wash system, which although designed to do the same job operated on a principle different from the pressure system. The court held that Buyer was not entitled to cover damages.

The preceding cases involved purchasers who were end users of the goods purchased. Are there different considerations present in cases of purchases for resale? Suppose a sales contract covered ladies gloves to be manufactured by Seller and delivered in time for the Fall sales season. The contract price was $4 a pair. Seller repudiated just before the delivery date. Buyer, a wholesaler, purchased substitute gloves for $6 a pair. The substitute gloves were similar in style and type but are of substantially better workmanship than Seller's gloves. Is Buyer entitled to damages under § 2–712: (1) if Buyer had contract commitments to supply gloves to retailers at $5 a pair and the substitute gloves were delivered in satisfaction of those commitments; and (2) if Buyer, not having any prior contract commitments, resold the substitute gloves to retailers for $7.50 a pair? If Buyer is not entitled to cover damages in either or both of these cases is there any other way of computing damages that is preferable?

DANGERFIELD v. MARKEL
Supreme Court of North Dakota, 1979.
278 N.W.2d 364.

ERICKSTAD, CHIEF JUSTICE. This appeal arises as a result of our decision in Dangerfield v. Markel, 252 N.W.2d 184 (N.D.1977), in which we held that Markel, a potato grower, breached a contract with Dangerfield, a potato broker, to deliver potatoes, thus giving rise to damages under the Uniform Commercial Code. On remand the district court awarded Dangerfield $47,510.16 in damages plus interest and costs * * *.

* * * By contract dated June 13, 1972, Markel (seller) contracted to sell Dangerfield (buyer) 25,000 cwt. of chipping potatoes during the 1972–1973 shipping season. The seller allegedly breached the contract by refusing to deliver 15,055 cwt. of potatoes during the contract period and the buyer was allegedly forced to purchase potatoes on the open market to fulfill a contract with potato processors. * * *

The primary issue on this appeal is whether or not the trial court made an erroneous award of damages to the buyer under the Uniform Commercial Code. The trial court in essence found that the buyer was entitled to damages pursuant to Section 2–712, for the amount expended by the buyer to purchase the 15,055 cwt. of potatoes still due under the contract:

"It appears to the Court that the Defendant [seller] * * * should be liable for the difference in price including freight, if any, between the quantity of the potatoes remaining to be delivered under the * * * contract after February 10, 1973 [date of breach], and the price including freight, if any, that the plaintiff [buyer] actually paid for potatoes to 'cover' the supply that the plaintiff, Dangerfield, had a right to expect to be delivered * * * under * * * [the] contract during the remainder of the 1972–73 potato shipping season."

The court determined that the buyer completed "covering" the contract on March 21, 1973, which was 38 days after the date of breach. During the first eighteen days of this cover period, the buyer's purchases averaged $4.41 per cwt. During the remaining twenty days, the buyer's purchases averaged over $5.41 per cwt., with many purchases made at $6.00 per cwt.

Seller argues in substance that thirty-eight days for the buyer to cover in a rapidly rising market is improper under Sections 2–711 and 2–712; therefore, he submits that Section 2–713 should have been used to compute damages.

*   *   *

The seller submits that the market price at the time of the breach was between $3.75 and $4.25 per cwt. He argues that a proper measure of damages pursuant to § 2–713 would be an average of $4.00 per cwt. minus the contract price at the time of the breach ($1.90), or damages of $31,615.50 as opposed to the present award of $47,510.16, a reduction of $15,894.66.

The buyer responds that due to the perishable nature of the product involved in this case and the installment nature of the contract, the cover period was not unreasonable pursuant to § 2–712; therefore, the damages are correct.

The pre-code measure of damages for a breach of contract for the sale of goods was to allow the aggrieved party the difference between his bargain (contract price) and the market price. Although this worked reasonably well in the majority of cases, practical problems arose in determining the market price as well as the related questions of "as of when" and "where." After the seller's breach, the buyer faced a dilemma, i.e. to ensure that he would be fully compensated for the seller's breach, the buyer had to make a substitute purchase that the finder of fact would later determine to be at the "market value." This "20–20 hindsight approach" by the factfinder produced questionable results. Therefore, Section 2–712 was added to the buyer's arsenal of remedies. This section allows the buyer to make a substitute purchase to replace the goods that were not delivered by the seller and the damages are measured by the difference between the cost of the substitute goods and the contract price.

*   *   *

The official comment to Section 2–712 states that "the test of proper cover is whether at the time and place the buyer acted in good faith and in a reasonable manner, and it is immaterial that hindsight may later prove that the method of cover used was not the cheapest or most effective."

In order for Section 2–712 to apply, the buyer must make a reasonable purchase in good faith without unreasonable delay. If a buyer fails to cover or covers improperly, e.g. waits an unreasonable length of time or buys in bad faith, he may still be entitled to some relief.

The seller argues that the buyer's purchases did not satisfy the criteria of Section 2–712; therefore, he is limited to the traditional measure of damages. Specifically, the seller argues that the buyer was obligated to purchase the entire cover on the date of the breach or shortly thereafter in order to mitigate his damages.

Although we have not dealt directly with the question of proper cover pursuant to Section 2–712, we stated in Jamestown Terminal Elevator, Inc. v. Hieb, 246 N.W.2d 736, 738 (N.D.1976), at Syl. 10 that the "determination of a reasonable time to 'cover' following a breach of contract rests in the discretion of the jury and generally will not be interfered with on appeal where there is substantial evidence to sustain the verdict." Although there was no jury present in this case, the question of reasonable time to cover following a breach of contract is still a question of fact and we are governed by the "clearly erroneous" standard of Rule 52(a), N.D.R.Civ.P.

Similarly, the criteria of good faith and reasonable purchase are also questions of fact and will not be set aside unless clearly erroneous. * * *

The record indicates that the buyer could not cover the balance of the contract on the date of the breach:

"Q. Once you learned you were not going to receive any more potatoes from Mr. Markel in February of 1973, did you attempt to buy potatoes to cover the shortage on the contract?

"A. I did.

"Q. Were you able to go out right at that time on February 12th or 13th, and buy quantity to cover the remaining balance on the contract?

"A. No, I was not able to.

"Q. Why was this?

"A. Well, we were continuing on rising market, no one wanted to commit more than one or two loads at any one time, so would load on basis whatever day they got car, they would accept whatever market was at that day.

"Q. If I understand what you are saying correctly, is that potatoes that were available at that time had to be bought and you would have to take delivery and ship them, that what you mean?

"A. That's correct.

"Q. That's correct?

"A. Right.

"Q. You were not able to buy potatoes in February for delivery in May?

"A. No.

"Q. Were you able to buy potatoes in middle of February for delivery say a month or two later?

"A. No.

"Q. Did you try to do this?

"A. Yes."

Furthermore, the trial court was obviously of the opinion that the buyer acted in good faith under the circumstances:

> "Based upon the foregoing facts and the Uniform Commercial Code as quoted above, the Court is of the opinion that the plaintiff having elected to 'cover' the defendant's breach was not obliged to purchase the entire cover as of the date of the breach since this contract called for installment deliveries over a period of months during the 1972, 1973 potato shipping season. In the absence of a showing of plaintiff so as to increase his damages against the defendant, the Court will view as reasonable a course of purchases of cover stocks from time to time. This ruling is particularly called for in this case where the subject of the contract is a bulky perishable commodity and the quantities must be warehoused at carefully controlled temperatures to avoid freezing or undue deterioration in holding. It would be unreasonable under these circumstances to hold the covering buyer to a February 10, 1973, market price date for immediate delivery of the entire amount of cover necessary to complete the contract of sale. This is particularly true where, as here, the quantity and bulk of goods in question is large and where the goods normally would flow into commerce upon delivery rather than into storage."

It is generally accepted that if the buyer complies with the requirements of Section 2–712, his purchase is presumed proper and the burden of proof is on the seller to show that cover was not properly obtained. Kiser v. Lemco Industries, Inc., supra at 589; Laredo Hides Co., Inc. v. H & H Meat Products Co., Inc., 513 S.W. 2d 210, 221 (Tex.Civ.App.1974).

In *Laredo,* a Texas Court of Appeals was presented with a similar question. The buyer sued the seller to recover damages for breach of contract for the sale of cattle hides. The buyer agreed, pursuant to the contract, to purchase the seller's entire cattle hide production from March through December 1972. The contract provided no specific quantity but provided that deliveries be made at least twice a month. On March 3, 1972, the first delivery of hides was made under the contract. On March 21, 1972, the seller refused to sell any more hides to the buyer because of a payment dispute. The Texas court found that the seller had waived any objection and therefore breached the contract. The buyer was forced to purchase hides on the open market in substitution for the hides that were to have been delivered under the contract. The court awarded damages to the buyer for the substitute purchase minus the contract price, even though the cover "purchases had to be made periodically throughout 1972 since Laredo Hides [buyer] had no storage facilities, and the hides would decompose if allowed to age," and even though "the market price for hides steadily increased following the execution of the contract in question."

In Farmer's Union Co-op Co. of Mead v. Flamme Bros., 196 Neb. 699, 245 N.W.2d 464 (1976), the Supreme Court of Nebraska was presented with a similar situation in which the seller argued that the buyer should not have been allowed to cover a breached corn contract over a 15-day-period in a rising market.

The Nebraska court rejected the argument:

"In the case at bar, the appellee did not go into the market and buy corn specifically to cover the contracts, but appellee did continue buying corn from its members, as was its normal practice until the three contracts were fulfilled. The trial court determined, as inherent in its verdict and judgment for appellee, that appellee did 'cover' the contract 'without unreasonable delay,' and under all the circumstances of this case, we affirm the trial court's judgment. Appellee did between the dates of January 2 and January 15, 1974, purchase over 111,000 bushels of corn and applied such purchases to the unfulfilled contracts. The comment following section 2–712 is particularly applicable to this case. That comment states, in part: '2. The definition of "cover" under subsection (1) envisages a series of contracts or sales, as well as a single contract or sale; * * * and contracts on credit or delivery terms differing from the contract in breach, but again reasonable under the circumstances. The test of proper cover is whether at the time and place the buyer acted in good faith and in a reasonable manner, and it is immaterial that hindsight may later prove that the method of cover used was not the cheapest or most effective.'

"The offended party is not bound by hindsight, and the practice used by appellee might have resulted in lower damages if the price over the time period had declined. Instead, the price fluctuated and the net result was that the damages were slightly higher than if the entire volume of corn had been purchased on January 2, 1974, at the $2.32 price. Appellee acted in good faith and made the 'cover' purchases without unreasonable delay, within the meaning of the Uniform Commercial Code." 196 Neb. at 706, 245 N.W.2d at 468.

* * *

White and Summers, in their Hornbook series on the Uniform Commercial Code, comment on Sections 1–106 and 2–712:

"If 2–712 is to be the remedy used by more aggrieved buyers than any other remedy, then the courts must be chary of finding a good faith buyer's acts unreasonable. The courts should not hedge the remedy about with restrictions in the name of 'reasonableness' that render it useless or uncertain for the good faith buyer. Indeed, one may argue that the courts should read very little substance into the reasonableness requirement and insist only that the buyer proceed in good faith. A question a lawyer might put to test his client's good faith under 2–712 is this: 'How, where, and when would you have procured these goods if you had not been covering and had no prospect of a court recovery from another?' If the client can answer truthfully that he would have spent his own money in the same way, the court should not demand more." J. White and R. Summers, Handbook of the Law under the Uniform Commercial Code, at p. 178.

We do not feel that the seller met his burden of showing that cover was improperly obtained in this case or that the district court's findings were clearly erroneous. Consequently, we affirm the district court judgment on this issue.

*   *   *

The district court's judgment is affirmed in all respects.

NOTE

In *Farmer's Union* discussed by the court in *Dangerfield*, the contract covered corn to be delivered during October, November, and December of 1973. The court found that not until the close of business on December 31, 1973 did Buyer know that Seller was not going to deliver. From January 2 to January 15, 1974 Buyer purchased from its regular customers corn, as it became available, in an amount equal to the amount Seller failed to deliver. Prices ranged from $2.31 to $2.45 a bushel. In holding that this was a valid cover under § 2–712 the court indicated that because prices were rising damages under § 2–712 were slightly higher than if they had been measured by market price of $2.32 at the time of breach. But the court also pointed out that damages would have been lower if prices had been falling. Suppose Buyer had purchased from its regular customers at prices less than $2.32. Would Buyer have been entitled to recover under § 2–713 based on market price of $2.32? Does Buyer's right to recover under § 2–713 depend upon whether Buyer covered? Kashi v. Gratsos, 790 F.2d 1050 (2d Cir.1986), holds that recovery under § 2–713 is not contingent upon the buyer's attempting to cover; that result is clearly supported by § 2–712(3). But can the seller defeat the buyer's action under § 2–713 by showing that the buyer in fact covered and that cover damages under § 2–712 are less than market damages under § 2–713? Comment 5 to § 2–713 states that a buyer who covers has no § 2–713 remedy, but the language of § 2–712 and § 2–713 does not specifically support Comment 5. Section 2–711(1)(a) and (b) is ambiguous. It can be read to mean that (a) the buyer can use either section or (b) that the buyer can either cover and use § 2–712 or not cover and use § 2–713. Comment 5 supports the latter interpretation but it causes difficulties. If a buyer's right to recover under § 2–713 is lost if the buyer covered, there will be a question of fact whether a particular purchase was a cover purchase. In the case of buyers who purchase for sale continuously as a regular part of their business—such as Buyer in *Farmer's Union*—is there any objective basis for deciding which, if any, of the purchases made after Seller's beach is a cover transaction? If Buyer in *Farmer's Union* was capable of reselling to other customers all grain purchased after Seller's breach, would any such purchase be a cover transaction? Could Buyer take the position that the failure of Seller to deliver resulted in lost sales by Buyer and that the proper relief is damages for lost profits under § 2–715? That issue is raised in *Hoefferle,* discussed in the next paragraph.

In Hoefferle Truck Sales, Inc. v. Divco–Wayne Corp., 523 F.2d 543 (7th Cir.1975), Plaintiffs (Eastland, Schmidt, and Fogelman) who were dealers in trucks manufactured by Divco, sued Divco for profits lost as a result of Divco's failure to deliver trucks it had contracted to sell to Plaintiffs. Divco in 1967 sold its manufacturing facilities to Highway Products who in turn sold to Transairco. It was intended that Transairco would manufacture the same type of trucks as had Divco. At the time of the sale by Divco the contracts with Plaintiffs had not yet been filled. There was a two-year time lag between the time Divco sold and Transairco began to produce trucks. All of the trucks that Plaintiffs had contracted to buy from Divco were eventually sold to Plaintiffs by Transairco. Divco argued that Plaintiffs were not entitled to recover lost profits because the trucks were eventually delivered. What is the basis for Plaintiffs' claim for lost profits? If Plaintiffs' purchases from Transairco are considered as cover transactions would Plaintiffs be entitled to recover for lost profits? In upholding Plaintiffs' claims the court stated:

> In any event, we think that the evidence introduced was sufficient to sustain liability for the loss of profits and that submission of the lost profits issue to the damage jury was not error.

> This conclusion, of course, does not fully reach the correctness of the district court's decision to set aside the damage verdicts. That decision was based upon testimony by representatives of all three plaintiffs that some or all of the

pending truck orders were turned over or resubmitted to Transairco, the eventual purchaser of Divco's manufacturing facilities, and later filled. But even if the plaintiffs received from Transairco trucks of the same specifications they had ordered from Divco, the liability jury was not precluded from concluding, as it apparently did, that Divco's abdication of its responsibilities and the two year delay in delivery amounted to a breach of contract. With liability thus established, the question of the extent or measure of damages is not a difficult one. Eastland's sales, after all, had averaged over 20 per month in the years before Divco ceased its manufacturing operations; Schmidt had sales of around 80 per year; and Fogelman's were about 25 per year. By every indication, this volume would have continued, subject only to available sources of supply. Transairco, though, had no obligation to accept Divco orders, and its subsequent sales to the plaintiffs would, in all likelihood, have been forthcoming regardless of the precise specifications of the trucks delivered. In such circumstances, damages for the dealers' lost profits on truck orders accepted by Divco and which Divco therefore had an obligation to deliver were wholly proper. Cf. Uniform Commercial Code §§ 2–712, 2–715.

b. ANTICIPATORY REPUDIATION

CARGILL, INC. v. STAFFORD
United States Court of Appeals, Tenth Circuit, 1977.
553 F.2d 1222.

[On July 31, 1973 Stafford as seller and Cargill as buyer made a contract for the sale of 26,000 bushels of wheat. The final date for performance by Stafford was September 30, 1973. On August 21 Stafford wrote Cargill stating that the contract was void. Cargill urged Stafford to perform but on September 6, 1973 Stafford told Cargill that he would not perform the contract. Cargill thereupon told Stafford that the contract was cancelled and that Stafford owed Cargill the difference between the contract price of the wheat and the price on September 6. The price of wheat rose from the end of July reaching a high point on August 21. Stafford refused to pay and Cargill brought suit for breach of contract.]

BREITENSTEIN, CIRCUIT JUDGE. * * * We agree with the trial court that the July 31 transaction resulted in a valid and enforceable contract which was breached by Stafford.

The remaining question is the damages to which Cargill is entitled. The trial court awarded damages in the amount of $27,300 plus interest which was the difference in the price of wheat on September 6 over that on July 31. September 6 is the day on which Cargill acted upon Stafford's statement that he would not perform. The court gave no reason for its selection of the September 6 date. The final day for performance was September 30.

Stafford repudiated the contract by an August 21 letter which was received by Cargill on August 24. Cargill argues alternatively that, (1) it should recover the difference between the price of wheat on August 24 and on July 31, and (2) the difference between the price on September 30 when performance was due and the price on July 31.

Section 2–711 provides that when a seller repudiates the buyer may (1) cover (buy substitute goods) and recover the difference in price, (2) recover damages for non-delivery under § 2–713, or sue for specific performance under § 2–716. Cargill has not attempted to obtain specific performance. The record contains scant, if any, evidence that Cargill covered the wheat. Section 2–713 relates to non-delivery and provides:

"Subject to the provisions of this article with respect to proof of market price (section 2–723), the measure of damages for nondelivery or repudiation by the seller is the difference between the market price *at the time when the buyer learned of the breach* and the contract price together with any incidental and consequential damages provided in this article (section 2–715), but less expenses saved in consequence of the seller's breach." (Emphasis supplied.)

The basic question is whether "time when buyer learned of the breach" means "time when buyer learned of the repudiation" or means "time of performance" in anticipatory repudiation cases. See discussion in J. White and R. Summers, Uniform Commercial Code, 197–202 (1972). The authors conclude, Ibid. at 201, that the soundest arguments support the interpretation of "learned of the breach" to mean "time of performance" in the anticipatory repudiation case. We agree for two reasons.

First, before the adoption of the Code in Colorado and other states, damages were measured from the time when performance was due and not from the time when the buyer learned of repudiation. * * * A clear deviation from past law would not ordinarily be accomplished by Code ambiguities.

Second, Code § 2–723(1) discusses when to measure damages in a suit for anticipatory repudiation which comes to trial before the time for performance. That section says:

"[A]ny damages based on market price (section 2–708 or section 2–713) shall be determined according to the price of such goods prevailing at the time when the aggrieved party *learned of the repudiation*." (Emphasis supplied.)

Thus, when the Code drafters intended to base damages on the date a party "learned of the repudiation," they did so by explicit language. We conclude that under § 2–713 damages normally should be measured from the time when performance is due and not from the time when the buyer learns of repudiation.

To support its contention that the time when it learned of the repudiation controls Cargill cites two cases. Sawyer Farmers Coop. Ass'n v. Linke, N.D., 231 N.W.2d 791 is not helpful because the date for determination of the market price was controlled by a contract provision and not by § 2–713. Oloffson v. Coomer, 11 Ill. App.3d 918, 296 N.E.2d 871, is more nearly in point. There the buyer contracted in 1969 with the seller-farmer for delivery of corn in 1970. In June 1970 the seller notified the buyer that he was not planting corn because of weather conditions and would not deliver in September. The buyer refused to cover and urged performance even though he knew there would be none. The court refused to award damages based on the September price but based its award on the price of corn on the June date when the seller notified the buyer that he would not deliver. In so doing the court pointed out that there was an easily accessible market for purchase of the grain, Ibid. 296 N.E.2d at 874, and that the words "for a commercially reasonable time" appearing in Code § 2–610(a) relating to anticipatory repudiation "must be read relatively to the obligation of good faith that is defined in Section 2–103(1)(b) and imposed expressly in Section 1–203." Ibid. 296 N.E.2d at 875.

This brings us to § 2–712 which provides that the buyer may "cover" by the reasonable purchase of substitute goods. A buyer is allowed to buy substitute goods so long as he does not delay unreasonably. Section 2–713 relates to a buyer's damages for nondelivery or repudiation. The official comment to that section says:

> "The general baseline adopted in this section uses as a yardstick the market in which the buyer would have obtained cover had he sought that relief."

We conclude that under § 2–713 a buyer may urge continued performance for a reasonable time. At the end of a reasonable period he should cover if substitute goods are readily available. If substitution is readily available and buyer does not cover within a reasonable time, damages should be based on the price at the end of that reasonable time rather than on the price when performance is due. If a valid reason exists for failure or refusal to cover, damages may be calculated from the time when performance is due.

Specifically, this means that Cargill had a reasonable time after the August 24 anticipatory repudiation to cover. This reasonable time expired on September 6 when Cargill cancelled the contract. The record does not show that Cargill covered or attempted to cover. Nothing in the record shows the continued availability or nonavailability of substitute wheat. On remand the court must determine whether Cargill had a valid reason for failure or refusal to cover. If Cargill did not have a valid reason, the court's award based on the September 6 price should be reinstated. If Cargill had a valid reason for not covering, damages should be awarded on the difference between the price on September 30, the last day for performance, and the July 31 contract price.

The judgment is affirmed except for the award of damages to Cargill under the July 31 transaction. The case is remanded for determination, in the light of this opinion, of the damages recoverable by Cargill.

OLOFFSON v. COOMER

Appellate Court of Illinois, Third District, 1973.
11 Ill.App.3d 918, 296 N.E.2d 871.

ALLOY, PRESIDING JUSTICE. Richard Oloffson, d/b/a Rich's Ag Service appeals from a judgment of the circuit court of Bureau County in favor of appellant against Clarence Coomer in the amount of $1,500 plus costs. The case was tried by the court without a jury.

Oloffson was a grain dealer. Coomer was a farmer. Oloffson was in the business of merchandising grain. Consequently, he was a "merchant" within the meaning of section 2–104 of the Uniform Commercial Code. Coomer, however, was simply in the business of growing rather than merchandising grain. He, therefore, was not a "merchant" with respect to the merchandising of grain.

On April 16, 1970, Coomer agreed to sell to Oloffson, for delivery in October and December of 1970, 40,000 bushels of corn. Oloffson testified at the trial that the entire agreement was embodied in two separate contracts, each covering 20,000 bushels and that the first 20,000 bushels were to be delivered on or before October 30 at a price of $1.12¾ per bushel and the second 20,000 bushels were to be delivered on or before December 15, at a price of $1.12¼ per bushel. Coomer, in his testimony, agreed that the 40,000 bushels were to be delivered but stated that he was to deliver all he could by October 30 and the balance by December 15.

On June 3, 1970, Coomer informed Oloffson that he was not going to plant corn because the season had been too wet. He told Oloffson to arrange elsewhere to obtain the corn if Oloffson had obligated himself to deliver to any third party. The price for a bushel of corn on June 3, 1970, for future delivery, was $1.16. In September of 1970, Oloffson asked Coomer about delivery of the corn and Coomer repeated that he would not be able to deliver.

Oloffson, however, persisted. He mailed Coomer confirmations of the April 16 agreement. Coomer ignored these. Oloffson's attorney then requested that Coomer perform. Coomer ignored this request likewise. The scheduled delivery dates referred to passed with no corn delivered. Oloffson then covered his obligation to his own vendee by purchasing 20,000 bushels at $1.35 per bushel and 20,000 bushels at $1.49 per bushel. The judgment from which Oloffson appeals awarded Oloffson as damages, the difference between the contract and the market prices on June 3, 1970, the day upon which Coomer first advised Oloffson he would not deliver.

Oloffson argues on this appeal that the proper measure of his damages was the difference between the contract price and the market price on the dates the corn should have been delivered in accordance with the April 16 agreement. Plaintiff does not seek any other damages. The trial court prior to entry of judgment, in an opinion finding the facts and reviewing the law, found that plaintiff was entitled to recover judgment only for the sum of $1,500 plus costs as we have indicated which is equal to the amount of the difference between the minimum contract price and the price on June 3, 1970, of $1.16 per bushel (taking the greatest differential from $1.12¼ per bushel multiplied by 40,000 bushels). We believe the findings and the judgment of the trial court were proper and should be affirmed.

It is clear that on June 3, 1970, Coomer repudiated the contract "with respect to performance not yet due." Under the terms of the Uniform Commercial Code the loss would impair the value of the contract to the remaining party in the amount as indicated. (§ 2–610) As a consequence, on June 3, 1970, Oloffson, as the "aggrieved party", could then:

> "(a) for a commercially reasonable time await performance by the repudiating party; or
>
> (b) resort to any remedy for breach (Section 2–703 or Section 2–711), even though he has notified the repudiating party that he would await the latter's performance and has urged retraction; ＊ ＊ ＊"

If Oloffson chose to proceed under subparagraph (a) referred to, he could have awaited Coomer's performance for a "commercially reasonable time." As we indicate in the course of this opinion, that "commercially reasonable time" expired on June 3, 1970. The Uniform Commercial Code made a change in existing Illinois law in this respect, in that, prior to the adoption of the Code, a buyer in a position as Oloffson was privileged to await a seller's performance until the date that, according to the agreement, such performance was scheduled. To the extent that a "commercially reasonable time" is less than such date of performance, the Code now conditions the buyer's right to await performance. § 2–610(a).

If, alternatively, Oloffson had proceeded under section 2–610(b) by treating the repudiation as a breach, the remedies to which he would have been entitled were set forth in section 2–711 which is the only applicable section to which section 2–610(b) refers, according to the relevant portion of 2–711:

> "(1) Where the seller fails to make delivery or repudiates or the buyer rightfully rejects or justifiably revokes acceptance then with respect to any goods involved, and with respect to the whole if the breach goes to the whole contract

(Section 2–612), the buyer may cancel and whether or not he has done so may in addition to recovering so much of the price as has been paid

> (a) 'cover' and have damages under the next section as to all the goods affected whether or not they have been identified to the contract; or

> (b) recover damages for non-delivery as provided in this Article (Section 2–713). * * *"

Plaintiff, therefore, was privileged under Section 2–610 of the Uniform Commercial Code to proceed either under subparagraph (a) or under subparagraph (b). At the expiration of the "commercially reasonable time" specified in subparagraph (a), he in effect would have a duty to proceed under subparagraph (b) since subparagraph (b) directs reference to remedies generally available to a buyer upon a seller's breach.

Oloffson's right to await Coomer's performance under section 2–610(a) was conditioned upon his:

> (i) waiting no longer than a "commercially reasonable time"; and

> (ii) dealing with Coomer in good faith.

Since Coomer's statement to Oloffson on June 3, 1970, was unequivocal and since "cover" easily and immediately was available to Oloffson in the well-organized and easily accessible market for purchases of grain to be delivered in the future, it would be unreasonable for Oloffson on June 3, 1970, to have awaited Coomer's performance rather than to have proceeded under Section 2–610(b) and, thereunder, to elect then to treat the repudiation as a breach. Therefore, if Oloffson were relying on his right to effect cover under section 2–711(1)(a), June 3, 1970, might for the foregoing reason alone have been the day on which he acquired cover.

Additionally, however, the record and the finding of the trial court indicates that Oloffson adhered to a usage of trade that permitted his customers to cancel the contract for a future delivery of grain by making known to him a desire to cancel and paying to him the difference between the contract and market price on the day of cancellation. There is no indication whatever that Coomer was aware of this usage of trade. The trial court specifically found, as a fact, that, in the context in which Oloffson's failure to disclose this information occurred, Oloffson failed to act in good faith. According to Oloffson, he didn't ask for this information:

> "I'm no information sender. If he had asked I would have told him exactly what to do. * * * I didn't feel my responsibility. I thought it his to ask, in which case I would tell him exactly what to do."

We feel that the words "for a commercially reasonable time" as set forth in Section 2–610(a) must be read relatively to the obligation of good faith that is defined in Section 2–103(1)(b) and imposed expressly in Section 1–203.

The Uniform Commercial Code imposes upon the parties the obligation to deal with each other in good faith regardless of whether they are merchants. The Sales Article of the Code specifically defines good faith, "in the case of a merchant * * * [as] honesty in fact and the observance of reasonable commercial standards of fair dealing in the trade." For the foregoing reasons and likewise because Oloffson's failure to disclose in good faith might itself have been responsible for Coomer's failure to comply with the usage of trade which we must assume was known only to Oloffson, we conclude that a commercially reasonable time under the facts before us expired on June 3, 1970.

Imputing to Oloffson the consequences of Coomer's having acted upon the information that Oloffson in good faith should have transmitted to him, Oloffson knew or should have known on June 3, 1970, the limit of damages he probably could recover. If he were obligated to deliver grain to a third party, he knew or should have known that unless he covered on June 3, 1970, his own capital would be at risk with respect to his obligation to his own vendee. Therefore, on June 3, 1970, Oloffson, in effect, had a duty to proceed under subparagraph (b) of Section 2–610 and under subparagraphs (a) and (b) of subparagraph 1 of Section 2–711. If Oloffson had so proceeded under subparagraph (a) of Section 2–711, he should have effected cover and would have been entitled to recover damages all as provided in section 2–712, which requires that he would have had to cover in good faith without unreasonable delay. Since he would have had to effect cover on June 3, 1970, according to section 2–712(2), he would have been entitled to exactly the damages which the trial court awarded him in this cause.

Assuming that Oloffson had proceeded under subparagraph (b) of Section 2–711, he would have been entitled to recover from Coomer under Section 2–713 and Section 2–723 of the Commercial

Code, the difference between the contract price and the market price on June 3, 1970, which is the date upon which he learned of the breach. This would produce precisely the same amount of damages which the trial court awarded him. [See § 2–723(1)].

Since the trial court properly awarded the damages to which plaintiff was entitled to this cause, the judgment of the circuit court of Bureau County is, therefore, affirmed.

Affirmed.

NOTE

In *Oloffson* there was an anticipatory repudiation of the contract by Seller. Anticipatory repudiation, which refers to a repudiation of the contract prior to the time performance by the repudiating party is due, is covered by § 2–610. "Repudiation" is not defined in the UCC. In *Oloffson* the court considered the statement by Seller of his intention not to perform to be unequivocal and therefore a clear repudiation.

In the event of repudiation by Seller, Buyer is given two options: Buyer may treat the repudiation as a breach of contract and resort to the remedies under § 2–711; or Buyer may forego for the time being the remedies under that section and simply await performance by the repudiating party "for a commercially reasonable time." With respect to the latter option it should be noted that § 2–611 provides for retraction by the repudiating party that has the effect, under the conditions stated in that section, of reinstating the repudiating party to the status of not being in breach of contract. Regardless of which option is chosen Buyer is not required to perform while the repudiation is effective.

Suppose Buyer does not immediately resort to the remedies under § 2–711 and awaits performance by Seller. By what standard can it be determined whether the time that Buyer waits is reasonable or unreasonable? What standard is used by the court in *Oloffson*? Does the reasonableness of Buyer's awaiting performance depend upon the likelihood that Seller might retract the repudiation? Suppose Seller had already planted the corn. Would a statement by Seller on June 3 that delivery would not be made because the market had risen have led to a different result? Does reasonableness depend upon the extent to which Buyer's delay in resorting to the remedies under § 2–711 has prejudiced Seller? In *Oloffson* the market on June 3 was $1.16 and in September when Buyer covered it was $1.35 and $1.49. Should this influence the decision concerning the reasonableness of Buyer's decision to await performance?

If Buyer decided to await performance and market price then rose, can Buyer be charged with knowledge that the market would rise? The latter question was presented in Ralston Purina Co. v.

McNabb, 381 F.Supp. 181 (W.D.Tenn.1974), which involved two contracts for the sale of soybeans to be delivered by November 30. Because of heavy rainfall and flooding of Seller's farm Seller delivered only 738 bushels of the 8,000 bushels promised. On November 30 the market price of soybeans was $3.695 a bushel and the contract prices, $3.29 and $3.33. Buyer gave to Seller a series of one-month extensions of the contracts for the months of December, January and February. § 2–209(1). During those months Seller delivered an additional 3,490 bushels. On March 8 Buyer covered for the undelivered soybeans at $6.25 a bushel. Held: Buyer was entitled to damages measured by the market price on November 30 ($1,497) rather than the cover price ($11,131). The court upheld a jury finding that the extensions granted by Buyer were not made in good faith. § 1–203. Seller alleged that Buyer urged Seller to accept the extensions so that, in the face of a foreseeably rising market it could maximize damages. The price of soybeans climbed steadily after November 30 because of a general shortage caused by severe weather. The court stated: "The jury determined that as early as November 30, 1972 Ralston Purina (1) had knowledge and (2) by the exercise of due diligence should have had knowledge that McNabb would not be able to complete his contract. Possessing such knowledge, Ralston Purina could not, in good faith, modify its contracts with McNabb in a way which would, in view of the past weather conditions and the trend in the market, almost inevitably result in compounding, rather than limiting, any injury to Ralston-Purina." Was there any advantage to Buyer in granting the extensions rather than covering immediately if it believed that it was likely that the market would go up?

If it is determined that Buyer has awaited performance by Seller for a time which is not "commercially reasonable" what is the effect on Buyer's rights? Although § 2–610 does not answer this question, Comment 1 to that section says that the effect is that Buyer "cannot recover resulting damages which he should have avoided." That comment may be directed at the following kind of situation: the sales contract covers goods that are in short supply and which Buyer is committed to resell; at the time of Seller's repudiation Buyer could have purchased substitute goods, but by awaiting Seller's performance Buyer loses the opportunity to cover; Buyer may be precluded from recovering consequential damages resulting from Buyer's failure to honor the resale contracts. § 2–715(2). Does the UCC Comment also apply to a case in which the market rises after repudiation? The issue will normally be presented when Buyer eventually resorts to the remedies under § 2–711, which will usually be an action for damages under § 2–712 or § 2–713. Consider the case of a cover transaction under § 2–712. That section requires that the cover occur "without unreasonable delay." What does "unreasonable delay" mean in the context of § 2–610? Suppose Buyer seeks damages under § 2–713 rather than under § 2–712. Section 2–713 says that market price is determined "at the time when the buyer learned of the breach." In *Oloffson* the court states that the quoted language refers to June 3, 1970 when the seller told the buyer that he was not going to perform, i.e. the time the buyer learned of the repudiation. But the court also held that on that date the buyer could have covered and, under § 2–610(b), could not have reasonably awaited performance by the seller. Thus, § 2–713 damages were measured by the market on that date. In *Cargill* the court states that the quoted language in § 2–713 means the time the performance was due under the contract. Thus, the cases disagree on the meaning of the quoted language. But the *Cargill* court also states that the buyer could await performance only for a reasonable time after learning of the repudiation. At the expiration of the reasonable time, which the court said was September 6, the buyer had to cover if cover was available. If the buyer failed to cover and sought market damages, market price on September 6 would determine § 2–713 damages. Thus both cases, by different routes, treat the expiration of the reasonable time under § 2–610(a) to await performance as the critical time for calculating damages under § 2–713.

In one case, involving an anticipatory repudiation by Buyer, Aura Orchards v. A. Peltz & Sons, Inc., 6 U.C.C. Rep. 149 (U.S. Dept. Agr. 1968), Seller was awarded damages measured by the difference between the contract price and the amount realized by Seller in resale of the goods. Seller did not resell at the time of Buyer's repudiation but waited until the time for Buyer's performance passed. Buyer objected on the ground that an earlier sale would have mitigated damages. The court stated "There is no merit in this contention. Under § 2–610 of the Uniform Commercial Code, [Seller] was not required to recognize [Buyer's] anticipatory breach of the contract but could await the time for performance by [Buyer] under the contract." If Seller's remedy under § 2–706 is considered to be the equivalent of Buyer's remedy under § 2–712 *Aura Orchards* is inconsistent with *Cargill* and *Oloffson,* because the latter cases suggested that Buyer was required to cover without unreasonable delay after learning of Seller's repudiation. But the time of measuring damages based on market price is not the same for buyers and sellers. In the case of a suit by a seller the market is taken at the time for tender. Compare § 2–708(1) and § 2–713. Is this a basis for distinguishing buyer-breach and seller-breach cases?

For full discussions of the problems raised by *Oloffson* and *Cargill* see White and Summers, Commercial Law 276–287 (3d ed. 1988) and Jackson, "Anticipatory Repudiation" and the Temporal Element of Contract Law: An Economic Inquiry into Contract

Damages in Cases of Prospective Nonperformance, 31 Stan.L.Rev. 69 (1978).

c. SPECIFIC PERFORMANCE

LACLEDE GAS CO. v. AMOCO OIL CO.
United States Court of Appeals, Eighth Circuit, 1975.
522 F.2d 33.

ROSS, CIRCUIT JUDGE.   The Laclede Gas Company (Laclede), a Missouri corporation, brought this diversity action alleging breach of contract against the Amoco Oil Company (Amoco), a Delaware corporation.   It sought relief in the form of a mandatory injunction prohibiting the continuing breach or, in the alternative, damages.   The district court held a bench trial on the issues of whether there was a valid, binding contract between the parties and whether, if there was such a contract, Amoco should be enjoined from breaching it.   It then ruled that the "contract is invalid due to lack of mutuality" and denied the prayer for injunctive relief.   The court made no decision regarding the requested damages.   Laclede Gas Co. v. Amoco Oil Co., 385 F.Supp. 1332, 1336 (E.D.Mo.1974).   This appeal followed, and we reverse the district court's judgment.

On September 21, 1970, Midwest Missouri Gas Company (now Laclede), and American Oil Company (now Amoco), the predecessors of the parties to this litigation, entered into a written agreement which was designed to provide central propane gas distribution systems to various residential developments in Jefferson County, Missouri, until such time as natural gas mains were extended into these areas.   The agreement contemplated that as individual developments were planned the owners or developers would apply to Laclede for central propane gas systems.   If Laclede determined that such a system was appropriate in any given development, it could request Amoco to supply the propane to that specific development.   This request was made in the form of a supplemental form letter, as provided in the September 21, agreement; and if Amoco decided to supply the propane, it bound itself to do so by signing this supplemental form.

Once this supplemental form was signed the agreement placed certain duties on both Laclede and Amoco.   Basically, Amoco was to "[i]nstall, own, maintain and operate * * * storage and vaporization facilities and any other facilities necessary to provide [it] with the capability of delivering to [Laclede] commercial propane gas suitable * * * for delivery by [Laclede] to its customers' facilities."   Amoco's facilities were to be "adequate to provide a continuous supply of commercial propane gas at such times and in such volumes commensurate with [Laclede's] requirements for meeting the demands reasonably to be anticipated in each Development while this Agreement is in force." Amoco was deemed to be "the supplier," while Laclede was "the distributing utility."

For its part Laclede agreed to "[i]nstall, own, maintain and operate all distribution facilities" from a "point of delivery" which was defined to be "the outlet of [Amoco] header piping." Laclede also promised to pay Amoco "the Wood River Area Posted Price for propane plus four cents per gallon for all amounts of commercial propane gas delivered" to it under the agreement.

Since it was contemplated that the individual propane systems would eventually be converted to natural gas, one paragraph of the agreement provided that Laclede should give Amoco 30 days written notice of this event, after which the agreement would no longer be binding for the converted development.

Another paragraph gave Laclede the right to cancel the agreement. However, this right was expressed in the following language:

> This Agreement shall remain in effect for one (1) year following the first delivery of gas by [Amoco] to [Laclede] hereunder. Subject to termination as provided in Paragraph 11 hereof [dealing with conversions to natural gas], this Agreement shall automatically continue in effect for additional periods of one (1) year each unless [Laclede] shall, not less than 30 days prior to the expiration of the initial one (1) year period or any subsequent one (1) year period, give [Amoco] written notice of termination.

There was no provision under which Amoco could cancel the agreement.

For a time the parties operated satisfactorily under this agreement, and some 17 residential subdivisions were brought within it by supplemental letters. However, for various reasons, including conversion to natural gas, the number of developments under the agreement had shrunk to eight by the time of trial. These were all mobile home parks.

During the winter of 1972–73 Amoco experienced a shortage of propane and voluntarily placed all of its customers, including Laclede, on an 80% allocation basis, meaning that Laclede would receive only up to 80% of its previous requirements. Laclede objected to this and pushed Amoco to give it 100% of what the developments needed. Some conflict arose over this before the temporary shortage was alleviated.

Then, on April 3, 1973, Amoco notified Laclede that its Wood River Area Posted Price of propane had been increased by three cents per gallon. Laclede objected to this increase also and demanded a full explanation. None was forthcoming. Instead Amoco merely sent a letter dated May 14, 1973, informing Laclede that it was "terminating" the September 21, 1970, agreement effective May 31, 1973. It claimed it had the right to do this because "the Agreement lacks 'mutuality.' "[1]

The district court felt that the entire controversy turned on whether or not Laclede's right to "arbitrarily cancel the Agreement" without Amoco having a similar right rendered the contract void "for lack of mutuality" and it resolved this question in the affirmative. We disagree with this conclusion and hold that settled principles of contract law require a reversal.

* * *

[Omitted is the portion of the opinion in which the court upheld the validity of the contract.]

Since he found that there was no binding contract, the district judge did not have to deal with the question of whether or not to grant the injunction prayed for by Laclede. He simply denied this relief because there was no contract. Laclede Gas Co. v. Amoco Oil Co., supra, 385 F.Supp. at 1336.

Generally the determination of whether or not to order specific performance of a contract lies within the sound discretion of the trial court. * * * However, this discretion is, in fact, quite limited; and it is said that when certain equitable rules have been met and the contract is fair and plain "specific performance goes as a matter of right." Miller v. Coffeen, 365 Mo. 204, 280 S.W.2d 100, 102 (1955), quoting, Berberet v. Myers, 240 Mo. 58, 77, 144 S.W. 824, 830 (1912). (Emphasis omitted.)

With this in mind we have carefully reviewed the very complete record on appeal and conclude that the trial court should grant the injunctive relief prayed. We are satisfied that this case falls within that category in which specific performance should be ordered as a matter of right. * * *

Amoco contends that four of the requirements for specific performance have not been met. Its claims are: (1) there is no mutuality of remedy in the contract; (2) the remedy of specific performance would be difficult for the court to administer without constant and long-continued supervision; (3) the contract is indefinite and uncertain; and (4) the remedy at law, available to Laclede is adequate. The first three contentions have little or no merit and do not detain us for long.

There is simply no requirement in the law that both parties be mutually entitled to the remedy of specific performance in order that one of them be given that remedy by the court.
* * *

---

1. While Amoco sought to repudiate the agreement, it resumed supplying propane to the subdivisions on February 1, 1974, under the mandatory allocation guidelines promulgated by the Federal Energy Administration under the Federal Mandatory Allocation Program for propane. It is agreed that this is now being done under the contract.

While a court may refuse to grant specific performance where such a decree would require constant and long-continued court supervision, this is merely a discretionary rule of decision which is frequently ignored when the public interest is involved. * * *

Here the public interest in providing propane to the retail customers is manifest, while any supervision required will be far from onerous.

Section 370 of the Restatement of Contracts (1932) provides:

Specific enforcement will not be decreed unless the terms of the contract are so expressed that the court can determine with reasonable certainty what is the duty of each party and the conditions under which performance is due.

We believe these criteria have been satisfied here. As discussed in part I of this opinion, as to all developments for which a supplemental agreement has been signed, Amoco is to supply all the propane which is reasonably foreseeably required, while Laclede is to purchase the required propane from Amoco and pay the contract price therefor. The parties have disagreed over what is meant by "Wood River Area Posted Price" in the agreement, but the district court can and should determine with reasonable certainty what the parties intended by this term and should mold its decree, if necessary accordingly.[3] Likewise, the fact that the agreement does not have a definite time of duration is not fatal since the evidence established that the last subdivision should be converted to natural gas in 10 to 15 years. This sets a reasonable time limit on performance and the district court can and should mold the final decree to reflect this testimony.

It is axiomatic that specific performance will not be ordered when the party claiming breach of contract has an adequate remedy at law. * * * This is especially true when the contract involves personal property as distinguished from real estate.

However, in Missouri, as elsewhere, specific performance may be ordered even though personalty is involved in the "proper circumstances." UCC § 2–716(1); Restatement of Contracts, supra, § 361. And a remedy at law adequate to defeat the grant of specific performance "must be as certain, prompt, complete, and efficient to attain the ends of justice as a decree of specific performance." National Marking Mach. Co. v. Triumph Mfg. Co., 13 F.2d 6, 9 (8th Cir. 1926). * * *

One of the leading Missouri cases allowing specific performance of a contract relating to personalty because the remedy at law was inadequate is Boeving v. Vandover, 240 Mo.App. 117, 218 S.W.2d 175, 178 (1949). In that case the plaintiff sought specific performance of a contract in which the defendant had promised to

3. The record indicates that Laclede has now accepted Amoco's interpretation and has agreed that "Wood River Area Posted Price" means Amoco's posted price for propane at its Wood River refinery.

sell him an automobile. At that time (near the end of and shortly after World War II) new cars were hard to come by, and the court held that specific performance was a proper remedy since a new car "could not be obtained elsewhere except at considerable expense, trouble or loss, which cannot be estimated in advance."

We are satisfied that Laclede has brought itself within this practical approach taken by the Missouri courts. As Amoco points out, Laclede has propane immediately available to it under other contracts with other suppliers. And the evidence indicates that at the present time propane is readily available on the open market. However, this analysis ignores the fact that the contract involved in this lawsuit is for a long-term supply of propane to these subdivisions. The other two contracts under which Laclede obtains the gas will remain in force only until March 31, 1977, and April 1, 1981, respectively; and there is no assurance that Laclede will be able to receive any propane under them after that time. Also it is unclear as to whether or not Laclede can use the propane obtained under these contracts to supply the Jefferson County subdivisions, since they were originally entered into to provide Laclede with propane with which to "shave" its natural gas supply during peak demand periods.[4] Additionally, there was uncontradicted expert testimony that Laclede probably could not find another supplier of propane willing to enter into a long-term contract such as the Amoco agreement, given the uncertain future of worldwide energy supplies. And, even if Laclede could obtain supplies of propane for the affected developments through its present contracts or newly negotiated ones, it would still face considerable expense and trouble which cannot be estimated in advance in making arrangements for its distribution to the subdivisions.

Specific performance is the proper remedy in this situation, and it should be granted by the district court.[5]

CONCLUSION

For the foregoing reasons the judgment of the district court is reversed and the cause is remanded for the fashioning of appropriate injunctive relief in the form of a decree of specific performance as to those developments for which a supplemental agreement form has been signed by the parties.

4. During periods of cold weather, when demand is high, Laclede does not receive enough natural gas to meet all this demand. It, therefore, adds propane to the natural gas it places in its distribution system. This practice is called "peak shaving."

5. In fashioning its decree the district court must take into account any relevant rules and regulations promulgated under the Federal Mandatory Allocation Program.

NOTE

In Copylease Corp. of America v. Memorex Corp., 408 F.Supp. 758 (S.D.N.Y.1976), a case involving the sale of toner for use in copying machines, the court stated that specific performance under § 2–716 would be appropriate if Buyer could prove that it could not obtain an alternative source of toner because other brands of toner are "distinctly inferior" to Seller's product. The court, however, indicated that the question of whether specific performance would be granted would depend upon how the court resolved other state policies limiting the remedy. It stated:

> If Copylease has no adequate alternative source of toner the Memorex product might be considered "unique" for purposes of § 2–716, or the situation might present an example of "other proper circumstances" in which specific performance would be appropriate.
>
> If such a showing is made it will be necessary to reconcile California's policy against ordering specific performance of contracts which provide for continuing acts or an ongoing relationship with § 2–716 of the Code. Although we recognize that the statute does not require specific performance, the quoted portion of the Official Comment seems clearly to suggest that where a contract calls for continuing sale of unique or "noncoverable" goods this provision should be considered an exception to the general proscription. Output and requirements contracts, explicitly cited as examples of situations in which specific performance may be appropriate, by their nature call for a series of continuing acts and an ongoing relationship. Thus, the drafters seem to have contemplated that at least in some circumstances specific performance will issue contrary to the historical reluctance to grant such relief in these situations. If, at the hearing, Copylease makes a showing that it meets the requirements of § 2–716, the sensible approach would be to measure, with the particulars of this contract in mind, the uniqueness or degree of difficulty in covering against the difficulties of enforcement which have caused courts to refrain from granting specific performance. It would be premature to speculate on the outcome of such analysis in this case.

2. DAMAGES FOR BREACH OF WARRANTY

AM/PM FRANCHISE ASSN. v.
ATLANTIC RICHFIELD CO.

Supreme Court of Pennsylvania, 1990.
526 Pa. 110, 584 A.2d 915.

CAPPY, JUSTICE.

* * *

We granted allocatur to determine whether the named appellants ("plaintiffs") have alleged sufficient facts to sustain a cause of action when they aver that the gasoline they purchased from the appellee ("ARCO") was not in conformance with the warranties made and resulted in their suffering economic harm.   In making such a determination, we address the question of whether such damages constitute a "loss of good will," and whether good will damages are too speculative as a matter of law to permit recovery.   For the reasons set forth herein, we find that the plaintiffs have alleged sufficient facts to entitle them to proceed with their claim and that the damages claimed are not good will nor so speculative as to deny them an attempt at recovery.

* * *

The Plaintiffs claim to represent a class of over 150 franchisees of ARCO that operated AM/PM Mini Markets in Pennsylvania and New York during a three and one-half year period.

ARCO entered into franchise agreements with the plaintiffs which were comprised of a premises lease, a lessee dealer gasoline agreement, and an AM/PM mini-market agreement.   The products agreement mandated that the franchisees sell only ARCO petroleum products.

The complaint sets forth the following facts: ARCO began experimenting with its formula for unleaded gasoline and provided its franchisees with an unleaded gasoline blended with oxinol, consisting of 4.5% methanol and 4.5% gasoline grade tertiary butyl alcohol (hereinafter "the oxinol blend") from early 1982 through September 30, 1985.

During this three and a half year period, the franchisees were required to sell the oxinol blend to their clients who desired unleaded gasoline.   The franchisees were given no opportunity to buy regular unleaded gasoline from ARCO during that period.

Plaintiffs claim that numerous purchasers of the oxinol blend gasoline experienced poor engine performance and physical damage to fuel system components.   Specifically, plaintiffs claim that the oxinol gasoline permitted an excess accumulation of alcohol and/or water which interfered with the efficiency of gasoline engines and, in certain vehicles, caused swelling of plastic or rubber components in the fuel delivery system and resulted in engine damage. The plaintiffs claim that the gasoline did not conform to ARCO's warranties about the product.

As the problems with the oxinol blend became known, the plaintiffs claim to have suffered a precipitous drop in the volume of their business and an attendant loss of profits. Specifically, plaintiffs point to the rise in sales from 1973 until 1982, when sales began to fall dramatically; allegedly due to defective oxinol blend gasoline.

In their complaint, plaintiffs allege three counts of Breach of Warranty, Breach of Implied Duty, Misrepresentation, and Exemplary Damages. They request damages for "lost profits, consequential and incidental damages."

* * *

Pursuant to the provisions of the U.C.C., plaintiffs are entitled to seek "general" damages, so-called, under section 2–714(2) and consequential damages as provided by section 2–714(3).

There has been substantial confusion in the courts and among litigants about what consequential damages actually are and what types of consequential damages are available in a breach of warranty case. Where a buyer in the business of reselling goods can prove that a breach by the seller has caused him to lose profitable resales, the buyer's lost profits constitute a form of consequential damages. We now hold that in addition to general damages, there are three types of lost profit recoverable as consequential damages that may flow from a breach of warranty: (1) loss of primary profits; (2) loss of secondary profits; and (3) a loss of good will damages (or prospective damages, as they are sometimes termed).

In order to alleviate the confusion that has developed concerning the various damages, we use an example to help illustrate the different types.

General damages in the case of accepted goods (such as occurred here) are the actual difference in value between the goods as promised and the goods as received. Thus, suppose a buyer bought five hundred tires from a wholesaler that were to be delivered in good condition, and in that condition would be worth $2,500. The tires were delivered with holes in them which rendered them worthless. The buyer would be entitled to $2,500 from the seller—the difference between the value of the tires as warranted and the value of the tires as received; those would be the general damages.

Consequential damages are generally understood to be other damages which naturally and proximately flow from the breach and include three types of lost profit damages: (1) lost primary profits; (2) lost secondary profits; and (3) loss of prospective profits, also commonly referred to as good will damages.

Lost primary profits are the difference between what the buyer would have earned from reselling the goods in question had there been no breach and what was earned after the breach occurred. Thus, if the buyer of the tires proved that he would have resold the tires for $5,000, he would be able to claim an additional $2,500 for loss of tire profits; the difference between what he would have earned from the sale of the tires and what he actually did earn from the sale (or lack of sales) from the tires.

If the buyer of the tires also sold, for example, hubcaps with every set of tires, he would also suffer a loss of hubcap profits. These types of damages are what we term "loss of secondary profits."

If the buyer's regular customers were so disgruntled about the defective tires that they no longer frequented the buyer's business and began to patronize a competitor's business, the buyer would have suffered a "loss of good will" beyond the direct loss of profits from the nonconforming goods; his future business would be adversely affected as a result of the defective tires. Thus, good will damages refer to profits lost on future sales rather than on sales of the defective goods themselves.

While this example provides a simple framework to understand the different types of possible damages in a breach of warranty case, it does not encompass the myriad of circumstances in which a claim for damages can arise, nor does it specify which of these different damages have been allowed in Pennsylvania.

In addition to recognizing general damages under § 2–714 of the Code, Pennsylvania allows consequential damages in the form of lost profits to be recovered.

* * *

Pennsylvania has, however, disallowed good will damages; finding them to be too speculative to permit recovery. In the cases disallowing good will damages, part of the reason we found them too speculative is that the damages were not contemplated by the parties at the time the contract was made.

In 1977, this court had occasion to re-examine sections 2–714 and 2–715 of the Uniform Commercial Code in the case of R.I. Lampus Co. v. Neville Cement Products Corp., 474 Pa. 199, 378 A.2d 288 (1977). Before the *Lampus* case, we required the party seeking consequential damages in the form of lost profits to show that there were "special circumstances" indicating that such damages were actually contemplated by the parties at the time they entered into the agreement. This rule, termed the "tacit-agreement" test, "permit[ed] the plaintiff to recover damages arising from special circumstances only if 'the defendant fairly may be supposed to have assumed consciously, or to have warranted the plaintiff reasonably to suppose that it assumed, [such liability] when the contract was made.'" *R.I. Lampus Co.*, supra, at 207,

378 A.2d at 291 (1977). (cites omitted) (brackets in original), quoting from J. White & R. Summers, Uniform Commercial Code (1972).

In *Lampus,* we overruled the restrictive "tacit-agreement" test and replaced it with the "reason to know" test; which requires that "[i]f a seller knows of a buyer's general or particular requirements and needs, that seller is liable for *the resulting consequential damages* whether or not that seller contemplated or agreed to such damages." Id. at 209, 378 A.2d at 292 (1977) (emphasis supplied).[6] Thus, in order to obtain consequential damages, the plaintiff need only prove that the damages were reasonably foreseeable at the time the agreement was entered into.[7]

Turning to the case at hand, we must determine whether the plaintiffs have alleged sufficient facts to permit them to proceed with a claim for consequential damages.

We note initially that the standard of review for preliminary objections is a limited one. As we stated in Vattimo v. Lower Bucks Hosp., Inc., 502 Pa. 241, 465 A.2d 1231, 1232–33 (1983):

> All material facts set forth in the complaint as well as all inferences reasonably deducible therefrom are admitted as true for [the purpose of this review.] Clevenstein v. Rizzuto, 439 Pa. 397, 266 A.2d 623 (1970). The question presented by the demurrer is whether, on the facts averred, the law says with certainty that no recovery is possible. Hoffman v. Misericordia Hospital of Philadelphia, 439 Pa. 501, 267 A.2d 867 (1970). Where a doubt exists as to whether a demurrer should be sustained, this doubt should be resolved in favor of overruling it. Birl v. Philadelphia Electric Co., 402 Pa. 297, 167 A.2d 472 (1960).

In this complaint, the plaintiffs have alleged, inter alia: that ARCO expressly warranted through its agreements, mailgrams and brochures that its oxinol gasoline was of high quality, better for the environment and would not damage new or older automobiles; that the oxinol gasoline was not merchantable because it damaged engines; that it was not fit for the ordinary purpose for which it was intended; that ARCO knew that the plaintiffs were relying on the skill of the defendants to select or furnish suitable gasoline; that ARCO's actions constituted a breach of express warranties which resulted in harm to the plaintiffs in the form of lost profits, incidental and consequential damages.

---

6. Lampus is in accord with section 2–715 of the U.C.C., comment 2 (1978), which states; "[t]he 'tacit agreement' test for the recovery of consequential damages is rejected."

7. Accord; U.C.C. § 2–715, comment 3 (1978).

Based on our standard of review as set forth above, we believe that the plaintiffs have set forth sufficient facts in their complaint to state a cause of action under the breach of warranty counts.

The plaintiffs seek lost profits, incidental and consequential damages.[8] The defendants and the lower courts, however, considered these damages to be lost good will. We believe that the lower courts and the defendants are in error in categorizing all the claimed damages as good will damages. We address separately the different types of damages claimed.

LOSS OF PROFITS FOR GASOLINE SALES

The first claim the plaintiff makes for damages is for the profits lost from the sales of gasoline. The plaintiffs claim that the breach of warranty by the defendant concerning the gasoline caused the plaintiffs to lose sales during a three and one half year period while they received nonconforming gasoline from ARCO. In the case of Kassab v. Central Soya, 432 Pa. 217, 246 A.2d 848 (1968), we permitted lost profits for cattle sales when the plaintiff showed that the defective feed caused harm to their cattle, causing the public to stop buying their cattle. The allegation here is similar. When the gasoline buying public discovered that the gasoline was defective, many stopped purchasing ARCO gasoline.

Employing the reasoning of Kassab and taking it one step further, we believe that the plaintiffs here are entitled to show that the gasoline buying community did not buy their gasoline from 1982 through 1985 because of the reasonable belief that the gasoline was defective and would harm their engines. The lost gasoline sales are comparable to the lost cattle sales in Kassab. The distinction between the two cases is that the Kassabs had bought the feed all at one time and thus all their livestock was affected. The instant plaintiffs bought their gasoline in regular intervals and could only earn a profit on what they could sell per month. The defendant's argument—that the plaintiffs sold all the gasoline they bought—misses the point. While they may have sold every gallon, they sold significantly fewer gallons during the period that ARCO allegedly delivered nonconforming gasoline. Thus, during this period, the plaintiffs' lost sales were just as directly attributable to the defective gasoline as the lost profits were attributable to the defective tires in the example we used previously.

Thus, if prior to the manufacture of defective gasoline the plaintiffs sold 100,000 gallons per month every month and then as a result of the defective gasoline, they sold only 60,000 gallons per month every month until ARCO discontinued that gasoline, then

---

8. The plaintiffs claim "lost profits, incidental and consequential damages." As we noted herein, however, "lost prof- its" are a type of consequential damage; not a separate category of damages.

the plaintiffs have lost the profits they would have received on 40,000 gallons per month for the three year claimed period. Lost profits are, in fact, the difference between what the plaintiff actually earned and what they would have earned had the defendant not committed the breach. Because the gasoline was allegedly not in conformance with the warranties, the plaintiffs may be entitled to lost profits for the gasoline on a breach of warranty theory. The lost gasoline sales are what we have termed "loss of primary profits," and they are recoverable pursuant to § 2–715 of the U.C.C. upon proper proof.

We note, furthermore, that the remedy of cover was unavailable to the plaintiffs. Section 2–715 of the U.C.C. limits a plaintiff's ability to recover when he could have prevented such damage "by cover or otherwise". Pursuant to the code, cover is defined as the buyer's purchase of substitute goods at a commercially reasonable price. * * *

The plaintiffs here, by their allegations, could not "cover;" they were contractually required to purchase all their gasoline from ARCO. In effect, they had to accept the allegedly nonconforming gasoline and had no possible way to avoid the attendant loss of profits. Thus, since they could not cover, the only remedy that was available to them was to file suit.

Furthermore, we note that Section 1–106 of the U.C.C. provides:

> [t]he remedies provided by this title shall be *liberally administered to the end that the aggrieved party may be put in as good a position as if the other party had fully performed* but neither consequential or special nor penal damages may be had except as specifically provided in this title or by other rule of law. (emphasis supplied).

The Code itself compels us to be liberal in our interpretation of the types of damages we permit. We would therefore allow the plaintiffs to proceed with their claims for lost gasoline profits during the period ARCO supplied allegedly nonconforming gasoline.

LOSS OF PROFITS FOR ITEMS OTHER THAN GASOLINE SALES

The plaintiffs allege that in addition to a loss of profits for sales of gasoline, they had a concomitant loss of sales for other items that they sold in their mini-marts during the period of time that ARCO supplied nonconforming gasoline. Their rationale is that when the number of customers buying gasoline decreased, so did the number of customers buying items at the mini-mart. In other words, related facets of their business suffered as a result of the defective gasoline. This type of injury is what we characterize as "loss of secondary profits;" meaning that the sales of other products suffered as a result of the breach of warranty. This court has not had an opportunity to address whether these types of damages are recoverable.

In the case before us, the essence of plaintiffs' allegations is that customers frequent the mini-marts because it is convenient to do so at the time they purchase gasoline. Customers of the mini-mart are foremost gasoline buying patrons; gasoline is their primary purchase and sundries are their incidental purchases. Here, the plaintiffs claim that the *primary product* sales so affected the incidental sales as to create a loss in other aspects of their business. It is reasonable to assume that if the gasoline sales dropped dramatically, there was a ripple effect on the mini-mart sales. Additionally, when a primary product does not conform to the warranty, we believe that it is foreseeable that there will be a loss of secondary profits. Thus, permitting these damages would correspond with the requirement of foreseeability as set forth in *Lampus,* supra, and the Code. It is much less foreseeable to assume there will be a loss of secondary profits when the nonconforming products are not the primary ones. We believe that unless it is a primary product that does not conform to the warranty, the causal relationship between the breach and the loss is too attenuated to permit damages for the loss of secondary profits.[12]

We also find that the fact situation before us presents a further problem in that the plaintiffs were not able to mitigate the harm in any way by buying substitute goods or "cover." Thus, the plaintiffs' primary product was defective and they were unable to remedy the situation by buying gasoline from another supplier.

We find that the present case presents compelling reasons for permitting damages for loss of secondary profits. Henceforth, in a breach of warranty case, when a primary product of the plaintiff is alleged to be nonconforming and the plaintiff is unable to cover by purchasing substitute goods, we hold that upon proper proof, the plaintiff should be entitled to sue for loss of secondary profits.[13]

12. As with all cases involving breach of warranty, the plaintiff is charged with the burden of proving that the defendant's breach is the proximate cause of the harm suffered. Thus, in order to proceed with their case, the plaintiffs here must prove that the alleged nonconformance of the gasoline caused both their loss of gasoline sales as well as their loss of mini-mart sales. This requirement is an arduous one and we render no opinion as to whether the plaintiffs can meet this burden. However, we note that this is for the trial court, in its wisdom, to decide whether the plaintiffs have met the threshold of proof to submit the case to the factfinder.

13. What constitutes a "primary product" will be dependent on the facts of each case. However, we would define a "primary product" as an item upon which the aggrieved party relies for a substantial amount of its revenue. The plaintiff must show that without that product, his business would be severely incapacitated.

LOSS OF GOOD WILL

Historically, Pennsylvania has disallowed recovery for loss of good will damages or prospective profits in breach of warranty cases. The cases generally relied upon for this proposition are Michelin Tire Co. v. Schulz, 295 Pa. 140, 145 A. 67 (1929); Harry Rubin & Sons, Inc. v. Consolidated Pipe Co. of America, 396 Pa. 506, 153 A.2d 472 (1959); and Kassab v. Central Soya, 432 Pa. 217, 246 A.2d 848 (1968).

The defendant and the lower courts rely on these cases for the proposition that the plaintiffs claims are for "good will damages" and thus too speculative as a matter of law to permit recovery. While this analysis is seductive in its simplicity, it ignores the nuances of each of these cases and the effect R.I. Lampus Co. v. Neville Cement Products Corp., has had on this area of law.

In fact, in the case of *Rubin & Sons,* supra, the court remarked "[i]ndeed if such were the holding [permitting good will damages], damages which the parties never contemplated would seem to be involved in every contract of sale." Id. at 513, 153 A.2d at 477.

With the advent of the *Lampus* "reason-to-know" test—which is a test of foreseeability—the holdings under each of these cases have much less precedential effect, since the *Lampus* test is much less restrictive than the tacit-agreement test.

Although the plaintiffs do not style their claim as one for good will damages, the Superior Court, the trial court, and the defendant have all characterized the claim for lost profits in this case as good will damages. What actually constitutes good will damages has caused much consternation to the courts and litigants. We in fact have serious doubts that the plaintiffs are even seeking good will damages. However, in order to determine that issue in the case before us, we must first discuss what good will damages are and whether they are allowable.

As one commentator aptly noted, "[l]oss of good will is a mercurial concept and, as such, is difficult to define. In a broad sense, it refers to a loss of future profits." [14] Other jurisdictions have considered loss of good will to be a loss of profits and reputation among customers.[15] Generally, good will refers to the reputation that businesses have built over the course of time that is reflected by the return of customers to purchase goods and the attendant profits that accompanies such sales. Thus the phrase "good will damages" is coextensive with prospective profits and loss of business reputation.

---

14. Anderson, Incidental and Consequential Damages, 7 J.L. & Com. 327, 420 (1987).

15. Texsun Feed Yards, Inc. v. Ralston Purina Co., 447 F.2d 660 (5th Cir. 1971).

Secondly, we must decide when good will damages arise in a breach of warranty situation. Essentially, damage to good will in a case in which the seller supplies a quantity dictated by the buyer's requirements arises only *after* the seller has ceased providing nonconforming goods—or the buyer has purchased substitute goods. Damage to good will in this case would refer to the loss of business sales that occurred after the buyer was able to provide acceptable goods to his customers; it does not refer to the period of time during which he is forced to sell the nonconforming goods.

Thirdly, we must address whether good will damages are too speculative to permit recovery, as we held in *Michelin, Rubin & Sons,* supra, and *Kassab,* supra. Although we disallowed good will damages in those cases, they are not recent. They were written in a time when business was conducted on a more simple basis, where market studies and economic forecasting were unexplored sciences.

We are now in an era in which computers, economic forecasting, sophisticated marketing studies and demographic studies are widely used and accepted. As such, we believe that the rationale for precluding prospective profits under the rubric of "too speculative" ignores the realities of the marketplace and the science of modern economics. We believe that claims for prospective profits should not be barred *ab initio.* Rather, plaintiffs should be given an opportunity to set forth and attempt to prove their damages.

Twenty years ago, the Third Circuit Court of Appeals noted in a case disallowing claims for prospective profits that damages once considered speculative may not be in the future:

> This is not to say we approve the Pennsylvania view or believe it will be the Pennsylvania position in the future [prohibiting good will damages]. Considering the advances made in techniques of market analysis and the use of highly sophisticated computers it may be that lost profits of this nature are no more speculative than lost profits from the destruction of a factory or hotel, and perhaps Pennsylvania will reconsider the reason for its rule in a future case. Neville Chemical Co. v. Union Carbide Corp., 422 F.2d 1205, 1227 (1970).

We believe the time has come to reconsider that rule. In doing so, we find our position on recovery for good will damages (or prospective profits) to be out of step with modern day business practices and techniques, as well as the law of other jurisdictions. As noted by Professor Anderson in his well-crafted article on incidental and consequential damages,

> [t]o date, only the Pennsylvania courts have categorically denied recovery for loss of goodwill under any circumstances, an issue which has been oft-litigated in Pennsylvania. If one removes the Pennsylvania cases from the count, a significant

majority of the cases have allowed for the recovery of lost goodwill in proper circumstances.[17]

Furthermore, our rule has been repeatedly criticized by other courts and commentators. In reviewing our case law on the issue of prospective profits, we have not had a significant case come before us since *Kassab* was decided in 1968. Since that time, astronauts have walked on the moon, engineers have developed computers capable of amazing feats and biomedical engineers and physicians have made enormous strides in organ transplantation and replacement. It is evident that the world of 1990 is not the same world as it was in 1929 when the *Michelin* case was decided, nor even the same world as it was in 1968 when *Kassab* was decided. While these rapid technological developments have not been without their concomitant problems, they have made possible many things that were not possible before; including the calculation of prospective profits.[19] For these reasons, we overrule *Michelin,* supra, *Rubin & Sons, Inc.,* supra, and *Kassab,* supra, to the extent they prohibit a plaintiff from alleging a claim for damage to good will as a matter of law.

Inextricably entwined with the issue of speculation is the difficulty in proving the damages are causally related to the breach. As we stated earlier, difficulty in proving causation should not operate as a bar to permitting plaintiffs to claim the damages. Furthermore, we note that pursuant to our case law and the Uniform Commercial Code, damages need not be proved with mathematical certainty. As long as the plaintiffs can pro-

---

17. Anderson, Incidental and Consequential Damages, 7 J.L. & Com. 327, 421 (1987).

19. Further curiosity is engendered by our extensive history of allowing claims for loss of prospective profits in breach of contract case. In Wilson v. Wernwag, 217 Pa. 82, 66 A. 242 (1907), this court said:

An examination of the well-considered cases will show that prospective profits may be recovered for the breach of a contract whenever they are susceptible of proof. They have been rejected by the courts as damages only because of the failure to prove them with sufficient certainty and definitiveness. There can be no good reason why they should not be recovered when they are capable of definite estimation." Id., at 94, 66 A., at 246.

* * * this court has recognized that although proof of prospective damages might be difficult, such difficulty should not operate as an absolute bar to the claim itself:

compensation for breach of contract cannot be justly refused because proof of the exact amount of loss is not produced, for there is judicial recognition of the difficulty or even impossibility of the production of such proof. What the law does require in cases of this character is that the evidence shall with a fair degree of probability establish a basis for the assessment of damages. Massachusetts Bonding & Insurance Co. v. Johnston & Harder, Inc., 343 Pa. 270, 280, 22 A.2d 709, 714 (1941).

The problem of proof in these breach of contract cases is really no different from the problems of proof in breach of warranty cases. In our attempt to craft law that is internally consistent as well as historically consistent, we must strive to reconcile differences as they become apparent. As such, we see no legitimate reason to prohibit prospective damages in breach of warranty cases when we never have in breach of contract cases.

vide a reasonable basis from which the jury can calculate damages, they will be permitted to pursue their case.

Thus, we now hold that plaintiffs should be entitled to try to prove good will damages; provided they are able to introduce sufficient evidence (1) to establish that such profits were causally related to a breach of warranty and (2) to provide the trier of fact with a reasonable basis from which to calculate damages.[20]

Turning to the facts of this case, we note that the plaintiffs have made no claim for good will damages, since none was incurred; ARCO having cured the breach by stopping the supply of the nonconforming gasoline. The damages claimed are only for the period of time that the plaintiffs were forced to purchase the gasoline with oxinol. Thus, we reverse the decision of the lower courts in holding that the plaintiffs' claim was for good will damages.

CONCLUSION

We now hold that there are three types of lost profits recoverable as consequential damages available under § 2–714 and § 2–715 of the Uniform Commercial Code: (1) loss of primary profits; (2) loss of secondary profits; and (3) good will damages, defined as a loss of prospective profits or business reputation. While this categorization of damages represents a new direction for the court, we believe it is the better direction.

As a final note, we do not find that this case should be decided on tort principles, but on warranty principles. The relationship between the parties is of a contractual nature and should be decided on contractual principles. For that reason, we uphold the decision of the court below dismissing the tort claims. Additionally, we do not believe that our case law or the Uniform Commercial Code authorizes a legitimate claim for exemplary damages and thus affirm the lower court's dismissal of such claim. Accordingly, we reverse the decision of the lower courts with respect to the breach of warranty claims and remand the case for proceedings consistent with the opinion.

[The concurring and dissenting opinion of
Justice Flaherty is omitted.]

---

20. There are a number of different ways that damages may be removed from the realm of speculation and be submitted to the jury with a rational basis from which the amount can be inferred. As long as the method of proof provides the jury with "a reasonable basis" for calculating damages, the issue should be submitted to the trier of fact. This is the approach taken by most jurisdictions.

B. SELLER'S REMEDIES

———

1. LOSS OF BARGAIN DAMAGES

———

a. DAMAGES MEASURED BY MARKET OR RESALE OF THE GOODS

———

COAST TRADING CO. v. CUDAHY CO.

United States Court of Appeals, Ninth Circuit, 1979.
592 F.2d 1074.

GRANT, DISTRICT JUDGE. This appeal involves an action by the plaintiff grain merchant against the defendant buyer for the anticipatory repudiation of a number of contracts for the purchase of barley.

Plaintiff, a Washington corporation, is a grain merchant with headquarters in Portland, Oregon. Its customers include other grain merchandisers, grain exporters, feed mills and processors and cattle feedlots. Defendant, a Delaware corporation, has its principal office in Phoenix, Arizona, and operated a feedlot for cattle in Sunnyville, Washington. From September 1973 through May 1974, the general manager of the feedlot was a Mr. Robin Van Woerden, having responsibility for day to day operations, including the purchase of supplies and feed. His compensation consisted of a salary and a bonus related to profits. Plaintiff had supplied feed grains to the feedlot since about 1954, and plaintiff was aware that the feedlot was owned by the defendant.

The trial court found that from 28 February to 2 April 1974, one of plaintiff's merchandisers and Van Woerden had executed 14 contracts for the sale of barley, totaling more than 10,000 tons. Van Woerden had been buying grain from other grain merchants in the same manner as from the plaintiff. The limited storage capacity at the feedlot (750–1,000 tons) required Van Woerden to arrange for outside storage. Because of that fact, plaintiff arranged for 1,500 tons of barley purchased by Van Woerden to be stored in Spokane, Washington.

In late May 1974, employees from defendant's home office first learned of the extent of barley purchases by the feedlot, and representatives of defendant met with plaintiff but no agreement could be reached. On 6 June 1974, defendant repudiated those contracts for which delivery had not been made on the basis that Van Woerden had no authority to bind defendant. Between 11 June and 19 June 1974, plaintiff allegedly sold over 10,000 tons of barley to eight purchasers and used those sales to compute resale prices for the barley repudiated by defendant. At the trial level, plaintiff argued that Van Woerden had both implied and apparent authority to bind his principal on all the contracts and plaintiff therefore sought the difference between resale prices and the prices in the repudiated contracts as damages under Section 2–706 of the Oregon Uniform Commercial Code.

The district court found that the general manager had implied authority to purchase reasonable amounts of barley for future delivery in order to assure a constant supply, but that this would not include authority for speculation in the barley market. The court concluded that in executing the 14 repudiated contracts, Van Woerden was speculating in the barley market and had exceeded his implied authority; likewise, that he had exceeded his implied authority in arranging for storage with plaintiff.

Addressing the apparent authority issue, the court found that Van Woerden had apparent authority to execute the contracts dated 28 February 1974 but that plaintiff could not rely on the apparent authority theory for contracts executed after 28 February 1974, because of changed market conditions. These conditions imposed a duty of inquiry on plaintiff regarding Van Woerden's authority in view of the continued orders of unprecedented size. Because plaintiff failed to make those appropriate inquiries, the court held that damages should be allowed for the repudiated contracts signed on 28 February 1974, but not for the repudiated purchase or storage contracts signed after that date.

The court then grappled with the measure of damages under Section 2–706 of the UCC which allows the difference between the contract price and the resale price but requires *inter alia* that the seller must give the repudiating buyer reasonable notice of the private resale. The court found that no reasonable notice had been given defendant by plaintiff regarding some of the resales, amounting to 1,500 tons, but that reasonable notice was given for later resales amounting to 3,000 tons. Therefore, plaintiff was partially entitled to damages provable under Section 2–706.

* * *

The parties present two main issues in this appeal: (1) the extent of the authority of Robin Van Woerden, and (2) the proper measure of damages.

THE AGENT'S AUTHORITY

* * *

We hold that the court did not commit reversible error in deciding the agency issue. In a case where different reasonable inferences may be drawn from the evidence, the question of the nature and extent of the authority of an agent is one of fact to be

determined by the trier of fact. * * * The instant case was
tried to the court sitting without a jury. Neither party has shown
such insufficiency of evidence as to require reversal. Therefore,
we affirm the trial court's ruling that Defendant Cudahy is liable
only for the barley purchase contracts entered into on 28 February
1974, amounting to 4,500 tons at an average of $128 per ton.

DAMAGES

The second and more difficult issue is whether the trial court
correctly measured the damages. In order to understand the
correct measure of damages, two sections of the Oregon Uniform
Commercial Code must be reviewed: Section 2–706, allowing resale damages, and Section 2–708(1), allowing market value damages. The seller in the case at bar has asserted that Section 2–706
should be the measure of damages. Under Section 2–706, if the
resale is made in good faith and in a commercially reasonable
manner, the seller may recover the difference between the resale
price and the contract price together with any incidental damages,
but less expenses saved in consequence of the buyer's breach.
Sale may be as a unit or in parcels and at any time and place and
on any terms, but every aspect of the sale including the method,
manner, time, place and terms must be commercially reasonable.
In addition, the resale must be reasonably identified as referring
to the broken contract, but it is not necessary that the goods be in
existence or that any or all of them have been identified to the
contract before the breach. Finally, if resale is at a private sale,
as in the case at bar, the seller must give the buyer reasonable
notification of his intention to resell.

* * *

Plaintiff contends that the trial court erred in holding, with
respect to the first two resale contracts, that plaintiff failed to give
reasonable notice of its intention to resell, in that defendant
received notice by telephone, by mailgram, and by direct mail.
Additionally, plaintiff avers that immediate sale was required by
accruing demurrage charges and because some of the barley was
in rail cars on track and in transit. Furthermore, plaintiff argues
its sales were commercially reasonable, in good faith, and that the
resold barley was properly identified to the repudiated contracts
on a ton for ton basis. Finally, plaintiff argues that if it is found
that damages cannot be calculated under a Section 2–706 resale
approach, then damages should be measured under a Section 2–
708 market value approach.

On the other hand, defendant argues that plaintiff failed to
prove damages and is not entitled to a resale measure of damages.
Defendant contends that plaintiff had a chance to sell the repudiated barley at higher prices than defendant would have paid and
indeed seized this opportunity; yet through sales manipulations,

fictional transactions, and disregard of the requisites of Section 2–706, plaintiff invented the claim that it suffered damages and in any event may not recover a resale measure of damages. It is further argued that plaintiff's resales were made neither in good faith nor in a commercially reasonable manner, and that the resale contracts were not reasonably identified to the repudiated contracts.

Several points are presented by defendant to support its contentions: (1) plaintiff charged defendant with costs for barley stored in a warehouse at Spokane, yet failed to credit defendant with any profit on the resale of that barley; (2) although plaintiff claims that 22 railroad cars of barley en route to the feedlot were included in the resales used to compute the damages—in fact, only ten of the cars were actually applied to plaintiff's resale damage calculation; (3) plaintiff failed to sell at reasonable prices because it sold prematurely while the market was at a temporary low, because over half the barley was sold at prices below the market price, and because plaintiff knowingly dumped all the barley on the market at once causing a depressive effect on prices, thereby failing to sell at a reasonable time; and (4) over half the barley plaintiff claims to have resold was merely a sham paper transaction with a related corporation, founded by plaintiff, and was cancelled nine days later by a re-purchase before any barley exchanged hands.

After reviewing the arguments and exhibits of both parties, we conclude that the trial court erred in allowing damages under Section 2–706 of the Oregon Uniform Commercial Code. In its 12 April 1976 Memorandum Opinion, the trial court insisted upon the reasonable notification requirement of Section 2–706, but failed to address the question of whether the other prerequisites had been fulfilled by the plaintiff. We find that, as a matter of law, the plaintiff did not satisfy the elements of good faith and commercial reasonableness, required in every aspect of every sale. The most striking example of commercial unreasonableness that suggests bad faith is the alleged resale contract between the plaintiff and a corporate purchaser entitled Montana Merchandisers, Inc. The total amount of barley involved in the repudiated contracts equals 10,343.11 tons. Of the 10,343.11 tons resold by plaintiff, 5,293.11 tons were supposedly sold to Montana Merchandisers, Inc., on 19 June 1974, as part of a 6,000-ton transaction. The sale price was $100 per ton, although the pertinent market price was $105 per ton. Nine days later, on 28 June 1974, the plaintiff signed a contract to purchase an identical amount (6,000 tons) of barley from Montana Mechandisers, Inc. This purchase agreement for the identical amount of grain stated only a $0.25 per ton increase in price and the instrument negated the earlier sale before any grain exchanged hands and even before written confirmation of the 18 June sale was received by plaintiff from

Montana Merchandisers, Inc. The trial court admitted defendant's exhibit showing what actually happened to the next 5,293.11 tons of barley that were sold by plaintiff after 28 June 1974. That exhibit reveals actual receipt of $133,566 more than that reported by plaintiff as receipts from the alleged sale to Montana Merchandisers, Inc. The defendant has characterized this sale to Montana Merchandisers, Inc., as a fictitious "wash" sale designed to inflate plaintiff's damage claim. We agree. The uncontroverted evidence has established that the Montana Merchandisers transaction was little more than a paper contract apparently intended to serve only as a basis for calculating resale damages under Section 2–706. The commercial unreasonableness is obvious and raises questions of bad faith. Plaintiff contends that it was totally independent of Montana Merchandisers, Inc., because their relationship had terminated a year earlier. We are not persuaded. Furthermore, plaintiff argues that "a seller *can* resell to himself under UCC 2–706", citing for authority Symonds v. Adler Restaurant Equipment Co., 10 U.C.C.Rept.Service 1179 (Okla.Ct.App.1971). However, *Symonds* deals with the law regarding *public* resales under Section 2–706 and the resales in the case at bar were *private* resales. Therefore, plaintiff's reliance on *Symonds* is misplaced. As Professor Nordstrom comments:

> A defaulting buyer ought to pay for the loss he caused, but he should not also be required to pay for those losses which the seller brought on himself through a careless resale (or even a friendly resale to a relative or acquaintance designed to set damages as high as possible).

Nordstrom, Handbook of the Law of Sales, § 173, at 522 (1970).

We find these words quite apt and therefore hold that the commercial unreasonableness of the resale of over fifty per cent of the barley involved in the repudiated contracts is of such magnitude that we need not further examine whether other aspects of the resales were in derogation of the safeguards required under Section 2–706. The plaintiff may not recover under Section 2–706.

The next question is whether the seller may then be allowed to recover market value damages under § 2–708(1). Official comment (2) of Section 2–706 states: "Failure to act properly under this section deprives the seller of the measure of damages here provided and relegates him to that provided in Section 2–708." * * * This comment will be followed by this court but, as noted in White and Summers' treatise,[9] the plaintiff-seller should not be allowed to obtain a greater amount in Section 2–708 damages than the seller actually lost:

9. White and Summers, Handbook on the Uniform Commercial Code (1972), pages 223, 224.

[W]e conclude that a seller who has resold at the time of trial should not be permitted to recover more under 2–708(1) than he could recover under 2–706. However, we would not cast the burden on the seller who sues under 2–708(1) to prove that 2–706 was less advantageous to him. Rather we would make it the buyer's burden to show that the seller had in fact resold, that this was not a lost volume case, and that 2–708(1) recovery would be greater than 2–706 recovery.

We adopt the White and Summers suggestion. In the case at bar, it is clear that the plaintiff, as a seller of grain on a commodity market, is not a volume seller of the kind contemplated in Section 2–708(2). Furthermore, the evidence admitted without objection at trial shows that the plaintiff in fact resold, and plaintiff's Illustrative Charts upon Oral Argument supply this court with plaintiff's version of how damages should be calculated under Section 2–708(1). The remaining factors have been supplied by the defendant and they are the components for the calculation of damages plaintiff actually suffered from its attempt to resell and recover under Section 2–706. The following chart was submitted by plaintiff to illustrate the amount received from the resale contracts:

RESALE CONTRACTS

Contract Number	Date of Resale Contract	Purchaser on Resale	FOB Yakima Contract Price	Contract Amount in Tons	Value
PBF 125	6/12/74	Western Farmers	$102.00	1,000	$ 102,000.00
PBF 126	6/11/74	Wheatheart Northwest Ind.	103.50	500	51,750.00
PBF 191	6/18/74	Cargill, Inc.	104.50	550	57,475.00
PBF 201	6/18/74	General Mills, Inc.	104.50	500	52,250.00
PBF 203	6/18/74	Continental Grain	101.00	1,000	101,000.00
PBF 207	6/18/74	Continental Grain	101.00	1,000	101,000.00
PBF 209	6/19/74	Wheatheart Northwest	103.50	500	51,750.00
PBF 226	6/19/74	Montana Merchandisers	100.00	5,293.11	529,311.00
				10,343.11	$1,046,536.00

Note: Contracts PBF 125, PBF 203, and PBF 207, were written on a FOB Coast basis. The contract prices above have been reduced by $4.00 per ton to adjust all resale contracts to a FOB Sunnyside basis.

This chart shows a value of $529,311.00 for the 5,293 tons of barley involved in the "wash" sale to Montana Merchandisers, Inc. Uncontroverted evidence supplied by defendant shows that the receipts from plaintiff's next actual sales of 5,293.11 tons of barley following the Montana Merchandisers transaction amounted to $662,877.00. That is a difference of $133,566.00. Plaintiff had originally calculated its Section 2–706 damages as follows:

Value of tons cancelled—	$1,227,403.85
Value of tons resold—	1,046,536.00
	$ 180,867.85

If this $180,867.85 figure is reduced by the unreported actual receipt of $133,566.00, then by the uncontroverted evidence, plaintiff actually suffered a loss of only $47,301.85, which would be the damages figure if damages could be measured under Section 2–706.

The market value damages for the 4,500 tons for which defendant is being held liable, are correctly calculated in plaintiff's Illustrative Charts upon Oral Argument:[12]

If, as Cudahy asserts, CTC's resales were all invalid, CTC's damages under 2–708 on the 4,500 tons compute as follows:[13]

Contract price —	4,403.85 T at $128/T —	$563,692.80
Market price	— 1,403.85 T at $101 (5/31) —	141,788.85
	— 1,500 T at $104 (6/30) —	156,000.00
	— 1,500 T at $126 (7/30) —	189,000.00
		$486,788.85
	TOTAL DAMAGES —	$ 76,903.95

If this court were to allow the full Section 2–708(1) measure of damages ($79,500), then plaintiff would receive a $32,198.15 windfall, which we will not sanction. Therefore, we hold that plaintiff is entitled to a compensatory damage award under Section 2–708(1), but only up to the amount of damages that could be recovered under Section 2–706, that is, plaintiff's actual losses. Plaintiff shall be granted a compensatory damage award of $47,301.85.

---

12. The three contracts entered into on 28 February 1978, call for May, June and July delivery, respectively, without further specifying a date for delivery. The plaintiff's resale damages are based on the highest market value prices during the months in question; therefore, the defendant will not be allowed to complain of the lack of specific delivery dates. We will use bid prices in our market value calculations. However, if the defendant has a yet unseen authority to support its argument that offer prices should be used, defendant may present this information to the district court which will already be required to re-examine the incidental damage award.

13. The parties concede that 96.15 tons of the 4,500 involved were accepted and paid for by Cudahy.

INCIDENTAL DAMAGES

We hold no incidental damages may be recovered for the costs of any resales because of the fact that plaintiff failed to fulfill the requirements of Section 2–706. Regarding other expenses plaintiff claims as incidental damages, such as storage and transit costs, we remand this portion of the case for a hearing to determine the amount of actual incidental damages resulting from defendant's repudiation of the 4,500 tons.

* * *

b. DAMAGES MEASURED BY LOSS OF PROFIT

NERI v. RETAIL MARINE CORP.

Court of Appeals of New York, 1972.
30 N.Y.2d 393, 334 N.Y.S.2d 165, 285 N.E.2d 311.

GIBSON, JUDGE. The appeal concerns the right of a retail dealer to recover loss of profits and incidental damages upon the buyer's repudiation of a contract governed by the Uniform Commercial Code. This is, indeed, the correct measure of damage in an appropriate case and to this extent the code (§ 2–708, subsection [2]) effected a substantial change from prior law, whereby damages were ordinarily limited to "the difference between the contract price and the market or current price". Upon the record before us, the courts below erred in declining to give effect to the new statute and so the order appealed from must be reversed.

The plaintiffs contracted to purchase from defendant a new boat of a specified model for the price of $12,587.40, against which they made a deposit of $40. They shortly increased the deposit to $4,250 in consideration of the defendant dealer's agreement to arrange with the manufacturer for immediate delivery on the basis of "a firm sale", instead of the delivery within approximately four to six weeks originally specified. Some six days after the date of the contract plaintiffs' lawyer sent to defendant a letter rescinding the sales contract for the reason that plaintiff Neri was about to undergo hospitalization and surgery, in consequence of which, according to the letter, it would be "impossible for Mr. Neri to make any payments". The boat had already been ordered from the manufacturer and was delivered to defendant at or before the time the attorney's letter was received. Defendant declined to refund plaintiffs' deposit and this action to recover it was commenced. Defendant counterclaimed, alleging plaintiffs' breach of the contract and defendant's resultant damage in the amount of $4,250, for which sum defendant demanded judgment. Upon motion, defendant had summary judgment on the issue of liability tendered by its counterclaim; and Special Term directed an assessment of damages, upon which it would be determined whether plaintiffs were entitled to the return of any portion of their down payment.

Upon the trial so directed, it was shown that the boat ordered and received by defendant in accordance with plaintiffs' contract of purchase was sold some four months later to another buyer for the same price as that negotiated with plaintiffs. From this proof the plaintiffs argue that defendant's loss on its contract was recouped, while defendant argues that but for plaintiffs' default, it would have sold two boats and have earned two profits instead of one. Defendant proved, without contradiction, that its profit on the sale under the contract in suit would have been $2,579 and that during the period the boat remained unsold incidental expenses aggregating $674 for storage, upkeep, finance charges and insurance were incurred. Additionally, defendant proved and sought to recover attorneys' fees of $1,250.

The trial court found "untenable" defendant's claim for loss of profit, inasmuch as the boat was later sold for the same price that plaintiffs had contracted to pay; found, too, that defendant had failed to prove any incidental damages; further found "that the terms of section 2–718, subsection 2(b), of the Uniform Commercial Code are applicable and same make adequate and fair provision to place the sellers in as good as position as performance would have done" and, in accordance with paragraph (b) of subsection (2) thus relied upon, awarded defendant $500 upon its counterclaim and directed that plaintiffs recover the balance of their deposit, amounting to $3,750. The ensuing judgment was affirmed, without opinion, at the Appellate Division, 37 A.D.2d 917, 326 N.Y.S.2d 984, and defendant's appeal to this court was taken by our leave.

The issue is governed in the first instance by section 2–718 of the Uniform Commercial Code which provides, among other things, that the buyer, despite his breach, may have restitution of the amount by which his payment exceeds: (a) reasonable liquidated damages stipulated by the contract or (b) absent such stipulation, 20% of the value of the buyer's total performance or $500, whichever is smaller (§ 2–718, subsection [2], pars. [a], [b]). As above noted, the trial court awarded defendant an offset in the amount of $500 under paragraph (b) and directed restitution to plaintiffs of the balance. Section 2–718, however, establishes, in paragraph (a) of subsection (3), an alternative right of offset in favor of the seller, as follows: "(3) The buyer's right to restitution under subsection (2) is subject to offset to the extent that the seller establishes (a) a right to recover damages under the provisions of this Article other than subsection (1)".

Among "the provisions of this Article other than subsection (1)" are those to be found in section 2–708, which the courts below did not apply. Subsection (1) of that section provides that "the measure of damages for non-acceptance or repudiation by the buyer is the difference between the market price at the time and place for tender and the unpaid contract price together with any incidental damages provided in this Article (Section 2–710), but less expenses saved in consequence of the buyer's breach." However, this provision is made expressly subject to subsection (2), providing: "(2) If the measure of damages provided in subsection (1) is inadequate to put the seller in as good a position as performance would have done then the measure of damages is the profit (including reasonable overhead) which the seller would have made from full performance by the buyer, together with any incidental damages provided in this Article (Section 2–710), due allowance for costs reasonably incurred and due credit for payments of proceeds of resale."

The provision of the code upon which the decision at Trial Term rested (§ 2–718, subsection [2], par. [b]) does not differ greatly from the corresponding provisions of the prior statute (Personal Property Law, § 145–a, subd. 1, par. [b]), except as the new act includes the alternative remedy of a lump sum award of $500. Neither does the present reference (in § 2–718, subsection [3], par. [a]) to the recovery of damages pursuant to other provisions of the article differ from a like reference in the prior statute (Personal Property Law, § 145–a, subd. 2, par. [a]) to an alternative measure of damages under section 145 of that act; but section 145 made no provision for recovery of lost profits as does section 2–708 (subsection [2]) of the code. The new statute is thus innovative and significant and its analysis is necessary to the determination of the issues here presented.

Prior to the code, the New York cases "applied the 'profit' test, contract price less cost of manufacture, only in cases where the seller [was] a manufacturer or an agent for a manufacturer" (1955 Report of N.Y.Law Rev.Comm., vol. 1, p. 693). Its extension to retail sales was "designed to eliminate the unfair and economically wasteful results arising under the older law when fixed price articles were involved. This section permits the recovery of lost profits in all appropriate cases, which would include all standard priced goods." (Official Comment 2 under Uniform Commercial Code, § 2–708.) Additionally, and "[i]n all cases the seller may recover incidental damages" (id., Comment 3). The buyer's right to restitution was established at Special Term upon the motion for summary judgment, as was the seller's right to proper offsets, in each case pursuant to section 2–718; and, as the parties concede, the only question before us, following the assessment of damages at Special Term, is that as to the proper measure of damage to be applied. The conclusion is clear from the record—indeed with mathematical certainty—that "the measure of damages provided in subsection (1) is inadequate to put the seller in as good a position as performance would have done" (Uniform Commercial

Code, § 2–708, subsection [2]) and hence—again under subsection (2)—that the seller is entitled to its "profit (including reasonable overhead) * * * together with any incidental damages * * *, due allowance for costs reasonably incurred and due credit for payments or proceeds of resale."

It is evident, first, that this retail seller is entitled to its profit and, second, that the last sentence of subsection (2), as hereinbefore quoted, referring to "due credit for payments or proceeds of resale" is inapplicable to this retail sales contract.[2] Closely parallel to the factual situation now before us is that hypothesized by Dean Hawkland as illustrative of the operation of the rules: "Thus, if a private party agrees to sell his automobile to a buyer for $2,000, a breach by the buyer would cause the seller no loss (except incidental damages, i.e., expense of a new sale) if the seller was able to sell the automobile to another buyer for $2000. But the situation is different with dealers having an unlimited suply of standard-priced goods. Thus, if an automobile dealer agrees to sell a car to a buyer at the standard price of $2000, a breach by the buyer injures the dealer, even though he is able to sell the automobile to another for $2000. If the dealer has an inexhaustible supply of cars, the resale to replace the breaching buyer costs the dealer a sale, because, had the breaching buyer performed, the dealer would have made two sales instead of one. The buyer's breach, in such a case, depletes the dealer's sales to the extent of one, and the measure of damages should be the dealer's profit on one sale. Section 2–708 recognizes this, and it rejects the rule developed under the Uniform Sales Act by many courts that the profit cannot be recovered in this case." (Hawkland, Sales and Bulk Sales [1958 ed.], pp. 153–154; and see Comment, 31 Fordham L.Rev. 749, 755–756.)

The record which in this case establishes defendant's entitlement to damages in the amount of its prospective profit, at the same time confirms defendant's cognate right to "any incidental damages provided in this Article (Section 2–710)" (Uniform Com-

2. The concluding clause, "due credit for payments or proceeds of resale", is intended to refer to "the privilege of the seller to realize junk value when it is manifestly useless to complete the operation of manufacture" (Supp. No. 1 to the 1952 Official Draft of Text and Comments of the Uniform Commercial Code, as Amended by the Action of the American Law Institute of the National Conference of Commissioners on Uniform Laws [1954], p. 14). The commentators who have considered the language have uniformly concluded that "the reference is to a resale as scrap under * * * Section 2–704" (1956 Report of N.Y.Law Rev.Comm., p. 397; 1955 Report of N.Y.Law Rev.Comm., vol. 1, p. 761; New York Annotations, McKinney's Cons.Laws of N.Y. Book 62½, Part 1, p. 606, under Uniform Commercial Code, § 2–708; 1 Willier and Hart, Bender's Uniform Commercial Code Service, § 2–708, pp. 1–180— 1–181). Another writer, reaching the same conclusion, after detailing the history of the clause, says that " 'proceeds of resale' previously meant the resale value of the goods in finished form; now it means the resale value of the components on hand at the time plaintiff learns of breach" (Harris, Seller's Damages, 18 Stanf.L.Rev. 66, 104).

mercial Code, § 2–708, subsection [2]). From the language employed it is too clear to require discussion that the seller's right to recover loss of profits is not exclusive and that he may recoup his "incidental" expenses as well (Proctor & Gamble Distr. Co. v. Lawrence Amer. Field Warehousing Corp., 16 N.Y.2d 344, 354, 266 N.Y.S.2d 785, 792, 213 N.E.2d 873, 878). Although the trial court's denial of incidental damages in the uncontroverted amount of $674 was made in the context of its erroneous conclusion that paragraph (b) of subsection (2) of section 2–718 was applicable and was "adequate * * * to place the sellers in as good a position as performance would have done", the denial seems not to have rested entirely on the court's mistaken application of the law, as there was an explicit finding "that defendant completely failed to show that it suffered any incidental damages." We find no basis for the court's conclusion with respect to a deficiency of proof inasmuch as the proper items of the $674 expenses (being for storage, upkeep, finance charges and insurance for the period between the date performance was due and the time of the resale) were proven without objection and were in no way controverted, impeached or otherwise challenged, at the trial or on appeal. Thus the court's finding of a failure of proof cannot be supported upon the record and, therefore, and contrary to plaintiffs' contention, the affirmance at the Appellate Division was ineffective to save it.

The trial court correctly denied defendant's claim for recovery of attorney's fees incurred by it in this action. Attorney's fees incurred in an action such as this are not in the nature of the protective expenses contemplated by the statute (Uniform Commercial Code, § 1–106, subd. [1]; § 2–710; § 2–708, subsection [2]) and by our reference to "legal expense" in Proctor & Gamble Distr. Co. v. Lawrence Amer. Field Warehousing Corp. (16 N.Y.2d 344, 354–355, 266 N.Y.S.2d 785, 792–793, 213 N.E.2d 873, 878–879, supra), upon which defendant's reliance is in this respect misplaced.

It follows that plaintiffs are entitled to restitution of the sum of $4,250 paid by them on account of the contract price less an offset to defendant in the amount of $3,253 on account of its lost profit of $2,579 and its incidental damages of $674.

The order of the Appellate Division should be modified, with costs in all courts, in accordance with this opinion, and, as so modified, affirmed.

JERICHO SASH & DOOR CO. v. BUILDING ERECTORS, INC.

Supreme Judicial Court of Massachusetts, 1972.
362 Mass. 871, 286 N.E.2d 343.

RESCRIPT. The defendant appeals from a final decree for the plaintiff on this bill in equity to reach and apply assets of the defendant to the plaintiff's claim of damages for breach of contract. The sole question presented is whether the trial judge erred in allowing damages for "profit (including reasonable overhead)" under UCC § 2–708(2), in the absence of evidence showing separate figures for profit and for overhead. The plaintiff delivered 1,420 pairs of assorted sizes of window sash, for which the defendant admitted liability, and the defendant then repudiated the undelivered balance of 5,580. The plaintiff introduced evidence showing the "weighted average sales price per pair" and the "weighted average direct cost per pair" of the delivered sash. Subtraction of cost from price gave "lost profit and overhead per unit," and multiplication by the number of undelivered units gave "total lost profit and overhead," and the judge awarded more than $21,000 on that account. There was no error. The judge followed the statutory injunction that the remedy "be liberally administered to the end that the aggrieved party may be put in as good a position as if the other party had fully performed." UCC § 1–106(1). Damages need not "be calculable with mathematical accuracy. Compensatory damages are often at best approximate: they have to be proved with whatever definiteness and accuracy the facts permit, but no more." Comment 1 to § 1–106(1) of the Uniform Commercial Code * * *. There was evidence that all the expenses that were saved as a result of the breach were included in direct cost except for a few relatively insignificant items. * * * There is no requirement that "overhead" be separated from "net profit" in the computation. As the plaintiff's witness and the judge clearly understood, "profit (including reasonable overhead)" in the statute is the equivalent of "gross profit," including fixed costs but not costs saved as a result of the breach.

Decree affirmed with costs of appeal.

PROBLEMS

1. Seller manufactures appliances which it sells for $80 each. Seller's plant is operated at full capacity at all times and Seller is unable to fill the entire demand for its appliances. X agreed to purchase 10,000 appliances at $80 each. Shortly after making the contract, X repudiated. To what damages is Seller entitled? How does § 2–708(2) apply to this case? Comment 2 to § 2–708(2). Does the application of § 2–708(2) depend upon whether the goods are "standard priced goods"? Compare Famous Knitwear Corp. v. Drug Fair, Inc., 493 F.2d 251 (4th Cir. 1974) in which the court stated:

> We are still left with the question of whether Famous Knitwear is a lost volume seller and, hence a seller for whom "the measure of damages provided in subsection (1) is inadequate." Due to the seasonal nature of the goods involved

(sweaters) and the long lead-time necessary for Famous Knitwear to secure goods from its suppliers, Drug Fair alleges that, but for its placement of such a large order with Famous Knitwear, the seller would not have had the necessary goods in stock to sell to other buyers subsequent to Drug Fair's breach. Famour Knitwear, on the other hand, contends that it could have fulfilled its contract with Drug Fair and procured additional goods for sale to the later buyers. Because there are no findings of fact by the district judge as to the conflicting assertions, we are unable to determine if Famous Knitwear is a lost volume seller and, as such, entitled to lost profits under 2–708(2).

2. In footnote 2 of *Neri* the court states that the words "due credit for ∗ ∗ ∗ proceeds of resale" at the end of § 2–708(2) were meant to apply only to cases in which a seller-manufacturer, who has sold uncompleted goods for junk value when completion was not feasible, is suing for lost profits. Consider this case. A contract provided for the sale of 100,000 widgets to be manufactured by Seller. The contract price was 27 cents a widget. Costs of manufacturing each widget exclusive of overhead costs were 20 cents. Buyer repudiated when the widgets were half completed, i.e., Seller had spent 10 cents and would have had to spend an additional 10 cents to complete each widget. Seller decided that completion of the widgets was not advisable and sold the partially completed widgets for 5 cents each. § 2–704(2). To what damages is Seller entitled under § 2–708(2)? Suppose Seller had elected to complete the widgets and then sold them to X for 27 cents each. If we assume that Seller had excess plant capacity, i.e. Seller could have manufactured widgets both for Buyer and for X, would § 2–706 or § 2–708(2) apply? If § 2–708(2) applies how must the words "due allowance for costs reasonably incurred and due credit for ∗ ∗ ∗ proceeds of resale" be read in order to put Seller "in as good a position as performance would have done"? Is there any basis for a different interpretation depending upon whether the goods are unfinished or finished? Is there a difference between cases in which the goods, whether finished or unfinished, are resold for more than cost and those in which they are resold for less than cost? When Seller resold the unfinished widgets for 5 cents Seller incurred a loss. Damages under § 2–708(2) comprise lost profit of 7 cents and 5 cents lost on resale. In effect Buyer is required to pay the cost of producing the unfinished widgets ("due allowance for costs reasonably incurred") but is given credit for resale proceeds that reduce Seller's net costs. Compare Seller's damages under § 2–706(1). If Seller does not seek to impose the cost of producing the unfinished widgets on Buyer, is Seller always entitled to receive the anticipated profit on Buyer's contract? Suppose Seller did not resell the unfinished widgets. If Seller seeks only anticipated profit, is the value to Seller of the unfin-

ished widgets relevant in calculating damages? Suppose the unfinished widgets were resold by Seller for 12 cents instead of 5 cents, i.e. at a profit. To what damages, would Seller be entitled? *Neri* suggests that in the case of completion of the widgets and resale at 27 cents Seller, as a lost volume seller, is entitled to recover the anticipated profit from Buyer without regard to the profit from X. If Seller is entitled to two profits when finished widgets are resold, is Seller also entitled to two profits if unfinished widgets are resold? If Seller is entitled to two profits in the latter case, what interpretation can be given to the "due allowance" clause of § 2–708(2)? Section 2–708(2) is thoroughly analyzed in Harris, A Radical Restatement of Seller's Damages: Sales Act and Commercial Code Results Compared, 18 Stan.L.Rev. 66 (1965). An economic analysis of § 2–708(2) with a critique of *Neri* is found in Goetz and Scott, Measuring Sellers' Damages: The Lost-Profits Puzzle, 31 Stan.L.Rev. 323 (1979).

3. Manufacturer made a contract to sell widgets to Buyer at $2 each. The contract called for delivery in November. Manufacturer's cost of producing widgets is $1.50. Thus, if the sale had been completed Manufacturer would have made a profit of 50¢ per widget. Because of the introduction into the domestic market of foreign-produced widgets in October the market price for widgets similar to those produced by Manufacturer precipitously dropped. At the time for tender in November the market price was $1.25. Buyer refused to take delivery. To what damages is Manufacturer entitled under § 2–708(1)? To what damages is Manufacturer entitled if § 2–708(2) applies? Which provision applies? In this regard consider the following quotation by the court in Nobs Chemical, U.S.A., Inc. v. Koppers Co., Inc., 616 F.2d 212 (5th Cir.1980):

> The plaintiffs argue, however, that in this case the measure of damages under UCC § 2–708(1) would adequately compensate them and therefore, according to the terms of UCC § 2–708(1), UCC § 2–708(2) does not control. This is an intriguing argument. It appears that the drafters of UCC § 2–708(1) did not consider the possibility that recovery under that section may be *more than* adequate. White & Summers, supra, § 7–12, at 232–233.

> It is possible that the code drafters intended UCC § 2–708(1) as a liquidated damage clause available to a plaintiff-seller regardless of his actual damages. There have been some commentators who agree with this philosophy. See, C. Goetz & R. Scott, Measuring Sellers' Damages: the Lost-Profits Puzzle, 31 Stan.L.Rev. 323, 323–324 n. 2 (1979); E. Peters, Remedies for Breach of Contracts Relating to the Sale of Goods Under the Uniform Commercial Code: A Roadmap for Article Two, 73 Yale L.J. 199, 259 (1963). But, this

construction is inconsistent with the code's basic philosophy, announced in UCC § 1–106(1), which provides "that the aggrieved party may be put in as good a position as if the other party had fully performed" but not in a better posture. White & Summers, supra, § 7–12, at 232. This philosophy is echoed in Texas case law. "The measure of damages for breach of contract is the amount necessary to place plaintiffs in a financial position equivalent to that in which it would have had [sic] if the contract had been fully performed by both parties." Little Darling Corp. v. Ald, Inc., 566 S.W.2d 347, 349 (Tex.Civ.App.1978). Moreover, White and Summers conclude that statutory damage formulas do not significantly affect the practices of businessmen and therefore "breach deterrence," which would be the purpose of the statutory liquidated damages clause, should be rejected in favor of a standard approximating actual economic loss. White & Summers, supra, § 7–12, at 232. No one insists, and we do not think they could, that the difference between the fallen market price and the contract price is necessary to compensate the plaintiffs for the breach. Had the transaction been completed, their "benefit of the bargain" would not have been affected by the fall in market price, and they would not have experienced the windfall they otherwise would receive if the market price-contract price rule contained in UCC § 2–708(1) is followed. Thus, the premise contained in UCC § 1–106(1) and Texas case law is a strong factor weighing, against application of UCC § 2–708(1).

2. ACTION FOR PRICE OF UNACCEPTED GOODS IN POSSESSION OF SELLER

INDUSTRIAL MOLDED PLASTIC PRODUCTS, INC. v. J. GROSS & SON, INC.

Superior Court of Pennsylvania, 1979.
263 Pa.Super. 515, 398 A.2d 695.

HOFFMAN, JUDGE. This is a breach of contract action brought by Industrial Molded Plastic Products, Inc. (Industrial) against J. Gross & Son, Inc. (Gross). In a non-jury trial below, the court awarded Industrial $2,494.52 damages representing lost profits. Industrial now contends that the proper measure of damages was the contract price of the goods. Gross has cross-appealed on the issue of liability, contending that the salesman who signed the contract lacked the authority to bind the corporate entity.

Industrial is in the business of manufacturing custom injection molded plastics by specification for various manufacturers. Industrial also manufactures various "fill-in" items during slack periods, such as electronic parts, industrial components, mirror clips, and plastic clothing clips. Industrial manufactured plastic clothing clips only for its house accounts of H. Daroff & Sons and Joseph H. Cohen & Sons. Gross is a wholesaler to the retail clothing industry, selling mostly sewing thread, but also other items such as zippers, snaps, and clips. Gross sold only a small amount of plastic clothing clips, never having more than $100–$200 worth of clips in inventory at any one time.

Sometime in the Fall of 1970, Mr. Stanley Waxman (Gross' President and sole stockholder) and his son Peter (a 22 year old salesman for Gross) appeared at the offices of Industrial's President, Mr. Judson T. Ulansey. They suggested to him that they might be able to market Industrial's plastic clothing clips in the retail clothing industry, in which they had an established sales force. At this initial meeting, there was no discussion of Peter Waxman's authority or lack thereof in the company. After this meeting, Stanley authorized Peter to purchase a "trial" amount of clips (not further specified) to test the market, but neither this authorization nor its limitation was communicated to Ulansey. All subsequent negotiations were between Ulansey and Peter Waxman only. Deceiving both his father and Ulansey, Peter held himself out as Vice-President of Gross, and on December 10, 1970, signed an agreement obligating Gross to purchase from Industrial five million plastic clothing clips during the calendar year of 1971, at a price of $7.50 per thousand units, delivery at Industrial's plant in Blooming Glen, Pennsylvania. Gross was granted an exclusive distributorship in the clips for the same time, excepting Industrial's two house accounts mentioned above. Before the execution of this agreement, Ulansey telephoned Stanley Waxman, who told Ulansey that Peter could act on behalf of Gross. There was no discussion of the specific terms of the agreement, such as the quantity purchased.

Industrial immediately began production of the five million clips during "fill-in" time. As they were manufactured, they were warehoused in Industrial's plant as per the contract. In February, 1971, Peter Waxman picked up and paid for 772,000 clips. Stanley Waxman, who had to sign Gross' check for payment, thought that this was the "trial amount" he had authorized Peter to buy. These were the only clips which Gross ever took into its possession. On numerous occasions during the year Ulansey urged Peter to pick up more of the clips, which were taking up more and more storage space at Industrial's plant as they were being manufactured. Peter told Ulansey that he was having difficulty selling the clips and that Gross had no warehousing capacity for the inventory that was being accumulated. At no time, however, did Peter repudiate the contract or request Industrial to halt production. By the end of 1971, production was completed and Industrial was warehousing 4,228,000 clips at its plant.

On January 19, 1972, Industrial sent Gross an invoice for the remaining clips of $31,710, less credit of $203.55, for a balance due of $31,506.45. However, Gross did not honor the invoice or pick up any more of the clips. Ulansey wrote to Stanley Waxman on February 7, 1972, requesting him to pick up the clips. Receiving no response, Ulansey wrote to Stanley Waxman again on February 23, 1972, threatening legal action if shipping instructions were not received by March 1, 1972. Finally, on March 30, 1972, Peter Waxman responded with a letter to Ulansey, which stated that Gross' failure to move the clips was due to a substantial decline in the clothing industry in 1971 and competition with new lower-cost methods of hanging and shipping clothes. The letter asked for Industrial's patience and predicted that it would take at least the rest of the year to market the clips successfully. At this point, Industrial initiated legal action. Stanley Waxman learned of the five million clip contract for the first time when informed by his lawyer of the impending law suit. Industrial filed its complaint in August of 1972, and at the same time Peter began an extended (four years) leave of absence from Gross.

Ulansey testified that Industrial was unable to resell any of the 4.2 million clips because of a lack of market generally. Additionally, Industrial lost its two house accounts for plastic clothing clips because Daroff went bankrupt and Cohen refused to do further business with Industrial, citing a close personal relationship with Stanley Waxman. Industrial, being a manufacturer, had no sales force to find new customers. However, Industrial did receive a small quantity of new orders from 1972 to 1976, for which new clips were manufactured.

Gross contends that it was not bound by the agreement to purchase the clips because Peter Waxman had no authority to sign the contract for Gross. * * * [We] affirm the conclusion of the court below that Gross was bound by the agreement to purchase the clips.

Industrial contends that the court below erred in entering judgment based upon its lost profits, on the grounds that the proper measure of damages was the unpaid balance of the contract price. The court below limited damages to lost profits because it found in fact that Industrial "did not make a good faith or reasonable effort to resell the goods * * * nor did he demonstrate the futility of any resale attempt."

It is true that in order to maintain an action for the contract price of goods which are merely *identified,* the seller must mitigate damages or show that such effort would be unavailing. Uniform Commercial Code § 2–709(1)(b). However, a seller of goods is also entitled to recover the contract price due for goods *accepted* by the buyer. § 2–709(1)(a). Under the Code, a buyer's acceptance of goods occurs, *inter alia,* when, after a reasonable opportunity to inspect the goods, the buyer fails to make an effective rejection of them. § 2–606(1)(b). To preserve his rights, the seller is only obligated to tender the goods in accordance with the terms of the contract. § 2–507(1). The seller is under no obligation to resell accepted goods in order to maintain his action for price. § 2–709(1)(a). * * *

Here, Industrial wholly performed its obligations under the contract, manufacturing five million clips and delivering them to its plant in Blooming Glen, Pennsylvania. For over a year, Industrial entreatied Gross to take possession of the growing pile of clips. Thus, Gross had ample opportunity to inspect, but never rejected the goods. In fact, even as late as March 30, 1972, Gross still indicated that it intended to market the clips, but would need more time to do so. As such, Gross accepted the clips and breached its contract by failure to pay for them. Since the goods were accepted, Industrial is entitled to the full unpaid balance of the contract price, notwithstanding its failure to attempt to resell the clips.

The order below is reversed and the court below is directed to enter judgment in favor of Industrial against Gross for $31,506.45, plus interest from January 19, 1972.

WALTER BALFOUR & CO. v. LIZZA & SONS, INC.

New York Supreme Court, Kings County, Trial Term, 1969.
6 U.C.C.Rep. 649.

HART, J. Plaintiff in this action seeks as damages the $16,000 price alleged to have been agreed upon in an oral contract to fabricate fourteen rolling steel doors for installation in a building which defendant had been in the process of erecting for itself at Seldon, New York. The principal defenses are (1) that no contract had been entered into, and (2) that the agreement, if made, was unenforcible since it was not in writing as required by the statute of frauds.

* * *

As to the defense of the statute of frauds plaintiff has established by a clear preponderance of the evidence that the doors were specially manufactured for defendant and are not suitable for sale to anyone else in the ordinary course of plaintiff's business. All steel rolling doors are fabricated with specific dimensions to fit designated openings, which vary from structure to structure. In fact, while all of the doors were approximately of the same dimensions, not all of them were specifically identical but some varied with respect to fractions of an inch. Plaintiff's proof clearly establishes that none of these massive doors are stocked but are "tailor-made" for each job as a contract is awarded. Accordingly, though the agreement here was not in writing, it is valid and enforcible as provided for in § 2–201, subdivision 3a, of the Uniform Commercial Code.

With respect to damages, plaintiff's proof satisfies the court that it is impractical to cut or adjust the doors for use at another site and that they now have only a scrap value of $630, and would have to be delivered by plaintiff to a scrap dealer at a cost of about $75 or $100. Plaintiff has satisfied the court that it has made a reasonable effort to resell the doors at a reasonable price, without success. The evidence clearly shows that there is no market or market value for the doors—but only scrap value. Accordingly, plaintiff is entitled to recover as damages the agreed price (§ 2–709, subdivision 1, of the Uniform Commercial Code). While the payment of the price would not have become "due" until the installation of the doors, where the defendant frustrates performance of a condition, the condition is waived and the payment is "due." Defendant, however, is entitled to a credit of the price of the two motorized doors, which were used by plaintiff as scrap to make repairs to doors of other customers. It was stipulated by the parties that this amounted to $2,476. Defendant is also entitled as a credit to the sum of $2,200, representing the moneys saved by plaintiff by the non-installation.

Plaintiff is therefore entitled to judgment against the defendant in the sum of $11,324, with interest from July 25, 1967. Plaintiff's claim for storage was not established to the satisfaction of the court and is disallowed. Defendant upon payment of the judgment is entitled either to the twelve doors in plaintiff's possession or the proceeds of any sale by plaintiff (UCC § 2–709, subdivision 2 ＊ ＊ ＊.)

NOTE

Suppose Seller in *Walter Balfour* had sold the doors for scrap for $630 and had incurred expenses of $100 in connection with the resale. Would Seller have been entitled to damages under § 2–706 or § 2–708(2)? Is the amount of damages affected by whether action is brought under those sections or § 2–709? Is it more advisable for Seller in a case of this kind to sue for the price or resell and sue for damages? Compare the requirements of § 2–706 and § 2–709. What course of action would you recommend to provide maximum protection to Seller? If the goods, though not resalable in their original condition, can be made resalable by alteration or reprocessing, is Seller required to make the necessary changes?

C. LIQUIDATED DAMAGES

FARMERS UNION GRAIN TERMINAL ASSN. v. NELSON

Supreme Court of North Dakota, 1974.
223 N.W.2d 494.

JOHNSON, JUDGE. This case involves two grain purchase contracts dated September 19, 1972, between Byron Nelson, a Hamberg, North Dakota, farmer, and the Farmers Union Grain Terminal Association, a cooperative marketing association with headquarters at Minneapolis, Minnesota (GTA). The contracts were printed forms prepared by GTA for the use of its "line" elevators. Under the terms of the contracts Nelson agreed to deliver 17,000 bushels of durum at $1.96 per bushel, and 47,000 bushels of hard wheat at $2.00 per bushel to the GTA-owned elevator at Hamberg, North Dakota. Each contract contained the following clause:

> "I agree to deliver said grain to Farmers Union Grain Terminal Association at its elevator at Hamberg, State of North Dakota, on or before 03 30, 1973 provided space is available to receive and store the same, and if not, as soon thereafter as space is available, and I agree that time is of the essence of this contract as to the delivery of said grain."

During November of 1972 and February of 1973 Nelson made partial deliveries of grain to the Hamberg elevator, totaling some 19,847.5 bushels. In March of 1973 he received two advances of $10,000 each as prepayments on the grain contracts. Nelson made a series of inquiries during the first part of the year as to when he could deliver the contracted grain yet in his possession but was informed each time that, due primarily to its inability to obtain a sufficient number of boxcars to make space available, the Hamberg elevator was unable to accept delivery. There was evidence that during the same period the elevator was purchasing substantial amounts of noncontracted or cash grain. In addition, the elevator had entered into a considerable number of other contracts for delivery of grain during this period. Nelson subsequently became heavily engaged in spring planting operations.

On June 6, 1973, the manager of the Hamberg elevator attempted to notify Nelson that he could commence hauling the grain yet to be delivered under his contracts. This message was not received by Nelson until the morning of June 9, and the evidence is conflicting as to whether he was told he could not deliver grain on that date. On June 13, 1973, Nelson notified the Hamberg elevator that he would not deliver the grain remaining under contract but would deliver it to another elevator. At the time he gave notice of his intentions, Nelson tendered a check payable to GTA in the sum of $26,555.05. This check represented a return of the $20,000 previously advanced, interest on that amount at the rate of five-sixths percent per month on the unpaid balance for the months of April and May, and the difference between the contract price and the market price on March 30, 1973.

Each of the grain purchase contracts in question contain the following clause regarding damages:

> "In case of default in the delivery of said grain, then and in that event, I agree to pay to Farmers Union Grain Terminal Association, as liquidated damages, the difference between the contract price herein and the market price of grain of like grade at the close of the market at the Minneapolis Grain Exchange on the 30th day of March, 1973, after making due deductions for freight from the above station to Minneapolis, Minnesota."

GTA refused the tender of damages and sued Nelson for the advances, plus damages based upon June 13 market prices which were substantially higher than the market on March 30. The matter was tried before a jury in the Wells County District Court, Fourth Judicial District, Judge Alfred A. Thompson, presiding. The jury found for GTA in the sum of $6,320.34 and awarded Nelson the sum of $220.76 as damages for storage of grain. Motions for judgments notwithstanding the verdict were made by both parties. The motion of GTA was granted. The court set aside the damages awarded to Nelson for grain storage and increased the award to GTA to the sum of $28,904.55.

I.

The primary dispute concerns the measure of damages to GTA for breach or cancellation of the contracts. Nelson is prepared to accept the damages formula specified under the contracts—the difference between the contract price and the market price on March 30. However, GTA contends that it is entitled to damages based upon market prices on June 13 when Nelson repudiated the contracts. The market prices on that date were substantially higher. Under the March 30 prices, the damages would be $6,220.34, while using June 13 prices resulted in damages of $28,904.55.

GTA relies primarily upon UCC § 2–719, to sustain its position.

* * *

GTA takes the position that (1) the agreement does not specifically provide that the damage provision is exclusive and, therefore, it is not, and (2) even if the contract provision is exclusive it has failed "of its essential purpose" and therefore is ineffective under the statute. The trial court accepted this position and instructed the jury that it should not use the contract clause in determining damages. The jury apparently used the March 30 market prices nonetheless, and the trial court ordered judgment notwithstanding the verdict.

We do not agree with the conclusions of the trial court on this question.

There are two principles of contract interpretation which should be given special weight in this situation. (1) A contract is construed most strongly against the party who prepared it, and who presumably looked out for his best interests in the process. * * * (2) An agreement which is essentially a "contract of adhesion" should be examined with special scrutiny by the courts to assure that it is not applied in an unfair or unconscionable manner against the party who did not participate in its drafting.

The traditional contract is a result of free bargaining between parties who are brought together by market conditions and who meet on a footing of approximate economic equality. In present-day commercial life, standardized, mass-produced contracts have appeared. These printed form agreements are used primarily by enterprises with strong bargaining power and position.

"The weaker party, in need of the goods or services, is frequently not in a position to shop around for better terms, either because the author of the standard contract has a monopoly (natural or artificial) or because all competitors use the same clauses. His contractual intention is but a subjection more or less voluntary to terms dictated by the stronger party, terms whose consequences are often understood only in a vague way, if at all." Kessler, Contracts of Adhesion—Some Thoughts About Freedom of Contract, 43 Colum.L.Rev. 629, 632 (1943).

* * * This is part of the background for the provisions of the Uniform Commercial Code regarding enforcement of unconscionable contract terms. See Section 2–302 and Official Comment.

The clause regarding determination of damages in these contracts is designed to provide an agreed method of computing loss in the event of breach. See Section 2–718. In the context of the agreement the clause appears clearly intended as an exclusive means of computing the loss in the event of failure to deliver. * * * For purposes of this action it may properly be construed against its author, GTA. It certainly is not a provision which was the subject of bargaining between GTA and Nelson.

There may or may not have been a mutual understanding to excuse a delay in taking delivery on the grain, but there was certainly no evidence of agreement on modification of the measure of damages. Mr. Nelson was entitled to rely on the measure of damages GTA had established under its form agreement. Taking the construction most favorable to the seller, we do not find that this clause had "failed of its essential purpose." While there had been a substantial increase in market price between March 30 and June 13 (some thirty-six cents a bushel for wheat and some seventeen cents a bushel for durum), that fact alone cannot be said to have caused the clause to have failed in its essential purpose. The clause was designed to provide a fixed date for determining damages in a market that varied from day to day. If Mr. Nelson had attempted to cancel the contract at an earlier time, when the market was lower than on March 30, it may be assumed that GTA would have claimed the March 30 market price for its measure of damages. The agreement contemplated that delivery might take place before or after March 30. The actual financial consequences visited upon GTA in having to "cover itself" in the event of rescission by a seller are also dependent upon the rise or fall of the grain market and could vary substantially. It appears from the record that GTA resold the grain on contract and was required to "buy back" its contract. It cannot be said that the contract provision had "failed of its essential purpose" merely because it had become more onerous to one of the parties.

We hold that the trial court erred in instructing the jury that it could not apply the damage clause of the agreement, and in granting judgment notwithstanding the verdict for additional damages claimed.

* * *

The judgment of the trial court is reversed and the case remanded for additional proceedings consistent with this opinion.

LEE OLDSMOBILE, INC. v. KAIDEN

Maryland Court of Special Appeals, 1976.
32 Md.App. 556, 363 A.2d 270.

POWERS, JUDGE. Lee Oldsmobile, Inc., as a part of its business operation at Glen Burnie, deals in Rolls-Royce automobiles, under the trade name of Gladding Rolls-Royce, Inc. Having learned through a dealer in Brooklyn, New York, that Gladding had on order as a part of its allotted quota of 10 or 11 automobiles for 1973 a Rolls-Royce of the style and color which she wanted, Mrs. Ada Kaiden of Hewlett, New York, sent to Gladding in August 1973, through her dealer, a $5,000 deposit on the purchase of the automobile. Lee Oldsmobile confirmed the request by transmitting a regular order form, which Mrs. Kaiden signed and returned. The price was $29,500.

Some of the correspondence, as well as a notation on Mrs. Kaiden's check, indicated that delivery was expected in November. The order form, however, specified no delivery date. Further, it contained a disclaimer of liability for failure to deliver or delay in delivery for a cause beyond the dealer's control, or without fault or negligence of the dealer.

On 21 November 1973 Mrs. Kaiden notified Lee Oldsmobile by telephone that she had purchased another Rolls-Royce elsewhere. She told the salesman to cancel her order. On 29 November, Lee Oldsmobile notified Mrs. Kaiden that the car was ready for delivery. She declined to accept delivery, and demanded the return of her deposit. The dealer refused. On 17 January 1974 Lee Oldsmobile sold the Rolls-Royce to a purchaser in Atlanta, Georgia, for $26,495.

A few months later Mrs. Kaiden, joined by her husband, filed a suit at law against Lee Oldsmobile, Inc., in the Circuit Court for Anne Arundel County, claiming damages of $5,000, plus interest.

Trial was held before Judge E. Mackall Childs, without a jury, on 24 April 1975. The ultimate result of the trial was that after receiving memorandum arguments from both sides the court, on 24 June 1975, entered judgment nisi and on 26 June 1975 entered judgment absolute in favor of the plaintiffs against Lee Oldsmobile, Inc. for $2,924.93. Lee Oldsmobile filed a timely appeal from that judgment and an appeal by the Kaidens followed.

                              *   *   *

* * * Counsel for Lee Oldsmobile argued, briefly, that there was uncontradicted evidence of a written retail order for an automobile, with no specific delivery date, and that plaintiff cancelled early, and bought another car. Counsel then said:

> "I needn't belabor the point, I don't believe. I would like, unless the Court requests me to do otherwise, to move on to the issue of damages. Does the Court wish me * * * to say anything else on the issue of liability?"

It is entirely clear to us that this argument was directed to the question of who breached the contract—whether it was Lee Oldsmobile, by failure to deliver as allegedly promised, or Mrs. Kaiden, either by an anticipatory breach, or by refusal to accept delivery when delivery was offered. In the background of this argument, and basic to the entire case, was the established fact that Lee Oldsmobile had received $5,000 from Mrs. Kaiden, for which she received nothing in return. If Lee Oldsmobile breached the contract, she was entitled to her money back. If she breached the contract, she was liable for whatever was found to be the proper amount of damages. Those damages could constitute either a partial or a complete set-off against the amount which Mrs. Kaiden, in the absence of damages, would be entitled to recover.

The argument of Lee Oldsmobile then proceeded to the issue of damages. Counsel said:

"I think that in the plaintiffs' case there is evidence to substantiate what appear as answer five to the plaintiffs' interrogatories listing the actual damages sustained by the defendant as a result of the plaintiffs' breach."

He then proceeded to itemize the figures. * * * The total was made up as follows:

Difference between contract price of $29,500 and sale price of $26,495	$3,005.00
Commission to salesman on second sale	601.00
Commission to broker on second sale	1,000.00
Floor plan interest on cost of car, 52 days	334.72
Transportation expenses [2]	139.35
Total	$ 5,080.07

Counsel further argued, as an alternative claim of damages, that under the liquidated damage clause of the written contract, Lee Oldsmobile was entitled, upon breach by the purchaser, to retain as liquidated damages the entire cash deposit.

* * *

It may be seen from our reference to the rulings made below, and from the issues raised in this appeal by the parties, that Lee Oldsmobile holds $5,000 of Mrs. Kaiden's money; that Mrs. Kaiden breached her contract to buy a Rolls-Royce automobile; and that whatever damages flowed from the breach should reduce, pro tanto, Mrs. Kaiden's right to get her money back. The question of law presented is how to determine the damages. The question of fact is their amount.

The order form signed by Mrs. Kaiden contained a clause providing that the dealer shall have the right, upon failure or refusal of the purchaser to accept delivery of the motor vehicle, to retain as liquidated damages any cash deposit made by the purchaser. The Uniform Commercial Code, as in force in Maryland, § 2–718(1) provides:

"Damages for breach by either party may be liquidated in the agreement but only at an amount which is reasonable in the light of the anticipated or actual harm caused by the breach, the difficulties of proof of loss, and the inconvenience or nonfeasibility of otherwise obtaining an adequate remedy. A term fixing unreasonably large liquidated damages is void as a penalty."

In Traylor v. Grafton, 273 Md. 649, 332 A.2d 651 (1975), the Court of Appeals reviewed at length numerous decisions dealing with liquidated damage clauses in contracts. Running through

---

2. This item of $139.35 was referred to as being listed in answers to interrogatories, but not placed in evidence. Whether inadvertently or not, Judge Childs allowed it as an expense in calculating the amount of the judgment. The Kaidens do not attack this specific item on that ground.

many of the cases is the rule that not only must the amount be a reasonable forecast of just compensation, but that actual damages from a breach must be incapable or very difficult of accurate estimation. As Judge O'Donnell said it for the Court in Traylor v. Grafton, at 662, 332 A.2d at 660:

> "If the sum agreed upon is a reasonable forecast of the just and fair compensation for the harm that would result by a breach of the contract and the resultant injury is difficult to estimate accurately or actual damages could not be easily ascertained, such a clause has been held enforceable as liquidated damages." (Citations omitted).

* * *

We reject the application of the liquidated damage clause in the present case, as the trial judge did below, because it is clear that the actual damages are capable of accurate estimation. We do not say this from hindsight made possible because the actual figures claimed were in evidence. We say it because at the time the contract was made, it was clear that the nature of any damages which would result from a possible future breach was such that they would be easily ascertainable.

We set out earlier a tabulation of the items of damages, and the amount of each, which Lee Oldsmobile claimed should be set off against Mrs. Kaiden's deposit. The itemized claims totaled $5,080.07. The trial judge did not allow the item of $3,005, the difference between the contract price of $29,500 and the resale price of $26,495. That is why Lee Oldsmobile complains. The court did allow the other items, which come to a total of $2,075.07, and set that amount off against the $5,000 deposit, resulting in the judgment for the Kaidens in the amount of $2,924.93. That is why the Kaidens complain.

Several sections of the Uniform Commercial Code govern our resolution of the remaining issues. Under § 2–703, where the buyer repudiates, the aggrieved seller may

> "(d) Resell and recover damages as hereafter provided (§ 2–706);
>
> (e) Recover damages for nonacceptance (§ 2–708)
> * * *."

For Lee Oldsmobile to be entitled to claim as damages the difference between the resale price and the contract price, the sum of $3,005 in this case, the resale must meet the requirements of § 2–706.

* * *

The trial court rejected as an item of damage the difference between the resale price and the contract price, because it held that the resale made by Lee Oldsmobile was not made in a commercially reasonable manner, and that no notification was given of its intention to resell at private sale. We need not decide whether the resale was made in a commercially reasonable manner. It is enough that Lee Oldsmobile did not give the Kaidens reasonable notification of its intention to resell. *   *   *

Deprived of the benefits of § 2–706 by its failure to give notice of its intention to resell at private sale, Lee Oldsmobile is still entitled to the remedy set out in § 2–703(e), to recover damages for nonacceptance, under § 2–708.

*   *   *

It will be seen that § 2–708(1) authorizes two kinds of damage to an aggrieved seller. The first, the difference between the market price at the time and place for tender and the contract price [6] was not claimed in this case, perhaps because Lee Oldsmobile's salesman testified in his deposition that the market price of a Rolls-Royce was the sticker price. For the incidental damages authorized in § 2–708(1), one turns to § 2–710 *   *   *.

Every item of damage claimed by Lee Oldsmobile which was allowable under §§ 2–708 and 2–710 was in fact allowed by the trial court as a set-off, to reduce the judgment entered against it. The contention of the Kaidens in their cross appeal that the incidental damages should not have been allowed, because the resale of the automobile was not made in a commercially reasonable manner, cannot prevail. Those incidental damages are allowable to an aggrieved seller under § 2–710, whether he gets there through § 2–706 or through § 2–708. It is only § 2–706 which imposes the condition of a commercially reasonable resale. The remedies under § 2–708 are not related to a resale. Under § 2–710, it is only the incidental damages, not an antecedent resale, which must be commercially reasonable. There is no contention here that the items of damage allowed were not commercially reasonable.

Judgment affirmed.

NOTES

1. Would the court that decided *Lee Oldsmobile* have given effect to the liquidated damages clause in *Farmers Union?* Why did Buyer in *Farmers Union* include the liquidated damages clause in its contract? Is a clause of this type useful in cases of anticipatory repudiation?

2. In Equitable Lumber Corp. v. IPA Land Development Corp., 38 N.Y.2d 516, 381 N.Y.S.2d 459, 344 N.E.2d 391 (1976), the New York Court of Appeals considered the validity of a clause in a sales contract requiring Buyer to pay the attorney's fees of Seller

---

6. This measure of damage appears to be authorized irrespective of whether the aggrieved seller actually covered himself by a resale, and irrespective, as well, of whether a resale, if made, brought more or less than market price.

in the event of breach by Buyer. The clause stated that in the case of an attorney's fee for collection of money, the fee would be 30%. The court held that under § 2–719(1) the parties could validly provide for any attorney's fee as an element of damages for breach of contract; however, the amount of the fee must comply with the restrictions of § 2–302 (unconscionability) and § 2–718. With respect to the latter section the court stated:

> The first sentence of subdivision (1) of section 2–718 focuses on the situation of the parties both at the time of contracting and at the time of breach. Thus, a liquidated damages provision will be valid if reasonable with respect to *either* (1) the harm which the parties anticipate will result from the breach at the time of contracting or (2) the actual damages suffered by the nondefaulting party at the time of breach * * *. Interestingly, subdivision (1) of section 2–718 does, in some measure, signal a departure from prior law which considered only the anticipated harm at the time of contracting since that section expressly contemplates that a court may examine the "actual harm" sustained in adjudicating the validity of a liquidated damages provision * * *. Thus, decisions which have restricted their analysis of the validity of liquidated damages clauses solely to the anticipated harm at the time of contracting have, to this extent, been abrogated by the Uniform Commercial Code in cases involving transactions in goods. * * *

> Having satisfied the test set forth in the first part of subdivision (1) of section 2–718, a liquidated damages provision may nonetheless be invalidated under the last sentence of the section if it is so unreasonably large that it serves as a penalty rather than a good faith attempt to pre-estimate damages * * *. Plaintiff may not manipulate the actual amount of damages by entering into any exorbitant fee arrangement with its attorney and, thus, it may be necessary to look beyond the actual fee arrangement between plaintiff and counsel to determine whether that arrangement was reasonable and proportionate to the normal fee chargeable by attorneys in the context of this case * * *.

> Our courts have, in the past, refused to enforce a liquidated damages provision which fixed damages grossly disproportionate to the harm actually sustained, or likely to be sustained, by the nonbreaching party. * * * In Wirth & Hamid Fair Booking v. Wirth, 265 N.Y. 214, 223, 192 N.E. 297, 301, this court noted that "[l]iquidated damages constitute the compensation which the parties have agreed must be paid in satisfaction of the loss or injury which will follow from a breach of contract. They must bear reasonable proportion to the actual loss. * * * Otherwise an agreement to pay a

fixed sum, upon a breach of contract, is an agreement to pay a penalty, though the parties have chosen to call it 'liquidated damages,' and is unenforceable."

* * *

Subdivision (1) of section 2–718 of the Uniform Commercial Code, however, is directly applicable in this case. At the time of contracting the attorney's fees were arguably incapable of estimation. The amount required for attorney's fees would vary with the nature of the defaulting party's breach. For instance, a greater amount would be charged in the event that litigation was necessitated as opposed to settlement; and additional charges might be required for possible appellate procedures.

Special Term ruled that the 30% figure was disproportionate to the amount of time and effort which, according to its estimate, was required by the plaintiff's claim. This approach did not, however, result in the proper measure of damages sustained by the plaintiff. Analysis of the harm suffered by the injured party is the focal point of subdivision (1) of section 2–718 of the Uniform Commercial Code. Under both the "actual" and "anticipated" harm tests, the time expended by the attorney in obtaining collection is not necessarily the correct measure of damages, since an attorney would be expected to bill his client on a contingent fee basis. The liquidated damages provision would prove to be a reasonable pre-estimate of anticipated harm if it is related to the normal contingent fee charged by attorneys in the collection context.

On the other hand, if plaintiff actually entered into a contingent fee arrangement with its attorney for 30%, then the actual harm suffered by plaintiff would be consistent with the liquidated damages provision. However, even if the "actual harm" test is satisfied, it is then necessary, pursuant to the second sentence of subdivision (1) of section 2–718, to determine whether the liquidated damages provision is so unreasonably large as to be void as a penalty. If plaintiff entered into an exorbitant fee arrangement with counsel, knowing that defendant would suffer the consequences, then the liquidated damages provision would be void as a "term fixing unreasonably large liquidated damages". The commercial practice of attorneys in the area of debtor-creditor relations is relevant if plaintiff did, in fact, agree to pay its attorney 30% of the amount recovered on its claim against the defendant. While plaintiff may enter into any fee arrangement it wishes with counsel, it should not be permitted to manipulate the actual damage incurred by burdening the defendant with an exorbitant fee arrangement.

This case, therefore, should be remitted for the resolution of these factual issues: (1) was a 30% fee reasonable in light of the damages to be anticipated by one in the plaintiff's position, that is, was the fee reasonably related to the normal fee an attorney would charge for the collection of plaintiff's claim; or, alternatively, (2) was the fee commensurate with the actual arrangement agreed upon by this plaintiff and its attorney? Even if the 30% fee did correspond to the actual arrangement between plaintiff and its attorney, the court on remand should determine whether the amount stipulated was unreasonably large or grossly disproportionate to the damages which the plaintiff was likely to suffer from breach in the event it did not rely on respondent's agreement to pay its attorney's fees. If the amount is found to be unreasonably large, then the provision is void as a penalty.

PROBLEM

Buyer purchased a television set for a price of $400, but did not want to take immediate delivery because the set was purchased for a house still under construction. Seller agreed to take $100 in partial payment and to hold the set for 60 days. The parties agreed that if the set was not called for in 60 days, Seller was authorized to sell it and keep the $100. After 60 days, Buyer repudiated the contract and demanded return of the $100. Seller refused. Buyer sued to recover the $100. What result? Suppose the agreement between Buyer and Seller had been silent on the question of what happened to the $100 after 60 days. What result? § 2–718(2).

D. SELLER'S RIGHT TO RECLAIM GOODS SOLD TO INSOLVENT BUYER

---

1. STOPPAGE IN TRANSIT

In most cases title to goods passes from the seller to the buyer when the goods are delivered or shipped to the buyer. In some cases, however, title may pass to the buyer before the seller has given up possession. For example, a contract might provide that the seller will hold the goods for the buyer who will take delivery at some time after the sale. In such a case, although title may have passed to the buyer at the time of the sale, if the buyer had not yet paid the price of the goods that was due, the common law recognized a lien in favor of the seller to withhold delivery of the goods until the buyer paid. The UCC does not refer to this seller's lien but § 2–703(a) states that if the buyer fails to make a payment due on or before delivery of the goods the seller may withhold delivery. This section is based on Uniform Sales Act

§ 53(a) which described the right to withhold as a "lien on the goods," a reference to the common law seller's lien. In the case of a credit sale the buyer is entitled to delivery without payment; however, if the buyer is insolvent the seller can refuse delivery. Professor Williston explained the right as follows: "This doctrine is only an application of a general principle in the law of contracts that when one party to a bilateral contract is incapacitated from performing his part of the agreement, the other party also is excused from performing. It should be noticed that insolvency does not dissolve the bargain; it merely revives the seller's lien." Williston, Sales § 507a (Rev. ed. 1948). This right is stated in § 2–702(1).

The right of stoppage in transit is an extension of the seller's lien and allows the seller to retake possession of goods shipped to the buyer and in the possession of the carrier. The right is now codified in § 2–705, but in a broader form. Events that terminate the right are stated in § 2–705(2). At common law the right to stop goods in transit could be exercised only by an unpaid vendor against the vendee and only in cases in which title to the goods had passed to the vendee. If the vendor had reserved title, there was no need for the right because the reserved title allowed the vendor to fully control the goods. See Williston, Sales § 521 (Rev. ed. 1948). The right arose only in the event of the insolvency of the vendee and it terminated when the transit ended, which in most cases occurred when goods were delivered to the vendee or into the vendee's control through possession by an agent of the vendee. The right originated in equity and was designed to avoid the injustice of allowing the buyer, who owned the goods, to acquire possession of them when they were not paid for and when the vendee could not pay for them because of insolvency. See Williston, Sales § 518 (Rev. ed. 1948). The right was first recognized in an English case, Wiseman v. Vandeputt, 2 Vern. 203 (1690), in which it was asserted against a buyer who became bankrupt. It was consistently recognized in cases arising under the Bankruptcy Act. See 4A Collier, Bankruptcy ¶ 70.40 (14th ed.).

IN RE NATIONAL SUGAR REFINING CO.

United States District Court, S.D. New York, 1983.
27 B.R. 565.

SAND, DISTRICT JUDGE.

Appellant National Sugar Refining Company appeals from an order of United States Bankruptcy Court Judge Edward J. Ryan, dated September 21, 1981, and from an oral order of the same court, dated November 9, 1981. Briefly stated, the September 21st order determined that appellee, C. Czarnikow, Inc. ("Czarnikow"), an unpaid seller of raw sugar to appellant, was entitled to exercise its right of stoppage in transit upon appellant's insolvency. The order also stated that Czarnikow had the right to dispose of the sugar in a commercially reasonable manner and to retain the proceeds pending the bankruptcy court's determination as to whether Bankers Trust Company ("Bankers"), an alleged secured creditor of appellant, or Czarnikow had a superior right to such proceeds. * * *

I. FACTS

Appellant purchased 6,550 long tons of raw sugar from Czarnikow pursuant to two contracts dated August 12, 1981 and August 26, 1981, both of which called for September delivery. On August 27, 1981, Czarnikow advised appellant that 6,550 tons of sugar then on board the vessel M/V Edispsos and for which Czarnikow held the negotiable bill of lading would be used to fulfill its obligations under the two contracts. At that point, title to the sugar passed from Czarnikow to appellant.

On September 3, 1981, appellant filed a Chapter 11 petition pursuant to the Bankruptcy Reform Act of 1978, 11 U.S.C. (the "Bankruptcy Code" or "Code") § 1101 et seq. in the United States Bankruptcy Court for the Southern District of New York.

On September 11, 1981, Czarnikow applied to the bankruptcy court and obtained on even date an order requiring appellant to show cause why it should not be required to assume or reject the two "executory" sugar contracts forthwith and, if the contracts were assumed, why appellant should not be required to provide Czarnikow with adequate assurance of payment. Czarnikow's application further stated that it was exercising its right of stoppage in transit pursuant to Uniform Commercial Code ("UCC") §§ 2–702(1), 2–705(1).

* * *

Appellant's answer and counterclaim to the Czarnikow application, filed September 16, 1981, asserted that the contracts were nonexecutory; that Czarnikow had no right of stoppage in transit; that the sugar should immediately be delivered to appellant; and that Czarnikow was restrained by the automatic stay provisions of Code § 362 from interfering with delivery of the sugar.

* * *

II. ISSUES

The central issue presented herein, one of apparent first impression, is whether Czarnikow's exercise of its right of stoppage in transit, under UCC § 2–702(1), subsequent to appellant's filing of a petition in bankruptcy constituted the creation of a "statutory lien" avoidable by the trustee or debtor-in-possession [1] under Bankruptcy Code § 545 or resulted in the creation of interest in the sugar in favor of Czarnikow subordinated to the rights of appellant under Bankruptcy Code § 544(a) and UCC § 9–301.

The second issue raised by appellant is whether Czarnikow's post-petition exercise of its right of stoppage violated the automatic stay provisions of Code § 362(a) and was accordingly void.

* * *

III. DISCUSSION

A. *Stoppage of Goods in Transit*

1. *Generally*

Section 2–702(1) of the Uniform Commercial Code provides:

"Where the seller discovers the buyer to be insolvent he may refuse delivery except for cash including payment for all goods theretofore delivered under the contract, and stop delivery under this Article * * *."

See also UCC § 2–705(1) ("The seller may stop delivery of goods in the possession of a carrier or other bailee when he discovers the buyer to be insolvent * * *.").

The right accorded a seller of goods pursuant to this provision is premised on the inequity of permitting the buyer to obtain possession of goods when there has been a prospective failure of the buyer's performance. When the buyer is insolvent and thus impaired in fulfilling its contractual obligation to pay, the seller rather than deliver the goods and seek to recover on the price, see UCC §§ 2–709(1), 2–607(1), may withhold or stop in transit the delivery of the goods—i.e., suspend his performance, see UCC § 2–705 Comment 1—until and unless he is assured of the buyer's payment in cash upon delivery, even though the contract may call for the extension of credit. See 3A R. Dusenberg & L. King, Sales & Bulk Transfers under the Uniform Commercial Code § 13.03[2], at 13–12 (1982).[2] This right persists so long as the goods are in the

---

1. A debtor-in-possession, such as appellant, is clothed with all the "avoiding" powers of a trustee, 11 U.S.C. § 1107(a). Accordingly, the two terms are used interchangeably in the text.

2. Czarnikow attempts to attach significance to its assertion that at no time did it instruct the Edipsos to deliver the sugar to appellant. * * * Even assuming the assertion as a fact, however, Czarnikow gains little: its actions would then constitute "withholding delivery", rather than stoppage in transit, the consequences of which under the

UCC are precisely the same. See 3A R. Dusenberg & L. King, Sales & Bulk Transfers under the Uniform Commercial Code, § 13.03[3], at 13–16 (1982); see also UCC § 2–702 Comment 6 ("After effective stoppage under this section, the seller's rights * * * are the same as if he had never made a delivery"). Moreover, because in either depiction of the events, there is no dispute that title passed to the appellant on August 27, 1981 and was thus part of the bankrupt's estate as of the petition date, we are of the view that under

hands of a carrier or any other bailee not holding for the buyer and is cut off by the buyer's attainment of actual or constructive possession. See UCC § 2–705(2).

The fact that Czarnikow had passed to appellant title to the sugar did not affect the former's right to stop in transit. As one commentator notes, "Under strict legal terminology, the right to stop goods where title has not passed should not be called stoppage in transitu. The vendor's rights are then much greater." 4A Collier on Bankruptcy ¶ 70.40, at 481 n. 2 (14th ed. 1978). See also UCC § 2–401; 78 C.J.S. Sales ¶ 403.

2. *Bankruptcy Code § 545*

Appellant asserts, however, that Czarnikow's stoppage in transit constitutes a statutory lien avoidable under Code § 545.

Section 545 provides, in relevant part: "Statutory liens. The trustee may avoid the fixing of a statutory lien on property of the debtor to the extent that such lien—

(1) first becomes effective against the debtor—

* * *

(D) when the debtor becomes insolvent;

* * *

(2) is not perfected or enforceable on the date of the filing of the petition against a bona fide purchaser that purchases such property on the date of the filing of the petition, whether or not such a purchaser exists * * *."

11 U.S.C. § 545(1)(D), (2).

A "statutory lien" is defined in the Bankruptcy Code as a

"lien arising solely by force of a statute on specified circumstances or conditions, or lien of distress for rent, whether or not statutory, but does not include a security interest or judicial lien, whether or not such interest or lien is provided by or is dependent on a statute or whether or not such interest of lien is made fully effective by statute;" 11 U.S.C. § 101(38).

Appellant maintains that the exercise of the right of stoppage in transit pursuant to UCC § 2–702(1) merely confers a vendor's lien upon the seller. In support of this position, appellant cites the following commentary:

"When delivery of goods is rightfully stopped by the seller, he is thereby revested with a lien in the same way as if possession of the goods had never been surrendered. The sale is not cancelled; if title had passed to the buyer * * * it remains in the buyer unless the seller thereafter makes a proper

Bankruptcy Code §§ 545, 544(a), it is immaterial whether Czarnikow literally stopped the goods in transit.

cancellation by virtue of the [Uniform Commercial] Code § 2–703."

2 Anderson, Uniform Commercial Code § 2–705:28, at 371 (2d ed. 1981); see also id. § 2–703:8, at 338. To the same effect, one treatise states:

> "Prior to the Uniform Commercial Code * * * the seller's right to withhold would not be dependent on his title in the goods, but he would be granted a seller's lien on the goods until payment of the purchase price. The seller's lien is nowhere mentioned in Article 2 of the Code and as a legal device it is omitted and presumably no longer exists. The consequences of it, however, are retained by the Code."

3A R. Dusenberg & L. King, Sales & Bulk Transfers under the UCC § 13.03, at 13–14 (1982) (emphasis supplied; footnote omitted). Because the right of stoppage in transit and the "lien" resulting from the exercise of such right become effective under UCC § 2–702(1) only at the time of the buyer's insolvency, appellant asserts that as a debtor-in-possession, it may avoid the "lien" under § 545(1).

* * *

4. *Relevancy of Code § 546(c)*

We are of the opinion, however, that appellant's arguments under both Code §§ 545 and 544(a) neglect the significance of Bankruptcy Code § 546(c) which states:

> "Limitations on avoiding powers
>
> " * * *
>
> "The rights and powers of the trustee under sections 544(a), 545, 547, and 549 of this title are subject to any statutory right or common-law right of a seller, in the ordinary course of such seller's business, of goods to the debtor to reclaim such goods if the debtor has received such goods while insolvent * * *."

The legislative history of this section expresses its purpose:

> "[§ 546(c)] specifies that the trustee's rights and powers under the strong arm clause, the successor to creditors provision, the preference section, and the post-petition transaction section are all subject to any statutory or common-law right of a seller, in the ordinary course of business, of goods to the debtor to reclaim the goods if the debtor received the goods on credit while insolvent * * *. The purpose of the provision is to recognize, in part, the validity of section 2–702 of the Uniform Commercial Code, which has generated much litigation, confusion, and divergent decisions in different circuits." H.R.Rep. No. 595, 95th Cong., 1st Sess. 371–372 (1977); S.Rep.

No. 989, 95th Cong., 2d Sess. 86–87 (1978), U.S.Code Cong. & Admin.News 1978, pp. 5787, 6327.

In light of this provision's denial of the avoidance powers conferred on a trustee under Bankruptcy Code §§ 544(a) and 545 as against a seller who delivers goods and then reclaims, we find it hardly likely that Congress intended to grant these very same powers as against a seller who succeeds in "reclaiming" the goods *prior* to delivery, by means of stopping them in transit.[3] In both instances, the property interest of the buyer in the goods that is affected by the post-petition acts of the seller is the same, namely, defeasible title. See 2 Anderson, Uniform Commercial Code, supra, § 2–705:28, at 371. There appears no rationale either in the legislative history or in case law construing UCC § 2–702(1) and the statutory antecedents to Code §§ 544(a) and 545, and appellant has suggested none, for holding that a seller's acts pursuant to UCC § 2–702(2) do not constitute the creation of a statutory lien, while those under UCC § 2–702(1) do.

Indeed, adoption of appellant's position would result in the anomaly of placing an unpaid seller who had withheld from the buyer constructive possession of the goods in a worse condition than one who has transferred such possession to the buyer, and would suggest that Czarnikow should have engaged in the rather absurd behavior of proceeding to deliver the goods to appellant and immediately thereafter issuing a written demand for reclamation pursuant to Code § 546(c).

Congress' silence in Code § 546(c) on the validity in bankruptcy law of a seller's right of stoppage in transit does not, as appellant argues, compel by negative implication a determination that Congress intended to subject such right to the trustee's avoidance powers. The more probable explanation for this silence lies in the apparently complete absence of case law, noted by both parties, suggesting that the seller's exercise of rights under subsection (1) of UCC § 2–702 constitutes the creation of a statutory lien or of lienor's rights junior to those enjoyed by the debtor-in-possession as a hypothetical lien creditor.

---

3. Apparently, one treatise writer has assumed the position that the statute itself excepts from the trustee's avoidance powers a seller's right of stoppage in transit, a position justified by construing the statute to encompass a right to reclaim title, as well as the goods themselves.

"*As long as the seller makes written demand for the goods* within ten days of or *prior to receipt by an insolvent debtor,* the trustee may be subject to any statutory or common law right to reclaim."

4 Collier on Bankruptcy § 546.01, at 546–4 (15th ed. 1980) (emphasis added). Of course, the seller cannot make a demand, written or otherwise, for goods that are not in the debtor's possession and, accordingly, the above-quoted statement should perhaps be read as requiring that a seller exercising a right of stoppage give written notice of same. Assuming such a requirement to exist, Czarnikow's filing of the Order to Show Cause on September 11, 1981 is fully adequate in this regard.

The lack of judicial consideration of UCC § 2–702(1) as creating a statutory lien or a subordinate security interest is paralleled by the secondary authorities on the subject. For example, one treatise, discussing the statutory antecedent of the Bankruptcy Code and the avoidance powers conferred therein on the trustee, states without qualification:

> "The bankruptcy courts recognize and give effect to the doctrine of stoppage *in transitu* * * *.

> " *   *   *

> "So far as the effect of bankruptcy is concerned, the right of stoppage *in transitu* may be exercised by a vendor where goods are shipped to a person who, unknown to the shipper, had gone into bankruptcy prior to the delivery of the goods to the carrier, or who went into bankruptcy while the goods were in transit."

4A Collier on Bankruptcy ¶ 70.40, at 481 (14th ed. 1978) (footnotes omitted). See also Buss v. Long Island Storage Warehouse, 64 F.2d 338 (2d Cir.1933) (L. Hand, J.). By contrast, the issue of UCC § 2–702(2) and its interrelationship with the trustee's avoidance powers under the former bankruptcy statute was marked by "much litigation, confusion, and divergent decisions in different circuits", see H.R.Rep. No. 595, supra; S.Rep. No. 989, supra, which prompted Congress to enact Code § 546(c). Accordingly, congressional silence regarding the seller's right of stoppage in transit as against the trustee's avoidance powers should be considered, if at all, more in the nature of an approval of the harmonious precedent in favor of the seller's right of stoppage rather than a disavowal by omission.[4]

In summary if, as appellant contends, stoppage in transit revests the unpaid seller with a vendor's lien, surely reclamation

---

4. We also take note of the numerous cases arising under the former bankruptcy statute and prior to the enactment of Bankruptcy Code § 546(c) holding that the seller's right of reclamation, set forth in UCC § 2–702(2), is not avoidable by the trustee in bankruptcy as an exercise of a statutory lien. See, e.g., In the Matter of Telemart Enterprises, Inc., 524 F.2d 761 (9th Cir. 1975), cert. denied, 424 U.S. 969, 96 S.Ct. 1466, 47 L.Ed.2d 736 (1976); In re Daylin, Inc., 596 F.2d 853 (9th Cir.1979); In the Matter of PFA Farmer's Market Ass'n, 583 F.2d 992 (8th Cir.1978); In re Federal's, Inc., 553 F.2d 509 (6th Cir. 1977); In the Matter of National Bellas Hess, Inc., 1 B.C.D. 926 (Bankr.S.D.N.Y. 1975). But see In re Giltex, 17 U.C.C. Rep. 887 (S.D.N.Y.1975).

The rationale of these cases, namely,

"that a state confers a priority repugnant to § 64 [11 U.S.C. § 545] only when it attempts to direct the disposition of assets to which the bankrupt has received a nondefeasible title."

In re Telemart Enterprises, supra, 524 F.2d at 765–66, is equally applicable to consideration of the issue whether the right of stoppage in transit constitutes a statutory lien. Because, as discussed above, appellant at the time of Czarnikow's stoppage of the goods had but a defeasible title, these cases support the conclusion that Czarnikow had the right to stop the sugar in transit at least as against appellant's rights under Code § 545.

is to the same effect. Congress' determination, as expressed in Code § 546(c), that the latter should not be countermanded by the Bankruptcy Code's statutory-lien provision or strong-arm clause persuades us that Congress would likewise have recognized the validity of a seller's right of stoppage as against a debtor-in-possession had the matter been placed in issue. Accordingly, the bankruptcy court correctly ruled that Czarnikow possessed the right to stop the delivery of the sugar in transit.

B. *The Automatic Stay*

Appellant further contends that Czarnikow's stoppage of the goods in transit violated the automatic stay provisions set forth in Bankruptcy Code § 362(a) and was accordingly "void and without effect".

*   *   *

Having concluded on the basis of the reasoning set forth above that under the Bankruptcy Code a seller has the right of stoppage in transit, we view appellant to be contending here that prior to exercising such right, Czarnikow must first have applied to the bankruptcy court for relief from the automatic stay pursuant to Code § 362 and * * * the Rules of Bankruptcy Procedure, and that the failure to so apply results in the nullification of the stoppage.

We are of the opinion, however, that Czarnikow was not required under Code § 362(a) to seek relief from the stay prior to exercising its right of stoppage. As a practical matter, establishing as a prerequisite to such exercise an application for relief would in many instances effectively deny to the seller the right of stoppage, in light of the often short period between the filing of the petition and actual or constructive delivery of the goods during which the right must be exercised.[5] Stoppage in transit, as

---

5. It may be argued that the seller's failure to obtain relief from the stay in time to stop delivery could be remedied by the seller's subsequent exercise of its right of reclamation under UCC § 2–702(2) and Code § 546(c). We are of the view, however, that forcing the seller to deliver and then to reclaim, rather than allowing it simply to suspend delivery, would result in waste that cannot be rationalized in light of the right and the opportunity afforded the trustee to assume contracts regardless whether the seller has exercised its right of reclamation or its right of stoppage in transit. Indeed, inasmuch as the respective rights of a seller and trustee subsequent to reclamation are governed by Code § 546(c)(2) (requiring the court to grant reclamation unless it grants seller's claim as a priority or lien on the estate), while those of a seller and trustee

subsequent to stoppage are governed by Code § 365(b)(1) (allowing the trustee to assume if it provides to the seller "adequate assurances of future performance"), the latter provision's less-favorable treatment of the seller suggests that, in general, trustees stand to be benefitted by having sellers resort to stoppage in transit rather than forcing them to the remedy of reclamation.

Moreover, we note that there exists some question as to a seller's right of reclamation under UCC § 2–702(2) where the seller has knowledge of the buyer's insolvency at or before the time of delivery. See In re Food Center of Delhi, Inc., 11 U.C.C.Rptg.Serv. 1186 (W.D.La.1973). If such knowledge does indeed preclude reclamation, then a seller who is unable to obtain relief from the automatic stay sufficiently in

opposed to any disposition of the goods so stopped, should be viewed as analogous to the written demand required of a reclaiming seller under Code § 546(c). It appears clear that the issuance of that demand—as much an "act" within the purview of Code § 362(a)(3), (4) and (5) as the stoppage in transit—need not be preceded by a grant of relief from the automatic stay. Cf. 4 Collier on Bankruptcy ¶ 546.04, at 546–12 (15th ed. 1980) (seller must obtain modification of stay before it "actually reclaims goods"). Accordingly, Czarnikow's failure here to apply for and obtain relief from the stay is immaterial and does not vitiate the proper exercise of its right of stoppage.

* * *

NOTES

1. Although the UCC does not specifically deal with the question of how the right of stoppage is affected by bona fide purchasers of the goods, the common-law cases distinguished between unilateral action by the buyer in reselling the goods and cases in which the seller assented to the resale and shipment of the goods to the subpurchaser. A typical case in which the right was lost is as follows: Buyer orders goods from Merchant who to fill the order buys the goods on credit from Manufacturer. At Merchant's request, Manufacturer ships the goods on a straight bill of lading directly to Buyer. Before the goods arrive Manufacturer learns of the insolvency of Merchant. The only right of Manufacturer is to stop delivery to the person who bought from Manufacturer, i.e., Merchant, but in this case no delivery to Merchant was contemplated so that right never arose. The shipment by Manufacturer to Buyer was treated by the courts as the equivalent of a delivery to Merchant and a reshipment by Merchant to Buyer. See Niemeyer Lumber Co. v. Burlington & Missouri River Railroad Co., 54 Neb. 321, 74 N.W. 670 (1898), and M. & L. R. Railroad Co. v. Freed, 38 Ark. 614 (1882). If the seller shipped to the buyer, the buyer could not unilaterally defeat the seller's right of stoppage by reselling the goods to a subpurchaser, but the seller could give up the right by shipping to somebody other than the buyer. "* * * when the vendor contemplates a transit to his purchaser, and ships accordingly, he cannot be defeated of his right by the conduct of the purchaser during the transit, without his assent, either express, or implied * * * Here he assents to a different destination before parting with his property; and if he thereby loses his right of stoppage, it is his voluntary act." M. & L. R.R.R. Co. v. Freed, supra at p. 623. This law was codified in Uniform Sales Act § 62. Comment 2 to § 2–705, which addresses the question of direct shipment to subpurchasers, is ambiguous with respect to the question of whether

advance to exercise its right of stoppage may effectively be denied not only that right but also the right of reclamation expressly recognized in Code § 546(c).

the right of stoppage is terminated 1) when the goods are received by the subpurchaser or 2) when the goods are shipped. Section 2–705 apparently intended to carry forward Uniform Sales Act § 62 which clearly incorporated the second interpretation.

2. Suppose in the example given in Note 1 it is Buyer rather than Merchant who becomes insolvent. Does Merchant have a right to stop delivery? Is Merchant able to stop delivery? § 2–705(1) and (3)(d).

2. RECLAMATION OF GOODS DELIVERED TO BUYER

Except to the extent bankruptcy law gives an avoiding power to the trustee in bankruptcy, the bankruptcy estate is subject to claims of third parties to property to the same extent as was the debtor just before bankruptcy. For example, if Debtor has converted goods of Owner, Owner can get them back if Debtor is in bankruptcy. The same result may occur in the case of voluntary transfers to the debtor. Suppose Transferor was obliged to transfer goods to X. Debtor fraudulently represented to Transferor that Debtor was X. Relying on that representation Transferor conveyed the goods to Debtor. If Debtor goes into bankruptcy the goods become part of the bankruptcy estate if under the state law Debtor got legal title. But Transferor is entitled to rescind the transfer of title to Debtor and reclaim the goods in bankruptcy if the rescission right is recognized by state law. The right to rescind is not a lien but rather an equitable right to undo the transaction by which Debtor acquired the legal title. Although this right could not be asserted against a person who purchased the goods from Debtor in good faith and for value (§ 2–403(1)) it could be asserted against a creditor of Debtor who acquired a judicial lien in the goods. Under Bankruptcy Code § 544(a) the trustee in bankruptcy has the rights of a judicial lien creditor to the goods, but does not have the rights of a bona fide purchaser for value. Thus, § 544(a) does not allow the trustee to defeat Transferor's claim to the goods.

Most cases in which rescission for fraud is asserted in bankruptcy involve sales transactions in which the goods were obtained on credit by a debtor who made a fraudulent misrepresentation of financial condition or who acquired the goods while insolvent. In these cases § 2–702(2) preempts the common law. It gives a right of reclamation to a seller who has sold goods on credit to an insolvent buyer. That section denies any other right to reclaim goods based on the buyer's fraudulent or innocent misrepresentation of solvency or intent to pay.

Another common case of buyer fraud involves cash sales. The buyer pays by check which is subsequently dishonored. This case is not covered by § 2–702. Rather, it is covered obliquely by § 2–

507(2) which states that when goods are sold for cash the right of the buyer to retain the goods is conditional upon making the payment due, and by § 2–511(3), which states that payment by check is conditional and defeated by later dishonor. Section § 2–403(1)(b) recognizes that in that case the buyer obtained a voidable title. The remedy of the seller is rescission and retaking of the goods. Frequently, dishonor of the check occurs because the buyer was insolvent when the goods were received. In that case, if the buyer is in bankruptcy the reclamation by the cash seller resembles that of the credit seller under § 2–702(2).

The cases that follow discuss how reclamation claims of sellers under § 2–702(2) and § 2–507(2) are affected by the bankruptcy of the buyer.

MATTER OF FLAGSTAFF FOODSERVICE CORP.

United States Bankruptcy Court, S.D. New York, 1981.
14 B.R. 462.

ROY BABITT, BANKRUPTCY JUDGE. This dispute between Flagstaff Foodservice Company New England, Inc. (Flagstaff or debtor), a Chapter 11 debtor and McCain Foods, Inc. (McCain) centers on the reach of Section 546(c) of the Bankruptcy Code, involving the rights Congress gave in that section to a seller of goods on credit to an insolvent purchaser.

Flagstaff, a distributor of food to institutional customers, filed its petition in this court on July 21, 1981 for the relief afforded by Chapter 11 of the Bankruptcy Code. * * * Upon learning of this filing, McCain, a seller on credit of $11,610 worth of frozen french fried potatoes, made a timely demand to reclaim these foodstuffs in accordance with Section 2–702(2) of New York's Uniform Commercial Code (U.C.C.). As this demand proved fruitless, McCain sought judicial aid in recovering the property sold to Flagstaff. * * *

McCain filed a complaint seeking reclamation * * * and alleged the sale on credit, the delivery of the potatoes, the debtor's insolvency, the filing of Flagstaff's Chapter 11 petition, the demand required by Section 2–702(2) of the U.C.C. and by Section 546(c)(1) of the Code, and the timeliness of the demand as prescribed by both of these sections.

Although Flagstaff's answer facially put some of these allegations in issue, its main defense was bottomed on the premise that McCain could reclaim only those potatoes in the debtor's possession and that, in any event, McCain could not receive payment for the value of such goods but would have to settle for priority status as an administrative expense creditor.[3]

3. Section 503 of the Code prescribes those claims, usually arising after a bankruptcy petition has been filed, which are given administrative expense status. As such, first priority is accorded in the Code's scheme of priorities

At the hearing, both sides agreed that there were no controlling facts in dispute save for the quantity of the potatoes from the specific sale still in the debtor's possession when the petition was filed, and as to that the parties could readily ascertain the quantity without the need for testimony.   *   *   *

  *   *   * McCain insists that it is entitled to an administrative claim under Section 546(c)(2)(A) for the full amount of its $11,610 shipment or a lien to that extent under Section 546(c)(2)(B), both without regard to whether any or all of the shipped foodstuffs could be retrieved by reclamation. The debtor insists that the discretion conferred by those sections may be exercised only to the extent it holds property which McCain could reclaim under applicable teachings.

For the reasons which follow the court concludes that the reading given to Section 546(c) of the 1978 Bankruptcy Code by the debtor is the proper one and that the plaintiff, McCain, is entitled to the administrative claim priority given by the scheme of the Code, but only to the extent of that portion of the foodstuffs delivered on July 13, 1981 which was in the debtor's possession on the date of McCain's demand.

I.

A SELLER'S PRE–1978 BANKRUPTCY CODE RIGHTS

Section 546(c) of the Code knows no antecedents in bankruptcy statutes as it appears to be Congress' first expression in the area it touches. But it cannot be said that Congress was unaware of non-federal statutes on the subject of the rights of sellers to recover property sold to insolvent purchasers and of the interfacing of those statutes with Congress' bankruptcy enactments as taught by federal judges. As so much is clear from the words of Section 546(c) itself and from its legislative history, the court does more than just assume that Congress knew of the state of the law before it wrote as it did.   *   *   *

Section 546(c) reads this way:

"The rights and powers of the trustee under sections 544(a), 545, 547 and 549 of this title are subject to any statutory right or common-law right of a seller, in the ordinary course of such seller's business, of goods to the debtor to reclaim such goods if the debtor has received such goods while insolvent, but—(1) such a seller may not reclaim any such goods unless such seller demands in writing reclamation of such goods before ten days after receipt of such goods by the debtor; and (2) the court may deny reclamation to a seller with such a right of

spelled out by Section 507(a). Section 726(a)(1) then provides for the distribution of the estate's property first to the   Section 507 priorities "in the order specified" in that section.

reclamation that has made such a demand only if court—(A) grants the claim of such a seller priority as an administrative expense; or (B) secures such claim by a lien."

As the section clearly recognizes a common law or nonbankruptcy statutory right of a seller to reclaim goods received by an insolvent, it is not inappropriate to consider what those rights were first at common law and, later, by statute. * * *

A. *AT COMMON LAW*

At common law, the right of a seller to reclaim his goods was governed by the law of contracts which permitted rescission by a seller who was induced to enter into a sales contract by a fraudulent or innocent misrepresentation. There were essentially four kinds of conduct which gave a seller at common law the right to rescind a sale based on the buyer's insolvency: (1) the buyer's concealment of insolvency with a demonstrable intent not to pay for the goods; (2) the buyer's concealment of insolvency where intent not to pay cannot be demonstrated; (3) the buyer's insolvency did not have to be proved but the buyer had materially misrepresented his financial status; and (4) the buyer's innocent misrepresentation. * * *

But the reach of the remedies flowing from rescission from the standpoint of the seller's ability to retrieve the property sold on application of common law principles yielded a melange of state court rulings. These turned on identification of the goods, their fungibility, commingling and the like where reclamation was not possible under applicable law because of problems of identification, the tracing of funds specifically allocable to the seller's goods yielded some solace in some places.

The lack of consistent and predictable handling of the dialogue between a seller and an insolvent purchaser and the absence of a standard which could harmonize the interests of both in an expanding economy has been noted, *inter alia,* in Weintraub & Edelman, Seller's Right to Reclaim Property Under Section 20702(2) of the Code Under the Bankruptcy Act: Fact or Fancy, 32 Bus.Law 1165, 1167 (1977).

B. *UNDER SECTION 2–702(2) OF THE UNIFORM COMMERCIAL CODE*

In large measure, the Uniform Commercial Code, and particularly relevant in this dispute, Section 2–702(2), were designed to afford certainty and completeness in preference to "those sources of 'general law' to which we were accustomed to resort in the days of Swift v. Tyson", to borrow the words of Judge Learned Hand in New York, N.H. & H.R. Co. v. Reconstruction Finance Corp., 180 F.2d 241, 244 (2d Cir. 1950). Today, 15 years after Judge Friendly made the observation in United States v. Wegematic Corp., 360

F.2d 674, 676 (2d Cir. 1966), the Uniform Commercial Code is with us as "a truly national law of commerce."

Section 2–702(2) of the U.C.C. is as follows:

"(2) Where the seller discovers that the buyer has received goods on credit while insolvent he may reclaim the goods upon demand made within ten days after the receipt, but if misrepresentation of solvency has been made to the particular seller in writing within three months before delivery the ten day limitation does not apply. Except as provided in this subsection the seller may not base a right to reclaim goods on the buyer's fraudulent or innocent mispresentation of solvency or of intent to pay."

As the Official Uniform Comment discloses, Section 2–702(2)

"takes as its base line the proposition that any receipt of goods on credit by an insolvent buyer amounts to a tacit business misrepresentation of solvency and therefore is fraudulent as against the particular seller. This Article makes discovery of the buyer's insolvency and demand within a ten day period a condition of the right to reclaim goods on this ground. The ten day limitation period operates from the time of receipt of the goods. An exception to this time limitation is made when a written misrepresentation of solvency has been made to the particular seller within three months prior to the delivery. To fall within the exception the statement of solvency must be in writing, addressed to the particular seller and dated within three months of the delivery".

And as to the goods involved in the seller's Section 2–702(2) quest, the rights there given bar all other remedies.

What emerges plainly from the section is that its predicate is the existence of the goods in the seller's possession and therefore able to be reclaimed. These must not have left the seller's possession as is clear from Section 2–702(3) making the rights of the seller seeking to recover subject to the rights of the purchasers there described.

Given the limitations on the seller's right to recover the goods and the problems inherent in tracing specific fungibles among others from the standpoints of the time of delivery of a given lot, it came as no surprise that the proceeds of a seller's identifiable goods would become the object of a seller's Section 2–702(2) claim. See 4A Collier on Bankruptcy (14th ed.) 70.39. That such a remedy going beyond Section 2–702(2) would cause problems is nowhere made more clear than in the several opinions coming from the Fifth Circuit Court of Appeals in Matter of Samuels & Co., Inc. There, after an earlier reversal and remand on other grounds by the Supreme Court, sub nom. Mahon v. Stowers, 416 U.S. 100, 94 S.Ct. 1626, 40 L.Ed.2d 79 (1974), the Court of Appeals divided in a dispute between a trustee in bankruptcy and a seller of cattle seeking to reclaim that which he could not get as the cattle had been slaughtered and butchered or, alternatively, seeking the proceeds attributable to the sale of the meat. 510 F.2d 139 (1975). Although the presence of a secured creditor loomed large, the majority opinion recognized that the cash seller's right to reclaim should not rest on the identity of the cattle as sold. 510 F.2d at 148. In short, reclamation on the facts there, was found to be "a futile gesture" contrary to "reason or logic." *Ibid.* Circuit Judge Godbold dissented, 510 F.2d at 154. Among other chidings, Judge Godbold took Section 2–702 of the Texas version of the U.C.C. to confer a right to reclaim and not a "right to go after proceeds." 510 F.2d at 157. Rehearing *en banc* was granted and the Court of Appeals, dividing 9–5, reversed the panel decision and adopted "as its opinion the dissenting opinion of Judge Godbold * * *". 526 F.2d 1238, 1240 (1976), reh. den. April 1, 1976, cert. denied sub nom. Stowers v. Mahon, 429 U.S. 834, 97 S.Ct. 98, 50 L.Ed.2d 99 (1976).

It would seem to follow, therefore, just from the tenor of the disparate views in the *Samuels* case itself and in others which need not be cited that the remedy of reclamation to a seller bringing himself within the plain language of U.C.C. Section 2–702(2) is secure as to the identifiable goods in the possession of the purchaser but much less so as to the proceeds yielded by the sale of those goods, for the tracing of specific funds attributable to specific sales is a formidable obstacle at best.

C. *BANKRUPTCY UNDER THE 1898 ACT AND ITS IMPACT ON U.C.C. SECTION 2–702(2)*

While the cup of the Section 2–702(2) seller was apparently full given the strictures of the section as to the goods sold and the questionable right to recover proceeds if they could be properly traced, a line of cases emerged where the purchaser's bankruptcy intervened which brought the seller's cup to overflowing.

[Some courts] * * * held for one reason or another that the right given by U.C.C. Section 2–702 collided impermissibly with rights given trustees in bankruptcy to denounce disguised priorities which looked like liens under state law. * * * Other courts however, sustained the vitality of Section 2–702(2) as against trustees in bankruptcy although they reached these results by different lines of reasoning. * * *

II.

A SELLER'S RIGHTS UNDER SECTION 546(c) OF THE 1978 BANKRUPTCY CODE

It is against this setting that Congress expressed itself in Section 546(c) of the Code in the matter of a seller's right to reclaim its goods where the purchaser had become subject to the provisions of the Bankruptcy Code.

What emerges plainly from the rather sparse legislative comments to Section 546 is that Congress was aware of the tension between U.C.C. Section 2–702 and the several rights given bankruptcy trustees by the 1898 Act to denounce certain pre-petition transactions. Swiftly and surely, Section 546(c) in its lead-in sentence resolves the disparate views of federal courts concerning the effect of bankruptcy on a reclaiming seller's U.C.C. or common law rights. Whatever weapons a bankruptcy trustee might have in his arsenal to gather the estate are subject to the U.C.C. statutory right or common law right of a seller to retrieve his goods.[8]

Congress explained this purpose of enacted Section 546(c) this way:

> "The purpose of the provision is to recognize, in part, the validity of section 2–702 of the Uniform Commercial Code, which has generated much litigation, confusion, and divergent decisions in different circuits."

S.Rep. No. 95–989, 95th Cong., 2d Sess. 86–7 (1978); H.Rep. No. 95–595, 95th Cong., 1st Sess. 371–2 (1977), U.S.Code Cong. & Admin.News 1978, pp. 5872–5873, 6328.

It is not necessary in the context of the specific dispute here to appraise Section 546(c) against Section 2–702(2) to determine whether a seller's right to seek reclamation depends on different conditions precedent where bankruptcy has come. ＊ ＊ ＊

Here the issue is whether, if reclamation is denied, and the court exercises its judgment to grant the seller a priority administrative claim or a lien, both authorized by Section 546(c)(2), the extent of either will exceed the value of the property which could be retrieved so that the full value of the goods sold will fix the reach of the priority or the lien.

Insofar as the discretion conferred on the court by Section 546(c)(2) expands the careful priority scheme outlined by Congress in Section 507(a) in which administrative claims under Section 503(b) lead all the rest, a legislative purpose to achieve greater expansion should be plainly expressed.

The conclusion emerging plainly is that the legislative history falls far short of what would be needed for the definitive answer that Section 546(c)(2) intended to give more to a reclaiming seller than he ever had either at common law or under U.C.C. Section 2–

---

8. The rights of the trustee given by bankruptcy law which are specifically defined to be subordinate to a reclaiming creditor's rights are those conferred by Section 544 of the Code—the trustee as lien creditor (the strong-arm power); by Section 545—avoidance of statutory liens; by Section 547—avoidance of preferential transfers; and by Section 549—avoidance of post-petition transfers.

702(2). * * * To the contrary, the identical statements by Congressman Edwards, the House sponsor of H.R. 8200, and by Senator DeConcini, on the Senate side, support this court's conclusion that the administrative claim or lien which could be granted are in lieu of the goods which the seller could retrieve and not in lieu of the total invoiced shipment. Both legislators saw Section 546(c)(2) as permitting the bankruptcy court to grant an administrative expense claim or a lien

"in lieu of turning over the property".

124 Cong.Rec.H. 11097 (daily ed. September 28, 1978); 124 Cong. Rec.S. 17414 (daily ed. October 6, 1978).

"These remarks, offered in lieu of a conference report by the principal sponsors of the Act, are entitled to great weight."

In re Spong; Pauley v. Spong, 661 F.2d 6 at 10 (2d Cir. 1981).

To be sure, the identical comments by both the House and the Senate relevant to an earlier version of enacted Section 546(c)(2) are ambiguous and could support plaintiff's argument were it not for the much surer comments made on the eve of passage of a revised bill, H.R. 8200, introduced on September 28, 1978. Both statements, which recognize the right given by U.C.C. Section 2–702, observe that that right (to reclaim) is subject to the court's power to grant an administrative expense priority in lieu of reclamation

"for his [the seller's] claim arising out of the sale of the goods."

S.Rep. No. 95–989, supra, at 87; H.Rep. No. 95–595, supra, at 372, U.S.Code Cong. & Admin.News 1978, pp. 5878, 6328.

At first blush, these quoted words suggest that a seller could be given his priority for the invoiced amount rather than for the value of the goods which he could actually recover. But this reading of these few words would require the court to ignore their context and to put at nought strong policy considerations which underlie bankruptcy principles.

The context of which the above statement is a part recognizes the continuing vitality of U.C.C. Section 2–702 or common law rights given reclaiming sellers. All Section 546(c)(1) does is assess a somewhat different procedural mode by requiring a written demand for reclamation within 10 days of the receipt of the goods by the debtor in a bankruptcy proceeding. There is absolutely nothing to show that Congress meant to expand rights given, absent bankruptcy, by state law or the common law. The plain language of all the legislative coments makes this clear.

All this aside, bankruptcy is governed by its own truths and those truths relevant here also require the court to construe Section 546(c)(2) in favor of the debtor and the overwhelming mass of the debtor's unsecured creditors for whom neither U.C.C. Section 2–702, the common law, nor Section 546(c) works.

First it must be recognized that Congress' scheme of priority creditors, while designed to achieve important policy aims thought relevant, nevertheless distorts one of the dominant schemes of bankruptcy—equality of distribution. * * * It follows, therefore, that if Congress meant to give the 10-day seller so much more than he ever had under non-bankruptcy law to the exclusion and detriment of the 11-day seller, it would have expressed itself far more clearly. Because any system of priorities ultimately attenuates the yield for those for whom Congress was less solicitous, the expressions of those priorities should be strictly read and not expanded unless plainly mandated.

The second truth is that reorganization under Chapter 11 is one of the desired aims of Congress for the financially pressed but honest debtor. The care Congress took in enacting Chapter 11 as "a carefully matured enactment", Guessefeldt v. McGrath, 342 U.S. 308, 319, 72 S.Ct. 338, 344, 96 L.Ed. 342 (1952), is reflected in the exhaustive discussions and numerous changes made before enactment of the final version. To achieve reorganization for the benefit of debtors and creditors alike, Congress gave the court the latitude Section 546(c)(2) gives it to ensure that the debtor's continued operation would not be adversely affected by the improvident grant to a seller of the right to retrieve its goods in the debtor's possession.

Section 546(c)(2) must therefore be read as striking a balance so that the debtor has the use of the goods it needs for its ongoing business while the seller has their value. To give the seller more, absent a clear indication that this should be so, cuts against the grain of compelling bankruptcy themes. In short, Congress' coverage of the reclaiming seller is vital to the Chapter 11 mission.
* * *

IV.

THE JUDGMENT

Judgment is rendered for the plaintiff to the extent its goods were in the debtor's possession on the filing date. The amount of that judgment is allowed as an administrative priority within the meaning of Section 503 of the Code. Unless it is paid within a reasonable period, the court will entertain a motion for an order directing it be paid pursuant to Section 503(a).

* * *

IN RE COAST TRADING CO.

United States Bankruptcy Court, D. Oregon, 1982.
31 B.R. 667.

FOLGER JOHNSON, BANKRUPTCY JUDGE.

This case involves three Washington growers who sold grain to the defendant, Coast Trading Company, and which grain was in turn sold by Coast Trading to Ralston Purina. Ralston did not pay for the grain as it was in doubt as to which party was entitled to receive payment. Coast brought suit against Ralston to obtain payment, and in response, Ralston filed an interpleader action and paid $29,762.24 into this court. Ralston was then relieved of any further liability, and its attorney was awarded $800.00 out of the money paid in as a fee for the interpleader.

Some of the grain was delivered to Coast at its facilities in the state of Washington, and some grain was sold to Coast FOB the grower's farm in Washington. It was admitted in the latter case that the ten-day reclamation period started to run from the date Coast picked up the grain from the grower's farm regardless of what date it reached Coast's storage facility.

It was also admitted that upon delivery of the grain to Coast, The Oregon Bank, which held a perfected security interest in Coast's inventory, acquired a lien on such grain as a good faith purchaser for value which would be superior to the reclamation rights of the growers. It was also admitted that the Bank of Nova Scotia has a valid security interest in accounts receivable of Coast. Where the grain was still held by Coast when the reclamation demand was received within the ten-day period, the grower insofar as Coast was concerned would have been entitled to receive either the grain or, if later sold by Coast, the market value of such grain on the date reclamation demand was received subject, of course, to the intervening claim of the banks and possibly, in some cases, Production Credit Associations. There is no conflict, however, between the growers and the PCA's so that any payment made to a grower would be deemed payment to the appropriate PCA also.

If the reorganization plan of Coast Trading is accepted and confirmed by the court and the two banks are paid in full as a result thereof, some of the case will become moot. If, however, there is insufficient money to pay both banks, a marshalling question may arise under the agreement whereby the Bank of Nova Scotia was given a subordinate lien on the assets claimed by The Oregon Bank under its perfected security agreement. The parties are not asking the court to decide the entire case at this time in view of the various contingencies but have asked that the court determine whether, without regard to the secured creditors, the three growers would have a right to claim the proceeds from the resale of grain by Coast before receipt of the reclamation demand where such proceeds were deposited into the court and hence are clearly traceable.

Another issue which arises if the court determines that the reclaiming sellers have no right to the proceeds where the grain had already been sold, is whether such sellers are entitled to an administrative priority for the amount of such proceeds under Bankruptcy Code § 546(c)(2).

Neither the Uniform Commercial Code, §§ 2–507 and 2–702, which discuss the right to reclaim goods nor § 546 of the Bankruptcy Code grant a right to the proceeds from resale of those goods by the buyer. Where a right or interest in proceeds is recognized by the UCC, it is recognized expressly such as in § 9–306. See Matter of Samuels Co., Inc., 526 F.2d 1238 (5th Cir. en banc 1976) wherein the sellers of cattle sought to reclaim cattle and assert a claim to the proceeds from the sale of the slaughtered cattle. The Court of Appeals in its final consideration of the case after an earlier reversal by the Supreme Court, held that sellers who could not reclaim goods could not then claim rights in proceeds. * * *

In the matter of Flagstaff Foodservice Corp., 14 B.R. 462 (Bkrtcy.S.D.N.Y.1981), Judge Babbitt denied reclamation of proceeds, saying that "the tracing of specific funds attributable to specific sales is a formidable obstacle at best." It would have been easy for the court to have stated, if such were its view, that when proceeds are traceable they can be claimed and when they are not traceable they can not be claimed, but the court voiced no such conclusion, leaving only an implication floating in the air which is dispelled by the court's approval of the *Samuels* case which held against the reclaiming seller.

* * *

In bankruptcy a reclaiming seller's UCC rights are altered by this section, restricting the use of any common-law right to the goods themselves. * * *

Section 546(c) gives a seller only a right to reclaim the goods. If the goods are still in the hands of the buyer at the time of reclamation and there is no intervening right of a secured creditor that would be superior to the seller's rights, the court must permit reclamation, unless the court finds that such goods are needed for the reorganization of the debtor and grants the seller instead an administrative expense priority or a lien on assets of the debtor to provide it adequate protection for its claim. If the buyer, before reclamation, has already sold the goods to a good faith purchaser for value, there is nothing to reclaim as the seller cannot demand a return of the goods from the ultimate purchaser. Since the seller has no right to the goods, he has no right to receive something in lieu of the goods. Whether the ultimate purchaser has yet paid for the goods or whether the proceeds paid by such purchaser can be clearly traced is immaterial. To the extent that In re Western Farmers Association, 6 B.R. 432 (Bkrtcy.W.D.Wash. 1980), holds to the contrary this court disagrees with such holding. There are many growers with unsecured claims against Coast and none should be given a preference unless provided by statute. Section 546(c) is unambiguous in granting a right to possession of the goods only and should be held to mean what it plainly expresses. Equity is out of place here in attempting to create a right not implied in the statute.

Even if the claims of The Oregon Bank and the Bank of Nova Scotia are satisfied in full out of other assets, the plaintiff-growers, Cliff Dopps, McCary Farms and Jake Pister, being unable to reach the goods at the time of reclamation, have no right to the traceable proceeds received from a good faith purchaser for value for the resale of such goods, nor are they entitled to any administrative expense priority or lien under § 546(c)(2) in lieu of such goods.

NOTES

1. In *Flagstaff* the court stated that "judgment is rendered for the plaintiff to the extent its goods were in the debtor's possession on the filing date." Earlier in the opinion the court stated that the plaintiff was entitled to an administrative claim based on its reclamation only to the extent that the goods were "in the debtor's possession on the date of McCain's demand." Thus, it is not clear what event determines the right of the reclaiming seller. This ambiguity was not important to the outcome in *Flagstaff* because the demand for reclamation and the filing of the bankruptcy petition occurred on the same day. In re Davidson Lumber Co., 22 B.R. 775 (Bkrtcy.Fla.1982), involved a timely demand for reclamation made on the debtor before bankruptcy. The goods were in the possession of the debtor when the demand was made. The debtor ignored the demand, sold the goods to buyers in ordinary course, and then filed in bankruptcy. The court held that the seller was entitled to an administrative expense claim for the value of the goods in the possession of the debtor at the time the demand was made. The court stated: "The debtor's reliance on the fact that there are intervening rights of good faith purchasers does not persuade me that the disposal of the goods by the debtor after a timely demand by the seller obliterates the seller's rights. The administrative claim which I find that the seller is entitled to is in lieu of the goods which the seller could reclaim."

2. The right, under § 2–507(2), of a cash seller to reclaim goods for which payment was made by a check subsequently dishonored can be compared to the right of a credit seller to reclaim goods delivered to an insolvent buyer. The right of the seller under § 2–507(2) exists regardless of whether the buyer is

insolvent, but in most of the litigated cases in which the right is asserted the buyer is insolvent. Unlike § 2–702(2), however, § 2–507(2) does not state any specific limitation with respect to the time period within which the seller must make a demand for return of the goods. Comment 3 to § 2–507. The first three sentences of Comment 3 have remained unchanged since the Comment was originally drafted. In the present version of Comment 3 the text appearing after the first three sentences was added by Permanent Editorial Board Commentary No. 1, dated March 10, 1990, in substitution for the following statement which appeared as the fourth sentence of Comment 3 as originally drafted: "The provision of this Article for a ten day limit within which the seller may reclaim goods delivered on credit to an insolvent buyer is also applicable here." The reference in the quoted words was to the 10-day limitation in § 2–702(2). Most courts followed the original Comment 3 and read a 10-day limitation into § 2–507(2). An example is Szabo v. Vinton Motors, Inc., 630 F.2d 1 (1st Cir.1980). The cases following this view involved reclamation claims against buyers who were in fact insolvent. Burk v. Emmick, 637 F.2d 1172 (8th Cir.1980), refused to read a 10-day limitation into § 2–507(2), but in that case the buyer was not insolvent. The present version of Comment 3 disapproves the result in *Szabo* and approves the result in *Burk*.

The dispute underlying the rewriting of Comment 3 to § 2–507 is of limited practical importance because in most cases in which a § 2–507(2) claim is asserted the goods were sold to an insolvent buyer and the buyer is in bankruptcy. In those cases the 10-day limitation will apply because Bankruptcy Code § 546(c) controls. The legislative history makes clear that § 546(c) was meant to apply to both cash and credit sales. See 124 Cong.Rec.S. 17,413–17,414 (remarks of Sen. De Concini) and 124 Cong.Rec.H. 11,097 (remarks of Rep. Edwards).

3. What is the purpose of the ten-day demand requirement? In In re Wathen's Elevators, Inc., 32 B.R. 912 (Bkrtcy.Ky.1983) the court stated: "Section 546 does not contain any explanation of why a ten-day demand must be made; neither does the legislative history provide its justification. Only one reported case, In re Samuels [526 F.2d 1238 (5th Cir.1976)] grapples with this issue unsuccessfully, and concludes that the notice must serve some function other than notifying third-party takers. The ten-day limit seems, at best, arbitrary."

4. In Montello Oil Corp. v. Marin Motor Oil, Inc., 740 F.2d 220 (3d Cir.1984), Montello sold more than one million gallons of gasoline to Marin. Marin agreed to pay within one day of delivery. The gasoline was delivered to a common carrier on April 10. The carrier delivered the gasoline to Marin on April 11. On April 16 an officer of Montello orally demanded payment or return of

the gasoline. On the same day Montello filed suit against Marin seeking attachment of the gasoline and an injunction against any resale of the gasoline. The injunction was issued and the order of the court was served on Marin on April 20. On April 21 Marin filed a petition in bankruptcy. Shortly after 11 p.m. of the same day Montello sent a telex demanding return of the goods. The telex was "electronically processed by Western Union" and received in the Western Union office nearest Marin a few minutes later. The telex "was physically received by Marin at approximately 9:04 a.m. on April 22 when Marin opened for business and turned on its telex machine." The court's holding that Montello made a demand for reclamation that complied with Bankruptcy Code § 546(c) was based on the following conclusions: (1) Neither the oral demand on April 16 nor the lawsuit brought on the same day satisfied the requirement of § 546(c) of a written demand for reclamation. The lawsuit was an action for damages and equitable relief rather than an action for reclamation. The prayer for attachment was simply a remedy designed to assure payment of any damages recoverable. (2) The ten-day period of § 546(c) started to run on April 11 when Marin got physical possession of the gasoline rather than on April 10 when it received title upon delivery to the common carrier. (3) Demand was made by Montello on April 21 when the telex was dispatched rather than on April 22 when it was received by Marin. The court adopted a "dispatch rule" rather than a "receipt rule" on grounds of certainty and ease of proof. The court imposed a requirement, however, that the method of communication be "commercially reasonable." The majority opinion concluded that it is easier to determine when a demand has been sent rather than when it is received. The concurring opinion emphasized the fact that a dispatch rule gave a greater degree of certainty to the seller.

PROBLEM

Retailer was in the business of selling furniture at retail. On February 5 it made five separate sales of furniture to customers on installment contracts. The total face value of the contracts was $4,800. Under each of the contracts the customer granted to Retailer a security interest in the furniture purchased to secure payment of the purchase price. The next day Retailer sold and delivered the five installment sale contracts to Finance Company for an aggregate price of $3,800. Immediate payment was made by a check drawn on Bank. Retailer promptly presented the check for payment to Bank which refused payment because of insufficient funds in the account of Finance Company. Retailer immediately made an oral demand on Finance Company that it pay the check or return the installment sale contracts. Finance Company refused to honor either demand. Two days later Finance Company filed a petition in bankruptcy under Chapter 7.

At the date of bankruptcy Finance Company was in possession of the installment sale contracts. Is Retailer entitled to return of the contracts?

This problem is based on In re Southern Industrial Banking Corp., 36 B.R. 1008 (Bkrtcy.Tenn.1984), but the facts have been modified.

IN RE HRT INDUSTRIES, INC.

United States Bankruptcy Court, S.D. New York, 1983.
29 B.R. 861.

BURTON R. LIFLAND, BANKRUPTCY JUDGE.

HRT Industries, Inc. ("HRT"), a Chapter 11 debtor, has moved to dismiss the complaints of the plaintiffs, Mr. Trio, Inc. ("Mr. Trio") and Crown Quilt Corp. ("Crown Quilt") * * * on the ground that the plaintiffs have failed to state a claim upon which relief can be granted. Plaintiffs, as unpaid vendors to a major department store chain undergoing reorganization, have filed complaints based upon common law theories of constructive fraud and conversion. Mr. Trio and Crown Quilt have thus requested special treatment in respect of the goods delivered to HRT outside the provisions of Section 546(c) of the Bankruptcy Code ("the Code"). Through its motion to dismiss, HRT has responded that the plaintiffs have failed to comply with the strict notice provisions of Section 546(c) and therefore are not entitled to any relief.

Essentially, the relief sought is the equivalent of reclamation, a remedy governed by Section 546(c). Plaintiffs concede an utter failure to comply with the notice provisions of Section 546(c) and acknowledge that their fraud complaints may not be in compliance with the pleading requirements for a constructive fraud and conversion. For example, plaintiffs have not alleged a fiduciary or confidential relationship nor pleaded the elements of fraud with the particularity required by Bankruptcy Rule 709 and Rule 9(b) of the Federal Rules of Civil Procedure. Also, as to conversion, plaintiffs have not, in the face of a sale of goods, shown the necessary elements of an intentional deprivation or interference with the dominion and control of the property of another. Plaintiffs hedge these deficiencies in pleading with a request for an opportunity either to amend, or to suffer dismissal without prejudice to an amended renewal of the suits. Defendant, on the other hand, urges dismissal with prejudice arguing that even if perfectly pleaded, these complaints would not entitle plaintiffs to relief since Section 546(c) of the Code provides the exclusive remedy for claimants in this type of situation.

No matter how the complaints of these unpaid vendors are clothed, the principal alternative relief sought of return of merchandise or money damages based on invoice price or an administrative claim is essentially the stuff of reclamation (a misnomer, as seldom if ever is property actually returned or reclaimed in a reorganization case in lieu of other available relief). Typically, fraud pleading is the last gasp of an unpaid vendor who has missed the ten-day notice requirement of Section 546(c) or of its nonbankruptcy state law analogue, Section 2–702 of the Uniform Commercial Code ("UCC"). This UCC section requires only that notice, whether oral or written, be given within 10 days of delivery of the goods. Section 546(c) requires that the notice be written. Courts have consistently viewed these fraud allegations for what they really are: masquerading reclamation claims. * * * The alleged basis for the relief sought is that HRT, at the time it accepted the goods, had already authorized its attorneys to file the petition for relief under Chapter 11 of the Code, or knew that such authorization would be given, and that had such information been supplied to plaintiffs, they would not have shipped goods on credit to HRT.

Additionally, plaintiffs allege that HRT's undertaking to render payment, knowing at the time it would not have been permitted to do so, constitutes obtaining property by false pretenses.

A motion to dismiss for failure to state a claim upon which relief can be granted should not be granted when the material allegations of the complaint, taken in their most favorable light, are legally sufficient to support a claim. * * * Therefore, the issue to be resolved by this motion to dismiss is whether plaintiffs have a right to any relief under any theory, even though they have not fulfilled the notice requirements of Section 546(c).

*   *   *

Based on the literal provisions of Section 546(c)(1), HRT argues that before reclamation or its equivalent can be granted, the specific notice requirements prescribed in subsection (1) of Section 546(c) must be met. HRT continues, reasoning that since the plaintiffs admit in their complaints that they did not comply with such notice requirements, the complaints for reclamation should be dismissed. Furthermore, the debtor reiterates the argument that Section 546(c) of the Code provides the exclusive remedy for reclaiming creditors and that, therefore, any cause of action based on common law fraud, i.e., misrepresentation of solvency or intent to pay for purchases, will not suffice where the plaintiff has not complied with the notice requirements.

On the other hand, plaintiffs argue that a better interpretation of Section 546(c) is that it provides the seller with a "safe harbor" against the trustee or debtor, but that it is not an exclusive remedy, and the vendor may rely on any other provisions or theories which would enable it to obtain the necessary relief. Plaintiffs argue strenuously for a detour around a statutory barricade. They argue in vain. The only road to relief is via route 546(c) and they have missed that turn.

Construing Section 2–702 of the Uniform Commercial Code and more recently Section 546(c), courts have been consistent in holding that the reclamation statutory scheme of relief is the sole remedy for an unpaid vendor when the buyer has filed for bankruptcy, thereby precluding any other common law rights a seller might have had. * * *

In In re Original Auto Parts Distributors, Inc., 9 B.R. 469 (Bkrtcy.N.Y.1981), a seller brought a fraud complaint seeking reclamation of goods sold on credit to a Chapter 11 debtor after the statutory ten-day period had expired. The court held that although the seller did not learn of the debtor's insolvency until more than ten days after the debtor had received goods on credit from the seller, the seller's failure to give timely written notice of its demand for recovery under Section 546(c) is fatal. * * * The court reasoned that the legislative history of Section 546(c) demonstrates that the drafters intended it to be the exclusive remedy for a reclaiming seller. *Original Auto Parts,* 9 B.R. at 471, quoting the Congressional Record as follows: "[A] demand for reclamation *must* be made in writing anytime before ten days after receipt of the goods by the debtor." 124 Cong.Rec.H. 11,097 (Sept. 28, 1978) (emphasis added). Other decisions within this Circuit are in accord with this holding. * * *

The Bankruptcy Appellate Panel of the First Circuit has also come to the conclusion that Section 546(c) is the exclusive remedy for reclaiming sellers. See In re Koro Corporation, 20 B.R. 241 (B.A.P. 1st Cir.1982). In *Koro,* the court found that "Section 546(c) is clear and unambiguous in its scope and its requirements," 20 B.R. at 242. The court went on to hold that any right to reclamation is contingent upon the seller "making a written demand within ten days of the Debtor's receipt of the goods." Id. at 243.

In sum, the substantial weight of authority holds that Section 546(c) represents an exclusive remedy, and that unless a seller meets the ten-day notice requirement, it has no other common law or statutory right of action. * * * But see In re A.G.S. Food Systems, Inc., 14 B.R. 27 (Bkrtcy.D.S.C.1980) (Section 546(c) held not to apply to seller who by making a timely oral demand one day prior to the filing of the bankruptcy petition complied with state law reclamation requirements).

Therefore, in the case at bar, plaintiffs' failure to give written notice of is demand for reclamation before the expiration of the statutory ten-day period requires that the court summarily deny their requests for relief.

Accordingly, HRT's motion to dismiss the plaintiffs' complaints is granted because their complaints fail to state a claim upon which relief can be granted.

INDEX

1247

†